The Catalogue of Antique Tools
Martin J. Donnelly Antique Tools

Table of Contents

www.mjdtools.com	2
Introduction	3
Marketing Your Antique Tools	3
Ordering Information	3
Antique Tools for Sale	4
Reference Books for Sale	281
Comprehensive Index	313

All Items in this Catalogue are for Sale

The Catalogue of Antique Tools

Martin J. Donnelly Antique Tools
PO Box 281 Bath, New York 14810-0281
Toll Free: (800) 869-0695
Telephone: (607) 566-2617
Fax: (607) 566-2575
E-mail: mjd@mjdtools.com
Web: www.mjdtools.com

President/CEO/Publisher
Martin J. Donnelly

Executive Managing Editor
Kathleen A. Donnelly

Senior Technical Advisor
Margaret A. Donnelly

Production Staff

Director of Photography and Design
Amber E. Budd

Office Manager
Nancy S. Walters

Warehouse & Book Division Manager
Velda C. Schmieg

Senior Production Assistant
Amanda M. Snyder

Production Assistants
Rebecca Ayer, Rebecca J. Beeman,
John Kukuk, Trevor Margeson,
Sean McKinley, Leanna VanZile,
Michelle Verhalen

Cover Photography
Sandra St. James & Michael Murray
White Light Studios, Spencerport, New York

Printed by
No Other Impressions, Inc.
Rochester, New York

The Catalogue of Antique Tools is published annually. If you did not purchase this book directly from Martin J. Donnelly Antique Tools, please contact us, toll free, at (800) 869-0695 to register. Registered subscribers are periodically notified of special discounts on unsold Catalogue items. In addition, subscribers receive our catalogues of reference books about tools and will receive notice of upcoming publications.

Copyright ©2000 Martin J. Donnelly Antique Tools

Don't Miss Our Award Winning Web Site!
Now with SECURE ONLINE ORDERING!!!

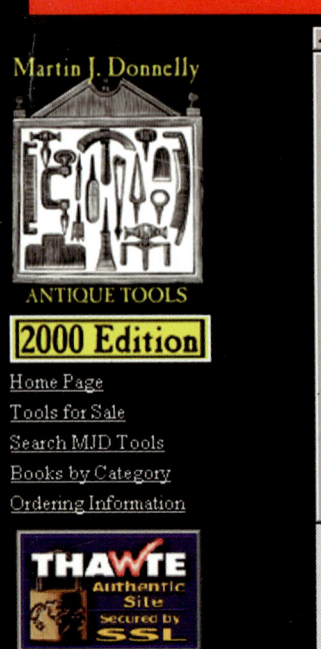

PO Box 281 Bath, NY 14810 Phone: **(800) 869-0695** FAX: **(607) 566-2575**

Now Shipping: The Catalogue of Antique Tools is Now ON SALE for Just $20.00, by Priority Mail. Ord

- **Click Here for Tools for Sale**
  More than 5000 tools! More every Tuesday and Thursday.
- **Click Here for Reviews of Books & Antique Value Guides**
  More than 600 titles. More coming every week.
- **Search our Site for Tools or Books**
  More than 5000 Tools and 600 Reference Books Available for Sale. Use our search engine for tool research.
- **Unsolicited Testimonials**
  Positive feedback from catalogue subscribers and web site visitors.
- **Register for Automatic Notification**
  Get an E-mail message every Tuesday and Thursday to remind you of the fresh postings.
- **Animal Testing**
  Your tool dealer with a social conscience, more or less.
- **Off Ramp**
  Other sites of interest to the antique tool afficianado.
- **E-mail**
  Contact us to brag, complain or tell us how wonderful we are.
- **Featured Focus**
  Whatever we feel like putting here.

www.mjdtools.com

More Hits Each Month Than All Other Antique Tool Web Sites Combined!

A Personal Note... *From the Publisher*

Welcome to the Millennium Edition of the Catalogue of Antique Tools. Once again, we believe we have met our commitment to bring you a "bigger and better" Edition than the previous year. Just for the record, this year's catalogue is 240 pages larger than the 1994 Edition, is printed in full color and costs just $10.00 more than the black & white 1994 Catalogue. For those who don't think it can get any bigger and better, just wait 'til next year.

This past year has been a busy one for us here at Martin J. Donnelly Antique Tools. We have moved into a new complex of buildings, substantially expanded our staff and, we believe, we are now more poised than ever to assist you in marketing your antique tools, whether you have a single item or a lifetime collection. I look forward to seeing many of you during the coming year. If you have tools that you are interested in selling, let's talk about how our unique print catalogue and dynamic web site (www.mjdtools.com) can help you realize the most value for your investment.

Martin J. Donnelly, Spring, 2000

Interested in Marketing Your Antique Tools?...Let's Talk

If you have a single item or a lifelong collection that you are interested in selling, we would like to discuss with you the many advantages of using our advanced, digital marketing capabilities to help you realize maximum market values for every item in your collection.

Because we have the most advanced antique tool database in the world, we can quickly organize, itemize and digitally photograph any individual tool or collection and then bring those items quickly to the attention of tens of thousands of potential buyers woldwide through our dynamic Internet site or through the medium of this catalogue.

If you would like to hear more, please give us a call, toll free, at (800) 869-0695. All inquiries will be held in the strictest confidence.

A NOTE ON CONDITION AND PRESENTATION:

The tools offered for sale in this catalogue have been individually selected for inclusion based on having met the exacting standard of quality and rarity of Martin J. Donnelly Antique Tools. Generally, items have been grouped for presentation based on function or similarity of function. Ratings shown in parentheses at the end of each description are based on The Standard Condition Classification of Antique Hand Tools, copyrighted by the Fine Tool Journal of Pownal, Maine. The vast majority of items included here are rated in FINE condition. Such tools, generally, are complete, flawless, totally useable and retain 90% or more of their original finishes on all surfaces. While it would be ideal to offer an entire catalogue of tools which meet the demanding test to be so classified, certain other items of great historical interest and/or rarity are featured as well, despite a lesser rating. In all instances I have attempted to carefully describe the positive features of each lot, while pointing out any flaws, or, more politely, apologies. Those who have an interest in an item are encouraged to call. We will be happy to describe the condition of any tool in much greater detail than the limited space here will allow. Prospective buyers have my personal assurance that the classic antique tools offered herein are of a level of quality available nowhere else.

ORDERING INFORMATION:

Those who wish to purchase items featured in this catalogue are encouraged to order by telephone, FAX.or E-Mail: mjd@mjdtools.com. Feel free to call between 6:00 a. m. and 11:00 p.m. E.S.T. (TOLL FREE: (800) 869-0695 or (607) 566-2617 FAX: (607) 566-2575. If you are really desperate to buy and the hour is late, call anyway. FAX orders may be sent at any time. Payment may be made in cash, by personal check, money order or feel free to use your VISA, MasterCard, Discover or American Express card. Every effort will be made to have a real live Human Being available to answer the phone at all times. However, in those rare instances where it becomes necessary to "not be able to come to the phone right now", the answering machine will be left on . If you reach the answering machine and you wish to reserve an item, or you have questions about a specific tool, please leave your name, telephone number and the catalogue number(s) of the item(s) in which you have an interest. Those lots will be held without obligation until we can speak with you personally. We will download electronic mail every ten minutes, at a minimum. E-Mail orders will be confirmed immediately by telephone, so a telephone number must be included for an order to be valid. Mail orders will, of course, be accepted, but it is highly recommended that you confirm the availability of tools you wish to purchase before sending payment.

ALL CORRESPONDENCE SHOULD BE DIRECTED TO:

MAIL: MARTIN J. DONNELLY ANTIQUE TOOLS
PO BOX 281
BATH, NY 14810-0281

SHIP: MARTIN J. DONNELLY ANTIQUE TOOLS
5223 COUNTY ROUTE 8
AVOCA, NY 14809

Phone: (800) 869-0695 or (607) 566-2617
Fax: (607) 566-2575 E-Mail: mjd@mjdtools.com

For sales within the United States, shipping costs are included in the purchase price of all items that would do less than $500.00 worth of damage to your automobile if dropped on it from a second story window. In matters of dispute, a Trial by Gravity may be arranged. Canadian customers will be assessed an additional fee to offset extra postage costs. Overseas shipments will be sent Air Mail at actual cost. Generally, items sold will be shipped upon receipt of payment. Reserved tools will be held 7 days pending receipt of payment. All items are subject to return within 5 days if you are not completely satisfied. If, for any reason, you are not satisfied with an item, please let us know as soon as possible. Sales tax at 8% is applicable to all New York State residents.

Group A1

A1-1. Rice, Royal B., Williamsburg, Mass: Muliple Imprint Molding Plane. Four Plane Makers Marks. See P-TAMPIA Vol. I, P. 87. Length: 9 1/2 Inches. *To pick up this plane is to hold history in the palm of one's hand. Its features, while seemingly not noteworthy from as short a distance as the far side of a room, come quickly into focus as one more closely examines the object. Even in the absence of any historical background on this tool, the fact that it has been boldly struck with the imprints of The Greenfield Tool Company of Greenfield, Massachusetts, J. Kellogg of Amherst, Massachusetts, H. Wells of Williamsburg, Massachusetts and the Union Tool Company of Goshen, Massachusetts would make it an extraordinary collectible curiosity. However, thanks to the tiny name stamp "R.B. Rice" on the toe of the plane and the research of Roger K. Smith, who has documented this very plane on page 87 of the Second Volume of "Patented Metallic & Transitional Planes in America", we know much, much more. We know that one Royal B. Rice of Williamsburg, Massachusetts was almost certainly the "R.B. Rice" and that he very likely used this "backing" plane in his work with the planemakers of the Connecticut Valley with whom he was associated and whose imprints appear on this tool. We also know that in addition to his planemaking, Rice was a bit of a Yankee inventor and was issued a patent on December 21, 1869 for a spur on a plow plane skate. In an exceptionally well preserved condition, this tool is as dramatic an example as we have yet seen as to how knowing the history of tools and toolmaking can transform an object that would appear nondescript to the uninitiated, into an important and exciting historical curiosity. Simply a great plane that captures within itself the essence of what all of this is all about. Highly recommended.* (GOOD+) **$1,950.00**

A1-2. Ziegler & Mc Curdy, Philadelphia, Etc.: Groesbeck's Calculating Machine. Patented March 18, 1870. Rare and Excellent. Length: 6 1/2 Inches. *While it can be demonstrated that the concept of mechanical calculating machines dates back to the earliest years of human civilization, the extension of the technology beyond a very, very limited few required the refinement of manufacturing techniques and the invention of technology to take advantage of those techniques. As was the case with nearly every area of invention and manufacturing, the aftermath U.S. Civil War brought about a huge leap forward in the quality and quantity of manufacturer. It was in those immediate post war years that Messrs. Ziegler & Mc Curdy of Philadelphia, Pennsylvania, produced for the world the Groesbeck's Calculating Machine. Patented on March 18, 1870, the Groesbeck calculator employed a series of five stylus driven semicircular wheels to activate a digital readout mechanism. Complete and mechanically perfect, although missing the stylus, this classic calculating device is a classic example from the earliest days of a March of Technology that would bring the power of calculation to everyone.* (GOOD+) **$3,450.00**

A1-3. Stanley Rule & Level No. 164: Low Angle Block Plane. Original P-TAMPIA Example. Near New Condition. Length: 9 Inches. *The publication of Roger Smith's classic "Patented Transitional and Metallic Planes in America" focused collectors on rare patented planes, including those manufactured by the Stanley Rule & Level Company, in a way that has not yet abated. What was true nearly 20 years ago when the book was released is still true today—most collectors first become acquainted with great metallic and transitional planes through this book. If they are lucky and work hard, they may actually see some of those planes. If they work very hard and are very lucky, they may eventually own some of the planes shown in the book. For most collectors however, the likelihood that they will one day own one of the specimens photographed for the book is one of those dreams that can be imagined, but never really believed. We are pleased to offer this, the original Stanley No. 164 low angle block plane that was photographed for and included in Roger Smith's book. Shown on page 246 in the Smith book, this plane was patented on September 27, 1927 by Edmund A. Schade of New Britain, Connecticut. It retains nearly all of its original black japan finish and is in superb collector quality condition. An extremely rare woodworking tool, an investment opportunity and a dream come true. Highly recommended.* (FINE) **$6,450.00**

A1-4. Chapin, Frank, Pine Meadow, Conn.: Presentation Masonic Folding Rule. Meridan Lodge No. 77. December 13, 1897. Length: 24 Inches. *In 15 years of serious looking, we have seen but three examples of the ivory Masonic ritual rule marked with the imprint of an American rulemaker and perhaps a dozen more without any maker markings. By any standard, this would be an extremely rare rule, but its historical interest and value to a collector are enhanced exponentially by the fact that sufficient documentation exists to establish historical provenance. Too often, such provenance consists of a story that, however well intentioned, cannot be linked absolutely to the tool. We know of a dealer in the State of Maine and another in the State of New Jersey who have each had the privilege of discovering in a barn, and an attic, respectively, the original surveying tools of George Washington. In this case, however, the strong historical association is etched onto the tool itself. Frank Chapin, very likely a grandson of Hermon Chapin, the tool manufacturing pioneer of Pine Meadow, Connecticut, had the foresight to have the center section of bright, white and exceptionally well preserved rule inscribed "Presented to Meriden Lodge No. 77 by Frank M. Chapin, Pine Meadow, Connecticut, December 13, 1897. What happened that day in 1897? Was Chapin a visitor at the lodge? Did he perhaps present other rules elsewhere that have not survived, or was this unique? Time may provide answers to these questions, and the publication of this information here will likely spur researchers to seek to answer those questions. That is how it should be. The seeking out of who we are by exploring where we have been and what we have made is important, but that search is not work. That search is antique tool collecting. An extraordinary presentation ivory Masonic rule from a major American rulemaker.* (FINE) **$5,450.00**

A1-5. Tanner & Davenport, Albany, N.Y.: Tanner's Patent Veneer Scraping Plane. Patented December 14, 1869. Rare and Excellent. Length: 6 Inches. *Patented by Richard W. Tanner of Albany, New York on December 14, 1869, the Tanner Patent Veneer Scraping plane is one of the least common of all patented woodworking planes. Fitted out with four turned and knurled brass adjusting and fixing screws, the Tanner patent was produced by Tanner in partnership with Samuel J. Davenport, also of Albany. This example is faintly marked with the Tanner & Davenport name, but is unmistakable in form. The original scraper blade is missing, but could be easily replaced. Only the second example of this rare and early-patented plane of which we are aware.* (GOOD+) **$3,450.00**

A1-6. Stanley Rule & Level: Special Transitional Planes. Rosewood and Boxwood. For U.S. Centennial? Length: 28 Inches. *One hundred years after the first reading of the Declaration of Independence, the spirit of America was on the rise. The memories of a destructive civil war were finally beginning to fade and there was a sense of optimism in the land. New cities were rising in the West and the great cities of the East were growing larger. Tools were needed to sustain the march of progress. No maker of hand tools was more at the center of that spirit of industry than the Stanley Rule & Level Company of New Britain, Connecticut. Stanley's business was being fueled by the dramatic success of the metallic planes invented by Leonard Bailey and manufactured at the Stanley Rule & Level Plant. Historical records show that a Great Centennial Exposition was held in Philadelphia in the year 1876 to commemorate one hundred years of independence. It is known that the Stanley Rule & Level Company put on a major display at that exhibition and period engravings exist of the elaborate Stanley display. What is not known, however, and will likely never be known, is the exact makeup of the Stanley display. We know from the few surviving examples of the work of other makers that companies often crafted special tools for these exhibitions to demonstrate mastery of their craft. While we have no specific documentation to associate the tools offered here with the Centennial Exposition, there is very strong evidence that these planes were crafted at precisely the time of the Philadelphia Centennial Exposition. Moreover, the extreme custom nature of these planes and the exotic materials of which they were made would have placed them outside the scope of the custom work Stanley would have been prepared to perform for customers. Crafted with bodies of beautifully grained Brazilian Rosewood and fitted with dovetailed soles of bright, yellow and grainless Turkish Boxwood, these pre-lateral transitional planes have been boldly struck at the junction of the rosewood and boxwood with the stylized eagle imprint and number imprint exactly as used beginning in the year 1874. The handles of these planes are formed of the same dark rosewood as the body, another extreme custom variation that would have required far more time and effort than could have been justified by a "special order". Retaining nearly all of their original lacquer finishes and shiny, black japan finish, this unique set consists of a jointer, fore, jack and smoothing plane. Only a tight crack in the boxwood of the throat of one plane and a crack at the base of the tote of another merit mention as "apologies". Otherwise these planes are in nearly new condition. Were these planes exhibited at the Centennial Exposition? We will likely never know. Should they have been part of that Exposition? We will lead it to the viewer to judge. Without question, the most important group of Stanley tools ever offered for sale. Highly recommended.* (FINE) **$36,500.00**

A1-7. Lane, E.S., Upton, Maine: Walking Wheel Log Caliper. Original Finish. Rare and Complete. Length: 48 Inches. *One of the most graphic and dramatic of all woodworking tools, the classic Maine "walking wheel" caliper is one of those tools that appeals to practically everyone, whether or not that individual has a predisposition to be interested in antique tools. This spectacularly well preserved example is imprinted with the mark of E.S. Lane who was one of only a few makers to produce tools of this style. Retaining nearly all of its original yellow lacquer finish and having the original Lane wheel that is intact and shows hardly any evidence of use, this tool is ready to serve as the focal point of conversation in any display of antique tools. Highly recommended.* (FINE) **$2,850.00**

A1-8. Ohio Tool Co., Columbus, Ohio: No. 111: Ivory Tip Plow Plane. With Centerwheel. Rare and Near New. Length: 11 1/2 Inches. *At the top of many lists of the most desirable collectible tools is found the center wheel adjusting cabinetmakers plow plane. These tools were offered exclusively by two Ohio makers, the Sandusky Tool Company and the Ohio Tool Company. It is odd that these exotic tools of such grace and beauty should have been made by makers who otherwise distinguished themselves by the quantity, rather than the quality, of their output. For years these tools were a fixture in the catalogs of both of these highly successful makers. Their cost, even at the "entry level" offering was far more than a month's wages for a successful cabinetmaker. To purchase a tool such as this solid Brazilian rosewood center wheel plow with six ivory tips would have required an investment of far more in money than could ever have been justified on the utilitarian value of the tool alone. These planes were, and remain, a grand indulgence that was symbolic of a commitment to quality and to the very best. Just as accomplished master woodworkers acquired for themselves the very, very best 125 years ago, so do collectors today actively seek out and fight for the few limited examples of these planes to appear on the market. An extremely rare and nearly perfectly preserved rosewood center wheel plow plane from the Ohio Tool Company. Magnificent.* (FINE) **$18,975.00**

A1-9. Nicholson, F., Wrentham: Reverse Ogee and Bead Molding Plane. Yellow Birch. Superb Patina. Length: 9 3/4 Inches. *This reverse ogee molder has been boldly struck with the imprint of Francis Nicholson, who is believed to have been the first commercial American planemaker. This plane which is also imprinted with the "Wrentham" designation measures 9 3/4" in length and likely dates from the 1740's. An exceptionally well preserved molding plane from America's first documented planemaker.* (GOOD+) **$4,750.00**

A1-10. Davis L. & T. Co., Springfield, Mass.: 12 Inch Inclinometer Level. Patented September 17, 1867. Original Pin Striping. Length: 12 Inches. *The fragility of early planes and levels made of cast iron is well known to those who have studied antique tools. The Davis Level & Tool Company made the breakage rate even higher by making some of the most elaborate castings attempted, before or since, from that same, early cast iron. Finding any Davis level without a sizeable chunk missing is a difficult task. A level such as that pictured here, then, becomes a Holy Grail of sorts for the serious level collector. With 99% of the paint, all of the original lacquer on the brass and nearly all of the original gold enamel ornamentation intact this 1867 patent inclinometer level is in near-new condition. An extraordinarily nice example of a highly collectible inclinometer level.* (GOOD+) **$1,175.00**

A1-11. Barlow, S.H., Lacona, New York: Stairbuilder's Tool Chest. All Original Tools. Superb Condition. Length: 48 Inches. *The full appreciation of antique tool collecting sometimes requires the skills of a detective. Such is the case with this complete set of tools. All of the tools in this set are imprinted with the initials "S.H.B." Further inspection reveals a billhead marked "S.H.Barlow, Lacona, New York". The billhead further states that Barlow was a "Builder and Manufacturer of Doors, Sash and Blinds", and that he further offered that "All Kinds of Building Material Furnished". Barlow's assumption of the role of manufacturer may explain much about this chest. In the chest are 25 wooden planes, 19 of which were made by the Sandusky Tool Company and appear to be in nearly new condition. The other planes are older and have been cared for, but have certainly been used. Such is the case with the rest of the tools—some are nearly unused and others are older and show more signs of use. All fitted into a paneled chest having a series of sliding trays and fixed compartments, including a pair of hinged doors on the inside of the top which appear to have been used to hold papers and drawing tools, this chest had been undisturbed for more than 80 years when the tools were carefully removed for this photograph. Given the dearth of information, speculation will be primarily just that, however, it seems likely that S.H. Barlow learned the woodworking trade from his father, perhaps acquired some tools of his own, and then decided to concentrate on the door and blind manufacturing business. As a consequence of his decision, this rare, complete set of carpenters tools from the end of the Nineteenth Century has been preserved for posterity in essentially the same condition as they were in when last put away many, many years ago. A rare opportunity to purchase an intact chest of carpenters tools.* (FINE) **$2,850.00**

A1-12. Stanley Rule & Level No. 42: Miller Patent Plow Plane. Patented June 26, 1870. Early and Near New. Length: 9 Inches. *The quintessential tool from the age of American Victorian excess, the Miller Patent combination plow, rabbet & filletster is generally regarded as the most beautiful tool ever produced by the Stanley Rule & Level Company. Produced under a patent granted to Charles Miller of Brattleborough, Vermont on June 28, 1870, these planes were of such quality and expense that they were purchased, primarily as a self indulgence, by a very limited few woodworkers. Most of the few examples that have survived have done so barely and are missing parts and finish and are severely damaged. It is very seldom that an example of the No. 42 gunmetal Miller Patent of this quality becomes available in the marketplace. Retaining nearly all of its original lacquer on the gunmetal and handle and complete with the original complement of nine cutting irons, this is, without question, the finest example of this rare plane that we have ever been privileged to sell. A quintessential Stanley collectible.* (FINE) **$7,450.00**

A1-13. Erlandsen, N., New York: American Miter Metallic Plane. Original Nickel Plating. Superb Example. Length: 9 Inches. *Metallic planes and other tools produced by the toolmakers who made tools for New York City's piano making industry in the Nineteenth Century are some of the finest American tools ever produced. They combine a distinct European flavor with the flair for innovation and technical improvement that is so characteristic of American tools. This mitre plane can be recognized as having been produced by the father and son planemakers, Napoleon and Julius Erlandsen, by its turned brass fixing screw and the manner of making of its throat adjustment. We know with certainty that the plane was produced by the elder Erlandsen as it is imprinted with his name on the front nose section. Some 85% of the original nickel plating remains, and the nickel that is missing is conspicuously absent from where the hand of the original owner would have been placed when using the tool. An exceptionally well preserved example of a classic New York City instrument makers miter plane.* (FINE) **$3,275.00**

A1-14. Stanley Rule & Level No. 1: Early Type Plane. With Beaded Knob. Extra Crisp and Clean. Length: 5 1/2 Inches. *Much sought after by collectors, examples of the earliest type of the coveted No. 1 plane become available for sale very seldom. When they do, the 140 year-old tools have generally deteriorated substantially from their original factory condition. This extraordinary example retains 98% of its original finishes on both wood and metal and has never been wet, dirty or cleaned. As nice an example of the early No. 1 plane as we have ever offered. Highly recommended.* (FINE) **$2,750.00**

Group B1

B1-1. Stanley Rule & Level No. 1: 5 1/2 Inch Smooth Plane. Ca. 1915 "V" Trademark. Near New Condition. Length: 5 1/2 Inches. *The Stanley No. 1 planes were produced beginning in 1867 and remained in the Stanley product line until 1943, when they were "temporarily" discontinued due to wartime exigencies, never again to return to be offered. Tool folklore has it that these tools were designed for the hands of children and marketed to "manual training" schools, where their smaller-than-life proportions would be just about right. For a story so oft-repeated, there seems to be no documentary evidence to support the claim that these were intended largely or solely for this specialized market. Whatever the case, the legend continues that these tools were sold in large numbers, all but a very few were consumed during the scrap metal drives of the First and Second World Wars. This one seems to have escaped the years with practically no battle scars. Imprinted with the "V" shaped trademark that Stanley used from 1915 to 1922, this plane retains more than 99% of its original black japan finish. An exceptionally well-preserved example in collector-quality condition.* (FINE) **$1,850.00**

B1-2. Sargent & Co., New Haven Conn.: No. 1508 1/2: "Ladybug" Rabbet Metallic Plane. All Proper Parts. Rare and Sound. Length: 7 Inches. *Complete with all original parts, this Sargent classic is one of the most easily recognizable tools ever produced. Referred to as the "Lady Bug" plane by modern collectors, it is not likely that Sargent sold very many of these. Of those that were sold, most quickly became separated from their principal parts and, at least for the sake of future collectors, deteriorated significantly in value. This complete example is proudly offered without apology.* (GOOD) **$2,350.00**

B1-3. Grangeret A Paris: 18th Century Trepanation Brace. Fitted Leather Case. Essentially Complete. Length: 12 Inches. *Designed for the once-common medical practice of trepanation—the removal of circular sections of bone from the skull to reduce pressure from swelling on the brain, this extraordinary French brace has been preserved in nearly new condition in its original leather bound case for more nearly 150 years. Fitted with a turned ebony head and elaborately forged to a decorative form, this brace includes three original bits as well as several saws and other accessories in the classic velvet-lined French fit case. A few accessories are missing, but the tool is essentially complete. A classic specialized medical brace of the type not generally available in the market today. Early and excellent.* (FINE) **$5,250.00**

B1-4. Sutton, Charles D., Kensico, N.Y.: Personal Model Caliper. With Scientific American Magazine. Patented January 3, 1860. Length: 10 Inches. *We have often repeated our belief that the greatest, the most desirable and the most collectible antique tools are those that embody within them ideas that failed. The American patent system encouraged individuals of great mechanical genius, such as L.S. Starrett and Leonard Bailey to protect their ideas from being copied and allowed them to build great enterprises that supported and improved the lives of thousands of others. However, for every Leonard Bailey, there were perhaps a hundred, or even a thousand Charles D. Suttons. The incredible tool offered here, was without a doubt the personal model for a caliper patented on January 3, 1860 by one Charles D. Sutton of Kensico, New York. It includes the original bronze caliper, a photocopy of the patent papers and an original copy of Scientific American Magazine that discusses the recent invention of Charles D. Sutton. Alas, it appears that Mr. Sutton's considerable mechanical talent, as is obvious from this model, and the publicity provided by the Scientific American article, were not enough to overcome that fact that this tool was perhaps too complex and of such limited utility that it failed, as did so many inventions, to find favor in the marketplace. We know little of Mr. Sutton, other than what can be gleaned from the contents of this ancient box, but we can speculate that within this wooden case are preserved the dreams of success and fame that must have seemed so near and so very real in those heady days following the publication of the Scientific American article. An idea whose time never came and an extraordinarily rare and collectible antique tool.* (FINE) **$3,285.00**

B1-5. Stanley Rule & Level No. 44: Miller Patent Plow Plane. Patented June 26, 1870. Rare "Slitter" Version. Length: 9 Inches. *The least common of the "Miller Patent" series, Stanley's No. 44 gunmetal plow plane offered nearly all of the aesthetic appeal of the No. 42, but lacked the optional filletster bed. Given the difference in the cost of the planes, taken with the fact that these tools were quite expensive to begin with, it is likely that very few buyers who had made a decision to indulge themselves in the luxury of such a fancy tool would have hesitated over the cost when deciding whether or not to purchase the No. 42 instead of the No. 44. Consequently, even among Miller Patent planes in gunmetal, which are extremely rare in any case, the No. 44 is by far the rarest of all. Moreover, it is likely that it was not necessary to produce additional runs of the No. 44 as new "improvements" were added to the rest of the Miller Patent Series. In all likelihood, examples from the earlier production runs of the No. 44 series were still being sold as late as the late 1880's. Stanley introduced the rear "slitter" as an improvement on the Miller Patent in 1882; however, it is not likely that this feature was added to the No. 44 until some time later. Making a new group of planes simply because an "improvement" had been added would not have made practical business sense. Consequently, it may have been as late as the end of the decade by the time the No. 44 series with the slitter feature was produced. By this time, these planes had declined in popularity and, by 1897, they would be eliminated from the product line altogether. This late example of the No. 44 is equipped with the rare "slitter" feature as well as a full box of cutting irons in their original box. Much of the original lacquer finish remains on this well preserved example. An exceptionally rare Millers Patent plane in top collector quality condition.* (FINE) **$6,750.00**

B1-6. Stanley Rule & Level No. 164: Low Angle Block Plane. 1926-1943 Only. Super Rare, Top Shelf. Length: 9 Inches. *What is it about the Stanley No. 164 that places it in the highest echelon of collectible Stanley planes? Rarity is, of course, a major factor in the appeal of these special purpose planes to collectors; but simply because there may have been only a few hundred examples manufactured in the initial, and, likely, final, production run, does not in and of itself explain the intense pride of ownership of the select few who have acquired the 164, or the fact that collectors of Stanley planes, almost without exception, have reserved a spot on their uppermost shelf for the Ultimate in their area of interest. As one who, as a general principal, operates under the dictum "If you have to take it apart or turn it upside down to know that it is rare, you had better not buy it", my personal and professional opinion is that the acquisition of rare items, simply because they are few in number, is neither a wise collecting philosophy, nor one that is likely to make the search for antique tools an avocation that will provide rewards to last a lifetime. Without belaboring the point, the Stanley No. 164, is at the top of everyone's want list because it has appeal in every one of the many qualities by which we evaluate an antique tool. It is Rare. These planes were offered for only 18 years, and it is likely that they were in such low demand that only a single run of planes was manufactured. It has aesthetic appeal. The No. 164, despite its relatively late period of manufacture, is constructed of nickel plated steel, lacquered brass, perfectly machined cast iron and figured Brazilian Rosewood in a combination of materials and form that please both the eye and the soul. It is mechanically intriguing. The adjustment mechanism of the No. 164 is unlike anything produced before or since. There is a sixth sense that comes over time to all collectors. Fifty experienced seekers after wood and iron can scan thousands of objects laid out on tables in a room and quickly converge to a few special items. Why? Because they are different, and because they represent something more than just an object; and this leads us into the ultimate answer to the question of why such planes as this are so much wanted...Rarity, form and function—separately they hold our interest for a moment or two; but when they converge, there is the stuff of which a Great Collectible Tool is made. Such a tool is the Stanley 164. Patented by Edmund A. Schade, a man whose name is synonymous with the technological innovation of Stanley Tools; manufactured with a degree of workmanship and finish far beyond that which had come to be accepted for the time; intended for the most specific of purposes—the planing of finely figured woods; possessed of a mechanical intricacy unlike anything else; and so very, very few in number. This tool is history, it is technology, it is art, it is the synthesis of all—and it is more...It is, quite simply put, what all of this is all about. It is not likely that a finer example of this most collectible Stanley tool has ever been offered for sale. This example retains 99% of its original finishes on all wood and metal surfaces. It is offered without apology and is recommended without reservation. Magnificent. Manufactured under a patent issued to prolific inventor Edmund A. Schade, of the Stanley Rule and Level Plant of the Stanley Works, the No. 164 Low Angle Block Plane had been introduced to the Stanley product line a full two years before the official patent date of September 27, 1927.* (FINE) **$5,850.00**

B1-7. Stanley Rule & Level No. 62: Low Angle Block Plane. As New Condition. Original Box. Length: 14 Inches. *Why is it that certain Stanley Tools seem never to be found in their original boxes, while others seem to be found no other way? The No. 49 bit gauge comes readily to mind as an example of the latter type. When tool collectors talk, there is a practiced cadence to their exchange of information. "Tool talk" takes many forms, including bragging, complaining, lies, and damned lies. One favored style of the genre that has attained the level of an art form begins with a minimalist statement, designed to bait and draw in other collectors with "so what's" and "yeah but's" only to send them reeling with a previously withheld tidbit of information. In the case of the tool offered here, such an exchange might go as follows: "Get anything?" "Yeah, a few things." "Anything good?" "Yeah... A 62". "Oh yeah, I've got three." (the question mark now passes ownership as the baiting collector swoops for the kill...) "In the box?" "Oh." It's over. A masterfully executed case of one-upmanship in a game that has as its only equivalent, the angler's tale of "the one that got away". A superb example of a most unusual collectible Stanley special purpose plane....In the box.* (FINE) **$2,175.00**

B1-8. Norris, London No. 17: Rosewood Infill Metallic Plane. Gunmetal Body. Rare and Excellent. Length: 8 Inches. *One of only a handful of these planes that have surfaced, this rare Norris plane employs the unusual combination of gunmetal cap iron and sides together with an annealed steel sole. Nicely stuffed with Brazilian rosewood, this tool is in excellent collector quality condition and could be put to use in the shop of a craftsman, if the new owner so desires. A rare Norris plane in excellent collector quality condition.* (GOOD+) **$2,450.00**

B1-9. Casella, L., London: Inclinometer Folding Rule. With Integral Compass. New Condition, Original Box. Length: 9 Inches. *A number of English makers produced finely finished specialty measuring and navigating tools for gentlemen. These tools are generally formed of boxwood and brass and were never intended for the rough and tumble world of day to day work. This extraordinarily well preserved example of that class of tools is imprinted with the mark of one L. Casella, a mathematical instrument maker of London. Complete and essentially unused in its original fitted case, this tool incorporates a compass, protractor, a pair of levels, an inclinometer function and a series of calculating tables into a single tool. As nice a representation of this genre of tools that we have offered, tools of this quality are simply not available in today's market. Rare and near new.* (FINE) **$2,475.00**

B1-10. Stanley Rule & Level No. 196: Curve Rabbet Plane. Complete and Excellent. 90%+ Original Plating. Length: 9 Inches. *Manufactured under a patent issued on December 13, 1910 to Judd. W. Montague of Columbus, Ohio, Stanley's No. 196 curved rabbet plane was included in the Stanley product line beginning in 1912 and continued to be offered for more that twenty years. It is not likely, however, that many of these highly-specialized tools were sold. The creation of elaborate curved moldings was the province of a select few who would have had the expertise to do the work using traditional methods and would not be inclined to purchase a "gizmo" to do the job. The market, then, would have been that limited few who would purchase the tool in the hope that it would provide them with the skill. As anyone who has attempted to actually use one of these devils can attest, no skill was supplied with the tool. This example is complete, clean and shiny, missing only a few spots of nickel on the upper surfaces. An excellent example of one of the most complex and least common of all tools produced by Stanley. Top shelf.* (GOOD+) **$2,345.00**

B1-11. Stanley Rule & Level No. 72 1/2: Patent Chamfer, Bullnose Plane and Beading Attachment. New Condition, Original Box. Length: 8 Inches. *For some reason, planes of the Stanley "Bedrock" series in their original boxes are almost impossible to find. Your author knows of less than 10 planes in collections anywhere that are complete with the distinctive red-labeled Bedrock box. This No. 603 comes complete with the box, which retains its full, distinctive red "Bedrock label". The corners of the box have separated at the front, but could be easily repaired. A very well preserved plane in an extra rare box.* (FINE) **$2,950.00**

B1-12. Unmarked: Knowles Type Metallic Plane. Rare Smoothing Plane. Rare and Excellent. Length: 9 Inches. *The world in which Yankee inventor Hazard Knowles of Colchester, Connecticut lived in 1827 was one in which virtually everything was made of wood. The superabundance of wood in the Great American Forest made it expendable and seemingly limitless. It was against this backdrop that Knowles submitted his patent for a metallic plane (Restored Patent No. 4859 X) and proclaimed that planes made of metal were superior in many respects to those fashioned from wood. Planes had been made from metal as early as Roman times, but Knowles' reinvention came at a time when the ability to precisely machine metal in a cost effective way was just becoming available on a widespread basis. It would take 50 years before it became the generally accepted fact that metal planes were superior, and another hundred years before wooden planes disappeared from catalogs, but the path of history was clearly charted by Knowles invention. This classic "Knowles Type" smoothing plane incorporates the cast iron wedge holding mechanism documented in the patent and is in clean, sound condition throughout. As is the case with all other known examples, this tool is not marked with the Knowles name or patent information, but is of the classic type. A rare and historically significant smoothing plane in excellent collector quality condition.* (GOOD+) **$2,850.00**

B1-13. Unmarked: Salesman's Sample Reversible Plow. N.H. Ca. 1880-1890. Perfectly Preserved. Length: 15 Inches. *Among some dealers in antiques, it is a common practice to characterize anything smaller than standard size as a "salesman's sample". We have seen many of the individual items from children's toolboxes put forward as "samples", despite the fact that they were of the very crudest construction. A true salesman's sample serves a very specific purpose: it allows a product representative to demonstrate the selling points of a large product, without it being necessary to bring the actual object to the potential customer or dealer. True salesman's samples are very highly detailed. Truly great salesman's samples have both a very high level of detail and are in nearly new condition. This superb 19th Century plow possesses all of those characteristics in ample measure. Retaining all original finishes and created as an exact model of the original adjustable plow it was intended to market, this extraordinary marketing item is at the very highest echelon of this class of collectible antique. A truly great salesman's sample.* (FINE) **$2,475.00**

B1-14. Stanley Rule & Level No. 12 3/4: Adjustable Scraper Plane. With Special Facing. "Sweetheart" Trademark. Length: 5 3/4 Inches. *This one is on the "short list" of every advanced Stanley collector, and rightly so. Very few examples of this special-purpose scraper plane have ever appeared in the antique tool market. This one, with over 95% of the original paint and finish, rates near the top level of condition. As is the case with other specimens, this plane has the casting mark, "12 1/2" in the body; but, as is the case with the few other known examples, the throat opening was refitted in the factory to a full 1 inch and specially fitted thick rosewood plates are affixed to the underside of the plane. Fitted brass receivers set into the special sole plates are the one necessary ingredient for positive identification of this very rare tool. Those receivers are present on this example and retain their original factory lacquer finish. Certainly one of the rarest of all Stanley planes. This one is as good as they get. Where do you find them?* (FINE) **$3,450.00**

B1-15. Chelor, Ce., Living in Wrentham: Early Fixed Sash Molding Plane. Replaced Iron. Extra Bold Stamp. Length: 10 Inches. *Imagine a freed slave engaged in private commerce as very likely the second professional planemaker ever to work in the American colonies; this, at a point some one hundred and ten years before the Great American Civil War that would settle the question of human slavery forever in this nation. That the tools of Cesar Chelor were works of art, better (some have offered than those of his master and his master's son) is unquestioned. The survival of several hundred known examples from this extremely early time indicates that Chelor produced a substantial number of planes which must have been eagerly sought out. Examples have been found in the most unlikely places throughout the U.S. and in foreign locations such as England and Texas. This example has been boldly struck with the imprint "Ce. Chelor, Living in Wrentham" in the style used by the first commercial American planemakers. This tool has seen some substantial use, and the cutting iron is a later replacement, but the strike on the toe is visible from across a room. Clearly marked, old as the hills and an important piece of American technological and cultural history. A rare and important American wooden plane.* (GOOD) **$2,550.00**

B1-16. Roberts, Edw., Grocers Alley, London: Rare 3 Slide Boxwood Slide Rule. B. Bennington, 1752. Early and Important. Length: 12 Inches. *One of the earliest boxwood slide rules we have offered, this extraordinary rule was made by Edw. D. Roberts, whose working location is inscribed on the inside of the slide as "...in Grocers Alley in Old Jewry LONDON". Beneath the slide on the reverse side has been inscribed, undoubtedly by Edward Roberts' hand, using the same stamps as for his own name, the inscription "*BENJAMIN:BENNINGTON Supervisor:1752*". In all likelihood, a bit of archival research could unearth the identity of Benjamin Bennington, reveal his occupation and perhaps shed some additional light on the type of person who would have used a slide rule in 1752. A rare and well preserved early dated slide rule having only a few spots of minor staining on its 250 year old body.* (GOOD+) **$2,275.00**

Group C1

C1-1. Stanley Rule & Level No. 42: Miller Patent Plow Plane. Patented June 28, 1870. With Set of Cutters. Length: 9 Inches. *Produced under a patent granted to Charles Miller of Brattleborough, Vermont on June 28, 1870, the "Miller's Patent" series of plow and filletster planes produced by the Stanley Rule & Level Company are generally regarded as among the most beautiful hand tools ever produced. This example of the top of the line No. 42 combination plow and filletster plane is an example of the style designated by collectors as "Type 6a" and it is equipped with the slitter and rear depth stop that were introduced on these planes. Complete with the original cast iron outside fence, the proper gunmetal "wraparound" fence as well as a full set of proper cutting irons in their original box, this plane has been carefully kept in a private collection for the past 25 years. A rare opportunity to acquire one of the rarest and most desirable of all Stanley planes.* (FINE) **$5,650.00**

C1-2. Greenfield Tool Co., Greenfield, Mass.: Rosewood Filletster Plane. Boxwood Arms and Nuts. Rare and Excellent. Length: 9 1/2 Inches. *Screw arm filletster planes by American makers are so scarce that many serious tool collectors with ten or twenty years of experience have never even seen one. These planes were a bit too specialized for the workaday world of the Nineteenth Century. When such planes are found, they are usually holding a place of honor in a collection. Those examples that have been found are generally the work Upstate New York makers or the major Ohio planemakers and are crafted of beech with boxwood arms and nuts. This extraordinary example of the configuration, which was recently acquired from an old-time New Hampshire collection bears the imprint of the Greenfield Tool Company of Greenfield Massachusetts and is crafted of dramatically grained Brazilian Rosewood. Arms and nuts of Turkish Boxwood provide a stark color contrast. The plane has only minor dings around the throat opening. The original wedge was sheared, and has been replaced by a masterfully executed replacement by master restorationist Robert Baker. An extremely rare screw arm filletster plane in a most appealing combination of exotic woods. Highly recommended.* (FINE) **$1,675.00**

C1-3. Unmarked: Ivory Tip Boxwood Plow Plane. Superb Patina. Ready to Use. Length: 11 Inches. *Handled boxwood plow planes with ivory tips on the stems are among the most visually appealing of all antique hand tools. Fashioned more for show than for functionality, these tools were meant to demonstrate a pride in craftsmanship, not only to the owner of the tool, but also to those for whom he practiced his trade, and to those who worked with him. This example, which has as its only detraction a tight crack through the fence that was carefully re-glued many years ago, possesses a dark golden patina that stands out among the steel gray and dark brown of so many antique tools. The threads on the arms have only minimal checking and the tips are in clean, bright white condition. Top shelf.* (GOOD+) **$1,150.00**

C1-4. Carpenter, E.W., Lancaster, Penna.: Improved Patent Plow Plane. Patented February 6, 1838. Varnall & McClure. Length: 7 Inches. *Students of planes and planemaking, the "science" that has given itself the lofty sounding designation as "Rhykenology" (from the Greek word for "plane"), will tell all who will listen that the development of wooden planeaking, as it moved from the Eighteenth to the Nineteenth Centuries, was one of standardization of styles, sizes and means of production. As is the case with all such historical truisms, however, there will be one or more who will attempt to run against that common thread. In the history of wooden planemaking there was no more striking exception to the trend than Emanuel W. Carpenter of Lancaster Pennsylvania. When other planemakers were moving quickly toward standardization in the 1830's and 1840's, Carpenter was defining his own unique style that would be carried on by his apprentices before they, too, were carried away by the tide of automation and uniformity. Carpenter's planes were frequently short, while others were making planes of a common 9 1/2" length. His planes featured dramatic oversized wedges when others were moving quickly toward mass produced wedges that sacrificed style to efficiency. Where Carpenter's planes deviated most from the norm, however, was when he produced the special purpose planes, such as plows, filletsters and sash planes where exotic materials and elaborate adjustments could be employed in large measure as a full indulgence of the Carpenter style. Working with rosewood, boxwood and other woods, Carpenter crafted a large number of spectacular tools that are today appreciated as much for their artistic merits as they are for their technological achievements. This spectacular boxwood plow, which employs the patent granted to E.W. Carpenter on February 6, 1838, but is not marked with the patent date, has been executed with adjustment screws of turned Brazilian Rosewood which provide a striking contrast to the rich golden color of the body and fence of grainless Turkish Boxwood. Most likely sold to a Philadelphia hardware dealer for resale, this plane is imprinted on the heel with the mark of Varnall & McClure, who marketed tools and hardware in Philadelphia in the 1840's. Clean, complete, boldly struck with the Carpenter imprint and having achieved a warm golden patina of age and careful use, we proudly offer this spectacular example of Emanuel W. Carpenter's unique and artistic planemaking style. Simply a great plow plane.* (GOOD+) **$5,450.00**

C1-5. Stanley Rule & Level No. 602 C: 7 Inch "Bedrock" Smooth Plane. Early Type. Super Rare. Length: 7 Inches. *As a newcomer to the tool world more years ago than are comfortable to remember, this writer made his first trip to the grand carnival known as the Brimfield Antique Market. More fascinating than the rush of people and the spectacle of the pageantry was an object that appeared in the booth of an antique dealer as he was setting out his merchandise during the initial panic of buying that defines the beginning of any Brimfield show. The tool collectors crowded around as the boxes were unpacked. Some items were purchased, others shunned and set aside. And then...then it appeared. There was a hush, followed by a low murmur of approval. It was the No. 602 early Bedrock plane with corrugated bottom—the rarest of the series, by far, and one of the most sought-after planes in all of Christendom. Soon the price became known: A THOUSAND DOLLARS! Amidst more murmuring and a fair share of dutiful harrumphing, the bargain hunters left in a huff. The serious people stayed, for it was indeed a magnificent tool—oh so rare, and in perfect condition. A novice gawked in the background. In due course, with longing looks, the serious people faded away saying things like "that's nice" or "just too much". The novice came back several times in the next hour to view the object of such interest and rarity and oh, yes, such cost. He was never alone when looking. At least one bargain hunter haranguing the dealer about excess or a collector lost in rapture was always in the booth. And then it happened. On the third or fourth trip back to the see the magical object, the space where it had been was empty! But what? "Sold," said the dealer. "Shazamm!" ,said the novice. Many years have passed since that day, and in all of that time, your enterprising author has seen nary an early model of the 602 C in travels both near and far. Nowhere...until now. The plane offered here retains 98% plus of its original finishes on all surfaces and is in never-need-to-upgrade condition. Feel free to turn back to this page and gawk. The picture will always be here.* (FINE) **$2,475.00**

C1-6. Campbell, Ja.: Ogee and Astragal Molding Plane. Yellow Birch Body. Very Early Appearance. Length: 10 1/4 Inches. *At the time of the production of the first commercially made planes in the then 13 Colonies in North America, it is likely that the first half dozen planemakers knew each other and may have worked together. The maker whose name appears on this tool, one "Ja. Campbell", is not documented in any reference we have seen, but the style and length of this plane as well as the Yellow Birch material from which it is fashioned make it likely that this plane was produced no later than 1750. Of an inordinately complex pattern and boldly struck with the maker's mark this plane has the characteristics of a manufactured plane from the very earliest period of planemaking. A rare opportunity to acquire a top quality example of the work of an early planemaker.* (FINE) **$1,475.00**

C1-7. Stanley Rule & Level No. 42: Miller's Patented Fillet Plane. Gunmetal Body. Recast Bronze Fence. Length: 10 Inches. *Complete with its original cast iron filletster bed and nicely patinated, this tool was originally missing the bronze "wraparound" fence, but it has been replaced by a recently recast gunmetal replacement that was produced using an original as a model. Differing only slightly in coloration from the original, this tool offers an opportunity for a collector to acquire a classic Miller Patent gunmetal plow plane at substantially less than market value. An opportunity.* (FINE) **$2,850.00**

C1-8. Dean, S., Dedham (Mass.): Early Bilection Molding Plane. Yellow Birch Body. AWP III: 4 Stars "A". Length: 9 1/2 Inches. *One of the very earliest of American planemakers, the S. Dean of Dedham, Massachusetts whose imprint has been boldly struck on the toe of this plane was likely Samuel Dean, who was listed as a joiner living in Dedham from 1737 to 1747. Dedham is only a few miles from Wrentham, Massachusetts, where Francis Nicholson and Cesar Chelor worked as the first documented American Planemakers and it seems likely that Dean would have known these contemporaries and competitors. Boldly struck with the "S* Dean/Dedham" mark that has been designated as imprint "A" in American Wooden planes, this early Yellow Birch molder is very likely more than 260 years old. A magnificent example of early American planemaking. Ex-Cooley Collection.* (GOOD+) **$2,250.00**

C1-9. Metallic Plane Co., Auburn, N. Y.: Early Filletster Metallic Plane. With Proper Fence. Rare and Excellent. Length: 10 Inches. *A prolific maker of patented metallic planes in the earliest days of the manufacture of such tools, the Metallic Plane Company of Auburn, New York was known for their innovative and artistically conceived tools. A wide range of bench planes, produced under the Palmer & Storkes patents were marketed, as were an array of other special purpose planes, including a plow, block planes and this graphic filletster plane. Notably susceptible to breakage owing to the lack of refinement at this stage of the casting process, this plane is completely sound, noting some minor flaking on the fence. The rear adjustment lever, in an "improvement" by an early owner, originally consisted of a lever, but it has been replaced by a forked lever regulated by a screw. The modification could be easily reversed. Seldom found in this condition with a complete cast iron fence, this example of the Metallic Plane Company filletster plane will be a credit to any collection of early patented planes.* (GOOD+) **$1,050.00**

C1-10. Fenn, J., Newgate St. (London): Early Patent Metallic Plane. "Bailey" Lever Cap. An Important Plane. Length: 6 3/4 Inches. *Patented by Joseph Fenn of London, England in 1844, this spring lock cap transitional plane anticipated, in many ways the lever cap and depth of cut adjustment features later patented by Leonard Bailey. It has been estimated by metallic plane researcher and author Roger K. Smith that less than half a dozen of these early patent planes are known to exist in the world. An early, well preserved and technologically important transitional plane.* (GOOD+) **$2,650.00**

C1-11. Stanley Rule & Level No. 51/52: Shute Board and Plane. Near New Condition. 99% Original Paint. Length: 22 Inches. *Finding the Stanley No. 51/52 Shoot Board and Plane Combination in complete condition is only slightly less difficult than succeeding in the search for the proverbial hen's teeth, but infinitely more rewarding for the collector of antique tools. This rare, complete example is in superb condition, with more than 95% of the original paint, although some flaking of the japanning has occurred on the plane body and some of the nickeled parts have dulled. This is a crisp example that could be significantly improved with some judicious cleaning. Extra hard to find.* (FINE) **$1,950.00**

C1-12. Stanley Rule & Level No. 1: Smooth Plane. "Sweetheart" Trademark. Near New Condition. Length: 5 1/2 Inches. *These diminutive gems were produced beginning in 1867 and remained in the Stanley product line until 1943, when they were "temporarily" discontinued due to wartime exigencies, never again to return to be offered. Tool folklore has it that these tools were designed for the hands of children and marketed to "manual training" schools, where their smaller-than-life proportions would be just about right. For a story so oft-repeated, there seems to be no documentary evidence to support the claim that these were intended largely or solely for this specialized market. Whatever the case, the legend continues that these tools were sold in large numbers, but all but a very few were consumed during the scrap metal drives of the First and Second World Wars. This one seems to have escaped the years with no battle scars whatsoever. Imprinted with the "Sweetheart" trademark that Stanley used from 1922 to 1933, this plane retains more than 99% of its orignal black japan finish. An exceptionally well-preserved example in collector-quality condition.* (FINE) **$1,695.00**

C1-13. Sanford, Levi, East Solon, N.Y.: Patent Transitional Metallic Plane. Patented November 26, 1844. 2nd Known Example. Length: 16 Inches. *In searching for their technological roots, the folks who put together "The Story of the Plane" as their Educational Chart No. 131 in the 1930's selected this obscure plane and featured it for its significance in moving planes to their "modern" form. Cited in Roger Smith's classic "Patented Metallic and Transitional Planes in America" as "one of the first major contributions" to improving the methods of adjusting and holding the cutter, what was then believed to be the only known example of this plane is illustrated on Page 17 of that book. Patented on November 26, 1844 by Levi Sanford of Solon, New York, it is likely that this important patent was retrofitted on a conventional jack or jointer plane. This example is imprinted only with the maker mark "JONES", stamped upside down on the toe. A rare and historically significant transitional plane that is clearly marked with the early and important patent date.* (GOOD) **$2,875.00**

C1-14. Woodrough & Mc Parlin: Rare Panther Head Saw. Carved Handle. Very Well Preserved. Length: 24 Inches. *As famous a tool as any that was ever produced, the Woodrough & McParlin panther head saw was featured in an article about antique tool collecting that was published in Smithsonian Magazine approximately 10 years ago. Based on a design patent issued to J.R. Woodrough on January 13, 1880, the saw has as its principal feature a handle that is carved in the shape of a panther's head. We are aware of less than a dozen examples of this rare saw. This one is sound and intact, but it is missing one of the saw bolts, which could be easily replaced, and the blade has seen some use. An extremely rare and graphic figural saw.* (FINE) **$1,850.00**

C1-15. Unmarked: Macassar Ebony Plow Plane. With 8 Cutting Irons. Made By Deforest? Length: 10 1/2 Inches. *All too often, the tools that we find in the markets, meetings and shops have about them a certain sameness and soulessness. The cognoscenti of the Tool World, in their flair for technical specificity, have properly characterized this accumulation of the woefully nondescript as "stuff". What a joy it is, when surveying the masses of mill-run tools to find among their number such an object of beauty as this extraordinary screw arm plow plane. Painstakingly crafted of exotic macassar ebony and apparently very little used, this plane has the color of a deliciously swirled mix of coffee brown, amber and dark, red wine. The pattern of the fence exactly matches that of the planes of Linson DeForest of Birmingham, Connecticut, who produced planes, including a number of very well made exotic wood plow planes, between 1850 and 1858. Absent any major evidence of wear and having only minor flaking from the turned boxwood arms, this spectacular plane comes complete with a full set of plane Sheffield cutting irons. As nice a plow plane as we have offered in some time. Top shelf.* (GOOD+) **$1,485.00**

C1-16. Union Mfg. Co., New Britain, Conn. No. 44: Cast Iron Bead Metallic Plane. 1/2 Inch Size. Rare and Excellent. Length: 8 Inches. *One of the most unusual of all cast iron planes offered by the competing makers of metallic planes at the beginning of this century, the No. 44 bead plane was offered in three sizes, of which this, the 1/2 inch size, was the largest. Little is know of the origins of this plane, although it bears a great similarity to the Gocher Patent cast iron bead plane and may have been inspired by, if not directly descended from, that tool.* (GOOD+) **$2,850.00**

C1-17. Lowell Plane & Tool Co.: Worall's Patent Metallic Plane. Patented June 23, 1857. Early and Extra Crisp. Length: 21 1/2 Inches. *A pioneering manufacturer of patented transitional planes who just happened to be a minister and the Pastor of the Mt. Holly Baptist Church in Mt. Holly, New Jersey. Thomas Worrall patented his first plane in 1854 and, shortly thereafter resigned his post and moved to Boston, leaving behind "disunion, financial troubles and pastoral indiscretions". Upon arriving in Boston, Worral was granted his second patent, the date of which is stamped on the toe and his third patent, which is cast into the body of the casting of this very well preserved fore plane. Complete, retaining 90% of its original japan finish and most of the original lacquer finish on the wood, this is the sort of patented plane that comes to market very, very seldom.* (FINE) **$1,475.00**

C1-18. Pool, H.M., Easton, Mass.: Classic "Y" Level. Engraved Imprint. Fitted Wood Case. Length: 17 Inches. *The Romance of the American Continent and the progress of civilization through a largely uninhabited and undeveloped wasteland was brought about through the efforts of the enterprising men who confronted the frontier. Working in concert with those who gave them the technology to conquer that frontier, these enterprising Americans brought a better quality of life to all. As symbols of the inexorable Westward movement of America, the surveyor and the railroad were always at front and center of this process. This classic "Y" level, from Easton, Massachusetts maker H.M. Pool incorporates, within a single object, both of those important participants in the taming of the West. Functionally complete and nicely aged to a patina of yellow gold, this classic surveyor's tool is engraved with the imprint of the Northern Pacific Railroad (N.P.R.R.) and must, most certainly, have been used in the process of laying railroads through the vast expanses of the North Plains States. Found in Northern Minnesota many years ago and carefully kept in a collection, this level, which retains what appears to be its original case, is ready to be proudly displayed among those who are not ashamed of America's heritage of greatness. An American classic.* (GOOD+) **$1,150.00**

Group D1

D1-1. Stanley, W. F., London (England): Boucher's Calculator. German Silver Case. Near New Condition. Length: 2 1/2 Inches. *Some of the earliest and most innovative slide rules were not slide rules at all, but the same principles were applied to producing, in circular format, the same scales that would have taken substantially more space on a wooden rule. Although they lacked the everyday practicality of basic calculating rules, these tools appealed to "gentlemen" as they could be kept in the vest pocket for ready access when needed. Because of their limited utility, few of these were likely sold. What is certain is that very few have survived. This extraordinarily well preserved example, which is marked "Boucher's Calculator" on the reverse side and it imprinted with the maker name of W.F. Stanley of London is fashioned from German silver and is in much the same condition as it would have been when new. Very likely dating to the earliest years of the Twentieth Century, this classic circular slide rule is ready for the vest pocket or a place of honor in a quality collection.* (FINE) **$1,175.00**

D1-2. Stanley Rule & Level (Unmarked) No. 58 1/2: Two Foot, Six Fold Folding Rule. Arch Joint, Full Bound. Extra Rare. Length: 24 Inches. *A step above the more common No. 58, Stanley's No. 58 1/2 added full brass binding in this top of the line six-fold rule. This unmarked example has seen very little wear and is clean, sound and ready to display. A very rare Stanley rule.* (GOOD+) **$975.00**

D1-3. Thornton, A. G., Manchester: Presentation Architect's Rule. R. J. Hughes From Joseph Owen, Original Box. Length: 24 Inches. *Among the most desirable of all collectible antique tools are those that were purchased as a presentation item for a colleague. Such tools are generally of extra quality, as they were generally meant to convey a level of achievement in one's trade of profession. This immaculate broad ivory folding rule is bright white condition in its original presentation box from instrument makers A.G. Thornton of Manchester, England. On the hinge, it is inscribed "R.J. Hughes from Joseph Owen". An exceptionally well preserved presentation ivory rule.* (FINE) **$845.00**

D1-4. Chadwick, J., Manchester: Engineer's Calculating Folding Rule. Rare "Chadwick" Scale. German Silver Fitting. Length: 24 Inches. *Fitted out with an arch joint and Gunter slide of German silver, this special engineer's rule was made to be something special at the time it was produced in the late Nineteenth Century. The face of the rule is imprinted with a form of Engineer's scale, designated as the "Chadwick" scale. It is similar in many respects to the more common Routledge scale, but very much less common. Apparently never used, or opened other than for inspection, this rare calculating rule is in absolutely immaculate condition. Highly recommended.* (FINE) **$945.00**

D1-5. Rabone & Sons, Makers, Birmingham: Ivory Architects Folding Rule. Early Style. Near New Condition. Length: 24 Inches. *Why it is that most of the tens of thousands of ivory rules that were produced quickly turned yellow or cracked, while others, such as this pristine example, were able to pass 100 years or more in essentially brand new condition will never be known. What is a certainty, however, is that this classic German silver and ivory two foot rule, which has been fashioned in the classic "Architect's" pattern with beveled inside edges, is nearly as sharp and white as it was when first produced by John Rabone in Birmingham, England in the 1880's. As nice an ivory rule as we have offered for some time.* (FINE) **$545.00**

D1-6. Greenleaf, F.M., Littleton, N.H.: Rare Cordwood Caliper. Original Finish. Near New Condition. Length: 48 Inches. *It is perhaps not particularly noteworthy that quality lumber caliper rules were produced by New Hampshire native F.M. Greenleaf in several locations in New England, and eventually, in the deep South. It is however, interesting to note that in addition to being a prolific producer of what are generally regarded as the best lumber calipers ever made, Greenleaf also put additional skills to use as the first violinist for the Boston Symphony Orchestra at the beginning of the Twentieth Century. Most noteworthy of all, however, is the fact that the multi-talented F.M. Greenleaf was known to friends as Flossie Greenleaf and that she was, without question, the most successful female maker of hand tools of all time. Having learned the trade from her father, who had practically invented these tools, Flossie continued to make tools of the same style, including this rare set of cordwood calipers, which are graduated with most unusual scales developed for this specialized task. Retaining nearly all of their original yellow lacquer finish and absent any evidence of use whatsoever, these are the finest set of these special purpose calipers that we have ever offered. Extra special.* (FINE) **$2,450.00**

D1-7. Stanley Rule & Level No. 40: One-Foot, Four Fold Folding Rule. Ivory and German Silver. Original Case. Length: 12 Inches. *Stanley's ivory rules are found today in only two levels of condition: Rare and Great. All surviving examples fall generally into the first category. There simply were not very many of these rules sold. The were intended from the very beginning to be indulgences and not considered useful for practical applications. Surviving rules that fit into the "Great" category have the following defining characteristics: They are bright white—ivory had a natural tendency to yellow with age. Those that did not are rare. They have tight, unsprung joints—these were presentation rules almost exclusively and using one would be akin to employing a commemorative groundbreaking shovel to plant your garden. This extraordinary example of Stanley's No. 40 one foot, four fold rule possesses both of those characteristics, thanks in large part to the presence of the original leather case that was supplied with the rule. Crisp, clean, bright white and absolutely perfect. Highly recommended.* (FINE) **$785.00**

D1-8. Gargory, James: Set of 6 Ivory Scale Rules. Fitted Leather Case. Rare and Excellent. Length: 2 Inches. *Specialized scale rules such as these would have been used by architects for laying out complex drawings. A fitted leather case has kept the full set of six rules in nearly new condition. All are absent any chips or yellowing. An exceptional set in top condition.* (FINE) **$325.00**

D1-9. Stanley Rule & Level No. 752: "Zig Zag" Folding Rule. Rare Size and Type. Ca. 1915. Length: 24 Inches. *The least common, by far, of all Stanley rules were those in the smaller sizes. It simply made no sense, to a woodworker considering making the transition from the standard two foot, four fold rule that had been in use for nearly 100 years to go to a lighter, less durable rule of the same length. The folks at Stanley Rule & Level seem to have come to this realization soon after the release of their "Zig Zag" line as the 2 foot rules were soon discontinued from the product line. What examples were sold were likely broken and discarded. This well marked example is marked with the early "ZZ" imprint and the "Victor" designation. A rare and highly collectible Stanley Zig Zag rule.* (GOOD) **$195.00**

D1-10. Taggart, Thomas, Grasmere, N.H.: Taggart's Saw Log Caliper. Mathematical Instrument Maker. With Ship Logo. Length: 36 Inches. *This spectacularly well preserved log caliper retains its full original paper label, which features an elaborate engraving of a ship and the signature of Thomas Taggart, "Mathematical Instrument Maker", of Grasmere, New Hampshire. An early and uncommon measuring instrument in superb condition. Highly recommended.* (FINE) **$765.00**

D1-11. Stanley Rule & Level (Unmarked?) No. 75: Early Advertising Folding Rule. Washington, D.C. Near New Condition. Length: 24 Inches. *The pentagonal pin at the joint is a sure indication that this very early advertising rule was produced by the Stanley Rule & Level Company for the Washington Hydraulic Press Brick Company of Washington, D.C., whose name appears on the outside of the rule. No. 75 rules are rare in their own right, as are advertising rules, especially those from the ca. 1880's period. This extraordinary example retains virtually all of its original finishes and is in essentially the same shape it would have been in when it left the Stanley factory. Extra special.* (FINE) **$545.00**

D1-12. Rabone & Sons, Makers, Birmingham No. 1167: Ivory Architects Folding Rule. R.G. Cooke, Wolverhampton. Near New Condition. Length: 24 Inches. *This spectacularly well preserved ivory architect's rule from premier makers John Rabone & Sons of Birmingham is also engraved with the name "R.G. Cooke, Wolverhampton" in a circular pattern on the German silver joint. The inside edges of the rule are beveled in the classic architect's pattern and the rule is bright white crisp and unused. A classic collectible ivory rule.* (FINE) **$550.00**

D1-13. Stanley Rule & Level: Rare Foot Measure Rule. Not Catalogued. Rare and Excellent. Length: 15 Inches. *The shoe measure rule was never offered in any Stanley catalog and at the time of the publication of Phil Stanley's book, Boxwood and Ivory, there was only one example known. This is the second or third specimen to surface and it is clearly marked and in top collector quality condition. A once in a lifetime opportunity for the serious rule collector.* (GOOD+) **$975.00**

D1-14. Stanley Rule & Level N1o. 39 M & E: One-Foot, Four Fold Folding Rule. Ivory and German Silver. With Metric Graduations. Length: 12 Inches. *This bright white Stanley No. 39 rule is graduated with the optional metric and English scales that were available to customers, but seldom ordered. Only a very tight, thin crack in the body requires mention on this spectacularly well preserved Stanley rule. Crisp, clean and clearly marked with the Stanley name.* (FINE) **$1,195.00**

D1-15. Cowgill, C.D.: Patent Rule Accessory. With H. Chapin Rule. Rare and Perfect. Length: 24 Inches. *Fitting into the category identified in Phil Stanley's classic "Boxwood and Ivory" as a "Purchaser Modified Rule", the Cowgill's Patent rule consists of a standard boxwood four-fold rule (in this case an H. Chapin rule), to which a patented attachment has been affixed to enable to function as an angle divider. Examples of this rule have been observed with Chapin-Stephens rules and also with Stanley rules, so it is likely that the manufacturer simply took what was available and refitted it with the patent attachment. This example is in excellent condition, clean and clearly marked. A rare rule attachment in excellent collector quality condition.* (GOOD+) **$895.00**

D1-16. Stanley Rule & Level No. 6: Two Foot, Two Fold Folding Rule. With Engineer's Tables. As New Condition. Length: 24 Inches. *Stanley offered its engineer's rule in both a bound and an unbound version. It only stands to reason that a prospective buyer of a relatively expensive, highly specialized rule would not concern himself with saving a few pennies to buy an unbound version. Consequently, the unbound No. 6 version is substantially less common than its full bound counterpart, the No. 16 Engineer's Rule, which is itself extremely scarce. The example of the No. 6 offered here retains 99% of its original finishes on both wood and metal. This rare rule is as shiny and clean as the day it was made. Top shelf.* (FINE) **$1,295.00**

D1-17. Perfection & Columbia Novelty Co.: Perfection Patent Rule. Patented January 8, 1895. Rare and Near New. Length: 12 Inches. *Imprinted with its early patent date and retaining the original paper label, this boxwood desk rule incorporates within its body a stylus-operated calculator and tally counter to facilitate mathematical calculations. One of the earliest examples, if not the earliest example, of this type of calculator that we have seen, this one hundred year old rule is in virtually the same condition as it was the day it was made. Perfect.* (FINE) **$625.00**

D1-18. Stanley Rule & Level No. 89: Two Foot, Four Fold Folding Rule. Double Arch Joint. Ivory and German Silver. Length: 24 Inches. *Stanley's top-of-the-line rule in the standard width, the No. 89 ivory and German silver rule was fitted with a pair of the highest quality "arch" joints. Such a tool as this would have likely been presented as a commemorative gift, as its cost and limited functionality made it impractical for everyday use. Only slight yellowing deserves mention on this rare and very high quality rule. Nice.* (GOOD+) **$1,150.00**

D1-19. Chapin, E.M. No. 64: Broad Ivory Folding Rule. With Arch Joint. White Ivory. Length: 24 Inches. *Among the rarest of all ivory rules are those of the extra quality "broad" width. Ivory rules were sold at a substantial premium price even during the days when it seemed there was an unlimited supply. The extra wide offerings, such as this E.M. Chapin No. 64, were exponentially more expensive. This well marked example has only slight yellowing and a single cross grain crack to the ivory worth noting as apologies. Bold, dramatic and ready to proudly display.* (GOOD+) **$745.00**

D1-20. Stearns & Co., E.A. No. 2: Engineer's Folding Rule. With Routledge Tables. Superb Condition. Length: 24 Inches. *A pioneer in the marketing of calculating rules for engineers, architects and builders, the E.A. Stearns Company offered a wide range of these tools in every conceivable configuration. This brass two foot, two fold rule is fitted out with a Gunter slide and engineers tables and is in nearly new condition. Practically perfect and highly recommended.* (FINE) **$1,295.00**

D1-21. Stanley Rule & Level No. 35: 2 Foot Bench Rule. With Board Scales. Extremely Rare. Length: 24 Inches. *One of the least common of all Stanley rules, the No. 35 bench rule was included in Stanley's product line from 1855 through 1892 only. During that time, very few examples were likely sold. Combining the function of a standard two foot bench rule with that of a board measure rule, the face of the tool was imprinted with both inch scales and board measure tables. In practical application its was likely too large and too fragile to be useful. The narrowness of the rule, in comparison to other board measuring devices, very likely lead to a level of breakage that has contributed to the rarity of this rule today. Clean, clearly marked with the Stanley name and missing only one of the brass end plates, this Stanley classic is in excellent collector quality condition. Extra special.* (GOOD+) **$1,450.00**

D1-22. Unmarked No. 0: 6 Inch, 2 Fold Folding Rule. Brass Joint and Tips. Advertising Rule? Length: 6 Inches. *A number of rules have been observed, both with the Stanley name imprint and without, that are imprinted with the number designation "0" or "00". Rule expert Phil Stanley has speculated that these rules were likely produced by Stanley from remaining ivory stock after the discontinuation of their lines of ivory rules as gifts for customers. This example is imprinted with the "No. 0" designation, but not the Stanley name. A rare ivory rule.* (GOOD+) **$695.00**

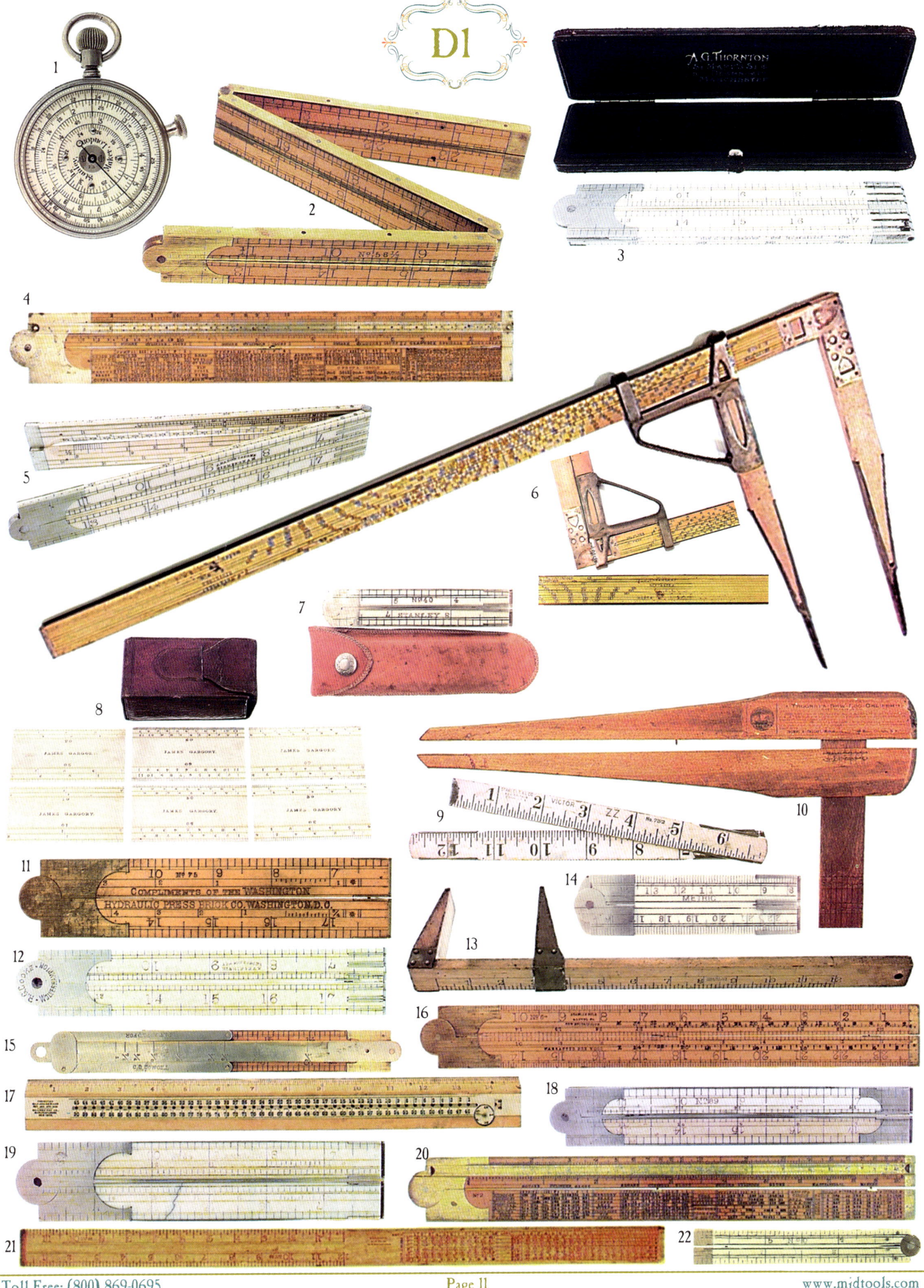

Group E1

E1-1. Stanley Rule & Level No. 44: Bit and Square Level. Patented November 16, 1886. Early Green Box. Length: 2 Inches. *Stanley probably didn't win any design prizes for these patented brass and glass levels. Designed to be screwed onto a bit brace, it seems unlikely that many skilled craftsmen would have gone for such a gizmo. This early example is in the early-type green pasteboard box and the level itself is in as-new condition. A rare level in top shape.* (FAIR) **$195.00**

E1-2. Stanley Rule & Level No. 85: Pivot Handle Scraper Plane. Patented April 11, 1905. Near New Condition. Length: 8 Inches. *This example of Stanley's rare pivoting handle scraper plane retains 99%+ of its original japan finish. Nicely grained Brazilian rosewood handles accent this rare collectible tool. Superb.* (FINE) **$975.00**

E1-3. Stanley Rule & Level No. 2: 7 Inch Cast Iron Smooth Plane. Prelateral Type. Early and Excellent. Length: 7 Inches. *Early examples of Stanley's No. 2 plane seem to be much less common in relation to other bench planes than is the case with later examples of the No. 2. Whatever the case, there is no question that this, the last of Stanley's four "prelateral" offerings is among the least common of all No. 2 size planes. Clean, complete and ready to proudly display. Rare.* (GOOD+) **$775.00**

E1-4. Stanley Rule & Level No. 98: "Scholar's" 1 Foot Rule. Rare Marked Example. Excellent Condition. Length: 12 Inches. *The No. 98 "Scholar's" rule was included in the Stanley product line from 1867 to 1933, but very few examples are known with the Stanley name marked on the body of the rule. This example appears to date from 1890 or thereabout. A rare Stanley rule.* (FINE) **$225.00**

E1-5. Stanley Rule & Level No. 2: Three Angle Rule Tool. Patented August 8, 1911. 1911-1935 Only. Length: 2 1/2 Inches. *Designed to fit onto a standard carpenter's rule, this patented gizmo was produced under a 1911 patent granted to W.H. Stanley. This example is in excellent collector quality condition.* (FINE) **$295.00**

E1-6. Stanley Rule & Level No. 110: "Shoe Buckle" Block Plane. Early Type 1. Rare and Sound. Length: 7 1/4 Inches. *Unquestionably one of the most graphically striking of all the planes produced by Stanley, this example of the early "shoebuckle" No. 110, unlike most that one encounters, retains most of its original shiny black paint. This is an example of the first production type of what was to become a mainstay of the Stanley line, albeit in substantially less decorated form. The original front knob is missing, and the cutting iron is a replacement, but the plane is otherwise in excellent overall condition. A rare Stanley plane.* (GOOD+) **$445.00**

E1-7. Stanley Rule & Level No. 72 1/2: Patent Chamfer Plane and Beading Attachment. With Bullnose. Length: 8 Inches. *Long popular among Stanley collectors due to their very special purpose and distinctive form, the No. 72 1/2 Chamfer Plane differs from its First Cousin, the No. 72, in that it includes an optional adjustable scratch beading attachment for the adding of decorative flourishes to chamfered beams or furniture. The example offered here is complete, together with five double-ended beading cutters for the beading attachment and is ready to provide dutiful service for a discriminating woodworker. Fully 98% of the original japan finish remains on the cast iron surfaces and the rosewood handles are in superb condition. Clearly marked with the April 21, 1885 date of the patent held on this tool by prolific Stanley inventor Justus A. Traut, this plane was likely one of the first to be sold together with the beading attachment, which was first offered in 1909. Crisp, complete, clean and ready to go to work. A nice plane.* (FINE) **$1,275.00**

E1-8. Stanley Rule & Level No. 1: Smoothing Plane. Ca. 1895. Sapwood Handle. Length: 6 Inches. *A dramatic handle formed of rosewood sapwood adds emphasis to this superb example of Stanley's No. 1 smooth plane, which dates from the very end of the Nineteenth Century. Nearly all shiny original finishes remain on this spectacularly well preserved example. Highly recommended.* (FINE) **$1,795.00**

E1-9. Stanley Rule & Level No. 1: Wood Level Sights. Early Green Box. New Condition, Original Box. Length: 2 1/4 Inches. *Stanley's "Green Box" period bracketed the turn of the century, making these ephemeral boxes more than 100 years old in some cases. The box is in excellent shape, with four intact corners, and the sights are in unused condition. A rare "green box" item.* (FINE) **$245.00**

E1-10. Stanley Rule & Level (Unmarked): Anderson Patent Lead Pipe Pliers. Patented May 5, 1896. Rare and Excellent. Length: 11 Inches. *Never imprinted with the Stanley name, these patented pliers were used for flaring the joints on lead pipe and were included in the Stanley line for a very brief period. A rare and interesting Stanley collectible.* (GOOD+) **$145.00**

E1-11. Stanley Rule & Level No. 10 1/2: Rare First Lateral Plane. With Adjustable Throat. Early and Excellent. Length: 8 Inches. *This early bench rabbet has the adjustable throat mechanism that was a feature of Stanley's early offerings of the No. 10 1/2. By turning the front knob, the user could precisely adjust the tightness of the throat to the requisite size. A tight crack to the tote was very carefully repaired a long time ago. A tough plane to find, especially in this condition.* (GOOD+) **$345.00**

E1-12. Stanley Rule & Level No. 340: Furring Plane. Early Arch Trademark. 90%+ Original Paint. Length: 10 Inches. *When the manufacturer of a tool encourages potential purchasers to employ the device being offered for "cleaning up rough surfaces" and "removing dirt and grit", its no surprise that finding an example in excellent condition, such as that offered here, would be a formidable task. Manufactured by Stanley under a patent issued to Jefferson Allen of Kennebunkport, Maine, on March 3, 1903, this very well preserved example of the rare No. 340 furring plane retains more than 90% of its shiny japan finish. Of distinctive profile, owing to its specialized purpose, the No. 340 is readily recognizable, yet seldom seen. Finished on all cast iron surfaces with shiny black japanning and retaining its bright yellow beechwood handles, the plane offered here is in excellent collector-quality condition and recommended without hesitation.* (GOOD+) **$1,695.00**

E1-13. Stanley Rule & Level No. 51/52: Shoot Board and Plane. Fully Complete. Rare and Excellent. Length: 22 Inches. *Finding the Stanley No. 51/52 Shoot Board and Plane Combination in complete condition is only slightly less difficult than succeeding in the search for the proverbial hen's teeth, but infinitely more rewarding for the collector of antique tools. This rare, complete example is in superb condition, with more than 95% of the original paint. A very tough plane to find.* (GOOD+) **$1,645.00**

E1-14. Stanley Rule & Level (Unmarked) No. 1: Rare "Type 1" Try Square. With Brass Frame. Rare Size and Type. Length: 4 Inches. *Stanley's early try squares are among the least common and most obscure of all Stanley collectible tools. Very few collectors are aware that the very first examples of the No. 1 try square, which were produced ca. 1871, featured a solid brass frame. This extremely well preserved example, which is unmistakable as a Stanley square but is not marked with the Stanley name, is in top collector quality condition. Extra rare and extra nice.* (GOOD+) **$875.00**

E1-15. Stanley Rule & Level: Replacement Handle for Transitional Plane. Original Shipping Tag. Rare and Near New. Length: 4 1/2 Inches. *The tool collecting world is one that is colored, almost exclusively, in shades of black and brown. Tools of those colors can be found at any major or minor tool meeting arrayed in formation looking much more like each other than anything else. Lost somewhere in their past was any sense of newness. The pride of ownership and the care of a craftsman have left them behind. They are wood and metal orphans—"things" or simply merchandise. Those who know take a glance at the tables and then at each other, and speak, almost in unison "just stuff". Once in a while, however, a discovery will proclaims itself among the mill run metal and wood will announce itself to all around like the bright light of sunshine finding its way to a clearing in the darkest of forests. There, among the "stuff" will be something so colorful, so new, so much like what it once was and so linked to the past as to still be there that all who see it will look on, shake their heads and utter an unconscious "wow". Such an object is this replacement handle for a Stanley transitional plane. Still fitted with the ageless factory tag that must have been applied before it was sent off to someone who ordered it in the State of New Hampshire nearly 100 years ago, this object captures in its bright paper and brilliant wood the spirit of newness that is so often missing from the objects that are our common quest. A graphic and colorful addition to any collection of Stanley tools or advertising, this seemingly simple plane handle and tag say more about the spirit of antique tool collecting than a hundred rows of a hundred black and brown planes. Highly recommended.* (FINE) **$345.00**

E1-16. Stanley Rule & Level No. 605 1/4: "Bedrock" Junior Jack Plane. Least Common Size. Rare and Excellent. Length: 11 1/2 Inches. *Other than the No. 602 series, the rarity prize for the "Bedrock" series goes to this, the equivalent, with the patent "Bedrock" features added, of the 5 1/4 Junior Jack Plane. Of those examples that have survived, many have been found as technical schools have sold them at auctions, often bringing "oohs" and "ahs" of amazement from a stunned auction crowd as a hand plane surpassed the hammer price of the power equipment that had been thought to be the prize of the sale. Auction crowd or not, this one will be sure to thrill and delight any crowd of serious antique tool enthusiasts, even if you're the only one in the crowd. A good one.* (FINE) **$795.00**

E1-17. Stanley Rule & Level No. 444: Dovetail Tongue and Groove Plane. Complete and Crisp. Fine Condition, Original Box. Length: 9 1/2 Inches. *Designed for precision planing of dovetail joints of every shape and size, this rare plane is in excellent overall condition. All parts, including the screwdriver and the original instruction booklet are included. The original chestnut box is intact, and the paper label is 60% present. The cutting irons are a set of exact replicas produced several years ago. An excellent example retaining 90%+ of its original nickel plating in its original box.* (GOOD+) **$1,385.00**

E1-18. Stanley Rule & Level No. 1: Rare "Battery" Pliers. Ca. 1930's Only. Rare and Excellent. Length: 7 Inches. *For a brief period in the 1930's, Stanley introduced a line of automotive tools at just about the time that Franklin Roosevelt was getting started at taking the bad economic situation that he inherited and making it far, far worse. The fact that unemployment in the United States was substantially higher in 1938 than it was in 1932 may have contributed to Stanley's decision to purge the automotive tools from their product line. Whatever the case, only a few examples of these Stanley battery pliers are known to exist. These are clean and clearly marked. Rare.* (GOOD+) **$345.00**

E1-19. Stanley Rule & Level No. 57: Core Box Plane. With 3 Sets of Extensions. Fitted Owner Box. Length: 14 Inches. *In theory, Stanley's No. 57 corebox plane could be fitted with an infinite set of nickel plated side extensions. In practice, however, most examples have but a single set of extensions, and those are generally missing. We are pleased to offer this exceptionally well preserved example complete with three sets of side extensions, three turnbuckles and all of the necessary fitting pins. A carefully crafted wooden box has kept the plane and extensions in excellent shiny condition, with nearly all of their original nickel plating intact. Only the extension rods and turnbuckles show any evidence of darkening. Complete with the original instructions and ready to display fully assembled or be stored in its well made box, this example of the No. 57 core box plane is among the finest we have ever offered—and the first with three pairs of extensions. Extra rare and nice. Highly recommended.* (FINE) **$1,850.00**

Group F1

F1-1. Staples, C.E., Worcester, Mass.: Locking Chuck Brace. Ca. 1860's. Early Appearance. Length: 12 1/2 Inches. *Apparently never patented, this very early and well made brace was produced by C.E. Staples of Worcester, Massachusetts. Turning the chuck causes a spring loaded locking mechanism to retract. When it is turned again, the mechanism locks the bit into place. According to the Directory of American Toolmakers, Staples ceased operations approximately 1860. A very rare early American brace.* (GOOD+) **$225.00**

F1-2. Davis Level & Tool Co. No. 1: "Mantle Clock" Level. Double Screw Adjust. Original Pinstriping. Length: 6 Inches. *Much of the original decorative gold pinstriping remains on this classic Davis "Mantle Clock" level, thanks in large part to the protection provided by the fitted mahogany box that has accompanied it through its 130+ years of existence. Absolutely free from any damage or evidence of wear, this level is as nice an example of this collectible classic as we have offered in several years. A rare and desirable patented inclinometer level in top collector quality condition. Highly recommended.* (FINE) **$845.00**

F1-3. Lovell Mfg. Co., The A.K., New York: Quick Adjust Nut Wrench. Patented June 7, 1892. Schulz No. 401. Length: 8 Inches. *The Lovell Wrench features a central helical screw that locks the jaw in place. Pushing on the brass button on the handle allows the jaw to travel freely to the desired size. An extremely rare wrench in excellent working order. Rare.* (GOOD) **$845.00**

F1-4. Unmarked: Early Full Body Caliper. Anatomically O.K. Victorian Style. Length: 6 1/2 Inches. *Among collectors of that select class of Nineteenth Century tools generally referred to as "lady-leg calipers", the forms most sought after are those having a high degree of detail and/or a full body figure. This classic pair features a Rubenesque form of woman having decorative "garters" applied to her legs, breasts more anthropomorphic than usual and a face that might make a skilled machinist work later than others. A classic example of this increasingly difficult to find genre.* (FINE) **$1,175.00**

F1-5. Smith, E.B., St. Louis, Missouri: "The Ideal" Patent Wrench. Patented May 9, 1893. Push Button Action. Length: 12 Inches. *A push button on the back of this patented quick adjust wrench releases a spring and allows the lower jaw to slide quickly into position. It is marked only with the patent date, but was patented by one E.B. Smith of St. Louis, Missouri. Never seen another.* (GOOD) **$775.00**

F1-6. Unmarked: Working Model of a Wrench. Carved From Wood. Patent Model? Length: 10 3/4 Inches. *Tools in their many forms are the physical manifestations of ideas—some very good, some very bad. We have in the past opined at length about the nature of invention and industry in a free society and how the celebration of a spirit of enterprise and industry led to the endless array of tools that collectors so avidly seek out today. Almost always, we see the ideas for tools in their final form, after the work has been done, the decisions (either good or bad) have been made and an assembly line has created thousands of nearly identical tools. For each tool, however, there is a beginning. In the case of the wooden model of a wrench shown here, the beginning was an idea, then perhaps a sketch or more detailed drawings, and then this working model. Unlike any wrench we have ever seen in production, this wooden model of a nut wrench includes a mechanism of a pair of springs to regulate the adjustment of the jaws. That we have not seen an actual tool of this configuration does not mean that it was never made, because the sheer complexity of the wrench virtually guaranteed that it would be a failure. Whatever the case, we are pleased and proud to be able to offer this snapshot of an idea in its earliest stages as an example of a world of invention now, sadly, gone.* (GOOD+) **$265.00**

F1-7. Mitteldorfer Straus: Patent Ceremonial Hammer. Patented January 10, 1928. "Goat Head" Design. Length: 8 1/2 Inches. *A superb bronze headed hammer which received a design patent from our own U.S. Government. The patent having been granted, the public was protected from any number of cheap, imitation goat head hammers that would likely have flooded the market. The real McCoy.* (FINE) **$395.00**

F1-8. Brown & Sharpe Mfg., Providence No. 1: Open Screw Thread Micrometer. "Sheet Metal Gauge". New Condition, Original Box. Length: 2 1/2 Inches. *Perhaps the most important technological advance in the history of precision machining was the availability, for general use, of precision measurement. This process was brought about in the United States through the introduction, by the Brown & Sharpe Manufacturing Company of Providence, Rhode Island of a "sheet metal gauge" micrometer based on the "Systeme Palmer" invented in France. Early examples of this quantum leap in precision measurement took the form of the tool offered here, having exposed screw threads along the length of the spindle and substantially smaller than the 1 inch to 2 inch micrometers that would soon become the standard. Protected from the elements by its slide top wooden box which is clearly imprinted with period advertising, this classic early micrometer is the quintessential example of a milestone of American technological achievement. Rare, important and in superb condition. Highly recommended.* (FINE) **$1,275.00**

F1-9. Grant, Thomas, (New York, N.Y.): Astragal, Cove/Astragal Molding Plane. I.S. Crowned Initials. Early Clear Mark. Length: 10 Inches. *One of the very first planemakers to work in New York City, Thomas Grant remains a bit of an enigma today, despite a great deal of research about his life and planemaking. Many of Grant's planes, as is the case with this example, were imprinted with "crowned initials", which consisted of individual letters stamped on the toe of the planes over each of which was the imprint of a small "crown" device. What evidence is known strongly suggests that these initials were applied by the planemaker at the request of the purchaser of the tool for identification purposes. In addition to Grant, American planemakers W. Raymond and L. Little and a handful of early English planemakers are known to have used the crowned initials device. This extra complex molder is in excellent collector quality condition and has a stronger than usual Thomas Grant imprint as well as the crowned initials "I.S." A great early plane in excellent collector quality condition. Ex-Cooley Collection.* (GOOD+) **$845.00**

F1-10. Greble, Turner & Co., Hamilton, Ohio: Boxed Set of 5 Try Squares. Original Paper Label. New Condition, Original Box. Length: 10 Inches. *According to Ken Cope's "Makers of American Machinists Tools", Greble, Turner & Company offered sets of squares in a fitted wooden case, but until the appearance of this extraordinarily well preserved example, we were unaware of the existence of any intact examples. Still retaining its original paper label and is essentially the same condition it would have been in when it left the factory in Hamilton, Ohio, this set is a classic example of the very best quality being produced by one of the many competitors of Starrett & Brown & Sharpe who were about to be left behind. A graphic set in mint condition.* (FINE) **$945.00**

F1-11. Stanley Rule & Level No. 72 1/2: Patent Chamfer Plane and Beading Attachment. Rare and Excellent. Length: 8 Inches. *Long popular among Stanley collectors due to their very special purpose and distinctive form, the No. 72 1/2 Chamfer Plane differs from its First Cousin, the No. 72, in that it includes an optional adjustable scratch beading attachment for the adding of decorative flourishes to chamfered beams or furniture. The example offered here is complete, together with six double-ended beading cutters for the beading attachment and is ready to provide dutiful service for a discriminating woodworker. Fully 99% of the original japan finish remains on the cast iron surfaces and the rosewood handles are in superb condition. This plane was likely one of the first to be sold together with the beading attachment, which was first offered in 1909. A nice plane in excellent working order.* (FINE) **$1,245.00**

F1-12. Brown & Sharpe Mfg. Co. No. 25: Patent "Digital" Micrometer. Patented August 22, 1911. Original Case. Length: 6 Inches. *Produced under a patent issued on August 22, 1911 to one F. Spalding of Providence, Rhode Island and assigned to the Brown & Sharpe Mfg. Company, this tool was one of the very first American micrometers to implement a digital readout. Complete with the original wrench in the original case, this tool has been used, but is in excellent working order. A very early, technologically significant and rare American micrometer caliper.* (GOOD+) **$875.00**

F1-13. Unmarked: Pair of Double Coach Planes. Compass and Bead. Ivory Soles. Length: 5 1/2 Inches. *The work of finish carpentry in the carriage maker's trade involved the application of decorative cuts on both curved and straight work to such an extent that in many cases the standard tools of the carpenter and cabinetmaker simply would not do. This volume is filled with specialized tools of every sort for cutting decorative beads or routing grooves for panels. The skill that was required to create the beautiful carriages of the Nineteenth Century was also brought to bear when it became necessary, as it often did, for the carriage maker to fashion his own tools by hand. Sometimes, for the sake of expediency, those tools took the form of standard, workaday tools. Other times, however, such as was the case with this spectacular pair of matched and complementary cove and bead double bladed planes, all of the carriage maker's skill was applied to the making of his tools. Fitted with ivory soles and possessed of sculptural "squirrel tail" bodies, these mahogany carriage planes are, without question, the finest examples of this type of tool that we have ever offered. Collected in the State of Vermont more than 50 years ago and then carefully set aside by former E.A.I.A. President Joe Link, we proudly offer these tools to a collector who will take up the task of safeguarding them for posterity. An extraordinary set. Highly recommended.* (GOOD+) **$1,895.00**

F1-14. Patent Level Co., Bridgeport, Conn.: Patent Inclinometer, Level. Patented May 8, 1866. Early and Excellent. Length: 6 Inches. *Produced under a patent issued on May 8, 1866 to A.J. Vandergrift, this elaborately cast bronze inclinometer preceded by two years the similarly-styled, if mechanically different, level to be patented and manufactured by L.L. Davis in the following year. Marked on the base of the body with the maker's name "Patent Level Co., Bridgeport, Conn." as well as the patent date, this level's resident genius was a glass-faced vial that was apparently to be filled with alcohol to the halfway point, where the 360 degree graduations would serve as both level and inclinometer. This level, as were the other two examples of which I am aware, has no fluid in the vial. There is no evidence of a break in either the glass or the seal, but the vial is dry, nonetheless. Complete with its porthole-type cover which locks back into position when the level is no longer needed, this classic early level is in extremely well-preserved condition. Simply a great antique tool.* (GOOD+) **$1,950.00**

F1-15. Kenney: Kenney's Patent Marking Gauge. Patented January 4, 1870. Complete and Excellent. Length: 9 1/4 Inches. *A perfectly preserved example of the Kenney patent of 1870. A brass beam, alternate rosewood and boxwood trammel heads and a precision adjust scribe make for one of the most complex tools ever devised. Complete with the original trammel point attachments. Magnificent.* (FINE) **$950.00**

F1-16. Unmarked: Walrus Tusk Handle Bow Drill. Triple Screw Lock. Knurled Ferrule. Length: 5 1/2 Inches. *The unmistakable longitudinal grain of the ivory handle of this spectacular marine ivory bow drill makes it a virtual certainty that it was formed from a walrus tusk. Further ornamented by a knurled brass ferrule and a turned chuck having three fixing screws, this precision Nineteenth Century tool was very likely used in the manufacture of musical instruments. An extraordinarily well made tool of miniature proportions.* (GOOD+) **$1,475.00**

F1-17. Assorted Makers: Set of Chair Maker's Tools. Adzes, Scorps, Etc. Rare and Excellent. Length: 12 Inches. *The making of chairs, particularly those of the Windsor style, has attracted a number of students in recent years who practice this craft as an avocation. We are particularly pleased to be able to offer this essentially intact kit of tools from the shop of a chairmaker of the last century. Included are a wide range of scorps, shaves, adzes auger bits and accessory tools. Nearly all of the tools are in excellent working condition and ready to be put immediately to use if the new owner so chooses. We highly recommend this set to a museum or restoration. This is the only such set we have ever offered or seen for sale. Simply a great set of tools.* (GOOD+ **$1,150.00**

F1-18. King, Arthur H., New York, N.Y.: Magnusun Patent Spoke Shave. Patented May 19, 1891. Rare and Extra Nice. Length: 9 Inches. *Arguably the most unusual spokeshave ever produced, the Magnusun Patent spokeshave combines a rabbeting feature, an adjustable tension cap and a pair of looped cast iron handles that adjust and lock in any desired angle in a single tool. Offered by a number of makers through less than 10 years of manufacture, these shaves have many of the qualities of great collectible tools: They are subject to breakage, a factor which contributed, no doubt to the second quality; they were not particularly popular—the fact is that most craftsmen don't want a tool that comes with an instruction manual; and, finally, they did what they did to indulge the inventive genius of the maker, not for any particularly compelling utilitarian reason. We have seen three examples of this rare tool in 15 years. This is by far the best. Extra special.* (GOOD+) **$895.00**

F1-19. Fuller & Field: Classic Halving Molding Plane. Yellow Birch Body. Superb Condition. Length: 10 Inches. *Writing in "American Wooden Planes" Emil and Martyl Pollak initially speculate that this obscure partnership was formed sometime in the late 1700's or early 1800's, but then immediately reverse themselves to conclude that the planes were made at a much earlier time. We agree. The 10 inch length of this plane, the decorative chamfering, the Yellow Birch body and the extra bold name stamp all point to a tool produced in the 1750's or earlier. Of the classic "halving" plane profile this magnificent example is in much the same condition as it would have been when first produced some 250 years ago. Extra nice and highly recommended. Ex-Cooley Collection.* (FINE) **$950.00**

Group G1

G1-1. Siegley Tool Company No. 2: Combination Plow Metallic Plane. Complete and Perfect. Original Nickel Plating. Length: 10 Inches. *Jacob Siegley, a German immigrant, began manufacturing planes in Wilkes Barre, Pennsylvania and continued until the business was sold to the Stanley Rule & Level Company in 1905. The tool offered here is an outstanding example of Siegley's highly successful line of combination planes. All original parts are included with this bright and clean patented plane in its original box. The cutters and cutter box are included. The finishes on the main body section are nearly 100% intact, clean and shiny. Absolutely extraordinary.* (FINE) **$775.00**

G1-2. Tower & Lyon, New York, N.Y.: Challenge Jointer Metallic Plane. Patented February 19, 1884. Rare Complete Example. Length: 23 Inches. *One of the most graphic and sought after of all patented planes, the "Challenge" planes were produced by New York City hardware and tool merchants Tower & Lyon under the patents granted to Washington, D.C. inventor Arthur T. Goldsborough. Writing in his classic "Patented Transitional & Metallic Planes in America, Volume I", author Roger Smith speculated that the Challenge planes were marketed almost exclusively in the growing markets of the American West. At the time of the publication of Smith's first book, only smooth and jack planes of the Challenge pattern were known to exist. Since that time, a number of jointer planes have come to light, all of which have been severely damaged or missing major parts. This example is clean, complete and absent any damage whatsoever. Unlike the smaller sizes, the patent information is cast in the body, as is the "Challenge" name. A spectacularly graphic and extremely rare patented jointer plane in excellent collector quality condition. Highly recommended.* (GOOD+) **$3,975.00**

G1-3. Bauge, J.L.: Patent Compound Mitre Box. Patented February 1874. Original Paint. Length: 19 1/2 Inches. *The last third of the Nineteenth Century produced some spectacular tools that incorporated mechanical ingenuity in combination with an artistry of design, but few did so as seamlessly as this extraordinary patented compound mitre box. Imprinted with the patent date and the maker's name in the casting on the working surface, a brass adjustment lever is rotated to free up the guide mechanism to move freely in two different planes and then be just as easily locked into place again. To ensure that the fittings of this mechanically complex tool stayed in place, a bronze wrench was provided, together with a fitted cast iron drawer (visible on the back of the tool on the left) to hold it. Retaining nearly all of its original finishes of red and black paint, this spectacular tool deserves a prominent place in an important collection, or perhaps in a museum, where all could marvel at the artistry of days gone by. A small repair to one of the cast iron legs, executed many years ago and invisible without close inspection is the only flaw in this otherwise perfect tool. A magnificent compound miter box. Highly recommended.* (FINE) **$2,950.00**

G1-4. Bailey and Company, L., Hartford No. 20: "Victor" Circular Metallic Plane. Cam-Type Cap Iron. Near New Condition. Length: 9 1/2 Inches. *Still retaining much of the original finish that would have been applied before it left the factory, this complete, sound and perfectly-preserved example of Leonard Bailey's "Victor" No. 20 circular plane is among the finest we have offered. Top shelf.* (FINE) **$895.00**

G1-5. Birmingham Plane Manufacturing Co: Iron Rabbet Metallic Plane. 8 Inch Overall Length. Patented April 1, 1884. Length: 8 Inches. *The Birmingham Plane Manufacturing Company of Derby, Conn. made a full line of cast iron planes in the 1870's that look as if they would be right at home in the Batcave. This, the smallest version of their bench rabbet plane series, is complete and in exceptionally nice condition. An appealing example of Americana.* (GOOD+) **$845.00**

G1-6. Fuller, Jo, Providence: Self-Regulating Plane. For Slitting. Yellow Birch Body. Length: 13 Inches. *Among the most fascinating of all tools are those that have the imprint of a well known maker, yet are of a form or type totally different than any other work known by that maker. The handled, self-regulating plane offered here clearly is numbered among those tools. Crafted of beech, oak and birch, this massive slitting plane bears the clear imprint of Eighteenth Century Providence, Rhode Island maker Joseph Fuller. Although it resembles in many respects the plow planes used by bookbinders, and one's initial reaction is to identify this planes as such, a more careful scrutiny reveals features inconsistent with such a plane. Most notably, a bookbinder's plow was designed to be held in a fixed groove and the wear pattern on this plane indicates that is was used in much the same manner as a bench plane or molder. The body is considerably less thick at the toe than at the heel and the fixing screw has been regularly locked at positions too wide and too narrow to be consistent with a bookbinder's plow plane. More likely is the possibility that this was designed for slitting of thin stock or veneer—something that would have been a regular task of the Providence cabinetmakers supplied by Fuller. One final and important observation should be made about this tool: Given Fuller's early working dates, it is very likely that this is the first known example of a fenced plane regulated by a threaded screw arm, a significant milestone in the development of the cabinetmaker's plow plane. A magnificent and historically significant slitting plow plane of graphic appearance. Extraordinary.* (GOOD) **$2,650.00**

G1-7. Munks, John & Sons, Sheffield (England): Early Patent Metallic Plane. Patented January 16, 1884. With Patent Date Imprint. Length: 6 1/2 Inches. *The making of patented metallic planes was an almost exclusively American indulgence. This example of the Munks Patent, produced under the specifications contained in English Patent No. 1511 is boldly marked with the January 16, 1884 patent on the cutting iron. Roger Smith, writing in Volume II of his classic series on patented planes, has noted the remarkable similarity between this tool and the "Challenge" plane, patented in 1883. A superb example of a most unusual and collectible early patent English plane.* (GOOD+) **$1,195.00**

G1-8. Unmarked: Rare Apothecary Plane. For Potions, Etc. Nickel Plated Brass Leg. Length: 9 1/2 Inches. *Intended for use behind the counter of the apothecary shop, this specialized plane would have been used for preparing curative mixtures from natural ingredients during the Nineteenth Century. Fitted with four cast brass legs that have been nickel plated, as has the rest of the tool, this device was obviously intended partly for show and partly for function. A rare special purpose plane in excellent overall condition.* (GOOD+) **$495.00**

G1-9. Spiers, Stewart, Ayr, Scotland No. 31: Parallel Side Smooth Metallic Plane. Original Spiers Iron. Dovetailed Sole. Length: 8 1/2 Inches. *Among the most sought after of all British metallic planes, the parallel side smoothing planes of Stewart Spiers have developed a well deserved reputation for excellence. This extra clean example retains its full original Spiers iron and is in excellent working order. A tight crack in the tote deserves mention, but could be easily repaired. A classic.* (GOOD+) **$895.00**

G1-10. Tobey, C., Hudson (N.Y.): 1/2 Inch Round Molding Plane. Yellow Birch Body. Ca. 1782 "A" Mark. Length: 9 3/4 Inches. *One of several who have competed for the honor of the designation of "New York's First Planemaker", little is known of Cornelius Tobey other than his listing as a "builder" in 1792. The known use of two distinct makers stamps, of which this is the earlier and most graphic example, would indicate that planemaking was more than just a sideline. Boldly struck, rare as clean Hudson River water and ready to brag about, we proudly offer this extremely rare early New York State molding plane.* (GOOD+) **$1,350.00**

G1-11. Bailey, Leonard No. 10: "Victor" Circular Metallic Plane. Uncommon Type. Complete and Excellent. Length: 10 1/2 Inches. *Complete examples of Leonard Bailey's "Victor" planes are among the most ardently sought out of all collectible tools. These planes combine decorative design with mechanical innovation in a way that their creator, inventive genius Leonard Bailey, seemed to do almost without effort. This, the less commonly encountered of the "Victor" circular planes has an elaborately cast fixing screw to lock the cap iron into place and a scalloped profile that signals the so-called "Era of Excess" in which it was produced. Protected by several of Bailey's patents and fitted with the Victor adjustment mechanism, this example is complete, original and ready to proudly display.* (GOOD) **$745.00**

G1-12. Ohio Tool Company No. 326 1/4: Pair of Cast Iron Metallic Planes. Also No. 328. 98% Original Paint. Length: 9 Inches. *Early in the Twentieth Century, the Ohio Tool Company absorbed the Auburn Tool Company of Auburn, New York and established two manufacturing locations. The history of the products of the merged firms is not well documented. What is known is that a series of bench planes, which employed a lateral adjustment mechanism and depth of cut adjustment similar to Stanley's patented designs of Leonard Bailey were put into production. These planes were very likely the result of the expiration of the Bailey patents. What is known for certain is that these planes used an obscure numbering system that expanded upon the Ohio Tool Company's use of fractional plane numbers. Included in this offering are an example of the No. 238 jointer plane, the equivalent of a Stanley No. 7, and the No. 326 1/4, which was more similar to Stanley's basic jack plane. Nearly 98% of the shiny black japan finish remains on these extremely well preserved planes. Most unusual.* (GOOD+) **$795.00**

G1-13. Unmarked: Double Tongue and Groove Plane. Rare Handled Type. Graphic Form. Length: 12 1/2 Inches. *One of the most graphic and interesting of all tools, the handled double tongue and groove plane has a look that appeals immediately to tool collectors and non-tool collectors alike. While it was intended to be used in a single direction only, the opposing handles suggest questionable functionality. This superbly executed craftsman made example is graced with a pair of exceptionally graceful horns to the carved totes and is in exceptionally well preserved condition. A dramatic plane that will captivate the interest of tool lovers and everyone else. Highly recommended.* (GOOD+) **$545.00**

G1-14. Davis Level & Tool Co.: Cast Iron Block Metallic Plane. Nickel Plated Body. Super Rare and Sound. Length: 6 Inches. *The cutting iron is unmarked, as were many of the originals, but was almost certainly the proper one for the tool. The rest of this Davis block plane noteworthy in that it was at one time nickel plated and it appears that the plating may well have been original. We know from having observed Davis levels that they certainly had the capacity for producing nickel plated tools, but this is the first such plane of which we are aware. A clean, sound and important Davis block plane.* (GOOD+) **$1,175.00**

G1-15. Stanley Rule & Level No. 72 1/2: Patented Chamfer, Bullnose Plane and Beading Attachment. Rare and Excellent. Length: 8 Inches. *Long popular among Stanley collectors due to their very special purpose and distinctive form, the No. 72 1/2 Chamfer Plane differs from its First Cousin, the No. 72, in that it includes an optional adjustable scratch beading attachment for the adding of decorative flourishes to chamfered beams or furniture. The example offered here is complete, together with five double-ended beading cutters for the beading attachment and is ready to provide dutiful service for a discriminating woodworker. Fully 90% of the original japan finish remains on the cast iron surfaces and the rosewood handles are in superb condition. This plane was likely one of the first to be sold together with the beading attachment, which was first offered in 1909. Crisp, complete, clean and ready to go to work. A nice plane.* (GOOD+) **$1,175.00**

G1-16. Bailey, L. No. 0 1/2: "Victor" Adjustable Metallic Plane. Ca. 1880-1888. Complete and Excellent. Length: 7 Inches. *Those who have taken the time to be able to distinguish, at a glance, the different varieties of the "Victor" block planes by their arcane numbering system, are to be commended for their achievement, and I hope they never corner me at a cocktail party. For the rest of us, who find the artistic majesty of these early cast iron tools sufficiently satisfying, and who have access to reference materials when necessary, this example of the adjustable No. 0 1/2 is a classic example of one of the most beautiful block planes ever produced. Fitted with the Bailey patent adjustment mechanism and the elaborately cast locking screw that was the trademark of these planes, this clean example retains nearly 90% of its original finishes. A superb example of a rare plane.* (GOOD+) **$485.00**

G1-17. Ohio Tool Co. (Unmarked) No. 105: Turkish Boxwood Plane. With Ivory Tips. Extra Crisp and Clean. Length: 9 Inches. *It is almost as if the makers of this tool (almost certainly the Ohio Tool Company, of Columbus, Ohio, whose No. 105 is inconspicuously embossed on the heel of the plane) thought it best to leave well enough alone when it came time to emboss their imprint on this magnificent solid boxwood plow plane. Carefully and precisely crafted from a single, grainless log of Turkish Boxwood this superbly patinated tool has the look and feel of polished marble. Only a slight chip from the side of the wedge detracts from an otherwise practically perfect ivory tipped plow plane. This tool that was from the very start meant to be something very special remains very much so today. Exotic wood plow planes in this kind of condition seldom become available in the open market. This one has been safely guarded in a collection for more than 20 years. We expect that it will quickly find a caring home. Extra special.* (GOOD+) **$1,750.00**

G1-18. Birmingham Plane Manufacturing Co.: Iron Block Metallic Plane. Original Marked Iron. Scarce and Excellent. Length: 4 Inches. *The Birmingham Plane Manufacturing Company of Derby, Conn. made a full line of cast iron planes in the 1870's. This most unusual boat-like miniature block plane is marked with the Birmingham imprint on the cutting iron. A rare and early metallic plane.* (GOOD) **$365.00**

G1-19. Erlandsen, N., New York (?): Set of Coachmakers Metallic Plane. Flat and Compass. Superb Condition. Length: 7 1/4 Inches. *Included in the early catalogues of the Hammacher & Schlemmer Company of New York City together with the precision instrument makers planes of Napoleon and Julius Erlandsen, it is likely that these classic tail handle coachmaker's planes were also produced by the Erlandsens. Each of these planes is clean, sound and retains much of its original black japan finish. The wedges and cutting irons are original. Sets of this sort become available in the market very infrequently. A classic and graphic set of coachmaker's planes. Ex-Cooley Collection.* (GOOD) **$825.00**

G1-20. Gocher, George: Gocher's Patent Bead Metallic Plane. Patented April 10, 1877. From Johnstown, Penn. Length: 9 Inches. *The Union Tool Company of New Britain, Connecticut introduced a series of metallic bead planes using the No. 44 designation in 1904. Writing in Patented Transitional & Metallic Planes in America, author Roger Smith speculates that the design may have been appropriated from this, the patented bead plane of George Gocher, of Johnstown, Pennsylvania, following the expiration of the patent. Examples of the Union No. 44 are extremely rare, but are certainly outdone in rarity by the original Gocher patent. The patent date is cast into the body of this plane and the reverse side has a uniform cross-hatch checkering pattern. A rare patented plane that may have been an inspiration.* (GOOD+) **$1,350.00**

G1-21. Unmarked: Wheelwright's Shoot Board Plane. For Wagon Spokes. Museum Quality. Length: 33 Inches. *We can imagine what a wheelwright's shop must have looked like some 200 years ago. We can smell the wood shavings and hear the pounding of the hammers and the sawing of saws. We can close our eyes and imagine the tools that we know in their places and in use in the making of wheels and the mending of carriages. Such images come into sharper focus, however, when a tool such as that offered here is found. Fitted with all manner of hand forged screws and obviously intended to be set in a fixed position on a bench, this specialty shoot board plane was recovered from a long closed wagon shop nearly 40 years ago and set away for keeping. Most likely used for the precise planing of wagon spokes, it is likely that similar tools that once existed were cast aside or relegated to the fireplace as having outlived their useful life. That this tool has survived is cause for celebration. It is a reason to imagine, and a reason to understand a world long ago. An extraordinary specialty woodworking tool of museum quality. Ex-Cooley Collection. Highly recommended.* (GOOD+) **$1,475.00**

G1-22. Unmarked: Miniature Ivory Smooth Plane. Appears Early. Rare and Excellent. Length: 1 1/2 Inches. *At less than 1 1/2 inches in length, this carved ivory smoothing plane could not possibly have been intended for performing a workaday task. Much more likely is the possibility that it was crafted in a few hours of idle time by a ship carpenter using the materials available to him and the skills that he possessed. Unquestionably old, but nearly perfectly preserved, this miniature tool is ready to add to a collection of tools that were made to be "something special".* (FINE) **$425.00**

Group I1

I1-1. Fenn, J., Newgate St. (London): "Ladies Size" Brace. Turned Rosewood Head. Near New Condition. Length: 13 Inches. *Clearly marked with the imprint of respected London maker J. Fenn, nicely accented with a turned rosewood head and retaining nearly all of its original finishes on both wood and metal, this classic undersize brace is the finest example of its type we have seen. Highly recommended.* (FINE) **$695.00**

I1-2. Stanley Rule & Level No. 20: Ratcheting Corner Brace. Rare Double Mark "Fray". Excellent Condition. Length: 18 Inches. *When the John Fray Company was eventually bought out by the Stanley Rule & Level Company a limited few braces from their product line were re-stamped with the "Stanley Rule & Level" designation and marketed under the Stanley name. This well preserved example is so marked and has also been stamped with the New Britain, Connecticut location. A rare Stanley/Fray brace.* (GOOD+) **$295.00**

I1-3. Flather, D., Solly Works, Sheffield: Classic Sheffield Brace. Push Button Chuck. Cleaned and Polished. Length: 13 1/2 Inches. *This classic brace has been cleaned and polished and is ready to be displayed. An eyecatcher.* (GOOD) **$115.00**

I1-4. Bloomer & Phillips: Registered Thumb Lever Brace. Registered October 10, 1847. Rare and Excellent. Length: 14 Inches. *The thumb lever on this brace was produced under the Registered Design of Bloomer & Phillips secured on October 10, 1847. A rare and important early brace.* (GOOD+) **$295.00**

I1-5. Unmarked: Sims Patent Type Brace. Ebony and Brass. Rare and Complete. Length: 13 1/2 Inches. *Among the rarest and most sought-after of all braces, the history of the manufacture "Sims-type" brace is simply not known. Writing in "The Ultimate Brace", author Reg Eaton observed "Neither the identity of the manufacturer of these rare and distinctive tools, nor indeed precisely when they were made, is by any means certain." Ken Roberts has suggested that the maker of these tools may have been made by Thomas Pilkington, whose "Pilkington" brace is well known for its elaborate ornamentation. Whatever the history of this tool, there is no doubt that it is among the most spectacularly beautiful of all braces, and indeed, of all tools. Comprised of a machined brass frame, stuffed with grainless black ebony and accented with a series of brass medallions, the Sims brace is unlike any other brace ever produced. A magnificent example of a most desirable collectible brace.* (GOOD+) **$1,850.00**

I1-6. Scholl, C.: 3 Stem Patent Marking Gauge. Patented March 8, 1864. Rosewood Body and Arms. Length: 8 Inches. *The C. Scholl patent involved a series of sliding shafts, all of which could be fixed in position by a single locking screw. This example of the solid rosewood version has three separate stems. It has been used, but is clearly marked and offered without apology. An interesting and aesthetically appealing gauge.* (GOOD+) **$295.00**

I1-7. Pope, W., Rralph: "Ultimatum" Trade Brace. With Ivory Ring. Macassar Ebony. Length: 13 Inches. *No apologies need be asked and none will be given for this excellent "Ultimatum" brace. Imprinted with the name of one W. Pope, this was likely a "trade" brace that was produced by one of the principal makers and then marked with the name of an "ironmonger" or hardware dealer. The full ivory ring, symbolic of the "Ultimatum" brace, is present in the head and the Macassar Ebony infill is in excellent condition. An accessory box of center spur bits, which have traveled with the brace throughout the years, are included with the tool. If you have been looking for "the" Ultimatum brace for your collection, look no further.* (GOOD+) **$685.00**

I1-8. Marples, William, Hibernia Works: Classic English Brace. Turned Ebony Head. Push Button Chuck. Length: 14 Inches. *A turned head of solid ebony provides a stark contrast to the beechwood body of this early English brace. A well preserved example that is clearly marked with the Marples imprint.* (GOOD+) **$195.00**

I1-9. Pilkington, C. T., Sheffield: Applied Frame Brace. With Patent Lever. Ca. 1857-1864. Length: 13 Inches. *Produced under a patent granted to Pedigor & Storrs in 1852, the "Pilkington" framed brace, which features an internal frame of brass as well as highly ornamented external plates of the same material, is one of the most appealing of all woodworking tools ever produced. This example, which bears the imprint of Charles Pilkington only, would have been produced in Sheffield between 1857 and 1864. A classic example of a most desirable collectible brace.* (GOOD+) **$1,675.00**

I1-10. Howarth, James, Sheffield, England: Rosewood Ultimatum Brace. With Lever Pad. Rare and Excellent. Length: 13 1/2 Inches. *Alone among makers of the "Ultimatum" brace not to offer a beech-stuffed version, James Howarth's braces are regarded at the highest quality braces of this type to have been produced. While none of the Howarth braces are at all common, this rosewood-filled offering is among the rarest of all. Crisp, clean and ready to display. A great brace.* (GOOD+) **$1,295.00**

I1-11. Simmons Hardware Co., St. Louis No. KR6: "Keen Kutter" Brace. Ratcheting Type. Rare 6 Inch Sweep. Length: 12 1/2 Inches. *Six inch braces by any maker are tough to find. This one is marked with the Keen Kutter name and product number. A good one.* (GOOD) **$75.00**

I1-12. Bower, W.: Classic "Sheffield" Brace. Unplated Type. Rosewood Head. Length: 14 Inches. *This "basic" wooden brace from a prominent Sheffield maker is in excellent working order and ready for use or display.* (GOOD+) **$195.00**

I1-13. Unmarked: Hand Forged Brace. Turned Walnut Head. Great Patina. Length: 12 3/4 Inches. *A turned walnut head and a grip formed to accommodate the fingers add character to this early hand forged brace. Different.* (GOOD) **$185.00**

I1-14. Cooper, Joseph: Joseph Cooper Patent Brace. Pull Lock Chuck. With Ivory Ring. Length: 15 Inches. *The application of technology to the all-metal brace was a nearly uniquely American phenomenon. The trend of development in English braces followed a decidedly more aesthetic path. The Joseph Cooper brace incorporates a unique chuck mechanism with an artistry of execution that is exceeded by few, if any, braces manufactured on either side of the Atlantic. Ornamented with an inlaid ivory ring in the pad and constructed on an oversize pattern, the Cooper brace stands out, even in the company of a number of extraordinary braces. An extremely rare and beautiful patented English brace.* (GOOD+) **$1,175.00**

I1-15. Unmarked: Solid Rosewood Brace. With Brass Plates. Check in Upper Body. Length: 13 1/2 Inches. *As collectors, we have become so accustomed to seeing an example of the "common" Sheffield brace, that has often been abused beyond reason, sitting on the shelf of our local antique shop, ridiculously overpriced and offering a not too flattering introduction to English woodworking tools to the novice. Contrasted with this spectacular rosewood-filled brace, which is exceedingly rare on either side of the Atlantic, that shopworn brace flatters by comparison. Unmarked with any maker's name and having only a small check in the upper body as a detraction, this showy brace is ready for display in a serious collection of woodworking tools.* (GOOD) **$475.00**

I1-16. Fenton & Marsden, Sheffield England: No. 986: "Registered" Head Brace. Spring Clip Chuck. Turned Ebony Head. Length: 14 1/2 Inches. *The plate on the top of the turned ebony head of this classic "Sheffield" brace is embossed with the Fenton & Marsden No. 986 designation. The bits are held in place by a spring clip. An uncommon Sheffield brace in excellent condition.* (GOOD+) **$295.00**

I1-17. Stanley Tools No. 2101 A: "Yankee" Heavy Duty Brace. 12 Inch Sweep. Best Brace Ever. Length: 13 1/2 Inches. *With regard to the "Yankee" brace, there were two classes of workmen: those who had one, and those who wished they did. A very nice example.* (GOOD+) **$65.00**

I1-18. Benjamin, G, Avoca, N.Y.: Early Patent Brace. Patented June 9, 1857. Elaborate Chuck. Length: 14 1/2 Inches. *Prominently featured in Paul Kebabian and Dudley Whitney's classic "American Woodworking Tools", the George Benjamin patented brace is one of only a handful of American braces formed primarily of wood. Patented on June 9, 1857, the Benjamin Patent employs a complex lever activated chuck mechanism to hold the bits in place. Assigned an "A" rating in Ron Pearson's book on patented American Braces, which signifies that less than 5 examples are known to exist, this tool is among the rarest of all American braces. An early break in the wood has been carefully repaired and is barely noticeable. The chuck is imprinted with the patent date. This dramatic brace is ready to serve as the centerpiece of a collection of patented American braces.* (GOOD) **$1,450.00**

I1-19. Hawke, H., Solly Works, Sheffield: Classic Sheffield Brace. Push Button Chuck. Eagle Medallions. Length: 13 1/2 Inches. *The "American eagle" imprints on this classic Sheffield style brace are strong evidence that it was intended for export to the American market. The nicely turned rosewood head is in excellent condition. A classic.* (GOOD+) **$225.00**

I1-20. Marples, William, 67 Spring Lane: Horn "Ultimatum" Brace. With Royal Crest. Superb Condition. Length: 14 1/2 Inches. *By far the rarest of all materials used as infill in the "Ultimatum" braces of William Marples was the Cape Buffalo horn used in this superb example. Nearly translucent and finely grained, the horn infill is found in perhaps one or two of every thousand of these tools produced. This superb example is essentially free of checking and retains its ivory ring in the head. The embossed logo of "67 Spring Lane" indicates that this was among the earliest of braces produced by William Marples.* (GOOD+) **$2,250.00**

I1-21. Bee, Wm., (Sheffield): Classic "Sheffield" Brace. Eagle Medallion. Brass Plates. Length: 14 Inches. *Sheffield maker James Bee was a major exporter of braces to the young United States of America. This classic plated Sheffield brace is fitted with an eagle medallion on the spring lock button for the chuck, an almost certain sign that this tool was crafted for the American market. Crisp, clean and retaining most of its original finishes, this superb brace is in top condition for a collection or use, or both. Extra nice.* (FINE) **$275.00**

I1-22. Marples, William, 67 Spring Lane: Rosewood "Ultimatum" Brace. With Royal Crest. Turned Rosewood Head. Length: 14 1/2 Inches. *Nearly all original finishes remain on this classic "Ultimatum" brace, which has as its "stuffing" darkly grained Brazilian rosewood. The head of the tool is imprinted is formed of much darker rosewood and was never fitted for the ivory ring found on many of these braces. Crisp, clean and retaining nearly all original finishes, this spectacular brace is ready to display and bedazzle. Nice.* (FINE) **$1,845.00**

I1-23. Keyworth: Sheffield Type Brace. Push Button Chuck. Not in Eaton. Length: 13 1/2 Inches. *Reg Eaton's classic "The Ultimate Brace" contains a listing of makers and dealers who imprinted their names on English and Scottish braces. Absent from the list is the name "Keyworth", which appears on this Sheffield brace. Fitted with a push button chuck and a turned head of lignum vitae, this brace is a classic example of the Sheffield type brace.* (GOOD+) **$185.00**

I1-24. Stanley Tools No. 2101 A: "Yankee" Heavy Duty Brace. 10 Inch Sweep. Best Brace Ever. Length: 13 1/2 Inches. *The "Yankee" line was purchased from the North Brothers Tool Company by Stanley in 1946 and the tools were included in the Stanley line for at least another 15 years. The 2101 A brace, which features ball bearing fittings, is regarded by many as the best working brace ever made. A superb example of a great brace.* (FINE) **$75.00**

I1-25. Hawke, H., Solly Works, Sheffield: Classic Sheffield Brace. Push Button Chuck. Eagle Medallions. Length: 14 Inches. *The "American eagle" imprints on this classic Sheffield style brace are strong evidence that it was intended for export to the American market. The nicely turned rosewood head is in excellent condition. A classic.* (GOOD+) **$165.00**

I1-26. Marples, William, Hibernia Works: Classic Sheffield Brace. Inlaid Plates. Push Button Chuck. Length: 14 Inches. *The "Sheffield" style of wooden brace was distinguished from the "common" brace by the presence of reinforcing brass plates. Evidence from observed examples indicates that the plates were not particularly effective in stemming breakage, and, in some cases, may have helped bring it about. This one is in excellent condition, free from any damage or signs of abuse, and ready to display.* (FINE) **$265.00**

I1-27. Arthur, Edinburgh (Scotland): Classic Scottish Brace. Push Button Chuck. Excellent Patina. Length: 14 1/2 Inches. *A spring catch holds the bits in place on this British classic that is imprinted with the name of an Edinburgh, Scotland tool maker who worked from 1793 to 1844. A nice example.* (GOOD+) **$225.00**

I1-28. Unmarked: 6 Violinmaker's Clamps. Full Working Set. Early and Excellent. Length: 8 Inches. *Used by violin makers for construction and repair, these specialty clamps are in excellent condition and could be put back to use if the purchaser so desired. Early and excellent.* (GOOD+) **$245.00**

I1-29. Hawke, H., Solly Works, Sheffield: Rosewood English Brace. With Lignum Head. Eagle Medallions. Length: 14 Inches. *Carefully formed of solid Brazilian Rosewood and capped with a head of turned lignum vitae, this spectacular brace from a prominent Sheffield maker has the classic "eagle" mark on the chuck button that is indicative of a brace intended for the American market. Undoubtedly made to be a cut above the common brace, a tool such as this would have been affordable by only the most successful of craftsmen. A tight check through the body is evidence that this tool was actually used, but it is thoroughly presentable and ready to proudly display. Very pretty.* (GOOD+) **$1,195.00**

I1-30. Unmarked: Classic Chairmaker's Brace. With One Original Bit. Rare and Excellent. Length: 15 1/2 Inches. *Fitted with a single spoon-type augur bit, this oversize chair maker's brace is an American classic. A tough brace to find, especially in this condition.* (GOOD+) **$245.00**

I1-31. Marples, William, Hibernia Works: Rosewood "Ultimatum" Brace. With Royal Crest. Superb Condition. Length: 14 1/2 Inches. *William Marples, for a time the "Sole Manufacturer of the Ultimatum Framed Brace", offered his line of strikingly beautiful tools stuffed with ebony, beech, rosewood and boxwood. Ebony filled examples were by far the most common. Boxwood and rosewood were both apparently not favored by the workmen of the day, although it could hardly have been on account of their outward appearance. The black-grained Brazilian Rosewood presents a stunning contrast to the bronze-yellow of the frame. A very rare and beautiful English brace from the premier maker of these classic tools. Highly recommended.* (FINE) **$1,950.00**

I1-32. Goodell-Pratt Company: Hollow Auger Brace. Uncommon Type. Ready to Use. Length: 18 Inches. *Here's a good working example of Goodell-Pratt's combination hollow augur and brace. A good one.* (GOOD) **$65.00**

I1-33. Flather & Sons, D., Sheffield: "American Mechanics" Brace. With Eagle Button. Rare and Excellent. Length: 13 1/2 Inches. *British makers produced a number of specialized tools for export to the "American Market", including this "American Mechanic's" brace. Nicely decorated with inlaid plates of brass in the classic Sheffield style, most of the original finishes remain on this clean and clearly marked export oddity. An extremely rare brace in excellent collector quality condition.* (GOOD+) **$1,175.00**

I1-34. Stanley Rule & Level No. 1: Smooth Plane. "Sweetheart" Trademark. Extra Crisp and Clean. Length: 5 1/2 Inches. *Every Stanley collector eventually hopes to add the rare and desirable No. 1 Smooth Plane to his or her collection. At only 5 1/2 inches in length, these diminutive planes appear even to those for whom the more esoteric elements of the tool menangerie seem incomprehensible. The "Sweetheart" era example offered here retains 98% of its original finishes on all surfaces. Almost all of the dark, black japanning remains on body and frog; the polished cap is cast with the "Stanley" name, the dark grained tote and knob of Brazilian Rosewood are smooth and shiny; and the cutter and chip breaker with bold "Sweetheart" trademark are full and very well preserved. For the collector who has been waiting for a No. 1 in top condition, this is the plane. A sweetheart.* (FINE) **$1,350.00**

I1-35. Unmarked: Classic Early Pad Brace. Fixed With Cut Nail. Rare and Excellent. Length: 17 1/2 Inches. *The pivoting head of this graphic early style wooden pad brace is held in place by a pin formed from a cut nail. A classic "primitive".* (GOOD+) **$195.00**

I1-36. Millers Falls Company No. 1: Rosewood Handle Spoke Shave. Full Nickel Plating. Near New Condition. Length: 10 Inches. *Early tools by the Millers Falls Company are noted for their exceptional finish and workmanship. This circular spokeshave is a classic example. Nearly all original finishes remain on this as-new example including shiny nickel plating, classic rosewood handles and period orange infill in the throat. Extra nice.* (FINE) **$135.00**

I1-37. Marples, Robert, Hermitage Works: Octagon Compound Brace. Registered No. 3954. Early and Excellent. Length: 14 1/2 Inches. *Much of the story of Reg Eaton's "The Ultimate Brace" details the rivalry between the firms of William Marples and "the other" Marples, Robert Marples. The Registered Design for this innovative brace, granted on March 3, 1857, was hilled as an "Improved Double-Bound Carpenters' Brace with Octagon Compound Lever Pad". It incorporated a new design for the plates and a distinctive spring-activated bit release mechanism. Eaton speculates that these innovations may have been designed to bypass the patents held by William Marples on the "Ultimatum Brace". The expiration of the William Marples patents a few years later allowed a number of imitators to flatter the more established Marples firm by copying their products. Robert Marples helped to lead the way. This rare transitional brace was apparently left behind in the rush to clone. An extremely rare and early Registered Design brace.* (GOOD+) **$1,550.00**

I1-38. Goodel Pratt Company No. 279: Heavy Duty Breast Drill. Leather Breast Pad. Heavy Duty Type. Length: 20 Inches. *The Goodell-Pratt Company specialized in hand and breast drills during their 30 something years of operation. This model, which features a leather breast plate and "D" handle, was one of the most elaborate they offered. An uncommon breast drill in well preserved condition.* (GOOD+) **$165.00**

I1-39. Preston & Sons, E.: Decorative Cast Iron Spoke Shave. Full Nickel Plating. Miniature Size. Length: 6 3/4 Inches. *Preston made this spokeshave in this size and a larger version. Both are spectacular in appearance. This one has nearly all of its original finishes.* (FINE) **$145.00**

I1-40. Unmarked: Classic English Brace. Rosewood Head. Check in Body. Length: 13 3/4 Inches. *There is a check through the body that has been glued, but this rosewood head Sheffield brace is otherwise in excellent condition. The head has been nicely turned from Brazilian Rosewood.* (GOOD) **$85.00**

Group H1

H1-1. Stanley Rule & Level No. 605 1/4: "Bedrock" Junior Jack Plane. With Manuals. New Condition, Original Box. Length: 11 Inches. *One of the rarest of Stanley's highly collectible "Bedrock" series, the No. 605 1/4 was like it's non-Bedrock equivalent, intended primarily for the smaller hands of youth at trade schools. "In the Box" items that are so coveted by collectors generally came to be preserved in that high condition for two reasons: either they were used one or two times and then stored in the box, or they were old hardware stock and never sold to a retail customer. Given the nature of the market for these manual training school planes, they would not likely have been stocked by a hardware dealer. As for the "used once and put away" option, it simply did not happen. When an order of these tools was received at the school, the boxes would have been thrown in the trash or used for something else—certainly not saved. For reasons unknown, this unused No. 605 1/4 has remained in nearly new condition throughout its approximately 75 years of existence. The box is clean and sound, noting only that a portion of the label has been chewed upon by silverfish, which had the good sense not to eat the portion marked with the product number, most likely owing to the bad taste of the ink. As rare a Bedrock series as we have ever offered. Brand new in the original box.* (FINE) **$2,875.00**

H1-2. Stanley Rule & Level (Unmarked?): Rare Prototype Router Plane. See "Stanley News". Marked "2314-1". Length: 7 Inches. *Were it not for the documentation published in the now-defunct "Stanley Collector News" few collectors would be aware of this prototypical Stanley router plane. Equipped with the standard issue handles and blade fixing yoke, the body of this experimental plane is marked with a casting number "2314-1". Only a few examples of this plane have been found, indicating that the plane was either distributed for testing, or that the original batch somehow found their way to the market after having been tried and found wanting by Stanley. Unmarked in any way, but of sufficient authenticity to warrant inclusion in the magazine that was for several years the Bible of Stanley Tool Collecting, we are proud to offer this rare experimental Stanley plane.* (GOOD+) **$1,295.00**

H1-3. Stanley Rule & Level No. 212: Adjustable Scraper Plane. Script Trademark. With Stanley Cutter. Length: 5 1/2 Inches. *Introduced by Stanley in 1911, when their product line seemed to be ever-expanding, the No. 212 scraper was designed to be used for specialized hand scraping such as would have been required of fine woodworkers, musical instrument makers, fishing rod makers and the like. Universally acclaimed for its utility, the No. 212 seems not to have generated sufficient demand among woodworkers of the time, and it was dropped from the product line a little more than twenty years later. It is not likely that many were sold during that time. This superb example is marked with Stanley's ca. 1915 tradmark on the cutting iron and the base is cast with the Stanley logo in the classic "script" trademark. Clean, crisp, complete and in top collector quality condition, we highly recommend this rare Stanley scraper.* (FINE) **$2,150.00**

H1-4. Unmarked: Set of Gunstocker's Floats. Mahogany Handles. Marked "H.Russell Co." Length: 10 Inches. *The task of precisely fitting the hardwood stock to the metal components of a rifle or shotgun was precision work that required precision tools. Each of the tools in this rare, complete set of gunstockers floats is fitted with a mahogany handle and imprinted with the maker's name on the shaft of the tool. An exceptionally nice set.* (FINE) **$565.00**

H1-5. Stanley Rule & Level No. 69: Patent Hand Beader. Beech Handle. Super Rare and Early. Length: 4 3/4 Inches. *Produced by Stanley for only a few short years, from 1898 to 1917, when it was discontinued "temporarily" for wartime purposes and then unceremoniously dumped, as were a number of slow selling items, when peacetime conditions again prevailed, the No. 69 beader is a rare and very collectible Stanley tool. Designed to be used in conjunction with a fixed fence of wood to cut decorative beading and fluting on wood, these tools apparently failed to produce sufficient demand in the marketplace. Accordingly, examples are quite rare. This example is in nearly new condition and retains some 98% of its shiny nickel plating. All of the original cutters are present in their original Stanley factory envelope. Extra special.* (FINE) **$945.00**

H1-6. Stanley Rule & Level: Turnbull's Patent Trammels. All Original Parts. Near New Condition. Length: 7 1/2 Inches. *Produced under a patent granted to Andrew Turnbull on March 2, 1909 these precision trammels were offered by Stanley between 1909 and 1935. The few sets that were sold were likely quickly separated and eventually discarded. In the past 15 years we have seen perhaps 10 full sets of these Stanley trammels and none in as well preserved condition as this exceptionally clean set. A rare set of trammels in top collector quality condition.* (FINE) **$595.00**

H1-7. Stanley Rule & Level No. 74: Floor Plane. Complete With Handle. 90% + Original Paint. Length: 10 Inches. *The heavy use for which they were intended and which most of them eventually performed made the No. 74 floor plane very susceptible to wear and damage. Generally, examples of this plane, when found, are totally missing the original handle, devoid of most paint and either rusted or broken. This superb example, has none of those flaws. Retaining fully 90% of its original paint as well as the original beech handle, this crispy clean floor plane is the finest example of this tool that we have offered in more than 10 years. If you wish to add a well preserved example of the No. 74 to your collection, this opportunity will not last long. Rare, and very highly recommended.* (GOOD+) **$1,650.0**

H1-8. Stanley Rule & Level No. 283: Adjustable Cabinet Scraper. With Rosewood Handles. New Condition, Original Box. Length: 9 1/2 Inches. *Among the least common of all of Stanley's scraper planes, the No. 283 features a pair of rosewood handes, one of which is attached to the cutting edge by a steel bracket that positively locks it into place. Because of the nature of these tools and the fact that it was necessary to disassemble them to get them to fit in the original box, examples of the box are nearly nonexistent. We are pleased and proud to offer this, the only "in the box" example of this rare scraper plane that we have ever seen. Rare and brand new. Highly recommended.* (FINE) **$1,595.00**

H1-9. Stanley Rule & Level No. 26: General Line Catalog. Aug 1900 Edition, 80 Page. 7 Inches X 5 Inches. Length: 7 Inches. *This, the first attempt by Stanley to provide a general line catalog to everyday woodworker, rather than just to hardware dealers, proved to be the basis for their incredible success in the first half of the Twentieth Century. In all likelihood, the No. 26 was distributed in limited numbers, but produced so much business that it led to the publication, beginning in 1905, of the annual No. 34 catalog that collectors know so well. This example shows only minor wear and is complete and unstained. A rare and historically significant Stanley catalog.* (GOOD+) **$265.00**

H1-10. Stanley Rule & Level No. G4 C: "Gage" Smoothing Plane. Patented February 17, 1920. New Condition, Original Box. Length: 9 Inches. *Stanley's short-lived venture in the expansion of the "Gage" line of planes began with their acquisition of the former Gage Tool Company of Vineland, New Jersey, in 1919, and culminated with the discontinuation of most of the Gage line in the 1930's, most likely as a result of the Roosevelt Depression, which would grow steadily worse until the beginning of the Second World War. Economic crash or not, the dearth of surviving examples suggests that these planes were not popular, even in the best of times. This example, it its original mustard-yellow Stanley box is one of those tools that is so rare that the sight of tool and box leads experienced tool collectors to do an exaggerated "double take" as they convince themselves that they've "never seen one of those before". A rare and pristine example of an under appreciated Stanley collectible. Worth two looks.* (FINE) **$1,945.00**

H1-11. Stanley Rule & Level No. 97: Cabinet Maker's Edge Plane. Early "Type 2". New Condition, Original Box. Length: 10 Inches. *The absolutely perfectly preserved No. 97 cabinetmaker's edge plane is dead right, and the box is the original; but the original label was missing and a previous owner has made use of color photocopying technology to replicate the original—a caveat emptor to all potential buyers of "in the box" tools. Whatever the case with the label, this plane is in top shelf condition and belongs on the very top shelf.* (FINE) **$845.00**

H1-12. Stanley Rule & Level No. 603: "Bedrock" Smoothing Plane. Red Label Box. New Condition, Original Box. Length: 8 1/2 Inches. *For some reason, planes of the Stanley "Bedrock" series in their original boxes are almost impossible to find. Your author knows of less than 10 planes in collections anywhere that are complete with the distinctive red-lebeled Bedrock box. This No. 603 comes complete with the box, the label of which has been torn, but is present and could be made more presentable. The plane has been used, but not abused. Most unusual.* (GOOD+) **$895.00**

H1-13. Stanley Rule & Level No. RG 1 1/2: Rare "Rubber Grip" Hammer. 16 Ounce Size. Excellent Condition. Length: 13 Inches. *Designated as the No. "RG" 1 1/2, this specialized Stanley hammer is fitted with a special rubber grip. It is not likely that many of these survived. A rare Stanley hammer.* (GOOD+) **$145.00**

H1-14. Stanley Rule & Level No. 4: Rare Bronze Trammels. Second Known Example. New Condition, Original Box. Length: 4 1/2 Inches. *At first glance, these Stanley trammel points appear, to the seasoned collector, to be a bronze recast of Stanley's No. 4 cast iron trammels. However, upon close inspection, the high degree of detail in the casting and the fact that the trammels are in new condition in their original box gives rise to suspicion that these might just be something far from the ordinary. If only a single example of these bronze trammels had appeared, it would still lead to questioning by serious collectors, who are naturally and rightly suspicious of something so different from the norm. A review of the Stanley Value Guide confirms, however, that at least one other pair of these special trammels are known. An exceptionally rare pair of Stanley No. 4 bronze trammels in new condition in their original box.* (FINE) **$1,175.00**

H1-15. Stanley Rule & Level No. 200: Adjustable Chisel Grinder. Patented December 10, 1912. Near New Condition. Length: 7 Inches. *Designed to facilitate the task of honing chisels and plane irons, this tool may have seemed like a good idea to its previous owner, but it appears that he used it very little, if at all. Nice.* (FINE) **$95.00**

H1-16. Stanley Rule & Level: Dowel Machine Cutter Head. Uncommon 5/16 Inch Size. New Condition, Original Box. Length: 2 3/4 Inches. *Arguably the least common of the dowel machine cutters, this example of the 5/16 inch size is in nearly new condition in its original box. A rare dowel cutter.* (FINE) **$225.00**

H1-17. Stanley Rule & Level No. 87: Cast Iron Scraper Plane. "Pat. Appl'd For". Rare and Near New. Length: 7 1/2 Inches. *A classic example of a tool of such limited utility in comparison to others in the Stanley's product line that collectors, possessed of the clarity of vision that hindsight bestows, are left to wonder why Stanley produced this plane at all. Similar in many respects to the No. 85 scraper plane, the No. 87 lacked the rabbet sides of the 85 as well as its versatile tilting handles. It appears that the folks in New Britain came to the conclusion themselves that this plane was never going to be popular and discontinued it from the product line after only 14 years in the catalogs. In all likelihood, perhaps one or two limited runs of production were made. This example, which is cast with the designation "Pat. Appl'd for" in the body is crisp, clean, complete and ready to display. The corners of the cutting iron have been slightly rounded with a file, most likely by the original owner. A rare Stanley plane in top collector quality condition.* (FINE) **$1,975.00**

H1-18. Stanley Rule & Level No. 1: Retractable Reel Plumb Bob. Patented April 28, 1874. Excellent Patina. Length: 4 Inches. *This, the larger of the Stanley retractable reel brass plumb bobs, is not marked with the maker name, but there's no mistaking who made it. Nicely patinated and hard to find.* (GOOD+) **$195.00**

H1-19. Stanley Rule & Level No. 14 NM: Nickel Plated Claw Hammer. 20 Ounce Size. Rare and Near New. Length: 14 Inches. *Stanley offered the No. 14 hammer for a brief period from 1911 to 1912. During that time, users were offered the option of purchasing the tool with a nickel plated head, designated as the 14 N, and with a mahogany handle, designated as the 14 NM. Apparently few opted for these additional features as these hammers are practically nonexistent in any condition. Examples such as this 20 oz. No. 14 NM, which is imprinted with the "Sweetheart" trademark and retains all of its original nickel plating and all of the lacquer on the mahogany handle are unheard of, until now. Absolutely perfect and a guaranteed showstopper. A magnificent Stanley hammer that comes very highly recommended.* (FINE) **$645.00**

H1-20. Stanley Rule & Level No. 1: 5 1/2" Smoothing Plane. Patent 1892 Trademark. Near New Condition. Length: 5 1/2 Inches. *The smallest version of its standard bench plane series, Stanley's No. 1 bench plane has always held a special place in the hearts of tool collectors. Of diminutive size and proportion that others less inclined to propriety would refer to a "cute", these planes appeal to far more than just the select few who are conversant with the arcana of tool collecting. This superb example is imprinted with the "Pat. 1892" trademark used ca. 1895 and is in clean, complete condtition, retaining 98% of original finishes on all parts. A prime example of a premier tool. Perfect.* (FINE) **$1,375.00**

H1-21. Stanley Rule & Level No. 10: Early 1st Lateral Plane. Beaded Front Knob. 95%+ Original Paint. Length: 12 1/2 Inches. *Students of the tools produced by the Stanley Rule & Level Company have documented the exact dates when specific technological innovations were introduced to the product line, making it relatively easy to determine, with a fair degree of accuracy, when a specific plane was produced. Early examples of Stanley's bench planes were not equipped with a lateral adjustment feature, making it necessary for the user to manually reset the iron to ensure that the cutting iron was set squarely in the plane. In 1885 a lever mechanism for lateral adjustment was introduced. This early adjustment was superceded, in 1888, by a more mechanically complex version. This crisp and clean example of the No. 10 carriage maker's rabbet plane is fitted with the distinctive lateral adjustment used from 1885 to 1888 only. A rare and nearly perfectly preserved bench rabbet plane from the 1880's. Rare.* (FINE) **$345.00**

H1-22. Stanley Rule & Level No. 312: 8 Inch Aluminum Try Square. Ca. 1925 Only. "Sweetheart" Trademark. Length: 9 1/2 Inches. *During the 1920's the Stanley Rule & Level began, and soon ended a questionably successful attempt to market tools produced largely from aluminum. After all, this once scarce metal had just become available in large quantities as a result of improvements in the process of extracting it from ore. It seemed only appropriate to use this strong and light material for tools. Looking backward, it appears that the tools were too susceptible to damage and weathering to stand up in comparison to their traditional competitors of steel and cast iron. As part of the initial rollout of the line, Stanley also included, for a very short time, a series of aluminum try squares. Initially included in advertising for the 1925 product line, these tools were soon dropped from production and are so scarce that many knowledgeable Stanley collectors are unaware of thier existence. This 8 inch model is marked with the "Sweetheart" imprint on the blade and is in excellent collector quality condition. A rare Stanley square in great shape.* (GOOD+) **$545.00**

H1-23. Stanley Rule & Level No. 12 1/4: Rosewood Handle Scraper. Sweetheart Trademark. New Condition, Original Box. Length: 10 Inches. *Stanley's No. 12 series of scrapers were planes that required a greater amount of assembly work than any others that the company offered. Consequently, very few were ever put back into their original boxes after having been used. If the No. 12 in the box is rare, and the No. 12 1/2 is rare in the box, it stands to reason that the No. 12 1/4, less common by far than either of the others would be an equal amount less common in the original box—and it is. This, the only such example of the 12 1/4 scraper we have ever offered is in brand new condition. The box is complete, but has been taped at the corners and the early "picture" label is about 95% complete. A rare plane in a very rare box.* (FINE) **$1,350.00**

Group J1

J1-1. Norris, London: 1 1/2 Inch Stuffed Shoulder Metallic Plane. Rosewood Infill. Original Norris Iron. Length: 7 1/2 Inches. *Nearly all of the original Norris cutting iron remains on this nearly perfectly preserved rabbeting plane from England's most highly respected maker. Tight at the throat and devoid of any evidence of wear, this plane is ready to provide years of service in a woodworking shop while adding an element of aesthetic appeal. Simply a great plane.* (FINE) **$695.00**

J1-2. Stanley Rule & Level No. 43: Miller Patent Plow Plane. Distinctive Design. Rare "Slitter" Type. Length: 9 Inches. *More than 90% of the shiny original black japan finish remains on this classic Millers Patent plow plane. The No. 43 differed from the No. 41 only in the absence of the filletster bed. A superb example.* (FINE) **$675.00**

J1-3. Hields, William, Nottingham: Set of 18 Hollow and Round Molding Planes. Skew Set Irons. Excellent Condition. Length: 95 Inches. *Full sets of hollow and round molding planes with skew set irons have become nearly impossible to find. This very well preserved set by William Hields of the fabled English City of Nottingham was made between 1830 and 1881. Crisp, clean and ready to use. Highly recommended.* (GOOD+) **$895.00**

J1-4. Unmarked: Classic "Chariot" Metallic Plane. Cupid's Bow Wedge. Excellent Condition. Length: 3 Inches. *A nicely proportioned brass bow and mahogany infill accent this well preserved chariot plane.* (GOOD+) **$295.00**

J1-5. Unmarked: Classic Spill Plane. Manufactured Type. Excellent Condition. Length: 9 1/2 Inches. *Obviously produced by a plane manufacturer, this classic "spill" plane was used to produced curled shavings that were used to transfer a light for a pipe or cigar from an open fire. It is in excellent condition.* (GOOD+) **$135.00**

J1-6. Norris, London No. 50: Precision Adjust Metallic Plane. Original Norris Iron. Near New Condition. Length: 9 Inches. *Nearly all original finishes remain on this Norris classic. Extra nice.* (FINE) **$795.00**

J1-7. Unmarked: Bronze "Chariot" Metallic Plane. With Ebony Wedge. Cupid's Bow Bridge. Length: 3 1/4 Inches. *A decorative "cupid's bow" bridge adds additional aesthetic appeal to this delightful bronze chariot plane.* (GOOD+) **$195.00**

J1-8. Norris, London No. A 5: Patent Smoothing Metallic Plane. With Patent Adjustment. Original Lacquer Finish. Length: 7 1/4 Inches. *Nearly all of the orignal lacquer finish remains on this crispy clean adjustable smoother from respected maker Norris of London. Extra nice.* (FINE) **$795.00**

J1-9. Norris, London: Rosewood Fill Smooth Metallic Plane. Mathieson Iron. Ready to Use. Length: 8 1/2 Inches. *Fitted out with a replacement iron from Scottish makers A. Mathieson & Son's, this classic parallel side pre-War dovetailed Norris smoothing plane is in excellent working order. A tight crack to the rosewood tote could be easily glued and a light cleaning to the new owner's standard is all that is needed to restore this plane to its former brilliance. A rare Norris plane in great working condition.* (GOOD+) **$745.00**

J1-10. Unmarked: Low Angle Miter Metallic Plane. Dovetailed Brass Body. Extra Low Angle. Length: 8 Inches. *Obtained this past summer in Scotland, this low angle mitre plane of dovetailed brass was an artist craftsman's workaday solution to the planing of end grain. A dramatic Scottish miter plane.* (GOOD+) **$425.00**

J1-11. Unmarked: Stuffed Smoothing Metallic Plane. Beechwood Infill. Robert Sorby Iron. Length: 7 3/4 Inches. *If you're looking for a good working infill smoothing plane and don't want to mortgage the house, this example, which is fitted with a full cutting iron by Robert Sorby, will fill the bill nicely. Crisp, clean and ready to use.* (GOOD+) **$295.00**

J1-12. Norris, London: No. 14: Rosewood Infill Metallic Plane. Original Iron. Superb Condition. Length: 7 1/4 Inches. *Nearly all of the original Norris cutting iron remains on this nearly perfectly preserved smoothing plane from England's most highly respected maker. Tight at the throat and devoid of any evidence of wear, this plane is ready to provide years of service in a woodworking shop while adding an element of aesthetic appeal. Simply a great plane.* (FINE) **$1,550.00**

J1-13. Spiers, Stewart, Ayr, Scotland: Stuffed Smooth Metallic Plane. Rosewood Infill. Ward & Payne Iron. Length: 8 Inches. *Spectacularly grained infill of Brazilian Rosewood adds visual appeal to this superb parallel sided smoother from legendary Scottish maker Stewart Spiers. The full original Ward & Payne cutting iron remains.* (FINE) **$785.00**

J1-14. Spiers, Stewart, Ayr, Scotland: Stuffed Panel Metallic Plane. Herring & Sons Iron. Superb Condition. Length: 14 Inches. *One look at the lines of this Scottish classic says that it was the work of master planemaker Stewart Spiers of Ayrshire. Dramatically grained infill of Brazilian Rosewood adds character to this well preserved panel plane. A good one.* (GOOD+) **$645.00**

J1-15. Spiers, Stewart, Ayr, Scotland: Rosewood Filled Metallic Plane. Brass Lever Cap. M. York Iron. Length: 8 Inches. *This well preserved Spiers smoother has a distinctive pebbled cap iron having the Spiers name in raised letters. Crisp, clean and ready to use.* (GOOD+) **$695.00**

J1-16. Unmarked: Classic Infill Metallic Plane. Mahogany Stuffed. Parallel Sides. Length: 7 1/2 Inches. *Here's a nearly perfectly preserved parallel side smoothing plane in excellent working order. A full cutting iron remains.* (FINE) **$445.00**

J1-17. Spiers, Stewart, Ayr, Scotland: No. 25: Rosewood Filled Smooth Metallic Plane. Spiers Parallel Iron. Dovetailed Sole. Length: 8 Inches. *Perhaps 30% of the planes produced by Stewart Spiers were fitted with cutting irons imprinted with the Spiers mark. The ready availability of superior irons by Ward, Mathieson and Sorby made it unnecessary for Stewart Spiers to concern himself with making his own, other than to save money—a concern not lost on any self respecting Scotsman. Indeed, we have heard a story, perhaps apocryphal, that Spiers, whose tailor had offered to reline his suits at no additional charge, once turned a suit inside out to seek to maximize the benefit of that generosity. Whatever the case, this Spiers classic retains a full Spiers marked iron and is in top collector quality condition. Extra nice.* (FINE) **$825.00**

J1-18. Spiers, Stewart, Ayr, Scotland: 3/4 Inch Shoulder Rabbet Metallic Plane. Proper "Ward" Iron. Extra Tight Throat. Length: 9 Inches. *One look at the profile of this well preserved and thoroughly usable rabbet plane and it is apparent that it was the work of Stewart Spiers, the preeminent Scottish planemaker. Fitted with its full Ward cutting iron and possessed of an extra tight throat, this plane is ready to go to work in the shop of a serious craftsman.* (GOOD+) **$385.00**

J1-19. Unmarked: Mahogany Infill Metallic Plane. Extra Tight Throat. Hearnsaw Brothers Iron. Length: 8 Inches. *A full iron bearing the imprint of edge tool makers Hernshaw Brothers is ready to help this pristine mahogany stuffed rabbet plane perform the function for which it was intended. Acquired this past Summer in the City of York in the North of England, this 19th Century plane is in nearly new condition.* (FINE) **$365.00**

J1-20. Norris, London No. A 5: Patent Smoothing Metallic Plane. With Patent Adjustment. Extra Crisp and Clean. Length: 7 1/4 Inches. *Complete with nearly all original finishes, a full Norris Iron and a throat that is as tight as the day it was made, this classic adjustable smoother is ready to provide a lifetime of service.* (FINE) **$745.00**

J1-21. Thackeray, J.W., Armley, Yorkshire: Scottish Stuffed Metallic Plane. Rosewood Infill. Gunmetal Cap and Body. Length: 9 Inches. *A product of planemaker J.W. Thackeray, who worked in Armley, near the Northern English City of Leeds, the Scottish influence is clearly visible in this rosewood-stuffed gunmetal smoothing plane. In excellent working condition, and a joy to behold, we proudly offer this classic infill plane.* (GOOD+) **$745.00**

J1-22. Norris, London No. A5: Adjustable Smoothing Metallic Plane. With Patent Adjustment. New Condition, Original Box. Length: 7 1/2 Inches. *As a working tool for precision hand planing, the patent adjustment planes manufactured by Norris of London have no equal. Rightly held in reverential esteem by woodworkers of every stripe, new Norris planes became unavailable when production was ceased shortly after World War II. Working examples quickly become the treasured possession of a serious craftsman. Finding usable Norris planes without major problems is difficult indeed. Finding the Norris plane in near-new condition, complete with the original box is practically impossible. This plane, an example of the immediate post-war work of the Norris firm, is in perfect condition and shows no evidence of use. We recommend this plane without hesitation to any serious woodworker. It's level of precison will add a different perspective to one's craft and provide a lifetime of satisfaction. The art of the impossible.* (FINE) **$1,195.00**

J1-23. Preston & Sons, E.: Bullnose Block Metallic Plane. With Rosewood Wedge. Scarce and Excellent. Length: 6 Inches. *A superb example of the Preston bullnose rabbet plane. This one has been very little used.* (GOOD+) **$225.00**

J1-24. Spiers, Stewart, Ayr, Scotland: No. 27: Rosewood Filled Smooth Metallic Plane. Mathieson Parallel Iron. Dovetailed Sole. Length: 8 1/2 Inches. *A full original parallel iron from from A. Mathieson & Sons makes this classic rosewood stuffed dovetailed smoother ready to last a lifetime, and then some. A classic.* (GOOD+) **$725.00**

J1-25. Norris, London No. 50: Precision Adjust Metallic Plane. Original Norris Iron. Ready to Use. Length: 9 Inches. *Absent the wooden infill that was the characteristic of more costly Norris planes, this functionally equivalent A 50 features the same precision cutter adjustment that was, and remains, the primary selling feature of their planes. A great working tool at a bargain price.* (GOOD+) **$575.00**

J1-26. Norris, London No. 50 G: Precision Adjust Metallic Plane. Original Norris Iron. Rare Gunmetal Type. Length: 9 Inches. *Early advertising indicates that the Norris Company introduced the non-stuffed No. 50 as a means of slightly lowering the price while allowing the inclusion of their legendary technical expertise without compromise. It does not necessarily follow that they would then price such a plane out of the reach of all but the most serious users by offering nearly the same tool with a gunmetal body, but that is exactly what they did. This No. 50 G features the Norris precision adjustment mechanism, a gunmetal body, rosewood infill and a sweated sole that appears never to have come into contact with wood. Nearly all original finishes remain on this pristine example of a sow's ear done up as a silk purse. A exceptionally well preserved and scarce Norris plane.* (FINE) **$1,395.00**

J1-27. Unmarked: Gunmetal Bullnose Metallic Plane. Rosewood Wedge. Iron by Buck. Length: 3 3/4 Inches. *This classic bronze bullnose is fitted with a full cutting iron imprinted with the mark of London maker Buck. A showpiece in excellent working order.* (GOOD+) **$145.00**

J1-29. Unmarked: Cast Iron Rabbet Metallic Plane. Decorative Infill. From North Scotland. Length: 5 Inches. *Even among the artistically inspired metallic planes of Scotland, this shoulder rabbet plane stands out for its dramatically sweeping lines. Recently collected in the town of Inverness, on the Northern tip of Loch Ness, this spectacular tool encapsulates the Scottish planemaking tradition within its bold and flowing form. Extra special.* (GOOD+) **$285.00**

J1-30. Spiers, Stewart, Ayr, Scotland: Parallel Side Metallic Plane. Dovetailed Sole. Spiers Cap and Iron. Length: 8 1/2 Inches. *Here's a Spiers classic in top working condition. It retains its original Spiers cutting iron. The tip of the tote has been professionally restored. An excellent example of a rare and very desirable dovetailed smoothing plane.* (GOOD+) **$745.00**

J1-31. Norris, London No. A 5: Patent Smoothing Metallic Plane. With Patent Adjustment. Original Engine Polish. Length: 7 1/4 Inches. *The patent adjustable planes of London maker Norris have rightly earned a worldwide reputation for quality and reliability. In most areas of collecting, it is the demand by collectors that determines the market price. With the Norris planes, however, especially the bench planes, user demand is so great, and supply is so limited, that it must realistically be said that the fact that user demand far exceeds collector interest is the sole reason for the limited supply of these tools. We offer a superb example which reatains nearly all of its original finishes. Complete with an original Norris iron, this plane is ready to provide a lifetime of useful service.* (FINE) **$845.00**

J1-32. Preston & Sons, E.: Handled Smooth Metallic Plane. Rosewood Infill. Dovetailed Sole. Length: 8 Inches. *Edward Preston & Sons were known for the uncompromising quality of their merchandise. This rosewood stuffed smoother is clearly marked with the Preston imprint on the cap iron and is ready to be immediately put to work. A full parallel iron by William Marples remains.* (FINE) **$765.00**

J1-33. Mathieson & Son, A., Glasgow: Handled Smooth Metallic Plane. Rosewood Infill. Dovetailed Body. Length: 7 1/2 Inches. *The infill planes produced by Alexander Mathieson & Sons of Glasgow, Scotland were the equal in performance and finish to the non-adjustable planes of Norris, but have yet to achieve their well deserved reputation. This classic dovetailed smoother is in nearly new condition and ready to be put immediately to work.* (FINE) **$865.00**

J1-34. Unmarked: Rosewood Infill Metallic Plane. With Parallel Iron. Near New Condition. Length: 9 Inches. *The turned finial on the cap iron of this parallel sided smoothing plane is evocative of those used by Alexander Mathieson of Glasgow. Fitted with a full parallel iron by W. Butcher, this plane is in excellent working order. A classic.* (FINE) **$625.00**

J1-35. Spiers, Stewart, Ayr, Scotland: Dovetailed Jointer Metallic Plane. Early Screw Sides. Ready to Use. Length: 20 1/2 Inches. *Nicely marked on its cast bronze cap iron with the imprint of respected Scottish maker Stewart Spiers, this superb 20 1/2 inch jointer plane is fitted with a fine iron of the proper type, but which is imprinted with the name of prominent English edge tool maker Ward. Showing only the level of wear that would be consistent with the working tools of a joiner, including a sheared horn to the tote, this well-preserved plane is in excellent order and ready to be returned to the tasks for which it was intended and at which it was employed for many years. The properly fitted iron retains nearly two inches of edge and leaves an opening barely the thickness of a sheet of paper when adjusted for work. Without question, this is the finest Spiers jointer plane we have ever offered. Extra nice and ready to provide a lifetime of service.* (GOOD+) **$1,475.00**

J1-36. Unmarked: Dovetailed Mitre Metallic Plane. Ward & Payne Iron. Mahogany Infill. Length: 9 1/2 Inches. *This classic mitre plane features a dovetailed sole, an extremely tight throat and a cutting iron from prominent edge tool makers Ward & Payne of Sheffield. Both the infill and the wedge are of mahogany. A classic "cupid's bow" pattern ornaments the hand-filed bridge. A classic woodworking in excellent condition for the shop or the collection.* (GOOD+) **$895.00**

J1-37. Fuller, Jo., Providence: Yellow Birch Bead Molding Plane. 10 Inch Overall Length. Superb Chamfers. Length: 10 Inches. *The 10 inch length of this plane is a sure sign that it was produced very early in the working period of Providence, Rhode Island planemaker Joseph Fuller. A classic Eighteenth Century plane.* (GOOD+) **$265.00**

J1-38. Unmarked: Gunmetal Rabbet Metallic Plane. Applied Steel Sole. Hearnshaw Brothers Iron. Length: 8 Inches. *This spectacular gunmetal rabbeting plane retains nearly all of its full original iron. There is some very light pitting to the applied steel sole, but this plane is otherwise in superb condition. A showstopper.* (GOOD+) **$585.00**

J1-39. Unmarked: Scottish Smooth Metallic Plane. Shield Cap Iron. "R.B. Mc Arthur". Length: 9 Inches. *The planes of Spiers and Mathieson were, in many ways, a case of life imitating art. In fashioning their classic lines of planes, they took the idiom of the artful Scottish infill plane and attempted to transform it into a manufactured product. They succeeded very well, and their planes are a joy to behold, but they could never quite capture the spirit of the real thing. This classic smoother, fitted with sculpted infill of tropical hardwood, decorative side panels and a bronze cap with an open "shield" pattern that is inscribed with the name "R.B. Arthur" is the sort of plane the great makers were attempting to produce, but, in so doing, they could produce only the words, and not the music. The real thing.* (GOOD+) **$645.00**

J1-40. Norris, London No. A 5: Patent Smoothing Metallic Plane. With Patent Adjustment. New Condition, Original Box. Length: 7 1/4 Inches. *A virtual guarantee that this plane will not only hold its value, but dramatically appreciate, the original box for this immediate postwar Norris classic is in excellent condition and retains nearly all of its original label. As a consequence of the presence the box, this plane is in immaculate condition. Absolutely perfect.* (FINE) **$1,295.00**

J1-41. Unmarked: Patternmaker's Metallic Plane. 10 Bases and Cutters. Very Well Made. Length: 11 1/2 Inches. *Complete with its full complement of 10 cutting irons and 10 interchangeable soles this spectacular patternmaker's plane is in essentially new condition. A fitted mahogany case has kept the 10 Buck Brothers cutting irons as clean and shiny as the day they were made. If you are looking for a classic patternmaker's plane in top shelf condition, we highly recommend this classic tool.* (FINE) **$685.00**

J1-42. Unmarked: Bronze Bullnose Metallic Plane. Mahogany Wedge. Owner "J.W. Jewell". Length: 3 1/2 Inches. *Time and the elements have worked their will on this bronze bullnose rabbet, but some judicious cleaning should easily bring it back to its original glory. A diamond in the rough.* (GOOD+) **$115.00**

J1-42. Stanley Rule & Level No. 98/99: Pair of Side Rabbet Planes. Patented January 29, 1895. Ready to Use. Length: 4 Inches. *These rosewood handled side rabbet planes are clean, complete and ready to go back to work. A pretty pair.* (GOOD+) **$245.00**

J1-43. Spiers, Stewart, Ayr, Scotland: Rosewood Filled Metallic Plane. Brass Lever Cap. Original Marples Iron. Length: 7 1/4 Inches. *This well preserved smoothing plane is imprinted with the mark of respected Scottish maker Stewart Spiers. Nearly all of the original William Marples cutting iron remains on this classic dovetailed smoothing plane.* (GOOD+) **$525.00**

J1-44. Unmarked: Scottish Mitre Metallic Plane. Rosewood Infill. Decorative Bridge. Length: 9 Inches. *What was it about Scotland and its woodworking tradition that virtually required that all craftsman made planes from that country be works of art? This spectacular cast iron low angle mitre plane has had its bridge formed in a a decorative form and has been nicely fitted with infill and wedge of Brazilian Rosewood. A great looking plane in excellent working order.* (GOOD+) **$445.00**

J1-45. Unmarked: Cast Iron Rabbet Metallic Plane. From Pattern Shop. Distinctive Form. Length: 7 1/2 Inches. *More than a few frustrated artists and sculptors found their way into pattern shops and foundries, a fact to which this early 20th Century rabbeting plane will bear witness. Artsy.* (GOOD+) **$115.00**

Group K1

K1-1. Stanley Rule & Level No. 50: Combination Beading Plane. With All Original Cutters. Fitted Wood Case. Length: 8 Inches. *This example of Stanley's light duty plow and bead plane adds functionality to a shop at considerably less weight than its more versatile cousins, the No. 45 and the No. 55. An owner made wooden box has protected the plane very well. Crisp, clean and ready to use.* (FINE) **$175.00**

K1-2. Stanley Rule & Level No. 39: Cast Iron Dado Plane. 1/4 Inch Size. "Sweetheart" Trademark. Length: 8 Inches. *The smallest of the No. 39 series, the 1/4 inch size is quite uncommon. This crispy clean example is in nearly new condition.* (FINE) **$325.00**

K1-3. Stanley Rule & Level No. 85: Pivot Handle Scraper Plane. Patented April 11, 1905. "Sweetheart" Trademark. Length: 8 Inches. *Nearly every example of the Stanley No. 85 tilt handle scraper plane that I have seen has been fitted with a thin steel scraper blade, which, while obviously original, was, for some reason, never imprinted with the Stanley logo. This pristine example of this rare, special purpose scraper plane retains nearly all of its original finshes on all surfaces. The body casting has the 1905 patent date cast into it and the cutter is boldly marked with the desirable "Sweetheart" trademark. A perfectly preserved example of a desirable Stanley tool. Highly recommended.* (FINE) **$985.00**

K1-4. Stanley Rule & Level No. 444: Dovetail Tongue and Groove Plane. Complete and Crisp. One Original Cutter. Length: 9 1/2 Inches. *Designed for precision planing of dovetail joints of every shape and size, this rare plane is in excellent overall condition. All parts, including spur blocks and the original instruction booklet are included. The wooden box is in sound condition and more than 60% of the original label remains. Three of the original four cutters are missing. Ready to use, if you choose.* (FINE) **$965.00**

K1-5. Stanley Rule & Level No. 9: Low Angle Block Plane. With Tail Handle. Damage to Side. Length: 9 Inches. *As was the case with many of Stanley's No. 9 cabinetmaker's block planes, the brittle casting on this example has been cracked through use. If the user so chose, it could be welded to restore it to its original magnificence. The tail handle mechanism, cap and blade are in good order and are worth the asking price of this tool as parts. A rare Stanley plane.* (GOOD) **$545.00**

K1-6. Stanley Rule & Level No. 65: Low Angle Block Plane. Nickel Plated Cap. Unused Condition. Length: 7 Inches. *A shiny nickel cap with nearly 100% japanning make this perfectly preserved No. 65 block plane a real showpiece. No apologies for this increasingly difficult to find plane.* (FINE) **$145.00**

K1-7. Stanley Rule & Level No. A4: Aluminum Smoothing Plane. With Stanley Decal. Rare and Excellent. Length: 9 Inches. *Finding examples of Stanley's "A" series planes, especially those that don't look like they've been buried for several months isn't easy. This one has never been in the ground, and its hardly been in the shop. Nearly all of the original Stanley decal remains. Crisp.* (FINE) **$395.00**

K1-8. Stanley Rule & Level No. 46: Skew Dado and Rabbet Plane. With Eight Original Cutters. Near New Condition. Length: 9 1/2 Inches. *This early and nearly perfectly preserved example of Stanley's desirable skew-bladed dado, rabbet and filletster plane includes eight original cutting irons. Extra nice.* (FINE) **$595.00**

K1-9. Stanley Rule & Level No. 283: Adjustable Cabinet Scraper. With Rosewood Handles. Sweetheart Trademark. Length: 9 1/2 Inches. *Nearly all original finishes remain on this pristine cabinet scraper which is clearly marked with the classic "Sweetheart" trademark. Choice.* (FINE) **$465.00**

K1-10. Stanley Rule & Level No. 10: Bench Rabbet Plane. Ca. 1915 Trademark. Ready to Use. Length: 12 Inches. *This clean and serviceable example of Stanley's longer bench rabbet plane is marked with the 1915 era "V" trademark. Clean, sound and ready to use.* (GOOD+) **$255.00**

K1-11. Stanley Rule & Level No. 92: 1 Inch Shoulder Rabbet Plane. Early "V" Trademark. 99% Original Plating. Length: 5 1/2 Inches. *Here's as nice an example of Stanley's 3/4 inch shoulder rabbet plane as you are likely to find. Some 98% of the shiny nickel plating remains on this ca. 1915 example. Top shelf.* (FINE) **$225.00**

K1-12. Stanley Rule & Level No. 2 C: 7 Inch Smoothing Plane. "Sweetheart" Trademark. Superb Condition. Length: 7 Inches. *For some reason, unlike the case with nearly every other Stanley bench plane, purchasers of the diminutive No. 2 smoother seemed not to prefer the corrugated sole version, which was offered beginning in 1897. Despite the 30 year production head start that the smooth bottom variety was given, there seems no apparent explanation for the lack of corrugated sole examples among all No. 2 planes produced since 1900. We proudly offer this excellent example of the 2 C which retains Some 98% of its original japan finish. Nearly all of the original decal remains on the handle. A great plane.* (FINE) **$525.00**

K1-13. Stanley Rule & Level No. 8: "Type 11" Jointer Plane. Ca. 1915 Trademark. 98% Origianl Paint. Length: 24 Inches. *The No. 8 jointer plane, at 24 inches in length is a tool that is not available from any contemporary manufacturer. This example incorporates the 1910 patent throat adjustment that dramatically improved the precision of the Stanley/Bailey planes and is marked behind the frog with two 1902 and the 1910 patent dates. We offer our best wishes for the speedy recovery of anyone who would prefer some of the junk being made today to one of these classic tools. Crisp, clean and ready to use.* (FINE) **$255.00**

K1-14. Stanley Rule & Level No. 9 1/2: Rare "Type I" Block Plane. Bailey Patent Iron. Ca. 1872. Length: 6 Inches. *Of a drastically different appearance than the later models and hardly similar to the "Type II" version that replaced it only two years later, this, the first model of the Bailey Patent No. 9 1/2 block plane is complete, very well preserved and in collector quality condition. Fitted with a simple screw for the throat adjustment and a cam lock lever for the cap that never appeared on any other Stanley planes, this tool is outdone only by the early models of the No. 110 block plane in its deviation from the form of other Stanley planes. A rare tool that very seldom comes onto the market. Opportunity knocks.* (GOOD+) **$675.00**

K1-15. Stanley Rule & Level No. 20: "Victor" Compass Plane. Full Nickel Plating. "Pat. '92" Trademark. Length: 9 1/2 Inches. *Here's a great combination: Stanley's best quality circular plane in the best condition you could ask for. Nearly all of the original shiny nickel plating remains.* (FINE) **$265.00**

K1-16. Stanley Rule & Level No. 72 1/2: Patent Chamfer, Bullnose Plane and Beading Attachment. Rare and Excellent. Length: 8 Inches. *Complete with its elusive bullnose attachment and the detachable beading attachment that earns a 1/2 number promotion from a 72 to a 72 1/2, this superb plane fails to achieve the coveted "Fine" grade solely for the want of its set of beading cutters, which are interchangeable with those found on the infinitely less common No. 66 hand beader. A rare and essentially complete Stanley tool with more than 95% of its original finishes. Nice.* (GOOD+) **$1,095.00**

K1-17. Stanley Rule & Level No. 603 C: "Bedrock" Smoothing Plane. With Corrugated Sole. Original Decal. Length: 8 1/2 Inches. *So little-used was this corrugated No. 603 Bedrock plane that it retains most of the original decal on the handle. A rare Stanley "Bedrock" plane in superb condition.* (FINE) **$395.00**

K1-18. Stanley Rule & Level No. 5 1/4: "Junior Jack" Plane. "Sweetheart" Trademark. Rosewood Handles. Length: 11 Inches. *The "Junior" jack plane, was the width of a No. 3 and just a bit shorter than a No. 5. Although these were marketed to manual training schools, these tools have found favor among latter-day woodworkers. This one is clean, complete, marked with 1920's era "Sweetheart" trademark and ready to put to work.* (FINE) **$195.00**

K1-19. Stanley Rule & Level No. 12: Early Patent Scraper Plane. With Bulbous Handles. Patented August 31, 1858. Length: 6 1/2 Inches. *Easily identifiable by the sharply angular nose and tail sections, and by the presence of the Bailey patent information on the adjustment nut, these tools were made from 1869 to 1874 only. These tools were fitted with a cutter having the edges filed at an angle of 45 degrees. The cutter in this example is proper, but is quite short. It can, however, be locked in the plane in such a way that it appears complete. A rare, early Stanley plane.* (GOOD+) **$445.00**

K1-20. Stanley Rule & Level No. 19: Early Knuckle Joint Plane. Patented December 28, 1886. Extra Crisp and Clean. Length: 7 Inches. *A very early and nicely preserved example of the No. 19 block plane. Those who have studied the variations of the knuckle joint plane could fill you in on whether this is a type II-c- iv (*) or an early version of the type III-a-i. In the absence of expert advice, I'll call it a nice early plane. A good one.* (FINE) **$115.00**

K1-21. Stanley Rule & Level No. 604: "Bedrock" Smooth Plane. "Sweetheart" Trademark. 98% Original Paint. Length: 9 Inches. *Here's a crispy-clean example of Stanley's "Bedrock" smoothing plane in the No. 4 (9 inch) size. A great working tool. Some 98% of the original paint remains and the Brazilian Rosewood handles are in excellent condition.* (GOOD+) **$295.00**

K1-22. Stanley Rule & Level No. 112: Handled Scraper Plane. Rosewood Handle, Knob. Near New Condition. Length: 9 Inches. *Looking for a top quality handled scraper plane to last a lifetime, or perhaps several? This No. 112 has its original iron and virtually all of its shiny original finishes. Nice.* (FINE) **$445.00**

K1-23. Stanley Rule & Level No. 8 C: 24 Inch Jointer Plane. Single 1910 Patent Date. Extra Crisp and Clean. Length: 22 Inches. *The presence of the single 1910 patent date on this perfectly preserved jointer plane identifies it as of the "Type 13" series, which was produced around 1925. As good as they get. Nice.* (FINE) **$285.00**

K1-24. Stanley Rule & Level No. 77: Hand Crank Dowel Machine. With Five Cutters. Ca. 1915 Trademark. Length: 9 Inches. *Complete with 5 original cutters and retaining nearly all of its original blue paint, this Stanley classic is ready to be put immediately to work or used to fill out an expanding collection of high quality Stanley tools. Nice.* (FINE) **$925.00**

K1-25. Stanley Rule & Level No. 191: Cast Iron Rabbet 1 1/4 Inch Width. Early Vine Casting. Patented November 18, 1884. Length: 10 1/2 Inches. *The earliest examples of Stanley's fixed and adjustable rabbeting and filletster planes featured this classic Victorian "vine" casting. This perfectly preserved example retains nearly all of its shiny black japanning. The crisp and shiny cutter is imprinted with the 1884 patent date. Mint.* (FINE) **$175.00**

K1-26. Stanley Rule & Level No. 604 1/2 C: "Bedrock" Smoothing Plane. Corrugated Sole. "Sweetheart" Trademark. Length: 10 Inches. *Here's an exceptionally well preserved example of the later "Bedrock" series. Of all the planes of the "Bedrock" series, it is the 604 1/2 wide smoothing plane that receives the best reviews from serious woodworkers. The distinctive feature of the Bedrock planes was the patented frog designed to eliminate "chatter" when working wood. It is in exactly the types of applications where a wide smoothing plane will be used that this problem is likely to occur. Those who have tried them, in overwhelming numbers, say that this is the tool for the job. We cannot disagree. This is the finest example of this rare and desirable plane that we have ever offered. Mint.* (FINE) **$875.00**

K1-27. Stanley Rule & Level No. 140: Skew Bladed Block Plane. 100% Paint. As New Condition. Length: 7 Inches. *One of the fixing screws on this skew bladed block plane has been finished with black japanning, which may indicate WW II era production.* (FINE) **$295.00**

K1-28. Stanley Rule & Level No. 3: Rare Type 3 Smooth Plane. "Arch" Trademark. Early and Excellent. Length: 9 Inches. *Leonard Bailey's association with the Stanley Rule & Level Company is well documented, but many collectors are not aware that the frog mechanism of the Type 3 bench plane was a Bailey innovation. The short-lived design, which very much resembles the design of Bailey's "Victor" planes, had the same flaw—a poor design which invited the breakage of the cast iron. Examples of the Type 3 are very uncommon. This crisp and clean example is of the No. 3 size. Fitted with an iron with the early arch trademark, this one is sound and ready for the collection.* (GOOD+) **$645.00**

K1-29. Stanley Rule & Level No. 95: Edge Trim Block Plane. Notch Rectangle Trademark. Unused Condition. Length: 6 Inches. *If you're looking for the No. 95 edge trim block plane, stop here. This one retains all of its original finishes and is in essentially unused condition. Nice.* (FINE) **$225.00**

K1-30. Stanley Rule & Level No. 605 1/4: "Bedrock" Junior Jack Plane. Rare and Excellent. Superb Condition. Length: 11 Inches. *Other than the No. 602 series, the rarity prize for the "Bedrock" series goes to this, the equivalent, with the patent "Bedrock" features added, of the 5 1/4 "Junior Jack Plane". Of those examples that have survived, many have been found as technical schools have sold them at auctions, often bringing "oohs" and "ahs" of amazement from a stunned auction crowd as a hand plane surpassed the hammer price of the power equipment that had been thought to be the prize of the sale. Auction crowd or no, this one will be sure to thrill and delight any crowd of serious antique tool enthusiasts, even if you'rе the only one in the crowd. A good one.* (FINE) **$845.00**

K1-31. Stanley Rule & Level No. 12 1/2: Adjustable Scraper Plane. Rosewood Bottom. 99% Original Paint. Length: 6 Inches. *This rosewood-faced scraper is in out-of-the-box-new condition. The original Stanley cutter is absolutely immaculate.* (FINE) **$295.00**

K1-32. Stanley Rule & Level No. 39: Cast Iron Dado Plane. 7/8 Inch Size. Early "V" Trademark. Length: 8 Inches. *A superb example of the tough to find 7/8 inch cast iron dado plane in extremely well preserved condition. Ready to fill out a collection that will never need an upgrade. Nice.* (FINE) **$285.00**

K1-33. Stanley Rule & Level No. 72: Adjustable Chamfer Plane. Patented April 2, 1885. Extra Crisp and Clean. Length: 9 Inches. *Designed to facilitate the planing of chamfers on the edges of boards and beams, these were a very specific special-purpose tool that would have been purchased by only a very limited number of woodworkers. Examples, accordingly, are rare. This nearly perfectly preserved example retains 98%+ of its original paint. The body of the plane has been cast with the 1885 patent date in the body. A very nice example.* (FINE) **$445.00**

K1-34. Stanley Tools No. 100 1/2: Model Maker's Block Plane. With Round Bottom. Near New Condition. Length: 3 Inches. *Stanley's convex sole modelmaker's plane belongs in every shop, and in every collection. This one is in excellent shape.* (FINE) **$155.00**

K1-35. Stanley Rule & Level No. 608 C: "Bedrock" Jointer Plane. Original Decal. Near New Condiiton. Length: 24 Inches. *This No. 608 C is, without question, the finest we have ever offered. Retaining more than 98% of its original Japan finish, as well as the original decal on the handle, this is as good as they get. Absolutely perfect and highly recommended.* (FINE) **$585.00**

K1-36. Stanley Rule & Level No. 122: "Liberty Bell Smooth Plane. 95% Original Paint. Rare and Excellent. Length: 8 Inches. *The smallest of Stanley's "Liberty Bell" series, this is also the least common. More than 95% of all original finishes remain. Crisp.* (FINE) **$135.00**

K1-37. Stanley Rule & Level No. 607: "Bedrock" Jointer Plane. Rosewood Handles. "Sweetheart" Trademark. Length: 22 Inches. *The principal distinction between the early and late incarnations of the "Bedrock" series was that the early models were affixed to the base of the plane directly by screws, and the later models were attached using cylindrical pins which where tightened into place using cone-shaped screws that functioned as wedges. A cosmetic difference between the two was the absence of the traditional rounded sides to the profile of the plane, as the later examples were cast with the upper rail parallel to the sole. At 2 inches shorter and 1/2 inch narrower than its big brother, the No. 608, this 22 inch jointer is somewhat lighter to use. This one is in near-new condition. Choice.* (GOOD+) **$345.00**

K1-38. Stanley Rule & Level No. 48: Tongue and Groove Plane. Swinging Fence. Apparently Unused. Length: 10 1/2 Inches. *A swinging fence determines whether the tongue cutter or the groove cutter is in use on this innovative Stanley plane. Nearly all original finishes remain on this nearly new example. Choice.* (FINE) **$225.00**

K1-39. Stanley Rule & Level No. 4 1/2: Wide, Heavy Smooth Plane. Rosewood Handle and Knob. Sweetheart Trademark. Length: 10 1/2 Inches. *This crispy clean No. 4 1/2 is marked with the ca. 1925 "Sweetheart" trademark and is in nearly new condition. Mint.* (FINE) **$215.00**

K1-40. Stanley Rule & Level No. 45: Combination Plane. With Instructions. New Condition, Original Box. Length: 12 Inches. *This example of Stanley's mainstay No. 45 plane is crisp, clean and complete in its original pasteboard box. All original parts, including the instruction manual are present on this shiny clean plane. Extra nice.* (FINE) **$445.00**

K1-41. Stanley Rule & Level No. 40: Beech Handle Scrub Plane. Sweetheart Trademark. Superb Condtiion. Length: 11 Inches. *Here's a crisp and little-used example of Stanley's ready to work "scrub" plane. This 1920's era version is fitted out with handles of lacquered beech. A great working tool in top condition.* (FINE) **$145.00**

K1-42. Stanley Rule & Level No. 71: Rare "Type 1" Router Plane. Patented March 4, 1884. 2 Original Cutters. Length: 8 Inches. *Nearly all original finishes remain on this clean and complete router plane which is cast with the March 4, 1884 patent date in the body and finished with black japanning, making it an example of the "Type I" version of this tool. A rare Stanley plane in top condition.* (FINE) **$225.00**

K1-43. Stanley Rule & Level No. 62: Low Angle Block Plane. "Sweetheart" Trademark. Rare and Excellent. Length: 14 Inches. *These were intended for precise planing of end-grain wood and were marketed to cabinetmakers as such. Their Achilles Heel was a fragile throat section that split out when pressured by a buildup of small shavings. This one is in perfect condition, but missing the throat adjustment lever.* (GOOD) **$445.00**

K1-44. Stanley Rule & Level No. 7 C: 22 Inch Jointer Plane. "Sweetheart" Trademark. Superb Condition. Length: 22 Inches. *Nearly all original finishes remain on this shiny clean jointer plane produced around 1925 by Stanley. A superb example of Stanley's best selling jointer plane.* (FINE) **$215.00**

K1-45. Stanley Rule & Level No. 55: Patent Universal Combination Plane. "Sweetheart" Trademark. New Condition, Original Box. Length: 11 1/2 Inches. *Advertised as "A Planing Mill Within Itself", the Stanley No. 55 Patent Universal Combination Plane can, with a bit of practice, be made to duplicate any molding profile ever made. This one is complete with all of the original parts, including the four boxes containing more than 50 specialized cutting irons. It comes in the original pasteboard box, which retains most of its original green paper label. Most original nickel plating remains and the rosewood fences and handles are in excellent condition. Were it possible to make these planes today, a working approximation of much lesser quality would cost thousands of dollars. A bargain.* (FINE) **$875.00**

K1

Group L1

L1-1. Chapin, E.M., Pine Meadow, Conn. No. 84 1/2: Three-Foot, Four-Fold Folding Rule. Arch Joint, Full Bound. "Mrs. H.A. Bronson 1". Length: 36 Inches. *A most unusual and interesting fully brass bound yard measure with the mark of E.M. Chapin (ca. 1880's). This one is inscribed and dated "Mrs. H.A. Bronson, 1889", indicating that it was likely a presentation rule. Presentation quality.* (GOOD) **$585.00**

L1-2. Stanley Rule & Level No. 40: One-Foot, Four-Fold Folding Rule. Square Joint, Full Bound. Ivory and German Silver. Length: 12 Inches. *Stanley's ivory rules have virtually disappeared from the market. This one foot, four fold has only slight yellowing and is in excellent condition, noting a tight hairline crack in the German Silver binding. A good one.* (GOOD+) **$345.00**

L1-3. Unmarked: Sectional Boxwood "A.Reynolds & C. Leeds". With Brass Joints. Original Case. Length: 10 1/2 Inches. *Rules such as this were assembled into a single section and used to estimate the amount of liquid that would be needed to fill a cask of a given size. Because they showed the amount that was "wanting" to fill the cask, they were known as "wantage" rods. A nice example that is complete in its original leather case.* (GOOD+) **$165.00**

L1-4. Tileston & Hollingsworth, Boston: Boxwood Caliper Rule. From Hardware Company? Early Appearance. Length: 4 1/2 Inches. *Tileston and Hollingsworth is a Boston partnership we have not previously encountered. The appearance of this caliper rule of distinctive configuration would suggest that it was made ca. 1890. A rare rule.* (GOOD+) **$125.00**

L1-5. Halden & Company: Ivory and German Silver Folding Rule. Architects Rule. Most Unusual Configuration. Length: 12 Inches. *"Architect's" rules are characterized by the presence of beveled edges on the inside faces, which were intended to facilitate their use for marking drawings and the like. Generally, these beveled edges are found only on two foot rules. This perfectly preserved one foot rule, which would have been limited in its practical application, is fitted out with the architect's beveled inside edges. Crisp, clean, bright white and ready to display. An extra special small size architects rule.* (FINE) **$495.00**

L1-6. Natural Ice Assn. of America: Promotional Advertising Rule. With Ice Weight Scale. Protects Public Health. Length: 36 Inches. *Back in the days when potentially deadly "artificial" ice was being foisted upon the unwitting consumer by conspirators at Frigidaire and the like, the good men and women of the Natural Ice Association of America took a stand for purity and promoted their cause through rules such as this, which features a catchy slogan on the front and an ice weight scale on the reverse.* (GOOD) **$225.00**

L1-7. Stanley Rule & Level (Unmarked) No. 39: One-Foot, Four Fold Folding Rule. Ivory and German Silver. Rare and Excellent. Length: 12 Inches. *Here's an example of Stanley's classic one foot, four fold caliper rule that is marked with the number, but not the name. Only very slight yellowing deserves mention on this crisp and clean ivory rule.* (GOOD+) **$395.00**

L1-8. Stanley Rule & Level No. 036: Inclinometer, Bevel Folding Rule. Rare "Stanley" Mark. Clean and Sound. Length: 12 Inches. *The Stanley Rule & Level Company was the last of a series of rulemakers to produce the Stephens patent combination rule, which was originally patented and produced in the 1850's. This example is imprinted with the "notched rectangle" logo used by Stanley in the 1930's. An uncommon rule in uncommonly nice condition.* (GOOD+) **$365.00**

L1-9. Stanley Rule & Level No. 56: One Foot, Four Fold Folding Rule. Arch Joint, Unbound. Extra Crisp and Clean. Length: 12 Inches. *No Stanley trademark but there's no question on this one. The number is slightly double struck. Extra crisp.* (FINE) **$445.00**

L1-10. Unmarked: Eight Fold Gauging Rule. Boxwood Body. Superb Condition. Length: 60 Inches. *This classic English gauging rule has a superb dark golden patina. No stains or mechanical problems. A great rule for the collection.* (GOOD+) **$595.00**

L1-11. Standard Rule Co., Unionville, Conn. No. 6: Two Foot, Two Fold Folding Rule. With Engineers Scales. Extra Rare and Excellent. Length: 24 Inches. *The equivalent in name and number to Stanley's No. 6 Engineer's Rule, this rule from the Standard Rule Company of Unionville, Connecticut is marked with complex engineer's tables of weights and measures on the reverse side. It is in excellent condition, noting a few small flakes from the edges of the boxwood.* (GOOD+) **$1,245.00**

L1-12. Stanley Rule & Level No. 83 C: Two Foot, Four Fold Folding Rule. "Sweetheart" Trademark. Early and Near New. Length: 24 Inches. *The No. 83 C was Stanley's only four-fold caliper rule, other than the No. 62 C, which was of a much narrower width. This one is in nearly new condition and marked with the ca. 1920's era "Sweetheart" trademark. Mint.* (FINE) **$425.00**

L1-13. Stephens & Co.: Patented School Rule. Patented July 3, 1883. Rare and Excellent. Length: 18 Inches. *Produced under a July 3, 1883 patent, this specially grooved "school" rule from Stephens is in nearly new condition. Rare and excellent.* (FINE) **$125.00**

L1-14. Upson Nut Co., Unionville, Conn. No. 100: 3 Inch Caliper Rule. Full Brass Bound. Rare and Excellent. Length: 3 Inches. *Unlike any rule produced by any other major rulemaker, this Upson nut caliper rule is formed from a single section of brass bound boxwood. It is in excellent collector quality condition.* (GOOD+) **$115.00**

L1-15. Stanley Rule & Level No. 62 E & M: Two Foot, Two Fold Folding Rule. English and Metric. Early Stanley Mark. Length: 24 Inches. *Stanley offered to provide any of its rules with metric graduations, if required by the user. This No. 62 with metric graduations is clean and ready to help fill out a collection of Stanley rules.* (GOOD+) **$115.00**

L1-16. Chapin-Stephens Co. No. 40: One Foot, Four Fold Folding Rule. Ivory and Geman Silver. Near New Condition. Length: 12 Inches. *Other than Stanley Rule & Level, the Chapin-Stephens Company was the last producer of Ivory rules in the United States. This extremely well preserved example is boldly marked with with the Chapin-Stephens name and the rule number. The sort of ivory rule you just can't find anymore.* (FINE) **$395.00**

L1-17. Stanley Rule & Level No. 72 1/2: Two Foot, Four Fold Folding Rule. Square Joint, Full Bound. Early and Excellent. Length: 24 Inches. *The No. 72 1/2 is distinguished from the No. 72 by being fully brass-bound. This one is in excellent condition and clearly marked.* (GOOD+) **$115.00**

L1-18. Upson Nut Co., Unionville, Conn. No. 6: Three Foot, Four Fold Folding Rule. With Yard Scales. Extra Crisp and Clean. Length: 36 Inches. *Most rule makers, unlike Stanley, imprinted their yard measure rules with fractional yards on the outside and inches on the inside. Stanley chose the opposite pattern. One advantage of the outside graduations, at least from the collector's perspective, is that outside graduated rules simply "look different" at first glance. This most unusual yard measure comes from the Upson Nut Company. Nearly all original finishes remain on this crisp, clean and clearly marked example.* (FINE) **$245.00**

L1-19. Stanley Rule & Level No. 036: Inclinometer, Bevel Folding Rule. Rare "Stanley" Mark. Clean and Sound. Length: 12 Inches. *The Stanley Rule & Level Company was the last of a series of rulemakers to produce the Stephens patent combination rule, which was originally patented and produced in the 1850's. This example is imprinted with the "notched rectangle" logo used by Stanley in the 1930's. An uncommon rule in uncommonly nice condition.* (GOOD+) **$395.00**

L1-20. Belcher Bros. & Co., New York: Brass-Bound Gunter Rule. Beveled Edge. Unusual Configuration. Length: 24 Inches. *The Belcher Brothers firm was one of the first commercially successful rule manufacturers in the U.S. They began in the 1830's and apparently succumbed to the economic vicissitudes of the 1870's. This classic "Gunter" rule was used by navigators for performing complex mathematical calculations. A nice example.* (GOOD+) **$225.00**

L1-21. Stearns & Co., E.A. No. 57: One Foot, Four Fold Folding Rule. Ivory and German Silver. Uncommon Type. Length: 12 Inches. *Before being bought out by Stanley, the E.A. Stearns Company, of Brattleboro, Vermont, enjoyed a run as America's pioneering and premier rule maker. This ivory one foot rule is marked with the Stearns name and is in clean, sound condition.* (GOOD) **$225.00**

L1-22. Stanley Rule & Level: Rare Half Meter Rule. With Metric Graduations. Extra Rare. Length: 19 Inches. *One of the least common of all Stanley rules, the half meter rule is so obscure that many knowledgeable collectors are unaware of its existence. According to the Stanley Value Guide, these rules were offered in 1919 only. This is only the second example of this rare rule that we have ever offered. Rare.* (GOOD) **$675.00**

L1-23. Unmarked: Broad Boxwood Folding Rule. Unfinished Graduations. Very Well Made. Length: 24 Inches. *For some reason this early appearing arch joint, half-bound boxwood rule did not complete the manufacturing process. It has no apparent defects and is in excellent condition. An interesting unfinished symphony from the world of folding rules.* (FINE) **$115.00**

L1-24. Lufkin Rule Co., The: Early Board Measure Folding Rule. 3 Fold Type. New Condition, Original Case. Length: 24 Inches. *The presence of the original leather case (which is itself in near new condition) has protected this early folding board measure rule and kept it in nearly new condition. This rule almost certainly was produced in E.T. Lufkin's Cleveland days at the end of the last century.* (FINE) **$285.00**

L1-25. Kerby & Bro., New York: Cordage Gauge Rule. "California Cordage". Early and Excellent. Length: 6 Inches. *Cordage rules were generally imprinted with advertising from the company who was promoting the sale of rope, or had some association with those who had a need for measuring rope and cable. This pristine cordage rule is marked on the edge with the name of rulemakers Kerby and Brother and on the ungraduated side with prominent advertising for the "California Cordage" company. A top quality collectible cordage rule.* (FINE) **$285.00**

L1-26. Cook, J.F. & Keller, A., New York: Patent Musical Rule. Patented December 22 , 1903. Rare and Near New. Length: 12 Inches. *Produced under a 1903 patent that must be a joy to read, this altogether different bench rule is fitted with a special slide that was used for laying out musical scores. Retaining nearly all original finishes and mechanically perfect, this is one of those rules that causes even the non-tool collector to take notice. Extra special.* (FINE) **$845.00**

L1-27. Stanley Rule & Level: Early 8 Inch Zig-Zag Folding Rule. For Advertising. Possibly Unique. Length: 8 Inches. *Not fitted with the folding joint that was the characteristic feature of Stanley's zig-zag line and showing no evidence of ever having featured such a hinge, this extremely early rule is nonetheless imprinted with the ZZ logo of the zig-zag line. Promotional items from the Stanley Rule & Level Company are scarce indeed. There can be no question that this rule was produced to promote the zig-zag line when it was first introduced at the beginning of this century. Rare.* (GOOD+) **$395.00**

L1-28. Chapin, H. No. 2: One Foot, Four Fold Folding Rule. Square Joint, Unbound. Rare and Excellent. Length: 12 Inches. *This No. 2 Chapin rule is the functional equivalent of Stanley's No. 65. A rare and early folding boxwood rule.* (GOOD+) **$95.00**

L1-29. Acme Rule Company: Patent Ivory Folding Rule. Applied Ivory Overlay. Rare and Excellent. Length: 12 Inches. *The patent for this most unusual early rule involved the application of the ivory body sections to the German silver frame. A nice clean example of an elusive early patented ivory rule.* (GOOD+) **$695.00**

L1-30. Chapin's Son Co., H. No. 14: Two Foot, Four Fold Folding Rule. Square Joint, Full Bound. Patented December 23, 1891. Length: 24 Inches. *During a transition from the H. Chapin Company to its eventual merger with Stephens & Company, the firm assumed a number of names, the least common of which is "H. Chapin's Son Company". This nicely preserved rule is clearly imprinted with this seldom-seen and historically significant rule. Rare and crispy clean.* (FINE) **$165.00**

L1-31. Unmarked: 4 Section Gauging Rule. For Cask Measure. Original Leather Case. Length: 10 Inches. *The original leather case has kept his classic English boxwood cask measure in top collector quality condition. Extra nice.* (GOOD+) **$245.00**

L1-32. Stearns & Co., E.A. No. 3: Two Foot, Two Fold Folding Rule. With Gunter Slide. Near New Condition. Length: 24 Inches. *A pioneer in the marketing of calculating rules for engineers, architects and builders, the E.A. Stearns Company offered a wide range of these tools in every conceivable configuration. This unbound two foot, two fold rule is fitted out with a Gunter slide and architect's scales and is in nearly new condition. Practically perfect.* (FINE) **$575.00**

L1-33. Chapin-Stephens Co., The No. 99 3/4: One-Foot, Four Fold Folding Rule. F.W. Duennebier. New Condition, Original Box. Length: 12 Inches. *In his introduction chapters to Boxwood & Ivory: Stanley Traditional Rules, 1855-1975, author Phil Stanley provides a narrative history of the principal rule makers of the United States and recounts the manufacturing process for both boxwood and ivory rules. Based on his collecting experience, Stanley suggests that the wide range of ivory rules offered by the principal makers between the 1850's and the beginning of the First World War would have been designed almost exclusively for presentation purposes, rather than actual utility. He points out the well known propensity of ivory to shrink and yellow over time, both qualities which would preclude any utilitarian function. The rule offered here, an unprecedented example of a presentation rule in its original presentation box, as prepared by the factory lends additional credence to Stanley's theory. The name "F. W. Duennebier" is written in ink on the outside of the ivory-colored pasteboard box with gilt edges. The inside of the No. 99 3/4 ivory and german silver 1 foot, four fold rule is also inscribed on the ivory face with the F.W. Duennebier name in carefully engraved block letters and filled with blacking in a way that could only have been accomplished in the Chapin-Stephens factory. The rule itself, a No. 99 3/4 inch caliper rule, is rare in its own right. The condition is as-new: the joints are tight, the ivory is bright white and all lacquer finishes remain on the german silver binding and joints. An extraordinary collectible rule in top collector quality condition. Magnificent.* (FINE) **$2,450.00**

L1-34. Halden & Co., Ltd., Manchester: Ivory and German Silver Folding Rule. Architects Rule. Near New Condition. Length: 24 Inches. *The inside edges of this spectacularly well preserved ivory rule are fitted with the beveled edges that were offered for use by architects and others doing very precise measuring against a drawing or map. The joints are tight, the ivory bright white and in perfect collector quality condition.* (FINE) **$475.00**

L1-35. Unmarked: "Pit Prop Gauge" Rule. For Mine Tunnels. Solid Boxwood. Length: 13 1/2 Inches. *This most unusual rule was used in the mining industry to gauge the size of wooden props used in mining. It is made of solid boxwood, unmarked with any maker's name and in unused condition.* (GOOD+) **$85.00**

L1-36. Unmarked No. 58: Two Foot, Six Fold Folding Rule. Arch Joint, Unbound. Extra Thick Body. Length: 24 Inches. *Unmarked in any way by its maker, this rare 6 fold rule has body sections that are noticeably thicker than other such rules that we have observed. A rare rule from an unknown maker.* (GOOD) **$585.00**

L1-37. C-S Co., The , Pine Meadow, Conn. No. 53: Two Foot, Four Fold Folding Rule. With Architect Scales. Near New Condition. Length: 24 Inches. *This top quality arch joint rule from Chapin Stephens is in top collector quality condition. An uncommon rule in great shape.* (FINE) **$145.00**

L1-38. Stanley Rule & Level No. 59: Two Foot, Four Fold Folding Rule. Double. Arch Joint, Unbound. Seldom Seen. Length: 24 Inches. *Differing from Stanley's double arch joint No. 60 rule only in the absence of full brass binding along the edges, the No. 59 was probably not given much consideration by those who were opting for a very high quality rule. The additional cost of binding would have been insignificant compared to the cost of the joints. A very rare Stanley rule.* (GOOD+) **$285.00**

L1-39. Weaver L. & Leiser, Z., Lock Haven: Patent Combination Folding Rule. Patented September 20, 1892. Complete and Excellent. Length: 15 Inches. *Combining the functions of marking gauge, scribe, bench rule and carpenter's rule into a single tool that most likely was not adequately up to performing any of its many functions from having assumed so many, this is the finest example of this rare patented carpenter's rule of which we are aware. Retaining most of the original finishes on both wood and metal and possessed of tight joints, this classic 1892 patented device is ready for display in a serious collection of measuring tools.* (GOOD+) **$1,175.00**

L1-40. Stephens & Co. No. 9: Two-Foot, Two-Fold Folding Rule. Square Joint, Unbound. With Extension Slide. Length: 24 Inches. *Two foot, two fold rules by the Riverton, Connecticut rule making firm of Stephens & Company have become increasingly difficult to find. This carpenter's calculation rule includes a Gunter slide and architects' scales. A nice example.* (GOOD+) **$145.00**

L1-41. Stanley Rule & Level No. 84: Two Foot, Four Fold Folding Rule. Square. Joint, Half Bound. Near New Condition. Length: 24 Inches. *Perhaps the second most common of Stanley's better-grade rules (to the full bound No. 62), the No. 84 was protected by brass binding on its outer edges only. This example is in practically perfect condition.* (FINE) **$65.00**

L1-42. Stanley Rule & Level No. 32: One-Foot, Four-Fold Folding Rule. "Mulconroy, Phila.". "Sweetheart" Trademark. Length: 12 Inches. *The reverse side of the Stanley caliper rule is imprinted with the designation "Mulconroy, Phila.". Mulconroy was likely a hardware dealer. The rule is in absolutely unused condition.* (FINE) **$110.00**

L1-43. Stanley Rule & Level No. 70: Two-Foot, Four-Fold Folding Rule. "Calcutta" Advertisised Most Unusual. Length: 24 Inches. *The extent to which the reach of Stanley Tools extends is illustrated by this No. 70 folding rule which is imprinted with advertising from "Clive Street, Calcutta". The No. 70 rule was discontinued from the Stanley line as of 1938, so we have a fairly good idea of the age of this most unusual advertising rule. An extremely rare Stanley advertising rule in excellent condition.* (GOOD+) **$295.00**

L1-44. Lufin Rule Co., The, Saginaw, Mich.: "Magic Pattern" Rule. For Tinsmith's, Etc. Original Box. Length: 49 Inches. *The Lufkin "Magic Pattern" rule was used for the laying out of complex patterns in tin. It applied principles of geometry that would have been well understood by Euclid and Mrs. Mac Dougall, my high school instructor in this arcane subject. Neither of the two possessed, to the best of my knowledge, any tinsmithing skills. An uncommon Lufkin rule, I would postulate.* (GOOD) **$115.00**

L1-45. Johnson Rule Mfg. Co., E. P. No. 45: One-Foot, Two-Fold Folding Rule. German Silver Body. Rare 12 Inch Length. Length: 12 Inches. *Most examples of the Johnson Patent rule, produced under a 1907 patent, are in the 6 inch length. Examples of this, the one-foot size are not often found, especially in this kind of condition. Crisp.* (FINE) **$295.00**

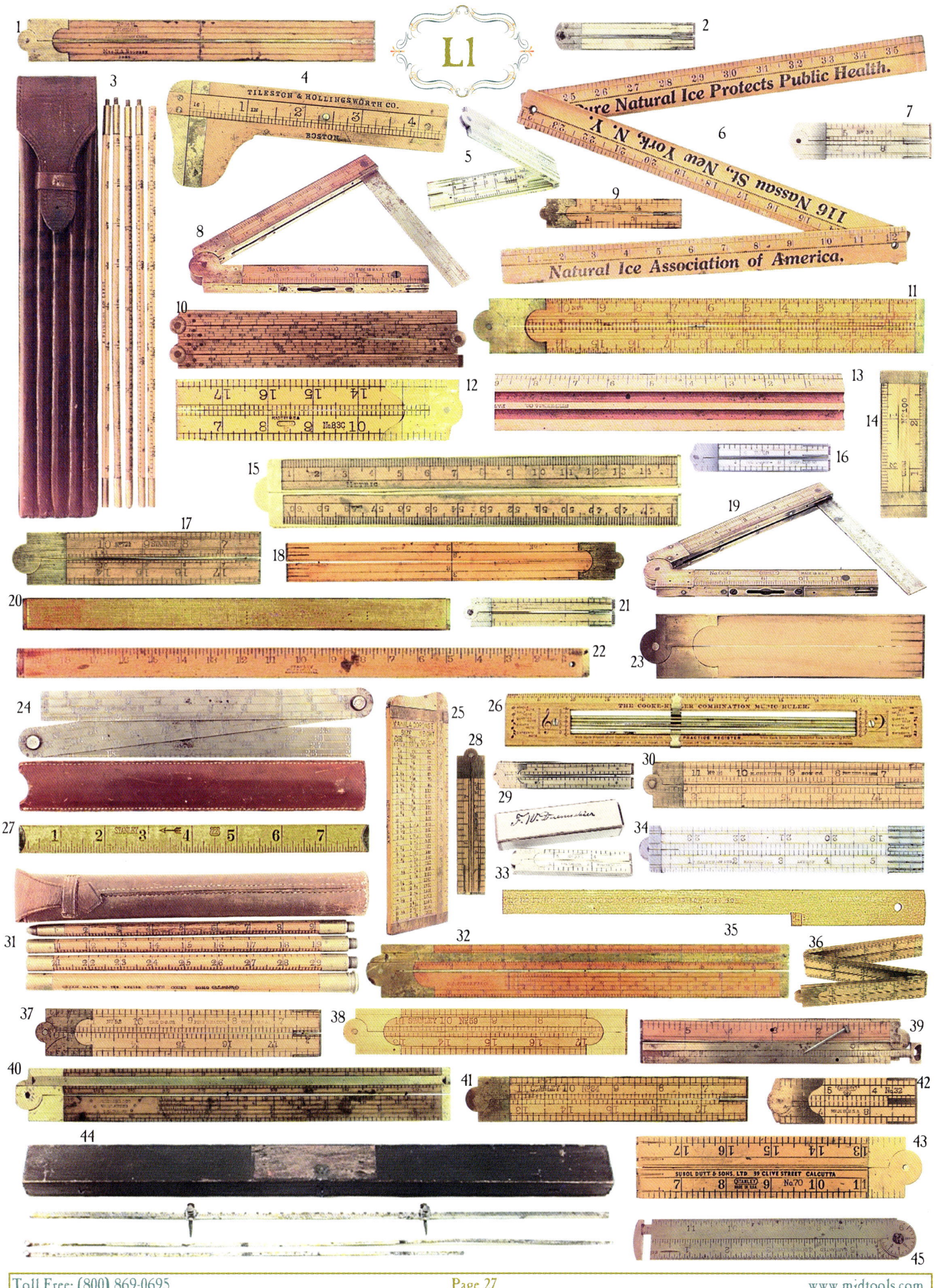

Group M1

M1-1. Unmarked: Decorative Bronze Trammels. With "Heart" Cutouts. Superb Patina. Length: 6 1/2 Inches. *Each of these spectacular trammels has a pair of heart shaped cutouts incorporated into its open cast body. Knurled screws can be loosened to remove either of the points. A very well preserved and dramatic pair of cast bronze Victorian trammels.* (GOOD+) **$645.00**

M1-2. Unmarked: Early Leg Caliper. Distinctive Form. Excellent Patina. Length: 2 1/2 Inches. *The precision with which the joint on these "ladyleg" calipers has been executed offers strong evidence that they were produced by a skilled machinist, almost certainly for his own use.* (GOOD+) **$45.00**

M1-3. Unmarked: Pair of Cast Brass Trammels. With Unusual Screws. Ready to Display. Length: 5 Inches. *The fixing screws on these solid brass trammels are fashioned like wing nuts. Different.* (GOOD+) **$75.00**

M1-4. Unmarked: Unusual "Ladyleg" Caliper. With Spike, Stilt Heels. Most Unusual Form. Length: 6 Inches. *Ask any ten seasoned tool collector what makes a great collectible tool and you will likely get the same answer from nine. That answer can be summed up in one word: Different. Different.* (GOOD+) **$950.00**

M1-5. Marble's Arms & Mfg. Co.: Pin on Miniature Compass. Solid Brass Body. Scarce and Excellent. Length: 1 3/4 Inches. *The Marble Arms & Manufacturing Company specialized in outfitting hunters, fishermen and the like. This compass, which was meant to be pinned to a jacket, was likely used in the "old days" when folks walked 8 miles to school each day. A nice example.* (GOOD+) **$45.00**

M1-6. Unmarked: Bronze "Ladyleg" Caliper. Owner "J. Massey". Excellent Patina. Length: 4 Inches. *A "garter belt" device was scribed onto one of the legs of these nicely patinated bronze "ladyleg" calipers. Very showy.* (GOOD+) **$225.00**

M1-7. Stanley Rule & Level No. 1: Bronze Metal Trammels. Smallest Size. With Pencil Clip. Length: 3 Inches. *Here's a crisp and clean example of Stanley's bronze cast trammel points in the smallest size offered. Complete with the original pencil clip. Perfect.* (GOOD+) **$115.00**

M1-8. Unmarked: "Perfect Pocket" Oil Can. Patented November 10, 1891. For Machine Mount. Length: 4 1/2 Inches. *This most unusual patent oiler has a housing that was designed by the manufacturer to be mounted on the side of a machine. The oiler was designed to be screwed into the housing so as to be out of the way when not in use.* (GOOD+) **$225.00**

M1-9. Wilkinson & Co., A. J., Boston, Mass.: Cast Bronze Trammels. With Integral Clip. Rare and Very Early. Length: 4 1/2 Inches. *Hardware dealers A.J. Wilkinson & Company operated in Boston in the last half of the Nineteenth Century. We have seen a number of tools imprinted with the Wilkinson name, including folding handle draw knives, wooden planes and hand saws. Thse trammels, which are imprinted with the Wilkinson name in an arch at the top of each of the trammels, are the first we have encountered. A rare pair in excellent condition.* (GOOD+) **$365.00**

M1-10. Unmarked: Presentation Set of Trammels. With Accessories. Original Fitted Case. Length: 13 1/4 Inches. *Obviously put together for presentation to a machinist, this set, which includes trammels, dividers and calipers is engraved with the initials "G.H." and is in new condition in its fitted velvet-lined case. Extraordinary.* (FINE) **$875.00**

M1-11. Unmarked: Set of Cast Brass Trammels. With Precision Adjustment. Composite Beam. Length: 36 Inches. *Here's a most interesting set of trammels with a precision adjustment mechanism set on the end of the beam. A mechanically interesting set of trammels.* (GOOD+) **$285.00**

M1-12. Unmarked: Miniature "Ladyleg" Caliper. Shapely Feet. External Joint. Length: 2 1/2 Inches. *in addition to their artistic effect, the extra long feet on this pair allow them to function as both an inside and an outside caliper. Pretty and petite.* (GOOD+) **$285.00**

M1-13. Unmarked: Miniature "Ladyleg" Caliper. With Copper Joint. Classic Form. Length: 2 1/2 Inches. *A copper washer serves as reinforcement on this diminutive pair while adding a dash of color. Nice.* (GOOD+) **$195.00**

M1-14. Unmarked: Massive Brass Trammels. Owner "A.F. Agnew". Excellent Patina. Length: 12 Inches. *We have it on very good authority that these trammels did not belong to the grandfather of the former Vice President, Spiro T. Agnew, a man believed, until very recent times, to have been the man who brought that office to the lowest level of public esteem in history. These huge trammels have a great look to them and are ready for display in the collection. A nice set.* (FINE) **$225.00**

M1-15. Stanley Rule & Level (Unmarked?): Early Cast Iron Trammels. With Brass Fittings. Black Japan Finish. Length: 4 Inches. *All of the shiny original finish remains on these spectacularly well preserved trammel points, which appear never to have been used.* (FINE) **$345.00**

M1-16. Cushman & Denison: "Star Oiler" Oil Can. Full Nickel Plating. Near New Condition. Length: 3 1/2 Inches. *Both the maker's name and the designation "Star Oiler" are imprinted on this crispy clean miniature oil can.* (FINE) **$85.00**

M1-17. Barnes, L.P.: Multi-Purpose Caliper. "Pat. Appl'd. For". Full Nickel Plating. Length: 3 1/2 Inches. *A most unusual early caliper which could function as inside, outside or hermaphrodite caliper, or as a pair of dividers. These are clearly marked with the maker's name and were apparently never used. Mint.* (FINE) **$225.00**

M1-18. Unmarked: Decorative Leg Caliper. With "Finger" Device. Distinctive Form. Length: 7 Inches. *Unlike any "leg" calipers we have ever seen, this most unusual variation on the theme incorporates a central leg of unknown function into the pattern. The longer end of the central "arm" has been formed in a serpentine pattern and the shorter end has been carefully filed into the form of a pointing finger. A dramatic craftsman made caliper in excellent condition.* (GOOD+) **$1,145.00**

M1-19. Unmarked: Cast Brass Trammels. Early Style Knurling. Owner Initials "JBO". Length: 4 1/4 Inches. *These have nicely knurled flat fixing screws and a soft patina of age. Nice.* (GOOD+) **$115.00**

M1-20. Unmarked: Copper "Ladyleg" Caliper. Owner "WLW". Distinctive Form. Length: 3 1/2 Inches. *Carefully filed from sheet copper, which has attained a rich, brownish-red patina, this pair has a simple joint formed from a small piece of copper pipe. Different.* (FINE) **$75.00**

M1-21. Stanley Rule & Level No. 1: Bronze Metal Trammels. Smallest Size. Near New Condition. Length: 3 Inches. *These well preserved examples of Stanley's smallest trammels are in excellent condition and mounted on a Mahogany beam. Nice.* (FINE) **$85.00**

M1-22. Unmarked: Cast Bronze Trammels. With Shield Cutouts. Superb Patina. Length: 6 Inches. *These oversize trammels feature a "shield" cutout pattern that may have been cast by a patriot-patternmaker. Different.* (GOOD+) **$225.00**

M1-23. Unmarked: Decorative Victorian Trammels. Bronze Bodies. Extra Small Size. Length: 2 1/2 Inches. *These unmarked trammels have an elaborate Victorian design cast into the bodies. They appear to date from the 1870's, or thereabout.* (GOOD+) **$65.00**

M1-24. Preston & Sons, Edward: Decorative Brass Trammels. With Pencil Clip. Elaborate Knurls. Length: 5 1/4 Inches. *Locking screws ornamented with decorative knurls highlight these brass trammels, which are imprinted with both the Preston name and logo. A nice set.* (FINE) **$165.00**

M1-25. Stanley Rule & Level No. 99: Patent Rule Trammels. Patented June 14, 1887. Rare, Complete and Excellent. Length: 1 1/2 Inches. *Stanley offered its rule trammels for nearly 45 years, but examples are scarce indeed. The lack of examples is likely attributable to the ease with which parts could be lost, and the fact that few could justify the purchase of such a tool. This set is in pristine condition and ready to display. A great set.* (FINE) **$465.00**

M1-26. Stanley Rule & Level No. 2: Bronze Metal Trammels. With Pencil Holder. Excellent Condition. Length: 4 1/2 Inches. *This perfect pair of Stanley's large bronze trammels are complete with the original pencil clip. Much of the original finish remains.* (GOOD+) **$85.00**

M1-27. Stanley Rule & Level No. 3: Bronze Metal Trammels. Victorian Casting. Largest Size. Length: 5 1/2 Inches. *At 5 1/2 inches in length, these were the largest size offered in Stanley's series of bronze trammels. They are clean, complete and ready to show.* (GOOD+) **$115.00**

M1-28. Unmarked: Brass "Ladyleg" Caliper. Oversize Round Joint. Most Unusual. Length: 3 1/2 Inches. *This most unusual pair of brass calipers has an extra heavy rounded joint. Colorful.* (GOOD+) **$235.00**

M1-29. Stanley Rule & Level No. 3: Bronze Metal Trammels. Victorian Casting. With Pencil Clip. Length: 5 1/2 Inches. *The original pencil clip has remained with these showy Stanley trammels throughout the last 125 years. A superb example of Stanley's largest trammels.* (FINE) **$115.00**

M1-30. Stanley Rule & Level No. 2: Bronze Metal Trammels. Victorian Design. Near New Condition. Length: 4 Inches. *These early trammels are still mounted on the "keeper" beam supplied by Stanley when they left the factory. Extra nice.* (FINE) **$115.00**

M1-31. Unmarked: Massive Bronze Trammels. Decorative Knurls. Superb Patina. Length: 7 Inches. *Decoratively turned and knurled fixing screws accent these massive cast bronze trammels, which are much more finely finished than the pattern shop types normally found in this large size. Extra special.* (FINE) **$345.00**

M1-32. A.M. Tool Co., Cleveland, Ohio: Set of Brass Trammels. With Pencil Holder. Rare Ohio Maker. Length: 4 3/4 Inches. *The back side of these bronze trammels is marked with the uncommon maker's name. A nice set.* (GOOD+) **$115.00**

M1-33. Smith & Co., E.S., Rockford, Ill.: Pair of Rule Trammels. October 24, 1876 Rule. Rare and Excellent. Length: 2 1/2 Inches. *The E.S. Smith combination patternmaker's rule is a rare tool, but less common still is it to find an example with the optional bronze trammels which were available with the tool. This clean pair will help to finish fitting out an example of the rule which may have lost those it came with. Rare.* (GOOD+) **$225.00**

M1-34. Unmarked: Early Full Body Caliper. Owner "H.P. Newhard". Near New Condition. Length: 4 1/2 Inches. *As clean and shiny as it was the day it was made, this early set appears to have been made by a metal worker of exceptional ability.* (FINE) **$425.00**

M1-35. Unmarked: Early Bronze Trammels. Turned Steel Screws. Superb Patina. Length: 4 Inches. *These bronze trammels feature nicely knurled caps. A good, clean set.* (FINE) **$85.00**

M1-36. Stanley Rule & Level No. 3: Bronze Metal Trammels. Victorian Casting. Early and Excellent. Length: 5 1/2 Inches. *At 5 1/2 inches in length, these were the largest size offered in Stanley's series of bronze trammels. They are clean, complete and ready to show.* (GOOD+) **$115.00**

M1-37. Unmarked: Massive Bronze Trammels. Superb Patina. With Original "Keepers". Length: 10 Inches. *At 10 inches in length, these would likely have been used for such tasks as the laying out of patterns for casting massive gear wheels and the like. Such tools would not have been available commercially and the skill of the craftsman would have been on display each time they were used. This pair is in magnificent overall condition, having achieved a most pleasant dark yellow patina of age. A magnificent set of early trammel points.* (GOOD+) **$695.00**

M1-38. Preston & Sons, Edward: Decorative Brass Trammels. Early Trademark. Elaborate Knurls. Length: 6 Inches. *The Preston logo is imprinted on one of these trammels, which are uncommon in that they are not fitted with a pencil clip. Different.* (GOOD+) **$85.00**

M1-39. Stanley Rule & Level No. 2: Bronze Metal Trammels. Victorian Pattern. Ca. 1880's. Length: 5 Inches. *No apologies for these well preserved and showy bronze trammels, which date from the 1880's, or thereabout.* (GOOD) **$85.00**

M1-40. Detroit Lock & Variety Works: Miller's Patent Trammels. Patented November 11, 1873. With Adjustable Leg. Length: 4 1/2 Inches. *The "Millers Patent" under which these trammels were produced was also applied to a pair of dividers from the same company. The patented feature was the screw-lock adjustment on one of the legs. It allowed the leg to be adjusted in height, or replaced with a pencil. A rare set in great shape.* (GOOD+) **$365.00**

M1-41. Stanley Rule & Level No. 2: Cast Bronze Trammels. With Patent Pencil Clip. Superb Condition. Length: 4 1/4 Inches. *A near-new set of Stanley's No. 2 bronze trammels, complete with the nickel plated, cast iron pencil grip. Clearly marked with maker name and number.* (FINE) **$145.00**

M1-42. Unmarked: Miniature Wood Trammels. Slide Lock Adjust. Excellent Patina. Length: 12 Inches. *One of these trammels is fixed to the end of the beam and the other can be adjusted by means of a wedge lock screw. A nicely patinated set of trammels.* (GOOD+) **$55.00**

M1-43. Unmarked: Pair of Bronze Trammels. With Pencil Clip. Uncommon Form. Length: 3 1/2 Inches. *A pair of circular brackets, which were likely intended to hold a pencil, have been cast into the body of these early bronze trammels.* (GOOD+) **$45.00**

M1-44. Unmarked: Rosewood and Brass Trammels. With Keeper Beam. Early Knurling. Length: 4 1/2 Inches. *Here's a great set of solid rosewood trammels set on a mahogany beam. Pretty.* (GOOD+) **$145.00**

M1-45. Preston & Sons, Edward: Decorative Brass Trammels. With Pencil Clip. Elaborate Knurls. Length: 6 Inches. *These showy trammels from Birmingham toolmaker Edward Preston & Sons are in nearly new condition. Choice.* (FINE) **$175.00**

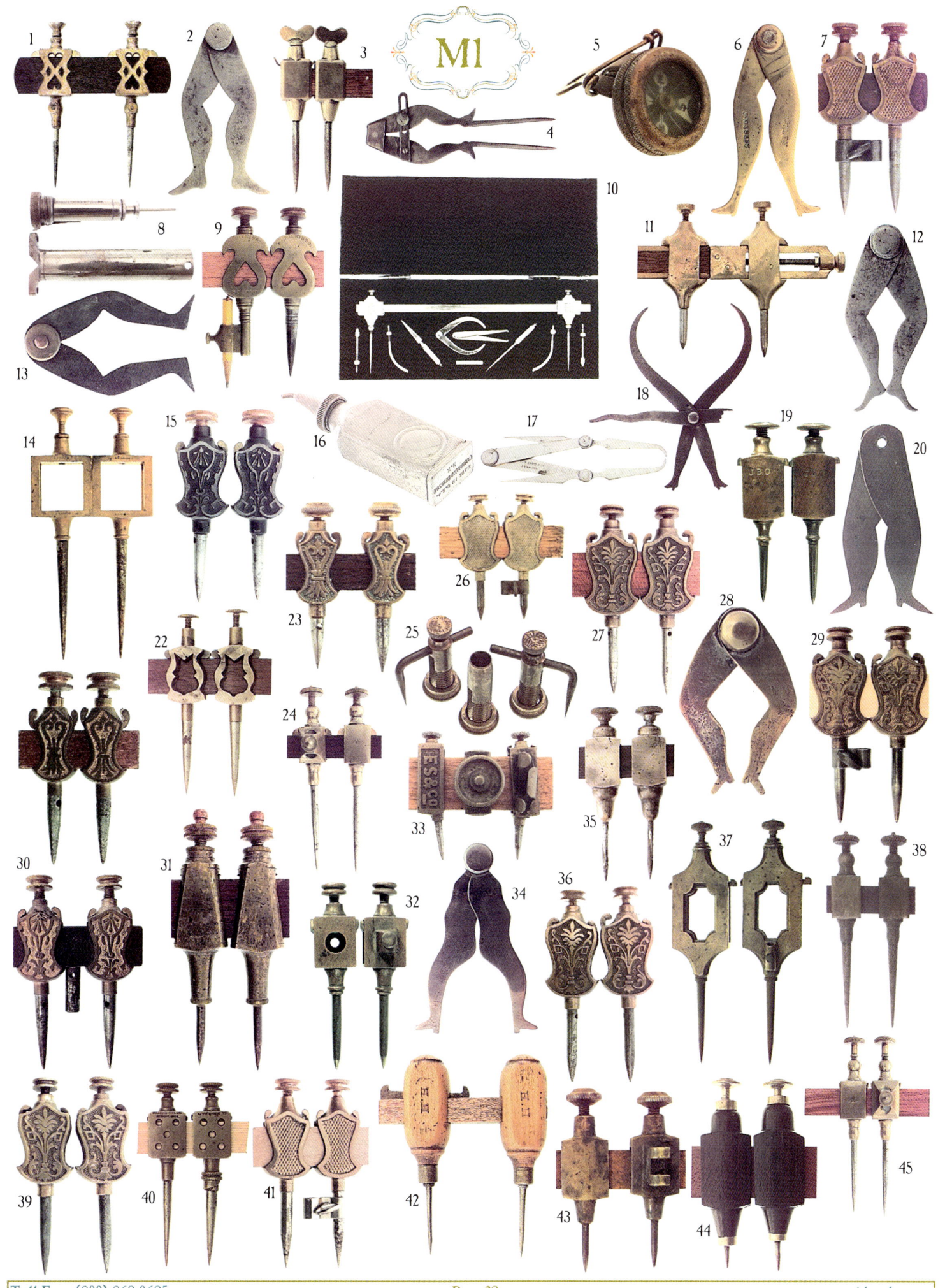

Group N1

N1-1. Keuffel & Esser Co., New York No. 4092-3: Double Cursor Slide Rule. In Original Case. Patented December 22, 1908. Length: 10 Inches. *The 1908 patent date is printed on the face of this most unusual "double cursor" slide rule. A tough rule to find.* (GOOD+) **$145.00**

N1-2. Tavella Sales Co., New York: Patent Circular Slide Rule. Copyright 1936. Original Pouch. Length: 4 Inches. *This early circular slide rule has been perfectly preserved by its leatherette case. A good one.* (GOOD+) **$45.00**

N1-3. Keuffel & Esser Co., New York, N.Y.: 8 Inch Mannheim Slide Rule. With Framed Cursor. Original Case. Length: 8 Inches. *The early style "framed" cursor on this K. & E. classic has been kept in excellent condition, thanks to the presence of the original leather slip case.* (GOOD) **$95.00**

N1-4. Keuffel & Esser Co., New York No. 4053-3: 10 Inch Manheim Slide Rule. In Original Case. New Condition, Original Box. Length: 10 Inches. *This early example of a K. & E. standard is in superb condition in its original case and protective pasteboard box. Mint.* (FINE) **$85.00**

N1-5. Keuffel & Esser Co., New York No. 4181-1C: Ivorite Slide Rule. With Instructions. New Condition, Original Box. Length: 8 Inches. *Complete in the original box with instruction manual, this "Ivorite" rule is in top collector quality condition.* (FINE) **$65.00**

N1-6. Mascot: "Vest Pocket" Slide Rule. Circular Type. With Instructions. Length: 2 3/4 Inches. *If you don't have a pocket watch, this would be just the thing to keep in your vest pocket. Complete with the original case and instruction manual. Different.* (FINE) **$65.00**

N1-7. Keuffel & Esser Co., New York No. 4058 W: "Beginner's" Slide Rule. With Instructions. New Condition, Original Box. Length: 11 Inches. *The "Beginner's" was included in the K. & E. line for many years. Here's a well preserved example in its original box.* (FINE) **$65.00**

N1-8. Faber, A.W., Germany: Early Patent Slide Rule. L.R.P. No. 206428. Covered Wood Case. Length: 11 1/2 Inches. *The original cursor is missing from this early Faber Mannheim slide rule, but the rule is otherwise clean and in excellent collector quality condition.* (GOOD+) **$65.00**

N1-9. Keuffel & Esser Co., New York No. 4097-C: 6 Inch "Ever There" Slide Rule. With Instructions. New Condition, Original Box. Length: 6 Inches. *The basic principal of the "Ever There" slide rule was that it could be placed in your pocket so as to be (you guessed it).... A nice example, complete with the original instructions.* (GOOD+) **$85.00**

N1-10. Keuffel & Esser Co., New York No. 4055: 10 Inch Merchants Slide Rule. In Original Case. With Instructions. Length: 10 Inches. *Another example of the short lived venture by K & E to expand its market. These appeared in the catalog for a brief time in the 1920's. Their basic feature was a substantial reduction in the number of scales, so as to be more appealing to the non-technically inclined. A marketing failure no doubt attributable to frustration on the part of grocers unable to ascertain the inverse hyperbolic cosecant of six sacks of flour. A collectible curiosity.* (FINE) **$115.00**

N1-11. Faber-Castell, Germany: "Electro" Slide Rule. For Electrical Calculations. Volts, Amps, Etc. Length: 12 Inches. *The special scales on this rule were intended for performing the complex calculations required of an electrical engineer. A nice example of an uncommon specialty slide rule.* (FINE) **$215.00**

N1-12. Slip Lens: Slide Rule Magnifying Lense. Uncommon Type. New Condition, Original Box. Length: 2 1/2 Inches. *A slide rule user with a need for corrective lenses might have opted instead for this special cursor, which incorporates a magnifying feature into its design. Never seen another.* (FINE) **$55.00**

N1-13. Amos, John P., Rochester, N.Y.: "Purification" Slide Rule. For Water Works. 1932 "Pat. Applied". Length: 12 Inches. *The enclosed documentation tells us all about the practical application of this rare work of genius, but little of its inventor. An educated guess would suggest that Mr. Amos was involved in the water works business and that this contribution to the advance of technology had been designed over many hours nestled amidst pipes and valves whilst being reimbursed for his efforts by the taxpayers. A recent survey of historic sites of the Rochester, New York area reveals no "Amos Mansion" or any other evidence of its inventor's having made it big with this brainchild, so we are probably correct in assuming that this, as was the case with so many such inventions, was one of those great ideas whose time never came.* (FINE) **$265.00**

N1-14. Assorted Makers: Group of 3 Assorted Slide Rules. Concrete, Etc. With Advertising. Length: 8 Inches. *Here's a bargain priced grouping of advertising slide rules from a range of makers. Opportunity knocks.* (FINE) **$25.00**

N1-15. Nestler, Albert: Mannheim Type Slide Rule. With Framed Cursor. Original Case. Length: 11 Inches. *This early rule from an uncommon maker has the classic style "framed" cursor. A good one.* (GOOD+) **$95.00**

N1-16. Keuffel & Esser Co., New York No. 4058 C: "Beginner's" Slide Rule. With Instructions. New Condition, Original Box. Length: 11 Inches. *A slide rule "newbie" could cut his or her teeth on this classic "beginners" rule from K. & E. The original instruction manual is present with this "in the box" example. Nearly new.* (FINE) **$85.00**

N1-17. Concise No. 300: Circular Slide Rule. Original Case. Made in Japan. Length: 4 1/2 Inches. *Here's a circular slide rule from a Japanese company that is complete and in much the same condition as it was when new.* (FINE) **$35.00**

N1-18. Assorted Makers: Group of 3 Slide Rules. Sterling, Pickett, E. "Acumath", Etc. Length: 10 Inches. *Here's a generous assortment of later style slide rules in top condition. First come, first serve.* (FINE) **$35.00**

N1-19. Keuffel & Esser Co., New York No. 4070-3: Duplex Slide Rule. In Original Case. Owner "Rich. Curran". Length: 10 Inches. *The original owner of this duplex classic from K. & E. tastefully engraved it with his name. Overall condition is excellent.* (FINE) **$65.00**

N1-20. Keuffel & Esser Co., New York No. 4053-3: 10 Inch Manheim Slide Rule. In Original Case. Early Type. Length: 10 Inches. *This early example of a K. & E. standard is in superb condition in its original case.* (GOOD+) **$35.00**

N1-21. Lawrence Eng. Svce., Peru, Indiana: Group of 5 Slide Rules. Various Styles. Original Cases, Etc. Length: 10 Inches. *Lawrence produced a wide range of slide rules of every conceivable type, of which this sampling gives an approximation. An opportunity lot.* (GOOD+) **$35.00**

N1-22. Dietzgen Co., Eugene, Chicago: Framed Cursor Slide Rule. Patented August 9, 1904. Early and Excellent. Length: 10 Inches. *This early Dietzgen rule is marked with a 1904 patent date and has the classic "framed" cursor. A nice example.* (GOOD+) **$75.00**

N1-23. Keuffel & Esser Co., New York No. 4181-3: Log Duplex Slide Rule. With Instructions. New Condition, Original Box. Length: 13 Inches. *This K. & E. classic is in brand new condition in its original box, complete with the instruction manual.* (FINE) **$35.00**

N1-24. Dietzgen Co., Eugene, Chicago No. 6025: Triple Cursor Slide Rule. Framed Type Cursor. Scarce and Excellent. Length: 10 Inches. *An extra wide "framed" cursor is the distinctive feature of this Dietzgen classic. Crisp, clean and clearly marked.* (GOOD+) **$115.00**

N1-25. Rabone & Sons, John, Birmingham No. 1206: Boxwood Cordage Rule. With Tables, Etc. Near New Condition. Length: 3 1/2 Inches. *The maker's name is imprinted on the edge of this classic "cordage" rule. Both sides of the rule are imprinted with tables showing the relative strength of ropes and cables. An uncommon rule in top condition.* (FINE) **$175.00**

N1-26. Gerber Scientific Co., The, Hartford No. TP-007100: Gerber Variable Scale Slide Rule. With Spring Extension. New Condition, Original Box. Length: 12 1/2 Inches. *A series of springs are at the heart of the mechanics of this specialty slide rule, which was apparently designed to calculate relative proportions. It is in excellent condition in its original box. Different.* (GOOD+) **$245.00**

N1-27. Raphaels, Ltd.: Orthop's Slide Rule. For Optician's Use. Apical Radii Project. Length: 7 Inches. *Designed for performing the complex mathematical calculations that were the daily bread of a practicing optician, this boxwood rule of English manufacture is clean and complete, noting a small stain on one face. A rare special function slide rule.* (GOOD+) **$125.00**

N1-28. Gilson (Unmarked): Patent Circular Slide Rule. Patented January 17, 1892. Original Case. Length: 4 Inches. *This early circular slide rule is of the classic "Gilson" pattern, but is marked only with the 1922 Gilson patent date. A highly collectible circular slide rule.* (GOOD+) **$65.00**

N1-29. Sun Hemmi, Japan: Magnifying Slide Rule. "U.S. Blue" Advertisement. Original Case. Length: 5 Inches. *These magnifying slide rules were apparently given away as promotional items by a Chicago manufacturer. Crisp and clean.* (FINE) **$65.00**

N1-30. Aston & Mander, Soho, London: Harrow Mark Reducer Slide Rule. For Grade Calculating. Solid Boxwood. Length: 33 Inches. *Those who lament the fact that standards are not quite so high in today's world may have their concern somewhat alleviated by the knowledge that the practice of grading on a "curve" had its beginning in the Nineteenth Century, as this specialty grading slide rule demonstrates. It may well have been that this slide rule also functioned as a "board of education" for use on students at the low end of the curve. This example is clean, complete and clearly marked. A classic.* (GOOD+) **$295.00**

N1-31. Lutz No. 151 C: Duplex Slide Rule. With Original Case. Marked "U.S.". Length: 14 Inches. *The "U.S." imprint on this Lutz Duplex slide rule may be a clue that it was originally purchased by the United States Government. A nice example.* (FINE) **$45.00**

N1-32. Stanley Rule & Level No. 34 1/4 VR: Two Way Bench Rules. Package of 1 Dozen. Unused Condition. Length: 12 Inches. *We have sold hundreds of "in the box" Stanley items over the past several years, but these are the first Stanley tools in their original wrapping paper we have ever been privileged to offer. All of these rules are in brand new condition. Perfect.* (FINE) **$345.00**

N1-33. Concise: Advertising Circular Slide Rule. "Mobil Oil". With Periodic Table. Length: 4 1/4 Inches. *Not exactly the kind of thing they would give you when you filled your car with gas (unless you were not wanted back), this 1960's era rule, which includes a slide-out copy of the Periodic Table of the Elements, was either distributed for use by Mobil's technical staff or given away to like minded sorts. Different.* (FINE) **$35.00**

N1-34. Unmarked: Early Boxwood Slide Rule. Sine and Tangent Scales. Ca. 1800. Length: 24 Inches. *There are no maker marks on this early boxwood calculating rule. The style and markings indicate that it was produced in the first quarter of the Nineteenth Century. A classic early slide rule.* (GOOD+) **$395.00**

N1-35. Stanley Rule & Level (Unmarked) No. 57: One Foot, Four Fold Folding Rule. Arch Joint, Full Bound. Extra Crisp and Clean. Length: 12 Inches. *Stanley may have made the No. 57 with its imprint applied thereto, but I have yet to see one. This example is exceptionally crisp and clean. Extra nice.* (FINE) **$165.00**

N1-36. Farmar: Reducing Slide Rule. Wine and Spirit Calculation. Near New Condition. Length: 12 1/2 Inches. *From personal experience of interaction with the English culture I am prepared to report that the practice of producing fermented and distilled spirits must be at least as prevalent as it was when this special calculating rule was produced. A nice example of an uncommon English special purpose slide rule.* (FINE) **$125.00**

N1-37. Faber, A.W., Germany: Early Patent Slide Rule. "Made In Bavaria". Original Case. Length: 11 1/2 Inches. *An extremely well preserved Manheim slide rule from the earliest days of slide rule making, this one is imprinted with the designation "Made in Bavaria". Nice.* (FINE) **$115.00**

N1-38. Nicholls & Co., J.A., London No. MK. VI: App. Obs. of Fire Slide Rule. Dated 1916. New Condition, Original Case. Length: 16 Inches. *Undoubtedly produced for use by artillery officers in the first world war, this aluminum slide rule of English manufacture is imprinted with its 1916 date of manufacture. The original case has kept it in top collector quality condition.* (FINE) **$295.00**

N1-39. Chapin, H., U. S. Standard No. 17 1/2: Two Foot, Four Fold Folding Rule. Architect Scales. Rare and Excellent. Length: 24 Inches. *The inside edges of this early and uncommon folding rule are beveled in the style of the classic "architect's" rule. A very nice example.* (GOOD+) **$185.00**

N1-40. Stanley Rule & Level No. 62: "Sweetheart" Era Folding Rule. Full Box of 6. New Condition, Original Box. Length: 24 Inches. *For a vision of what a hardware store would have been like in the 1920's, just open this box of six immaculate No. 62 rules. All original finishes remain on all of the rules in the box, which is in sound condition with a full paper label. A rarity.* (FINE) **$595.00**

N1-41. Lufkin Rule Co., The, Saginaw, Mich. No. 8120: Rare Shoe Measure Caliper. Maple Body. Crisp and Clean. Length: 14 1/2 Inches. *We have sold the more elaborate boxwood folding shoe caliper by Lufkin in the past, but this is the first "standard pattern" shoe caliper from Lufkin that we have seen. A rare Lufkin rule.* (GOOD+) **$185.00**

N1-42. Unmarked: Japanese Advertising Slide Rule. Canadian Westinghouse. Missing Cursor. Length: 6 Inches. *The leather case has protected this advertising rule, but has not kept its original cursor with it.* (GOOD+) **$35.00**

N1-43. Concise No. 28 N: Circular Slide Rule. Original Case. With Instructions. Length: 3 1/4 Inches. *This later style circular slide rule comes complete with its original instruction manual.* (FINE) **$45.00**

N1-44. Stanley Rule & Level No. 5: Two Foot, Two Fold Folding Rule. Architect's Scales. Superb Condition. Length: 24 Inches. *Stanley offered the No. 5 two foot carpenter's rule from 1854 to 1942, but examples in this condition are very seldom seen. Nearly new.* (FINE) **$255.00**

N1-45. Stanley Rule & Level No. 83 C: Two Foot, Four Fold Folding Rule. With Caliper. "Sweetheart" Trademark. Length: 24 Inches. *The No. 83 C was Stanley's only four-fold caliper rule, other than the No. 62 C, which was of a much narrower width. This one is in nearly new condition and marked with the ca. 1920's era "Sweetheart" trademark. Mint.* (FINE) **$295.00**

N1-46. Faber, A.W., Newark, N.J.: Early Boxwood Slide Rule. With "Dial" Cursor. Original Case. Length: 11 Inches. *We are uncertain as to the function of the unique "dial" mechanism on the cursor of this early Faber slide rule. The boxwood body has been kept in fine condition, thanks to the presence of the original box. The glass cursor has a crack, which could be easily repaired.* (FINE) **$245.00**

Group O1

O1-1. Springfield Level & Tool Co.: Cast Iron Plumb Level. Decoritive Filigree. Chip from Lower Corner. Length: 12 Inches. *There is a 1/2 inch x 1 inch chip from the rail at one corner of this showy level, but it is otherwise excellent. A dramatic early level.* (GOOD+) **$225.00**

O1-2. Modern Utilities Co., Harrisburg,: "Perfection" Patent Level. Patented April 21, 1914. New Condition, Original Box. Length: 3 3/4 Inches. *This patent specialty level was meant to be mounted on a straight edge. It has never been used. Absolutely perfect.* (FINE) **$85.00**

O1-3. Athol Machine Co., Athol, Mass.: 6 Inch Cast Iron Plumb and Level. With Dual Plumbs. Near New Condition. Length: 6 Inches. *This pristine example of the smallest size plumb and level from the Athol Machine Company, L.S. Starrett's former business associates, is in new condition and clearly marked.* (FINE) **$165.00**

O1-4. Patent Level Co., Bridgeport, Conn.: Patent Inclinometer, Level. Patented May 8, 1866. Early and Excellent. Length: 6 Inches. *Produced under a patent issued on May 8, 1866 to A.J. Vandergrift, this elaborately cast bronze inclinometer preceded by two years the similarly-styled, if mechanically different, level to be patented and manufactured by L.L. Davis in the following year. Marked on the base of the body with the maker's name "Patent Level Co., Bridgeport, Conn." as well as the patent date, this level's resident genius was a glass-faced vial that was apparently to be filled with alcohol to the halfway point, where the 360 degree graduations would serve as both level and inclinometer. This level, as were the other two examples of which I am aware, has no fluid in the vial. There is no evidence of a break in either the glass or the seal, but the vial is dry, nonetheless. Complete with its porthole-type cover which locks back into position when the level is no longer needed, this classic early level is in extraordinarily well-preserved condition. Simply a great antique tool.* (FINE) **$2,650.00**

O1-5. Unmarked: Ebony Sighting Level. With Brass Fittings. Missing Stadia. Length: 12 Inches. *The stadia, or "cross hairs" are missing from this most unusual ebony and brass sighting level, but it is otherwise in superb, collector quality condition. A most unusual level with a pronounced Scottish look. Very nice.* (GOOD+) **$245.00**

O1-6. Unmarked: Cast Iron Plumb and Level. Elaborate Casting. Original Pinstriping. Length: 7 Inches. *Who defines the limits of where work ends and art begins? Or are there any limits? Mark Twain, through the words of Tom Sawyer, told us that "Work is what a body is obliged to do, and play is what a body is not obliged to do". Is this level, then, judged in light of that observation, just a waste of time, some fool's folly that took valuable time and energy away from the real work to be done? Should something so carefully crafted and elaborately decorated have been made at all? Why would someone go to all this trouble when a block of iron or wood with a glass vial fitted into it would be good enough? If you find yourself agreeing with any of these observations, you will probably never be a tool collector. You will probably never experience the absolute delight that the discovery of an object such as this level can bring. The feeling of seeing something so wondrous and immediately being able to see far beyond its outward appearance to a long forgotten world will be an experience you will never share. You will content yourself by doing that which you are "obliged to do". For others, perhaps not so inclined, we offer this spectacular cast iron level with elaborate Victorian era decoration. Play.* (FINE) **$850.00**

O1-7. Starrett Co., L.S., Athol, Mass. No. 130: Bench Level. 3 1/2 Inch Size. Early Red Box. Length: 3 1/2 Inches. *An excellent example of Starrett's 4 inch bench level. All original finishes remain on this "in the box" example. Perfect.* (FINE) **$55.00**

O1-8. Stanley Rule & Level No. 187: Precision Line Level. Enameled Metal Case. Near New Condition. Length: 3 1/4 Inches. *The original hinged top orange box has kept this Stanley classic in top collector quality condition. An uncommon Stanley level, especially in this condition.* (FINE) **$45.00**

O1-9. Melick, W.B.: "Clinometer Gravity" Level. Patented December 3, 1889. Rare and Excellent. Length: 24 Inches. *Produced under a patent granted on December 3, 1889 to St. Louis, Missouri inventor W.B. Melick, this wood-bodied inclinometer features a spring-activated inclinometer that can be stopped at a specific measurement by a push button in the back of the tool. An excellent example of a rare Nineteenth Century precision level.* (GOOD) **$895.00**

O1-10. Fitchburg Tool Co. Fitchburg, Mass.: 12 Inch Cast Iron Level. Open Filligree Casting. Double Plumb Vial. Length: 12 Inches. *The levels of the Fitchburg Tool Company are easily distinguishable by their reticulated filigree casting surrounding a central, rectangular housing of a level and two plumb vials. This one is in excellent condition. A good one.* (GOOD+) **$395.00**

O1-11. Stanley Rule & Level No. 39 1/2: Machinist's Bench Level. Sweetheart Trademark. Excellent Condition. Length: 6 Inches. *This extra-clean machinist's level features the popular "Sweetheart" trademark. Nice.* (GOOD+) **$45.00**

O1-12. Acme Level Company, Toledo, Ohio. No. 24: 24 Inch Inclinometer Level. Copper Finish. New Condition, Original Box. Length: 24 Inches. *Toledo's Acme Level Company produced a line of copper finished steel levels that included an inclinometer function on many types. Generally, when found, these tools have deteriorated significantly from their original level of finish. Thanks to the presence of the original box, which retains its original label, this level has been protected throughout its long life from exposure of any kind to the elements. Retaining all of its original finish and without question the finest example of the Acme inclinometer level we have ever seen, we proudly offer this pristine tool.* (FINE) **$745.00**

O1-13. Stanley Rule & Level No. 31: Hexagonal Machinist's Level. Ca. 1910. Excellent Condition. Length: 3 1/2 Inches. *This early example of Stanley's No. 31 machinist's level has a slight split in the body, but is otherwise in excellent condition. A good one.* (GOOD) **$45.00**

O1-14. Davis & Cook, Watertown, N. Y. No. 01: 16 Inch Mahogany Level. Original Nickel Plating. Uncommon Type. Length: 16 1/2 Inches. *Sufficient numbers of the larger sizes of the Davis & Cook wooden levels have been found to convince collectors and researchers that these levels were quite popular in their day. However, examples of the smaller sizes of these levels are not often found. This 16 inch mahogany example is in excellent collector quality condition. An uncommon Davis & Cook level.* (GOOD+) **$245.00**

O1-15. Unmarked: Macassar Ebony Level. Classic Scottish Style. Superb Condition. Length: 6 Inches. *The combination of the reddish black Macassar ebony and the brass fittings of this superb Scottish level is more beautiful than even a full color photograph can convey. Really pretty.* (FINE) **$155.00**

O1-16. Stanley Rule & Level (Unmarked) No. 42: Solid Brass Square Level. Unused Condition. Rare and Perfect. Length: 3 1/4 Inches. *Offered in Stanley's catalogs from 1859 through 1917 only, these solid brass square levels may have been a bit too expensive and a bit less showy than Stanley's other tools in this area. Whatever the case, these are quite scarce. This example is unmarked, but unmistakable and has developed a dark golden patina over time. A rare Stanley level.* (FINE) **$165.00**

O1-17. Stanley Rule & Level No. 41: Ornate Brass Top Level. Patented June 23, 1896. With Embossed Imprint. Length: 3 Inches. *The top plate on this variation of the No. 41 is particularly ornately embellished. Classic, and classy.* (GOOD+) **$55.00**

O1-18. Jennings & Co., C.E., New York, N.Y.: Rare Square Level. Full Nickel Plating. Owner "W.J.F.". Length: 4 Inches. *We have offered these square levels from a wide variety of makers, but this is the first example from the C.E. Jennings Company that we have seen. Rare.* (GOOD+) **$195.00**

O1-19. Springfield Level & Tool Co.: Cast Iron Plumb Level. Graphic Form. Crack Through Top. Length: 24 Inches. *This level has a tight crack through the body adjacent to the vial, but it is otherwise complete, sound and ready to display. A bargain.* (GOOD) **$95.00**

O1-20. Davis Level & Tool Co.: Miniature Machinist Level. With Brass Finials. Extra Rare and Nice. Length: 2 1/4 Inches. *It may have been their limited utility that caused the tool buying public to opt for larger sizes that makes these diminutive levels so rare today. What few were produced and sold were undoubtedly lost or broken over the years. Whatever the case very few examples of this, the smallest level produced by the Davis Level & Tool Company have survived. This example retains nearly all of its original nickel plating and is in excellent collector quality condition. A very rare Davis level.* (GOOD+) **$875.00**

O1-21. Springfield Level & Tool Co.: Cast Iron Plumb Level. Nickel Plated Vials. 85% Original Paint. Length: 12 Inches. *Most of this original paint remains on this graphic level from a Davis Level & Tool successor. Nearly all of the shiny nickel plating remains on the vials. Very showy.* (GOOD+) **$265.00**

O1-22. Marples & Co., William, Sheffield: Figured Rosewood Level. "Shamrock" Logo. Near New Condition. Length: 10 Inches. *A sheltered corner of a tool box has protected this pristine rosewood and brass level from any apparent wear or weathering. Choice.* (FINE) **$175.00**

O1-23. Davis, L.L., Springfield, Mass. No. 11: Decorative Post Level. Rare Small Size. Early and Uncommon. Length: 4 Inches. *Here's a nice example of the Davis post level that is ready for the collection.* (FINE) **$475.00**

O1-24. Hibbard, Spencer & Bartlett Co. No. 100: "O.V.B." Brand Level. Solid Rosewood. Extra Crisp and Clean. Length: 26 Inches. *Rosewood levels from any maker are far from common. After the end of the Nineteenth Century, the production of these levels was severely curtailed, most likely owing to the rising cost of the wood. This 26 inch rosewood level from the "Our Very Best" line of Hibbard, Spencer & Bartlett was very likely made for them by the Baker McKillen Company. A rare rosewood level.* (GOOD+) **$225.00**

O1-25. Richardson, C.F., Athol, Mass.: 4 Inch Machinist's Level. Superb Condition. 99% Nickel Plating. Length: 4 Inches. *The C.F. Richardson Company was eventually assumed by machinist tool manufacturing giant L.S. Starrett & Company. Richardson levels were considered among the very best. This most uncommon nickel plated hexagonal brass machinist's level is in superb condition. Nice.* (FINE) **$85.00**

O1-26. Millers Falls Company No. 21: Machinist's 4 Inch Level. Discontinued Ca.1915. Extra Rare and Fine. Length: 4 Inches. *One of the least common of all small cast iron levels, the Millers Falls No. 21 was featured in several early catalogs, but seems not to have been a popular item. This is only the second example that we have been able to buy and offer for sale in the past 15 years. 95% of the paint and nearly all of the original nickel plating remain. A rare level.* (FINE) **$675.00**

O1-27. Davis Level & Tool Co. No. 1: 7 Inch Inclinometer Level. Patented September 17, 1867. Crisp and Clean. Length: 7 Inches. *The Davis "mantel clock" inclinometers have a special appeal for collectors, especially when they are absent the cracks and chips so often found in these tools, as is the case with this example. This well preserved example has been cleaned and polished by a previous owner and is ready to display. A rare and desirable level.* (GOOD+) **$445.00(**

O1-28. Stanley Rule & Level No. 264: Aluminum Torpedo Level. New Condition, Original Box. Length: 9 Inches. *This aluminum level is in new condition in its original 1950's era "Christmas" box. A good, clean level in a tough to find box.* (FINE) **$85.00**

O1-29. Stanley Rule & Level No. 98: 9 Inch Machinist's Level Level. Least Common Size. "Sweetheart" Trademark. Length: 9 Inches. *Stanley offered their No. 98 series of levels in a full range of sizes from 6 inches to 24 inches. This example of the 9 inch size, which some claim to be the least common size of the bunch, retains 99% of all original finishes on all surfaces. The desirable "Sweetheart" trademark is embossed on the top plate and the tools is absent any nicks or dings whatever. A glorious example of a great Stanley level.* (FINE) **$975.00**

O1-30. Stratton Bros., Greenfield, Mass. No. 10: 10 Inch Rosewood Level. Full Brass Bound. With End Vial. Length: 10 Inches. *Nearly all original finishes remain on this classic rosewood level from a top American maker. If you are looking for a representative Stratton level in top condition, this is it. Nice.* (FINE) **$775.00**

O1-31. Stratton Bros., Greenfield, Mass. No. 10: Rosewood Plumb and Level. Patented March 1, 1870. Early and Excellent. Length: 8 Inches. *This early type brass bound level is fitted with the classic end-view plumb bob. There is a small gouge from the wood on the base, but it would be invisible when displayed. A nice example.* (GOOD+) **$565.00**

O1-32. Springfield Level & Tool Co.: Cast Iron Plumb Level. 95% Original Paint. Graphic Form. Length: 24 Inches. *Nearly all of the original shiny black japanning remains on this cast iron filigree level from an important New England maker. A rare and graphic collectible level.* (GOOD+) **$265.00**

O1-33. Starrett Co., L.S., The, Athol, Mass. No. 199: Master Precision Level. For Precise Work. New Condition, Original Box. Length: 16 1/2 Inches. *Designed for the most exacting work, this "Master Precision Level" was intended to be stored in its fitted wooden box to keep it properly calibrated. Not for every machinist, we have seen only a few examples of these levels in the past ten years. A quality tool in top condition.* (FINE) **$265.00**

O1-34. Goodell-Pratt Company: 12 Inch Macinist's Bench Level. 98% Original Finish. "V" Groove Base. Length: 12 Inches. *Nearly all of the Goodell-Pratt machinist levels are quite scarce. This example of the 12 inch size is in great shape.* (FINE) **$65.00**

O1-35. Stratton Bros., Greenfield, Mass. No. 10: Rare 6 Inch Machinist's Level. Most Unusual Imprint. With Inside Vial. Length: 6 Inches. *Here's an exceptionally clean example of the 8 inch rosewood version of the Stratton No. 10 brass-bound level. Unlike most levels in this side, which feature the machinist's type plumb vial set in the end of the tool, this example has the inside plumb vial of a carpenter's level. A rare Stratton level.* (GOOD+) **$795.00**

O1-36. Stanley Rule & Level No. 34: "Eclipse" Level. 4 Inch Size. Original Green Box. Length: 4 Inches. *Examples of Stanley's classic "Eclipse" bench levels are tough to find in any size. This perfectly preserved 4 inch version retains all of its original finishes. One end of the early green box is missing, but the tool and box are otherwise perfect. Rare.* (FINE) **$365.00**

O1-37. Unmarked: Mahogany Spirit Level. "J. Fenwick, 1870". Fitted Leather Case. Length: 12 Inches. *A custom made leather slip case has kept this classic mahogany spirit level in much the same condition as when it was fashioned by one J. Fenwick and engraved with "1870", the year of its completion. A classic collectible tool.* (FINE) **$295.00**

O1-38. Stanley Rule & Level No. 43: Machinist's Pocket Level. 1863 To 1879 Only. Super Rare. Length: 9 Inches. *Included in Stanley's product line from 1863 to 1879 only, the demand for these cast iron machinist's levels must have been so slight that Stanley eliminated them from their ever-expanding product line. This example is not marked with the Stanley name, as is the case with every example that we have observed, but it is clean, sound and ready to display. A very rare Stanley level.* (GOOD) **$785.00**

O1-39. Tower & Lyon, New York, N.Y.: Patent Inclinometer Level. Patented March 31, 1891. Near New Condition. Length: 2 1/2 Inches. *Designed to fit on the edge of a framing square or try square, this very well made patented device from New York City makers Tower & Lyon was designed to turn any such tool into a functioning inclinometer. Because of their small size and fragility, most examples of this tool were quickly broken or degraded in condition. This one is in much the same condition as the day it was made. Crisp, clean, clearly marked and ready to display.* (FINE) **$225.00**

O1-40. Stanley Rule & Level No. 31: Hexagonal Machinist's Level. Ca. 1910. Unused Condition. Length: 3 Inches. *All of the original nickel plating remains on this hexagonal pocket level from Stanley. A tough level to find, especially in this condition.* (FINE) **$45.00**

O1-41. Preston & Sons, E.: Rosewood and Brass Level. Original Lacquer. Near New Condition. Length: 8 Inches. *This classic bench level from English makers Edward Preston & Sons is in nearly new condition. Choice.* (FINE) **$85.00**

O1-42. Davis Level & Tool Co. No. 03: Level. Patented September 17, 1867. Crisp and Clean. Length: 30 Inches. *Nicely cleaned and restored by a previous owner, this classic inclinometer level has been polished to a showy brilliance and the japan finish has been lightly enhanced to make it a virtual showstopper. An eyecatcher.* (FINE) **$445.00**

O1-43. Helb, Edward, Railroad, Penn.: Patent Inclinometer Level. Patented July 12, 1904. Excellent Condition. Length: 24 Inches. *Here's an excellent example of the Helb inclinometer level that is clean, sound and in excellent working order. Contrary to popular misconception, these are not "Railroad" levels, they were made in the City of Railroad, Pennsylvania and have no more likely to be associated with trains than a patented brace produced in Buffalo, New York would be intended to be employed in some inhumane manner on an American Bison. A most unusual level, but not for the train crowd.* (GOOD+) **$575.00**

O1-44. Preston & Sons, Edward: Ebony and Brass Bench Level. With Steel Facing. Fitted Brass Case. Length: 12 1/2 Inches. *Having been protected from wear of any kind by virtue of the fitted brass box in which it was kept, this immaculate ebony level is a superb example of the very best work of prominent English makers Edward Preston & Sons. Highly recommended.* (FINE) **$525.00**

O1-45. Davis & Cook, Watertown, N. Y.: 24 Inch Cast Iron Level. Patented December28, 1886. Fifty per cent Original Paint. Length: 24 Inches. *The Davis & Cook Company of Watertown, New York (no association with L.L. Davis) produced a highly collectible line of wood, cast iron and aluminum levels. The elaborate, cast iron levels are among the most graphic of all cast iron levels. Their reticulated castings, sometimes referred to as "pretzel-type" did not lend themselves to rough use. This clean and sound example of the uncommon 24 inch cast iron level retains more than half of its original paint and is marked with the patent date. Much of the shiny nickel plating remains on the vial covers and the casting is as it was the day it was made. A rare and graphic patented level.* (GOOD) **$445.00**

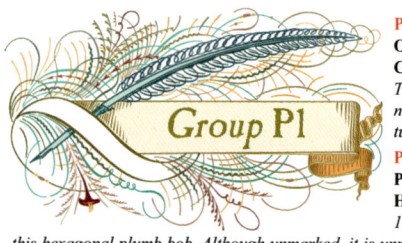

Group P1

P1-1. Braunsdorf-Mueller Co. No. 50: 8 Ounce Brass Plumb Bob. Picture Box. New Condition, Original Box. Length: 5 Inches. *This Braunsdorf-Mueller Company bob has never been used. Complete with its original picture box. A superb example.* (FINE) **$125.00**

P1-2. Millers Falls Co. (Unmarked): Nickel Plated Plumb Bob. Removable Cap. Hexagonal Body. Length: 3 Inches. *Fully 100% of the original nickel plating remains on this hexagonal plumb bob. Although unmarked, it is unmistakably an example of the standard carpenter's plumb bob produced by the Millers Falls Tool Company. Mint, and a good old fashioned bargain.* (FINE) **$15.00**

P1-3. Unmarked: Early Turnip Shape Plumb Bob. Knurled Cap. Excellent Patina. Length: 4 Inches. *A decoratively knurled cap accents this well patinated bob in the classic "turnip" shape.* (FINE) **$265.00**

P1-4. Unmarked: Solid Brass Plumb Bob. With Hanger Bracket. Early and Excellent. Length: 2 Inches. *This basic bob dispenses with the finery of a threaded cap and is attached fishing weight style to the string.* (GOOD+) **$25.00**

P1-5. Unmarked: Millwright's Brass Plumb Bob. With Acorn Finial. Original Finish. Length: 7 Inches. *This classic millwright's plumb bob has only a bit of oxidation on its brass body to its detriment, otherwise, as-new. An American classic.* (GOOD+) **$235.00**

P1-6. Unmarked: Distinctive Brass Plumb Bob. With Plated Brass Cap. Most Unusual. Length: 4 1/2 Inches. *The nickel-plated thimble type cap on this brass bob is new to me. Obviously manufactured, but unmarked. Found in the Great State of Illinois.* (GOOD+) **$185.00**

P1-7. Unmarked: 12 Ounce "Carrot" Plumb Bob. Black Japan Finish. New Condition, Original Box. Length: 5 Inches. *We would suspect the presence of brass beneath the japan finish, but have not taken a core sample. A most interesting plumb bob with a finish we have not seen before. Different.* (FINE) **$35.00**

P1-8. Berger, C.L. No. 416: 16 Ounce "Retracta Bob" Plumb Bob. Original Sleeve. "Only New Design". Length: 7 1/2 Inches. *The tip of this most unusual bob is fitted with a spring which causes it to retract when substantial force is exerted upon it. An innovative design from the prominent maker of surveyor's tools. New and in the box.* (FINE) **$125.00**

P1-9. Stevens A. & T. Co., C. Falls, Mass.: Lead Filled Plumb Bob. Full Nickel Plating. Rare and Excellent. Length: 4 Inches. *The J. Stevens Arms & Tool Company offered several plumb bobs for sale during the course of their history, all of which are extremely rare. This narrow, nickel plated version derives its weight from small lead shot, a material that might have been available to a manufacturer of firearms. A rare bob with a bold maker mark.* (GOOD+) **$395.00**

P1-10. Keuffel & Esser Co., New York: Internal Reel Plumb Bob. Perfect Mechanical Condition. Crisp and Clean. Length: 4 Inches. *This internal reel plumb bob is adjusted by turning the knurled screw at the point where the thread enters the bob. Mechanically perfect and tough to find, especially in this condition.* (GOOD+) **$325.00**

P1-11. Unmarked: Ovate Brass Plumb Bob. Steel Tip. Excellent Patina. Length: 4 Inches. *This one is as broad as it is long. Early, nicely patinated and ready to display.* (GOOD+) **$225.00**

P1-12. Unmarked: Millwright's Plumb Bob. No. 2 1/2 Size. Great Patina. Length: 6 1/2 Inches. *This classic bob in the millwright's style has a few light toolbox dings, but is nicely patinated and ready to display. A classic.* (GOOD+) **$265.00**

P1-13. Unmarked: Ovate Brass Plumb Bob. With Early Reel. Distinctive Form. Length: 2 1/4 Inches. *An early hand made reel complements this miniature bob with a thicker than normal neck.* (FINE) **$285.00**

P1-14. Unmarked No. 3: Hexagonal Cap Plumb Bob. Elongated Body. Excellent Patina. Length: 3 1/4 Inches. *The makers of this unusual and nicely patinated bob dispensed with the concept of decorative knurling for the cap and instead fashioned it in the shape of a hexagon. Never seen another.* (FINE) **$115.00**

P1-15. Unmarked: 16 Ounce Brass Plumb Bob. Decorative Rings. Distinctive Form. Length: 3 Inches. *The lack of elaborate ornamentation on this bob is indicative of very early manufacture. This plumb bob has achieved a most appealing patina over its many years of life.* (GOOD+) **$85.00**

P1-16. Unmarked: Early Style Plumb Bob. Decorative Cap. Elongated Steel Tip. Length: 3 1/2 Inches. *A wider than usual cap is treaded on the top of this early plumb bob. Ex-Cooley Collection.* (GOOD+) **$185.00**

P1-17. Unmarked: Massive Bronze Plumb Bob. Oblong Shape. Ex-Beecher Collection. Length: 5 Inches. *This spectacularly well preserved bob features a double ring of knurls at its cap. Much of the original finish remains on this showstopper from the Mark Beecher Collection.* (FINE) **$385.00**

P1-18. Unmarked No. 00: Miniature Brass Plumb Bob. With Brass Reel. Distinctive Form. Length: 2 Inches. *The presence of a knurled brass spool makes it likely that this bob was intended for the finer sorts of work that might be encountered in the management of a home, rather than the rough and tumble world of building construction. Pretty.* (GOOD+) **$135.00**

P1-19. Unmarked: Massive Art Deco Plumb Bob. Solid Brass Body, 4 Pounds. Full Nickel Plating. Length: 8 Inches. *At a full four pounds in weight, this massive nickel-plated bob would have been used for the laying out of bridges or large buildings where its massive size would have resisted attempts by the wind to complicate the efforts of the engineers. Incorporating a level of design that dates it to the 1920's, this oversize and unusual plumb bob will add interest to any serious collection.* (FINE) **$365.00**

P1-20. Unmarked: Unusual Carrot-Shape Plumb Bob. Early Spiral Knurls. Excellent Condition. Length: 4 1/2 Inches. *Longer and leaner than your average garden-variety plumb bob. Decidedly different.* (GOOD+) **$85.00**

P1-21. Unmarked: Internal Reel Plumb Bob. Distinctive Cap. Superb Patina. Length: 6 1/2 Inches. *Among the most sought-after of all plumb bobs are those which seek to change the basic design (a design determined by gravity at the beginning of time) and somehow "improve" upon it. At the forefront of such efforts have been attempts to incorporate some means of storing and/or regulating the release of the cord that was the necessary, if admittedly less aesthetically appealing, partner in the plumb bob's working relationship with Newton's laws. We offer here an example of one of those efforts with which we have heretofore been unfamiliar. Incorporating a bobbin-like mechanism housed in its hollow central core, the operator of this precision plumb bob can release as little or as much cord as desired, simply by turning the elaborately-knurled cap. A most unusual and mechanically interesting plumb bob in excellent condition.* (GOOD+) **$645.00**

P1-22. Unmarked: Early Brass Plumb Bob. Decorative Knurls. Excellent Patina. Length: 1 1/2 Inches. *Classic spiral knurling on the cap gives this diminutive bob a most appealing ornamented look. Early and perfectly patinated.* (FINE) **$165.00**

P1-23. Stanley Rule & Level No. 2: Retractable Reel Plumb Bob. Brass Body and Reel. With Stanley Mark. Length: 4 Inches. *An excellent example of the largest of Stanley's retractable reel plumb bobs. This one is boldly marked with the maker name on the reel. Extra nice.* (FINE) **$245.00**

P1-24. Unmarked: Early Cast Iron Plumb Bob. Partial Nickel Plating. Classic Style. Length: 2 1/2 Inches. *Much of the original nickel plating remains on this classic cast iron bob.* (GOOD+) **$15.00**

P1-25. Unmarked: Classic Pear Shape Plumb Bob. Owner "D. Kelley". Excellent Patina. Length: 7 Inches. *The original owner of this massive pear shaped bob was so proud of it he imprinted it with his name. A classic.* (GOOD+) **$465.00**

P1-26. Unmarked: Turned Brass Plumb Bob. Polished Body. Distinctive Form. Length: 3 Inches. *This highly polished bob has elements of design from the first quarter of the Twentieth Century. Nice.* (GOOD+) **$45.00**

P1-27. Unmarked: Early Style Plumb Bob. Decorative Turning. Excellent Patina. Length: 6 Inches. *This massive bob was turned long ago into a decorative shape that we have not previously encountered. A classic early plumb bob from the collection of Mark Beecher, who specialized in these tools.* (GOOD+) **$345.00**

P1-28. Unmarked: Early Brass Plumb Bob. Extended Neck. Dark Metal Patina. Length: 5 Inches. *The narrow neck and extra wide body of this early bob kept its center of gravity low and minimized the effect of the wind on the force of gravity. An appealing dark gold patina has developed over the years.* (GOOD+) **$285.00**

P1-29. Unmarked: Reversible Brass Plumb Bob. With Spiral Knurling. Most Unusual Form. Length: 4 Inches. *The spindle of this double knurled classic is set up so that it can be reversed, if necessary, and the narrow, pointed tip will be at the bottom. A pretty plumb bob.* (GOOD+) **$225.00**

P1-30. Unmarked: Massive Bronze Plumb Bob. "Turnip" Form. Distinctive Neck. Length: 7 Inches. *In a departure from the standard pattern, the shaft for this massive plumb bob was incorporated into the casting, rather than being fitted with a tip as part of the finishing process. A most unusual plumb bob.* (FINE) **$345.00**

P1-31. Unmarked: Spectacular Turned Plumb Bob. Ornamental Knurls. Superb Patina. Length: 6 Inches. *In the last century, there were no "trade schools" for machinists. The wall opposite the master metalworker's bench would not have been adorned with certificates of mastery of certain aspects of the trade. To be sure, each man in a shop would have completed an apprenticeship, for which there were certain standards, but the evaluation of the level of skill achieved by an individual craftsman would have been best determined by an examination of his work. What better way for a master to showcase his mastery of his trade than by the tools he used in his work, and which would be on constant display to those with whom he might be involved in business. The name of the master machinist who crafted this magnificent plumb bob will likely never be known, but the measure of excellence in his trade lies perfectly preserved in this stunning and timeless tribute to his skill. A glorious thing.*(FINE) **$695.00**

P1-32. Unmarked: Massive Millwright's Plumb Bob. Elaborate Knurls. Superb Patina. Length: 7 Inches. *A series of complimentary knurls ring the upper shaft of this early and nicely patinated plumb bob. Extra special.* (GOOD+) **$425.00**

P1-33. Unmarked: Classic Millwright's Plumb Bob. Knurled Cap. Excellent Patina. Length: 6 Inches. *This massive bob is formed in the classic "millwright's" pattern. Time has favored it with a most appealing golden patina.* (GOOD+) **$285.00**

P1-34. Wms. Mfg. Co., H.A., Boston, Mass.: Early Brass Plumb Bob. Extra Small Size. Near New Condition. Length: 2 Inches. *The Williams Manufacturing Company produced these decorative bobs in a wide range of sizes of which this, the 2 inch size, was the smallest. A most attractive miniature plumb bob.* (FINE) **$265.00**

P1-35. Unmarked: Early Rounded Plumb Bob. Reversible Tip. Great Patina. Length: 4 Inches. *This heavy duty bob is a bit more spherical in shape than most of its brethren. It has a very early appearance. Different.* (GOOD+) **$285.00**

P1-36. Perfection: "Perfection" Patent Plumb Bob. Patented April 2, 1905. Fine Condition, Original Box. Length: 3 3/4 Inches. *The original wooden box has kept this patented bob in excellent collector quality condition through nearly 100 years of existence. The top of the knurled cap is imprinted with the maker name and patent date.* (GOOD+) **$295.00**

P1-37. Unmarked: Massive 4 1/2 Pound Plumb Bob. Decorative Knurling. Early Appearance. Length: 5 1/4 Inches. *The form and finish of this decorative large bob suggest that it was made in the 1870's, or thereabout. Minor toolbox wear adds, rather than detracts, from the character of this classic Victorian bob.* (GOOD+) **$285.00**

P1-38. Kuker- Ranken Inc., Seattle, Wash. No. K32: Solid Brass Plumb Bob. 2 Pound Size. New Condition, Original Box. Length: 9 1/4 Inches. *A massive extra-long brass plumb bob in new condition in its original box. An unusual find.* (FINE) **$225.00**

P1-39. Cedarberg Mfg. Co., Minneapolis: "Dandee" Reel and Plumb Bob. With Clip For Bob. Most Unusual. Length: 4 Inches. *Integral reels of any type are tough to come by. This combination bob and chalk line is the first of its type in my experience. Reel interesting.* (GOOD) **$155.00**

P1-40. Spot Bob, Santa Ana, C.A.: Ink Marking Plumb Bob. Most Unusual. New Condition, Original Box. Length: 5 Inches. *Just when you thought it was safe to go back in the water, along comes the "spot bob". This work of genius was designed to mark the exact location of the plumb line. The best (and only) marking plumb bob we have ever offered. Different.* (FINE) **$115.00**

P1-41. Unmarked: Round Brass Plumb Bob. Extra Thick Point. Knurled Cap. Length: 5 Inches. *An extra thick shaft is the distinctive feature of this distinctly formed 5 inch bob. An oversize plumb bob with character.* (GOOD+) **$185.00**

P1-42. Unmarked: Early Brass Plumb Bob. Dated "1891". Ex-Beecher Collection. Length: 5 Inches. *The maker of this nicely knurled Nineteenth Century bob left no doubt as to when it was made by imprinting it with "1891". A superbly patinated dated 19th Century plumb bob.* (GOOD+) **$325.00**

P1-43. Unmarked: Wallpaper Plumb Bob. Decorative Form. With Miniature Bob. Length: 3 Inches. *Most likely designed for laying out the lines for hanging wallpaper, this elaborately decorated bob was designed with indoor use in mind. Very pretty.* (FINE) **$165.00**

P1-44. Unmarked: Top Shaped Brass Plumb Bob. Spiral Knurl Cap. Excellent Patina. Length: 4 1/2 Inches. *The knurled rings on the cap of this early brass bob are complemented by an identical pair of extruded rings around the center of the tool. Extra early and nicely patinated.* (GOOD+) **$225.00**

P1-45. Berger, C.L. No. 412: 12 Ounce "Retracta Bob" Plumb Bob. Original Sleeve. "Only New Design". Length: 6 Inches. *This example of C.L. Berger's "Retracta Bob" has never been used. New and in the original box.* (FINE) **$115.00**

Group Q1

Q1-1. Unmarked: Advertising Hook Rule. J.C. Pennoyer Co. Uncommon Type. Length: 6 Inches. *The configuration of this unusual advertising is not one that is easily recognizable as a product of an American rulemaker. An unusual hook end advertising rule in top condition.* (FINE) **$65.00**

Q1-3. Cleveland Twist Drill Co.: Burring Reamer. Bit Brace Shank. New Condition, Original Box. Length: 3 1/2 Inches. *This specialty deburring tool was intended to fit in a bit brace. It has never been used. Mint in the box.* (FINE) **$15.00**

Q1-4. Gould Prod. Co., Oakland, Calif.: "Gould" Multi Tooth Saw Set. Original Advertising Card. "Pat. Appld. For". Length: 8 Inches. *The idea behind this work of genius from the Gould Products Corporation, of America's Left Coast, was to set multiple saw teeth simultaneously by driving this device between them. The fact that the store display card is still completely full gives some indication of the level of enthusiasm with which this "innovation" was received. A lasting monument to an idea whose time never came.* (FINE) **$165.00**

Q1-5. Stanley Rule & Level: Brass Advertising Tape Measure. "Bundles For Britain". Rare and Excellent. Length: 36 Inches. *We have it on good authority that these rules were produced by Stanley, a leading participant in the "Bundles for Britain" program to provide assistance to the British people before America's entry into the Second World War, in appreciation for contributions by those who participated in the program. The case is decorated with enameled British and American flags together with the "Bundles for Britain" name. A rare and important collectible Stanley tape measure.* (GOOD+) **$285.00**

Q1-6. Bigelow & Dowse Co., Boston, Mass.: Axe Handle Crate Stencil. "Best Lumbermen". Solid Brass. Length: 32 Inches. *Originally used for stenciling crates of axe handles, this Nineteenth Century brass stencil will make a great decoration for the tool room. Graphic.* (GOOD+) **$195.00**

Q1-7. Tiffany & Co.: Sterling Silver Poin Rule. With Pencil. Rare and Excellent. Length: 12 Inches. *It had to happen, I guess, that the name of Tiffany and Company would come to be associated with Martin J. Donnelly Antique Tools. It seems, in retrospect, inevitable, that their products would someday be offered here. Alas, they have always been envious of our high standard of quality, but their efforts, until now, have fallen short of the mark for inclusion within the hallowed pages of these volumes. It is with great pleasure that we offer this most unusual Sterling Silver mechanical pencil, pointing device and extension rule combination. A Tiffany Collectible of Martin J. Donnelly Quality.* (FINE) **$275.00**

Q1-8. Bradley Smith Co.: Cigar Box Hammer. For 108 Cigars. Classic Form. Length: 4 1/4 Inches. *The carpenter's hammer was a common theme for the makers of cigar box opening hammers. This one is from the Bradley Smith Company. Different.* (GOOD+) **$35.00**

Q1-9. Warren Paint Co., Warren, Ohio: Promotional Foot Rule. With Brass Edge. Ca. 1890's. Length: 12 Inches. *This one foot rule is imprinted with advertising from an Ohio maker. The quality level is much better than standard.* (FINE) **$35.00**

Q1-10. Starrett Co., The L.S., Athol, Mass: Advertising Pin. With Tools Trademark. Early and Excellent. Length: 3/4 Inch. *This advertising pin is bright red in color and is decorated with the famous "tools" logo. Crisp, clean and graphic.* (FINE) **$25.00**

Q1-11. Starrett Co., The L.S., Athol, Mass.: Bronze Advertising Sign. Raised Cast Letters. Unused Condition. Length: 9 Inches. *This large sign was used for mounting on the Starrett Display cases that hung in hardware stores. It is made of cast bronze. The background is unfinished and the raised letters have been highly polished. It is in unused condition. A dramatic Starrett advertising item.* (FINE) **$165.00**

Q1-12. Disston & Sons, Henry, Philadelphia, Penn.: Promotional Advertising Watch Fob. With Red Enamel. Keystone Pattern. Length: 2 Inches. *For the serious collector, there is no more cherished item than one that was originally intended to promote the company that is the subject of his collection. This enameled watch fob, from Henry Disston & Sons, is exactly that. Top shelf.* (GOOD+) **$195.00**

Q1-13. Lufkin Rule Co., The, Saginaw, Mich.: Advertising Bronze Sign. Raised Letters. Unused Condition. Length: 6 1/2 Inches. *Here's an absolute essential for the Lufkin collector—a cast bronze sign in brand new condition. It was apparently intended to be mounted on a Lufkin display case.* (FINE) **$225.00**

Q1-14. Snap On Tools Corp, Kenosha, Wiss.: Open End Wrench Tie Clasp. Unused Condition. Length: 2 3/4 Inches. *Mechanics could show their loyalty to Snap On by wearing these clasps on their ties. Most of the mechanics we are aware of who wore ties while working around fan belts and the like are referred to with the designation "the late" preceding their name.* (FINE) **$35.00**

Q1-15. Early American Industries Association: Commemorative Medallion. Sterling Silver. Very Well Made. Length: 1 1/2 Inches. *These extremely well made medallions were produced for the Early American Industries Association Fiftieth Anniversary in 1983. This is the only example I have ever seen offered for sale.* (FINE) **$125.00**

Q1-16. Lancaster: Advertising Key Ring. For Lancaster Braces. Dated 1896. Length: 2 Inches. *The Lancaster Brace Company was in business for a short time in the Buffalo, New York area ca. 1900. This Key chain is scarcer than their rare line of braces. An early advertising collectible in top condition.* (GOOD+) **$135.00**

Q1-17. Starrett Co., L. S., Athol, Mass.: Promotional Pencil. Retractable Tip. Excellent Condition. Length: 4 1/4 Inches. *This safety pencil is square in cross section. Nice markings, a pencil that works, but we wouldn't bet on the eraser. An interesting Starrett advertising item.* (GOOD+) **$25.00**

Q1-18. Amer. Mfg. Concern, Rochester, N.Y: "Clark Bar" Advertising Rule. Children's Weight and Height Scale. "Millions Are Happy". Length: 12 Inches. *Writing in the subdued advertising style of the first quarter of the Twentieth Century, this promotional one foot rule proclaims that "Millions are Happy", no doubt due to their consumption of Clark Bars.* (FINE) **$45.00**

Q1-19. Escher & Sons, J.G.: Unused Razor Hone. Fitted Mahogany Case. Early and Excellent. Length: 10 1/2 Inches. *All of the original label remains on this graphic German razor hone, thanks to the presence of the fitted mahogany case. Very nice.* (FINE) **$125.00**

Q1-20. Eagle Square Mfg. Co.: Miniature Advertising Square. Rustproof Squares. With Eagle Imprint. Length: 6 Inches. *Too small to be functional, this Eagle square, which is imprinted with information about their rustproof squares, was likely given out as an advertising promotion. An uncommon advertising item.* (GOOD) **$85.00**

Q1-21. Chesterman, Sheffield: Combination Rule and Knife. T. & W. Farmilowe, L. Dual Blades. Length: 3 Inches. *This combination of penknife and machinist's precision rule bears the advertising of a company who most likely gave it away to one of its best customers. We're selling it.* (FINE) **$35.00**

Q1-22. Snap On Tools Corp, Kenosha, Wiss.: Screwdriver Tie Clasp. Original Case. Unused Condition. Length: 2 3/4 Inches. *We don't know the story of how one qualified for one of these tie clips from the Snap On man, or whether or not they were available for sale from the catalog. Here at Martin J. Donnelly Antique Tools, we will provide a free Snap On tie clasp to anyone who purchases more than $10,000.00 worth of tools from this volume. Hurry, supply is limited.* (FINE) **$35.00**

Q1-23. Stanley Rule & Level: Advertising Tape Measure. Savings Bank of New Britian With Magnifying Case. Length: 2 3/4 Inches. *When the Savings Bank of New Britain, Connecticut went looking for a promotional item to give to their customers, they didn't have to go very far. This Stanley tape measure is in new condition in its original magnifying case.* (FINE) **$65.00**

Q1-24. Lufkin Rule Co., The, Saginaw, Mich: Advertising Sample Rule. "Why Stock Two?" Scarce and Excellent. Length: 6 Inches. *Apparently designed to promote Lufkin's line of "Zig-Zag" rules, this one neither zigs nor zags, but it does encourage retailers to abandon the folding rules offered by the "other" maker of such tools. A nice example.* (FINE) **$45.00**

Q1-25. Modern Woodmen of America: Fraternal Charm. With Axe Logo. Ca. 1920's. Length: 3/4 Inch. *A member of the Modern Woodmen of America would have been able to demonstrate his affiliation by wearing one of these on his lapel. Never seen another.* (GOOD+) **$35.00**

Q1-26. Lufkin Rule Co., The, Saginaw, Mich.: Advertising Sample Rule. "Lufkin For Every Job". Scarce and Excellent. Length: 6 Inches. *The inscription on this rule informs us that there is a "Lufkin for Every Job", including advertising. A scarce Lufkin advertising rule.* (GOOD+) **$45.00**

Q1-27. Atkins, E.C., Indianapolis, Indiana: Advertising Combination Original Sleeve. Scarce and Excellent. Length: 4 1/4 Inches. *The original sleeve has kept this aluminum advertising comb in the shape of a saw in top collector quality condition. A great Atkins collectible.* (FINE) **$75.00**

Q1-28. American Institute, New York: Invention Medallion. Blind Mortising Machine. Dated 1869. Length: 2 Inches. *In a modern age where those who build and create are more often held up to scorn and shame as "capitalists" and "polluters", it is difficult for some to imagine the sense of progress and enthusiasm that greeted the same endeavors in the Nineteenth Century. We offer this high relief medallion, produced by the American Institute in New York, which shows Liberty surrounded by the fruits of American invention as evidence of a once proud time in this Great Nation. The reverse side is dated 1869 and embossed with the inscription "Awarded to Martin Buck for Blind Mortising Machine".* (FINE) **$285.00**

Q1-29. Millers Falls Company: Advertising Stand For Screwdriver Bits. Hardware Store Type. Near New Condition. Length: 9 Inches. *Nothing dresses up the tool room like period advertising. This display stand from Millers Falls has the full M.F. logo and is in great collector quality condition.* (FINE) **$110.00**

Q1-30. Simonds Saw and Steel Co., The: Promotional Charm. In Saw Shape. "...Are The Best". Length: 1 Inch. *There probably weren't many sawmill operators wearing charm bracelets when the Simonds Saw Company produced these advertising handouts, but they must have produced a number of them as I have seen other, different examples. Charming.* (FINE) **$55.00**

Q1-31. Starrett Co., The L.S., Athol, Mass.: No. 130: 3 1/2 Inch Bench Level. Cast Iron Body. New Condition, Original Box. Length: 3 1/2 Inches. *An excellent example of Starrett's 4" bench level. All original finishes remain on this "in the box" example. Perfect.* (FINE) **$55.00**

Q1-32. Unmarked No. 186: Cast Iron Tractor Tool Box. With Cast "Neptune". Oil Can Holder. Length: 11 Inches. *An image of Neptune, the God of the Sea, is cast into the cover of this very early tractor tool box. The semicircular casting on the side of the tool box was designed to hold an oil can. Different.* (GOOD) **$275.00**

Q1-33. Coes Wrench Co., Worcester, Mass.: Promotional Wrench Stick Pin. Original Card. "Pin to Your Memory". Length: 3 Inches. *The original backing and paper sleeve, which is imprinted with the slogan "Pin the Name to Your Memory" remain with this brand new old stock advertising pin from the Coes Wrench Company. An uncommon tool advertsing collectible.* (FINE) **$65.00**

Q1-34. Disston & Sons, H., Philadelphia, Penn.: Advertising Display For Saws. "Keystone Saws". Ca. 1920's. Length: 26 Inches. *Imagine, if you would, a bustling major city hardware store in the 1920's. There would be tools arrayed on the high shelves in their original boxes and there would be display cases with every imaginable plane and chisel and saw. And, of course, there would be promotional displays, including this extraordinarily well preserved example from Henry Disston & Sons, which was designed to hold samples of the "Keystone" line of hand saws. An excellent item for the saw collector or any collector intent on turning a tool room into a hardware store lookalike. Rare and excellent.* (GOOD+) **$795.00**

Q1-35. Hull, Grummond & Company: Cigar Box Hammer. Full Nickel Plating. "Havana Cigars". Length: 6 Inches. *In the old days, they used these pointed objects to open cigar boxes. Today they are used to persuade those who choose to speak out against the oppressive Castro government to change their mind. We offer it as a collectible only.* (FINE) **$35.00**

Q1-36. Nicholson File Co., Providence, R.I.: Promotional Stand. For Hack Saw Blades. High Speed and Standard. Length: 11 1/2 Inches. *The Nicholson File Company was America's premier maker of such tools. Their advertising would have been a fixture in any hardware store. Here's a nice example.* (FINE) **$45.00**

Q1-37. Stanley Rule & Level No. 41: Ornate Brass Top Level. Patented June 23, 1896. With Embossed Imprint. Length: 3 Inches. *The top plate on this variation of the No. 41 is particularly ornately embellished and marked with the 1896 patent date. Classic, and classy.* (FINE) **$65.00**

Q1-38. Ford Motor Co., Dearborn, Mich.: "Fordson" Factory Tool Check. Used in Factory. With Worker ID. Length: 1 1/2 Inches. *The use of specialized tools from the Fordson Tractor plane required that you provide the keeper of the "tool cage" with one of these checks, which were marked with your ID number. If you didn't bring the tool back, they knew where to find you. Fordson ceased U.S. Operations in 1926. A rare tool and tractor collectible.* (FINE) **$15.00**

Q1-39. Stanley Rule & Level: Advertising Pencil. Tool Box of The World. New Condition. Length: 7 Inches. *Stanley's "Tool Box of the World" campaign began in the 1920's. This carpenter's pencil, which must have been produced early in the campaign, given its "10 (don't bother looking for a "cent" sign on a computer keyboard) cent Value" notation, is in brand new condition and ready to add to a collection of Stanley advertising memorabilia. Different.* (FINE) **$25.00**

Q1-40. Dunn Edge Tool Co., Oakland, Maine: Copper Print Block. With Axe Logo. Highly Detailed. Length: 3 Inches. *Apparently used for catalog or newspaper advertising, this print block shows an embossed felling axe from the Dunn Edge Tool Company—an axe that we have never seen before. A nice accent to a collection of embossed axes.* (FINE) **$35.00**

Q1-41. Modern Woodmen of America: Fraternal Pin. With Axe and Maul. Ca. 1920's. Length: 3/4 Inch. *What better way to promote the local lodge than by wearing a button showing the Modern Woodmen of America logo on your lapel. It would be a sure conversation starter and it wouldn't be long before others became interested in carrying an aluminum axe and engaging in secret rituals. This pin will only be sold to someone who mails or faxes us a photo of the secret handshake.* (GOOD+) **$45.00**

Q1-42. Irwin Augur Bit Co., The: Letter Opener From Auger Bit. Promotional Item. Decidedly Different. Length: 7 1/2 Inches. *If you opened the Mail at Martin J. Donnelly Antique Tools, you might not be too happy if someone gave you this hand mangler as a "gift". A scarce and interesting advertising letter opener.* (FINE) **$85.00**

Q1-43. Mandery, Joseph, Rochester, N.Y.: Promotional Advertising Level. "Business on the Level". As New Condition. Length: 3 1/2 Inches. *Mr. Joseph Mandery made a promise to his customers and gave them a tool to gauge his commitment. Some antique tool dealers of questionable adherence to ethical standards might consider giving out inclinometers in like fashion. An interesting small collectible level.* (FINE) **$110.00**

Q1-44. Starrett Co., L. S., Athol, Mass.: No. 63136: Key Chain Tape Measure. Ca. 1960's. Brand New Condition. Length: 3 1/2 Inches. *The original shrink wrap has kept this Starrett keepsake in brand new condition.* (FINE) **$15.00**

Q1-45. Starrett Co., The L.S., Athol, Mass.: Advertising Display Sign. Shown in 1919 Catalogue. Brand New Condition. Length: 12 3/4 Inches. *This highly polished new old stock advertising sign was featured in Starrett's 1919 catalog to encourage dealers to display the sign in their store. This sign is in nearly new condition.* (FINE) **$85.00**

Group R1

R1-1. Stanley Rule & Level No. 6: 18 Inch Fore Plane. Rosewood Handles. 98% Original Paint. Length: 18 Inches. *Half jack plane and half jointer, the 18 inch No. 6 can do some of the work of each. This one is about as good as they get. Some 98% of all original finishes remain.* (FINE) **$115.00**

R1-2. Stanley Rule & Level No. 39: Cast Iron Dado Plane. 3/4 Inch Size. Rare 1st Model. Length: 8 Inches. *This "Type 1" No. 39 is out of the box crisp and clean. Ready to help fill out a set of early examples or to use every day in the shop.* (FINE) **$325.00**

R1-3. Stanley Rule & Level No. S 4: Steel Body Jack Plane. Small "N" Sweetheart Trademark. 98% Original Paint. Length: 9 Inches. *A number of these all-steel planes have turned up at the disbursement of manual training schools. Having lived through the days where "shop" was one of those rituals of Junior High, when it was still acceptable, nay—expected, that shop teachers would holler and act like drill instructors, no matter what, I can see that one of those sorts might have been inclined to dash off an order to Stanley for half a dozen of these after some knucklehead smashed a 605 1/2 C on the classroom floor. Apparently not enough orders were dashed off, however. These were not long in the Stanley line and examples are rare indeed, especially in this kind of condition.* (FINE) **$345.00**

R1-4. Stanley Rule & Level No. 93: 1 Inch Shoulder Rabbet Plane. "Made in USA". Near New Condition. Length: 6 Inches. *A crisp, clean and ready to use example of Stanley's 1 inch shoulder plane, with the coveted "Made in U.S.A." imprint. Extra nice.* (FINE) **$225.00**

R1-5. Stanley Rule & Level No. 39: Cast Iron Dado Plane. 1/4 Inch Size. Near New Condition. Length: 8 Inches. *Here's the smallest size of the No. 39 series in pristine condition. More than 99% of the original finishes remain. A great plane.* (FINE) **$325.00**

R1-6. Stanley Rule & Level No. 39: 1/2 Inch Width Dado Plane. "Sweetheart" Trademark. Extra Crisp and Clean. Length: 8 Inches. *A picture perfect 1/2 inch cast iron dado plane imprinted with the 1920's era "Sweetheart" trademark. 99% original finishes. Very nice.* (FINE) **$245.00**

R1-7. Stanley Rule & Level No. 101: Early "Toy" Block Plane. Circular Trademark. 95% Original Paint. Length: 3 1/4 Inches. *This extremely early No. 101 block plane has the "Stanley Rule & Level" circular mark. At least 110 years old. A good one.* (GOOD+) **$65.00**

R1-8. Stanley Rule & Level No. 40: Beech Handle Scrub Plane. Sweetheart Trademark. Extra Crisp and Clean. Length: 11 Inches. *The roughing out of virgin stock before the jack and smooth plane went to work was the task assigned to these workaday planes, which were fitted with convex cutting irons to literally "scoop" out the wood. A great working example that is fitted with the nicely contrasting beechwood handles.* (GOOD+) **$125.00**

R1-9. Stanley Rule & Level No. 603: Bedrock Smoothing Plane. Later Style. Ready to Use. Length: 8 Inches. *A great working example of Stanley's later style "Bedrock" smother in the tough to find 8 inch size. Crispy clean.* (GOOD+) **$295.00**

R1-10. Stanley Rule & Level No. 135: Liberty Bell Smooth Plane. With Lever Adjust. Nicely Repainted. Length: 10 Inches. *A previous owner did a respectable job of dressing up this "Liberty Bell" transitional plane and bringing it back. A survivor.* (GOOD) **$55.00**

R1-11. Stanley Rule & Level No. 604 C: "Bedrock" Smooth Plane. Corrugated Bottom. 98% Original Paint. Length: 9 Inches. *Traces of the original decal and nearly all of the orignal paint remain on this superb smoothing plane from Stanley's legendary "Bedrock" series.* (FINE) **$285.00**

R1-12. Stanley Rule & Level No. 147: Rare Double Tongue and Groove Plane. For 5/8 Inch Stock. Superb Condition. Length: 9 Inches. *Stanley made this plane in three sizes, this size for 5/8 inch stock and the No. 146, for 1/2 inch stock are rare. The No. 148 is more frequently found as it was originally intended for stock lumber. This one is in clean and complete condition. A nice example of a rare plane.* (GOOD+) **$325.00**

R1-13. Stanley Rule & Level No. 110: Cast Iron Block Plane. "Sweetheart" Trademark. Original Decal. Length: 7 Inches. *Here's a perfectly preserved example of Stanley's best selling non-adjustable block plane. It is marked with the ca. 1920's "Sweetheart" trademark and retains nearly all of its original decal. Mint.* (FINE) **$45.00**

R1-14. Stanley Rule & Level No. 40: Rosewood Handle Scrub Plane. Ca. 1935. Excellent Condition. Length: 9 1/2 Inches. *Stanley offered its scrub plane with rosewood handles during the later years of its production. These were intended for rough duty work and usually saw a lot of it. This one didn't. Extra crisp and clean.* (GOOD+) **$125.00**

R1-15. Stanley Rule & Level No. 608 C: "Bedrock" Jointer Plane. With Corrugated Sole. Superb Condition. Length: 24 Inches. *A superb example of the largest size Bedrock, this one is fitted with the grooved sole. More than 90% of the original paint remains and all parts in perfect repair. A good one.* (GOOD+) **$395.00**

R1-16. Stanley Rule & Level No. 171: Door Trim Router Plane. Patented December 26, 1911. Complete with 1 Cutter. Length: 11 1/2 Inches. *Introduced by Stanley in the early years of this century, when business was booming, power tools were not even imagined and the average workman could afford such niceties, Stanley may have produced a tool that was a bit too specialized in function for it to achieve any significant market success. This example, which is complete with one of the original 3 cutting irons retains more than 95% of its original shiny black japan finish. A superb example of a rare Stanley plane.* (FINE) **$445.00**

R1-17. Stanley Rule & Level No. 78: Duplex Filletster Plane. With Lever Adjust. Superb Condition. Length: 9 1/2 Inches. *Here's a superb working example of an increasingly desirable Stanley classic in never-need-to-upgrade condition. No apologies for this extra clean and complete plane.* (FINE) **$95.00**

R1-18. Stanley Rule & Level No. 604 1/2 C: "Bedrock" Smoothing Plane. Corrugated Sole. Superb Condition. Length: 10 Inches. *Of all the planes of the "Bedrock" series, it is the 604 1/2 wide smoothing plane that receives the best reviews from serious woodworkers. The distinctive feature of the Bedrock planes was the patented frog designed to eliminate "chatter" when working wood. It is in exactly the types of applications where a wide smoothing plane will be used that this problem is likely to occur. Those who have tried them, in overwhelming numbers, say that this is the tool for the job. This one is in excellent overall condition and ready to be put immediately to use. A very nice example.* (GOOD+) **$685.00**

R1-19. Stanley Rule & Level No. 3 C: "Type 11" Smooth Plane. Rosewood Handles. 98% Original Paint. Length: 9 Inches. *This crispy-clean example of Stanley's corrugated sole 8 inch smoothing plane is proudly offered without apology. This is the scarce and desirable "Type 11" version, which many woodworkers believe represents the high point of technical functionality and aesthetic appeal. After this point, goes the logic, Stanley compromised on quality to improve production methods. A superb example of a rare and desirable Stanley plane.* (FINE) **$155.00**

R1-20. Stanley Rule & Level No. 271: World War II Era Router Plane. Black Japan Finish. Unused Condition. Length: 3 Inches. *A growing number of collectors have taken an interest in the modifications made to Stanley's product line due to wartime (World War II) exigencies. This No. 171 router plane was finished with black japanning instead of the standard nickel plating. It is in nearly new condition.* (FINE) **$65.00**

R1-21. Stanley Rule & Level No. 8: Cast Iron Jointer Plane. Patented April 19, 1910. Near New Condition. Length: 24 Inches. *The No. 8 jointer plane, at 24 inches in length is a tool that is not available from any contemporary manufacturer. We offer our best wishes for the speedy recovery of anyone who would prefer some of the junk being made today to one of these classic tools. This is an example of the "Type 13" version, which is imprinted with the 1910 patent date in the casting. The cutting iron is a ca. 1930's era Stanley cutter.* (FINE) **$225.00**

R1-22. Stanley Rule & Level No. 20: "Victor" Compass Plane. Full Nickel Plating. "Pat. '92" Trademark. Length: 9 1/2 Inches. *Long the circular plane of choice among discriminating woodworkers, the No. 20 was included in the Stanley product line for nearly 100 years. This one dates from the turn of the century, but the condition is extremely nice.* (GOOD+) **$265.00**

R1-23. Stanley Rule & Level No. 40 1/2: Rare 10 1/2 Inch Scrub Plane. Uncommon Type. Ready to Use. Length: 10 1/2 Inches. *Stanley produced its rough duty "scrub" planes in two sizes, of which this was the larger, and far less common size. Apparently those who were going to be doing the rough and dirty work that these planes were intended to perform couldn't find a reason to justify the extra expense. Stanley apparently figured this out, eventually, as the Stanley Value Guide tells us that the 40 1/2 was discontinued from the product line some 15 years before the smaller No. 40. A tough plane to find.* (GOOD+) **$115.00**

R1-24. Stanley Rule & Level No. 98/99: Pair of Side Rabbet Planes. With Depth Stops. Near New Condition. Length: 4 Inches. *A fitted case has kept these side rabbet planes in nearly new condition. These are the "type 3" planes, which incorporate the adjustable depth stops that were not included in the earlier offerings. A pretty pair.* (FINE) **$365.00**

R1-25. Stanley Rule & Level No. 112: Handled Scraper Plane. Rosewood Handles. 98%+ Original Paint. Length: 9 Inches. *Another clean and ready to use example of Stanley's finest adjustable cabinet scraper plane. Crisp, clean, complete and ready to use.* (FINE) **$385.00**

R1-26. Stanley Rule & Level No. 9 1/4: Cast Iron Block Plane. Non-Adjustable Throat. Clean and Sound. Length: 6 Inches. *The No. 9 1/4 block plane was the functional equivalent of the No. 9 1/2, with the exception of the absence of a throat adjustment mechanism. This one is in top shape.* (GOOD+) **$35.00**

R1-27. Stanley Rule & Level No. 71 1/2: Nickel Plated Router Plane. Patented October 29, 1901. Complete and Excellent. Length: 7 1/2 Inches. *All original cutters are present with this well preserved example of Stanley's closed throat router plane. A great working tool.* (GOOD+) **$115.00**

R1-28. Stanley Rule & Level No. 5 C: Rosewood Handle Jack Plane. Ca. 1930's. Unused Condition. Length: 14 Inches. *This ca. 1930's era jack plane appears never to have been used. Absolutely perfect.* (FINE) **$125.00**

R1-29. Stanley Rule & Level No. 148: Tongue and Groove Plane. "Sweetheart" Trademark. Superb Condition. Length: 9 Inches. *No apologies for this pristine example of Stanley's stock-lumber version of its 140 series of double tongue and groove plane. These are becoming increasingly difficult to find. Examples in this condition have always been scarce. A good one.* (FINE) **$225.00**

R1-30. Stanley Rule & Level No. 4: "Type 12" Smooth Plane. With 3 Patent Dates. 99% Original Paint. Length: 9 Inches. *The "Type 12" bench plane was distinguished from its predecessor by the presence of the "tall" front knob, a feature that was introduced in 1919. We offer and need not offer any apologies for this pristine example. Choice.* (FINE) **$145.00**

R1-31. Stanley Rule & Level No. 20: Cast Iron Circular Plane. "Sweetheart" Trademark. 98% Original Paint. Length: 10 Inches. *This japan-finished example of Stanley's most popular adjustable compass plane is in top condition. Some 98% of all original finishes remain. A great working tool from the 1920's in superb condition.* (FINE) **$295.00**

R1-32. Stanley Rule & Level No. 49: Swing Fence Match Plane. Cuts 3/16 Inch Groove. Early Japan Finish. Length: 10 Inches. *Early examples of Stanley's swinging fence match plane with the 3/16 inch cutter are seldom found, especially examples that retain some 95% of their original shiny japan finish, as does this example. The fence is imprinted with the date of the July 6, 1875 patent granted to Charles G. Miller, the same Miller whose patents were applied to Stanley's 41-44 series of combination planes. A rare plane in excellent condition.* (GOOD+) **$345.00**

R1-33. Stanley Rule & Level No. 35: Handled Transitional Plane. Patented 1892 Trademark. Crisp and Clean. Length: 8 1/2 Inches. *Nearly all original finishes remain on this well preserved transitional smooth plane. A nice example.* (GOOD+) **$85.00**

R1-34. Stanley Rule & Level No. 5 1/4: "Junior" Jack Plane. "Sweetheart" Trademark. Near New Condition. Length: 13 Inches. *Stanley's "Junior Jack Plane" is nearly a cross between the No. 5 and the No. 3. Like so many hybrids, this one retains the best features of each: It is long enough to be more than just a smooth plane and narrow enough to work precisely. A great working tool from Stanley's ca. 1920's "Sweetheart" era.* (FINE) **$115.00**

R1-35. Stanley Rule & Level No. 606: Bedrock Fore Plane. Later Style. "Sweetheart" Trademark. Length: 18 Inches. *In essentially the same condition as it was when first produced in the 1920's, this "Sweetheart" era later Bedrock is as crisp and clean as they come. Some 95% of the original japan finish remains. A very nice example of a tough "Bedrock" plane to find.* (GOOD+) **$245.00**

R1-36. Stanley Rule & Level No. 607: "Bedrock" Jointer Plane. 98% Original Paint. Near New Condition. Length: 22 Inches. *This later style Bedrock jointer plane is a good as they get: 98% original finishes remain. Nice.* (FINE) **$425.00**

R1-37. Stanley Rule & Level No. 90: Cast Iron Bullnose Plane. Early and Excellent. Patented August 3, 1897. Length: 4 Inches. *A fitted craftsman made wooden case has kept this early example of the No. 90 bullnose rabbet plane in top collector quality condition. Mint.* (FINE) **$165.00**

R1-38. Stanley Rule & Level No. 46: Skew Blade Combination Plane. Complete With 7 Cutters. Full Nickel Plated. Length: 10 1/2 Inches. *For sheer pleasure, try setting up a Stanley 46 skew-blade combination plane and having at the hardest piece of wood you can find. Complete with six original cutters and ready to go to work.* (GOOD+) **$425.00**

R1-39. Stanley Rule & Level No. 45: Combination Plane. Complete, Original Box. Near-New Condition. Length: 12 Inches. *This superb example of Stanley's No. 45 combination has been sheltered from the elements by its original pasteboard box. A great working tool that is complete with all original parts and the original instruction manual and is in perfect working order. Nice.* (FINE) **$465.00**

R1-40. Stanley Rule & Level No. A4: Aluminum Smoothing Plane. With Stanley Decal. Rare and Excellent. Length: 9 Inches. *Finding examples of Stanley's "A" series planes, especially those that don't look like they've been buried for several months isn't easy. This one has never been in the ground, and it has hardly been in the shop. Nearly all of the original Stanley decal remains. Crisp, clean and highly recommended.* (FINE) **$425.00**

R1-41. Stanley Rule & Level No. 140: Skew-Blade Block Plane. With Removable Side. "Sweetheart" Trademark. Length: 7 Inches. *The No. 140 has a skew-set iron and a removable side to facilitate rabbeting. Most of the original nickel plating remains on the cap. A nice "Sweetheart" era example in excellent usable condition.* (FINE) **$225.00**

R1-42. Stanley Rule & Level No. 5: Rosewood Handle Jack Plane. Ca. 1950's. 99%+ Original Paint. Length: 14 Inches. *Unlike planes used for more precise work, jack planes derive limited utility from the later technological improvements in the adjustment of metallic planes. This shiny clean example dates from the 1950's and has the distinctive orange filled cap iron. Mint.* (FINE) **$115.00**

R1-43. Stanley Rule & Level No. 9 1/2: Adjustable Throat Plane. With Precision Adjust. Near New Condition. Length: 6 Inches. *Here's a great working example of Stanley's mainstay No. 9 1/2 block plane in nearly new condition. Extra crisp and clean.* (FINE) **$65.00**

R1-44. Stanley Rule & Level No. 5 1/2: Heavy Jack Plane. Ca. 1915 "V" Trademark. Extra Crisp and Clean. Length: 14 1/2 Inches. *Stanley's No. 5 1/2 plane is approximately the length of the No. 5, but as wide as its big brother, the No. 7 jointer. This immediate pre World War I example has been very little used. A great working tool in top condition.* (FINE) **$165.00**

R1-45. Stanley Rule & Level No. 7 C: Rosewood Handle Jointer Plane. "Pat. '92" Tradmark. Crisp and Clean. Length: 22 Inches. *This crispy clean jointer would likely have been made sometime between 1895 and 1902. Overall condition is excellent. Ready to go to work.* (GOOD+) **$145.00**

Group S1

S1-1. Marshall Wells Hdwe Co.: No. 3851: "Zenith" Folding Rule. Similar to Stanley 66 1/2. Most Unusual. Length: 36 Inches. *From their base in the Minnesota sunbelt city of Duluth, the Marshall Wells Hardware Company offered a wide range of tools under their "Zenith" brand name. This No. 66 1/2 rule is the first folding rule we have offered with the "Zenith" imprint.* (GOOD) **$95.00**

S1-2. Stanley Rule & Level No. 72 1/2: Two Foot, Four Fold Folding Rule. Square Joint, Full Bound. Early and Excellent. Length: 24 Inches. *The No. 72 1/2 is distinguished from the No. 72 by being fully brass-bound. This one is in excellent condition and clearly marked with the early Stanley imprint.* (FINE) **$255.00**

S1-3. Stearns & Co., E.A.: Six Inch, Two Fold Folding Rule. With Brass Section. Rare and Excellent. Length: 6 Inches. *The entire upper section of this most unusual rule from Brattleboro, Vermont rule makers E.A. Stearns & Company is fashioned from brass. Crisp, clean and clearly marked with the Stearns imprint. A very rare Stearns rule.* (GOOD+) **$325.00**

S1-4. Bruin & Co., Bristol (England): Boxwood Folding Square. Unused Condition. Uncommon Maker. Length: 18 Inches. *Of extra-thick construction, this boxwood folding square in unused condition is imprinted with the mark of Bruin and Company, who were likely dealers in the port city of Bristol, England. The finest folding boxwood square we have ever offered. Choice.* (GOOD) **$125.00**

S1-5. Smallwood, I. & D., Birmingham: Rope Caliper Rule. With Brass Slide. Druntons, Scotland. Length: 4 1/2 Inches. *The advertising of a Scottish company is imprinted on the brass caliper head of this classic "cordage" caliper. These were used by sailors and merchants for gauging the thickness of rope and cable.* (FINE) **$145.00**

S1-6. Chapin-Stephens Co., The: No. 036: Patent Inclinometer Folding Rule. With Level, Bevel, Etc. Crisp and Clean. Length: 12 Inches. *The Chapin Stephens Company was the last of a series of makers who produced the Stephens Patent Combination Rule that was originally patented by L.C. Stephens in 1858. This example is in new condition in its original pasteboard box. A portion of one side of the box is missing, but it is otherwise complete and intact. As good as they get.* (GOOD+) **$245.00**

S1-7. C-S Co., The, Pine Meadow, Conn.: No. 53 1/2: Two-Foot, Four-Fold Folding Rule. Arch Joint, Unbound. Uncommon Type. Length: 24 Inches. *Every major rulemaker produced an "architect's" rule. This type was distinguished by having beveled inside edges and a series of proportional scales used by architects and builders. This example from one of the last of the rulemakers is in excellent collector quality condition.* (GOOD+) **$95.00**

S1-8. Lufkin Rule Co., The, Saginaw, Mich.: No. 863 L: Combination Folding Rule. With Level, Protractor. Most Unusual. Length: 24 Inches. *Lufkin's 863 L rule features an integral inclinometer and level. The 863 version was distinguished by brass binding on the outside edge. This one is clean, sound and ready to display.* (GOOD) **$155.00**

S1-9. Lufkin Rule Co., The, Saginaw, Mich.: No. 026: Six Inch Caliper Rule. Uncommon Configuration. Excellent Condition. Length: 6 Inches. *A most unusual Lufkin caliper rule. They alone apparently made rules of this configuration. A scarce Lufkin rule.* (GOOD+) **$345.00**

S1-10. Ainsley, J.D., South Shields: Boxwood Rope Gauge Rule. With Brass Caliper. English Ironmonger. Length: 3 1/2 Inches. *This side of this well made and perfectly preserved cordage rule is imprinted with the name of an English "ironmonger", or hardware dealer. Extra nice.* (FINE) **$265.00**

S1-11. Stanley Rule & Level No. 31 1/8: Early Shrinkage Folding Rule. Early Stanley Mark. Extra Crisp and Clean. Length: 24 Inches. *An early Stanley mark is imprinted on this rare folding shrinkage rule. A shrinkage of 1/8 inch was the standard for cast iron. This extra early example is in essentially unused condition.* (FINE) **$325.00**

S1-12. Stanley Rule & Level No. 31 1/2: Early Shrinkage Folding Rule. 1/4 Inch Shrinkage. Rare and Extra Nice. Length: 24 Inches. *This rare Stanley folding shrinkage rule has graduations that correspond to 1/4 inch per foot. A tough rule to find, especially in the 1/4 inch size.* (FINE) **$465.00**

S1-13. Stanley Rule & Level No. 70: Two-Foot, Four-Fold Folding Rule. Square Joint, Unbound. Extra Crisp and Clean. Length: 24 Inches. *Stanley offered a wide range of "broad" rules, that were of wider widths than its standard two foot rules in its No. 70 series. This square joint, unbound "broad" rule was at the lower end of a range of quality rules, which included the No. 78 1/2, which was fully bound and included a pair of the high quality "arch" joints. This example is in excellent condition.* (FINE) **$185.00**

S1-14. Standard Rule Co., Unionville, Conn.: No. 36: Six Inch, Two Fold Folding Rule. Early Union Imprint. Rare and Excellent. Length: 6 Inches. *Rules of any kind from the Standard Rule Company should be considered scarce. This six inch, two fold rule is clearly marked with the Standard name and working location and is in excellent condition.* (GOOD+) **$225.00**

S1-15. Stanley Rule & Level No. 75: Two Foot, Four Fold Folding Rule. "Sweetheart" Trademark. Near New Condition. Length: 24 Inches. *Production of Stanley's arch-joint No. 75 rule was discontinued in 1933 and sales prior to that time must have been very sporadic. This "Sweetheart" vintage example is in top collector quality condition. Rare and mint.* (FINE) **$395.00**

S1-16. C-S Co., The, Pine Meadow, Conn.: No. 60: Two-Foot, Four-Fold Folding Rule. Double Arch Joint. Rare Configuration. Length: 24 Inches. *Double arch joint rules of any type may legitimately be called rare. This, the equivalent of Stanley's No. 60, is from Chapin Stephens Company. It appears unused, but has a small black stain in the center of the rule. Rare.* (FINE) **$145.00**

S1-17. Thrall & Son, Willis, Hartford, Conn.: One Foot, Four Fold Folding Rule. Rare Configuration. Extra Rare and Early. Length: 12 Inches. *A hardware dealer, tool merchant and likely tool manufacturer in Hartford, Connecticut during the 1830's, 40's and 50's, Willis Thrall's line of tools were characterized by an extremely high level of quality and finish. This fully brass bound boxwood rule is clearly imprinted with the Thrall name and is in excellent condition.* (GOOD+) **$395.00**

S1-18. Stanley Rule & Level No. 59: Two-Foot, Four-Fold Folding Rule. Double Arch Joint, Unbound. Seldom Seen. Length: 24 Inches. *Differing from Stanley's double arch joint No. 60 rule only in the absence of full brass binding along the edges, the No. 59 was probably not given much consideration by those who were opting for a very high quality rule. The additional cost of binding would have been insignificant compared to the cost of the joints. A very rare Stanley rule.* (GOOD+) **$225.00**

S1-19. C-S Co., The, Pine Meadow, Conn.: No. 15: Two Foot, Four Fold Folding Rule. Square Joint, Full Bound. Near New Condition. Length: 24 Inches. *Two foot, two fold rules were easily broken or otherwise abused. Finding examples in this kind of condition has become increasingly difficult. This uncommon Chapin Stephens rule is clean, clearly marked and ready to display.* (GOOD+) **$265.00**

S1-20. Stephens & Co., Riverton, Conn.: Special Order? Folding Rule. 10th of an Inch. Superb Condition. Length: 24 Inches. *A most unusual folding rule, this offering from J. Stephens & Company is not imprinted with any number designation, and is graduated in 10ths of an inch, making it likely that this was a special order rule. A rare Stephens rule.* (GOOD+) **$125.00**

S1-21. Unmarked: Patent Rule Attachment. Patented May 12, 1901. With Cam Lock. Length: 3 Inches. *A number of collectors have taken to collecting the wide range of tools that were designed for use in conjunction with folding rules. This cam lock accessory, which is imprinted with a 1901 patent date, is the first example of this tool that we have seen. Rare.* (GOOD+) **$425.00**

S1-22. Lufin Rule Co., The, Saginaw, Mich.: No. 478: One-Foot, Four-Fold Folding Rule. Full Bound, Square Joint. Stanley 65 1/2 Equivalent. Length: 12 Inches. *Lufkin's equivalent to Stanley's basic No. 65 1/2 is unmistakable as such, owing to the prominent imprinting of the Stanley equivalent number on the face of the rule. Examples of this rule by Stanley are quite difficult to find. This is the first of these that we have ever offered.* (FINE) **$245.00**

S1-23. Stanley Rule & Level No. 64: One Foot, Four Fold Folding Rule. Rare 'Stanley' Mark. Superb Condition. Length: 12 Inches. *One rule that almost never is found with the "Stanley" imprint imprinted in the boxwood is the No. 64, which is distinguished from the No. 65 by the presence of brass edge plates at the center joint. A one-time, no upgrade opportunity for the seeker of "one of each".Nice.* (FINE) **$395.00**

S1-24. Stanley Rule & Level No. 61 1/2: Two Foot, Four Fold Folding Rule. Square Joint, Unbound. Rare and Extra Crisp. Length: 24 Inches. *The No. 61 1/2 is graduated on both its faces and sides. Clean examples are hard to come by. This one is especially clean, noting a very slight bow to the body.* (FINE) **$195.00**

S1-25. Stanley Rule & Level No. 66: Three-Foot, Four-Fold Folding Rule. Arch Joint, Unbound. Early and Near New. Length: 36 Inches. *Stanley's No. 66 yard measure rule was imprinted on the inside edge with graduations of fractions of a yard. Because of their large size and the stress on the wood and joints that was applied when they were fully extended, these rules deteriorated quickly from use. This one apparently was used very little, if ever. The nicest example of this rule that we have ever offered.* (FINE) **$445.00**

S1-26. Stanley Rule & Level No. 60: Two-Foot, Four-Fold Folding Rule. Double Arch Joint, Full Bound. Early and Near New. Length: 24 Inches. *Stanley offered three rules featuring their highest quality "double arch joint": the No. 78 1/2, the No. 97 (ivory) and the No. 60. Only the No. 60 was of the "standard" width. An uncommon Stanley rule in absolutely perfect condition. Highly recommended.* (FINE) **$365.00**

S1-27. Stanley Rule & Level No. 94: Three-Foot, Four-Fold Folding Rule. Arch Joint, Full Bound. "Sweetheart" Trademark. Length: 36 Inches. *Three foot rules placed an incredible strain on the joints, and the body sections as well. If they were used much, it is quickly apparent. This example of the full bound, arch joint carriagemaker's rule is in nearly new condition and marked with the ca. 1920's era "Sweetheart" trademark.* (FINE) **$395.00**

S1-28. Rabone & Sons, Makers, Birmingham: Two-Foot, Two-Fold Folding Rule. With Gunter Slide. Engineer's Tables. Length: 24 Inches. *The steel tips on the end of this engineer's rule from English maker John Rabone are an indication of relatively early manufacture. The scales were used in conjunction with the Gunter slide rule to perform engineering calculations. This example is in top condition. Choice.* (FINE) **$345.00**

S1-29. Jones & Co., S.A., Hartford, Conn.: Two-Foot, Two-Fold Folding Rule. Arch Joint, Unbound. With Gunter Slide. Length: 24 Inches. *S.A. Jones and company manufactured carpenter's tools in Hartford in the years before the Civil War. This classic calculating rule is in excellent condition, noting a few small stains and a "hang hole" through the brass plating of one joint. Extra early.* (GOOD) **$265.00**

S1-30. Stanley Rule & Level No. 7: "Blind Man's" Folding Rule. With English Graduations. Excellent Condition. Length: 24 Inches. *The printed letter format of the Blind Man's rules left them particularly susceptible to wear. This one retains all of its original lacquer finishes on brass and boxwood and is marked with the early Stanley logo. A very rare rule in this condition.* (FINE) **$225.00**

S1-31. Stanley Rule & Level No. 26: Two-Foot, Two-Fold Folding Rule. Middle, Edge Scales. Crisp and Clean. Length: 24 Inches. *Stanley's No. 26 folding rule features a Gunter slide on a square joint, full bound rule. This example is crisp, clean and clearly marked. A nice example of an increasingly difficult rule to find.* (GOOD+) **$285.00**

S1-32. Preston & Sons, Edward: Ironmonger's Folding Rule. Multiple Scales. Rare and Near New. Length: 24 Inches. *Designed as a pocket rule for those in the hardware trade, this rare three fold rule from Edward Preston & Sons is imprinted with all manner of charts and tables to facilitate computation. It is in new condition.* (FINE) **$495.00**

S1-33. Chapin-Stephens Co., The: No. 036: Patent Inclinometer Folding Rule. With Level, Bevel, Etc. Superb Condition. Length: 12 Inches. *The Chapin Stephens Company was the last of a series of makers who produced the Stephens Patent Combination Rule that was originally patented by L.C. Stephens in 1858. This example is in nearly new condition. Extra nice.* (FINE) **$345.00**

S1-34. Lufkin Rule Co., The, Saginaw, Mich.: No. 873 L: Combination Folding Rule. With Level, Protractor. Near New Condition. Length: 24 Inches. *This protractor/level/rule combination was apparently Lufkin's attempt to provide some level of innovation to the folding rule market, even as they copied nearly every offering being produced by market leader Stanley Rule & Level. The dearth of surviving examples indicates that they failed to catch on with the rule buying market, many of the inhabitants of which were busy abandoning traditional rules for tape measures and the "zig-zag" style just as Lufkin was entering the market. A rare combination rule in top collector quality condition.* (FINE) **$275.00**

S1-35. Unmarked No. 11: Two Foot, Two Fold Folding Rule. Extra Thick Body. Unknown Maker. Length: 24 Inches. *The extra thick body and the style of lettering of this rule indicate that it was produced quite early. The only marking on the rule is the designation "No. 11". Never seen another.* (GOOD+) **$115.00**

S1-36. Stanley Rule & Level: 1/8 Inch Shrinkage Folding Rule. Uncommon Type. Superb Condition. Length: 24 Inches. *In addition to its full range of shrinkage rules in the two-foot size, Stanley offered a series of folding rules for a very short period. They were apparently not a big seller. A rare rule in near-new condition* (FINE) **$285.00**

S1-37. Stanley Rule & Level No. 82: Two Foot, Four Fold Folding Rule. Arch Joint, Full Bound. With Board Tables. Length: 24 Inches. *The arch joint, full bound No. 82 was Stanley's top-of-the-line folding board measure rule. This one has seen very little use and the board measure scales on the inside face are in excellent condition. A previous owner has imprinted his initials in the wood. A rare lumber rule from America's premier maker.* (GOOD+) **$345.00**

S1-38. Stanley Rule & Level No. 94: Four-Foot, Four-Fold Folding Rule. Arch Joint, Full Bound. For Carriage Use. Length: 48 Inches. *Their designation as "Carriage maker's" rules would indicate that these rules were intended for hard use. This one has some evidence of use, but is clearly marked and mechanically sound. An uncommon Stanley rule.* (GOOD+) **$165.00**

S1-39. Rabone & Sons, J., Birmingham: No. 1 P M11: "Ullage" Rule. Solid Brass. With Ebonite Inlay. Length: 12 Inches. *This heavy duty rule from Rabone is designated on the body as an "ullage" rule. This is our first such rule and we are unfamiliar with their function.* (GOOD+) **$95.00**

S1-40. Upson Nut Co., Unionville, Conn.: No. 75: Two Foot, Four Fold Folding Rule. Arch Joint. Very Rare Type. Length: 24 Inches. *Equivalent in all respects to the Stanley No. 75 equivalent, the Upson Nut Company No. 75 is perhaps ten times as scarce. A rare rule.* (GOOD+) **$245.00**

S1-41. Stanley Rule & Level No. 22: Two Foot, Two Fold Folding Rule. With Board Tables. Metric and English Scales. Length: 24 Inches. *A very nice example of the only two-foot rule Stanley offered with the board scales used by the timber industry. All scales are sharp and readable on this rare rule.* (GOOD) **$295.00**

S1-42. Rabone & Sons, John, Birmingham: Broad Arch Joint Folding Rule. With Extension Slide. Early and Extra Nice. Length: 24 Inches. *The "bitted" center joint, the width of the rule and the presence of the highest quality "arch" joint are indications that this was made to be a top quality rule by Rabone. It still is.* (FINE) **$165.00**

S1-43. Stanley Rule & Level No. 66 3/4: Three-Foot, Four Fold Folding Rule. Arch Joint, Full Bound. Early Stanley Mark. Length: 36 Inches. *A nice clean example of Stanley's 3 foot, full-bound folding rule with an extra early trademark. Excellent.* (GOOD+) **$95.00s**

S1-44. Stanley Rule & Level No. 3: One-Foot, Four-Fold Folding Rule. Square Joint, Full Bound. Crisp and Clean. Length: 12 Inches. *The one foot, full bound caliper rule is among the rarest of Stanley one foot rules. This one has been used, but very little, and it is in excellent condition. A tough rule to find.* (GOOD+) **$345.00**

S1-45. Unmarked: Early Gunter Slide Folding Rule. Double Thick Body. Superb Condition. Length: 24 Inches. *The boxwood body of this early calculating rule is nearly twice as thick as later rules produced by Stanley and their competitors. The section beneath the Gunter slide is graduated with architect's scales.* (FINE) **$265.00**

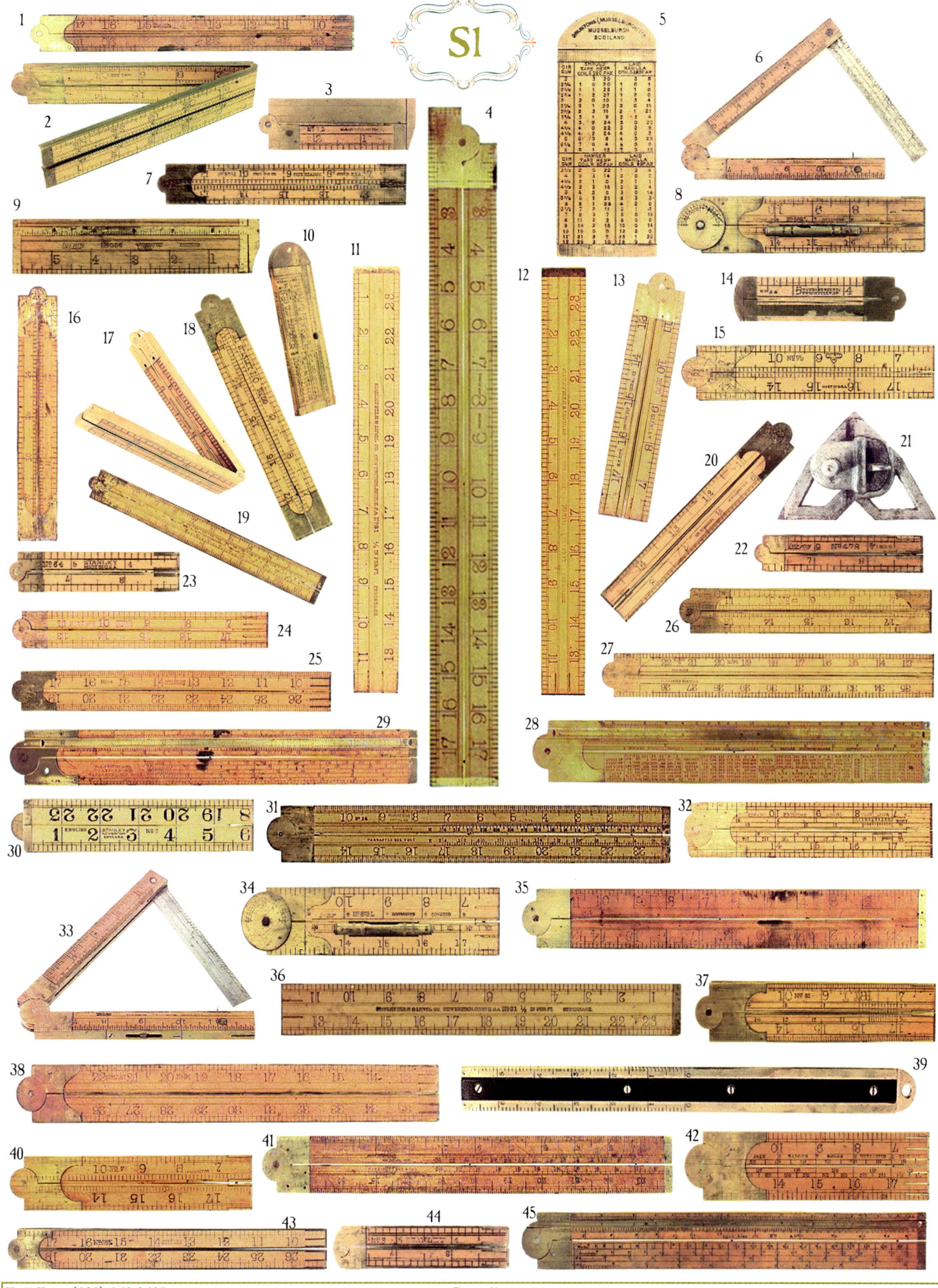

Group T1

T1-1. Otto & Sons, F.C., 64 Chatham, N.Y.: No. 3: Doctor Drescher's Patent Quackery Device. Patented November 4, 1879. Complete and Perfect. Length: 7 1/2 Inches. *This most interesting medical quackery apparatus is as complete and well preserved an example of a device of this genre in my experience. Included are all of the original parts, which include an electrical coil; a pair of fired carbon crucibles formed to accept a solution of mercury and water; zinc electrodes to be suspended in the solution to generate a chemical reaction; the wires to route the electricity generated by the reaction; a wooden roller looped with wire that was designed to be rolled over the body parts of the afflicted victim; and turned handles of beech, rosewood and brass to be affixed to the roller. All of these are fitted in a lacquered mahogany case with hinged doors that also holds the sockets where the wires to the roller are attached. The inside of one of the doors contains the original green paper engraved label marked with the maker/marketer's name, patent information and an engraving of the device. Also included is a flyer illustrating and describing the full range of devices offered by Dr. Otto, and proclaiming the relative merits of each. In the pamphlet, we learn that this, the No. 3 device, and the top of the line, sold for a whopping $9.00 in 1879. An enormous sum for that period. Complete, perfect and absolutely fascinating.* (FINE) **$795.00**

T1-2. Unmarked: Early Proportional Divider. For Navigation Use. Brass Body Sections. Length: 6 Inches. *The genius of these proportional dividers is based on a geometric principle that any 10th grader knows very well. Ask one to explain it to you. A pretty pair having brass body sections.* (GOOD+) **$55.00**

T1-3. Lufin Rule Co., The, Saginaw, Mich.: "Finger" Lumber Gauge. Brass Body. Scarce and Sound. Length: 3 Inches. *Looking not unlike a single "brass knuckle", this tool was used for measuring the thickness of sawn lumber and could be carried in the pocket of the user.* (GOOD) **$65.00**

T1-4. Stanley Rule & Level No. 44: Bit and Square Level. Patented November 16, 1886. New Condition, Original Box. Length: 2 Inches. *Stanley probably didn't win any design prizes for these patented brass and glass levels. Designed to be screwed onto a bit brace, it seems unlikely that many skilled craftsmen would have gone for such a gizmo. This early example is in the early-type green pasteboard box and the level itself is in as-new condition. A rare level in top shape.* (FINE) **$225.00**

T1-5. Gurley, W. & L.E., Troy, N.Y.: Folding Balance Scale. Precision Type. For Military Use? Length: 19 Inches. *This specialized bronze scale folds into a flat, compact shape when not in use. It might originally have been intended for field surveying or military use. An uncommon Gurley scale.* (FINE) **$95.00**

T1-6. Robertson & Sons, James L.: Willis Improved Planimeter. Patented July 9, 1895. With Horsepower Attachment. Length: 15 Inches. *In addition to the Willis Planimeter, this offering also includes the optional, and rare, German silver horsepower attachment. All original finishes remain, and the horsepower attachment includes one of the original trammel points. A most unusual planimeter in top collector quality condition.* (FINE) **$145.00**

T1-7. Hoerner, John S., Highland, Illinois: Early Patent Tool Sharpener. Patented January 17, 1899. Rare and Graphic. Length: 6 Inches. *A copy of the original patent papers is included with this most unusual Illinois patent "tool sharpener". The body of the tool is made of wood, which is fitted out with nickel plated fittings. Condition is near new. A rare patented sharpening device that we have not previously encountered.* (FINE) **$675.00**

T1-8. White Dental Mfg. Co., The S.S.: No. 3,4,5,6: Set of Early Dental Scalers. With Pewter Ferrules. New Condition, Original Box. Length: 7 1/2 Inches. *A late Nineteenth Century dentist would have found these "Rigg's Scalers" available from a medical equipment supplier of the time. Each of the four sizes represented is in new condition. Classic dental tools from a bygone time.* (FINE) **$675.00**

T1-9. Unmarked: Early Drafting Trammels. German Silver. Original Case. Length: 4 1/2 Inches. *These well preserved trammels are unmarked, but obviously produced by a quality maker.* (GOOD+) **$85.00**

T1-10. Rex Wrench Co., Boston, Mass.: "Rex T" Adjustable Wrench. Patented May 8, 1906. Fine Conditon, Original Box. Length: 9 1/4 Inches. *Unlike any wrench we have ever offered, this early automotive set has a "U" shaped hook to allow it to attach in different angles to the socket, wrench or screwdriver. A most unusual set in clean complete condition in its original box.* (GOOD+) **$115.00**

T1-11. Deming, F.B., Calais, Maine: "Dirigo Ink" Rule. Patent Applied For. Original Paper Label. Length: 12 Inches. *A specialized lining rule from the unlikely location of Calais, Maine, this unusual tool retains a substantial portion of its original paper label. Very different.* (FINE) **$225.00**

T1-12. Starrett, L.S., Athol, Mass.: No. 362: Patent Draughtsmans Protractor. With Tools Trademark. New Condition, Original Box. Length: 10 Inches. *The Brown & Sharpe Company offered a nearly identical protractor for many years. This equivalent from L.S. Starrett is in perfect collector-quality condition in its original box. Different.* (FINE) **$125.00**

T1-13. Topp & Co., G.A., Indianapolis, Indiana: Topps Framing Tool Try Square. Patented November 1, 1892. With Horsehead Trademark. Length: 9 1/2 Inches. *An excellent example of the Topp's Patent Framing Tool, nearly all of the elaborate early etching remains, including the trademark horse's head. An interesting measuring and calculating tool in superb condition.* (FINE) **$225.00**

T1-14. Unmarked: Ivory, German Silver Drafting Set. With Descriptive Book. Brass and Rosewood Box. Length: 7 1/2 Inches. *A period book on the uses of instruments was apparently included with this ca. 1880's drafting set and remains with it today. Crisp, clean complete and ready to display. A very nice set.* (FINE) **$325.00**

T1-15. Putz, J., N.Y.: Special Purpose Device. From Instrument Maker. Unknown Function. Length: 2 1/2 Inches. *The presence of a location on this tool in addition to the maker's mark make it highly likely that this tool was manufactured for resale. Fitted out with a total of ten pointed pins that are sequentially numbered, but are apparently not of different sizes, this special purpose tool is a genuine mystery.* (FINE) **$35.00**

T1-16. Unmarked: Early Drafting "T" Square. Ebony and Brass Heads. Diamond Plates. Length: 17 1/2 Inches. *Everything about this ebony head drafting "T" squares says that it is of very early manufacture, perhaps as early as 1850. A series of diamond shaped brass plates are set into the head as functional ornamentation.* (GOOD+) **$165.00**

T1-17. Starrett, L.S., Athol, Mass.: Early Patent Combination Square. Patented May 6, 1879. Rare Small Size. Length: 4 Inches. *This early square is imprinted with the date of L.S. Starrett's 1879 patent. A nice example.* (GOOD+) **$145.00**

T1-18. Starrett Co., L.S., The, Athol, Mass.: No. 8 M: Rare 60 Centemeter Blade Combination Square. Oversize Head and Blade. 99% Original Paint. Length: 24 Inches. *This massive oversize square from Starrett is rare in any condition, but to find an example in essentially new condition that is also graduated with metric scales is a rare occurrence indeed. Absolutely perfect and highly recommended.* (FINE) **$365.00**

T1-19. Dixon Crucible Co., Jersey City, N.J.: No. 500 A: Box of Lumber Crayon Holders. With Crayons. Old Store Stock. Length: 6 Inches. *One wouldn't want to go out in the woods to mark lumber without a lumber crayon, and one certainly wouldn't want to use a lumber crayon without a lumber crayon holder, so we offer a box of each. A lifetime supply, now available on a first come, first serve basis.* (FINE) **$35.00**

T1-20. Otto & Reynders, New York: Set of Surgical Knives. Ebony Handles. Silver Ferrules. Length: 15 Inches. *Knives such as this were used in the amputation of limbs from human beings in the days before anaesthesia. The necessary components for a proper amputation were sharp knives, a strong surgeon and a pair of equally strong assistants to persuade the patient that the surgeon was not his enemy. These knives are clearly marked with the maker's name and are fitted with handles of checkered ebony. A great set.* (GOOD+) **$265.00**

T1-21. Unmarked: Surgeon's Double Saw. African Blackwood Handle. Convex and Straight Blades. Length: 6 3/4 Inches. *This one has flat and convex blades on opposite sides of the business end. Very well preserved.* (GOOD) **$155.00**

T1-22. Stanley Rule & Level: Medical Use Hand Drill. Missing Chuck. "Medical Dept. U.S.A." Length: 10 Inches. *Undoubtedly produced by Stanley as part of the war effort in World War I, this rare medical drill is missing its original chuck, but is otherwise excellent. Clearly marked with the Stanley name.* (GOOD) **$145.00**

T1-23. Unmarked: Ivory Sector Folding Rule. For Navigation. and Calculation. Length: 6 Inches. *The sector rule was used in conjunction with a pair of dividers to perform complex mathematical computations in the days before the slide rule came into widespread use. This elephant ivory example would likely have come from the kit of a ship's navigator. A rare, early calculating rule in top condition.* (FINE) **$165.00**

T1-24. Sherman, S.J., New York, N.Y.: Early Patent Square Level. Patented July 19, 1853. Unused Condition. Length: 3 1/2 Inches. *This, one of the earliest of a series of levels designed to attach to a framing square, is marked with the maker name and patent date on a piece of paper under the vial. Early and unusual.* (FINE) **$85.00**

T1-25. Keuffel & Esser Co., New York: Draughtsman's Dotting Pen. With Accessory Wheels. Fine Condition, Original Box. Length: 4 Inches. *One of the more mechanically interesting of drafting tools, these dotting pens consisted of an extension arm holding an ink pen that was moved up and down by interaction with one of a series of cam-shaped drive wheels, leaving a mark at an exact distance from the previous mark as it moved across a piece of paper. A perfectly preserved example.* (GOOD+) **$225.00**

T1-26. Unmarked: Miniature Glass Beaker. "Minim Measure". New Condition, Original Box. Length: 2 Inches. *The inscriptions "minim measure" has been stamped in gold lettering on the top of the leather case that holds this miniature beaker. A most unusual and early liquid measuring device.* (FINE) **$45.00**

T1-27. Unmarked: Assorted Early Drafting Tools. Rules, Dividers, Etc. To Fill a Set. Length: 6 Inches. *Nearly every drafting set one encounters is missing a piece or two. Here's a generous lot assorted drafting tools, including a boxwood and an ivory scale to fill the set you have or to keep on hand for when you might need them.* (GOOD+) **$65.00**

T1-28. Gardam & Son, Wm., New York, N.Y.: Early Patent Section Liner. Patented September 2, 1884. New Condition, Original Box. Length: 14 Inches. *Of the many works of mechanical ingenuity that were designed to facilitate the drawing of a series of parallel lines on a piece of paper, this 1884 patent device is the most mechanically complex. Complete in the original box with the original instruction and in new condition, this gizmo employed a series of special interchangeable wheels to regulate the distance between each line. Simply a great drafting tool in near-new condition.* (FINE) **$575.00**

T1-29. Unmarked: Patent Pill-Making Device. Patented March 18, 1873. Walnut and Brass. Length: 12 1/2 Inches. *Back in the old days, the pharmacist, or, rather, the apothecary, might well have mixed together all manner of chemicals and herbs, mashed them to a pulp with a mortar & pestle and then rolled them into pills with one of these. The accessory device is for cutting the strips into pill-sized pieces. A most unusual antiquarian curiosity.* (GOOD+) **$395.00**

T1-30. Unmarked: Early Style Tooth Key. For Extraction. Pivoting Head. Length: 6 1/2 Inches. *A rosewood handle provides a touch of aesthetic appeal on this early tooth "key", which functioned as a lever working in conjunction with the fulcrum of the jawbone to remove teeth that had outlived their usefulness. An early dental tool, but not for the faint of heart.* (GOOD+) **$185.00**

T1-31. Unmarked: Surgeon's Locking Saw. For Blade Tension. Most Unusual Form. Length: 12 Inches. *The handle on this medical saw serves as a spring clamp to lock the blade in place and keep it taut. A rare saw in new condition.* (FINE) **$95.00**

T1-32. Millers Falls Company No. 3: Spring Tension Hand Vise. 5 Inch Size. New Condition, Original Box. Length: 5 Inches. *A new old stock example of the M.F. No. 3 hand vise in its original pasteboard box. Perfect.* (FINE) **$65.00**

T1-34. Sawyer Tool Co., Fitchburg, Mass.: Oversize 12 Inch Combination Square. With Fitchburg Imprint. Rare and Excellent. Length: 12 Inches. *Markedly larger in size than a standard combination square, we have seen less than a handful of these Fitchburg-made squares in the last 20 years. A rare Sawyer square in excellent condition.* (GOOD+) **$285.00**

T1-35. Keuffel & Esser Co., New York: "Paragon" Drafting Rule. 4 Beveled Edges. Original Leather Case. Length: 6 Inches. *The original leather case has kept this top of the line drafting rule in nearly new condition.* (GOOD+) **$15.00**

T1-36. De Wolf, Lucien: Patent Model(?) Combination Tool. Rule, Divider/Bevel. With Specifications. Length: 9 1/2 Inches. *Complete in its original fitted mahogany case, this abomination of tool design is one of the most outrageous examples of the maxim that "Bad Ideas Make Great Tools" that we have ever seen. The accompanying specifications, which indicate that the intention of producing this monstrosity was to apply for a patent, go on, ad nauseum, to recount the technical specifications and supposed advantages contained in this tool. Embodying, in a single tool, the functions of a pair of dividers, a bevel, try square, miter square and more, there is no evidence that this tool ever progressed beyond the design stage. Oversize, awkward, sharp to the point of being dangerous and difficult even to get back into the box, this brainchild was doomed as a useful tool from the outset. Luckily for tool collectors, however, this patent design has survived to remind us, from time to time, that the search for that "something different" sometimes leads to discovery. A great tool.* (FINE) **$795.00**

T1-37. Unmarked: Early Drafting Template. Patented January 31, 1888. Rare and Excellent. Length: 4 1/2 Inches. *A glance at the patent papers should quantify the genius embodied in this early patented device. In all likelihood, it was intended for the draughtsman to facilitate the rendering of shapes not easily drawn by standard instruments using established techniques. Different.* (FINE) **$145.00**

T1-38. Suffell, 132 Long Acre (London): Ivory Draughtsman's Rule. With Rolling Parallel. Early and Unusual. Length: 6 Inches. *Very likely produced for the gentleman draughtsman, or perhaps even a ship's captain, this ivory rule is graduated with a wide range of scales and fitted with an ivory rolling parallel rule. A most unusual rule configuration in excellent collector quality condition.* (GOOD+) **$345.00**

T1-39. Unmarked: Patent Hexagonal Drafting Rule. Patented December 1, 1885. Multiple Scales. Length: 18 Inches. *The patented feature of this India rubber drafting rule was likely the six scales that radiate from its center. A rule having one to three scales was the standard for this type of work, so three more must have sounded like a good idea. The only example of which we are aware. Rare.* (FINE) **$275.00**

T1-40. Unmarked: Adjustable Parallel Rule. Original Sleeve. Unusual Type. Length: 11 Inches. *This is the first of these parallel rules we have seen. Its function is not known. Different.* (FINE) **$15.00**

T1-41. Dentist Supply Co., The, New York: "Twentieth Century" Tooth Shade Guide. Marked "T C". Most Unusual. Length: 4 Inches. *If there's anything worse than a toothless smile, its a bright, white, false tooth in the middle of a mouthful of tobacco and blueberry stained teeth. Thank goodness for the "Twentieth Century" Tooth Shade Gauge. Opportunity knocks.* (FINE) **$55.00**

T1-42. Boes Co., The W.W., Dayton, Ohio: Astro Compass. Mk II Design. New Condition, Original Box. Length: 9 1/2 Inches. *A full original copy of the instructions accompany this specialized precision compass, which has been protected by a fitted case from the wear and tear of time.* (GOOD+) **$165.00**

T1-43. Gurley, W. & L.E., Troy, N.Y.: Folding Balance Scale. Precision Type. For Military Use? Length: 19 Inches. *This specialized bronze scale folds into a flat, compact shape when not in use. It might originally have been intended for field surveying or military use. An uncommon Gurley scale.* (GOOD+) **$95.00**

T1-44. Unmarked: Assorted Brass Turning Tools. From Watchmaker. Early Appearance. Length: 16 Inches. *Rescued intact from a single shop these tools and the accompanying lather have an 1870's-ish appearance and are in excellent condition.* (GOOD+) **$975.00**

T1-45. North Bros. Mfg. Co., Philadelphia, Penn.: No. 105: "Yankee" Radio Tool Kit. With No. 23 Driver. New Condition, Origianl Box. Length: 7 1/2 Inches. *In addition to the regular "Yankee" screwdriver and slotted screwdriver bits, these kits included a range of specialized tools for working with a radio chassis. This well preserved set includes all original tools. Rare and near new.* (FINE) **$395.00**

T1-46. Alteneder & Sons, Theo, Philadelphia, Penn.: Draughtsman's Trammels. E.G. Soltmann Tag. Solid German Silver. Length: 4 Inches. *E.G. Soltmann operated a tool and instrument supply business in New York City. These perfectly preserved trammels from Theodore Alteneder were apparently sold by them. A great set.* (FINE) **$165.00**

Group U1

U1-1. Hinckley, A.: 18th Century Carpenter's Slick. Undocumented Maker. Extra Crisp and Clean. Length: 23 Inches. *The name "A. Hinckley" has been boldly struck on this early carpenter's slick. A well made tool from an undocumented maker.* (GOOD+) **$165.00**

U1-2. Sargent & Co., New Haven, Conn.: No. 12: Polished Steel Framing Square. Uncommon Size. Extra Crisp and Clean. Length: 12 Inches. *This Sargent framing square is a crisp clean example of a most uncommon size. Clearly marked with the maker's name and number. Crisp.* (GOOD+) **$35.00**

U1-3. Unmarked: Classic Carpenter's Adze. Unused Condition. Original Handle. Length: 33 Inches. *This classic adze is in essentially the same condition as it was the day it was made. Perfect.* (FINE) **$95.00**

U1-4. Unmarked: Classic "T" Handle Carpenter's Slick. Octagonal Shaft. Extremely Well Made. Length: 22 1/2 Inches. *A leather "keeper" has kept this "T" handle slick in top condition. The quality of the forging, evident in the joint of the shaft to the blade, is of superior quality. Never been dirty, never been cleaned.* (FINE) **$295.00**

U1-5. Goodell Pratt Company No. 1306: Precision Mitre Box. With Saw and Attachments. New Condition, Original Box. Length: 37 Inches. *Complete in its original box and in essentially, new condition, this Goodell Pratt Mitre Box is a high precision tool that just happens to be a bit more poetic than a "chop saw". A refined woodworking tool.* (FINE) **$395.00**

U1-6. Powell Tool Co., Cleveland, Ohio: 12 1/2 Broad Axe. Original Handle. Ready to Use. Length: 26 Inches. *The Powell Tool Company of Cleveland, Ohio is a name that is new to us, but we have some experience with quality edge tools. This 12 1/2 inch broad axe retains its original handle and the blade is in excellent working order. This extra large precision tool has the "ring" when struck that is a sign of a top quality edge tool. Nice.* (GOOD+) **$185.00**

U1-7. Sorby, Robert, Sheffield No. 1: Polled Carpenters Adze. Octagonal Poll. Ca. 1820's. Length: 20 1/2 Inches. *This excellent working adze has been boldly struck with the I. Sorby imprint. An excellent working tool.* (GOOD+) **$75.00**

U1-8. Unmarked: Classic Deep Hollowing Adze. For Shipwright. Early and Near New. Length: 32 Inches. *Although they are commonly referred to as "gutter" adzes, these tools were used primarily in the shipbuilding industry and are most frequently found in areas where wooden shipbuilding took place. This example is in excellent working order.* (GOOD+) **$185.00**

U1-9. Peck, Stow & Wilcox Co.: No. 1 EX: 3 Inch Blade Carpenter's Slick. Original Handle. Excellent Patina. Length: 30 1/2 Inches. *This well made slick retains its original handle and is thoroughly clean and sound. There is some light pitting on the underside, but the tool is otherwise excellent.* (GOOD) **$135.00**

U1-10. Unmarked: Early Patent Spiral Boring Machine. Patented June 2, 1872. Adjustable Angle. Length: 28 Inches. *This most unusual patented boring machine dates from the 1870's and appears to be fully functional today. A rare patented boring machine in collector quality condition.* (GOOD+) **$495.00**

U1-11. Unmarked: Early Patent Spiral Boring Machine. Patented June 2, 1872. Adjustable Angle. Length: 34 Inches. *Only slightly larger than the machine shown as U1-10 adjacent, this tool was produced under the same patent and is in equally well preserved condition. A rare patented boring machine.* (GOOD+) **$550.00**

U1-12. Buck Bros., Millbury, Mass.: 3 Inch Blade Carpenter's Slick. Turned Mahogany Handle. Ready to Use. Length: 32 Inches. *There's no doubt that the quality invested by the Buck Bros. firm of Millbury, Mass. in their smaller edge tools is also to be found in this 3 inch carpenter's slick. The underside has been precision machined to be absolutely true. Crisp, clean and ready to use. Nice.* (GOOD+) **$185.00**

U1-13. Eagle Square Mfg. Co.: No. 100: Patent "Takedown" Square. Patented January 22, 1907. Near New Condition. Length: 24 Inches. *This square must have been produced shortly before the Stanley firm acquired the Eagle Square Company. This one is clean and complete. Very nice and clearly marked with the patent date.* (FINE) **$165.00**

U1-14. Burge: Early Hewing Adze. Usable Condition. Early Handle. Length: 27 Inches. *This early appearing octagonal poll adze is imprinted only with the name "Burge", an edge tool maker we have not previously encountered. An exceptionally boldly struck early hand forged tool.* (GOOD) **$95.00**

U1-15. Maddock, E., Watertown (N.Y.): Early "D" Handle Carpenter's Slick. Nicely Forged. Early and Excellent. Length: 25 Inches. *The conventional wisdom has it that these "D" handle slicks were used for separating radially-sawn clapboards in sawmills. I don't believe it. This example is boldly struck with the imprint of obscure Watertown, New York maker "E. Maddock". Simply a great early edge tool.* (GOOD+) **$325.00**

U1-16. Plumb, Philadelphia, Penn.: Lipped Carpenter's Adze. 5 Inch Cut. Unused Condition. Length: 32 1/2 Inches. *The Philadelphia firm of Fayette R. Plumb offered a full line of edge tools. including this lipped carpenter's adze. This one has apparently never been used. Mint.* (FINE) **$125.00**

U1-17. Unmarked: Classic Logger's Picaroon. With "Hook" Handle. Found in Maine. Length: 15 Inches. *The lumberman who carved the handle for this classic Maine picaroon put a bit more artistic effor than most into the tip of the handle. A classic lumber tool.* (GOOD+) **$65.00**

U1-18. Peck, Stow & Wilcox Co.: No. 1 EX: 3 Inch Blade Carpenter's Slick. Original Handle. Unused Condition. Length: 30 1/2 Inches. *This is as nice a Peck Stow & Wilcox slick as we have ever offered. Absolutely perfect.* (FINE) **$265.00**

U1-19. New Haven Edge Tool Co.: 3 1/2 Inch Width Carpenter's Slick. Extra Crisp and Clean. Ready to Use. Length: 30 Inches. *The New Haven Edge Tool Company produced a full line of chisels, gouges and other edge tools, including this well preserved slick. A great working tool from a quality maker.* (GOOD+) **$245.00**

U1-20. Eagle Square Mfg. Co.: Rare 6 Inch "Framing" Square. With Eagle Imprint. Early and Excellent. Length: 6 Inches. *Eventually assumed by the Stanley Rule & Level Company, the Eagle Square Company produced a wide range of squares from their Shaftesbury, Vermont location . This scarce 6 inch framing square is in top condition.* (FINE) **$85.00**

U1-21. Peck, Stow & Wilcox Co.: No. 1 EX: 3 Inch Blade Carpenter's Slick. Original Handle. Extra Crisp and Clean. Length: 30 Inches. *This Southington firm specialized in edge tools for timber framers. Their edge tools are of exceptional quality. This well made slick is an excellent example of their best work.* (GOOD+) **$245.00**

U1-22. Unmarked: 3 Inch Socket Type Carpenter's Slick. Straight and Sharp. Ready to Use. Length: 19 Inches. *This well made slick has been fitted with a handle like that found on a framing chisel. It is in excellent working condition.* (GOOD+) **$145.00**

U1-23. Witherby, T.H.: 3 1/4 Inch Wide Laminate Carpenter's Slick. Extra Crisp Condition. Extra Long Blade. Length: 32 1/2 Inches. *Here's a crisp, clean and ready to use Witherby slick. No apologies for this one.* (GOOD+) **$295.00**

U1-24. Stanley Rule & Level No. R100B: Patent "Takedown" Square. Patented August 18, 1914. 1915 Era "V" Trademark. Length: 24 Inches. *An especially well preserved example of Stanley's patent "takedown" square. Clean and clearly marked. A rare and interesting Stanley collectible.* (GOOD+) **$165.00**

U1-25. Marsh & Sons, Oakland, Maine: Massive Felling Axe. With Advertising Paper. 7 Inch Edge. Length: 8 Inches. *Original advertising for Marsh & Sons, the maker of this axe, came with it and will stay with it. The oversize axe head is very similar to that shown in the accompanying brochure, which features the world champion woodcutter.* (GOOD+) **$115.00**

U1-26. Brown & Sharpe Mfg. Co., Providence: Massive 24 Inch Try Square. With Beveled Edge. Fitted Wood Case. Length: 24 Inches. *A fitted owner-made case has kept this massive try square in perfect condition. If they still make tools like this, they are probably pretty expensive. This one is a bargain.* (FINE) **$225.00**

U1-27. Unmarked: Classic Nailmaker's Bench. For Hand Cut Nails. Early and Excellent. Length: 26 Inches. *Many, many years ago, farmers earned "hard" money during the winter by cutting nails at a bench like this for long hours. One of the legs is an early replacement, but this bench is otherwise in excellent condition. A piece of history.* (GOOD+) **$185.00**

U1-28. Beatty, J.: Early 3 Inch Carpenter's Slick. Original Handle. Near New Condition. Length: 31 1/2 Inches. *This perfectly preserved carpenters slick has been beveled at the top in the classic style of the Beatty family of Southeastern Pennsylvania. Condition is nearly new.* (FINE) **$345.00**

U1-29. Greenlee Tool Co., Rockford, Illinois: 3 Inch Blade Carpenter's Slick. Turned Beech Handle. Near New Condition. Length: 29 Inches. *The Greenlee Tool Company produced quality edge tools for many years. This 3 inch carpenter's slick is in essentially unused condition. Ready to go to work.* (FINE) **$225.00**

U1-30. Witherby, T.H.: 3 Inch Wide Laminated Carpenter's Slick. Extra Crisp Condition. Original Beech Handle. Length: 29 1/2 Inches. *This one has achieved a light brownish blue patina from years of careful use. It has never been wet, rusted or abused in any way. A quality tool from a quality maker that is in ready to use condition.* (GOOD+) **$265.00**

U1-31. Swan Co., The James, Seymour, Conn.: Adjustable Angle Boring Machine. With 2 Inch Bit. Near New Condition. Length: 26 Inches. *This classic adjustable boring machine is in nearly new condition. Ready to use or add to a top level collection of tools from this important maker of high quality tools. Comes with the original 2 inch bit.* (FINE) **$345.00**

U1-32. Mann, William, Lewistown, Penn.: "Red Warrior" Broad Axe. Original Decal. Rare and Excellent. Length: 31 Inches. *The axes produced by William Mann at his factory in Lewistown, Pennsylvania are legendary for their quality. This "Red Warrior" broad axe retains its original gold paint and American Indian decal. A rare axe in great shape.* (GOOD+) **$265.00**

U1-33. Swan Co, The James: Heavy Socket Framing Chisel. Turned Walnut Handle. Rare "Bevel Back". Length: 29 1/2 Inches. *Chisels by the James Swan Company are spoken of in hushed, reverent terms by those who have used them. This rare "bevel back" example in the 1 7/8 inch size has been fitted with a slick-like handle of turned black walnut. A classic.* (GOOD+) **$115.00**

U1-34. Witherby, T.H.: 3 Inch Wide Laminated Carpenter's Slick. Framing Chisel Handle. Usable Condition. Length: 17 Inches. *The Witherby name is held in special reverence by those who work with edge tools. Their tools were meant to take and hold a fine cutting edge. This one is in excellent condition and ready to go to work.* (GOOD) **$165.00**

U1-35. Unmarked: Carpenter's Adze. With Hickory Handle. Ready to Use. Length: 34 Inches. *The owner of this adze was apparently in the process of fitting the handle when he was interrupted. All that needs to be done is to trim the handle at the base and fit a wedge to lock it tight on the handle. A classic.* (GOOD+) **$65.00**

U1-36. Unmarked: Early Hand Forged Adze. With Laminated Edge. Usable Condition. Length: 24 1/2 Inches. *This one appears to have left the shop long before the practice of tool makers marking their tools became commonplace. An excellent working adze having an early appearance.* (GOOD) **$45.00**

U1-37. Witherby, T.H.: 3 Inch Wide Laminated Carpenter's Slick. Extra Crisp Condition. Original Beech Handle. Length: 15 Inches. *Chisels and working edge tools are one area of collecting where user demand drives the value higher than collector interest. Working tools like this T.H. Witherby slick in top condition are simply not available for any price. Tools now produced are nowhere near the quality of this tool, and equally expensive, or more so. Extra, extra nice.* (FINE) **$295.00**

U1-38. Brown, C.: Classic Hollowing Adze. For Shipwrights Use. Laminated Edge. Length: 32 1/2 Inches. *These tools function as a large gouge and were commonly used by shipwrights. This one is clean, sound and ready to be put back to use.* (GOOD+) **$125.00**

U1-39. Ogden, R.C., N.Y.: Polled Carpenters Adze. Unused Condition. Original Gold Paint. Length: 11 Inches. *This shipwright's adze was never "hung" on a handle and consequently never used. Most of the original gold paint remains.* (FINE) **$55.00**

U1-40. Simmons Hardware Co., St. Louis: "Keen Kutter" Broad Axe. With Embossed Logo. Super Rare. Length: 22 Inches. *The "Keen Kutter" people marked everything they sold with their trademark logo. This extremely rare embossed broad axe has a mark that could be seen a country mile away. A good one.* (GOOD) **$550.00**

U1-41. Peck, Stow & Wilcox Co. No. S-100: "Pexto" "Takedown" Square. Screw Lock Mechanism. Extra Crisp and Clean. Length: 24 Inches. *A locking screw holds this classic "takedown" square precisely in position once it is assembled.* (GOOD+) **$115.00**

U1-42. Walker, Isaac, Peoria, Illinois: Walker's "Perfect" Axe. Deep Embossed Type. Dated "1842". Length: 7 Inches. *The date on this most unusual deep embossed felling axe very likely refers to the beginning date of the business of Peoria's Isaac Walker. A rare embossed axe that we have never offered before.* (FINE) **$325.00**

U1-43. Staatsburg, Staatsburg, N.Y.: Classic Ice Hatchet. Marked "Sher. Ice Co.". Near New Condition. Length: 11 Inches. *For a look at what an ice hatchet looked like when it left the factory, take a look at this tool from an obscure maker of edge tools. Mint.* (FINE) **$85.00**

U1-44. Southington Hardware Co.: "The Standard" Square. Takedown Framing. Copyright 1912. Length: 24 Inches. *This copyrighted "takedown" square has a slotted tongue joint to ensure the trueness of the angle. An uncommon square in well preserved condition.* (GOOD+) **$65.00**

U1-45. Collins & Co., Hartford, Conn.: Shipwright's Lipped Adze. 5 Inch Blade. Near New Condition. Length: 29 Inches. *Edge tools made by Collins & Company of Hartford, Connecticut are regarded by many as the finest ever made. This classic shipwright's lipped adze, which retains its full, original handle, has been kept in essentially new condition, thanks to the presence of a leather "keeper" over the blade. Extra special.* (FINE) **$165.00**

Group V1

V1-1. Multiform Molding Plane Co.: Handle for Patent Plane. Beech Handle. Rare and Near New. Length: 4 1/2 Inches. *Manufactured under a patent granted on August 29, 1854 to Thomas Worrall who at that time was pastor of the Baptist church of Mt. Holly, New Jersey, the Multiform Molding Planes had as their patented feature interchangeable soles with differing molding cuts which utilized a common, removable handle. We offer a rare example of the handle that could be attached to any of the soles. In nearly new condition, these handles become available very seldom and stay available for a short time indeed.* (FINE) **$545.00**

V1-2. Arthington, Manchester: Square, Cove/Astragal Molding Plane. Nicely Boxed. Most Unusual Profile. Length: 9 1/2 Inches. *This extra complex molder is the sort of molding plane that has become virtually impossible to find. John Arthington produced molding planes in Manchester, England, from 1836 to 1856.* (GOOD+) **$365.00**

V1-3. Unmarked: Pair of Bullnose Planes. "J.W. Cocking". Ibbotson Irons. Length: 3 1/2 Inches. *This pristine pair of bullnose planes retain nearly all of their original blued finish on their full irons, which are boldly struck with the imprint of planemaker Thomas Ibbotson. A great pair.* (FINE) **$345.00**

V1-4. Unmarked: Patternmaker's Set of Planes. Fruitwood Bodies. Two are Dated. Length: 10 Inches. *Crafted in the classic European style by a patternmaker who must, most certainly have been a recent immigrant to the United States, these exceptionally well preserved planes have a distinctive style that makes it immediately apparent that they were executed by the same hand, despite their dissimilarity of function.* (FINE) **$475.00**

V1-5. Richardson: Pencil Sharpener Plane. With Original Box. Advance Machine Company. Length: 2 3/4 Inches. *A presentation inscription is written on the box for this early pencil sharpener plane, which is imprinted with advertising from the Evanston Christian Sunday School. Most unusual and nearly new.* (FINE) **$165.00**

V1-6. Hammond, I., New Haven, Conn.: Pair of Carriage Molding Planes. Curve, Straight Cove. Rare and Excellent. Length: 7 Inches. *An extraordinarily well preserved pair of carriage maker's half-round planes in a straight and curved profile. Both planes are clearly and boldly stamped with the imprint of Issac Hammond, a planemaker who worked in New Haven, Connecticut from 1840-1845. An uncommon set of planes in near-new condition.* (FINE) **$550.00**

V1-7. Unmarked: Rosewood Sole Toothing Plane. Buck Brothers Cutter. Ready to Use. Length: 6 3/4 Inches. *Perhaps to minimize wear or perhaps to take advantage of the natural lubricating qualities of rosewood, someone, sometime, for some reason, fitted this beech toothing plane with a sole of Brazilian rosewood. A full Buck Brothers iron is in place and ready to use. A nice plane.* (GOOD+) **$115.00**

V1-8. Fuller, Jo.: 3/8 Inch Hollow Molding Plane. Yellow Birch Body. Superb Patina. Length: 10 Inches. *This classic molder from Providence, Rhode Island Jo. Fuller has been artfully chamfered and boldly struck with the Fuller imprint. A nice example.* (GOOD+) **$115.00**

V1-9. Douglass, N.Y.: Cove and Astragal Molding Plane. Ca. 1799. Earliest New York Maker. Length: 9 1/2 Inches. *Quite possibly the least common imprint of a New York City planemaker, the brothers Douglass, who used the mark, are documented to have been working in 1796 and quite likely worked much earlier. A nice mold on a very rare and clearly marked plane.* (GOOD+) **$595.00**

V1-10. Howland & Co., A., Auburn, N.Y.: No. 189: Handled Nosing Plane. Double Iron Type. Crisp and Clean. Length: 12 Inches. *Designed for the workaday task of applying the rounded "nosing" to stair treads and the like, this handled example from Auburn Prison planemaker A. Howland is in excellent working order. A good one.* (GOOD+) **$75.00**

V1-11. Wells, R.: Quirk Ovolo and Astrgal Molding Planes. Rosewood Boxing. Ca. 1830-1840. Length: 9 1/2 Inches. *Upstate New York maker C.R. Wells kept unusually detailed accounts of his planemaking activities, providing for rhykenological scholars a treasure trove of information about Nineteenth Century planemaking. These three complex molders, which were rescued many years ago and safely set away, are fitted with boxing of dark lignum vitae or rosewood. Extra nice.* (GOOD+) **$525.00**

V1-12. Kennedy, L., Hartford: Reed and Follow Molding Plane. Triple Boxed. Marked "3". Length: 9 1/2 Inches. *Reed and follow planes were designed to cut a single reeding groove, and then to use that initial groove as a fence for cutting a series of additional parallel grooves. This early example is in excellent working condition.* (FINE) **$165.00**

V1-13. Bartlett, S.B., Watertown, N.Y.: Double Cove and Bead Molding Plane. Rare and Undersize. AWP IIII 3 Stars. Length: 7 Inches. *In addition to being the first double cove and bead molding plane we have ever seen, this is also the first plane bearing the mark of Watertown, New York maker S.B. Bartlett that we have offered. One of the cutting irons and one of the wedges are missing, but are well worth restoring to bring this most unusual "coming and going" plane back to its initial splendor. A great molding plane.* (GOOD+) **$385.00**

V1-14. Sym, I.: Pair of Snipe Bill Molding Plane. Ca. 1753-1803. Nicely Boxed. Length: 9 1/2 Inches. *This excellent working pair of snipe bill molders are imprinted with the mark of John Sym, who hung up his planemaker's float for the last time in 1803. Clean, early and clearly marked.* (FINE) **$255.00**

V1-15. Deforest, Birmingham (Conn.): Screw Arm Filletster Plane. Boxwood Arms and Nuts. Rare and Excellent. Length: 10 Inches. *Screw arm filletster planes from American makers are rare indeed. This nicely side boxed example from Connecticut maker Linson Deforest is crisp, clean and thoroughly usable. A very nice example.* (GOOD+) **$425.00**

V1-16. Martin & Shaw, (Birmingham, England): Steep Ovolo, Bead Molding Plane. Ca. 1840's. Extra Crisp and Clean. Length: 9 1/2 Inches. *A wide beading cut complements this steep, wide quirk ovolo molding plane by British planemakers Martin & Shaw.* (FINE) **$165.00**

V1-17. Chelor, Ce., Wrentham: Yellow Birch Bead Molding Plane. Replaced Wedge. AWP III "A1" Imprint. Length: 10 Inches. *Imagine a freed slave engaged in private commerce as very likely the second professional planemaker ever to work in the American colonies; this, at a point some one hundred and ten years before the Great American Civil War that would settle the question of human slavery forever in this nation. That the tools of Cesar Chelor were works of art, better (some have offered than those of his master and his master's son) is unquestioned. The survival of several hundred known examples from this extremely early time indicates that Chelor produced a substantial number of planes which must have been eagerly sought out. Examples have been found in the most unlikely places throughout the U.S. and in foreign locations such as England and Texas. This example, which has a properly replaced wedge of yellow birch has seen some wear in its nearly two hundred fifty years of existence,but it is boldly marked with what has been designated as the "B" imprint. Clearly marked, old as the hills and an important piece of American technological and cultural history and our contribution to Black History Month. A good one.* (GOOD) **$1,395.00**

V1-18. Mathieson & Son, A, Glasgow: Quirk Ogee and Bevel Molding Plane. Scottish Double Iron. Classic Pattern. Length: 9 1/2 Inches. *Double iron complex molding planes were a specialty of Scottish planemakers and Scottish planemakers don't get any more Scottish than Alexander Mathieson. This clean molder in the classic ogee and bevel pattern is clean, clearly marked and ready to use.* (GOOD+) **$115.00**

V1-19. Sanborn, D.P., Littleton N.H.: Screw Lock Plow Plane. Sculptural Form. Superb Example. Length: 8 1/2 Inches. *Graced with the classic "tombstone" depth stop and carefully hand-cut fixing screws, this magnificent plow plane has proportions that make it appear more an art object than a functional device. Boldly struck with the imprint of Littleton, New Hampshire, planemaker David Page Sanborn, this most visually appealing tool is ready to proudly display. Extra nice.* (GOOD+) **$375.00**

V1-20. Malloch, D., Perth (Scotland): Boxed Bead Molding Plane. Marked "3/4". Appears Unused. Length: 9 1/2 Inches. *Three quarter inch bead planes are becoming increasingly difficult to obtain. This one is in excellent working order. Nice.* (FINE) **$35.00**

V1-21. Hill, J.V., Gray's Inn Road(London): Pair of Side Snipe Molding Planes. Fully Boxed. Distinctive Wedges. Length: 9 1/2 Inches. *A nice working pair of snipe bill molding planes with oversize wedges shaped so as to facilitate adjustment and extraction of the cutting irons. These were designed for cleaning up molding cuts and serve that purpose equally well today.* (GOOD+) **$225.00**

V1-22. Unmarked: Whimsical Horn Plane. With Secret Box. Dated "1902". Length: 4 3/4 Inches. *Fashioned in the shape of a European-style horned scrub plane, this keepsake box was more than likely fashioned for a child by his cabinetmaker father. The tool is inscribed with the date "1902". Cute.* (GOOD+) **$125.00**

V1-23. Haines & Smith, Portland, Maine: Handled Smoothing Plane. Portland Hardware Dealer. 5 Star Mark. Length: 9 Inches. *The Haines and Smith imprint rates Five Stars in American Wooden Planes. The mark is weak, but readable. A most unusual Maine plane.* (GOOD) **$245.00**

V1-24. Brooks, P.: Double Tongue and Groove Plane. Rare Handled Type. Marked "Patented". Length: 15 Inches. *What makes a tool collectible? Is it simply the fact that few examples were made and that we should therefore acquire without consideration those tools identified by experts as being "rare". What a joyless, uninspiring world tool collecting would be if that were the case. As one who has frequently offered as advice to new collectors to take to heart the Tool Aphorism "If you have to take it apart or turn it upside down to know if it is rare, you probably shouldn't buy it", my answer to the question of collectibility would be that one should simply collect what appeals to his or her personal tastes. This is, after all, supposed to be fun, not some mercantile exchange where tools are acquired and let go with the same impersonal matter of factness as if they were soybeans or pork bellies. This tool has a distinctively different form that appeals almost universally to collectors of every stripe. The thousands of planes that we see almost invariably have the same generic look: rear handle, front handle, cutter, etc. etc., so when something as distinctively different as a double handled plane comes our way, we instinctively know that it is something rare , different and worthy of saving. Stamped with the imprint "BROOKS/ PATENT" on two lines on the toe of the tool, this plane is the work of Peter Brooks of East Hartford, Connecticut. Despite the patent markings, no patents records have been found. A rare, interesting and collectible plane.* (GOOD+) **$950.00**

V1-25. Clark, H., Utica, N.Y.: No. 16: Hollow Molding Plane. Extra Rare Mark. Crisp and Clean. Length: 9 1/2 Inches. *Emil Pollak's essential reference, American Wooden Planes, suggests that Clark may have left Utica to come to Wisconsin. Judging from the style of the imprint, it appears that Mr. Clark may have apprenticed with the prominent Utica maker, John Reed. A very rare imprint.* (GOOD+) **$265.00**

V1-26. Sym, I.: Pair of Side Rabbet Molding Plane. Ca. 1753-1803. Near New Condition. Length: 9 1/2 Inches. *These most unusual side rabbet molding planes have been artfully fitted with full boxwood reinforcements along their soles to further their useful life. A great working pair in top condition.* (FINE) **$225.00**

V1-27. Sheneman & Bro., B., Philadelphia Penn.: Quirk Ogee, Bevel Molding Plane. Rare Double Iron. Clean, Crisp Mark. Length: 9 1/2 Inches. *This massive Philadelphia molder is fitted with dual cutting irons to facilitate the execution of the wide moldings it was crafted to create. Very different.* (GOOD+) **$325.00**

V1-28. Storer, J.P., Brunswick, Maine: Lignum Vitae Jointer Plane. Highly Figured Grain. Rare Marked Example. Length: 22 Inches. *The Maine seacoast produced a style of toolmaking that is unlike that of anywhere else. The shipbuilding industry required woodworking tools in great abundance and the heavy, tropical hardwood that was often used as ballast in ships from the tropics provided just the stuff from which to make them. Most of the classic Maine planes of ebony or lignum vitae are not imprinted with makers marks, or, when they are, the density of the wood renders the imprint all but unreadable. This magnificent woodworking plane possesses all of the characteristics of a great Maine plane: The wood has been selected with an artist's eye for color; the making of the plane has been executed by a master planemaker, working in a most challenging material; the elements have not been unduly harsh on the tool and the name and working location of Brunswick, Maine maker J.P. Storer has been boldly struck on the toe of the plane. A tool for working wood, or a work of art? Or is it both? Absolutely magnificent and highly recommended.* (FINE) **$695.00**

V1-29. Unmarked: "Yankee" Plow Plane. Yellow Birch Body. Early Riveted Skate. Length: 9 Inches. *A classic example of the "Yankee" plow plane, this unmarked but aesthetically appealing early plane features hand-cut fixing screws, a riveted skate and is otherwise nicely fashioned from yellow birch. A superb example of the principal working tool of the early American cabinetmaker. Very nice.* (GOOD+) **$225.00**

V1-30. Wetherell, H., Chatham: Reverse Ogee, Astragal Molding Plane. With "Cartouche". Early and Excellent. Length: 9 3/4 Inches. *Boldly struck with the "cartouche" of dual crowns that was his trademark, this example of the work of Henry Wetherell of Chatham, Connecticut, features a complex cut not often found on planes from this early period of manufacture. An early and clearly marked complex molding plane.* (GOOD+) **$365.00**

V1-31. Providence Tool Co.: Full Set of 8 Plow Plane Irons. Marked "Cast Steel". Ready to Use. Length: 9 Inches. *The Providence Tool Company provided plane irons for a large number of American planemakers. Here's a well preserved full set of 8 cutting irons for a plow plane. A nice set.* (GOOD+) **$155.00**

V1-32. Bartlett, A.C. No. 113: Double Iron Nosing Molding Plane. Marked "1 1/4". Made by Sandusky. Length: 9 1/2 Inches. *The planes marketed by A.C. Bartlett were produced by the Sandusky Tool Company, as is evident from the distinctive wedge finials. This nosing plane is in nearly new condition. Nice.* (FINE) **$55.00**

V1-33. Cumings, S., (Providence, R.I.): Classic Astragal Molding Plane. Marked "5/8". Unused Condition. Length: 9 1/2 Inches. *Astragal molders are in high demand and short supply. This 5/8" example dates from ca. 1830. Extra nice.* (FINE) **$115.00**

V1-34. Unmarked: 18th Century Filletster Plane. With Pewter Fittings. Distinctive Form. Length: 9 3/4 Inches. *It goes without saying that the world of the Eighteenth Century was markedly different from that which followed. One look at this extraordinarily well preserved moving fillester plane adds increased emphasis to that truism. Fitted with a massive relieved wedge, characterized by graphic wide, flat chamfers and accented by a most unusual wide depth stop that has pewter stops to complement those on the fence, this two hundred year old plane has only the presence of four worm holes to detract from its otherwise pristine state of preservation.* (FINE) **$155.00**

V1-35. Unmarked: Classic Lignum Smoot Plane. D.R. Barton Iron. Near New Condition. Length: 9 Inches. *The D.R. Barton Company would have had the materials available and were known to be willing to accommodate their customers in any way that they could, so it is not inconceivable that this lignum vitae smoother, which has been fitted with a Barton cutting iron, could have been made on special order by Barton. The body of the plane is not marked. A dramatic lignum vitae smoothing plane.* (FINE) **$115.00**

V1-36. Heald, Addison, Milford, N.H.: Razee Type Smooth Plane. Lignum Strike. Bold "A" Mark. Length: 10 Inches. *A lignum vitae strike button adds accent and emphasis to this well made handled smoothing plane. A light cleaning is all that is necessary to restore it to its full glory.* (GOOD) **$85.00**

V1-37. Cox, I., (Birmingham, England): Boxed Bilection Molding Plane. Early Initials "SC". Marked "3/4". Length: 9 1/2 Inches. *A crisp and clean cove and bead molder with the boldly struck imprint of Eighteenth Century English maker I. Cox. A nice profile on a nicely patinated early plane with character.* (GOOD+) **$125.00**

V1-38. Malloch, D., Perth (Scotland): Full Boxed Bead Molding Plane. Marked "3/16". Scarce and Near New. Length: 9 1/2 Inches. *Bead planes, especially the narrower widths, have a tendency to wear away their boxing, making them no longer usable. This 3/16 inch bead is fitted with a full strip of boxwood to minimize the possibility of that eventuality. Ready to use.* (FINE) **$45.00**

V1-39. Manchester, P.H.: Rare "Linenfold" Molding Plane. For Door Panels. Unused Condition. Length: 9 1/2 Inches. *This early fenced molder is formed in the classic "linenfold" pattern that was used for ornamenting the edges of door panels. Its condition is nearly new. Rare and excellent.* (FINE) **$225.00**

V1-40. Unmarked: Special Purpose Slitting Plane. For Horizontal Work. Most Unusual. Length: 11 1/2 Inches. *Here's a real enigma: this handled slitting plane has a wide, flat iron that is intended to cut along the edge of the plane to the inside of the workman. The presence of a handle that is not offset indicates that clearance for the user's hand was not a problem; however, holding one's hand on the grip causes it to extend beyond the reach of the cutting iron. This was either poorly designed, or intended for some very specific function. Any ideas? A fascinating plane in great condition.* (GOOD+) **$165.00**

V1-41. Unmarked: Razee Trying Plane. Mahogany Handle. Found in Maine. Length: 17 Inches. *A favorite of shipbuilders, "razee" type planes featured a recessed rear and/or front section on a bench plane. This classic example, which comes to us from the State of Maine, is fitted with a mahogany handle and is in nearly new condition. A classic.* (FINE) **$55.00**

V1-42. Unmarked: Classic Razee Smooth Plane. D.R. Barton Iron. Extra Crisp and Clean. Length: 10 1/4 Inches. *This handled razee type smoother is not imprinted with a maker's mark, but the cutting iron is marked with the imprint of Rochester, New York planemaker D.R. Barton. Other than a dab of green paint on one side, it is in superb condition. Nice.* (GOOD+) **$65.00**

V1-43. Stevens, J., Boston, Mass.: Fixed Rabbet Molding Plane. With Integral Fence. Near New Condition. Length: 9 1/2 Inches. *This most unusual fixed fence rabbeting plane from prominent Boston planemaker J. Stevens is in perfectly preserved condition with a bold maker imprint. Nice.* (FINE) **$135.00**

V1-44. Unmarked: Massive Rabbet Plane. With Hand Guide. Length: 43 Inches. *At nearly four feet in length, this extremely early European plane is difficult not to notice. A groove, apparently original, has been cut in the plane to accommodate the user's thumb. A rare and early tool.* (GOOD+) **$245.00**

V1-45. Shiverick, (Brooklyn, N.Y.): Pair of Adjustable Throat Bench Planes. Ca. 1865-1867. Most Unusual Configuration. Length: 19 Inches. *Unlike any American bench planes we have ever offered, each of these planes from Brooklyn planemaker Shiverick has been fitted with a wooden throat adjustment mechanism. Each has been boldly marked with the maker's name and is in showroom new condition. Mint and highly recommended. Ex-Link Collection.* (FINE) **$645.00**

Group W1

W1-1. Lowentraut, P., Newark, N.J.: Patented Brace Wrench. Johnston's Patent. Patented December 4, 1894. Length: 12 Inches. *These multi-purpose brace/wrenches were aggressively marketed by the Lowentraut company. The handle comes out to become a screwdriver. If you've been waiting for a good one of these to come along, here's your chance. This is the nicest example we have ever offered for sale.* (FINE) **$225.00**

W1-2. Lovell Wrench Co., Bridgeport, Conn.: Lovell Bicycle Wrench. Patented May 12, 1896. Schulz No. 815. Length: 5 1/4 Inches. *One of the least common of all adjustable bicycle wrenches, the Lovell Wrench Company listed the merits of their wrench as "thin jaws" for use on sprocket and pedal nuts, strength and quick adjustment. The square opening is 7/16 inch in diameter, but closing the jaw will reduce the sides proportionately to take any size of nut. A most unusual patented bicycle wrench in excellent collector quality condition.* (GOOD+) **$345.00**

W1-3. Coes Wrench Co., Worcester, Mass.: Promotional Wrench Stick Pin. Original Card. "Pin to Your Memory". Length: 3 Inches. *The rough and tumble crowd who used Coes' wrenches probably didn't have much use for stickpins. Here's a nice example, nonetheless.* (FINE) **$65.00**

W1-4. Carabel, Carlo: Massive Double Coach Wrench. Continental Style. Superb Condition. Length: 15 Inches. *The classic Continental "double coach wrench" remained the standard form for more than 100 years in Europe while American inventors were pushing the bounds of sanity to outdo each other in creativity. A classic.* (GOOD+) **$175.00**

W1-5. Schrader, Frederick, Bridgeport, Conn.: Combination Spanner Wrench. Patented May 11, 1897. Schulz No. 21. Length: 5 Inches. *Unmarked with the maker's name, the patent information informs us that the lower jaw serves to regulate the spanner wrench against lock nuts of various sizes. A rare patented bicycle wrench in excellent collector quality condition.* (FINE) **$115.00**

W1-6. Ellis: Nickel Plated Nut Wrench. With Pivot Head. Patented November 3, 1903. Length: 6 Inches. *An extremely well preserved an fully functional example of the "Ellis" patent pivoting jaw wrench in the smallest and most desirable size. Rare and excellent.* (GOOD+) **$365.00**

W1-7. Bornstein, H.: Worlds Exposition Wrench. Chicago, 1893. Patented July 26, 1892. Length: 5 Inches. *If you attended the World's Exposition in Chicago in 1893, you might have picked up one of these wrenches at the Bornstein booth. If you were otherwise occupied, or perhaps not yet at the twinkle in the eye stage, we have just the wrench for you. A rare and very well preserved commemorative bicycle wrench. Rare. Ex-Cooley Collection.* (GOOD+) **$425.00**

W1-8. Joy, A.P., Rockingham, N.H.: "Joy Patent" Buggy Wrench. Nickel Plated 10 Inches. New Condition, Original Box. Length: 10 Inches. *The box for this perfectly preserved wrench has succumbed to the forces of time, but the graphics are in great shape, as are the original instructions. A rare wrench in this condition. Nice.* (FINE) **$295.00**

W1-9. Stanley Rule & Level: "The Triplet" Wrench. Patented August 19, 1913. Rare and Excellent. Length: 5 1/2 Inches. *The listing of this wrench on a Stanley packing slip confirms that these were offered to hardware dealers by Stanley. How they came to be included, if only briefly, in the product line remains a mystery.* (GOOD+) **$225.00**

W1-10. Portland Wrench Company: Combination Nut and Buggy Wrench. Smallest Size. Patented October 16, 1883. Length: 5 1/2 Inches. *This was the smallest size of "buggy" wrench offered by this firm. A baby carriage wrench, perhaps? A rare wrench in a most desirable size.* (GOOD+) **$165.00**

W1-11. Billings & Spencer Co., The No. 0: "Barwick Patent" Wrench. Patented June 6, 1871. Full Nickel Plating. Length: 8 1/2 Inches. *There was a fellow walking around at a recent tool meeting with the original patent papers for this wrench. He was looking for a wrench to go with the papers, which were not for sale, unless you had $1,000.00. An uncommon patented wrench in top collector quality condition.* (FINE) **$195.00**

W1-12. Lozier Mfg. Co., Cleveland, Ohio: "Wakefield Cycle" Wrench. "Cleveland Cycles". Rare and Excellent. Length: 6 Inches. *This was apparently a giveaway when you bought a bicycle from the Cleveland Cycle company. Most unusual.* (GOOD+) **$245.00**

W1-13. Merrick, S.: Merrick's Patent Nut Wrench. Patented August 17, 1835. Schulz No. 832. Length: 12 Inches. *The Merrick patent was one of the first patents granted for wrenches. This one is marked with the Merrick name, but not the patent date. A clean, sound, working example of an historically significant early wrench. A good one.* (GOOD+) **$325.00**

W1-14. Utility Wrench Co., New York: Patent Lever Adjust Wrench. Patented August 18, 1878. Rosewood and Nickel. Length: 4 1/2 Inches. *The Utility Wrench Company of New York City, the manufactures of this, "Atwater's Tiger Wrench", are believed by many to have produced the very finest precision adjustment wrenches ever made. This, the smallest size offered by this short-lived company, features a handle of Brazilian Rosewood and 80% of its original shiny nickel plating. The precision adjustment mechanism is in superb working condition. For the collector of small wrenches, we offer this as the cornerstone of a fine collection. Simply a great wrench.* (GOOD+) **$545.00**

W1-15. Holt Co., The G.L., Hartford, Conn.: Double Adjustable Wrench. Patent Applied For. Schulz No. 108. Length: 4 Inches. *The Holt company excelled at the manufacture of tools of many types. Although not their original intention, they entered the field of collectible wrench making when they put their name on this ill-advised invention.* (GOOD+) **$265.00**

W1-16. Billings & Spencer Co., The: Side Adjust Bicycle Wrench. Patented January 15, 1895. Made For Pope Manufacturing Company. Length: 5 1/2 Inches. *Here's a great example of a tool that is completely different from everything else. There are literally hundreds, if not thousands of variations on the bicycle wrench theme, but this seems to be the only one to have found it necessary to use the face of the wrench as a receiver for the adjustment screw. These were specially made for the Pope Manufacturing Company, undoubtedly for inclusion with their line of bicycles. A rare and unusual wrench.* (FINE) **$265.00**

W1-17. Baxter, William, Newark, N.J.: "Baxter's Patent" Wrench. Early Patent. Very Scarce Size. Length: 6 Inches. *A nice example of the early Baxter patent wrench. This one is clean, mechanically perfect and ready to display. A tough size to find.* (GOOD+) **$155.00**

W1-18. Bristol, C.B.: Revolving Nut Wrench. Patented June 26, 1855. Schulz No. 556. Length: 10 Inches. *A clean and extra-early rotating head nicely marked with the patent date. A survivor from the earliest age of wrench manufacture.* (GOOD+) **$245.00**

W1-19. Kone, G.W.: Patent Model(?) Wrench. With Original Tag. "Pat. Allowed". Length: 9 Inches. *The name G.W. Kone is inscribed on this wooden model for a wrench as is the notation "Pat. Allowed". While we are not of the sort likely to call anything that is not a tool, but looks like a tool, a "patent model", we note that one G.W. Kone did patent several wrenches, including one identical to this model. A rare model of a wrench that was patented.* (FINE) **$345.00**

W1-20. Smith & Co., H.D., Plantsville, Conn.: "Perfect Handle" Nut Wrench. Rare 21 Inch Size. Extra Crisp and Clean. Length: 21 Inches. *The products of the Perfect Handle Tool Company of Plantsville, Conn. were characterized by exceptional quality and finish, included their trademark wooden infill on the handles. The "monkey" wrenches made by this company were apparently quite popular, judging from the number that have survived. Examples of this, the largest size offered, at 21 inches, are scarce indeed. This is the only the second example we have had. The other is in the Donnelly collection. A rare "Perfect Handle" wrench.* (GOOD+) **$125.00**

W1-21. Coes & Co., L., Worcester, Mass.: 32 Inch Key Lock Wrench. Patented October 20, 1903. Excellent Condition. Length: 32 Inches. *A sliding wedge behind the jaw was the "Key" described in the patent papers. This 32 inch monster was by no means the largest size offered. Coes is known to have made a 6 foot version of this wrench, but we have yet to have an answer to our standing offer to pay $2500.00 for one of the big ones: (800) 869-0695.* (GOOD+) **$385.00**

W1-22. Gellman Wrench Corp. No. 61: Patented Adjustable Wrench. "Polly". Patented April 17, 1923. Length: 6 Inches. *This was the smallest of the quick-adjust "Polly" series produced by the Gellman Company. A great example in a desirable size.* (GOOD+) **$85.00**

W1-23. Wright Wrench Forging Co., The: Quick Adjust Nut Wrench. Patented March 15, 1904. Rare Small Size. Length: 6 Inches. *The "Wright" quick-adjust wrench had a practical design and was very well-made. Pushing on the back of the lower jaw depresses a spring that unlocks the jaw so it can slide freely into place. This was the smallest size offered.* (FINE) **$150.00**

W1-24. Parmenter, Geo. A., Boston, Mass.: Quick Adjust Combination Wrench. Patented October 6, 1915. With Instructions. Length: 7 Inches. *This small quick-adjust wrench has a pair of serrated jaws which are adjusted by means of a sliding, spring-lock jaw. The manufacturer advertised this tool as a combined pipe and nut wrench, but I wouldn't use it on either. Sometimes trying to do things ensures that neither one will be done adequately. An uncommon patented wrench, complete with the orignal instructions.* (FINE) **$295.00**

W1-25. Mossberg Co., Frank, Attleboro, Mass.: No. 2600: Boxed Set of Socket Wrenches. With Accessory Tools. New Condition, Original Box. Length: 16 Inches. *Here's a great set of Mossberg socket wrenches in their original fitted wooden box. A pair of cotter pin pullers add interest to this extra large set.* (FINE) **$235.00**

W1-26. B.W. Co., Newark, N.J.: Double End Adjustable Wrench. Patented December 1, 1868. Rare Small Size. Length: 4 Inches. *We would conjecture that this Baxter Patent wrench was made by the Baxter Wrench Company, who may have used the initials "B.W." A rare marked example in excellent condition.* (GOOD+) **$165.00**

W1-27. L. & S. Company, Cleveland, Ohio: "Steel Bicycle" Wrench. Desirbable Small Size. Rare and Excellent. Length: 5 Inches. *Why it is that one of the few bicycle wrenches ever made to have a wooden handle, rather than steel, should bill itself as the "Steel Bicycle" wrench is beyond my grasp. An uncommon small wrench in nice condition.* (GOOD) **$115.00**

W1-28. Imperial, Bloomington, Illinois: "Imp. Angle" Wrench. Patent Applied. For. Schulz No. 311 "B". Length: 9 Inches. *The Imperial Angle wrench is of the class of wrenches designated by the late Al Schulz as "Angle Wrenches". Here's a nice example of one mechanically interesting member of that class.* (GOOD+) **$85.00**

W1-29. Mossberg, Frank No. 74: Bicycle Monkey Wrench. Screw Adjust With Sleeve. Schulz No. 870. Length: 4 1/2 Inches. *A somewhat heavier duty version of the Frank Mossberg's more common bicycle wrenches, this one is clearly imprinted with the maker name and number designation. A good one.* (FINE) **$45.00**

W1-30. Johnson, Iver, Fitchburg, Mass.: Nickel Plated Bicycle Wrench. With Screwdrivers. "Pat. Appld. For". Length: 4 1/4 Inches. *This interesting and unusual bicycle wrench is fitted with a screwdriver accessory at the base of the handle. Most original nickel plating remains.* (GOOD+) **$245.00**

W1-31. Stanley Rule & Level: "The Triplet" Wrench. Patented August 19, 1913. Rare and Excellent. Length: 5 1/2 Inches. *The listing of this wrench on a Stanley packing slip confirms that these were offered to hardware dealers by Stanley. How they came to be included, if only briefly, in the product line remains a mystery.* (GOOD+) **$245.00**

W1-32. Trimont Mfg. Co., Roxbury, Mass.: No. A 6: Combination Pipe Wrench. With Screwdriver Tip. Rare and Excellent. Length: 6 Inches. *The tip of the handle removes to reveal a secret screwdriver. These are rare.* (GOOD+) **$345.00**

W1-33. Whitman & Barnes: "Bull Terrier" Alligator Wrench. Patented March 26, 1901. Not in Schulz. Length: 7 Inches. *Just when you thought you had seen them all, along comes the "Bull Terrier" wrench. This invention of questionable utility tool the classic "alligator" wrench, which was designed to be a "one size fits all" tool, and made it adjustable. Had this proved to be a marketing success, they undoubtedly would have gone on to produce sets of fixed size "Crescent" wrenches. A rare wrench.* (GOOD+) **$295.00**

W1-34. Bullard No. 0: Self-Adjusting Pipe Wrench. Patented October 27, 1903. Schulz No. 661. Length: 5 1/2 Inches. *According to Antique & Unusual Wrenches, the Bullard wrench was offered in a wide range of sizes. This, the smallest size ever offered, and by far the rarest of the bunch, is about as good as they get. A great collectible wrench in new condition.* (FINE) **$265.00**

W1-35. Park Metalware Co., Inc.: Multi-Head Wrench. "Xcel Multi-Head". Patented April 29, 1925. Length: 8 Inches. *This well made wrench features a series of interchangeable heads. It seems like a good idea, but in actual practice, the heads were probably quickly misplaced. All of the original components of this set are in new condition in their original box. Mint.* (FINE) **$110.00**

W1-36. Craftsman Tool Co., Conneaut, Ohio: Quick Adjust Pipe Wrench. With Rolling Wheel. Patented November 12, 1907. Length: 6 Inches. *Here's a well preserved example of the smallest size of the rolling-jaw Craftsman wrench. Nice.* (FINE) **$185.00**

W1-37. Amer. Circular Loom Co., Chelsea,: Electroplated Wrench. For Enameled Pipe. New Condition, Original Box. Length: 11 Inches. *Why a Loom Company would have produced a wrench is news to me. This early example is in new condition in its original box. Nice.* (FINE) **$165.00**

W1-38. Klein, Hilary: G.B. Phillips Patent Wrench. Patented July 21, 1857. Fitted Wooden Case. Length: 4 3/4 Inches. *Iowan Hillary Klein has spent most of the last twenty winters in his private machine shop producing high quality miniature replicas of classic patented wrenches. Each Spring, he brings out ten or so of each creation for distribution to those who are on his select "list". Fitted in the hinged walnut box that is a Klein tradmark, this example of the G.B. Phillips patent replica is in perfectly preserved condition. A rare contemporary collectible wrench.* (FINE) **$445.00**

W1-39. Blue Point No. C 70: Set of Open and Box End Wrenches. Original Pouch. Unused Condition. Length: 7 Inches. *The saying "they don't make 'em like they used to" applies to many things that were made within the memory of the readers of this volume. These early style "Blue Point" wrenches are in new condition in their original pouch. They don't make 'em like they used to.* (FINE) **$115.00**

W1-40. Reed Mfg. Co., Erie, Penn.: Twist Handle Nut Wrench. Distinctive Form. Rare and Excellent. Length: 5 1/2 Inches. *Turning the handle on this miniature nut wrench adjusts the width of the jaws. A rare "bicycle" size nut wrench in collector quality condition.* (GOOD+) **$285.00**

W1-41. Guild Machine Co., C.D., Attleboro: Quick Adjust Nut Wrench. "The Allright". Patented February 28, 1899. Length: 4 1/2 Inches. *This one features a sliding quick-adjust lower jaw that is locked into place when the nut is engaged. An uncommon quick-adjust wrench.* (FINE) **$145.00**

W1-42. Unmarked: Combination Jack and Buggy Wrench. Patented November 27, 1900. Unused Condition. Length: 21 Inches. *They probably didn't give out an award for the Most Stupid Idea in the category of Wrenches back in 1900, but if they had, this monstrosity would not have had to hug and congratulate anybody when the emcee opened the final envelope. Of all the idiotic ideas we have seen, the concept of a wrench for removing wheels also serving as a jack to lift them into place for removal seems so outwardly self defeating that we wonder what sort of person might have come up with such a hare brained concept. The copy of the original advertising, which is included in the makeshift case in which this tool came gives no clue as the name is nowhere to be found. Shame is a humbling thing. Apparently never used (we can imagine someone with a wheel in need of removing taking this thing out, thinking...thinking some more... and then whirling it golf club style into the adjacent woods in frustration) this collectible classic is in essentially new condition. A stupid idea and a really great wrench.* (FINE) **$675.00**

W1-43. Phillips, George B., Albany, N.Y.: Massive 25 Inch Patent Wrench. Patented May 3, 1859. Schulz No. 614. Length: 25 Inches. *The pre-Civil war patent of Albany, New York inventor George Phillips featured a sliding lower jaw mechanism. This example, at 25 inches in length, is the largest we have yet seen.* (GOOD+) **$225.00**

W1-44. Kraut, Henry, Summit, New Jersey: Prototype Wrenches. For Kraut Patent. Two Examples. Length: 9 3/4 Inches. *Those who have frequented past volumes of this publication are aware of the special delight that we take in analyzing the merits of any of the thousands of patented wrenches that history has bequeathed to the tool collecting community. Students will note that we find far fewer merits than we do flaws. If you are expecting a change in that pattern as we dissect the creative genius of Mr. Henry Kraut (we may need a microscope), then you are in line for disappointment. Shown complete with the patent papers which "protected" this monstrosity (and, apparently, its single-headed cousin, shown juxtaposed) from copying by technological highwaymen, this is the only instance of this rare patented wrench of which we are aware. Patented on September 17, 1912, the patent specifications go on, ad nauseum, to describe in technical detail the many merits of a tool that common sense dictates should never have been made. It may well be that Mr. Kraut though better of his "better mousetrap" and never sought to put it into production. In all likelihood, these two wrenches are the only models ever produced. A classic patented collectible wrench that fuses in a single object the twin spirits of invention and reckless enterprise that have been so much a part of American history, much to the delight of antique tool collectors.* (FINE) **$950.00**

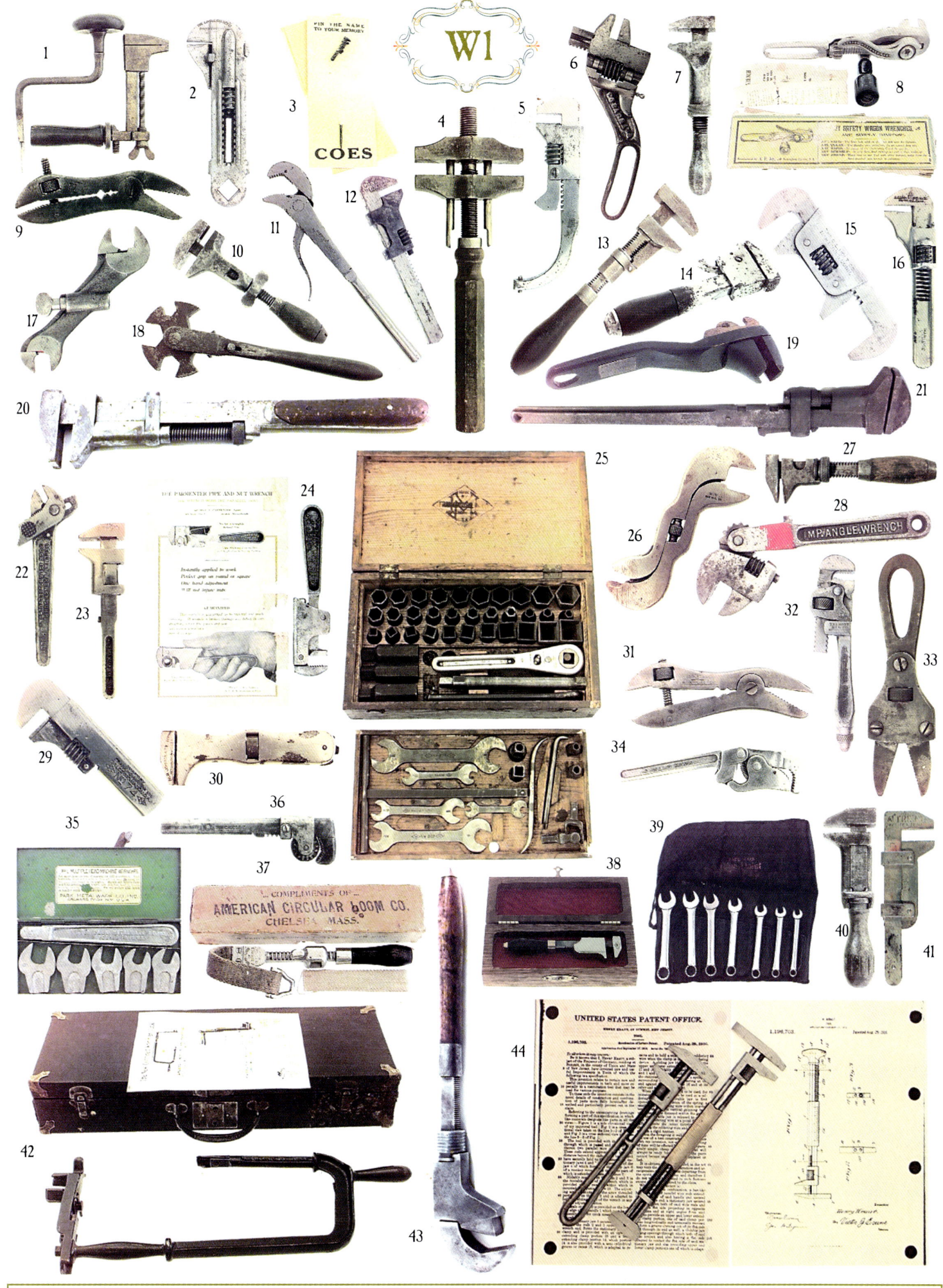

Group X1

X1-1. Lufkin Rule Co., The: No. 7181: Maple Wantage Rod. Extra Rare. Superb Condition. Length: 37 1/2 Inches. *An extra crisp and clean cask wantage rod by a maker who apparently made very few such rules. As good as they get.* (FINE) **$345.00**

X1-2. Hjorth Lathe and Tool Company No. 2: Precision Adjust Depth Gauge. Complete. New Condition, Original Box. Length: 7 Inches. *In addition to its line of machinery, the Hjorth Company briefly offered a line of precision measuring tools. This, the larger of their micrometer adjusting depth gauges is in new condition in the original box.* (FINE **$225.00**

X1-3. Keuffel & Esser Co., New York, N.Y. No. 83 0010: Surveyor's Brass Plumb Bob. With Retracting Reel. "Gammon Reel". Length: 6 Inches. *A brightly colored combination target and retractable plumb bob reel is attached to this well preserved surveyor's plumb bob from K. & E. This is the first we have seen of the "Gammon" reel.* (GOOD+) **$45.00**

X1-4. Chloride of Silver Battery Co., BA: Early Patent Electric Meter. Patented July 20, 1869. Original Paper Label. Length: 6 Inches. *Early electrical tools have a "look" about them that suggests their designers were aware that the technology with which they were working would change the world forever. This early patent meter retains its full original paper label on the underside and is clearly marked with several early patent dates. Nearly all original lacquer remains on the brass fittings. A classic of early technology.* (FINE) **$225.00**

X1-5. Stanley, W. F., London (England): Special Purpose Compass. Fitted Leather Case. Unknown Function. Length: 5 Inches. *A heavy leather case has kept this special function compass in excellent condition. We are not certain of its function.* (FINE) **$55.00**

X1-6. General Electric Corp., Schenectad: Surface Roughness Scale. Sight and Feel Scale. New Condition, Original Box. Length: 6 Inches. *The surface of this most unusual gauging device has been machined to a variety of different degrees of roughness. It was apparently used by engineers to evaluate metal finishes. This example has never been used. Mint.* (FINE) **$75.00**

X1-7. Marshall, I.: Early Carpenter's Name Stamp. With Scalloped Border. 18th Century Appearance. Length: 3 Inches. *At nearly every tool show the careful observer can find examples of the stamps that carpenters of the last century used to mark their tools. Examples from the Eighteenth Century, however are extremely rare. This classic stamp bears the imprint of one I. (probably John) Marshall and is bracketed with the classic "zig zag" border preferred by planemakers. Early and most unusual.* (GOOD+) **$185.00**

X1-8. Evans & Co., Old Change, London: Early Bronze Scarificator. Decorated Body. Original Case. Length: 2 3/4 Inches. *A German inscription on the case of this extra early blood letting device may be a clue as to the country of its manufacture. Etched on its bronze body with a decorative floral pattern and retaining nearly all of its original retinue of accessories, this early medical tool is in superb collector quality condition.* (FINE) **$485.00**

X1-9. Unmarked: Early Style Compass. With Mahogany Case. Uncommon Type. Length: 3 Inches. *The lens on this compass has a tight crack, but it is clear enough to see the very early printing on the face below.* (GOOD) **$55.00**

X1-10. Gurley, W. & L.E., Troy, N.Y.: Surveyor's Compass. Ca. 1895. New Condition, Original Box. Length: 17 Inches. *This pristine surveyor's compass lay undisturbed for more than a century before being discovered this past summer. Complete with its original tripod and protected by its original box, this tool retains 100% of all original finishes. A magnificent example of a classic American surveying instrument.* (FINE) **$2,475.00**

X1-11. Unmarked: Early Carpenter's Name Stamp. Owner "G. Mitchell". Chamfered Edges. Length: 3 Inches. *The name "G. Mitchell", in early-style lettering, could be imprinted with this carpenter's name stamp.* (GOOD+) **$25.00**

X1-12. Woods, A.W., Lincoln, Nebraska: "Steel Square Key" Calculator. With Tangent Table. Original Case, Instructions. Length: 4 Inches. *In my days on this earth I have met some house framers—the 28 ounce hammer in the leather holster on the belt types. You get the picture. Can you begin to imagine one of them sitting down with this Mr. Wizard gizmo before going to work? I don't think so. A carpenters tool for the mathematician.* (FINE) **$125.00**

X1-13. Strange, J.W., Bangor, Maine: Navigator's Brass Protractor. Near New Condition. Patented June 13, 1876. Length: 16 Inches. *Patented in 1876 and manufactured shortly thereafter, one would assume, a cache of the J.W. Strange navigator's protractors was discovered about 15 years ago in brand new condition. This example was one of the original find. It is in brand new condition and clearly marked with the patent date. A rare navigational tool.* (GOOD+) **$395.00**

X1-14. Brown & Sharpe Mfg. Co.: Patent Micrometer Depth Gauge. Patented January 11, 1896. Near New Condition. Length: 6 Inches. *A spring mechanism allows this one to be set in place with a plunger action, then locked with the turn of a screw. A previous owner, one "J.A.S." has lightly marked it with his initials, but in a barely visible way.* (FINE) **$85.00**

X1-15. Harling, W.H., London: Surveyor's Alidaide. Boxwood Base. Dated 1918. Length: 16 Inches. *The original leather case, together with an apparently total absence of use, has kept this boxwood surveyor's alidaide in the same condition as it was on the day it was made. Perfect.* (FINE) **$225.00**

X1-16. Haley & Son, London: Ivory Sector Folding Rule. For Navigation. Early and Excellent. Length: 12 Inches. *Sector rules were used in conjunction with a pair of dividers to perform precise mathematical calculations. This folding sector of ivory and German silver would have been found among the tools of a ship's navigator. A well preserved example of an early calculating device.* (GOOD+) **$165.00**

X1-17. Stephenson Mfr., A.M., Joliet, Illinois: Stylus Operated Calculator. "Agents Wanted". Near New Condition. Length: 3 1/2 Inches. *The reverse side of this stylus operated calculator (missing the stylus) is inscribed with the maker's name and the words "Agents Wanted". An uncommon early calculating device.* (FINE) **$85.00**

X1-18. Stanley Rule & Level: Surveyor's Set of Tools. Level, Stand and Sight. Uncommon Find. Length: 12 Inches. *Stanley offered this assortment as a group in its 1920's era catalogs for those who would be doing layout work. This working set has survived in essentially unused condition. All tools are in unused condition. A most unusual set. Highly recommended.* (FINE) **$585.00**

X1-19. Lufkin Rule Co., The No. 594: Surveyors Arrows. 10 Inch Size. New Condition, Original Box. Length: 10 Inches. *We have it on questionable authority that these were used by surveyors at the end of a hard day's work to prepare meat for roasting. These are new and in their original box. Mint.* (FINE) **$115.00**

X1-20. General Hardware Mfg. Co. No. 800: Brass Surveyor's Plumb Bob. Rmovable Tip. Near New Condition. Length: 4 Inches. *This later style bob is in unused condition. Mint.* (FINE) **$25.00**

X1-21. Unmarked: Carpenter's Name Stamp. "R. Cornell". Ca. 1890's. Length: 3 Inches. *"R. Cornell" was the name of the carpenter who used this stamp to mark his tools.* (GOOD+) **$15.00**

X1-22. F. Mc C.: Boxwood Surveyors Rules. Full Set of 10. With Matching Offsets. Length: 12 Inches. *In the days before computer-assisted design programs removed the need for manual skill in the practice of drafting and surveying, maps were drawn with sets such as this. Comprised of a series of 5 rules (numbered 1A through 1E), each with its own graduation scale, expressed in feet to the portion of an inch, together with a corresponding "offset" rule which was used to facilitate the drawing of lines that deviated from the perpendicular, this magnificent set of rules is in absolutely unused condition. Complete with the original green felt-lined fitted mahogany case, this set of precisely graduated boxwood rules is a classic example of the high quality tools that were once a necessary accessory for draughtsmen and surveyors. Mint.* (FINE) **$225.00**

X1-23. Brown & Sharpe Mfg. Company: No. 250: Precision Caliper and Micrometer. Uncommon Type. New Condition, Original Box. Length: 4 Inches. *This uncommon precision tool combined the function of caliper and micrometer in a tool that appears a little bit of each. Condition is perfect.* (FINE) **$145.00**

X1-24. Keuffel & Esser Co., New York: No. 83-0310: "Surveyor's" Machete. Made By Collins. New Condition, Original Box. Length: 28 Inches. *The collecting of tools in their original boxes has been much decried by self-styled purists and much celebrated by those for whom such tools hold special appeal. Whatever one's perspective, most would agree that the presence of the original box, imprinted with the words "Surveyor's Machete" on this otherwise common yet perfectly-preserved tool captures the spirit of the world of the surveyor as it once was. Images of a member of a team of engineers, involved in preparations to leave some sheltered city location for the laying out of a bridge or dam site in a tropical location, stopping into the distributor's salesroom and leaving with one of these under his arm come rushing to mind. Still wrapped in its original "Collins & Co." paper wrapping, this tool comes complete with the original box that has not only sheltered the tool, but also captured images of atime that was.* (FINE) **$295.00**

X1-25. Stanley Rule & Level No. 38: Cast Iron Leveling Stand. For Surveying. For Use With Stake. Length: 5 1/2 Inches. *Produced under a patent granted on August 24, 1915 to E.A. Schade of the Stanley Rule & Level Company, this leveling stand was included in the Stanley product line for more than 20 years. Complete examples are very difficult to find. Clean, complete and rare.* (GOOD+) **$195.00**

X1-26. Keuffel & Esser Co., New York, N.Y.: No. 89 1098: Surveyor's Clamp Handle. For Tape Measure. New Condition, Original Box. Length: 2 3/4 Inches. *As a maker of tape measures and the accoutrements of surveying, K. & E. would have been remiss if they did not produced one of these stretching devices for surveyor's tapes. They were not. New and in the box.* (FINE) **$65.00**

X1-27. Crosby Steam Gage & Valve, Boston: Precision Steam Gauge. Rules, Diagrams, Etc. New Condition, Original Box. Length: 12 1/2 Inches. *Without question the finest example of this precision tool that we have ever seen, the Crosby Steam Gauge was used for precision calculation of horsepower. Retaining all of its original shiny nickel plating and complete in a fitted oak box, this gauge comes with a series of pads used for making readings and a series of rules for performing calculations. Imprinted with a number of ca. 1880's patents, this 100 year old gauge is in essentially the same condition as the day it was made. Museum quality.* (FINE) **$845.00**

X1-28. Brown, Jas., St. Vincent St., Glas: Sykes' Hydrometer. With Book of Tables. New Condition, Original Box. Length: 9 1/2 Inches. *The Sykes Hrdrometer was used in the distilling industry to determine the alcohol level of a given product. Examples are relatively common. However, this superb example, which is imprinted with the name of a Scottish maker, also includes the book of original tables used in conjunction with the instrument. A rare and complete example of the Sykes Hydrometer.* (FINE) **$395.00**

X1-29. Keuffel & Esser Co., New York No. 999026: "Linemaster" Plumb Bob Reel. Crank Reel Type. New Condition, Original Box. Length: 3 1/4 Inches. *If you were one of those unfortunate enough to have a plumb bob without an internal winding reel (most were), this gizmo would provide you with additional functionality. An uncommon accessory to the world of Plumb Bobbery.* (FINE) **$65.00**

X1-30. Brown & Sharpe Mfg., Providence: No. 1: Open Screw Thread Micrometer. Patented April 22, 1878. Early and Excellent. Length: 2 1/2 Inches. *Perhaps the most important technological advance in the history of precision machining was the availability, for general use, of precision measurement. This process was brought about in the United States through the introduction, by the Brown & Sharpe Manufacturing Company of Providence, Rhode Island of a "sheet metal gauge" micrometer based on the "Systeme Palmer" invented in France. Early examples of this quantum leap in precision measurement took the form of the tool offered here, having exposed screw threads along the length of the spindle and substantially smaller than the 1" to 2" micrometers that would soon become the standard. The reverse side of this historically and technologically important tool is marked with the April 22, 1878 patent date and it is in excellent overall condition. Rare and important.* (GOOD+) **$485.00**

X1-31. Unmarked: Verner's Patent Sketching Pad. For Surveyor's Use. Original Pouch. Length: 10 Inches. *One of the most interesting of surveyor's tools, these devices were intended for use by a man on horseback, using a roll of paper mounted on the side reels, to produce a general sketch of the lay of the land in advance of a more precise survey. The leather strap was intended to attach to the forearm. A heavy leather case has kept this tool in brand new condition. Mint.* (FINE) **$385.00**

X1-32. Keuffel & Esser Co., New York: No. 6482: Brass Plumb Bob. For Surveyor's. 8 Oz. Size. Length: 5 Inches. *This K. & E. Classic was intended to be used by surveyors. It is clean and clearly marked with the K. & E. name.* (GOOD+) **$45.00**

X1-33. Hjorth Lathe and Tool Company: No. 1: Micrometer Adjust Depth Gauge. Rare Small Size. New Condition, Original Box. Length: 4 Inches. *This was the smaller of two sizes of micrometer depth gauges produced by this company. It is in new condition in its original box.* (FINE) **$225.00**

X1-34. Unmarked: "Pat. Pend." Stamp. Bold Block Letters. Unknown Function. Length: 4 Inches. *We will require certification of good character before this stamp is sold. Membership in the Arkansas Bar Association is not, in and of itself, sufficient proof for our purposes. A nice stamp, President's Honor.* (GOOD+) **$85.00**

X1-35. Gurley, W. & L.E., Troy, N.Y.: Surveyor's Level. With Integral Compass. New Condition, Original Box. Length: 13 1/2 Inches. *This most unusual and massive surveyors level features a compass mounted atop the level. Condition is as new. Complete with the original box and tripod.* (FINE) **$1,850.00**

X1-36. Unmarked: Cast Iron Plumb Bob. For Surveying? Original Lacquer Finish. Length: 2 Inches. *This is identical to the bob provided with Starrett's engineer's level. A good one.* (GOOD+) **$15.00**

X1-37. Fowler & Co., Manchester (England): Fowler's Textile Calculator. Short Scale Type. Marked "Patent". Length: 2 3/4 Inches. *The Fowler Company produced a line of circular calculators for many years. This specialized "Textile" calculator was used for the unique ciphering required in a textile mill. A rare calculator.* (FINE) **$345.00**

X1-38. Unmarked: Classic Surveyors Plumb Bob. Polished Brass Body. Elongated Form. Length: 5 1/2 Inches. *The form of this surveyor's bob is just a bit different from that normally encountered. A variation on a theme.* (GOOD) **$45.00**

X1-39. Cleveland Autmatic Machine Co.: No. 1 3/8: Brass Surveyor's Plumb Bob. Removable Cap. Original Box. Length: 4 Inches. *This is our first experience with the Cleveland Automatic Machine Company, but hey appear to have produced a high quality plumb bob. New and in the box.* (FINE) **$55.00**

X1-40. Gurley, W. & L.E., Troy, N.Y.: No. 18: Precision Surveyor's Chain. Extra Thin Wire. With Unusual Attachment. Length: 7 Inches. *A most interesting surveying accessory, this specialized chain is formed of extra thin wire and is fitted with a specialized tensioning attachment of unknown function. The loops at the end of the chain appear to have been designed to facilitate a hand grip. A rare and interesting surveyor's chain in excellent condition.* (FINE) **$745.00**

X1-41. Keuffel & Esser Co., New York: No. 6486: Surveyor's Brass Plumb Bob. Extra Large Size. Superb Condition. Length: 8 Inches. *This oversize plumb bob from K. & E. is clearly marked with their name. It is in top collector quality condition.* (FINE) **$225.00**

X1-42. Williams, Brown & Earle, Inc.: Calculating Instrument Catalogue. 12 Pages Ca. Slide Rules, Etc., E. Length: 9 Inches. *Slide rules from this company are quite scarce. If you get one, you can identify it with this.* (FINE) **$75.00**

X1-43. Standard Engineering Wks.: No. 6419-14: Surveyor's Plumb Bob. Removable Tip. Excellent Patina. Length: 5 3/4 Inches. *This plumb bob is the first tool we have offered from this company. A good one.* (GOOD+) **$35.00**

X1-44. Richardson, C.F., Athol, Mass.: Cast Iron Sighting Level. Patented August 16, 1887. Fine Condition, Original Box. Length: 36 Inches. *An early and extremely well preserved sighting level from Athol maker C.F. Richardson. Nearly all finishes remain on tube and level. Comes with the leveling stand in the original wooden box. A rare, early level in great shape.* (FINE) **$495.00**

X1-45. Webb, C.H., New York (Unmarked): Early Patent Calculator. Nickel Plated Case. Rare and Excellent. Length: 6 1/4 Inches. *The C.H. Webb calculator was, despite its complexity, a very successful and popular stylus operated calculator. This well preserved and mechanically perfect example is not marked with the maker's name, but is unmistakable owing to its distinctive form.* (GOOD+) **$395.00**

X1-46. Keuffel & Esser Co., New York: No. 83 0038: Surveyor's Brass Plumb Bob. In Green Box. New Condition, Original Box. Length: 6 Inches. *A perfectly preserved bob found in the same location the smaller size shown adjacent.* (FINE) **$85.00**

X1-47. Woods, A.W., Lincoln, Nebraska: "Steel Square Key" Calculator. With Tangent Table. Original Case, Instruction. Length: 4 Inches. *In my days on this earth I have met some house framers—the 28 ounce hammer in the leather holster on the belt types. You get the picture. Can you begin to imagine one of them sitting down with this Mr. Wizard gizmo before going to work? I don't think so. A carpenters tool for the mathematician.* (FINE) **$125.00**

X1-48. Lufkin Rule Co., The: "Bell System" Tape Measure. On Hand Reel. 200 Feet Length. Length: 12 Inches. *A most uncommon "Bell System" item, this extra long tape measure in in excellent overall condition. Scarce.* (GOOD+) **$55.00**

Group Y1

Y1-1. Reed, Utica (N. Y.): Pair of Quirk Ovolo, Astragal Planes. Marked 1/2 and 5/8. Double Boxed. Length: 9 1/2 Inches. *Here's a very well preserved pair of extra complex molding planes from a prominent Upstate New York maker. Ex-Cooley Collection.* (GOOD+) **$295.00**

Y1-2. Soule, L.S., Waldoboro, Maine: Cove and Bevel Molding Plane. With Applied Fence. AWP Iii: 3 Stars (B). Length: 9 1/2 Inches. *A reworked sole, an applied sole and some other evidence of use have not affected the bold imprint of Waldoboro, Maine maker L.S. Soule on this complex molding plane. A rare Maine mark.* (GOOD) **$75.00**

Y1-3. Sandusky Tool Co., Sandusky, Ohio: No. 124: Handled Beech Plow Plane. Boxwood Arms and Nuts. Extra Crisp and Clean. Length: 12 Inches. *The Sandusky Tool Company was very successful at the marketing of tools for the simple reason that the tools they produced were of extremely high quality. This handled beech plow with boxwood arms and nuts is a classic example of their best work. Crisp, clean and ready to use.* (FINE) **$295.00**

Y1-4. Routledge, 64 Bull St., Birmingham: Pair of Side Rabbet Molding Plane. Near New Condition. Ready to Use. Length: 9 1/2 Inches. *This perfectly preserved pair appear never to have been used. As good as they get.* (FINE) **$135.00**

Y1-5. Howland & Co., A., Auburn, N.Y.: No. 158: Boxed Bilection Molding Plane. Marked "3/4". Dated "1869". Length: 9 1/2 Inches. *A clean and usable boxed bilection plane by the last of the New York makers to employ prison contract labor. A very nice plane.* (GOOD+) **$210.00**

Y1-6. Reed, Utica (N. Y.): Special Purpose Bevel Molding Plane. For Sash Work? Rare and Near New. Length: 9 1/2 Inches. *Unlike any molding plane we have previously encountered, this special function skew rabbet molder has a sharp bevel to its sole that was made that way at the Reed factory. Undoubtedly designed for some special function, we are likely to be left to speculate about its intended use. Apparently never used for the task for which it was intended, this tool is in essentially new condition. Ex-Cooley Collection.* (FINE) **$475.00**

Y1-7. Unmarked No. 187: Pair of Table Joint Molding Planes. Marked "1/2". Manufactured Type. Length: 9 1/2 Inches. *Only the designation "No. 187" is imprinted on these fenced table joint molding planes in the 1/2 inch size. They are in excellent working order. Crisp, clean and ready to use.* (GOOD+) **$325.00**

Y1-8. Denison, J. & L., Saybrook, Conn.: Quirk Ogee and Square Molding Plane. 3 1/2 Inch O.A. Width. Extra Crisp and Clean. Length: 9 1/2 Inches. *This extra wide molder has an extra wrinkle to its profile and has been bored with a pair of holes through the body so that it can be pulled over the work with the assistance of some "carpenter's helpers". A dramatic wide molding plane excellent condition.* (GOOD+) **$215.00**

Y1-9. Rowell, S., Troy, N.Y.: Steep Quirk Ovolo, Astragal Molding Plane. Ca. 1828-1832. Near New Condition. Length: 9 1/2 Inches. *Molding profiles of the 1820's and 1830's were decidedly steeper and more complex than those of the 1840's and later. This perfectly preserved molder is a classic example of the earlier and more elaborate pattern.* (FINE) **$345.00**

Y1-10. Mc Master, Z. J., Auburn, N. Y.: Quirk Ovolo, Bead Molding Plane. Marked "3/8". Fully Boxed Bead. Length: 9 1/2 Inches. *A fully boxed bead profile is an indication that this ca. 1830's complex molder was made to be a bit better than most. A nice plane.* (GOOD+) **$125.00**

Y1-11. Peckham, P.M., Fall River, Mass.: Adjustable Sash Molding Plane. Rosewood Screws. Extra Bold Imprint. Length: 9 1/2 Inches. *A dramatic pair of rosewood screws provide a striking contrast to the light beech body and golden boxing on this self adjusting sash plane. Perry Mumford Peckham worked in Fall River from 1850 to 1860.* (GOOD+) **$265.00**

Y1-12. Copeland, D. & M.: Ovolo, Cove/Astragal Molding Plane. Marked "6/8". Uncommon Profile. Length: 9 1/2 Inches. *Here's a crisp, clean molder with a profile having that "something extra" that makes for a great molding profile. A most unusual configuration in excellent condition.* (GOOD+) **$285.00**

Y1-13. Malloch, D., Perth (Scotland): Classic Toothing Plane. Original Iron. Near New Condition. Length: 7 Inches. *Here's an excellent working toothing plane from a prominent Scottish maker in top working order. Nice.* (FINE) **$95.00**

Y1-14. Lyon & Smith, Cincinnati Ohio: Quirk Ogee Molding Plane. Ca. 1850's. AWP Iii: 2 Stars. Length: 9 1/2 Inches. *Joseph Lyon and John Smith are known to have made planes in Cincinnati from 1849 to 1853. This molder is missing a small piece of boxing in the back but is otherwise clean, sound and clearly marked.* (GOOD+) **$95.00**

Y1-15. Bartlett, A.C. No. 119: Handled Beechwood Plow Plane. Made By Sandusky. Right Hand Handle. Length: 10 Inches. *The handle of this handled beech plow is contoured to accommodate the hand of a right-handed user. Most likely made for Bartlett by the Sandusky Tool Company, it is in excellent condition and ready to use, if you choose.* (GOOD+) **$195.00**

Y1-16. Fisk, S.: Panel Raising Plane. Early Appearance. Yellow Birch Body. Length: 12 1/2 Inches. *The maker mark "S. Fisk" has been boldly struck on the end of this Yellow Birch panel raiser, which is lacking its wedge and iron, but is otherwise excellent. Two other examples of this imprint are known. A legitimate Five Star plane.* (GOOD+) **$345.00**

Y1-17. Unmarked: Early Cove, Astragal Molding Plane. Figured Beech Body. Decorative Chamfers. Length: 9 Inches. *This craftsman made 18th Century molder is in excellent working order. A bargain.* (GOOD+) **$115.00**

Y1-18. Baldwin, A. & E., New York: Steep Quirk Ovolo, Bevel Molding Plane. Marked "1 1/4". Crisp and Clean. Length: 9 1/2 Inches. *This oversize molder produced by New York City planemakers Austin and Elbridge Gerry Baldwin is in great condition and clearly marked with the makers' imprint. Nice.* (GOOD+) **$165.00**

Y1-19. Moore, William, (New York): Quirk Ogee, Bevel Molding Plane. Undocumented Mark. Marked "4/8". Length: 9 1/2 Inches. *William Moore was a hardware dealer in New York City from 1844 to 1847, he may have been a planemaker in Baltimore, Maryland before that time. This molder is in great working order and clearly marked. A rodent sampled the side of the wedge at one point, but then moved on to something more palatable.* (GOOD+) **$95.00**

Y1-20. Parkhurst, J., (Springfield, N.J.): Steep Cove, Astragal Molding Plane. Ca. 1850's. Rare N.J. Imprint. Length: 9 1/2 Inches. *One of New Jersey's least common planemakers, Charles Parkhurst worked in Newark from 1835 to an undetermined time. This complex molder has a wedge shape that is distinctly different from that shown in American Wooden Planes.* (GOOD+) **$165.00**

Y1-21. Semple & Bro., A.B., Louisville, Kentuky: 1/2 Inch Groove Molding Plane. Ca. 1839-1859. AWP Iii: 3 Stars. Length: 9 1/2 Inches. *The mark of this Louisville hardware dealership rates 3 stars for rarity in American Wooden Planes. A tough mark to find.* (GOOD+) **$95.00**

Y1-22. Benson & Mockridge: Steep Cove and Astragal Molding Plane. Marked "7/8". Extra Crisp and Clean. Length: 9 1/2 Inches. *This massive cove and astragal molder dates from 1830-1831, when this obscure partnership worked in Albany, New York. A dramatic complex molder from an obscure Albany planemaking partnership.* (FINE) **$245.00**

Y1-23. Manchester, P.H., (Providence, R.I.): Pair of Snipe Bill Molding Planes. Ca. 1843-1859. Near New Condition. Length: 9 1/2 Inches. *Snipe bill molding planes by American makers are just a bit more common than chicken teeth. These are very nicely boxed, clearly marked and in excellent working order. A pretty pair.* (FINE) **$225.00**

Y1-24. Baldwin, A. & E., New York: 1/2 Inch Dado Molding Plane. Adjustable Depth. Ready to Use. Length: 9 1/2 Inches. *Here's a crispy clean adjustable dado plane in the desirable 1/4 inch size. Ready to use.* (GOOD+) **$55.00**

Y1-25. Unmarked: Quadruple Reed Molding Plane. With Adjustable Fence. Owner "A. Johnson". Length: 8 1/2 Inches. *A cast iron fence regulate the distance from the edge of the work on this early and interesting quadruple reed plane. it looks like it would be a handy working tool. Ready to use.* (GOOD+) **$165.00**

Y1-26. Moss, Wm., Birmingham, England: Early Complex Molding Plane. Ca. 1775-1797. Spectacular Profile. Length: 9 1/2 Inches. *A photograph can not do justice to the complexity of the profile of this 18th Century molding plane. Most likely produced for use on picture frame moldings, it forms an extremely elaborate cut. Extra nice.* (GOOD+) **$395.00**

Y1-28. Collins, Utica: Quirk Ovolo and Bevel Molding Plane. Marked "5/8". Ready to Use. Length: 9 1/2 Inches. *Here's an excellent wide molder in excellent working condition from a prominent Upstate New York planemaker. Ready to use.* (GOOD+) **$95.00**

Y1-29. Danberry, E., N. Brunswick, N. J.: 1/2 Inch Boxed Bead Molding Plane. Ca. 1850. Rare Full Boxing. Length: 9 1/2 Inches. *Bead planes were subjected to such hard use that it is surprising that more of them were not ordered with the optional "full boxing". Examples such as this are quite uncommon. Extra nice.* (GOOD+) **$85.00**

Y1-30. Unmarked: Yellow Birch Smooth Plane. With Double Iron. Imprint "G.W.P.". Length: 7 3/4 Inches. *Only the maker's initials "G.W.P." are imprinted on this classic yellow birch molder. A classic.* (GOOD+) **$65.00**

Y1-31. Unmarked: Massive Rabbet Plane. With Brass Depth Stop. Imprint "S.E.". Length: 17 Inches. *An adjustable fence regulates the width of the cut on this classic handled rabbeting plane. A stylized imprint of the initials "S.E." has been struck on the toe.* (GOOD) **$165.00**

Y1-32. Reed, Utica (N. Y.): Massive Ogee Molding Plane. Marked "8/8". Near New Condition. Length: 9 1/2 Inches. This massive ogee molder has been boldly struck with the Reed imprint. It is in nearly new condition. *Ex-Cooley Collection.* (FINE) **$175.00**

Y1-33. Mc Master, Z. J., Auburn, N. Y.: Ovolo, Cove/Bead Molding Plane. Marked "3/8". Extra Crisp and Clean. Length: 9 1/2 Inches. *Narrow complex molding planes in this condition have become nearly impossible to find. This one is as good as they get. Highly recommended. Ex-Cooley Collection.* (FINE) **$265.00**

Y1-34. Sandusky Tool Co., Ohio: No. 152: Quadruple Reed Molding Plane. Marked 3/8 Inch. With Applied Fence. Length: 9 1/2 Inches. *A previous owner of this well made fenced reeding plane bored a "hang hole" in the back to keep this well made tool within easy reach. This was acquired at the Phipps Tool Museum auction together with a number of similar fenced reeding planes.* (GOOD+) **$245.00**

Y1-35. Marley, New York: Intricate Complex Molding Plane. Ovolo, Cove/Astragal. Most Unusual Profile. Length: 9 1/2 Inches. *This extra-complex molder by Luke Marley has more dips and drops than most. A nice one.* (GOOD+) **$275.00**

Y1-36. Currie, Glasgow, Scotland: Pair of Tongue and Groove Molding Planes. 3/4 Inch Size. Crisp and Clean. Length: 9 1/2 Inches. *Here's a crispy clean and ready to use pair of tongue and groove molders from Scottish maker Daniel Currie.* (GOOD+) **$85.00**

Y1-37. Reed, Utica (N. Y.): Adjustable Door Molding Plane. Screw Adjustment. Near New Condition. Length: 9 1/2 Inches. *Used for the specialized task of making paneled doors, these planes were not found among the tools of the average carpenter. This example seems to have been very little used. Ex-Cooley Collection.* (FINE) **$345.00**

Y1-38. Baldwin, A. & E., New York: Quirk Ogee With Bevel Molding Plane. Marked 3/4. Ca. 1830-1841. Length: 9 1/2 Inches. *This Baldwin molder has a steeper than normal cut to its wide profile. A classic molding plane.* (FINE) **$225.00**

Y1-39. Creagh & Pickard, Cincinnati, Ohio: Steep Quirk Ovolo, Bevel Molding Plane. Ca. 1829. AWP Iii: 2 Stars. Length: 9 1/2 Inches. *One of the many planemaking partnerships formed in the dynamic Western city of Cincinnati, Ohio, Creagh & Pickard are known to have worked around 1829 only. This elaborate molder was likely used to build one of the early "great houses" of that city. A dramatic complex molding plane.* (GOOD+) **$255.00**

Y1-40. Mc Master, Z. J., Auburn, N. Y.: Classic Bilection Molding Plane. Marked "3/8". Extra Crisp and Clean. Length: 9 1/2 Inches. *Here's an excellent small bilection molder in top collector quality condition. Nice.* (FINE) **$165.00**

Y1-41. Fuller, Jo., Providence: Quarter Round Molding Plane. Yellow Birch Body. Marked "3/8". Length: 10 Inches. *Executed with the planemaking artistry that characterizes the early work of this maker, this Yellow Birch molder has been boldly struck with the Jo. Fuller imprint. A very nice early plane. Ex-Cooley Collection.* (GOOD+) **$445.00**

Y1-42. Reed, Utica (N. Y.): Steep Quirk Ogee, Bevel Molding Plane. Marked "3/4". Near New Condition. Length: 9 1/2 Inches. *Wide complex molding planes in this condition are not often found. This one has been very little used. Ex-Cooley collection.* (FINE) **$165.00**

Y1-43. Scovill, J. (Johnstown, N.Y.): 7/8 Inch Rabbet Molding Plane. Ca. 1827-1838. AWP Iii: 1 Star. Length: 9 1/2 Inches. *The distinctive imprint of Johnstown, New York planemaker John Scovill appears on the toe of this clean rabbet plane. Scovill eventually abandoned planemaking for a career as an Episcopal priest.* (GOOD+) **$65.00**

Y1-43. Kirk & Asling, Nottingham: Compass Sole Smooth Plane. With Boxwood Stop. Ca 1880's. Length: 7 1/2 Inches. *Nosing planes were used for rounding the edges of wide boards, such as stair treads. This example, which was intended for use with 1 3/8 Inch stock lumber, is in very crisp, clean condition.* (GOOD+) **$85.00**

Y1-44. Scott, W., Pittsburgh, Penn.: Quirk Ovolo/Astragal Molding Plane. Extra Steep Profile. AWP Iii: 3 Stars. Length: 9 1/2 Inches. *This extraordinarily well preserved complex molder dates from the earliest days of Pittsburgh history. Scott worked from 1819 to 1839. A rare Pennsylvania complex molding plane.* (GOOD+) **$345.00**

Y1-45. Oothoudt, J.: Ovolo, Bevel/Cove, Astragal Molding Plane. Rare N.Y.(?) Maker. Excellent Example. Length: 9 1/2 Inches. *The obscure Ooothoudts were planemakers who most likely worked in Upstate New York. This extraordinarily complex molder has been boldly struck with the J. Oothoudt imprint. Only a small sliver of wood from the base deserves mention as an apology. Ex-Cooley Collection.* (GOOD+) **$345.00**

Y1-46. Wetherell, H., Chatham: Panel Raising Plane. With "Cartouche". Yellow Birch Body. Length: 12 1/2 Inches. *Missing its original wedge and iron, which may account for the superb condition in which it is found today, this early Yellow Birch molder has the classic "cartouche" mark adjacent to the Wetherell, Chatham imprint. A classic early plane and a potential project.* (GOOD+) **$185.00**

Group Z1

Z1-1. Buck Bros., Millbury, Mass.: 3/4 Inch Crank Neck Chisel. Extra Clean and Sharp. Ready to Use. Length: 12 1/2 Inches. *Here's an older style bevel edge crank neck chisel in the desirable 3/4 inch size. Crisp, clean and ready to use.* (GOOD+) **$55.00**

Z1-2. White, L. & I.J., Buffalo, N.Y.: Special Purpose Chisel. Unknown Function. As New Condition. Length: 6 Inches. *A thorough search through all the L. & I.J. White literature we have found no mention of this specialized edge tool, which features a handle welded to a short, chisel-like device. Most unusual and absolutely perfect.* (FINE) **$85.00**

Z1-3. Buck Bros., Millbury, Mass.: 1/8 Inch Crank Neck Chisel. Extra Clean and Sharp. Original Fruitwood Handle. Length: 11 3/4 Inches. *This 1/8 inch crank neck chisel retains its original turned fruitwood handle and is in superb working order. A tough size to find in this configuration.* (FINE) **$55.00**

Z1-4. Addis & Sons, J. B., Sheffield: Pair of Front Bent Carving Tool. Marked "28" and "30". Excellent Condition. Length: 8 Inches. *Both of these tools came from the kit of the same woodcarver, both are in essentially new condition. Mint.* (FINE) **$125.00**

Z1-5. Sorby, I. , (England): Tang Mortise Chisel. 1/2 Inch Size. Boxwood Handle. Length: 13 Inches. *These English tang chisels are great working tools. This one is ready to use.* (GOOD+) **$45.00**

Z1-6. Taylor Ltd., Henry, Sheffield: Group of 5 Assorted Carving Tools. From Single Owner. Ready to Use. Length: 9 Inches. *Here's a nice assortment of carving tools from Sheffield maker Henry Taylor. All are in excellent working order.* (GOOD+) **$115.00**

Z1-7. Addis, S.J., London: Set of 4 Flat Gouge Carving Tools. From Single Owner. Ready to Use. Length: 9 Inches. *The blades of this flat gouges are clean and shiny and the edges are sharp.* (GOOD+) **$75.00**

Z1-8. Marples & Son, Wm., Sheffield: Lock Mortise Chisel. 1/2 Inch Size. Original Decal. Length: 18 Inches. *Another nice mortise chisel. This one has part of the original decal on the side not shown in the photograph. I'm the guy who takes the pictures at the family reunion where half of everybody's head is cut off. A nice chisel, trust me.* (GOOD+) **$75.00**

Z1-9. Buck Brothers: Heavy Socket Chisel. 1 Inch Size. Near New Condition. Length: 15 Inches. *Nearly all finishes remain on this heavy socket framing chisel from quality makers Buck Brothers of Millbury, Massachusetts. Ready to use.* (FINE) **$75.00**

Z1-10. Buck Bros., Millbury, Mass.: Group of 4 Assorted Carving Tools. Original Handles. Ready to Use. Length: 9 1/2 Inches. *Each of these pristine Buck Brothers carving tools retains its original fruitwood handle and is in nearly new condition. Nice.* (FINE) **$95.00**

Z1-11. Stanley Rule & Level: Set of 3 Stanley Cold Chisels. Stanley and Atha. Extra Crisp and Clean. Length: 5 Inches. *Each of these cold chisels is marked with the Stanley imprint, including one with the elusive "Atha" mark. All are in excellent condition.* (FINE) **$35.00**

Z1-12. Stanley Rule & Level No. 750: Set of 7 Bevel Edge Chisels. Extra Crisp and Clean. Ready to Use. Length: 9 Inches. *Here's a nice working set of Stanley's bevel edge butt chisels. Ready to use.* (GOOD+) **$185.00**

Z1-13. Jessop: Removable Handle Chisel. "Pat. Pending". Very Rare. Length: 12 Inches. *The idea here was to have one handle and many chisel blades. Never seen another.* (GOOD+) **$85.00**

Z1-14. Swan Co., The James, Seymour, Conn.: Heavy Socket Mortise Chisel. 5/16 Inch Size. New Old Stock. Length: 15 1/2 Inches. *Here's an extra crisp and clean mortise chisel from a highly respected maker.* (FINE) **$55.00**

Z1-15. Addis, S. J., London: Piar of Front Bent Carving Tools. Extra Deep Cuts. Ready to Use. Length: 9 1/4 Inches. *These front bent gouges have steeper than usual cuts. Both are in excellent working condition.* (GOOD+) **$115.00**

Z1-16. Stanley Rule & Level No. 750: Bevel Edge Socket Chisel. 1 1/4 Inch Width. Brand New Condition. Length: 10 Inches. *This 1 1/4 inch butt chisel has never been used. Perfect.* (FINE) **$45.00**

Z1-17. Assorted Makers: Group of 10 Assorted Carving Tools. Gouges, Etc.. Ready to Use. Length: 9 1/2 Inches. *Here's a nice assortment of carving tools from a variety of makers, including a few that are not marked. All are in usable condition.* (GOOD+) **$145.00**

Z1-18. Unmarked: 2 Inch Laminated Framing Chisel. Extra Heavy Type. Excellent Condition. Length: 15 3/4 Inches. *Heavy socket chisels are used by timber framers for cleaning up large mortise joints. This one is in ready to use condition.* (GOOD+) **$55.00**

Z1-19. Underhill: 1/2 Inch Socket Mortise Chisel. For Framing. Ready to Use. Length: 15 1/2 Inches. *The blade on this uncommon 1/2 inch socket mortise chisel is straight, sharp and ready to use. A well preserved chisel from a top maker.* (GOOD+) **$55.00**

Z1-20. Douglass Mfg. Co.: Heavy Socket Corner Chisel. 1 Inch Size. Applied Steel Edge. Length: 16 Inches. *An exceptionally clean socket corner chisel from a prominent New England Maker. The original handle is also in excellent shape.* (GOOD+) **$65.00**

Z1-21. Maiers, C.: Set of 30 Assorted Carving Tools. From Single Owner. Respected Maker. Length: 8 Inches. *Painstakingly assembled by a single carver who regarded this maker as the very best, these carving tools include a wide variety of shapes and sizes. All are in excellent working order and ready to use.* (GOOD+) **$465.00**

Z1-22. Stanley Rule & Level No. 720: 7/8 Inch Bevel Edge Chisel. Unused Condition. Rare and Excellent. Length: 14 Inches. *This extra long No. 720 chisel has never been used. Mint.* (FINE) **$65.00**

Z1-23. New Haven Edge Tool Co.: Heavy Socket Corner Chisel. Rare 1/2 Inch Size. As New Condition. Length: 15 1/2 Inches. *Corner chisels in the 1/2 inch size are tough to come by in any condition. This one is brand new. Perfect.* (FINE) **$165.00**

Z1-24. Union Hardware Co., Torrington, Conn.: Heavy Socket Framing Chisel. 1 Inch Size. New Condition. Length: 16 Inches. *This one was packed in the original cosmoline when it came into my hands. The chisel is now clean, but my hands are not. A great tool now cleansed of this hellish goo.* (FINE) **$75.00**

Z1-25. Herring Bros., London (England): Group of 6 Carving Tool. Bent Gouges, Etc.. Ready to Use. Length: 9 Inches. *Each of these Herring Brothers carving chisels came from the tools of a single woodcarver. All are in excellent working condition.* (GOOD+) **$155.00**

Z1-26. Sears, Roebuck & Co.: Mortise Boring Chisel Sets. For Drill Press. Unused Condition. Length: 8 Inches. *Never having bought any of these things new, we would imagine that they are quite expensive. A bargain.* (FINE) **$65.00**

Z1-27. Addis, S.J., London: 3 Deep Gouge Carving Tool. From Single Owner. Ready to Use. Length: 8 1/2 Inches. *Each of these gouges is a bit steeper and wider than usual. All are in excellent working order.* (GOOD+) **$125.00**

Z1-28. Addis, S.J., London: 4 Front Bent Gouge Carving Tools. From Single Owner. Ready to Use. Length: 9 3/4 Inches. *These front bent gouges came from a single drawer in a chest of carving tools, where they must have been kept together for ease of use. A very nice set.* (GOOD+) **$165.00**

Z1-29. Union Hardware Co.: Heavy Socket Corner Chisel. 1 Inch Size. Unused Condition. Length: 16 Inches. *This one inch heavy socket corner chisel appears never to have been used. An old tool in new condition.* (FINE) **$85.00**

Z1-30. Barton & Co., D.R., Rochester, N.Y.: 1 3/4 Inch Flat "Tang" Chisel. Original Handle. Extra Crisp and Clean. Length: 16 Inches. *There was a time when we found these in the toolboxes of patternmakers, back when we found toolboxes full of patternmakers tools. This classic tang chisel is in working condition. It dates from ca. 1880 or thereabout.* (FINE) **$55.00**

Z1-31. Buck Bros., Millbury, Mass.: Massive 2 Inch Paring Chisel. Fruitwood Handle. Extra Crisp and Clean. Length: 17 Inches. *Here's a 2 inch paring chisel to last a lifetime. Absolutely perfect and ready to use. A classic.* (FINE) **$75.00**

Z1-32. Unmarked: Heavy Socket Framing Chisel. 1 1/2 Inch Size. Crisp and Clean. Length: 15 1/2 Inches. *Someone has taken the trouble to fit this one out with a brass ferrule and it is otherwise in great condition. A good working tool at a bargain price.* (FINE) **$45.00**

Z1-33. Peck, Stow & Wilcox Co.: Heavy Socket Framing Chisel. 2 Inch Width. Ready to Use. Length: 17 Inches. *No apologies whatsoever for this very well preserved heavy socket corner chisel in the desirable 2 inch size. Ready to use.* (GOOD+) **$75.00**

Z1-34. Buck Brothers: 1 Inch Crank Neck Chisel. Desirable Size. Ready to Use. Length: 15 1/2 Inches. *Complete with its original turned fruitwood handle, this 1 inch crank neck paring chisel is ready to be put immediately to work.* (FINE) **$85.00**

Z1-35. Chapin, A., Troy (N.H.?): Early Socket Chisel. Uncommon Maker. Excellent Condition. Length: 15 Inches. *The Directory of American Toolmakers reports an A. Chapin mark from Troy on a cooper's drawknife, but is uncertain of the location. There is a Troy in both New York and New Hampshire. The chisel that launched a thousand ships.* (GOOD) **$65.00**

Z1-36. Stanley Rule & Level No. 99: "Atha Brand" Cold Chisel. 5/8 Inch Size. Scarce and Excellent. Length: 6 Inches. *Stanley's acquisition of the Atha Tool Company of Newark, New Jersey was intended to provide them a prominent position in the manufacture of metalworking tools. The reality of the Roosevelt Depression of the 1930's made them quickly reduce the Atha line. By the end of the Second World War, it had been virtually eliminated.* (GOOD+) **$25.00**

Z1-37. Blue Point: Set of "Supreme" Punches and Chisels. Original Pouch. Unused Condition. Length: 4 1/2 Inches. *Early brand name automotive tools are becoming increasingly collectible. These "Blue Point" chisels are the type of tool that the collectors are looking for. Perfectly preserved in the original pouch.* (FINE) **$115.00**

Z1-38. Stanley Rule & Level No. 720: Set of 4 Socket Chisel. Extra Long Type. 1 1/2 Inch, 1 Inch, 3/4 Inch, 1/2 Inch. Length: 14 Inches. *Here's an excellent working set of Stanley's extra long No. 720 paring chisels. Ready to be put immediately to work.* (GOOD+) **$145.00**

Z1-39. Assorted Makers: Group of 7 Assorted Carving Tools. Gouges, Etc. Ready to Use. Length: 9 1/2 Inches. *Sizes and shapes of every sort are included in this hodgepodge for the wood carver. A nice set.* (GOOD+) **$95.00**

Z1-40. Berg, Erik, Eskilstuna, Sweden: 1 3/4 Inch "Shark" Chisel. Bakelite Handle. Superb Condition. Length: 8 1/2 Inches. *The later type "Shark" chisels employed the more resilient, if aesthetically challenging bakelite handles, but the steel was always of the very first quality. A top quality chisel.* (FINE) **$45.00**

Z1-41. Buck Bros., Millbury, Mass.: 3/4 Inch Crank Neck Chisel. Extra Clean and Sharp. Fruitwood Handle. Length: 12 Inches. *Most of the original blued finish remains on this perfectly preserved bevel edge paring chisel.* (FINE) **$75.00**

Z1-42. Unmarked: Set of "Riffler" Rasps. For Carving, Etc. Ready to Use. Length: 7 Inches. *Designed to fit into nooks and crannies formed by the carver's chisels and gouges, these "riffler" rasps are in excellent working order and ready to do just that.* (FINE) **$35.00**

Z1-43. Assorted Makers: Set of Front Bent Carving Tools. Addis, Marples, Etc. Excellent Condition. Length: 11 Inches. *Here's an excellent working set of front bent gouges from top edge tool makers. Crisp, clean and ready to use.* (GOOD+) **$145.00**

Z1-44. Buck Bros., Millbury, Mass.: 3/8 Inch Crank Neck Chisel. Extra Clean and Sharp. Original Fruitwood Handle. Length: 11 3/4 Inches. *This 3/8 inch crank neck chisel is as good as they get. Ready to be put immediately to use.* (FINE) **$55.00**

Z1-45. Addis, S.J., London: 3 Flat Gouge Carving Tools. From Single Owner. Ready to Use. Length: 8 1/2 Inches. *These wide, flat gouges are crisp, clean and ready to use. Addis quality.* (GOOD+) **$95.00**

Z1-46. Ash & Co., Wm.: Special Purpose Gouge. 180 Degree Bend. Early and Excellent. Length: 12 1/2 Inches. *This most unusual woodcarving gouge forms a "U" shape at the tip. Wm. Ash & Company worked at the end of the 18th and the beginning of the 19th Centuries.* (GOOD+) **$95.00**

Z1-47. Unmarked: Solid Steel Corner Chisel. Octagonal Shaft. Ready to Use. Length: 16 Inches. *This extra heavy duty corner chisel is forged from a single piece of steel. The shaft and head have a most appealing octagonal form. A most unusual corner chisel in ready to use condition.* (GOOD+) **$75.00**

Z1-48. Maiers, C.: Set of 27 Assorted Carving Tools. From Single Owner. Respected Maker. Length: 8 Inches. *All of these chisels were assembled by a single carver over a long career because he believed that these were the very best chisels made. A great working set of carving tools in top working order. Ready to use.* (GOOD+) **$445.00**

Z1-49. Mayhew Steel Products, Inc., Mass. No. 840: Set of "All Steel" Chisel. Original Decals. New Condition, Original Box. Length: 9 1/2 Inches. *These Mayhew chisels are in exactly the same condition as they were when they were made. New and in the original box.* (FINE) **$95.00**

Z1-50. Addis, S.J., London: Set of 18 Assorted Carving Tools. Owner "Hodgkins". Fruitwood Handles. Length: 9 Inches. *All of the tools in this superb set of carving tools from S.J. Addis are imprinted with the name of their owner, one "Hodgkins", on the handles. A great working set in absolutely top condition. Nice.* (FINE) **$645.00**

Group A2

A2-1. Unmarked: Early Chisel Axe. With "Cartouche". Rare and Excellent. Length: 18 Inches. *This early hand forged chisel axe was the first cousin of the twybil. Both edge tools are of ancient origin and are the tools from which modern edge tools were derived. This example has been boldly marked with a stylized "cartouche" by its maker. Rare, early and ready to display.* (GOOD) **$365.00**

A2-2. White, H.G.: Rare "Claw" Felling Axe. Near New Condition. Original Handle. Length: 34 Inches. *And now for something completely different....This is our first-ever claw axe. Any ideas about its use, or who H.G. White might have been? The imprint is most definitely that of a manufacturer. A rare variation on a pair of discordant themes.* (FINE) **$285.00**

A2-3. Blood, I., Ballston, N.Y.: 12 Inch Broad Axe. Early Offset Handle. Ready to Use. Length: 23 1/2 Inches. *The axes made by Isaiah Blood at Ballston Spa, New York were particularly respected in their day for their high quality. Here's a nice example in ready to use condition.* (GOOD+) **$225.00**

A2-4. Unmarked: "American Beauty" Axe. Rare Double Bit. Extra Crisp Logo. Length: 9 Inches. *The "American Beauty" is not mentioned in the embossed axe book and there is no indication of who made them on the axe head. We have had several single bit axes so-marked, but this is the only double bit bearing this logo that we have seen. A good one.* (GOOD+) **$295.00**

A2-5. Norton Tool Co.: Promotional Hatchet. Atlantic City, 1903. Rare and Excellent. Length: 12 Inches. *If you missed the big hardware dealers convention in Atlantic City in 1903, here's your last chance for a souvenir. A rare promotional item.* (GOOD+) **$125.00**

A2-6. Unmarked: "Fulton Clipper" Axe. Deep Embossed. Rare and Excellent. Length: 29 Inches. *This example of the "Fulton Clipper" embossed axe is the only one I have ever seen. Artfully decorated and ready to add to a collection of these American originals.* (GOOD+) **$345.00**

A2-7. Kelley-How-Thomson Co., Duluth, Minn.: "Hickory" Embossed Axe. From North Minnesota. Uncommon Imprint. Length: 36 Inches. *The "Hickory" logo on this one will not require a magnifying glass to read. An uncommon imprint that is clean and clearly legible.* (GOOD) **$145.00**

A2-8. Baker, Hamilton & Co., San Francisco, Calif.: "Stilletto" Axe. Embossed Head. Extra Crisp and Clean. Length: 27 1/2 Inches. *This California hardware dealer offered a full line of tools with the "Stilletto" tradmark. We don't know if any knives were so-marked. An uncommon embossed axe.* (GOOD+) **$145.00**

A2-9. Hibbard, Spencer & Bartlett Co.: "Our Very Best" Axe. With Etched Logo. Uncommon Type. Length: 7 Inches. *Here's the basic felling axe offered by the "Our Very Best" crowd at H.S. & B.* (GOOD) **$35.00**

A2-10. Williams, J.L., Philadelphia, Penn.: Classic Cooper's Axe. Offset Handle. Bold Maker Mark. Length: 16 Inches. *The Directory of American Toolmakers lists a Williams as having worked in Philadelphia as an edge tool maker, but states that the two reported examples had obscured makers marks and the initial could not be read. This well preserved example is clearly marked. A rare Philadelphia cooper's axe.* (GOOD+) **$165.00**

A2-11. Preveron, Pontarion: French Style Axe. Marked "Acier Fondue". Excellent Patina. Length: 16 1/2 Inches. *The head of this well preserved French axe is marked "Acier Fondue", in addition to the maker's name. A nicely shaped handle with a bulbous end complements the tool. Only some evidence of worm in the handle detracts from this otherwise superb tool.* (GOOD+) **$195.00**

A2-12. Unmarked: "Pry Axe" For Fire Use. Original Sheath. Length: 18 Inches. *This specialty axe was apparently marketed to fire departments. It has been used, but is intact and retains its original belt sheath.* (GOOD) **$25.00**

A2-13. Hicks, J.: Post Mortise Axe. Early Apperance. Excellent Condition. Length: 21 1/2 Inches. *The J. Hicks whose name appears on this early post mortise ax was one Jason Hicks of Elizabeth Town, New Jersey, which is now known as Elizabeth. An interesting and unusual early New Jersey tool.* (GOOD+) **$95.00**

A2-14. Jones & Co., M.H., Cohoes, N.Y.: 13 Inch Edge Broad Axe. Original Handle. Near New Condition. Length: 28 Inches. *The makers of this superb condition axe produced edge tools in Cohoes, New York during the years 1874-1876, before they were taken over by A.G. Peck & Company. An extraordinarily well preserved axe from an obscure Upstate New York edge tool maker.* (FINE) **$245.00**

A2-15. Haw Hdwe. Co., Ottumwa, Iowa: "Haws" Embossed Axe. With "H" Logo. Uncommon Type. Length: 36 Inches. *Before this embossed axe arrived at World Headquarters, we were unaware of the Haw Hardware Company of Ottumwa, Iowa, an important tool making city, where, incidentally, there was a 50 foot tall likeness of a bird in the front yard of a motel the last time I was in town. A rare embossed axe.* (GOOD) **$185.00**

A2-16. Unmarked: Specialty Fire Axe. "M.F.D." From Milford, N.H. Length: 29 Inches. *The fact that this axe was acquired at an auction in Milford, New Hampshire leads us to suspect that the M.F.D. imprinted upon it stands for the Milford Fire Department. Because we never discuss sources and methods, information beyond that will not be released. An interesting combination fire axe and adze.* (GOOD+) **$65.00**

A2-17. Plumb, Fayette R., Philadelphia, Penn.: "Plumb Champion" Axe. With Embossed Logo. Excellent Condition. Length: 30 Inches. *One of the most elaborately etched embossed axes, examples of the "Plumb Champion" are not rare, but examples as well-preserved as this one most certainly are.* (GOOD+) **$225.00**

A2-18. Kelly Axe & Tool Works, Charleston: Embossed Felling Axe. Oil Whetted and Hand Honed. Rare and Excellent. Length: 7 Inches. *There is no mention of this "Oil Whetted and Hand Honed" embossed axe in the embossed axe book, nor have I ever seen another. It has some light surface rust, but should clean fairly easily. A rare axe.* (GOOD) **$345.00**

A2-19. Kelley-How-Thomson Co., Duluth, Minn.: "Hickory" Embossed Axe. From North Minnesota. Uncommon Imprint. Length: 36 Inches. *The "Hickory" logo on this one will not require a magnifying glass to read. An uncommon imprint that is in collector-quality condition.* (GOOD+) **$245.00**

A2-20. Collins & Company, Hartford, Conn.: No. 2: Carpenter's Hatchet. New Old Stock. Original Decal. Length: 12 3/4 Inches. *This absolutely brand new carpenter's hatchet from prominent Connecticut makers Collins & Company was recently discovered in the State of Michigan. A great example that is as good as they get.* (FINE) **$95.00**

A2-21. Richards & Co., J.F., Kansas City: "1857 Pioneer" Axe. Commemorative Date. Rare and Excellent. Length: 9 Inches. *The J.F. Richards Company was merged with the Conover Hardware Company in 1924. The 1857 date may have something to do with the date of their founding. A rare embossed axe.* (GOOD) **$285.00**

A2-22. Kelly Axe & Tool Works, Charleston: "Forest Ranger" Axe. Opposed Blades. Marked "FS" and "NHFD". Length: 34 Inches. *The late Bill Kannia, a dealer in bear traps, triple-claw hammers and fascinating stories to accompany each item in his inventory, referred to these as "Forest Ranger Axes". That's good enough for me. An uncommon form. The "F.S." imprint on this tool may refer to "Forest Service".* (GOOD+) **$75.00**

A2-23. Stanley Tools: Combination Hatchet, Wrench. Marked "Bell System". Crisp Stanley Mark. Length: 16 Inches. *Stanley produced these lineman's hatchets for the Bell System for many years. I'm not really sure what the hatchet did, because they were never sharpened. The square opening served as a wrench. This one is marked "Stanley". A good one.* (GOOD+) **$65.00**

A2-24. Hibbard, Spencer & Bartlett Co.: "Our Very Best" Axe. Deep Etched Logo. Uncommon Type. Length: 7 Inches. *You can see the "O.V.B." logo on this one from across the room. An excellent example of an uncommon embossed axe.* (GOOD+) **$85.00**

A2-25. Yerkes & Plumb, Philadelphia, Penn.: Laminated Edge Broad Axe. 12 Inch Cutting Edge. Ready to Use. Length: 27 Inches. *This early Philadelphia broad axe is in great working condition and retains its original handle. Ready to go back to work.* (GOOD+) **$145.00**

A2-26. Bigelow & Dowse Co., Boston, Mass.: Deep Etched Felling Axe. "Special Temper". Excellent Condition. Length: 28 Inches. *This company also produced, at a later date, tools bearing the "Worth" brand logo. This much earlier axe is a most uncommon acquisition.* (GOOD+) **$165.00**

A2-27. Beatty & Co., W., Chester, Penn.: 11 1/2 Inch Broad Axe. With Bovine Logo. Ready to Use. Length: 20 Inches. *This extra sharp and ready to use broad axe is imprinted with the logo of Chester, Pennsylvania maker William Beatty.* (GOOD+) **$165.00**

A2-28. Sheffield, J.M. & Palmer, Stanford: Early Masting Axe. Rare Connecticut Imprint. Not in EAIA Dirctory. Length: 26 1/2 Inches. *The Directory of American Toolmakers lists a James Sheffield in Stamford, Connecticut from 1849 to 1859 and a number of Palmers who were edge tool makers, but there is no mention of this partnership. An extremely well preserved masting axe from a previously undocumented partnership.* (GOOD+) **$185.00**

A2-29. Hibbard, Spencer & Bartlett Co.: "Our Very Best" Axe. Deep Etched Logo. Superb Condition. Length: 36 Inches. *Here's the basic felling axe offered by the "Our Very Best" crowd at H.S. & B.* (GOOD+) **$175.00**

A2-30. Kruse & Baulmann Hdwe. Co., Cincinnati, Ohio: "Cutsure" Embossed Axe. Uncommon Maker. Extra Crisp and Clean. Length: 6 3/4 Inches. *This "Cutsure" embossed axe is the first bearing this imprint that we have offered. Apparently this was the trade name of the Kruse & Baulmann Hardware Company of Cincinatti, Ohio. A rare embossed axe.* (GOOD+) **$225.00**

A2-31. Belknap Hardware Co., Louisville: "Bluegrass" Embossed Axe. With Bell Logo. Deep Embossed. Length: 13 1/2 Inches. *The distinctive "bell" logo of the Belknap Hardware Company is embossed in this well preserved example of their "Bluegrass" line. A scarce hatchet to find.* (GOOD+) **$85.00**

A2-32. Unmarked: Special Function Axe. With Center "Poll". Unknown Purpose. Length: 8 1/2 Inches. *We are uncertain whether or not this graphic axe had a functional or ceremonial purpose. If we said it was an Indian axe, some tribe would sue us for sure and we'd lose it and the interest it would have generated for the last two hundred years. A most unusual axe head.* (GOOD) **$65.00**

A2-33. Unmarked: Extremely Early Axe. With Decorative Edge. Offset Blade. Length: 28 Inches. *The offset blade on this early axe is reminiscent of the "goosewing" style of Southeastern Pennsylvania. The neck has been forged with a series of folds and there is a "nib" cast in the back of the lower part of the blade.* (GOOD) **$345.00**

A2-34. Plumb: "Super Scout" Axe. Partial Original Label. Scarce and Near New. Length: 24 Inches. *Most of the original paper label remains on this ca. 1950's "Super Scout" Boy Scout axe from Fayette R. Plumb. We've seen our share of Boy Scout hatchets, but very few of these.* (FINE) **$85.00**

A2-35. Matchless: "Matchless" Embossed Axe. Refined Silver Steel. Most Unusual Type. Length: 7 Inches. *The now out-of-print book "Embossed American Axes" is silent about this one, and I've never seen another. A rare embossed axe.* (GOOD+) **$295.00**

A2-36. American Ax & Tool Co., Glassport,: "Will Wear" Embossed Axe. "Crucible Steel". Rare and Excellent. Length: 0 Inches. *Hardware stores apparently found it essential to offer an embossed axe head bearing their logo. This is the first example of the Masbach Hardware imprint that I have seen. A rare axe.* (GOOD) **$395.00**

A2-37. Richards & Co., J.F., Kansas City,: "1857 Pioneer" Axe. Commemorative Date. Uncommon Type. Length: 9 Inches. *The J.F. Richards Company was merged with the Conover Hardware Company in 1924. The 1857 date may have something to do with the date of their founding. A rare embossed axe.* (GOOD) **$65.00**

A2-38. Plumb, Fayette R., Philadelphia: "Plumb Champion" Axe. With Embossed Logo. Uncommon Type. Length: 28 Inches. *One of the most elaborately etched embossed axes, examples of the "Plumb Champion" are not rare, but examples as well-preserved as this one most certainly are. An axe that has never seen its embossed face used as a hammer.* (GOOD+) **$85.00**

A2-39. Teneyck Mfg. Co., Cohoes, New York: Early 12 Inch Broad Axe. Original Offset Handle. Ready to Use. Length: 20 Inches. *The ready availability of water power in the area north of Albany, New York made that area the home of a number of edge tool makers. The Teneyck Manufacturing Company worked in Cohoes from 1866 to 1880. This axe retains its original handle and is in excellent working order.* (GOOD+) **$225.00**

A2-40. Kelly Axe & Tool Works, Charleston: "Forest Ranger" Axe. Opposed Blades. Marked "U.S.F.S.". Length: 34 Inches. *A dual leather keeper has protected both cutting edges of this "Forest Ranger" axe. A very nice example.* (GOOD+) **$85.00**

A2-41. Kelly Axe & Tool Works, Charleston: Kelly "Registered" Axe. Register No. 18722. Dated "1912". Length: 7 Inches. *This Kelly "Registered axe has a distinctive form to its head that is only very slightly flared from the eye to the edge. A clean and clearly marked embossed axe.* (GOOD+) **$125.00**

A2-42. Unmarked: Classic Early Axe. Applied Edge. Usable Condition. Length: 21 Inches. *There are no maker marks on this early broad axe, but the presence of an applied steel edge indicate that it was the product of a skilled edge tool maker. A nice early axe in excellent working condition.* (GOOD+) **$125.00**

A2-43. Unmarked: "Goosewing" Type Axe. With Arrows, Heart. Early and Excellent. Length: 24 Inches. *This well preserved "goosewing" type axe is marked with stylized arrows and hearts. A great example of a classic style.* (GOOD+) **$485.00**

A2-44. Lee, Coit & Anderson Hdwe., Omaha: Embossed Felling Axe. Ca. 1900. Rare Western Axe. Length: 9 Inches. *A most uncommon hardware mark is boldly embossed on this double bit axe head. A light cleaning and this one will be visible half a block away. Most unusual.* (GOOD) **$365.00**

A2-45. Champion Fitzall: Salesman's Sample Axe and Hammer Handles. Original Felt Roll. Original Labels. Length: 14 Inches. *Here's a great set of salesman's display sample axe handles in their original felt roll. The original paper labels remain on all of the full scale samples. Rare and excellent.* (FINE) **$125.00**

Group B2

B2-1. Riverside Tool Co., New York, N.Y.: No. 4 1/2: Wide Smooth Metallic Plane. Uncommon Imprint. Near New Condition. Length: 9 1/2 Inches. *We are on record as having recommended the No. 4 1/2 size as an appropriate subject for a collection. These planes were only made by high quality makers, they display well because they are both short and wide and the search keeps tool hunting interesting. This example bears the distinctive logo of the Riverside Tool Company of New York. This is the first Riverside plane of any type we have ever offered. Rare and nearly new.* (FINE) **$195.00**

B2-2. Union Mfg. Co., New Britain, Conn.: No. 41: Tongue and Groove Metallic Plane. Similar to Stanley 47/4. Brand New Condition. Length: 11 Inches. *The Union Manufacturing Company, Stanley's cross-town competitor tried hard, but failed to achieve a substantial market share. The quality of their products was not to blame. This tongue and groove plane is an example of their best work. A very well made metallic plane in brand new condition.* (FINE) **$225.00**

B2-3. Ohio Tool Co., Columbus, Ohio: No. 09 1/2: Adjustable Block Metallic Plane. With Lever Adjust. Uncommon Type. Length: 6 Inches. *This early Ohio Tool Company Block plane features their distinctive throat adjustment mechanism. More than 90% of the original paint remains.* (GOOD+) **$165.00**

B2-4. Record, Sheffield, England: No. 044: Light Duty Plow Metallic Plane. With Original Cutters. New Condition, Original Box. Length: 8 Inches. *These light duty plows are equally as functional as Stanley's No. 50 beading plane and can be had much cheaper. Complete with all cutters in the original box.* (FINE) **$155.00**

B2-5. Davis Level & Tool Co.: Cast Iron Block Metallic Plane. Distinctive Profile. Rare "Davis" Imprint. Length: 6 Inches. *We have offered a half dozen examples of the Davis Level & Tool Company block plane over the years, but never once, until now, have we had one that was imprinted with the Davis name on the cutting iron. This example, which retains more than 70% of its original black japan finish, is very boldly struck on the cutting iron with both the maker name and working location. A very, very rare Davis block plane.* (GOOD+) **$545.00**

B2-6. Unmarked: Stuffed Smoothing Metallic Plane. With Ward Iron. Distinctive Form. Length: 10 Inches. *Most likely the product of the artistic creativity of the pattern shop, this early appearing cast iron plane is nicely stuffed with dark hardwood. The contoured rear handle serves double duty as a brace for the elongated cutting iron. A very early plane of dramatic appearance.* (GOOD+) **$325.00**

B2-7. Unmarked: Carriage Rabbet Metallic Planes. Cast Gunmetal. Flat and Compass. Length: 7 1/2 Inches. *Carriagemakers rabbet planes cast in bronze have a most appealing look to them and this pair even more so. A warm, golden patina accents the shadows on the open castings of this set of flat and compass soled planes. One of the original mahogany wedges has been replaced by an acceptable stand in that appears to be made of oak. A superb set of visually stunning planes.* (GOOD+) **$525.00**

B2-8. Marsh No. M 2: "No. 2" Size Metallic Plane. With Fulton Cutter. Rare and Excellent. Length: 7 Inches. *The Marsh Tool Company of Rockford, Illinois offered a full range of bench and block planes in direct competition with the major planemakers. At only 7 inches in length, this No. M 2 plane was the smallest size offered and the rarest of the Marsh planes to find today. The original cutting iron has been replaced by that from a Fulton Tool Company plane, but the tool is otherwise complete, sound and ever so rare.* (GOOD+) **$475.00**

B2-9. Union Mfg. Co., New Britain, Conn.: No. 4: 10 Inch Smooth Metallic Plane. Mahogany Handles. 95% Original Paint. Length: 7 1/2 Inches. *The Union Manufacturing Company, Stanley's cross-town competitor tried hard, but failed to achieve a substantial market share. The quality of their products was not to blame. This smoothing plane is every bit as well made as the Stanley equivalent.* (GOOD+) **$75.00**

B2-10. Union Mfg. Co., New Britain, Conn.: No. 515: Transitional Metallic Plane. Patented June 28, 1904. Near New Condition. Length: 10 Inches. *Produced under a patent granted on June 28, 1904 to George E. Trask and John W. Carleton of New Britain, Connecticut, this nearly new transitional plane incorporates a lever adjustment mechanism that was unique to Union's transitional plane. Retaining nearly all of its shiny, black japanning and 99% of the shiny yellow lacquer on its beech body, this is the way most patented transitional planes looked when they left the factory and the way few of them look today. Rare and near new.* (FINE) **$445.00**

B2-11. Vaughn & Bushnell, Chicago, Illinois: No. 905: Forged Steel Metallic Plane. "Unbreakable". Near New Condition. Length: 14 Inches. *Nearly all of the original finishes remain on the V. & B. "unbreakable" jack plane. These tools were forged from heavy grade sheet metal and nickel plated on the bed and sides. This is one of the nicest examples we have yet encountered.* (GOOD+) **$175.00**

B2-12. Union Mfg. Co., New Britain, Conn.: Transitional Metallic Plane. Similar to Stanley No. 21. With Lever Adjust. Length: 7 Inches. *The equivalent in size and form to Stanley's No. 21 transitional plane, this is the first example of the Union Manufacturing Company equivalent we have offered. This one has been rejapanned, but a rare plane nonetheless.* (GOOD) **$85.00**

B2-13. Standard Rule Co., Unionville, Conn.: No. 3: Cast Iron Metallic Plane. Early Patent. Rare and Excellent. Length: 8 Inches. *Only slightly larger than the "No. 2" size planes, this example of the Standard Tool Company's No. 3 offering is fitted with the trademark massive knurled adjusting nuts and the adjustment mechanism produced under the October 30, 1883 patent of Solon and Arthur Rust. A rare type of plane in an especially rare size by an important 19th Century planemaker.* (GOOD+) **$725.00**

B2-14. Unmarked: "Knowles Type" Metallic Plane. Mahogany Tote and Wedge. Rejapanned Body. Length: 10 Inches. *Someone has repainted the body of this early, Knowles type plane with black lacquer and the front knob is not original, but this ca. 1830's metallic plane, which embodies the design specified in Hazard Knowles' 1827 patent, is otherwise in excellent condition and worthy of inclusion in any serious collection of patented planes.* (GOOD+) **$645.00**

B2-15. Unmarked: Cast Bronze Metallic Plane. Decorative Form. From Carriage Shop? Length: 7 Inches. *We have no specific information on the history of this cast bronze rabbeting plane, but it is likely that this was the proud possession of a practitioner of the carriage makers trade. A wedge with an ovate finial adds to the dramatic profile.* (GOOD+) **$225.00**

B2-16. G.T.L.: Cast Bronze Metallic Plane. With Screw Adjustment. From England. Length: 9 Inches. *This precision adjustable plane in solid bronze was likely the product of an English planemaker. It is in excellent condition and appears well suited for the work for which it was designed.* (GOOD+) **$245.00**

B2-17. Union Mfg. Co., New Britain, Conn.: No. 2 C: 7 1/2 Inch Smoothing Metallic Plane. Mahogany Handles. 95% Original Paint. Length: 7 1/2 Inches. *Stanley "competitor" matched their cross town neighbor nearly plane for plane, but Union's tools seem not to have caught on with woodworkers of the day. They are rare. This example of Union's "No. 2" size plane with corrugated sole is in excellent collector quality condition. A nice example of a very scarce plane.* (GOOD+) **$550.00**

B2-18. Gage Tool Co., Vineland, N.J.: No. 2: Patent Transitional Metallic Plane. Patent 1886. 95% Original Finishes. Length: 9 Inches. *At 9 inches in length, this diminutive plane was the second smallest size produced by the Gage Tool Company of Vineland, New Jersey. Examples of this particular Gage offering are scarce indeed. This one is in superb condition, retaining nearly all finishes on the knob and cap. The rear handle, however, has cracked as have so many Gage planes. It could be repaired fairly easily, however as the handles of all planes produced by the Gage Tool Company are interchangeable with each other. A superb example of a rare Gage plane having a very prominent Achilles Heel.* (GOOD+) **$145.00**

B2-19. Preston & Sons, Edward: Cast Iron Hand Beader. With 5 Double Irons. 3 Orignal Fences. Length: 13 1/2 Inches. *This Preston classic includes five original double cutters and three fences. A superb example of an uncommon and desirable Preston beader. Highly recommended.* (GOOD+) **$245.00**

B2-20. Birmingham Plane Manufacturing Co: "B Plane" Metallic Plane. Patented October 22, 1889. Transitional Type. Length: 14 3/4 Inches. *Here's a transitional plane that incorporates an 1889 patent. The listing of plane patents in the back of Roger Smith's Patented Transitional and Metallic Planes in America, Vol. II, lists two patents for this date, one by George Mosher and one by Solon Rust, both of which were assigned to the Birmingham Plane Company. A crispy clean plane that has had a light coat of protective lacquer applied.* (GOOD+) **$85.00**

B2-21. Ohio Tool Company No. 05 C: Patent Cast Iron Metallic Plane. Patented August 20, 1907. Rare and Excellent. Length: 9 Inches. *This scarce patented plane incorporates the throat adjustment patent granted to Richard Marks on August 20, 1907, which featured a raised yoke cast into the bed of the plane. This example is in clean, sound condition and ready to fill out a collection of patented planes.* (GOOD) **$225.00**

B2-22. Bailey, L. No. 0 1/2: "Victor" Adjustable Metallic Plane. Ca. 1880-1888. Complete and Excellent. Length: 7 Inches. *Those who have taken the time to be able to distinguish, at a glance, the different varieties of the "Victor" block planes by their arcane numbering system, are to be commended for their achievement, and I hope they never corner me at a cocktail party. For the rest of us, who find the artistic majesty of these early cast iron tools sufficiently satisfying, and who have access to reference materials when necessary, this example of the adjustable No. 0 1/2 is a classic example of one of the most beautiful block planes ever produced. Fitted with the Bailey patent adjustment mechanism and the elaborately cast locking screw that was the trademark of these planes, this clean example retains nearly 90% of its original finishes. An excellent example of a very rare plane.* (GOOD+) **$625.00**

B2-23. Siegley Tool Company: Sielgley Adjustable Block Metallic Plane. Uncommon Type. Rare and Excellent. Length: 6 Inches. *This early cast iron block plane is imprinted with the Siegley Tool Company. Most unusual.* (GOOD+) **$75.00**

B2-24. Jennings & Co., C.E., New York, N.Y.: No. A1: Beech Handle Scraper. Near New Condition. Most Unusual Type. Length: 15 Inches. *We have offered a wide range of products from the C.E. Jennings Company, but this is the first example of this specialty scraper we have encountered. It appears never to have been used. A very rare scraper in nearly new condition.* (FINE) **$85.00**

B2-25. Record Ridgway Tools Ltd.: No. 075: Bullnose Block Metallic Plane. With Original Decal. Ready to Use. Length: 4 Inches. *This equivalent to Stanley's No. 75 bullnose rabbet is in new condition, complete with its original decal.* (GOOD+) **$35.00**

B2-26. Union Mfg. Co., New Britain, Conn.: No. 50: Bullnose Block Metallic Plane. Similar to Stanley 75. 98% Original Paint. Length: 4 Inches. *The equivalent to the Stanley No. 75, this cast iron bullnose plane has the Union name and product number cast in the rear portion of the tool body.* (FINE) **$75.00**

B2-27. Rubelmann, Geo., St. Louis, Missouri: Stranahan's Patent Metallic Plane. For Blind Nailing. Patented July 20, 1886. Length: 6 Inches. *Designed to lift a sliver of wood so that a nail could be set in the opening and then have the sliver of wood glued back over it, the William Stranahan Blind Nailing Plane is unique among patented planes. This well preserved example is clearly marked with the patent date and ready to display. Different.* (GOOD+) **$795.00**

B2-28. Unmarked: Solid Cast Iron Metallic Plane. "V" Cut Profile. Graphic Form. Length: 8 3/4 Inches. *Looking in profile like something that might have been conjured up in the woodworking shop of Jules Verne, this specialty plane has a "V" shaped bed and a pointed cutter. It was likely created in a pattern shop for the making of fillet. A great looking owner made plane.* (GOOD+) **$165.00**

B2-29. Shapleigh Hardware Co.: No. 4 1/2 C: Wide Heavy Smooth Metallic Plane. Patented July 13, 1909. "Diamond Edge" Br. Length: 10 Inches. *The Shapleigh Hardware Company offered a full range of bench planes under their "Diamond Edge" brand, but we have seen very few examples of this, the No. 4 1/2 size. The July 13, 1909 patent refers to a patent for a "tool handle for planes" granted to Charles B. Stanley of New Britain, Connecticut. The Stanley patent stands as absolute confirmation that these planes were produced for Shapleigh by Stanley Rule & Level. A nice example.* (GOOD+) **$195.00**

B2-30. Marshall Wells Hardware Co.: No. 776 X: "Zenith" Transistion Metallic Plane. Similar to Stanley No. 21. "Fulton" Cutter. Length: 7 1/2 Inches. *This diminutive transitional plane is imprinted with the "sunrise" logo of Duluth, Minnesota hardware dealers Marshall Wells. It is the equivalent in size to Stanley's No. 21 and much less common. A rare transitional plane of the smallest size offered.* (GOOD) **$225.00**

B2-32. Siegley Tool Company No. 2: Combination Plow Metallic Plane. Uncommon Type. Ca. 1890's. Length: 9 1/2 Inches. *Other than a few chips around the fixing screw, this early example of the Siegley No. 2 plow plane is in excellent condition. These graphic Nineteenth Century planes have become increasingly difficult to find.* (GOOD+) **$265.00**

B2-33. Ohio Tool Co., Columbus, Ohio: No. 0130: Double End Block Metallic Plane. Uncommon Type. Extra Crisp and Clean. Length: 8 Inches. *The Ohio Tool Company attempted, for a short time, to match the products of industry giant Stanley Rule & Level. Their product line failed to catch on among the woodworkers of the day in the way that the surviving examples have inspired latter-day collectors, who recognize their rarity. This double end block plane, the equivalent to Stanley's No. 130, is the first of this type that we have offered. Rare.* (GOOD+) **$145.00**

B2-34. Union Mfg. Co., New Britain, Conn.: No. 21: Patent Transitional Metallic Plane. Patented October 22, 1889. Rare and Complete. Length: 7 Inches. *The smallest of the Union transitional planes, the number 21 is equally as rare as its Stanley counterpart. An extremely scarce transitional plane.* (GOOD) **$155.00**

B2-35. Unmarked: Bronze Core Box Metallic Plane. Original Red Paint. From J.J. Kjelleberg. Length: 6 1/2 Inches. *We have observed a sufficient number of planes identical to this example to conclude that they were manufactured for sale to patternmakers sometime in period from 1880 to 1910. This example retains some 90% of the original japanning and was included with the tools of J.J. Kjelleberg, whose other patternmaking tools are offered elsewhere in this volume.* (GOOD+) **$225.00**

B2-36. Riverside Tool Co., New York, N.Y.: No. 4 C Size Metallic Plane. With Anvil Logo. Scarce and Excellent. Length: 9 Inches. *The Riverside Tool Company of New York City produced planes imprinted with their distinctive "anvil" logo. This well preserved example retains more than 90% of its original black japan finish.* (GOOD+) **$135.00**

B2-37. Hibbard, Spencer & Bartlett Co.: No. 36: Transitional Smooth Metallic Plane. Similar to Stanley 36. "Revonoc" Brand. Length: 9 Inches. *The cutting iron is marked "REVONOC", a trademark of the Hibbard, Spencer and Bartlett Company, which has something to do with their affiliation with the Conover hardware company. One need only to spell CONOVER backwards to come up with the "REVONOC" trademark. The only thing backward about this plane is the logo. Probably made for H.S.B. by the Union Tool Company, it is in excellent condition. Rare.* (FINE) **$185.00**

B2-38. Union Mfg. Co., New Britain, Conn.: Bullnose Block Metallic Plane. Equivalent to Stanley 75. Scarce and Excellent. Length: 4 Inches. *This Union bullnose block plane is not imprinted with the product number, but it matches the specifications of the Union No. 50. Some 95% of the original japanning remains.* (GOOD+) **$55.00**

B2-39. Fulton, New York, N.Y. No. 5329: Adjustable Combination Metallic Plane. Manufactured by Sargent & Co. New Condition, Original Box. Length: 11 Inches. *A line of tools bearing the "Fulton" name was marketed in the early days of Sears, Roebuck & Company, long before they adopted their "Craftsman" trademark. This rare "Fulton" combination plane must most certainly have been produced for Fulton at about the same time they introduced their No. 1080 combination plane, as it is identical to that tool in all but name. Complete with the original instructions and screwdriver, this early combination plane is in top collector quality condition.* (FINE) **$395.00**

B2-40. Tower & Lyon, New York, N.Y.: Chaplin's Patent Metallic Plane. India Rubber Handles. Crisp and Clean. Length: 18 Inches. *The later versions of the O.R. Chaplin patent planes, as offered by the Tower & Lyon Company of New York City were distinguished by having handles formed of hard India rubber, beds that were corrugated on the upper surface and by having a distinctive profile to the rails. This fore plane is a classic example of the type. Crisp, clean and ready to display.* (GOOD+) **$195.00**

B2-41. Stearns & Co., E.C., Syracuse, N.Y.: Cast Iron Jointer Gauge. Nickel Plated Fence. Extra Crisp and Clean. Length: 9 Inches. *Of essentially the same design as the jointer gauges offered by the Millers Falls Company, those made by the E.C. Stearns Company are equally useful. A nice example of an excellent working tool.* (GOOD+) **$85.00**

B2-42. Fulton Tool Company: "No. 2" Size Metallic Plane. 7 Inch Length. Made By Sargent? Length: 7 Inches. *Those seeking to fill out a collection of the diminutive "No. 2" size planes might wish to consider this well preserved example of the Fulton Tool Company's product. A good one.* (GOOD+) **$135.00**

B2-43. Buck Brothers: Cast Iron Smooth Metallic Plane. Ca. 1960's. Uncommon Type. Length: 8 1/2 Inches. *Fitted with a contoured handle and knob of domestic plastic, this ca. 1960's era plane is imprinted with the name of Buck Brother, the legendary Millbury, Massachusetts edge tool maker. It appears never to have been used.* (FINE) **$35.00**

B2-44. Unmarked: Model Maker's Block Metallic Plane. Unmarked Cutter. Early Appearance. Length: 3 1/4 Inches. *The body of this plane appears to be an early version of the Stanley No. 101 block plane, but the cutter is not marked in any way. A clean and ready to use block plane.* (GOOD+) **$25.00**

B2-45. Ohio Tool Company, Columbus, Ohio: No. 024: Transitional Smooth Metallic Plane. With "World" Logo. Excellent Condition. Length: 8 Inches. *The side of this uncommon Ohio Tool Company transitional plane is imprinted with the well known "World" logo used by this toolmaking concern.* (GOOD+) **$65.00**

B2-46. Bailey, L. No. 7: "Victor" Patent Metallic Plane. Cast Iron Handle. Refinished Body. Length: 22 Inches. *This Bailey No. 7 patent metallic plane, one of the least common and most desirable of all patented planes has the "look" of a Bailey classic, but has had some restoration. The body has been nicely rejapanned and the iron is short, although it can be mounted to appear complete, and the original chip breaker is missing and has been replaced. These planes have become so difficult to find in any condition that this plane might be worth its highest value as parts. An opportunity.* (GOOD) **$445.00**

Group C2

C2-1. Farrand Sales Corp., New York, N.Y.: "Farrand" Patent Tape Measure. Patented January 3, 1922. Uncommon Type. Length: 2 1/2 Inches. *This Farrand rule has seen some use, but it is clean, mechanically sound and retains its original box.* (GOOD+) **$125.00**

C2-2. Lufkin Rule Co., The: Decorative Tape Measure. Masterbuilt Floors. Master Builders, Cleve. Length: 60 Inches. *In the 1920's and 30's, the Lufkin Rule Company offered a range of decorative advertising tape measures, many of which have become highly collectible in today's market. Among the most sought-after are those with embossed cases, such as this example from Masterbuilt Floors, which features an image of a floor finisher. The reverse side is imprinted "Compliments of The Master Builders Co., Cleveland, Ohio". Never seen another.* (GOOD+) **$145.00**

C2-3. Farrand, Hiram A., Inc., Berlin, N.H.: Early Patent Tape Measure. Patented January 3, 1922. New Condition, Original Box. Length: 72 Inches. *This early patent tape measure from master marketer Hiram Farrand of new Hampshire is in new condition in its original box, complete with the instruction manual. Mint.* (FINE) **$295.00**

C2-4. Rule Products Co., Stratford, Conn.: "Set-A-Rule" Tape Measure. For Tool Setup. New Condition, Original Box. Length: 2 1/2 Inches. *This combination tape measure and machine setup gauge is as unusual a tape measure we have encountered in some time. The body of the device is a pyramid-like series of scales of fixed graduations which house a tape measure. Rare.* (FINE) **$185.00**

C2-5. Keuffel & Esser Co., New York No. N7936: Surveyor's Tape Measure Clamp. Cam Lock Feature. New Condition, Original Box. Length: 3 Inches. *Holding a tape measure tight enough to be accurate without slicing open the hand was facilitated by the use of one of these clamps. This one is in new condition in its original box. Nice.* (FINE) **$85.00**

C2-6. Lufkin Rule Co., The No. 584: Tape Measure Clamp Handle. Nickel Plated Brass. Excellent Condition. Length: 3 Inches. *These were used by surveyors for tensioning tape measures over long distances. A nice example of an uncommon accessory tool.* (FINE) **$75.00**

C2-7. Unmarked: Direct Reading Tape Measure. "Chemical Proof" Advertisement. Near New Condition. Length: 2 1/4 Inches. *This direct reading tape measure is marked "Chemical Proof", but it was likely and advertising giveaway from that company. Different.* (FINE) **$35.00**

C2-8. Farrand, Hiram A., Inc., Berlin, N.H.: Early Patent Tape Measure. Patented January 3, 1922. Solid Brass Case. Length: 72 Inches. *This Farrand tape measure has seen some use and has some "pocket wear" but it is clearly legible and in excellent working order. A rare and collectible tape measure.* (GOOD+) **$45.00**

C2-9. Dietzgen Co., Eugene, Chicago No. 5360 C: "Columbia" Tape Measure. 50 Foot Length. New Condition, Original Box. Length: 600 Inches. *Not to be done in the quest to provide tape measures with names wholly unrelated to measures, measurement or the work they were intended to perform, the Eugene Dietzgen Company marketed this "Columbia" brand 50 foot tape measure. It appears never to have been used. Hail Columbia.* (FINE) **$65.00**

C2-10. Stanley Rule & Level No. 1260: "Defiance" Tape Measure. Marked "Automatic Rule". Early and Uncommon. Length: 72 Inches. *This 1950's era tape measure features a "Wings" device on the case. A superb example in clean, sound condition.* (GOOD) **$25.00**

C2-11. Stanley Rule & Level No. 6386: "Direct Reading" Tape Measure. 6 Foot Length. Metric and English. Length: 72 Inches. *A rare variation, this "Direct Reading" tape measure is graduated with both English and metric measurements.* (FINE) **$225.00**

C2-12. Ralph Williams, Inc., Boston, Mass.: Record-O-Meter Tape Measure. With Sliding Stops. Includes Instruction. Length: 2 1/2 Inches. *Think tape measures are simple enough that there would be no need to "improve" them? Think again. The outside of this New Standard for the class includes a series of sliding gauges on the outside of the case to record specific measurements in feet, inches and portions thereof. The original instructions are included in the box.* (FINE) **$65.00**

C2-13. Stanley Rule & Level No. 6386: "Direct Reading" Tape Measure. 6 Foot Length. Near New Condition. Length: 72 Inches. *These "Direct Reading" tape measures were one of many Stanley innovations. This one is in excellent collector quality condition.* (FINE) **$65.00**

C2-14. Lufkin Rule Co., The No. X686: Inside, Outside Tape Measure. Patent Pending. Near New Condition. Length: 72 Inches. *These were designed to overcome one of the shortcomings of the tape measure compared to its competition, the folding rule. The tape measure, in its circular form, was incapable of making accurate inside measurements. This rather clumsy attempt by Lufkin was a market disaster and a collectible hit. These are rare.* (FINE) **$145.00**

C2-15. Unmarked: German Military Tape Measure. Mit Der Swastika. Solid Brass Case. Length: 4 1/2 Inches. *While they were on their way to world conquest, one member of the "Master Race" carried this 25 meter tape measure which is imprinted with the German Federal Eagle and the swastika symbol. An uncommon German military tape measure.* (GOOD+) **$65.00**

C2-16. Montgomery Ward & Co. No. 84-2025: "Lakeside" Brand Tape Measure. 6 Foot Length. New Condition, Original Box. Length: 2 1/2 Inches. *This is the first "Lakeside" rule we have encountered. New and in the box.* (GOOD+) **$25.00**

C2-17. Lufkin Rule Co., The No. C 9210: "Chrome Clad" Tape Measure. 10 Foot Length. New Condition, Original Box. Length: 72 Inches. *The last half of Lufkin's four digit product number gave the length of the rule in feet.* (FINE) **$35.00**

C2-18. Roe & Sons, Justus, Patchogue, N.Y.: Nickel Plated Tape Measure. 50 Foot Length. Unused Condition. Length: 3 1/4 Inches. *The Justus Roe & Sons Company were early producers of high quality tape measures. This one is in top condition.* (FINE) **$45.00**

C2-19. Keuffel & Esser Co., New York: "Favorite Wyteface" Tape Measure. 100 Foot Length. Excellent Condition. Length: 5 Inches. *If you're looking for a top quality 100 foot tape measure and don't want to pay an arm and a leg, here's your chance. A good one.* (GOOD+) **$45.00**

C2-20. Starrett Co., The L.S., Athol, Mass. No. 530: 25' Steel Tape Measure. Red Leatherette Case. New Condition, Original Box. Length: 300 Inches. *As with everything else they made, this 25 foot tape measure from the L.S. Starrett Company is of the highest quality. New and in the box.* (FINE) **$45.00**

C2-21. Stanley Rule & Level No. 7366: Brass Advertising Tape Measure. "Bundles For Britain". Rare and Excellent. Length: 36 Inches. *We have it on good authority that these "Bundles for Britain" tape measures were produced by Stanley for those who participated in the privately arranged pre-World War II effort to help the English resist the Nazi blitz. This example is in excellent condition and retains much of the lamination on the U.S. & British flags. A rare and highly collectible tape measure.* (GOOD+) **$275.00**

C2-22. Lufkin Rule Co., The: "Metallic" Tape Measure. 100 Foot Length. Original Box. Length: 7 1/2 Inches. *This example of Lufkin's "Metallic" tape measure, which, incidentally, was made of cloth, is in new condition in its original box, which is missing its label.* (FINE) **$65.00**

C2-23. Unmarked: "Mechanic's Pal" Tape Measure. Nickel Plated Case. Near New Condition. Length: 2 3/4 Inches. *The mechanics pal was meant to be an inexpensive alternative to Lufkin and Stanley. It still is.* (FINE) **$15.00**

C2-24. Carlson & Sullivan, Monrovia, Cal. No. 21 P: Diameter Measure Tape Measure. "Hobby" Brand. Uncommon Type. Length: 2 Inches. *The Carlson Company also produced tape measures bearing the name of the Henry Disston Company, although we don't know the exact business relationship. Here's a nice example of their "Hobby" brand.* (GOOD+) **$35.00**

C2-25. Stanley Rule & Level No. 7506 N: Nickel Plateed Tape Measure. With Horizontal No.'s. Excellent Condition. Length: 72 Inches. *The "N" designation is for nickel plating, all of which still remains. The numbers on the tape are arranged for horizontal reading, an uncommon variation.* (FINE) **$65.00**

C2-26. Carlson & Sullivan, Monrovia, Cal. No. 2210: 10 Foot Steel Tape Measure. "Chief" Brand. New Condition, Original Box. Length: 2 Inches. *A prime competitor with Lufkin in the contest to come up with the stupidest names for tape measures, Carlson & Sullivan offered this "Chief" tape measure in a fire engine red box, perhaps hoping to appeal to the heads of fire departments. Different.* (FINE) **$15.00**

C2-27. Master Rule Mfg. Co., Inc.: "Lady's Man" Tape Measure. See "Art Of Fine Tools." New Condition, Original Box. Length: 2 Inches. *Popularized by its prominent inclusion in Sandor Nagyzlanzy's "The Art of Fine Tools", the "Lady's Man" tape measure captures the spirit of 20th Century tape measure collecting. A nice example.* (FINE) **$95.00**

C2-28. Disston & Sons, H., Philadelphia, Penn.: Commemorative Tape Measure. 125th Anniversary, 1965. With Keystone Logo. Length: 2 1/4 Inches. *Henry Disston founded the firm in 1840, so this commemorative dates to 1965. Never seen another.* (FINE) **$85.00**

C2-29. Mayhew Steel Products, Inc.: Early Steel Tape Measure. Shelburne Falls, Mass. Excellent Condition. Length: 72 Inches. *The Mayhew Company dates from the earliest days of manufacturing in the Greenfield/Millers Falls/Shelburne Falls area. Their specialty was forged tools. This tape measure is an uncommon example.* (FINE) **$25.00**

C2-30. Lufkin Rule Co., The: "Mezurall" Tape Measure. 6 Foot Length. New Condition, Original Box. Length: 2 Inches. *An early yellow box and a pamphlet complement this brand new, but old, Lufkin tape. Mint.* (FINE) **$35.00**

C2-31. Farrand, Hiram A., Inc., Berlin, N.H.: Early Patent Tape Measure. Patented January 3, 1922. Heavy Duty Grip. Length: 72 Inches. *This example of the Farrand Patent features spring tension release levers on the sides to facilitate the extension and retraction of the tape. Different.* (GOOD+) **$55.00**

C2-32. Squangle Corporation, Lynwood, Wa.: "Line Master" Plumb Bob Reel. With Wall Hanger. New Condition, Original Box. Length: 3 1/2 Inches. *An extension pin allows this plumb bob reel to be secured in a wall or beam when being used. This is our first offering of a product from the Squangle Corporation. Unusual.* (FINE) **$65.00**

C2-33. Unmarked: Bakelite Case Tape Measure. Marked "Germany". Similar to "Farrand". Length: 72 Inches. *Nearly identical to the Hiram Farrand patent that was produced by Stanley, this German-made example features a Bakelite case. Different.* (GOOD+) **$25.00**

C2-34. Farrand, Hiram A., Inc., Berlin, N.H.: Early Patent Tape Measure. Patented January 3, 1922. New Condition, Original Box. Length: 72 Inches. *Hiram Farrand was one of the first to recognize the market potential of the tape measure. He later sold his business to the Stanley Rule & Level Company. This superb example is in new condition in its original box, complete with the original instructions.* (FINE) **$245.00**

C2-35. Disston-Carlson, Philadelphia, Penn. No. 76: "Chieftan" Tape Measure. 6 Foot Length. New Condition, Original Box. Length: 72 Inches. *This 6 foot measure was apparently intended for marketing to the upper echelons of the American Indian hierarchy. An uncommon tape from a prominent American toolmaker.* (FINE) **$45.00**

C2-36. Master Rule Mfg. Co., Inc.: Promotional Advertisement Tape Measure. Singer: 1851-1951. Near New Condition. Length: 1 1/2 Inches. *If you missed the Singer Centennial in 1951, here's your chance to pretend you were there. A rare commemorative advertising tape measure.* (FINE) **$85.00**

C2-37. Starrett Co., L. S., Athol, Mass. No. C504: 12 Foot Tape Measure. With Crank Handle. Near New Condition. Length: 144 Inches. *The L.S. Starrett Company didn't make anything other than the finest quality. This tape measure meets their high standard.* (FINE) **$45.00**

C2-38. Stanley Rule & Level No. 6386: "Direct Reading" Tape Measure. 6 Foot Length. Near New Condition. Length: 72 Inches. *This No. 6386 tape measure retains nearly all of its shiny nickel plating. Extra nice.* (FINE) **$65.00**

C2-39. Lufkin Rule Co., The No. C 926: " Chrome Clad" Tape Measure. 8 Foot Length. New Condition, Original Box. Length: 2 1/4 Inches. *This eight-foot Lufkin rule is in new condition in its original box. Mint.* (FINE) **$45.00**

C2-40. Lufkin Rule Co., The No. C216: "Anchor" Steel Tape Measure. Original Carton. 100 Foot Length. Length: 4 Inches. *Once again, we are confounded by Lufkin's choice of names for its tape measures. The word "Anchor" has about as much to do with measurement as guard rails have to do with strawberries. The reason of the very well preserved condition of this tape may be attributable to the fact that no one could justify buying something with such a confusing name. New and in the box.* (FINE) **$55.00**

C2-41. Lufkin Rule Co., The No. 926 T A: Printer's "Mezurall" Tape Measure. 6 Foot Length. New Condition, Original Box. Length: 72 Inches. *Tape measures were produced for nearly every task that had previously been accomplished with a conventional rule. Here's a most unusual printer's tape measure.* (FINE) **$55.00**

C2-42. Keuffel & Esser Co., New York No. 7445 T: Woven Tape Measure. "Dartmouth" Brand. New Condition, Original Box. Length: 6 Inches. *Perhaps attempting to appeal to the "old school" crowd with their tape measure naming convention, K. & E. offered the "Dartmouth" to a less than eager buying public. This one is in new condition in its original box.* (FINE) **$75.00**

C2-43. Master Rule Mfg. Co., Inc. No. 306: "Tufboy" Tape Measure. 6 Foot Lentgth. New Condition, Original Box. Length: 2 Inches. *The practice of giving stupid names to tape measures was not the exclusive bailiwick of Lufkin. This "Tufboy" rule is in nearly new condition in its original packaging.* (GOOD+) **$15.00**

C2-44. Lufkin Rule Co., The No. C 928: " Chrome Clad" Tape Measure. 6 Foot Length. New Condition, Original Box. Length: 72 Inches. *A bright blue box distinguishes this perfectly preserved Lufkin classic.* (FINE) **$45.00**

C2-45. Lufkin Rule Co., The: "Banner" Steel Tape Measure. 50 Foot. Graduations in 10th's. New Condition, Original Box. Length: 4 Inches. *In keeping with their practice of giving tape measures names that have absolutely nothing to do with the tool, the folks at Lufkin designated this as the "banner" tape measure. This one is in new condition in its original box.* (FINE) **$65.00**

Group D2

D2-1. Winchester Repeating Arms Co. No. W 68: Two Foot, Two Fold Folding Rule. With Round Joint. Rare and Excellent. Length: 24 Inches. *Winchester tools having product numbers beginning with the number "W" date from the later years of Winchester's failed experiment in merchandising. This two foot rule is in new condition. Mint.* (FINE) **$225.00**

D2-2. Winchester Repeating Arms Co. No. 9532: One Foot, Four Fold Folding Rule. With Caliper Slide. Rare and Excellent. Length: 12 Inches. *Among the least common "Winchester" tools are examples of the limited line of folding boxwood carpenters rules that they offered. This one foot, four fold rule is clearly marked with both the Winchester name and the product number. A rare Winchester rule.* (FINE) **$375.00**

D2-3. Winchester Repeating Arms Co. No. 6022: 13 Ounce Bell Face Claw Hammer. With Original Handle. Rare and Excellent. Length: 12 Inches. *This uncommon 13 ounce hammer retains its original handle, which is marked on the end with the Winchester product number.* (GOOD+) **$95.00**

D2-4. Winchester Repeating Arms Co. No. 9777: Cast Iron Butt Marking Gauge. Patented February 28, 1911. Complete and Excellent. Length: 3 Inches. *We have offered several Winchester marking gauges in the past, but this is the first butt mortise gauge we have encountered. The body of the tool is cast with the Winchester logo.* (FINE) **$245.00**

D2-5. Winchester Repeating Arms Co. No. 4033: 1 Inch Butt Chisel. Original Handle. Extra Crisp and Clean. Length: 10 Inches. *This well preserved butt chisel retains its original handle and is clean and clearly marked. Extra nice.* (FINE) **$75.00**

D2-6. Winchester Repeating Arms Co.: Classic "Camp" Hatchet. Original Case. Superb Condition. Length: 13 1/2 Inches. *We have seen our share of Winchester hatchets, but this is the first example with the original sheath we have had the opportunity to offer. The snap lock on the sheath is imprinted with the Winchester logo.* (GOOD+) **$365.00**

D2-7. Winchester Repeating Arms Co. No. 4841: 1/4 Inch Socket Chisel. Original Handle. "Pocket" Chisel Type. Length: 9 1/2 Inches. *"Pocket" chisels were the middle size between butt chisels and the full size offering. This one retains its original handle.* (GOOD+) **$55.00**

D2-8. Winchester Repeating Arms Co. No. 7101: 2 Inch Blade Screwdriver. Crisp and Clean. Brass Ferrule. Length: 6 Inches. *This classic Winchester screwdriver was the smallest size offered. Rare.* (GOOD+) **$45.00**

D2-9. Winchester Repeating Arms Co. No. 4572: 1/4 Inch Cape Chisel. Uncommon Type. Near New Condition. Length: 5 1/2 Inches. *This is the first example of this rare metalworking chisel we have seen bearing the Winchester name. New old stock.* (FINE) **$75.00**

D2-10. Winchester Repeating Arms Co.: 1/2 Inch Socket Chisel. Original Handle. Near New Condition. Length: 10 1/2 Inches. *If you're looking to fill out a set of Winchester chisels, this one will help you along the way. Even if you're not, you may want to start with this one. Nice.* (FINE) **$75.00**

D2-11. Winchester Repeating Arms Co. No. 7160: Miniature Slotted Screwdriver. Black Lacquerd Handle. Brass Ferrule. Length: 3 Inches. *In their advertising, Winchester referred to these as "pocket" screwdrivers. Rare.* (GOOD+) **$165.00**

D2-12. Winchester Repeating Arms Co. No. 4983: 1/2 Inch Socket Chisel. Original Handle. Bevel Edge Type. Length: 11 1/2 Inches. *The original handle is present in this well preserved Winchester chisel.* (GOOD+) **$65.00**

D2-13. Winchester Repeating Arms Co. No. 3045: Transitional Jack Metallic Plane. 90% Original Paint. Clean and Sound. Length: 15 Inches. *Transitional planes were subject to a level of wear and a susceptibility to dirt and grime, that was not the case with the darker colored cast iron planes. This one has survived quite well, retaining some 90% of its original paint. A good one.* (GOOD+) **$115.00**

D2-14. Winchester Repeating Arms Co.: "October Special" Pliers. 6 Inch Size. 90% Original Plating. Length: 6 Inches. *Although I know some collectors who are old enough to remember Winchester's "October Special" promotions in the 1920's, I never asked what they were all about. These pliers were apparently available at a bargain price as part of the hoopla. A nice example.* (GOOD+) **$65.00**

D2-15. Winchester Repeating Arms Co. No. 2495: 5 1/2 Inch Slip Joint Pliers. Full Nickel Plating. Extra Crisp and Clean. Length: 5 1/2 Inches. *These nearly perfectly preserved pliers have been forged with checking on the handle in a way that is evidence that they were of the very highest quality. A pretty pair.* (FINE) **$115.00**

D2-16. Winchester Repeating Arms Co. No. 7126: 5 Inch Heavy Duty Screwdriver. With Brass Fittings. Scarce and Excellent. Length: 10 Inches. *Winchester's screwdrivers were characterized by their prominent brass ferrule. This example is clean and clearly marked.* (GOOD+) **$55.00**

D2-17. Winchester Repeating Arms Co. No. 9827: 30 Inch Mahogany Level. Original Decal. Near New Condition. Length: 24 Inches. *Nearly all of the original decal remains on this perfectly preserved Winchester level. Near mint.* (FINE) **$245.00**

D2-18. Winchester Repeating Arms Co. No. W 91: Cast Iron Spoke Shave. Proper Cutting Iron. Rare and Excellent. Length: 10 Inches. *As was the case with tools of nearly every type, Winchester offered a full line of spoke shaves. This cast iron, gull wing offering is clean, complete and ready to fill out a collection. A rare Winchester item.* (GOOD+) **$225.00**

D2-19. Winchester Repeating Arms Co. No. 4703: 1/2 Inch Socket Chisel. Original Handle. "Butt" Chisel Type. Length: 7 1/2 Inches. *This example of Winchester's butt chisel is very clean, clearly marked and retains its original handle.* (GOOD+) **$45.00**

D2-20. Winchester Repeating Arms Co. No. 2365: Countersink Auger Bit. Clearly Marked. Uncommon Type. Length: 5 Inches. *Sometimes finding the small, obscure Winchester items is the most rewarding. This is the first example of this countersink bit that we have encountered. Rare.* (GOOD+) **$85.00**

D2-21. Winchester Repeating Arms Co. No. 2795: Cotter Pin Puller. Most Unusual Type. Near New Condition. Length: 9 Inches. *Apparently never used for the purpose for which it was produced, this most unusual Winchester item was intended for the mechanic to be used in extracting cotter pins. Never seen another. Mint.* (FINE) **$145.00**

D2-22. Winchester Repeating Arms Co. No. F1431: Full Set of Spur Auger Bits. In Added Case. A Rare Set. Length: 10 Inches. *This full set of Winchester bits has been stored in a case from a set of Russell Jennings bits. The bits in this set are complete, but have some evidence of pitting on the shafts.* (GOOD) **$185.00**

D2-23. Winchester Repeating Arms Co. No. 5350: Shingling Hatchet. With Hammer End. Extra Crisp Imprint. Length: 15 1/4 Inches. *This uncommon shingling hatchet is boldly marked with the Winchester name. The handle may not be the original. A nice example.* (GOOD+) **$85.00**

D2-24. Winchester Repeating Arms Co. No. 2166: Pair of 6 Inch End Cutters. Uncommon Type. Excellent Condition. Length: 6 Inches. *These end cutting pliers have been boldly struck with the Winchester logo. An essential tool for the "one of each" collector.* (GOOD+) **$85.00**

D2-25. Winchester Repeating Arms Co. No. 9811: 24 Inch Mahogany Level. Partial Original Decal. Rare and Excellent. Length: 24 Inches. *Much of the original decal remains on this well preserved mahogany level. The level that won the west.* (GOOD+) **$85.00**

D2-26. Winchester Repeating Arms Co.: Chip Breaker and Cutting Iron. For No. 4, 5, and 6. Extra Crisp and Clean. Length: 12 Inches. *If you have a Winchester plane that is missing the cutting iron, here's your chance to make it right. The chip breaker is a Stanley, but the cutter has the Winchester trademark.* (FINE) **$35.00**

D2-27. Winchester Repeating Arms Co. No. W3624: Cast Iron Plumb and Level. 99% Original Paint. Near New Condition. Length: 24 Inches. *Nearly all original finishes remain on this rare cast iron Winchester level. Rare and excellent.* (FINE) **$395.00**

D2-28. Winchester Repeating Arms Co. No. 9726: Cast Iron Mitre and Try Square. 6 Inch Blade. Copper Flash Plating. Length: 6 Inches. *The body of this well preserved cast iron try square was apparently finished with copper plating when new. A rare and graphic Winchester square.* (GOOD+) **$185.00**

D2-29. Winchester Repeating Arms Co.: Single Bit Felling Axe. Crisp, Clear Logo. Original Handle. Length: 32 1/2 Inches. *The bold "Winchester" logo is clearly legible on this classic felling axe, which retains its original handle.* (GOOD) **$65.00**

D2-30. Winchester Repeating Arms Co.: Nested "Plumber's" Saw. With 4 Original Blades. Rare and Near New. Length: 20 Inches. *The ambitious plans of the Winchester Repeating Arms Company to enter the hardware business are well documented, but the scope of their initial commitment to the enterprise, and the later depth of their failure, becomes more apparent when one begins to appreciate the wide range of products they produced after starting virtually from scratch. This spectacularly well preserved kit of "plumber's" saws is in virtually unused condition, except for one blade, in its orignal case. Each of the saws is etched with the Winchester name the master handle is absolutely perfect. For the saw collector or Winchester enthusiast, this exceptional set will serve as a focal point of a collection for many, many years. Highly recommended.* (FINE) **$1,850.00**

D2-31. Winchester Repeating Arms Co. No. 9778: Double Rod Marking Gauge. With Steel Roller. Raised Cast "W". Length: 7 Inches. *An excellent double beam marking gauge with the Winchester "W" in raised casting on the body. A good one.* (GOOD+) **$165.00**

D2-32. Winchester Repeating Arms Co. No. 3504: 12 Inch Sweep Brace. Rosewood Handle, Pad. Superb Condition. Length: 12 Inches. *This 12 inch sweep brace retains virtually all of its original nickel plating. A rare Winchester tool.* (GOOD+) **$225.00**

D2-33. Winchester Repeating Arms Co. No. 3533: 10 Inch Sweep Brace. Beech Handle and Pad. Scarce and Sound. Length: 12 Inches. *Winchester offered this ratcheting brace in three sizes, of which this was the middle size.* (GOOD+) **$115.00**

D2-34. Winchester Repeating Arms Co. No. 2901: 14 Inch Blade Meat Saw. Original Blade. Near New Condition. Length: 18 Inches. *Meat saws were the sort of tool that either quickly degraded in condition due to the sort of work they performed, or didn't. This one didn't.* (GOOD+) **$225.00**

D2-35. Winchester Repeating Arms Co. No. 2184: 5 Inch Round Nose Pliers. Scarce Type. Near New Condition. Length: 5 Inches. *To eliminate confusion on the part of the buying public, the obscure product number of these F2184M pliers was changed to W890R5 in 1926. Huh? A rare pair.* (FINE) **$165.00**

D2-36. Winchester Repeating Arms Co. No. 3004: No. 4 Equivalent Metallic Plane. Mahogany Handles. Complete and Sound. Length: 9 Inches. *We are prepared to certify that this Winchester plane is marked in 3 places and therefore qualifies as a Winchester plane. The japan finish has been enhanced by a previous owner, but it is otherwise clean and sound.* (GOOD) **$115.00**

D2-37. Winchester Repeating Arms Co. No. 2499: 10 Inch Slip Joint Pliers. Full Nickel Plating. Most Unusual Size. Length: 10 Inches. *Much larger than the commonly encountered Winchester pliers, these oversize slip joint pliers feature jaws that are slightly offset. Nearly all original nickel plating remains.* (GOOD+) **$95.00**

D2-38. Winchester Repeating Arms Co. No. 9776: Double Beam Marking Gauge. Beechwood Body. Near New Condition. Length: 8 1/2 Inches. *Nearly all of the original decal remains on the Winchester gauge. Nice.* (FINE) **$145.00**

D2-39. Winchester Repeating Arms Co.: Double End Screwdriver. Special Design. Rare and Near New. Length: 6 Inches. *A thorough search through all Winchester reference materials in the Donnelly Library failed to turn up any mention of this double end screwdriver. A rare Winchester tool in new condition.* (FINE) **$145.00**

D2-40. Winchester Repeating Arms Co. No. 8733: Double Speed Breast Drill. With Built in Level. Original Decal. Length: 16 Inches. *A most unlikely Winchester tool, this breast drill retains nearly all of its original decal and much of its subdued mint colored paint. A rare Winchester tool.* (GOOD+) **$345.00**

D2-41. Winchester Repeating Arms Co. No. 9616: 24 Inch Framing Square. Copper Plate Finish. Rare and Excellent. Length: 24 Inches. *Copper plating adds a bit of color to this rare Winchester square. A good one.* (GOOD+) **$185.00**

D2-42. Winchester Repeating Arms Co. No. 3083: Adjustable Dado Metallic Plane. Rare 1 Inch Size. Clean and Complete. Length: 8 Inches. *These were made for Winchester by Sargent & Company of New Haven, Connecticut. The reverse side is ornamented with a stylized pattern of decoration. Of the four sizes offered in this series, this is the largest and the rarest. A tough Winchester plane to find.* (GOOD+) **$545.00**

D2-43. Winchester Repeating Arms Co. No. F1431: Full Set of Spur Auger Bit. In Added Case. A Rare Set. Length: 10 Inches. *The roll in which these bits are kept does not appear original, but it has kept this full set of Winchester bits in excellent condition for the collector. A nice set.* (GOOD+) **$285.00**

D2-44. Winchester Repeating Arms Co. No. 3006: No. 4 1/2 Equivalent Metallic Plane. Mahogany Handles. Near New Condition. Length: 10 Inches. *This is as nice an example of the Winchester Line as we have ever offered. All original finishes remain on wood and metal surfaces. No apologies for this one. Top shelf.* (FINE) **$445.00**

D2-45. Winchester Repeating Arms Co. No. W 27 1/2: Combination Mitre Try Square. 6 Inch Blade. Near New Condition. Length: 6 Inches. *Nearly all of the original bluing remains on this later-style Winchester try and mitre square.* (FINE) **$195.00**

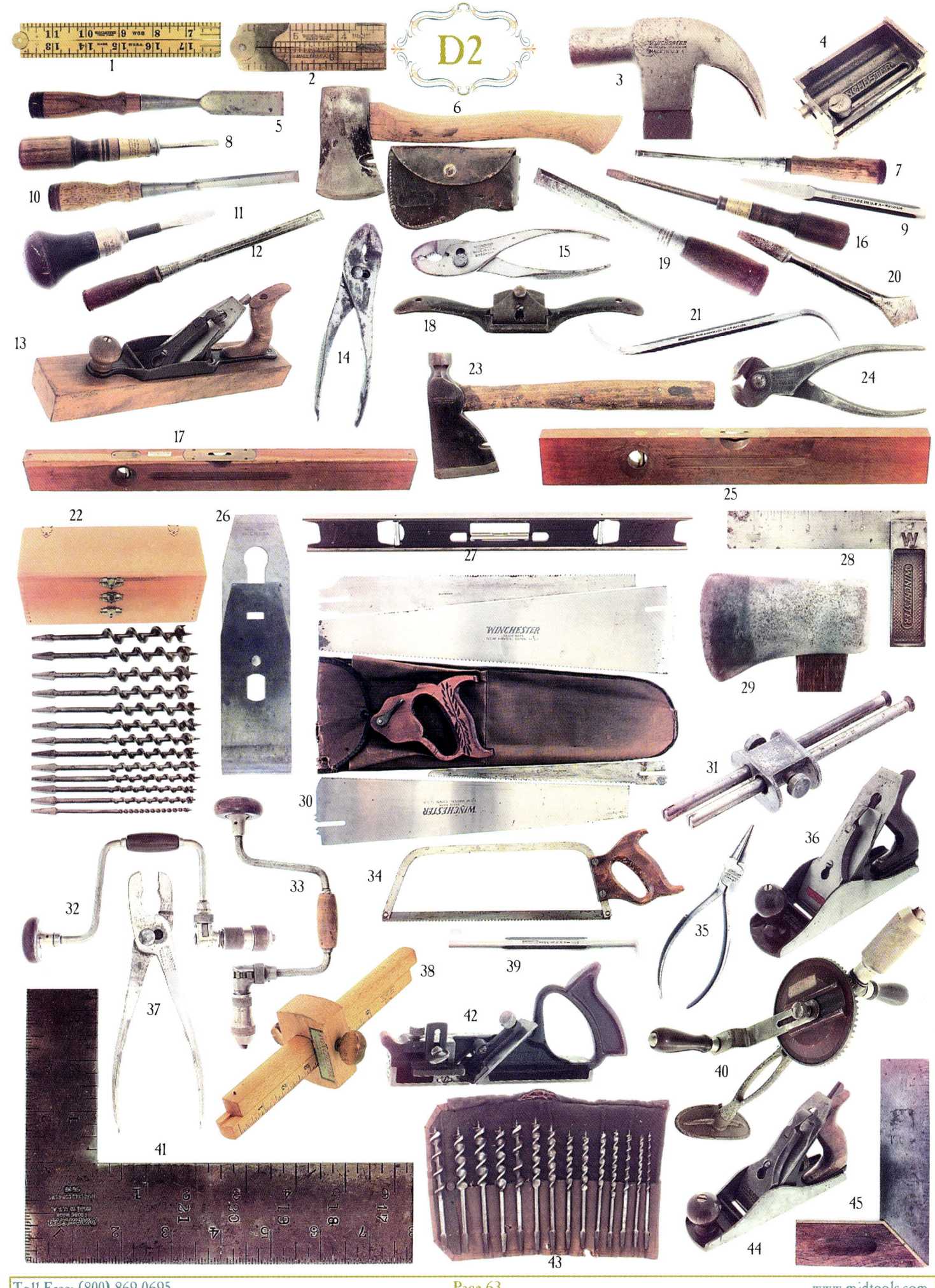

Group E2

E2-1. Stanley Rule & Level No. 42: Precision Adjust Saw Set. Cast Iron Body. New Condition, Original Box. Length: 6 1/2 Inches. *The No. 42 was Stanley's best sawset. This one is in unused condition in its original box with all original finishes intact. Ready to use or display.* (FINE) **$55.00**

E2-2. Stanley Rule & Level No. 42: Precision Adjust Saw Set. Cast Iron Body. Near New Condition. Length: 6 1/2 Inches. *The No. 42 was Stanley's best sawset. This one is in unused condition in its original box with all original finishes intact. Ready to use or display.* (FINE) **$45.00**

E2-3. Smith, S.: Early Patent Saw Set. Patented October 4, 1859. Rare and Excellent. Length: 12 Inches. *This example of the Seymour Smith patent has spent some time in the woods, but it is complete and ready to display. A graphic saw set of very early manufacture.* (GOOD+) **$165.00**

E2-4. Croissant & Bro., C., Albany, N.Y.: Early Patent Saw Set. Patented May 30, 1877. Excellent Condition. Length: 8 1/2 Inches. *This example of Charles Crosissant's 1884 patent is clean and complete. An excellent addition to any collection of mechanically interesting saw sets.* (GOOD+) **$85.00**

E2-5. Stanley Rule & Level No. 43: Heavy Duty Saw Set. Original Advertising. New Condition, Original Box. Length: 8 1/2 Inches. *The average woodworker would have little cause to purchase one of these oversize saw sets. Saw sets are frequently found in boxes because they were generally stored away in those boxes and placed on a shelf or in a drawer. A tool like this, however, would have been used in the woods or in a specialized sharpening shop, where use would have been much more frequent. A most unlikely "in the box" item.* (FINE) **$95.00**

E2-6. Marples & Sons, Wm., Hibernia: Boxwood Handled Saw Set. English Type. Excellent Condtion. Length: 9 1/2 Inches. *This classic English saw wrest is boldly struck with the imprint of William Marples' Hibernia Works. A nice example.* (GOOD+) **$35.00**

E2-7. Noepal & Assman, Newark, N.J.: Early Patent Saw Set. Patented April 21, 1868. Rare Unmarked Exmple. Length: 8 Inches. *Unmarked with either the patent date or the maker name, this is unquestionably an example of the Noepal & Assman patent of April 21, 1868. A very rare saw set.* (GOOD) **$245.00**

E2-8. Unmarked: "Wrest" Type Saw Set. For Large Crosscut Saws. Ca. 1880's. Length: 8 Inches. *There are no marks on this one, but it is similar to the early saw sets produced by Henry Disston & Sons. A nice example.* (GOOD+) **$45.00**

E2-9. True, Moses, Oakfield, New York: Early Patent Saw Set. Patented March 24, 1874. Multiple Adjustment. Length: 11 1/2 Inches. *The Moses True patent saw set of 1874 features enough screws and adjustments to confound even the seasoned sawyer. A rare saw set in excellent collector quality condition.* (GOOD+) **$95.00**

E2-10. Boynton, E.M.: Early Patent Saw Set. Patented November 25, 1873. Rare Large Size. Length: 11 Inches. *This is the patent of William Boynton of Battle Creek, Michigan. A plier type device that receives a "UC" rating in the now out of print Friberg book. Different.* (GOOD+) **$85.00**

E2-11. Holt Co., The G.L., Hartford, Conn.: Adjustable Saw Set. Patented October 8, 1901. With Patent Date. Length: 7 Inches. *The G.L. Holt company made tool handles, a pad saw that is quite uncommon, and braces. This is the first saw set bearing their name that I have seen.* (GOOD+) **$55.00**

E2-12. Sears, Roebuck & Company No. 4886: Cast Iron Saw Set. Uncommon Type. New Condition, Original Box. Length: 5 1/2 Inches. *Sears offered this workaday saw set for the home saw setter. New and in the box.* (FINE) **$35.00**

E2-13. Atkins & Co., E.C., Indianapolis: Patent Stump Anvil Saw Set. Patented Decemcer 6, 1881. Rare and Excellent. Length: 5 1/2 Inches. *Not unlike the classic German dengelstock, this patented saw setting device was designed to be mounted in a stump for use. A rare patented saw set in excellent condition.* (GOOD+) **$285.00**

E2-14. Holt Co., The G.L., Hartford, Conn.: Adjustable Saw Set. Patented October 8, 1901. Marked "Patent Pending". Length: 7 Inches. *The patent on this one was issued in the name of Gardner Holt, of Hartford, Connecticut. A good one.* (GOOD+) **$45.00**

E2-15. Borthwick, John, Atlantic City, N.J.: "Borthwick's Patent." Saw Set. Patented June 23, 1885. Most Unusual Mechanism. Length: 8 Inches. *Adjustment of this one is relatively simple, but was accomplished by building the simplicity into a well machined tool that might have taken many days wages to purchase. Mechanically interesting and uncommon.* (GOOD+) **$85.00**

E2-16. Borthwick, John, Atlantic City, N.J.: "Borthwick's Patent." Saw Set. Patented June 23, 1885. Superb Example. Length: 8 Inches. *Adjustment of this one was accomplished by building the simplicity into a well machined tool that is mechanically interesting and uncommon. This is by far the nicest example of this mechanically interesting saw set that we have ever offered..* (FINE) **$115.00**

E2-17. Rust, W.O., Gt. Falls, N.H.: Early Forged Saw Set. Patented August 22, 1854. Superb Condition. Length: 9 Inches. *One of the earliest, most graphic and most collectible of all saw sets, this example of the W.O. Rust patent is in excellent collector quality condition.* (GOOD+) **$365.00**

E2-18. Disston & Sons, H., Philadelphia, Penn. No. 8: "Triumph" Saw Set. Largest Size. Superb Condition. Length: 7 Inches. *This great working set bears the mark of Henry Disston & Sons, the saw people.* (FINE) **$65.00**

E2-19. Borthwick, John, Atlantic City, N.J.: "Borthwick's Patent" Saw Set. Patented June 23, 1885. Most Unusual Mechanism. Length: 8 Inches. *These mechanical marvels are unlike any other saw set ever produced. A gizmo.* (GOOD+) **$75.00**

E2-20. Morrill, Charles, Jersey City, N.J: Early Cam-Type Saw Set. Patented December 14, 1886. Friberg: "R" Rating. Length: 5 1/2 Inches. *The later Morrill patent was one of the most successful of all saw sets. Apparently Morrill "cut his teeth" on this earlier invention. A rare saw set.* (GOOD+) **$165.00**

E2-21. Leopold: "Leopold's Patent" Saw Set. Patented October 11, 1887. Near New Condition. Length: 7 1/2 Inches. *There are no maker marks apparent on this one, but the patent information clearly demonstrates that this is the June 5, 1891 patent of Charles Leopold of Philadelphia. A scarce and mechanically interesting sawset.* (FINE) **$115.00**

E2-22. Taintnor Mfg. Co., New York No. 7: Patent Spring Saw Set. Full Nickel Plating. Patented May 5, 1891. Length: 6 1/2 Inches. *Arguably the most successful saw set of all time, the Taintnor patent was popular for a reason—it did the job it was intended to do very well. A great example in fine working condition.* (FINE) **$35.00**

E2-23. Lloyd, W.S.: "Leach's Improved" Saw Set. Patented January 19, 1869. Original Gold Paint. Length: 12 1/2 Inches. *Nearly all of the original gold lettering that identified this set to would-be buyers as the "Leach's Improved" is bright and clearly visible. A clean and early patented sawset.* (GOOD+) **$75.00**

E2-24. Frisk, O., Kiron, Iowa: "The Buller" Saw Set. Patented February 26, 1924. Clean and Complete. Length: 12 1/2 Inches. *These graphic saw sets were intended for use on very large saws. A nice example.* (GOOD+) **$25.00**

E2-25. Unmarked: "Leach's Patent" Saw Set. Patented January 19, 1869. Early and Excellent. Length: 7 Inches. *A mechanically interesting and visually appealing saw set with a lean and early look. Cassius and carry.* (GOOD+) **$15.00**

E2-26. B. Mfg. Assoc.: Patent Adjustable Saw Set. Patented April 5, 1904. Superb Condition. Length: 8 1/2 Inches. *Another clean and mechanically interesting saw set, this one was patented by Joseph Lester of Norwich, Connecticut. Nearly all original nickel plating remains. Nice.* (FINE) **$55.00**

E2-27. Atkins & Co., E.C., Indianapolis No. 3: Circular and Band Saw Set. Sheffield Saw Works. New Condition, Original Box. Length: 9 Inches. *For the saw set collector, or the would-be saw-setter, we offer this fully equipped kit. Complete with instructions.* (FINE) **$45.00**

E2-28. Unmarked: Hand Forged Saw Set. Made From File. With Screwdriver. Length: 7 Inches. *Worn out files provided the raw material for producing all manner of tools, including this well made "wrest" type saw set.* (GOOD+) **$25.00**

E2-29. Geer, John, Holden, Mass.: Geer's Patent Saw Set. Patented July 9, 1867. Friberg: "NS" Rating. Length: 6 Inches. *Patented on July 9, 1867 by one John Geer of Holden, Massachusetts, this one is marked with the patent date, but not the maker name.* (GOOD+) **$295.00**

E2-30. Unmarked: Early Mechanical Saw Set. Complete and Sound. Most Unusual. Length: 17 Inches. *Most likely used for setting the teeth of band saws, this cast iron device has the look of a tool made in the 1870's or early 1880's. It is mechanically in excellent condition.* (GOOD) **$95.00**

E2-31. Stanley Rule & Level No. 43: Heavy Duty Saw Set. For Crosscut Saws. Superb Condition. Length: 8 1/2 Inches. *This oversize saw set, which was acquired in the State of Kansas this fall is imprinted with the initials "U.P.R.R.", which, one would assume stands for the Union Pacific Railroad, the venerable concern from which it was stolen. A nice example in top condition.* (FINE) **$45.00**

E2-32. Unmarked: Filigree Inlay Saw Set. Pewter Inlay. Classic Form. Length: 8 1/2 Inches. *Fitted with a rosewood handle and ornamented with pewter inlay in a style that was popular at the very beginning of the Nineteenth Century, this is the most aesthetically pleasing saw set we have ever offered. Very pretty.* (GOOD+) **$195.00**

E2-33. Bach & Co., S.F.L., Boston, Mass.: Early Patent Saw Set. Patented January 19, 1869. Excellent Condition. Length: 7 Inches. *An exceptionally early and clearly marked saw set in excellent collector quality condition. A angular brass fence provides visual appeal. Nice.* (GOOD+) **$115.00**

E2-34. Kohler, F.: Fager's Patent Saw Set. Patented March 3, 1891. Multiple Adjustment. Length: 7 1/2 Inches. *The essential elements of a good saw set were a provision for multiple settings, facility of adjustment and ease of use. Sometimes one got in the way of the other. This one looks O.K. on points 1 and 3, but one might need an instruction manual to get it lined up properly. Clean and clearly marked.* (GOOD+) **$95.00**

E2-35. Stanley Tools No. 432: "Defiance" Saw Set. 99.9 % Original Finish. Brand New. Length: 6 Inches. *All this one needs is the original box. Shiny, clean and brand new. Perfect.* (FINE) **$35.00**

E2-36. Rust, W.O., Gt. Falls, N.H.: Early Forged Saw Set. Patented August 22, 1854. Rare and Excellent. Length: 9 Inches. *Marked with the patentee's name but not the patent date, this example of the Rust patent set is in top collector quality condition. All original parts remain. A good one.* (FINE) **$425.00**

E2-37. Disston & Sons, H., Philadelphia, Penn.: "Triumph" Saw Set. Precision Adjust. Superb Condition. Length: 7 Inches. *This crispy-clean example of the smaller size of Disston's "Triumph" line is in excellent condition for use or for a growing collection.* (GOOD+) **$25.00**

E2-38. Buller: "The Buller" Saw Set. For Larger Saws. New Condition, Original Box. Length: 12 1/2 Inches. *The original box has kept this later version of the Buller saw set in top condition. Complete with the original green paint, which was apparently intended to keep it from getting lost in the woods.* (FINE) **$45.00**

E2-39. Stanley Rule & Level No. 42: Precision Adjust Saw Set. Cast Iron Body. Near New Condition. Length: 6 1/2 Inches. *The No. 42 was Stanley's best sawset. This one is in unused condition. Ready to use or add to a "one of each" Stanley collection.* (FINE) **$35.00**

E2-40. Unmarked: "The Star" Patent Saw Set. Patented December 24. Trip Lever Activated. Length: 6 Inches. *This was apparently designed to be mounted to a bench with a cord attached to the trip lever extending through the bench. The first of this type that we have offered.* (GOOD+) **$65.00**

E2-41. Unmarked: Classic Hand Made Saw Set. With Screw Adjustment. Superb Patina. Length: 6 Inches. *Fashioned from available materials by some long forgotten craftsman, this well made and perfectly proportioned saw set is a classic example of the ingenuity and artistry of the 19th Century.* (GOOD+) **$55.00**

E2-42. Stearns & Co., E.C., Syracuse, N.Y. No. 2: "Taintnor Pattern" Saw Set. Full Nickel Plating. Uncommon Type. Length: 6 Inches. *All of the original nickel plating remains on this immaculate example of one of the most popular and well made saw sets of all time.* (FINE) **$45.00**

E2-43. Stanley Rule & Level No. 43: Heavy Duty Saw Set. For Crosscut Saws. New Condition, Original Box. Length: 8 1/2 Inches. *Complete in the original box with the Stanley advertising pamphlet, this oversize saw set is in top collector quality condition. An uncommon "in the box" item.* (FINE) **$75.00**

E2-44. Chase, R.G.: "O.K" Patent Saw Set. Patented February 13, 1866. Complete and Excellent. Length: 6 Inches. *Patented by one R.G. Chase in the year following the end of the American Civil War, the "O.K." saw set featured a pistol grip mechanism unlike anything else made before that time. This example is complete, mechanically perfect and clearly marked. A rare collectible saw set.* (GOOD+) **$285.00**

E2-45. Unmarked: Classic Beech Handle. Saw Set. "Wrest Type". Excellent Condition. Length: 9 Inches. *Fitted with a series of notches that were used as lever to bend saw teeth to the precise angle of set, these "saw wrests" were in much more common use in England than in the New World, where gizmocity was the order of the day.* (GOOD+) **$30.00**

Group F2

F2-1. Nicholson File Co., Providence, R.I. No. 4: Set of Needle Files. "Wiss Pattern". New Condition, Original Box. Length: 4 1/4 Inches. *A great working set of files of the quality that is nowhere available today. Ready to use.* (FINE) **$45.00**

F2-2. Buck & Hickman, (London): Elaborate Bench Level. For Machinist Use. New Condition, Original Box. Length: 5 Inches. *Complete with its original pasteboard box, which has kept it in brand new condition, this oversize brass machinists bench from London tool merchants Buck & Hickman is the first example of this tool that we have seen. Rare and brand new.* (FINE) **$345.00**

F2-3. Esterbrook Steel Pen Mfg. Co. No. 8: Patent Sliding Compass. With Instructions. New Condition, Original Box. Length: 3 1/2 Inches. *Apparently not content with the design that had been perfected sometime after the reign of Amenhotep IV, the Esterbrook brought out this "improvement", complete with a fitted metal box and literature proclaiming the triumph of technology over wisdom. There weren't many takers. A rare tool in excellent condition.* (FINE) **$115.00**

F2-4. Petersen Mfg. Co., Dewitt, Nebraska No. 8 R: "Vise-Grip" Wrench. For Sheet Metal. New Condition, Original Box. Length: 8 Inches. *An extra wide jaw facilitate the use of these specialty vise grips with sheet metal. The original instruction manual is included with this "in the box" set.* (FINE) **$45.00**

F2-5. Sandvik, Sweden: Coromant Cutting Tool. With Hard. Steel Tips. For Metal Lathe? Length: 6 Inches. *This special purpose lathe cutting tool comes complete with a series of hardened tips of Swedish steel. Try buying something like this new.* (GOOD+) **$25.00**

F2-6. Murcott, John H., Inc., St. Albans No. 76: "Baby Terrier" Hammer. Crate Openers. New Condition, Original Box. Length: 7 Inches. *For the collector of crate and box opening tools (yes, they're out there) we offer this ultimate prize: A full box of miniature crate opening hammers. These were sold under the "Baby Terrier" brand name. Where else but Martin J. Donnelly Antique Tools?* (FINE) **$155.00**

F2-7. Crescent Tool Co., Jamestown, N.Y. No. 20: 4 1/2" Flat Nose Pliers. With Cushion Grip. New Condition, Original Box. Length: 4 1/2 Inches. *These specialty pliers feature the optional rubberized "cushion grip". New and in the box.* (FINE) **$35.00**

F2-8. Mayhew Steel Prod. Co., Shelburne No. 388: Taper Reamer. For Bit Brace. New Condition, Original Box. Length: 6 Inches. *This perfectly preserved reamer was intended for use in a bit brace. Absolutely unused.* (FINE) **$25.00**

F2-9. Sawyer Tool Co., Fitchburg, Mass. No. 27: Keyseat Rule Blocks. Original Blued Finish. New Condition, Original Box. Length: 2 Inches. *Makers of machinist tools in the last century must most certainly have sold their tools individually boxed, as was the custom, but very few seem to have survived. Here's a pristine example of the packaging used by the Sawyer Tool Company of Fitchburg, Mass. Rare.* (FINE) **$125.00**

F2-10. Eden Specialty Co., The: The Eden Plumb And Level. Patented June 17, 1924. New Condition, Original Box. Length: 6 Inches. *This add-on level also features a plumb vial. If you choose, you could be the first to remove it from the original box. Brand new.* (FINE) **$95.00**

F2-11. North Bros Mfg. Co., Philadelphia. No. 41: Automatic Push Push Drill. Original Decal. New Condition, Original Box. Length: 10 Inches. *By the time the tool makers got around to figuring out that these things were obsolete, this was the only one still being made. It gave the knockout punch to Goodell Pratt's "Mr. Punch" and many others. A great example, new in its original box.* (FINE) **$55.00**

F2-12. Stanley Rule & Level No. 22: Dowel Sharpener. For Electric Drill. New Condition, Original Box. Length: 2 1/4 Inches. *This most unusual "straight shaft" dowel sharpener was apparently intended for use in an electric drill. Condition is unused. A rare Stanley "in the box" item.* (FINE) **$45.00**

F2-13. Keuffel & Esser Co., New York No. 932: "Anvil" Railroad Pen For Draughtsman. New Condition, Original Box. Length: 5 1/2 Inches. *These double tipped "railroad" pens were used for drawing parallel lines two at a time. New and in the box.* (FINE) **$55.00**

F2-14. Heller Bros. Co., Newark, N.J.: Set of Asstorted Needle Files. No. 0 Cut. New Condition, Original Box. Length: 5 1/2 Inches. *Here's a set of small "needle files" in new condition in their original box. Better than new.* (FINE) **$65.00**

F2-15. Unmarked: Massive Arkansas Oilstone. Fitted Walnut Box. Ready to Use. Length: 9 Inches. *This oversize whetstone is flat, clean and ready to be immediately put to work. A great working stone in a handsome walnut case.* (GOOD+) **$115.00**

F2-16. Stanley Rule & Level: Box of "Ready Edge" Cutting Irons. For Patented Cutter. Rare and Excellent. Length: 2 1/2 Inches. *The "Ready Edge" plane irons marketed by Stanley in the 1920's were the disposable razor's of a previous era. Changing the habits of a time-honored trade isn't easy, as Stanley found out. These are rare. Track 1.* (FINE) **$95.00**

F2-17. Millers Falls Company No. 106: Flexible Bench Rule. On Display Card. Unused Condition. Length: 6 Inches. *A colorful card was employed by Millers Falls' marketers to attract interest to this steel machinists rule. Brand new.* (FINE) **$25.00**

F2-18. Conn. Valley Mfg. Co.: "Clark's Pattern" Auger Bit. Expansive-Bit. New Condition, Original Box. Length: 8 Inches. *The box for this classic pattern auger bit is in excellent condition. The tool has been used, but not abused.* (GOOD+) **$25.00**

F2-19. Mc Gillis, Brown & Pratt Mfg. Co.: The "Perfection" Tack Puller. Old Hardware Stock. With Original Handbill. Length: 6 Inches. *One of the fascinating qualities of antique tools is their ability to evoke the reality of an era very long ago, if not so very far away. Imagine a world where anyone could, and many did, set their hand to creating a "new and useful device", and then very quickly obtain a patent for same. To be sure, many of these patents were a waste of good paper, but a world so rich with opportunity seems to have motivated a great many to achieve extraordinary things. This "Perfection" tack puller, although undated, appears to date from the 1880's, or possibly even earlier. It has never been used, nor was it ever unwrapped from the paper sleeve/handbill in which it has lain protected from a century of weather and dirt, until it was carefully taken out for this photograph. According to the papers, this tack puller was prepared for offering to the market, despite the fact that numerous other tack pullers were available, because it was the "...superior of any other made". Moreover, the "Perfection" puller is identified in the accompanying description as "...the only tool of the kind ever manufactured from such high quality material". It may well be that this tool was simply too nice to use; or it might more likely be that the expenditure of time and money for materials and distribution on something so mundane as a tack puller may have proved prohibitively expensive for Mssrs. McGillis, Brown & Pratt of Menominee, Michigan. Whatever the case, we thank them, one and all, for having created this magical link to a bygone time, and for having sealed, so long ago, within the protective paper wrapper, a piece of the dream that resides in each of us. Extra special.* (FINE) **$55.00**

F2-20. Utica Drop Forge & Tool Corp. No. 20: 4 1/2" Flat Nose Pliers. Fully Polished. New Condition, Original Box. Length: 4 1/2 Inches. *A graphic "picture box" complements these well preserved flat nose pliers from an important New York State maker. Nice.* (FINE) **$35.00**

F2-21. Athol Machine Co., Athol, Mass.: Pair of Machinist's Setup Blocks. In Fitted Wood Case. Original Paper Box. Length: 3 1/2 Inches. *Perhaps the most interesting feature of this set of machinists blocks in a fitted wooden box is the snippet of ribald verse found in the bottom of the box. In consideration of the many children who are encouraged (and rightly so) to read from the pages of these volumes that their education might thereby be more complete, we will not quote from this writing in print. Suffice it to say that the nature of humor in the workplace has not changed much in one hundred years. A potential article of evidence in a lawsuit against Mitsubishi Motors.* (FINE) **$125.00**

F2-22. Diamond Tool And Horseshoe Co. No. D76: 6" "Diamalloy" Wrench. "Crescent" Type. New Condition, Original Box. Length: 6 Inches. *This classic 6" "Crescent" wrench has never been used. Brand new.* (FINE) **$45.00**

F2-23. Crescent Tool Co., Jamestown, N.Y. No. 24: 7" "Knitter's" Pliers. Most Unusual Type. New Condition, Original Box. Length: 7 Inches. *These "knitters" pliers are new to us. They are in new condition in their original box.* (FINE) **$65.00**

F2-24. Millers Falls Company: Set of 3 Chuck and Drill Assortments. For Screwdrivers. New Condition, Original Box. Length: 3 Inches. *If you ever need to outfit your collection of Millers Falls push drills and screwdrivers with the proper accessories, here's just what you need. Six different sets for six different drills.* (FINE) **$75.00**

F2-25. Numberall Stamp & Tool Co.: Rotating Wheel Number Stamp. Patented December 31, 1918. Original Wood Box. Length: 3 1/2 Inches. *No need to reach back into a box of stamps every time the number changes—a simple click of the wheel with this work of genius and work continues apace. Different.* (GOOD+) **$75.00**

F2-26. Brown & Sharpe Mfg., Providence No. 573: Precision Key Seat Rule. With Inserts. New Condition, Original Box. Length: 3 1/2 Inches. *This specialty rule from Brown & Sharpe is in new condition in its original box.* (GOOD+) **$45.00**

F2-27. Sears, Roebuck And Company No. 4186: "Craftsman" Doweling Jig. Ca. 1950's. New Condition, Original Box. Length: 8 Inches. *This well made doweling jig features a rotating turret to select the size of dowel and comes with an auger bit depth stop. New and in the box.* (FINE) **$55.00**

F2-28. Favor, Ruhl & Co., Chicago, Illinois: Ackron's Beam Compass. Graduated Beam. New Condition, Original Box. Length: 10 Inches. *Here's a most unusual adjustable precision compass in new condition is an interesting pasteboard box. Different.* (FINE) **$55.00**

F2-29. Millers Falls Company: Cutting Iron For No. 85 Plane. Fits Stanley No. 78. New Condition, Original Box. Length: 4 1/2 Inches. *This Millers Falls cutting iron will also fit Stanley's No. 78 plane. Brand new in the original box.* (FINE) **$25.00**

F2-30. Lufkin Rule Co., The No. 584: Clamp Handle For Tape Measures. Fully Nickel Plated. New Condition, Original Box. Length: 3 1/4 Inches. *This Lufkin tape measure clamp is in perfect condition in its original box. Mint.* (FINE) **$125.00**

F2-31. Stanley Rule & Level No. 49: Auger Bit Depth Gauge. Nickel Plated Finish. New Condition, Original Box. Length: 2 1/2 Inches. *This auger bit depth stop from Stanley has been protected through the years by its original pasteboard box. All original nickel plating remains.* (FINE) **$55.00**

F2-32. Diamond Tool And Horseshoe Co. No. C79: 9" Monkey Wrench. Nickel Plated. New Condition, Original Box. Length: 9 Inches. *This monkey wrench classic has never been used. Absolutely perfect.* (FINE) **$65.00**

F2-33. Kearney & Foote: Box of Slim Taper Triangular Files. "Double Extra Slim". For Saw Filing?Length: 6 1/2 Inches. *Kearney & Foote were eventually bought out by the Nicholson File Company. These files, which appear to be the proper size for saw filing, are in brand new condition.* (FINE) **$35.00**

F2-34. Lenk Mfg. Co., Newton Lower Falls, Mass. No. 350: Deluxe Automatic Blowtorch. Original Decal. New Condition, Original Box. Length: 7 3/4 Inches. *All of the original decal remains on this unused blowtorch. Complete in the original box with instructions.* (FINE) **$55.00**

F2-35. Whitney Metal Tool Co., Rockford No. 5 JR.: "Whitney" Metal Punch. All Original Parts. Fine Condition, Original Box. Length: 8 1/2 Inches. *This classic "Whitney" metal punch appears complete and ready to use.* (FINE) **$65.00**

F2-36. Nicholson File Co., Providence, R.I. No. 4: Surface File Holder. For Body Work? New Condition, Original Box. Length: 17 1/2 Inches. *This holder for large files was likely intended for use by auto body workers. This one is in absolutely unused condition.* (FINE) **$65.00**

F2-37. Coes Wrench Co., Worcester, Mass.: Promotional Wrench Stick Pin. Original Card. "Pin to Your Memory". Length: 3 Inches. *The rough and tumble crowd who used Coes' wrenches probably didn't have much use for stickpins. Here's a nice example, nonetheless.* (FINE) **$65.00**

F2-38. Starrett Co., L. S., Athol, Mass. No. 436RL: 3" to 4" Micrometer. Complete and Near New. Original Box. Length: 9 Inches. *No apologies for this precision micrometer in the uncommon 3" to 4" size.* (GOOD+) **$35.00**

F2-39. Stanley Rule & Level: "No. 1" Cutting Iron. "Sweetheart" Trademark. Original Wax Sleeve. Length: 5 Inches. *The original wax sleeve has kept this "Sweetheart" era cutting iron in brand new condition. Mint.* (FINE) **$65.00**

F2-40. Nicholson File Co., Providence, R.I: Box of Files and File Handles. Unused Condition. Great Graphics. Length: 7 1/2 Inches. *If you're looking to set up a shop, here's a supply of files that will last you a good long time. Offered complete with a set of handles. Now is the time.* (FINE) **$55.00**

F2-41. Lufkin Rule Co., The, Saginaw, Mich. No. 9 A: Height Gauge Attachment. Blued Steel Finish. New Condition, Original Box. Length: 2 3/4 Inches. *Never having seen one of these tools at all, we are particularly pleased to offer an example that is in new condition in its original box. An unusual item for the growing number of collectors of Lufkin machinists tools.* (FINE) **$55.00**

F2-42. Millers Falls Company No. 172: Pipe Burring Reamer. For Bit Brace. New Condition, Original Box. Length: 4 1/2 Inches. *This tool was made to fit in a bit brace where it could be used to take the sharp burr off the inside edge of a recently cut piece of pipe. Brand new.* (FINE) **$25.00**

F2-43. Gohm Mfg. Co., Saginaw, Mich.: "Gohm" Butt Mortiser. For Electric Drill. New Condition, Original Box. Length: 8 Inches. *And now for something completely different, here's a butt mortise device that was designed to work in conjunction with an electric drill to facilitate the tedious task of hanging doors. New and in the box.* (FINE) **$25.00**

F2-44. Nicholson File Co., Providence, R.I.: Special Promotional Files. "Two File Special". For National Hardware Week. Length: 13 1/2 Inches. *As part of the "National Hardware Week" celebration, retailers teamed with the Nicholson to offer this boxed set of files. A nice pair in new condition in their original box.* (FINE) **$85.00**

F2-45. Unmarked: Multi Purpose Combination Tool. From Japan. New Condition, Original Box. Length: 11 1/2 Inches. *In the years following the Second World War, the designation "made in Japan" was synonymous with inexpensive tools of questionable quality. This high gizmocity factor combination tool meets that standard. Very different.* (FINE) **$45.00**

Group G2

G2-1. Eagle Mfg. Co.: Boxed Complex Molding Plane. Possible Rework. APW III: 3 Stars (A). Length: 9 1/2 Inches. *There is speculation that this imprint may have been a trade name used by the H.L. James Manufacturing Company, a planemaking enterprise located in Williamsburg, Massachusetts. The sole may have been reworked on this plane, which rates 3 stars for rarity.* (GOOD+) **$95.00**

G2-2. Lindsey, J.F. & G.M., Warranted: Roman Ogee Molding Plane. Marked "7/8". Owner "S.A. Cushno". Length: 9 1/2 Inches. *This 7/8" roman ogee from a prominent Huntington, Massachusetts planemaker is in excellent working condition. A nice plane.* (GOOD+) **$55.00**

G2-3. Auburn Tool Co., Auburn, N.Y. No. 189: Double Iron Nosing Molding Plane. Marked "Inch 1/4". Extra Crisp and Clean. Length: 9 1/2 Inches. *This double iron nosing plane was intended for working with what is today known as "5/4" lumber. Clean and clearly marked.* (GOOD+) **$75.00**

G2-4. Unmarked: Classic Coachmakers Router. Owner "C.T.". Superb Condition. Length: 11 1/2 Inches. *This classic coachmaker's double router combines an artistry of execution with a warm patina burnished to a light, golden brown through years of careful use. The owner initials, "C.T.", which appear on the end grain, are sufficiently stylish that they may well be a maker's imprint. Extra-nice.* (FINE) **$125.00**

G2-5. J.T.O.: Square, Cove & Astragal Molding Plane. Round Chamfers. Uncommon Cut. Length: 9 1/2 Inches. *The initials "J.T.O." are the only mark on this early and well preserved complex molding plane.* (GOOD+) **$215.00**

G2-6. Chapin, H., Union Factory No. 124: Set of 3 Double Bead Molding Planes. 1/2", 3/8" and 3/4". Scarce and Excellent. Length: 9 1/2 Inches. *Acquired this past summer at the dispersal of a cabinet making shop, this is the first stepped set of double bead planes that we have ever offered. Nicely boxed and in excellent working condition, these ca. 1840's planes are ready to be put back to use or accent a collection of Chapin planes. A great set.* (GOOD+) **$645.00**

G2-7. Pirce, J.W.: Screw Arm Sash Molding Plane. Dated "1840". Early and Excellent. Length: 9 1/2 Inches. *This early plane from Fall River, Massachusetts is dated "1840", which would coincide with the earliest known working dates of Fall River maker "J.W. Pearce", who spelled his name "Pirce" early-on. A rare Fall River plane in nearly new condition.* (FINE) **$275.00**

G2-8. Danberry, E., N. Brunswick, N. J.: 7/8" Rabbett Molding Plane. Ca. 1850. APW III: * *. Length: 9 1/2 Inches. *A nice, clean mark on a nice, clean plane. Planes by Danberry are much underrated for rarity.* (GOOD+) **$55.00**

G2-9. J. & J. Gibson, Albany: Quirk Ovolo and Bead Molding Plane. Ca. 1837-1838 Only. AWP III: 1 Star. Length: 9 1/2 Inches. *This crisp molder from an early Albany, New York planemaking partnership is in top working order. Nice.* (FINE) **$175.00**

G2-10. Bewley, Warranted: Special Cove Molding Plane. For Sash Work? Uncommon Type. Length: 9 1/2 Inches. *This elongated cove molder may have had a window sash making application. Crisp and clean.* (GOOD+) **$65.00**

G2-11. Unmarked: Oriental Pull Plane. Tropical Hardwood Body. Excellent Condition. Length: 6 1/2 Inches. *This oriental plane is formed from a highly figured tropical hardwood. The cut is accomplished on the pull stroke. A most unusual Eastern plane in excellent working order.* (FINE) **$95.00**

G2-12. Fuller, Jo., Providence: Early Ogee Molding Plane. Yellow Birch Body. Marked "6/8". Length: 10 Inches. *This 10" yellow birch molder was produced early in the planemaking career of prominent Providence, Rhode Island maker Jo. Fuller.* (GOOD+) **$425.00**

G2-13. Unmarked: Early Tongue Molding Plane. Brand "W.H. Chapman". 10 Inch Overall Length. Length: 10 Inches. *"W.H. Chapman" is the undocumented maker mark on this early 10" tongue plane.* (GOOD+) **$45.00**

G2-14. Lourie, (Edinburgh, Scotland): Steep Ogee and Bead Molding Plane. Ca. 1774-1813. Uncommon Profile. Length: 9 1/2 Inches. *The name of Scottish planemaker William Lourie, who worked from 1874 to 1813 in Edinburgh, is boldly struck on the toe of this early complex molder.* (GOOD) **$145.00**

G2-15. Emir, London: Beech Smoothing Plane. Partial Original Decal. Near New Condition. Length: 8 Inches. *A portion of the original decal remains on this crispy clean smoothing plane from a prominent English maker. Crisp, clean and ready to use.* (FINE) **$55.00**

G2-16. Unmarked: Classic Beech Try Plane. Moulson Brothers. Iron. Ready to Use. Length: 22 Inches. *Only a chipped tote detracts from this otherwise crisp, clean and usable trying plane. The Moulson Brothers cutting iron is in excellent condition.* (GOOD+) **$45.00**

G2-17. Fuller, C., Causeway St., Boston: 7/8" Round Molding Plane. Wrong Order Imprint. Extra Crisp Condition. Length: 9 1/2 Inches. *This historical curiosity provides insight into the world of planemaking in a pre-automated world. Unlike other examples of the Fuller imprint that have surfaced, this example is marked with the "Boston" mark preceding the "Causeway St." imprint. While this was most certainly a workman's error, the fact that it could happen gives us a bit better picture of the processes used in wooden plane making. Most interesting and unusual.* (GOOD+) **$65.00**

G2-18. Buell, F.A., St. Paul (Minn.?) No. 52: Center Bead Molding Plane. Manufactured by Sandusky. Not in APW III. Length: 9 1/2 Inches. *A pair of holes for an adjustable are the only apology for this full boxed center bead that was made by the Sandusky Tool Company for this undocumented St. Paul, Minnesota hardware concern.* (GOOD+) **$145.00**

G2-19. Marples & Co., William, Sheffield: Classic Beech Smooth Plane. Double Cutting Iron. Great Working Condition. Length: 8 Inches. *If you're looking for a good working smoothing plane, this one will fill the bill nicely. A well made plane in great working order.* (GOOD+) **$45.00**

G2-20. Hayden, Syracuse, N.Y.: Cove and Bead Molding Plane. Uncommon Profile. Excellent Condition. Length: 9 1/2 Inches. *This most unusual molder is imprinted with the mark of Syracuse, New York planemaker Joseph Hayden, who worked from 1850 to 1851. A nice profile on a rare imprinted plane. There are holes in the side from a screwed on fence, but the plane is otherwise in excellent condition.* (GOOD+) **$95.00**

G2-21. Spencer: Boxed Bead Molding Plane. Marked '"3/8". Rare and Excellent. Length: 9 1/2 Inches. *This boxed bead molder from Connecticut maker Benjamin Spencer of Saybrook is crisp, clean and clearly marked.* (GOOD+) **$45.00**

G2-22. Unmarked: Boxwood Smooth Plane. Fruitwood Handle. Decorative Wedge. Length: 10 Inches. *A carved wedge nicely accents this solid boxwood smoothing plane. Very pretty and in excellent working condition.* (GOOD+) **$165.00**

G2-23. Unmarked: Classic Coachmaker's Plane. With Rosewood Sole. Excellent Patina. Length: 6 1/2 Inches. *A rosewood sole provides a nice contrast to the beechwood body of this well preserved coachmaker's "T" rabbet. There is a "hang" hole in the elongated handle, which may have been put there by the maker of the tool. Pretty.* (GOOD+) **$145.00**

G2-24. Parker Hubbard & Co., Conway, Mass: Screw Lock Plow Plane. Solid Beech Body. Boxwood Screws. Length: 8 Inches. *Boxwood fixing screws lock the arms precisely into position on this adjustable beech plow plane from an uncommon Central Massachusetts maker.* (FINE) **$175.00**

G2-25. Unmarked: Unfinished Block Plane. Professionally Made. Very Different. Length: 8 Inches. *The stock for this block plane was formed roughly to shape, but it was never fitted for an iron. Finish the job yourself or keep it as a collectible curiosity.* (FINE) **$65.00**

G2-26. Ogontz Tool Company No. 19: 22" Jointer Plane. With Lignum Strike. Extra Crisp and Clean. Length: 22 Inches. *The Ogontz Tool Company was a trade name used by the Sandusky Tool Company. Its name was taken from the name of an Indian chief who lived in the Sandusky area. A lignum vitae strike button indicates that this plane was a cut above normal quality.* (GOOD+) **$55.00**

G2-27. Unmarked: Early "Transitional" Plane. With Brass Cam Cap. Dwights & French Iron. Length: 9 1/2 Inches. *Perhaps anticipating a trend in wood plane innovation, the maker of this early "transitional" plane fitted the throat with a "U" shaped brass cam to lock the cutting iron into place. Most unusual and very graphic.* (GOOD+) **$185.00**

G2-28. Sandusky Tool Co., Sandusky, Ohio No. 117: Beechwood Plow Plane. Boxwood Arms and Nuts. Replaced Wedge. Length: 8 Inches. *The wedge on this unhandled beechwood plow plane is a replacement, but the body and boxwood arms and nuts are in excellent condition.* (GOOD+) **$55.00**

G2-29. Casey & Co., Auburn, N.Y.: Quirk Ovolo, Bevel Molding Plane. Ca. 1857 Only. Marked "1/2". Length: 9 1/2 Inches. *According to "American Wooden Planes", Casey & Company produced planes in Auburn Prison for a single year, 1857. This complex molder is marked with the number "1/2" on the reverse. Crisp and clean.* (FINE) **$115.00**

G2-30. Sims, London: Compass Smooth Plane. Script Trademark. Uncommon Type. Length: 6 1/2 Inches. *This diminutive plane from a prominent London maker has a compass shape to its sole. It is imprinted with Sims' script logo.* (GOOD+) **$55.00**

G2-31. Buell, F.A., St. Paul (Minn.?) No. 47: 1/4 Boxed Bead Molding Plane. Manufactured by Sandusky. Not in APW III. Length: 9 1/2 Inches. *A small hang hole in the front is the only apology for this previously undocumented Minnesota mark. Boldly struck with the name "F.A. Buell/St. Paul", this rare imprint was found recently in the most unlikely location of Eastern Ohio. Latter-day archeologists and others will certainly have a field day with this tidbit of data, which may indicate that the truism of Westward migration is no more than historical supposition. Whatever the case, this is a rare, important and previously undocumented imprint on an American wooden plane. The tool was obviously made by the Sandusky Tool Company. First come, first serve.* (GOOD+) **$245.00**

G2-32. Denison & Co., G.W., Winthrop, Conn.: Pair of Table Joint Molding Plane. A. Hammacher & Co. Extra Crisp and Clean. Length: 9 1/2 Inches. *The heel ends of these table joint molding planes are imprinted with the mark of A. Hammacher, an early New York City Hardware dealer. A rare pair in ready to use condition.* (GOOD) **$325.00**

G2-33. Gibson, J., Albany (N.Y.): Steep Quirk Ovolo, Bevel Molding Plane. Marked "7/8". Ca. 1823-1824. Length: 9 1/2 Inches. *This early molder has the steepness of pitch that was characteristic of the 1820's. By the 1830's and 1840's, standard molding profiles had become much flatter. A nice plane.* (GOOD+) **$145.00**

G2-34. Cumings & Gale, (Providence, R.I.): Quirk Ovolo, Cove/Astragal Molding Plane. Marked "3/8". Uncommon Profile. Length: 9 1/2 Inches. *A clean and sharp molder with a steep cabinet profile. A nice working plane by a partnership that operated in Providence, Rhode Island for a few short years in the early 1830's. A good one.* (GOOD+) **$125.00**

G2-35. Barnes, R. (Orange, Mass.): 1 1/4" Torus Bead Molding Plane. Side Boxed. Extra Crisp Condition. Length: 9 1/2 Inches. *This massive torus bead plane is in excellent collector quality condition. It could be put immediately to use if the new owner so chose.* (GOOD+) **$95.00**

G2-36. Unmarked: Patternmaker's Plane. With 3 Soles. Brass Plates Sides. Length: 10 Inches. *A patternmaker fashioned this tailed plane for shaping concave cuts. Three of the original soles remain.* (FINE) **$125.00**

G2-37. Barton & Co., D.R., Rochester, N.Y.: 5/8 Boxed Bead Molding Plane. Extra Crisp and Clean. Extra Crisp Imprint. Length: 9 1/2 Inches. *This perfectly preserved boxed bead plane has been boldly struck with the early "zig zag border" imprint of D.R. Barton & Company.* (FINE) **$55.00**

G2-38. Buell, F.A., St. Paul (Minn.?) No. 54: 7/8" Quarter Round Molding Plane. Manufactured by Sandusky. Not in APW III. Length: 9 1/2 Inches. *This clean quarter round plane was made by the Sandusky Tool Company for the undocumented St. Paul, Minnesota hardware dealer F.A. Buell. A rare mark on a pretty plane from the Sandusky Tool Company.* (GOOD+) **$225.00**

G2-39. Hills & Winship, Springfield, Mass.: Beech Smoothing Plane. Single Cutting Iron. Uncommon Type. Length: 7 1/2 Inches. *Hills and Winship were prolific makers of wooden planes, but this is the first smoothing plane bearing their name that we have offered. An uncommon smoothing plane.* (GOOD) **$25.00**

G2-40. Tileston, T., Boston (Front St.): Classic Smooth Plane. Uncommon Type. James Cam Iron. Length: 7 1/2 Inches. *We have sold a wide range of molding planes and bench planes bearing the imprint of 1830's and 1840's era Boston maker Timothy Tileston, but this is the first smoothing plane we have ever offered for sale.* (GOOD+) **$65.00**

G2-41. Unmarked: Dark Rosewood Jointer Plane. With Beech Handle. Ready to Use. Length: 23 Inches. *This dark rosewood jointer plane has the look of a well used plane, perhaps because it was being used on a regular basis up until the time it was consigned for inclusion here. A heavy working plane with character.* (GOOD+) **$85.00**

G2-42. Unmarked: Compass Smooth Plane. Applied Steel Sole. Early and Uncommon. Length: 7 1/2 Inches. *This compass soled smoothing plane has been fitted with a steel sole to minimize wear. It was most likely used by a cooper for shaping barrel staves.* (GOOD) **$25.00**

G2-43. Stickeley, I. No. 16: Early Hollow Molding Plane. Goodman: Ca. 1800. Extra Bold Imprint. Length: 9 1/2 Inches. *This British planemaker worked around 1800, according to Goodman's "British Planemakers from 1700". A boldly struck example of an uncommon early English plane.* (GOOD+) **$35.00**

G2-44. Unmarked: Classic Astragal Molding Plane. Early Wide Chamfers. Sleeper Style Wedge. Length: 10 Inches. *This early astragal molding plane cuts a 1 1/8" profile. A Sleeper-style wedge and wide, flat chamfers accent this ca. 1780's plane.* (GOOD+) **$125.00**

G2-45. Davis, G., (Birmingham): Massive Cove, Bevel Molding Plane. 3 1/2" Overall Width. Superb Patina. Length: 9 1/2 Inches. *No apologies for this well preserved English molder. A crisp, clean plane in an extra large size.* (GOOD+) **$145.00**

Group H2

H2-1. Unmarked: Hand Forged Double Adze. Grooving and Flat. Early Handle. Length: 9 Inches. *Designed to serve dual functions as both a standard adze and a hollowing adze, this early hand forged tool remains in excellent working order today.* (GOOD+) **$165.00**

H2-2. Unmarked: Miniature "Peavey". With Hook and Point. Early Appearance. Length: 17 1/2 Inches. *No idea of the function of this graphic Peavey-like device. Early and nicely patinated.* (GOOD+) **$55.00**

H2-3. Unmarked: Miniature Hand-Forged Cant Hook. With "Heart" Finial. Early and Unusual. Length: 16 Inches. *An interesting miniature cant hook that has as its most appealing feature, a heart-shaped rivet that holds the hook to the extension arm. A classic primitive with an appealing early look.* (GOOD+) **$475.00**

H2-4. Unmarked: Hand Forged Riving Froe. Rare Small Size. 5" Blade. Length: 13 Inches. *With a blade only 5" in length and a much longer handle, this special function froe is unlike any we have encountered before. We would welcome information about its specific function. A rare froe.* (GOOD+) **$115.00**

H2-5. Evansville Tool Works, Evansville: Post Mortise Axe. Apparently Unused. Partial Paper Label. Length: 15 1/2 Inches. *Post mortise axes were more often the product of the early South Eastern Pennsylvania makers. This one, from Western Indiana has been little, if ever, used. Part of the original paper label remains. A most unusual tool from the American Mid-West.* (FINE) **$155.00**

H2-6. Unmarked: Classic Filemaker's Hammer. Broad Arrow Imprint. Superb Patina. Length: 9 1/2 Inches. *The only imprint on this classic filemakers hammer is a bold, broad arrow imprint. The early and original handle has developed an excellent patina from years of use. A rare hammer in excellent collector quality condition.* (GOOD+) **$345.00**

H2-7. Unmarked: Early Wood Compass. With Steel Joint. Excellent Patina. Length: 15 Inches. *The compass was used for all manner of layout work by carpenters. This early example is clean and nicely patinated.* (GOOD) **$55.00**

H2-8. Unmarked: Hand Forged Riving Froe. Early Handle. 12" Blade. Length: 18 Inches. *We are pleased to offer an excellent batch of top quality froes. These tools are extremely handy around the woodworking shop. This one is in excellent condition and ready to go to work.* (GOOD+) **$95.00**

H2-9. Unmarked: Early Style Compass. Wood Spring Joint. Excellent Patina. Length: 16 Inches. *Formed from bent wood and showing evidence of many years of use, this early compass would likely have been used in a cooper's shop. A good one.* (GOOD+) **$85.00**

H2-10. Unmarked: Hand Forged Riving Froe. Early Handle. 12" Blade. Length: 16 Inches. *A nice early handle and an extra clean blade make this working tool a good choice for the would be wood butcher. A good one.* (GOOD+) **$145.00**

H2-11. Unmarked: Connecticut Hand Adze. Symbol of M-WTCA. Superb Example. Length: 11 Inches. *The official symbol of the Mid-West Tool Collector's Association, the Connecticut hand adze, or a variation thereof, is used in nearly every country on the face of the earth. This particularly graphic example features a closed grip that was apparently designed to improve the hold of the user on the tool. A classic collectible tool in excellent condition.* (GOOD+) **$345.00**

H2-12. Unmarked: Classic Burl Mallet. With Lead Inserts. Ready to Use. Length: 7 Inches. *In a "best of both worlds" scenario, a previous user of this burl mallet has bored holes in the top and poured in some lead to give to tool a bit more heft. It is in excellent working order.* (GOOD+) **$25.00**

H2-13. Unmarked: Carver's Lignum Mallet. Great Grain Pattern. Unused Condition. Length: 11 1/2 Inches. *This classic lignum vitae carver's mallet has never been used. New, but old.* (FINE) **$65.00**

H2-14. Unmarked: Classic Form Ice Chopper. Beechwood Handle. Excellent Condition. Length: 10 Inches. *Back in the days before electric refrigerators, a wide range of tools were offered to assist with the management of ice in the home. A woman, having learned that her neighbor, and not she, was the first on the block to get a new Frigidaire, could render a big block of ice to tiny fragments in seconds using one of these. A kitchen collectible.* (GOOD+) **$15.00**

H2-15. Unmarked: Rare Curved Froe. Early Handle. For Cooper's Use. Length: 12 Inches. *Among the rarest of all coopers tools, this curved froe is in excellent condition, either to display or put to use.* (GOOD+) **$165.00**

H2-16. Unmarked: Hand Forged Riving Froe. Early Handle. Near New Condition. Length: 17 Inches. *This is, without a doubt the finest froe we have ever been privileged to offer. Nicely forged, sharp and ready to use. A dandy.* (FINE) **$145.00**

H2-17. Unmarked: Rare Curved Froe. Early Handle. Excellent Patina. Length: 11 Inches. *Used almost exclusively by white coopers splitting out staves for barrels, examples of the curved froe are few and far between. Such tools were subjected to severe use and they were of far more specialized use than their straight-pattern cousins, hence their extreme rarity today. A nice example.* (GOOD+) **$155.00**

H2-18. Unmarked: Hand Made Scorp. With Finger Holes. Superb Patina. Length: 6 1/4 Inches. *The sort of tool that almost certainly has a fascinating story locked inside of it, we unfortunately know only the recent history of this spectacular woodworking tool. Carefully carved in such a way that it would perfectly accommodate the hand of its creator, this one of a kind tool captures the spirit of a long forgotten craftsman. Nicely patinated to a rich, golden brown from years of use and proper care, this tool was acquired by the consignor at the Elmer Keith tool auction, held in 1952, and has been a treasured possession since that time. A classic "primitive" that puts most manufactured tools to shame. Highly recommended.* (GOOD+) **$545.00**

H2-19. Unmarked: Specialized Cobble Tool?. From Phipps Museum. Most Unusual. Length: 36 Inches. *This most unusual tool was obtained at the auction of the Phipps Tool Museum of Burton, Ohio. When on display, it had been displayed as a specialized tool for laying cobblestones. We have had Macadam surfaces for so long here in downtown Bath that I can't offer an opinion one way or another. A most unusual oversize tool.* (GOOD+) **$115.00**

H2-20. Unmarked: Special Purpose Woodworking Scorp. Hand Forged Cutter. With Wooden "Guide". Length: 5 Inches. *A most unusual scorp which combines the handle with a guide to regulate the depth of cut. A most appealing "primitive" tool.* (GOOD+) **$245.00**

H2-21. Unmarked: Yoke for Ox Horns. Hand Forged Chain. Found in Canada. Length: 18 Inches. *This most unusual ox yoke has been carved to fit around a pair of very large horns. A hand forged chain is hooked to the center of the yoke. Different.* (GOOD+) **$145.00**

H2-22. Unmarked: Hand Forged Riving Froe. Early Handle. Ready to Use. Length: 12 Inches. *Years of use have given the handle of this classic hand forged riving froe a golden patina. Ready to use.* (GOOD) **$75.00**

H2-23. Unmarked: Hand Forged Riving Froe. With Original Mallet. Excellent Patina. Length: 18 Inches. *Author Eric Sloane educated collectors on the use of the froe for the riving of clapboards for the siding of early houses. The passage of time has not been kind to the partnerships established between these early edge tools and the heavy-duty wooden tools used to make them work. Here's a rare and very well preserved example of a pair that began together and remain together.* (GOOD+) **$165.00**

H2-24. Unmarked: Classic Farrier's Butteris. With Leather Pad. Superb Patina. Length: 18 Inches. *A padded leather fitting on the shoulder brace of the butteris adds additional character to this graphic hand forged tool. For those of you who don't know, these tools were used for trimming the hooves of horses. The loop handle was used as a grip to guide the tool and the force was applied by applying pressure with the shoulder. A nice example.* (GOOD+) **$55.00**

H2-25. Unmarked: Hand Forged Riving Froe. Early Handle. 11" Blade. Length: 14 Inches. *If you have a hankerin' to do some old time woodwork, Eric Sloane style, here's just the tool you need. The only other thing you will need is a piece of wood to drive it. A good one.* (GOOD+) **$95.00**

H2-26. Unmarked: "Travisher" Type Spoke Shave. Ready to Use. Excellent Patina. Length: 6 1/2 Inches. *The steep curve of this shave makes it an ideal tool for the work of forming the hollows in chair seats. A scarce tool in usable condition.* (GOOD) **$85.00**

H2-27. Unmarked: Belt Holder For Sythe Stone. From Cow's Horn. Early and Extra Nice. Length: 7 1/4 Inches. *Fitted with a hand forged loop that is riveted to the body, this cow horn was converted by an early pioneer for use as a holder for the sharpening stone for his scythe. A classic early farm tool having an excellent patina of age and use.* (GOOD+) **$145.00**

H2-28. Unmarked: Rare Curved Froe. For Firkin Staves?. Excellent Patina. Length: 9 1/2 Inches. *Almost without exception, the curved froes that we have encountered have been of a much larger size and a noticably less pronounced curve. Much smaller sized barrels would have required a proportionately smaller blade and a proportionately more acute angle to the curve of the blade. This example retains its original handle and is in top working order.* (GOOD+) **$225.00**

H2-29. Unmarked: Basket Maker's Froe. Superb Patina. Ready to Use. Length: 5 1/2 Inches. *The same principle that was used for the riving of clapboards for houses applied to this splitting of splints for baskets. This well preserved example retains its original handle and is in top working condition.* (GOOD+) **$185.00**

H2-30. Unmarked: Flax Swingle Knife. With Carved Opening. Rare and Excellent. Length: 24 Inches. *This flax "swingle" knife has been carved with an opening in the center, perhaps to provide an aerodynamic advantage. A rare agricultural tool in great condition.* (GOOD+) **$165.00**

H2-31. Unmarked: Classic "Bowl" Adze. 6" Cutting Edge. Original Handle. Length: 10 Inches. *These rounded edge tools were used for hollowing out wooden vessels in a much simpler time. This one retains what appears to be its original handle. A good one.* (GOOD) **$145.00**

H2-32. Unmarked: Hand Forged Riving Froe. Early Handle. Superb Condition. Length: 19 Inches. *Here's an excellent working froe for those of you whose homes are in need of siding this year. There's a bit of Roy Underhill in each of us and these are just the thing to bring it out. A nice working tool.* (GOOD+) **$135.00**

H2-33. Atkins & Co., E.C., Indianapolis: Adjustable Ram's Horn Scraper. Laminated Body. Unused Condition. Length: 12 Inches. *In much the same condition as it would have been when it left the Atkins factory, this is by far the nicest example of the Atkins "ram's horn" scraper that we have ever offered. In great shape to use and pretty enough to use as a centerpiece, we highly recommend this quality tool.* (FINE) **$225.00**

H2-34. Unmarked: Classic Grafting Froe. Fruitwood Handle. Distinctive Form. Length: 10 Inches. *A nicely turned fruitwood handle ornaments this early grafting froe. A graphic example of a classic American tool.* (GOOD+) **$65.00**

H2-35. Saybarger, J., Cincinnati., Ohio: Classic Grafting Froe. Undocumented Maker. Early and Excellent. Length: 12 Inches. *The name and working location of one J. Saybarger is boldly imprinted on this early grafting froe, but there is no documentation of this maker in the Directory of American Toolmakers. An early froe from an undocumented maker.* (GOOD+) **$85.00**

H2-36. Bartlett & Co. No. 71: Post Mortise Axe. 2" Cutting Edge. Excellent Condition. Length: 21 1/2 Inches. *The Directory of American Toolmakers lists a number of Bartletts, but none that made edge tools. This post mortise axe is in excellent condition and retains its original handle.* (GOOD+) **$95.00**

H2-37. Caspar, A., Sooutah, Ill.: Mill Bill Holder. For Dressing Wheels. Rare Marked Example. Length: 18 Inches. *The cleaning and sharpening of grindstones was accomplished with the use of a diamond-shaped hardened steel cutter which was held in a device such as this. Generally, these tools were made by hand. This uncommon example is marked with the name of an undocumented Illinois maker.* (GOOD+) **$85.00**

H2-38. Unmarked: "Woman's Tooth" Router Plane. Cast Brass Mechanism. Crisp, Clean and Usable. Length: 9 Inches. *An oversize brass screw is used to adjust the cutting iron of this well made router, which was most likely produced in a patternmaking shop as an apprentice project.* (GOOD+) **$55.00**

H2-39. Unmarked: Miniature Bowl Adze. Early Handle. Ready to Use. Length: 6 Inches. *This extra small size bowl adze is in excellent working condition and ready to be put back to use.* (GOOD+) **$225.00**

H2-40. Unmarked: Whittler's Plier Whimsy. Working Jaws. Most Unusual. Length: 4 Inches. *What was this all about? A knife, some time, and an idea have given us an object that gives rise to wonder. Who, why, when? Was this simply a carver's sampler? Or were the two pairs of pliers in one the physical manifestation of that deep, dark, primal instinct that exists in every man: the need, somehow, before his limited time on earth has passed, to fashion, by whatever means are at his disposal, a wrench that embodies his vision of mechanical perfection? For some, the avenues of creative outlet have been so limited that innate urge has been forever suppressed. Good men, talented men, men who might, with the help of The Almighty and a milling machine have solved forever the ancient riddle of the single-hand quick-adjust spring activated nut wrench, or removed forever from the collective experience of humankind the frustration of quickly and easily removing a faucet fixture, have, instead, been driven by the suppression of what is good and Natural to bitter ends, to evil ends, to despair. What, then, of this tool? We will never know. But the optimist deep within says that this is nothing less than the physical manifestation of one now-forgotten individual's effort to come to terms with a spark deep within that, for want of other circumstances, might well have been a flame.* (GOOD+) **$45.00**

H2-41. Unmarked: Classic Corn Husking Peg. With Leather Strap. New Old Stock. Length: 5 Inches. *Come harvest time this fall, you can be the first to use this husking peg. Having spoken to those who have done so, I can not recommend the practice.* (FINE) **$15.00**

H2-42. Unmarked: Flax Swingle Knife. Formed from Oak. Superb Patina. Length: 22 1/2 Inches. *The processing of flax required the use of this "swingle" which I understand was used in some way to strike the flax, although I have never observed the process.* (GOOD+) **$95.00**

H2-43. Unmarked: Primitive Form Router Plane. Wedge Lock Blade. Most Unusual. Length: 13 Inches. *Dispensing with the finery of carved throats and precisely fitted wedges, the maker of this early router was apparently inclined to get directly to work. A classic primitive that tells a story about itself.* (GOOD) **$25.00**

H2-44. Chevillon A Auxerre: Massive French Bowl Adze. With Hammer Feature. Extra Crisp and Clean. Length: 10 Inches. *The forming of bowls from hardwood is a craft that was born of necessity. In order to accomplish the task as efficiently as possible, specialized tools were required. This massive, curved bowl adze, which has markings that indicate French provenance, is fitted with an accessory hammer to multiply the functionality of the tool. The blade is in superb condition, clean and sharp and could be quickly put to use if the owner so chose. A rare tool in top condition.* (FINE) **$365.00**

H2-45. Iowa Novelty Co., Burlington: Bronze Concrete Edger. Rosewood Handle. Rare and Excellent. Length: 6 Inches. *A handle of Brazilian Rosewood accents this cast bronze scraper from an obscure Iowa maker of mason's tools. Never seen another* (GOOD+) **$65.00**

Group 12

12-1. Unmarked: Cast Iron Door Metallic Plane. "Patent Applied For". "The Green Plane". Length: 8 1/2 Inches. *An example of this rare cast iron plane appears in the "Interesting non-Patented Planes" section of P-TAMPIA, where it is described as being used for door hinge gains. This one is as nice as they come, with all of the original dark green japanning. A nice example of artistic casting in an elusive plane. Tough to find.* (FINE) **$485.00**

12-2. Unmarked: Classic Victorian Router Plane. Decorative Knurls. Ca. 1870's. Length: 5 Inches. *The creator of this early cast iron router plane indulged a flair in its making. A nicely knurled brass locking screw accents the sculptural quality of the tool. Very, very pretty.* (FINE) **$225.00**

12-3. Unmarked: Cast Iron Block Metallic Plane. With Tail Handle. Unknown Maker. Length: 5 Inches. *These handled block planes have been found in a wide range of sizes, but it has never been precisely documented who made them.* (GOOD+) **$45.00**

12-4. Metallic Plane Co., Auburn, N. Y.: Palmer's Patent Metallic Plane. "Triple Lever" Adjustment "W. Butcher" Iron. Length: 15 Inches. *This is by far the most complex adjustment mechanism ever to be fitted to a metallic plane. It is only half in jest that it has been suggested that a degree in mechanical engineering may have been a necessary and essential prerequisite to operate one of these competently. A mechanical marvel in clean, sound and complete original condition, noting only a chip to the tote.* (GOOD+) **$265.00**

12-5. Unmarked: Miniature Block Metallic Plane. Similar to Metalic Plane Company. Most Unusual. Length: 3 3/4 Inches. *Similar in many respects to the non-adjustable block plane produced by the Metallic Plane Company of Auburn, New York, this unmarked plane is quite a bit smaller. A mystery.* (GOOD+) **$165.00**

12-6. Unmarked: Patternmaker's Router Plane. Precision Adjust. Very Well Made. Length: 3 3/4 Inches. *Small router planes offer a great opportunity for the potential collector. They are infinitely variable, easily displayed and appealing, even to those courser souls who have not yet come to understand tools.* (GOOD+) **$155.00**

12-7. Sears, Roebuck & Co.: Low Angle Block Metallic Plane. Made by Sargent. Superb Condition. Length: 9 Inches. *Produced for Sears by Sargent & Company of New Haven, Connecticut in the 1930's, this high quality low angle block plane is in nearly new condition.* (FINE) **$85.00**

12-8. Brown Quality Machine Co. (Unmarked) No. 001: "Brown's Toboggan" Metallic Plane. Uncommon Type. All Original. Length: 7 Inches. *The finish on this well preserved and well named metallic plane appears to be original. A very nice example of a rare and graphic plane.* (GOOD) **$145.00**

12-9. Union Mfg. Co., New Britain, Conn. No. 42: Tongue and Groove Metallic Plane. With Swing Fence. Near New Condition. Length: 11 Inches. *The Union No. 42 was the equivalent of Stanley's No. 47 swinging fence match plane. This example is in fine condition.* (FINE) **$145.00**

12-10. Mitchell & Co., Hudson, N. Y.: "Evans Patent" Metallic Plane. Patented January 28, 1862. Mouldson Brothers Iron. Length: 10 1/2 Inches. *Patented in 1862, and quite successful in the marketplace, the Evans patent was certainly the first commercially viable metallic compass plane. Roger Smith observes in his first book that Stanley may have purchased the operations of the Mitchell firm. He does not elaborate, but this plane bears a striking resemblance to the mechanism on Stanley's No. 13 compass plane, which entered their product line in 1871, approximately the time that Mitchell & Company ceased operations.* (GOOD+) **$345.00**

12-11. Union Plane Co., New Britain, Conn. No. 100: Squirrel Tail Block Metallic Plane. 95% Original Paint. Uncommon Type. Length: 4.5 Inches. *The equivalent of Stanley's No. 100 "squirrel tail" block plane, this example from the Union Plane Company is at least twenty times less common.* (GOOD+) **$85.00**

12-12. Siegley Tool Company No. 2: Combination Plow Metallic Plane. Complete and Excellent. Ca. 1880's. Length: 9 1/2 Inches. *The plow planes of Jacob Siegley are far more visually interesting than the line of bench planes he produced. This may be attributable to the fact that he had personally invented and patented the plows. This example of the Siegley No. 2 plow is in excellent overall condition. One original cutting iron remains. A graphic tool.* (GOOD+) **$345.00**

12-13. Metallic Plane Co., Auburn, N. Y.: Cast Iron Block Metallic Plane. "Excelsior" Cutter. Early and Excellent. Length: 5 1/2 Inches. *This "basic" block plane of the Metallic Plane Company has a look about it that says "antique". One of the best examples we have encountered.* (GOOD+) **$225.00**

12-14. Ohio Tool Co., Columbus, Ohio No. 03: Cast Iron Smooth Metallic Plane. Uncommon Number. With "World" T.M.. Length: 8 Inches. *The Ohio Tool Company went head to head with Stanley in the production of metallic planes. The only difference in the product numbers was the presence of the letter "O" in front of each of the Ohio products. Other than the No. 2 size (O2 in Buckeye parlance), which is rare by any maker, the No. 03 is the least common of the Ohio Tool bench planes. A nice example.* (GOOD+) **$125.00**

12-15. Unmarked: Cast Router Metallic Plane. Brass Handles and Stop. Miniature Size. Length: 3 Inches. *At only 3 inches in width, this artistically-conceived miniature router must have been as much a craftsman's indulgence as it was a functional tool. It most certainly would have been a joy to use, and it would have done its job very well, but its seems, somehow, to be just a bit too nice. A great tool with a story locked within.* (GOOD+) **$225.00**

12-16. Shapleigh Hardware, St. Louis No. DE04C: "Diamond Edge" Metallic Plane. Patented November 22, 1904. Buckeye Saw Vise Co.. Length: 9 1/2 Inches. *Produced under a patent granted on November 22, 1904 to John Muehl of Cleveland, Ohio, this uncommon patented plane was marketed both as the "Buckeye" plane and also by the Shapleigh Hardware Company under their "Diamond Edge" trade name. This one is complete, sound, and in need of just a bit of a cleaning.* (GOOD) **$345.00**

12-17. Mongomery Ward & Company No. 85: Duplex Rabbet Metallic Plane. Made by Millers Fall. Near New Condition. Length: 9 1/2 Inches. *The Millers Falls duplex rabbet plane was every bit as well made of a tool as the Stanley equivalent. This one was made for the Montgomery Ward Company, very likely as part of their high end "Lakeside" line. Perfect.* (FINE) **$75.00**

12-18. Union Mfg. Co., New Britain, Conn.: Rare Knuckle Joint Metallic Plane. With "Stanley" Cutter. Superb Condition. Length: 7 Inches. *Before their acquisition by cross town neighbor, The Stanley Rule & Level Company, The Union Manufacturing Company produced an expanding line of metallic planes, including equivalents to Stanley's "knuckle joint" block planes. This uncommon example has all Union characteristics, but is fitted with a ca. 1915 Stanley cutting iron. A likely transitional example.* (GOOD+) **$115.00**

12-19. Unmarked: Cast Iron Jack Metallic Plane. Appears Manufactured. Early Appearance. Length: 15 Inches. *Unmarked in any way with a patent date or maker's mark. This ca. 19th Century plane has characteristics that make it likely it was a manufactured tool. Both the adjustment screws and the frog mechanism have been professionally nickel plated and the machining on the metal parts is much more precise than one would expect from a tool thrown together in a shop. Reminiscent, in many ways of the planes of John Gage and imitators, this enigmatic plane is in excellent condition and worthy of inclusion in any collection of patented metallic planes. Rare and excellent.* (GOOD+) **$385.00**

12-20. Unmarked: Cast Iron Router Plane. Distinctive Handles. Excellent Condition. Length: 4 1/2 Inches. *The handles on this plane are evocative of those on the Hazard Knowles block plane featured in Roger Smith's first book. An early and appealing router plane.* (GOOD+) **$265.00**

12-21. Ohio Tool Co., Columbus, Ohio No. 08: Cast Iron Jointer Metallic Plane. Uncommon Number. Unused Condition. Length: 24 Inches. *Apparently someone bought this one and never put it to use. This metallic jointer plane is in practically new condition. Fully 99% of all shiny original finishes remain. Super nice.* (FINE) **$365.00**

12-22. Mitchell & Co., Hudson, N. Y.: "Evans Patent" Metallic Plane. Patented January 28, 1862. Early and Uncommon. Length: 10 1/2 Inches. *Patented in 1862, and quite successful in the marketplace, the Evans patent was certainly the first commercially viable metallic compass plane. Roger Smith observes in his first book that Stanley may have purchased the operations of the Mitchell firm. He does not elaborate, but this plane bears a striking resemblance to the mechanism on Stanley's No. 13 compass plane, which entered their product line in 1871, approximately the time that Mitchell & Company ceased operations.* (GOOD) **$225.00**

12-23. Unmarked: Patternmakers Fillet Metallic Plane. Early Appearance. Similar to Metallic Plane Company. Length: 7 Inches. *We have never attempted to subdue our enthusiasm for tools made in pattern shops for patternmakers. These tools were made not only to be used, but also to demonstrate mastery of one's trade to other professionals. This "fillet" cutting plane is an example of such a tool. Nicely cast in a short, squat style and fitted with a carved tote and turned front knob, this was an ideal tool in both form and function for the cutting of the strips that were used to form contours on 90 degree joints. A most appealing craftsman made tool.* (GOOD) **$385.00**

12-24. Belknap Hardware Co., Louisville No. BG 79: Adjustable Block Metallic Plane. Similar to Stanley 9 1/4. Near New Condition. Length: 7 Inches. *As a major distributor of tools, the Belknap Hardware Company of Louisville, Kentucky, was in a position to purchase tools from major makers, such as Stanley, and have them imprinted with their "Bluegrass" brand name. This equivalent to Stanley's No. 9 1/4 block plane is a classic example. Some 98% of original japanning remains.* (FINE) **$55.00**

12-25. Ohio Tool Company No. 05: Cast Iron Jack Metallic Plane. With World Trademark. Unused Condition. Length: 14 Inches. *Retaining fully 99% of its original shiny black japan finish, this is the finest example of an Ohio Tool Company bench plane that we have ever offered. Mint.* (FINE) **$195.00**

12-26. Stubs, P.S. (?): Ebony Stuffed Metallic Plane. Bullnose and Rabbet. Owner "Louis Krause". Length: 8 1/2 Inches. *The iron in this most unusual ebony stuffed metallic plane is marked P.S. Stubs, suggesting that it may have been of English manufacture, but there's no mistaking who owned it: The side of the plane has been carefully and tastefully etched with the owner's name, location and the date. He was careful to note that it was 1894 A.D., lest someone find the plane and think it belonged to a contemporary of Hammurabi. A most appealing plane.* (GOOD+) **$595.00**

12-27. Siegley Tool Company No. 5 C: 14" Jack Metallic Plane. Rosewood Handles. 99% Original Paint. Length: 14 Inches. *The Siegley Tool Company produced a line of metallic planes in direct competition with Stanley and the other principal makers during the last quarter of the Nineteenth Century. For a discussion of Siegley's planemaking, we recommend Patented Transitional & Metallic Planes in America, Volume I. This exremely well preserved jack plane is clean, complete and ready to add to a collection of metallic planes.* (GOOD+) **$225.00**

12-28. Unmarked: Applewood Router Plane. Carved Body, Brass Sole. From J.J. Kjellberg. Length: 6 Inches. *Sometimes, we see a tool and wonder. We wonder who made it, and when; and we wonder how the maker of that tool came to have the skill and the artistic inclination to creatively invest himself in its making. Usually we just wonder. In the case of this sculpted applewood patternmaker's router, we don't have all the answers, but we know a little. This object was acquired together with a group of tools from the tool kit of one J.J. Kjellberg of Fitchburg, Massachusetts, and we know that Kjellberg was a patternmaker, and we know that he marked some of his tools with dates, and from those dates we know that he worked from the 1880 into the beginning of the Twentieth Century. Beyond that, we are left to speculate. We are left to ponder why Mr. Kjellberg was not content with factory made tools, or simply to "make do" with the tools he made himself. We wonder, and we delight. We delight in this wonderful object that has within it a bit of someone long ago. Someone who put more of himself into his creation and, in so doing, achieved a measure of immortality. A spectacularly well preserved craftsman made router plane of sculptural form. Highly recommended.* (FINE) **$345.00**

12-29. Unmarked: Handled Block Metallic Plane. Unknown Maker. Interesting Form. Length: 5 Inches. *There is a Nobel prize in Tooldom waiting out there for the person or persons who can divine the manufacturers of these handled block planes. A mystery plane in excellent condition.* (GOOD+) **$55.00**

12-30. Unmarked: Fruitwood Router Plane. Dated "1903". From J.J. Kjellberg. Length: 7 Inches. *One of a number of tools recently acquired from the patternmaking tools of one J.J. Kjelleberg, a patternmaker from central Massachusetts, this nicely detailed router plane is imprinted with the date "1903" on its applewood body. A classic example of the tool making artistry of the patternmaking trade.* (FINE) **$195.00**

12-31. Siegley Tool Company: Transitional Fore Metallic Plane. 2 3/8" Width. Similar to Stanley No. 27. Length: 21 Inches. *The triple "S" marking on the cutting iron was the distinctive marking, and the only marking used on transitional planes produced by the Siegley Tool Company. This one retains much of its original finishes on both wood and metal. An uncommon transitional plane.* (GOOD+) **$225.00**

12-32. Ohio Tool Co., Columbus, Ohio No. 0103: Adjustable Block Metallic Plane. With "World" Logo. Rare and Excellent. Length: 5 1/2 Inches. *The Ohio Tool Company attempted, for a short time, to match the products of industry giant Stanley Rule & Level. Their product line failed to catch on among the woodworkers of the day in the way that the surviving examples have inspired latter-day collectors, who recognize their rarity. This lever-adjust block plane is in excellent overall condition.* (GOOD+) **$65.00**

12-33. Union Mfg. Co., New Britain, Conn. No. 43: Combination Rabbet and Fillet Metallic Plane. All Original Parts. Unused Condition. Length: 10 Inches. *Not to be intimidated by next door neighbor Stanley Rule & Level, the Union Plane Mfg. Company wasn't about to follow the Stanley naming convention, even if it confounded collectors in later years. Even though Stanley had called its duplex rabbet plane the No. 78 for 40 years and other makers were doing the same thing, the folks at Union opted for the No. 43. This example is in unused condition.* (FINE) **$125.00**

12-34. Tower & Lyon, New York, N.Y. No. 1211: Chaplin's Patent Metallic Plane. India Rubber Handles. Extra Crisp and Clean. Length: 24 Inches. *The later versions of the O.R. Chaplin patent planes, as offered by the Tower & Lyon Company of New York City were distinguished by having handles formed of hard India rubber, beds that were corrugated on the upper surface and by having a distinctive profile to the rails. This jointer plane is a classic example of the type. Crisp, clean and ready to display.* (GOOD+) **$325.00**

12-35. Kelley-How-Thomson Co., Duluth, Minn.: "Hickory" Low Angle Metallic Plane. By Ohio Tool Company. Rare and Near New. Length: 6 1/2 Inches. *This low angle block plane is identical in form to the Stanley No. 60. It was undoubtedly manufactured for the K.H.T. People by the Ohio Tool Company under the patent granted to Edward Marks of Auburn, New York on August 6, 1901. A rare plane with an uncommon dealer imprint in top condition.* (FINE) **$325.00**

12-36. Fulton, New York, N.Y. No. 5320: Patent Block Metallic Plane. Patented March 21, 1893. New Condition, Original Box. Length: 5 1/2 Inches. *The Fulton Tool Company of New York City produced quality tools for sale in the late 19th and early 20th Centuries. This equivalent to Stanley's 102 block plane is in new condition in its original box, which is marked with an early patent date.* (FINE) **$115.00**

12-37. Tower & Lyon, New York, N.Y.: Chaplin's Patent Metallic Plane. Non-Adjustable Throat. Corrugated Sole. Length: 8 1/2 Inches. *Most of the original nickel plating remains on this Chaplin's Patent plane. The cutting iron is marked with the imprint of the Tower & Lyon Hardware Company of New York City, who produced and distributed the plane.* (FINE) **$265.00**

12-38. Lewin: The Lewin Universal Metallic Plane. Similar to Stanley 45. With 18 Original Cutters. Length: 12 Inches. *Here's an extremely well made British combination plane, complete and in excellent condition in its original wooden box. These have received very good grades for usability from those I have spoken with who have experience with them. An excellent working tool.* (FINE) **$265.00**

12-39. Metallic Plane Co., Auburn, N. Y. No. CORR: Palmer's Patent Metallic Plane. "Triple Lever" Adjustment. Complete, Excellent. Length: 9 1/2 Inches. *These mechanical marvels never cease to amaze. They have, arguably, the most complex adjustment mechanism ever fitted to a metallic plane, yet they were apparently a commercial success. Has anyone ever used one of these? A most interesting tool* (GOOD+) **$425.00**

12-40. Gage Tool Co., Vineland, N.J. No. 4: Patent Transitional Metallic Plane. Patent 1886. Complete and Near New. Length: 10 Inches. *Finding a Gage plane with any handle at all is sometimes quite a challenge. Finding one with its original handle intact and retaining all of its shiny nickel plating is a rare happening indeed. Nearly all original finishes remain on this pristine example of the Gage Tool Company's No. 4 size plane. Magnificent.* (FINE) **$345.00**

12-41. Fulton, New York, N.Y. No. 55334: Knuckle Joint Block Metallic Plane. Patented February 3, 1891. New Condition, Original Box. Length: 7 Inches. *Another unusual Fulton plane in its original box. This is the only knuckle joint plane I have seen with their mark. Most unusual.* (FINE) **$125.00**

12-42. Metallic Plane Co., Auburn, N. Y.: Palmer & Storkes Patented Metallic Plane. With Lever Adjustment. Adjustable Throat. Length: 14 1/2 Inches. *The folks at the Metallic Plane Company apparently changed the design on all of their planes several times each week, more often if conditions warranted. This example of one of the many "Palmer & Storkes" patents, features a lever adjustment for the cutter and an adjustable throat mechanism. A rare plane in very well preserved condition.* (GOOD+) **$365.00**

12-43. Siegley Tool Company No. 7: Cast Iron Jointer Metallic Plane. Mahogany Handles. Scarce and Excellent. Length: 22 Inches. *Looking for all the world like its Stanley equivalent, this jointer plane differed only in that it has a non-Stanley adjustment lever and is imprinted with the Siegley triple "S" on the cutting iron.* (FINE) **$125.00**

12-44. Pond, W.H., New Haven, Conn.: Classic Double Router Plane. For Coachmaker. Excellent Patina. Length: 18 1/2 Inches. *The end of the handle of this classic double pistol router is marked with the imprint of W.H. Pond, who specialized in the making of tools for carriagemakers in New Haven, Connecticut.* (GOOD+) **$345.00**

12-45. Langdon Mitre Box Co., M.F., Mass.: "Perfection" Brand Jointer Gauge. Pre-Millers Falls. Early Pasteboard Box. Length: 10 Inches. *Not only did they manufacture the mitre box from which they took their name, the Langdon company also produced this cast iron jointer fence. All of their products were eventually merged with the Millers Falls Tool Company. This gauge continued in production for more than 50 years. The only example in the box that we have seen.* (GOOD+) **$225.00**

Group J2

J2-1. E.F.B. & Co.: Precision Watchmakers Caliper. German Silver Body. Very Well Made. Length: 3 1/2 Inches. *These watchmakers' calipers are imprinted with the name E.F.B. Co., an entity about whom we have limited information.* (FINE) **$65.00**

J2-2. Stubs, P.S.: Jeweler's Hand Vise. 4" Size. Early and Excellent. Length: 4 Inches. *P.S. Stubs supplied tools of the finest quality for the American market. An interesting small sized hand vise.* (GOOD+) **$25.00**

J2-3. Unmarked: Pair of Brass Magnifying Glasses. For Textile Use? Early Appearance. Length: 1 Inches. *These specialty magnifying glasses came together. We suspect that they were used for gauging cotton fabric in a mill. Interesting and unusual.* (GOOD+) **$55.00**

J2-4. Unmarked: Jeweler's Stake Anvil. Round, Square Horns. Ready to Use. Length: 4 1/4 Inches. *Here's an extremely well preserved "stake" anvil having a pair of extra fine horns. Ready to use.* (GOOD+) **$65.00**

J2-5. Unmarked: Piano Tuner's Listening Device. Patented January 16, 1906. Most Unusual. Length: 16 Inches. *This most unusual mechanical marvel came together with a group of piano tuner's tools. According to a purported "expert" these were used to somehow listen to the piano to gauge its pitch by placing the wooden end against the ear. A patent date is marked on the tool, so it shouldn't be too hard to figure out.* (GOOD+) **$75.00**

J2-6. Vernier, J.J., Toledo, Ohio: Sharpener for Engraver's Tools. Early and Excellent. Full Nickel Plating. Length: 4 1/2 Inches. *We offer here another one of those ideas whose time never came. This very well-made device was intended to take the requisite skill out of the gravers used to engrave metal. The problem was, that if an engraver wasn't sufficiently skilled at his craft to be able to keep his tools sharpened properly, he might as well be doing paint-by-number work. His limited business acumen notwithstanding, Mr. Vernier has, nonetheless, given us a great collectible tool, which we proudly offer, complete with the original instruction sheet. Very different.* (FINE) **$375.00**

J2-7. O.W.B. & Co.: Jeweler's Punch Pliers. "Patent Applied For". Early and Unusual. Length: 5 Inches. *Early jeweler's tools are among the most unappreciated of all collectible tools, often being lumped into a box of pliers and open end wrenches, rather than with the precision tools, where they belong. This company is not one with which we are familiar, but their product is of the highest quality. Early and excellent.* (GOOD+) **$55.00**

J2-8. Unmarked: Jeweler's Precision Micrometer. With Chain Drive. Very Well Made. Length: 3 1/4 Inches. *The drive mechanism of this small spring activated micrometer is a very well made small chain. Appearance is quite early (ca. 1860) and condition is superb. Never seen another.* (FINE) **$185.00**

J2-9. Unmarked: Special Purpose Watch Tool. Adjustable Legs. Brass Fixing Screw. Length: 3 1/4 Inches. *No idea what these things were for, but I think it has something to do with watch repair. A nice one, whatever it is.* (GOOD+) **$25.00**

J2-10. Unmarked: Turned Handle Hand Vise. Uncommon Type. Owner "W. Field". Length: 8 Inches. *Hand vises make a great collectible. They are small, infinitely variable and mechanically interesting. Here's one to start with.* (GOOD+) **$65.00**

J2-11. Unmarked: Classic Jeweler's Hammer. Polished Head. Marked "20 G". Length: 8 Inches. *The only mark on the head of this delicate jewelers hammer is the designation "20 G". A cynic would suggest that it was the amount expended by the U.S. Military for a single fountain pen. We say its a nice hammer.* (FINE) **$45.00**

J2-12. Unmarked: Precision Jeweler's Hammer. Mahogany Handle. Superb Condition. Length: 9 Inches. *The narrow neck on this hammer was likely intended to give it some play as it was being worked. Overall condition is excellent.* (FINE) **$75.00**

J2-13. Unmarked: Jeweler's Planishing Hammer. Decorative Filework. With Original Handle. Length: 9 1/2 Inches. *These visually appealing hammers are a perennial favorite of tool collectors. We simply can't find enough of them. First come, first serve.* (GOOD+) **$65.00**

J2-14. Unmarked: Bronze Jeweler's Caliper. Round Central Joint. Excellent Patina. Length: 3 Inches. *Here's an extra nice jeweler's caliper that looks to be as accurate today as it was when new.* (FINE) **$65.00**

J2-15. Unmarked: Early Jeweler's Hammer. Hand Filed Head. Extraordinary Form. Length: 8 1/4 Inches. *The head of this very well made miniature jeweler's hammer has been carefully hand filed into a most appealing form. A delicate and pretty jewelers hammer.* (GOOD+) **$155.00**

J2-16. Unmarked: Jeweler's Handled Hand Vise. With Brass Ferrule. Uncommon Type. Length: 7 Inches. *This interesting variation on the hand vise theme has been fitted with a wooden handle having a brass ferrule. A nice vise.* (GOOD+) **$75.00**

J2-17. Unmarked No. 3: Jeweler's Staking Pliers. Patented May 31, 1898. Scarce and Complete. Length: 5 1/2 Inches. *This patented jeweler's tool features a rotating disk to accommodate different sizes of work. A small chip of the ebony handle is missing, otherwise perfect.* (GOOD+) **$55.00**

J2-18. Unmarked: Bronze Double Caliper. With Central Joint. For Jeweler. Length: 5 Inches. *This double caliper has been fashioned from bronze, perhaps by the artisan who used it. Cute.* (GOOD+) **$55.00**

J2-19. Unmarked: Miniature "Dental" Hammer. Maul Shape Head. Unknown Function. Length: 8 Inches. *We have had a number of these including some that were marked as "dental" hammers, but have never really figured out how they were used. Open wide...* (GOOD+) **$45.00**

J2-20. Unmarked: Precision Jeweler's Hammer. Extra Delicate. Near New Condition. Length: 8 Inches. *This extra delicate hammer weighs in at about one ounce. It is in nearly new condition.* (FINE) **$115.00**

J2-21. Unmarked: Miniature Jewelers Hammer. Rosewood Handle. Excellent Condition. Length: 5 1/2 Inches. *A nicely grained handle of Brazilian Rosewood complements the polished head of this extra small jewelers hammer. Choice.* (FINE) **$85.00**

J2-22. Goodell Pratt Company No. 2: Early Steel Glass Cutter. Uncommon Type. Distinctive Form. Length: 5 1/2 Inches. *An early (ca. 1895) glass cutter that was originally produced by the Goodell Brothers Company Shelburne Falls, Massachusetts. Clean and clearly marked.* (GOOD+) **$45.00**

J2-23. Hemsley, R., Montreal, P.Q, Canada: Early Patent Jeweler's Tool. Patented September 29, 1885. For Spreading. Length: 5 1/4 Inches. *Pushing on the metal at the end of the handle causes the spring-activated arms to separate. A most unusual patented tool from a most unlikely location. No idea whether the patent is American or Canadian. Different.* (FINE) **$95.00**

J2-24. Unmarked: Precision Jeweler's Hammer. Extra Long Handle. Superb Condition. Length: 11 1/4 Inches. *The extra long handle on this delicate hammer seems out of proportion to the weight of the head, but makes for an aesthetically appealing tool.* (FINE) **$65.00**

J2-25. Unmarked: Set of 5 Jeweler's Hammer. Burnished Faces. Ready to Use. Length: 11 Inches. *The faces on these jewelers hammers have been burnished to a brilliant shine. A great working set of tools for the would-be metalworker.* (GOOD+) **$195.00**

J2-26. Unmarked: Early Jeweler's Hand Vise. With Octagon Handle. Unusual Type. Length: 7 1/2 Inches. *A graceful octagonal handle adds to the appeal of this delicate jewelers vise.* (GOOD+) **$25.00**

J2-27. Unmarked: Precision Optical Caliper. Brass and Steel. Metric Graduations. Length: 6 1/2 Inches. *These were apparently used in the glass grinding trade. This one appears to be of French origin. A nice example.* (GOOD+) **$45.00**

J2-28. Unmarked: Classic Jeweler's Saw. Adjustable Length. Brass Finial. Length: 10 1/2 Inches. *This extra nice jeweler's saw has been fitted with a coping saw blade, but it is otherwise in excellent working order. A detailed brass finial accents the end of the upper arm—a sign of a tool that was made to be special. Special.* (GOOD+) **$55.00**

J2-29. Unmarked: Unusual Assembly Tool. Unknown Purpose. Very Well Made. Length: 9 Inches. *This is one of those things that is made up for some very special purpose and then forgotten. I couldn't pass it by. The handles activate a spring that separates and pushes, then pulls. Hours of fun for a pittance. The crowd at the "whatsit" table will slap your back and shake your hand. Fifteen Minutes of Fame.* (FINE) **$25.00**

J2-30. Unmarked: Special Purpose Scribe. Turned Ivory Handle. Unused Condition. Length: 4 1/2 Inches. *This ivory handled scribe is in brand new condition. Its function is unknown.* (FINE) **$45.00**

J2-31. Vigor, Switzerland: Jeweler's Precision Vise. German Silver Body. New Condition, Original Box. Length: 2 1/2 Inches. *The reason for the legendary reputation of Swiss craftsmanship is evident in this well made jewelers vise of German silver.* (FINE) **$85.00**

J2-32. Unmarked: Jeweler's Ring Cutter. Very Well Made. Ca. 1900. Length: 6 1/4 Inches. *The preferred mode of using this tool was when the ring was removed from the finger, but it was designed in such a way that it would work to remove a ring stuck on a swollen finger. Just the thing for an emergency.* (GOOD+) **$35.00**

J2-33. Unmarked: Jeweler's Thread and Tap Tool. Multiple Adjustment. Rare and Near New6. Length: 6 1/2 Inches. *This specialized threading and tapping tool is unlike anything we have ever encountered. It is fitted with all manner of adjustment screws and threaded dies. It very likely had something to do with lathe work on a metal lathe, but we have no absolute information. Rare and nearly new.* (FINE) **$345.00**

J2-34. Stevens & Co.: Bronze Watch Caliper. With Attachments. Early and Excellent. Length: 3 1/4 Inches. *Stevens & Co. is the maker name imprinted on this most unusual bronze watchmaker's caliper, which comes complete with a variety of accessories.* (GOOD+) **$45.00**

J2-35. Unmarked: Patent Parallel Jaw Punch. Patented March 18, 1877. Early and Near New. Length: 7 1/2 Inches. *Clearly marked with the early patent date and in nearly-new condition, this early parallel jaw jeweler's punch is as nice as they come. A rare item from an under appreciated area of collecting.* (FINE) **$175.00**

J2-36. Millers Falls Company No. 4: Jeweler's Hand Drill. Elaborate Paint. Rosewood Handle. Length: 8 Inches. *Here's a superb example of the Millers Falls diminutive jeweler's hand drill. Nearly all original paint remains on this rosewood handled tool. Nice.* (FINE) **$225.00**

J2-37. Simmons Hardware Co., St. Louis: "Keen Kutter" Scissors. With Brass Lock. Early and Uncommon. Length: 4 1/2 Inches. *These most unusual scissors are imprinted with the E.C. Simmons Company's "Keen Kutter" logo and are fitted with a brass locking mechanism. Very different.* (GOOD+) **$85.00**

J2-38. K. & D.: Jewler's Staking Tool. Mahogany Case. Approximatly 100 Tools. Length: 9 Inches. *More than 100 tools remain with this American made jewelers staking tool. Near new.* (FINE) **$115.00**

J2-39. Unmarked: Jeweler's Staking Pliers. "Acier Fondue". Marked "France". Length: 7 Inches. *This one is marked "Acier Fondue", which my five years of training in the French language tells me translates, roughly, as "metal dipped in cheese". I may be wrong, but c'est la vie. A nice early set of staking pliers, sans fromage.* (FINE) **$55.00**

J2-40. Unmarked: Jewelers Staking Pliers. With Pins. Superb Condition. Length: 6 1/2 Inches. *Here's a clean but unmarked pair of jeweler's staking pliers. Condition is near new.* (FINE) **$45.00**

J2-41. Unmarked: Special Purpose Gauge. British Institute Standard. Near New Condition. Length: 4 Inches. *This unusual gauge was meant to fold up and fit in one's pocket. I'm really not sure what it was for, but its very well made.* (FINE) **$65.00**

J2-42. Waltham Watch Co., Waltham, Mass.: "Waltham" Leather Gauge. Patented November 24, 1903. Excellent Condition. Length: 9 1/2 Inches. *The experience of the Waltham Watch Company with the use and making of precision tools most likely led them to produce this precision caliper for use in the shoemaking industry.* (GOOD+) **$65.00**

J2-43. Unmarked: Jeweler's Stake Anvil. Round, Square Horns. Ready to Use. Length: 4 1/4 Inches. *This classic stake anvil is in excellent working condition. These have become nearly impossible to find.* (GOOD+) **$55.00**

J2-44. Atkins & Co., E.C., Indianapolis: Tin of Silver Solder. Embossed Logo. Scarce and Excellent. Length: 0 3/4 Inches. *For the collector who has everything, we offer this full tin of silver solder from the "Atkins Silver Steel" people. The Atkins logo is nicely embossed on the lid.* (GOOD+) **$35.00**

J2-45. Unmarked: Combmaker's Graille Quannet. For Tortoise Shell. Rare and Excellent. Length: 13 1/2 Inches. *The making of combs from tortoise shells required highly specialized tools, including these seldom seen devices known as a graille (the long, flat tool) and quannet (the tool with the angular handle). Each tool has a file-like facing that was used for precision shaping of the material. Seldom found available for sale, these tools have been set away in a prominent Connecticut collection for nearly 50 years. Museum quality tools available on a first come, first serve basis.* (GOOD+) **$365.00**

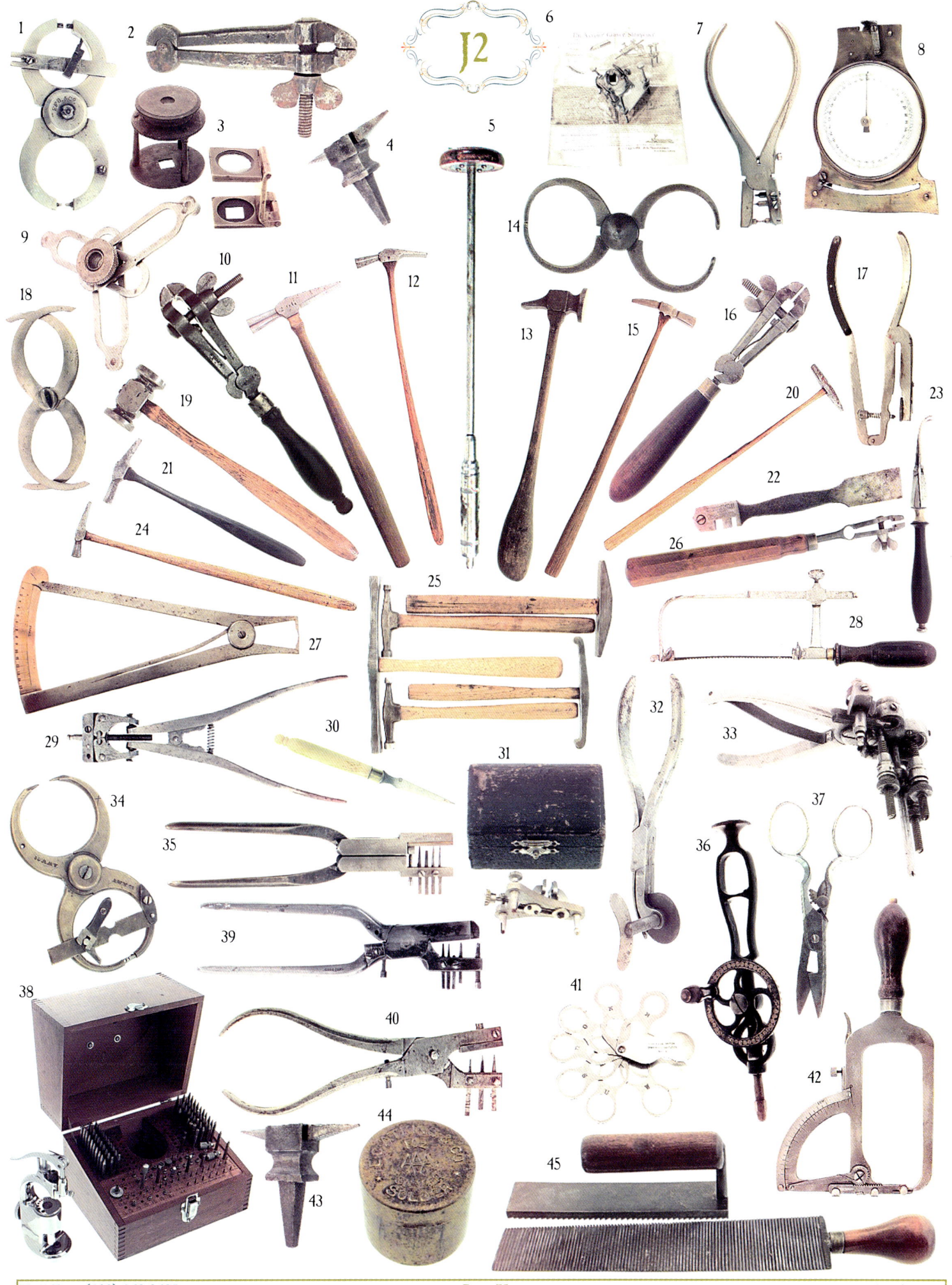

Group K2

K2-1. Chapin-Stephens Co., The No. 036: Patent Inclinometer Folding Rule. With Level, Bevel, Etc. Extra Crisp and Clean. Length: 12 Inches. *The Chapin Stephens Company was the last of a series of makers who produced the Stephens Patent Combination Rule that was originally patented by L.C. Stephens in 1858. This example is in excellent collector quality condition and ready to proudly display.* (GOOD+) **$295.00**

K2-2. Lufkin Rule Co., The, Saginaw, Mich. No. 386: Arch Joint, Unbound Folding Rule. With Caliper Slide. Extra Crisp and Clean. Length: 12 Inches. *No apologies, clean and well preserved caliper rule from Lufkin. A good one.* (GOOD+) **$55.00**

K2-3. Stephens & Co., Riverton, Conn. No. 99: One Foot, Four Fold Folding Rule. With Caliper. Uncommon Type. Length: 12 Inches. *This is the first example of this most unusual Stephens caliper rule that we have offered. A rare Stephens rule.* (FAIR) **$45.00**

K2-4. Stanley Tools No. 136: 4" Caliper Folding Rule. Later Production. Near New Condition. Length: 4 Inches. *This later Stanley caliper rule features printed lettering on its face. It appears never to have been used.* (FINE) **$15.00**

K2-5. Stephens & Company No. 100: Six Inch, Two Fold Folding Rule. Extra Wide, with Caliper. Rare Configuration. Length: 6 Inches. *The equivalent in configuration to Stanley's scarce No. 13 rule, this Stephens rule is the first of its type that we have offered. Rare.* (GOOD) **$125.00**

K2-6. Stanley Rule & Level No. 32: One-Foot, Four-Fold Folding Rule. Arch Joint, Unbound. With Caliper. Length: 12 Inches. *Nearly every carpenter kept a rule such as this in his (or her, if you insist) vest pocket. This one is marked with the Stanley trademark in use at the very beginning of the Twentieth Century.* (GOOD+) **$45.00**

K2-7. Lufkin Rule Co., The, Saginaw, Mich. No. 171: Six Inch, Two Fold Folding Rule. With Caliper. Stanley No. 36 Equivalent. Length: 6 Inches. *Lufkin's answer to Stanley's No. 36 caliper rule, this clean example retains nearly all of its original lacquer finish. A nice example.* (GOOD+) **$45.00**

K2-8. C-S Co., The No. 65: One Foot, Four Fold Folding Rule. Square Joint, Unbound. Uncommon Number. Length: 12 Inches. *The equivalent of Stanley's No. 65 square-joint, boxwood rule has seen some wear, but is otherwise in excellent condition.* (GOOD) **$35.00**

K2-9. Stanley Rule & Level No. 36: Six-Inch, Two-Fold Folding Rule. Square Joint, Caliper. Early Example. Length: 6 Inches. *This early caliper rule has some evidence of "pocket wear" but it is otherwise in sound condition and not too bad for a 100 year old rule.* (GOOD) **$25.00**

K2-10. Stanley Rule & Level No. 3: One-Foot, Four-Fold Folding Rule. Square Joint, Full Bound. Uncommon Type. Length: 12 Inches. *The one foot, full bound caliper rule is among the rarest of Stanley one foot rules. This one has some heavy staining, but the maker name and number are clearly visible.* (GOOD) **$135.00**

K2-11. Stanley Rule & Level No. 36: Six-Inch, Two-Fold Folding Rule. Square Joint, Caliper. Early Imprint. Length: 6 Inches. *This perfectly preserved caliper rule features a very early Stanley imprint. Examples of the No. 36 are becoming increasingly difficult to find.* (GOOD+) **$55.00**

K2-12. Stanley, W. F., London (England) No. 249: Cased Marquois Rules. Original Mahogany Case. Superb Condition. Length: 12 Inches. *This matching cased set of boxwood rules from the W.F. Stanley firm of London were intended for military calculations in gunnery. All of the rules and the fitted mahogany box, which features a bright yellow Stanley label, are marked with the incuse assembly number "249". A rare set of rules in superb condition in the original box. Extra nice.* (FINE) **$375.00**

K2-13. Rabone & Sons, John, Birmingham No. 1167: Three Foot Folding Rule. With Printed Letters. Crisp and Clean. Length: 36 Inches. *Here's a clean and sound example of Rabone's classic "blind man's" rule in the 3 foot size. A good one.* (GOOD) **$45.00**

K2-14. Lufkin Rule Co., The No. 2062: Two-Foot, Three-Fold Folding Rule. "Patent Pending". With Integral Level. Length: 24 Inches. *A crisp and clean example of Lufkin's larger, unbound level/rule combination. This one has seen some wear, but it is without damage and clearly marked.* (GOOD) **$245.00**

K2-15. Rabone & Sons, John, Birmingham No. 1167: Three Foot Folding Rule. With Printed Letters. Crisp and Clean. Length: 36 Inches. *A later example of the Rabone line, this rule features the printed "blind man's" lettering that was offered for the nearsighted. The main hinge pin has been replaced by a tack.* (GOOD+) **$35.00**

K2-16. Stanley Rule & Level No. 53 1/2: Two-Foot, Four-Fold Folding Rule. Arch Joint, Unbound. Architect's Rule. Length: 24 Inches. *This early example of Stanley's bevel-edged architect's rule features the block lettering of the 1890's era. A very well preserved early rule. It has seen a bit of use and has some staining, but a rare rule nonetheless.* (FAIR) **$25.00**

K2-17. Stanley Rule & Level No. 66 3/4: Three-Foot, Four-Fold Folding Rule. "Sweetheart" Trade Mark. Crisp Condition. Length: 36 Inches. *A nice clean example of Stanley's 3 foot, full-bound folding rule with a bold Sweetheart trademark. Excellent.* (GOOD+) **$115.00**

K2-18. Stephens & Co., Riverton, Conn. No. 44 3/4: Two Foot, Four Fold Folding Rule. Arch Joint, Narrow. Uncommon Type. Length: 24 Inches. *This is the first example of this uncommon Stephens rule that we have encountered. It features an arch joint and a narrower than usual width to the body. A rare rule.* (GOOD+) **$115.00**

K2-19. Stanley Rule & Level No. 66 1/2: Three Foot, Four Fold Folding Rule. Arch Joint, Unbound. Near New Condition. Length: 36 Inches. *Stanley basic three-foot rule in uncommonly nice condition. This one dates from the latter days of Stanley production. Extra crisp and clean.* (FINE) **$45.00**

K2-20. Starrett, L.S., Athol, Mass.: Folding Advertising Rule. Troy Paper Corp. Uncommon Type. Length: 12 Inches. *The Troy Paper Corporation apparently contracted with L.S. Starrett & Company to produce this folding rule bearing their advertising. An uncommon advertising rule.* (GOOD+) **$35.00**

K2-21. Stanley Rule & Level No. 66 1/2: Three Foot, Four Fold Folding Rule. Arch Joint, Unbound. Superb Condition. Length: 36 Inches. *Stanley basic three-foot rule in uncommonly nice condition. This one dates from the latter days of Stanley production. A previous owner "Earl" has etched his name in the back and there is a small chip from the edge on the reverse side, but this rule is otherwise in superb condition.* (GOOD+) **$35.00**

K2-22. Lufkin Rule Co., The No. 1206: Aluminum Zig-Zag Folding Rule. Flat Rolled Metal. Uncommon Type. Length: 72 Inches. *Lufkin offered an extensive line of aluminum rules. This one is in excellent condition. A nice example.* (GOOD+) **$15.00**

K2-23. Stanley Rule & Level No. 57: Three-Foot, Four-Fold Folding Rule. Arch Joint, Unbound. Yard Measure Scales. Length: 36 Inches. *Unmarked with the Stanley mark, as was the case, apparently, with every example ever produced, this full-bound, arch-joint rule has a warm golden patina achieved from years of careful use. A good one.* (GOOD+) **$165.00**

K2-24. Stanley Rule & Level No. 36: Six-Inch, Two-Fold Folding Rule. Square Joint, Caliper. "Made In Usa" Mark. Length: 6 Inches. *This well preserved caliper rule features an early Stanley imprint with the "Made in U.S.A. designation. Examples of the No. 36 are becoming increasingly difficult to find, especially in this condition.* (GOOD+) **$55.00**

K2-25. Rabone & Sons, John, Birmingham No. 1377: Three Foot Folding Rule. With Metric Graduations. Uncommon Type. Length: 39 1/4 Inches. *Reluctantly metrified as the English have been, they were forced, early on, to contend with a "progressive" Europe that was more than willing to throw away its traditional standards of measurement. English rule makers responded with a wide range of metric rules, of which this four-fold meter rule is a classic example. A good one.* (GOOD) **$55.00**

K2-26. Stanley Rule & Level No. 32: One-Foot, Four Fold Folding Rule. Arch Joint, Unbound. Early Trademark. Length: 12 Inches. *This one has seen some pocket wear, but is otherwise intact. A good one.* (GOOD) **$35.00**

K2-27. C-S Co., The, Pine Meadow, Conn. No. 36 1/2: One Foot, Two Fold Folding Rule. With Caliper. Uncommon Number. Length: 12 Inches. *This Chapin-Stephens caliper rule is crisp, clean and ready to fill out a collection or put immediately to use.* (GOOD+) **$55.00**

K2-28. Stanley Rule & Level No. 6: Engineer's Folding Rule. With Calculating Tables. Rare and Excellent. Length: 24 Inches. *Stanley offered its engineer's rule in both a bound and an unbound version. It only stands to reason that a prospective buyer of a relatively expensive, highly specialized rule would not concern himself with saving a few pennies to buy an unbound version. Consequently, the unbound No. 6 version is substantially less common than its full bound counterpart, the No. 16 Engineer's Rule, which is itself extremely scarce. The example of the No. 6 offered has seen some use, but not much. An excellent example of a scarce Stanley calculating rule.* (GOOD+) **$845.00**

K2-29. Simmons Hardware Co., St. Louis No. 620: "Redline" Folding Rule. Similar to No. 62. Near New Condition. Length: 24 Inches. *The E.C. Simmons "Redline" rules were most likely produced for them by Stanley or Chapin to compete directly with the products of those companies. One of the few examples of this rule that we have encountered. Perfectly preserved.* (FINE) **$115.00**

K2-30. Belcher Brothers Makers, New York: Two-Foot, Two-Fold Folding Rule. With Gunter Slide. Steel Tips. Length: 24 Inches. *The Belcher Brothers rule making enterprise dates to the 1830's, when they became one of the first makers of high quality boxwood and ivory rules in the United States. This early calculating rule has some staining on its face, but it is otherwise clean and sound. A rare rule from a prominent early American maker.* (GOOD) **$365.00**

K2-31. Stanley Rule & Level No. 36 1/2 R: One Foot, Two Fold Folding Rule. Right Hand Graduations. With Caliper Rule. Length: 12 Inches. *This right hand caliper rule is in nearly perfectly preserved condition. This one features the printed graduations that were employed very late in Stanley's production.* (FINE) **$25.00**

K2-32. Stanley Rule & Level No. 62 C: Two-Foot, Four Fold Folding Rule. "Sweetheart" Trade Mark. Near New Condition. Length: 24 Inches. *The basic 62 rule was offered with the caliper option, but few seem to have survived. This one is a good as they get. Nice.* (FINE) **$335.00**

K2-33. Johnson Rule Mfg. Co., E. P. No. 45: One-Foot, Two-Fold Folding Rule. German Silver Body. Rare 12" Length. Length: 12 Inches. *Most examples of the Johnson Patent rule, produced under a 1907 patent, are in the 6 inch length. Examples of this, the one-foot size, are not often found, especially in this kind of condition. Crisp.* (FINE) **$325.00**

K2-34. Upson Nut Co., Unionville, Conn. No. 62: Two-Foot, Four-Fold Folding Rule. Square Joint, Full Bound. Near New Condition. Length: 24 Inches. *This example of the Upson Nut Company's mainstay full bound boxwood rule is in nearly new condition. Choice.* (FINE) **$115.00**

K2-35. Stanley Rule & Level (Unmarked) No. 36 1/2: One Foot, Two Fold Folding Rule. With Caliper. Early and Excellent. Length: 12 Inches. *This one foot Stanley caliper rule dates from the first quarter of this century, but is in very well preserved condition.* (GOOD+) **$25.00**

K2-36. Stanley Rule & Level No. 62: Two-Foot, Four-Fold Folding Rule. Square Joint, Full Bound. Architect Scales. Length: 24 Inches. *This extra-clean example of one of Stanley's more popular rules has an early "block letter" trademark. A good one.* (GOOD+) **$45.00**

K2-37. Stanley Rule & Level No. 7: "Blind Man's" Folding Rule. With English Graduations. Uncommon Type. Length: 24 Inches. *The printed letter format of the Blind Man's rules left them particularly susceptible to wear. This one has seen some outside wear, but is otherwise in excellent condition.* (GOOD) **$55.00**

K2-38. Stanley Rule & Level No. 84: Two Foot, Four Fold Folding Rule. Square Joint, Half Bound. Early Trademark. Length: 24 Inches. *Perhaps the second most common of Stanley's better-grade rules (to the full bound No. 62), the No. 84 was protected by brass binding on its outer edges only. This example is in excellent overall condition.* (GOOD+) **$45.00**

K2-39. C-S Co., The , Pine Meadow, Conn. No. 62: Two-Foot, Four-Fold Folding Rule. Square Joint, Full Bound. Architect Scales. Length: 24 Inches. *The Chapin-Stephens equivalent to Stanley's popular No. 62 was similarly numerically designated by their principal competitor. A nice example.* (GOOD+) **$45.00**

K2-40. Stanley Rule & Level No. 62 1/2: Two Foot, Four Fold Folding Rule. Full Brass Bound. "Sweetheart" Trade Mark. Length: 24 Inches. *The configuration of this rule is identical to the No. 62, except for the narrow width. This one has a few stains and is a bit sprung, but is otherwise in sound condition.* (GOOD+) **$55.00**

K2-41. Stanley Rule & Level No. 52: Two-Foot, Two-Fold Folding Rule. Arch Joint, Half Bound. Uncommon Type. Length: 24 Inches. *According to Phil Stanley's classic "Boxwood & Ivory: Stanley Traditional Rules, 1855-1975", these were offered from 1859 to 1917 only. This one is in well preserved condition.* (GOOD) **$45.00**

K2-42. Stanley Rule & Level No. 68: Two-Foot, Four-Fold Folding Rule. Round Joint, Unbound. Horizontal Read. Length: 24 Inches. *This later style No. 68 features the horizontal read numbers introduced near the end of production of this tool.* (GOOD+) **$25.00**

K2-43. Stanley Rule & Level (Unmarked) No. 61: Two Foot, Four Fold Folding Rule. "Sweetheart" Trade Mark. "T. Riggs Frame Department". Length: 24 Inches. *Here's an early example of Stanley's No. 61 rule imprinted with the classic "Sweetheart" imprint. A previous owner, imprinted the rule with the designation "T. Riggs, Frame Department". A good one.* (GOOD) **$25.00**

K2-44. Chapin-Stephens Co., Pine Meadow, No. 72 1/2: Two Foot, Four Fold Folding Rule. Sqare Joint, Full Bound. Early and Excellent. Length: 24 Inches. *This broad square joint, full bound rule was the equivalent to Stanley's offering of the same number. An uncommon Chapin-Stephens rule.* (GOOD+) **$135.00**

K2-45. Master Rule Mfg. Co.: "Interlox" Folding Rule. Sliding Zig Zag. Patented November 2, 1915. Length: 72 Inches. *The "Interlox" rule features a sliding adjustment that is handy for inside measurements. This well preserved example has only a slight sliver missing from one section that deserves mention.* (GOOD) **$35.00**

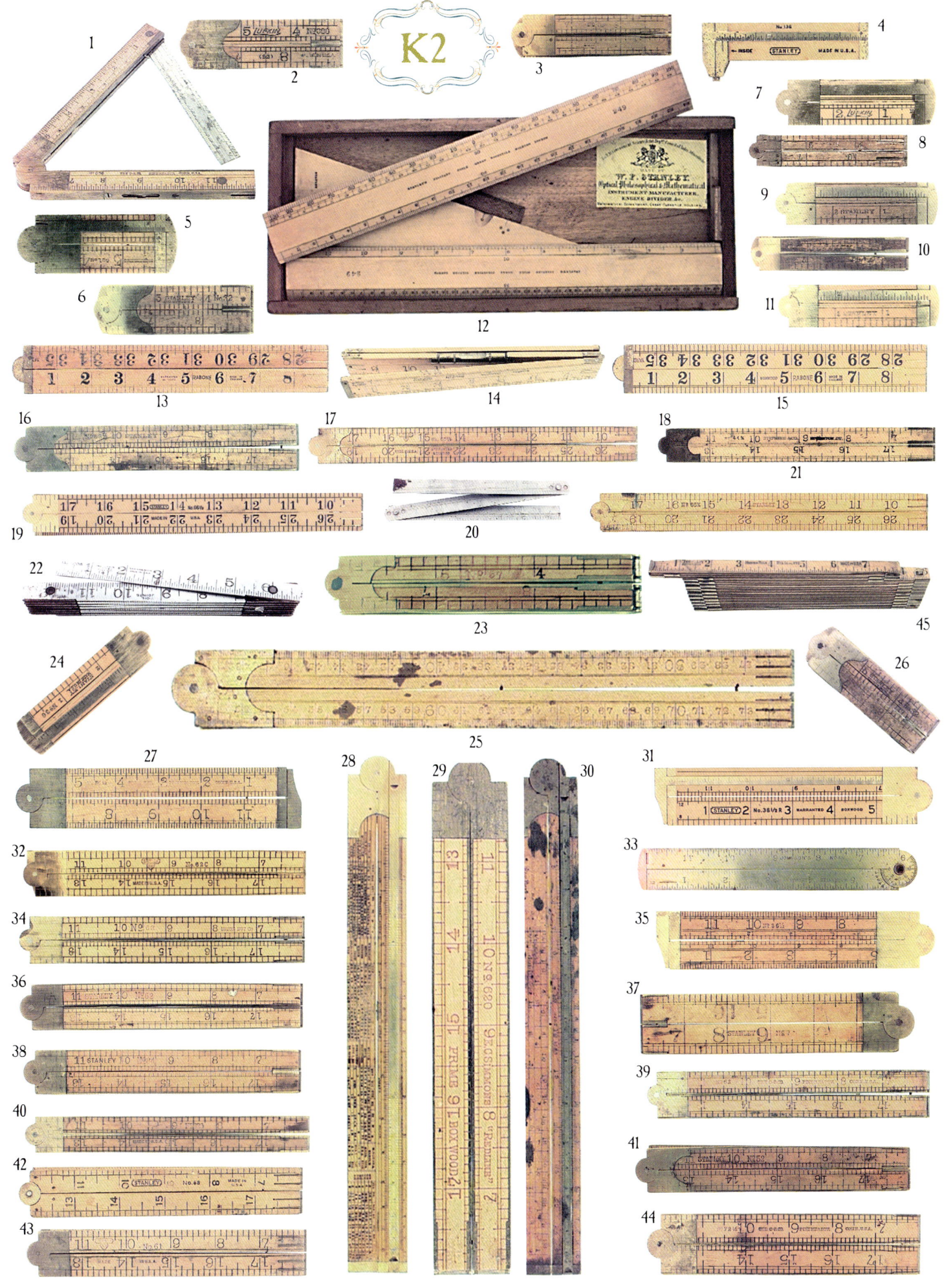

Group L2

L2-1. Assorted Makers: Set of 8 Assorted Tracing Wheels. Rosewood Handles. Gomph, Osborne, Etc.. Length: 5 Inches. *Here's a great set of tracing wheels from the recently-acquired set of leather working tools. All are from top makers and in great working condition. Extra nice.* (GOOD+) **$255.00**

L2-2. Solidhed Company, Hoboken, N.J.: Combination Eyelet Pliers. With Punch Awl. New Condition, Original Box. Length: 4 1/2 Inches. *These specialty pliers don't say so on the box, but they were very likely produced by the William Schollhorn Company, who produced the "Bernard" line of specialty pliers. New and in the box.* (FINE) **$85.00**

L2-3. Charlton, J., Newark, N.J.: Rosewood and Brass Draw Gauge. Ca. 1850's. Rare Maker. Length: 5 1/2 Inches. *John Charlton's international reputation as a toolmaker of exceptional skill has not survived with time, nor have many of his tools. A clean and clearly marked example of a tool that is becoming increasingly collectible.* (GOOD+) **$235.00**

L2-4. Aiken, F.H.: Aiken's Patent Leather Splitter. Early Knurling. Scarce and Complete. Length: 7 1/2 Inches. *F.H. Aiken was a prominent pre-Civil War inventor and manufacturer of tools in his native state of New Hampshire. This leather splitter was apparently designed to be mounted on a bench. Extra early and clearly marked with the maker's name.* (GOOD) **$125.00**

L2-5. Assorted Makers: Set of 10 Assorted Crease Tools. Rosewood Handles. Gomph, Osborne, Etc.. Length: 5 Inches. *Here's a great working set of crease tools from major makers, there are five doubles and the rest are singles. A great lot from a recently-acquired chest.* (GOOD+) **$225.00**

L2-6. Kelley, A.D.: Patent Heel Gauge. Patented March 20, 1854. Extra Early and Rare. Length: 8 Inches. *One of the earliest patented tools we have been privileged to offer. This leatherworker's heel cutter was patented on March 20, 1854 and has that date imprinted into its cast iron base. It is also imprinted with the name of its inventor, one A.D. Kelley. Of exceptionally graphic form, complete and ready to display, the A.D. Kelley heel cutter and form captures the essence of mechanical ingenuity and limited machining ability that is so characteristic of pre-Civil War tools. A classic.* (GOOD+) **$265.00**

L2-7. Sargent & Co., New Haven Conn. No. 190: 6 1/2" Eyelet Punch. "Triumph" Model. New Condition, Original Box. Length: 6 1/2 Inches. *Sargent & Company absorbed the products of the New Haven, Connecticut maker Schollhorn & Company into their line. This specialty punch is in new condition in its original box. Mint.* (FINE) **$55.00**

L2-8. Osborne, Late Dodd, Newark, N.J.: Early Brass and Rosewood Draw Gauge. Ca. 1850's. With Hook Handle. Length: 4 1/2 Inches. *The imprint on this tool would indicate that it was produced sometime in the 1850's, shortly after C.S. Osborne acquired the leather working tool business of William Dodd. A rare draw gauge having an historically significant mark.* (GOOD+) **$225.00**

L2-9. Adams, Z., Philadelphia., Penn..: Half Moon Leather Knife. Uncommon Maker. Excellent Condition. Length: 6 Inches. *This is the first time we have encountered the leather tool maker "Z. Adams", whose name is imprinted on this knife. The Directory of American Toolmakers makes no mention of this name. Rare.* (GOOD+) **$85.00**

L2-10. Unmarked: Early Patent Leather Tool. Patented July 1, 1879. Unusual Type. Length: 5 1/4 Inches. *This specialty leather trimming tool is imprinted with a July 1, 1879 patent date. An early and unusual specialty leather working tool.* (GOOD+) **$165.00**

L2-11. "Uneedme" Tool Co., Col's., O.: Special Function Stretcher. "Pat. Apld. For". Early and Unusual. Length: 16 Inches. *This was probably used for something relating to barrels, but I'm not sure. An early appearing tool with an unlikely name.* (GOOD+) **$95.00**

L2-12. Webster, W., E. Jaffrey, N.H.: Early Patent Leather Knife. Patented April 29, 1880. Uncommon Type. Length: 5 Inches. *One Wilbur Webster of Jaffrey, New Hampshire is listed as the patentee and manufacturer of this uncommon leather tool in "Instruments of Change", published by the New Hampshire Historical Society. A rare patented leather knife that is clean and clearly marked.* (GOOD+) **$55.00**

L2-13. Champion Dearment, Meadville, Penn.: Rare Cobbler's Hammer. With Original Decal. Near New Condition. Length: 10 Inches. *The Champion Company produced a wide range of products including this cobbler's hammer, which retains its original decal. Nearly new.* (FINE) **$85.00**

L2-14. Osborne & Co., C.S., Newark, N.J. No. 216: Grommet Setting Kit. With Die and Punch. New Condition, Original Box. Length: 6 Inches. *Here's a most unusual leatherworking tool from the Big Enchilada in the leather working tool business, the C.S. Osborne Company of Newark, New Jersey.* (FINE) **$65.00**

L2-15. Christensen, A.M., Brockton, Mass. No. 8: Special Purpose Leather Tool. Solid Bronze Head. Clearly Marked. Length: 5 1/2 Inches. *This one obviously served some purpose in the shoemaking industry. It is clearly marked with the Christensen imprint. Different.* (GOOD+) **$65.00**

L2-16. Unmarked: Assorted Floats and Scribes. For Bookbinding? Early Appearance. Length: 8 Inches. *We are uncertain as to the function of these obviously very early tools. They were apparently designed to fit into a tang type handle.* (GOOD+) **$35.00**

L2-17. Snell & Co., L.S., Bridgeport: Early Patent Leather Tool. Adjustable Cut. Patented 1860. Length: 6 Inches. *This early patent leather tool had some specialized function in the shoe manufacturing trade. A good clean example.* (FINE) **$55.00**

L2-18. Unmarked: Classic Cobbler's Hammer. Original Handle. Near New Condition. Length: 9 1/2 Inches. *This classic cobbler's hammer appears to have been very little, if ever, used. A nice example.* (FINE) **$45.00**

L2-19. Unmarked: Violin Maker's Perfiling Tool. Adjustable Brass Head. Rare and Near New. Length: 5 1/2 Inches. *These tools were used for scribing a band around the edge of a piece of woodwork for the purpose of inlaying an ornamental strip of veneer. This example features an adjustable brass head and is in nearly new condition.* (FINE) **$195.00**

L2-20. Unmarked: Special Purpose Reamer. With Knife Blade. Solid Brass Cone. Length: 7 1/2 Inches. *This specialty tool was apparently intended for some reaming/trimming function. Most unusual.* (GOOD+) **$25.00**

L2-21. Osborne & Co., C.S., Newark, NJ: Cast Iron Leather Draw Gauge. Screw Lock. Crisp and Clean. Length: 5 Inches. *This basic all-steel draw gauge is in fine working order. Ready to use.* (GOOD+) **$45.00**

L2-22. Boudreau & Co., L.: Early Patent Leather Stretcher. Patented December 3, 1872. Clear Patent Imprint. Length: 11 Inches. *The tools of the leather working trades have become increasingly collectible as collectors have expanded their range of interest beyond merely woodworking tools. Here's an early and clearly marked webbing stretcher from L. Boudreau & Company, a name we have not previously encountered.* (GOOD+) **$45.00**

L2-23. Unmarked: Set of Four Special Purpose Leather Tools. For Edging? Rare and Excellent. Length: 6 1/2 Inches. *These extraordinary leather working tools were apparently intended for some sort of edging work. All have extremely complex shapes that we have not previously encountered on such tools. Acquired in the State of Maine as part of the deaccession of a private museum. A great set.* (GOOD+) **$365.00**

L2-24. Unmarked: Moody's Patent Leather Tool. Dual Perforator. Patented April 20, 1880. Length: 5 1/2 Inches. *These performed some specialized leather working function. This one was never put to work. Brand new.* (FINE) **$55.00**

L2-25. Crawford, J., Newark, N.J.: Rosewood and Brass Draw Gauge. Early N.J. Mark. Hand Scribed Beam. Length: 5 1/2 Inches. *The Crawford name must have been well-respected in its time. Alexender Farnham notes in his book on New Jersey tool makers that several makers simultaneously claimed to be the sole successor to Crawford, and this despite the fact that Crawford was himself still in business at the time! A good one.* (GOOD+) **$185.00**

L2-26. Hanover, J. C., Cincinatti, Ohio: "Moody's Patent" Leather Tool. Patented April 20, 18880. Double Perforated Wheel. Length: 5 3/4 Inches. *A most interesting patented leather perforator, well marked and in superb condition.* (FINE) **$85.00**

L2-27. Bauer, P.: Patented Buttonhole Cutter. Patented July 16, 1872. Cast Brass Tip. Length: 9 1/2 Inches. *This early patent buttonhole cutter was once fitted with a steel spring on one of the arms that is now missing, but is otherwise in good overall condition. An uncommon early patent leather working tool.* (GOOD) **$55.00**

L2-28. Osborne & Co., C.S., Newark, N.J. No. 0150: 1 3/4" Strap End Punch. Pointed Tip. Ready To Use. Length: 6 3/4 Inches. *This was used for cutting a pointed tip on the end of a harness strap. Condition is near new.* (FINE) **$55.00**

L2-29. Osborne & Co., C.S., Newark, N.J.: Leather Worker's Pricking Iron. Hardened Steel. Unused Condition. Length: 4 1/4 Inches. *Tools such as this were known as "pricking irons" and were used for laying out a series of stitches in leather. The points are cut at a 45 degree angle to set the pattern for the sewing. An uncommon leather working tool in excellent condition.* (FINE) **$35.00**

L2-30. Brown & Sharpe Mfg. Co., The No. 771: Adjustable Tension Punch. With Brass Sleeve. Scarce and Near New. Length: 5 1/2 Inches. *By turning the knurled ring on the top of this automatic punch, the amount of force that would be applied by the spring acting in conjunction with the tip could be regulated. A great working tool and an uncommon B. & S. item in excellent condition.* (FINE) **$55.00**

L2-31. Unmarked: Harnessmaker's Rein Rounder. Lever Type Lift. Early and Excellent. Length: 14 Inches. *This tool was designed to be mounted on a bench where leather reins would be drawn through the appropriately undersized opening to form them into a rounded shape. A nice example.* (GOOD+) **$195.00**

L2-32. Unmarked: Early Leather Splitter. Working Condition. Uncommon Type. Length: 13 Inches. *This early leather splitting device was likely mounted to a bench by a pair of threaded rods. Early and excellent.* (GOOD+) **$55.00**

L2-33. Leypoldt, F.C., Philadelphia, Penna. No. 3: Early Patent Leather Cutter. Patented December 18, 1860. Spring Lever Action. Length: 6 1/2 Inches. *These cast iron and brass leather cutting tools were, I believe, used for cutting button holes in leather. This one is clearly marked with the early patent date.* (FINE) **$145.00**

L2-34. Whitcher, Boston, Mass. No. 3: "Crispin" Shoemaker' Hammer. Superb Examle. Original Label. Length: 9 1/2 Inches. *Much of the original label remains on this classic "Crispin" shoemaker's hammer from the Whitcher Company of Boston. A top quality cobbler's hammer from the very best maker.* (FINE) **$55.00**

L2-35. Unmarked: Assorted Shoemmaker' Tools. Anvil, Cutter, Etc.. Early Appearance. Length: 5 Inches. *This assortment of tools came from the working kit of a shoemaker. A nice assortment.* (GOOD+) **$25.00**

L2-36. "Uneedme" Tool Co., Col's., O.: Special Function Stretcher. "Patent Applied For". Early and Unusual. Length: 16 Inches. *This was probably used for something relating to barrels, but I'm not sure. An early appearing tool with an unlikely name.* (GOOD) **$85.00**

L2-37. Kraeuter & Co., Newark, NJ: Set of Heavy Duty Leather Punches. Set of 11 Punches. Essentially Unused. Length: 7 Inches. *Having looked, by accident, from time to time, at the prices of some of the more obscure hand tools that are still available today, I shudder to think what might be the cost of a set of leather punches such as this magnificent set offered here. Artfully forged and boldly stamped with the mark of prominent Newark, New Jersey maker Kraeuter & Company, these punches, which cut large circular holes from 3" down, have apparently never been used. For a craftsman with a use for fine tools of this sort or the collector with a different perspective, we recommend this superb set.* (FINE) **$225.00**

L2-38. Arlindo: Set of 3 Leather Burnishers. From One Kit. Marked "Arlindo". Length: 5 1/2 Inches. *The name "Arlindo" is carved into one of these three burnishing artistically inspired tools which came from the same working set. Visually appealing, perfectly patinated and ready to display. A great set. Highly recommended.* (GOOD+) **$295.00**

L2-39. Assorted Makers: Set of Oval Leather Punches. Osborne, Etc.. Excellent Condition. Length: 5 1/2 Inches. *These oval punches were used by harness makers for punching holes for straps. All are in excellent working order.* (GOOD+) **$145.00**

L2-40. Osborne & Co., C.S., Newark, N.J.: Oval Leather Punch. 1 1/4" Size. New Condition, Original Box. Length: 5 3/4 Inches. *This oblong ovoid punch from C.S. Osborne is in new condition in its original box. A most unusual Osborne tool in top shape.* (FINE) **$125.00**

L2-41. Osborne & Co., C.S., Newark, N.J.: Pair of Channel Leather Tool. Rosewood Handles. Near New Condition. Length: 5 1/2 Inches. *Each of these leather channeling tools is in excellent collector quality condition. Nice.* (FINE) **$75.00**

L2-42. De Lacy, G., N.Y.: Full Set of 1/8" Numbers and Letters. For Bookbinding. Seriph Type Characters. Length: 8 Inches. *This early and perfectly preserved set of bookbinder number and letter stamps is complete and ready to be put back to use. The letters are ornamented with seriphs in classic Nineteenth Century style. A great set.* (FINE) **$365.00**

L2-43. Unmarked: Leather Worker's Graining Board. From E. Pepperell Mass. Rare and Excellent. Length: 19 Inches. *This extremely rare and nicely patinated graining board was used by a leather worker to smooth the surface of leather. Consigned from a prominent Connecticut collection, where it has resided for some 50 years, this is the first example of this uncommon leather working tool that we have ever seen offered for sale.* (GOOD+) **$225.00**

L2-44. Sargent & Co., New Haven, Conn.: Wheel Type Leather Punch. Excellent Order. Ready To Use. Length: 8 1/2 Inches. *All of the cutters are in excellent order on this turret type leather punch from Sargent. Nearly new.* (FINE) **$25.00**

L2-45. Unmarked: Pair of Hand Forged Leather Dies. With "Pinking" Edge. Made From Files. Length: 6 1/2 Inches. *Each of these leather working tools has been hand forged from a discarded file. Most unusual.* (GOOD+) **$65.00**

L2-46. Mann, J.B., Bridgewater, Mass.: Salesman's Case of Leather Tools. Many Special Tools. Ca. 1860-1880. Length: 13 Inches. *The presence of an engraved brass tag bearing the imprint "J.B. Mann" on the outside of this box of specialty leather tools, together with the fact that the tools are permanently fastened to the inside of the case, leaves little doubt that this was a salesman's display case, perhaps even the personal display case of the company owner. Filled with a wide variety of highly specialized tools, all of which are in top collector quality condition, this is the first intact tool salesman's kit we have been privileged to offer. Whether you are a collector of leather working tools or assembling a general collection of extraordinary tools, this spectacular set comes very highly recommended. A great set of tools.* (FINE) **$675.00**

Group M2

M2-1. Starrett, L.S., Athol, Mass. No. 89: Combination Caliper and Divider. Patented September 24, 1889. Complete and As New. Length: 9 Inches. *This multi-purpose divider and caliper is clearly marked with the patent date and includes all original parts. Minty crispy nice.* (FINE) **$225.00**

M2-2. Stevens A. & T. Co., J.: Stevens' Patent Divider. Patented March 9, 1886. With Spring Joint. Length: 6 Inches. *This 1886 patent divider is marked on the top of the spring joint, which may well be the patent feature. An extremely clean early machinists divider.* (FINE) **$95.00**

M2-3. Unmarked: Early Wing Divider. With Slitter Tip. Unknown Function. Length: 7 1/2 Inches. *The form of this specialty divider is one that we have not encountered previously. The manner in which the cutting tip on the adjustable leg is sharpened would indicate that this tool was intended for the leather worker.* (GOOD+) **$85.00**

M2-4. Wagor, D.: Massive Wing Divider. Turned Brass Handle. Superb Patina. Length: 26 Inches. *This extraordinary pair of dividers is surmounted by a turned finial of brass that has achieved a rich golden patina of age. Of oversize proportions, the precise adjustment of the legs is regulated by a semicircular protractor that is not graduated with angle measurements. Generally, a divider of this size would have been used by a metalworker, however the form of this tool suggests that it might have belonged to a clockmaker or other precision craftsman. An extraordinarily graphic and nearly perfectly preserved pair of dividers. Highly recommended.* (FINE) **$2,850.00**

M2-5. Unmarked: Pair Of Wing Dividers. Decorative Forging. Ca. 1800. Length: 8 1/2 Inches. *This decoratively filed divider looks to date from the end of the Eighteenth Century. A nice example.* (GOOD) **$35.00**

M2-6. Standard Tool Co., Athol, Mass.: Bellows Patented Square, Bevel. Patented March 11, 1884. Rare and Excellent. Length: 9 Inches. *Another of the patents of Stephen Bellows, the prolific inventor of the Standard Tool company, this one is among the most elusive of all early machinist tools. Clearly marked with the 1884 patent date and possessing the proper Standard Tool Company 9 inch rule, these are as rare as they come. A piece of American technological history.* (GOOD+) **$550.00**

M2-7. Stevens & Co., J., C. Falls, Mass.: Pratt's Patent Divider. Patented February 23, 1886. Near New Condition. Length: 4 Inches. *This micrometer-adjusting precision divider is in essentially unused condition. Clearly marked with the early patent date.* (FINE) **$265.00**

M2-8. D. & S., Bangor, Maine: 4" Bench Rule. Graduated in 50ths, Inch. Rare Early Mark. Length: 4 Inches. *This crispy clean example of the work of pioneering precision machinist tool makers Darling & Swartz, of Bangor, Maine, is in nearly new condition. Highly recommended.* (FINE) **$125.00**

M2-9. Unmarked: Rare Triple Leg Divider. Early Appearance. Superb Patina. Length: 6 Inches. *Among the rarest of drafting tools, these three legged dividers would have been included in only the most extensive kits of tools. This example is in excellent condition, noting only slight tarnish to the legs. Rare.* (GOOD+) **$365.00**

M2-10. Sawyer Tool Mfg Co.: "Beeswax Joint" Caliper. Hermaphrodite Type. Patented August 22, 1906. Length: 6 1/2 Inches. *Marked with its "beeswax joint" designation, these friction-joint calipers were produced under a 1906 patent. Rare.* (GOOD+) **$25.00**

M2-11. Unmarked: Elaborate Scribe and Caliper. With Precision Adjust. Early and Unusual. Length: 10 Inches. *An exquisitely detailed multi-purpose caliper in superb condition. The precision adjustments on this carefully hand-filed tool are unlike anything I have ever seen. Choice.* (GOOD+) **$265.00**

M2-12. Schmidt & Moellenhoe: Early Style Divider. Decorative Form. German Make? Length: 6 1/2 Inches. *The makers of this pair of dividers are names that we have not previously encountered. One would suspect that they are of German origin. A pretty pair.* (GOOD+) **$55.00**

M2-13. Starrett Co., L. S., Athol, Mass. No. 18-B: Machinist's Center Punch. Spring Loaded. Ready to Use. Length: 6 Inches. *This spring activated punch has the the amount of force to be applied regulated by turning a knurled ring at the top of the punch. An uncommon Starrett tool in excellent working order.* (GOOD+) **$35.00**

M2-14. Brown & Sharpe Mfg. Co.: Machinist's Pocket Tool Kit. With Caliper and Rule. Original Pouch. Length: 2 1/2 Inches. *A most interesting caliper and rule combination in a leather pouch marked with the Brown & Sharpe Logo. An advertising item? Different and near-new.* (FINE) **$135.00**

M2-15. Unmarked: Craftsman-Made Caliper. Brass and Steel. Marked: "O.E. Reed". Length: 7 1/2 Inches. *A particularly nice craftsman made caliper with an inlaid brass name plate tastefully inscribed with the owner's mark. Different.* (GOOD) **$95.00**

M2-16. Unmarked: 4" "Call's Patent" Caliper. With Bow Mechanism. Early and Excellent. Length: 4 Inches. *No markings on this one, but is unquestionably the 1861 patent of John Call. As new.* (FINE) **$75.00**

M2-17. Unmarked: Draughtsman's Divider. With Crown Finial. Early and Excellent. Length: 5 1/2 Inches. *This drafting tool has a very early look about it. The brass finial screw is unlike anything I have seen. Early and excellent.* (GOOD+) **$195.00**

M2-18. Standard Tool Co., Athol, Mass. No. 553: "Never Slip" Surface Gauge. With Precision Adjust. Rare and Excellent. Length: 10 Inches. *An excellent example of one of the later offerings of the Standard Tool Company, this rare gauge is in excellent collector quality condition.* (GOOD+) **$425.00**

M2-19. Bell, J.: Pair Of Outside Calipers. Early Appearance. Owner Made? Length: 9 Inches. *These well preserved calipers came from a chest of early machinist tools and were likely owner made.* (FINE) **$45.00**

M2-20. Unmarked: Machinist's Pocket Tool. Taps, Reamers, Etc. Near New Condition. Length: 3 Inches. *A most interesting machinist's accessory, this tap, die, reamer and screwdriver set was possibly intended for use by those fitting gas pipes. A most unusual combination tool in excellent condition.* (FINE) **$65.00**

M2-21. Smith, E. G., Columbia, Penn. No. 128: Adjustable Slide Caliper. 6" Length. Excellent Condition. Length: 6 Inches. *These calipers were marketed as a sort of "poor man's precision tool". Their quality level was lower than that of Starrett and the like, but sufficient for all work except that requiring the closest tolerances. A well-preserved pair.* (GOOD+) **$65.00**

M2-22. Starrett, L.S., Athol, Mass.: Fay's Patent Caliper. Patented June 2, 1885. Oversize Adjustable Screw. Length: 6 Inches. *This example of the Fay patent caliper can be precisely locked into position after being adjusted with the oversize adjustment screw. An uncommon variation* (FINE) **$65.00**

M2-23. Mass. Tool Co., Greenfield, Mass.: Assorted Dividers and Calipers. Quick Adjust, Etc.. One Users Set. Length: 7 Inches. *The Massachusetts Tool Company was later assumed into the Goodell-Pratt Company. This set of dividers and calipers came from the working tools of a single machinist. An interesting set.* (FINE) **$245.00**

M2-24. Stevens & Co.: Early Spring Joint Caliper. Rare 3" Size. Extra Early. Length: 3 Inches. *This spring joint caliper is of a size smaller than that usually encountered. A good one.* (GOOD) **$45.00**

M2-25. Brown & Sharpe Mfg. Co.: Precision Adjust Depth Gauge. Patented June 21, 1904. With Spring Adjustment. Length: 6 Inches. *A spring mechanism allows this one to be set in place with a plunger action, then locked with the turn of a screw. Yet another of the many patents of Frank Spalding. Pristine.* (FINE) **$85.00**

M2-26. Athol Machine Co., Athol, Mass.: 4" Hermaphrodite Caliper. Slide Adjust Leg. Uncommon Type. Length: 4 Inches. *A mechanically interesting caliper from an early cross-town competitor of the L.S. Starrett Company.* (FINE) **$45.00**

M2-27. Unmarked: Precision Adjust Caliper. With Metric Scale. Early and Unusual. Length: 8 Inches. *There are no maker marks on this early Metric precision caliper. It appears to date from the 1870's. Condition is as-new. A great early machinist tool.* (FINE) **$115.00**

M2-28. Corning, Arthur W., New York: Direct Reading Caliper. With Advertising. Scarce and Excellent. Length: 3 Inches. *The reverse side of this indicating caliper is marked with the name of its maker (or dealer) Arthur W. Corning. The Acorn Oil & Grease people apparently gave these away. We're selling it.* (FINE **$55.00**

M2-29. Unmarked: Early Beam Micrometer. With Exposed Screw Thread. Uncommon Type. Length: 4 Inches. *The shaft on this unusual and apparently early beam micrometer appears to have been shortened. The mechanism is new to me. Different.* (GOOD+) **$85.00**

M2-30. Starrett Co., L. S., Athol, Mass.: Fay's Patent Spring Divider. With Knurled Handle. Near New Condition. Length: 3 Inches. *A nice example of the Fay patent divider in a much later manifestation. A nice set in nice condition.* (FINE) **$25.00**

M2-31. Reizenstein & Moller: German Wing Divider. Distinctive Form. Early and Excellent. Length: 8 Inches. *To the best of my knowledge, this style is no more common in Germany than it is here. Clean, early and very nicely marked.* (GOOD+) **$95.00**

M2-32. Darling Brown & Sharpe: Early Vernier Caliper. Graduated in 100ths. Crisp & Clean. Length: 4 1/2 Inches. *An early precision tool in excellent condition. Nicely marked.* (GOOD+) **$90.00**

M2-33. Millers Falls Company No. June 19, 1935: Set Of Feeler Gauges. Assorted Sizes. New Old Stock. Length: 3 1/2 Inches. *These feeler gauges and thread gauge came from one owner's kit of tools. All are in excellent condition.* (FINE) **$25.00**

M2-34. Stubs, P.S.: Early Wire Gauge. Number Sizes. Uncommon Type. Length: 5 Inches. *P.S. Stubs produced a wide range of tools. This rectangular wire gauge is the first we have seen bearing his imprint. A nice example.* (GOOD) **$15.00**

M2-35. King, W.H., Athol, Mass.: Early Patent Depth Gauge. Patented June 7, 1881. Rare and Excellent. Length: 3 Inches. *Designed to fit on a twist auger bit to serve as depth stop, this bronze gizmo was patented in 1878 by one W.H. King of Athol, Massachusetts, who most likely knew L.S. Starrett when he was just getting started. A good one.* (GOOD) **$125.00**

M2-36. Unmarked: Precision Slide Caliper. Marked "Tokyo". Original Leather Case. Length: 12 Inches. *The only mark on these precision calipers is the word "Tokyo", which is indicative of a pre-WW II manufacture. A well made tool from the Land of the Rising Sun.* (FINE) **$115.00**

M2-37. Starrett Co., The L.S., Athol, Mass. No. 188: English Standard Gauge. For Wire. Uncommon Type. Length: 3 1/4 Inches. *This one has a few broken teeth but is otherwise excellent.* (GOOD) **$15.00**

M2-38. Goodell-Pratt Company No. 925: Machinists Feeler Gauge. Uncommon Type. Near New Condition. Length: 4 Inches. *Goodell Pratt marketed and then assumed manufacture of the machinist tools of Massachusetts Tool Company. This "feeler" gauge is in new condition.* (FINE) **$35.00**

M2-39. Starrett Co., L.S., The, Athol, Mass. No. 284: Screw Thread Gauge. 29 Degree Thread. Scarce and Excellent. Length: 3 1/2 Inches. *This specialty thread gauge was used for measuring threads cut to the Acme Standard, which differed from standard threads are set at an angle of 14 1/2 degrees, for an included angle of 29 degrees. An uncommon Starrett tool.* (FINE) **$35.00**

M2-40. Woburn Machine Co., Woburn, Mass. No. 2: Leather Thickness Gauge. With Beech Handle. Scale In Milimeters & Ounces. Length: 10 1/2 Inches. *These were used for estimating the thickness of leather in the shoe and leather manufacturing factories of New England. This one has a nicely turned beech handle and retains nearly all of its original plating. An interesting and unusual precision tool.* (FINE) **$75.00**

M2-41. Unmarked: Early Wire Gauge. With Metric Graduates. Decorative Form. Length: 9 Inches. *This ornamentally filed wire gauge has both metric and English graduations. Most unusual.* (GOOD+) **$45.00**

M2-42. Goodell-Pratt Company: Parallelogram Center Gauge. Nickel Plated. Patented July 3, 1906. Length: 6 Inches. *This patented tool applies a basic geometric principle to automatically scribe a line at the center of a piece of wood. Because the central brace is fixed at the center of each of the two side pieces and the scribe is at the center point of the central brace we could very easily prove that the scribe will always end up in the center of the work being scored. Wouldn't Euclid be proud?* (GOOD+) **$55.00**

M2-43. Lufkin Rule Co., The: Precision Inside Micrometer. Single Side Adjust. New Condition, Original Box. Length: 2 1/2 Inches. *This perfectly preserved micrometer comes complete with its original adjustment wrench. The original box is missing its label. Nice.* (FINE) **$55.00**

M2-44. D.B. and S., Providence, R.I.: Machinist's Bench Rule. Near New Condition. Owner "G.F Tyler". Length: 12 Inches. *Another of the tools of the machinist, G.F. Tyler, this D.B. and S. classic is in new condition. Mint.* (FINE) **$95.00**

M2-45. Eagle Pencil Co., New York: Early "School" Compass. Decorative Design. New Conditon, Original Box. Length: 5 1/4 Inches. *When you went to school at the turn of the century, you would have taken one of these along, where it could have been turned into a formidable weapon in a crowded hallway. Early and near new.* (FINE) **$55.00**

Group N2

N2-1. Nicholson File Co., Providence, R.I.: Files For The Farm Catalog. 1953. 47 Pages. Length: 8 1/4 Inches. *Most of the major toolmakers produced pamphlets such as these, which purported to offer advice, but actually attempted to market the manufacturer's product. In this case, the products were the files of the Nicholson File Company.* (FINE) **$35.00**

N2-2. Crafts & Co., Arthur A., Boston, Mass.: Diamonds In Tools Catalog. For Machinists and Jewelers. 32 Pages, Ca. 1921. Length: 9 1/2 Inches. *Everything you need to know about the use of diamonds in tools is included in this catalog from a Boston company.* (FINE) **$35.00**

N2-3. Ward, Vern: 31 Fine Tool Journal Catalogs. 1983-1986. Much Information. Length: 11 Inches. *For a look at the way things used to be in the tool world, as well as for some very interesting tool prices, we recommend a read through these periodicals, which date from the earliest days of the entry of yours truly into the tool business. Things have changed.* (GOOD+) **$25.00**

N2-4 Ward, Vern: Iron Horse Antiques Catalogs. 1972-1976. Group Of 15. Length: 8 1/2 Inches. *These early catalogs of tools for sale are filled with objects priced at ridiculously high and ridiculously low prices. For a look at how much the tool world has changed in 20 years, we recommend these periodicals from the early days of tool collecting.* (GOOD+) **$95.00**

N2-5. Brown & Sharpe Mfg. Co. No. 32: Price Lists Catalog. 1935 Edition. Full Product Line. Length: 6 3/4 Inches. *This early Brown & Sharpe catalog has only a tear to its binding to offer as an apology. A great reference to a major line of machinists tools.* (GOOD) **$25.00**

N2-6. Stanley Tools No. 34: General Line Catalog. 1955 Edition. 216 Pages. Length: 5 Inches. *Only a minor tear near the binding on the front cover. Nice.* (GOOD+/FINE) **$65.00**

N2-7. Starrett Co., L. S., Athol, Mass. No. 21: General Line Catalog. Ca. 1913. 336 Pages. Length: 7 Inches. *A picture of the Starrett factory, ca. 1913 graces the cover of this full line catalog.* (FINE) **$145.00**

N2-8. Stanley Rule & Level No. 34: General Line Catalog. 1912 Edition. 128 Pages. Length: 7 1/2 Inches. *This one is missing the back cover, but is otherwise excellent.* (FAIR/FINE)**$45.00**

N2-9. Platt Co., The Frank S.: Root's Bee Keepers Supplies. January 1, 1912, 101st. Edition, 42nd Year, 64 Pages Length: 9 Inches. *All manner of supplies and accessories of the beekeeper are included in this ca. 1912 catalog. Included are smokers, clothing and the world's most famous whatsit—the knife from removing the wax from the top of the honeycomb.* (FINE) **$55.00**

N2-10. Stanley Rule & Level No. 34: General Line Catalog. August, 1925 Edition. 178 Pages. Length: 7 Inches. *One of the very first catalogs of the "Sweetheart" era. The 1925 catalog is a tough one to find. Scarce.* (GOOD) **$115.00**

N2-11. Starrett Co., L. S., Athol, Mass. No. 25: 50th Anniversary Catalog. 1930 Edition. 382 Pages. Length: 7 Inches. *The spot on the cover is where some idiot put a price tag. No, it wasn't me, but thanks for asking. Otherwise excellent.* (GOOD+) **$65.00**

N2-12. Nicholson File Co., Providence, R.I.: File Filosophy and How To Get The Most. Use Of Files, 1956. Twentieth Edition,49 Pages Length: 9 Inches. *Most people today don't have the slightest idea how to properly use files. Reading this pamphlet is a good place to start.* (GOOD+) **$25.00**

N2-13. Stanley Rule & Level No. 34: General Line Catalog. 1927 Edition. 192 Pages. Length: 7 Inches. *A good clean example of an uncommon Stanley catalog.* (GOOD+) **$125.00**

N2-14. Stanley Rule & Level: Pamphlet Type Catalog. Ca. 1900. 16 Pages, 3 1/2 X 6.Length: 6 1/2 Inches. *Stanley's trademark 'imp" is featured on the cover of this early Stanley advertising pamphlet.* (GOOD+) **$45.00**

N2-15. Nicholson File Co., Providence, R.I.: File Filosophy and How To Get Most Out Of Files, 18th Edition First Printing, 1954. Length: 9 Inches. *This version of Nicholson's famous "File Filosophy" pamphlet dates from some 45 years ago.* (FINE) **$25.00**

N2-16. Brown & Sharpe Mfg. Co. No. 32: Price Lists Catalog. 1935 Edition. Full Product Line. Length: 6 3/4 Inches. *The entire Brown and Sharpe line as well as their price listings are included in this catalog which dates from the early years of the Roosevelt Depression.* (GOOD+) **$35.00**

N2-17. Ward, Vern: Iron Horse Antiques Catalog. 1972-1981. Rare and Excellent. Length: 8 1/2 Inches. *In the "Good Old Days" of tool collecting, ignorance was the coin of the realm. Before much had been discovered about what tools had been produced, and before much thought had been given to what was good, what was great and what was awful, a virtual stampede of buying took place. That stampede is documented here in these early catalogs, which include some extraordinary bargains and many items that now sell for a tenth of their perceived value at the time. For an interesting, nostalgia filled look at the way tool collecting used to be, spend a few evenings going through these interesting books of tools for sale.* (GOOD+) **$115.00**

N2-18. Goodell-Pratt Company No. 16: General Line Catalog. Ca. 1926. 400 Pages. Length: 5 3/4 Inches. *A clean and complete guide to the full product line of "1500" good tools. They were, and are.* (GOOD+) **$75.00**

N2-19. Buck Bros., Millbury, Mass. No. 36: Price List And Catalog. With Addendum. Ca. 1936. Length: 10 Inches. *This price list and catalog illustrates the entire Buck Brothers line as it existed in 1936.* (GOOD+) **$45.00**

N2-20. Arnold & Walker, London No. 1-6: Early Antique Tool Catalog. Ca. 1970's. Very Well Preserved. Length: 8 1/4 Inches. *The Arnold & Walker catalogues of the 1970's are credited by many with bringing a level of "respectability" to the collecting of antique tools. Filled with exquisite photographs of graphic tools and very well documented, these catalogs have themselves become highly collectible. A rare set.* (GOOD+) **$295.00**

N2-21. Marples & Son, Wm., Sheffield: 1928 General Line Catalog. Centenary Edition. 237 Pages, Clothbound. Length: 11 Inches. *This was the 100th Anniversary Catalog of the important English toolmaking firm of William Marples & Company. An excellent and historically important catalog.* (GOOD+) **$125.00**

N2-22. Stanley Rule & Level No. 34: General Line Catalog. April, 1938 Edition. 180 Pages, With Supplement Length: 7 Inches. *This mid-Depression issue of the No. 34 is not a common catalog.* (GOOD+) **$110.00**

N2-23. Starrett Co., L. S., Athol, Mass. No. 21: General Line Catalog. Ca. 1913. 336 Pages. Length: 7 Inches. *Pre-war prosperity apparently warranted this sooner-than-usual new catalog. A great reference to a great line of tools.* (GOOD+) **$125.00**

N2-24. Disston & Sons, H., Philadelphia, Penn.: General Line Catalog. 1921 Edition. 153 Pages. Length: 6 1/4 Inches. *This handbook contains all sorts of information for the logger and lumberman, as well as a pitch to buy Disston Tools.* (GOOD+) **$110.00**

N2-25. Stanley Rule & Level No. 34: General Line Catalog. August, 1925 Edition. 178 Pages. Length: 7 Inches. *Very minor soiling on the front cover, otherwise excellent.* (GOOD+/GOOD+) **$125.00**

N2-26. Stanley Tools No. 34: General Line Catalog. 1949 Edition. 192 Pages. Length: 7 Inches. *A single fold in the cover and some minor color fading are the only problems with this one. Otherwise perfect.* (GOOD+/FINE) **$70.00**

N2-27. Dixon, William, Newark, N.J.: "Worth Looking Into", Fine Tools and Dixon Supplies. 1909, 672 Pages Length: 7 1/4 Inches. *A single fold in the cover and some minor color fading are the only problems with this one. Otherwise perfect.* (GOOD+) **$75.00**

N2-28. Keuffel & Esser Co., N.Y. No. 37240: Measuring Tape Catalog. With Rules and Plumb Bob. Ca. 1944. Length: 8 1/2 Inches. *All manner of tapes and surveying accessories are illustrated in this excellent reference.* (FINE) **$65.00**

N2-29. Dixon, William, Newark, N.J.: 1939 Dealer Catalog. "Art Metal Crafts". With 1940 Price List. Length: 12 Inches. *Here's a great reference to the world of metalworking, painting, and drawing as it existed 60 years ago.* (FINE) **$85.00**

N2-30. Stanley Tools No. 34: General Line Catalog. 1953 Edition. 208 Pages. Length: 7 Inches. *Very slight fading and a fold in the lower outside corner are the only apologies for this one. A good, clean catalog.* (GOOD+/FINE) **$75.00**

N2-31. Hammacher Schlemmer & Co., N.Y. No. 355: Tools For All Trades And Supplies. General Line Catalog. 5th Edition, 1145 Pages Length: 8 Inches. *This extensive catalog from the prominent New York City hardware dealer dates from the 1920's. A great reference.* (GOOD+) **$195.00**

N2-32. Starrett Co., L. S., Athol, Mass. No. 23: General Line Catalog. Ca. 1924. 348 Pages. Length: 7 Inches. *A bit scuffed, but intact and ready for the library. Starrett by the numbers.* (GOOD) **$65.00**

N2-33. American Fork & Hoe Company: A Book About True Temper Tools. 1927, Form No. 537. 136 Pages Length: 9 Inches. *The American Fork & Hoe Company was the principal manufacturer of high quality hand tools for garden use at the beginning of the Twentieth Century. This catalog illustrates their full line as it existed in 1927.* (GOOD+) **$55.00**

N2-34. Starrett Co., L. S., Athol, Mass. No. 26: General Line Catalog. Copyright 1938. 282 Pages. Length: 7 Inches. *"Depend upon it, Sir, when a man knows he is to be hanged in a fortnight, it concentrates his mind wonderfully." Samuel Johnson's observation may explain the Starrett firm's substantial paring of their product line in this Depression Era catalog. Economic history without the boredom.* (GOOD+) **$45.00**

N2-35. Stanley Rule & Level No. 34: General Line Catalog. July, 1936 Edition. 208 Pages. Length: 7 Inches. *Only a few minor folds on a bright blue cover. Otherwise perfect.* (GOOD+/FINE) **$130.00**

N2-36. Starrett Co., L. S., Athol, Mass. No. 26: General Line Catalog. Copyright 1938. 282 Pages. Length: 7 Inches. *An excellent illustration of Starrett's tool line as more and more of the skill was being built into the machines.* (GOOD+) **$45.00**

N2-37. Stanley Rule & Level No. 28: 1902 Dealer Catalog. With Color Plates. Rare and Complete. Length: 11 1/2 Inches. *One of the rarest of all Stanley dealer catalogs, including those from the Nineteenth Century, the No. 28 catalog features a series of color illustrations of the line of Stanley Rules. Rare.* (GOOD) **$225.00**

N2-38. Stanley Rule & Level No. 34: General Line Catalog. May, 1940 Edition. 240 Pages. Length: 7 Inches. *An uncommon catalog in excellent condition.* (GOOD+) **$125.00**

N2-39. Nicholson File Co., Providence, R.I.: Smiles... That Sell Files. 1951 Edition. 39 Pages, Softbound. Length: 9 Inches. *This 1950's era catalog of files includes a cover illustration that might not pass muster in today's world. The publishers and artist are perhaps now undergoing "sensitivity training" in Purgatory or worse. A graphic early advertising pamphlet that is offered as an historical curiosity.* (FINE) **$145.00**

N2-40. Stanley Rule & Level No. 34: General Line Catalog. July, 1926 Edition. 192 Pages. Length: 7 Inches. *This one has had a price tag removed from the front corner, but is otherwise complete. An excellent reference.* (GOOD/GOOD+) **$85.00**

N2-41. Stanley Tools No. 34: General Line Catalog. 1950 Edition. 192 Pages. Length: 7 Inches. *The first of Stanley's "baby blue" catalogs, this one is in excellent condition.* (GOOD+) **$85.00**

N2-42. Strelinger & Co., Charles, Detroit: 1895 Metal Work Catalog. Excellent Commentary. 520 Pages. Length: 7 Inches. *The Strelinger catalogs were filled with highly opinionated commentary delivered in pontificatorial style, a practice of which of which we do not approve. A great read and highly recommended.* (GOOD+) **$225.00**

N2-43. Stanley Rule & Level No. 34: General Line Catalog. September 1929 Edition. 192 Pages Length: 7 Inches. *Pre-Stock Market Crash. A great reference to the expanding Stanley line during economic good times.* (GOOD+) **$110.00**

N2-44. Stanley Tools No. 34: General Line Catalog. 1948 Edition. 192 Pages. Length: 7 Inches. *The change from everything that had gone before is evident in the transformed appearance of this post-war issuance and those that followed. A nice example.* (GOOD/FINE) **$65.00**

N2-45. North Bros. Mfg. Co., Philadelphia, Penn.: General Line Catalog. With Price List. Ca. 1915. Length: 6 Inches. *This superb example features the entire pre-WW I "Yankee" line. Pristine.* (FINE) **$285.00**

Group O2

O2-1. Millers Falls Company No. 77: Closed Throat Router Plane. With All Original Irons. Near New Condition. Length: 9 Inches. *Millers Falls' early efforts at planemaking intended, at the very least, to meet, if not exceed, the quality standard set by the dominant market force, Stanley Tools. They did. This closed-throat router is in essentially unused condition.* (FINE) **$115.00**

O2-2. Millers Falls Company No. 4: Bullnose Block Metallic Plane. Removable Nose. Near New Condition. Length: 4 1/2 Inches. *Here's a later incarnation of the Millers Falls equivalent to Stanley's mainstay No. 75 pocket bullnose rabbet plane. As new.* (FINE) **$55.00**

O2-3. Millers Falls Company No. 17: Cast Iron Block Metallic Plane. Similar to Stanley No. 15. Scarce and Excellent. Length: 7 Inches. *Matching Stanley plane for plane in the competition for the woodworking tool dollar, the Millers Falls Company went to great expense in tooling up to produce such obscure tools as this 7" equivalent of Stanley's uncommon No. 17 block plane. These are even less common from Millers Falls. A rare block plane.* (GOOD+) **$75.00**

O2-4. Millers Falls Company No. 1980: Patent Ratcheting Hand Drill. Multiple Speed. Ready To Use. Length: 15 1/2 Inches. *This was the Millers Falls Company's top-of-the-line hand drill, and Millers Falls was the premier hand drill maker. This example is in excellent working order.* (GOOD+) **$55.00**

O2-5. Millers Falls Company No. 47: Low Angle Block Metallic Plane. Knuckle Joint Cap. Rare Type and Excellent. Length: 7 Inches. *The Millers Falls got into the manufacturing of metallic planes at just about the time the Great Depression settled in for a stay. Their ambitious attempt to match many of Stanley's offerings was pared back in short order. This was likely one of the first to go. These are rare. Pristine.* (FINE) **$145.00**

O2-6. Millers Falls Company No. 206: Solid Steel Metallic Plane. For School Shops. Near New Condition. Length: 6 Inches. *These pressed steel planes were designed for rough duty, such as might have been encountered in a high school wood shop class. This one looks to have been spared any abuse. A rare plane in top condition.* (FINE) **$85.00**

O2-7. Millers Falls Company No. 570: Spiral Ratchet Screwdriver. Uncommon Size. Crisp and Clean. Length: 12 Inches. *Smaller in size than the spiral ratchet screwdrivers more commonly encountered, this tool was designed to compete with the North Brothers "Yankee" line.* (GOOD+) **$25.00**

O2-8. Millers Falls Company No. 48: Clark's Expansive Auger Bit. 1 3/4" To 3". New Condition, Original Box. Length: 9 1/2 Inches. *This oversize expansion bit is complete with the accessory cutter blade. New and in the box.* (FINE) **$45.00**

O2-9. Millers Falls Company No. 2: Deep Throat Fret Saw. With Extra Blades. New Condition, Original Box. Length: 12 Inches. *Clean and clearly marked with the Millers Falls name, this high quality coping saw is a top shelf collectible. Rare, new and in the original box.* (FINE) **$165.00**

O2-10. Millers Falls Company No. 814: Cast Iron Jack Metallic Plane. Equivalent To Stanley No.5. New Condition, Original Box. Length: 14 Inches. *Most of the original decal remains on this ca. 1950's Millers Falls jack plane in its original box. Nice.* (FINE) **$95.00**

O2-11. Millers Falls Company: Patent Portable Mitre Box. Patented February 5, 1902. Near New Condition. Length: 8 Inches. *Much of the original decal remains on this patented folding miter box from the Millers Falls Company. These were designed to allow the stock being cut to serve as a brace for the saw bracket.* (FINE) **$85.00**

O2-12. Millers Falls Company No. 55: Wood Scraper. With Interchangable Blades. New Condition, Original Box. Length: 6 Inches. *A nice special purpose scraper in its original box from Millers Falls. Complete with three original blades and in new condition.* (FINE) **$55.00**

O2-13. Millers Falls Company No. 88: Original Box Jointer Gauge. For Wood And Iron Planes. Length: 10 Inches. *This one has a bit of pitting on the working face, but it should not affect its utility. A bargain.* (GOOD) **$35.00**

O2-14. Millers Falls Company No. 4: Pratt's Patent Auger Handle. Removeable Handle. Heavy Duty. Length: 15 Inches. *These ratchet handle augur handles were produced by Millers Falls as "Pratt's Patent Augur Handle" for many years. The longevity of this tool is solely attributable to the fact that it performed the work for which it was designed very well. A great working tool.* (GOOD+) **$55.00**

O2-15. Millers Falls Company: Extension Auger Bit. With Barber Chuck. 24" Length. Length: 24 Inches. *This early extension auger bit includes its own "Barber Type" chuck. These types were soon supplanted by extension bits that employed a bit holder narrower than the bore of the bit being used. These are rare.* (GOOD+) **$85.00**

O2-16. Millers Falls Company: Cast Iron "Buggy" Wrench. Full Nickel Plating. Near New Condition. Length: 8 Inches. *These were never marked, but they were advertised in the catalogs of the Millers Falls Company for more than 50 years. A particularly fine example of a mechanically interesting wrench.* (FINE) **$75.00**

O2-17. Millers Falls Company No. 77: Gear-Driven Hand Drill. Original Carton. Early Red Box. Length: 12 1/2 Inches. *This ca. 1920's era hand drill includes a flyer showing some other Millers Falls tools. New and in the box.* (FINE) **$65.00**

O2-18. Millers Falls Company: Handle For Drill and Brace Combination. With Fixing Screw. Rosewood Handle. Length: 7 Inches. *If one of the Millers Falls braces in your collection is drilled and tapped to receive a screw just above the chuck, it may well have been for the purpose of accommodating this drill handle. A rare part.* (GOOD+) **$45.00**

O2-19. Millers Falls Company No. 2500: Hardwood Handle Hand Drill. Ca. 1930's. New Condition, Original Box. Length: 11 1/2 Inches. *This uncommon Millers Falls drill is in new condition in its original box. Nice.* (GOOD+) **$85.00**

O2-20. Millers Falls Company No. 52: Ratchet Corner Brace. Extension Handle. Rare Type and Excellent Length: 23 Inches. *Designed for the rough and tumble work of boring through floor joists to fit electrical wire and pipe, these tools were subjected to much abuse. This example has survived intact and in excellent working order.* (GOOD) **$75.00**

O2-21. Millers Falls Company No. 207: Cast Iron Bench Drill. With Screw Feed. Crisp and Clean. Length: 18 Inches. *Bench mounted drill presses, in addition to being a graphic addition to the shop, are extremely useful tools. Here's a very well preserved example.* (GOOD+) **$245.00**

O2-22. Millers Falls Company No. 227: Adjustable Butt Marking Gauge. Goodell Pratt Item. New Condition, Original Box. Length: 3 3/4 Inches. *Originally marketed by the Goodell Pratt Company, this style of butt marking gauge was merged into the Millers Falls Company product line when the two toolmakers merged in the early 1930's. New and in the box.* (FINE) **$45.00**

O2-23. Millers Falls Company No. 106: Flexible Bench Rule. On Display Card. New Condition, Original Box. Length: 6 Inches. *This advertising rule is on its original display card, which in turn is in its original box. Brand new.* (FINE) **$55.00**

O2-24. Millers Falls Company No. 11: "Junior Jack" Metallic Plane. Stanley 5 1/4 Equiv. Near New Condition. Length: 11 Inches. *Identical in size to Stanley's No. 5 1/4 "Junior Jack" plane, these tools were intended for trade schools. Luckily, the kids never got their hands on this one. Extra nice.* (FINE) **$165.00**

O2-25. Millers Falls Company No. 65: Handled Adjustable Scraper. With Rosewood Sole. Rare And Excellent. Length: 6 1/2 Inches. *The Millers Falls Company's short-lived, but ambitious entry into the market for metal planes came at a most inopportune time. For an excellent discussion, see Patented Transitional and Metallic Planes in America, Volume II . This example of the No. 65, which was the equivalent of Stanley's No. 12 1/2, is in excellent collector quality condition. A rare Millers Falls plane.* (GOOD+) **$495.00**

O2-26. Millers Falls Company No. 10: Wide Smoothing Metallic Plane. Similar to Stanley 4 1/2. Rosewood Handles. Length: 10 Inches. *Millers Falls sought to match Stanley plane-for-plane when they entered the competitive world of metallic plane manufacturing in the 1920's. Despite a Rocky Balboa-like effort, the folks from Millers Falls couldn't go the distance. This wide, smoothing plane is the functional equivalent of Stanley's No. 4 1/2. Yo... Adrian, a great working tool.* (GOOD+) **$115.00**

O2-27. Millers Falls Company No. 85: "Radio" Hand Drill. Original Decal. New Condition, Original Box. Length: 12 1/2 Inches. *The designation "Radio" on this drill may have to do with the fact that its production coincided with the Ham radio craze in the United States. In the old days, accommodating parts to a radio chassis often required the drilling of holes. This example is in new condition in its original box.* (FINE) **$145.00**

O2-28. Millers Falls Company No. 33: "Toy" Size Metallic Plane. 99% Original Paint. Ready To Use. Length: 3 1/2 Inches. *As crisp and clean as it was when it left the factory, this early Millers Falls plane is ready for a lifetime of service. Perfect.* (FINE) **$35.00**

O2-30. Millers Falls Company: Early Cast Iron Hand Drill. Early Type Chuck. Rare and Excellent. Length: 13 1/2 Inches. *These very early hand drills were undoubtedly very fragile, owing to the lightness of their castings. Very few have survived. A survivor.* (GOOD+) **$85.00**

O2-30. Millers Falls Company No. 67: Open Throat Router Plane. With All Original Irons. Original Box. Length: 9 Inches. *Unlike their No. 77 router, the No. 67 featured an open throat that would allow the cutting iron to be worked facing outward in very close situations. Clean, complete and in the original box.* (GOOD+) **$165.00**

O2-31. Millers Falls Company No. 3: Handled Block Metallic Plane. For Model Makers. Most Unusual Type. Length: 4 1/2 Inches. *A legitimately rare Millers Falls plane, the No. 3 "squirrel tail" block was the equivalent of Stanley's No. 100 block plane. Crispy clean.* (FINE) **$115.00**

O2-32. Millers Falls Company No. 52: Ratchet Corner Brace. Extension Handle. Rare Type and Excellent Length: 23 Inches. *The wooden handle on this joist brace can be loosened and maneuvered into position for wood boring jobs that generally fell to the electrician's assistant. An uncommon Millers Falls brace.* (GOOD+) **$85.00**

O2-33. Millers Falls Company No. 3: "Rogers'" Auger Handle. 16" Length. Excellent Condition. Length: 16 Inches. *Another example of the Millers Falls line. These were strong and simple, yet fully functional. Ready to use.* (FINE) **$45.00**

O2-34. Millers Falls Company No. 5: Gear Driven Hand Drill. Ball Bearing Action. New Condition, Original Box. Length: 13 Inches. *A pristine example of Millers Falls' best small hand drill in new condition. Complete with the decal in an early box with picture label. Highly recommended.* (FINE) **$115.00**

O2-35. Millers Falls Company No. 07: Skew Blade Block Metallic Plane. With Removable Side. Superb Condition. Length: 7 Inches. *Millers Falls was a very late entrant into the competition for the woodworker's plane-buying dollar. Early on, they attempted to duplicate nearly every plane in the Stanley line. This functional equivalent to Stanley No. 140 skew-blade block plane features a removable side plate to allow for close rabbeting work. Apparently little, if ever, used.* (FINE) **$175.00**

O2-36. Millers Falls Company No. 5: Non Adjustable Block Metallic Plane. Early Appearance. 98% Original Paint. Length: 5 1/2 Inches. *The raised lettering in the casting of this obscure Millers Falls block plane is an indication that it was produced early in the Millers Falls planemaking venture. Given the scarcity of these tools, there was not likely a second run. Rare.* (FINE) **$75.00**

O2-37. Millers Falls Company No. 2: Rosewood Handle Hand Drill. Precision Movement. Superb Condition. Length: 14 1/2 Inches. *The Millers Falls No. 2 hand drill features a hollow rosewood handle with a screw top cap that can be removed to gain access to the internal magazine for drills. This well preserved example has seen very little use. The side handle is a replacement, but the tool is otherwise excellent. A joy to use.* (GOOD+) **$45.00**

O2-38. Millers Falls Company No. 7: 7" Smooth Metallic Plane. Equivalent To Stanley No. 2. Rare and Excellent. Length: 7 Inches. *One of the least common and very likely the last "No. 2" size plane introduced to the market, The Millers Falls No. 7 was produced by Millers Falls as part of their short lived effort to compete with Stanley Rule & Level in the market for metallic planes. This one is in excellent overall condition.* (GOOD+) **$675.00**

O2-39. Millers Falls Company: Steel Rod Adjustment Boring Machine. Ready To Use. Near New Condition. Length: 30 Inches. *An extra clean boring machine in top shape. These machines are extremely well made and intended for years of tough work. The choice of timber framers. Complete with one bit.* (FINE) **$645.00**

O2-40. Millers Falls Company No. 151: Expansive Auger Bit. Screw Adjustment. New Condition, Original Box. Length: 8 Inches. *This precision adjustable auger bit is in new condition in its original box. Choice.* (FINE) **$65.00**

O2-41. Millers Falls Company No. 900: Cast Iron Smooth Metallic Plane. Equivalent To Stanley No.4. New Condition, Original Box. Length: 10 Inches. *This later style Millers Falls plane is in new condition in its original box, which is also in great shape. A collectible.* (FINE) **$95.00**

O2-42. Millers Falls Company No. 75: Adjustable Block Metallic Plane. Similar To Stanley No. 220. Unused Condition. Length: 7 Inches. *The Millers Falls equivalent to Stanley's No. 220 adjustable block plane, this one is in nearly new condition.* (FINE) **$45.00**

O2-43. Millers Falls Company No. 206: Solid Steel Metallic Plane. For School Shops. New Condition, Original Box. Length: 6 Inches. *These pressed steel planes were designed for rough duty, such as might have been encountered in a high school wood shop class. This one looks to have been spared any abuse. A rare plane in new condition in its original box.* (FINE) **$145.00**

O2-44. Millers Falls Company No. 35: 24" Extension Auger Bit. With Locking Chuck. New Condition, Original Box. Length: 24 Inches. *These extension bits are in big demand by furniture makers and other modern craftsmen. This one is in new condition in its original box.* (FINE) **$45.00**

O2-45. Millers Falls Company No. 66: Rare Extra-Long Jointer Gauge. Raised Cast Letters. Not In Millers Falls Catalogs. Length: 16 Inches. *The Donnelly Library has just about every Millers Falls catalog issued, going back to the 1880's and continuing until they were making power tools in the 1960's. I can find no mention of this huge jointer gauge. There can be no question that this is the way that it came from Millers Falls as it is cast with the Millers Falls name in the body of the fence. A rare and possibly unique jointer gauge.* (GOOD+) **$345.00**

O2-46. Millers Falls Company No. 1405: Heavy Duty Awl. Black Painted Handle. Unused Condition. Length: 7 Inches. *This hardwood handle awl from the Millers Falls Company is in nearly new condition.* (FINE) **$15.00**

Group P2

P2-1. Clerline, Weedsport, N.Y.: Bellows Action Dust Remover. For Hand Saws. With Instructions. Length: 3 Inches. *The next time you're sawing a board by hand and despair of the buildup of sawdust on the cutoff line you so carefully scribed, remember that the Clerline (clever, eh?) Company of beautiful Weedsport, New York could have solved that problem for you by fitting you out with one of these. Designed to be mounted on the top of the blade of the handsaw, this device includes a gravity-activated bellows that huffs and puffs away the sawdust, leaving your line as clear as need be. A great collectible tool, complete with the original detailed instructions in new condition in its original box.* (FINE) **$35.00**

P2-2. Unmarked: Set Of Early 5/8" Number Stamps. With Seriphs. With Hammer. Length: 5 Inches. *These stamps and hammer came together from a kit of tools where they were apparently used in conjunction with each other. A nice, early set of stamps and the power to use them.* (GOOD+) **$65.00**

P2-3. Stanley Rule & Level No. 100: Full Roll Of Jenning Auger Bits. Near New Condition. Ready To Use. Length: 10 Inches. *The original roll has kept these auger bits in essentially new condition. Perfect.* (FINE) **$85.00**

P2-4. Millers Falls Company No. 48: Clark's Expansive Auger Bit. 1 3/4" To 3". New Condition, Original Box. Length: 9 1/2 Inches. *This oversize expansion bit is complete with the accessory cutter blade. Perfect.* (FINE) **$45.00**

P2-5. Stanley Rule & Level No. 112: Handled Scraper Plane. Rosewood Handles. Originial Stanley Cutter. Length: 9 Inches. *Collectors have been aghast as serious woodworkers have bought up the few available examples of Stanley's No. 112 scraper. Once thought to be a common plane, examples are now nearly impossible to obtain. This example is about as good as they get. Retaining 99% of the original paint and all other finishes. Choice.* (FINE) **$435.00**

P2-6. Stanley Rule & Level No. 59: Precision Doweling Jig. With 6 Original Cutters. New Condition, Original Box. Length: 5 Inches. *Here's a clean and complete working example of Stanley's best doweling jig. Virtually unused, complete with the original instructions and ready to use.* (FINE) **$55.00**

P2-7. Unmarked: Massive Initial Stamp. From Log Hammer. Initials "B.S.". Length: 5 Inches. *All this log hammer needs is a handle and you're ready to ship your timber down river. A nice example.* (GOOD+) **$85.00**

P2-8. Stanley Rule & Level No. 75: Bullnose Rabbet Plane. Ready To Use. Near New Condition. Length: 4 1/2 Inches. *This pristine example of Stanley's smallest "bullnose" plane retains nearly every bit of its original finish. Nice.* (FINE) **$55.00**

P2-9. Stanley Rule & Level: 1/2" Bevel Edge Chisel. Original Handle. Ready To Use. Length: 9 1/2 Inches. *Another complete and usable hollow augur, this one with a rotating wheel to accommodate a multitude of sizes. Nice and clean.* (GOOD+) **$35.00**

P2-10. Aldrich, Milton, Lowell, Mass.: Group Of 3 Wood Clamps. Stamped On Ends. Early and Excellent. Length: 8 Inches. *Each of these small and well preserved clamps is imprinted on the end grain with the maker's name and working location. Early and excellent.* (GOOD+) **$65.00**

P2-11. Wood & Sons Co., The A.A., Atlanta: Adjustable Hollow Auger. Complete and as New. Ready To Use. Length: 6 3/4 Inches. *Those seeking to purchase a fine working example of the A.A. Wood top-of-the-line hollow augur would be well advised to purchase this clean example. Complete with a full blade and the often-missing depth gauge.* (GOOD+) **$110.00**

P2-12. Holt Mfg. Co., Springfield, Mass.: Pair Of Screw Adjust Clamps. "Patent Applied For". Uncommon Maker. Length: 6 Inches. *Here's a great working pair of clamps from a top quality maker. Ready to use.* (GOOD+) **$55.00**

P2-13. Sears, Roebuck & Co. No. 4873: "Dunlap" Aluminum Saw Set. Uncommon Type. New Condition, Original Box. Length: 6 Inches. *This solid aluminum saw set is imprinted with Sears' "Dunlap" trade name. New and in the box.* (FINE) **$35.00**

P2-14. Unmarked: Adjustable Depth Spoke Pointer. 2" Maximum Cone Width. Excellent Condition. Length: 4 1/2 Inches. *A graduated shaft allows precise adjustment of the variable size spoke pointer. Crisp, clean and ready to use.* (FINE) **$55.00**

P2-15. Unmarked: Cast Iron Bench Stop. With Dial Adjust. Spring Action. Length: 4 Inches. *There seems to be no end to the number of variations on the theme of adjustable bench stops. This one features a dial mechanism that works in conjunction with a spring to regulate the adjustment of the stop edge from the bench. Ready to put back to work or add to a growing collection.* (GOOD+) **$45.00**

P2-16. Unmarked: Miniature Boxwood Spoke Shave. 1 1/8" Cutter. Superb Condition. Length: 5 Inches. *This miniature boxwood spoke shave is in excellent working condition. A good one.* (GOOD+) **$65.00**

P2-17. Lufkin Rule Co., The No. 1306 D: Aluminum Zig-Zag Folding Rule. Decimal Graduations. With Hook End. Length: 72 Inches. *The "D" designation on this Lufkin aluminum rule is for decimal graduations. It is also fitted with a hook end. Nearly new.* (FINE) **$35.00**

P2-18. Assorted Makers: Set Of 5 Countersink Auger Bit. Single Collection. Different Styles. Length: 4 Inches. *This group of countersink bits was assembled by a single collector. All are in excellent condition.* (GOOD+) **$55.00**

P2-19. Stanley Rule & Level No. 9 1/2: Adjustable Throat Plane. With Precision Adjust. Clean and Ready To Use. Length: 6 Inches. *This precision adjust block plane is in nearly new condition, retaining 98% of its original finish. A great working tool in top shape.* (FINE) **$65.00**

P2-20. Unmarked: Double Tine Fish Spear. Hand Forged Type. Early and Excellent. Length: 8 Inches. *This fish spear was found in the state of Maine. The fish, we understand, were glad to see it leave.* (GOOD) **$85.00**

P2-21. Stanley Rule & Level No. 101: "Toy" Block Plane. Red Lever Cap. 99% Original Paint. Length: 3 1/4 Inches. *As a handy tool for use around the shop, these Stanley planes can't be beat. Near new condition.* (FINE) **$35.00**

P2-22. Stanley Rule & Level No. 604: "Bedrock" Smooth Plane. Later Type, Sqanre Side. "Sweetheart" Trade Mark. Length: 9 Inches. *The original decal is present on the handle of this extremely well preserved "Bedrock" smoothing plane that dates from the 1930's. Choice quality.* (FINE) **$395.00**

P2-23. Unmarked: 4" Blade Draw Knife. Hand Forged Blade. Ready To Use. Length: 6 1/2 Inches. *This small drawknife is in great shape and ready to be put back to use. A rare tool in this size.* (GOOD+) **$115.00**

P2-24. Unmarked: Early Cast Iron Clamp. With Spring Clip. "Patent Applied For". Length: 3 1/2 Inches. *This early cast iron clamp has a pair of holes where it could be mounted to the wall. No idea what function it was intended to perform, but it is in nice shape and retains much of its original gold embellishment.* (GOOD+) **$45.00**

P2-25. Stanley Rule & Level No. 271: Nickel Plated Router Plane. Crisp and Clean. "Made In U.S.A.". Length: 3 Inches. *Nearly all of the original nickel plating remains on this American made miniature router plane. Crisp, clean and ready to use.* (GOOD+) **$45.00**

P2-26. The Simonds Saw Works: Simonds Guide For Carpenters, 1914. Useful Rules and Illustrations 64 Pages. Length: 5 Inches. *This giveaway for carpenters included all sorts of information including the secret of who made the best saws (Simonds). An interesting little book.* (GOOD+) **$15.00**

P2-27. Swan Co, The James: Boring Machine Auger Bit. 1 1/2" Size. Near New Condition. Length: 13 Inches. *This boring machine auger bit is imprinted with the name of the highly respected James Swan company. Nearly new.* (FINE) **$65.00**

P2-28. Millers Falls Company (Unmarked) No. 88: Cast Iron Jointer Gauge. With Cam Lock. Near New Condition. Length: 9 Inches. *The Millers Falls jointer gauge differed from that offered by Stanley in that the M.F. version attached to the side rails of the plane with a pair of circular cams. Users report that they both work equally well.* (FINE) **$55.00**

P2-29. Stanley Rule & Level No. 607: "Bedrock" Jointer Plane. Early Style. Crisp and Ready To Use. Length: 22 Inches. *This classic early style "Bedrock" jointer plane is in excellent condition and retains more than 95% of its original japan finish. A good one.* (GOOD+) **$295.00**

P2-30. Unmarked: Quick Adjust Bench Stop. With Lever Action. Rare and Excellent. Length: 3 Inches. *This innovative bench stop features a spring lock mechanism to hold the sliding dog precisely in place. When it is no longer needed, it can be pushed back flush with the bench. A different way of doing things.* (FINE) **$45.00**

P2-31. Millers Falls Company No. 1440: Pocket Ratchet Screwdriver. 1 1/2" Blade. Unused Condition. Length: 5 Inches. *This perfectly preserved ratchet screwdriver has never been used. Perfect.* (FINE) **$55.00**

P2-32. Stanley Rule & Level No. 18: Adjusable Cast Iron Bevel. 10" Size. Near-New Condition. Length: 8 Inches. *Here's a crisp and clean example of Stanley's adjustable locking bevel. Ready to use.* (GOOD+) **$45.00**

P2-33. Stanley Rule & Level No. 750: 1/2" Bevel Edge Chisel. Original Handle. Ready To Use. Length: 9 1/2 Inches. *This well preserved "red handle" chisel is ready to fill out a set or be put immediately to work. Extra crisp & clean.* (GOOD+) **$35.00**

P2-34. Millers Falls Company: 2" Bench Vise. Original Decal. Near New Condition. Length: 7 1/2 Inches. *All of the original decal remains on this perfectly preserved bench vise from the Millers Falls Company. A nice vise.* (FINE) **$45.00**

P2-35. Alaska Freezer Co., Winchendon, Mass.: "Gem" Folding Mitre Box. Original Label. New Condition, Original Box. Length: 14 Inches. *We could accept the fact that a Massachusetts Company that produced iceboxes might want to conjure up images of ice and bitter cold by selecting the "Alaska" name for their company, despite the 4000 miles that separated them from the frozen North. However, we suspect that that connection began to lose something once the Alaska name was applied to a folding mitre box. Whatever the case, this most unusual tool appears to have been kept on ice throughout its long life and is in excellent overall condition, complete with its original decal.* (FINE) **$45.00**

P2-36. Unmarked: Set Of Chinese Textile Tools. Ca. 1980's. Most Unusual. Length: 9 Inches. *This extraordinary set of tools was acquired by the consignor during the 1970's on a trip to China, after causing a minor political incident as a result of an offer to "buy" the tools. In keeping with the policies of "scientific socialism", the tour guide and party member were able to obtain the tools so that the poor peasant was not exposed to the evils of capitalism and the six months of wages that the prospective purchaser would have given for the tools. We have no word on whether or not the purchase price eventually found its way into the coffers of the "People's Republic".* (FINE) **$95.00**

P2-37. Millers Falls Company: Precision Cast Iron Combination Square. 6" Rule. Near-New Condition. Length: 6 Inches. *Apparently never put to use at the tasks for which it was designed, this 6" combination square is complete with its original scribe and ready to go to work.* (FINE) **$65.00**

P2-38. Cincinnati Tool Co., The: Decorative Cast Iron Spoke Shave. Raised Lettering. Hargrave Cutter. Length: 10 1/2 Inches. *The Cincinnati Tool Company was a prolific maker of spokeshaves, both under the "Hargrave" brand name and the "Martin" brand name. Here's a nice example of the adjustable throat cast iron version. A good one.* (GOOD+) **$55.00**

P2-39. Goodell Tool Co., Shel. Falls, Mass.: Patent Butt Marking Gauge. Patented December 18, 1894. Near New Condition. Length: 3 1/4 Inches. *A clean and as new example of the Goodell Brothers' offering in the butt gauge market. Nicely made and clearly marked with the patent date.* (FINE) **$65.00**

P2-40. Smith & Hemenway, Jamestown, N.Y. No. 159: Seavey Patent Mitre Box. Patented March 28, 1899. New Condition, Original Box. Length: 8 Inches. *The original pasteboard picture box has kept this example of the Seavey patent mitre box of 1899 in nearly new condition. A rare patented mitre box in top condition.* (FINE) **$145.00**

P2-41. Stanley Rule & Level No. 763: Cast Iron Bench Vise. "Sweetheart" Trade Mark. Uncommon Type. Length: 6 Inches. *This example of Stanley's bench mounted vise retains much of its original black and orange paint. The jaw is imprinted with Stanley's ca. 1920's era "Sweetheart" trademark. A good one.* (GOOD) **$35.00**

P2-42. Unmarked: Early Patent Hog Holder. Patented December 29, 1874. For Hog Snouts. Length: 15 Inches. *The gentle art of persuasion, when it came to dealing with petulant porcines, involved the use of one of these, which was extended over the snout and then directed in the angle that the farmer wanted the pig to go. This particular example contains the seeds of a sufficient amount of genius that it was protected by a U.S. Patent.* (GOOD+) **$85.00**

P2-43. Superior: Set Of 1/24" Number Stamps. Most Unusual Size. Complete and Near New. Length: 3 Inches. *At only 1/24" in height, these are the smallest number stamps we have ever offered, or observed, for that matter.* (FINE) **$65.00**

P2-44. Stanley Rule & Level No. 604 1/2: "Bedrock" Smoothing Plane. Early Type. 99% Original Paint. Length: 10 Inches. *This early style Bedrock plane retains fully 99% of its original paint and is in top working condition. Without question, this is the best example of this rare plane that we have ever offered.* (FINE) **$745.00**

P2-45. Stearns & Co., E.C. (Unmarked): Adjustable Hollow Auger. O.V.B. Sales Tag. Superb Condition. Length: 7 Inches. *The original hardware store tag remains on this patented hollow auger from the E.C. Stearns Company of Syracuse, New York. Extra nice.* (FINE) **$125.00**

P2-46. Aldrich, Milton., Lowell, Mass.: Group Of 2 Wood Clamps. Stamped On Ends. Ready To Use. Length: 11 Inches. *Milton Aldrich produced clamps in Lowell, Massachusetts between 1853 and 1860. These examples of his work are boldly marked on the end grain.* (GOOD+) **$45.00**

P2-47. Stanley Rule & Level No. 30: Angle Divider Bevel. Ca. 1930's. Complete and Excellent. Length: 7 1/2 Inches. *Only a "hang" hole in the lower bar detracts from this otherwise perfect angle divider. Choice.* (FINE) **$85.00**

P2-47. Osborne & Co., C.S., Newark, N.J. No. 4: Rivet Header. Uncommon Osborne. Near New Condtion. Length: 4 1/2 Inches. *These were used for producing the even rounding at the end of a professionally installed rivet. This is the first example we have encountered with the C.S. Osborne imprint.* (FINE) **$45.00**

P2-48. Stanley Rule & Level No. 386: Adjustable Jointer Gauge. With Rosewood Handle. 99% Nickel Plating. Length: 14 Inches. *Stanley's jointer gauge was a great seller for 60 years for the simple reason that it was the best there was. This one is in nearly new condition.* (FINE) **$165.00**

Group Q2

Q2-1. **Maydole, D., Norwich, N.Y.: 2 Ounce Ball Pein Hammer. Original Handle. Early Imprint. Length: 9 Inches.** *This extra small and well preserved hammer dates from the earliest days of David Maydole's hammer making career.* (GOOD+) **$45.00**

Q2-2. **Peters, P.F., Natick, Mass.: Patented Lasting Hammer. Patented January 22, 1878. Complete With Spring. Length: 7 1/2 Inches.** *These were intended for the leather working trade, where the spring apparently provided some calculated advantage in the manufacture of shoes. A rare and visually appealing hammer. The shoemaking trade apparently didn't warm to this tool the way collectors have.* (GOOD+) **$295.00**

Q2-3. **Cheney Corp., H., Little Falls, Ny No. 944: Straight Claw Ripping Hammer. With Nail Holder. Rare and Near New. Length: 13 Inches.** *Here's a most unusual straight claw ripping hammer that includes the famous Cheney nail holding feature. Condition is near new. A rare hammer.* (FINE) **$195.00**

Q2-4. **Unmarked: Early Iron Hammer. Decorative Handle. Most Unusual Form. Length: 8 Inches.** *The handle of this early hand forged hammer has been nicely ornamented by its maker. Made to be something special and still the case.* (GOOD+) **$225.00**

Q2-5. **Stanley Rule & Level: 4 Ounce Ball Pein Hammer. Partial Original Decal. Excellent Condition. Length: 10 Inches.** *Most of the original Stanley decal remains on this well preserved small ball pein hammer. Nice.* (FINE) **$25.00**

Q2-6. **Cheney Corp., H., Little Falls, Ny: Long Nose Farriers Hammer. Early Cheney Mark. Uncommon Type. Length: 12 1/2 Inches.** *The name Cheney is most commonly associated with their nail-holding hammers, but the Cheney name goes back well into the last century. This artfully forged tool was designed to meet the needs of the horseshoer, and most likely did the job fairly well.* (GOOD+) **$45.00**

Q2-7. **De Sancon, B.F.: Unused Metalwork Hammer. Decorative Form. "Acier Fondue". Length: 9 1/2 Inches.** *The French words Acier Fondue (for cast steel) is imprinted on the head of this unused and nicely formed metalworking hammer. Extra nice.* (FINE) **$85.00**

Q2-8. **Vulcan: Illinois Central R.R. Hammer. "Vulcan Bell Face". Original Handle. Length: 13 Inches.** *We have not previously encountered the "Vulcan" name before, although it might well have been a product of the Vaughn & Bushnell Company of Chicago. This one is also imprinted with the initials of the Illinois Central Railroad, from whence it was "accidentally" carried home in a lunch box.* (GOOD+) **$65.00**

Q2-9. **Belknap Hardware Co., Louisville No. 47 1/2: 16 Ounce Claw Hammer. Original Handle. Extra Crisp and Clean. Length: 13 Inches.** *A number of years ago, I met a collector who was looking for a "Bluegrass" hammer to put in the pocket of a friend when the friend was buried. We have had no word on whether there was an urgent need for the hammer. We finally have one. First come, first serve.* (GOOD+) **$35.00**

Q2-10. **Unmarked: Cast Iron Hammer. From Tool Kit? Most Unusual. Length: 10 Inches.** *The head of this classic small hammer has a rivet through it to keep it where it belongs.* (GOOD+) **$15.00**

Q2-11. **Maydole, David, Norwich, Ny No. 13: 7 Ounce Claw Hammer. Original Handle. Crisp and Clean. Length: 12 Inches.** *The original handle, the bottom of which is marked with the product number, remains on this uncommon 7 ounce claw hammer from America's most respected hammer maker.* (GOOD+) **$45.00**

Q2-12. **Unmarked: Cross Pein Hammer. For Metalwork. Excellent Condition. Length: 9 1/2 Inches.** *This early metalworking hammer is in nearly new condition. A great example.* (FINE) **$55.00**

Q2-13. **Cheney Corp., H., Little Falls, Ny No. 16: 5 Ounce Claw Hammer. Unused Condition. Rare and Perfect. Length: 11 Inches.** *Less common than their highly collectible cousins, the 7 ounce claw hammer, the 5 ounce claw hammer is not often encountered. This example is imprinted with the Legendary H. Cheney name.* (FINE) **$125.00**

Q2-14. **Cheney Corp., H., Little Falls, Ny No. 76: 6 Ounce Tinner's Hammer. Uncommon Type. Near New Condition. Length: 11 Inches.** *This classic tinner's hammer appears never to have been used. Perfect.* (FINE) **$85.00**

Q2-15. **Cheney Corp., H., Little Falls, Ny: Unmarked Hammer. From Little Falls. Christmas Gift? Length: 13 Inches.** *We have it on good authority that the employees of the Cheney Hammer Corporation in Little Falls, New York, were presented with hammers at Christmas time that were not marked with the Cheney name. One can imagine the thrill of those who, having toiled for 364 days of the year pounding out hammers, were the proud recipients of this largesse. We suspect that there was a reason why shoemaker's children went without. Whatever the case, this oversize hammer features the Cheney nail holding feature and is in excellent overall condition. Merry Christmas.* (GOOD+) **$125.00**

Q2-16. **Unmarked: Early Machinists Hammer. Faceted Head. Distinctive Form. Length: 7 1/2 Inches.** *The sides of this hammer have been carefully filed into a "faceted" shape, no doubt by the apprentice machinist who made it as a demonstration of his mastery of his chosen trade.* (GOOD+) **$45.00**

Q2-17. **Unmarked: Multi Purpose Combination Tool. Patented September 28, 1909. From Minneapolis. Length: 13 1/2 Inches.** *This one was apparently designed to serve as a hammer, wrench, screwdriver, pry bar and who knows what else. A look at the patent papers should set everyone straight. There being no evidence to suggest that these tools quickly displace the traditional utensils that were incorporated into its ingenious design, we might rightly suspect that this was a questionable business success. A great collectible hammer.* (GOOD+) **$235.00**

Q2-18. **Unmarked: Special Function Hammer. With Point, Chisel Tips. Most Unusual. Length: 9 Inches.** *Both of the working ends of this specialty hammer taper to a very thin, flat working end. Function unknown.* (GOOD+) **$65.00**

Q2-19. **Unmarked: Early Hand Forged Hammer. Bulbous Handle. Distinctive Form. Length: 14 Inches.** *The bulbous handle on this hammer may have been intended to improve the grip while leaving some spring in the handle. A graphic and well preserved hammer.* (GOOD+) **$55.00**

Q2-20. **Peck, Stow & Wilcox Co. No. 12 1/2: "Pexto" 12 Ounce Claw Hammer. Original Handle. Excellent Condition. Length: 13 Inches.** *This smaller than usual hammer from the Peck, Stow & Wilcox Company of Southington, Connecticut is imprinted with their "Pexto" brand name.* (FINE) **$55.00**

Q2-21. **Unmarked: Early 7 Ounce Hammer. Distinctive Form. Extra Long Handle. Length: 13 Inches.** *There are no maker marks on this nicely patinated 7 oz claw hammer. A pretty tool.* (GOOD+) **$45.00**

Q2-22. **Maydole, D., Norwich, Ny No. 124: 20 Ounce Ball Pein Hammer. Original Handle. Original Label. Length: 15 Inches.** *Nearly all of the original label remains on this pristine ball pein hammer from Norwich hammer making entrepreneur David Maydole.* (FINE) **$85.00**

Q2-23. **Cheney Corp., H., Little Falls, Ny No. 988: 16 Ounce Carpenter's Hammer. With Bell Face. Original Decal and Label. Length: 13 Inches.** *This classic carpenter's hammer incorporates the trademark Cheney nail holding feature and retains both of its original decals.* (FINE) **$165.00**

Q2-24. **Unmarked: Special Purpose Hammer. Long Wedge Pein. Extra Long Handle. Length: 12 1/2 Inches.** *The extra long pein of this early hammer tapers to a narrow wedge shape. Its function is not known.* (GOOD+) **$115.00**

Q2-25. **Unmarked: Specialized Metalwork Hammer. Owner "C.P. Boynton". Early and Excellent. Length: 12 3/4 Inches.** *This miniature hammer is imprinted with the owner's name "C.P. Boynton". An excellent early metalworking hammer.* (GOOD+) **$45.00**

Q2-26. **Cheney Corp., H., Little Falls, Ny No. 899 1/2: Ball Pein Machinist Hammer. Original Label. Original Black Finish. Length: 9 Inches.** *This small machinists hammer features the black painted handle that was a Cheney option. Most of the original decal remains.* (GOOD+) **$85.00**

Q2-27. **Dasco No. 399: Combination Chisel and Hammer. Uncommon Type. Excellent Condition. Length: 8 Inches.** *The end of this multi purpose hammer also serves as a chisel. Different.* (GOOD+) **$25.00**

Q2-28. **Evansville Tool Works, Evansville: Farrier's Hammer. Early Mark. Rare Type. Length: 12 Inches.** *Another nice farrier's hammer bearing the early mark of the Evansville Tool Works, who made a superb line of hammers and edge tools.* (GOOD) **$45.00**

Q2-29. **Cheney Corp., H., Little Falls, Ny: 2 Ounce Ball Pein Hammer. As New Condition. Nickel Plated Head. Length: 8 Inches.** *The head on this top quality Cheney ball pein hammer was nickel plated in the factory. Top quality.* (FINE) **$115.00**

Q2-30. **Unmarked: Special Horn Head Hammer. For Napping? Near New Condition. Length: 11 Inches.** *This specialty hammer consists of a piece of horn mounted on a stick. There is a possibility that this was a napping hammer for working with flint, but we have no documentation to back that up.* (FINE) **$65.00**

Q2-31. **Unmarked: Early Metalworking Hammer. Elaborate Repair. Soldered Brass Key. Length: 9 1/4 Inches.** *The previous owner of this early hammer thought so much of it that when it cracked, he fitted it with a dovetailed key and brazed it back to one piece. An interesting early hammer with a story.* **$45.00**

Q2-32. **Unmarked: Patent Tack Hammer. Patented June ???. With Extended Neck. Length: 10 Inches.** *The patent date on this unusual hammer has been applied so lightly that it is not legible. An uncommon patented hammer.* (GOOD+) **$55.00**

Q2-33. **Belknap Hardware Co., Louisville No. 8017: 7 Ounce Claw Hammer. Rare Size. Near New Condition. Length: 11 Inches.** *A growing number of collectors have set themselves to assembling "one of each" of the varieties of 7 ounce claw hammer. This example of Belknap Hardware's "Bluegrass" line is in superb collector quality condition.* (FINE) **$85.00**

Q2-34. **Unmarked: Early Style Hammer. With Adze Eye. Excellent Patina. Length: 8 Inches.** *This classic hand forged hammer dates from the early days of the "adze eye" innovation. A nice example.* (GOOD) **$15.00**

Q2-35. **Unmarked: Early Claw Hammer. Extra Long Nose. Most Unusual. Length: 8 1/2 Inches.** *This early long nose hammer lacks the "adze eye" that was developed in the 1850's and quickly became the standard. A nice early hammer.* (GOOD+) **$35.00**

Q2-36. **Maydole, D., Norwich, N.Y. No. 266: 6 Ounce Tinner's Hammer. Original Handle. Rare Size and Type. Length: 10 Inches.** *This small tinner's hammer retains its original handle, which is marked on the end with the Maydole product number.* (GOOD+) **$55.00**

Q2-37. **Cheney Corp., H., Little Falls, Ny No. 139 1/2: Cross Pein Machinist Hammer. Origina Label. Rare Type. Length: 10 Inches.** *Nearly all of the original label remains on this Cheney cross pein machinists hammer.* (FINE) **$165.00**

Q2-38. **Unmarked: Miniature Ball Pein Hammer. Original Handle. Early and Excellent. Length: 6 1/2 Inches.** *The head of this early hammer has the degree of detail that suggests it was produced by an apprentice machinist as a demonstration of his mastery of filework.* (GOOD+) **$45.00**

Q2-39. **Unmarked: Special Purpose Brass Hammer. With Pointed Peen. Near New Condition. Length: 7 3/4 Inches.** *This special purpose brass hammer was apparently designed for some very specific purpose, but we have no information as to what that purpose was. A great example.* (FINE) **$65.00**

Q2-40. **Unmarked: Miniature Metalwork Hammer. With Cross Pein. Early Handle. Length: 8 1/4 Inches.** *This early metalworking hammer has a nicely shaped head and handle. A good one.* (GOOD) **$35.00**

Q2-41. **Cheney Corp., H., Little Falls, Ny No. 76: 6 Ounce Tinner's Hammer. Original Decal. Near New Condition. Length: 11 Inches.** *This tinner's hammer is a classic example of Cheney quality. Brand new.* (FINE) **$115.00**

Q2-42. **Unmarked: Special Purpose Hammer. With Rosewood Handle. Near New Condition. Length: 11 Inches.** *A nicely turned handle of Brazilian rosewood adds accent to this special purpose hammer, which looks almost too good to use.* (GOOD+) **$145.00**

Q2-43. **Billings & Spencer Co., The: Multi-Purpose Small Hammer. Superb Quality. Unusual Tip. Length: 7 1/2 Inches.** *A look through the 1883, 1909 and 1925 of the Billings & Spencer Company didn't reveal one of these. It includes a tack puller and various other functions.* (GOOD+) **$65.00**

Q2-44. **Unmarked: Special Purpose Hammer. Turned Poll. Ca. 1700's. Length: 7 Inches.** *The ornamentation on the nose of this specialty hammer suggests that it may date to the Eighteenth Century, or thereabout.* (GOOD) **$165.00**

Q2-45. **Osborne & Co., C.S., Newark, Nj No. 5: Rosewood Handle Hammer. Near New Condition. Rare & Excellent. Length: 11 Inches.** *This leatherworking hammer is fitted with a rosewood handle. Condition is nearly new.* (FINE) **$125.00**

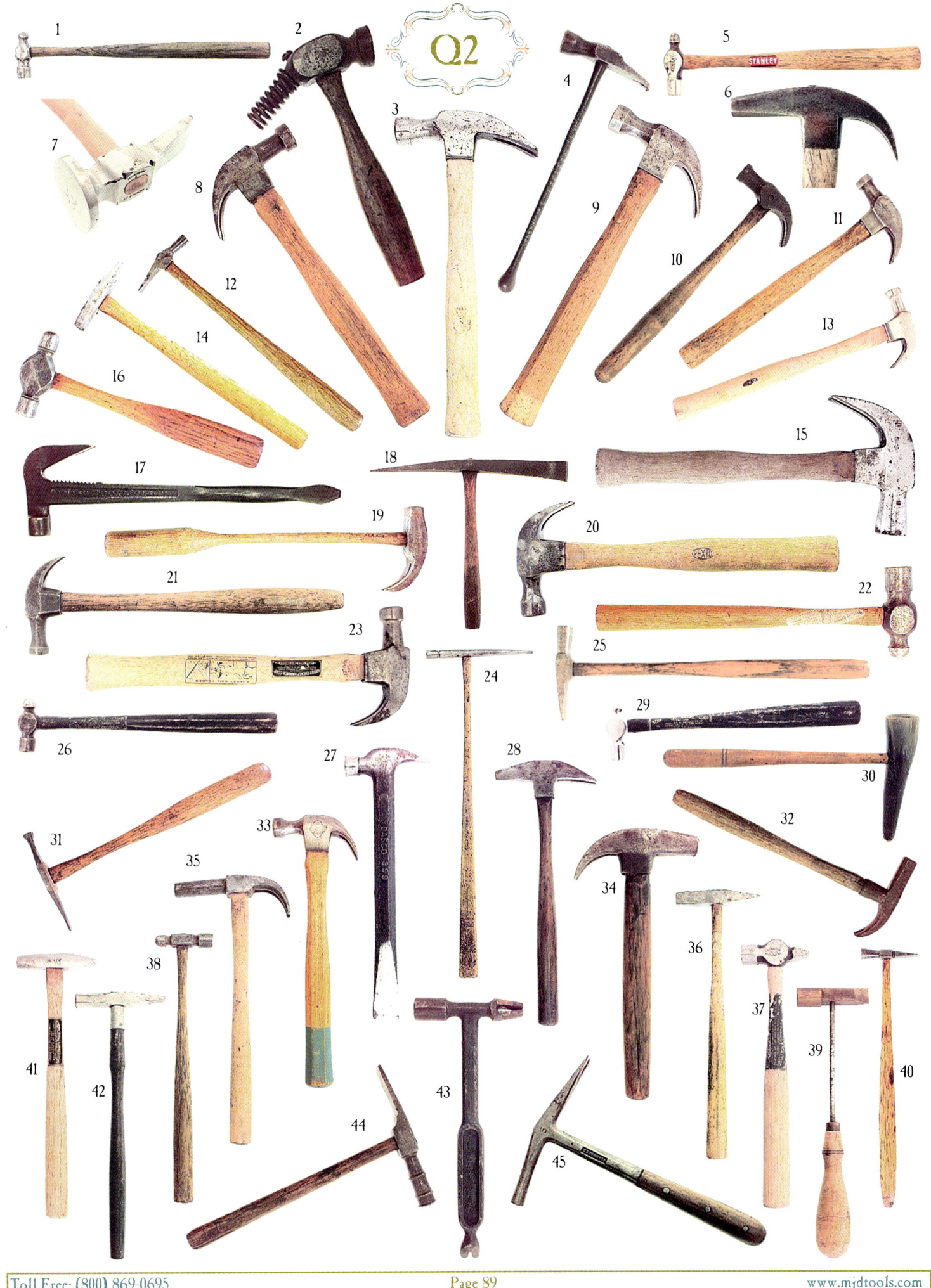

Group R2

R2-1. F.W.S., N.Y.: Massive Cast Iron Spoke Pointer. 2 1/2" Maximum Diameter. For Twig Furniture. Length: 6 1/2 Inches. *This one is marked F.W.S., although it is obviously a product of the E.C. Stearns Company. It was likely purchased by a hardware dealer for marketing in their store.* (GOOD+) **$65.00**

R2-2. Stearns & Co., E.C., Syracuse, N.Y.: Patent Adjustable Hollow Auger. Patented June 5, 1900. Precision Adjustment. Length: 7 Inches. *A precision adjustment mechanism on the base of this E.C. Stearns hollow auger allows precise adjustment of the cutting iron. Clean, complete and ready to use.* (GOOD+)**$95.00**

R2-3. Wood & Sons Co., The A.A., Atlanta: Rare Large Size Hollow Auger. With Depth Stop. For Rustic Furniture. Length: 7 Inches. *A dowel pointer of this size is essential for the making of rustic furniture. This one is complete with the often missing depth stop and ready to use.* (GOOD+) **$215.00**

R2-4. Unmarked No. 1: 1" Cast Iron Hollow Auger. With Depth Stop. Ready To Use. Length: 6 Inches. *This hollow auger is fixed at the 1" size. Clean, complete with the depth stop, and in excellent working order.* (GOOD+) **$45.00**

R2-5. Unmarked: Adjustable Depth Spoke Pointer. 2" Size. Excellent Condition. Length: 5 Inches. *The adjustable shaft of this unmarked spoke pointer is graduated in 1/8" increments. A good one.* (FINE) **$55.00**

R2-6. Millers Falls Company No. 3: Adjustable Hollow Auger. 1/4 To 1 1/4" Cut. Extra Crisp and Clean. Length: 7 Inches. *This hollow auger from the Millers Falls Company is in nearly new condition, complete and ready to go to work. A very well made hollow auger from a top quality toolmaker.* (FINE) **$115.00**

R2-7. Unmarked: Adjustable Depth Spoke Pointer. Cast Iron Body. Ready To Use. Length: 5 Inches. *The width of the tenon to be cut can be regulated by using the locking screw to slide the adjustable shaft into position. A well made tool in ready to use condition.* (GOOD+) **$45.00**

R2-8. Unmarked: Cast Iron Hollow Auger. Patented July 17, 1866. Early and Unusual. Length: 6 Inches. *This oversize hollow auger is of a form we have not previously encountered. According to Jim Prices "Sourcebook for United States Patents for Bitstock Tools", the patent for this auger was granted to one J.H. Smith of Pineville, Pennsylvania. A rare and early patented hollow auger.* (GOOD) **$165.00**

R2-9. Goodell-Pratt Company: Patent Adjustable Hollow Auger. Patented December 8, 1911. Ready To Use. Length: 7 Inches. *As is the case with almost every tool they made, this offering from the Goodell-Pratt Company is cleverly designed, perfectly machined and nicely finished. A substantial tool in excellent condition.* (GOOD+) **$110.00**

R2-10. Stearns, George, H., Syracuse, N.Y.: Early Patent Hollow Auger. Patented September 8, 1863. 5 Interchangeable Cutters. Length: 7 1/2 Inches. *This 1863 patent hollow auger comes complete with 5 interchangeable cutters to accommodate different diameters of stock. A rare patented hollow auger in excellent condition.* (GOOD+) **$155.00**

R2-11. North Bros. Mfg. Co., Phila., Penn. No. 2992: "Yankee" Machinist's Vise Holder. Rare and Excellent. Unused Condition. Length: 9 3/4 Inches. *These were offered by North Brothers to hold their line of machinist's bench vises in place when working with metalworking machinery. Clearly marked and numbered. A rare tool in unused condition.* (FINE) **$85.00**

R2-12. Unmarked: Adjustable Depth Spoke Pointer. 3" Size. Excellent Condition. Length: 6 Inches. *This adjustable-depth spoke pointer is in near-new condition. Nice.* (FINE) **$85.00**

R2-13. Stearns & Co., E.C., Syracuse, N.Y.: Adjustable Hollow Auger. Complete and Excellent Ready To Use. Length: 7 Inches. *A previously unused but ready to use hollow augur from a company that specialized in such tools. A great working tool.* (FINE) **$135.00**

R2-14. Sargent & Company, New Haven, Conn.: Early Patent Hollow Auger. Complete and Sound. Patented March 30, 1887. Length: 6 3/4 Inches. *This early hollow auger from Sargent is clean, complete and imprinted with the 1887 patent date. Rare and excellent.* (GOOD) **$55.00**

R2-15. Unmarked: Cast Iron Spoke Pointer. Fixed Size Cut. Ready To Use. Length: 4 Inches. *This fixed size spoke pointer is ready to go back to work. A good one.* (GOOD) **$35.00**

R2-16. Wood & Sons Co., The A.A., Atlanta: Adjustable Hollow Auger. With Depth Stop. Superb Condition. Length: 6 1/2 Inches. *Another nice example of the Wood hollow augur, this one is in near new condition. Choice.* (FINE) **$155.00**

R2-17. Wood & Sons Co., The A.A., Atlanta: Large Cast Iron Spoke Pointer. Fixed Size. Unused Condition. Length: 6 Inches. *This extra large fixed width spoke pointer is in nearly new condition. A rare tool in top condition.* (FINE) **$75.00**

R2-18. Unmarked: Cast Iron Spoke Pointer. With Fluted Casting. From E.C. Stearns? Length: 2 Inches. *This is the smallest example of the Stearns spoke pointer that we have encountered. Rare.* (GOOD) **$45.00**

R2-19. Wood Mfg. Co.: Early Patent Hollow Auger. Patented May 7, 1878. Scarce and Complete. Length: 7 Inches. *We have sold scores of the hollow augers produced by the A.A. Wood & Sons Company of Atlanta, Georgia, but this is the first time we have encountered the Wood Manufacturing Company. It is likely that this company was founded after A.A. Wood left the employ of E.C. Stearns and that the company was later moved to Georgia and renamed. The patent was issued to George N. Stearns on May 7, 1878. A rare, early hollow auger.* (GOOD+) **$75.00**

R2-20. Wood & Sons Co., The A.A., Atlanta: Adjustable Hollow Auger. With Depth Stop. Superb Condition. Length: 6 1/2 Inches. *These precision tools are our largest selling hollow auger, as they have been among woodworkers since they were first manufactured. The Best.* (GOOD+) **$155.00**

R2-21. Preston & Sons, Edward: Nickel Plated Dowel Pointer. Most Unusual Item. Near New Condition. Length: 2 3/4 Inches. *Identical in form to the brace-mounted spoke pointer offered by Stanley, this product of Edward Preston & Sons is the first we have encountered bearing their distinctive trademark. Condition is near new.* (FINE) **$65.00**

R2-22. Goodell-Pratt Company No. 248 1/2: Patent Adjustable Hollow Auger. Patented December 5, 1911. Near New Condition. Length: 7 1/2 Inches. *Here's a perfectly preserved example of the Goodell-Pratt hollow auger in nearly new condition. This was the nearest (we would say better) in quality to the A.A. Wood version. An extremely well made tool.* (FINE) **$125.00**

R2-23. Dole, I.A., Salem, O.R.: Dole's Patent Hollow Auger. Patented January 10, 1860. Brass Adjustable Ring. Length: 5 1/2 Inches. *This mechanically intricate early patented hollow auger is fitted with a knurled brass adjusting ring to regulate the diameter of the cut. Crisp, clean and clearly marked, this is a rare and desirable hollow auger.* (GOOD+) **$285.00**

R2-24. Unmarked: Adjustable Depth Spoke Pointer. Cast Iron "Key". Ready To Use. Length: 5 Inches. *This ready to use spoke pointer is fitted with a cast iron "key" for locking and unlocking the adjustable depth stop. A good one.* (GOOD+) **$45.00**

R2-25. Unmarked: Forged Steel Dowel Maker. Adjustable Blade. Uncommon Type. Length: 6 Inches. *Here's a nicely made dowel turning device that incorporates an adjustment screw to regulate the thickness of the dowel. A well made tool that looks like it would work.* (GOOD+) **$25.00**

R2-26. Stearns, George, H., Syracuse, N.Y.: Early Patent Hollow Auger. Patented September 8, 1863. Interchangeable Cutters. Length: 9 Inches. *The Stearns Company of Syracuse, New York produced an exceptionally high grade of hollow augur. This uncommon offering, which was produced under an 1863 patent, includes a series of interchangeable cutters to accommodate different sizes of stock. A rare hollow auger in excellent condition.* (GOOD+) **$145.00**

R2-27. Goodell Pratt Company: Bench Mounted Drill Press. With Vise. Feed Screw Drive. Length: 16 Inches. *Mounting one of these in the shop adds to the overall effect, even if you never use it. These were made to be used, however, and are handy tools. This uncommon example was fitted with an integral vise. There is a small chip from the vise holding clamp, but the tool is otherwise excellent.* (GOOD+) **$285.00**

R2-28. Stearns & Co., E.C. (Unmarked): Adjustable Depth Spoke Pointer. Fluted Body. Near New Condition. Length: 5 1/2 Inches. *Here's a great working spoke pointer from the E.C. Stearns Company of Syracuse, New York.* (GOOD+) **$65.00**

R2-29. Wood & Sons Co., The A.A., Atlanta: Large Cast Iron Spoke Pointer. With Adjustable Depth. For Larger Timbers. Length: 7 Inches. *Substantially larger than the spoke pointers normally encountered, these were designed for work with larger stock, such as that used in the making of rustic furniture. A tough tool to find, especially in this condition.* (GOOD+) **$195.00**

R2-30. Unmarked: Cast Iron Hollow Auger. Integral Depth Stop. Early and Unusual. Length: 6 Inches. *This unmarked hollow auger is identical in many respects to the July 17, 1866 patent granted to J.H. Smith of Pineville, Pennsylvania. A rare and early hollow auger.* (GOOD+)**$115.00**

R2-31. Peck, Stow & Wilcox Co.: Fixed Size Hollow Auger. 5/8" Diameter. Early and Excellent. Length: 6 Inches. *This uncommon offering from the "Pexto" people is the first we have ever offered bearing their name. The size is fixed at 5/8". Scarce and excellent.* (GOOD+) **$35.00**

R2-32. Wood & Sons Co., The A.A., Atlanta: Adjustable Hollow Auger. Complete and Near New. Ready To Use. Length: 6 3/4 Inches. *Those seeking to purchase a fine working example of the A.A. Wood top-of-the-line hollow augur would be well advised to purchase this clean example. Complete with a full blade and the often-missing depth gauge. Nearly new.* (FINE) **$155.00**

R2-33. Unmarked: Cast Iron Bench Stop. With Dial Adjust. Spring Action. Length: 4 Inches. *There seems to be no end to the number of variations on the theme of adjustable bench stops. This one features a dial mechanism that works in conjunction with a spring to regulate the adjustment of the stop edge from the bench. Ready to put back to work or add to a growing collection.* (GOOD+) **$45.00**

R2-34. Stearns & Co., E.C., Syracuse, N.Y.: Adjustable Hollow Auger. Complete and Excellent Ready To Use. Length: 7 Inches. *This adjustable hollow auger can be locked into a range of diameters of cut in increments of 1/8". Complete and nearly perfectly preserved.* (FINE) **$125.00**

R2-35. Stanley Rule & Level No. 22: Dowel Sharpener. For Electric Drill. New Old Stock. Length: 2 1/4 Inches. *This most unusual "straight shaft" dowel sharpener was apparently intended for use in an electric drill. Condition is unused. A rare Stanley "in the box" item.* (FINE)**$15.00**

R2-36. Douglass Mfg. Co.: Fixed Size Hollow Auger. 5/8" Diameter. Early and Excellent. Length: 6 Inches. *This fixed size hollow auger is imprinted with the name of the Douglass Manufacturing Company, who were well known as makers of edge tools. A nice example.* (GOOD+) **$45.00**

R2-37. Unmarked: Quick Release Bench Stop. With Spring Clip. Most Unusual. Length: 3 Inches. *Here's a quick release bench stop that allows the stop to be quickly set back to flush with the bench stop when it is not being used. Crisp, clean and ready to use.* (GOOD+) **$55.00**

R2-38. Stearns & Co., E.C., Syracuse, N.Y.: Cast Iron Drill Press. Bench Mounted. Very Early Type. Length: 26 Inches. *This heavy duty drill press from a prominent Syracuse, New York maker was intended to be mounted on the edge of a bench. A feed screw made it an ideal tool for boring through thick metal. Scarce and in clean, complete condition.* (GOOD+) **$115.00**

R2-39. Unmarked: Cast Iron Spoke Pointer. Fixed Size Cut. Ready To Use. Length: 4 1/2 Inches. *This early spoke pointer is clean, sound and ready to use. A good one.* (GOOD) **$35.00**

R2-40. Stearns, E.C. (Unmarked): Adjustable Depth Spoke Pointer. Cast Iron Body. Fluted Body. Length: 6 Inches. *These spoke pointers from E.C. Stearns were generally unmarked, but are easily recognizable from the fluted sides to the casting. A great working tool that looks just a bit better than most.* (GOOD+) **$55.00**

R2-41. Wood & Sons Co., The A.A., Atlanta: Adjustable Hollow Auger. With Depth Stop. Superb Condition. Length: 6 1/2 Inches. *The A.A. Wood hollow augers were much more precisely machined that nearly all of the competitors, which may account for their long lasting popularity. Simply the best.* (FINE) **$155.00**

R2-42. North Bros Mfg. Co., Philadelphia. No. 991: "Yankee" Machinist Vise. With Jaw Insert. New Condition, Original Box. Length: 5 Inches. *This classic North Brothers tool is in new condition in its original box, complete with the original jaw insert. Nearly all of the original decal remains.* (FINE) **$225.00**

R2-43. Stearns & Co., E.C., Syracuse, N.Y. No. 209: Bronze Edging Tool. Uncommon Type. Near New Condition. Length: 6 Inches. *This mason's edging tool is cast in solid bronze. It appears to have been very little used, if ever. Never seen another.* (FINE) **$85.00**

R2-44. Wood & Sons Co., The A.A., Atlanta: Patent Adjustable Hollow Auger. Precision Adjust. Complete and Excellent. Length: 6 1/2 Inches. *A clean working example of the acknowledged finest spoke tenoning tool or hollow augur. Perfect.* (GOOD+) **$135.00**

R2-45. Unmarked: Quick Release Bench Stop. With Spring Clip. Most Unusual. Length: 3 Inches. *A spring clip allows this flush mounted depth stop to be raised and lowered nearly effortlessly. A good idea and a great working tool.* (GOOD+) **$55.00**

Group S2

S2-1. Disston, Henry, Philad'a: Early Tenon Saw. With Eagle Medallion. Ca. 1850's. Length: 17 Inches. *One of the very first of Henry Disston's saws, this one features an embossed eagle imprint on the handle. It has seen some use, but the handle is complete and the markings fully legible.* (GOOD) **$45.00**

S2-2. Jennings & Co., C.E., New York, N.Y.: Nested "Plumber's" Saws. Original Pouch. Near New Condition. Length: 17 1/2 Inches. *It seems that all the principal saw makers offered sets roughly corresponding to that offered here. They were designed for electricians or plumbers who had to work in tight situations and might require all manner of wood and metal saws. If anyone has ever tried their hand at it, they will not argue that plumbing is very hard work indeed....Hard, and dirty. That such a set as this could have passed in essentially new condition through ninety-odd years of existence is a virtual minor miracle. Clean, pristine, complete and highly recommended.* (FINE) **$575.00**

S2-3. Drummond, J., Edinburgh: Open Handle Dovetail Saw. 10" Blade. Straight and True. Length: 14 Inches. *The name Drummond is a Scottish as Loch Lomond, but we have not previously encountered it imprinted on a saw. An excellent brass back dovetail saw in top working order.* (GOOD+) **$115.00**

S2-4. Stanley Rule & Level: Commemorative Saw. 150th Anniversary. 1853-1993. Length: 30 Inches. *Perhaps the finest made and, we would argue, the best long term investment of the Stanley 150th anniversary collectibles, this beautifully made saw is complete in its original pasteboard box and its tooled leather sheath. The fact that a major producer could and would make tools of this quality, even if only as part of the commemoration of an anniversary, as recently as 1993 is, in a way encouraging. However, the fact that the promotion did not work to Stanley's bottom line advantage probably means that we will not see it again. A great Stanley collectible and highly recommended.* (FINE) **$375.00**

S2-5. Atkins & Co., Indianapolis, Ind.: 8" Dovetail Saw. With Atkins Logo. Straight and True. Length: 13 Inches. *Eight inch dovetail saws have become increasingly difficult to find-especially those from prominent American makers. This Atkins classic is straight, sharp and ready to use.* (GOOD+) **$75.00**

S2-6. Jackson: Open Handle Tenon Saw. 10" Blade Length. Straight and True. Length: 14 1/2 Inches. *Disston's "Jackson" line was a step below their top of the line, but as a working tool its aeons ahead of anything made today. A good working saw at a bargain price.* (GOOD+) **$55.00**

S2-7. Disston & Sons, Henry, Philada, Penna: "Keystone" Saw. With Etched Logo. Near New Condition. Length: 18 Inches. *This is simply a great saw. Never illustrated in any Disston catalog, it was either part of a Disston child's tool kit or possibly offered as a promotional item. Portions of the original decal remain. The detailed etching on the blade shows a man in ca. 1920's garb sawing a board. Finished with an orange and black handle and essentially in new condition, this rare saw belongs in the collection of a Disston enthusiast.* (FINE) **$245.00**

S2-8. Jennings & Co., C.E., New York, N.Y. No. 10: Metal Cutting Saw. Legible Etching. Carved Apple Handle. Length: 18 Inches. *One of the principal producers and marketers of tools in the New York City area at the beginning of the Twentieth Century, the Jennings Company did not compromise on quality. This metal cutting saw retains much of its original etching. A rare wood handled hack saw in collector quality condition.* (GOOD+) **$75.00**

S2-9. Jackson: 10" Dovetail Saw. Straight and Sharp. "S.C. U.S.A.". Length: 14 1/2 Inches. *This "Jackson" dovetail saw from Henry Disston & Sons is also imprinted "S.C.U.S.A." and acronym for the Signal Corps, United States Army. We have seen a number of tools with this marking, but this is the very first handsaw. An excellent working saw that once cost the government several thousands of dollars.* (FINE) **$75.00**

S2-10. Bishop & Co., Geo. H., Cincinnati No. 10: 16" Blade Cabinet Saw. Adjustable Depth Stop. Patented January 9, 1906. Length: 16 Inches. *A crisp, clean and ready to use example of the 1906 Bishop Patent Cabinet Saw. These would serve as a back saw, to cut stopped dados, dovetails or whatever. They still will. A nice saw in great condition.* (GOOD+) **$135.00**

S2-11. Disston & Sons, Henry, Philidelphia, Penn. No. K 4: 11 Point Cutoff Saw. Unused Condition. Uncommon Size. Length: 18 Inches. *Finding saws like this one, virtually unused and complete with all original finishes and etching, carries with it a responsibility for ensuring that the tool is not allowed to degrade in condition while it is in our care. It is a responsibility we take seriously. Our special Saw Vault is monitored 24 hours a day for temperature and humidity. Three levels of air baffles ensure that no stray particles of dust ever reach the Inner Chamber. A great saw....Honest.* (FINE) **$85.00**

S2-11. Bishop & Co., Geo. H. No. 10: Patent Depth Stop Saw. 12" Cutting Edge. Near-New Condition. Length: 17 1/2 Inches. *A crisp, clean and unused example of the 1906 Bishop Patent Cabinet Saw. These would serve as a back saw, cut stopped dados, dovetails or whatever. They still will. A nice saw in mint condition.* (FINE) **$185.00**

S2-12. Simonds Saw and Steel Co., The No. 62: Skew Back Crosscut Saw. Original Blue Etching. Nearly New Condition. Length: 29 Inches. *The shiny-new blade of this pristine Simonds crosscut saw retains virtually all of its original blue and black etching and the handle is almost exactly as it was when it left the Fitchburg factory location on its way to a sheltered life. Choice.* (FINE) **$275.00**

S2-13. Simmons Hardware Co., St. Louis No. 88: 26" "Keen Kutter" Saw. Applewood Handle. 10 Point Crosscut. Length: 15 1/2 Inches. *All of the original etching and nearly all original finishes remain on this "Keen Kutter" hand saw, which features a carved applewood handle—the sure sign of a high quality saw. No apologies.* (FINE) **$155.00**

S2-14. Penn Saw Co., Frackville, Penn.: 26" 5 1/2 Point Rip Saw. Applewood Handle. Straight and True. Length: 29 1/2 Inches. *Having traveled through Frackvile, I don't recall having seen a saw factory there, but, then again, I wasn't really looking. This well made saw features an applewood handle and the classic "sway" back. Crisp, clean and ready to use.* (GOOD) **$85.00**

S2-15. Disston & Sons, Henry No. D 7: 24" 8 Point Crosscut Saw. Marked "Lightweight". Near New Condition. Length: 27 1/2 Inches. *This unused saw has the word "lightweight" etched on the blade. A great working saw that is far, far better than anything being made today.* (FINE) **$85.00**

S2-16. Atkins & Co., E. C. No. 100: Flooring Saw. Lacquered Beech Handle Extra Crisp and Clean. Length: 22 Inches. *These special purpose saws were curved to allow a cut to be started on a flat surface. The pointed tip could also start a cut from a small hole. This example never participated much, if at all, in the dirty and difficult work of installing flooring. Much original etching remains. An uncommon saw in excellent condition.* (GOOD+) **$125.00**

S2-17. Unmarked: Early Patent. Crosscut Saw. Patented January 26, 1885. With Copper Handle. Length: 25 Inches. *A copper bracket secures the handle to the blade of this saw, which is imprinted with its January 26, 1885 patent date. A rare saw in excellent condition.* (FINE) **$115.00**

S2-18. Simmons Hardware Co., St. Louis No. 88: 26" "Keen Kutter" Saw. Applewood Handle. 5 1/2 Point Rip. Length: 29 1/2 Inches. *All of the original etching and nearly all original finishes remain on this "Keen Kutter" rip saw. The carved applewood not only looks great, but was much easier on the hand than the plywood handled saws offered today. Highly recommended.* (FINE) **$145.00**

S2-19. Groves & Sons, R., Sheffield: 14" Tenon Saw. Shapely Handle. Extra Crisp and Clean. Length: 18 3/4 Inches. *This well made tenon saw hails from the saw making city of Sheffield, England, where quality was an absolute requirement for all who imprinted that name on their tools. Sheffield quality.* (GOOD+) **$75.00**

S2-20. Sandvikens Jernverks, A.B. No. 270: 26" 10 Point Crosscut Saw. Best Quality. Elaborate Handle. Length: 29 1/2 Inches. *The Sandvik Company was Sweden's largest and best sawmaker. They ended up having the last laugh as they ended up buying up the Henry Disston & Sons Company. This superb quality saw, which features an elaborately carved handle and etched blade is the only example of this saw we have encountered. It appears to date from the 1920's, or earlier. Condition is near new.* (FINE) **$265.00**

S2-21. Disston & Sons, Henry No. D 7: Early 9 Point Crosscut Saw. Straight and Sharp. Extra Crisp Condition. Length: 26 Inches. *This extremely well made Disston hand saw is straight, sharp and reatins nearly all of its original etching. A great working saw in top condition.* (FINE) **$85.00**

S2-22. Pierce & Co.: "Eureka" Logo Saw. With Golden Bear. Early and As New. Length: 14 Inches. *There can be little question that the "Eureka" logo and golden bear etched on this immaculately preserved hand saw were meant to appeal to California customers. Pierce & Company was likely a major hardware dealer who purchased saws from the Richardson Company of New Jersey. Absolutely perfect and highly recommended. Simply a great collectible saw.* (FINE) **$445.00**

S2-23. S.H. Co.: Etched "Gladiator" Saw. Disston Keystone Screw. Near New Condition. Length: 29 Inches. *Produced and marketed by the Simmons Hardware Company of St. Louis, Missouri, whose "S.H. Co." name is etched on the blade, this saw has also been artfully etched with a single "Gladiator" logo. We who are about to buy salute you. Perfect and highly recommended.* (FINE) **$245.00**

S2-24. Simonds Saw And Steel Co., The No. 51: Embossed Blade Xcut Saw. Filed With O Set. With Price Button. Length: 29 1/2 Inches. *The blade of this most unusual Simonds saw is etched with both the price and the warning "Do Not Set Correct Filing is Essential". A rare saw in excellent condition.* (GOOD+) **$245.00**

S2-25. Unmarked: Set Of Lucite Handle Saws. With Wheat Carving. Owner Enhancent. Length: 28 Inches. *And now for something completely different...This set of four saws, with handles that are every bit as nice as the applewood hand grips available then on only the very best saws, are in perfect condition, down to the carefully executed "wheat" pattern carvings on the handles. Made up from blades of saws by Atkins and Disston, these saws must most surely have a story behind them that time may yet reveal. A great set of saws.* (FINE) **$395.00**

S2-26. Shurly - Dietrich- Atkins No. 152: 10 Point Crosscut Saw. Patent Ground. Secret Temper. Length: 20 Inches. *A nice new-old stock item from North of the border. The Hardware firm of Shurley-Dietrich sold only the finest hand tools and this nicely etched saw is no exception. This one possesses the "Secret Temper" if we are to believe the engraving. No secret about the quality of this one.* (FINE) **$95.00**

S2-27. Disston & Sons, Henry, Philadelphia, Penn. No. 7: 26" 5 Point Rip Saw. Early Style "Nib". Ready to Use. Length: 29 Inches. *This early Disston saw predates the "D" numbering system. The presence of the "nib" near the tip indicates an especially early saw. Straight, sharp and ready to use. A very nice saw.* (GOOD+) **$65.00**

S2-28. Atkins & Co., E. C. No. 100: Flooring Saw. Lacquered Beech Handle Unused Condition. Length: 22 Inches. *Nearly all of the original finish remains on the handle of this example of the hard to find Atkins flooring saw. All of the original etching is intact. Absolutely perfect.* (FINE) **$165.00**

S2-29. Peace, Harvey W.: 24" 6 Point Rip Saw. With Patent Handle. Patented July 8, 1883. Length: 27 1/2 Inches. *The underside of the handle of this early and well preserved saw has a metal bracket that is imprinted with the July 8, 1883 patent date. The apparent purpose of the patent was to keep the saw handle from breaking at its weakest point. It seems to have had the opposite effect: nearly every example I have encountered has been cracked in the vicinity of the "protective" bracket. This one is a rare survivor. A scarce saw in excellent condition.* (GOOD+) **$75.00**

S2-30. Disston & Sons, H., Philadelphia, Penn. No. D 12: 24" 7 Point Rip Hand Saw. Applewood Handle. Straight and Sharp. Length: 27 Inches. *The D 12 saws of Henry Disston & Sons were made with special "London Crucible Steel" and among the very best saws Disston offered. This pristine rip saw retains nearly all original finishes on the carved applewood handle and the blade is absolutely straight and sharp. Extra nice.* (FINE) **$135.00**

S2-31. Disston & Sons, H., Philadelphia, Penn. No. 8: Rare Half Back Saw. With Ogee Blade. 16" Blade. Length: 21 1/2 Inches. *Among the least common of all American made saws, the half back saw was perhaps so perfectly positioned in the middle between a standard saw and a back saw that few woodworkers of the time could justify the considerable expense to purchase one. The truth of that theory seems to be reinforced by the fact that, of the few examples we have encountered, nearly all were in excellent condition. Such is the case with this perfectly preserved example. Crisp, clean and ready to proudly display.* (GOOD+) **$385.00**

S2-32. Montague, Woodrough Saw Co.: Patent Combination Saw. Patented September 4, 1888. Near New Conditon. Length: 29 Inches. *One of the most unusual hand saws we have offered in some time, this Nineteenth Century patented saw is filed with a distinctive tooth pattern that the etching informs us is guaranteed for crosscut, rip and mitre work. It is in nearly new condition. Highly recommended.* (FINE) **$445.00**

S2-33. Lakeside Saw & Tool Co., Chicago, No. L 100: 26" 11 Point Crosscut Saw. Original Etching. Carved Fruitwood Handle. Length: 29 Inches. *No idea who the Lakeside Saw & Tool Company was, but it sure wasn't the people who brought us the Montgomery Ward "Lakeside" line. This crispy-clean saw dates from the turn of the century, but it has aged hardly at all since that time. Nice.* (FINE) **$95.00**

S2-34. Disston & Sons, Henry (Unmarked): 24" Gladiator Saw. Full Original Etching. Near New Condition. Length: 27 1/2 Inches. *This "Gladiator" saw was the product of the Henry Disston Company, but it is not imprinted with their name. Disston offered a range of what were then "lesser quality" saws bearing decorative etching. This is the first of this type that we have encountered.* (FINE) **$110.00**

S2-35. Groves & Sons, R., Sheffield: 26" 8 Point Rip Saw. Straight and True. Early Appearance. Length: 29 Inches. *English-made saws have a greater heft to them and a stiffer feel to the blade. It is neither good nor bad, only different. Many woodworkers prefer the English saws for this reason. Here's one to try out. A clean, early saw in top shape.* (GOOD+) **$95.00**

S2-36. Assorted Makers: Pair Of Carpenter's Saw. Disston D 23 and Atkins 65. 5 1/2 Rip and 11 Xcut.. Length: 30 Inches. *Just because he apparently liked to keep his tools "nice", the previous owner of this pair of saws, one Disston and one Atkins, fashioned a hinged case in which to keep them. Unlike so many saws that have been ruined by even limited exposure to dust and moisture, these are in much the same condition as they were when new. A pretty pair in a case made to keep them that way.* (FINE) **$195.00**

S2-37. Disston & Sons, Henry, Toronto No. D 8: 26" 5 1/2 Point Rip Saw. With Contour Handle. Unused Condition. Length: 29 Inches. *This Disston rip saw features the special contoured handle that was designed to facilitate overhand rip sawing. Absolutely perfect and ready to put directly to use.* (FINE) **$95.00**

S2-38. Disston & Sons, Henry No. D 7: Early 5 1/2 Point Rip Saw. With Early "Nib". Extra Crisp and Clean. Length: 29 Inches. *Here's a very well preserved early Disston rip saw having the characteristic early "nib". Straight, sharp and ready to use.* (FINE) **$65.00**

S2-39. Disston & Sons, Henry, Toronto No. D 8: 26" 5 1/2 Point Rip Saw. With Contour Handle. Unused Condition. Length: 29 Inches. *This Disston rip saw features the special contoured handle that was designed to facilitate overhand rip sawing. Absolutely perfect and ready to put directly to use.* (FINE) **$85.00**

S2-40. Atkins & Co., E. C. No. 53: 20" 12 Point Crosscut Saw. Decorative Handle. Straight and Sharp. Length: 23 Inches. *Nearly all of the original finish remains on the handle of this high quality handsaw from one of America's premier saw makers.* (GOOD+) **$85.00**

S2-41. Disston & Sons, Henry No. D 7: 22" 12 Point Crosscut Saw. Early Appearance. Extra Crisp and Clean. Length: 26 Inches. *Henry Disston's "Standard" grade of saw was several cuts above ony saw being made now or in recent memory. This 12 point beauty is ready to serve as a faithful workshop companion for years to come.* (GOOD+) **$45.00**

S2-42. Jackson & Gorham No. 29: Combination Square and Saw. With Original Scribe. Rare and Excellent. Length: 30 Inches. *The straight back of this saw is set at a 90 degree angle to the handle and etched with graduations to facilitate its use as a square or straight edge. The original brass-tipped scribe remains on this very early saw from Jackson & Gorham, which was apparently a Disston brand name. A rare saw in excellent condition.* (GOOD+) **$625.00**

S2-43. Simonds Saw & Steel Co. No. 72: 22" 10 Point Crosscut Saw. Carved Apple Handle. "$1.75 Price." Length: 25 Inches. *This Simonds saw has the original price of $1.75 cast into the saw "button". Straight and ready to use. There is a tight crack in the handle, but this tool is otherwise in excellent condition. A bargain.* (GOOD+) **$25.00**

S2-44. Atkins & Co., E.C., Indianapolis No. 51: 26" 10 Point Crosscut Saw. Carved Apple Handle. Straight and True. Length: 29 Inches. *This high quality Atkins crosscut features the "wheat" carving that was symbolic, for all major saw makers, of a very high quality saw. Straight, sharp and ready to use.* (FINE) **$65.00**

S2-45. Disston & Sons, Henry, Philadelphia Penn. No. D 8: 20" 12 Point Crosscut Saw. Applewood Handle. Near New Condition. Length: 22 1/2 Inches. *You couldn't get someone to say something bad about this superb quality saw on a bet, a dare or a threat. A perfect saw. We dare you to buy it.* (FINE) **$115.00**

Group T2

T2-1. Tower & Lathrop: Early 13" Bevel. From Millbury, Mass. Rare Partnership. Length: 13 Inches. *We have seen a number of bevels imprinted with the name "H. Tower", a Millbury, Massachusetts maker in the 1840's and 1850's. However this "Tower & Lathrop" imprinted tool is the first we have encountered. The maker name is absent from the Directory of American Toolmakers. A rare bevel from an obscure early partnership.* (GOOD) **$115.00**

T2-2. Star Tool Company (Unmarked): Patent Carpenter's Bevel. Solid Bronze Body. Patented November 5, 1867. Length: 6 Inches. *Here's an upgrade opportunity for those with a clean blade for a Howard Patent bevel. First come, first serve.* (GOOD+) **$165.00**

T2-3. Stanley Rule & Level No. 14: Adjustable Try Square. Early Japan Finish. Patented October 24, 1882. Length: 4 Inches. *Stanley totally changed the design of these squares in later years. This one is clean and clearly marked with the early patent date.* (GOOD+) **$135.00**

T2-4. Howard, L.D.: "Howard Patent" Bevel. Patented November 5, 1867. Elaborate Cast Brass. Length: 8 Inches. *The Howard Patent bevel incorporated a level within the body of a bevel. This superb example is cast in gunmetal with an elaborate, Victorian pattern that incorporates the November 5, 1867 patent date into the design. A rare bevel in excellent condition.* (GOOD+) **$345.00**

T2-5. St. Johnsbury Tool Co.: Rosewood and Steel Bevel. Patented June 14, 1870. 15" Blade. Length: 15 Inches. *Produced under an 1870 patent, the locking bevels of the St. Johnsbury Tool Company contain a perfect combination of technological innovation and aesthetic appeal. This, an example of the largest size offered in the all-steel rosewood filled bevel is in superb collector-quality condition. Crispy clean and nice.* (FINE) **$895.00**

T2-6. Unmarked: Special Function Bevel. With Hanger, Handle. Most Unusual. Length: 15 1/2 Inches. *There may be someone in our studio audience who knows the function of this must unusual special purpose bevel. If so, we would like to know. Fitted out with a hanger on one end and a locking bevel on the other, nothing comes immediately to mind as the likely purpose of this mystery tool. Decidedly different.* (GOOD+) **$85.00**

T2-7. Disston & Morss (Unmarked): 6" "T" Bevel. Elaborate Screw. Early and Near New. Length: 6 Inches. *This early Disston & Morss bevel is in absolutely new condition. A perfectly preserved 150 year old bevel.* (FINE) **$55.00**

T2-8. Unmarked: Handmade Cam-Lock Bevel. Dated January 30, 1925. Excellent Condition. Length: 6 Inches. *Artfully fashioned with an oversize cam-lock mechanism and dated with its apparent date of completion, this mechanically interesting craftsman-made tool is the kind of tool you never find, but sometimes do. Very nice.* (GOOD+) **$225.00**

T2-9. Southington Hardware Company: Patent "Holdfast" Bevel. Full Nickel Plating. Smallest Size Made. Length: 6 Inches. *Fitted with a blade that is only 6 inches in length, this example of the Southington "Holdfast" bevel is the smallest size they offered. It is in new condition. Immaculate.* (FINE) **$125.00**

T2-10. Lufkin Rule Company, The, Saginaw, Mich. No. 66: Machinist's Adjust Bevel. Angled Blade. Superb Condition. Length: 3 Inches. *This uncommon Lufkin machinist's bevel is in excellent overall condition, noting that one "Walter Rogers" demonstrated his pride of ownership by tastefully scribing his name on the back in flowing script. An uncommon Lufkin bevel.* (GOOD+) **$35.00**

T2-11. Disston & Sons, Henry (Unmarked): 6" Rosewood & Brass Bevel. Lever Locking Screw. Ready To Use. Length: 6 Inches. *The steel locking lever is an instant clue that this bevel was produced by Henry Disston & Sons. A closer look reveals the high level of overall quality that was a Disston hallmark.* (GOOD+) **$45.00**

T2-12. Star Tool Company (Unmarked): Patent Carpenter's Bevel. With Integral Level. Patented November 5, 1867. Length: 5 Inches. *This patent bevel from the Star Tool Company includes an integral level. It incorporates the November 5, 1867 Howard Patent. The blade appears to be a replacement.* (GOOD+) **$245.00**

T2-13. Hall & Knapp, New Britain, Conn.: Rosewood and Brass Bevel. 8" Blade. Stanley Precursor. Length: 8 Inches. *A major expansion of Augustus Stanley's rule manufacturing business took place when he, and the other principals of A. Stanley & Company purchased the Hall & Knapp Company of New Britain, Connecticut, a manufacturer of high quality, levels, bevels and try squares. To help spread the word about the broadening of the product line, the name of A. Stanley's company was changed to the "Stanley Rule & Level Company". The rest is history. This extremely early bevel with an extra-thin blade is boldly struck with the imprint of the Hall & Knapp Company. A very rare bevel.* (GOOD+) **$295.00**

T2-14. Goodell-Pratt Company: Rosewood Infill Bevel. With Brass Body. Rare and Excellent. Length: 8 Inches. *Among the most difficult of the Goodell-Pratt Company's diverse line of tools to obtain, and also one of the most beautiful, this example of the rosewood infill bevel is in superb condition. Condition is near new. Highly recommended.* (FINE) **$345.00**

T2-15. Stanley Rule & Level No. 18: Adjusable Cast Iron Bevel. 9" Size. Near-New Condition. Length: 8 Inches. *This classic example of Stanley's mainstay "Eureka" patent flush T bevel is in essentially unused condition. Ready to provide several lifetimes of use for a discriminating woodworker. Nice.* (GOOD+) **$35.00**

T2-16. Millers Falls Company No. 98: 8" Mahogany Handle Bevel. Uncommon Type. New Condition, Original Box. Length: 8 Inches. *This obscure bevel from the Millers Falls Company is in new condition in its original box. Never seen one in the box before. A rare bevel.* (FINE) **$95.00**

T2-17. Stanley Tools No. 25: Rosewood Body Bevel. 12" Blade. Near New Condition. Length: 12 Inches. *This extra large size Stanley bevel is in excellent condition and ready to be put to use for the tasks for which it was designed. Nice.* (GOOD+) **$35.00**

T2-18. Stanley Rule & Level No. 1225: "Defiance" Bevel. Bakelite Handle. Rare and Excellent. Length: 6 Inches. *Stanley's "Defiance" line of tools included a wide range of products, a fact that has attracted a number of devoted collectors to this product line. This bakelite handled bevel is in excellent collector quality condition.* (GOOD+) **$55.00**

T2-19. Kershaw Bros. Mfrs., Clevland, Ohio: 6" "Eagle" Patent Bevel. Patented February 9, 1892. Near New Condition. Length: 6 Inches. *One of the most graphic of all patented bevels, these tools have their name boldly cast into the body. A crisp, clean example of a desirable patent bevel.* (FINE)**$185.00**

T2-20. Stanley Tools No. 18: 10" Cast Iron Bevel. Full Nickel Plating. Excellent Condition. Length: 10 Inches. *A great working example of Stanley's best locking bevel. Ready to use.* (GOOD+) **$35.00**

T2-21. Stanley Rule & Level No. 18: 8" Blade Bevel. Cast Iron Body. Ready To Use. Length: 8 Inches. *No apologies for this crisp, clean example of Stanley's flush-lock "T" bevel. A good one.* (GOOD+) **$25.00**

T2-22. Topp & Company, G.A., Indianapolis, Indiana. Topps Framing Tool Try Square. Rare First Model. Crisp and Clean. Length: 9 1/2 Inches. *This was the first, less elaborate incarnation of the Topp's Framing Tool. Nearly all of the original etching remains on this rare patent bevel.* (GOOD+) **$265.00**

T2-23. Stanley Tools No. 25: Rosewood Handle Bevel. Ca. 1930's. Near New Condition. Length: 10 Inches. *All of the blued finish and the gold lettering remains on this well preserved example of a classic Stanley tool.* (FINE) **$35.00**

T2-24. Unmarked: Miniature Rosewood Bevel. 4 1/2" Blade. Blued Steel Finish. Length: 4 1/2 Inches. *There are no maker marks on this diminutive 4 1/2" bevel, but it has a decided manufactured look.* (GOOD+) **$45.00**

T2-25. Stanley Rule & Level No. 30: Angle Divider Bevel. Apparently Unused. Complete and Excellent. Length: 7 1/2 Inches. *Perfect is the best way to describe this Stanley angle divider. A very rare tool in this condition. Perfect.* (FINE) **$135.00**

T2-26. Unmarked: Ebony and Brass Bevel. "Sandwich" Type. Solid Brass Frame. Length: 9 Inches. *Formed from laminated brass and ebony, this showy bevel is in superb condition. Nice.* (FINE) **$135.00**

T2-27. Howard, L.D. (Unmarked): "Howard Patent" Bevel. Patented November 5, 1867. Cast Bronze Body. Length: 8 Inches. *Cast in bronze in a most appealing pattern and fitted with an integral level to multiply its functionality, this example of the L.D. Howard patent bevel is one of the most spectacular patent bevels ever produced. A great looking tool.* (GOOD+) **$645.00**

T2-28. Kershaw Bros. Mfrs., Clevland, Ohio: "Eagle" Patent Bevel. Patented February 9, 1892. Raised Letter Cast. Length: 8 Inches. *This graphic patented bevel from Cleveland makers Kershwa Brothers has its name cast into the body of the tool. A nice example.* (GOOD+) **$95.00**

T2-29. Wickmann, W.: Machinist's Locking Bevel. Multi Angle. Unique Design. Length: 9 1/2 Inches. *A series of angles are scribed on the blade of this adjustable blade bevel. The only marking is "W. Wickmann/Maker". Different.* (FINE) **$85.00**

T2-30. Johnson & Conaway, Philadelphia, Penn.: Rosewood and Brass Bevel. Early Philadelphia Imprint. Scarce Type. Length: 8 Inches. *Johnson & Conaway were hardware dealers and tool merchants in the dynamic 19th Century city of Philadelphia. This well preserved bevel is clearly marked with their imprint.* (GOOD) **$55.00**

T2-31. Langlais: Langlais' Patent Bevel. For Angle Dividing. Patented June 12, 1894. Length: 8 Inches. *This patented angle divider and bevel has a pair of gears which mesh at the joint of the two body sections to facilitate adjustment of the angle. Once the adjustment is made, the blade is locked into position by two cam levers at the pivot points of the gears. Mechanically interesting and clearly marked. A rare bevel.* (GOOD+) **$325.00**

T2-32. Southington Hardware Company: Patent "Holdfast" Bevel. Patented December 15, 1914. Rare Wood Handle. Length: 6 Inches. *Fitted with a blade that is only 6 inches in length, this example of the Southington "Holdfast" bevel is the smallest size they offered. It is in nearly new condition. A difficult to find patented bevel in top collector quality condition.* (FINE) **$65.00**

T2-33. Stanley Rule & Level No. 18: 6" Blade Bevel. Cast Iron Body. Ready To Use. Length: 6 Inches. *Here's a nice working example of a Stanley classic at a bargain price. First come, first serve.* (GOOD+) **$35.00**

T2-34. Stanley Rule & Level: Traut's Patent Bevel. Patented May 9, 1871. Excellent Condition. Length: 10 Inches. *This extraordinary example of the Traut patent bevel of May 9, 1871 is unique in that it does not have, nor did it ever have provision for, the central feature of the patent. The specifications for the Traut patent apply to a conical locking mechanism at the principal joint. However, this tool has a bronze wing nut mechanism in its place and the joint was never machined to accommodate the patent feature. Also, the wing support at the base of the bevel is not present, nor is the body wide enough to accommodate that feature. Could this have been an attempt to use up the castings for the Traut patent after it was discontinued from the product line? We may never know, but there can be no question that this most unusual variation is one of the rarest of all Stanley bevels.* (FINE) **$465.00**

T2-35. Disston & Sons, H., Philadelphia Penn.: Rosewood Handle Bevel. 8" Blade. Early Fixing Screw. Length: 8 Inches. *This early Disston bevel features the ornate brass fixing screw that was also employed on the on the cam. 1860's Fisher patent bevel. Condition is nearly new.* (FINE) **$35.00**

T2-36. Kershaw Bros. Mfrs., Clevland, Ohio: "Eagle" Patent Bevel. Patented February 9, 1892. Raised Letter Cast. Length: 12 Inches. *A particularly graphic bevel bearing the imprint of an early manufacturer. This one has red paint infill on the body that we have not previously observed. A scarce patented bevel in a seldom encountered size.* (GOOD+) **$85.00**

T2-37. Stanley Rule & Level No. 24: Combination Try Square and Bevel. Patented April 5, 1864. Uncommon Size. Length: 10 Inches. *Here's an excellent example of an uncommon combination tool from Stanley's earliest days. Scarce.* (GOOD) **$125.00**

T2-38. Bailey, Leonard: Patent Cam-Lock Bevel. Patented March 19, 1872. Superb Condition. Length: 10 Inches. *Leonard Bailey's non-plane patented tools were unfailingly invested with manifestations of his mechanical genius and his sense of style—a style that was very much home in the Victorian "Age of Excess". A clean, clearly marked and mechanically perfect example of Bailey's 1872 patent bevel.* (FINE) **$475.00**

T2-39. Stanley Rule & Level No. 25: Rosewood Handle Bevel. Unused Condition. Blued Steel Blade. Length: 10 Inches. *The purchaser of this tool will be the very first to use it for its intended purpose. Absolutely perfect.* (FINE) **$35.00**

T2-40. Stephens & Co., Riverton, Conn. No. 31: Shipwright's Folding Bevel. Early Example. Excellent Patina. Length: 12 Inches. *This double-blade bevel from the Stephens Rule Company is clean and clearly marked.* (GOOD+) **$115.00**

T2-41. Melhuish Sons & Co., Fetter Lane: Ebony and Brass Bevel. Blued Steel Blade. Near New Condition. Length: 7 1/2 Inches. *Nearly all original finishes remain on this ebony and brass bevel, which is embossed with the Melhuish imprint on the body. Nearly new.* (FINE) **$95.00**

T2-42. Stanley Tools No. 25: Rosewood Body Bevel. 12" Blade. Near New Condition. Length: 12 Inches. *Here's a very nice example of Stanley's basic bevel that retains nearly all of its original finishes. A tough size to find in this condition.* (FINE) **$45.00**

T2-43. Southington Hardware Co.: Rosewood Handle Bevel. 8" Size. Unused Condition. Length: 8 Inches. *This Rosewood bevel is in new condition and is imprinted with the name of the Southington Hardware Company, a principal Connecticut maker of try squares, bevels, levels and more.* (FINE) **$35.00**

T2-44. Disston & Morss (Unmarked): 6" "T" Bevel. Elaborate Screw. Early and Near New. Length: 6 Inches. *This early bevel has seen very little use. Nearly all original lacquer remains on the brass fittings and the blade retains nearly all of its original blued finish.* (FINE) **$45.00**

T2-45. Unmarked: Miniature Boxwood Bevel. Made From Larger Bevel. Added Graduations. Length: 4 Inches. *This miniature bevel appears to have been produced by an innovative craftsman from a larger shipwright's bevel. Once started on the creative path, he apparently continued by adding 1" graduations to the body. An interesting curiosity.* (GOOD+) **$25.00**

Group U2

U2-1. G.E.: Farrier's Clincher. Uncommon Tool. Apparently Unused. Length: 13 Inches. *This miniature bevel appears to have been produced by an innovative craftsman from a larger shipwright's bevel. Once started on the creative path, he apparently continued by adding 1" graduations to the body. An interesting curiosity.* (FINE) **$45.00**

U2-2. Unmarked: Classic Double Caliper. All Hand Forged. Early and Excellent. Length: 12 Inches. *This smaller than average double caliper appears to have been put together by one with an eye for metalwork. Graphic.* (GOOD+) **$145.00**

U2-3. Unmarked: Early Wheelwrights Traveler. Nicely Hand Forged. Great Patina. Length: 13 1/4 Inches. *This early traveler has a distinctively shaped loop handle and a forged wheel.* (GOOD) **$115.00**

U2-4. Unmarked: Early Harpoon Head. With Tang Handle. From Coastal Conn. Length: 11 1/4 Inches. *The fact that this tool was obtained from an old time Connecticut collection from coastal Connecticut makes it quite likely that this is a domestically produced harpoon for the American whaling industry. A rare piece of American history and a souvenir of a once flourishing trade.* (GOOD+) **$345.00**

U2-5. Unmarked: Hand-Forged Blacksmiths Butteris. With Basket Forging. Superb Patina. Length: 13 1/2 Inches. *A farrier would have possessed the skill at the forge necessary to fashion a tool such as this, although most were apparently content with just enough to get by. Someone, sometime, a long time ago, took the time to make something special. A graphic example art of the blacksmith.* (GOOD+) **$285.00**

U2-6. Goodell-Pratt Company: Farrier's Butteris. Made By Wells Tool. Rare and Excellent. Length: 16 Inches. *This nicely machined farrier's butteris was unquestionably the finest made in this country. This one is clearly marked with the Goodell-Pratt imprint.* (GOOD+) **$115.00**

U2-7. Parsons Bros. Slate Co., Pen Argyl: Lever Arm Slate Cutter. With Perforating Tool. Solid Brass Frame. Length: 22 Inches. *This device was used for cutting and perforating slate for roofing. The body is cast from brass or bronze. Condition is near new.* (FINE) **$155.00**

U2-8. Unmarked: Fireman's Pike Point? Early Hand Forged. Unused Condition. Length: 12 Inches. *This hand forged spike was intended to be mounted in some sort of wooden receiver. My sources tell me that the twisted tip was designed to be stuck into the boards of burning buildings, twisted until fast and then pulled back so as to control the fire. In short, this is purported to be the point for a fireman's pike, and is offered as such. Apparently never used.* (FINE) **$115.00**

U2-9. Unmarked: Miniature Double Caliper. Early Appearance. Graphic Form. Length: 8 Inches. *This smaller than usual double caliper includes its own hanging hook. A nice example.* (GOOD+) **$95.00**

U2-10. Lufkin Rule Co., The, Saginaw, M.I. No. 1085: Blacksmith's Folding Rule. Solid Brass Blades. Unused Condition. Length: 24 Inches. *The working conditions in the blacksmith's shop demanded a more forgiving material and one that would not rust. These brass folding rules were the answer. This one is in unused condition.* (FINE) **$135.00**

U2-11. Albertson & Co., Poughkeepsie, N.Y.: Early Slater's Tool. Uncommon Maker. Extra Strong Imprint. Length: 20 1/2 Inches. *This extra early slater's tool is boldly struck with the name of Pokeepsie (sic), New York edge tool maker. We have seen axes and adzes with Albertson mark, but this is the first slater's tool we have seen.* (GOOD) **$95.00**

U2-12. Unmarked: Blacksmith Tongs and Cutters. For Flat and Curved. Ready To Use. Length: 24 Inches. *All of these tools were acquired together when a blacksmith shop was dispersed this summer in New Hampshire. A nice set of working tools for the would-be metalworker.* (GOOD) **$55.00**

U2-13. Unmarked: Laminated Handle Traveler. With Brass Ponter. Graphic Appearance. Length: 12 Inches. *The handle of this futuristic traveler is made up of a laminated series of rings of brass, aluminum and some sort of red laminate. Very unusual and quite showy.* (GOOD+) **$285.00**

U2-14. Unmarked: Early "Paving" Hammer. For Cobblestones. Scarce and Excellent. Length: 15 1/2 Inches. *These tools were used for the precise positioning of the cobblestones that once served as paving for the major streets of most major cities. This example has a particularly appealing form, having chamfers at the neck of the poll end and a squared striking face. As nice a paving hammer as we have ever offered.* (GOOD+) **$165.00**

U2-15. Unmarked: Unusual Hand Forged Eel Spear. Socket Type Handle. Distinctive Form. Length: 16 1/2 Inches. *Here's a forged iron eel spear in a pattern we have not previously encountered. Thanks in large part to Marcel Salive's study "Ice Fishing Spears", the number of collectors for such tools has burgeoned recently while the supply has plummeted. Examples of this quality are not often available.* (GOOD) **$285.00**

U2-16. Unmarked: Classic Farrier's Butteris. For Hoof Trimming. Turned Beech Handle. Length: 16 Inches. *A nicely turned handle ornaments this early farriers butteris. A good one.* (GOOD+) **$25.00**

U2-17. Unmarked: Pair Of Early Clapboard Gauges. Fruitwood Handles. Distinctive Form. Length: 5 1/2 Inches. *Designed for the workaday task of hanging sawn clapboards, these early clapboard gauges have a most appealing "look" that immediately arouses curiosity. A rare pair in superb condition.* (FINE) **$145.00**

U2-18. Atha Tool Co. No. 20: Farrier's Hammer. With Horseshoe Logo. Unusual and Excellent. Length: 13 Inches. *The Atha Tool Company specialized in farriers tools. It should come as no surprise that they made an excellent farrier's hammer. Nice.* (GOOD+) **$45.00**

U2-19. Tyzak & Son, S., Sheffield: Specialty Mason's Tool. Also Marked. "Goldblatt. Very Well Made. Length: 8 Inches. *The American makers of Masons' tools apparently imported these striking tools from England, as this one is imprinted with the name of respected Sheffield maker S. Tyzak.* (GOOD+) **$25.00**

U2-20. Peck & Smith Co, Southington: Early Tinsmith's Beading Tool. Brass Fittings. Early and Excellent. Length: 27 Inches. *A product of one of the many early partnerships that eventually became the Peck, Stow & Wilcox Company, this well preserved tinsmith's tool is fitted on a wooden base and appears to be in excellent working order.* (GOOD+) **$295.00**

U2-21. Unmarked: Early Double Caliper. Decorative Form. Superb Condition. Length: 30 Inches. *This massive double caliper would have been used in the shop of a blacksmith or wood turner to gauge progress in the duplication of work. Early and excellent.* (GOOD+) **$365.00**

U2-22. Unmarked: Filemaker's Hammer. With Thumb Wear. Rare and Excellent. Length: 9 1/2 Inches. *The handle just behind the head of this early file maker's hammer has been worn from the constant pressure of the user's thumb to appear to have been cast into a contour shape. A rare hammer with much character.* (GOOD+) **$245.00**

U2-23. Unmarked: Early "Double" Caliper. For Blacksmith Use. Excellent Patina. Length: 13 Inches. *This graphic "double" caliper would have been used in a blacksmith shop. A nice example.* (GOOD+) **$55.00**

U2-24. Unmarked: Hand Forged Butteris. For Blacksmith Use. Classic Form. Length: 16 1/2 Inches. *This hand forged butteris has a particularly graphic appearance. A nice example.* (GOOD) **$35.00**

U2-25. Burnham Co., The George, Worcester: Blackmith Drill Catalog. 40 Pages, Ca. 1894. Bench Mounted Drills. Length: 6 Inches. *This illustrates the full line of blacksmith's post drills offered by the Burnham Company.* (GOOD+) **$65.00**

U2-26. Atha Tool Co., Newark, N.J.: Rare "Napping" Hammer. For Stone Work. Most Unusual. Length: 12 1/2 Inches. *The Atha Tool Company name is cast into the head of this most unusual "napping" hammer. These tools were used for the facing of stone. This is the only maker marked example of this type of hammer that we have ever sold.* (GOOD+) **$110.00**

U2-27. Unmarked: Hand Forged Butteris. For Blacksmith Use. Classic Form. Length: 19 1/2 Inches. *The maker/user of this early butteris might well have been inspired in his design by previous experience as a gunsmith. Different.* (GOOD) **$25.00**

U2-28. Fordham, J., Sag Harbor (N.Y.): Early Hand Forged Eel Spear. With 8 Tines. Socket Handle. Length: 12 Inches. *This early eel spear is imprinted with the name of an early Long Island maker. Graphic.* (GOOD) **$145.00**

U2-29. Unmarked: Sawtooth Pattern Eel Spear. With 6 Tines. Extra Long Shaft. Length: 11 1/2 Inches. *To forge this spear, the smith apparently flattened a piece of bar stock and then cut it into strips, which were then struck with a chisel to form the tines. Extra early and very graphic.* (GOOD) **$125.00**

U2-30. Unmarked: Massive Proportional Calipers. For Sculptor's Use. Ready To Use. Length: 56 Inches. *Tools such as this were used by sculptors working from clay models to transfer proportional measurements to the actual work. This graphic tool is in excellent condition.* (GOOD+) **$145.00**

U2-31. Unmarked: Wheelwright's Traveler. Forged Iron Pointer. Early and Excellent. Length: 13 Inches. *These tools were used for measuring the length of the metal "tire" that surrounded a wooden wagon wheel. The wheelwright needed only to count the number of revolutions and then transfer the pattern to the a piece of flat steel which would the be formed into a hoop, heated and shrunk to fit around the wheel. Watching this process was a major source of entertainment for children in the days before Sesame Street and Ritalin. Here's a nice example for the tool room.* (FINE) **$85.00**

U2-32. Unmarked: Set Of Foundryman's Tampers. For Sand Molds. Graphic Form. Length: 13 1/2 Inches. *Looking not unlike the stone figures found on certain South Pacific islands, these graphic tools were use for shaping the sand that was used for forming castings in brass and cast iron. A superbly patinated set with great visual appeal.* (GOOD) **$165.00**

U2-33. Stanley Rule & Level No. 17: Brass Blacksmith's Folding Rule. Early Trademark. Extra Crisp and Clean. Length: 24 Inches. *A nice example of the Stanley brass blacksmiths' rule with a crisp early trademark. Uncommon.* (FINE) **$95.00**

U2-34. Unmarked: Lignum Vitae Tamper. For Sand Casting. Unused Condition. Length: 8 Inches. *Designed to be used in the foundry for packing the sand into molds for casting, this lignum vitae tamper appears never to have been called upon to perform that task. Unused.* (FINE) **$35.00**

U2-35. Unmarked: Hand Forged Fish Spear. Decorative Form. Socket Type Handle. Length: 11 3/4 Inches. *The bluntness of the tines on this spear would lead one to suspect that it is an eel spear and intended to catch its prey between, rather than on the end of the tines.* (GOOD) **$115.00**

U2-36. Williams & Co., J.H., Brooklyn: Metalwork Knurling Tool. With 2 Sets of Knurls. Ready To Use. Length: 5 Inches. *This machinist's knurling tool comes complete with an extra set of spiral knurls.* (FINE) **$35.00**

U2-37. Pierce, W.F.: Early Set Of Metalworking Tools. All Single Owner. Ca. 1850's. Length: 15 Inches. *All of these early tools are imprinted with the owner's name "W.F. Pierce" and it is very likely that they were fashioned by him. An early set of tools in excellent condition.* (GOOD+) **$225.00**

U2-38. White, L. & I.J., Buffalo, N.Y.: Patent Cooper's Raising Iron. Apparently Unused. Rare and Excellent. Length: 7 1/2 Inches. *One of the less common of coopers' tools, this raising iron is in unused condition. Rare.* (FINE) **$85.00**

U2-39. Unmarked: Sawtooth Pattern Eel Spear. With 5 Tines. Uncommon Type. Length: 9 1/2 Inches. *Here's an early hand forged eel spear having a graphic sawtooth pattern. Bold.* (GOOD) **$115.00**

U2-40. Unmarked: Hammer and Hook Combination Tool. For Loading Dock. With Nail Puller. Length: 10 Inches. *Crate hammers, box openers and the like have attracted a growing number of collectors. This unusual variation on the theme includes a hammer, nail puller and hook. Never seen another.* (GOOD) **$75.00**

U2-41. Unmarked: Assorted Bronze Founder's Tools. Spoons, Corners, Etc. Hard To Find. Length: 8 Inches. *Here's a well preserved set of founders tools for sand casting. Most are formed from cast bronze. A brass and leather box has kept these tools together through the years. A nice set.* (GOOD+) **$145.00**

U2-42. Unmarked: Set Of 65 Assorted Chasing Tools. For Metalwork. Elaborate Designs. Length: 2 1/2 Inches. *This working set of chasing tools includes a wide range of decorative patterns for the decorating of metalwork. All are in excellent working order. A great set.* (GOOD+) **$545.00**

U2-43. Unmarked: Plumber's Flaring Tool. Solid Boxwood. Superb Patina. Length: 4 Inches. *In the days before plastic pipe, a plumber would use one of these to flare the end of a lead pipe for fitting. An interesting curiosity from the world of old time waterworks.* (GOOD+) **$35.00**

U2-44. Unmarked: Classic Hand Forged Eel Spear. Nicely Formed. With 6 Tines. Length: 15 Inches. *This well preserved eel spear has a graphic pattern of six external hooks and a thin central spear. Bold and starkly beautiful.* (GOOD) **$185.00**

U2-45. Unmarked: Hand Forged Bark Spud. Very Well Made. Superb Patina. Length: 17 1/2 Inches. *Bark spuds were used for removing bark to facilitate the drying of the wood and also to remove bark being harvested for use in the tanning process. This hand forged example is in excellent condition and ready to use, if desired.* (GOOD+) **$45.00**

Group V2

V2-1. Buck Bros., Millbury, Mass.: Set of 5 Bevel Edge Chisels. 1/4" to 1 1/2". Unused Condition. Length: 13 Inches. *No apologies whatsoever for these perfectly preserved bevel edge chisels from one of America's premier makers. A set to last a lifetime.* (FINE) **$225.00**

V2-2. Assorted Makers: Group of 6 Assorted Carving Tools. Gouges, Etc. Ready to Use. Length: 9 Inches. *Each of these assorted carving chisels and gouges are in excellent working order. A great working set.* (GOOD+) **$135.00**

V2-3. Peck, Stow & Wilcox Co. No. 1 EX.: Heavy Socket Framing Chisel. 1 3/4" Size. Original Handle. Length: 17 1/2 Inches. *This uncommon framing chisel is of the in-between 1 3/4" size. Condition is near new.* (FINE) **$85.00**

V2-4. Marples & Co., William, Sheffield No. 20: Front Bent Gouge. Extra Deep Cut. Near New Condition. Length: 11 1/4 Inches. *This steep, front bent gouge bears the imprint of William Marples & Company, the respected Sheffield edge tool makers. It appears never to have been used. Mint.* (FINE) **$85.00**

V2-5. Underhill Bros., Boston, Mass.: Early Hand-Forged Gouge. Rare Imprint. Excellent Patina. Length: 21 Inches. *This early gouge has been shaped to its current form by repeated blows from a triphammer. The maker mark was applied after the forging process was completed. An interesting early gouge with a decidedly different texture.* (GOOD+) **$95.00**

V2-6. Barton, D.R., Rochester No. 9: Deep Bent Gouge Carving Tool. Original Handle. Extra Crisp and Clean. Length: 9 Inches. *This extra deep gouge from Rochester, New York's D.R. Barton Company is in nearly new condition. A very well preserved carving tool.* (FINE) **$65.00**

V2-7. Addis, J.B., Sheffield: Pair. of Front Bent Carving Tools, Flat & Skew. Near New Condition. Length: 8 1/2 Inches. *This pair of Addis carving tools includes two front bent tools, one having a straight edge and the other skewed. Absolutely mint.* (FINE) **$125.00**

V2-8. Butcher, W., Sheffield (England): Set of 3 Flat Chisels. Octagon Handles. Excellent Patina. Length: 8 1/2 Inches. *Sheffield quality needs no introduction, nor does the name W. Butcher, a maker of top quality edge tools for more than 150 years. A very well preserved set of chisels from ca. 1810. Nice.* (FINE) **$85.00**

V2-9. Assorted Makers: Group of 9 Assorted Carving Tool. Gouges, Etc.. Ready to Use. Length: 9 1/2 Inches. *This opportunity lot of carving tools includes a wide range of gouges of varying sweeps. A great set at a bargain price.* (GOOD+) **$165.00**

V2-10. Unmarked: Heavy Socket Framing Chisel. 2" Size. Ready to Use. Length: 12 Inches. *An unmarked, but clean and ready to use framing chisel. A good one.* (GOOD+) **$55.00**

V2-11. Buck Brothers: 1" Crank Neck Chisel. With Flat Sides. Ready To Use. Length: 13 Inches. *Here's a crispy-clean crank-neck with flat sides. The back side has a mirror polish. Nice.* (FINE) **$55.00**

V2-12. Swan Co., The James, Seymour, Conn.: Heavy Socket Framing Chisel. 3/4" Size. New Old Stock. Length: 15 Inches. *Here's a great working tool that wants only for a steel ferrule for the top of the handle. A nice chisel from a respected maker.* (FINE) **$55.00**

V2-13. White, L. & I.J., Buffalo, N.Y.: Shipwright's Mortise Chisel. 2" Width. Unused Condition. Length: 16 Inches. *All this perfectly preserved chisel from prominent 19th Century Buffalo, New York edge tool makers L. & I.J. White needs is a handle. Absolutely perfect and unused.* (FINE) **$155.00**

V2-14. Peck, Stow & Wilcox Co.: Heavy Socket Framing Chisel. 3/4" Width. New Old Stock. Length: 11 1/2 Inches. *Crispy clean and ready for years of service. Excellent.* (FINE) **$75.00**

V2-15. Swan Co, The James: Rare 1/2" Corner Chisel. Excellent Condtion. Ready to Use. Length: 10 3/4 Inches. *Chisels by the James Swan Company are spoken of in hushed, reverent terms by those who have used them. This rare 1/2" corner chisel is an example of why that is so. Perfect.* (FINE) **$135.00**

V2-16. Shapleigh Hardware, St. Louis: "Diamond Edge" Corner Chisel. Rare 1/2" Size. Original Handle. Length: 15 1/2 Inches. *Perhaps because of their susceptibility to breakage, very few corner chisels in the 1/2" size have survived. This excellent example from St. Louis based hardware dealer Shapleigh features their top of the line "Diamond Edge" logo. Nice.* (GOOD+) **$115.00**

V2-17. Unmarked: Heavy Socket Framing Chisel. 1 1/2" Size. Crisp and Clean. Length: 11 1/4 Inches. *No maker marks on this clean and usable corner chisel, but it is sound and ready to pound.* (FINE) **$55.00**

V2-18. Stanley Rule & Level No. 750: Bevel Edge Socket Chisel. 1" Width. Unused Condition. Length: 10 Inches. *No apologies whatsoever for this essentially unused pocket chisel from Stanley's "red handle" line. Perfect.* (FINE) **$55.00**

V2-19. Davenport: Heavy Socket Framing Chisel. 1 1/4" Width. Superb Condition. Length: 19 Inches. *A good clean working chisel in an uncommon size.* (GOOD+) **$65.00**

V2-20. Sears, Roebuck & Co.: Set of 4 Bevel Edge Chisel. With Socket Handles. Near New Condition. Length: 10 1/2 Inches. *A great example of the sort of quality which was characteristic of early examples of the "Craftsman" line. Good tools.* (FINE) **$55.00**

V2-21. Crossman, A.W.: Heavy Socket Framing Chisel. 1/2" Size. Near New Condition. Length: 15 Inches. *An extra crisp and clean socket framing chisel from the Massachusetts edge tool firm A.W. Crossman. A very nice chisel.* (FINE) **$65.00**

V2-22. Belknap Hardware Co., Louisville: Set of 6 Bevel Edge Chisels. 1/4" to 2". With Original Decals. Length: 14 Inches. *The Belknap Hardware Company of Louisville, Kentucky became famous for their "Bluegrass" line of tools. This set of 6 long, bevel edge chisels is clear evidence that that notoriety was well deserved. A great set in top condition.* (FINE) **$325.00**

V2-23. Buck Brothers No. 39: Straight "V" Gouge Carving Tool. Octagon Handle. Clean and Sharp. Length: 5 Inches. *The nicely formed octagonal handle of the "V" gouge has attained a warm patina from years of use. Sharp and ready to use.* (GOOD+) **$45.00**

V2-24. Mephisto: 2" "Everlasting" Chisel. Pat. Feb. 23, 1909. Rare and Excellent. Length: 12 1/2 Inches. *Most likely produced for this obscure Connecticut tool line by the Wood Manufacturing Company, who were bought out by Stanley to acquire the "Everlasting" chisel line, this rare chisel is imprinted with the Mephisto mark and the early patent date. Rare and excellent.* (GOOD+) **$115.00**

V2-25. Stanley Rule & Level No. 60: Set of 6 Bevel Edge Chisel. "Permaloid" Handles. Original Pouch. Length: 8 Inches. *The original pouch, which bears Stanley's "Tool Box of the World" slogan, has kept these chisels in nearly new condition. A great working set of chisels that can trace their lineage to Stanley's early "Everlasting" chisels. Perfect.* (FINE) **$115.00**

V2-26. Barton, D.R., Rochester: Bent Gouge Carving Tool. Fruitwood Handle. Usable Condition. Length: 10 Inches. *This deep gouge is fitted with a fruitwood handle and has a pronounced angle to the blade. Ready to use.* (GOOD) **$45.00**

V2-27. Fulton, New York, N.Y.: Heavy Socket Corner Chisel. 1" Size. Extra Crisp & Clean. Length: 1 Inches. *The Fulton Tool Company of New York City offered high quality edge tools and woodworking planes at the beginning of the Twentieth Century. This nearly new corner chisel is boldly struck with the Fulton mark, but it may well have been made for Fulton by one of the prominent Connecticut makers such as Witherby or Peck, Stow & Wilcox. A very well made corner chisel in top condition.* (FINE) **$95.00**

V2-28. Douglass Mfg. Co.: Heavy Socket Corner Chisel. 1" Size. Ready to Use. Length: 16 1/2 Inches. *This heavy-duty corner chisel is in fine working condition. A good one.* (GOOD+) **$65.00**

V2-29. Ash & Co., Wm.: Pair of Carving Chisels. Extra Narrow. From Single Owner. Length: 8 1/4 Inches. *These narrow, flat tang-handle carving tools are imprinted with the name of English maker William Ash, whose career spanned the Eighteenth and Nineteenth Centuries. Very old and near new.* (FINE) **$45.00**

V2-30. Marples & Co., William, Sheffield No. 46: Bent "V" Gouge Carving Tool. 1/2" Max Width. Near New Condition. Length: 10 1/4 Inches. *This "V" gouge measures 1/2" across at the widest part. It is in immaculate condition.* (FINE) **$65.00**

V2-31. Buck Bros., Millbury, Mass.: Pair of Slight Sweep Carving Tools. Marked "3" & "4". Fruitwood Handles. Length: 12 Inches. *These flat gouges have a very slight sweep to their cut and identical turned handles. A pretty pair.* (GOOD+) **$135.00**

V2-32. Addis, J.B., Sheffield No. 10: Flutaroni Gouge Carving Tool. 1/4" Width. Near New Condition. Length: 9 Inches. *This flutaroni carver has a width of 1/4" inch. It is in nearly new condition. A rare carving tool.* (FINE) **$85.00**

V2-33. Addis & Sons, J. B., Sheffield: Pair of Wood Carving Tools. Straight & Skewed. Fruitwood Handles. Length: 9 1/4 Inches. *These carving tools from respected London maker J.B. Addis came together from the same kit of tools. Nearly new.* (FINE) **$135.00**

V2-34. Underhill Edge Tool Co.: Heavy Socket Framing Chisel. 1/4" Size. Unused Condition. Length: 15 Inches. *If you are the lucky purchaser, you can be the first to take this chisel to wood in anger. Absolutely unused.* (FINE) **$85.00**

V2-35. Union Hardware Co., Torrington, Ct: Heavy Socket Framing Chisel. 1" Size. New Condition. Length: 16 Inches. *This one was packed in the original cosmoline when it came into my hands. The chisel is now clean, but my hands are not. A great tool now cleansed of this hellish goo.* (FINE) **$75.00**

V2-36. Unmarked: O. Hanks Patent? Tool Holder. Pat. May 31, 1870. For Chisel Grinding?. Length: 0 Inches. *The limited patent records we have available here at the Donnelly Tool Repository and Research Center list one O. Hanks as having patented what was described as a "tool holder" on May 31, 1870, but there is no picture to associate with this most unusual tool. Machined from solid bronze, with a steel rolling wheel attached to the base and a locking screw at the top on which is marked the 1870 patent date, it appears that this could be one of the earliest examples of a manufactured "honing guide" to come to light. A rare and interesting patented tool in superb condition.* (FINE) **$235.00**

V2-37. Buck Bros., Millbury, Mass.: Set of 3 Tang Chisels. Beechwood Handle. Near New Condition. Length: 10 Inches. *Here's an excellent set of square sided tang chisels by prominent maker Buck Brothers. Extra crisp and clean.* (FINE) **$55.00**

V2-38. Union Hardware Co., Torrington, Conn.: Heavy Socket Framing Chisel. 1" Size. New Condition. Length: 16 Inches. *This one inch heavy socket framing chisel has never been used. An old tool in new condition.* (FINE) **$75.00**

V2-39. Buck Bros., Millbury, Mass.: 1 1/2" Crank Neck Chisel. Extra Clean and Sharp. Ready to Use. Length: 13 1/2 Inches. *An exceptionally nice, wide bevel-edge chisel that has an early-style fruitwood handle imprinted with the Buck's head logo. Nice.* (FINE) **$75.00**

V2-40. Unmarked: Offset Patternmaker' Chisel. With Octagonal Handle. Near New Condition. Length: 19 Inches. *Fitted with a handle that retains all of its original lacquer and having a nicely chamfered shaft jointed to a bevel edged blade, this superb tool came from a kit of patternmakers' tools from the State of New Jersey. A most unusual chisel in perfectly preserved condition. Highly recommended.* (FINE) **$165.00**

V2-41. Buck Bros., Millbury, Mass.: 3/4" Crank Neck Chisel. Extra Clean and Sharp. Fruitwood Handle. Length: 12 Inches. *This crank neck in the desirable 3/4" size is in perfect working order. A tough size to find.* (FINE) **$85.00**

V2-42. Buck Bros., Millbury, Mass.: 3/8" Crank Neck Chisel. Extra Clean and Sharp. Fruitwood Handle. Length: 12 Inches. *Here's an extra nice 3/8" crank neck chisel imprinted with the distinctive Buck Brothers logo. The handle is original as well, and marked with the "Buck" trademark. Ready to use.* (FINE) **$75.00**

V2-43. Addis, J.B., Sheffield: Group of 4 Flat Carving Tools. Extra Wide Sizes. Ready to Use. Length: 9 Inches. *These wide gouges are all marked with the name of Sheffield edge tool maker J.B. Addis. Crisp, clean and ready to provide a lifetime of service.* (GOOD+) **$165.00**

V2-44. Addis, S.J., London: Macaroni Gouge Carving Tool. Early Octagon Hdle.. Ready to Use. Length: 9 1/2 Inches. *The macaroni gouge is distinguished by having squared corners and a flat base. We have only had a handful of these in the last 10 years. Rare and excellent.* (GOOD+) **$75.00**

V2-45. Addis, S.J., London: Set of 4 Assorted Carving Tools. From Single Owner. Ready to Use. Length: 9 3/4 Inches. *Here's an interesting assortment of carving tools in ready to use condition.* (GOOD+) **$85.00**

V2-46. Addis, S.J., London: Set of 4 "V" Cut Carving Tools. From Single Owner. Ready to Use. Length: 8 1/2 Inches. *These "V" cut carving tools came from the chest of a single carver and represent a series variations on the same shape. A nice working set for the carver.* (GOOD+) **$195.00**

V2-47. Addis, J.B., Sheffield No. 30: Wide Spoon Gouge Carving Tool. 1" Width. Extra Deep Bend. Length: 9 Inches. *This massive carving gouge has an extra wide bend at the business end. Nearly perfectly preserved.* (FINE) **$95.00**

V2-48. Addis, J.B., Sheffield No. 31: Spoon Gouge Carving Tool. 1" Width. Near New Condition. Length: 9 1/2 Inches. *This wide spoon gouge is in nearly new condition. A rare carving tool.* (FINE) **$85.00**

V2-49. Taylor Ltd., Henry, Sheffield: Massive Bent Gouge Carving Tool. 2" Width. Extra Crisp and Clean. Length: 12 1/2 Inches. *This extraordinary spoon gouge measures 2" across the opening. Ready to use, if you choose.* (GOOD+) **$115.00**

V2-50. Assorted Makers: Group of 9 Assorted Carving Tools. Addis, Etc.. Ready to Use. Length: 9 1/2 Inches. *All 9 of these chisels were the property of a single woodworker and came together when the tools were dispersed. We are not inclined to break them up. A nice working set.* (GOOD+) **$125.00**

Group W2

W2-1. Card, S.W., Mansfield, Mass. No. 7: Horsefield Tap Wrench. Sizes 3/16" To 1/2". New Cond., Orig. Box. Length: 11 1/2 Inches. *This well made die stock from Massachusetts maker S.W. Card is in new condition in its original box. Mint.* (FINE) **$55.00**

W2-2. Rast Prod. Corp., New York, N.Y.: "Fits All" Wrench. Forged Iron Body. Uncommon Type. Length: 6 Inches. *From here, I can count a total of four sizes that could be accommodated in this "Fits All" wrench—not too many as wrenches go. A nice example.* (GOOD) **$25.00**

W2-3. North Bros Mfg. Co., Phila. (St) No. 251 A: "Yankee" Ratchet Tap Wrench. Smallest Size. New Cond., Orig. Box. Length: 5 Inches. *These were, without question, the finest ratcheting tap wrenches ever made. A total of three sizes were made. This was the second largest size. New and in the box.* (FINE) **$85.00**

W2-4. Unmarked: Turned Steel Tap Wrench. Checkered Handle. Ready To Use. Length: 8 1/2 Inches. *The adjustable end of this well made tap wrench has been checkered in a lathe to improve the grip of the user. An excellent working tool.* (GOOD+) **$15.00**

W2-5. Prefer: "Prefer" French Wrench. "Modele Depose". Very Well Made. Length: 4 1/2 Inches. *This extremely well made wrench is marked "Prefer" and "Modele Depose", sure signs that it is of French origin. A nice example.* (GOOD+) **$65.00**

W2-6. Coes Wrench Co., Worcester, Mass.: Promotional Wrench Stick Pin. Original Card. "Pin To Your Memory". Length: 3 Inches. *The rough and tumble crowd who used Coes' wrenches probably didn't have much use for stickpins. Here's a nice example, nonetheless.* (FINE) **$65.00**

W2-7. Starrett Co., The L.S., Athol, Mass. No. 1: Adjustable Jaw Cutnippers. 7" Size. Extra Crisp & Clean. Length: 7 Inches. *These were apparently used for nipping off wire, the tips of small bolts and the like. These are in excellent condition. A nice, early example.* (GOOD+) **$35.00**

W2-8. Whitman & Barnes Mfg. Co., Boston: "Ben Hur" Bicycle Wrench. With Fluted Sides. Most Unusual. Length: 5 Inches. *We have it on good authority that this wrench was used by Charlton Heston to tighten his chariot wheels. A most unusual bicycle wrench.* (GOOD+) **$20.00**

W2-9. Unmarked No. 2: Pipe Jaw Wrench Insert. For Monkey Wrench. Rare &excellent. Length: 3 1/2 Inches. *These could be bolted to the jaw of your monkey wrench to make it into a pipe wrench. The evidence is that they were not big sellers. Rare.* (FINE) **$55.00**

W2-10. Rown, W., Sheffield: English Twist Hdle. Wrench. With Screwdriver Tip. Most Unusual Type. Length: 6 Inches. *The elongated tip of this twist handle wrench serves double duty as a tack puller and a screwdriver. Never have seen another.* (GOOD+) **$55.00**

W2-11. Utica Tools, Utica, N.Y. No. 92-12: Crank Adj. "Crescent Wrench. With Quick Adjust. Most Unusual. Length: 12 Inches. *This "improvement" on the standard "Crescent" wrench included an adjustable handle that would allow the user to quickly adjust the jaw to size and then lock it in place. They may have proved impractical in everyday usage. An uncommon adjustable wrench* (FINE) **$65.00**

W2-12. Unmarked: Hand Forged Spanner Wrench. Forged From File. Most Unusual. Length: 7 1/4 Inches. *This split wrench was hand forged for use in a bit brace. Function unknown.* (GOOD+) **$85.00**

W2-13. Bullard No. 0: Self-Adjusting Pipe Wrench. Patented Oct. 27, 1903. Schulz No. 661. Length: 5 1/2 Inches. *This is the smallest of the Bullard series which ranged from the sublime, as illustrated here, to the ridiculous (huge). Cute.* (GOOD+) **$95.00**

W2-14. Victor: "The Victor" Wrench. Patented Aug. 25, 1903. Thumb Lever Adjust. Length: 8 Inches. *This turn of the Century patent pipe wrench featured a quick adjust lower jaw that would slide into place with the action of the thumb. A nice example.* (GOOD+) **$95.00**

W2-15. Billings & Spencer Co., The: "Billings Patent" Wrench. Patented Jan. 18, 1879. Uncommon Type. Length: 5 1/2 Inches. *This early patent wrench has the black finish that was always an option on adjustable wrenches from the Billings & Spencer Company. This one is marked with the 1879 patent date.* (GOOD) **$45.00**

W2-16. Gearench Mfg. Co., Houston, Texas. Adjustable Pipe Wrench. "Gearench". Patented June 1, 1926. Length: 8 Inches. *The "Gearwrench" is a cam activated self adjusting pipe wrench that looks as though it would have worked fairly well and been quite expensive to produce. They apparently were not produced for very long. A scarce wrench.* (GOOD+) **$165.00**

W2-17. Coes Wrench Co.: Steel Handle Wrench. Patented Dec. 24, 1901. Smallest Size. Length: 5 Inches. *These metal handled wrenches are more common than their wood-handled cousins in the same size, but are nevertheless uncommon. A well preserved example.* (GOOD+) **$85.00**

W2-18. Attwood Mfg. Co., The, Conneaut, Ohio: 10" "Craft" Wrench. Patented Nov. 12, 1907. Schulz No. 663. Length: 10 Inches. *We have offered a number of examples of the quick adjusting "Craft" wrench, but this is the first we have seen imprinted with the Attwood Mfg. Company name.* (FINE) **$65.00**

W2-19. Hayden's Patent: Bicycle Monkey Wrench. Center Adjust. Patented June 15, 1880. Length: 4 1/4 Inches. *One of the earliest of "bicycle" type wrenches, the Hayden Patent was issued in 1880, long before many bicycles were in use.* (GOOD+) **$115.00**

W2-20. Petersen Tool Co., Eldorado, Kansas: "Helix" Slide Adjust Wrench. Pat. No. 3555939. Near New Condition. Length: 8 Inches. *A later, but mechanically interesting slide jaw wrench. It's not in Kansas anymore. Different.* (FINE) **$65.00**

W2-21. Unmarked: Screw Adjust Nut Wrench. With Threaded Shaft. Most Unus. Type. Length: 6 Inches. *This small wrench features a threaded handle which must have been none too comfortable to use. This is the only example of this wrench that we have encountered.* (GOOD+) **$55.00**

W2-22. Petersen Tool Co., Eldorado, Ks: "Helix" Slide Adjust Wrench. Pat. No. 3555939. Near New Condition. Length: 8 Inches. *The "Helix" wrench is one of those classic "engineer designed" wrenches that apply a mechanical principal to the science of nuts and bolts without due consideration of the possibility of non-laboratory conditions. An effortlessly adjustable central spiral screw works just great under design and test conditions, but hardly at all when filled with the dust and dirt that those who use such tools encounter each and every day. This thing probably made the inventor's mother proud, but not too many were sold, especially on the recommendation of someone who had used one.* (FINE) **$195.00**

W2-23. Vandegrift Mfg. Co., Shelbyville No. 11: Quick Adjust Nut Wrench. Wedge Lock Adjustment. Schulz No. 546. Length: 8 Inches. *These are generally not marked, as is the case with this cast iron wrench, but research has revealed this to be the output of the Vandegrift Wrench Company of Shelbyville, Indiana. A wood handled model was also manufactured. This one is in excellent working order. A good one.* (GOOD+) **$225.00**

W2-24. Grannis, J.: Revolving "Buggy" Wrench. Patented April 21, 1896. Original Gold Paint. Length: 9 Inches. *The crank handle on this early patent carriage wrench can be locked into a slot on the reverse side to maximize leverage. When the nut is loose, the crank can be employed to full extent. Never seen another.* (GOOD+) **$475.00**

W2-25. La Gripper Wrench Co., Battle Creek, Michigan: Quick Adjust Nut Wrench. Patented June 28, 1898. Schulz No. 689. Length: 7 Inches. *Looking not unlike some ancient marine predator, these are less common than most endangered species. A most interesting double grip adjustable wrench with a pre-1900 patent date.* (GOOD) **$325.00**

W2-26. Hinkle, J.N., Columbus, O. No. 0: Quick Adjust Pipe Wrench. Reversed "S". Most Unus. Type. Length: 8 Inches. *The "S" on the word "Columbus" on this wrench is reversed. It is hard to believe that this could have happened by accident, so we'll assume it was a marketing ploy that didn't work. An uncommon wrench.* (GOOD+) **$65.00**

W2-27. Starrett Co., L. S., Athol, Mass. No. 240: Adjustable Plier Wrench. Early Type. "Pat. Appl'd For". Length: 7 Inches. *This is the earlier version of the Starrett plier wrench, which was apparently fitted with a fine adjustment as an improvement in later models.* (GOOD+) **$75.00**

W2-28. Simplex Wrench Co., New York, N.Y. No. 14: "Simplex Ratchet" Wrench. Patented Jan. 1, 1924. Most Unusual. Length: 6 1/4 Inches. *We have seen a number of stupid ideas masquerading as tools, but this "Simplex" scores as both simplistic and stupid. The general idea here was to allow one open end wrench to function as several sizes by cutting a series of notches in the same opening. Anyone who has ever used one of these tools to simultaneously break the head off from a bolt and remove a substantial amount of skin from the knuckles knows what I mean. Looks more like the Simpleton wrench to me.* (GOOD) **$35.00**

W2-29. Unmarked: Hand Forged Nut Wrench. Early Square Style. Very Well Made. Length: 6 1/2 Inches. *Mastery of the blacksmith's craft is evident in this brace-mounted wrench for square nuts. It was most likely made for use in a wagon shop.* (GOOD+) **$35.00**

W2-30. Wright Wrench Forging Co., The: 8" "Wright" Wrench. Patented March 15, 1904. Crisp & Clean. Length: 8 Inches. *One of the best made of the successful quick adjust wrenches, the "Wright Wrench" features a set of precise notches machined into the back of the body. A well preserved example of a well made wrench.* (GOOD+) **$85.00**

W2-31. Tite Grip Wrench Co., Milwaukee, Wisconsin: Nickel Plated Nut Wrench. Screw Adj. Handle. Full Nickel Plating. Length: 6 1/2 Inches. *There are no patent marks on this most unusual small nickel plated wrench, but it appears to have been manufactured. The adjustment of the jaws is brought about by turning the handle. Never seen another.* (GOOD+) **$345.00**

W2-32. Portland Wrench Company: Comb. Nut And Buggy Wrench. Patented Oct. 16, 1883. Extra Crisp & Clean. Length: 5 1/2 Inches. *This, the smallest size of the Portland buggy wrench is in top collector quality condition. An excellent example.* (FINE) **$225.00**

W2-33. Crescent Tool Co., Jamestown, N.Y.: "Crestoloy" Adjustab Wrench. With Slide Lock Featur. Uncommon Type. Length: 8 Inches. *This unusual Crescent product includes a sliding lock to positively hold the jaw in place. These apparently didn't sell very well—examples are scarce.* (FINE) **$25.00**

W2-34. Gordon: Quick Adj. "Crescent Wrench. Spring Activated. "Pat. Applied For". Length: 6 Inches. *The "Gordon Automatic" monkey-type wrench was relatively popular, however this "Crescent" type cousin apparently never caught on. A rare quick adjust wrench.* (GOOD+) **$195.00**

W2-35. Unmarked: Nickel Plated Nut Wrench. Pat. Appl'd. For. 85% Nickel Plating. Length: 5 Inches. *"Pat. Appl'd. For" is the only mark on this early appearing nut wrench, which is formed from a "sandwich" of two nickel plated sides and a central core. A very well made wrench in excellent condition.* (FINE) **$195.00**

W2-36. Smith Co., H.D., The: "Perfect Handle' Wrench. 1 1/8" Opening. Marked "5/8". Length: 9 Inches. *There must be a story as to why many "Perfect Handle" wrenches were marked with one size, but measure at another. There is no evidence that this tool has been modified in any way.* (GOOD+) **$45.00**

W2-37. Gordon: Quick-Adjust Nut Wrench. "Gordon Automatic". Schulz No. 493. Length: 7 1/4 Inches. *The Gordon Automatic is a mechanical marvel of springs and gears. The idea was to open the jaw, lock it into place, then push the button for it to lock around the nut. A gizmo.* (GOOD+) **$135.00**

W2-38. Elgin: " The Elgin" Wrench. Patented June 8, 1897. Schulz No. 35 B. Length: 7 Inches. *How would you like to use one of these on a $600.00 mountain bike? They apparently served their purpose as the evidence suggests they were quite popular. An excellent example.* (FINE) **$35.00**

W2-39. Springfield Drop Forging Co.: Bicycle Monkey Wrench. Side Adjust. Full Nickel Plating. Length: 5 1/2 Inches. *Nearly all original nickel plating remains on this turn of the century classic. A nice wrench.* (GOOD+) **$35.00**

W2-40. Wakefield Wrench Co., Worcester, Mass. No. 3: Comb. Tire Iron & Wrench. "Patents Pending". Rare & Excellent. Length: 5 Inches. *The narrowed and angled end of this bicycle wrench also functions as a tire iron when the wrench is fully closed. An uncommon Wakefield wrench.* (GOOD+) **$165.00**

W2-41. Trimont Mfg. Co., Roxbury, Mass. No. 1: Patent Chain Wrench. Smallest Size. Patented 1894 "Bull Dog". Length: 6 Inches. *At only 6" in length, this was the smallest size offered in this chain-type wrench. The range of sizes included wrenches up to four feet in length. Cute.* (GOOD+) **$115.00**

W2-42. Cornwell Quality Tools Co.: Circular Motion Wrench. For Round Stock. "Pat. Appl'd. For". Length: 6 1/2 Inches. *This most unusual wrench set includes a series of sockets, each of which is fitted with a series of cylinders that function as cams. When the wrench is turned, the cams lock on to the nut or bolt. I sure this idea appealed to the engineers, but might have been impractical in the greasy and gritty world of the auto mechanic.* (GOOD+) **$85.00**

W2-43. Lavigne & Scott Mfg. Co., The: Patented Bicycle Wrench. "Sandow" Brand. Patented Feb. 5, 1895. Length: 5 1/4 Inches. *This interesting bicycle wrench features an opened handle to hold the nut and upper jaw extension. It was patented in 1895. An interesting early bicycle wrench.* (GOOD+) **$85.00**

W2-44. Bessey: "Bessey" Self Adjust Wrench. "Made In Germany". Near New Condition. Length: 9 1/4 Inches. *This variation on one of the most popular quick adjusting wrench schemes—the self-adjusting wrench—comes to us by way of Germany. A nice example.* (FINE) **$35.00**

W2-45. Snap On Tools Corp, Kenosha, Wisconsin: "Ferret" & "Midget" Wrench. F70 N & M70 M. Fitted Wood Box. Length: 7 Inches. *Back in the days before sensitivity to endangered species and the height challenged, the folks at Snap On had the audacity to name tools in an ill-considered way. Part of the proceeds from the sale of these tools will be used to send someone at Snap On to sensitivity training in Cambodia. A rare pair.* (GOOD+) **$165.00**

Group X2

X2-1. Stanley Rule & Level (Unmarked) No. 73: Boxwood Marking Gauge. With Sliding Scribe. Excellent Condition. Length: 6 Inches. *As was the case with most examples of Stanley's uncommon No. 73 boxwood gauge, there is no maker mark on this tool. As is not the case with the other examples, this one is in near new condition. Perfect.* (FINE) **$85.00**

X2-2. Scholl, C.: 3 Stem Patent Marking Gauge. Patented March 8, 1864. Rosewood Body, Arms. Length: 8 Inches. *This 3 stem version of the Scholl 1864 patent features six circular wear strips inlaid in the face of the head. A tough gauge to find.* (FINE) **$425.00**

X2-3. Scholl, C.: 3 Stem Patent Marking Gauge. Patented March 8, 1864. Rosewood Body, Arms. Length: 8 Inches. *This 3 stem version of the Scholl 1864 patent features six circular wear strips. A tough gauge to find.* (GOOD+) **$395.00**

X2-4. Blaisdell, A.H.: Blaisdell's Patent Marking Gauge. Patented June 23, 1868. Near New Condition. Length: 8 Inches. *Certainly one of the most complex of all marking gauges, the Blaisdell's patent has all the qualities of a great collectible tool: exotic materials finely crafted and finished; bold maker and patent imprints; and a level of mechanical intricacy far beyond what is necessary for the task. They don't get much better.* (FINE) **$725.00**

X2-5. Sorby, Robert, Sheffield: Rosewood Mortise & Marking Gauge. Original Decal. Near New Condition. Length: 8 Inches. *Nearly all of the original decal, featuring Sorby's classic "Kangaroo" logo, remains on this classic English gauge. Nearly new.* (FINE) **$85.00**

X2-6. Curtis, F., Stockbridge, Mass.: Rosewood and Brass Marking Gauge. With Eagle Imprint. Early and Uncommon. Length: 8 Inches. *The Western Massachusetts Village of Stockbridge seems initially to have been an unlikely location for a toolmaker in that it is situated far from any major population centers. However, in the 1830's and 1840's, when this tool was likely made, the Connecticut river, which passed through Western Massachusetts, was a major artery for commerce. Little is known of Curtis, other than that he produced quality marking gauges and imprinted them with a stylized eagle touchmark in keeping with the spirit of those revolutionary times. This well made gauge is nicely inlaid with brass and ornamented with a hand-filed locking screw and decoratively turned adjustment screw. A nice gauge from an uncommon early maker.* (GOOD+) **$95.00**

X2-7. Stanley Rule & Level No. 61: Classic Beechwood Marking Gauge. Graduated in 16ths. Unused Condition. Length: 9 Inches. *This example of one of Stanley's mainline offerings is in top condition.* (FINE) **$15.00**

X2-8. Stanley Rule & Level No. 77: Rosewood Mortise and Marking Gauge. Sweetheart Trade Marked. Near New Condition. Length: 7 Inches. *All original finishes remain on this well preserved example of Stanley's extra-high quality rosewood mortise gauge. Only a slight sliver of rosewood detracts from its appearance, but not from its functionality.* (FINE) **$75.00**

X2-9. Unmarked: Mahogany Panel Marking Gauge. With Brass Facing. Rosewood Wear Strip. Length: 22 Inches. *This finely crafted mahogany panel gauge is fitted with an inlaid brass strip to protect the beam from the fixing screw. The head of the gauge has an inlay of rosewood to serve as a wear strip. A classic gauge in great condition.* (GOOD+) **$65.00**

X2-10. Kenney: "Kenney's Patent" Marking Gauge. Patented January 4, 1870. Complete and Excellent. Length: 9 Inches. *A perfectly preserved example of the Kenney patent of 1870. A brass beam, alternate rosewood and boxwood trammel heads and a precision adjust scribe make for one of the most complex tools ever devised. The trammel tips are professionally turned replacements that are identical in all respects to the original. An extremely rare gauge in top collector quality condition.* (GOOD+) **$585.00**

X2-11. Unmarked: Miniature Boxwood and Rosewood Marking Gauge. Chamfered Screw. Owner "W.H.M.". Length: 6 1/2 Inches. *Sometimes a tool is far more than just "an extension of the hand". Sometimes tools, such as that offered here, embody an extension of the soul of the maker. Painstakingly crafted from Brazilian rosewood and contrasting, yet complimentary, Turkish boxwood, this miniature mortise and marking gauge is topped with a carefully chamfered fixing screw that stands a lasting testimony to the skill of the maker. Tastefully imprinted with the initials "W.H.M.", this unpretentious yet spectacular tool captures the spirit of a long forgotten woodworker within the simple artistry of its form. Extra nice.* (FINE) **$115.00**

X2-12. Marples & Co., William, Sheffield: Rosewood Slitting Marking Gauge. Full Brass Face. Extra Crisp and Clean. Length: 9 Inches. *This classic slitting and marking gauge from respected English maker William Marples features a full brass wear plate on the face of the head. A very well made and thoroughly usable English tool.* (GOOD+) **$125.00**

X2-13. Stanley Rule & Level No. 265: Ungraduated Boxwood Marking Gauge. "Sweetheart" Trade Mark. Uncommon Type. Length: 8 1/2 Inches. *Stanley offered its principal Boxwood marking gauge in an ungraduated version for patternmakers and manual training shops. Apparently, few were sold. This uncommon example with the "Sweetheart" logo is in excellent condition and needs only a light cleaning. A collector's opportunity.* (GOOD+) **$95.00**

X2-14. Mc Master, T. J., Auburn, N. Y.: Beechwood Mortise and Marking Gauge. Early Imprint. With Slide Mechanism. Length: 8 Inches. *In addition to a full line of wooden planes, New York's prison planemakers, among whom Truman J. McMaster was numbered, produced a line of marking gauges. This one is boldly struck with the McMaster mark. It is in excellent condition, clean and very boldly struck.* (GOOD+) **$125.00**

X2-15. Unmarked: Rosewood and Walnut Marking Gauge. Classic Style. Excellent Condition. Length: 18 Inches. *The maker of this rosewood and mahogany panel marking gauge set out to make a beautiful tool and succeeded. Very pretty.* (GOOD+) **$55.00**

X2-16. Stanley Rule & Level No. 72: Unfaced Beech Marking Gauge. With Double Scribe. "Sweetheart" Trade Mark. Length: 8 Inches. *The Stanley No. 72 gauge was a poor man's version of the brass faced boxwood alternative. This one is clearly marked with the Sweetheart mark and in excellent condition. Very nice and clearly marked.* (GOOD+) **$55.00**

X2-17. Mathieson & Son, A., Glasgow: Rosewood and Brass Marking Gauge. Screw Adjust Scribe. Uncommon Maker. Length: 6 3/4 Inches. *One of the less common tools to be found with the Mathieson imprint, this brass-faced mortise gauge is in fine working order. Nice.* (GOOD+) **$175.00**

X2-18. Moulson Brothers, (England): Boxwood and Brass Slitting Gauge. Full Brass Facing. Screw Adjust Type. Length: 7 Inches. *This substantial gauge features a fully-faced head and a screw adjustment for the mortise slide. An uncommon boxwood gauge.* (GOOD) **$65.00**

X2-19. Stanley Rule & Level No. 73: Boxwood Marking Gauge. Rare "Stanley" Mark. Superb Condition. Length: 6 Inches. *Finding the No. 73 boxwood marking gauge with a "Stanley" mark, or even the number mark is almost impossible. This one has both and is in superb condition.* (FINE) **$225.00**

X2-20. Unmarked: Macassar Ebony Slitt Marking Gauge. Full Brass Face. Excellent Condition. Length: 9 1/2 Inches. *This fully brass faced slitting and marking gauge has been formed from a spectacular piece of Macassar Ebony. Very pretty.* (GOOD+) **$115.00**

X2-21. Unmarked: Boxwood Marking Gauge. With Wedge Lock. Golden Patina. Length: 6 Inches. *According to R.A. Salaman's "Dictionary of Woodworking Tools", this was known as a "grasshopper" marking gauge and was used for "..straight and circular marking over obstructions, e.g. over the top of a stair rail". This superb example has been formed from solid boxwood, which has achieved a bright, golden patina from age and use. The body of the tool has been decorated with a series of "starburst" patterns. Simply a beautiful tool.* (FINE) **$110.00**

X2-22. Unmarked: Special Purpose Marking Gauge. Nicely Chamfered. Unknown Function. Length: 7 1/2 Inches. *Try as they might, the experts here at the Donnelly Institute for Advance Tool Studies have been unable to fathom the function of this special function gauge. We're offering a free T Shirt and a hearty handshake to anyone who can fill us in. A most interesting marking gauge.* (GOOD+) **$45.00**

X2-23. Stanley Rule & Level No. 71: Double Beam Marking Gauge. Beech Head and Beam. Extra Crisp and Clean. Length: 8 1/2 Inches. *The original patent for this sliding gauge was issued in 1864. A nicely marked example of a mainstay of the Stanley line.* (FINE) **$125.00**

X2-24. Stanley Rule & Level (Unmarked) No. 85 1/2: Rosewood Panel Marking Gauge. Patented August 5, 1873. Near New Condition. Length: 21 Inches. *Stanley offered the No. 85 1/2 rosewood panel gauge for many years, beginning in the 1870's. Few examples are marked with the Stanley logo, however. This one does not have the Stanley name, but it is boldly struck with the August 5, 1873 patent date.* (FINE) **$145.00**

X2-25. Unmarked: Rosewood Head Marking Gauge. Solid Brass Stem. Near New Condition. Length: 7 1/2 Inches. *For sheer aesthetic appeal among marking gauges, it is difficult to best these brass-stemmed, solid brass faced gauges that were produced by the Sheffield toolmakers of the Nineteenth Century. This spectacular example features a spectacularly grained rosewood head and brass fittings that retain nearly all of their original lacquer finish. A spectacular tool for the shop or the collection.* (FINE) **$225.00**

X2-26. Scholl, C.: 4 Stem Patent Marking Gauge. Patented March 8, 1864. Rosewood Body, Arms. Length: 8 Inches. *Here's the 4 stem Scholl patent in mahogany with circular plates set into the working face as wear strips. A nice example of a rare gauge.* (GOOD) **$215.00**

X2-27. Chapin, H. (Unmarked): Solid Mahogany Marking Gauge. Circular Brass Inserts. Early and Excellent. Length: 9 Inches. *Existing historical evidence shows that the H. Chapin Company offered a full line of mortise and marking gauges. Most examples, however, were not imprinted with the Chapin name. This example, formed from solid mahogany, is fitted with the distinctive circular inserts that make these tools immediately identifiable to knowledgeable collectors.* (GOOD+) **$65.00**

X2-28. Unmarked: Precision Woodwork Marking Gauge. With Screw Shaft. Locking Ring. Length: 7 Inches. *The idea behind this specialty gauge was that it could be screwed into place and then locked into place by the companion locking "nut". Never seen another.* (GOOD+) **$45.00**

X2-29. Stanley Rule & Level No. 77: Rosewood Mortise and Marking Gauge. Ca. 1910. Near New Condition. Length: 7 Inches. *A perfectly preserved example of Stanley's mainstay mortise gauge. No apologies.* (FINE) **$85.00**

X2-30. Fenton & Marsden, Sheffield (England) No. 970: Rare "Registered" Marking Gauge. Screw Adjust Head. With Embossed Button. Length: 9 Inches. *Unlike anything that preceded it or followed, the Fenton & Marsden "Registered" gauge features a brass shaft fitted with a precision adjustment mechanism and an ebony head decorated with an elaborately embossed button. An extremely rare and desirable mortise gauge.* (GOOD+) **$675.00**

X2-31. Dunbar, D.: Early Center Gauge Gauge. Ebony and Mahogany. Dated "1856". Length: 11 Inches. *Comprised of a mahogany head into which is precisely dovetailed a rule of Gabon ebony, this centering gauge is imprinted with the mark of the maker, a forgotten D. Dunbar, and dated "1856". A classic handmade tool.* (FINE) **$110.00**

X2-32. Stanley Rule & Level No. 73: Boxwood Marking Gauge. Rare "Stanley" Mark. Superb Condition. Length: 6 Inches. *Finding the No. 73 boxwood marking gauge with a "Stanley" mark, or even the number mark is almost impossible. This one has both and is in superb condition.*(FINE) **$165.00**

X2-33. Star Tool Company: Cam-Lock Mortise Marking Gauge. Patented April 21, 1868. Rosewood and Brass. Length: 8 Inches. *Much less common than the standard non-mortise scribe equipped version also offered by this maker, this gauge features an adjustable mortise scribe. The head is locked into place by twisting it against the cam-shaped beam. A rare patented marking gauge.* (GOOD+) **$345.00**

X2-34. Stanley Rule & Level No. 74: Double Beam Marking Gauge. Boxwood Body and Beam. Full Brass Face. Length: 8 Inches. *Here's a good example of Stanley's double beam mortise gauge with full brass facing. A tough one to find.* (GOOD+) **$185.00**

X2-35. Unmarked: English Rosewood Marking Gauge. Inlaid Brass Trim. Near New Condition. Length: 8 Inches. *This classic English mortise gauge looks almost too good to use, and it appears that the previous owner may have felt that way as well. Absolutely perfect.* (FINE) **$115.00**

X2-36. Unmarked: Pair Of Early Marking Gauges. From Single Chest. Hand Filed Screws. Length: 8 1/2 Inches. *These hand made marking gauges have a very early appearance that is emphasized by their dramatic hand filed fixing screws. The combination of woodwork and metalwork, particularly the presence of a central, threaded screw in the mortise gauge indicate that these tools were fashioned by a craftsman with considerable skill and versatility.* (GOOD+) **$85.00**

X2-37. Unmarked No. 18: Classic Veneer Gauge. With Globular Adjust. Appears Manufactured. Length: 22 1/2 Inches. *This spectacular veneer slitting and marking gauge is imprinted only with the number "18" designation. A distinctive globular fixing screw adds character to this extremely well preserved woodworking tool.* (FINE) **$115.00**

X2-38. Unmarked: Brazilian Rosewood Slitting Gauge. With Boxwood Wedges. A Showpiece. Length: 16 Inches. *This spectacular slitting gauge was crafted long ago from the complimentary, but contrasting materials of Brazilian Rosewood and Turkish Boxwood. A spectacularly beautiful tool.* (FINE) **$225.00**

X2-39. Scholl, C.: 4 Stem Patent Marking Gauge. Patented March 8, 1864. Rosewood Body, Arms. Length: 8 Inches. *Here's the 4 stem Scholl patent in mahogany with circular plates set into the working face as wear strips. A great example of a rare gauge. Nearly new.* (FINE) **$525.00**

X2-40. Unmarked: English Rosewood Marking Gauge. Inlaid Brass Trim. Extra Crisp and Clean. Length: 8 Inches. *The presence of the extra long original scribes on this adjustable mortise and marking gauge is strong evidence that is was very little used. A great gauge.* (FINE) **$85.00**

X2-41. Lyon & Co., D.M., Newark, N.J.: Rosewood and Brass Marking Gauge. Ca. 1850's. Excellent Condition. Length: 8 Inches. *The D.M. Lyon Company was part of the dynamic pre-Civil War hand tool industry of Newark, New Jersey that has been so well documented in Alexander Farnham's books on New Jersey tools.* (GOOD+) **$65.00**

X2-42. Unmarked: Ebony and Brass Marking Gauge. Full Brass Face. Superb Condition. Length: 7 Inches. *This mortise gauge can be precisely adjusted by using a turnscrew in the end of the handle. The fully brass faced head is solid ebony. Magnificent.* (GOOD+) **$145.00**

X2-43. Star Tool Company: Cam Lock Rosewood Marking Gauge. Patented April 21, 1868. Early And Excellent. Length: 8 1/2 Inches. *A well marked and well preserved example of the cam-lock marking gauge from the Star Tool Company of Middletown, Connecticut A good one.* (GOOD+) **$185.00**

X2-44. Stanley Rule & Level No. 98: Double Mortise and Marking Gauge. "Old English" Castin. Near New Condition. Length: 7 Inches. *This clean and well preserved example of Stanley's double beam, cast iron gauge features the script logo that was in use ca. 1907-1915. A tough gauge to find, especially in this condition.* (FINE) **$145.00**

X2-45. Johnson, W., Newark, New Jersey: Solid Boxwood Marking Gauge. Graduated Beam. Scarce and Excellent. Length: 8 Inches. *The beam of this boxwood classic has been graduated with measurements in 1/16" increments. A bold boxwood gauge from a top New Jersey maker.* (GOOD+) **$65.00**

Group Y2

Y2-1. North Bros. Mfg. Co. No. 3400: Offset Ratchet Screwdriver. With Slotted Tip. Extra Crisp and Clean. Length: 3 3/4 Inches. *These were designed for those constricted spaces designed by malevolent engineers as a boon to the specialty tool design market and as a curse to the home handyman. This one is in excellent condition. A rare screwdriver.* (FINE) **$25.00**

Y2-2. North Bros. Mfg. Co. No. 3800: Offset Ratchet Screwdriver. With Slotted Tip. Uncommon Type. Length: 4 1/2 Inches. *The No. 3800 offset ratchet screwdriver is distinguished from its cousin, the No. 3400, by being exactly 3/4" longer and having slightly larger tips.* (FINE) **$45.00**

Y2-3. North Bros. Mfg. Co., Philadelphia Penn. No. 90: "Yankee" Slotted Screwdriver. 2" Blade. Near New Condition. Length: 14 Inches. *The "Yankee" screwdriver featured a lacqured hardwood handle and a steel ferrule with a knurled edge to facilitate turning. Many believe that these were the finest screwdrivers ever produced. Mint.* (FINE) **$25.00**

Y2-4. Stanley Tools No. 130 A: Spiral Ratchet Screwdriver. "Yankee" Trademark. New Condition, Original Box. Length: 18 Inches. *These automatic screwdrivers were a standard tool in many trades until the advent of the electric screwdriver. They have quickly made the transition from obsolescence to collectibility. New and in the box.* (FINE) **$45.00**

Y2-5. Millers Falls Company No. 1: Ratchet Screwdriver. 1 Original Blade. Rosewood Handle. Length: 15 Inches. *This was the first ratcheting screwdriver produced by the Millers Falls Company. A lever mechanism could be activated by the thumb to change the direction of the ratchet. Complete with one original blade. Early and excellent.* (GOOD+) **$85.00**

Y2-6. North Bros Mfg. Co., Philadelphia No. 100: Boxed Set Or 3 Screwdrivers. Black Metal Finish. New Condition, Original Box. Length: 12 Inches. *Nearly all original finishes remain on the screwdrivers in this boxed set from the North Brothers Company of Philadelphia. The absence of nickel plating indicates that these were produced in the early days of the Second World War.* (FINE) **$225.00**

Y2-7. Booth & Son, John, Philadelphia Penn.: Massive Cabinet Screwdriver. 24" Blade. Early and Unusual. Length: 34 1/2 Inches. *This is by far the largest screwdriver we have encountered from this Philadelphia area toolmaker and dealer. A good one.* (GOOD) **$55.00**

Y2-8. Millers Falls Company No. 1440: Pocket Ratchet Screwdriver. 1 1/2" Blade. Unused Condition. Length: 5 Inches. *Finding ratchet screwdrivers in this condition has become an increasingly difficult task. This one is as good as they get. Perfect.* (FINE) **$55.00**

Y2-9. Billings & Spencer Co., Hartford: Billings' Patent Screwdriver. Patented March 15, 1892. Multiple Blades. Length: 4 Inches. *The Billings patent screwdriver featured four retractable blades, any one of which could be used while the others were folded away. Here's an especially clean example. Nice.* (FINE) **$85.00**

Y2-10. Johnson, Iver, Fitchburg, Mass.: Loop Handle Screwdriver. With Embossed Mark. Rare and Excellent. Length: 8 Inches. *This most unusual screwdriver has the "Iver Johnson" name forged into the body of the tool. Nearly all original nickel plating remains on this very unusual screwdriver.* (GOOD+) **$85.00**

Y2-11. Millers Falls Company No. 1440: Pocket Ratchet Screwdriver. 1 1/2" Blade. New Condition, Original Box. Length: 5 Inches. *The presence of the original pasteboard box has kept this diminutive ratchet screwdriver in pristine condition. Perfect.* (FINE) **$85.00**

Y2-12. North Bros. Mfg. Co., Philadelphia Penn. No. 80: Screw Eye Driver Screwdriver. Smallest Size. Rare and Excellent. Length: 5 1/2 Inches. *Among the least common and most sought-after tools of the North Brothers Tool Company are those that were designed to perform highly specialized functions. Near the top of the list of those tools is this "screw eye driver", which was designed for driving cup hooks and eyes. Only the second example we have ever offered. Rare.* (GOOD+) **$165.00**

Y2-13. Unmarked: Early Hand Forged Screwdriver. Forged From File. Distinctive Form. Length: 15 Inches. *The creator of this 19th Century classic employed many hours of filework to fashion this graphic pattern. Bold and beautiful.* (GOOD+) **$85.00**

Y2-14. Millers Falls Company No. 1440: Pocket Ratchet Screwdriver. 1 1/2" Blade. Unused Condition. Length: 5 Inches. *No apologies for this brand new ratcheting screwdriver from top quality maker Millers Falls Tool Company. Mint.* (FINE) **$55.00**

Y2-15. Irwin: "Perfect Handle" Screwdriver. Square Shank Blade. Apparently Unused. Length: 9 1/2 Inches. *The inlaid wood handle style was introduced by the H.D. Smith Company of Plantsville, Connecticut, but was imitated by many others for the simple reason that it was a great idea. This fifty year old example bears the name of the Irwin Auger Bit Company. Brand New.* (FINE) **$45.00**

Y2-16. Booth & Mills, Philadelphia, Penn.: Early Cabinet Screwdriver. N.Y. and Phildelphia Institutes. Rare and Extra Nice. Length: 8 1/4 Inches. *This early offering from Philadelphia's Booth & Mills Company bears their trademark "New York and Philadelphia Institutes" imprint on the handle. An uncommon early screwdriver.* (GOOD+) **$65.00**

Y2-17. Unmarked: Early Hand-Forged Screwdriver. Forged From File. Artistic Design. Length: 14 Inches. *Artfully executed from a used-up file, this is one of the nicer file-forged tools we have offered. A good one.* (GOOD+) **$155.00**

Y2-18. Unmarked: Early Hand Forged Screwdriver. Serpentine Pattern. Excellent Patina. Length: 12 Inches. *An early craftsman crafted this visually appealing screwdriver with an undulating pattern that is most pleasing to the eye. Early and unusual.* (GOOD) **$45.00**

Y2-19. Millers Falls Company No. 1440: Pocket Ratchet Screwdriver. 1 1/2" Blade. Unused Condition. Length: 5 Inches. *This pocket sized ratcheting screwdriver has never been used. Mint.* (FINE) **$55.00**

Y2-20. North Bros Mfg. Co., Philadelphia No. 95: "Yankee" Slotted Screwdrivers. 2 1/2", 3 1/2" and 5". Near New Condition. Length: 8 1/4 Inches. *Each of these classic "Yankee" screwdrivers is in nearly new condition. A great set of what many believe to be the finest screwdrivers ever produced.* (FINE) **$85.00**

Y2-21. Bowser & Co., S.F., Ft. Wayne, Indiana : Spiral Ratchet Screwdriver. Brass Fittings. Excellent Patina. Length: 13 1/2 Inches. *An excellent example of the Bowser patent screwdriver in collector-quality condition.* (GOOD+) **$115.00**

Y2-22. Stanley Rule & Level: "Hurwood" Slotted Screwdriver. "Sweetheart" Trademark. Rare Size and Excellent. Length: 4 Inches. *We don't have much information about this early automotive tool maker. Observation of the few tools that we have encountered indicates that they were a producer of extremely high quality tools.* (GOOD+) **$35.00**

Y2-23. Unmarked: Early Screwdriver. Turned Ivory Handle. Rare and Excellent. Length: 4 Inches. *Alas, we have nothing to report of the history of this extraordinary screwdriver, as there must be a very interesting story in its background. Capped with a mahogany pad and ornamented with an ivory shaft buttressed by a pair of brass ferrules, this tool was unquestionably made to be a showpiece. If only tools could talk...Exceptional.* (GOOD+) **$445.00**

Y2-24. Millers Falls Company No. 909-12: Hardwood Handle Screwdriver. 12" Blade. Unused Condition. Length: 19 Inches. *This Millers Falls screwdriver is in unused condition. A high quality tool.* (FINE) **$25.00**

Y2-25. Unmarked: Massive Early Screwdriver. Decorative Handle. Distinctive Form. Length: 24 Inches. *The creator of this graphic early screwdriver gave it more than just a touch of character by turning the handle on a lather. The shaft and tip have seen some wear, but this tool is otherwise in excellent condition.* (GOOD+) **$25.00**

Y2-26. N.Y. Manufacturers Co., New York: "Electric" Spiral Screwdriver. Patented November 24, 1874. Rare and Excellent. Length: 11 1/2 Inches. *There is no evidence that this tool was ever fitted with an extension cord or batteries, so we believe that we are safe in assuming that the "Electric" designation has to do with the 19th Century meaning of the term. The brass shaft is clearly marked with the maker's name and patent date. A rare and extremely early patent ratchet screwdriver.* (GOOD+) **$115.00**

Y2-27. North Bros Mfg. Co., Philadelphia. No. 35 A: Spiral Ratchet Screwdriver. With 1 Original Bit. Unused Condition. Length: 12 Inches. *The tools produced by the North Brothers Tool Company were distinguished by having an exceptionally high degree of finish. This unused example demonstrates their very best work. Perfect.* (FINE) **$35.00**

Y2-28. Decatur Coffin Co., Decatur, Illinois. Patented Spiral Ratchet Screwdriver. Patented October 7, 1884. Unused Condition. Length: 11 Inches. *I'll repeat the story only if you don't quote me as the source: Legend has it that these spiral screwdrivers only turn screws in one direction because they were marketed by the Decatur Coffin Company and you only turn screws in one direction when dealing with coffin lids.* (FINE) **$145.00**

Y2-29. Vlchek Tool Co., The: Lacquered Hdle. Screwdriver. Slotted Style. Uncommon Type. Length: 9 Inches. *We don't have much information about this early automotive tool maker. Observation of the few tools that we have encountered indicates that they were a producer of extremely high quality tools.* (GOOD+) **$10.00**

Y2-30. Unmarked: Early Carved Handle Screwdriver. With Steel Ferrule. Rosewood Handle. Length: 11 1/4 Inches. *The handle of this screwdriver has been carved with an interesting pattern by a woodworker of bygone days. Most unusual.* (GOOD+) **$35.00**

Y2-31. Millers Falls Company No. 852: 10" Blade Screwdriver. "Permaloid" Handle. Unused Condition. Length: 16 1/2 Inches. *Another nice screwdriver with the early plastic handle. Pristine.* (FINE) **$15.00**

Y2-32. Millers Falls Company No. 63: Reversible Ratchet Screwdriver. 3" Blade. Unused Condition. Length: 8 Inches. *The Millers Falls Company made a mid-1920's foray into the ratchet screwdriver market and produced some excellent tools. This pristine example appears never to have been used. Choice.* (FINE) **$35.00**

Y2-33. Millers Falls Company No. 41: Spiral Ratchet Screwdriver. Patented March 21, 1893. Early and Excellent. Length: 9 Inches. *Millers Falls produced a spiral ratchet screwdriver before the arrival on the scene of the North Brothers Tool Company, but the M.F. tool was no match for the North Brothers "Yankee" line. Consequently, these early offerings are quite scarce. This on is in top condition.* (FINE) **$65.00**

Y2-34. Smith & Co., H.D., Plantsville, Conn: "Perfect Handle" Screwdriver. 9" Length. "Triple Blade". Length: 9 Inches. *These were designed for use in constricted areas by placing additional tips at right angles to the main blade and at right angles to each other. They usually broke off around the first time they were used. These didn't. A rare screwdriver, especially in this condition.* (FINE) **$175.00**

Y2-35. Stanley Rule & Level No. 1001: "100 Plus" Screwdriver. 3" Blade. "Bell System" Mark. Length: 8 Inches. *Ma Bell purchased only the highest quality tools for her installers. They thanked her by taking them home in their lunch boxes. Here's a most uncommon Stanley "100 Plus" screwdriver that is also imprinted with the "Bell System" mark.* (GOOD) **$35.00**

Y2-36. Smith & Co., H.D., Plantsville, Conn: 5" "Perfect Handle" Screwdriver. For Slotted Screws. Excellent Condition. Length: 10 Inches. *For a look at what the tools of the H.D. Smith Company's "Perfect Handle" line looked like as they rolled off the assembly line, take a look at this perfectly preserved screwdriver. Scarce and nearly new.* (FINE) **$55.00**

Y2-37. Unmarked: Early Patent Spiral Screwdriver. Patented April 16, 1889. Rare and Perfect. Length: 10 1/2 Inches. *We are not aware of the patentee or the manufacturer of this early screwdriver, which is of a design we have not previously encountered. Rare and clearly marked.* (GOOD+) **$135.00**

Y2-38. Reid, A. H., Philadelphia Penn.: Patent Archimedian Screwdriver. Patented December12,1882. Cocobolo Head. Length: 15 Inches. *An excellent example of the Reid patent push screwdriver/brace. A nicely turned head of tropical hardwood provides a contrast to the nickeled metal. A good one.* (GOOD+) **$85.00**

Y2-39. Smith & Co., H.D., Plantsville, Conn No. 6: "Perfect Handle" Screwdriver. With Wing Extensions. Rare and Excellent. Length: 11 1/2 Inches. *The manufacturing enterprise of the H.D. Smith & company of Plantsville, Connecticut, produced an extremely well made line of tools under the "Perfect Handle" trademark. This winged handle screwdriver is boldly struck with their imprint.* (GOOD+) **$45.00**

Y2-40. Thayer, W.E.: Early Patent Ratchet Screwdriver. Patented December 25, 1883. Rosewood Handle. Length: 9 1/2 Inches. *One of the hardest to find of all early patent screwdrivers, this example of the 1883 patent of W.E. Thayer includes one original cutter. A rare and extremely early patented screwdriver.* (GOOD) **$75.00**

Y2-41. Stanley Rule & Level No. 2701/2702: No. 1 and 2 Phillips Screwdrivers. Uncommon Type. Excellent Condition. Length: 9 Inches. *Nearly all of the original lacquer finish remains on the handles of these uncommon Stanley phillips head screwdrivers. A pretty pair.* (GOOD+) **$55.00**

Y2-42. Unmarked: Classic Hand Forged Screwdriver. With "Basket" Handle. Excellent Patina. Length: 10 1/2 Inches. *An innovative blacksmith of days past produced this most unusual screwdriver by heating and then twisting a series of wire rods. The lower portion was hammered into a blade and the tip was upset into a ball shaped finial. Interesting and unusual.* (GOOD+) **$145.00**

Y2-43. Smith & Co., H.D., Plantsville, Conn: "Perfect Handle" Screwdriver. "Triple Lever". Rare And Excellent. Length: 9 Inches. *The handles can move into any position to provide leverage or snap tightly together in the form of a standard screwdriver. This one is in excellent condition, clean and clearly marked.* (GOOD+) **$145.00**

Y2-44. Unmarked: Early Hand Forged Screwdriver. Distinctive Form. Superb Patina. Length: 21 Inches. *Preserved through perhaps 150 years from exposure to the elements, this artfully forged screwdriver was intended from the day it was made to be something very special. It still is. Nicely patinated, perfectly preserved and highly recommended.* (GOOD+) **$115.00**

Y2-45. Smith & Co., H.D., Plantsville, Conn: "Perfect Handle" Screwdriver. "Triple Lever". Uncommon Type. Length: 9 Inches. *These would have come in very handy when there was a need for extra torque to persuade a reluctant fastener. The fact that there were other, less expensive ways of coping with the same problem may account for the rarity of these tools today. A good one.* (GOOD) **$85.00**

Group Z2

Z2-1. Stanley Rule & Level No. 278: Rabbet and Filletster Plane. Ca. 1915. New Condition, Original Box. Length: 7 Inches. *A complete and perfect No. 278 rabbet and filletster in a clean sound box. The box is sound and the label is 85% complete. A rare tool in top collectible condition.* (FINE) **$785.00**

Z2-2. Stanley Rule & Level No. 9 1/2: Adjustable Throat Plane. "Sweetheart' Trademark. New Condition, Original Box. Length: 6 Inches. *Only a dollop of orange paint on the front knob detracts from this otherwise excellent block plane in its original box. A copy of the original Stanley advertising brochure is included.* (FINE) **$95.00**

Z2-3. Stanley Rule & Level No. 190: Cast Iron Rabbet Plane. Original Decal. New Condition, Original Box. Length: 10 1/2 Inches. *Nearly all of the original decal remains on this pristine Stanley rabbet plane. Perfect.* (FINE) **$165.00**

Z2-4. Stanley Rule & Level No. 9 1/4: Cast Iron Block Plane. Non-Adjustable Throat. Fine Condition, Original Box. Length: 6 Inches. *The No. 9 1/4 block plane was the functional equivalent of the No. 9 1/2, with the exception of the absence of a throat adjustment mechanism. The presence of the original box has kept this one in top shape.* (FINE) **$85.00**

Z2-5. Stanley Rule & Level No. 50: Combination Beading Plane. With All Original Cutters. New Condition, Original Box. Length: 8 Inches. *This English-manufactured version of Stanley's No. 50 light plow and rabbeting plane comes complete with its original complement of rabbeting and beading cutters and instruction book. A great plane to use.* (FINE) **$165.00**

Z2-6. Stanley Rule & Level No. 65: Low Angle Block Plane. "Sweetheart" Trademark. New Condition, Original Box. Length: 7 Inches. *Here's a crispy clean example of Stanley's best wide, low-angle block plane. All of the shiny nickel plating remains on the knuckle joint cap. New in the original box.* (FINE) **$215.00**

Z2-7. Stanley Rule & Level No. 4: 9" Smoothing Plane. Orange Infill Cap. New Condition, Original Box. Length: 9 Inches. *All original finishes remain on this perfectly preserved Stanley No. 4 smooth plane. Mint in the box.* (FINE) **$185.00**

Z2-8. Stanley Rule & Level No. 49: Swing Fence Match Plane. Cuts 3/16" Groove. New Condition, Original Box. Length: 10 Inches. *This absolutely brand new tongue and groove plane has been protected through the years by the presence of its original box. The box has some tape on the corners, but is otherwise excellent. Extra nice.* (FINE) **$365.00**

Z2-9. Stanley Rule & Level No. 40: Rosewood Handle Scrub Plane. Ca. 1930's. New Condition, Original Box. Length: 9 1/2 Inches. *Stanley's scrub plane was one of those tools that was purchased when it was needed. The box was incidental and was very likely discarded immediately. We have offered only a very few boxed examples of the No. 40 in the past 10 years. This pristine example, complete in a well preserved box is as good as we have seen. Perfect.* (FINE) **$255.00**

Z2-10. Stanley Rule & Level No. 102: Fixed Angle Block Plane. Original Price Imprint. Fine Condition, Original Box. Length: 5 1/2 Inches. *The original price imprint from a hardware store is visible on the cap of this small Stanley block plane. New and in the box.* (FINE) **$65.00**

Z2-11. Stanley Rule & Level No. 90: Bullnose Rabbet Plane. "Made In Usa". New Condition, Original Box. Length: 4 Inches. *This brand new No. 90 bullnose rabbet plane includes its original box and a copy of the Stanley pamphlet "How to Use Special Purpose Planes".* (FINE) **$185.00**

Z2-12. Stanley Rule & Level No. 82: Adjustable Head Scraper. Maroon Handles. New Condition, Original Box. Length: 12 Inches. *All original finishes remain on this adjustable scraper. The box has weathered a bit, but is intact.* (GOOD+) **$55.00**

Z2-13. Stanley Rule & Level No. 78: Duplex Rabbet, Fillet Plane. With Advertising. New Condition, Original Box. Length: 10 Inches. *A great early example of the popular No. 78 rabbet and filletster plane in absolutely pristine condition it its original box. As advanced collectors know very well, and woodworkers would be well advised to learn, tools found in their original boxes are almost invariably in perfectly preserved condition. Choice.* (FINE) **$115.00**

Z2-14. Stanley Rule & Level No. 67: Universal Spoke Shave. Complete and Excellent New Condition, Original Box. Length: 9 1/2 Inches. *A clean and complete (including the seldom seen edge guide) example of Stanley's "Universal" rosewood handled spokeshave. Picture perfect in its original pasteboard box.* (FINE) **$265.00**

Z2-15. Stanley Rule & Level No. OH 20: "Two Tone" Plane. Yellow and Black. New Condition, Original Box. Length: 6 1/2 Inches. *Stanley had the good fortune to tool up for production of the "Two Tone" line about six months before the entire country tooled up to produce arms and war materials for a sustained period. A perfect example of a tool that was casually swept aside by the winds of war. A rare plane in superb condition.* (FINE) **$195.00**

Z2-16. Stanley Rule & Level No. 605: "Bedrock" Jack Plane. Ca. 1930's. New Condition, Original Box. Length: 14 Inches. *We have had the privilege of offering less than a handful of Stanley's "Bedrock" planes in their original red-labeled boxes. This example of the No. 5 size is a good as they get. The box has seen some light wear, but the label is intact and the tool is in pristine condition. Top shelf.* (FINE) **$975.00**

Z2-17. Stanley Rule & Level No. OH 4: "Two Tone" Metallic Plane. Red and Grey. New Condition, Original Box. Length: 9 Inches. *This "Two Tone" plane from Stanley is in new condition in its original box, which has split slightly at the corners, but could be easily repaired.* (FINE) **$225.00**

Z2-18. Stanley Rule & Level No. 1213: "Defiance" Smooth Plane. Ca. 1929-1941. Original Box. Length: 9 1/2 Inches. *This classic "Defiance" plane is in new condition in its original box, which has seen some wear but is complete.* (GOOD+) **$115.00**

Z2-19. Stanley Rule & Level (Canada) No. 45: Patent Combination Plane. "Sweetheart" Trademark. New Condition, Original Box. Length: 11 Inches. *Both the box and the plane are in absolutely perfect condition on this classic No. 45 combination plane. As nice an example as we have ever offered. Mint.* (FINE) **$575.00**

Z2-20. Stanley Rule & Level No. 192: Cast Iron Rabbet Plane. "Sweetheart" Trademark. New Condition, Original Box. Length: 10 1/2 Inches. The No. 192 was the narrowest size of the Stanley rabbet plane series. This one is in new condition in its original box. Nearly all of the original decal remains. Mint. (FINE) **$245.00**

Z2-21. Stanley Rule & Level No. 1247: "Defiance" Block Plane. With "Defiance" Decal. New Condition, Original Box. Length: 7 Inches. *Stanley's "Defiance" line was meant to compete with the mail order companies and hardware dealers who where offering tools at a grade below professional specifications. This example of the No. 1247 block plane is in the same condition as it was when new. Perfect.* (FINE) **$85.00**

Z2-22. Stanley Rule & Level No. 9 1/2: Adjustable Throat Plane. With Precision Adjust. New Condition, Original Box. Length: 6 Inches. *Fitted with an adjustable throat mechanism as well as independent lateral adjustment and depth-of-cut features, the No. 9 1/2 block plane was a mainstay of the Stanley line for many years. This one is in top condition thanks to the presence of the protective original box.* (FINE) **$115.00**

Z2-23. Stanley Rule & Level No. 171: Door Trim Router Plane. Complete with 3 Cutters. New Condition, Original Box. Length: 11 Inches. *Those who have made it their vocation to acquire Stanley tools in new condition in their original boxes are aware of an essential fact: The likelihood of a tool being found in its original box is inversely proportional to the degree of difficulty in returning that tool to the box after it is first assembled. Block planes are often found with their original carton for the simple reason that it made a handy storage place. Accordingly, except in the case of the rarest planes, block planes in the box do not command much of a premium. On the other hand, the tool offered here is close to the top of the list of collectible "in the box" Stanley tools. Not only is it impossible to get it back in the box without fully disassembling it, it is nearly impossible to get it back in the box after it is completely taken apart. The small parts, including the instruction and the two additional cutting irons were consequently very quickly lost as the plane deteriorated in quality for that want of protection. This was true in most cases, but not all. We offer an exceptionally well preserved example complete with all cutters and instructions in its original box with full paper label. Mint and boxed, and offered without apology.* (FINE) **$1,395.00**

Z2-24. Stanley Rule & Level No. 95: Edge Trimming Plane. Ca. 1930's. New Condition, Original Box. Length: 6 1/2 Inches. *If you're looking for the No. 95 edge trim block plane, stop here. This one retains all of its original finishes and is in essentially unused condition in the original box.* (FINE) **$345.00**

Z2-25. Stanley Rule & Level No. 75: Bullnose Rabbet Plane. "Sweetheart" Trademark. New Condition, Original Box. Length: 4 1/2 Inches. *This pristine example of Stanley's smallest "bullnose" plane is imprinted with the desirable "Sweetheart" logo. Nice.* (FINE) **$85.00**

Z2-26. Stanley Rule & Level No. 5: Rosewood Handle Jack Plane. Crisp and Clean. Fine Condition Original Box. Length: 14 Inches. *All of the shiny black japan finish remains on this excellent rosewood handled jack plane. A great example.* (FINE) **$185.00**

Z2-27. Stanley Rule & Level No. OH 4: "Two Tone" Metallic Plane. Maroon and Yellow. New Condition, Original Box. Length: 9 Inches. *A complete and undamaged original box has protected this scarce maroon and yellow "Two Tone" plane through its more than 60 years of existence. Mint.* (FINE) **$225.00**

Z2-28. Stanley Rule & Level No. 203: Adjustable Block Plane. Rosewood Knob. New Condition, Original Box. Length: 5 Inches. *Essentially a scaled-down version of the No. 220, the No. 203 was marketed to manual training schools. Here's an example of this elusive plane in top collector-quality condition in its original box.* (FINE) **$215.00**

Z2-29. Stanley Rule & Level No. 61: Low Angle Block Plane. Rare, Early Type. Excellent Condition, Original Box. Length: 6 Inches. *The No. 61 featured a non-adjustable throat and a nickel plated cap. Here's an excellent example with 95% of the original finishes, complete in its original box. A rare "in the box" tool.* (GOOD+) **$475.00**

Z2-30. Stanley Rule & Level No. 66: Universal Hand Beader. Shiny Nickel Plating. Original Box. Length: 12 Inches. *This complete example of Stanley's highly-desirable scratch beader is complete with the both fences and five double-ended cutters in its original box. Extra crisp and clean.* (FINE) **$265.00**

Z2-31. Stanley Rule & Level No. 100: Squirrel Tail Block Plane. "Sweetheart" Trademark. New Condition, Original Box. Length: 4 Inches. *The working partner of the 101 1/2, this version has the squirrel tail handle, but with a flat sole. A superb example of a most underrated plane in new condition in its original box.* (FINE) **$265.00**

Z2-32. Stanley Rule & Level No. 4: 9" Smoothing Plane. Unused Condition. New Condition, Original Box. Length: 9 Inches. *This fifty year old smooth plane appears never to have been used. An excellent example.* (FINE) **$155.00**

Z2-33. Stanley Rule & Level No. 220: Adjustable Block Plane. Hardwood Knob. Fine Condition, Original Box. Length: 7 Inches. *A clean and essentially unused example of Stanley's basic screw-adjust block plane in its original box. The box is missing one side, but the plane is perfect. Nice.* (GOOD+) **$55.00**

Z2-34. Stanley Rule & Level No. 10: Bench Rabbet Plane. "Made In Canada". New Condition, Original Box. Length: 13 Inches. *Both the cutting iron and the label of this 1920's era No. 10 rabbet plane are marked with the imprint of Stanley's Canadian arm, The Roxton Pond Tool Company of Roxton Pond, Quebec. A perfectly preserved Stanley tool in an uncommon picture box.* (FINE) **$645.00**

Z2-35. Stanley Rule & Level No. 4: Method 1 A Package Plane. Stock No. 41P1452. Unopened Box. Length: 10 Inches. *This most unusual Stanley plane, which must, most certainly, have been produced for military use, is covered with heavily waxed paper and has never been opened. We do know that there is a No. 4 plane inside, but little else about this most unusual Stanley "in the box" item. Very, very different.* (FINE) **$395.00**

Z2-36. Stanley Rule & Level No. 78: Duplex Rabbet, Fillet Plane. With Advertising. New Condition, Original Box. Length: 10 Inches. *This perfectly preserved Stanley duplex rabbet plane is in new condition in its original box. Perfect.* (FINE) **$135.00**

Z2-37. Stanley Rule & Level No. 48: Tongue And Groove Plane. "Sweetheart" Trademark. New Condition, Original Box. Length: 9 Inches. *A swinging fence determines whether the tongue cutter or the groove cutter is in use on this innovative Stanley plane. New in the original box.* (FINE) **$345.00**

Z2-38. Stanley Rule & Level No. 194: Fibre Board Beveling Plane. With Adjustable Fence. New Condition, Original Box. Length: 8 1/2 Inches. *One of the first to enter the line of fibre board tools that was uniquely the province of Stanley Tools, this beveling plane was also one of the last to leave. This one is perfectly preserved in top collector-quality condition in its original box. Mint.* (FINE) **$255.00**

Z2-39. Stanley Rule & Level No. 98: Side Rabbet Plane. With Depth Stop. New Condition, Original Box. Length: 5 Inches. *The box on this No. 98 side rabbet plane shows a bit of wear, but the plane, which includes the desirable depth stop feature, is in brand new condition.* (FINE) **$255.00**

Z2-40. Stanley Rule & Level No. 45: Combination Plane. "Sweetheart" Trademark. Original Box. Length: 12 Inches. *This superb example of Stanley's No. 45 combination has been sheltered from the elements by its original pasteboard box. A great working tool that is complete with all original parts and the original instruction manual and is in perfect working order. Nice.* (FINE) **$395.00**

Z2-41. Stanley Rule and Level No. 2: 7" Smooth Plane. High Knob. New Condition, Original Box. Length: 7 Inches. *For the advanced collector of manufactured tools, merely having "one of each" is not enough. The very best collections are distinguished by tools of exceptional quality, rarity and, above all else by being in exceptionally well-preserved condition. While some objects are so rare that the likelihood of finding another is remote and inclusion of a less than perfect example may be warranted, most seasoned collectors will wait for a tool of very high quality rather than become trapped by constantly having to "upgrade" one's collection. Tools of collector-quality condition are defined here as those that are in very nearly the same condition as they were when they were first offered for sale following their manufacture. The highest level of tools then, are those that are in all respects the same as they were when they were new. It necessarily follows that even a tool in new condition is subject to upgrade when an example in the original box is found. In the case of the No. 2 Stanley plane offered here, no upgrade will likely be necessary. The "Sweetheart" trademark plane with nickel plated, orange-infill is in new condition in a very well preserved box. Absolutely top shelf. A good one.* (FINE) **$975.00**

Z2-42. Stanley Rule & Level No. 118: Low Angle Block Plane. Solid Steel Body. New Condition, Original Box. Length: 6 Inches. *Here's a crispy-clean example of the No. 118 block plane in new condition in the original box. A nice example of a plane that is becoming increasingly difficult to find.* (FINE) **$95.00**

Z2-43. Stanley Rule & Level No. 118: Low Angle Block Plane. Solid Steel Body. New Condition, Original Box. Length: 6 Inches. *Here's a crispy-clean example of the No. 118 block plane in new condition in the original box. A nice example of a plane that is becoming increasingly difficult to find.* (FINE) **$95.00**

Z2-44. Stanley Rule & Level No. 83: Adjustable Scraper Plane. With Lignum Wheel. Patented February 4, 1896. Length: 9 1/2 Inches. *Stanley offered these rolling wheel scrapers for approximately 40 years, from 1896 to 1935. This one is in much the same condition as it was when new. The original box, label and some sides, has protected it during its long life.* (FINE) **$245.00**

Z2-45. Stanley Rule & Level No. 100 1/2: Squirrel Tail Block Plane. With Convex Sole. New Condition, Original Box. Length: 3 1/2 Inches. *A previous owner has tastefully etched his initials on the side of this convex sole block plane, but it is otherwise in top condition. A scarce "in the box" item.* (FINE) **$255.00**

Group A3

A3-1. Carter, Edward, Troy, N.Y.: Moving Filletster Molding Plane. With Screw Depth Stop. Near New Condition. Length: 9 1/2 Inches. *This nice plane from the Carter family of Troy, N.Y. has full boxing along the working edge and appears to have been very little used. Filletster planes have become almost impossible to find in this condition.* (FINE) **$195.00**

A3-2. Unmarked: Pair of Boxwood Coach Planes. Owner "W. Adamson". Great Early Patina. Length: 3 3/4 Inches. *The owner of these miniature boxwood coachmaker's planes was so proud of them that he marked them with his name on both the bodies and the wedges. A superb set.* (GOOD+) **$245.00**

A3-3. Kellogg, J., Amherst, Mass.: Tiger Striped Boxwood Plow Plane. Superb Grain. Near New Condition. Length: 8 Inches. *The boxwood of this unhandled screw arm plow has a distinctive tiger striping that must have been selected especially for this tool. The threads are virtually without chips and only minor evidence of use needs to be noted on this crispy clean plow plane.* (FINE) **$425.00**

A3-4. Moseley & Son, John, London: Boxed Bead Molding Plane. 7/8" Size. Extra Crisp and Clean. Length: 9 1/2 Inches. *Here's a good clean boxed bead plane in excellent working order.* (GOOD+) **$35.00**

A3-5. Veal, I., (England): Ogee and Bead Molding Plane. Possible Rework. Uncommon Maker. Length: 9 1/2 Inches. *Someone has tacked a fence on this molder, and the profile may have been slightly altered, but it is in working order and priced to sell.* (GOOD) **$25.00**

A3-6. Unmarked: Coachmaker's Rabbet Plane. With Tail Feature. Extra Small Size. Length: 5 Inches. *Those who worked at building the fancy horse drawn conveyances of the Nineteenth Century would have required considerable woodworking skills and a bit of an artistic flair. The coachmaker who fashioned this diminutive rabbet plane apparently had an ample share of each. A pretty plane.* (GOOD+) **$125.00**

A3-7. Unmarked: Razee Type Try Plane. Brazilian Rosewood. Decorative Wedge. Length: 18 Inches. *This classic trying plane has been artfully shaped from a massive piece of Brazilian Rosewood. Extra special.* (FINE) **$125.00**

A3-8. Crane, D.O., Utica, N.Y.: Massive Cove and Astragal Molding Plane. Marked "9/8". Early and Excellent. Length: 9 1/2 Inches. *David Orville Crane was a former apprentice planemaker to Leonard Kennedy in Hartford, Connecticut, who relocated to Utica, New York where he was self-employed as a planemaker in the 1830's. This massive cove and astragal molder is boldly struck with his imprint and in top, collector quality condition.* (FINE) **$245.00**

A3-9. Unmarked: Tropial Hardwood. Smooth Plane. Spear & Jackson Iron. Double Cutter. Length: 7 3/4 Inches. *This classic smoother features a cutter and chip breaker by English makers Spear and Jackson and a body and wedge of a beautifully grained tropical hardwood.* (GOOD) **$45.00**

A3-10. Ohio Tool Co., Columbus, Ohio No. 37: Boxed Bead Molding Plane. Marked "3/4". Ready to Use. Length: 9 1/2 Inches. *Here's a crisp, clean bead plane in the desirable 3/4" size. Ready to use.* (GOOD+) **$45.00**

A3-11. Auburn Tool Co., Auburn, N. Y. No. 167: Screw Arm Sash Molding Plane. Triple Boxed. Excellent Condition. Length: 9 1/2 Inches. *The presence of additional boxing at the points of the most wear indicates that this screw arm sash plane was made to be better than common quality. It is in excellent condition for the shop or for the collection.* (GOOD+) **$110.00**

A3-12. Unmarked: Razee Type Fore Plane. Buck Brothers Cutter. Ready to Use. Length: 21 Inches. *"Razee" planes seem to be found much more often among the tools of shipwrights, although there seems to be no specific reason for that fact. This well used but sound example has a tight throat and a clean, sharp iron from Buck Brothers. Ready to use.* (GOOD+) **$45.00**

A3-13. Ohio Tool Co., Columbus, Ohio: Beechwood Jointer Plane. Auburn Tool Iron. Ready to Use. Length: 22 Inches. *To preserve the longevity of this workaday plane, the previous owner repaired the throat with an inlaid piece of hardwood. A working plane with character.* **$25.00**

A3-14. Arthur, Edinburgh (Scotland): Ovolo, Cove, Bevel Molding Plane. Most Unusual Profile. Double Iron Type. Length: 9 1/2 Inches. *This extra-steep Scottish molder has a fixed depth stop to regulate the cut. Most unusual.* (GOOD+) **$325.00**

A3-15. Unmarked: Yellow Birch Rabbet Plane. Uncommon Type. Ca. 1790's. Length: 6 3/4 Inches. *This Yellow Birch rabbet is a classic 18th Century plane. A narrow check along the side is a mark of character and not a flaw.* (GOOD) **$65.00**

A3-16. Dryburgh, Toronto (Canada): Fenced Quirk Ogee Molding Plane. Rare Canadian Maker. Massive Form. Length: 9 1/2 Inches. *This massive and boldly struck molder bears the imprint of Canadian maker Dryburgh and his uncommon "Toronto" working location. A great collectible plane with a desirable Canadian mark.* (GOOD+) **$355.00**

A3-17. Osborn, Henry, Southhampton (England): Compass Sole Rabbet Plane. For Coachmaker. Superb Example. Length: 6 1/2 Inches. *The sole of this coachmaker's rabbet plane has a compassed profile. Henry Osborn began work in Southampton in 1884.* (GOOD+) **$75.00**

A3-18. Unmarked: Beechwood Jack Plane. Isaac Graves Cutter. Ready to Use. Length: 17 Inches. *This classic jack plane is in excellent working condition and rates at the highest level of condition classification. Nice.* (FINE) **$45.00**

A3-19. Unmarked: Early Reverse Ogee Molding Plane. Wide Flat Chamfers. Excellent Patina. Length: 9 1/4 Inches. *This steep reverse ogee molder has a pronounced 18th Century look, including extra wide, flat chamfers. A nice plane in working order.* (GOOD+) **$45.00**

A3-20. Unmarked: Fixed Bevel Molding Plane. With Rem. Fence. Most Unusual. Length: 9 1/2 Inches. *Complete with a removable side fence and a manufactured look, this plane performed some specialized function, but I'm not quite sure what that was.* (GOOD) **$65.00**

A3-21. Read, M., Boston, Mass.: Quirk Ogee and Bevel Molding Plane. Marked "1/2". Full Boxed Bevel. Length: 9 1/2 Inches. *A strip of inlaid boxing adds additional appeal to this extra-clean complex molder from the 1840's. The M. Read mark is particularly bold. As you like them.* (GOOD+) **$225.00**

A3-22. Nelson (Richard), York, England: "Badger" Rabbet Plane. With Brass Depth Stop. Ready to Use. Length: 9 1/2 Inches. *A classic English plane that is not often found in the United States, the badger plane's skew set iron would have been much more useful working with the hardwoods that predominated in British woodworking, rather than the pervasive pine that was the lot of the American carpenter. A nice example in fine working order.* (GOOD+) **$95.00**

A3-23. Unmarked: Early Wide Astragal Molding Plane. Owner "H. Jones". Ready to Use. Length: 9 1/4 Inches. *This massive astragal molder is in excellent working order, but someone has driven some wood screws through the body, perhaps to repair a check in the wood.* (GOOD+) **$35.00**

A3-24. Machin, Thos., Toronto (Canada): 1 3/4" Rabbet Plane. Rare Canadian Maker. Owner "Isaac Skeith". Length: 9 1/2 Inches. *Thomas Machin was listed as a planemaker in Birmingham, England in 1854, and later in London (1863). By 1885 he was making planes in Toronto. There is no subsequent mention of his name after 1886. Planes with his Toronto mark are quite scarce. This particular plane incorporates a name stamp used in England with a subscript "TORONTO" mark. A good one.* (GOOD+) **$175.00**

A3-25. Stiles, J., Kingston, N.Y.: Quirk Ovolo, Bevel Molding Plane. Extra Steep Profile. AWP III: "D" Imprint. Length: 9 1/2 Inches. *The profile of this ovolo molder is so steep and pronounced that it might rightly be called a bevel & bevel. A clean molder with the desirable imprint of a family of Hudson River planemakers.* (GOOD+) **$165.00**

A3-26. Griffiths, Norwich (England): Set of Coachmakers Planes. Convex, Concave and Flat . Scarce and Excellent. Length: 6 1/2 Inches. *This set of coachmakers smoothing planes includes a one each of a concave, convex and flat profile. All are in excellent collector quality condition.* (GOOD+) **$345.00**

A3-27. Reed, Utica (N. Y.): Q. Ovolo, Cove/Astragal Molding Plane. Marked "1/2". Near New Condition. Length: 9 1/2 Inches. *This pristine complex molder has a most uncommon cove profile in the middle of its cut. Condition is as new. A great plane. Ex-Cooley Collection.* (FINE) **$365.00**

A3-28. Unmarked: Classic "T" Rabbet Plane. For Coachmaker. Marked "5". Length: 7 Inches. *The only mark on this well preserved coachmaker's "T" rabbit is the number "5". A nice plane.* (GOOD+) **$65.00**

A3-29. Creagh & Williams, Cincinnati, Ohio: Extra Steep Ogee Molding Plane. Ca. 1831. AWP III: 2 Stars (B). Length: 9 1/2 Inches. *This early Cincinnati plane has a decidedly complex profile that is much steeper than normal. The maker mark rates two stars for rarity.* (GOOD+) **$295.00**

A3-30. Unmarked: 18th C. "Thumbnail" Molding Plane. Wide Flat Chamfers. Relieved Wedge. Length: 8 3/4 Inches. *This classic 18th Century "thumbnail" molder is in excellent working order. Ready to use.* (GOOD+) **$115.00**

A3-31. Warren, C., Nashua (N.H.): Pair of Table Joint Molding Planes. Ca. 1860's. Missing Cutter. Length: 9 1/2 Inches. *One of the cutting irons is missing, but these table planes by New Hampshire maker Cyrus Warren are otherwise in new condition. Choice.* (FINE) **$335.00**

A3-32. Denison, C.H., Freeport, Maine: "V" Cut Molding Plane. For Ship Work. Near New Condition. Length: 9 1/2 Inches. *Chests of shipwrights tools often contain shapes and sizes of planes and other tools that stand out as being "different". This "V" shaped grooving double beveling obviously served some specific function in ship construction, but we are at a loss to explain exactly what. Boldly struck with the imprint of obscure, Freeport, Maine maker C.H. Denison, this one is is top collector quality condition. Nice.* (FINE) **$135.00**

A3-33. Child, J. E., Providence, R.I.: Fixed Grooving Molding Plane. With Integral Fence. As New Condition. Length: 9 1/2 Inches. *No matter what the birds think of it, we like this most unusual fenced grooving plane from Providence maker J. Edwin Child. Different.* (FINE) **$110.00**

A3-34. Dean, S., Dedham (Mass.): Early Reverse Ogee Molding Plane. Yellow Birch Body. AWP III: 4 Stars "A". Length: 9 1/2 Inches. *One Samuel Dean is known to have lived and worked in Dedham, Massachusetts from 1737 to 1747 where his occupation was listed as "joiner". This example which is boldly imprinted with the mark designated as the "A" mark in American Wooden Planes, has a steep reverse ogee profile that is consistent with the working dates of Samuel Dean. A contemporary of Francis Nicholson and Cesar Chelor, Dean's home town of Dedham is less than twenty miles from Wrentham, Massachusetts and he may well have known these planemakers. A clearly marked and very well preserved plane from the earliest days of American planemaking.* (GOOD+) **$2,250.00**

A3-35. Jones, John N.: York Pitch Molding Plane. With Planemaker Label. Dual Lignum Boxing. Length: 9 1/2 Inches. *The discovery of a new planemaker's imprint is all the more exciting when that planemaker used a paper label to identify his work. Never intended to serve as a lasting record of his output, planemaker John F. Jones probably applied these labels so that hardware dealers could reorder, if they so desired. Most would have fallen off the first day on the job or been consciously removed by the workman. This one, miraculously, survived and provides us with additional information to add to the history of American planemaking.* (GOOD+) **$335.00**

A3-36. Ponder, S., London No. 13: Hollow Molding Plane. Ca. 1788-1826. Ready to Use. Length: 9 1/2 Inches. *According to Goodman's "British Planemakers", S. Ponder worked in London in the 40 years bracketing 1800. A good clean molding plane.* (GOOD+) **$35.00**

A3-37. George, M.: Early Round Molding Plane. Undocumented Maker. Distinctive Imprint. Length: 9 1/2 Inches. *This early appearing round molding plane is imprinted with the mark of one "M. George" an undocumented maker we have not previously encountered. Rare.* (GOOD) **$45.00**

A3-38. Kellogg, J., Amherst, Mass.: Special Tongue and Grove Molding Planes. With Fixed Depth. 1/4" Groove. Length: 9 1/2 Inches. *These special purpose match planes performed some specific function, the nature of which I am not aware. They may have been used for forming dust proof joints. Different.* (FINE) **$165.00**

A3-39. Doscher Plane & Tool Co., The: Classic Toothing Plane. Near New Condition. Ready to Use. Length: 9 1/2 Inches. *This classic toothing plane from the Doscher Plane & Tool Company is in nearly new condition. A superb example and the way you wish they all were. Mint.* (FINE) **$95.00**

A3-40. Taylor, W.W. No. 11: Round Molding Plane. Undocumented Maker. Owner "M. Drew". Length: 9 1/2 Inches. *The maker's mark "M. Drew" appears on the toe of this No. 11 round molding plane. A boldly struck plane by an undocumented maker.* (GOOD+) **$55.00**

A3-41. Unmarked: Mahogany Try Plane. Shapely Handle. Ready to Use. Length: 18 Inches. *The maker of this classic razee-type trying plane added a metal plate at the throat to keep it permanently tight and functional. A nice looking plane that is ready to be put right to work.* (GOOD+) **$55.00**

A3-42. Scott, W., Pittsburgh Allegany Town: Quirk Ogee/Astragal Molding Plane. Extra Steep Profile. AWP III: 3 Stars. Length: 9 1/2 Inches. *This extraordinarily well preserved complex molder dates from the earliest days of Pittsburgh history, when part of it was referred to as "Allegany Town". Scott worked from 1819 to 1839. A rare Pennsylvania plane.* (GOOD+) **$445.00**

A3-43. Ohio Tool Co., Columbus, Ohio: Pair of Tounge and Groove Molding Plane. 1/2" Size. Extra Crisp and Clean. Length: 9 1/2 Inches. *These 1/2" tongue and groove planes are in excellent condition. For some reason, someone has bored holes in the top of each plane, but they are otherwise excellent. A pretty pair.* (GOOD+) **$65.00**

A3-44. Clark, D.: Early Style Molding Plane. Distintive Point Finial. See AWP III. Length: 9 1/2 Inches. *This imprint on this boldly marked plane is identical to that shown in "American Wooden Planes", as is the pointed wedge finial. A nice example of a very rare planemaker's stamp.* **$185.00**

A3-45. Brooks, P., E. Hartford (Conn.): Double Iron Sash Molding Plane. With Central "Nicker". Extra Crisp and Clean. Length: 9 1/2 Inches. *This clean sash plane features full boxing on one working face and an adjustable slitter that fits through the center of the body, most likely for scoring the cut to be planed. An exceptionally nice sash plane.* (FINE) **$185.00**

Group B3

B3-1. Sloane, Eric: "Look at The Sky" Book. Rare Sloane Book. Published 1961, 76 Pages. Length: 9 1/4 Inches. *An extremely rare Eric Sloane book, this obscure offering continues Sloane's fascination with clouds and the sky that began with his very first book in the 1940's.* (GOOD+) **$195.00**

B3-2. Sloane, Eric: "American Yesterday" Book. Roads, Bridges, Etc. Published 1956, 123 Pages. Length: 10 Inches. *Originally published in 1956, this Sloane classic further develops his continuing American themes of roads, bridges and forgotten ways of yesterdays past.* (FINE) **$45.00**

B3-3. Oliver Chilled Plow Works: The Professor's Adventures in Ohio and Indiana; In Search of Information, 18 Pages. Length: 6 1/2 Inches. *This original pamphlet was published as an advertising promotional item by the Oliver Chilled Plow Works. This example is in nearly new condition.* (FINE) **$45.00**

B3-4. Grier, William: The Mechanic's Pocket Dictionary. 6th Edition, 1840. 547 Pages. Length: 7 Inches. *Filled with every fact and trick that a "mechanic" would need to know in 1840, this little book is a look back in time. A rare early book. The spine is worn, but the book is intact.* (GOOD+) **$275.00**

B3-5. Sloane, Eric: "3 By Eric Sloane" Books. Boxed Edition. Diary, Reverence, Etc. Length: 12 1/2 Inches. *This boxed set includes those books most likely to appeal to a tool collector: "A Reverence for Wood", "Diary of an Early American Boy" and "A Museum of American Tools".* (FINE) **$295.00**

B3-6. Stanley Rule & Level: Framing Squares Brochure. Ca. 1949, 48 Pages. 3 1/2" X 6". Length: 6 Inches. *These were given away with Stanley squares and probably were available in the hardware store. It includes everything (actually more) that anyone would want to know about framing squares and their uses.* (GOOD+) **$25.00**

B3-7. Sloane, Eric: "Clouds, Air & Wind" Book. Early Sloane Book. Published 1941, 76 Pages. Length: 12 1/2 Inches. *The very first book ever published by prominent American artist Eric Sloane, this book was published just at the outset of the Second World War, which may account for the very limited number of surviving examples. A rare Sloane book.* (GOOD+) **$465.00**

B3-8. Rixford, O. S.: Axes, Scythes, Snaths, and Stones. Catalog. 68 Pages. Length: 6 1/2 Inches. *The product line of this Vermont maker of edge tools is documented in this original catalog, which appears to date from the 1890's. A very well preserved early catalog.* (FINE) **$45.00**

B3-9. Sloane, Eric: The Sound of Bells 1966. A Doubleday Prebound. Edition, 58 Pages. Length: 9 1/2 Inches. *A favorite Sloane theme, "bells", is developed in this rare Eric Sloane book.* (FINE) **$165.00**

B3-10. Davidson, Marshall & Namuth, Hans: American Woodworking Tool Book. Published 1975. 65 Pages, Illustrated. Length: 12 1/2 Inches. *More art book than tool reference, this out-of-print coffee table book includes some excellent black & white photographs of primarily "primitive" tools, together with commentary. An interesting look at tool collecting...the way it was.* (FINE) **$115.00**

B3-11. Sloane, Eric: "Do's and Don'ts" Book. Boxed Edition. Published 1972. Length: 7 1/2 Inches. *This boxed set contains one volume of positive advice and one volume of negative advice, all illustrated in the way that only Eric Sloane could. A great set.* (FINE) **$165.00**

B3-12. American Steel & Wire Company: Ellwood Fences; Different Kinds of Fences. 31 Pages. Length: 6 1/4 Inches. *All manner of fences are illustrated in this catalog from the late 1800's. An interesting piece of period advertising.* (FINE) **$35.00**

B3-13. Lufkin Rule Co., The, Saginaw, Mich.: The Amazing Story of Measurement. Cartoon, 1959. 23 Pages. Length: 7 1/2 Inches. *Published as a promotional item by the Lufkin Rule Company, this "comic book" style publication documents the development of measurement until (you guessed it) that science achieves its apotheosis with the rise of the Lufkin Rule Company. A scarce tool related book in top condition.* (FINE) **$35.00**

B3-14. Walker Turner Co., Plainfield, New Jersey: "Woodworkers Handbook" Projects, Etc. Ca. 1932, 128 Pages. Length: 9 Inches. *Walker Turner produced power woodworking tools of the very best quality. This 1932 publication is filled with information and projects. It most likely came free when you purchased a piece of shop equipment.* (FINE) **$35.00**

B3-15. Proudfoot, Christopher & Walker,: "Woodworking Tools" Book. Christies Publication. Ca. 1984, 160 Pages. Length: 10 Inches. *Originally published in 1984, this classic book on tools has long been out of print.* (FINE) **$75.00**

B3-16. Connecticut Valley Mfg. Co.: Wood Boring Tools Book. Catalog No. 11. 12 Pages. Length: 9 Inches. *This original catalog illustrates the full ca. 1930's line of this Connecticut manufacturer.* (FINE) **$15.00**

B3-17. Sellens, Alvin: "The Stanley Plane" Book. 1st Edition, 1975. Signed by Sellens. Length: 9 1/2 Inches. *This First Edition of Al Sellens' "The Stanley Plane" was autographed by Sellens at the 1976 Mid-West Tool Collectors Meeting. Scarce.* (GOOD+) **$185.00**

B3-18. Sloane, Eric: The Second Barrel Book. Compare To "Cracker Barrel" Published. 1969, 104 Pages. Length: 11 Inches. *A follow up to his "Cracker Barrel" book, Sloane provided more of the same in this 1969 publication.* (FINE) **$55.00**

B3-19. Sloane, Eric: A Reverence For Wood Book. Signed by Sloan. 112 Pages, Hardbound. Length: 11 Inches. *An original Eric Sloane illustration of a bird perched on a hatchet stuck in a stump is etched on the inside of this copy of "A Reverence for Wood". A rare signed and illustrated Eric Sloane classic.* (FINE) **$575.00**

B3-20. Sloane, Eric: A Museum of Early American Tools. 1964. 105 Pages. Length: 11 1/2 Inches. *This extremely important book was largely responsible for the first surge of interest in tool collecting. The research that it sparked continues today. A classic.* (FINE) **$55.00**

B3-21. Sloane, Eric: "Our Vanishing Landscape" Book. Roads, Bridges, Etc. Published 1955, 95 Pages. Length: 10 Inches. *Nicely illustrated with color and black & white illustrations, this 1955 classic addresses familiar themes of buildings, tools and American life.* (FINE) **$45.00**

B3-22. Tunis, Edwin: Colonial Living Book. First Edition, 1957. 155 Pages. Length: 12 1/2 Inches. *Long out of print, this volume by William Tunis chronicles, in illustrations and text, the way of life of pioneer Americans.* (FINE) **$65.00**

B3-23. Scientific American: Group of 6 Issues. From 1867-1880. Interesting Read. Length: 16 1/2 Inches. *For a glimpse inside the world of Nineteenth Century technology, we recommend a read through these early issues of Scientific American. All are in excellent condition and include many advertisements and articles about tools and technology.* (GOOD+) **$85.00**

B3-24. Sloane, Eric: Diary of an Early American Boy. Noah Blake, 1805. January 1973 Edition, 108 Pages. Length: 11 Inches. *An illustrated look at the life of Noah Blake, a real American boy, through the interpretive eyes and pen of Eric Sloane. A classic.* (GOOD+) **$75.00**

B3-25. Smith, Joseph: Explanation or Key, to the Various Manufacturers of Sheffield... 1975. The Early American Industries Association. Length: 11 1/4 Inches. *Originally republished in 1975 this Sheffield "pattern book" illustrated in great detail the tools, hardware and household devices that were being produced in mid-Nineteenth Century Sheffield. An essential reference for the collector's library and long out of print.* (FINE) **$75.00**

B3-26. Mateaux, C. L.: The Wonderland of Work- Book. 312 Pages. The Making of Everything Length: 10 1/2 Inches. *This splendid book looks at how things were made in the late 1800's and both describes and illustrates those processes. An interesting look at technology.* (GOOD+) **$225.00**

B3-27. Sloane, Eric: "Seasons of America Past" Book. Signs of Seasons. Published 1958, 150 Pages. Length: 11 Inches. *Eric Sloane paints the American landscape in the color's of the seasons in the 1958 classic.* (FINE) **$95.00**

B3-28. Goodman, W. L.: The History of Woodworking Tools. Out of Print Book. Near New Condition. Length: 10 Inches. *Long out of print, this book provided my introduction to the world of tools and I recommend it without hesitation to anyone who really wants to understand. A great book from an interesting man.* (FINE) **$125.00**

B3-29. Bedini, Silvio A.: Early American Scientific Instruments. Smithsonian Instruments. 1964, Bulletin 231. Length: 9 1/4 Inches. *A pioneering publication on the topic of scientific instruments in the United States, this book has itself become highly collectible. Rare and in excellent condition.* (FINE) **$385.00**

B3-30. Sloane, Eric: "Museum of Early Book". 100+ Folk Tools. Published 1964, 104 Pages. Length: 11 1/4 Inches. *This extremely important book was largely responsible for the first surge of interest in tool collecting. The research that it sparked continues today. A bit of tape on the dust jacket deserves mention. A classic.* (GOOD+) **$85.00**

B3-31. Sloane, Eric: "The Sound of The Bells" Book. Rare Sloane Book. Published 1966, 58 Pages. Length: 9 1/2 Inches. *This obscure Eric Sloane offering was published in 1966 and may not have been a big seller. Examples are very rare.* (FINE) **$175.00**

B3-32. Sloane, Eric: I Remember America, Book. 1975 Edition. Great Color Photos. Length: 14 Inches. *In a book that is very much a personal retrospective, Sloane looks at the America of his youth and captures it in sketches and paintings in this coffee table classic.* (GOOD+) **$95.00**

B3-33. Rural Industries Bureau: The Blacksmith's Craft, An Introduction to Smithing, Reprinted. 1955, 108 Pages. Length: 9 Inches. *Reprinted in 1955 to document the practice of blacksmithing, this book remains an excellent reference today.* (GOOD+) **$35.00**

B3-34. Sellens, Alvin: "The Stanley Plane" Book. 1st Edition, 1975. Original Dust Jacket. Length: 9 1/2 Inches. *This book, which started the Stanley collecting craze, is no longer in print, nor are there any plans to reprint it. A First Edition copy of a contemporary classic.* (FINE) **$125.00**

B3-35. Sloane, Eric: Diary of An Early American Boy Book. Noah Blake, 1805. Published 1962, 108 P. Length: 11 Inches. *In a text and series of drawings that recount the day to day adventures of one Noah Blake, Sloane captures in this book the reality of early American life from the perspective of a boy.* (FINE) **$85.00**

B3-36. Sloane, Eric: "Seasons of America Book". Signs of Seasons. Published 1958, 150 Pages. Length: 11 Inches. *Filled with examples of Sloane's mastery of art, this book captures glimpses of America at its very best throughout the year.* (GOOD+) **$85.00**

B3-37. Sloane, Eric: Don't: A Book. 1968. 72 Pages, Hardbound. Length: 7 1/4 Inches. *Illustrations of what NOT to do are contained in this listing of advice from an Eighteenth Century perspective.* (FINE) **$95.00**

B3-38. Roberts, Kenneth D.: Wooden Planes in 19th Century America Volume I. Original Dust Jacket. 307 Pages, Clothbound. Length: 12 Inches. *Author Ken Roberts of New Hampshire, was, in large measure, responsible for the first surge of interest in antique tool collecting that took place some 25 years ago. Through his research, his writings and the original catalogs of manufacturers that he produced, Roberts inspired thousands to learn the history of the tools that built Western Civilization. We are pleased to offer his classic volume that was largely responsible for the interest in wooden planes that continues today.* (GOOD+) **$95.00**

B3-39. Stanley Rule & Level: How to Work With Tools and Wood. 1927 Edition, 190 Pages . Great Photographs. Length: 9 Inches. *This early version of Stanley's "how to" book for the home shop is filled with excellent period photographs of Stanley tools in use. A classic.* (FINE) **$95.00**

B3-40. Sloane, Eric: Diary of An Early American Boy Book. Noah Blake, 1805. January 1973 Edition, 108 Pages. Length: 11 Inches. *In a text and series of drawings that recount the day to day adventures of one Noah Blake, Sloane captures in this book the reality of early American life from the perspective of a boy.* (FINE) **$85.00**

B3-41. Nicholson File Co., Providence, R. I.: File Filosophy and How To Get The Most Out of Files, 17th Edition. 1950, 2nd Printing. Length: 9 Inches. *This version of Nicholson's famous "File Filosophy" pamphlet dates from some 50 years ago.* (GOOD) **$25.00**

B3-42. Sloane, Eric: "American Barns & Covered Bridges" Book. Barns, Bridges, Etc. Published 1954, 112 Pages. Length: 10 Inches. *Eric Sloane's fascination with barns and covered bridges is indulged to the reader's delight in this classic from 1954.* (FINE) **$45.00**

B3-43. Goodman, W. L.: The History of Woodworking Tools. Out of Print Book. Original Dust Jacket. Length: 10 Inches. *Long out of print, this book provided my introduction to the world of tools and I recommend it without hesitation to anyone who really wants to understand. A great book from an interesting man.* (FINE) **$125.00**

B3-44. Lukin, James, Ed.: Turning Lathes: A Manual For Technical Schools and Apprentices. Third Edition, 1892. Length: 8 Inches. *A great original reference on Lathes and the science of turning, this book has been reprinted and is available through our booklist.* (FINE) **$95.00**

B3-45. Sloane, Eric: "Folklore of American Weather" Book. Rare Sloane Book. Published 1963, 63 Pages. Length: 9 1/4 Inches. *Another extremely uncommon Eric Sloane book, this "Weather Almanac" recounts and illustrates all manner of conventional wisdom about everyone's favorite topic of conversation: The Weather.* (FINE) **$175.00**

B3

 1
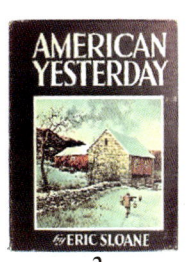 2
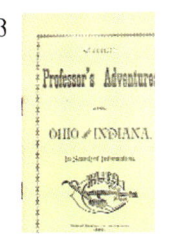 3
 4
 5
 6
 7

 8
 9
 10
 11
 12
 13
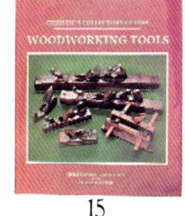 14
15

 16
17
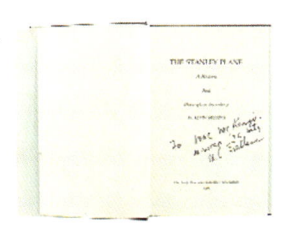 18
 19
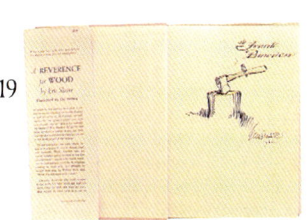 20

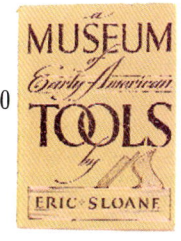 21
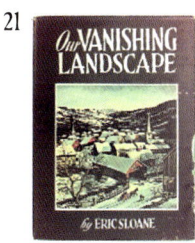 22
 23
24
 25

 26
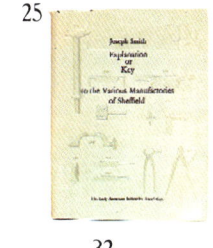 27
28
 29
 30
 31
32

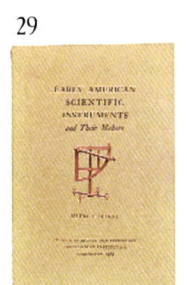 33
34
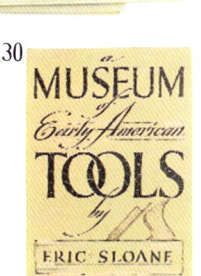 35
 36
 37
 38
 39

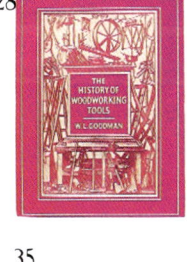 40
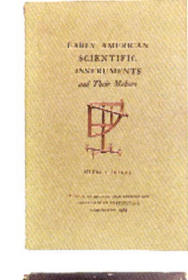 41
42
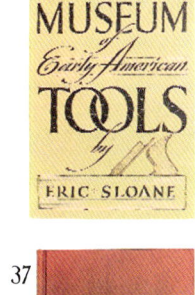 43
 44
 45

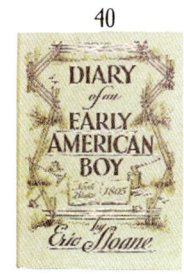

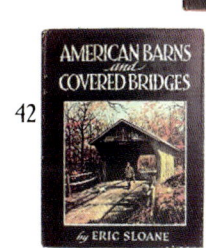

Toll Free: (800) 869-0695   Page 111   www.mjdtools.com

Group C3

C3-1. Unmarked: Rare Cooper's Windlass. Tightening Barrels. Superb Patina. Length: 14 1/2 Inches. *The cooper's windlass was used for drawing together the barrel staves for final fitting and assembly. This is the first example we have ever offered for sale. A rare collectible coopers tool from a prominent Connecticut collection.* (GOOD+) **$225.00**

C3-2. Unmarked: Chairmaker's Hollow Shave. With Wooden Gauge. Early and Excellent. Length: 10 Inches. *The work of the chairmaker required the hollowing of the seat to accommodate the contour of the body. Precise regulation of the cutting iron when addressing such a task was largely left to the skill of the workman. In this instance, however, a wooden guide has been mortised into the body in a way that suggests that different sized stops could be used interchangeably depending upon the nature of the work. An interesting and unusual shave.* (GOOD+) **$165.00**

C3-3. Unmarked: Basket Splint Cutter. For Grass Baskets? Superb Patina. Length: 14 Inches. *This classic primitive has a serrated cutting iron on the underside of the movable arm that was used for splitting reeds for the making of grass baskets. Nicely pegged together and tastefully chamfered, this tool has developed a rich, warm patina from years of careful use. Museum quality.* (GOOD+) **$385.00**

C3-4. Unmarked: Chairmaker's Hollow Scorp. Original Leather Handle. Superb Patina. Length: 7 Inches. *This classic chairmaker's scorp is fitted with the original leather strap that held it in place in the user's hand. A classic hand made tool having a golden patina of age and use. Nice.* (FINE) **$265.00**

C3-5. Unmarked: Combination Croze and Howell. Superb Patina. Uncommon Form. Length: 15 1/2 Inches. *This combination cooper's tool combines two barrel making functions into a single device. There are no maker marks on this one, but it appears to have been manufactured.* (GOOD+) **$135.00**

C3-6. Bailey, L., Boston, Mass.: Cooper's Heavy Spoke Shave. 18 Inch Length. 4" Cutter. Length: 18 Inches. *A previous owner marked this early Leonard Bailey spokeshave with red paint to make sure that no one made off with it. Someone did. Rare.* (GOOD) **$65.00**

C3-7. Unmarked: Classic Chairmakers Scorp. Extra Deep Cut. Early and Excellent. Length: 6 Inches. *The steepness of the curve of this tool distinguishes it as a chairmaker's scorp from the much flatter cooper's inshave. A nice example in excellent usable condition.* (GOOD+) **$45.00**

C3-8. Unmarked: Dry Cooper's Hoop Driver. For Wooden Hoops. Wrapped Head. Length: 4 1/2 Inches. *The tip of this hoop driver has been bound with twine to minimize the possibility of the "mushroom" head so common to these tools. This driver was likely used to drive wooden hoops on barrels intended for the storage of dry materials. A classic.* (GOOD+) **$45.00**

C3-9. Unmarked: Chairmaker's Travisher. Excellent Condition. Ready to Use. Length: 11 1/2 Inches. *The blade on this travisher is clean and will take and hold an edge. A great working tool. Rare.* (GOOD+) **$225.00**

C3-10. Barton & Co., D.R., Rochester, N.Y: Cooper's Sun Plane. Fruitwood Body. Near New Condition. Length: 13 Inches. *This cooper's sun plane is about as god as they come. Its applewood body is virtually without dings and nearly all of the original finish remains on the cutting iron. Top shelf.* (FINE) **$215.00**

C3-11. White, L. & I.J., Buffalo, N.Y. No. 241: Cooper's Sun Plane. Beech Body. Extra Crisp and Clean. Length: 13 Inches. *Only a "hang hole" in the back detracts from this otherwise perfect cooper's sun topping plane. A nice example of a classic collectible.* (FINE) **$155.00**

C3-12. Wiser, C., Cincinnati, Ohio: Basketmaker's Splitter. Screw Adjust Type. Extra Crisp and Clean. Length: 4 3/4 Inches. *This basket maker's splitter bears the imprint of its maker, one C. Wiser of Cincinnati, Ohio. A strong spring between the wood handle and the steel facing keeps constant pressure against the material as it is being cut.A rare basket making tool from a maker who does not appear in the Directory of American Toolmakers.* (GOOD+) **$225.00**

C3-13. Collins & Co., Hartford, Conn.: "Legitimus" Cooper's Adze. Rare Collins Imprint. Near New Condition. Length: 9 1/2 Inches. *Boldly struck with the Collins name and trademark, this rare Collins cooper's adze was apparently never used. Mint.* (FINE) **$135.00**

C3-14. Unmarked: Special Purpose Cooper's Croze. For Apple Barrels. From Central N.Y.. Length: 33 1/2 Inches. *This specialty cooper's croze comes from the apple growing region of Central New York. The depth of the cut is adjustable by a wedge mechanism. The extra long length of the tool allows it to work with barrels of many sizes. Most unusual.* (GOOD+) **$195.00**

C3-15. Billings, J.P., Clinton, Maine.: Early Cooper's Adze. Uncommon Maker. Excellent Condition. Length: 9 Inches. *John P. Billings produced edge tools in Clinton and, later, in Hallowell, Maine from 1825 to 1872. This cooper's adze likely dates from his early period as it lacks the "adze eye" that would soon revolutionize the making of hammers and adzes. It has been boldly struck with the Billings name and the Clinton location.* (GOOD+) **$185.00**

C3-16. Unmarked: Classic Chairmakers Scorp. Unusual Form. Excellent Condition. Length: 13 Inches. *This superbly patinated chairmaker's scorp has an extra deep angle to its cut. The cutting iron is in excellent condition and could be put back into use if the owner so desired.* (GOOD+) **$225.00**

C3-17. Unmarked: Classic Cooper's Driver. With Steel Ring. Distinctive Form. Length: 9 1/4 Inches. *This manufactured cooper's hoop driver was fitted with a steel ring to keep it from splitting. Condition is excellent.* (GOOD+) **$45.00**

C3-18. Unmarked: Cooper's Bung Mallet. Classic Form. Excellent Condition. Length: 23 1/2 Inches. *The split hickory handles of these tool allowed them to apply the appropriate amount of pressure to insert a bung without damaging the barrel. This classic example is in excellent condition. A good one.* (GOOD+) **$95.00**

C3-19. Unmarked: Early Firkin Croze. Yellow Birch Body. Pewter Fittings. Length: 8 Inches. *We have observed many coopers tools over the course of the last 15 years, including a goodly number of the croze family. This yellow birch example is the first firkin size croze we have yet encountered. Inscribed with the owner's initials "I.L", accented with pewter fittings to the cutting blade, decoratively chamfered and possessed of a rich, warm patina, this tool virtually shouts "Eighteenth Century". An extraordinary find.* (GOOD+) **$265.00**

C3-20. Mowry, B.R., Union, Maine: Early Cooper's Adze. Hand Forged Head. With Decorations. Length: 9 1/2 Inches. *A series of stylized "starburst" decorations highlight this early cooper's adze, which bears the imprint of maker B.R. Mowry. Mowry is listed in the Directory of American Toolmakers as having produced edge tools in Union, Maine between 1820 and 1860. He appears to have specialized in the making of cooper's adzes.* (GOOD+) **$85.00**

C3-21. Unmarked: Hand Forged Cooper's Adze. Very Early Type. Excellent Patina. Length: 8 Inches. *This early hand forged cooper's adze has the classic characteristics of a very early tool. The lack of the precise forming of later tools of this type adds an element of character that evokes the spirit of a less technologically complex time. A classic.* (GOOD) **$55.00**

C3-22. Unmarked: Cooper's Bung Mallet. From Phipps Museum. Hickory Handle. Length: 20 1/2 Inches. *This very well preserved cooper's bung mallet was acquired at the recent auction of the Wayne Phipps tool museum near Cleveland, Ohio. Museum quality.* (GOOD+) **$95.00**

C3-23. Unmarked: Classic Chairmaker's Scorp. Extra Deep Cut. Usable Condition. Length: 6 1/2 Inches. *Formed from a single piece of white oak and colored to a rich, brown patina from years of use, this chairmaker's scorp remains in excellent usable condition, despite 175 or more years of existence.* (GOOD+) **$175.00**

C3-24. Unmarked: Carriagemkrs Draw Knife. With Router Blade. Early and Near New. Length: 11 Inches. *The narrow, single cutter on this carriagemaker's drawknife is a new one to me. Nicely forged and very well preserved. Crispy clean.* (FINE) **$65.00**

C3-25. Fuller, C., Causeway St., Boston: Classic Stair Shave. With Cast Fence. Crisp and Clean. Length: 11 1/2 Inches. *The end of this classic stair shave is imprinted with the name of Boston planemaker Charles Fuller. Missing the cutting iron, but otherwise excellent. A rare woodworking tool.* (GOOD+) **$85.00**

C3-26. Stortz, J., Philadellphia Penna.: Cooper's Scorp. Crisp and Clean. Turned Handles. Length: 7 1/2 Inches. *J. Stortz was a prominent Philadelphia tool merchant and hardware dealer. This cooper's inshave which bears his name is ornamented with a series of concentric rings on the handles, which also served to improve the grip of the user. A good one.* (GOOD+) **$65.00**

C3-27. Sorby, Robert, Sheffield: Cooper's Howell. Partial Original Decal. Near New Condition. Length: 14 Inches. *Part of the original decal remains on this cooper's howell from prominent English maker Robert Sorby of the tool making city of Sheffield. A classic tool in excellent condition.* (FINE) **$165.00**

C3-28. Unmarked: Classic Cooper's Adze. Unusual Small Size. Usable Condition. Length: 7 1/2 Inches. *This cooper's adze is considerably smaller and lighter than the type usually encountered. Ready to use or display.* (GOOD+) **$55.00**

C3-29. Barton & Co., D.R., Rochester, N.Y: Cooper's Sun Plane. Fruitwood Body. Extra Bold Stamp. Length: 14 Inches. *This immaculate cooper's sun plane has been boldly struck with the imprint of important 19th Century maker D.R. Barton & Company. A classic.* (FINE) **$225.00**

C3-30. Unmarked: Specialized Basket Spoke Shave. Tenon Handles. Excellent Condition. Length: 8 Inches. *Designed for splitting splints for baskets, this specialized shave has been fitted with a pair of turned oak handles, each of which has been mortised to the side of the main body. Most unusual.* (GOOD+) **$145.00**

C3-31. Unmarked: Cooper's Hoop Driver. With "Peened" Head. Superb Patina. Length: 6 Inches. *This hoop driver was intended for driving the wooden hoops that were used on non-watertight barrels. The head has been mushroomed over from use. Early and nicely patinated.* (GOOD+) **$35.00**

C3-32. Routledge, 64 Bull St., Birmingham: Wheelwright's Jarvis. For Rounding. Scarce and Excellent. Length: 12 Inches. *The wheelwright's "jarvis" was used for rounding and precision fitting of wheel spokes. This example is in excellent condition and clearly imprinted with the name of its maker, Birmingham, England planemaker Richard Routledge. A tough tool to find.* (GOOD+) **$135.00**

C3-33. Barton & Co., D.R., Rochester, N.Y: Cooper's Sun Plane. With Clear Mark. Fruitwood Body. Length: 14 Inches. *The top of this classic sun plane is boldly imprinted with the mark of Rochester, New York maker D.R. Barton & Company. A classic tool that has a rich, dark patina.* (GOOD+) **$145.00**

C3-34. Unmarked: Early Bung Cutter. Heart-Shape Nut. Excellent Patina. Length: 13 Inches. *This most unusual bung hole cutter features an adjustment screw to regulate the size of the opening. A distinctively different cooper's tool.* (GOOD+) **$75.00**

C3-35. Unmarked: Classic Cooper's Head Shave. With Double Iron. Very Well Made. Length: 15 1/2 Inches. *The cooper's head shave was the hardest working of the entire range of spokeshave tools. This double iron offering is extremely well made and well preserved. A good one.* (GOOD+) **$45.00**

C3-36. Unmarked: Special Basket Splitter. Spring Jaw Cutters. "V" Shape. Length: 4 1/2 Inches. *The cutting edges of this basket splitter are fitted with springs to regulate pressure on the material being cut. An uncommon basket maker's tool in great working order.* (GOOD+) **$115.00**

C3-37. Unmarked: Cooper's Bung Cutter. With Threaded Tip. Most Original Finish. Length: 9 Inches. *Nearly all of the original finishes remain on this classic bung cutting tool. Nice.* (FINE) **$55.00**

C3-38. Unmarked: Chairmakers Travisher. Excellent Condition. Ready to Use. Length: 12 Inches. *Here's an extra wide travisher in excellent condition and ready to be put immediately to work.* (GOOD+) **$225.00**

C3-39. Unmarked: Elongated Birch Hoop Driver. For Dry Cooper. Great Patina. Length: 6 3/4 Inches. *This dry cooper's driver has been fashioned from native Yellow Birch and may date from the Eighteenth Century. Early and excellent.* (GOOD+) **$65.00**

C3-40. Unmarked: Chairmaker's Scorp. 1 1/2" Cutter. Ready to Use. Length: 7 Inches. *The cutting edge on this classic chairmaker's scorp is in excellent condition and ready to be put back to use.* (FINE) **$65.00**

C3-41. Drew & Co., C., Kingston, Mass.: Cooper's Nantucket Hoop Driver. With Drew Mark. Unused Condition. Length: 9 1/4 Inches. *Edge tool makers C. Drew & Company of Kingston, Massachusetts were well respected for the quality of their forge work. This unused hoop driver is a classic example of why they deserved that respect. Perfect.* (FINE) **$55.00**

C3-42. Unmarked: Massive Fruitwood Scraper. With Ogee Cutter. Superb Patina. Length: 24 Inches. *Decidedly different from any other scraper we have previously encountered, this oversize fruitwood scraper plane is fitted with an ogee shaped iron, which has been almost completely used up. The chamfered beech wedge, which is likely early replacement, nicely accents this beautifully patinated tool. A most interesting special purpose tool.* **$85.00**

C3-43. White, L. & I.J., Buffalo, N.Y. No. 241: Cooper's Sun Plane. Beech Body. Extra Crisp and Clean. Length: 13 Inches. *Given the hard work to which these tools were subjected, it is a wonder that any of them survive at all. This classic example from prominent Buffalo, New York makers L. & I.J. White appears to have been very little used. A classic collectible tool in top condition.* (FINE) **$185.00**

C3-44. Unmarked: Early Chairmaker's Scorp. Forged From File. Usable Condition. Length: 8 1/2 Inches. *The creator of this early scorp made use of a discarded file from which to fashion the tool. An interesting bit of forge work that is in excellent usable condition.* (GOOD+) **$45.00**

C3-45. Sandusky Tool Co., Sandusky, Ohio No. 239: Cooper's Sun Plane. Tropical Hardwood. Rare Type. Length: 14 Inches. *Formed from extra heavy tropical hardwood, this rare Sandusky plane has seen much use, but is clean and clearly marked.* (GOOD) **$225.00**

Group D3

D3-1. Unmarked: Quick Adjust Nut Wrench. Spring Activated. With Screwdriver. Length: 5 Inches. *An unmarked, but mechanically interesting wrench with a lever adjustment mechanism behind the lower jaw. Different.* (GOOD) **$395.00**

D3-2. Chandler Co, Cedar Rapids, Iowa: Special "Yoke" Wrench. Unknown Function. "Patent Pending". Length: 12 Inches. *We know from the writing on the side of the tool that this is a "yoke" wrench, but it's specific use is not known. We would suspect that it was a tool of the wheelwright.* (GOOD+) **$45.00**

D3-3. American Plierwrench Co., Chicago: "Eifel Geared" Plier Wrench. Quick Adjust Jaw. 3 Original Jaws. Length: 9 Inches. *A contender for the title of "most popular quick-adjust wrench of all time", the "Eifel Geared" (whatever that means) Plier wrench might likely have had its own Infomercial if it were being marketed today. The basic idea is that opening the jaws to their full extension allows the moving jaw to be quickly positioned for use on fasteners of every sort. This one is in great working order, complete with three original interchangeable jaws, and ready to be placed on the shelf next to your "Pocket Fisherman" and "Veg-O-Matic".* (FINE) **$45.00**

D3-4. Walden, Worcester, Mass. No. 4: Combination Wrench Set. Original Leather Case. Complete and Excellent. Length: 11 Inches. *The early days of automobiles produced a wide range of specialty wrenches, including this cased ratchet wrench set from the Walden Wrench Company of Worcester, Massachusetts, a principal maker of early automotive tools. Complete and well preserved sets of automotive tools have become increasingly difficult to find. A great set.* (FINE) **$145.00**

D3-5. Lever Wrench Co.: Lever Action Nut Wrench. "Heimbach Patent". Patented in 1919. Length: 10 Inches. *A look through the Wrench Forest to be found in Al & Lucille Schulz' Antique & Unusual Wrenches would likely find this one among the "Lever Adjust Nut Wrenches", in the company of many dozens of similar aberrations of human creativity. This one is in excellent order and in never-need-to-upgrade condition. A good one.* (FINE) **$225.00**

D3-6. Tower & Lyon, New York, N.Y.: " Gem" Pocket Wrench. 3" Size. Near-New Condition. Length: 3 Inches. *These "pocket" wrenches were apparently quite popular, although I can't imagine using one. Tough to find this nice.* (FINE) **$225.00**

D3-7. Standard Tool Company, Athol, Mass: Quick Adjust Nut Wrench. Patented 1880. Rare and Excellent. Length: 6 Inches. *This one slides quickly and smoothly into place with a push of the button at the rear of the lower jaw. Crisp, clean and clearly marked. A good one.* (GOOD+) **$225.00**

D3-8. Pazzano Wrench Co., Waltham, Mass: Specialty Battery Wrench. With Serrated Jaws. Multiple Function. Length: 8 Inches. *This is the first we have encountered this specialty tool maker from the Boston, Massachusetts area. A very well made pair of battery pliers.* (GOOD+) **$35.00**

D3-9. Mossberg Co., Frank: Bicycle Monkey Wrench. Superb Condition. "Sterling". Length: 5 Inches. *Mossberg's mainstay bicycle wrench the way you like to find them, but seldom do.* (FINE) **$35.00**

D3-10. Seabers Mach.Co., J.A.W., Malden, Mass.: "Bornstein Patent" Wrench. With Octagon Handle. Not in Schulz. Length: 5 Inches. *The Bornstein patent wrenches are among my favorites. They are mechanically interesting, clearly marked and very well made. This one is a great example of all of those features and has the added benefit of being imprinted with the name of the manufacturer as well as that of the patentee. Nice.* (GOOD+) **$245.00**

D3-11. Billings & Spencer Co., The No. A: Bicycle Monkey Wrench. Center Adjust. Crisp and Clean. Length: 4 1/4 Inches. *This "A" series wrench was available in nickel, polish or painted finish. This one came with the black paint.* (GOOD+) **$35.00**

D3-12. Utility Wrench Co., New York: Quick-Adjust Nut Wrench. Patented August 13, 1878; September 4, 1883. Schulz No. 542. Length: 7 1/2 Inches. *Here's a superb, small size example of one of the finest wrenches ever produced. A good one.* (GOOD+) **$425.00**

D3-13. Canuck Tool Co., Toronto, Canada: Pivot Head Nut Wrench. "Canuck Patent". Rare and Excellent. Length: 10 Inches. *A most unusual pivoting head wrench from Canada. Nicely marked with the interesting company name. Never seen another.* (GOOD+) **$245.00**

D3-14. Hall: Patent Screw Adjust Wrench. With Pivoting Head. Patented March 13, 1894. Length: 5 1/2 Inches. *A superb example of a rare patent adjustable wrench in its smallest size and finest condition. Nearly all original nickel plating remains and the markings are as crisp and clear as the day they were made. A great addition to a collection of small wrenches. Highly recommended.* (FINE) **$465.00**

D3-15. Reedman & Co., C.H., Newark, NJ: Pipe and Nut Wrench. Thumb Lever Lock. 14" Size. Length: 14 Inches. *Self-tightening through the action of the upper jaw, and adjustable by a thumb lever. Missing the serrated insert on the lower jaw.* (FAIR) **$35.00**

D3-16. H. & E. Wrench Co., New Bedford, Mass.: Slide Adjust Pipe Wrench. Patented March 27, 2023. Near-New Condition. Length: 13 Inches. *The mathematicians would put it this way: (High Quality Manufacture+Exceptional Materials) x Stupid Idea=Great Collectible. The equation balances for this sliding jaw gizmo in new condition.* (FINE) **$195.00**

D3-17. Cressy, J.: Screw Adjust Pipe Wrench. Patented March 7, 1876. Schulz No. 595. Length: 14 Inches. *The lower jaw of the Cressy patent rocks on what appears to be a brass spring. A rare and early wrench.* (GOOD+) **$195.00**

D3-18. Portland Wrench Company: Combination Nut and Buggy Wrench. Rare 5" Size. Patented October 16, 1883. Length: 5 Inches. *This was the smallest size of "buggy" wrench offered by this firm. A baby carriage wrench, perhaps? The fixing nut at the base of the handle is marked with a patent date, but it may have come from another tool. A rare wrench.* (GOOD) **$115.00**

D3-19. A. & M., Buffalo, NY: Bicycle Monkey Wrench. Center Adjust. Center Sleeve. Length: 5 Inches. *No idea who the A. & M. people might have been, but they made a nice wrench.* (GOOD+) **$65.00**

D3-20. Calef: Calef's Patent Samson Wrench. Patented April 13, 1880; March 6, 1883. Schulz No. 323. Length: 12 Inches. *Here's a most unusual early self-adjusting wrench with a nice wooden handle. Great wrenches are becoming increasingly difficult to acquire.* (GOOD+) **$345.00**

D3-21. Tower & Lyon, New York, N.Y.: "Involute" Wrench. Patented October 30, 1900. Not In Schulz. Length: 5 3/4 Inches. *A combination wrench and screwdriver with a primeval profile. This appears to have been another attempt (and successful at that) to patent a basic mechanical principle. A rare patented wrench.* (GOOD+) **$85.00**

D3-22. Iron Age: Cast Iron "Cutout" Wrench. 11/16" Open End. 5/8" Square. Length: 6 1/2 Inches. *This was the second, and smaller, size of the Iron Age wrench. A good example.* (GOOD+) **$65.00**

D3-23. Portland Wrench Company: Combination Nut And Buggy Wrench. 10" Size. Patented October 16, 1883. Length: 10 Inches. *Here's a nice carriage wrench from an important maker. A good one.* (GOOD) **$75.00**

D3-24. Bemis & Call, Springfield, Mass.: Double Pipe and Nut Wrench. 6" Size. Super Rare and Excellent. Length: 6 Inches. *A clean and perfectly presentable example of the rare and desirable double pipe and nut wrench. A good one.* (GOOD) **$595.00**

D3-25. Unmarked: Early Brass Nut Wrench. "Economy Faucet". Graphic Appearance. Length: 4 3/4 Inches. *Anyone who has been to the hardware store recently and paid several dollars for a half-dozen brass screws will likely be puzzled by the inscription on this showy wrench. Never seen another.* (GOOD) **$15.00**

D3-26. Windsor Mfg. Co., Windsor, Vermont: Screw Adjust Nut Wrench. Patented January 24, 1860. Schulz No. 427. Length: 10 Inches. *A great early patent wrench from the Green Mountain State that is clearly marked with the maker name and the early patent date. Just for the record, these were manufactured in the same building that now houses the American Precision Museum. Rare.* (GOOD) **$195.00**

D3-27. Williams & Co., J.H., Brooklyn: "Twin Bulldog" Wrench. No. 1 and No. 2 Sizes. Uncommon Type. Length: 12 Inches. *The "Twin Bulldog" features a pair of small alligator wrenches. We have long opined about the utter uselessness of the "alligator" type wrenches and offer as our only comment that this example incorporates insult and injury in a single so-called.* (GOOD+) **$25.00**

D3-28. Trimont Mfg. Co., Roxbury, Mass. No. A 6: Combination Pipe Wrench. With Screwdriver Tip. Rare and Excellent. Length: 6 Inches. *The tip of the handle removes to reveal a secret screwdriver. These are rare.* (GOOD+) **$365.00**

D3-29. Coes Wrench Co.: Monkey Wrench. Wood Handle. Coes "No. 1". Length: 4 3/4 Inches. *Just as every plane collector wants a Stanley No. 1 plane, every wrench collector wants one of these. A nice example.* (GOOD+) **$325.00**

D3-30. Bullard No. 0: Self-Adjusting Pipe Wrench. Spring Activated. Patented October 27, 1903. Length: 5 1/2 Inches. *This is the smallest of the Bullard series which ranged from the sublime, as illustrated here, to the ridiculous (huge). Cute.* (FINE) **$225.00**

D3-31. Lowentraut, P., Newark, NJ: Patented Brace Wrench. Johnston's Patent. Patented December 4, 1894. Length: 12 Inches. *These multi-purpose brace/wrenches were aggressively marketed by the Lowentraut company. The handle comes out to become a screwdriver. A good clean example.* (GOOD) **$175.00**

D3-32. Mossberg Wrench Co, Attleboro, Mass. No. C: Bicycle Monkey Wrench. Center Adjust. Patented November 19, 1895. Length: 5 Inches. *Here's a collector-quality example of the B. & S. "C" wrench. Nice.* (GOOD+) **$65.00**

D3-33. Tower & Lyon, New York, N.Y.: Quik Adjust Bicycle Wrench. Patented August 23, 1892. Schulz No 101 (C). Length: 5 Inches. *A sliding lever at the back of the jaw allows the rapid adjustment of this early patent "bicycle" wrench. This was patent number 481, 389, issued to one E.A. Cochran.* (GOOD) **$495.00**

D3-34. Carpenter, D. H.: Adjustable Spanner Wrench. Patented February 10, 1891. Not in Schulz. Length: 5 Inches. *This patented adjustable wrench is also marked "cycle grip". Small and mechanically interesting.* (FINE) **$165.00**

D3-36. Universal Wrench Co., Detroit: Lever Adjust Nut Wrench. Patented June 3, 1919. Schulz No. 530 (A). Length: 6 Inches. *These well made wrenches combined the features of the classic "Crescent" wrench with the convenience of a quick adjust wrench. This one is in excellent collector quality condition.* (GOOD+) **$85.00**

D3-37. Wakefield Wrench Co.: Wrench. Spring Activated. Patented June 30, 1891. Length: 9 Inches. *This clean working example of the Wakefield patent is in top working order. A good one.* (GOOD+) **$85.00**

D3-38. Mathews, Dayton, Ohio: "Neverstall" Combonation Wrench. Patented September 14, 1909. Schulz No. 818. Length: 10 Inches. *The "Never Stall" name probably came about because that would have been the constant prayer of anyone who had to rely on one of these monstrosities in the event of an emergency. Fitted out with every feature except its own kitchen sink, this classic boondoggle was set up to do many things equally poorly. They apparently sold very well. Another Veg-O-Matic of the tool world.* (GOOD+) **$65.00**

D3-39. Universal Wrench Co., Detroit: Quick Adjust Nut Wrench. Patented June 3, 1919, July 22, 1919. Schulz No. 530. Length: 8 Inches. *Another interesting crescent-type wrench, this one has a lever lock mechanism. A nice, clean example.* (FINE) **$90.00**

D3-40. Tower & Lyon, New York, N.Y.: Boardman's Patent Wrench. 6" Combination Wrench. Excellent Condition. Length: 6 Inches. *The Boardman's patent was a relatively popular wrench, especially for one so totally devoid of any redeeming value as a usable tool. This example of the rare, 6 inch size is in nearly-new condition. Ex-Donnelly collection (I flipped a coin). A great wrench.* (FINE) **$395.00**

D3-41. Gellman Wrench Corp. No. 61: Patented Adjustable Wrench. "Polly". Patented April 17, 1923. Length: 6 Inches. *This was the smallest of the quick-adjust "Polly" series produced by the Cellman Company. A great example in a desirable size.* (GOOD) **$55.00**

D3-42. Abingdon No. 1: Bicycle Monkey Wrench. Center Adjust. "King Dick". Length: 4 Inches. *This classic nut wrench is clean and clearly marked.* (GOOD+) **$55.00**

D3-43. Bauman & Sons, Frank W. No. 1-14: "Baumo" Patent Pipe Wrench. Patented April 23, 1935. Schulz No. 651. Length: 14 Inches. *Pushing in the thumb lever allows quick adjustment of this Pennsylvania patent wrench.* (GOOD+) **$95.00**

D3-44. Edmonds-Metzel Mfg. Co., Chicago: Double Alligator Wrench. Patented July 10, 1906; August 14, 1906. Schulz No. 9 (A). Length: 9 Inches. *Composed of a series of identically-shaped plates held together with screws, these wrenches were designed to be able to be repaired with replacement parts easily. When the selling point of a tool is "what to do when it breaks", one would be well-advised not to buy it. Most took the advice. A rare wrench.* (FINE) **$165.00**

D3-45. Syracuse No. Z2: Cast Iron Implement Wrench. Raised Lettering. Excellent Condition. Length: 10 1/2 Inches. *Four wrenches and a hammer on this cast iron tool with forged-in maker mark. Missing the plow.* (GOOD+) **$35.00**

D3-46. M.W. & Co., Framingham, Mass.: Patent Pivot Jaw Wrench. Patented June 15, 1897. Superb Condition. Length: 10 Inches. *This most unusual patented wrench features a spring-activated upper jaw that locks on to the pipe or nut before final adjustments are made. Crisp, clean and clearly marked. A rare wood-handled quick adjust wrench. Nearly new.* (FINE) **$265.00**

Group E3

E3-1. Stanley Rule & Level No. 45: Early Combination Plane. Original Chestnut Box. Complete Original Label. Length: 12 Inches. *A previous owner has "enhanced" the original japan finish, but it appears that it might not have been necessary to do so. Complete in the original box and ready to use or display.* (GOOD) **$225.00**

E3-2. Stanley Rule & Level No. 98/99: Pair of Side Rabbet Plane. With Depth Stops. Ready to Use. Length: 4 Inches. *A good clean pair of side rabbet planes, including the desirable depth stops. One of the stops is a brass replacement, but the tools are otherwise in excellent condition. Ready to add versatility to a woodworker and a woodworking shop. Nice.* (GOOD+) **$285.00**

E3-3. Stanley Rule & Level No. 92: 1" Shoulder Rabbet Plane. Complete and Sound. Usable Condition. Length: 5 1/2 Inches. *At 1/4" narrower than the its cousin, the No. 93, these were suited to lighter duty tasks. This one has been given a coat of lacquer by a previous owner, but is otherwise clean, sound and usable.* (GOOD+) **$125.00**

E3-4. Stanley Rule & Level No. 55: Patent Combination Plane. With 4 Boxes Cutters. Extra Crisp and Clean. Length: 12 Inches. *Advertised as "A Planing Mill Within Itself", the Stanley No. 55 Patent Universal Combination Plane can, with a bit of practice, be made to duplicate any molding profile ever made. This one is complete with all of the original parts, including the four boxes containing more than 50 specialized cutting irons.. Nearly all original nickel plating remains and the rosewood fences and handles are in excellent condition. Were it possible to make these planes today, a working approximation of much lesser quality would cost thousands of dollars. A bargain.* (FINE) **$845.00**

E3-5. Stanley Rule & Level No. 100 1/2: Model Maker's Block Plane. With Round Bottom. Near-New Condition. Length: 3 Inches. *Topped off with a nicely-contrasting red lever cap, this example of Stanley's convex bottom model maker's block plane is in mint condition. Perfect.* (FINE) **$155.00**

E3-6. Stanley Rule & Level No. 9 1/2: Adjustable Throat Plane. With Precision Adjustment. Patented October 12, 1897. Length: 6 Inches. *Fitted with an adjustable throat mechanism as well as independent lateral adjustment and depth-of-cut features, the No. 9 1/2 block plane was a mainstay of the Stanley line for many years. This one has some light pitting on the sole, but is otherwise in good shape.* (GOOD) **$25.00**

E3-7. Stanley Rule & Level No. 271: Nickel Plated Router Plane. Original Carton. 'Made In England". Length: 3 Inches. *This Stanley classic is in new condition in its original box. A tough tool to find in any condition.* (FINE) **$45.00**

E3-8. Stanley Rule & Level No. 39: Cast Iron Dado Plane. 1/4" Size. Complete and Usable. Length: 8 Inches. *This one has seen some use, but it is clean, sound and ready to use or display. A good one.* (GOOD) **$110.00**

E3-9. Stanley Rule & Level No. 3 C: 8" Smoothing Plane. Rosewood Handles. With Corrugated Sole. Length: 9 Inches. *The name of the previous owner and the inscription "1942 Hawaii" have been tastefully etched on the side of the "Type 11" No. 3 C smoothing plane. An excellent working plane with a tropical past.* (GOOD+) **$110.00**

E3-10. Stanley Rule & Level No. 113: Adjustable Compass Plane. Early Wheel Type. Ready to Use. Length: 11 Inches. *Early versions of Stanley's No. 113 circular plane are among the most visually appealing of all Stanley metallic planes. This early example features the early patent dates on the cutter and the distinctive "side wheel" mechanism. A previous owner "enhanced" the black japanning, but the plane is otherwise complete and sound.* (GOOD) **$115.00**

E3-11. Stanley Rule & Level No. 148: Tongue and Groove Plane. For 7/8" Stock. Superb Condition. Length: 9 Inches. *No apologies for this pristine example of Stanley's stock-lumber version of its 140 series of double tongue and groove plane. These are becoming increasingly difficult to find. Examples in this condition have always been scarce. A good one.* (GOOD) **$255.00**

E3-12. Stanley Rule & Level No. 71: Open Throat Router Plane. Patented September 10, 1907. With Depth Stop. Length: 8 Inches. *This open throat router plane is complete and in fine working order. The adjustable fence is affixed to the bottom of the plane. One original cutter included.* (GOOD+) **$65.00**

E3-13. Stanley Rule & Level No. 140: Skew Bladed Block Plane. WW II Type. Ready to Use. Length: 7 Inches. *Stanley discontinued the No. 140 skew bladed block plane in 1943, so this black japan finished model , undoubtedly produced under wartime restrictions that precluded use of the nickel plating process, would have been the final version ever sold. This one is clean, complete and ready to use.* (GOOD+) **$125.00**

E3-14. Stanley Rule & Level No. 71 1/2: Nickel Plated Router Plane. Patented October 29, 1901. With 2 Original Irons. Length: 7 1/2 Inches. *Both the 1/4" and 1/2" cutter are present with this tough to find closed throat router plane. First come, first serve.* (GOOD+) **$110.00**

E3-15. Stanley Rule & Level No. 78: Duplex Rabbet, Fillet Plane. Patented June 7, 1910. Absolutely Brand New. Length: 10 Inches. *A good, clean working example of Stanley's mainstay bullnose/rabbet & filletster plane. A nice "Sweetheart" trademark on an absolutely unused plane. Mint.* (FINE) **$165.00**

E3-16. Stanley Rule & Level No. 27: Transitional Jack Plane. 95% Original Paint. Extra Crisp and Clean. Length: 15 Inches. *One of the more common of Stanley's "Transitional" planes, very few have survived in this condition. Crisp, clean and ready to display or use.* (FINE) **$125.00**

E3-17. Stanley Rule & Level No. 72: Adjustable Chamfer Plane. 98% Paint. Superb Condition. Length: 7 Inches. *If you're looking for a good working model of Stanley's patented chamfer plane that just happens to be in top collector quality condition, stop here. A very nice example.* (FINE) **$345.00**

E3-18. Stanley Rule & Level No. 57: Core Box Plane. With One Set Extension. Orignal Turnbuckle. Length: 10 Inches. *This example of Stanley's large size core box plane has seen some use, but it retains its original turnbuckle and one full set of extensions, plus an extra.* (GOOD) **$265.00**

E3-19. Stanley Rule & Level No. 171: Door Trim Router Plane. Patented December 26, 1911. Complete with 1 Cutter. Length: 11 1/2 Inches. *Introduced by Stanley in the early years of this century, when business was booming, power tools were not even imagined and the average workman could afford such niceties, Stanley may have produced a tool that was a bit too specialized in function for it to achieve any significant market success. This example, which is complete with one of the original 3 cutting irons retains some 98% of its original shiny black japan finish. A superb example of a rare Stanley plane.* (FINE) **$465.00**

E3-20. Stanley Rule & Level No. 40: Cast Iron Scrub Plane. With Beech Handles. Ca. 1930's. Length: 9 1/2 Inches. *This ca. 1930's era scrub plane has much of the yellow lacquer on the handles and a good 98% or more of the original paint. A good one.* (FINE) **$135.00**

E3-21. Stanley Rule & Level No. 22: 8" Transitional Plane. Patented 1892 Trade Mark. Clean and Complete. Length: 8 Inches. *This No. 22 retains much of its original finishes. Crisp, clean and ready to fill out a collection or use in the shop.* (GOOD+) **$75.00**

E3-22. Stanley Rule & Level No. 605 C: "Bedrock" Jack Plane. Corrugated Bottom. Ready to Use. Length: 14 Inches. *This clean and sound "Bedrock" jack plane has a corrugated sole and miles of use remaining. A good one.* (GOOD+) **$265.00**

E3-23. Stanley Rule & Level: "Defiance" Steel Block Plane. With "Defiance" Cutter. Scarce and Excellent. Length: 6 Inches. *These workaday planes were were produced from japan finished sheet metal and offered as a "household", or second quality, line of tools by Stanley in the 1930's. This one is in excellent condition and clearly marked with the Defiance name on the cutting iron.* (GOOD+) **$65.00**

E3-24. Stanley Rule & Level No. 4 1/2: Wide, Heavy Smooth Plane. Rosewood Handle and Knob. Ca. 1910. Length: 10 1/2 Inches. *A clean and ready to use wide, heavy smoothing plane. Someone sprayed a bit of lacquer on this one, but it is otherwise in great working condition. An increasingly tough plane to find.* (GOOD+) **$145.00**

E3-25. Stanley Rule & Level No. 605: "Bedrock" Jack Plane. "Sweetheart" Trade Mark. Excellent Condition. Length: 14 Inches. *Bearing the No. 605 designation of Stanley's respected "Bedrock" series, this was, without question the very best jack plane ever offered. This example has been so little used that nearly all of its original decal remains on the handle.* (GOOD+) **$285.00**

E3-26. Stanley Rule & Level No. 71: Open Throat Router Plane. With Depth Stop. "V" Shap Cutter. Length: 8 Inches. *This open throat router plane retains 98% of its original finishes and comes complete with its original "v" shaped cutting iron.* (GOOD+) **$35.00**

E3-27. Stanley Rule & Level No. 289: Skew-Blade Rabbet Plane. Complete and Original. "Sweetheart" Trademark Length: 8 1/2 Inches. *There is no question that these skew-bladed rabbet and filletster planes would have become the standard had they not required such precise machining and hand-fitting in the Stanley factory, resulting in what proved to be a prohibitively expensive plane for the average woodworker. This one is complete and ready to go to work effortlessly planing end grain or easily working figured woods. Not for the average woodworker. Pristine.* (FINE) **$445.00**

E3-28. Stanley Rule & Level No. 3: 8 1/2" Smooth Plane. From Hardware Store. Unused Condition. Length: 8 1/2 Inches. *This example of Stanley's 8" smoother is in unused condition, a fact that is emphasized by the existence of the bottom portion of the original box. A superb example of Stanley's ca. 1930's rosewood handle No. 3 that was recently discovered among old hardware store stock.* (FINE) **$115.00**

E3-29. Stanley Rule & Level No. 604 1/2 C: "Bedrock" Smoothing Plane. Early Style. 99% Original Paint. Length: 10 Inches. *Here's an exceptionally well preserved example of the early-style "Bedrock" series. Of all the planes of the "Bedrock" series, it is the 604 1/2 wide smoothing plane that receives the best reviews from serious woodworkers. The distinctive feature of the Bedrock planes was the patented frog designed to eliminate "chatter" when working wood. It is in exactly the types of applications where a wide smoothing plane will be used that this problem is likely to occur. Those who have tried them, in overwhelming numbers, say that this is the tool for the job. We cannot disagree. A great working tool.* (FINE) **$595.00**

E3-30. Stanley Rule & Level No. 95: Edge Trim Block Plane. "Sweetheart" Trademark. Original Decal. Length: 6 Inches. *If you're looking for the No. 95 edge trim block plane, stop here. This one retains all of its original finishes as well as the original decal. Minty crispy nice.* (FINE) **$245.00**

E3-31. Stanley Rule & Level No. 5: "Bedrock" Fore Plane. Early Type 2. Ground Off Patent Date. Length: 15 Inches. *The japanning that covers the ground off 1895 patent date at the rear of this plane indicates that this is one of the earliest examples of Stanley's "Bedrock" plane series. A chipped tote and hang hole require mention on this otherwise excellent, early and uncommon Stanley plane.* (FINE) **$195.00**

E3-32. Stanley Rule & Level No. 72: Adjustable Chamfer Plane. Patented April 21, 1885. With Bullnose Attachments. Length: 9 Inches. *Designed to facilitate the planing of chamfers on the edges of boards and beams, these were a very specific special-purpose tool that would have been purchased by only a very limited number of woodworkers. Examples, accordingly, are rare. This nearly perfectly preserved example retains 98%+ of its original paint. This one comes complete with the uncommon "bullnose" attachment. A rare Stanley plane in top condition.* (FINE) **$545.00**

E3-33. Stanley Rule & Level No. 8: "Type 13" Jointer Plane. "Sweetheart" Trademark. With Frog Adjustment. Length: 24 Inches. *The No. 8 jointer plane, at 24" in length is a tool that is not available from any contemporary manufacturer. This example incorporates the 1910 patent throat adjustment that dramatically improved the precision of the Stanley/Bailey planes. We offer our best wishes for the speedy recovery of anyone who would prefer some of the junk being made today to one of these classic tools. Crisp, clean and ready to use.* (GOOD+) **$215.00**

E3-34. Stanley Rule & Level No. 605: Early "Bedrock" Plane. Extra Crisp and Clean. 90%+ Original Paint. Length: 14 Inches. *Bearing the No. 605 designation of Stanley's respected "Bedrock" series, these were, without question the very best jack planes ever offered. Ready to put back to use.* (GOOD+) **$185.00**

E3-35. Stanley Rule & Level No. 90: Bullnose Rabbet Plane. "Made in USA". Usable Condition. Length: 4 Inches. *This American-made bullnose has a nickel finish that is a bit dulled, but it is otherwise in ready to use condition.* (GOOD) **$75.00**

E3-36. Stanley Rule & Level No. 2: 7 1/2" Smoothing Plane. "Sweetheart" Trademark. Crisp and Clean. Length: 7 1/2 Inches. *This 1920's era example of the No. 2 smooth plane retains 95% of its original black japan finish and is clean and complete. A good one.* (GOOD+) **$255.00**

E3-37. Stanley Rule & Level No. 4 1/2: "Type 13" Smooth Plane. Rosewood Handle and Knob. Ready to Use. Length: 10 1/2 Inches. *Looking for a great working heavy smoothing plane. Here's an exceptionally nice No. 4 1/2 fitted out with handles of Brazilian Rosewood. A great working tool that is ready to provide several lifetimes of service. The ca. 1930's era cutting iron is in new condition on this desirable "Type 13" version.* (GOOD+) **$215.00**

E3-38. Stanley Tools No. 79: Double Side Rabbet Plane. Cast Iron Body. Nickel Plated 2nd Model. Length: 5 Inches. *Stanley introduced the second type No. 79 shortly after the Second World War. This one is clean and ready to use.* (GOOD+) **$95.00**

E3-39. Stanley Tools (England) No. 130: Double End Block Plane. Ca. 1960's. 99% Original Paint. Length: 8 Inches. *This double end block plane retains nearly all of the dark blue finish that was used by Stanley at the very end of their U.S. production of planes. A great working plane in top condition.* (FINE) **$45.00**

E3-40. Stanley Rule & Level No. 75: Bullnose Rabbet Plane. "Sweetheart" Trademark. New Condition. Length: 4 1/2 Inches. *This pristine example of Stanley's smallest "bullnose" plane is imprinted with the desirable "Sweetheart" logo. Nice.* (FINE) **$75.00**

E3-41. Stanley Rule & Level No. 31: Transitional Jointer Plane. With "Mattison" Brand. With No. 00 Level. Length: 24 Inches. *The previous owner of these two tools boldly branded them with his name. In keeping with what one would expect from someone so justifiably proud of his tools, they have been kept through the years in nearly new condition. A pretty pair with a story.* (FINE) **$235.00**

E3-42. Stanley Rule & Level No. 62: Low Angle Block Plane. Ca. 1915. Precision Lapped Sole. Length: 14 Inches. *This crisp No. 62 plane has been precision lapped by a previous owner and it is in top working order. These low angle planes were extremely susceptible to breakage as a result of a design flaw that caused the small end-grain shavings that a plane of this sort would produce, to accumulate under the cutter and exert pressure at the rear of the mouth. Almost invariably, these planes have a chip or crack at that weak point. While some may advertise these planes for sale with what they call the "usual throat chip", here at Martin J. Donnelly Antique Tools, we will offer only those that are without damage. Not only is this example without damage, it has been precisely tuned by a previous owner and is ready to use. A great plane.* (GOOD+) **$545.00**

E3-43. Stanley Rule & Level No. 4 1/2: Wide, Heavy Smooth Plane. Rosewood Handle and Knob. Ca. 1890's. Length: 10 1/2 Inches. *This early No. 4 1/2 plane is clean and sound, but just a bit dirty. Worth the time and trouble to clean up.* (GOOD+) **$110.00**

E3-44. Stanley Rule & Level No. 97: Cabinet Maker's Edge Plane. "Sweetheart" Trademark. Near-New Condition. Length: 10 Inches. *Another of the Stanley planes with an "Achilles Heel" the Stanley No. 97 might better be referred to as the "cabinetmaker's broken edge plane". This superb example has the later-style high knob and is marked with the "Sweetheart" trademark on the shiny cutting iron. Nearly all of the original shiny black japan finish remains on the metal parts and the original lacquer is intact on the rosewood knob. An absolute top shelf example. Highly recommended.* (FINE) **$625.00**

Group F3

F3-1. Stover Mfg. Co., Freeport, Ill. No. 22: Folding Cast Iron Saw Vise. Early and Complete. Distinctive Form. Length: 12 Inches. *A graphic and interesting early saw vise which bears a striking resemblance to a vise later marketed by Disston. This is my first experience with the Stover company, but their product line was probably not limited to this one tool, given the bold "No. 22" cast into the body of the tool in great Victorian lettering. A superb collectible tool.* (FINE) **$85.00**

F3-2. Simmons Hardware Co., E.C.: Fruitwood Saw Handle. With Keen Kutter Logo. New Old Stock. Length: 6 Inches. *We wouldn't recommend mounting this Keen Kutter saw handle on your best saw, or any saw. It's just too nice the way it is. Brand new, but quite old.* (FINE) **$55.00**

F3-3. Unmarked: Cast Iron Washer Cutter. Early Appearance. 90% Original Paint. Length: 5 Inches. *Most of the original paint remains on this early cast iron washer cutter. The cutting edges are adjusted by means of slotted screws.* (FINE) **$55.00**

F3-4. Stevens, G.M., Portland, Maine: Stevens' Patent Mitre Box. Patented May 7, 1872. Rare and Excellent. Length: 24 Inches. *This early patent Mitre Box from the state of Maine features a reinforcing bracket with finials formed in a fleur de lis pattern. A rare early patent that is clean and clearly marked.* (GOOD+) **$255.00**

F3-5. Atkins & Co., Indianapolis, Ind.: Pair of Handles. For Crosscut Saw. Near New Condition. Length: 12 Inches. *If your two man crosscut saw is in need of handles, we are at your service. Complete in unused condition with the original decals.* (FINE) **$45.00**

F3-6. Unmarked: Faucett Handle Washer Cutter. Apparently Unused. Most Unusual Type. Length: 5 Inches. *Nearly all of the original black japanning remains on this decidedly different cutter. Most unusual and in superb condition. Shiny new.* (FINE) **$115.00**

F3-7. Unmarked: Early Open Saw Handle. Stylized Design. Ready to Use. Length: 7 Inches. *If you're looking to dress up your dovetail saw, this early handle should do the trick nicely.* (GOOD+) **$25.00**

F3-8. Disston & Sons, Henry No. 3: Embossed Brass Saw Screws. New Condition, Original Box. Length: 4 Inches. *Here's a lifetime supply of Disston saw screws. A rare Disston "in the box" item.* (FINE) **$55.00**

F3-9. Wentworth No. 3: Wentworth's Patent Saw Vise. Patented April 8, 1879. Ready to Use. Length: 12 Inches. *This classic saw vise is imprinted with the date of the patent in raised cast letters on the body. An excellent working tool that is ready to be returned to use.* (GOOD+) **$35.00**

F3-10. Unmarked: Cast Iron Washer Cutter. 4 Lug Wing Nut. Scarce and Excellent. Length: 5 1/2 Inches. *A central wing nut with four appendages is the means by which this graphic washer cutter is adjusted. Loosening the screws allows the arms to be adjusted to the requisite length.* (GOOD+) **$85.00**

F3-11. Palmer, A.J.: Cast Iron Washer Brace. With Cupid Design. Masonic Emblem. Length: 12 Inches. *A.J. Palmer of Carlton, New York State, was granted a patent for this "improved washer cutting brace" on December 3, 1878. The patent drawings offer no explanation for the Masonic symbol and cupid with arrows that appear in raised castings on the body of the tool. A clean and visually appealing example of a tool that combined function and art. This has received the "B" rating, in the Pearson book, denoting that less than twenty examples are known to exist. Complete and excellent.* (GOOD+) **$295.00**

F3-12. Clipper Tool Co., Buffalo, N.Y.: Patented Bench Mount Saw Vise. Patented February 20, 1906. Scarce and Excellent. Length: 11 Inches. *There seems to be no end to the number of variations on the "saw vise" theme that exist in the world of tools. This patented vise was produced by an obscure Buffalo, New York maker. Never seen another.* (GOOD+) **$45.00**

F3-13. Unmarked: Early Cast Iron Washer Cutter. Original Gold Paint. Screw Lock Adjustment. Length: 4 Inches. *Yet another variation on the washer cutter theme, this unmarked example retains all of its original gold paint. This is the first example of this pattern that we have ever offered.* (GOOD+) **$75.00**

F3-14. Atkins & Co., E.C., Indianapolis No. 500: Cast Iron Saw Tool. Large Saw Jointer. Raised Letter Casting. Length: 5 Inches. *In the old days, if you needed to set and file the teeth of your saw, you could go to the hardware store and buy one of these. Today, they're available in hardware store new condition from Martin J. Donnelly Antique Tools.* (FINE) **$25.00**

F3-15. Unmarked: Brace Type Washer Cutter. Cast Iron Body. Original Orange Finish. Length: 8 1/2 Inches. *Most tools of this type were intended to fit in the chuck of a standard bit brace. This one was designed to save the user the trouble by including the brace with the tool. Most unusual.* (GOOD+) **$135.00**

F3-16. Unmarked: Early Cast Iron Washer Cutter. Cast Iron Nuts. Most Unusual Type. Length: 4 Inches. *Here's a particularly early appearing washer cutter that retains nearly all of its original factory japan finish. A good one.* (FINE) **$55.00**

F3-17. Prutton Mfg. Co., D.H., Cleveland,: "Ace" Brand Saw Vise. With Cam Grip. New Condition, Original Box. Length: 11 Inches. *For the collector of saw vises, we recommend this "Ace" brand offering from Cleveland's obscure Prutton Manufacturing Company. Most unusual.* (FINE) **$35.00**

F3-18. Unmarked: Early Appearing Washer Cutter. Appears Hand Forged. As New Condition. Length: 4 Inches. *Try spending ten or fifteen minutes closely examining a tool of this sort sometime. Carefully hand-filed and fitted and precisely graduated perhaps as long as 160 years ago, this early washer cutter is in near-new condition. More than meets the eye.* (FINE) **$95.00**

F3-19. Disston & Sons, H., Philadelphia, Penna. No. 2: "Conqueror" Saw Swage. With Instructions. New Condition, Original Box. Length: 3 1/2 Inches. *This Disston saw swage appears unused. Shiny new and in the original wooden box with instructions.* (FINE) **$75.00**

F3-20. Unmarked: Early Patent Washer Cutter. Patented October 11, 1875. Twist Lock Handle. Length: 9 Inches. *This one is clearly marked with the early patent date. Twisting the handle locks the knives into place. Different.* (GOOD) **$75.00**

F3-21. Unmarked: Set of 5 Sash Miter Templates. For Scribing and Trim. Excellent Condition. Length: 6 1/2 Inches. *Here's a nice grouping of sash mitre templates of varying types. A great working set for the collector or the window maker.* (GOOD+) **$65.00**

F3-22. Unmarked: Double Blade Washer Cutter. Appears Manufactured. Complete and Unusual. Length: 4 1/2 Inches. *This precision washer cutter features a pair of cutter arms arranged at right angles to each other. Without a doubt, a manufactured product, but unmarked in any way. Very different.* (GOOD+) **$65.00**

F3-23. Karle, Geo. J., Buffalo, N.Y.: Combination Saw Jointer. Patented April 23, 1912. New Condition, Original Box. Length: 10 1/2 Inches. *Here's a most unusual saw jointer, which incorporates a grindstone into its design. Patented on April 23, 1912, this one is in new condition in its original box, complete with the original instructions.* (FINE) **$65.00**

F3-24. Disston & Sons, H., Philadelphia, Penna. No. 3: Box of Saw Screws. 3 Original Screws. Brass and Nickeled. Length: 3 Inches. *This original Henry Disston & Sons box contains 5 original saw screws. An interesting and unusual find.* (FINE) **$35.00**

F3-25. Unmarked: Faucet Handle Washer Cutter. Rare Nickel Plated Version. Most Unusual Type. Length: 5 Inches. *Nearly all of the original nickel plating remains on this interesting variation on the washer cutter theme.* (GOOD+) **$85.00**

F3-26. Van Camp Hardware & I. Co. No. 50: Cam Lock Saw Vise. With Folding Bench Clamp. Rare and Excellent. Length: 12 Inches. *Don't try to hold your saw in your lap when you sharpen it. A good saw vise will help ensure that the teeth are properly filed. This one is clean, complete and ready to use.* (GOOD+) **$55.00**

F3-27. Atkins & Co., E.C., Indianapolis: Cast Iron Saw Tool. Large Saw Jointer. Raised Letter Casting. Length: 5 Inches. *This device was intended to hold a file while it was run over the tips of saw teeth before filing. It was called a "jointer" because it functioned in the same way as a jointer plane, making the surface completely flat. When saws are filed without jointing, the teeth can have varying heights, making it difficult going through the wood. This early example from a prominent maker is in excellent condition and ready to use.* (GOOD+) **$15.00**

F3-28. Osborne & Co., C.S., Newark, N.J.: Adjustable Washer Cutter. With Brass Stops. For Bit Brace. Length: 5 Inches. *The C.S. Osborne Company, as the leading manufacturer of leatherworking tools, would have a ready market for tools such as this. Examples are not common, however. Nicely marked and ready to use, if you choose.* (GOOD+) **$75.00**

F3-29. Prutton Mfg. Co., D.H., Cleveland: "Ace" Brand Saw Vise. With Cam Grip. New Condition, Original Box. Length: 11 Inches. *For the collector of saw vises, we recommend this "Ace" brand offering from Cleveland's obscure Prutton Manufacturing Company. Most unusual.* (FINE) **$25.00**

F3-30. Osborne & Co., C.S., Newark, N.J.: Nickel Plated Washer Cutter. Patented August 16, 1881. Full Nickel Plating. Length: 4 Inches. *These tools were intended for working with leather, so it is no surprise that the Osborne firm would offer such an appealing product. Nicely marked with the patent date and in superb condition.* (FINE) **$75.00**

F3-31. General Hardware Mfg. Co.: "Pawood" Circle Cutter. 5/8" to 2 1/2" Size. New Condition, Original Box. Length: 3 1/4 Inches. *This "Pawood" circle cutter was apparently meant to fit in a drill press where it would perform its woodworking function. New and in the box.* (FINE) **$35.00**

F3-32. Disston & Sons, H., Philadelphia, Penna. No. 3: "Conqueror" Saw Swage. Smallest Size. Original Box. Length: 4 Inches. *A swage was used to level the teeth by hammering them head-on. This was the mid-size version of the "Conqueror" series.* (GOOD+) **$35.00**

F3-33. Smith, Otis A., Rockfall, Conn.: Early Patented Washer Cutter. Patented October 24, 1865. Near New Condition. Length: 4 Inches. *Otis Smith of Rockfall, Conn., was a prolific inventor, having also patented a plow plane and auger bit countersink, among other things. This adjustable washer cutter is marked with his name and patent date. Complete and nearly new.* (FINE) **$95.00**

F3-34. Unmarked: Central Washer Cutter. Dual Slide Scribes. Early and Excellent. Length: 5 Inches. *This graphic washer cutter is complete and in excellent collector-quality condition.* (GOOD+) **$65.00**

F3-35. Pike Mfg. Co., Pike, N.H. U.S.A.: "Perfect" Saw Jointer. With Catalog. New Condition, Original Box. Length: 5 Inches. *The original box has kept this New Hampshire made saw jointer in new condition. Complete with a miniature catalogue of Pike products.* (FINE) **$95.00**

F3-36. Simonds Saw & Steel Co., Fitchburg No. 100: Pair of Crosscut Saw Handles. For One, Two Man. Ready to Use. Length: 12 Inches. *Here's just the thing to put your crosscut saw back into working order. Brand new.* (FINE) **$35.00**

F3-37. Lose Wrench Works, Corry, Penn.: Patented Folding Saw Vise. Patented July 15, 1895. "Bickerd Patents". Length: 14 Inches. *A collector seeking to obtain "one of each" in area of saw vises will face a daunting task. There seems to be no end to the number of variations on this theme. This patented example is intended to fold out of the way when not in use. Most unusual.* (GOOD+) **$85.00**

F3-38. Sears, Roebuck & Co. No. 4920: "Dunlap" Saw Filing Saw Vise. Unused Condition. New Condition, Original Box. Length: 11 Inches. *At one time or another, Sears, Roebuck and Company offered every imaginable type of tool. In some cases they offered two or more examples of each, under their "Craftsman" and "Dunlap" trade names. This "Dunlap" version is in new condition in its original box. Nice.* (FINE) **$45.00**

F3-39. Lowntraut Mfg. Co., P., Newark, N.J.: Adjustable Washer Cutter. With Graduated Face. With Adjusting Screws. Length: 5 Inches. *We have offered washer cutters from this company before, but this example is decidedly more complex than the others we have offered. Its features include a graduated beam and replaceable and adjustable cutting tips. A rare washer cutter.* (FINE) **$85.00**

F3-40. Unmarked: Pair of Crosscut Saw Handles. Excellent Condition. Ready to Use. Length: 13 1/2 Inches. *There are no marks to indicate the maker of these well preserved crosscut saw handles, but they are very well made and in excellent condition.* (GOOD+) **$35.00**

F3-41. Sears, Roebuck & Co. No. 4920: Saw Filing Device. With Instructions. New Condition, Original Box. Length: 10 Inches. *The first cousin to the saw vise, the filing device inspired nearly as much wasted creativity. This offering, from Sears' "Dunlap" line is in new condition in its original box, complete with instruction manual. Mint.* (FINE) **$45.00**

F3-42. Unmarked: Early Cast Iron Washer Cutter. Dual Adjusting Screws. Calibrated Base. Length: 5 Inches. *The graphic "mousketeer" wing nuts on this cast iron washer cutter make it immediately evident that this is a very early example of this type of tool. Nearly new.* (FINE) **$65.00**

F3-43. Millers Falls Company No. 82: Precision Adjust Washer Cutter. For Gasket Work. New Condition, Original Box. Length: 5 Inches. *Fitted with a graduated and a pair of slotted and knurled screws to lock the cutters into place, this well made washer cutter was introduced at about the time these tools were becoming obsolete. New and in the original box.* (FINE) **$55.00**

F3-44. Disston & Sons, H., Philadelphia, Penna. No. 222: Pair of Crosscut Saw Handles. Excellent Condition. Ready to Use. Length: 13 1/2 Inches. *If you need a pair of handles for your Disston two man crosscut saw, here's a pair in unused condition. Perfect.* (FINE) **$45.00**

F3-45. Disston & Sons, Henry, Philadelphia, Penna. No. 6: Patented Folding Saw Vise. Patented December 27, 1910. Extremely Clean Condition Length: 15 Inches. *An, exceptionally well preserved saw vise, this one bears the prestigious Disston name in raised cast lettering on the jaw. The patent date is also cast into the body. More than 90% of the shiny black japanning remains. A good one.* (FINE) **$125.00**

Group G3

G3-1. Nylint No. 911-Z: Steel Body Stanley Truck. Promotional Item. New Condition, Original Box. Length: 22 Inches. *This well made solid steel truck is imprinted with Stanley's "Do Things Right" logo. It is in new condition in its original box.* (FINE) **$115.00**

G3-2. Stanley Rule & Level: Sleeve for "Ready Edge" Blades. 1 3/4" Size. Scarce Stanley Item. Length: 6 3/4 Inches. *This sleeve was intended to fit over a box of Stanley's rare "Ready Edge" cutting irons, which featured a replaceable cutting tip. Great graphics on a striking piece of Stanley ephemera.* (GOOD+) **$65.00**

G3-3. Stanley Rule & Level: Commemorative Marking Gauge. 150th Anniversary. 1853-1993. Length: 9 Inches. *In a daring move that was popular with tool collectors, but apparently very few others, Stanley Tools produced a line of classic tools to commemorate its 150th Anniversary in 1993. Because of their high quality, these tools quickly became collectible. This marking gauge from the series is in new condition.* (FINE) **$145.00**

G3-4. Stanley Tools: Powerlock Tape Telephone. Promotional Item. New Condition, Original Box. Length: 8 Inches. *Offered as part of a series of devices in the form of Stanley's "Powerlock" tape series, this telephone is in new condition and could be put to use, if the owner so desired.* (FINE) **$45.00**

G3-5. Stanley Rule & Level No. 60: Multiple Guide Doweling Jig. Total Of 9 Guides. New Condition, Original Box. Length: 5 1/2 Inches. *This is the No. 60 doweling jig, the equivalent to the No. 59 shown below, but with several extra guides for different size bits. Box is intact but in need of help. The gauge is perfect and housed in a fitted wood box.* (FINE) **$110.00**

G3-6. Stanley Tools No. 1530-A: "Yankee" Ratcheting Hand Drill. New Condition, Original Box. Length: 11 Inches. *Originally manufactured by the North Brothers Tool Company, this multiple speed ratcheting drill was, without question, the finest small hand drill ever produced. Brand new and in the box.* (FINE) **$225.00**

G3-7. Stanley Rule & Level No. 49: Auger Bit Depth Gauge. Nickel Plated Finish. New Condition, Original Box. Length: 2 1/2 Inches. *Stanley's standard auger bit depth stop in excellent condition in its original box.* (FINE) **$35.00**

G3-8. Stanley Rule & Level No. 199: Commemorative Knife. 150th Anniversary. 1853-1993. Length: 10 Inches. *A replica of its classic No. 199 aluminum knife, this commemorative item was cast in solid bronze. Complete with the original commemorative paperwork.* (FINE) **$145.00**

G3-9. Stanley Tools No. 257: Laminated Pine Level. Non-Adjustable. New Condition, Original Box. Length: 24 Inches. *This late but most unusual level is in absolutely new condition. Levels like this are found in this condition about as often as transitional planes are; that is to say, almost never. Never say never again.* (FINE) **$125.00**

G3-10. Stanley Tools: Powerlock Tape Radio. Promotional Item. New Condition, Original Box. Length: 8 Inches. *If you wanted to discretely listen to music while working at your carpentry job, this would be just the thing. Brand new.* (FINE) **$45.00**

G3-11. Stanley Rule & Level No. 49: Auger Bit Depth Gauge. Nickel Plated Finish. New Condition, Original Box. Length: 2 1/2 Inches. *These were used for boring holes of a fixed depth, such as those used for stopped mortises. A perfectly preserved example in new condition in the original box.* (FINE) **$45.00**

G3-12. Stanley Rule & Level No. 82: Adjustable Head Scraper. With 2 Cutters. New Condition, Original Box. Length: 12 Inches. *Both original cutters remain with this adjustable scraper, as are the original instructions. The box is in clean, sound condition.* (FINE) **$85.00**

G3-13. Stanley Tools No. 30-176: "Bicentennial" Tape Measure. With Liberty Bell. New Condition, Original Box. Length: 4 Inches. *As did most major companies, Stanley produced a commemorative item for the United States Bicentennial in 1976. This tape measure is in new condition in its original packaging.* (FINE) **$95.00**

G3-14. Stanley Rule & Level No. 45: Box for Plane. Early Chestnut Box. Complete Original Label. Length: 12 Inches. *If you have a clean, early No. 45, here's just what you need.* (GOOD+) **$65.00**

G3-15. Stanley Rule & Level: Advertising Tape Measure. Savings Bank of New Britain With Magnifying Case. Length: 2 3/4 Inches. *Stanley no doubt contracted with the nearby Bank of New Britain to produce these advertising tape measures. This one is complete with its original magnifying glass case. An uncommon Stanley tape measure with close to home advertising.* (FINE) **$65.00**

G3-16. Stanley Rule & Level No. 25M: Set Of "Matched" Screwdriver. With Golf Logo. New Condition, Original Box. Length: 11 Inches. *The inside of the box for these most unusual "matched" screwdrivers features a golfing illustration. A great set.* (FINE) **$295.00**

G3-17. Stanley Rule & Level: Commemorative Belt Buckle. 150th Anniversary. 1853-1993. Length: 10 Inches. *The design for this cast bronze commemorative belt buckle was taken from the cover of a Nineteenth Century Stanley catalog. Part of a limited edition, this was Number 2795. Why did the Stanley collector wear a bronze buckle on his belt?...* (FINE) **$155.00**

G3-18. Stanley Rule & Level: Commemorative Transitional Plane. No. 136 of 2000. Limited Edition. Length: 15 1/2 Inches. *To commemorate their 150th Anniversary Stanley offered a series of commemorative tools of which this restored and numbered transitional plane was one. The original intent was to produce a series of 2000 planes, each individually serial numbered. Word has it that Stanley sold all that were offered, but, owing to supply problems, was only able to provide slightly more than 1000. This one, numbered 136 of 2000, is sure to appreciate even more in value in the coming years. One of only one offered here.* (FINE) **$365.00**

G3-19. Stanley Rule & Level No. 59: Cast Iron Doweling Jig. With 6 Bit Guides. Fine Condition, Original Box. Length: 5 Inches. *This ready to use doweling jig is the equal of any doweling device on the market today. For the woodworker who doesn't want a tool that requires an engineering degree to set up and use, we recommend this Stanley stalwart. A fine working tool in top condition.* (FINE) **$65.00**

G3-20. Stanley Rule & Level: Commemorative Level. 150th Anniversary. 1853-1993. Length: 12 Inches. *This classic 12" level was produced for Stanley's 150th Anniversary celebration in 1993. Brand new.* (FINE) **$165.00**

G3-21. Stanley Rule & Level: Commemorative Tape Measure. 150th Anniversary. 1853-1993. Length: 2 Inches. *The reverse side of this commemorative tape measure is decorated with the same elaborate pattern that surrounds the outside edge of the front. A well made Stanley collectible tape measure.* (GOOD) **$95.00**

G3-22. Stanley Rule & Level No. 264: Aluminum Torpedo Level. Silver and Yellow Box. New Condition, Original Box. Length: 9 Inches. *The orange and aluminum covered box was apparently only produced for this level. An uncommon tool in a rare box.* (FINE) **$115.00**

G3-23. Stanley Rule & Level: Commemorative Dovetail Saw. 150th Anniversary. 1853-1993. Length: 8 Inches. *The blade of this commemorative dovetail saw is etched with an imprint of Stanley's tool factory. An uncommon member of this series.* (FINE) **$225.00**

G3-24. Stanley Tools No. 1201: "Defiance" Brand Awl. Full Box of 12. Most Unusual Find. Length: 4 1/2 Inches. *Stanley's "Defiance" brand awl was offered for a scant twenty years. Finding an example in top condition is an uncommon occurrence. Here's a full box in mint condition. Extra special.* (FINE) **$285.00**

G3-25. Stanley Rule & Level: Commemorative Bevel. 150th Anniversary. 1853-1993. Length: 8 Inches. *Marked "Special Edition" on the body, these bevels were not included in the 150th Anniversary promotion, but were given to employees and the attendees at the Stanley Tool Collectors Convention held to commemorate the anniversary.* (FINE) **$245.00**

G3-26. Stanley Rule & Level No. 289: Skew Blade Rabbet Plane. With Original Decal. New Condition, Original Box. Length: 9 Inches. *The original "picture box" has a ca. 1910 illustration of the skew bladed plane it contained. This tool is in immaculate, unused condition and ready to proudly display. A rare boxed item.* (FINE) **$945.00**

G3-27. Stanley Rule & Level: Commemorative Try Square. 150th Anniversary. 1853-1993. Length: 10 Inches. *This 150th Anniversary collectible features a brass blade. It is in new condition.* (FINE) **$125.00**

G3-28. Stanley Tools No. 1221: Gear Driven Hand Drill. 0 to 1/4" Chuck. New Condition, Original Box. Length: 11 1/2 Inches. *This drill was included in Stanley's "Defiance" line and was produced from 1951 to 1953 only. A rare and underrated hand drill in top condition. New and in the box.* (FINE) **$95.00**

G3-29. Stanley Rule & Level: Commemorative Tape Measure. 150th Anniversary. 1853-1993. Length: 2 Inches. *The reverse side of this Stanley commemorative rule has an elaborate decoration formed into the metal. Here's an opportunity to obtain a souvenir of Stanley's 150th Anniversary if you missed it the first time.* (FINE) **$95.00**

G3-30. Stanley Rule & Level No. 95 1/2: Butt Mortise Marking Gauge. Rare Small Size. New Condition, Original Box. Length: 2 1/2 Inches. *We have seen less than a dozen of these small size Stanley butt mortise gauges. This is the first "in the box" example we have encountered. A rare Stanley gauge.* (FINE) **$145.00**

G3-31. Stanley Rule & Level No. 78: Duplex Rabbet, Fillet Plane. Complete and Excellent. New Condition, Original Box. Length: 10 Inches. *A Stanley mainstay for many years, this plane was designed to serve as both a rabbet plane and a bullnose plane. In the last years of the manufacture of this tool, a severe degradation in quality took place. This one dates from the 1930's, when the quality of Stanley tools was near its peak. The box has seen some wear, but the plane is in new condition.* (FINE) **$145.00**

G3-32. Stanley Rule & Level No. 20: Rosewood and Brass Try Square. 8" Size. New Condition, Original Box. Length: 9 1/2 Inches. *The original box has kept this Stanley classic in brand new condition. Mint.* (FINE) **$85.00**

G3-33. Stanley Rule & Level No. 68: Cast Iron Rabbet Spoke Shave. Sweetheart T.M. New Condition, Original Box. Length: 11 Inches. *The hard to find patternmaker's spoke shave in crispy clean condition in a clean and sound original box. Seldom seen in this condition. Choice.* (FINE) **$425.00**

G3-34. Stanley Tools No. 42-320: Commemorative Mason's Level. For Eaia Anniversary. New Condition, Original Box. Length: 24 Inches. *Produced by Stanley to commemorate the 50th Anniversary of the Early American Industries Association in 1983, this level is fitted with a medallion in the form of the 50th Anniversary logo. New and in the box. A rare commemorative Stanley collectible.* (FINE) **$245.00**

G3-35. Spalding: Stanley Promotional Basketball. Unused Condition. Uncommon Item. Length: 12 Inches. *If you're a Stanley collector who wants "one of each", you'll need one of these. Different.* (FINE) **$75.00**

G3-36. Stanley Rule & Level No. 20: Rosewood and Brass Try Square. 10" Size. New Condition, Original Box. Length: 12 Inches. *The original box has kept this 10" rosewood handle try square in new condition. Mint.* (FINE) **$95.00**

G3-37. Stanley Rule & Level No. 163: Light Duty Folding Rule. 1941 to 1943 Only. New Condition, Original Box. Length: 24 Inches. *These light-duty rules were produced during WW II and discontinued after a short run. This one is in brand new condition in its original box. Mint.* (FINE) **$145.00**

G3-38. Stanley Tools No. 1526: 26" 8 Point Crosscut Saw. "Handyman" Brand. New Condition, Original Box. Length: 29 Inches. *Stanley's "Handyman" brand is sometimes colored by perceptions of what was available on the shelves in recent memory. This early "Handyman" saw is well made and in new condition in its original box.* (FINE) **$145.00**

G3-39. Stanley Rule & Level No. OH 20: "Two Tone" Plane. Yellow and Black. New Condition, Original Box. Length: 6 1/2 Inches. *Stanley had the good fortune to tool up for production of the "Two Tone" line about six months before the entire country tooled up to produce arms and war materials for a sustained period. A perfect example of a tool that was casually swept aside by the winds of war. A rare plane in superb condition.* (FINE) **$195.00**

G3-40. Stanley Rule & Level No. 22: Dowel Sharpener. For Electric Drill. New Condition, Original Box. Length: 2 1/4 Inches. *The original box has kept this most unusual "straight shaft" dowel sharpener in brand new condition. A rare Stanley "in the box" item.* (FINE) **$35.00**

G3-41. Stanley Rule & Level No. 1240: "Defiance" Wedge Vise. Original Display Box. Scarce and Unused. Length: 11 1/2 Inches. *This "Defiance" series wedge vise is complete in its original box with the original hardware store display advertising materials. A most unusual Stanley Defiance item in top collector quality condition.* (FINE) **$95.00**

G3-42. Stanley Rule & Level: Commemorative Chisel Set. 150th Anniversary. 1853-1993. Length: 15 Inches. *This superb set from Stanley's 150th Anniversary series features a set of 3 "Everlasting" type chisels and a mallet in a fitted wooden box. A great set.* (FINE) **$375.00**

G3-43. Corgi Toys, Ltd., Swansea (England No. C906/6: "Stanley Tools" Toy Truck. Cast Iron Body. New Condition, Original Box. Length: 7 1/2 Inches. *These recently-produced toy trucks were a hit with Stanley collectors. Here's a perfectly preserved example. First come, first serve.* (FINE) **$125.00**

G3-44. Stanley Works: Promotional Hinge Display. Oak Stand. Ca. 1950's. Length: 6 1/4 Inches. *This hardware store display stand folds out to demonstrate the mechanical advantages of Stanley hinges. An uncommon Stanley promotional item.* (FINE) **$95.00**

G3-45. Stanley Rule & Level: Set Of 3 Commemorative Posters. From Stanley Convention. Unused Condition. Length: 20 Inches. *Attendees at the Stanley Tool Collector's convention received these commemorative posters. Here's a set with one extra poster.* (FINE) **$115.00**

Group H3

H3-1. Chatillon, New York, N.Y.: Circular Spring Scale. Marked "Milk Scale". Early And Excellent. Length: 10 Inches. *This classic brass faced scale from prominent New York City maker Chatillon is marked "milk scale", and it must have been intended for weighing milk cans. An interesting antique and a potential decorator collectible.* (GOOD+) **$65.00**

H3-2. Unmarked: Miniature Broom. With Pencil Shaft. Very Well Made. Length: 9 1/2 Inches. *A consignor inadvertently included this well made broom and pencil combination in his package of planes and chisels. We have included it under the general heading of "kitchen tool" and ask our readers to note that it also qualifies under the "miniature" listing.* (GOOD+) **$35.00**

H3-3. Unmarked: Hand Forged Stove Lifter(?). With "Heart" Design. Early Appearance. Length: 11 Inches. *This graphic piece of forge work appears to have been crafted for purpose of lifting the lid from a wood stove. Visually interesting and unusual.* (GOOD+) **$55.00**

H3-4. Peck, Stow & Wilcox Co.: Brass Faced Hardware Scale. Decorative Design. Most Unusual. Length: 5 Inches. *A bold five-pointed star and a stylized P.S. & W. logo accent this uncommon scale. Different.* (GOOD) **$45.00**

H3-5. Lagomarcino-Grupe Co., Iowa: Sauerkraut Tool. With Rubber Blade. Most Unusual. Length: 10 Inches. *Apparently a promotional item from the Lagomarcino Company, this "Sauerkraut Tool" features a rubber blade not unlike a squeegee. Exactly who might have a use for such a device is not made clear by any instructions on the tool. Whatever its specific function, we are pleased to add a sauerkraut tool to our ever expanding Menagerie of Tooldom. Really different.* (FINE) **$45.00**

H3-6. Unmarked: Craftsman Made Box. With Slide Top. Mahogany Body. Length: 4 Inches. *This hinged top box of mahogany is filled with wax and may have performed some function in a woodworking shop. Early and unusual.* (FINE) **$55.00**

H3-7. Johnson: "Johnson's Patent" Carpet Stretcher. With Tack Driver. Original Paint. Length: 7 Inches. *We have become enamored of the class of tool used for simultaneously stretching and tacking carpeting into place. The same sort of mechanically ingenious and thoroughly impractical sorts who set their hands to the making of wrenches also found solace in the world of flat carpeting. This particular example is one of the smaller examples of this genre that we have seen. Much of the original green paint remains, as does the stenciled patent and manufacturer markings. A nice example.* (FINE) **$65.00**

H3-8. Unmarked: Hammer Head Cane. From Courser Collection. Decidedly Different. Length: 36 Inches. *Half shillelagh and half sledgehammer, this whimsical cane came from the collection of New Hampshire collector Fred Courser. Different.* (GOOD+) **$145.00**

H3-9. Root Co., The C.J., Bristol, Conn.: "Elm City" Counter. Patented 1881. With Integral Bell. Length: 7 Inches. *This early patent counter could be activated by hand or machine. An attached bell could be set to announce whatever increment of which the user desired to be kept informed. Most unusual.* (GOOD+) **$115.00**

H3-10. Unmarked: Solid Bronze Webbing Stretcher. With Compound Jaw. Very Well Made. Length: 10 Inches. *The task of stretching webbing and/or upholstery material seems to have attracted more than its share of those for whom practicality and mechanical ingenuity operated in different orbits. This solid bronze example is so complex in design that it seems unlikely to have been cost productive to manufacture. Whatever the case, we are pleased to offer this apparition of mechanical gizmocity. Highly unusual.* (FINE) **$115.00**

H3-11. Unmarked: Early Bristle Brush. With Turned Handle. Tapered Pattern. Length: 12 Inches. *This specialized bristle brush is tapered nearly to a point. A nicely turned handle adds accent to its overall form.* (FINE) **$35.00**

H3-12. Unmarked: Early Style Sugar Nippers. Hand Forged Body. Graphic Form. Length: 8 1/2 Inches. *These sugar nippers are of the simple but classic Eighteenth Century style.* (GOOD+) **$195.00**

H3-13. Unmarked: Early Style Sugar Nippers. Similar to Winterthur E. Graphic Form. Length: 6 3/4 Inches. *The consignor of these early sugar nippers noted that he had observed a nearly identical set on display among the artifacts at the DuPont Winterthur Museum in Delaware. A great set in excellent collector quality condition.* (GOOD+) **$165.00**

H3-14. Unmarked: Folding Coat Hanger. "Pat. Appld. For.". Excellent Condition. Length: 9 Inches. *"Pat. Appl'd. For" is the only mark on this unusual folding coat hanger. Different.* (GOOD+) **$15.00**

H3-15. Detroit Shear Co.: Compound Lever Shears. "Pat. Pending". Uncommon Type. Length: 8 Inches. *There's probably an engineer out there somewhere, maybe several, given the sorts of folks this hobby attracts, who could explain in great detail why these shears are mechanically superior to the garden variety. The "tin knockers" probably wouldn't bring him along for a beer after work, but engineering has its own rewards. Special shears.* (GOOD) **$65.00**

H3-16. Unmarked: Early Patent Shellfish Opener. Patented June 2, 1867. For Knee Mount. Length: 6 1/2 Inches. *We have not consulted the patent records, but it appears likely from the design of this early patent tool that its purpose was for the opening of clams, oysters or both. Fitted out with a leather strap (the original remains), this device was meant to be clamped on the thigh of the user for convenience. We would assume that the patent feature is the leg strap, the lever action or a bit of both. A milestone of technological achievement of the sort to be expected from Martin J. Donnelly Antique Tools.* (GOOD+) **$225.00**

H3-17. A.P.W. Paper Co., Albany, N.Y.: "Albany Oval" Paper Dispenser. For Wall Mount. Patented May 1, 1894. Length: 5 Inches. *We are pleased and proud to offer this early patent tissue dispensing device which was intended to be mounted on the wall of a public restroom. This is the first such device ever included in the Catalogue of Antique Tools. A necessary artifact of the human condition, offered by popular demand.* (GOOD+) **$45.00**

H3-18. Mc Bee: Conductor's Ticket Punch. With Unusual Escapemnet. Ready to Display. Length: 5 1/2 Inches. *This classic ticket punch features a receptacle for holding the punched tabs, lest they clutter the floor of the train car. Different.* (GOOD) **$15.00**

H3-19. Booth, J., (Philadelphia): Early Oyster Knife. With "Star" Device. Uncommon Imprint. Length: 8 1/2 Inches. *This early oyster knife bears the imprint of Philadelphia hardware dealer J. Booth. This is the first such tool we have seen imprinted with the Booth mark.* (GOOD) **$45.00**

H3-20. Unmarked: Hand Forged Shepherd's Crook. Most Unusual. Great Patina. Length: 5 1/2 Inches. *Never having seen a shepherd's crook, it is difficult to say if this is such an animal, but it has the long handle and it looks as though this would do the trick in grabbing a sheep by the leg and getting it to go where you want it to. In today's world, Certified Sheep Counselors, employed by the United States Department of Agriculture would work with the errant ovine creatures to persuade them to comply with rational shepherd-given directions, provided those directions were in accordance with the provisions of the Federal Sheep Management Act. Anyone caught in possession of such a device would be subject to strict Federal penalties. Contraband.* (GOOD+) **$95.00**

H3-21. Unmarked: Special Purpose Winch, Pawl and Ratchet. Mortised Body. Length: 14 Inches. *Fitted together with precise mortise and tenon joints fixed by wooden pegs and outfitted with a hand forged ratchet mechanism, this device was likely intended for use in drawing water from a well. A warm patina of age and use adds to its appeal.* (GOOD+) **$145.00**

H3-22. Davis Instrument Mfg. Co., Baltimore: Wind Speed Gauge. From Illinois. Missing Dial. Length: 5 Inches. *Acquired at an auction in the community of Pana, Illinois, this wind speed gauge would have been used in one of the coal mines that operated at one time in that area. Manufactured by an obscure Baltimore company, this brass gauge is in excellent condition, although one of the pointers is missing from one of the indicator dials.* (GOOD) **$185.00**

H3-23. Reading Hardware Co., The: Patent Cast Iron Apple Parer. Patented March 5,1872. Superb Condition. Length: 12 Inches. *My sources tell me that this variation on a theme from the Reading, Pa. area is one of those more commonly encountered, however the condition of this example sets it a step above. Nicely cast, extremely well preserved and retaining nearly all of its original gold paint.* (FINE) **$155.00**

H3-24. Unmarked: Decorative Sugar Tongs. 18th C. Style. Great Condition. Length: 7 1/2 Inches. *A practitioner of the blacksmith's art certainly plied his craft well in producing these graphic and extremely early sugar tongs. Condition is superb.* (FINE) **$225.00**

H3-25. Millers Falls Company No. 1500: Set of 1/8" Letter Stamps. Complete and Clean. Ready to Use. Length: 5 1/2 Inches. *Here's a full set of letter stamps that are ready to be put to use.* (FINE) **$55.00**

H3-26. Stark, Molly, Bennington, Vermont: "Molly Stark" Mop Ringer. Elaborate Casting.. Complete And Sound. Length: 21 Inches. *Anyone who has driven through Bennington, Vermont knows that it is impossible to move twenty yards in any direction without encountering a business, monument, or National Park commemorated to the memory of the heroine of the Battle of Bennington. After the war, despite her fame, Molly was probably back in the kitchen, mop in hand, using one of these excessively elaborate and mechanically interesting mop wringers commemorating her Fifteen Minutes of Fame. A visually interesting piece of casting from your Official Molly Stark Antique Tool Catalogue.* (GOOD) **$245.00**

H3-27. Unmarked: Cast Victoraian Tack Puller. Decorative Form. Fruitwood Handle. Length: 6 1/4 Inches. *You won't find anything like this hanging on a hook in a shrink-wrapped package. A Victorian classic, this graphic tool evokes images of a world supposedly more simple than ours, but apparently, in many ways, far more complex. A treasure.* (GOOD+) **$165.00**

H3-28. Unmarked: Collection of Calf Weaning Devices. Patented, Etc. Graphic Form. Length: 8 Inches. *Looking not unlike Medieval instruments of torture, these accoutrements of animal husbandry were employed to promote the dissolution of bonding between mother and child of the bovine variety. We are pleased to offer this graphic collection, which was assembled by a single collector, as part of the Catalogue of Antique Tools.* (GOOD+) **$225.00**

H3-29. Burke Tobacco Co., R.M., Utica: Cigar Clipping Tamper. With Original Sacks. "The King of Chews". Length: 12 1/2 Inches. *All of these tools were salvaged from the long defunct Burke Tobacco Company where the bin-like device was used for filling bags of cigar clippings which were marketed as chewing tobacco. The wooden device was used to tamp the clippings into the bag and the cutting device was used to trim the ends of the cigars, thereby producing the "clippings". An interesting artifact from the days before the Nanny State took away our cherished Freedom in the name of "health".* (GOOD+) **$345.00**

H3-30. Unmarked: Retractable Ink Eraser. Early Appearance. Excellent Condition. Length: 5 1/2 Inches. *In the early days of penmanship, when paper was much more dear than it is today, mistakes could be separated from the paper with a device such as this knife-like "eraser" by being scraped away. This uncommon variation on this theme includes a retractable blade that stores inside of the handle. Most unusual.* (GOOD+) **$75.00**

H3-31. Unmarked: Presentation Yard Rule. "Clara N. Austin". From "Unknown". Length: 36 Inches. *"Just a basic, Nineteenth Century hickory yardstick", or so it was, until someone, "Unknown", as he billed himself, used it as a means to demonstrate the measure of his devotion to one "Clara N. Austin". We can assume, from the presence of the heart shapes on the inlaid brass plate that this "present" was meant to symbolize more than we will ever know. That this rule was found in the State of Maine, not far from the City of Skowhegan, this past Spring is all that we know for certain. But who were these people? How and when did they live. What became of Clara Austin and her admirer? We will probably never know, but the images that arise from our speculation about these people and this tool that celebrates the intersection of their lives on this earth, know no limits save those that can be supplied from seeking out the individuals through historical records and the limits of time that the style of this rule will provide. People, tools, time, and emotions. These are themes that constantly interact in the great drama of history and imagery that is found in every rule, every wrench, every plane and every unanswered question that are the facninating world of antique tool collecting. For those who see only an object here, move on; for those who find, in this simple rule, something wonderful beyond measure, welcome home. A great rule.* (GOOD+) **$395.00**

H3-32. Unmarked: "Takedown" Carpet Stretcher. With Brass Ferrule. Near New Condition. Length: 32 Inches. *This classic carpet stretcher is fitted with a central brass ferrule which allows it to be put away for storage and forgotten—a fate that apparently befell this well preserved example.* (FINE) **$65.00**

H3-33. Canastota Knife Company, The No. 50: Ivory Handle Nut Pick. Ca. 1890's. New Condition, Original Box. Length: 5 1/4 Inches. *Nut picks with ivory handle evoke images of a world of Victorian opulence that seems larger than life, but which the artifacts of material culture demonstrate was very real indeed. The pasteboard box and high class nut pick are in new condition, despite their 100+ years of existence.* (FINE) **$115.00**

H3-34. Mc Gillis, Brown & Pratt Mfg. Co.: The "Perfection" Tack Puller. Old Hardware Stock. With Original Handbill. Length: 6 Inches. *One of the fascinating qualities of antique tools is their ability to evoke the reality of an era very long ago, if not so very far away. Imagine a world where anyone could, and many did, set their hand to creating a "new and useful device", and then very quickly obtain a patent for same. To be sure, many of these patents were a waste of good paper, but a world so rich with opportunity seems to have motivated a great many to achieve extraordinary things. This "Perfection" tack puller, although undated, appears to date from the 1880's, or possibly even earlier. It has never been used, nor was it ever unwrapped from the paper sleeve/handbill in which it has lain protected from a century of weather and dirt, until it was carefully taken out for this photograph. According to the papers, this tack puller was prepared for offering to the market, despite the fact that numerous other tack pullers were available, because it was the "...superior of any other made". Moreover, the "Perfection" puller is identified in the accompanying description as "...the only tool of the kind ever manufactured from such high quality material". It may well be that this tool was simply too nice to use; or it might more likely be that the expenditure of time and money for materials and distribution on something so mundane as a tack puller may have proved prohibitively expensive for Mssrs. McGillis, Brown & Pratt of Menominee, Michigan. Whatever the case, we thank them, one and all, for having created this magical link to a bygone time, and for having sealed, so long ago, within the protective paper wrapper, a piece of the dream that resides in each of us. Extra special.* (FINE) **$85.00**

H3-35. Disston & Sons, Henry, Philada, Penna. No. 6: De-Horning Saw. Original Blade. Superb Condition. Length: 15 1/2 Inches. *Here's a great example of the Disston No. 6 De-Horning saw. A rare Disston saw in superb condition.* (FINE) **$115.00**

H3-36. Youngstown Kitchens: Youngstown Kitchen Rule. 25 Ft. Sliding Rule. For Kitchen Layout. Length: 42 Inches. *When the Youngstown Kitchen Cabinet salesman came to your home, he could make sense of your kitchen in a matter of minutes and have you committed to long term indebtedness within an hour using this tool alone. A versatile measuring device that appears to date from the 1940's—nearly 60 years ago.* (FINE) **$115.00**

H3-37. Unmarked: Early Patent Cherry Pitter. Patented October 10, 1871. Rare and Complete. Length: 4 1/4 Inches. *Patented in 1871, this scissors type cherry pitter features a number of prongs, which may allow it to function as a raisin seeder as well. An early kitchen tool in clean, sound condition.* (GOOD) **$165.00**

H3-38. Brinkerhoff & Son, Upper Sandusky: Patent "Universal" Husker. Patented February 21, 1888. Adjustable Size. Length: 4 1/2 Inches. *This patented corn husker is boldly imprinted with the maker's name and patent information. With only a pair of pliers, a resourceful owner could make double duty out of this outside the harvest season by refashioning it into a shoehorn.* (FINE) **$65.00**

H3-39. Assorted Makers: Collection of Scissors. For Lamp Wicks, Etc.. Boker and Badger.Length: 4 1/4 Inches. *These specialized scissors were designed for the task of trimming the wicks on oil lamps—an everyday necessity in many parts of the country until well into the first quarter of this century. An interesting collection.* (GOOD+) **$95.00**

H3-40. Smith Co., H.D., Plantsville, Conn.: "Perfect Handle" Meat Hook. Patented "Union Hook". Most Unusual. Length: 9 1/2 Inches. *There's no mistaking the "circle S" trademark of the H.D. Smith Company on this rare meat or hay hook which features their trademark inlaid wood handle. The only example I've seen. Rare.* (GOOD+) **$165.00**

H3-41. Larkin: Special Purpose Brushes. Patented February 15, 1876 and September 18, 1883. Length: 6 Inches. *These may well be stenciling brushes, although I must confess that I haven't had time to do the research. Acquired at the tag sale conducted before the auction of the Fred Courser collection, a betting man would wager big money that their patentees resided in the State of New Hampshire. Very, very different.* (FINE) **$115.00**

H3-42. Assorted Makers: Collection of 16 Name Stamps. From 19th Century. Early and Excellent. Length: 4 1/2 Inches. *We are aware that an increasing number of collectors have taken to accumulating the name stamps that were kept by nearly every Nineteenth Century woodworker for the express purpose of diminishing the potential future collectibility of their tools. Here's a mother lode of 16 different stamps. First come, first serve.* (GOOD+) **$295.00**

H3-43. Union Hardware Co., Torrington, Conn: "Union" Skate Sharpenter. With Extension Handle. New Condition, Original Box. Length: 3 1/2 Inches. *The Union Hardware Company of Torrington, Connecticut seems to have specialized in producing hardware novelties, including a wide range of patented tools. This early skate sharpener is in new condition in its original box.* (FINE) **$45.00**

H3-44. Unmarked: Early Carpenter's Initial Stamp. Initials "JG". Uncommon Find. Length: 2 1/2 Inches. *This early owner's initial name stamp has a look not unlike the initials found on the toes of Eighteenth Century molding planes. A rare, early stamp in superb condition.* (FINE) **$95.00**

H3-45. Peck, Stow & Wilcox Co.: "Mother's Own" Tool Kit. For Kitchen Use. Rare and Excellent. Length: 10 Inches. *Evocative in an instant of the world of the 1950's, this "Mother's Own" tool set is the sort of thing that would never have been possible before the social changes brought about by the Second World War. One can imagine an episode of "Leave it to Beaver" where Wally and the Beaver, under the evil influence of Eddie Haskell, appropriate June Cleaver's tools and cause them irreparable harm, prompting a paternal lecture from Ward. Luckily, the boys didn't get to this classic set and they are in nearly new condition. A legitimately rare set of tools from an increasingly collectible tool maker.* (GOOD+) **$445.00**

Group 13

13-1. Unmarked: Patternmaker's Pinch Dogs. Assorted Sizes. Ready to Use. Length: 4 Inches. *These "pinch dogs" were driven into the end grain of two boards to hold them together when gluing. Here's a lifetime supply.* (GOOD+) **$55.00**

13-2. American Tool. Co., Pawtucket, R.I.: Special Function Bench Clamp. With Ratchet Locking Mechanism. Interesting. Length: 9 Inches. *Here's a gizmo that is shown from directly above. The lever has a ratchet lock mechanism that moves and locks the jaws on the body next to each other. No idea what it is for, but it is very well made.* (FINE) **$95.00**

13-3. S.M.: Precision Machinist Clamp. European Style. Extremely Well Made. Length: 4 1/2 Inches. *The only mark on this well made clamp are the letters "S.M." inside an oval. A nice clamp.* (FINE) **$25.00**

13-4. Onions & Co.: Set of Plow Plane Cutting Irons. "Governor Brand". Original Roll. Length: 10 1/2 Inches. *Here's a full set of cutting irons from an obscure English maker in excellent condition in their original roll. Nice.* (FINE) **$110.00**

13-5. Unmarked: Wagon Spring Greaser. Full Nickel Plating. Uncommon Type. Length: 6 Inches. *These were wedged into the springs of wagons and then tightened to wedge the springs apart so grease could be inserted. Thanks to these tools, the phrase "the squeaky wagon spring gets the grease" has not entered into common usage.* (FINE) **$25.00**

13-6. Tolor Mfg. Co., J.L., P'kpsie, N.Y.: Sliding Bar Clamp. With Screw Adjust. Very Well Made. Length: 11 Inches. *Here's an excellent working clamp from a maker we have not previously encountered.* (GOOD+) **$15.00**

13-7. Stanley Rule & Level No. 89: Pair of Adjustable Gauges. Patent July 6, 1886. For Clapboards. Length: 7 Inches. *These specialized tools were used for the hanging of sawn clapboards on the sides of houses. They are in excellent order and clearly marked with the patent date. Nice.* (FINE) **$65.00**

13-8. Unmarked: Pair of Precision Clamps. Marked "40" and "70". Brass Facing. Length: 6 Inches. *Manufactured with a painstaking eye for detail, these clamps may well be of German origin and the number may be the width, in milimeters, of the clamp opening. A great set.* (FINE) **$45.00**

13-9. Greenfield Tap & Die Corp., Mass.: Assorted Taps and Tap Wrenches. 13 Assorted Taps. Ready to Use. Length: 8 1/4 Inches. *Here's a great working set of taps, dies and the holders for each from Greenfield Tap & Die. A bargain.* (FINE) **$35.00**

13-10. Unmarked: Early Hand Forged Die Stock. "Cl. Charroux". Decorative Form. Length: 20 1/2 Inches. *The maker of this artistically inspired die stock, one "Cl. Charroux", who has carefully imprinted it with his name, invested it with more character than one would have thought possible of such a tool. A nicely hand forged die stock with character to spare. Very nice.* (GOOD+) **$225.00**

13-11. Goodell-Pratt Company: Pair of Clapboard Gauges. Graphic Wing Nut. Scarce and Complete. Length: 8 Inches. *A frequent visitor to the "whatsit" table, these graphic devices were used in pairs to facilitate the hanging of sawn clapboards on the sides of buildings. These need a light cleaning, but are otherwise complete and sound. A rare pair.* (GOOD+) **$55.00**

13-12. Starrett Co., The L.S., Athol, Mass. No. 815: Tool and Die Makers Hammer. With Magnifying Glass. New Condition, Original Box. Length: 7 Inches. *The Starrett Company has been responsible for some of the great innovations in machinist's tools, but this combo tool falls a bit short in the ingenuity category. How it came to pass that a hammer with a principal part made of glass is beyond me. I must admit that I've never seen a broken one, but then there aren't many around. A rare tool in new condition in its original box.* (FINE) **$165.00**

13-14. North Bros Mfg. Co., Philadelphia No. 990: "Yankee" Machinists Vise. With Insert. New Condition, Original Box. Length: 7 3/4 Inches. *Complete with its original jaw insert, this "Yankee" classic is in new condition in its original box. Nice.* (FINE) **$125.00**

13-15. Unmarked: Classic Early Die Stock. With Diamond Adjusting Screw Circa 1820's. Length: 22 Inches. *A relic from the days when metalwork began by making the first tool, which then made the second tool, which then worked together to produce subsequent tools, this early hand forged die stock has a look that says it was made at the very beginning of the Nineteenth Century. A great hand made tool.* (GOOD+) **$25.00**

13-16. Boker, H., Germany: Early Screw Plate. With "Tree" Brand. Nice Filework. Length: 8 Inches. *Products marked with the Boker name were always of the highest quality. This one is in perfect condition.* (FINE) **$55.00**

13-17. Unmarked: Hand Forged Bench Stop. Serrated Stop. Uncommon Type. Length: 4 Inches. *The tip of this early bench stop has been filed with a series of serrations to improve its functionality.* (GOOD+) **$65.00**

13-18. Unmarked: Joiner's Bench Stop. "Y" Shaped Forging. Distinctive Form. Length: 6 Inches. *Carefully hammer welded together and hand filed to proportional perfection. This bench stop is a classic "primitive" tool that is anything but.* (FINE) **$65.00**

13-19. Unmarked: Joiner's Bench Stop. Hand Forged. Ready to Use. Length: 6 Inches. *Why some workaday tools could and were transformed into works of art while most others were just "stuff" is what makes the search for antique tools so infinitely interesting. Nice.* (FINE) **$55.00**

13-20. Unmarked: Early Adjustable Washer Cutter. Screw Lock Type. Original Nickel Plating. Length: 3 1/2 Inches. *A locking screw holds a pair of triangular beams precisely in place on this early washer cutter. It is in nearly new condition.* (FINE) **$45.00**

13-21. Dobson: Set of 6 Sand Moulder's Tools. For Pattern Shop. Double End Type. Length: 7 1/2 Inches. *These highly specialized tools were used by sand casters in the making of molds in foundry work. An uncommon set.* (GOOD+) **$85.00**

13-22. Harrison, J. & H., Newcastle (England): 1/2" Fruitwood Die Stock. With Original Tap. Ready to Use. Length: 8 Inches. *This fruitwood tap and die set is in nearly new condition and ready to be put back to work. Choice.* (FINE) **$125.00**

13-23. Unmarked: Joiner's "U" Shape Bench Stop. Early Appearance. Ready to Use. Length: 6 Inches. *The very old bench stop is in excellent working condition. Ready to use, if you choose.* (GOOD+) **$45.00**

13-24. Unmarked: Early Hand Forged Bench Stop. Elaborate Form. Early and Excellent. Length: 8 Inches. *The forging of bench stops for carpenters gave way to artistic release for a number of blacksmiths. This early example is of a form we have not previously encountered. Graphic.* (GOOD+) **$65.00**

13-24. Josef, E.E., Buffalo, N.Y.: Patent Cast Iron Clamp. Patent April 8, 1890. Unknown Function. Length: 9 Inches. *We have seen several of these special purpose clamp-like devices, which have a worm gear like grinding on the reverse side to lock the sliding jaw, but do not know their specific function. Different.* (GOOD+) **$35.00**

13-25. Unmarked: 1 Inch Tap and Die Stock. Rosewood Body. Ready to Use. Length: 6 Inches. *A turned boxwood handle nicely complements this rosewood die stock, which includes the matching tap. Very pretty and fully functional.* (GOOD+) **$215.00**

13-26. Unmarked: Early Hand Forged Clamp. Forged From File. Distinctive Form. Length: 4 1/2 Inches. *This artfully hand forged and filed clamp has a look about it that says its maker wanted it to be something special. Something special.* (GOOD+) **$55.00**

13-27. Lothrop, G.M., Norwood, Mass.: Early Patent Sanding Block. Patent May 11, 1880. For Sharkskin?. Length: 5 Inches. *Clearly marked on one of the brass edges with both the maker's name and patent date, this most unusual device, which was patented in 1880, allows a piece of sandpaper to be locked into place by turning the handle. An extremely well made patented sanding block. Most unusual.* (GOOD+) **$225.00**

13-28. Unmarked: Joiner's "U" Shape Bench Stop. Decorative Filework. Early and Excellent. Length: 8 Inches. *The maker of this "U" shaped bench stop was not content to stop at the attainment of functionality, but added a decorative effect with filework at the junction of the "U" and the extended arm. First class.* (FINE) **$95.00**

13-29. Unmarked: Early Cast Iron Clamp. With Spring Clip. "Pat. Appld. For". Length: 3 1/2 Inches. *This early appearing cam action clamp was apparently meant to be screwed to a wall or other surface for holding something in place. A mystery.* (GOOD+) **$45.00**

13-30. Saunders' Sons, D.: Early Patent Die Stock. Patent April 25, 1876. Multiple Sizes. Length: 16 Inches. *The resident genius of this one appears to have been the multiple sizes of dies that were ready at a moment's notice. The "two men and a boy" required to lug it around may have compromised its practicality somewhat. A nice looking tool.* (GOOD+) **$85.00**

13-31. Unmarked: Single Section Bench Stop. Owner "C.P. Boynton". Distinctive Form. Length: 6 1/2 Inches. *A most unusual variation on the theme, this hand forged bench stop is imprinted with the name of "C.P. Boynton" a Connecticut machinist and "mechanic" of the 1850's and 1860's. Extra special.* (FINE) **$85.00**

13-32. Wood & Sons Co., The A.A., Atlanta: Cast Iron Spoke Pointer. Fixed Size. Ready to Use. Length: 4 1/2 Inches. *The Wood & Sons Company were the established leader in the manufacture and marketing of doweling tools. This superb example of their best spoke pointer is in excellent working condition.* (GOOD+) **$45.00**

13-33. Wiley & Russell Mfg. Co. No. 1122: Screw Plate Die Stock. Uncommon Type. Original Wood Box. Length: 12 1/2 Inches. *This specialized set of taps and dies includes a most unusual tap that was intended to be mounted in a bit brace. Most of the original blued finish remains, but a few of the objects have some spots of oxidation, which should respond well to a light cleaning. An uncommon set of taps and dies in their original box.* (GOOD+) **$85.00**

13-34. Nicholson File Co., Providence, R.I.: Special Promotional Files. "Two File Special". For National Hardware Week. Length: 13 1/2 Inches. *As part of the "National Hardware Week" celebration, retailers teamed with the Nicholson to offer this boxed set of files. A nice pair in new condition in their original box.* (FINE) **$85.00**

13-35. Cincinnati Tool Co., The No. 55-P: "Hargrave" "C" Clamps. 3" Opening. New Condition, Original Box. Length: 5 Inches. *Two of the original "C" clamps remain in their original picture label box. Hardware store new.* (FINE) **$35.00**

13-36. Starrett Co., L. S., Athol, Mass. No. 298: Pair of Key Seat Rule Clamps. Blued Steel Finish. New Condition, Original Box. Length: 1 1/2 Inches. *Here's a nice set of Starrett key seat rules in brand new condition. Special.* (GOOD) **$45.00**

13-37. Brown & Sharpe Mfg. Co., The No. 756-B: Adjustable Machinist Clamp. "Patent Pending". Near New Condition. Length: 2 1/2 Inches. *"Patent Pending" has been stamped on this most unusual triple screw clamp from the Brown & Sharpe Company. We do not know if a patent was ever awarded.* (FINE) **$25.00**

13-38. Tyzak & Son, S., 34 Old St, London: Solid Boxwood Screw Box. With Matching Tap. Ready to Use. Length: 4 1/2 Inches. *Here's an excellent working screwbox and tap in the desirable 1/2" size. The boxwood body has developed a rich golden patina. A beautiful tool in excellent working order.* (GOOD+) **$145.00**

13-39. Unmarked: Special Purpose Tool. Canopener. Made With Thimble. Length: 12 Inches. *The ferrule on this early can opener type device has been formed from what appears to be a discarded thimble.* (GOOD+) **$45.00**

13-40. Stanley Rule & Level No. 22: Dowel Sharpener. For Electric Drill. Original Wrapper. Length: 2 1/4 Inches. *This most unusual "straight shaft" dowel sharpener was apparently intended for use in an electric drill. Condition is unused.* (FINE) **$15.00**

13-41. Mossberg Co., Frank No. 607: Early Rotary Valve Grinder. Auto Tool Maker. Uncommon Type. Length: 4 1/2 Inches. *We have offered a wide range of valve grinding devices in the past. This is the first example we have seen from the Frank Mossberg Company.* (GOOD+) **$35.00**

13-42. Lufkin Rule Co., The, Saginaw, Mich.: Two Foot, Two Fold Rule. Solid Brass. With Circumference Scales. Length: 24 Inches. *The reverse side of this uncommon Lufkin rule, which is not marked with a Lufkin number, is imprinted with circumference scales, such as those used by tinsmiths. Different.* (FINE) **$95.00**

13-43. Mathieson & Son, A., Glasgow: Solid Boxwood Tap and Die Stock. 1/2" Size. Superb Condition. Length: 3 3/4 Inches. *Working pairs of taps and dies for wood are helpful tools in the modern shop. This one is in excellent working order and boldly marked with the imprint of Scottish maker Alexander Mathieson. A good one.* (FINE) **$115.00**

13-44. Marples & Co., William, Sheffield: Set of Plow Plane Cutting Irons. With "Shamrock" T.M. Extra Crisp and Clean. Length: 9 Inches. *Here's a full set of shiny and clean plow plane cutting irons from one of England's top makers. Nice.* (FINE) **$135.00**

13-45. Wells Tool Co., Greenfield, Mass.: Assorted Taps and Dies. New Condition, Original Boxes. Length: 2 Inches. *If you have use for taps and dies, here's a wide range of both in all sorts of sizes—all in new condition in their original boxes. At military procurement prices, the cost of these tools could send several of you on a world cruise. A bargain.* (FINE) **$85.00**

Group J3

J3-1. Assorted Makers: Set of 3 Auger Bits. 1 1/4", 1 1/2", 2". Early Wood Box. Length: 14 Inches. *A fitted wooden case has kept these boring machine auger bits in nearly new condition. Mint.* (FINE) **$225.00**

J3-2. Assorted Makers: Group of Spoon, Shell Auger Bits. Excellent Condition. Ready to Use. Length: 8 Inches. *These spoon and shell auger bits came from the same tool box. All are in working order and ready to get back to the tasks for which they were made.* (GOOD+) **$75.00**

J3-3. Unmarked: Massive 3" Auger Bit. With Square Shank. Excellent Condition. Length: 24 Inches. *If you plan to use one of these, bring some help along. The clean, White Pine that would allow one man to effortlessly bore through a beam with this 3" auger is about gone. An uncommon bit in excellent condition.* (GOOD+) **$55.00**

J3-4. Starrett Co., The L. S. S.: Counter Sink Auger Bit. Specialty Tip. Most Unusual Type. Length: 4 Inches. *Here's a crisp and clean example of the only countersink bit ever offered by Starrett. A good one.* (GOOD+) **$35.00**

J3-5. Assorted Makers: Set of 5 Countersink Auger Bit. Single Collection. Different Styles. Length: 4 Inches. *All of these countersink bits were accumulated by a Connecticut collector with an eye for detail. A nice assortment.* (GOOD+) **$55.00**

J3-6. Unmarked: Set of 3 Auger Bits. Fitted Mahogany Box. 1", 1 1/2" and 2" Size. Length: 16 Inches. *Here's a nice working set of boring machine auger bits in a craftsman fitted box. All are in excellent shape and appear very well made.* (GOOD+) **$145.00**

J3-7. Assorted Makers: Asstorted Center Spur Auger Bits. Extra Large Sizes. Ready to Use. Length: 5 1/2 Inches. *Finding center spur auger bits in these large sizes can be a challenge. Challenge met.* (GOOD+) **$45.00**

J3-8. Stanley Rule & Level No. 100: Russell Jennings Auger Bit. 3 Tiered Box. Unused Condition. Length: 10 Inches. *None of the bits in this set of 13 has ever been used. A classic set of Jennings bits in new condition.* (FINE) **$225.00**

J3-9. Jennings Mfg. Co., The Russell No. 100: Boxed Set of Auger Bits. With Original Label. Two Broken Shafts. Length: 10 Inches. *Two of the shafts on the auger bits in this Jennings set have truncated shafts, most likely because they were removed to use the bits in a power drill. A nearly complete set in excellent working order.* (GOOD+) **$85.00**

J3-10. Jennings & Co., C.E., New York, N.Y.: "Steer's Patent" Auger Bit. With 3 Original Tips. Near New Condition. Length: 8 Inches. *William Steers of Brattleborough, Vermont, patented a very successful adjustable auger bit on April 1, 1884. This example, which is marked with the name of C.E. Jennings & Company, who likely manufactured and distributed it, is in nearly new condition.* (FINE) **$95.00**

J3-11. Nurse, C., 32 Mill St. (London): Countersink Auger Bit. Original Straw Temper. Unused Condition. Length: 4 1/4 Inches. *All of the original "straw temper" finish remains on this London made countersink bit.* (FINE) **$15.00**

J3-12. Starrett Co., The L. S. S.: Counter Sink Auger Bit. Specialty Tip. Unused Condition. Length: 4 Inches. *This early Starrett Countersink bit has never been used. Mint.* (FINE) **$45.00**

J3-13. Snell Mfg. Co., Fiskdale, Mass.: Boring Machine Auger Bit. 2" Width. Ready to Use. Length: 12 Inches. *The Snell Manufacturing Company seems to have specialized in bits for boring machines. This 2" example is in top condition and ready to use. Nice.* (FINE) **$45.00**

J3-14. Assorted Makers: Assorted Center Spur Auger Bits. With Square Shanks. Ready to Use. Length: 5 1/2 Inches. *This appears to be a full working set of center spur bits. Just the thing to accent your Sheffield or Ultimatum brace.* (GOOD+) **$45.00**

J3-15. Mayhew Co., H.H., Shelburne Falls: Box of Countersink Auger Bits. Unused Condition. "Diamond" Brand. Length: 5 1/2 Inches. *If you had gone to the hardware store in 1890 and asked for a countersink bit, the clerk would likely have reached into a box like this one and offered you one of these. Now you can get every one of them. Absolutely perfect.* (FINE) **$85.00**

J3-16. Wayne Mfg. Co. (Unmarked.): C. Meister Patent Angle Boring Tool. Patented January 14, 1896. Superb Condition. Length: 12 Inches. *Christian Meister, of Allentown, Pennsylvania, described this tool as an "angle boring tool for dentists and mechanics". We can be relatively certain that the example offered here, imprinted with the mark of the Wayne Manufacturing Company, was of the sort not intended for dental use. A variation on a common theme, this tool was designed to redirect rotary motion into an otherwise unreachable area. We remain confident that such tools were not capable of being used by a single human being fitted out with the standard complement of two arms and two hands. So confident are we, in fact, that we will offer a free copy of Dr. Jim Price's excellent book on patented bitstock tools to anyone who is able to successfully complete the rewiring of the Donnelly warehouse using this tool. An uncommon patented boring device in excellent condition.* (GOOD+) **$115.00**

J3-17. Unmarked: Boring Machine Auger Bit. 1 3/4" Size. Scarce and Near New. Length: 11 1/2 Inches. *Finding the odd sizes of boring machine bits can be a challenge. This 1 3/4" bit is in nearly new condition and ready to go back to work. Perfect.* (FINE) **$55.00**

J3-18. Unmarked: 1 1/2" Twist Auger Bit. For Boring Machine. Ready to Use. Length: 11 Inches. *Here's a 1 1/2" boring machine bit in excellent working order. A good one.* (GOOD+) **$45.00**

J3-19. Snell Mfg. Co., Fiskdale, Mass.: 1 1/2" Boring Mach. Auger Bit. Near New Condition. Ready to Use. Length: 12 Inches. *In essentially the same condition as it would have been when it left the Snell factory, this 1 1/2" bit is in perfect condition. Ready to use.* (FINE) **$55.00**

J3-20. Crossman & Co., C.P., Fitchburg, Mass: Early Patent Auger Handle. With 2 Original Bits. Patented November 1850. Length: 15 1/2 Inches. *This very early patent augur handle comes complete with two of the bits that were specific to this tool. The handle is very nicely marked with the patent date. A great example of an early patented "T" augur.* (GOOD+) **$125.00**

J3-21. Gibbs, I.H., N.Y.: Patent Adjustable Auger Bit. Patented June 17, 1855. Early and Excellent. Length: 9 Inches. *One of the earliest of expansion augur bits, this mechanically interesting tool from a Washington, D.C. inventor was also one of the most complex. A great example of a rare augur bit.* (FINE) **$195.00**

J3-22. Unmarked: 5/8" Spoon Auger Bit. Unused Condition. Ready to Use. Length: 8 Inches. *Here's a 5/8" spoon auger bit in mint condition. Perfect, and ready to use.* (FINE) **$85.00**

J3-23. Unmarked: Hand Forged Reamer Auger Bit. Forged From File. Graphic Appearance. Length: 6 1/2 Inches. *Evidence of its former life is still visible on this countersink bit.* (GOOD+) **$25.00**

J3-24. Remington Tool & Machine Co., Boston: Early Drill Grinding Gauge. Rare Marked Example. Excellent Condition. Length: 5 1/2 Inches. *Ken Cope's Makers of American Machinist's Tools notes that no examples of this obscure maker's work have been observed. We are pleased and proud to offer what may be the only extant example of the work of this patent grinding gauge from the little known Remington Tool & Machine Company. Extra rare and excellent.* (GOOD+) **$345.00**

J3-25. Morse Twist Drill & Machine Co. No. 2 A: Patent Machine Drill Chuck. Patented September 6, 1864. Early and Excellent. Length: 7 Inches. *This patented drill bit is marked with an early patent date, which may apply to the "Morse taper" of its shank. A rare and early drill chuck.* (GOOD+) **$75.00**

J3-26. Sorby, I.: Set of 5 Spoon Auger Bits. Extra Deep Cut. Ready to Use. Length: 8 Inches. *Here's a great working set of spoon bits from respected maker I. Sorby of Sheffield, England. Near new.* (FINE) **$115.00**

J3-27. Jennings & Co., C.E., New York, N.Y.: Patent Adjustable Auger Bit. Patented March 1, 1910. Rare and Excellent. Length: 9 Inches. *Patented by Archer B. Jennings of Wallingford, Connecticut, this uncommon bit was manufactured by the family tool business. An uncommon expansion bit.* (GOOD+) **$55.00**

J3-28. Assorted Makers: Set of 4 Spoon, Spur Auger Bits. French Type. Ready to Use. Length: 6 1/2 Inches. *These extra large spoon auger bits are in superb working condition and ready to be put immediately to use. Spoon auger bits in this size have become nearly impossible to find.* (GOOD+) **$185.00**

J3-29. Assorted Makers: Set of 3 Spoon Auger Bits. Excellent Condition. Ready to Use. Length: 6 1/2 Inches. *These spoon bits came from the same drawer of a tool chest where they had been placed by the last person to use them. A nice set.* (GOOD+) **$75.00**

J3-30. Clark, William A.: Clark's Expansive Auger Bit. Patented May 11, 1858. Fitted Wood Box. Length: 10 Inches. *The Clark's patent bit was a successful tool that continued to be produced well into the Twentieth Century. It is easy to forget how early are its origins. This classic example, which as been preserved by a craftsman made wooden case, complete with a "stopper", is clearly marked with the May 11, 1858 patent date. A classic.* (GOOD+) **$55.00**

J3-31. Sorby, I. & H.: Pair of Spoon Auger Bit. Unused Condition. Ready to Use. Length: 8 1/4 Inches. *These crispy clean large spoon auger bits are in brand new condition. Mint.* (FINE) **$145.00**

J3-32. Irwin Augur Bit Co., The No. 886-R: Set of "Speedbor" Auger Bit. Original Roll. New Condition, Original Box. Length: 9 Inches. *The transition from hand to power tools and to a totally different way of doing things is evident in this set of "Speedbor" bits in new condition in their original box. The early graphics on the box label is in marked contrast to the plastic case and the unrefined bits.* (FINE) **$65.00**

J3-33. Derby Bit Co., Ansonia, Conn.: Set of Extra Long Auger Bits. Patented May 31, 1881. Fitted Mahogany Box. Length: 18 Inches. *Anyone who has ever looked in to buying even one extra long auger bit at the hardware store, and survived without going in to cardiac arrest, will appreciate this early set of 12 extra long bits from the Derby Bit Company of Ansonia, Connecticut. All are in excellent working order and marked with the date of the 1881 patent granted to John Parmalee of Ansonia.* (GOOD+) **$275.00**

J3-34. Buck & Hickman, (London): Full Set of Auger Bits. Spoon, Spur Etc. Original Straw Temper. Length: 8 Inches. *Nearly all of the original "straw temper" finish remains on this magnificent set of spoon, spur, countersink and reamer auger bits. A superb set to complement a classic English brace in new condition in their original roll. Extra nice.* (FINE) **$195.00**

J3-35. Unmarked: Early Patent Auger Handle. Patented April 15, 1888. Ready to Use. Length: 15 Inches. *The 1888 patent date is the only marking on this early "T" auger. Ready to use.* (GOOD) **$35.00**

J3-36. Stanley Rule & Level: Countersink Auger Bit. With Depth Stop. Full Nickel Plating. Length: 4 Inches. *Nearly all original finishes remain on this fully nickel plated example of Stanley's countersink with depth stop. The shank is clearly marked with the Stanley name.* (FINE) **$55.00**

J3-37. Greenlee Tool Co., Rockford, Ill. No. 6: "Setfast" Expansive Auger Bit. 1 3/4" to 3" Size. New Condition, Original Box. Length: 8 Inches. *Here's a great expansion augur bit that adjusts like a "Crescent" wrench. Brand new in the box.* (FINE) **$55.00**

J3-38. Hugenot, L., Tussot (France): Spring Action Hand Vise. With Faceted Head. Near New Condition. Length: 4 Inches. *We have offered a wide range of hand vises, but this is the first example is the first we have seen from this French maker. A very well made hand vise in top condition.* (FINE) **$65.00**

J3-39. Unmarked: Early Style "T" Auger Bits. Hand Riven Handles. Great Condition. Length: 25 Inches. *Some idle time in New Hampshire last summer offered an opportunity for a drive through the country. Ever the one to keep an eye out for business, I spotted a roadside sale that had the look of something more than a permanent display of a family's worn out clothing, so on went the brakes. The man tending to the sale was in the process of emptying the contents of large wooden tool chest on the ground. To make a long story short, the rush of adrenaline wasn't quite worth it. It was a "real" chest and it had some real tools, including this extra early set of "T" augers, but the man tending the sale was an antique dealer who had a fairly good idea of what was going on. We discussed the chest and concluded that it had been "picked" many years ago of nearly anything of perceived merit. Anyway, after some spirited discussion, I was able to purchase this set of extra long auger bits, two of whichhave their early hand-hewn handles. All are in great working order and ready to be put immediately to work. A great working set, with a story.* (GOOD+) **$125.00**

J3-40. Unmarked: Set of Wide Spoon Auger Bits. For Chairmaker's Use. Rare and Ready to Use. Length: 5 1/2 Inches. *Without question, this is the finest set of spoon auger bits we have ever offered for sale. Obtained when a set of carpenters tools was dispersed in New Hampshire this past spring, These bits had been kept safely hidden away in a drawer of the carpenter's chest. A magnificent set of spoon augur bits in fine working order.* (GOOD+) **$395.00**

J3-41. Unmarked: Drill and Countersink Auger Bit. Very Well Made. Ca. 1880's. Length: 6 Inches. *Virtually untouched by the forces of time and the elements, this most unusual drill and countersink bit has the look of a patented tool, but it is not marked in any way. A rare and perfectly preserved countersink bit.* (FINE) **$115.00**

J3-42. Peck, Stow & Wilcox Co.: Patent Auger Handle. Patented March 20, 1888. With 3 Original Bits. Length: 17 1/2 Inches. *This classic "T" handle auger bit comes complete with 3 original bits, all of which are in nearly new condition. A great working set.* (FINE) **$125.00**

J3-43. Jennings Mfg. Co., The Russell: Set of 9 Auger Bit. In Fitted Case. With Original Label. Length: 10 Inches. *All of the bits in this cased set of nine are in excellent condition and ready to use. Nearly new, but old.* (FINE) **$135.00**

J3-44. Assorted Makers: Group of Early Auger Bits. Spoon, Pod, Spur, Etc. Excellent Condition. Length: 6 Inches. *The bits in this grouping came together from the same chest and will be kept together. Included are a number of spoon bits, a working set of center bits, countersinks, reamers and more. A veritable grab bag of boring accessories.* (GOOD+) **$85.00**

J3-45. Assorted Makers: Assorted Auger Bits. Twist, Reamer, Etc. Ready to Use. Length: 9 Inches. *Each of the bits in this assortment is in very well preserved condition and ready to be put back into use.* (GOOD+) **$15.00**

J3-46. Jennings Mfg. Co., The Russell: Set of 13 Auger Bits. Tiered Wooden Box. Extra Crisp and Clean. Length: 10 1/2 Inches. *All of the original bits remain in this early fitted case, which retains its original paper label. A set like new, but quite old.* (GOOD+) **$285.00**

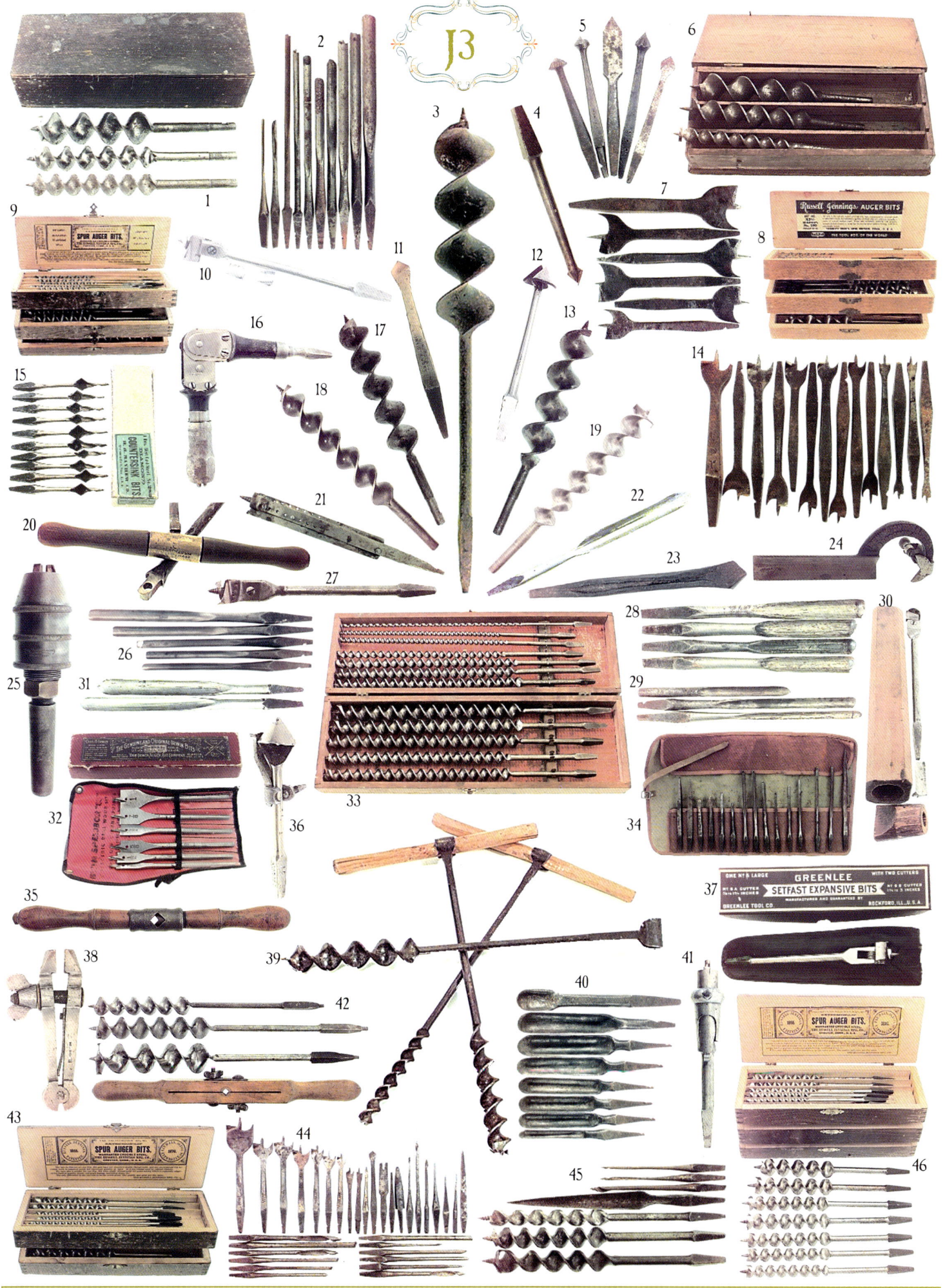

Group K3

K3-1. Stanley Rule & Level: Chip Breaker and Cutting Iron. For No. 2 Plane. Patented 1892 Trademark. Length: 7 Inches. *This ca. 1895 cutting iron and chip breaker are in excellent working order.* (GOOD+) **$45.00**

K3-2. Stanley Rule & Level: Unused Arm For No. 64 1/2 Marking Gauge. With Extra Drill Hole. Factory Reject? Length: 8 Inches. *The top side of this marking gauge beam has been bored for a scribe—not only where the hole should be, but also directly above the trademark, where it shouldn't. The nearness to new condition of this part may be a result of an error having been made in the factory. A Stanley collectible curiosity.* (FINE) **$35.00**

K3-3. Stanley Rule & Level: Replacement Sole For No. 12 1/2 Plane. Brazilian Rosewood. Tough to Find. Length: 6 1/2 Inches. *A number of No. 12 1/2's that we have seen look like the user was using his scraper on protruding nail heads. Here's a retread in brand new out of the hardware store condition.* (FINE) **$65.00**

K3-4. Unmarked: Handle For Block Plane. Cast Bronze Yoke. For 9 1/2 or 15. Length: 4 1/2 Inches. *A long time ago, someone used a tail handle from a Stanley block plane to fashion this bronze copy. Ready to use on your 9 1/2 to give it the functionality of a 9 3/4 or 15 1/2 without the added cost.* (GOOD+) **$45.00**

K3-5. Stanley Rule & Level: Frog Mechanism For Stanley No. 2. "Pat. 1888" on Lever. Clean and Sound. Length: 5 1/2 Inches. *The 1888 patent date that applied to the lateral adjustment mechanism is imprinted on this No. 2 frog. A nice part to have when you need it.* (GOOD+) **$45.00**

K3-6. Stanley Rule & Level: Removable Steel Side. For No. 140 Plane. Near New Condition. Length: 6 1/2 Inches. *If your Stanley No. 140 is missing its removable side, here's what you need. Nice.* (FINE) **$55.00**

K3-7. Stanley Rule & Level: Frog Mechansim For Bedrock Plane. 4 1/2, 6, 7. Near New Condition. Length: 5 Inches. *If your later Bedrock No. 4 1/2, 6 or 7 needs a new frog, here it is. Crisp and clean.* (FINE) **$65.00**

K3-8. Stanley Rule & Level: Brand New 1 5/8" Cutting Iron. For No. 2 Size. "Sweetheart" Trademark. Length: 7 Inches. *This brand new cutting iron for the No. 2 plane bears the ca. 1920's "Sweetheart" logo. New.* (FINE) **$55.00**

K3-9. Stanley Rule & Level: Stanley No. 2 Cutting Iron. Ca. 1915 Trademark. Unused Condition. Length: 6 Inches. *This cutting iron for a No. 2 size plane is in brand new condition. It dates to about 1915, when Stanley introduced the "V" shaped logo. Mint.* (FINE) **$55.00**

K3-10. Stanley Rule & Level: Scrub Plane Cutting Iron. For Stanley 40 1/2. Unused Condition. Length: 6 Inches. *This "Sweetheart" era cutting iron for a No. 40 scrub plane is in new condition. Crisp, clean and ready to use.* (FINE) **$45.00**

K3-11. Stanley Rule & Level No. 235: Sextuple Reeding Cutting Iron. Special Order Item. Unused Condition. Length: 3 3/4 Inches. *This wide reeding cutter for a Stanley No. 45 or No. 55 plane is in brand new condition in its original Stanley mailing box. Rare and brand new.* (FINE) **$85.00**

K3-12. Stanley Rule & Level: Set of 10 Cutting Irons. For Stanley No. 46. Near New Condition. Length: 3 Inches. *Try writing to Stanley to get them to send you a set of these. A complete and perfect set. First come, first serve.* (FINE) **$245.00**

K3-13. Millers Falls Company: Cutting Iron For No. 4 Rabbet Plane. Fits Stanley No. 75. Unused Condition. Length: 4 1/2 Inches. *The Millers Falls Company was thoughtful enough to model their planes exactly after the Stanley equivalents, making this cutting iron work just fine for a Stanley No. 75 bullnose rabbet. Brand new.* (FINE) **$15.00**

K3-14. Stanley Rule & Level: Cutting Iron For No. 2 Size Plane. With Chip Breaker. "Sweetheart" Trademark. Length: 6 Inches. *Complete with its original chip breaker, this "Sweetheart" era cutting iron is in excellent condition and could be lightly cleaned to dramatically improve its appearance.* (GOOD+) **$55.00**

K3-15. Stanley Rule & Level No. 215: Sextuple Reeding Cutting Iron. Special Order Item. Unused Condition. Length: 3 3/4 Inches. *There was a time when you could order these from Stanley. You can't any more. Rare and near new.* (FINE) **$55.00**

K3-16. Stanley Rule & Level: Set of 11 Cutting Irons. For Stanley No. 50. Ready to Use. Length: 3 1/4 Inches. *A fitted wood case has kept these cutting irons for Stanley's No. 50 plane in top condition. Ready to use.* (FINE) **$75.00**

K3-17. Millers Falls Company: Cutting Iron for No. 85 Plane. Fits Stanley No. 78. Unused Condition. Length: 4 1/2 Inches. *This new old stock cutting iron will also fit your Stanley No. 78 plane. Perfect.* (FINE) **$15.00**

K3-18. Stanley Rule & Level: Scrub Plane Cutting Iron. For Stanley No. 40 1/2. Unused Condition. Length: 6 Inches. *This cutting iron for a No. 40 1/2 scrub plane has never been used. Mint.* (FINE) **$45.00**

K3-19. Stanley Rule & Level: Cap Iron For "Bedrock" Plane. For 6, 7, 4 1/2 Size. Scarce and Excellent. Length: 5 1/2 Inches. *If you have a later style "Bedrock" plane with the wrong lever cap, here's the chance to make it right.* (FINE) **$85.00**

K3-20. Unmarked: Replacement Handle For Wooden Plane. New Old Stock. Ready to Use. Length: 4 1/2 Inches. *Whether you're planning to make your own plane or fix up one with a sheared tote, this brand new (but old) handle is just the thing you need.* (FINE) **$15.00**

K3-21. Stanley Rule & Level: "No. 1" Cutting Iron. "Sweetheart" Trademark. Unused Condition. Length: 5 Inches. *This No. 1 cutter comes to us from a consignor who found it in a Chicago hardware store. New, but old.* (FINE) **$55.00**

K3-22. Howarth, James, Sheffield, England: Set of Plow Plane Cutting Irons. Numbers 1-8. Fitted Felt Roll. Length: 9 1/2 Inches. *The imprint of respected Sheffield maker James Howarth has been boldly stamped on this extra clean set of cutting irons. A full set of plow irons in top condition.* (FINE) **$155.00**

K3-23. Stanley Rule & Level: Stanley No. 39 5/8" Cutting Iron. Near New Condition. Rare Stanley Part. Length: 3 1/4 Inches. *The simple screw lock adjustment on the No. 39 series of dado planes made it very easy for the cutter and the plane to become separated. This cutting iron for the 5/8" size is in nearly new condition. A tough part to find when you need one.* (FINE) **$75.00**

K3-24. Stanley Rule & Level: Frog Mechanism For No. 608 Plane. 90%+ Original Paint. Ready to Use. Length: 5 Inches. *If you need a later style frog mechanism for your "Bedrock" jointer, here it is. Clean, sound and ready to use.* (GOOD+) **$65.00**

K3-25. Stanley Rule & Level: Cutting Iron For H104 Smooth Plane. Manufactured 1964 Only. Unused Condition. Length: 1 1/4 Inches. *Just in case you were one of the folks who bought your H104 in 1964 (the year they were introduced and the year that they were discontinued), you might be due for a replacement. This one is in brand new condition.* (FINE) **$25.00**

K3-26. Stanley Rule & Level: Frog Assembly For No. 2 Plane. 95% Original Paint. Uncommon Part. Length: 4 1/2 Inches. *Here's a complete and flawless frog for your Stanley No. 2 plane. Much of the original lacquer remains on the adjustment screw.* (FINE) **$65.00**

K3-27. Goodell Pratt Company: Original Screwdriver Bit. For G.P. Screwdriver. Unused Condition. Length: 4 Inches. *If you need a screwdriver bit for your G.P. spiral drive screwdriver, here it is. A tough part to find. First come, first serve.* (FINE) **$8.00**

K3-28. Stanley Rule & Level: Cap Iron For Bedrock No. 608. Black Infill Type. Scarce and Excellent. Length: 4 1/2 Inches. *This style of "Bedrock" cap has been observed on both the early and the late styles. A tough part to find.* (GOOD+) **$65.00**

K3-29. Stanley Rule & Level: Auxiliary Center Bottom Attachment. For Stanley No. 55. Often Missing. Length: 5 1/2 Inches. *Everyone needs one and this is all I have to offer. Complete and excellent. First come, first serve.* (GOOD+) **$95.00**

K3-30. Stanley Rule & Level: 3 "Four Square" Handles. For Chisel and File. With Original Decals. Length: 4 1/2 Inches. *If your "Four Square" collection needs dressing up, these handles will help you along the way.* (GOOD+) **$35.00**

K3-31. Stanley Rule & Level: Cap Iron For No. 2 Plane. "Stanley" Casting. Extra Crisp and Clean. Length: 5 Inches. *The "Stanley" name is cast into this crispy clean cap iron for a No. 2 plane. A rare part in top shape.* (FINE) **$65.00**

K3-32. Siegley Tool Company: 2 7/16" Width Cutting Iron. For No. 12 Plane. Unused Condition. Length: 7 Inches. *If you happen to still be using your Siegley bench plane, you're in luck. Even though the hardware store can't get you a cutter, we can. Brand new.* (FINE) **$45.00**

K3-33. Stanley Rule & Level: Stanley No. 8 Cutting Iron. Ca. 1915 Trademark. Unused Condition. Length: 8 Inches. *An apparently unused cutting iron for Stanley's No. 8 or No. 608 series jointer planes.* (GOOD+) **$65.00**

K3-34. Stanley Rule & Level: 2 3/8" "Stanley" Cutting Iron. For 6, 7, 4 1/2, Etc. New Old Stock. Length: 7 3/4 Inches. *Here's a brand new cutter for your Stanley jointer plane. Mint.* (FINE) **$15.00**

K3-35. Stanley Rule & Level: "No. 2" Size Cutting Iron. Notch Trademark. Original Oil Coating. Length: 6 1/4 Inches. *This ca. 1930's era cutter is in unused condition. Perfect.* (GOOD+) **$45.00**

K3-36. Stanley Rule & Level: Stanley No. 140 Cutting Iron. Early Arch Trademark. Ready to Use. Length: 5 Inches. *This early cutting iron for a No. 140 block plane is in excellent condition. Ready to use.* (GOOD+) **$45.00**

K3-37. Stanley Rule & Level: Original Cap Iron for No. 2 Plane. With "Stanley Logo. Uncommon Part. Length: 5 Inches. *The next time you see a No. 2 for sale with a broken lever cap, buy it. Assuming, of course, that you buy this first.* (FINE) **$75.00**

K3-38. Stanley Rule & Level: Side Stop Attachment For Stanley Mitre Box. Patented October 31, 1916. Often Missing. Length: 5 Inches. *Here's a Stanley part that often ends up on the "whatsit" table. Its purpose was to regulate the rods that served as stops on Stanley's best mitre boxes.* (FINE) **$35.00**

K3-39. Stanley Rule & Level: Set of "Millers Patent" Cutting Irons. 8 Original Cutters. With Filletster Iron. Length: 3 1/2 Inches. *Here's a nearly complete set of cutting irons, including the filletster cutter, for your Millers Patent plane. Rare.* (GOOD) **$465.00**

K3-40. Kunz: 2 7/8" Scraper Cutting Iron. For 12, 12 1/2, 112. Ready to Use. Length: 5 Inches. *If you need a replacement scraper cutter for your Stanley scraper, this will do the trick. New.* (FINE) **$25.00**

K3-41. Stanley Rule & Level: Set of Pins and Screws For Bedrock Plane. Excellent Condition. Ready to Use. Length: 1 Inches. *These pins and screws came from a No. 608 "Bedrock". We believe that they are interchangeable with others in the series.* (FINE) **$35.00**

K3-42. Bridge Tool Co., St. Louis, Missouri: No. 2 Size Cutting Iron. With Chip Breaker. Rare and Excellent. Length: 6 Inches. *The Bridge Tool Company was a St. Louis hardware and tool dealer who marketed a line of tools under their brand name. If your Bridge No. 2 is missing its cutting iron, here's the part you need. Rare.* (GOOD+) **$55.00**

K3-43. Stanley Rule & Level: Rare "Ready Edge" Cutting Iron. Patented January 2, 1923. With Chip Breaker. Length: 6 1/2 Inches. *A rare example of Stanley's short-lived "Ready Edge" cutting iron, which featured removable edges for quick replacement without grinding and honing. Complete with the proper cap iron. An idea whose time never came.* (GOOD+) **$295.00**

K3-44. Unmarked: Set of 8 Plow Plane Cutting Irons. Fitted Craftsman Box. Excellent Condition. Length: 10 Inches. *Here's a full set of plow plane cutting irons in excellent condition, thanks in large part to the presence of a fitted wooden box. A great set that we won't have for long. First come, first serve.* (FINE) **$165.00**

K3-45. Kellett: "Kellet's Patent" Plane Iron. Patented September 16, 1884. Near New Condition. Length: 8 1/2 Inches. *This patent plane iron has a number of precision adjustments which I have yet to figure out. Crisp, clean and clearly marked.* (FINE) **$125.00**

K3-46. Stanley Rule & Level: Chip Breaker For No. 8 Size Plane. Uncommon Size. Ready to Use. Length: 5 3/4 Inches. *This one has seen some use, but it will do if you need one. A tough part to find.* (FAIR) **$15.00**

Group L3

L3-1. Dunham, S.C. & Mc Master, T.J.: Quirk Ovolo and Astragal Molding Plane. Early Prison Partner. Extra Crisp and Clean. Length: 9 1/2 Inches. *A particularly steeply cut complex molder imprinted with the mark of early prison contract partners Dunham & McMaster. A great example of an early New York State plane with an extra-complex cut. A good one.* (GOOD+) **$255.00**

L3-2. Mathieson & Son, A., Glasgow: Lignum Sole Smooth Plane. Original Decal. Rare and Near New. Length: 7 1/2 Inches. *Scottish planemaker Alexander Mathieson offered smoothing planes of the very highest quality that were fitted with a dovetailed lignum sole. Most collectors' experience with these planes has been through research. We are pleased to offer an example of one of these rare extra quality planes in much the same condition as it would have been when it left the Mathieson factory. Complete with nearly all original finishes and much of the original decal, this spectacular plane is ready to be used and admired, either alternately or consecutively.* (FINE) **$165.00**

L3-3. Griffiths, Norwich (England): Wedge Arm Plow Plane. Brass Depth Stop. Ready to Use. Length: 8 Inches. *This classic English plow has been fitted with four brass tips, a sign of extra quality. Crisp, clean and clearly marked.* (GOOD+) **$75.00**

L3-4. Greenslade, W., Bristol (England): Classic Toothing Plane. Ibbotson Iron. Near New Condition. Length: 7 1/2 Inches. *Here's a very well preserved toothing plane from one of England's top planemakers. Crisp, clean and ready to use.* (FINE) **$85.00**

L3-5. Wilson, H., Newcastle (England): Handled Beech Plow Plane. Brass Tips and Fitting. Replaced Wedges. Length: 11 1/2 Inches. *Handled plow (or plough) planes from British makers are much common than those on this side of "the pond". This brass tipped offering from a Northern maker is in excellent condition. The wedges that lock the arms are replacements, but well executed.* (GOOD) **$95.00**

L3-6. Potter, C.: Q. Ovolo, Bevel/Assorted Molding Plane. Undocumented Maker. Uncommon Type. Length: 9 1/2 Inches. *This complex molding plane, which appears professionally made, is marked "C. Potter", a maker's name we have not previously seen. It was found in the Mohawk Valley. Ex-Cooley Collection.* (GOOD+) **$145.00**

L3-7. Mc Master, Z. J., N.Y. No. 10: Pair of Hollow and Round Molding Planes. Extra Bold Stamps. Ready to Use. Length: 9 1/2 Inches. *These clean hollow and round planes have been boldly struck with the imprint of prison labor contractor Zalmon J. McMaster. A nice working pair.* (GOOD+) **$75.00**

L3-8. Mathieson & Son, A., Glasgow No. 8: Fully Boxed Sash Filletster Plan. Boxwood Arms and Nuts. Superb Condition. Length: 9 Inches. *The tools of Mathieson & Sons of Glasgow, Scotland have inspired a large and growing cadre of collectors, and for good reason. Mathieson's tools were always part art and part tool, in the grand Scottish tradition. This fully boxed filletster is a classic example. Fitted with artfully turned boxwood arms, notched fixing screws and in much the same condition as it was when new, this classic plane is ready to add accent to any collection of top quality woodworking tools.* (FINE) **$265.00**

L3-9. Sargent & Co., New Haven Conn.: Set of Cutting Irons. For 1080 Plane. Elaborate Case. Length: 9 1/2 Inches. *We are pleased to offer what we believe to be the most elaborate holder for combination plane cutting irons ever constructed. Each of the cutters in this full set of Sargent cutting irons has been individually fitted into a mahogany case, which is fitted with brass facing on all sides. Whether or not you need any cutting irons, we heartily recommend this special boxed set.* (FINE) **$225.00**

L3-10. Collins, Utica No. 4: Pair of Hollow and Round Molding Planes. Nearly New Condition. Ready to Use. Length: 9 1/2 Inches. *Here's a great working pair of No. 4 hollow and round planes in nearly new condition. Choice.* (FINE) **$85.00**

L3-11. Unmarked: Cove and Astragal Molding Plane. Rosewood Boxing. Uncommon Profile. Length: 9 1/2 Inches. *Decorative rosewood boxing accents this cove and astragal complex molding plane.* (GOOD+) **$85.00**

L3-12. Wells, R.: Special Purpose Molding Plane. "Washboard" Type. Extra Crisp and Clean. Length: 9 1/2 Inches. *A previous owner has applied a fence to the sole of this unusual "washboard" profile plane, which could be easily removed. A nice molder from an uncommon maker.* (FINE) **$165.00**

L3-13. Littell, T. & Atkinson, T., Louisville: Rare Louisville Molding Plane. Ca. 1838-1839 Only. AWP III: 3 Stars. Length: 9 1/2 Inches. *The partnership of Thomas Littell and T. Atkinson lasted two short years. Planes imprinted with their mark rate 3 stars for rarity. A rare Kentucky imprint.* (GOOD+) **$185.00**

L3-14. Salmen's, A.B. Successors, Ltd.: Beech Toothing Plane. Original Decal. Unused Condition. Length: 7 1/2 Inches. *Nearly all of the original decal remains on this apparently unused English toothing plane. Brand new.* (FINE) **$95.00**

L3-15. Mathieson & Son, A., Glasgow: Adjustable Chamfer Plane. Adjustable Fence. Apparently Unused. Length: 5 Inches. *The side of this classic fenced adjustable chamfer plane has been struck with the distinctive half moon logo of A. Mathieson & Sons. Rare and extra nice.* (FINE) **$185.00**

L3-16. Howland & Co., A., Auburn, N.Y. No. 93: Handled Screw Arm Plane. Boxwood Arms, Nuts. With 6 Cutting Irons. Length: 12 Inches. *This Howland plow planes comes with a mixed set of 6 cutting irons by assorted makers. A dirty but sound working plane at a bargain price.* (GOOD+) **$95.00**

L3-17. Gardner & Murdock, Boston, Mass.: Rare 3/16 Inch Dado Molding Plane. Marked. 1/8, 1/16. Extra Crisp and Clean. Length: 9 1/2 Inches. *Perhaps because they were temporarily missing the proper stamp, this 3/16 inch dado plane was marked "1/8" and "1/16" on the heel, causing confused woodworkers to quickly find the least common denominator. A well preserved plane from respected planemakers.* (GOOD+) **$65.00**

L3-18. Geer, D.S. & S.P., Syracuse, N.Y. No. 14: Round Molding Plane. Ca. 1853-1865 Only. AWP III: 2 Stars. Length: 9 1/2 Inches. *The obscure partnership whose imprint appears on this plane supposedly produced planes for 12 years, but the dearth of surviving examples suggests that they marked very few of them with their own mark. A rare maker imprinted plane* (GOOD+) **$145.00**

L3-19. Little, L., (Boston): Massive Complex Molding Plane. Lignum Boxing. AWP III: 3 Stars (A). Length: 9 1/2 Inches. *This early complex molder has the first Levi Little mark, which rates 3 stars for rarity in AWP III. The profile is so complex as to defy description. The sort of molding plane you don't find anymore.* (GOOD+) **$445.00**

L3-20. King, Josiah, 373 Bowery, N.Y.: Boxed Bead Molding Plane. Marked 3/8". Ready to Use. Length: 9 1/2 Inches. *Josiah King was a prolific producer of quality wooden planes in New York City in the 1840's through the 1880's.* (GOOD) **$35.00**

L3-21. Mathieson & Son, A., Glasgow: Boxed Bead Molding Plane. Marked "1/2". Unused Condition. Length: 9 1/2 Inches. *This boxed bead from Alexander Mathieson has apparently never been used. Mint.* (FINE) **$65.00**

L3-22. Auburn Tool Co., Auburn, N.Y. No. 90: Handled Beechwood Plane. Boxwood Arms and Nuts. Extra Crisp and Clean. Length: 11 Inches. *Handled plow planes, especially those with boxwood arms and nuts in good working order have virtually disappeared from the market. This one is in excellent working order. Ready to use.* (GOOD+) **$225.00**

L3-23. Mathieson & Son, A., Glasgow: Pair of Tongue and Groove Molding Planes. Rare 1/4 Inch Size. Unused Condition. Length: 9 1/2 Inches. *Finding chicken teeth is a more rewarding search than coming up with a pair of 1/4 inch tongue and groove molding planes. These exceptionally clean planes from A. Mathieson & Sons are in nearly new condition. Rare and near new.* (FINE) **$125.00**

L3-24. Nurse, C., Walworth Road, London: Pair of Snipe Bill Molding Plane. Fully Boxed. Near New Condition. Length: 9 1/2 Inches. *The firm of C. Nurse & Co. commenced operation in 1841 and remained in business for nearly 100 years, that longevity no doubt attributable to the production of tools such as that offered here. These fully boxed snipe bill molding planes, which appear to date from around 1890, are in nearly new condition.* (FINE) **$165.00**

L3-25. Moss, Wm., Birmingham, England: Early Boxed Bead Molding Plane. Ca. 1775-1797. Replaced Wedge. Length: 9 1/2 Inches. *Here's a genuine bargain on a well used but honest 18th Century molding plane.* (FAIR) **$25.00**

L3-26. Collins & Robbins, Utica: 1 1/4 Inch Hollow Molding Plane. Ca. 1829-1830. AWP III: 2 Stars. Length: 9 1/2 Inches. *Collins & Robbins worked in Utica, New York for two years only. This plane, which is missing its iron, is boldly struck with their mark. A bargain.* (GOOD+) **$15.00**

L3-27. Mathieson & Son, A., Glasgow: Set of 3 Boxed Bead Molding Planes. 1/4 Inch, 1/2 Inch and 5/8 Inch. Near New Condition. Length: 9 1/2 Inches. *The original decals remain on two of the three boxed bead planes in this exceptionally well preserved set. Mint.* (FINE) **$165.00**

L3-28. Rowell, S., Albany, N.Y.: Pair Quirk, and Ovolo, Bevel Molding Planes. Extra Steep Profiles. Marked "5/8" and "3/4". Length: 9 1/2 Inches. *Here's a nice working pair of molders from Simeon Rowell, an early planemaker in Albany, and Troy, New York. The steepness of the profiles of these planes is consistent with Rowell's 1820's era working dates. A nice set.* (GOOD+) **$285.00**

L3-29. Ohio Tool Co., N.Y. No. 119 1/2: 2 1/2 Inch Skew Rabbet Plane. With Side Nicker. Near New Condition. Length: 16 Inches. *This massive skew blade rabbeting plane is in nearly new condition and boldly marked with the Ohio Tool name. A great plane.* (FINE) **$95.00**

L3-30. Sarjent, W., West Street, Reading: Full Boxed Bead Molding Plane. Uncommon 1/8 Inch Size. Near New Condition. Length: 9 1/2 Inches. *Smaller bead planes that were not fitted with full boxing soon became unusable. This fully boxed 1/8 inch bead is in nearly new condition and ready to last a lifetime.* (FINE) **$65.00**

L3-31. Colton, J., Market St./Philadelphia: Fenced Hand Rail Molding Plane. Owner Brand "Simon". Near New Condition. Length: 7 Inches. *A previous owner by the name of "Simon" has branded his name, Philadelphia style, on the toe of this adjustable stair rail plane. Overall condition is nearly new.* (FINE) **$295.00**

L3-32. Vincent, J., Stratford On Avon: Center Bead Molding Plane. Uncommon Maker. Replaced Cutter. Length: 9 1/2 Inches. *There may not have been people still alive in Stratford on Avon when this plane was made who actually knew William Shakespeare, but we would venture that there were those who claimed that they had known him. An early plane with an uncommon English imprint.* (FAIR) **$25.00**

L3-33. Tileston, T., Boston (Front St.): Massive Steep Ovolo Molding Plane. Ca. 1841-1866. Marked "Inch 1/2". Length: 9 1/2 Inches. *Here's a spectacularly steep complex molding plane from the planemaker who produced many of the tools that build the great mansions of Boston. A most unusual cut on a very well preserved plane.* (GOOD+) **$385.00**

L3-34. Coughtry, J., Albany: Applewood Plow Plane. Rare Albany Maker. Near New Condition. Length: 10 Inches. *One of the least common of all New York State planemakers, J. Coughtry produced wooden planes for a brief period in Albany, New York in the 1850's. This imprint has been designated as his "B" mark and includes the Albany location. The arms have a pattern that we have not previously seen, and the applewood body and boxwood arms are in spectacularly well preserved condition. Highly recommended.* (FINE) **$445.00**

L3-35. Mathieson & Son, A., Glasgow: Classic Beech Smooth Plane. Half-Moon Logo. Unused Condition. Length: 8 Inches. *This perfectly preserved smoothing plane is in the same condition as it was when it left Mathieson's Glasgow factory perhaps 100 years ago. Dead mint.* (FINE) **$65.00**

L3-36. Moseley & Son, John, London: Boxed Torus Bead Molding Plane. Marked "5/8". Ready to Use. Length: 9 1/2 Inches. *A pair of extra wide strips of boxing were fitted into the sole of this plane to ensure its longevity. It is in excellent working order.* (GOOD+) **$65.00**

L3-37. Tolman, J.R. , Hanover, Mass.: Center Bead Molding Plane. Marked "1/4". Full Boxed. Length: 9 1/2 Inches. *This plane has been photographed from the side to show the squared off escapement that was used almost exclusively by Tolman and a few other Southeastern Massachusetts coastal makers. An interesting plane in near-new condition.* (GOOD+) **$85.00**

L3-38. Mathieson & Son, A., Glasgow: Classic Scottish Plow Plane. Full Set of Irons. Decorative Form. Length: 10 1/2 Inches. *This graphic plow plane has turned finials on the arms and cruciform lock nuts that say without looking that it was produced by Mathieson of Glasgow. The Mathieson mark has been boldly struck on the toe of this well preserved plow, which includes a full set of cutting irons. The No. 2 iron is quite short from use. A classic Scottish plow that is warranted for use or display, or both. Nice.* (GOOD+) **$365.00**

L3-39. Doscher Plane & Tool Co., The: 3/8 Inch Dado Molding Plane. Unusual Nicker Wedge. Extra Crisp and Clean. Length: 9 1/2 Inches. *This 3/8 dado from a prominent New York City maker is fitted with an oversize wedge for the front nicker. Straight, sharp and ready to cut.* (FINE) **$75.00**

L3-40. Kendall, I., Bristol: Early Dado Molding Plane. Ca. 1780's. 11/16 Inch Width. Length: 9 1/2 Inches. *This well preserved dado plane is in a most unusual size. Crisp, clean and ready to use.* (GOOD+) **$95.00**

L3-41. Atkin & Sons, Birmingham (England): Set of Plow Plane Cutting Irons. Full Set of 8. Ready to Use. Length: 8 1/2 Inches. *If you have a plow plane in need of a set of irons, these are complete and in great working order.* (GOOD+) **$115.00**

L3-42. See, C. S., (New York): Boxed Bead Molding Plane. With Eagle Trademark. Marked "3/16". Length: 9 1/2 Inches. *The trademark eagle imprint of C.S. See has been boldly struck on the toe of this boxed bead plane.* (GOOD) **$35.00**

L3-43. Unmarked: Fenced Hand Rail Plane. Solid Lignum Vitae. From Coastal Maine. Length: 13 1/2 Inches. *This spectacular handled lignum vitae handrail plane comes to us from the Maine coast, where planes of this material were the preference of local woodworkers. The tip of the tote has a longitudinal crack, but is bent, and not broken. A dramatic special purpose plane.* (GOOD+) **$285.00**

L3-44. Tileston, T., Boston (Front St.): Rare Cluster Bead Molding Plane. Uncommon Profile. AWP III: "F" Imprint. Length: 9 1/2 Inches. *The cluster bead is a profile that was produced in the 1830's and 1840's and neither before nor since. It is in excellent collector quality condition and clearly marked.* (GOOD+) **$365.00**

L3-45. Appleton, Thos., Boston: Combination Tongue and Groove Plane. Gladwin's Patented June 9, 1857. Rare 1/2 Inch Size. Length: 11 Inches. *Marked only with the "Thos. Appleton/Boston" "A" mark, this is undoubtedly an example of Gladwin's patent Tongue and Groove plane. A missing grooving cutter may account for its extraordinarily well preserved condition. Crisp.* (FINE) **$295.00**

Group M3

M3-1. Moir, G.D.: Craftsman Made Calipers. Innovative Style. Early and Excellent. Length: 9 1/2 Inches. *Sometimes, in our quest for tools imprinted with the names of historically significant manufacturers, we make the mistake of overlooking those tools that the manufactured tools displaced. Certainly, the importance of manufactured tools increased dramatically, beginning in the 1860's, until virtually no machinists made their own tools by the beginning of this Century. But what of the time before the manufactured tools came, and what of the transition? The pair of calipers offered here offers us a glimpse of the level of mechanical artistry that a skilled machinist could produce in the creation of tools that were, at the same time, a testament of his skill and the means by which he earned his livelihood. Marked only with the maker's name, "G.D. Moir", these fixed outside and precision adjusting calipers have a distinctive style that is unlike any manufactured tool. Perfectly preserved, boldly marked and distinctively different, these owner-crafted tools capture within them the spirit of creativity and self reliance that built a mighty nation; they capture within them the soul of G.D. Moir. Extraordinary.* (FINE) **$225.00**

M3-2. Brown & Sharpe Mfg. Co.: Early Precision Caliper. With "Tools" Trademark. 100th of an Inch. Length: 4 Inches. *Engine dividing machinery developed by J.R. Brown and Lucien Sharpe was still in use some 70 years after it was invented. This early caliper has been graduated in 100ths of an inch using equipment based on the early prototype. An excellent example.* (GOOD+) **$35.00**

M3-3. Starrett, L.S., Athol, Mass.: Early Screw Adjust Caliper. Inside, Outside Measurment. Ca. 1895. Length: 5 1/2 Inches. *A classic example of the Starrett Company's early work. Complete and excellent.* (FINE) **$95.00**

M3-4. Starrett , L. S., Athol, Mass. No. 231: 0 - 1 Inch Micrometer Caliper. With Ratchet Adjust. Locking Mechanism. Length: 4 3/4 Inches. *This mechanically perfect micrometer has the optional ratchet adjustment.* (GOOD+) **$40.00**

M3-5. Unmarked: Early Machinist Caliper. Fleur De Lis Pointer. Dated "1854". Length: 3 Inches. *This hand-filed gauging caliper has a brass joint, a delicately filed pointer with an elaborate point and is dated 1854. Condition is superb. Extraordinary and highly recommended.* (GOOD+) **$265.00**

M3-6. Unmarked: Machinists Center Gauge. Elaborate Form. "A. Lombardo". Length: 9 1/2 Inches. *Elaborate filework by a forgotten "A. Lombardo" has transformed this "basic" center gauge into a work of art. A magnificent craftsman made machinist's tool. Highly recommended.* (GOOD+) **$165.00**

M3-7. Brown & Sharpe Mfg., Providence: Patent Caliper Rule. Patented June 14, 1892. Near New Condition. Length: 3 Inches. *The small knurled cylinder inset into the body of the rule locks the caliper in place. An uncommon rule in great shape.* (FINE) **$95.00**

M3-8. Starrett Co., The L.S., Athol, Mass. No. 83: "Yankee" Spring Divider. 6 Inch Size. New Condition, Original Box. Length: 6 Inches. *A perfectly preserved pair of "Yankee" dividers in their original box.* (FINE) **$45.00**

M3-9. Unmarked: Early German Caliper. "A. Reulsback" Owner. Nicely Decorated. Length: 5 1/4 Inches. *These most unusual calipers have a tastefully engraved owner's mark that does not sound Irish.* (GOOD+) **$65.00**

M3-10. Smith, E.G., Columbia, Penn. No. 128: Adjustable Slide Caliper. 6 Inch Length. Excellent Condition. Length: 6 Inches. *The E.G. Smith Company offered a full line of calipers and related tools. This one is clean, complete and clearly marked.* (FINE) **$85.00**

M3-11. Unmarked: Machinist's Depth Gauge. Quick Adjust Feature. Appears Manfactured. Length: 3 1/4 Inches. *Identical in many ways to a quick adjust depth gauge produced by the Standard Tool Company, this crispy clean "push button" depth stop is in top condition.* (FINE) **$145.00**

M3-12. Mc Grath, St. Paul, Minnesota: Machinist's Combination Gauge. Uncommon Type. Excellent Condition. Length: 4 1/2 Inches. *No doubt patterned after a similar tool produced by L.S. Starrett, this Minnesota combination gauge includes taper and feeler gauges and wire gauges.* (GOOD+) **$35.00**

M3-13. Wyke & Co., E. Boston, Mass.: "Wyke's Patent" Gauge. Patented September 11, 1882. Complete and Excellent. Length: 2 1/2 Inches. *A clean, complete and clearly marked example of the Wyke multi-purpose machinist's gauge of 1882. A rare and mechanically interesting tool in excellent condition.* (FINE) **$145.00**

M3-14. Assorted Makers: Assortment of Feeler Gauges. Moore & Wright, Etc. Excellent Condition. Length: 7 Inches. *These gauges came from the chest of a Canadian machinist and include an assortment of British makers. A handy set.* (FINE) **$25.00**

M3-15. Starrett Co., L. S., Athol, Mass. No. 494: Toolmaker's Locating Buttons. Uncommon Tool. Near New Condition. Length: 2 Inches. *These "toolmaker's buttons" served some special purpose which has never been adequately explained to me. Usually, about halfway through the information sharing session, I see someone three tables over opening a box of tools. The rest, as they say, is history. A nice example of an uncommon tool.* (FINE) **$65.00**

M3-16. Darling, Brown & Sharpe: Machinist's Center Gauge. Standard Type. Early and Excellent. Length: 2 1/2 Inches. *A good, clean center gauge with a desirable maker mark. An early owner's stamp "Hill" adds character.* (FINE) **$25.00**

M3-17. Bemis & Call Co., Springfield, Mass: Precision Inside Caliper. Patented May 28, 1861. Early And Excellent. Length: 6 Inches. *Maker-marked examples of the early output of the Bemis & Call Company are not common, especially when imprinted with the early patent date. Choice.* (FINE) **$75.00**

M3-18. Lorsch, Albert & Co., New York, N.Y.: Brass Slide Caliper. Metric Graduates. Ca. 1900. Length: 3 1/2 Inches. *An interesting brass sliding caliper with the mark of an unfamiliar maker. Any information? Early and unusual.* (GOOD+) **$65.00**

M3-19. Stevens & Co., J., C. Falls, Mass.: Screw Lock Divider. With Dumbell Lock. Scarce and Sound. Length: 10 Inches. *Stevens offered this "lever lock" mechanism on a range of calipers and dividers. It seems to have become the standard on the larger calipers and dividers that Stevens produced.* (GOOD+) **$45.00**

M3-20. Starrett Co., The L.S., Athol, Mass. No. 274: Toolmaker's Inside Caliper. With Spring Joint. New Condition, Original Box. Length: 4 Inches. *The original box has protected this pair of "Toolmaker's" calipers from any aging or abuse. Mint in the box.* (FINE) **$45.00**

M3-21. Chesterman & Co., Ltd., Sheffield No. 770: Precision Vernier Caliper. With Instructions. New Condition, Original Box. Length: 16 1/2 Inches. *This precision caliper from a prominent British toolmaker is in much the same condition as it was when new. Extra nice, and ready to use.* (FINE) **$85.00**

M3-22. Unmarked: Early Machinist's Protractor. "George Thumshirn". Ca. 1860's. Length: 8 Inches. *The owner/maker of this protractor employed a pattern that was being produced at this time by J.R. Brown & Sharpe. The maker, one "George Thumshirn", engraved his name on his creation in elaborate script. A classic.* (GOOD+) **$115.00**

M3-23. Brown & Sharpe Mfg., Providence: Precision Adjust Caliper. Integral Spring. Early and Excellent. Length: 4 Inches. *A spring formed from the bracket arm of this caliper serves to regulate its adjustment. An uncommon and mechanically interesting early machinist tool.* (FINE) **$45.00**

M3-24. Brown & Sharpe Mfg. Co. No. 715: Gear Tooth Gauge. With "Tools" Trademark. Crisp and Clean. Length: 2 1/2 Inches. *There was no margin for error in the making of gear teeth—either the gears would mesh, or the factory would be a place filled with loud noises, broken metal and non-functioning machines. This pocket caliper would allow a machinist to quickly check the size of a given gear.* (FINE) **$45.00**

M3-25. Spiers, Stewart, Ayr, Scotland: Machinist's Double Caliper. Dated "1917". WW I Production? Length: 5 Inches. *When Great Britain tooled up for the First World War, the Scottish planemaking firm of Stewart Spiers joined the war effort. These most unusual double calipers are imprinted with the "Spiers/Ayr" imprint and dated 1917. A most unusual Spiers collectible.* (GOOD+) **$175.00**

M3-26. Brown & Sharpe, J.R.: Early Screw Lock Caliper. Ca. 1850's or Before. Excellent Condition. Length: 5 Inches. *Tools imprinted with the mark of Providence, Rhode Island maker J.R. Brown & Sharpe date from the 1850's and 1860's. This caliper is clean and clearly marked with the name. Rare.* (GOOD+) **$145.00**

M3-27. Brown & Sharpe Mfg. Co.: Number Drill Gauge. Sizes 61-80. Uncommon Type. Length: 2 Inches. *The ca. 1915 "tools" trademark of B. & S. has been boldly stamped on this pristine drill gauge.* (FINE) **$25.00**

M3-28. Starrett, L.S., Athol, Mass.: 6 Hermaphrodite Caliper. Patented January 6, 1885. Extra Early and Fine. Length: 10 Inches. *A good, clean example of Starrett's precision adjust 1885 patent.* (FINE) **$55.00**

M3-29. Assorted Makers: Assortment of 6 Calipers. Starrett, Etc. Inside and Outside. Length: 10 Inches. *All of these calipers were included among the working tools of a single machinist. A nice set.* (GOOD+) **$45.00**

M3-30. Consolidated Tool Co., New York, N.Y.: 7 Inch Outside Caliper. "Pilot" Brand. Ship Wheel Logo. Length: 7 Inches. *This company sold planes, chisels and drills. This is the first machinist tool I've seen with their mark. Most unusual.* (GOOD+) **$45.00**

M3-31. Stevens & Co., J.: Quick Adjust Caliper. Patented November 20, 1888. Near New Condition. Length: 5 Inches. *A split adjustment screw allows it to slide easily into place. The spring in the caliper holds it in place to be turned for precise adjustment. A great example.* (FINE) **$95.00**

M3-32. Starrett Co., L. S., Athol, Mass.: Promotional Pencil. Retractable Tip. Excellent Condition. Length: 4 1/4 Inches. *To protect the point, this Starrett pencil holder would allow you to store the pencil inside the handle when not in use. A nice example of an uncommon Starrett promotional item.* (GOOD+) **$25.00**

M3-33. Assorted Makers: Group of Small Gauges. Starrett, Etc. Radius, Etc. Length: 1 1/2 Inches. *Here's an interesting assortment of radius, gear tooth and other gauges. All were rescued from the same chest. An interesting lot.* (FINE) **$25.00**

M3-34. Slocomb, J.T., Providence, R.I.: Massive 5 -6 Inch Micrometer. Original Decal. Excellent Condition. Length: 10 1/2 Inches. *J.T. Slocomb produced precision measuring equipment from the 1890's into the first quarter of the 20th Century. The level of quality rivaled that of the major producers. A well preserved example of the work of an under appreciated maker.* (GOOD+) **$35.00**

M3-35. Stubs, P.S. No. 1: Early Double Caliper. Extremely Well Made. Superb Condition. Length: 6 Inches. *The English and German maker P.S. Stubs produced metalworking tools of the very highest quality. This double caliper is an example of their best work. Choice.* (FINE) **$85.00**

M3-36. Nash Co., George, New York, N.Y.: Machinists Center Gauge. Rare Maker. Crisp and Clean. Length: 4 Inches. *Designed to implement a principle of geometry known to every fifteen year old and then quickly forgotten, this device allows the user to quickly find the center of a spherical object by scribing intersecting lines. The maker is new to us. Most unusual.* (GOOD+) **$35.00**

M3-37. Stevens & Co.: Early Spring Joint Caliper. Rare 2 Inch Size. Extra Early and Nice. Length: 2 Inches. *This early spring joint caliper a size or two smaller than that usually encountered. A well preserved early caliper in top collector quality condition.* (FINE) **$125.00**

M3-38. Unmarked: Triangular Machinist Bevel. Marked. "Pat. Apl'd For". Most Unusual. Length: 3 Inches. *A triangular bevel and gauging tool of early appearance. No maker name, but obviously manufactured.* (FINE) **$85.00**

M3-39. Unmarked: Early Hand Forged Compass. With Pin Joint. Excellent Patina. Length: 11 3/4 Inches. *These early dividers have a "primitive" look to them.* (GOOD) **$45.00**

M3-40. Starrett Co., L. S., Athol, Mass. No. 18-AA: Machinist's Center Punch. Spring Loaded. Ready to Use. Length: 3 3/4 Inches. *By turning the cap on this precision center punch, the amount of force applied when the punch is activated can be regulated. A great working tool in excellent condition.* (GOOD+) **$35.00**

M3-41. Starrett Co., L. S., Athol, Mass.: Double Joint Caliper. With Divider Legs. Excellent Condition. Length: 6 1/2 Inches. *The pivoting legs on this caliper allow it to function as an inside or outside caliper, or as a divider. Different.* (GOOD+) **$45.00**

M3-42. Starrett Co., The L.S., Athol, Mass. No. 178 B: Folding Radius Gauge. Multiple Sizes. Excellent Condition. Length: 3 Inches. *Both inside and outside radius gauges are included on this handy tool. A nice example.* (GOOD+) **$25.00**

M3-43. Wood & Reynolds, Boston, Mass.: Farrier's Angle Gauge. Precision Adjust. Full Nickel Plating. Length: 7 Inches. *Infinitely more elaborate than the equipment of the barnyard farrier, this precision gauge was used for calculating and gauging the exact placement of horseshoes. Clean, clearly marked with the maker's name and much earlier than other tools of this type that we have observed.* (GOOD+) **$185.00**

M3-44. Brown & Sharpe Mfg., Providence No. 601: Precision Adjust Depth Gauge. With Lever Lock. Near New Condition. Length: 9 Inches. *Depressing the lever on the side of this precision depth gauge allows it to be quickly adjusted. Condition is nearly new.* (FINE) **$85.00**

M3-45. Modern Tools, Japan No. MT-12A: Precision Adjust Caliper. 0 - 7 Inch Scale. Original Case. Length: 8 Inches. *We are not familiar with this post War Japanese maker, but the degree of detail on this caliper suggests a quality maker. A bargain.* (FINE) **$35.00**

Group N3

N3-1. Richards, W.G.: Early Patent Speed Indicator. Patented September 26, 1882. Fitted Leather Case. Length: 3 Inches. *Marked only with the patent date, which is embossed in tiny letters on the reverse side of this early indicator, this tool is in extraordinarily well-preserved condition in a leather sleeve that was most likely original. An ebony handle provides a nice contrast to the bright nickel plating. A great early indicator in new condition.* (FINE) **$345.00**

N3-2. Unmarked: English "Turnip" Plumb Bob. Marked "Sheffield". Nicely Turned. Length: 3 Inches. *Here's an English classic imprinted with the name of a city that is renowned for uncompromising quality. A nice one.* (GOOD+) **$115.00**

N3-3. Hjorth Lathe And Tool Company: Precision Adjust Surface Gauge. Rare Small Size. Unused Condition. Length: 4 1/2 Inches. *Topped by a micrometer adjustment, this specialty ca. 1900 surface gauge from from this Massachusetts maker was meant to be and is a highly precise measuring tool. Condition is as new.* (FINE) **$285.00**

N3-4. Assorted Makers: Caliper and Speed Indicators. Starret and Mibro. From Single Chest. Length: 7 1/2 Inches. *Another bargain lot from a machinist's chest, this grouping includes a pair of speed indicators and a caliper.* (GOOD+) **$25.00**

N3-5. Unmarked: Massive Brass Plumb Bob. Marked "1". Distinctive Form. Length: 7 Inches. *More verbally effusive sorts than are found here have designated this form of plumb bob as the "arrow through the apple" form. This massive example has an "arrow" much thicker than is usually encountered. A massive and nicely patinated bob having a distinctive shape.* (FINE) **$365.00**

N3-6. Unmarked: Oil Tank Plumb Bob. With Graduations. Crisp and Clean. Length: 6 1/2 Inches. *Lufkin was the likely maker of this oil tank gauging bob. It is in new condition.* (FINE) **$35.00**

N3-7. Unmarked: Adjustable Surface Gauge. Early Appearance. Nicely Knurled. Length: 6 Inches. *No marks on this one, but its very nicely made. The type of tool that deserves more attention than it gets.* (GOOD+) **$75.00**

N3-8. Unmarked No. 2: Turned Brass Plumb Bob. With "S" In Shield. Unused Condition. Length: 2 1/2 Inches. *This miniature brass plumb bob is in unused condition. Choice.* (GOOD+) **$75.00**

N3-9. Unmarked: Small Brass Plumb Bob. Rounded Cap. Excellent Patina. Length: 2 1/4 Inches. *This "basic" bronze plumb bob has a most appealing shape.* (GOOD+) **$35.00**

N3-10. Stanley Rule & Level No. 1: Retractable Reel Plumb Bob. Patented April 28, 1874. Near New Condition. Length: 4 Inches. *The date of the 1874 patent granted to Justus Traut for the friction activated reel is imprinted on the body of this early and exquisite example. Nearly all original finishes remain. Choice.* (FINE) **$285.00**

N3-11. Starrett, L.S., Athol, Mass. No. 52: Precision Adjust Surface Gauge. Rare First Model. 80% Original Paint. Length: 12 Inches. *Easily recognized by its distinctive base, this classic gauge is ready to add accent to any collection. A seldom seen example of the first model of Starrett's premier surface gauge in their early years.* (GOOD) **$395.00**

N3-12. Chandler, C.E., Boston, Mass.: Early Patent Speed Indicator. Patented July 31, 1883. Fitted Wood Case. Length: 6 1/2 Inches. *Patented by S.E. Chandler in 1883, These were marketed by S.E. Chandler of Boston, Mass. One would suspect some connection to the hardware firm of Chandler and Farquar, also of Boston. These are extremely scarce, especially in the clean condition offered here. Almost all of the original finishes remain. Nice.* (GOOD+) **$265.00**

N3-13. Unmarked: Classic Brass Plumb Bob. Removable Top. Golden Patina. Length: 3 Inches. *This distinctively shaped bob has achieved a dark, golden patina. Nice.* (GOOD+) **$25.00**

N3-14. Billings & Spencer Co., The: "Billings Patent" Surface Gauge. Patented August 1, 1882. Super Rare. Length: 8 Inches. *An extremely well preserved and clearly marked example of the surface gauge marketed by the Billings and Spencer Company of Hartford, Conn. and patented by Charles E. Billings on August 1, 1882. Most of the nickel plating remains. Very, very rare.* (GOOD+) **$775.00**

N3-15. Unmarked: Conical Cast Iron Plumb Bob. With Brass Cap. Uncommon Style. Length: 3 1/4 Inches. *A brass cap crowns this cast iron plumb bob. Different.* (GOOD+) **$25.00**

N3-16. Unmarked: Special Function Speed Indicator. With Instructions. New Condition, Original Box. Length: 1 1/2 Inches. *The original instructions are included with this most unusual variation on the speed indicator theme. Appearance is ca. 1920's.* (FINE) **$65.00**

N3-17. Unmarked: 5 1/2 Lb. Brass Plumb Bob. Decorative Knurls. For Bridge Work? Length: 8 Inches. *Looking as much like a howitzer shell as it does a plumb bob, this extra heavy plumb bob was likely used for major construction jobs, like building bridges, where movement of a bob by the wind could be a factor. An interesting plumb bob from the State of California.* (GOOD+) **$165.00**

N3-18. Starrett, L.S., Athol, Mass. No. 55: Early Patent Surface Gauge. Patented March 17, 1896. Rare and Excellent. Length: 12 1/2 Inches. *A most extremely rare surface gauge, this is the elusive No. 55 manufactured by the L.S. Starrett firm. These had disappeared from the catalog by the turn of the century and only a few examples are known. This is the larger of two sizes offered.* (GOOD+) **$325.00**

N3-19. Unmarked: Early Precision Speed Indicator. With Brass Dial. Nickel Plated. Length: 3 3/4 Inches. *There seems to be no end to the number of variations on a common theme that the speed indicator can generate. This one is just different enough to be...different.* (GOOD+) **$45.00**

N3-20. Veeder Mfg. Co., Hartford, Conn.: Patent Speed Indicator. Patented November 6, 1907. With Digital Reading. Length: 3 Inches. *These folks also made those counters that fit on machines to tally the number of endless repetitions. I worked in a factory for several summers. By August, the world of academia seemed somehow more attractive than the memories of spring had indicated. An uncommon speed indicator.* (FINE) **$95.00**

N3-21. Stanley Rule & Level No. 2: Retractable Reel Plumb Bob. Brass Body and Reel. Clean and Shiny. Length: 4 Inches. *A clean and shiny but unmarked example of Stanley's larger brass integral reel plumb bob.* (GOOD+) **$165.00**

N3-22. Starrett Co., The L.S., Athol, Mass.: Mercury Filled Plumb Bob. Patented October 16, 1906. With Integral Reel. Length: 6 Inches. *This classic mercury filled plumb bob is in excellent collector quality condition. A good one.* (GOOD+) **$55.00**

N3-23. Thompson, A.L. Mfr., Lowell, Mass. No. 8: Early Brass Plumb Bob. Maker Marked. 99% Original Lacquer. Length: 6 Inches. *A later fitted wooden case has kept this A.L. Thompson plumb bob in essentially the same condition as it was the day it was made. Nearly all original finishes remain. Absolutely mint and highly recommended.* (FINE) **$385.00**

N3-24. Unmarked: Ovate Brass Plumb Bob. Knurled Cap Lip. Highly Polished. Length: 3 Inches. *A knurled tip facilitates the removal of the cap on this classic brass bob. A good one.* (GOOD) **$35.00**

N3-25. Tabor Mfg. Co., N.Y.: Machinist's Speed Indicator. Patented September 8, 1885. Original Carton. Length: 4 Inches. *The original pasteboard box, which has itself degraded over time, has kept this early patent indicator in new condition. Absolutely perfect.* (FINE) **$95.00**

N3-26. Hebert, J.R., Brooklyn, N.Y.: "The Duplex" Speed Indicator. "Pat. Appl'd. For". New Condition, Original Box. Length: 4 1/4 Inches. *If you intend to put this rare American speed indicator to use, the original instructions may be of help. This tool is marked "Patent Applied For", but we can find no record that a patent was granted. The maker name appears in neither of Ken Cope's books on machinists tools makers.* (FINE) **$295.00**

N3-27. Unmarked: Machinist's Speed Indicator. With Bell Mechanism. New Condition, Original Box. Length: 4 3/4 Inches. *Substantially different in form from the "bell" sounding speed indicator normally encountered, this unmarked example is in new condition in its original box. The only example of this rare tool that we have seen. Rare and near new.* (FINE) **$550.00**

N3-28. Unmarked: Carrot Shape Plumb Bob. Removable Tip. Golden Patina. Length: 2 Inches. *This tip of this "carrot shape" bob is removable, most likely to facilitate replacement. A good one.* (GOOD+) **$25.00**

N3-29. Unmarked: Decorative Handmade Surface Gauge. Acorn Finials. Near-New Condition. Length: 6 Inches. *This superbly hand-crafted surface gauge was obviously made by a machinist of considerable skill. The acorn finials at the top of the beam and on the fixing screw are especially well executed. Extra nice.* (FINE) **$165.00**

N3-30. Unmarked: "Carrot" Type Plumb Bob. Brass Body. Superb Patina. Length: 3 Inches. *This early bob makes no pretensions to style, but it is honest and has the golden patina of age. Ex-Cooley Collection.* (GOOD+) **$65.00**

N3-31. Unmarked: Squat Brass Plumb Bob. With Knurled Cap. Great Patina. Length: 3 Inches. *A decorative spiral knurl accents the cap of this nicely patinated bob.* (FINE) **$85.00**

N3-32. Sheffield Machine & Tool Co., Dayt: Deming Precision Indicator. Rare and Excellent. New Condition, Original Box. Length: 4 1/2 Inches. *This early dial indicator is in superb collector-quality condition in its original box. All original finishes remain on this rare and complete example.* (FINE) **$225.00**

N3-33. Unmarked: Early Machinists Surface Gauge. Very Well Made. Turned Brass Base. Length: 11 Inches. *A turned brass base supports this classic Nineteenth Century craftsman made surface gauge.* (GOOD+) **$85.00**

N3-34. Starrett Co., The L.S., Athol, Mass. No. 5150: Brass Gauging Plumb Bob. Precision Graduated Edge. Near New Condition. Length: 7 Inches. *These were designed to fit on the end of Starrett's oil gauging tape measures. It is in new condition.* (FINE) **$85.00**

N3-35. Unmarked: Reversible Tip Plumb Bob. For Storage. Early and Excellent. Length: 4 Inches. *Perhaps a personal experience of the creator of this ingenious plumb bob was the impetus behind the design of this reversible-tip version. By reversing the tip for storage, both the tool and its owner would be protected. A most unusual plumb bob.* (GOOD+) **$185.00**

N3-36. Unmarked: Early Beet Shape Plumb Bob. Decorative Cap. Great Patina. Length: 2 1/2 Inches. *The cap of this classic "beet shape" bob has been turned into an interesting shape. An early and nicely patinated plumb bob.* (GOOD+) **$85.00**

N3-37. Lintner & Sporborg, Gloversville: Early Patent Speed Indicator. Patented December 31, 1869. Rare and Near New. Length: 9 Inches. *We have offered a number of speed indicators over the years that were manufactured in Gloversville, New York. All were affiliated in some as yet undocumented way with the makers of this tool, which differs markedly in form and size from the other examples we have observed. The more common Gloversville indicators are fitted with a decorative handle of black India rubber and imprinted with patent dates from the 1880's and 1890's. This oversize device, however, has a polished steel handle and is marked with a much earlier patent date. It is likely that this was the initial product of Lintner and Sporborg. A rare early indicator in top condition.* (FINE) **$675.00**

N3-38. Unmarked: Millwright's Plumb Bob. Owner Initials "T.F.T.". Classic Form. Length: 6 Inches. *This classic millwright's plumb bob was designed to have the tip protrude from either end. This clean and shiny example was tastefully stamped with this initials of its original owner, one "T.F.T.". A classic.* (GOOD) **$195.00**

N3-39. Woodman: "Woodman's Patent" Speed Indicator. With Floral Design. Patented September 12, 1876. Length: 3 1/2 Inches. *The fleur de lis pattern of the Woodman patent speed indicator is among the more common seen on early indicators, but there is nothing common about the exceptional condition of this one. Crisp clean.* (FINE) **$65.00**

N3-40. Greene, Tweed & Co., New York, N.Y.: Ringing Bell Speed Indicator. In Presentation Box. Patented November 22, 1892. Length: 3 3/4 Inches. *Those who thought that the expression "bells and whistles" as a description of excessive complexity in mechanical invention was derived from an imaginary degree of excess had best take a second look at the pocket speed indicator offered here—or maybe just listen. Every 100 revolutions a bell contained in the semi-spherical housing on the reverse side, strikes a resonant tone, perhaps so as to be heard over the factory whistle? The original box is imprinted with the inscription "with James Hernden & Company's Compliments". Rare and excellent.* (FINE) **$265.00**

N3-41. Starrett Co., L. S., Athol, Mass. No. 87: Mercury Filled Plumb Bob. 6 Inch Length. New Condition, Original Box. Length: 6 Inches. *Starrett's top of the line plumb bob has been kept in new condition by the presence of its original box. Nice.* (FINE) **$65.00**

N3-42. Shapleigh Hardware, St. Louis: "Diamond Edge" Plumb Bob. Hexagonal Steel. With Imprinted Logo. Length: 3 1/2 Inches. *The Shapleigh Hardware produced a wide range of tools under their "Diamond Edge" trademark. This bob is clearly marked with their logo.* (GOOD+) **$35.00**

N3-43. Engineering Products Ltd., London No. MS 14: "Oldak" Dial Indicator. Uncommon Type. New Condition, Original Box. Length: 4 1/2 Inches. *If you're a dial indicator guy and you're serious enough to want "one of each", you simply can't be without one of these.* (FINE) **$25.00**

N3-44. Unmarked: Early Bronze Plumb Bob. Turned Body. Knurled Cap. Length: 3 3/4 Inches. *A single ring of knurls on the cap contrasts with the series of rings turned into the body by the maker of this early bob. A nice early bob having a rich, golden patina.* (GOOD+) **$265.00**

N3-45. Unmarked: Early Craftsman Made Surface Gauge. Acorn Finial. Decorative Knurling. Length: 8 1/2 Inches. *No marks on this early and visually appealing gauge. Nice.* (FINE) **$165.00**

N3-46. Moore & Wright, Sheffield (England) No. 405: Precision Surface Gauge. Uncommon Type. Original Case. Length: 13 Inches. *Moore & Wright entered the machinists tool business in the early part of the 20th Century in response to an effort by the British government to develop, for national security reasons, a domestic machine tool industry. Their products largely copied the products of the American toolmaking giants, Starrett and Brown & Sharpe. This surface gauge is in excellent condition in its original case.* (GOOD+) **$35.00**

N3-47. Starrett Co., The L.S., Athol, Mass. No. 177: Solid Steel Plumb Bob. Integral Reel. Extra Crisp and Clean. Length: 4 1/2 Inches. *An integral reel at the top of this solid steel plumb bob was designed to facilitate the storage of string. A nice example.* (GOOD+) **$35.00**

Group O3

O3-1. Stanley Rule & Level No. 73: "Razor Edge" Spoke Shave. Rare Cast Iron Type. 2 1/2 Inch Cutter. Length: 11 Inches. *The bulk of Stanley's "Razor Edge" spokeshave line was discontinued after WW I. This extremely rare example of the wider of the two cast iron, japan-finished versions is in excellent, collector quality condition.* (GOOD+) **$445.00**

O3-2. Unmarked: Solid Steel Spoke Shave. Distinctive Form. Extra Crisp and Clean. Length: 10 1/2 Inches. *A craftsman made shave fashioned from a solid piece of steel stock. Shiny clean and razor sharp.* (FINE) **$55.00**

O3-3. Snell & Atherton, Brockton, Mass.: Convex Sole Spoke Shave. Adjustable Brass Fence. Unused Condition. Length: 7 1/2 Inches. *This convex sole spokeshave from Massachusetts maker Snell & Atherton retains nearly all of its original black japanning and all of the shiny lacquer finish on its adjustable fence. A classic tool in brand new condition.* (FINE) **$45.00**

O3-4. Unmarked: Miniature Boxwood Spoke Shave. 1 Inch Cutter. Superb Condition. Length: 4 Inches. *The 1 inch cutting iron on this miniature boxwood shave was intended for very precise work. It remains in excellent working order.* (GOOD+) **$85.00**

O3-5. Cincinnati Tool Co., The: Decorative Cast Iron Spoke Shave. Raised Lettering. Hargrave Cutter. Length: 10 1/2 Inches. *This superb example of the early work of the Cincinnati Tool Company retains more than 75% of its original black japan finish on all surfaces. A nice example of a graphic spokeshave.* (GOOD+) **$75.00**

O3-6. Stearns, G.N., Syracuse (Unmarked): Early Patent Spoke Shave. Patented December 13, 1870. Rare and Excellent. Length: 9 Inches. *There are no marks on this distinctively-shaped spokeshave, but it is clearly the tool patented on December 13, 1870 by G.N. Stearns. Stearns was apparently somehow related to E.C. Stearns, who continued the manufacture of spoke shaves, hollow augers, and other tools well into this century. A rare shave.* (GOOD+) **$115.00**

O3-7. Unmarked: Carriagemaker's Spoke Shave. Cast Iron Body. Unused Condition. Length: 12 Inches. *It is likely that this oversize carriage maker's spokeshave was intended to be mounted with handles, but wasn't. It appears never to have been used.* (FINE) **$85.00**

O3-8. Stanley Rule & Level No. 60: Double Blade Spoke Shave. Sweetheart Trademark. Superb Condition. Length: 11 Inches. *This convex and straight-blade shave was produced in Stanley's heyday in the 1920's and bears the famous "Sweetheart" trademark. Perfect.* (GOOD+) **$75.00**

O3-9. Stanley Rule & Level?: Cast Iron Spoke Shave. Adjustable Throat. 95% Original Paint. Length: 10 Inches. *This very well preserved adjustable throat spokeshave is unmarked, other than on the cutting iron, which is imprinted with the early "arch" trademark of the Stanley Rule & Level Company. However, the pattern doesn't seem to fit with anything we have seen in print, and that includes the new spokeshave book. A most unusual early spokeshave.* (FINE) **$145.00**

O3-10. Stanley Rule & Level No. 65: Adjustable Chamfer Spoke Shave. Early "Arch" Trademark. Extra Crisp and Clean. Length: 10 Inches. *This example of Stanley's adjustable chamfer spokeshave features the extra-early "arch" trademark. Extra crisp and clean.* (GOOD+) **$165.00**

O3-11. Bailey Tool Co., Woonsocket, R.I. No. 1: Patent Cam-Lock Spoke Shave. Patented July 26, 1870. Rare and Complete. Length: 10 Inches. *We are pleased to offer one of the least common and most desirable of all patented spokeshaves. This, the 1870 patent cam lock shave of Selden Bailey is in clean, sound condition and clearly marked with the patent date. A rare early spokeshave.* (GOOD) **$225.00**

O3-12. Cincinnati Tool Co., The: Decorative Cast Iron Spoke Shave. Raised Lettering. Excellent Condition. Length: 10 1/2 Inches. *There is no mistaking the maker of this early cast iron spokeshave as it has been cast in bold Victorian lettering on the cap iron. An uncommon early shave in great shape.* (GOOD+) **$65.00**

O3-13. Morrill, B., Bangor, Maine: Stair Builder's Spoke Shave. Ogee Form. Rare Type and Maker. Length: 11 1/2 Inches. *This early stair builder's shave is boldly struck on the end of the handle with the imprint of B. Morrill, the Bangor, Maine planemaker, who worked from 1832 to 1851. The profile of the cutting iron exactly matches that of the tool, but appears to be a later replacement. An extra rare tool from a very specialized line of woodworking.* (FINE) **$225.00**

O3-14. Stanley Rule & Level No. 151 M: Malleable Iron Spoke Shave. Sweetheart Trademark. As New Condition. Length: 10 Inches. *The "unbreakable'" version of the double-adjustable spokeshave. Just the thing for those with a cement floor in the workshop. Never been used.* (FINE) **$55.00**

O3-15. Stanley Rule & Level No. 152: Double Adjustable Spoke Shave. Rare Flat Body. Sweetheart Trademark. Length: 10 Inches. *The No. 152 differed from the 151 in having a body that was totally flat, as opposed to the "gull wing" style of the 151. The gull wing design was a good idea and not many of these were sold. Most uncommon.* (FINE) **$90.00**

O3-16. Stanley Rule & Level No. 53: Adjustable Throat Spoke Shave. "Sweetheart" Trademark. Near New Condition. Length: 10 1/2 Inches. *Turning the adjustment screw at the top regulates the adjustment of the throat of this precision Stanley spokeshave. A popular spokeshave for the modern woodworking shop.* (FINE) **$55.00**

O3-17. Unmarked: Rosewood and Brass Spoke Shave. Distinctive Form. Superb Condition. Length: 14 Inches. *The most unusual adjustment mechanism on this nearly new rosewood bodied shave features a pair of screws tapped into the body to precisely lock the blade in place. Extra nice.* (FINE) **$115.00**

O3-18. Geral No. 0: Carriagemaker's Spoke Shave. For 3/8 Inch Round. Cast Bronze Body. Length: 9 Inches. *This most unusual bronze spokeshave is illustrated in the new spokeshave book in advertising produced by a company under the trade name "Geral". Apparently no documentation exists as to where and when these tools were manufactured. A superb example in top condition.* (FINE) **$65.00**

O3-19. Unmarked: Side Rabbet Spoke Shave. Cast Bronze Fence. Most Unusual Type. Length: 12 3/4 Inches. *A pentagonal cast bronze fence serves both to regulate the cut and to buttress the wedge lock irons. A showy and uncommon carriagemaker's shave in excellent condition.* (GOOD+) **$195.00**

O3-20. Unmarked: Pair of Bronze Spoke Shaves. Flat and Curve. With Stanley Cutters. Length: 5 1/4 Inches. *Making do with what was available, a coachmaker or patternmaker fashioned these bronze shave around a pair of spoke shave irons. A great set.* (GOOD+) **$115.00**

O3-21. Unmarked: Double Bronze Spoke Shave. Graphic Form. Most Unusual. Length: 3 3/4 Inches. *Different in form from any other spokeshave we have ever offered, this double-bodied, double-bladed bronze shave includes both a flat and a convex cutting iron. Most unusual.* (GOOD+) **$225.00**

O3-22. Nurse, C., 32 Mill St. (London): Set of Coachmaker's Spoke Shaves. Working Set. Near New Condition. Length: 9 1/2 Inches. *Still retaining nearly all of the original finishes on both wood and metal surfaces, this magnificent set of coachmakers tools are in essentially the same condition as they were when they were first produced. Boldly marked with the imprint of prominent London toolmaker C. Nurse & Company, this is the finest set of coachmakers' shaves that we have ever offered for sale. Magnificent.* (FINE) **$775.00**

O3-23. Unmarked: Solid Rosewood Spoke Shave. Unused Condition. Distinctive Form. Length: 12 1/2 Inches. *Workaday spokeshaves were generally fashioned from beech, or, in the case of better quality shaves, of boxwood. We have offered a few ebony and rosewood shaves over the years, but never an example in this condition. In absolutely brand new condition and retaining all of its original finishes, this magnificent shave is ready to be carefully put to use or serve as the centerpiece of a collection. Perfect.* (FINE) **$145.00**

O3-24. Unmarked: Pair of Coachmaker's Spoke Shaves. Cast Bronze Bodies. Never Handled. Length: 9 Inches. *Apparently never fitted with the wooden handles which they appear to have been designed to accept, these coachmakers or stairbuilders spokeshaves are in near new condition. Like new, but old.* (FINE) **$195.00**

O3-25. Unmarked: Double Coachmaker's Spoke Shave. Brass Body and Stops. Very Well Made. Length: 16 1/2 Inches. *Turned and decorated mahogany handles add an appealing contrast to this particularly presentable carriagemaker's tool. As found and extra nice. Highly recommended.* (GOOD+) **$195.00**

O3-26. Unmarked: Precision Adjust Spoke Shave. With Brass Screws. Near New Condition. Length: 10 Inches. *This precision adjusting spokeshave is in unused condition with a full iron. A great working tool in ready to use condition.* (FINE) **$65.00**

O3-27. Unmarked: Early Patent Spoke Shave. Patented November 17, 1868. Full Nickel Plating. Length: 10 Inches. *Patented on November 17, 1868, these shaves were intended for use in the shoe making industry of New England. Much of the shiny original nickel plating remains on this well preserved example.* (GOOD+) **$115.00**

O3-28. Nurse, C., Walworth Road, London: Solid Boxwood Spoke Shave. 1 3/4 Inch Cutter. Near New Condition. Length: 10 Inches. *This precision shave from a prominent London maker is in essentially unused condition. Nice.* (FINE) **$45.00**

O3-29. Unmarked: Adjustable Rosewood Spoke Shave. Brass Adjustable Screws. Well Used Iron. Length: 10 Inches. *Much of the iron on this rosewood shave has been used, but the tool is otherwise in working order. A cutting iron from an adjustable beech shave could quickly restore this tool to top working condition.* (GOOD) **$85.00**

O3-30. Stanley Rule & Level No. 85: "Razor Edge" Spoke Shave. Narrow Boxwood. Excellent Condition. Length: 11 1/2 Inches. *Stanley offered its "Razor Edge" line of spokeshaves for 30 years, beginning in 1905. They were designed for especially close work. This magnificent example of the 2 1/2 inch cutter boxwood version appears to have been very little used. A rare Stanley spokeshave.* (GOOD+) **$245.00**

O3-31. Field, Alfred, Sheifield: Working Pair of Spoke Shaves. 2 Inch and 1 1/2 Inch Cutters. Near New Condition. Length: 10 Inches. *These as-new spokeshaves have cutters of complimentary sizes to fit you out for all of your woodworking needs. A nice set.* (FINE) **$95.00**

O3-32. Unmarked: 3 Inch Precision Spoke Shave. With Screw Lock. Ready to Use. Length: 11 Inches. *This 3 inch shave is fitted with the desirable screw lock mechanism for the cutting iron. Ready to use.* (FINE) **$35.00**

O3-33. Unmarked: 2 1/2 Inch Precision Spoke Shave. With Screw Lock. Extra Tight Throat. Length: 11 Inches. *Once the cutting iron is adjusted on this precision 2 1/2 inch shave, it can be precisely locked into position by a pair of fixing screws. A precision tool.* (GOOD+) **$45.00**

O3-34. Stanley Rule & Level No. 81: Razor Edge Spoke Shave. Rosewood Body. Patented February 19, 1901. Length: 11 Inches. *Only some minor dulling of the nickel plating detracts from this otherwise perfectly preserved example of Stanley's 'Razor Edge" line of patented spokeshaves. A very nice example.* (FINE) **$295.00**

O3-35. Mathieson, Glasgow: Lacquered Beech Spoke Shave. 3 Inch Cutting Iron. Original Decal. Length: 12 Inches. *Most of the original decal remains on this classic shave from Scotland's premier toolmaker. A classic.* (FINE) **$55.00**

O3-36. Unmarked: Solid Ebony Spoke Shave. 3 Inch Cutting Iron. Great Working Order. Length: 9 Inches. *The handles on this wide, solid ebony shave were likely shortened at one point to facilitate working in cramped quarters. An uncommon ebony shave in excellent working order.* (GOOD+) **$65.00**

O3-37. Unmarked: Adjustable Rosewood Spoke Shave. 2 1/2 Inch Cutter. Excellent Condition. Length: 11 Inches. *This rosewood "tang" style shave features a 2 1/2 inch cutting iron and is in ready to use condition.* (GOOD+) **$115.00**

O3-38. Unmarked: Classic Boxwood Spoke Shave. 2 Inch Cutting Iron. Ready to Use. Length: 9 3/4 Inches. *A few stains to the boxwood do not detract from the utilitarian value of this crisp, clean and ready to use shave. Ready to use.* (GOOD+) **$25.00**

O3-39. Unmarked: Precision Adjust Spoke Shave. Dual Brass Screws. Near New Condition. Length: 10 3/4 Inches. *A pair of brass screws serve to adjust the width of the opening and hence the amount of the throat opening on this very well preserved spokeshave.* (FINE) **$85.00**

O3-40. Stanley Rule & Level No. 84: "Razor Edge" Spoke Shave. Narrow Boxwood. Sweetheart Trademark. Length: 11 1/2 Inches. *A good clean example of Stanley's boxwood razor edge shave in excellent condition. These are tough to find, period. A good one.* (GOOD+) **$195.00**

O3-41. Healy, Chas., Sheffield: Adjustable Beech Spoke Shave. Brass Adjustable Screws. 3 1/4 Inch Cutting Iron. Length: 11 1/2 Inches. *A pair of brass adjustment screws allow the precise adjustment of the width of the throat on this shave from an obscure Sheffield toolmaker.* (GOOD+) **$65.00**

O3-42. Millers Falls Company No. 1: Rosewood Handle Spoke Shave. Most Original Paint. Ready to Use. Length: 10 Inches. *Early tools by the Millers Falls Company are noted for their exceptional finish and workmanship. This circular spokeshave is a classic example. Most original finishes remain on clean example of the nickel plating, classic rosewood handles and period red infill in the throat. A nice example.* (GOOD+) **$115.00**

O3-43. Unmarked: Cast Iron Spoke Shave. Rabbeting Type. Appears Manufactured. Length: 10 Inches. *Similar in form to Stanley's No. 68 pattern maker's shave, this unusual cousin bears no maker marks whatsoever. An interesting and very well preserved spokeshave.* (GOOD+) **$35.00**

O3-44. Unmarked: Coachmakers Rabbet Spoke Shave. With Skew Set Blades. Solid Boxwood. Length: 12 1/2 Inches. *A center fence of dark Brazilian Rosewood provides a dramatic contrast to the rich golden patina of this solid boxwood coachmaker's shave. The cutting irons have been angled to facilitate use with hardwoods. Highly recommended.* (GOOD+) **$265.00**

O3-45. Stanley Rule & Level No. 58: Flat Cast Iron Spoke Shave. "Sweetheart" Trademark. Excellent Condition. Length: 10 Inches. *These flat handled shaves were designed for situations where there was plenty of room to move, a circumstance that the craftsman could not always expect; they are therefore less common than the No. 53, which had raised handles, just in case. This one is in fine, collector quality condition and is marked with the Stanley "Sweetheart" trademark. A good one.* (GOOD+) **$85.00**

Group P3

P3-1. North Bros Mfg. Co., Philadelphia: No. 1003: Automatic Feed Bench Drill. Smallest Size. 98% Original Paint. Length: 18 Inches. *Only a tight crack in the casting where the crank is attached to the gear wheel needs mention as an apology on this otherwise perfect example of the smallest bench drill produced by the North Brothers Company. The function of the tool does not seem to be affected by the minor flaw. A rare drill in excellent working order.* (FINE) **$285.00**

P3-2. Edgerton, H.S., German, N.Y.: Spectacular Brass Breast Drill. Early Appearance. Very Well Made. Length: 12 1/2 Inches. *The number of surviving examples of brass or bronze breast drills indicates that these were standard shop tools in the 1870's. Generally, these tools were made in th shop where they were used. This particularly artful example, which may be one of the very first manufactured gear driven drills, is imprinted with the maker mark of "H.S. Edgerton" and the location "German, N.Y." A rare, important and aesthetically pleasing brass hand drill.* (GOOD+) **$485.00**

P3-3. Goodell-Pratt Company No. 2: Box For Automatic Push Drill. Printed Tin Box. Ca. 1890's. Length: 9 3/4 Inches. *Great graphics from the turn of the Century are very well preserved on this early tin box. Rare.* (GOOD+) **$25.00**

P3-4. Tollner, C., 209 Bowery, N.Y.: Brass Framed Bow Drill. Rosewood Handle. Uncommon N.Y. Maker. Length: 9 1/2 Inches. *C. Tollner is known to have produced piano makers tools in New York City, including a marked mitre plane. This rosewood handled bow drill, which is clearly marked with the Tollner name, is the first such tool by this maker of which we are aware. The brazing that joins the chuck to the spool may have been reinforced with solder at some point. A rare New York City bow drill.* (GOOD) **$445.00**

P3-5. Stanley Rule & Level No. 624: Gear Driven Hand Drill. Uncommon Type. With Dual Gears. Length: 13 3/4 Inches. *Dual drive gears and a magazine handle characterize this uncommon Stanley drill. A nice example.* (FINE) **$45.00**

P3-6. Stanley Rule & Level No. 984: Corner Ratchet Brace. Rosewood Handle, Knob. Near New Condition. Length: 9 Inches. *Stanley's entry in the go anywhere brace competition. This one is in super shape, with nearly all original finishes. Nice.* (FINE) **$115.00**

P3-7. Unmarked: Classic Early Brace. With Brass Sleeve. Most Unusual. Length: 11 1/2 Inches. *The head of this early forged brace is fitted with an aesthetically appealing ferrule of polished brass. A pretty brace.* (GOOD+) **$145.00**

P3-8. Goodell-Pratt Company No. 385: High Speed Hand Drill. Aluminum Body. Most Unusual. Length: 15 1/2 Inches. *A genuine Goodell-Pratt rarity, this one, which features an aluminum body, is among the hardest to find of all gear driven drills. Used, but not abused.* (GOOD+) **$145.00**

P3-9. Goodell-Pratt Company: Hollow Auger Brace. Rare and Excellent. Ready to Use. Length: 18 Inches. *This marriage of convenience is in excellent shape for the collection or the shop. A nice example.* (GOOD+) **$125.00**

P3-10. Unmarked: Early Pump Hand Drill. With Bronze Wheel. Complete and Original. Length: 14 Inches. *A turn-of-the-century pump drill that is complete with all original parts. Graphic.* (GOOD+) **$115.00**

P3-11. Unmarked: Early Brass Framed Hand Drill. Distinctive Form. Superb Condition. Length: 16 Inches. *An especially showy and visually appealing brass-framed drill in very well preserved condition. Nicely turned and patinated mahogany handles complement this handsome tool.* (GOOD+) **$275.00**

P3-12. Goodell-Pratt Company: Mechanical Bench Drill. Cast Iron Base. Rare and Near New. Length: 14 Inches. *This miniature Goodell Pratt bench drill, which can be adjusted to a wide variety of angles and incorporates holes so that it can be screwed to a bench, is so rare that we have not even observed an illustration of it in a G.P. catalog. An extremely rare bench drill in nearly new condition.* (FINE) **$345.00**

P3-13. Stanley Rule & Level No. 921: 6 Inch Sweep Ratchet Brace. Patented October 14, 1902. Near New Condition. Length: 13 1/2 Inches. *Those seeking a collecting opportunity in collecting Stanley's under appreciated brace line would be well advised to invest in tools that are of the quality of this superb 6 inch version of the No. 919 ratcheting brace. This one is marked with Stanley trademark and is in near new condition. Nice.* (FINE) **$235.00**

P3-14. Fray & Co., John S. No. 114: 14 Inch Sweep "Spofford" Brace. Rosewood Head, Handle. Superb Condition. Length: 10 1/2 Inches. *A classic "Spofford" patent brace, this one features an uncommon 14 inch sweep. The reinforcing rings on the handles of these braces were formed from pewter. Crisp and clean.* (FINE) **$135.00**

P3-15. Vaughn & Bushnell, Chicago, Ill.: No. 222: 8 Inch Heavy Duty Ratchet Brace. With Rosewood Handles. Ready To Use. Length: 12 1/2 Inches. *The Vaughn & Bushnell Company of Chicago, Illinois, produced and marketed a wide range of tools under their own name. This extremely well preserved brace is fitted with a raised "V. & B." logo as a dust seal over the chuck mechanism. A very well made brace in top working order.* (GOOD+) **$45.00**

P3-16. Shannon & Co., Philadelphia, Penn.: Cast Iron Bench Drill Press. With Screw Feed. Manufactured by Goodell-Pratt. Length: 18 Inches. *This cast iron bench drill was obviously manufactured by the Goodell-Pratt Company for the Shannon Hardware Company of Philadelphia. This one is nicely accented with a keystone plate riveted to the body bearing the Shannon trade name. A graphic bench drill in excellent condition.* (GOOD+) **$225.00**

P3-17. Goodell Bros. Co., Greenfield, Mass: Rosewood Handle Push Drill. For Standard Drills. Ready To Use. Length: 10 Inches. *The screw lock chuck on this early rosewood handle drill is designed to work with standard twist drills of various sizes. Nice.* (FINE) **$35.00**

P3-18. Peck, Stow & Wilcox Co. No. 516: Hollow Handle Hand Drill. Ca. 1930's. Extra Crisp and Clean. Length: 12 1/2 Inches. *P.S. & W. produced a wide range of tools, but we have seen very few hand drills of their manufacture. This one is in top condition with its full complement of original bits.* (FINE) **$35.00**

P3-19. Goodell Tool Co., Shelburne Falls,: "Goodell's Patent" Brace. Patented December 27, 1892. APB: "B" Rating. Length: 15 Inches. *Fully 95% of the shiny nickel plating remains on this example of the Goodell Patent brace. A most uncommon patented brace.* (FINE) **$85.00**

P3-20. Millers Falls Company No. 502: Right Angle Corner Brace. Lacquered Beech Handle. Nickel Plated Body. Length: 19 1/2 Inches. *Boring a hole in a corner was no easily accomplished task in the days before the electric drill. The installation of electrical wiring in at the beginning of the century inspired the inventive genius of many. This was the basic design that evolved, here represented on an especially clean example.* (FINE) **$95.00**

P3-21. Dixon, William, Newark, N.J.: Nickel Plated Hand Drill. With Rosewood Handle. Near New Condition. Length: 7 3/4 Inches. *The Millers Falls Company produced a nickel plated example of their No. 4 jeweler's hand drill which is extremely rare. This nearly identical drill from Wm. Dixon of Newark, New Jersey, has an adjustable chuck that is imprinted with the Dixon name. A rare miniature drill in top condition.* (FINE) **$125.00**

P3-22. Unmarked: Handle For Bow Drill. Early Appearance. Often Missing. Length: 31 Inches. *Here's a real honest to goodness bow drill handle. These are often missing when the drills are found.* (GOOD) **$75.00**

P3-23. Unmarked: Archimedian Type Hand Drill. With Brass Driver. Saw Type Frame. Length: 11 1/2 Inches. *This unusual Archimedian drill features a "bow" device that was most likely designed to steady the tool when in use. A shiny brass driver adds color to this graphic and interesting tool.* (GOOD+) **$115.00**

P3-24. Unmarked: Ebony Handle Bow Drill. With Ebony Handle Bow. Turned Brass Spool. Length: 37 1/2 Inches. *This miniature ebony handled bow drill comes with a matching ebony handled bow. A showy bow drill in excellent collector quality condition.* (GOOD+) **$345.00**

P3-25. Goodell-Pratt Company No. 99: Ratcheting Hand Drill. Hardened Feed Screw. 3/8 Inch Chuck. Length: 6 Inches. *Designed from boring through heavy steel or cast iron, this ratcheting drill from Goodell-Pratt was designed to have pressure applied to it as it was working. An uncommon ratcheting drill from a top maker.* (GOOD) **$35.00**

P3-26. Unmarked: Whitney Patent Hand Drill. Original Striping. Rare and Excellent. Length: 10 1/2 Inches. *The Whitney patent drill is among the most beautifully decorated of all tools. Its practicality was perhaps another question. Examples that retain as much of their original pin striping as this example are rare indeed.* (GOOD+) **$135.00**

P3-27. North Bros Mfg. Co., Philadelphia No. 41: Automatic Push Push Drill. All Original Bits. New Condition, Original Box. Length: 10 Inches. *The Stanley "Yankee" No. 41 was the first choice of those who used these tools a lot. Still a great working tool. New and in the box.* (FINE) **$55.00**

P3-28. Johnson & Tainter: Early Patent Push Drill. Original Tin Box. Early and Excellent. Length: 9 Inches. *A wooden "plunger" which guides and regulates the tension of the spring was the genius behind this early patent push drill, which was among the very first examples of this type of tool.* (GOOD) **$25.00**

P3-29. Wright, S.J., Ellsworth, N.Y.: Combination Wrench and Brace. Patented December 16, 1873. Complete and Excellent. Length: 14 1/2 Inches. *The S.J. Wright patent brace/wrench combination was one of those "great ideas" that take two or more simple and practical tools (in this case the brace and the wagon wrench) and combine them so ingeniously into a single device as to render the resulting hybrid totally useless. In this case the compromises produced a brace of insufficient strength, owing to its accommodation of wrench features and a wrench impractical in its adjustment owing to having been mated with a brace. The original owner of this one apparently gave up in frustration early on, preserving this extra clean example for posterity. A most interesting early patented brace in top collector quality condition.* (GOOD+) **$115.00**

P3-30. Stanley Tools No. 2101-10: "Yankee" Ratchet Brace. 10 Inch Sweep. "Best Brace Made". Length: 10 Inches. *The "Yankee" line of braces manufactured by the North Brothers Tool Company and, after 1946 by Stanley were unquestionably the finest functional braces ever made. This one is in excellent condition and ready to complement the workshop of a master craftsman, or just a wannabe.* (GOOD+) **$55.00**

P3-31. North Bros Mfg. Co., Philadelphia: No. 1530: Multi Speed "Yankee" Hand Drill. Removable Handle. Fine Working Condition. Length: 7 Inches. *There's nothing like the convenience of having a small hand drill to address simple problems of home maintenance. The Yankee 1530 multiple speed drill is the only drill you'll ever need. A very well made drill in excellent condition.* (GOOD+) **$55.00**

P3-32. North Bros Mfg. Co., Philadelphia: No. 1500: "Yankee" Chain Drill. 3 Jaw Chuck. New Condition, Original Box. Length: 11 Inches. *Chain drills were meant to be fitted around a pipe or a beam and then tightened progressively with each turn of the drill. This version, from the North Brothers Tool Company, helped do the tightening for you. It is in new condition in its original box.* (FINE) **$85.00**

P3-33. Unmarked: Early Patent Breast Drill. "Pat. June 15". Decorative Casting. Length: 14 Inches. *The only mark on this early cast iron breast drill is the designation "Pat. June 15" that is cast in the body. Appearance is ca. 1880's. Rare.* (GOOD+) **$145.00**

P3-34. Millers Falls Company No. 4: Cast Iron Hand Drill. For Jewelers. With Rosewood Handle. Length: 8 1/2 Inches. *Most of the original paint remains on this early "jeweler's" hand drill. Nice.* (GOOD+) **$75.00**

P3-35. Consolidated Tool Co., New York, N.Y.: No. 210: 7 Inch Outside Brace. "Pilot" Brand. Ship Wheel Logo. Length: 14 Inches. *The tools from this obscure New York City maker were marked with their "Pilot" brand and imprinted with a ship's wheel. This brace is the first we have seen bearing that mark. A scarce brace.* (FINE) **$85.00**

P3-36. Unmarked: Whitney Patent Hand Drill. Original Striping. Rare and Excellent. Length: 10 1/2 Inches. *Another example of the artfully embellished Whitney patent hand drill with much of its original pin-striping intact. A good one.* (GOOD+) **$115.00**

P3-37. Millers Falls Company No. 97: Ratcheting Breast Drill. Patented August 4, 1911. Immaculate Condition. Length: 17 Inches. *Hours of fun can be had just testing the multiple adjustments on this mechanical marvel. It pivots, ratchets, bores, drills and entertains. The full original decal and virtually all original finishes remain. Mint, and highly recommended.* (FINE) **$345.00**

P3-38. Goodell-Pratt Company No. 677: Heavy Duty Breast Drill. With Leather Strap. Aluminum Housing. Length: 18 Inches. *A leather strap protects the user from the breastplate on this uncommon Goodell-Pratt drill. Rare & near new.* (FINE) **$345.00**

P3-39. Jo Mfg. Co., So. Gate, Calif.: "Joic" Hand Drill. Multiple Angle. Near New Condition. Length: 9 Inches. *The inventor of this California-made adjustable hand drill most likely put together the details of his creation in the wake of attempting to drill a hole in an inaccessible spot. Despite the fact that you can position this tool to fit in any conceivable nook or cranny, the matter of how to turn the crank once it is there seems not to have been addressed. A rare adjustable drill in new condition.* (FINE) **$85.00**

P3-40. Unmarked: Rosewood and Brass Bow Drill. Elaborate Knurling. Early and Near New. Length: 13 1/4 Inches. *Unlike any bow drill we have previously offered for sale, this spectacular rosewood and brass example features a narrow drive spool filled with turned rosewood, an extra long shaft, a decoratively knurled ferrule and a sectional rosewood handle that can be disassembled for adjustment. Nearly all original finishes remain on this beautiful woodworking tool. Highly recommended.* (FINE) **$895.00**

P3-41. Millers Falls Company No. 445: Automatic Push Drill. With Rosewood Handle. Near New Condition. Length: 10 1/2 Inches. *This uncommon rosewood handled push drill is marked with the Millers Falls product number. A rare M.F. item in top condition.* (FINE) **$45.00**

P3-42. Stanley Tools No. 1530-A: "Yankee" Ratcheting Hand Drill. Near New Condition. Ready to Use. Length: 11 Inches. *Originally manufactured by the North Brothers Tool Company, this multiple speed ratcheting drill was, without question, the finest small hand drill ever produced. Brand new.* (FINE) **$65.00**

P3-43. Goodel Pratt Company: "Giant" Breast Drill. With Oversize Chuck. Complete and Original. Length: 19 Inches. *One of the least common of the entire Goodell Pratt line of bench drills, this massive tool, which was marketed under the name "Giant", is fitted with a gearing mechanism to allow multiple speeds.* (FINE) **$285.00**

P3-44. Millers Falls Company No. 2A: Gear Driven Hand Drill. With Magazine Handle. Original Decal. Length: 14 1/2 Inches. *The Number 2 and 2A drills were the Millers Falls Company's premier "full size" hand drills. This example is in new condition and retains nearly all of its original finish.* (FINE) **$85.00**

P3-45. North Bros. Mfg. Co., Philadelphia, Penn.: No. 1545: Reversible Ratchet Hand Drill. With Magazine Handle. Unused Condition. Length: 15 1/2 Inches. *Virtually all original finishes remain on this ratcheting drill, which could be set to 5 different settings. A mechanical marvel in top condition.* (FINE) **$245.00**

P3-46. Millers Falls Company No. 182: Combination Drill and Brace. With Ratchet Drive. Original Decal. Length: 14 1/2 Inches. *Much of the original decal remains on this very well preserved example of the Millers Falls combination drill and brace. A rare tool in this condition.* (FINE) **$225.00**

Group Q3

Q3-1. **Lufkin Rule Co., The No. 7122: Classic Yard Measure Rule. With Brass Tips. Unused Condition. Length: 36 Inches.** *Nearly all original finishes remain on this heavy duty yard measure from Lufkin. Nice.* (FINE) **$45.00**

Q3-2. **Lufkin Rule Co., The, Saginaw, Mich.: No. 7127: 45 Inch Bench Rule. Beveled Edges. Uncommon Type. Length: 45 Inches.** *Both sides of this special purpose rule are beveled to facilitate marking of the material being measured. This example is clearly marked with the Lufkin name and product number.* (GOOD+) **$55.00**

Q3-3. **Unmarked: Specialty Board Rule. Brass Hook Ends. Decorative Style. Length: 38 1/4 Inches.** *There are no numeric graduations on this unusual rule, only a pair of hook ends. The width between the scales on the rule bears no relation to any unit of measurement we have seen before. Different.* (GOOD+) **$65.00**

Q3-4. **Stanley Rule & Level No. 46 1/2: Square Lumber Rule. Rare "Stanley" Mark. Unused Condition. Length: 24 Inches.** *Stanley imprinted very few of its board and log measures with the "Stanley" imprint. This near-new example is marked with both the name and the number. Absolutely perfect and highly recommended.* (FINE) **$675.00**

Q3-5. **Youglove, G.T., Fitchburg, Mass.: Hook End Board Measure Rule. Uncommon Maker. Original Hardware Label. Length: 25 Inches.** *The handle of this early board measure rule is imprinted with the name of this obscure Fitchburg, Massachusetts rulemaker and the original store price tag is affixed to the handle.* (GOOD+) **$165.00**

Q3-6. **Lufkin Rule Co., The, No. 55: "Merritt Hypsometer" Rule. For Timber Cruising. "Biltmore Stick". Length: 38 Inches.** *The markings on this tool designate it as both a "Merritt Hypsometer" and a "Biltmore Stick". It was apparently used to combine the functions of measuring and calculating the potential yield of timber. A rare Lufkin rule in excellent condition.* (GOOD+) **$125.00**

Q3-7. **Stanley Rule & Level No. 30: Early Shrinkage Rule. Ca. 1880's. New Condition. Length: 24 Inches.** *Up until 1892, Stanley's No. 30 shrinkage rule was produced for an allowance of 1/8 inch shrinkage per foot (the standard for cast iron) only. Rules produced after this time included the No. 30 imprint as well as size designation. This perfectly preserved example appears to date from the 1880's.* (FINE) **$125.00**

Q3-8. **Nicholl, R., High Holborn, London: Engine Divided Rule. 1/1200 Scale. Solid Boxwood. Length: 12 Inches.** *This boxwood drafting scale rule is in new condition and absent any chips or cracks. A good one.* (FINE) **$25.00**

Q3-9. **Stanley Rule & Level No. 48 1/2: Octagon Log Cane Rule. With Stanley Mark. Crisp and Clean. Length: 36 Inches.** *Both the Stanley name and the product number are marked on this well preserved Stanley log cane. A nice example.* (FINE) **$275.00**

Q3-10. **Stanley Rule & Level No. 34 V: Vertical Read Bench Rule. With Brass Tips. Unused Condition. Length: 24 Inches.** *The "V: designation on these rules was for the vertical graduations of the numbers. Generally, these are found in the 12 Inch length.* (FINE) **$45.00**

Q3-11. **Unmarked: Board Measure Rule. Classic Form. Superb Patina. Length: 24 Inches.** *These rules were employed in sawmills and lumber yards to gauge the number of board feet of wood contained in a board. This manufactured but unmarked example is in excellent condition.* (GOOD+) **$75.00**

Q3-12. **Rabone & Sons, John, Birmingham: No. 1034: Boxwood Yard Measure Rule. Circular Body. Extra Crisp and Clean. Length: 36 Inches.** *Here's an unusual English yard measure that is circular in form. It is clearly marked with the early imprint of Birmingham makers John Rabone & Sons. Extra nice.* (FINE) **$65.00**

Q3-13. **Federal Land Bank of Springfield: Lumber Cruising Rule. Original Case and Instructions. Near New Condition. Length: 36 Inches.** *One shudders at the thought of the Federal Government being involved in banking of any kind, but such is the imprint on this set of lumber gauging rules. They were apparently provided to landowners and other amateur woodsmen to estimate the potential yield of their forests. Complete with the original instruction manual in nearly new condition.* (FINE) **$155.00**

Q3-14. **Lufkin Rule Co., The No. 7132: Heavy Gauge Yard Rule. Uncommon Type. Near New Condition. Length: 36 Inches.** *If your experience with yard sticks is limited to what you find today, seeing this Lufkin yard measure will be an eye opener. Extra thick in construction, precisely graduated and in nearly new condition, this yard measure was designed to last several lifetimes.* (FINE) **$45.00**

Q3-15. **Unmarked: Narrow Metric Rule. Solid Boxwood. Unused Condition. Length: 39 1/2 Inches.** *This four fold, one meter rule is in brand new condition. Mint.* (FINE) **$65.00**

Q3-16. **Lufkin Rule Co., The No. 7112 Maine: One Meter Rule. With English Graduates. Near New Condition. Length: 39 Inches.** *Those who would exhort us to renounce the Sacred Standards of Measurement that our common heritage have been mercifully silent of late. Here's a nice 39.27 in top collector quality condition. You don't find these by the firkin-full.* (FINE) **$55.00**

Q3-17. **Kerby & Bro., New York (Unmarked.): Classic Wantage Rule. With Stencil Numbers. "J. Studebaker", Minneapolis. Length: 36 Inches.** *This half-size wantage rule is imprinted with the advertising of one J. Studebaker of Minneapolis, Minnesota.* (FINE) **$125.00**

Q3-18. **Stanley Rule & Level No. 34 VR: Vertical Read Bench Rule. With Brass Tips. Maple Body. Length: 24 Inches.** *Here's a 24 inch vertical read rule from Stanley. Condition is nearly new.* (FINE) **$45.00**

Q3-19. **Kerby & Bro. (Unmarked.), New York: Firkin Size Wantage Rule. With Stencil Numbers. Superb Patina. Length: 17 Inches.** *This smaller size wantage rule has the distinctive "stencil" numbers that were used by Kerby and Brother, the prominent New York City rulemakers. It is in top collector quality condition. Mint.* (FINE) **$195.00**

Q3-20. **Lufkin Rule Co., The: No. 34 1/4 V: Vertical Reading Rule. Uncommon Type. Unused Condition. Length: 12 Inches.** *The "V" in the product number relates to the vertical read required by the manner of imprinting of the numbers. These were largely used in schools. This one has never been used at all. Brand new.* (FINE) **$35.00**

Q3-21. **Stanley Rule & Level No. 240: Inside Measure Rule. 2-4 Feet Extension. Unused Condition. Length: 24 Inches.** *Stanley's extension measures were offered in a full range of sizes from 2 feet to 12 feet. The numbers of the rules described the range of extension of the rule: This, the 240 extends from 2 to 4 feet; the 612 from 6 to 12 feet, etc. ad nauseum. This one has never been used. Mint.* (FINE) **$65.00**

Q3-22. **Kerby & Bro., New York (Unmarked.): Maple Wantage Rule. George F. Bauer, Philadelphia. Unused Condition. Length: 36 Inches.** *Kerby & Brother were well known as specialty rulemakers who would produce a rule to the user's specifications and/or imprint that rule with advertising. This unused wantage rule, designed for measuring the amount "wanting" to fill a barrel, was ordered by Philadelphia's George F. Bauer Cooperage works, but apparently never used or given away. Absolutely brand new.* (GOOD+) **$225.00**

Q3-23. **Lufkin Rule Co., The, Saginaw, Mich.: No. 22 1/2: Handled Lumber Measure Rule. Scribner's Decimal C. Extra Crisp and Clean. Length: 42 Inches.** *This later-style rule is imprinted with the "Scribner's Decimal C" scale. Unused.* (FINE) **$145.00**

Q3-24. **Unmarked: "Holland" Scale Log Rule. Brass Hook Tip. Extra Crisp and Clean. Length: 36 Inches.** *This 3 foot rule is graduated with the "Holland" scale that was used primarily in the State of Maine. The tip is fitted with a brass hook to facilitate its use.* (GOOD+) **$55.00**

Q3-25. **Unmarked: Classic Oak Timber Caliper. With "Tally" Pegs. Excellent Patina. Length: 48 Inches.** *A series of pegs in one of the caliper legs were used to keep track of the amount of timber being purchased. This well made and graphic caliper has no maker marks of any kind. A classic collectible.* (GOOD+) **$185.00**

Q3-26. **Kerby & Bro., New York (Unmarked): Advertising Wantage Rule. Budde & Westerman, N.Y. Near New Condition. Length: 17 Inches.** *Surviving examples suggest that New York City rulemakers Kerby & Bro. produced, as a percentage of their total output, more advertising rules than any other maker. This small gauging rule is imprinted with the name "Budde & Westerman", a partnership with which we are not familiar. In all likelihood, they were wine makers or wine merchants. The rule has never been used. Mint.* (FINE) **$225.00**

Q3-27. **Haselton, R.B., Groton, N.H.: 24 Inch Maple Board Measure. 14 Scales. Brass Tips. Length: 24 Inches.** *This is the earlier Haselton mark from Groton, N.H. (the firm relocated to Contoocook, N.H. in 1881). Minor discoloration on the body, otherwise excellent.* (GOOD+) **$145.00**

Q3-28. **Gurley, W. & L.E., Troy, N.Y.: Heavy Duty Yard Rule. Brass Hook Tip. Rare and Near New. Length: 36 Inches.** *The ends of this extra heavy duty yard scale are fitted out with brass plates which could be hooked over the edge of a counter. The Gurley imprint has been boldly struck on the side of the tool. A rare and well made rule from a prominent maker of surveying instruments.* (FINE) **$195.00**

Q3-29. **Fabian Son, Derby, Maine: Holland Scale Rule. 11 to 30 Foot Sizes. Original Paper Label. Length: 48 Inches.** *A nearly perfectly preserved example of the work of one of the mainstay makers of log and lumber rules. This one retains nearly all of its original paper label. Very nice.* (FINE) **$225.00**

Q3-30. **Lufkin Rule Co., The, Windsor, Ontario: 4 1/2 Foot Log Measure Rule. With Doyle Scale. Superb Condition. Length: 54 Inches.** *This pristine Canadian-made lumber rule is of the long-handled sort used in the big tree forests. This one appears never to have made it into the woods.* (FINE) **$235.00**

Q3-31. **Belcher, Z., Sheffield: Shoe Measure Folding Rule. Father of Belchers? Early and Important. Length: 15 Inches.** *This extra early shoe measure rule is imprinted with the name of Sheffield maker Z. Belcher. We would be interested in knowing if this Belcher was related in any way to the Belcher Brothers who began producing rules in New York City in the 1840's.* (GOOD+) **$225.00**

Q3-32. **Stanley Rule & Level No. 30: 1/8 Inch Per Foot Shrin Rule. Early Type. Near New Condition. Length: 24 Inches.** *This designation of shrinkage rule was for use with the most common material for casting, cast iron. A nice example in top collector quality condition.* (FINE) **$85.00**

Q3-33. **Whitcher Co., Frank W., Boston, Mass.: Early Patent Rule. Patented April 13, 1880. Early and Excellent. Length: 17 Inches.** *This most unusual rule is imprinted with the patent information and maker name. It apparently was a shoe sizing rule, which would mean that it still is a shoe sizing rule. Rare.* (FINE) **$115.00**

Q3-34. **Welch Mfg. Co., W.M., Chicago: Metric and English Rule. Full Meter Length. Uncommon Imprint. Length: 39 1/2 Inches.** *This metric-English is imprinted with the name of a Chicago maker that is new to us. Different.* (GOOD+) **$35.00**

Q3-35. **Unmarked: Brazilian Rosewood Rule. Straight Edge? Great Grain Pattern. Length: 24 Inches.** *This rule has been cut from a strikingly figured piece of Brazilian rosewood and graduated in inches by the maker. Pretty.* (GOOD+) **$35.00**

Q3-36. **Stanley Rule & Level No. 41: Maple Yard Rule. Ca. 1910 Trademark. Near-New Condition. Length: 36 Inches.** *Stanley's ca. 1910 trademark is imprinted on this well preserved yard measure. A nice example in top collector quality condition.* (FINE) **$45.00**

Q3-37. **Stanley Rule & Level (Unmarked.) No. 46: Octagon Lumber Rule. With 16 Separate Scales. Excellent Condition. Length: 24 Inches.** *Unmarked, but obviously made by Stanley, this multi-faceted rule is in superb condition and has a rich, golden patina.* (GOOD+) **$145.00**

Q3-38. **Stanley Rule & Level (Unmarked) No. 45: 36 Inch Wantage Rod Rule. Maple Body. Superb Condition. Length: 36 Inches.** *Stanley produced the No. 45 wantage rule for use in the wine industry to gauge the amount "wanting" to fill a barrel. This example is in excellent condition, noting a small hang hole. A rare Stanley rule in excellent condition.* (FINE) **$245.00**

Q3-39. **Lufkin Rule Co., The, Saginaw, Mich.: No. 7166: Sliding Extension Rule. 6-12 Foot Span. Rare and Excellent. Length: 72 Inches.** *We know from personal experience that these 6 to 12 foot extension rules can help one to unintentionally make enemies in elevators. This example is in nearly new condition. A rare Lufkin rule.* (FINE) **$125.00**

Q3-40. **Stanley Rule & Level (Unmarked) No. 46 1/2: Square Lumber Rule. Circular Brass End. Rare and Excellent. Length: 24 Inches.** *This clean Stanley lumber rule is in excellent condition and is imprinted with the Stanley number, but not the Stanley name. Crisp and clean.* (GOOD+) **$195.00**

Q3-41. **Haselton, R. B., Contoocook, N.H.: Lumberfman's Tally Rule. With Original Counter. Near New Condition. Length: 24 Inches.** *Used to maintain a cumulative count of the number of potential board feet of timber, this classic rule retains one of its original tally pegs. A series of holes on the edge have graduations. Placing the peg in a specific hole "marked off" a fixed amount of lumber. This rule is boldly struck with the Haselton name and working location.* (FINE) **$255.00**

Q3-42. **Stanley Rule & Level No. 41: Maple Yard Rule. With Sweetheart Trademark. Near New Condition. Length: 36 Inches.** *Stanley's ca. 1920's "Sweetheart" trademark is imprinted on this well preserved yard measure. A nice example.* (FINE) **$45.00**

Q3-43. **Unmarked: Narrow Metric Rule. Inside Marked "Rijnland". Unused Condition. Length: 39 1/2 Inches.** *The designation "Rijnland" appears on the intside of this comparative scale rule, which has had its maker's mark removed in the factory. The outside of the rule has metric graduations. A rare comparative scale rule in unused condition.* (FINE) **$85.00**

Q3-44. **Lufkin Rule Co., The: No. 1069: Counter Measure Rule. Solid Brass. With Countersunk Holes. Length: 36 Inches.** *This brass counter measure was likely intended for a yard goods store. An unusual Lufkin rule.* (GOOD+) **$75.00**

Q3-45. **Stanley Rule & Level No. 48 1/2: Octagon Log Cane Rule. With Stanley Mark. Extra Crisp and Clean. Length: 36 Inches.** *The early imprint of the Stanley Rule & Level Company has been boldly marked on this classic log gauging cane. These tools functioned as an estimating device while serving to steady the footing of the user. Marked examples, especially in this kind of condition, are quite scarce. A good one.* (GOOD+) **$365.00**

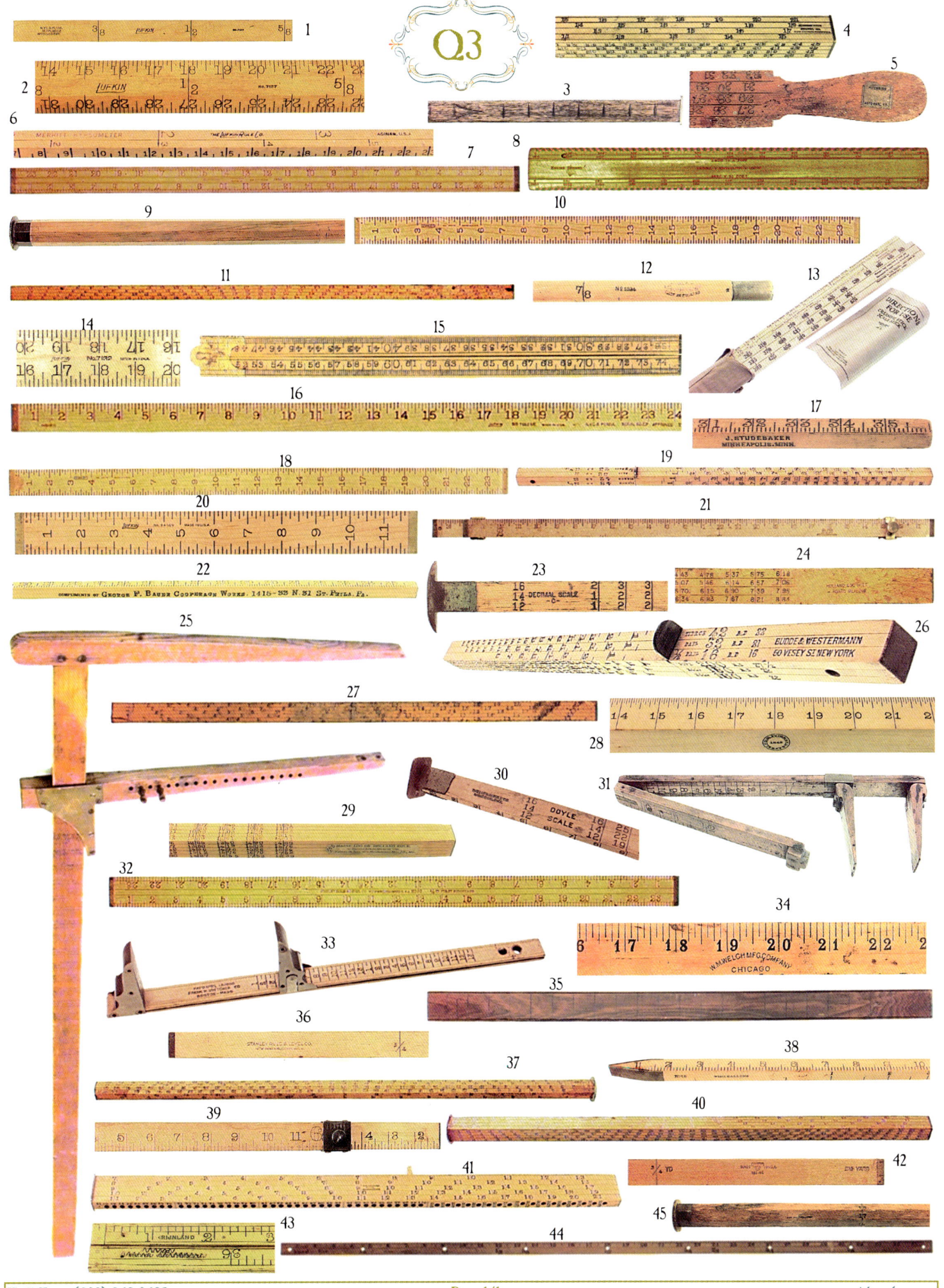

Group R3

R3-1. Davis Level & Tool Co. No. 1: 7 Inch Inclinometer Level. Patented September 17, 1867. Superb Condition. Length: 7 Inches. *In addition to their "Mantle Clock" level, the Davis Level & Tool Company offered a full range of cast iron levels with the inclinometer feature. This, the 7 inch No. 1 inclinometer was the smallest size offered. This extra-clean example retains nearly all of its original black japan finish. The level mechanism is clean, sound and in generally perfect condition. A superb example of a very desirable collectible inclinometer level.* (FINE) **$695.00**

R3-2. Stratton Bros., Greenfield, Mass. No. 11: Brass Bound Mahogany Level. Narrow Width. Rare and Excellent. Length: 24 Inches. *Full brass binding and a body of reddish brown mahogany give this narrow-bodied level from Stratton Brothers a striking visual appeal.* (GOOD+) **$165.00**

R3-3. Stanley Rule & Level No. 98: Brass-Bound Rosewood Level. 12 Inch Size. Original Decal. Length: 12 Inches. *Stanley offered their No. 98 series of levels in a full range of sizes from 6 inches to 24 inches. This example of the 12 inch size retains 99% of all original finishes on all surfaces. The desirable "Sweetheart" trademark is embossed on the top plate, retains its full original decal and the tool is absent any nicks or dings whatever. A glorious example of a great Stanley level.* (FINE) **$895.00**

R3-4. Unmarked: Early Cast Iron Level. With Triple View. Uncommon Form. Length: 9 3/4 Inches. *Of sufficiently complex design to suggest that it was manufactured, this cast iron level is not marked with a maker's imprint of any kind. Unusual.* (GOOD+) **$65.00**

R3-5. Unmarked: Ebony "Torpedo" Level. Uncommon Style. Miniature Size. Length: 4 Inches. *At only 4 inches in length, this ebony level can rightly be called "cute".* (GOOD+) **$95.00**

R3-6. Helb, Edward, Railroad, Penn.: Patent Inclinometeri Level. Patented July 12, 1904. Complete and Sound. Length: 24 Inches. *Here's another example of the Helb level that is clean, sound and in excellent working order. Contrary to popular misconception, these are not "Railroad" levels, they were made in the City of Railroad, Pennsylvania and have no more likely to be associated with trains than a patented brace produced in Buffalo, New York would be intended to be employed in some inhumane manner on an American Bison. A most unusual level, but not for the train crowd.* (GOOD) **$475.00**

R3-7. Davis L. & T. Co., Springfield, Mass.: Pedestal Level. For Carpenters Square Rare and Excellent. Length: 4 Inches. *The smaller bench levels of the Davis Level and Tool Company are among the least common and most eagerly sought-after of all collectible tools. Unmarked with any maker's markings, in many cases, only a few short years ago, these levels were often found on flea market tables in mid-afternoon as the general level of appreciation for such classics had not yet reached the fever pitch of current times. This special purpose pedestal level was designed to serve as a standard bench level, or when desired, be fixed to the blade of a try square, bevel or framing square to multiply its usefulness. Clean, complete, and absent any evidence of the breakage to which all Davis levels are susceptible, this one is ready to set on a shelf at eye level for all to admire. A great small level.* (GOOD+) **$345.00**

R3-8. Unmarked: Mahogany Sighting Level. "Patent Applied For". Original Label. Length: 12 Inches. *A number of these levels have appeared over the years, but no one seems to know exactly who made them. A sighting tube through the body partly focuses on a mirror so that the user can gauge whether or not the line he is viewing is properly oriented. An excellent example of a rare, early level.* (FINE) **$165.00**

R3-9. Staney Rule & Level No. 40: Cast Iron Level. Decorative Casting. For Use On Square. Length: 3 Inches. *This cast iron pocket and square level is in excellent condition. A good one.* (GOOD+) **$35.00**

R3-10. Rabone & Sons, J., Birmingham: Rosewood "Torpedo" Level. Decorative Plates. Extra Clean and Nice. Length: 9 Inches. *This classic English "torpedo" level features artfully formed top plates of polished brass. It is in top collector quality condition. Nice.* (FINE) **$115.00**

R3-11. Stanley Rule & Level No. 36: Double Plumb and Level. Smallest Size. Crisp and Clean. Length: 6 Inches. *Stanley offered these levels in every possible size, ranging in size from 6 inches to 30 inches. Here's a crisp and clean example of the least common 6 inch variety. A good one.* (GOOD+) **$45.00**

R3-12. Smallwood, I. & D., Birmingham: Tropical Hardwood Level. Billiard Table Advertising. "E.J. Riley, London". Length: 10 Inches. *Nicely embossed with the advertising from the maker of billiard tables, it is very likely that this perfectly-preserved rosewood and brass level was intended for leveling slate billiard tables. A curious and interesting collectible level.* (FINE) **$165.00**

R3-13. Davis, L.L., Springfield, Mass. No. 37: Early Machinist's Level. Marked With Name, Number. Superb Condition. Length: 3 1/2 Inches. *Here's a great example of the Davis cast iron bench level. This one is marked with the Davis number designation and the name.* (GOOD+) **$425.00**

R3-14. Unmarked: Early Adjustable Plumb and Level. Decorative Vial Covers. Spring Regulated. Length: 29 1/2 Inches. *Levels such as this one were manufactured in the Hudson River area of New York State and are found with various maker names. This unusual variation has brass plumb vial covers cast in a honeycomb pattern. The level vial is set on springs to facilitate adjustment.* (GOOD+) **$125.00**

R3-15. Stratton Bros., Greenfield, Mass.: 28 Inch Mahogany Level. Full Brass Bound. Rare and Excellent. Length: 28 Inches. *The Stratton Brothers Company was extremely successful for one reason: they made great levels, people bought them and people used them. This fully brass bound example is in excellent overall condition and ready to accent any display of classic antique tools.* (GOOD+) **$195.00**

R3-16. Stanley Rule & Level No. 0: Solid Cherry Level. "Made In Canada". New Condition, Original Box. Length: 18 Inches. *This Canadian-made version of Stanley's basic cherry level is in new condition in its mustard-yellow box. An oddity.* (FINE) **$85.00**

R3-17. Starrett Co., L. S., Athol, Mass.: Double Plumb Level. Cast Iron Body. 98% Original Paint. Length: 6 Inches. *This precision machinist's level was produced in the first quarter of this century. Nearly all original paint remains.* (FINE) **$65.00**

R3-18. Jennings & Co., C.E., New York, N.Y.: 18 Inch Cast Iron Level. Filigree Design. Clean And Sound. Length: 12 Inches. *Manufacturers of the celebrated "Arrowhead" brand of tools, the C.E. Jennings Company of New York City, produced a product line of exceptionally high quality. In keeping with the custom of the time, their cast iron levels incorporated a degree of elaborate design and finish that, while unquestionably beautiful, seems somehow excessive to modern perceptions. This example of their 18 inch carpenter's plumb and level is in excellent condition and retains more than 90% of its original paint.* (GOOD+) **$115.00**

R3-19. Lyon & Co., D.M., Newark, N.J. No. 7: 30 Inch Cuban Mahogany Level. Distinctive Vials. Extra Early and Nice. Length: 30 Inches. *Daniel M. Lyon produced levels in Newark, New Jersey from 1857 to 1863. This extra heavy Cuban Mahogany specimen features a pair of showy circular plumb vial covers. It is in excellent collector quality condition. Nice.* (GOOD+) **$225.00**

R3-20. Unmarked: Brass Machinist's Level. In "Keeper" Case. Extra Crisp and Clean. Length: 4 Inches. *A locking metal case, that looks as though it may have been designed to hold a cigar, has kept this small brass level in nearly new condition. Nice.* (FINE) **$45.00**

R3-21. Unmarked: Mahogany Sighting Level. Full Brass Facing. Missing Plumb Vial. Length: 8 Inches. *Needing only a replacement plumb vial, which could be easily fitted, this classic English-style sighting level is a bargain waiting to happen. A good one.* (GOOD+) **$95.00**

R3-22. Unmarked: Brass Presentation Level. "Thos. Foulkes, 1875". Fitted Boxwood Case. Length: 3 Inches. *Unfortunately, the boxwood case was not sufficient to keep the vial from going dry on this brass presentation level. Dated 1875 and nicely engraved, this level is worthy of restoration. Nice.* (GOOD) **$135.00**

R3-23. Stratton Bros., Greenfield, Mass.: 24 Inch Mahogany Level. Full Brass Bound. Very Well Preserved. Length: 24 Inches. *A clean and clearly marked example of the fully brass bound Stratton carpenter's mahogany level. A good one.*(GOOD) **$95.00**

R3-24. Stanley Rule & Level No. 38: "Oil Burner" Level. Cast Iron Body. Orange Japan Finish. Length: 6 Inches. *A very well preserved example of Stanley's "oil burner" level that retains nearly all of its original orange japanning. Colorful.* (FINE) **$65.00**

R3-25. Richardson, C.F., Athol, Mass.: 12 Inch Double Plumb and Level. Cast Iron Body. 95% Original Paint. Length: 12 Inches. *This early level has the "Richardson" mark. The pattern is identical to levels later offered by Goodell Pratt. A good, clean level.* (FINE) **$115.00**

R3-26. Disston & Sons, Henry, Philadelhia, Penn. No. 70: Brass Bound Mahogany Level. Patented October 29, 1912. Scarce Size and Excellent. Length: 12 Inches. *Disston's smaller brass-bound levels are difficult to find, especially in as well preserved condition as is this one. Clean and ready to display.* (GOOD+) **$255.00**

R3-27. Goodell Pratt Company No. 509: Precision Cast Iron Level. "Open End" Style. Excellent Condition. Length: 18 Inches. *Goodell Pratt offered these cast iron levels with squared, flat ends and in this lighter version. They are not common.* (GOOD+) **$65.00**

R3-28. Stanley Rule & Level No. 5: Laminated Cherry Level. Ca. 1900. Near New Condition. Length: 28 Inches. *This Stanley classic is in essentially unused condition. All original finishes remain on this turn of the century level.* (FINE) **$75.00**

R3-29. Stanley Rule & Level No. 36 G: Cast Iron Plumb and Level. 12 Inch Size. Unused Condition. Length: 12 Inches. *This example of the cast iron No. 36 G retains more than 99% of its original black japan finish. Mint.* (FINE) **$95.00**

R3-30. Mathieson & Son, A., Glasgow No. 7 C: Ebony and Brass Level. Full Brass Face. Sliding Top Plate. Length: 9 Inches. *A sliding brass plate moves to the side when this level is called into action. It is marked with both the Mathieson name and product number. The vial may be an early replacement.* (GOOD+) **$85.00**

R3-31. Unmarked: Classic English Spirit Level. Solid Brass Body. Green Glass Vial. Length: 10 Inches. *This is identical to the spirit levels offered in the catalogs of Edward Preston & Sons. A classic brass level with a most appealing green coloration to the vial. A nice tool.* (FINE) **$125.00**

R3-32. Stanley Rule & Level No. 31: Hexagonal Machinist' Level. Ca. 1930's. Near New Condition. Length: 3 1/2 Inches. *All of the original nickel plating remains on this hexagonal pocket level from Stanley. A tough level to find.* (FINE) **$35.00**

R3-33. Stanley Rule & Level No. 41: Ornate Brass Top Level. Patented June 23, 1896. With Embossed Imprint. Length: 3 Inches. *The top plate on this variation of the No. 41 is particularly ornately embellished and marked with the 1896 patent date. Classic, and classy.* (GOOD+) **$45.00**

R3-34. Starrett Co., L. S., Athol, Mass. No. 134: Cross Test Level. Angle Shape. Superb Condition. Length: 3 1/4 Inches. *An extremely well preserved example of a Starrett level of uncommon form. Very nice.* (GOOD+) **$85.00**

R3-35. Chapin-Stephens Co., The, No. 506: Inclinometer Level. With Boxwood Dial. Near New Condition. Length: 28 Inches. *Nearly all original finishes remain on wood and metal of this early inclinometer. The body is clearly stamped with the C-S product number. When these do show up, they generally look as though they had come by boat, having been used as an oar in the process. Not so this one. Highly recommended.* (FINE) **$245.00**

R3-36. Stanley Rule & Level No. 41: Brass Top Level. Replaced Screw. With Embossed Imprint. Length: 3 Inches. *Embellished, yet in a way that post-Victorian sensitivities could accept, this later version of the No. 41 level is in excellent condition for the collection. A good one.* (GOOD+) **$45.00**

R3-37. Stanley Rule & Level No. 36: 6 Inch Cast Iron Level. Patented August 4, 1896. 98% Original Nickel. Length: 6 Inches. *Nearly all of the original nickel plating and japan finish remain on this crispy clean double plumb and level in the uncommon 6 inch size.* (GOOD+) **$35.00**

R3-38. Williamsburg Mfg. Co., Wmsburg, Mass.: Rare 4 Inch Pocket Level. Hexagon Shape. Near New Condition. Length: 4 Inches. *Somewhere, somebody knows the full story of the relationship of the many level manufacturers who operated in Western Massachusetts and had some relationship to the Davis Level and Tool Company, or, at the very least, produced products remarkably similar to the Davis line. The Williamsburg Manufacturing Company was one such company. Examples of their small machinists levels are scarce indeed. This one is in superb, collector-quality condition.* (FINE) **$145.00**

R3-39. Mathieson & Sons, A., Saracen Tool No. 21 C: 12 Inch Rosewood Level. Full Brass Top. Excellent Condition. Length: 12 Inches. *The Saracen Tool Works was located in Glasgow, Scotland. At the time this level was made, Mathieson was the largest tool manufacturer in the British Isles. A clean and clearly marked small level.* (GOOD+) **$65.00**

R3-40. Stanley Rule & Level No. 38 1/2: Machinist's Bench Level. "Sweetheart" Trademark. Near New Condition. Length: 4 Inches. *This shiny bench level has weathered the passage of time unscathed. Perfect.* (FINE) **$65.00**

R3-41. Stanley Rule & Level No. 36: 18 Inch Cast Iron Level. Patented June 23, 1896. Early Type. Length: 18 Inches. *This early cast iron level from Stanley has the 1896 patent date cast into the body. A nice example.* (GOOD+) **$55.00**

R3-42. Stanley Rule & Level No. 93: Brass Bound Mahogany Level. With Original Decal. Sweetheart Trademark. Length: 30 Inches. *Stanley's brass-bound levels are treasures when found in factory-new condition. This one is absolutely mint, complete with the original decal.* (FINE) **$225.00**

R3-43. Chapin, H., Union Factory No. 294: Laminated Fruitwood Level. Early Example. Near New Condition. Length: 24 Inches. *Despite the prolific output of the Chapin Union Factory, certain tools with their early mark are not often seen. Such is the case with their wooden levels, of which this example, marked with the maker name and product number, is an excellent example. Nearly new.* (FINE) **$125.00**

R3-44. Huber Mfg. Co., The, Marion, O.: Beechwood Level. With Brass Top. Uncommon Maker. Length: 8 Inches. *A Huber Manufacturing Company is documented in the Directory of American Toolmakers as having produced machinists tools, including the Woodman Patent speed indicator, in Marion, Ohio in the 1870's. It is likely that this small level was intended as an advertising promotion for their business. A rare level.* (GOOD+) **$65.00**

R3-45. Williamsburg Mfg. Co., Williamsburg, Mass.: Cast Iron Plumb and Level. Filigree Design. Extra Crisp and Clean. Length: 18 Inches. *Somewhere, somebody knows the full story of the relationship of the many level manufacturers who operated in Western Massachusetts and had some relationship to the Davis Level and Tool Company, or, at the very least, produced products remarkably similar to the Davis line. The Williamsburg Manufacturing Company was one such company. This filigree-cast carpenter's level is in excellent condition without any damage to the casting. A classic Nineteenth Century level.* (GOOD+) **$165.00**

Group S3

S3-1. Sargent & Co., New Haven, Conn.: General Line Catalog. 1911 Edition. 250 Pages, Hardbound. Length: 8 1/4 Inches. *Every tool offered by Sargent at the peak of their production is illustrated and described in this catalog. A great reference tool.* (GOOD+) **$195.00**

S3-2. Sargent & Co. (Unmarked): Locksmith's Screwdriver. Rosewood Head. Multiple Sizes. Length: 4 1/4 Inches. *This classic rosewood handle locksmith's screwdriver from Sargent complemented their hardware line, which included a substantial number of door locks. This example is clean and clearly marked with the Sargent name.* (GOOD+) **$95.00**

S3-3. Sargent & Co., New Haven, Conn. No. 29: Bench Rabbet Metallic Plane. Similar to Stanley 10 1/2. Near New Condition. Length: 9 Inches. *Sargent's equivalent to the Stanley No. 10 1/2 is rare in any condition. This one is absolutely mint. A great plane.* (FINE) **$550.00**

S3-4. Sargent & Co., New Haven, Conn. No. 107: Early Block Metallic Plane. Complete and Proper. 99%+ Original Paint. Length: 6 Inches. *More than 99% of the shiny original black japanning remains on this early Sargent block plane. Nice.* (FINE) **$55.00**

S3-5. Sargent & Company No. 8: 8 Inch Machinists Divider. Precision Adjust. Uncommon Mark. Length: 8 Inches. *Sargent offered a full line of "mechanic's" tools. Here's a nicely marked pair of dividers.* (GOOD+) **$25.00**

S3-6. Sargent & Co., New Haven, Conn.: Steel Multi Wrench. For Locks?. Near New Condition. Length: 7 Inches. *The Sargent hardware company offered all manner of metallic tools and hardware, so it is not surprising that a wrench would bear their imprint. Different.* (FINE) **$25.00**

S3-7. Sargent & Co., New Haven, Conn.: Adjustable Punch. "Bernard" Type. Unused Condition. Length: 6 1/2 Inches. *No one has ever used this adjustable punch from Sargent, which was continued as part of the "Bernard Patent" line.* (FINE) **$45.00**

S3-8. Sargent & Co., New Haven, Conn. No. 40: Polished Steel Framing Square. Uncommon Size. Marked "S. & Co.". Length: 6 Inches. *The abbreviation for the Sargent name on this minty crispy nice 6 inch square may be attributable to the fact that the full name would not fit. Extra nice.* (FINE) **$95.00**

S3-9. Sargent & Co., New Haven, Conn. No. 306: Adjustable Block Metallic Plane. Patented July 6, 1897. New Condition, Original Box. Length: 6 Inches. *This example of Sargent's answer to Stanley's No. 9 1/2 block plane has been used, but is clean, complete and retains its original box. It is marked with the 1897 patent date.* (GOOD) **$195.00**

S3-10. Sargent & Co., New Haven Conn. No. 307: Adjustable Throat Metallic Plane. Similar to Stanley 15. Scarce and Excellent. Length: 7 Inches. *A bit longer than the standard block plane, this 7 inch offering from Sargent was the equivalent to Stanley's No. 15 block plane. A scarce Sargent block plane in top collector quality condition.* (FINE) **$85.00**

S3-11. Sargent & Co., New Haven, Conn. No. 2204: All-Steel Metallic Plane. With V.B.M. Logo. Near New Condition. Length: 4 1/4 Inches. *These were offered by Sargent from 1913 to 1947. This one appears to date from the earliest years of that production run, as it is imprinted with the "V.B.M." logo. A very nice example.* (FINE) **$185.00**

S3-12. Sargent & Co.: 6 Inch Beech Handle Draw Knife. Marked " V B M". Rare and Excellent. Length: 11 1/2 Inches. *Sargent's early catalogues offered high quality such as that illustrated here. This one is clearly marked with the Sargent V.B.M. mark. Extra crisp and clean.* (GOOD+) **$65.00**

S3-13. Sargent & Co., New Haven Conn. No. 606: Low Angle Block Metallic Plane. Similar to Stanley 60 1/2. Rare Sargent Type. Length: 6 Inches. *This, Sargent & Company's equivalent to Stanley's No. 60 series is clean and complete, and retains its original Sargent cutting iron. Try as we might, we cannot get the throat adjustment mechanism to work, otherwise excellent.* (GOOD+) **$115.00**

S3-14. Sargent & Co., New Haven, Conn. No. 710: "Autoset" Patent Metallic Plane. "V.B.M." Trademark. Near New Condition. Length: 10 Inches. *This "Autoset" bench plane is in nearly new condition. Nice.* (FINE) **$265.00**

S3-15. Sargent & Co., New Haven Conn.: Parallel Jaw Pliers. With Wire Cutter's. "Schollhorn" Type. Length: 8 Inches. *Sargent incorporated the Schollhorn Company's line of "Bernard Patent" pliers and cutter into their line. These parallel jaw pliers with wire cutters are one example of the diverse line. These are in top collector quality condition.* (FINE) **$45.00**

S3-16. Sargent & Co., New Haven, Conn. No. 710: "Autoset" Patent Metallic Plane. "V.B.M." Trademark. Near New Condition. Length: 10 Inches. *Sargent's "Autoset" planes were a later, but most interesting, entry in the competition to produce the most involved adjustment mechanism on a metallic plane. This example of the equivalent of Stanley's No. 4 plane is in near-new condition. For a great collectible plane, we recommend this Autoset No. 710.* (FINE) **$265.00**

S3-17. Sargent & Co., New Haven, Conn.: "V.B.M." Camp Hatchet. With Original Sheath. Rare and Near New. Length: 14 Inches. *Sargent's "V.B.M." line (Very Best Made) included a wide range of tools. This hatchet, which includes the original sheath, is the first example of this tool that we have offered. Rare.* (FINE) **$125.00**

S3-18. Sargent & Co., New Haven, Conn. No. 5206: Adjustable Low Angle Metallic Plane. Pressed Steel Body. Uncommon Type. Length: 6 Inches. *This was the Sargent equivalent, of a sort, to Stanley's 118 pressed steel block plane. This one is in excellent overall condition.* (GOOD+) **$55.00**

S3-19. Sargent & Co., New Haven, Conn.: Specialized Crimping Pliers. "Bernard's Patent". Rare and Excellent. Length: 7 Inches. *These specialty crimping pliers form a 3/8 inch circle when fully closed. Most unusual.* (FINE) **$65.00**

S3-20. Sargent & Co., New Haven Conn. No. 81: "Show Case Rabbet" Metallic Plane. Patented July 21, 1914. Rare and as New. Length: 4 1/2 Inches. *Protected by its original box with the most curious label "Show Case Rabbet Plane" still intact in great shape, this perfectly preserved example of Sargent's double side rabbet is in top collector-quality condition. Superb.* (FINE) **$425.00**

S3-21. Sargent & Co., New Haven, Conn.: Laminated Cherry Level. Partial Paper Label. Made By Disston. Length: 26 Inches. *Part of the original paper label remains on this cherry level from Sargent, which was undoubtedly made for them by Henry Disston & Sons. An uncommon Sargent level.* (GOOD+) **$65.00**

S3-22. Sargent & Co., New Haven Conn. No. 2204: All-Steel Metallic Plane. With V.B.M. Logo. New Condition, Original Box. Length: 4 1/4 Inches. *The presence of the original box has kept this "pocket" block plane in essentially the same condition as it was when it was made. A rare Sargent "in the box" item.* (FINE) **$385.00**

S3-23. Sargent & Co., New Haven, Conn. No. 1607: Low Angle Block Metallic Plane. Nickel Plated Cap. Rare and Excellent. Length: 7 Inches. *Sargent & Company matched competitor Stanley nearly plane for plane, but they didn't make it easy for collectors by adopting the Stanley numbering system—those who would master the esoterica of Sargent will need to do some studying. This low angle block plane was the equivalent of Stanley's No. 60. A rare Sargent plane.* (GOOD+) **$45.00**

S3-24. Sargent & Co., New Haven, Conn.: Belt Cutting Pliers. "Bernard's Patent". Rare and Excellent. Length: 6 1/2 Inches. *These specialty pliers, which were designed to cut and join leather belts, such as the type found on sewing machines, includes a cutter, a piercing device and a pair of pliers. Nearly all original nickel plating remains.* (GOOD+) **$45.00**

S3-25. Sargent & Co., New Haven, Conn. No. 5206: Adjustable Low Angle Metallic Plane. Pressed Steel Body. Crisp and Clean. Length: 6 Inches. *Someone has inscribed his initials in the body of this plane, but it is otherwise in excellent condition. A tough Sargent plane to find.* (GOOD+) **$55.00**

S3-26. Sargent & Co., New Haven, Conn. No. 160: Cast Iron Scrub Metallic Plane. Hollow Cast Body. Rare and Excellent. Length: 10 Inches. *Sargent offered these unusual cast iron scrub planes in three sizes: rare, rarer and ain't-never-seen-one (which featured a dual cutting iron assembly). The double cutter thing apparently did for the plane what the sidecar does for the motorcycle. This example of the more common of the series is in clean, sound condition and is fitted out with its full complement of original parts.* (GOOD) **$345.00**

S3-27. Sargent & Co., New Haven Conn. No. 18: Rare "Shaw Patent" Metallic Plane. Patented July 3, 1906. Near New Condition. Length: 18 Inches. *Whatever its merits in functionality, Sargent's "Shaw Patent" planes were extremely difficult to disassemble, owing to the complexity of the frog mechanism. This pristine example of the No. 18 (Stanley No. 6 equivalent) is in great shape. Nice.* (FINE) **$375.00**

S3-28. Sargent & Co., New Haven Conn.: Asstorted Leather Punches. "Bernard" Type. Extra Crisp and Clean. Length: 6 1/2 Inches. *All of these "Bernard Patent" tools came from the same tool kit—an indication that the original owner found the quality level of these tools to his liking. All are in superb condition.* (FINE) **$155.00**

S3-29. Sargent & Co., New Haven Conn. No. 9: Rare "Shaw Patent" Metallic Plane. Patented July 3, 1906. Excellent Condition. Length: 9 Inches. *The short-lived "Shaw Patent" featured a complex frog adjustment mechanism that was very likely not very practical. Examples that employ this mechanism are quite scarce. This example is in nearly perfectly preserved condition and features dramatically grained handles. Extra nice.* (FINE) **$245.00**

S3-30. Sargent & Co., New Haven Conn.: Combination Cutters and Pliers. "Bernard" Type. Excellent Condition. Length: 4 3/4 Inches. *Try buying a pair of parallel jaw pliers at the store sometime—they are not available. This pair incorporate a wire cutting mechanism into the tool.* (FINE) **$35.00**

S3-31. Sargent & Company, New Haven, Conn.: Early Patent Hollow Auger. Complete and Sound. Patented March 30, 1887. Length: 6 3/4 Inches. *This early hollow auger from Sargent is clean, complete and imprinted with the 1887 patent date. Rare and excellent.* (GOOD+) **$115.00**

S3-32. Sargent & Co., New Haven, Conn. No. 5306: Knuckle Joint Block Metallic Plane. Adjustable Throat. Superb Condition. Length: 6 1/2 Inches. *This rare knuckle joint block plane is in excellent collector quality condition. A good one.* (FINE) **$75.00**

S3-33. Sargent & Co., New Haven, Conn. No. 32: Rare 1/4 Inch Dado Metallic Plane. Crisp and Clean. Floral Casting. Length: 8 Inches. *Sargent's cast iron dado planes are among the prettiest ever produced. This 1/4 inch size dado is in excellent overall condition. A rare plane.* (FINE) **$365.00**

S3-34. Sargent & Co., New Haven Conn. No. 81: "Show Case Rabbet" Metallic Plane. Patented July 21, 1914. New Condition, Original Box. Length: 4 1/2 Inches. *Protected by its original box with the most curious label "Show Case Rabbet Plane" still intact in great shape, this perfectly preserved example of Sargent's double sided rabbet is in top collector-quality condition. Superb.* (FINE) **$485.00**

S3-35. Sargent & Co., New Haven Conn. No. 2606: Vacuum Ticket Punch. "Bernard" Brand. New Condition, Original Box. Length: 5 Inches. *The "Bernard" line of tools that Sargent acquired from the Schollhorn Company is becoming an increasingly popular collectible. Here's a pristine example of an uncommon type. New and in the box.* (FINE) **$45.00**

S3-36. Sargent & Co., New Haven, Conn.: Smooth Plane Cutting Iron. For No. 407/707. Early and Excellent. Length: 6 Inches. *If your "No. 2" size Sargent plane is in need of a cutting iron, here it is. It is marked with Sargent's "oval" logo. Scarce.* (FINE) **$65.00**

S3-37. Sargent & Co., New Haven, Conn. No. 107: Cast Iron Block Metallic Plane. Patented Feb. 3, 1891. New Condition, Original Box. Length: 6 Inches. *The original box has kept this Sargent block plane in top collector quality condition. Missing the back flap from the box, but otherwise mint.* (FINE) **$110.00**

S3-38. Sargent & Co., New Haven, Conn. No. 5307: Knuckle Joint Block Metallic Plane. Extra Crisp and Clean. Stanley No. 19 Equivalent. Length: 7 Inches. *The Stanley No. 19, at 1 inch longer in size than its more common cousin, is a scarce plane. The equivalent "knuckle joint" plane from Sargent is less common still. This one is clean, sound and ready to fill out a Sargent collection.* (GOOD+) **$45.00**

S3-39. Sargent & Co., New Haven, Conn. No. 500 B R: Black Finish Square. 95% Original Finish. With Rafter Scale. Length: 24 Inches. *Here's an example of Sargent's "black" finish square in nearly new condition. Perfect.* (FINE) **$75.00**

S3-40. Sargent & Co., New Haven, Conn. No. 1068: Tongue and Groove Metallic Plane. Patented October 22, 1912. Albert Page Patent. Length: 9 Inches. *Here's a clean and sound example of Albert Page's 1912 patented nightmare. The only tool in its class. Another bad idea that makes a great collectible tool.* (GOOD+) **$275.00**

S3-41. Sargent & Co., New Haven Conn. No. 76: Adjustable Circular Metallic Plane. Elaborate Knob. Near New Condition. Length: 10 Inches. *Fitted with an ornately cast nickel-plated front knob and retaining nearly all of its original finishes, this example of the Sargent No. 76 is the finest we have seen in many years. A great plane.* (FINE) **$455.00**

S3-42. Sargent & Company No. 72: Expansive Auger Bit. Original Box. With 2 Cutters. Length: 9 1/2 Inches. *Both of the original cutters are present with this adjustable auger bit from Sargent. First come, first serve.* (FINE) **$15.00**

S3-43. Sargent & Co., New Haven, Conn. No. 718: Autoset Fore Metallic Plane. With Pivoting Knob. Superb Condition. Length: 18 Inches. *Finding Sargent's Autoset planes in top condition is not a common occurrence. Finding one with the pivoting front knob in nearly new condition is a Red Letter Day. Celebrate.* (FINE) **$365.00**

S3-44. Sargent & Co., New Haven, Conn. No. 411: "Junior Jack" Metallic Plane. Uncommon Size. Superb Condition. Length: 11 Inches. *Not to be outdone by fellow Nutmeg State planemaker Stanley Rule & Level, Sargent offered the full range of bench planes, including this, the equivalent to Stanley's No. 5 1/4 "Junior Jack Plane". This example is in top collector quality condition.* (FINE) **$245.00**

S3-45. Sargent & Company No. 1080 PB: Combination Metallic Plane. Nickel Plated Body. Complete, Original Box. Length: 11 3/4 Inches. *This crispy clean combination plane from Sargent has been kept in top condition, thanks to the presence of the original box. All original parts, including the original instructions, remain. A small sliver of wood from the side of the tote needs mention, but barely so. A well made combination plane in top working order.* (FINE) **$185.00**

Group T3

T3-1. Stanley Rule & Level No. 45: Multi Purpose Combination Plane. Ca. 1950's. New Condition, Original Box. Length: 9 Inches. *All original parts as well as the original instruction manual and screwdriver remain with this exceptionally well preserved example of Stanley's No. 45 combination plane. Nearly all of the original paper label remains on this shiny and crispy clean example from the early 1950's. The nicest No. 45 we have offered in some time. Choice.* (FINE) **$525.00**

T3-2. Greenlee Tool Co., Rockford, Illinois: No. V 200 D: Set of Bevel Edge Chisels. 1/2 Inch to 1 1/2 Inch. Original Pouch. Length: 9 Inches. *Here's a nearly new set of socket chisels from a prominent American maker in new condition in their original pouch. A nice set.* (FINE) **$85.00**

T3-3. Assorted Makers: Opportunity Box Lot. Square, Bits, Rule, Files, Brace, Etc. Length: 10 Inches. *This hodgepodge of whatnot came from the bottom of a tool chest. All tools, including a ratcheting brace and a Disston cast iron square, are in workable condition. A bargain.* (GOOD+) **$35.00**

T3-4. Stevens Walden, Inc., Worcester, Mass.: Mechanic's Tool Kit. Wrenches, Screwdriver. Original Roll. Length: 13 Inches. *The Walden Wrench Company of Worcester, Massachusetts was an early maker of specialty automotive tools. We have never heard of the company that produced this specialty mechanic's set, but it is likely that they were in some way affiliated.* (GOOD+) **$145.00**

T3-5. Bridgeport Gun Implement Co., The: No. 99: Patent Gun Implement Set. Full Set of Implements. Patented February 25, 1890. Length: 12 1/2 Inches. *The original pasteboard box has kept this set of gun accessories in superb condition, despite their nearly 110 years of age. Everything you need to clean and load your shotgun. An exceptionally nice set.* (FINE) **$295.00**

T3-6. Millers Falls Company: "Home Maintenance" Tool Kit. Most Original Tools. Original Case. Length: 18 Inches. *This Millers Falls kit, which retains nearly all of its original complement of tools likely dates from the late 1950's or early 1960's. An uncommon set.* (GOOD+) **$285.00**

T3-7. Union Hardware Co.: Set of 3 "Samson" Chisels. 1/2 Inch, 3/4 Inch and 1 Inch. New Condition, Original Box. Length: 14 1/2 Inches. *The original box has kept these heavy socket chisels in new condition throughout their long life. As good as they get.* (FINE) **$175.00**

T3-8. Peck, Stow & Wilcox Co.: Framer's Set of Chisels. 1 Inch, 1 1/4 Inch, and 1 1/2 Inch. Near New Condition. Length: 17 1/2 Inches. *Protected by a carpenter's chest and their fitted roll through some 100 years of existence, each of the chisels in this set of heavy socket framing chisels from one of America's premier makers of framing tools in in essentially new condition. If you're looking for a set of chisels to last several generations, we recommend this perfectly preserved stepped set without hesitation.* (FINE) **$525.00**

T3-9. Currier-Koeth Mfg. Co.: Koeths's Comb. Kit Wrench. Jack of All Trades. New Condition, Original Box. Length: 8 1/2 Inches. *If you looked at this assortment of metal and someone told you it was a handy tool, what would you say? We have seen a few of these in collections and almost all are in their original boxes. Perhaps these were sold at Christmas time to women as gifts for their husbands. The Electric Socks of the 1890's. An uncommon wrench.* (FINE) **$195.00**

T3-10. Ward & Payne: Set of Bevel Edge Chisels. Extra Long Blades. Ready to Use. Length: 15 Inches. *English makers Ward & Payne of Sheffield produced edge tools of the very highest quality. Each of the chisels in this full set of 11 is in excellent working order and ready for a lifetime of service. One of the handles shows some evidence of wear, but the others are in great shape. The sort of set you dream about. A dream come true.* (GOOD+) **$545.00**

T3-11. Lufkin Rule Co., The, Saginaw, Mich.: Oak Machinist's Tool Box. Original Plaque and Decal. Excellent Condition. Length: 20 Inches. *As part of their rollout of the Lufkin machinist's tool line, Lufkin offered these oak machinists chests. This example is in excellent condition and retains its full original Lufkin decal. Rare and excellent.* (GOOD+) **$445.00**

T3-12. Addis, S.J., London: Set of 6 Assorted Carving Tools. From Single Owner. Ready to Use. Length: 8 1/2 Inches. *These extra small carving tools from English maker S.J. Addis are in great working order and ready to use.* (GOOD+) **$145.00**

T3-13. Assorted Makers: Opportunity Box Lot. Dividers, Pliers, Oil Can, Wrench, Etc. Length: 10 Inches. *Here's an interesting batch of tools in excellent condition that were rescued from a tool box after some 75 years of captivity. A bargain.* (GOOD+) **$45.00**

T3-14. Hammacher, Schlemmer & Co.: Quarter Sawn Oak Tool Chest. With Original Keys. Near New Condition. Length: 22 1/2 Inches. *Hammacher Schlemmer offered a wide variety of tool boxes such as this one, either with or without the tools. This one is in nearly new condition with its original brass plaques, but lacks the tools. There is no more challenging or rewarding task than refitting one of these with its original tools. Here's a good start.* (FINE) **$245.00**

T3-15. Unmarked: Multi Purpose Tool Kit. Marked "Germany". Unused Condition. Length: 6 Inches. *This crispy clean tool kit from pre-War Germany is complete in a doeskin case with its full complement of original tools, including a wrench. A classy kit in mint condition.* (FINE) **$165.00**

T3-16. Unmarked No. CS-34: United States Army Signal Corps Tool Kit. Pliers and Knife. For Belt Mount. Length: 8 Inches. *Here's a pair of pliers and a knife, complete with their original case, that were stolen from the United States Army. At this price, the crime will be repeated when you purchase it from us.* (GOOD+) **$35.00**

T3-17. Stanley Rule & Level No. 66: Patent Cast Iron Beader. 8 Original Cutters. New Condition, Original Box. Length: 12 Inches. *Complete in its original box with eight original cutters, including the double router cutter, this pristine beader is ready to be put immediately to work. A rare and desirable Stanley plane.* (FINE) **$265.00**

T3-18. Unmarked: Complete Veneer Kit. Special Saws, Hammers. Near New Condition. Length: 14 Inches. *The craft of applying wood veneer can be as complex or as simple as the craftsman doing the work wishes it to be. For the home woodworker, the tools used in veneering are make-do at best. For the professional woodworker, however, especially one that specializes in this high form of the woodworker's art, specialized tools are a necessity. Generally these tools appear sporadically in the antique tool market, with a hammer found here, a saw there and so forth. The possibility of finding an intact kit of veneering tools has been, until now, essentially unthinkable. However, with the consignment of a major collection came this complete and virtually unused set of tools that were brought to the Utica, New York area from France around 1910 and then set away and forgotten. Included are a wide range of saws, hammers, scrapers and knives of every possible shape and size. For the generalist collectorseeking an extraordinary grouping of the tools of a particular craft or for the serious artist craftsman with the intention of putting these tools to use, we highly recommend this special set.* (FINE) **$685.00**

T3-19. Flash Sales Corp., The, Chicago, Illinois: "Eifel Gear Plierench" Tool Kit. With Instructions. Original Pouch. Length: 8 1/2 Inches. *This is, without question, the finest example of this popular combination tool that we have offered. Complete with all original jaws, the instruction booklet and the original carrying case, nearly all original finishes remain on the tool. Extra nice.* (FINE) **$115.00**

T3-20. North Bros Mfg. Co., Philadelphia: No. 105: "Yankee" Radio Tool Kit. With All Original Tools. Complete, Original Box. Length: 7 1/2 Inches. *I haven't counted all the parts, but this example of the rare "Yankee" Radio Tool Kit appears to be substantially intact. The box is dark, but complete, and much of the paper label remains. A tough tool to find.* (FINE) **$295.00**

T3-21. Lufkin Rule Co., The, Saginaw, Mich: No. 576: Tape Measure Rule Repair Kit. Leatherette Case. Most Unusual. Length: 9 Inches. *Just in case your Lufkin tape measure failed under use, this special kit from Lufkin, which includes a punch, riveter and extra end sections for the tapes, would have you back in action in no time. An essential for the collector of tape measures. Rare.* (FINE) **$115.00**

T3-22. Unmarked: Brass Hanging Scale. With Troy Ounce Weights. Ca. 1890's. Length: 6 3/4 Inches. *Here's an interesting small Troy measure scale that looks to date from the late 1890's. Different.* (GOOD+) **$85.00**

T3-23. North Bros. Mfg. Co., Philadadelphia, Penn.: No. 1431 A: Single Speed Hand Drill. 3 Jaw Chuck. New Condition, Original Box. Length: 10 Inches. *Acquired at a recent estate auction, this tool was a "new old stock" item purchased from a hardware store in the vicinity of Cleveland, Ohio. The North Brothers Company offered this drill and a range of other tools to cater to the Ham radio craze in the 1920's. Absolutely brand new.* (FINE) **$265.00**

T3-24. Unmarked: Special Purpose Tool Kit. "Ecoration De Ouir". For Leather Work? Length: 11 1/2 Inches. *We don't get many of these, whatever they are. It has a French look, and the word repousse comes to mind, but I'm not really sure. I know that there are a number out there waiting to pounce immediately when my pontification exceeds the bounds of truth or logic, so have at it. A free T Shirt will be provided to the first to accurately correct my ignorance. This applies only to the instant case, as I realize that a general correction would require a much more substantial effort.* (GOOD+) **$245.00**

T3-25. Assorted Makers: Opportunity Box Lot. Gauges, Chisles, Cutter, Tape Measure, Pliers. Length: 6 Inches. *If you need a bunch of tools, here's an opportunity grab bag that includes one of each.* (GOOD+) **$35.00**

T3-26. Millers Falls Company No. 1: Alford Hand Vise. Rosewood. With 8 Attachments. Length: 7 1/2 Inches. *The "Alford Patent" hand vise combined the functions of a hand vise, tool handle, trammel points and drill chuck into a single tool. The example is complete and in top collector quality condition.* (FINE) **$195.00**

T3-27. Record No. 50 A: Combination Metallic Plane. With Original Cutters. New Condition, Original Box. Length: 9 3/4 Inches. *The No. 50 A combination plane was distinguished from the No. 50 by the presence of a precision adjustment mechanism on the blade. This one is clean, complete and ready to use. The original box has kept it in nearly new condition.* (FINE) **$225.00**

T3-28. H. Gerstner & Sons, Dayton, Ohio: Large Machinist's Tool Box. With Front Cover. Ready to Use. Length: 26 Inches. *Here's a ready to use machinists tool box from the premier maker of these chests.* (GOOD+) **$115.00**

T3-29. North Bros Mfg. Co., Philadelphia: No. 106: "Yankee" Radio Tool Kit. With Radio Drill. Fine Condition, Original Box. Length: 10 Inches. *A number of serious and sophisticated collectors have been drawn, in recent years, to the tools produced by the North Brothers Tool Company of Philadelphia. The output of this pioneering company was characterized by a degree of quality and finish equalled by very few other toolmakers. Among the most desirable tools are special sets of tools, which sometimes include tools that are quite rare in their own right. A classic example is this "Radio Tool Kit", which was likely assembled for marketing to amateur radio operators in the 1920's. Retaining its full complement of original tools and in nearly new condition in its original box, this Yankee classic is a North Brothers collectible classic. Highly recommended.* (FINE) **$595.00**

T3-30. Assorted Makers: Opportunity Box Lot. Chisel, Wrench, Etc. From Auction. Length: 11 Inches. *If anyone can deduce a common theme from the hodgepodge assembled in this lot, we are willing to listen, but we will be disinclined to believe. A melange.* (GOOD+) **$35.00**

T3-31. Johnson Tool Co., Warren, Penn.: Screwdriver Handle Tool Kit. Patented December 9, 1913. Original Pouch. Length: 7 Inches. *These patented tool kits were provided in a number of configurations, including some with hammers and full sets of socket wrenches. This one has a range of screwdrivers and the wedge shaped device used to remove the blades. A nice example.* (GOOD+) **$115.00**

T3-32. Assorted Makers: Opportunity Box Lot. Machinist Tools. Starrett, B. & S. Length: 4 1/2 Inches. *These tools came from the same machinists chest and will stay together. An excellent buying opportunity.* (GOOD+) **$45.00**

T3-33. Waycott, Paignton: Set of 18 Hollow and Round Molding Planes. Skew Set Irons. Ready to Use. Length: 9 1/2 Inches. *The cutting irons on the planes in this well preserved set from English maker Waycott are set at a skew to facilitate their use with hard woods. A great set in ready to use condition.* (GOOD+) **$845.00**

T3-34. Allen & Co., (Providence, R.I.): "Allen Universal" Wrench. Pivoting Ratchet. New Condition, Original Box. Length: 10 1/2 Inches. *Produced by the same company that gave us the six sided wrench that will forever bear their name, this specialized pivoting ratchet wrench never made it to that level of popularity. All of the original parts are present in a fitted wood box. An interesting early wrench from an important maker.* (GOOD+) **$65.00**

T3-35. Millers Falls Company No. 106: Boxed Set of Carving Tool. Green Lacquer Handle. New Condition, Original Box. Length: 7 Inches. *Whether you are a would-be woodcarver or a collector of fine tools, this "in the box" set from the Millers Falls Company is highly recommended. Mint.* (FINE) **$95.00**

T3-36. Stanley Rule & Level No. 750: Set of 8 Bevel Edge Chisels. Original Handles. Ready to Use. Length: 9 Inches. *A protective case provided by the previous owner has kept these Stanley classics in top working order. Crisp, clean and ready to use.* (GOOD+) **$265.00**

T3-37. Unmarked: Oilstone in Carved Holder. Rock Maple Construction. Old But Near New. Length: 7 Inches. *A decorative pattern around the footed base of this early oilstone, as well as a molding pattern around the top of the case, make it look almost too good to use, although it is still perfectly usable. A classic.* (FINE) **$145.00**

T3-38. Currier- Koeth Mfg. Co.: Koeths's Combination Kit Wrench. Jack of All Trades. Fine Condition, Original Box. Length: 10 1/2 Inches. *These have got to be one of the stupidest ideas ever put into production. How many times do you need a pair of pliers and have time to disassemble the pair you are using and then reassemble another pair? They probably looked great under the Christmas tree. An ideal gift for a tool collecting friend.* (GOOD+) **$265.00**

T3-39. Brown & Sharpe Mfg. Co.: Apprentice's Tool Kit. Folding Case. Complete and Excellent. Length: 7 Inches. *Nearly every manufacturer of machinists tools offered these "apprentice kits". Here's a perfectly preserved offering from the folks in Providence. Complete and excellent.* (FINE) **$225.00**

T3-40. Nicholson File Co., Providence, R.I.: Special Advertising Tool Box. With Nicholson Plaque. Protective Cover. Length: 33 1/2 Inches. *At nearly 3 feet in length, it is a virtual certainty that this case was not used for Nicholson's traditional line of files. The box is velvet lined, fitted with a brass plaque and includes a fitted padded cover, which has kept this interesting curiosity in top condition.* (FINE) **$95.00**

T3-41. Record No. 405: Combination Metallic Plane. With Hollow and Round Attachments. Near New Condition. Length: 12 Inches. *Unquestionably the best modern attempt to replicate the quality and functionality of the Stanley No. 45 combination plane, the Record No. 405 has, because of that quality, become collectible itself. A woodworker seeking to purchase a high quality, investment grade, working tool would be well advised to consider this immaculate and complete example, which also includes the optional hollow and round attachments. As nice an example of this desirable plane as we have ever offered. Highly recommended.* (FINE) **$645.00**

T3-42. Starrett Co., The L.S., Athol, Mass.: Apprentice's Tool Kit. All Original Tools. Ca. 1910. Length: 12 Inches. *This apprentice's kit from the L.S. Starrett Company contains enough tools to get a beginning machinist started (on buying Starrett tools, if you get the picture). Nice.* (FINE) **$285.00**

T3-43. Millers Falls Company: Complete Home Tool Kit. 20 Original Tools. Original Case. Length: 18 Inches. *A home handyman of the late 1950's or early 1960's might well have purchased one of these for the cellar workshop. This example is in top collector quality condition.* (FINE) **$225.00**

T3-44. Union Steel Chest Corp., Leroy, N.Y.: Machinist's Tool Chest. With 7 Sliding Drawers. Ready to Use. Length: 21 Inches. *Here's a heavy duty steel machinists tool chest made the way they used to be. It is in excellent condition and includes the cover for the front of the sliding doors. Ready to use.* (GOOD+) **$75.00**

T3-45. Stanley Tools: "Defiance" Tool Chest. For Farm and Home. Excellent Condition. Length: 24 Inches. *Nearly all of the original paper label, as well as the outside label, remain on this "Defiance" classic. A nice example.* (FINE) **$85.00**

Group U3

U3-1. Unmarked: Early Hollow Molding Plane. Yellow Birch Body. Owner "Griswold". Length: 10 Inches. *This classic Yellow Birch molder has the wide, flat chamfers of an early plane, but lacks the sophistication of execution that would indicate that it was produced by a professional planemaker. The owner's name "Griswold" has been branded on the side. A well preserved early molding plane.* (GOOD+) **$55.00**

U3-2. Reed, Utica (N. Y.): Quirk Ovolo, Cove/Astragal Molding Plane. Marked "5/8". Missing Cutting Iron. Length: 9 1/2 Inches. *Even if you don't have the cutting iron to replace the one missing from this crispy complex molder, it would be well worth the time to grind a new one. Nice.* (GOOD+) **$115.00**

U3-3. Unmarked No. 4: Early Hollow Molding Plane. Wide Flat Chamfers. Ready to Use. Length: 9 1/2 Inches. *Here's an extra early molder in excellent working order. Appearance is ca. 1810.* (GOOD+) **$25.00**

U3-4. Collins & Robbins, Utica: Quirk Ogee With Bevel Molding Plane. Ca. 1829-1830. AWP III: 2 Stars. Length: 9 1/2 Inches. *Collins & Robbins worked in Utica, New York for two years only. This wide molding plane is boldly struck with their mark. An excellent wide molder from a rare New York State maker.* (GOOD+) **$245.00**

U3-5. Greenfield Tool Co., Greenfield, Mass. No. 101: Boxed Bead Molding Plane. 3/8 Inch Size. Extra Crisp and Clean. Length: 9 1/2 Inches. *Finding bead planes in this condition has become more and more of a challenge. Challenge met.* (GOOD+) **$45.00**

U3-6. Auburn Tool Co., Auburn, N.Y.: Handled Boxwood Plane. Boxwood Arms, Nuts. Superb Condition. Length: 11 Inches. *A rich patina of weathered gold adds visual appeal to this classic solid boxwood plow. Whether you are a tool collector looking to add to your collection or a traditional woodworker seeking a classic usable tool, this well preserved plow will more than fill the bill. Extra crisp and clean.* (GOOD+) **$445.00**

U3-7. Gibson, J., Albany (New York): Boded Bead Molding Plane. Ca. 1823-1835. AWP III: "A" Mark. Length: 9 1/2 Inches. *This crisp and clean bead plane has been boldly struck with the graphic "J.Gibson" mark. The kind of plane you don't find any more.* (GOOD+) **$35.00**

U3-8. Reed, Utica (N. Y.): 5/8 Inch Astragal Molding Plane. Uncommon Type. Extra Crisp and Clean. Length: 9 1/2 Inches. *Astragal molders by American makers are exceptionally difficult to obtain. This pristine example is in much the same condition it was in when it left the Reed planemaking enterprise. Nice.* (FINE) **$85.00**

U3-9. Kellogg, J., Amherst, Mass.: Screw Lock Arm Plow Plane. Near New Condition. Owner "I. Titcomb". Length: 9 Inches. *One Isaac Cummings Titcomb was listed as a cabinetmaker, born September 8, 1813 in Newburyport, Massachusetts. It is entirely conceivable, that Titcomb could have purchased this J. Kellogg plow plane during his working life. Kellogg began making planes in 1835, when Titcomb would have been 22 years old, and ceased in 1867, when Titcomb would have been 54. Beyond the maker's mark, we have no information on the provenance of this tool, but the Titcomb name is so closely associated with woodworking and the Newburyport area that this scenario is more that just speculation. A perfectly preserved plow that may well have been the possession of a New England cabinetmaker.* (FINE) **$365.00**

U3-10. Unmarked: Reverse Ogee Molding Plane. Early Flat Chamfers. Ready to Use. Length: 9 1/2 Inches. *Here's a classic reverse ogee molder that has been nicely side boxed to preserve its working life. Wide, flat chamfers are indicative of early manufacture.* (GOOD+) **$55.00**

U3-11. Unmarked: Miniature Rabbet Plane. Fence and Depth Stop. Yellow Birch Body. Length: 8 3/4 Inches. *Differing in appearance from any plane we have previously offered, this special undersize rabbeting plane is formed from native Yellow Birch and incorporates a series of depth stops into its design. It has been used, but is in excellent collector quality condition.* (GOOD+) **$165.00**

U3-12. Casey, Kitchell & Co., Auburn, N.Y.: Massive Quirk Ovolo, Bevel Molding Plane. Marked "Inch". Ca. 1830's. Length: 9 1/2 Inches. *Finding wide molders that have not been buried or left overnight in a barrel of oil has become a challenge of late. This wide ovolo and bevel combination is exceptionally crisp and clean. A good one. Ex-Cooley Collection.* (GOOD+) **$185.00**

U3-13. Collins, Utica: Wide Quirk Ovolo and Bevel Molding Plane. Missing Boxing. Easily Restored. Length: 9 1/2 Inches. *A section of boxing, which could be easily replaced by a halfway competent woodworker, is missing from this exceptionally steep ovolo and bevel molder. An extra wide and steep molder bearing a most uncommon imprint.* (GOOD) **$115.00**

U3-14. Unmarked: Early Yellow Birch Molding Plane. Wide Flat Chamfers. 1 3/4 Inch Hollow. Length: 9 3/4 Inches. *All too often the planes we find have been battered about to the point that it is not apparent that they were once precision tools. This classic Eighteenth Century molder has escaped much of that abuse and its consequences. A classic.* (GOOD+) **$65.00**

U3-15. Stewart: Double Iron Molding Plane. Cove and Bead. Near New Condition. Length: 9 1/2 Inches. *One of the cutting irons is missing from this classic double iron Scottish molder, but it could be easily be replaced. A classic Scottish plane in top collector quality condition. Nice.* (FINE) **$165.00**

U3-16. I.D.F.: Cove, Bead/Bevel Molding Plane. Uncommon Profile. Early Appearance. Length: 9 1/2 Inches. *This early complex molder is imprinted with the initials "I.D.F." and has the characteristics of a well made plane. A classic molder from ca. 1800. Ex-Cooley Collection.* (GOOD+) **$145.00**

U3-17. Harris & Shepherd, L. Falls, N.Y.: Wide Flat Ogee Molding Plane. Ca. 1868-1869. AWP III: 3 Stars. Length: 9 1/2 Inches. *Rated at 3 Stars for rarity in American Wooden Planes, this wide ogee molder dates from the years 1868-1869, when Isaac Harris and Alexander Shepherd operated a hardware dealership in Little Falls, New York. Rare.* (GOOD+) **$115.00**

U3-18. Fitch, W.: Yellow Birch Rabbet Molding Plane. With Relieved Wedge. Early Appearance. Length: 9 1/2 Inches. *We can find no documentation of a W. Fitch, or any other Fitch having worked as a planemaker. This early Yellow Birch molder has been boldly struck with the Fitch name.* (GOOD) **$45.00**

U3-19. Reed, Utica (N. Y.): 5/16 Inch Dado Molding Plane. Fixed Depth of Cut. Extra Crisp and Clean. Length: 9 1/2 Inches. *Essentially untouched by the ravages of time and weather, this uncommon 5/16 inch dado is in superb shape for the tool collector or the woodworker. Nice.* (FINE) **$75.00**

U3-20. Reed, Utica (N. Y.): 7/8 Inch Astragal Molding Plane. Uncommon Type. Ready to Use. Length: 9 1/2 Inches. *Here's a 7/8 inch astragal molder in excellent working order. A tough plane to find, especially in this condition. Nice.* (GOOD+) **$65.00**

U3-21. Stothert, Bath (England): Fenced Rabbet Molding Plane. Marked "3/8". Ca. 1784-1841. Length: 9 1/2 Inches. *Planemaker George Stothert seems to have specialized in exporting planes to the United States. This fenced rabbet molder was found in the Mohawk Valley of New York State. Extra nice. Ex-Cooley Collection.* (FINE) **$65.00**

U3-22. Stothert, Bath (England): Quirk Ovolo, Bevel Molding Plane. Marked "3/8". Ca. 1784-1841. Length: 9 1/2 Inches. *This small cabinet molder is in excellent working order and ready to be put back in to use. A nice plane.* (GOOD+) **$65.00**

U3-23. Gladding, R.: Early Groove Molding Plane. Relative of J. Gladding? Ca. 1800's. Length: 9 1/2 Inches. *A J. Gladding, Jr. is known to have produced wooden planes in Saybrook, Connecticut in the 1830's and 1840's. This groove molder may well have been made by a relative. A clean plane from an undocumented maker.* (GOOD+) **$65.00**

U3-24. E.R:: Early Quarter Round Molding Plane. Wide Flat Chamfers. Owner "E. Adams". Length: 9 Inches. *Only the stylized mark "E.R" in a large zig-zag border designates the maker of this early and very well made quarter round molding plane. A classic.* (GOOD+) **$65.00**

U3-25. Delve, I.: Fenced Quirk Round Molding Plane. Early Appearance. Ready to Use. Length: 9 1/2 Inches. *The maker mark on this fenced quarter round is one that we have not previously encountered. It is in excellent working order and appears to date from the 1820's or thereabout.* (GOOD+) **$55.00**

U3-26. Delve, I.: Bead and Bevel Molding Plane. Early Appearance. Uncommon Profile. Length: 9 1/2 Inches. *We are aware of at least one other example of this imprint, which appears to date from the first quarter of the Nineteenth Century.* (GOOD+) **$85.00**

U3-27. Mathieson, A., Glascow (Scotland): Sash Filletster Plane. Replaced Wedge and Boxing. Early Imprint. Length: 9 Inches. *Both the boxing and the wedge have been replaced on this Scottish sash filletster, but it is otherwise sound and in working order.* (GOOD) **$65.00**

U3-28. Casey, Clark & Co., Auburn, N.Y. No. 158: Massive Quirk Ogee, Bevel Molding Plane. Marked "Inch". Crisp and Clean. Length: 9 1/2 Inches. *This extra-wide prison-made plane is boldly struck with the imprint of the partnership who held the planemaking contract for Auburn Prison in the 1840's. A nice molding plane.* (GOOD+) **$195.00**

U3-29. Greenslade, W., Bristol (England): Classic Toothing Plane. "Ex. Medals", Etc. Ready to Use. Length: 7 1/2 Inches. *Here's a clean working toothing plane from one of England's top planemakers. Ready to use.* (GOOD+) **$75.00**

U3-30. Spring, T.: Early Rabbet Molding Plane. Yellow Birch Body. Distinctive Imprint. Length: 10 Inches. *This early Yellow Birch molder is imprinted with the name of a maker we have not previously encountered. It was found in Central New York State. A well made plane from an undocumented maker.* (GOOD+) **$55.00**

U3-31. Reed, Utica (N. Y.): Snipe Bill Molding Plane. Fully Boxed. Near New Condition. Length: 9 1/2 Inches. *This snipe bill molder is in much the same condition as it was when it was first made. Snipe bill molders by American makers are very scarce. Rare.* (FINE) **$55.00**

U3-32. Sandusky Tool Co., Sandusky, Ohio No. 146: 2 Inch Skew Rabbet Molding Plane. Extra Crisp and Clean. Ready to Use. Length: 9 1/2 Inches. *Skew blade rabbet planes are handy tools for the shop that just happen to be fun to use. Here's a nice working example in top collector quality condition.* (FINE) **$55.00**

U3-33. Harris & Shepherd, L. Falls, N.Y.: Massive Ogee Molding Plane. Ca. 1868-1869. AWP III: 3 Stars. Length: 9 1/2 Inches. *In addition to its massive ogee profile, this oversize molder cuts a small bevel adjacent to the fence. A great wide molder bearing an uncommon Upstate New York imprint.* (GOOD+) **$215.00**

U3-34. Reed, Utica (N. Y.): 7/8 Inch Dado Molding Plane. Brass Screw Adjust. Near New Condition. Length: 9 1/2 Inches. *Thanks to the foresight of a collector, this plane was rescued from a tool chest many years ago and set away for safe keeping. Having been kept in virtually new condition through the efforts of two owners, we ask for a third to take up the task. Ex-Cooley Collection.* (FINE) **$125.00**

U3-35. Collins, Utica No. 4: Pair of Hollow and Round Molding Planes. Ca. 1831-1834. Near New Condition. Length: 9 1/2 Inches. *Here's a working pair of hollow and round molding planes in nearly new condition. Choice. Ex-Cooley Collection.* (FINE) **$85.00**

U3-36. Reed, Utica (N. Y.): Adjustable Door Molding Plane. Screw Adjustment. Near New Condition. Length: 9 1/2 Inches. *This screw adjust molder cuts a steep ogee mold for door panels. It is in excellent working order. Ex-Cooley Collection.* (GOOD+) **$275.00**

U3-37. Reed, Utica (N. Y.): Classic Ogee Molding Plane. Marked "7/8". Ready to Use. Length: 9 1/2 Inches. *This classic ogee molder has a steeper than usual cut and is in excellent working order. A good one.* (GOOD+) **$115.00**

U3-38. Kellogg, J., Amherst, Mass.: Beech Smooth Plane. Lignum Strike Button. AWP III: 2 Stars (A). Length: 8 1/2 Inches. *This well preserved molder has been boldly struck with the first imprint used by prolific Amherst, Massachusetts planemaker J. Kellogg. A lignum vitae strike button indicates that this was meant to be a tool of extra quality.* (GOOD+) **$65.00**

U3-39. Taylor, Wm. No. 9: Hollow Molding Plane. Undocumented Maker. Owner "M. Drew". Length: 9 1/2 Inches. *The name "Wm. Taylor" is the first we have seen on a molding plane. A clean plane from an undocumented maker.* (GOOD+) **$25.00**

U3-40. Martin & Corey (Made For): 7/8 Inch Groove Molding Plane. N.Y.C. Ca. 1857-1865. Uncommon Imprint. Length: 9 1/2 Inches. *Howard Martin and William Corey were hardware dealers in New York City from 1857 to 1865. A previous example of this imprint was double struck with a J. Denison mark. This example has only the Martin & Corey stamp. A rare American imprinted molding plane in top condition.* (FINE) **$85.00**

U3-41. Kellogg, J., Amherst, Mass.: Quirk Ovolo With Bevel Molding Plane. Marked "8/8". Crisp and Clean. Length: 9 1/2 Inches. *This classic profile molder is in excellent working condition. Ready to go back to work.* (GOOD+) **$85.00**

U3-42. Unmarked: Early Astragal Molding Plane. 3/4 Inch Width. Yellow Birch Body. Length: 9 1/2 Inches. *This early Yellow Birch molder cuts a classic 3/4 inch astragal profile. A well preserved early molder in excellent working condition.* (GOOD+) **$65.00**

U3-43. White, L. & I.J., Buffalo, N.Y.: Boxed Bead Molding Plane. Marked 6/8 Inch. Extra Crisp Condition. Length: 9 1/2 Inches. *This 3/4 inch boxed bead has seen very little use. A very nice example in ready to use condition.* (GOOD+) **$45.00**

U3-44. Reed, Utica (N. Y.): Skew Rabbet Molding Plane. 1 7/8 Inch Width. Ready to Use. Length: 9 1/2 Inches. *Here's a great working skew rabbet from a prominent Upstate New York maker.* (GOOD+) **$45.00**

Group V3

V3-1. Millers Falls Company No. 192: Combination Drill and Brace. With Ratchet Drive. Rare Side Handle. Length: 14 1/2 Inches. *Substantially less common than the more commonly encountered version of this brace, which was designated as the No. 182, the No. 192 is fitted with an auxiliary handle that would adjust the drill mechanism into 3 separate positions, or allow it to be removed altogether. A rare Millers Falls brace in excellent condition.* (GOOD+) **$345.00**

V3-2. Unmarked: Classic "Gentleman's" Brace. Decorative Turning. Screw Lock Chuck. Length: 11 Inches. *A turnscrew serves to lock the bits into place on this classic "Gentleman's" brace. These tools were intended for the casual user. Their extra ornamentation was intended to improve their marketability, rather than their functionality.* (GOOD) **$45.00**

V3-3. Millers Falls Company: Patent Adjustable Corner Brace. Patented February 18, 1890. Full Nickel Plating. Length: 20 Inches. *Nearly all original nickel plating remains on this crispy clean example of one of the least common and most complicated of all corner braces. Nice.* (GOOD+) **$645.00**

V3-4. North Bros Mfg. Co., Philda. No. 2010-10: "Yankee" Wimble Brace. Never Nickel Plated. With "Bell System" Mark. Length: 14 Inches. *Here's a clean, sturdy and ready to use example of "the best brace ever made". A great brace.* (FINE) **$75.00**

V3-5. Millers Falls Company: 6 Inch Sweep Ratchet Brace. Rosewood Handles. Excellent Condition. Length: 12 Inches. *A tough brace to find in any condition, this example of the 6 inch sweep brace (which has a crank that deviates only 3 inch from the center) is in excellent collector quality condition.* (GOOD+) **$115.00**

V3-6. Atkins & Co., E.C., Indianapolis: Rare Patent Corner Brace and Drill. Patented October 10, 1905. Bennett and Bloedel, Penn. Length: 24 Inches. *This rare corner brace bears a maker's mark of the Atkins Tool Company, a famous saw maker. The patent was issued to Alexander Bennet and Philip Bloedel of Buffalo, New York for a combination brace that was manufactured by the Lancaster Tool Company. This one is missing the crank, but otherwise excellent. Different.* (GOOD) **$195.00**

V3-7. American Ratchet: L.C. Wilcox Patent Brace. Patented May 27, 1890. Pearson: "A" Rating. Length: 16 Inches. *Patented by Lewis C. Wilcox of Buffalo, New York on May 27, 1890, this brace has received the "A" rating for less than 5 examples known, in the Pearson book on braces. The patent applies to an extremely complex chuck mechanism that may have required an engineering degree to assemble and reassemble—a likely reason for its rarity.* (GOOD+) **$395.00**

V3-8. Unmarked: Classic Early Brace. With Screw Lock Chuck. Elaborate Turned Handle. Length: 12 1/2 Inches. *Of much the same form as the so-called "Penny Brace", this one is much more elaborate in design and, unlike the cheap braces, is of full-size construction. A nice looking brace.* (GOOD+) **$145.00**

V3-9. Stanley Tools No. 2101 A: "Yankee" Heavy Duty Brace. 8 Inch Sweep. "Bell System" Mark. Length: 13 1/2 Inches. *Still retaining the leather strap and clip that held it to a lineman's belt, this classic "Yankee" brace is in nearly new condition. A great working tool.* (FINE) **$85.00**

V3-10. Goodell Tool Co., Shelburne Falls,: "Goodell's Patent" Brace. Patented December 27, 1892. APB: "B" Rating. Length: 13 1/2 Inches. *Here's a clean and presentable example of the 1892 Patent granted to A.D. Goodell. This imprint precedes the production of this tool by the Goodell Pratt Tool Company. Most original nickel plating remains. Pearson: B Rating. A tough brace to find.* (FINE) **$65.00**

V3-11. Wright, S.J., Ellsworth, N.Y.: Combination Wrench and Brace. Patented December 16, 1873. Complete and Excellent. Length: 14 1/2 Inches. *Here's a clean and well preserved example of the S.J. Wright combination brace that was produced under an 1873 patent.* (GOOD+) **$125.00**

V3-12. Stackpole, Greenleaf, New York, N.Y.: Early Patent Brace. Patented April 2, 1867. Pearson: "B" Rating. Length: 13 Inches. *A spiral locking mechanism is the genius behind this early patent granted to Greenleaf Stackpole of the City of New York. A nice example of a rare, early brace.* (GOOD+) **$285.00**

V3-13. Stanley Rule & Level No. X-3: Rare "Fray" 6 Inch Sweep Brace. Marked "O.D. Usa". Early Trademark. Length: 12 Inches. *Following Stanley's purchase of the John S. Fray company, the Fray association with the United States Government was continued under the Stanley name. This 6 inch sweep brace marked "O.D. U.S.A." is in nearly new condition. A rare brace in new condition.* (FINE) **$225.00**

V3-14. Goodell Tool Co., Shelburne Falls,: Angular Corner Brace. Nickel Plate Chuck. Scarce and Excellent. Length: 12 1/2 Inches. *There seems to be no end to the various devices designed to facilitate the boring of holes in inconvenient places. This offering by Greenfield, Massachusetts maker Goodell-Pratt features a 2 jaw chuck and a level of finish found in the tools of few other makers. Extra crisp and clean.* (GOOD+) **$95.00**

V3-15. Vom Berg, Gebr: Classic Forged Brace. Octagonal Frame. Spring Catch Chuck. Length: 11 1/4 Inches. *The spring locking catch on this early German brace was designed to hold bits securely in place. We are not familiar with this maker, but the tool is of excellent quality.* (GOOD+) **$125.00**

V3-16. Davis L. & T. Co., Springfield, Mass.: 10 Inch Sweep Ratchet Brace. Patented October 14, 1884. Early Example. Length: 15 Inches. *Everyone knows that the Davis Level & Tool Company made great levels. Here's a clearly marked example of one of their less often seen tools.* (GOOD) **$145.00**

V3-17. Stanley Rule & Level No. 10: "Fray" Combination Drill and Brace. With Stanley Mark. Rare and Excellent. Length: 14 1/2 Inches. *For a short period after the acquisition of the Fray Company in 1909, Stanley distributed this brace and drill combination (No. 10DB) for only a very short period. This example is in clean, sound and complete condition and retains more than 75% of its finishes on all surfaces. A rare tool.* (GOOD+) **$475.00**

V3-18. Stanley Tools No. 2101A-14: "Yankee" Ratchet Brace. Rare 14 Inch Sweep. Near New Condition. Length: 14 1/2 Inches. *Finding the "Yankee" brace in the 14 inch sweep does not happen often. These tools were designed for very hard work and, when found, those remaining usually show the consequences of their hard life. This one seems to have escaped the hard life of its brethren. A rare brace in excellent condition.* (FINE) **$95.00**

V3-19. Stanley Rule & Level No. 8: 10 Inch Sweep Brace. Japanned Finish. Marked Ordinance Department U.S.A. Length: 11 Inches. *There must be a story here. I am aware of at least three of these early Fray-type braces marked with the Stanley mark and imprinted with the "Ord. (for ordnance) Dept. U.S.A. Mark. All are in the same nearly new condition as is this example. The fixing screw is nicely nickel-plated. A great Stanley collectible.* (FINE) **$145.00**

V3-20. Shepardson, Shelburne Falls, Mass.: Early Patent Bit Brace. Patented March 1, 1870. Pearson: "B" Rating. Length: 12 1/2 Inches. *A most visually interesting brace, this hails from Shelburne Falls, Massachusetts, where invention was apparently a local pastime. Issued in the name of H.E. Shepardson, this segmented jaw brace gives the impression that it would not have been a particularly functional tool in the workplace.* (GOOD+) **$245.00**

V3-21. Hildreth, S.W., Athol Depot, Mass.: Royall Hildreth Patented Brace. Patented February 1, 1871. Rarity Rating "B". Length: 13 Inches. *The mechanically distinct feature of the Royall Hildreth patent brace is spring-activated locking chuck. All that was necessary was for the workman to draw back on the chuck, thus compressing the spring(s) inside and insert the bit. Releasing his grip, the bit was then locked securely in place. A good idea, but most likely of sufficient difficulty to manufacture that it could not compete with the simple "Barber Patent" braces being turned out just to the West at the fledgling Millers Falls Company. A good one.* (GOOD+) **$265.00**

V3-22. Fray, J.S.: Early Patent Brace. Patented June 24, 1884. Pearson "A" Rating. Length: 14 Inches. *The cam adjust mechanism for this rare brace was patented by John S. Fray on June 24, 1884. According to the Pearson book on patented braces, it is one of less than 5 examples known extant. A rare patented American brace.* (GOOD) **$345.00**

V3-23. Unmarked: Early Barber Type Brace. 6 Inch Sweep. Excellent Condition. Length: 12 Inches. *An attractive early brace of the sort marketed as a "Gentleman's" or light duty brace. This one apparently found its way into the hands of a real gentleman. Extra clean.* (FINE) **$85.00**

V3-24. Fray & Co., John S. No. 107: 7 Inch Sweep "Spofford" Brace. Rosewood Head, Handle. Excellent Condition. Length: 10 Inches. *Nearly all of the original nickel plating remains on this classic "Spofford Patent" brace from the John S. Fray Company. Confirming the time-tested truth of tool making, that simple ideas are very often the best, this brace, with its single screw chuck that was no more than a glorified clamp, remained in production for more than 80 years.* (GOOD+) **$45.00**

V3-25. Millers Falls Company No. 14: 6 Inch Sweep Barber Patented Brace. Non-Ratcheting. Patented January 14, 1868. Length: 12 1/2 Inches. *This non-ratcheting brace is fitted with the 1868 patent Barber chuck that became the standard mechanism within a very short time. A rare collectible brace in a most desirable size.* (GOOD) **$45.00**

V3-26. Fray & Co., John S., Bridgeport, Conn.: "Wimble" Type Brace. Rosewood Handles. Uncommon Type. Length: 13 Inches. *The "wimble" brace was designed to be turned by both hands simultaneously while suspended high atop a pole. Many of those who mastered their use went on to a career in the circus. A nice early example in Big Top Condition.* (GOOD) **$145.00**

V3-27. Stanley Rule & Level No. 921: 10 Inch Ratcheting Bit Brace. Ca. 1930's. Extra Crisp and Clean. Length: 14 Inches. *Those seeking a collecting opportunity in collecting Stanley's under appreciated brace line would be well advised to invest in tools that are of the quality of this superb 10 inch version of the No. 921 ratcheting brace. This one is marked Stanley trademark and is in very clean condition. Nice.* (FINE) **$95.00**

V3-28. Davis L. & T. Co., Springfield, Ma: 14 Inch Sweep Ratchet Brace. Patented May 25, 1886. Rare Size and Type. Length: 15 Inches. *The basic patent on this brace, for a ratcheting chuck mechanism, was granted to Lawrence Bolen of Springfield, Massachusetts. They were distributed by the Davis Level & Tool Company. The handles on this brace are formed from Gutta Percha. A rare brace in excellent condition.* (GOOD+) **$115.00**

V3-29. Millers Falls Company No. 14: 6 Inch Sweep Barber Patented Brace. Non-Ratcheting. Patented January 14, 1868. Length: 12 1/2 Inches. *This non-ratcheting brace is fitted with the 1868 patent Barber chuck that became the standard mechanism within a very short time. A rare collectible brace in a most desirable size. Condition is excellent.* (FINE) **$85.00**

V3-30. Millers Falls Company No. 733 A: 8 Inch Ratcheting Brace. Original Decal. Near New Condition. Length: 13 Inches. *Nearly all of the original decal remains on this well preserved 8 inch sweep brace from the Millers Falls Company. Extra nice.* (FINE) **$65.00**

V3-31. White, H.O., Hebron, Conn. No. 3: Jeremy Taylor Patent Brace. Patented June 30, 1836. Early and Excellent. Length: 12 1/4 Inches. *The patent date on this early and extremely well-preserved brace has been identified by research as one issued to J.W. White of Hebron, Connecticut on June 30, 1836. Records of the patent were apparently destroyed in the great Patent Office Fire of the 1830's. A great early brace.* (GOOD) **$115.00**

V3-32. Peck, Obed & Powers, D.: Early Patent Bit Brace. Patented February 11, 1879. With Fluted Chuck. Length: 14 1/2 Inches. *The Peck and Powers patent brace of 1879 features a chuck housing that looks as if it should be topped by a Corinthian capital. The patent feature is a single piece spring lock chuck. A good one.* (GOOD+) **$155.00**

V3-33. Stanley Rule & Level No. 3 X: 6 Inch Ratchet Bit Brace. Not Listed By Stanley. "O.D. U.S.A.". Length: 12 Inches. *There is no mention of the "3 X" brace in Stanley catalogs or the Stanley Value Guide. This well preserved example dates from the first quarter of this century and is essentially unused condition. A Rare brace.* (GOOD+) **$225.00**

V3-34. Unmarked: Classic Gentlemans Brace. Turned Lignum Head. Heart Shape Screw. Length: 9 1/2 Inches. *An artfully turned head of lignum vitae and a locking screw forged in the shape of a heart are indications that this early brace was made to be something special. Nearly all original finishes remain on this classic early brace. Extra nice.* (FINE) **$195.00**

V3-35. Stanley Tools No. 2101 A: "Yankee" Heavy Duty Brace. 10 Inch Sweep. Best Brace Ever. Length: 13 1/2 Inches. *With regard to the "Yankee" brace, there were two classes of workmen: those who had one, and those who wished they did. A very nice example.* (FINE) **$85.00**

V3-36. Stanley Rule & Level No. 923 A: 12 Inch Sweep Ratchet Brace. Aluminum Head and Handles. Rare Size and Type. Length: 13 1/2 Inches. *Stanley offered a line of braces with aluminum fittings from 1934 to 1942. Examples are quite scarce, especially in this condition.* (GOOD+) **$115.00**

V3-37. Fray & Co., John S. (?) No. 59 1/2: 6 Inch Sweep Brace. Ordinance Department U.S.A. Rare and Excellent. Length: 12 Inches. *This extra small size brace from the John Fray Company is also marked with the imprint "Ordnance Dept. U.S.A." It is in excellent collector quality condition.* (GOOD+) **$115.00**

V3-38. Stanley Rule & Level No. 8: 10 Inch Sweep Brace. Heavy Duty Chuck. Scarce and Excellent. Length: 14 Inches. *Stanley offered this heavy duty brace between 1911 and 1947, but there were apparently few takers. A rare Stanley brace.* (GOOD+) **$75.00**

V3-39. Stanley Rule & Level No. 923: 10 Inch Sweep Ratchet Brace. Rosewood Handles. Full Nickel Plating. Length: 14 1/2 Inches. *Looking for a good working brace? Stanley's "900" series featured rosewood handles and a ratcheting mechanism that was comparable to anything on the market. A brace to last a lifetime.* (FINE) **$95.00**

V3-40. Stanley Rule & Level No. 929: 8 Inch Sweep Brace. With Aluminum Handles. 1926-1933 Only. Length: 13 Inches. *Stanley offered an expanded line of tools using aluminum components during the 1920's and quickly scaled back in the early 1930's. This brace was one of the tools that was removed from production. A rare Stanley brace.* (GOOD+) **$225.00**

V3-41. Goodell Bros. Co., Greenfield, Mass.: Patented Corner Brace. Patented May 9, 1905. Near New Condition. Length: 11 Inches. *There seems to be no end to the various devices designed to facilitate the boring of holes in inconvenient places. This offering by Greenfield, Massachusetts maker Goodell-Pratt features a 3 jaw chuck and a level of finish found in the tools of few other makers. This example is clean, complete and ready to display.* (GOOD) **$225.00**

V3-42. Stanley Tools No. 2101 A: "Yankee" Heavy Duty Brace. 8 Inch Sweep. "Bell System" Mark. Length: 14 Inches. *This classic "Yankee" brace is in nearly new condition. A great working tool.* (FINE) **$115.00**

V3-43. Holt Mfg. Co., Springfield, Mass.: Extension Shaft For Brace. Patented December 14, 1880. Rare and Excellent. Length: 17 Inches. *In the years before the standard pattern for these bit brace extensions was developed, a number of innovative ideas were tried. Unfortunately, most had the problem of having the mechanism for holding the bit being wider than the bore of the bit. This early patent extension is an example of a tool with that Achilles heel. A rare bit extension.* (GOOD+) **$115.00**

V3-44. Vaughn & Bushnell, Chicago, Ill. No. 222: 10 Inch Heavy Duty Ratch Brace. With Rosewood Handles. Ready to Use. Length: 12 1/2 Inches. *The Vaughn & Bushnell Company of Chicago, Illinois, produced and marketed a wide range of tools under their own name. This extremely well preserved brace is fitted with a raised "V. & B." logo as a dust seal over the chuck mechanism. A very well made brace in top working order.* (FINE) **$65.00**

V3-45. Dumont Tool Co.: Dumont Patent Corner Brace. Patented September 10, 1901. Rarity Rating "A". Length: 18 Inches. *This mechanically interesting corner brace was patented by Charles DuMont of Buffalo, New York at the beginning of this century. This example, which is one of less than five known examples, based on the "A" rating assigned in Dr. Ron Pearson's book, is clean, sound condition. A rarity.* (GOOD) **$245.00**

Group W3

W3-1. **Mathews, Dayton, Ohio: "Neverstall" Combination Wrench. Patented September 14, 1909. Schulz No. 818. Length: 10 Inches.** *This one does it all: Hammer, wrench, pliers, tack puller, screwdriver, etc., etc.... With only one of these and a Veg-O-Matic, a man could live comfortably in the wilderness for weeks on end. A nice example.* (GOOD+) **$65.00**

W3-2. **Whitman & Barnes Mfg. Co., Boston: "Improved Bicycle" Wrench. Full Nickel Plating. Rare and Excellent. Length: 4 Inches.** *We have encountered less than a handful of these cast iron, nickel plated bicycle wrenches from Whitman & Barnes in the past several years. This one retains nearly all of its shiny nickel plating. A rare wrench.* (FINE) **$225.00**

W3-3. **Shaw Propeller Co. No. 4/6: Set of Alligator Wrenchs. Leatherette Pouch. Patented April 26, 1910. Length: 4 Inches.** *What a great idea! Ensure success for your questionably capable wrench invention by getting everyone to buy two of them. Any takers? A rare wrench set in top collector quality wrench.* (GOOD+) **$115.00**

W3-4. **S.D.: Nickel Plated Bicycle Wrench. "Pat. Appl'd For". Keyed Screw Mechinism. Length: 5 1/2 Inches.** *We are unfamiliar with this maker and this is the first bicycle wrench bearing this mark that we have encountered. A scarce small wrench for the bicycle wrench collector.* (FINE) **$55.00**

W3-5. **Cochran: "The Speednut" Wrench. Patented May 2, 1916. Excellent Condition. Length: 9 Inches.** *These were the standard among self-adjusting wrenches. This clean example is in great working condition.* (GOOD+) **$45.00**

W3-6. **Unmarked: Combination Saw and Wrench. Double Open End. Near New Condition. Length: 8 Inches.** *The inventor of this one probably had several Stupid Idea plaques on the wall of his office. A perfectly preserved example of an idea whose time never came. Crispy clean.* (FINE) **$65.00**

W3-7. **Sheldon Axle Company: Special Purpose Nut Wrench. For Carriage Wheels? Embossed Casting. Length: 10 Inches.** *One needn't go too far out on a limb to speculate that this wrench, from the Sheldon Axle Company, was intended for use on the wheels of horse drawn conveyances. It is the first example by this maker that we have encountered.* (GOOD) **$35.00**

W3-8. **Ideal: Cast Iron Buggy Wrench. With Spring Lock. Patented April 28, 1903. Length: 9 Inches.** *About the last thing you would want when removing the nut from the wheel of a horseless carriage would be to have the grease covered nut fall into a pile of dirt. A spring mechanism inside the square opening of this classic "buggy" wrench was designed to prevent that eventuality. An uncommon patented wrench in clean, sound condition.* (GOOD) **$35.00**

W3-9. **Renchall: Combination Nut, Plier Wrench. USA and Foreign Patents . Length: 8 1/2 Inches.** *This extremely well made potential hand-mangler of apparent British manufacture gives reassurance to those who fear that the desire to create wrenches that are wholly impractical from a utilitarian perspective may be regional in nature and attributable primarily to noxious gasses emanating from American swamps. Misery loves company.* (GOOD+) **$185.00**

W3-10. **Wiard Plow Company: Multi Size Plow Wrench. Dated 1894. Excellent Condition. Length: 11 Inches.** *The Wiard Plow Company produced this cast iron wrench to adjust the specialized fittings on the agricultural equipment they produced.* (GOOD+) **$45.00**

W3-11. **"King Dick": Center Screw Bicycle Wrench. As-New Condition. Rare 3 Inch Size. Length: 3 Inches.** *This example of the smallest of the "King Dick" series is in perfect condition.* (FINE) **$85.00**

W3-12. **Unmarked: Screw Lock Buggy Wrench. Cast Iron Frame. Most Unusual Type. Length: 10 1/2 Inches.** *A locking screw that projects from the side of the lower jaw is the immediately distinguishable feature of this early buggy wrench. An open end wrench at the end of the jaw adds extra functionality. Most unusual.* (GOOD+) **$265.00**

W3-13. **Reed & Co., Higganum, Conn.: "Remington" Buggy Wrench. Patented May 21, 1878. Schulz No. 226. Length: 8 Inches.** *Having a profile not unlike a musical instrument, the Remington buggy wrench is easily recognizable among a crowd of wrenches. A rare, early wrench in excellent condition.* (GOOD+) **$225.00**

W3-14. **Diamond Horseshoe Caulk Co.: Combination Pliers and Wrench. With Screwdriver. Near New Condition. Length: 6 Inches.** *The folks at the Diamond Horseshoe Company must have figured it wasn't hard enough to use a pair of pliers to loosen the object of its use, so they added a "crescent" wrench to the end of one of the handles at the precise location where the application of force in the use of the pliers would cause the most pain. As for the adjustable wrench, these things are imprecise enough without the added burden of a pair of pliers to stick you in the eye. Offered as an historical curiosity unless you're stupid enough to try and use this thing. Caveat Emptor.* (FINE) **$65.00**

W3-15. **Boardman, B., Norwich, Conn.: Combination Hammer and Wrench. Center Adjust Pipe, Nut. Patented July 10, 1866. Length: 6 Inches.** *An excellent example of this multi-purpose combination tool that includes a hammer, screwdriver, pipe wrench, nut wrench, nail puller and God knows what else. An early patent combination tool in excellent condition.* (GOOD+) **$125.00**

W3-16. **Keystone Mfg. Co., Buffalo, N.Y. No. 74: 4 Inch " Westcott" Wrench. " S" Handle Crescent. Rare, Small Size. Length: 4 Inches.** *The Keystone Manufacturing Company produced a wide range of sizes of this "S" handle wrench. In all likelihood, there was limited demand for examples in this, the smallest size offered. Those that were sold were most likely found impractical and discarded. Whatever the case, these small wrenches are extremely rare and much sought after by knowledgeable wrench collectors.* (GOOD+) **$325.00**

W3-17. **Baxter, William, Newark, N.J.: 12 Inch Baxter Patent Wrench. Double Nut Wrench. Schulz No. 462. Length: 8 1/2 Inches.** *This unmarked double-end wrench was produced under the second of three patents granted to New Jersey inventor William Baxter for adjustable, double-end wrenches. An excellent example in fine working order.* (FINE) **$115.00**

W3-18. **Mossberg, Frank No. 74: Bicycle Monkey Wrench. Screw Adjust With Sleeve. Schulz No. 870. Length: 4 1/2 Inches.** *A somewhat heavier duty version of the Frank Mossberg's more common bicycle wrenches, this one is clearly imprinted with the maker name and number designation. A good one.* (FINE) **$55.00**

W3-19. **Efficient Wrench Co., Cleveland, Ohio: "The Efficient" Wrench. Rack Adjust Type. Rare and Excellent. Length: 7 Inches.** *The genius of the "efficient" wrench is a gear rack cut into the back of the shaft that allows positive adjustment of its "alligator" type jaws in the precise position necessary to mangle a piece of pipe. Another stupid idea incarnated as a wrench.* (GOOD+) **$155.00**

W3-20. **Unmarked: Cast Iron Buggy Wrench. With Lever Handle. Wing Nut Adjust. Length: 9 1/2 Inches.** *Unlike any carriage wrench we have previously encountered, this double buggy and nut wrench employs an oversize wing nut to facilitate adjustment of the dual jaws. A cast iron "spinner" would facilitate loosening of the wheel nut. Most unusual.* (GOOD+) **$385.00**

W3-21. **Diamond Wrench Co., Portland, Maine: Patent Carriage Wrench. Patented October 16, 1883. Smallest Size. Length: 5 1/2 Inches.** *This, the smallest size of the Diamond combination carriage and nut wrench, is imprinted with the 1883 patent date. A nice example of a rare wrench.* (GOOD+) **$145.00**

W3-22. **Diamond Tool And Horseshoe Co.: 18 Inch "Monkey" Wrench. New Old Stock. Most Unusual. Size. Length: 18 Inches.** *This was apparently the largest size "monkey" wrench offered by the folks at the Diamond Tool Company in Minnesota. It has never been used. Mint.* (FINE) **$35.00**

W3-23. **H. & E. Wrench Co., New Bedford, Mass.: Slide Adjust Pipe Wrench. Patented March 27, 1923. Near-New Condition. Length: 13 Inches.** *A worm gear drive screw activated by the steel band around the body of the wrench was the resident work of genius on this patented wrench. Different.* (FINE) **$95.00**

W3-24. **Unmarked: Early Patented Bicycle Wrench. Patented March 26, 1895. Early and Excellent. Length: 6 Inches.** *Only the patent date is imprinted on this perfectly preserved early bicycle wrench, which retains nearly all of its original plating. A rare bicycle wrench in top condition.* (FINE) **$115.00**

W3-25. **Toledo Plow Co.: Cast Iron Plow Wrench. 3/4 Inch and 1 Inch. Uncommon Brand. Length: 10 Inches.** *Never having found the need to adjust a plow, we have no way of knowing whether or not the specialized wrenches included with nearly every piece of agricultural equipment ever produced added any improvement in functionality. What we do know is that these wrenches have become much sought-after by the "one of each" crowd. This one is just a bit different.* (GOOD) **$45.00**

W3-26. **Keystone Mfg. Co., Buffalo, N.Y.: Patent Ratchet Wrench. Patented November. 6, 1883. Excellent Working Order. Length: 9 Inches.** *One of the earliest attempts at producing a practical ratchet wrench, the "Keystone" patent of 1883 employed adjustable jaws, rather than the interchangeable sockets that were to become the standard. Clean, clearly marked and ready to fill out a wrench collection.* (GOOD) **$75.00**

W3-27. **Unmarked: Early Forged Iron Wrench. With Twist Handle. Uncommon Type. Length: 9 1/2 Inches.** *This screw adjust nut wrench has a decidedly early look. A bend in the shaft could be easily straightened by the new owner, if desired.* (GOOD) **$35.00**

W3-28. **Walden, Worcester, Mass.: Early Patent Ratchet Wrench. Patented July 20, 1900. Uncommon Type. Length: 9 Inches.** *The early days of automobiles produced a wide range of specialty wrenches, including this fixed ratchet wrench from the Walden Wrench Company of Worcester, Massachusetts, a principal maker of early automotive tools.* (GOOD) **$25.00**

W3-29. **Coes Wrench Co.: 4 5/8 Inch Nut Wrench. Bulbous Metal Handle. Most Unusual. Length: 4 1/2 Inches.** *While the cast metal handle on this Coes nut wrench appears to be an owner modification, it has been so well executed as to leave open the possibility that it was produced that way at the factory. Different.* (GOOD+) **$85.00**

W3-30. **Bemis & Call Co., Springfield, Mass.: 6 Inch S-Handle Pipe Wrench. Rare Type and Size. Similar to Schulz No. 860. Length: 6 Inches.** *In an effort to add increased functionality to their line of "S" handle wrenches, the Bemis & Call Company added an "alligator type" pipe jaw feature that could not have worked well in practical applications. A rare pipe wrench in excellent condition.* (GOOD+) **$85.00**

W3-31. **Diamond Tool And Horseshoe Co.: 12 Inch "Crescent" Wrench. Forged Steel Type. Ready to Use. Length: 12 Inches.** *In addition to their line of horseshoe caulk wrenches, the Diamond Tool Company also tried its hand at the production of "Crescent" type wrenches. This example is in new condition.* (FINE) **$15.00**

W3-32. **Coes & Co., A.G, Worcester, Mass.: Screw Adjust Nut Wrench. Patented March 6, 1866. Rare Early Patent. Length: 10 Inches.** *This early product of the Coes Company is imprinted with only a single patent mark. Early and unusual.* (GOOD+) **$115.00**

W3-33. **Griplock, Norfolk, Nebraska: "Griplock" Plier Wrench. Patented January 22, 1924. Schulz No. 261. Length: 7 Inches.** *Looking not unlike a not particularly happy arranged marriage between a nutcracker and a shock absorber, this early precursor of the "Vise Grip" wrench has found favor with collectors of wrenches, but apparently not with the tool buying public.* (GOOD+) **$65.00**

W3-34. **Bemis & Call Co., Springfield, Mass. No. 75: Crescent Type Wrench. With Straight Handle. Uncommon Style. Length: 6 Inches.** *Bemis & Call manufactured a wide range of tools of every sort. This is the first example of this wrench that we have seen. A good one.* (GOOD+) **$55.00**

W3-35. **Reinhard-Mc Cabe Co., Minneapolis No. 1 C: Lever Adjust Wrench. "Pat. Pend". Uncommon Type. Length: 10 Inches.** *In the days before the "Vise Grip" wrench joined the hammer and duct tape as the Three Universal Tools, a number of wannabes appeared on the scene, including this lever locking dandy from a Minnesota maker. An uncommon universal plier wrench.* (GOOD+) **$45.00**

W3-36. **Lorain Wrench Co.: "Gates' Bull" Wrench. Patented February 15, 1887. Schulz No. 391. Length: 10 Inches.** *This example of the "Gates' Bull" wrench is clearly marked with the patent date on the lower jaw. An uncommon quick adjust wrench.* (GOOD+) **$145.00**

W3-37. **Diamond Tool And Horseshoe Co.: 11 Inch "Monkey" Wrench. New Old Stock. All Original Finish. Length: 11 Inches.** *Nearly all of the original finish remains on this classic "monkey" wrench from a principal American wrench maker.* (FINE) **$15.00**

W3-38. **Hall Co., The Chas. E., Buffalo, N. Y. No. 15: Dual Function Nut Wrench. With Hook End. Full Nickel Plating. Length: 7 Inches.** *Pondering about the potential purpose of the pointed tip on this most unusual wrench gave rise to memories of a friend who worked as a tour guide in one of the local wineries during summer breaks from college. At the end of the tour, guests were seated in a great hall for a tasting. Arrayed on the wall behind the guide, whose purpose it was to direct the tasting, was an extensive display of the corkscrews used to open wine and champagne bottles. Many of these knives were equipped with brushes to remove the sediment from the neck of the bottle. It would invariably happen that one of the tourists would ask my friend why the corkscrews were equipped with brushes. He would smile, utter a reassuring "good question!" to the guest, and then launch into a well-rehearsed dissertation about how it was necessary for wine to "breathe" after being decanted. Fair enough. The story then continued that it had been discovered that the appropriate time for this aeration to take place had been determined to be roughly equal to the time it took a man to shave in Nineteenth Century America. The brush, he would recount, with a completely straight face, was there so that the man could lather up and attend to personal grooming while waiting for the wine to be ready to serve. The sandal and Bermuda-clad guests would make note of this most interesting fact and depart, content that they were somewhat wiser about the ways and workings of olden times. Who knows to what extent the "facts" shared during the wine tasting were recounted as the Gospel Truth in a geometric progression of ignorance that likely continues today. The point of all this is, from the perspective of the student of wrenches, to accept information tentatively, and verify whenever possible. Know-it-all's usually don't. A great wrench fitted on one end with an avocado pit extractor.* (GOOD+) **$110.00**

W3-39. **Unmarked: Quick Adjust Nut Wrench. With Thumb Adjust. Uncommon Type. Length: 8 Inches.** *The spring activated lower jaw on this innovative wrench can be moved into position with the thumb of the operator. An uncommon wrench.* (FINE) **$25.00**

W3-40. **Whitman & Barnes: Early Patent Pipe Wrench. Patented May 19, 1891. Double Lower Jaw. Length: 9 Inches.** *The patent feature of this early pipe wrench appears to be a "double" lower jaw that could be rotated when the serrations on one edge had been sufficiently mangled as to be incapable of doing further damage to pipe. The patent drawings show it to have been the brainchild of one F.S. Cook of Jamestown, New York.* (GOOD+) **$35.00**

W3-41. **Gesch, E.S., Germany: "Elite" Double Nut Wrench. With Magazine Handle. Uncommon Type. Length: 6 1/2 Inches.** *German engineering may be the reason for the incorporation of a receptacle in the handle of this unusual double adjust wrench from Germany. Most unusual.* (GOOD+) **$45.00**

W3-42. **Bryan Plow: Bryan Plow Wrench. Multiple Sizes. Unusual Maker. Length: 10 Inches.** *This classic implement wrench incorporates a total of five openings into a single wrench casting. While not documented in the owner's manual, these tools could easily be converted, by a frustrated plow owner, into a percussion tool or aerial projectile. This one seems to have escaped the conversion process. An uncommon implement wrench.* (GOOD) **$55.00**

W3-43. **Vandegrift Mfg. Co., Shelbyville No. 11: Quick Adjust Nut Wrench. Wedge Lock Adjustment. Schulz No. 546. Length: 8 Inches.** *These are generally not marked, as is the case with this cast iron wrench, but research has revealed this to be the output of the Vandegrift Wrench Company of Shelbyville, Indiana. A wood handled model was also manufactured. This one is in excellent working order. A good one.* (GOOD) **$55.00**

W3-44. **Joy, A.P., Rockingham, N.H.: Adjustable Buggy Wrench. Patented February 1, 1898. Schulz No. 221. Length: 10 Inches.** *The A.P. Joy Company made this functional wrench which was apparently quite popular. A good working example.* (GOOD+) **$45.00**

W3-45. **Walworth & Co., Boston: Pivot Jaw Pipe Wrench. Unusual Type. Precision Adjust. Length: 12 Inches.** *As the marketers of the highly successful "Stillson" wrench, which was destined to become the standard for pipe wrenches, one would have thought that the Walworth Wrench Company would have stayed with the tried and true. However, this innovative sliding nut wrench offers evidence that this was not the case. Apparently the wrench buyers of the time preferred the "Stillson" type. These are rare.* (GOOD) **$55.00**

Group X3

X3-1. Norton, S.S., Colchester, Conn.: Boxwood and Brass Marking Gauge. With Graduations. Brass Wear Strips. Length: 8 Inches. *The marking gauges of S.S. Norton are distinguished by the bold styling of the numbers and the general high quality of the tool. This is a classic example.* (GOOD+) **$110.00**

X3-2. Unmarked: Boxwood Mortise Marking Gauge. Unique Head Scribe. Utellme. Length: 4 Inches. *A short stemmed boxwood gauge with an adjustable scribe fitted inside of the head of the gauge. The head mounted gauge is adjusted with a screwdriver. Very different.* (GOOD) **$125.00**

X3-3. Kenney: "Kenney's Patent" Marking Gauge. Patented January 4, 1870. Complete and Excellent. Length: 9 Inches. *A spectacular example of the Kenney Patent marking gauge and trammel combination tool. This one is complete with both the rosewood and boxwood head and all parts are in working order. The central screw is missing, but this set is otherwise in excellent condition.* (GOOD+) **$595.00**

X3-4. Stanley Rule & Level No. 73: Boxwood Marking Gauge. Rare "Stanley" Mark. Superb Condition. Length: 6 Inches. *Finding the No. 73 gauge with a "Stanley" mark, or even the number mark is almost impossible. This one has both and is in superb condition.* (FINE) **$215.00**

X3-5. Stanley Rule & Level No. 64 1/4: Rare Beechwood Marking Gauge. 1911-1917 Only. Rare and Excellent. Length: 8 Inches. *These were listed in the Stanley catalog for a very brief period preceding the First World War. At that point they disappeared from the catalog, and from everywhere else for that matter. This is only the second example of which I am aware. As rare as turkey teeth.* (GOOD+) **$550.00**

X3-6. Unmarked: Brass Faced Mahogany Slitting Gauge. With Boxwood Screw. Superb Condition. Length: 8 1/2 Inches. *No markings on this very well constructed marking gauge that appears to be of English manufacture. The mahogany head and body are nicely complemented by a carved boxwood fixing screw. Unfortunately, we can't offer a reference book on marking gauges and their many makers.* (GOOD+) **$65.00**

X3-7. Wheatcroft, I,, New York, N.Y.: Brass Faced Boxwood Marking Gauge. With Mortise Slide. Extra Rare Mark. Length: 8 Inches. *This one has some wear to the head, but is offered as a significant historical find. The I. Wheatcroft mark most likely has some connection to the Wheatcroft brothers of New Jersey and New York City. A rarity.* (GOOD) **$115.00**

X3-8. Unmarked: Multi Scribe Butt Marking Gauge. Beechwood and Brass. Patented February 23, 1886. Length: 4 Inches. *Complete, nicely patinated and clearly marked, this early marking gauge is in top collector quality condition.* (FINE) **$165.00**

X3-9. Unmarked: Precision Adjust Marking Gauge. Unusual Locking Mechanism. Rosewood Head. Length: 10 Inches. *Everything about this most unusual rosewood marking gauge says that it was a manufactured tool except for the fact that nothing about it, at least in writing, says that it was a manufactured tool. A well made scribe from an unknown maker.* (FINE) **$145.00**

X3-10. Stanley Rule & Level No. 92: Rosewood and Brass Marking Gauge. " Pat. Pending". Superb Condition. Length: 9 1/2 Inches. *As nice an example of Stanley's No. 92 butt and mortise gauge as we have offered. This one has a bold "Patent Pending" stamp on the head of the gauge.* (FINE) **$165.00**

X3-11. Nester: "Nester's Patent" Marking Gauge. Patented December 31, 1867. Rare and Excellent. Length: 12 Inches. *This example of the Nester's Patent clapboard gauge has been cleaned and is ready to display. An excellent example of a rare, early marking gauge.* (GOOD+) **$475.00**

X3-12. Unmarked: Classic English Marking Gauge. Rosewood and Brass. Near New Condition. Length: 6 1/2 Inches. *Comprised of a cast brass frame stuffed with exotic wood, these English gauges were locked into place with a slotted screwdriver. A classic jointer's tool in excellent condition.* (FINE) **$115.00**

X3-13. Unmarked: Pattern and Casting For Marking Gauge. From Pattern Shop. Rare Combination. Length: 8 Inches. *We have seen quite a few panel gauges that were cast or made from mahogany in a patternmaker's shop, but this it the first gauge head and pattern combination we have been privileged to offer. An interesting combination.* (FINE) **$125.00**

X3-14. Unmarked: "Grasshopper" Marking Gauge. Marked "1" and "2". Early and Uncommon. Length: 8 Inches. *This gauge was apparently marked to keep the parts in the right slots. A classic early gauge with a dark patina of age and use.* (GOOD) **$25.00**

X3-15. Jones & Co, S. A., Hartford, Conn.: Boxwood Mortise and Marking Gauge. Full Brass Face. Nicely Marked. Length: 7 1/2 Inches. *This darkly patinated boxwood gauge is boldly struck with the S.A. Jones name. An excellent early gauge.* (GOOD+) **$95.00**

X3-16. Marples & Co., William, Sheffield: Solid Rosewood Marking Gauge. Brass Mortise Slide. Original Decal. Length: 8 1/2 Inches. *A clean and early rosewood marking gauge from William Marples. Most of the original decal remains. Nice.* (GOOD) **$55.00**

X3-17. Vinall, J.J., Cleveland, O.: Classic Clapboard Marking Gauge. With Planemaker Imprint. Extra Rare. Length: 9 1/2 Inches. *Directories for the City of Cleveland indicate that an English-born J.J. Vinall was employed at planemaking there for approximately 10 years in the 1840's and 1850's. Planes with the Vinall mark are extremely rare. Among marking gauges, manufactured clapboard gauges are scarce. Those marked with the name of a documented planemaker are practically unheard of. This one is boldly struck with the J.J. Vinall imprint. A great early gauge in superb condition.* (GOOD+) **$975.00**

X3-18. Watts, G: Boxwood Mortise and Marking Gauge. Slide Adjustment. Graphic Form. Length: 7 Inches. *"G. Watts", stamped in a very stylized manner is the only marking on this most unusual gauge. The central shaft is fitted with a circular wooden slide to regulate the scribing of mortises. A most unusual and appealing marking gauge.* (GOOD+) **$195.00**

X3-19. Stanley Rule & Level No. 77: Rosewood Mortise and Marking Gauge. Unused Condition. Rare Stanley Mark. Length: 6 1/2 Inches. *All original finishes remain on this perfectly preserved example of Stanley's extra-high quality rosewood mortise gauge. As nice an example of this desirable gauge as we have ever offered. Mint.* (FINE) **$145.00**

X3-20. Stanley Rule & Level (Unmarked) No. 85 1/2: Rosewood Panel Marking Gauge. Patented August 5, 1873. Excellent Condition. Length: 21 Inches. *This one is not marked, but the patent date and style of manufacture make it a certainty that this is Stanley's No. 85 1/2 panel gauge. A nice example.* (GOOD+) **$95.00**

X3-21. Phillips (Unmarked): "Phillips' Patent" Marking Gauge. Patented January 15, 1867. Rare and Excellent. Length: 9 Inches. *Here's a clean and complete example of the 1867 Phillips patent that is clearly imprinted with the patent date. A good one.* (FINE) **$185.00**

X3-22. Star Tool Company: Cam Lock Boxwood Marking Gauge. Patented April 21, 1868. Rare Boxwood Example. Length: 8 1/2 Inches. *Much less common than the standard non-mortise scribe equipped version also offered by this maker, this gauge features an adjustable mortise scribe. The head is locked into place by twisting it against the cam-shaped beam. Nearly every example of this rare gauge that we have observed was made of rosewood. This boxwood example is an order of magnitude less common than any Star gauge we have ever offered. Extra rare.* (GOOD+) **$345.00**

X3-23. Stanley Rule & Level No. 70 1/2: Handled Slitting Marking Gauge. Complete and Excellent. A Rare Gauge. Length: 8 1/2 Inches. *These handled slitting gauges apparently found little favor among woodworkers. This is only the third example of this elusive tool that we have had the opportunity to offer for sale. A seriously underrated collectible.* (GOOD+) **$265.00**

X3-24. Unmarked: Patent Rosewood Marking Gauge. Patented January 14, 1873. Cam-Lock Mechanism. Length: 8 Inches. *At first glance, this early patent marking gauge appears to be an example of the cam-lock gauge offered by the Star Tool Company. Upon closer inspection, however, the mechanism is revealed to be altogether different. An eccentric insert on the inside of the head is engaged by turning the beam to lock the tool precisely into place. A series of inlaid brass disks serve as wear plates to protect the working surface. A rare, early and very well made patented marking gauge.* (FINE) **$265.00**

X3-25. Scholl, C. No. 268: Rosewood 3 Stem Marking Gauge. Patented March 8, 1864. Rare "No." Marking. Length: 8 Inches. *This most interesting and unusual example of the C. Scholl patent marking gauge is also marked "No. 268". Given that there was no "Scholl Tool Company" we are led to suspect that the Scholl's patent may have been produced by a major manufacturer. The presence of circular inset wear plates on some known examples, plates that are nearly identical to those found on gauges produced by Hermon Chapin at his "Union Factory", lead one to suspect that the Scholl's patent was marketed and distributed by H. Chapin for C. Scholl. A great gauge in top collector-quality condition.* (FINE) **$445.00**

X3-26. Curtis, F., Stockbridge, Mass.: Boxwood and Brass Marking Gauge. Decorative Knurls. Early and Uncommon. Length: 8 Inches. *The Western Massachusetts Village of Stockbridge seems initially to have been an unlikely location for a toolmaker in that it is situated far from any major population centers. However, in the 1830's and 1840's, when this tool was likely made, the Connecticut river, which passed through Western Massachusetts, was a major artery for commerce. Little is known of Curtis, other than that he produced quality marking gauges and imprinted them with a stylized eagle touchmark in keeping with the spirit of those revolutionary times. This well made gauge is nicely inlaid with brass and ornamented with a hand-filed locking screw and decoratively turned adjustment screw. A nice gauge from an uncommon early maker.* (GOOD+) **$125.00**

X3-27. Unmarked: Multiple Adjust Marking Gauge. Similar to Marsden. With Slitting Feature. Length: 7 1/2 Inches. *This gauge is very similar to Marsden, and may in fact be an earlier type. This one is fitted with a wedge-lock slitting scribe above the fence. Very different.* (GOOD+) **$195.00**

X3-28. Auxer & Remley, Lancaster, Penn.: Rosewood and Boxwood Marking Gauge. Carpenter Style. Superb Condition. Length: 8 1/2 Inches. *One glance at this tool immediately brings to mind one thing: "E.W. Carpenter". Samuel Auxer billed himself as the "successor to E.W. Carpenter". This magnificent gauge leaves no doubt that that succession came because of a perception that the quality of the work would continue at the high Carpenter Standard. Boldly marked, aesthetically magnificent and historically significant, this superb gauge is one of the treasures that tool collecting yields all too infrequently.* (FINE) **$695.00**

X3-29. Wheatcroft, Geo., Newark, N.J.: Boxwood and Brass Marking Gauge. Precision Graduation. Full Brass Face. Length: 8 Inches. *A nice boxwood mortise gauge from George Wheatcroft, a Newark maker noted for exceptionally well made gauges. Nice.* (GOOD+) **$145.00**

X3-30. Unmarked: Rosewood and Brass Marking Gauge. Screw Adjust Scribe. Cast Brass Sleeve. Length: 7 Inches. *There are no maker markings on this heavy and mechanically perfect rosewood and brass gauge. A good one.* (GOOD+) **$125.00**

X3-31. Stanley Rule & Level No. 77: Rosewood Mortise and Marking Gauge. With Brass Facing. Ready to Use. Length: 7 Inches. *Stanley kept this rosewood mortise gauge in their product line long after many of their specialy gauges had disappeared from their product line. This one is in clean and ready to use condition.* (GOOD+) **$55.00**

X3-32. Lyon, D.M., Newark, N.J.: Boxwood Mortise and Marking Gauge. Full Brass Face. With Graduations. Length: 8 Inches. *This brass-faced gauge is in collector quality condition, clean and clearly marked. Circa 1860. Ready to use or display.* (GOOD+) **$85.00**

X3-33. Carpenter, E.W., Lancaster, Penn.: Beechwood Mortise and Marking Gauge. Fitted Wooden Slide. Clearly Marked. Length: 8 Inches. *Lancaster, Pennsylvania planemaker E.W. Carpenter had a distinctive style that has attracted a number of collectors. This gauge is boldly marked with his imprint.* (GOOD+) **$125.00**

X3-34. Marples & Co., William, Sheffield No. 1598: "Registered" Marking Gauge. "Spring Lane" Marked Registered March 23, 1818. Length: 7 Inches. *The closest English equivalent to the patent markings that seem to be found on nearly every American tool, "Registered" English tools are far, far less common. This most unusual gauge from the William Marples Company is imprinted with the Registration date of March 23, 1818. Early and near-new.* (FINE) **$495.00**

X3-35. Phillips: Early Patent Marking Gauge. Patented January 15, 1867. Rare Boxwood Body. Length: 9 Inches. *Very few examples of the Phillips patent gauge are known with boxwood beams. This one is clean and clearly marked. Rare.* (GOOD+) **$245.00**

X3-36. Stanley Rule & Level No. 80: Rare Boxwood Marking Gauge. Patented October 22, 1872. Extra Crisp and Clean. Length: 6 1/2 Inches. *Included in the Stanley product line for a short period of less than 30 years, the No. 80 boxwood mortise gauge was discontinued in 1897. This example is marked with the 1872 patent date of Justus Traut, which applied to the "moustache" face plate. A rare Stanley marking gauge.* (GOOD+) **$255.00**

X3-37. Scholl, C.: 3 Stem Patent Marking Gauge. Patented March 8, 1864. Mahogany Body, Arms. Length: 8 Inches. *The equivalent, in mahogany to the rosewood 3 stem gauge, this one is clean and clearly marked with the patent date and maker name.* (GOOD+) **$345.00**

X3-38. Unmarked: Screw Lock Rosewood Marking Gauge. Extra Crisp and Clean. Hand Graduated. Length: 8 1/2 Inches. *No marks on this one, but the head of the gauge has a striking pattern of color. A beautiful tool.* (FINE) **$55.00**

X3-39. Unmarked: Boxwood and Lignum Marking Gauge. 11 3/4 Inch O. A. L. Superb Patina. Length: 11 3/4 Inches. *This dramatic gauge has a boxwood head and a lignum vitae beam. The color contrast is most appealing to the eye.* (FINE) **$95.00**

X3-40. Phillips: Patented Mortise Marking Gauge. Patented January 15, 1867. Excellent Condition. Length: 9 Inches. *In addition to the double sliding brass stops, this example also has the mortise slide. Complete, early and well-marked.* (FINE) **$285.00**

X3-41. Stanley Rule & Level No. 62: Beech and Boxwood Marking Gauge. "Sweetheart" Trademark. Unused Condition. Length: 9 Inches. *Nicely marked with the classic "Sweetheart" logo, this uncommon Stanley gauge is in new condition. Mint.* (FINE) **$85.00**

X3-42. Stanley Rule & Level No. 77: Rosewood Mortise and Marking Gauge. Sweetheart Trademark. Near New Condition. Length: 7 Inches. *A perfectly preserved example of Stanley's mainstay rosewood mortise gauge. Extra clean and clearly marked.* (FAIR) **$85.00**

X3-43. Unmarked: Early Patent Marking Gauge. Adjustable Bronze Face. Patented October 20, 1890. Length: 9 Inches. *The maker mark is not listed on this one but the patent date is clearly marked on the complex bronze adjusting head. Absolutely brand new. A rare patented marking gauge.* (FINE) **$550.00**

X3-44. Phillips, J., Cincinnati, O.: Rosewood Mortise Marking Gauge. Superb Craftsmanship. Excellent Condition. Length: 8 3/4 Inches. *Early, extraordinarily well made and in super condition, this gauge from an obscure Mid-Western maker is an example of the highest level of the tool maker's art. The steep spiral knurling at the base of the fixing and mortise screws is evidence of pre-Civil War manufacture. A sweetheart.* (FINE) **$395.00**

X3-45. Unmarked: Rosewood and Brass Marking Gauge. Solid Brass Head. With Mortise Slide. Length: 10 Inches. *This classic mortise gauge with solid, cast-brass head is in excellent condition, either for use or as a collectible.* (GOOD+) **$145.00**

Group Y3

Y3-1. Stanley Rule & Level No. 25M: Set of "Matched" Screwdrivers. With Golf Logo. New Condition, Original Box. Length: 11 Inches. *The inside of the box for these most unusual "matched" screwdrivers features a golfing illustration. A great set.* (FINE) **$295.00**

Y3-2. Millers Falls Company No. 850: Phillips Head Screwdriver. # 4 Size, 8 Inch Blade. New Condition, Original Box. Length: 14 1/2 Inches. *The Phillips head design is a very recent innovation. I would guess that this "Permaloid"-handled screwdriver dates from the 1950's. Brand new in its original box.* (FINE) **$45.00**

Y3-3. Unmarked: Patent Double End Screwdriver. Patented July 2, ????. Uncommon Type. Length: 9 Inches. *The year of the patent date on this double head screwdriver is not legible, but it looks to date from 1900, or thereabout. Never seen another.* (GOOD+) **$65.00**

Y3-4. Stanley Tools No. 130 A: Spiral Ratchet Screwdriver. "Yankee" Trademark. New Condition, Original Box. Length: 18 Inches. *These automatic screwdrivers were a standard tool in many trades until the advent of the electric screwdriver. They have quickly made the transition from obsolescence to collectibility. Extra crisp and clean.* (FINE) **$45.00**

Y3-5. North Bros Mfg. Co., Philadelphia. No. 95: "Yankee" Slotted Screwdriver. 6 1/2 Inch Blade. Unused Condition. Length: 10 Inches. *This early "Yankee" screwdriver is in brand new condition. A nice example of a very well made screwdriver.* (FINE) **$35.00**

Y3-6. Unmarked: Early Beech Handle Screwdriver. Classic Form. Excellent Condition. Length: 5 Inches. *Back when screwdrivers like this were being used, they were called "turnscrews". Now they're called rare.* (GOOD+) **$15.00**

Y3-7. Smith Co., The H.D.: "Perfect Handle" Screwdriver. "Triple Lever". Crisp and Clean. Length: 9 Inches. *These could be adjusted to be used in any position except one that was comfortable. A nice example of an uncommon perfect handle tool. A good one.* (GOOD+) **$125.00**

Y3-8. Disston & Son, Henry, Philadelphia, Penn.: Hardened Steel Burnisher. Beechwood Handle. Unused Condition. Length: 9 Inches. *If you're looking for a high quality burnisher for use on scraper blades and the like, you won't find it at the hardware store. A high quality product from the Disston hand-saw folks. Brand new.* (FINE) **$15.00**

Y3-9. Stanley Rule & Level No. 1001: "100 Plus" Screwdriver. 5 Inch Blade. "Sweetheart" Trademark. Length: 11 1/2 Inches. *Here's a most uncommon Stanley "100 Plus" screwdriver that is imprinted with the "Sweetheart" trademark.* (GOOD+) **$65.00**

Y3-10. North Bros. Mfg. Co. No. 20: Reciprocating Archimedian Drill. Patented October 3, 1911. Removable Jaw. Length: 15 1/2 Inches. *Among the rarest most desirable of all of the North Brothers line of "Yankee" tools, this most unusual variation on their standard archimedian drill was fitted with a removable drill chuck which could be replaced by a screwdriver blade. We have not observed another example. It is in excellent mechanical condition.* (GOOD+) **$445.00**

Y3-11. Decatur Coffin Co., Decatur, Il: Patented Spiral Ratchet Screwdriver. Patented October 7, 1884. Uncommon Type. Length: 9 1/2 Inches. *I'll repeat the story only if you don't quote me as the source: Legend has it that these spiral screwdrivers only turn screws in one direction because they were marketed by the Decatur Coffin Company and you only turn screws in one direction when dealing with coffin lids. An uncommon screwdriver that is clearly marked with the patent date. Nice.* (GOOD+) **$45.00**

Y3-12. Unmarked: Spiral Twist Screwdriver. Hand Forged Type. Uncommon Form. Length: 12 Inches. *Made to be just a bit different, this early screwdriver was evenly heated and then twisted into its current form. There are no marks, but it certainly looks manufactured. Never seen another.* (GOOD+) **$85.00**

Y3-13. Shelton: Multi Blade Screwdriver. Similar to Billings Patent. New Condition, Original Box. Length: 4 1/2 Inches. *This specialty screwdriver is essentially the same design as that offered by the Billings & Spencer Company 90 years before, except that this one is fitted with a ratchet mechanism. It is in new condition in its original box.* (FINE) **$35.00**

Y3-14. Millers Falls Company No. 1440: Pocket Ratchet Screwdriver. 1 1/2 Inch Blade. Unused Condition. Length: 5 Inches. *Finding ratchet screwdrivers in this condition has become an increasingly difficult task. This one is as good as they get. Perfect.* (FINE) **$55.00**

Y3-15. Unmarked: Set of 11 Assorted Gimlets. From Single Collection. Uncommon Assortment. Length: 4 Inches. *Why one person would have accumulated this many gimlets is a question that will likely never be answered. We are asking that the purchaser of this set write down his reason for so doing lest the same dead end be reached in another few years. A full Clinton dozen. First come, first serve.* (GOOD+) **$15.00**

Y3-16. North Bros Mfg. Co., Philadelphia No. 95: "Yankee" Slotted Screwdriver. 1 1/2 Inch Blade. New Condition, Original Box. Length: 4 Inches. *This extra small "Yankee" screwdriver is in new condition in its original box. Absolutely Mint.* (FINE) **$95.00**

Y3-17. Irwin: "Perfect Handle" Screwdriver. 6 Inch Blade. Apparently Unused. Length: 11 Inches. *The inlaid wood handle style was introduced by the H.D. Smith Company of Plantsville, Connecticut, but was imitated by many others for the simple reason that it was a great idea. This fifty year old example bears the name of the Irwin Auger Bit Company. Brand New.* (FINE) **$55.00**

Y3-18. Howard & Son, F. A., Belfast, Maine: Patented Reverse Spiral Screwdriver. Patented March 1, 1892. Rare Small Size. Length: 7 1/2 Inches. *Perhaps the shipbuilding industry along the Maine coast was responsible for the plethora of patented screwdrivers originating in that area in the last quarter of the 19th century. Simple artistry combined with a mechanically complex form.* (GOOD) **$45.00**

Y3-19. Stanley Rule & Level No. 215: 3 Inch Blade Ratchet Screwdriver. Patented November 24, 1925. Sweetheart Trademark. Length: 8 Inches. *Second only to the flashlight version in the hierarchy of Stanley screwdriver rarity, the No. 200 series ratcheting screwdrivers were fitted with rosewood handles, ratchet mechanisms and marked with the patent date and "Sweetheart" trademark. This one is in great shape.* (FINE) **$125.00**

Y3-20. Shephardson & Co., Shelburne Falls: Multiple Blade Screwdriver. Beech Body. Rare and Excellent. Length: 8 Inches. *A most unusual early variation on the screwdriver theme, this multiple blade tool was likely produced by the the company of the same name who made patented braces in Shelburne Falls, Massachusetts.* (GOOD+) **$285.00**

Y3-21. North Bros Mfg. Co., Philadelphia No. 95: "Yankee" Slotted Screwdriver. 3 1/2 Inch Blade. Unused Condition. Length: 7 1/2 Inches. *Someone apparently set this one away in the back of the workshop and forgot about it. It is in brand new condition.* (FINE) **$35.00**

Y3-22. Callendar & Co., B., Boston, Mass.: Cabinet Maker's Screwdriver. 4 Inch Blade. Most Unusual Type. Length: 9 Inches. *B. Callendar was a hardware & tool dealer in Boston, Massachusetts from 1862 through 1887 who also imprinted wooden planes with the same mark. An uncommon 19th Century screwdriver.* (GOOD) **$85.00**

Y3-23. Millers Falls Company No. 852: 10 Inch Blade Screwdriver. "Permaloid" Handle. New Condition, Original Box. Length: 16 1/2 Inches. *Here's a slotted, square shank screwdriver from the M.F. people. Brand new and in the box.* (FINE) **$35.00**

Y3-24. North Bros Mfg. Co., Phila. No. 27: Industrial Use Screwdriver. For Assembly Work. Rare and Excellent. Length: 15 1/2 Inches. *In addition to its line of tools for carpenters and mechanics, the North Brothers Company offered several industrial assembly tools of which this is an example. Missing some of the lacquer on the handle, this one is otherwise in excellent condition. A mechanically perfect example of a very rare "Yankee" tool.* (GOOD+) **$165.00**

Y3-25. North Bros Mfg. Co., Phila. No. 10: Ratchet Screwdriver. 8 Inch Blade. With "Keeper" Tip. Length: 13 1/2 Inches. *The North Brothers No. 10 screwdriver is rare enough on its own, but this one has the optional screw holder tip. Most unusual.* (GOOD+) **$145.00**

Y3-26. North Bros. Mfg. Co. No. 50: Reciprocating Archimedian Drill. Maroon Head. Original Box. Length: 15 Inches. *The North Bros. Mfg. Co. of Philadelphia made a full line of drills, braces, screwdrivers and other tool specialties before being purchased by Stanley Tools in 1946. Their products are among the best tools ever produced. Knowledgable collectors have long sought out choice examples of the "Yankee" line. The reciprocating archimedian drill offered here illustrates the appeal of the North Bros. tools: It is mechanically complex, precisely machined and artfully finished. New in the original box.* (FINE) **$265.00**

Y3-27. Marples & Sons, Wm., Hibernia Wks.: Boxwood "T" Handle Screwdriver. Uncommon Type. Early Appearance. Length: 5 1/2 Inches. *This English screwdriver is the first we have seen in this pattern. A nicely patinated boxwood handle gives it a most appealing look.* (GOOD+) **$55.00**

Y3-28. Simmons Hardware Co., E.C.: Spiral Ratchet Screwdriver. Patented December 13, 1892. Rosewood Handle. Length: 11 1/2 Inches. *The innards of this unusual ratcheting screwdriver need some fine tuning, but the tool is otherwise in excellent condition and retains nearly all of its original nickel plating. A rare screwdriver.* (GOOD) **$35.00**

Y3-29. Furbish & Hamlin, Augusta, Maine: Early Patent Ratchet Screwdriver. "The Maine Screwdriver." Early and Extra Rare. Length: 10 Inches. *The metal band around the handle of this early screwdriver is marked with the maker name and its designation as the screwdriver of the Pine Tree State.* (GOOD) **$145.00**

Y3-30. Stanley Rule & Level No. 177: Wood Handle Screwdriver. Gold Stanley Name. Scarce and Excellent. Length: 3 Inches. *An unused example of a scarce Stanley screwdriver. The red and black painted handle is marked with the "Stanley" name in gold lettering. Choice.* (FINE) **$35.00**

Y3-31. North Bros. Mfg. Co. No. 15 A: Reverse Ratchet Screwdriver. 4 Inch Blade. Unused Condition. Length: 6 3/4 Inches. *All of the original finishes remain on this crispy clean classic from the North Brothers Tool Company. Mint.* (FINE) **$55.00**

Y3-32. Crescent Tool Co., Jamestown, N.Y.: Folding T Handle Screwdriver. "4 In One". Scarce and Excellent. Length: 7 1/2 Inches. *For convenience, the blades on these screwdrivers would snap back out of the way into the handle. A nice example.* (FINE) **$55.00**

Y3-33. Peck, Stow & Wilcox Co. No. 2: Rare "Solbar" Screwdriver. "Pat. Apl'd For". 2 1/2 Inch Blade. Length: 6 1/2 Inches. *"Solid Bar" was the name of a line of wrenches manufactured by the P.S. & W. Company. This is only the second example of a screwdriver bearing that designation that we have seen. A most unusual screwdriver.* (GOOD+) **$55.00**

Y3-34. Stanley Rule & Level No. 6: "Hurwood" Awl. 3 Inch Point. Original Decal. Length: 6 Inches. *Stanley's "Hurwood" line was an extension of the manufacturing process used to produce their "Everlasting" line of chisels. All "Hurwood" tools had a central steel shaft that went from the tip of the tool to the top of the handle. This awl is in brand new condition.* (FINE) **$65.00**

Y3-35. Stanley Rule & Level: "Hurwood" Slotted Screwdriver. 5 Inch Blade. "Sweetheart" Trademark. Length: 10 1/4 Inches. *Stanley's "Hurwood" line featured tools that were solid steel from the tip to the end of the handle. Here's a well preserved example with an early trademark.* (GOOD+) **$15.00**

Y3-36. Stanley Rule & Level No. 216: 2 Inch Blade Ratchet Screwdriver. Patented November 24, 1925. "Sweetheart" Trademark. Length: 6 Inches. *Stanley's "200" series ratcheting screwdrivers were distinguished by a patented ratchet mechanism and rosewood handles. They were apparently not up to the competition from North Brothers and Millers Falls. A rare Stanley screwdriver.* (FINE) **$135.00**

Y3-37. Smith & Co., H.D., Plantsville, Conn.: Perfect Handled Screwdriver. Rare 1 Inch Size. As-New Condition. Length: 8 Inches. *These could have the handles folded up to serve as a standard screwdriver, or folded down for extra leverage. Rare.* (GOOD) **$145.00**

Y3-38. North Bros Mfg. Co., Phila. No. 95: "Yankee" Slotted Screwdriver. 5 1/2 Inch Blades. Unused Condition. Length: 9 1/2 Inches. *This early "Yankee" screwdriver is in brand new condition. A nice example of a very well made screwdriver.* (FINE) **$35.00**

Y3-39. North Bros. Mfg. Co No. 43: Light Duty Automatic Hand Drill. Rare and Excellent. Original Carton. Length: 9 3/4 Inches. *Among the least common of the North Bros. line, this light duty hand drill is in superb condition in its original box. A very well preserved example.* (GOOD+) **$115.00**

Y3-40. Assorted Makers: Set of 3 Push Drills. Original Tips. P. & C., Millers Falls. Length: 10 1/2 Inches. *Here's a buyer opportunity lot of push drills, including one marked "P. & C.". Different.* (GOOD+) **$45.00**

Y3-41. Stanley Tools No. 20: Set of 6 " Hurwood" Screwdriver. 8 Inch Blades. New Condition, Original Box. Length: 15 Inches. *Here's a full box of Stanley's "top of the line" screwdrivers in brand new condition. An investment.* (FINE) **$155.00**

Y3-42. North Bros Mfg. Co., Philda. No. 135: Spiral Ratchet Screwdriver. All Original Bits. New Condition, Original Box. Length: 12 Inches. *Slightly smaller in size than its seemingly ubiquitous older cousin, the No. 30, examples of the No. 135 are much less common, especially in this kind of condition. Choice.* (FINE) **$55.00**

Y3-43. Assorted Makers: Screwdrivers, Scribe Cutters, Etc. From Single Chest. Ready to Use. Length: 4 Inches. *We are pleased to offer the contents of a single drawer of a tool chest. We are aware of the function of all items except the one on the far right.* (GOOD+) **$15.00**

Y3-44. Irwin Auger Bit Co., Wilmington, O No. 300 S: Set of "Nu Series" Screwdrivers. Set of 5 Tools. New Condition, Original Box. Length: 16 1/2 Inches. *Each of these screwdrivers is in brand new condition. A great set in new condition in the original box.* (FINE) **$65.00**

Y3-45. Reid, A.H., Philadelphia: Archimedian Push Screwdriver. Superb Condition. Patented December 12, 1882. Length: 16 1/2 Inches. *This was the younger brother of the larger Reid patent screwdriver. These are much less common. This one is complete and ready to display.* (GOOD+) **$65.00**

Group Z3

Z3-1. Stanley Rule & Level No. 52: Cast Iron Spoke Shave. "Sweetheart" Trademark. Superb Condition. Length: 9 3/4 Inches. *This classic spokeshave is imprinted with the 1920's era "Sweetheart" logo. An underrated Stanley spokeshave.* (GOOD+) **$75.00**

Z3-2. Stanley Rule & Level No. 66: Patented Scratch Beader. Early Japan Body. Fitted Wood Box. Length: 11 1/2 Inches. *Nearly 99% of the original black japan finish remains on this complete, early example of the No. 66 scratch beader. All original parts, including both fences and six cutters are included in a period wood box. Choice.* (FINE) **$225.00**

Z3-3. Stanley Rule & Level No. 984: Patented Corner Ratchet Brace. Rosewood Handles. "Sweetheart" Trademark. Length: 9 Inches. *Stanley spent only a short time in the corner ratchet brace business before ceding the territory to the electric drill. This is an excellent example of one of the two types of such braces offered by Stanley. Nearly 95% of the original nickel plating remains on this example, which bears the ca. 1920's "Sweetheart" trademark.* (GOOD+) **$155.00**

Z3-4. Stanley Rule & Level No. 36: 12 Inch Cast Iron Level. "Sweetheart" Trademark. Near New Condition. Length: 12 Inches. *Stanley's "Sweetheart" trademark is imprinted on the vial protector of this perfectly preserved cast iron level.* (FINE) **$12.00**

Z3-5. Stanley Rule & Level No. 41: Brass Top Level. With "Stanley" Imprint. Near New Condition. Length: 3 Inches. *Designed for all the Monday to Friday tasks that a working carpenter might devise for it, including, if necessary, being mounted on a try or framing square, this elaborately embossed level comes dressed in its Sunday best. Retaining nearly all of its century-old japan and lacquer finishes, this extraordinary level is as fine an example as we have offered.* (FINE) **$65.00**

Z3-6. Stanley Rule & Level No. 2: Winterbottom's Patented Try Square. Patented June 20, 1869. Scarce and Excellent. Length: 6 Inches. *Stanley purchased the Winterbottom patent to begin the manufacture of these combined try and miter squares. This "Type 1" example is marked with the patent date and in excellent condition for the collector.* (GOOD+) **$125.00**

Z3-7. Stanley Rule & Level No. 40: Cast Iron Patent Level. For Use on a Square. Patented June 23, 1896. Length: 3 Inches. *These cast iron levels for mounting on a framing square or try square are becoming increasingly difficult to find. A nice example.* (GOOD+) **$35.00**

Z3-8. Stanley Rule & Level No. 2: 2 Inch Traut's Patent Try Square. Patented May 26, 1874. Smallest Size Made. Length: 3 Inches. *Produced under an 1874 Justus Traut patent that applied to the means of affixing the blade to the handle, the No. 2 try square was later designated as the No. 12. As is the case with the later No. 12, which featured a nickel-plated body, the version of the No. 2 having a 2 inch blade is by far the rarest of the line. This is the only example of the two inch size of the No. 2 Traut Patent that we have ever offered for sale and only the second example of which we are aware. In excellent collector quality condition and clearly marked with the patent date, this extraordinarily rare and well-preserved square is the sort of tool that makes even the most experienced Stanley collectors utter that reflexive "wow". Wow.* (GOOD+) **$595.00**

Z3-9. Stanley Tools No. 450: "Victor" Soldering Iron. With Holder. New Condition, Original Box. Length: 13 Inches. *You won't find a better example of Stanley's "Victor" soldering iron. New and in the box.* (GOOD+) **$45.00**

Z3-10. Stanley Tools No. 1220: "Defiance" Hand Drill. With Original Decal. Near New Condition. Length: 11 1/2 Inches. *Nearly all original finishes and all of the original decal remain on this uncommon "Defiance" brand drill. Nice.* (FINE) **$85.00**

Z3-11. Stanley Rule & Level No. 22: Dowel Pointer. Full Nickel Plating. Apparently Unused. Length: 3 1/4 Inches. *All original finishes remain on this classic brace-mounted dowel sharpener. A tough tool to find, especially in this condition.* (FINE) **$35.00**

Z3-12. Stanley Tools: Advertising Knife. Sectional Part. Uncommon Type. Length: 6 Inches. *This obscure Stanley knife was produced rather late in Stanley's production, but is the first of its type we have seen. Different.* (FINE) **$15.00**

Z3-13. Stanley Rule & Level No. 25: Rosewood Handle Bevel. Rare 14 Inch Blade. Patented March 16, 1897. Length: 14 Inches. *A nice working bevel in the desirable and hard to find 14 inch size. The rarest of the No. 25 series.* (GOOD+) **$145.00**

Z3-14. Stanley Rule & Level No. 198: Blade Holder and Honer. As-New Condition. Rare and Underrated. Length: 5 Inches. *These specialized tools designed for honing spokeshave irons are among the rarest of the Stanley line. Introduced very late in Stanley's history, and offered for a very few years, from 1936 to 1943, while sales were diminished by the Twin Devils of impending World War and the continuing Roosevelt Depression, it is surprising to find an extant example—especially one in such superb condition. An extremely rare, special-purpose Stanley collectible in pristine condition. Highly recommended.* (FINE) **$255.00**

Z3-15. Stanley Tools No. 42-189: Bakelite Pocket Level. Patent D228942. With Pencil Clip. Length: 5 Inches. *We have no idea when these were produced, but its the first one we have encountered. Most unusual.* (GOOD+) **$45.00**

Z3-16. Stanley Rule & Level (Unmarked.) No. 2: Plumb and Level Try Square. Ca. 1863-1887 Only. Extra Scarce. Length: 9 Inches. *Stanley offered the No. 2 combination try square, plumb and level for a few short years beginning in 1863. Easily recognizable by the distinctive Stanley brass escutcheon, this example is not imprinted with the Stanley name. A rare Stanley tool.* (GOOD) **$295.00**

Z3-17. Stanley Rule & Level No. 18: 8 Inch Blade Bevel. Cast Iron Body. New Condition. Length: 8 Inches. *No apologies whatsoever for this pristine bevel from America's top toolmaker. A great working tool in new condition. Try buying something as nice today and see what you pay.* (FINE) **$55.00**

Z3-18. Stanley Rule & Level No. 5 1/2: Wide Jack Plane Plane. Rosewood Handles. New Condition, Original Box. Length: 14 1/2 Inches. *An excellent example of a Stanley bench plane that is seldom found in its original box. An absolutely immaculate example. All original finishes remain on the body, cap and rosewood handles.* (FINE) **$255.00**

Z3-19. Stanley Rule & Level No. 70: Patented Adjustable Box Scraper. Patented April 4, 1876. Near New Condition. Length: 13 Inches. *Stanley offered this pivoting-head box scraper for more than eighty years, beginning in 1877. This one is marked with the Traut & Richards patent date of April 4, 1876. Condition is nearly new. Nice.* (FINE) **$115.00**

Z3-20. Stanley Rule & Level No. 1: 5 1/2 Inch Smoothing Plane. "Sweetheart" Trademark. As-New Condition. Length: 5 1/2 Inches. *Is there any better way to begin a list consisting entirely of Number 1 tools than with the most popular Number 1 of all time—The Stanley No. 1 Smooth Plane? These diminutive gems were produced beginning in 1867 and remained in the Stanley product line until 1943, when they were "temporarily" discontinued due to wartime exigencies, never again to return to be offered. Tool folklore has it that these tools were designed for the hands of children and marketed to "manual training" schools, where their smaller-than-life proportions would be just about right. For a story so oft-repeated, there seems to be no documentary evidence to support the claim that these were intended largely or solely for this specialized market. Whatever the case, the legend continues that these tools were sold in large numbers, but all but a very few were consumed during the scrap metal drives of the First and Second World Wars. This one seems to have escaped the years with practically no battle scars. Only a slight sliver of rosewood missing from the side of the top of the tote. Imprinted with the "Sweetheart" trademark that Stanley used from 1922 to 1933, this plane retains more than 99% of its orginal black japan finish. An exceptionally well-preserved example in collector-quality condition.* (FINE) **$1,645.00**

Z3-21. Stanley Rule & Level No. 60: Concave, Convex Spoke Shave. 1 1/2 Inch Cutters. New Condition, Original Box. Length: 11 Inches. *This convex and straight-blade shave was produced shortly after the end of World War II and is marked with the "notched rectangle" trademark. Perfect.* (FINE) **$125.00**

Z3-22. Stanley Rule & Level No. 1: Wood Level Sights. Patented May 7, 1889. Extra Crisp and Clean. Length: 2 Inches. *Designed to be mounted on either end of a wooden level to allow that tool to function as a surveyor's level, these sights are in nearly new condition.* (FINE) **$45.00**

Z3-23. Stanley Rule & Level No. 49: Auger Bit Depth Gauge. Nickel Plated Finish. New Condition, Original Box. Length: 2 1/2 Inches. *This auger bit depth stop from Stanley has been protected through the years by its original pasteboard box. All original nickel plating remains.* (FINE) **$35.00**

Z3-24. Stanley Rule & Level No. 31: Hexagonal Machinist' Level. Ca. 1915. Near New Condition. Length: 3 1/2 Inches. *All of the original nickel plating remains on this hexagonal pocket level from Stanley. A tough level to find, especially in this condition.* (FINE) **$55.00**

Z3-25. Stanley Rule & Level No. 61: Two Foot, Four Fold Folding Rule. Full Box of 6. New Condition, Original Box. Length: 24 Inches. *All of the original six No. 61 rules remain in this original box. Full boxes of folding rules are becoming nearly impossible to find.* (FINE) **$295.00**

Z3-26. Stanley Rule & Level No. 2: Three Angle Rule Tool. Patented August 8, 1911. 1911-1935 Only. Length: 2 1/2 Inches. *Designed to fit onto a standard carpenter's rule, this patented gizmo was produced under a 1911 patent granted to W.H. Stanley. This is as nice an example of this rare tool as we have seen. Mint.* (FINE) **$295.00**

Z3-27. Stanley Tools No. 41: "Yankee 100 Plus" Push Drill. With Magazine Handle. 6 Original Bits. Length: 10 Inches. *The Stanley "Yankee" No. 41 was the first choice of those who used these tools a lot. Still a great working tool. Six original bits remain.* (FINE) **$25.00**

Z3-28. Stanley Rule & Level No. 1299: "Defiance" Carpenter Knife. Cast Iron Body. Unused Condition. Length: 4 1/4 Inches. *Stanley's newer carpenters' knives are no match for these cast iron workaday tools. A nice example.* (FINE) **$35.00**

Z3-29. Stanley Rule & Level No. 386: Adjustable Cast Iron Jointer Gauge. Rosewood Handle. Ready to Use. Length: 11 Inches. *Stanley's jointer gauge was a great seller for 60 years for the simple reason that it was the best there was. This one is complete and is in excellent working order* (GOOD+) **$145.00**

Z3-30. Stanley Rule & Level No. 30: Carpenter's Plumb and Level. Dual Brass Plumbs. Cleaned and Polished. Length: 30 Inches. *These levels are easily recognized by their dual circular brass-faced plumb vials. This early example has been cleaned and is ready to display.* (GOOD+) **$65.00**

Z3-31. Stanley Rule & Level: Rosewood Leather Burnisher. Rare "Stanley" Mark. Superb Condition. Length: 5 Inches. *A most unusual rosewood leather burnisher clearly imprinted with the mark "Stanley Rule & Level Co." Quite possibly added to the Stanley line as a wartime exigency during the First World War. A rare Stanley tool.* (FINE) **$125.00**

Z3-32. Stanley Rule & Level No. 77: Rosewood Mortise and Marking Gauge. "Sweetheart" Trademark. Near New Condition. Length: 7 Inches. *Stanley kept this rosewood mortise gauge in their product line long after many of their specialty gauges had disappeared from their catalog. This one is in catalog-new condition, and ready to use or display. Perfect.* (GOOD+) **$65.00**

Z3-33. Stanley Rule & Level No. 35: Handled Transitional Plane. "Sweetheart" Trademark. Original Decal. Length: 8 1/2 Inches. *Nearly all of the original decal remains on this crispy clean transitional plane from Stanley. As good as they get.* (FINE) **$395.00**

Z3-34. Stanley Rule & Level No. 645: Rare "Atha" Center Punch. Ca. 1930's. Superb Condition. Length: 4 Inches. *Stanley's "Atha" brand name has been boldly struck on this rare center punch. Obscure, but very scarce.* (FINE) **$45.00**

Z3-35. Stanley Rule & Level No. 282: Handled Wood Scraper. With Instructions. New Condition, Original Box. Length: 13 1/2 Inches. *This pristine example of Stanley's handled scraper is in new condition, with instructions and both cutter in the original box. Mint.* (FINE) **$125.00**

Z3-36. Stanley Rule & Level No. 66: Patented Scratch Beader. Early Japan Body. Unused Condition. Length: 11 1/2 Inches. *An cutlery box has sheltered the components of this extra early No. 66 beading plane from exposure to the elements during its 110 years of life. This plane is in essentially the same condition as it would have been when new. Absolutely perfect and highly recommended.* (FINE) **$245.00**

Z3-37. Corgi Toys, Ltd., Swansea (England No. C906/6: "Stanley Tools" Toy Truck. Cast Iron Body. New Condition, Original Box. Length: 7 1/2 Inches. *These recently-produced toy trucks were a hit with Stanley collectors. Here's a perfectly preserved example. First come, first serve.* (FINE) **$110.00**

Z3-38. Stanley Rule & Level No. SR100: Stainless Steel Framing Square. "Sweetheart" Trademark. Near New Condition. Length: 24 Inches. *Stanley offered the stainless steel framing square in its catalogs during the 1920's, but there were apparently very few takers. This example is, as one might expect, stainless, and ready to help fill out a collection of Stanley squares. A rare tool in excellent condition.* (FINE) **$195.00**

Z3-39. Stanley Rule & Level No. 207: Nickel Plated Bench Stop. With Spring Stop. Scarce and Near New. Length: 3 3/4 Inches. *Here's a pristine example of Stanley's uncommon spring-activated bench stop in new condition. Extra nice.* (FINE) **$35.00**

Z3-40. Stanley Rule & Level No. 93: Nickel Plated Adjustable Marking Gauge. With "Sweetheart" Trademark. Near New Condition. Length: 4 Inches. *The No. 93 was discontinued from the Stanley product line in 1942. This one has the 1920's era "Sweetheart" logo. Pristine.* (FINE) **$55.00**

Z3-41. Stanley Rule & Level No. 41: Brass Top Level. For Square or Level. Near New Condition. Length: 3 Inches. *Nearly all original finishes remain on this perfectly preserved Stanley classic.* (FINE) **$55.00**

Z3-42. Stanley Rule & Level No. 917: Ratcheting Bit Brace. Full Nickel Plating. New Condition, Original Box. Length: 13 1/2 Inches. *The original pasteboard box has kept this Stanley classic in top collector quality condition. Extra nice.* (FINE) **$165.00**

Z3-43. Stanley Rule & Level No. 4: 9 Inch Smoothing Plane. Rosewood Handles. New Condition, Original Box. Length: 9 Inches. *This example of Stanley's mainstay smoothing plane appears to date from the early 1950's, when it was set on a shelf and forgotten. Perfectly preserved.* (FINE) **$125.00**

Z3-44. Stanley Rule & Level No. 2: "Excelsior" Tool Handle. Patented March 29, 1867. With 2 Original Bits. Length: 3 1/2 Inches. *Stanley's earliest catalogs featured this Clement's patent tool handle. Here's one in clean, sound condition, including two of the original bits.* (GOOD) **$65.00**

Z3-45. Stanley Rule & Level No. 34: General Line Catalog. May, 1937 Edition. 208 Pages. Length: 7 Inches. *One fold in the cover and some fading inside. Otherwise complete and excellent.* (GOOD/GOOD+) **$115.00**

Group A4

A4-1. **Riverside Tool Co., New York, N.Y.: No. 10: Boxed Bits and Brace. Label Inside and Out. German, English Institute. Length: 14 Inches.** *A most unusual boxed brace and set of bits. With a name like "Yankee Boy", it must certainly have been intended for domestic sale. Half of the label features a description of the product in German. Different. A multicultural marvel.* (FINE) **$295.00**

A4-2. **Stanley Rule & Level No. 41: Miller's Patent Plane. With Filletster Bed. For Parts. Length: 10 1/2 Inches.** *Missing the "wraparound" fence and the outside fence, we offer this sound but dirty example of the No. 41 Millers Patent for its parts, including the highly desirable filletster bed.* (GOOD) **$525.00**

A4-3. **Stanley Rule & Level No. S5: Steel Jack Plane. Rosewood Handle and Knob. Nicely Refinished. Length: 14 Inches.** *Thanks to the efforts of a previous owner who "enhanced" the japan finish, this example of Stanley's S 5 steel body plane appears nearly new. A tough plane to find.* (GOOD+) **$250.00**

A4-4. **Stanley Rule & Level No. 45 E: Export Model Combination Plane. Rare Red Box. Rare and Near New. Length: 12 Inches.** *For some reason that has yet to be documented, examples of the Stanley No. 45 combination plane exported to the British Isles are imprinted with the number designation "45 E". They are functionally equivalent to their American equivalent in every way. That they were in some way modified so as to accommodate those accustomed to driving on the left side of the road is one possible reason, but it is so ridiculous that we will not raise it here. A rare, collectible Stanley plane with the turn signal on the right hand side of the steering wheel.* (FINE) **$545.00**

A4-5. **Buck Brothers: Set of 8 Out Cannel Gouges. With "Buck Logo". Near New Condition. Length: 12 1/2 Inches.** *Acquired recently when an extraordinary ca. 1900 chest of tools was broken up and disbursed at auction, all of the gouges in this set from the respected Millbury, Massachusetts maker Buck Brothers are in nearly new condition. The kind of set you don't find anymore. Highly recommended.* (FINE) **$345.00**

A4-6. **Stanley Rule & Level No. 10 1/2: "Union" Brand Rabbet Plane. Mahogany Handles. New Old Stock. Length: 9 Inches.** *It is well documented that the Stanley Rule & Level Company bought out and assumed the operations of the crosstown Union Plane Manufacturing Company. Scholars who have studied the merger have concluded that Stanley was primarily interested in acquiring the plant and equipment of Union, rather than their line of tools. However, the tools would needed to be disbursed. This brand new Union No. 10, which has been fitted with a Stanley "Sweetheart" cutting iron offers strong evidence that Stanley marketed the Union planes under their own name until the stock was diminished. A rare Union plane under any circumstances, the Stanley connection adds a substantial boost to the desirability of this exceptionally well preserved tool. Mint.* (FINE) **$595.00**

A4-7. **Auxer, Samuel, Lancaster, Penn.: Rosewood and Boxwood Marking Gauge. Carpenter Style. Superb Condition. Length: 8 1/2 Inches.** *The fact that Samuel Auxer learned his toolmaking as an apprentice to legendary Lancaster County planemaker E.W. Carpenter is immediately evident in this rosewood and boxwood mortise gauge. A rare and beautiful gauge in nearly new condition. Extra special.* (FINE) **$345.00**

A4-8. **Rabone & Sons, John, Birmingham: Brass Faced Bench Level. With Sighting Feature. Uncommon Type. Length: 12 Inches.** *A pair of levels and a sighting tube allow this bench level to function as a hand held inclinometer of a sort. It has been cleaned and polished and is ready to show. Showy.* (GOOD) **$225.00**

A4-9. **North Bros Mfg. Co., Philadelphia.: No. 95: "Yankee" Slotted Screwdriver. 3 1/2 Inch Blade. New Condition, Original Box. Length: 7 1/2 Inches.** *Someone apparently set this one away in the back of the workshop and forgot about it. It is in brand new condition.* (FINE) **$95.00**

A4-10. **Metallic Plane Co., Auburn, N.Y.: Palmer's Patent Metallic Plane. Non-Adjustable Type. Complete, Excellent. Length: 14 1/2 Inches.** *This early non-adjustable example of the Palmer & Storkes patent plane is in sound condition, but the cutting iron is marked "Sandusky Tool Company" and there is a tight crack in the tote. Otherwise complete and excellent. A scarce early plane.* (GOOD) **$185.00**

A4-11. **Stanley Rule & Level No. 48: Fixed Dado Plane. 7/8 Inch Size. Rare Early Type. Length: 9 1/2 Inches.** *Only the very early examples of the No. 48 swinging fence match plane were finished with black japanning and only the early models had the distinctive "vine" casting. Here's an excellent example to fill out a Stanley collection.* (GOOD+) **$225.00**

A4-12. **Unmarked: Cast Iron Block Metallic Plane. Decorative Casting. Early Appearance. Length: 3 Inches.** *Enough of these have turned up to make it quite certain that they were manufactured and marketed, but the lack of any markings, other than the distinctive wave casting and cast iron washer beneath the fitting screw for the cutter, leave even the serious searchers wondering. Obviously of pre-20th Century manufacture, this is an excellent example of this early plane.* (FINE) **$245.00**

A4-13. **Stanley Rule & Level No. 608: "Bedrock" Jointer Plane. Early Style. 98% Original Paint. Length: 24 Inches.** *One of the most popular of all the Bedrock series, the No. 608 would perform work under circumstances where the "chatter" that it was supposed to prevent would be most likely to occur. This superb example retains nearly all of its original paint and is in nearly perfectly preserved condition. As good as they get.* (FINE) **$585.00**

A4-14. **Scholl, C.: 4 Stem Patent Marking Gauge. Patented March 8, 1864. Rosewood Body, Arms. Length: 8 Inches.** *The C. Scholl patent involved a series of sliding shafts, all of which could be fixed in position by a single locking screw. This example of the solid rosewood version has four separate stems. An interesting and aesthetically appealing gauge in top collector quality condition.* (FINE) **$475.00**

A4-15. **Union Mfg. Co., New Britain, Conn.: No. X No. 8: Patent Jointer Metallic Plane. Patented December 8, 1903. Near New Condition. Length: 24 Inches.** *The also-ran planemakers, such as the Ohio Tool Company, Sargent, and Union had to resort to mechanical gimmickry to compete with the market dominance of Stanley's Bailey Patent plane. Evidence suggests that they failed to make much of a mark. (For a thorough overview of patented planes and the world in which they were made, see Roger Smith's Volume I and Volume II.) This wannabe offering from the Union Tool Company, also of New Britain, featured a "vertical post" mechanism similar to those offered on early Leonard Bailey planes. Produced under a patent issued in 1903, examples of these planes are not common, especially in the perfectly preseved condition in which this example of the largest (24 inch) size is found. Retaining nearly all of its original finishes and absolutely crisp and clean, this plane is very highly recommended.* (FINE) **$295.00**

A4-17. **Stanley Rule & Level No. 51: Cast Iron Spoke Shave. With Screw Cap Lock. Ready to Use. Length: 10 Inches.** *This example of the No. 51 shave has the later style casting with the "checkered" handles, that were designed to improve the grip of the user.* (GOOD+) **$25.00**

A4-18. **Stanley Rule & Level No. 1: Smooth Plane. "Sweetheart" Trademark. Original Oil Glaze. Length: 5 1/2 Inches.** *Every Stanley collector eventually hopes to add the rare and desirable No. 1 Smooth Plane to his or her collection. At only 5 1/2 inches in length, these diminutive planes appeal even to those for whom the more esoteric elements of the tool menangerie seem incomprehensible. The "Sweetheart" era example offered here retains 99% of its original finishes on all surfaces. Almost all of the dark, black japanning remains on body and frog; the polished cap iron, chip breaker and cutting iron all retain a brownish glaze from the coat of oil finish that would have been applied to the tool when it left the factory; the dark grained tote and knob of Brazilian Rosewood are smooth, flawless and shiny; and the cutter is imprinted with a bold "Sweetheart" trademark. For the collector who has been waiting for a No. 1 in top condition, this is the plane. A sweetheart.* (FINE) **$1,675.00**

A4-19. **Shelton: Patent Metallic Plane. Patent No. 1914609. Last Major Patent. Length: 8 1/2 Inches.** *The only marking ever applied to these planes was the patent number on the cap iron. Accordingly, they prompt more inquiries than any metallic plane ever made. This example has had its japanning "enhanced" and appears nearly new.* (FINE) **$45.00**

A4-20. **Stanley Rule & Level No. 66: Universal Scratch Beader. Complete With 2 Fences. 8 Double Cutters. Length: 11 Inches.** *The No. 66 scratch beader was the best tool of its type on the market and it remains the most versatile and functional available today. This example is complete with all original cutters and both fences. A classic.* (GOOD+) **$225.00**

A4-21. **Stanley Rule & Level No. 100 1/2: Squirrel Tail Block Plane. With Convex Sole. 99% Original Paint. Length: 3 1/2 Inches.** *Topped off with a nicely-contrasting red lever cap, this example of Stanley's convex bottom model maker's block plane is in mint condition. Perfect.* (FINE) **$185.00**

A4-22. **Stanley Rule & Level No. A5: Aluminum Jack Plane. Sweetheart Trademark. Rosewood Handle and Knob. Length: 14 Inches.** *Here's an exceptionally clean example of the No. A 5 jack plane. The handles have been nicely refinished, but it is otherwise excellent.* (GOOD+) **$325.00**

A4-23. **Unmarked No. 1205: Chaplin's Improved Metallic Plane. Corrugated Sole. Length: 9 1/2 Inches.** *This later Chaplin's Patent plane is complete and sound. a good one.* (GOOD+) **$225.00**

A4-24. **Stanley Rule & Level No. 39: Cast Iron Dado Plane. 1/4 Inch Size. New Condition, Original Box. Length: 8 Inches.** *The original box has kept this rare 1/4 inch dado plane in brand new condition. Absolutely immaculate.* (FINE) **$445.00**

A4-25. **Millers Falls Company No. 3: Adjustable Hollow Auger. 1/4 to 1 1/4 Inch Cut. New Condition, Original Box. Length: 5 1/4 Inches.** *Here's an example of the Millers Falls No. 3 Hollow auger in very little-used condition in its original pasteboard box. An excellent tool in a box with a clean picture label.* (FINE) **$185.00**

A4-26. **Goodell-Pratt Company: Bench Mounted Drill Press. With Feed Screw. Complete and Excellent. Length: 21 Inches.** *Looking for something to add a touch of class to your shop? Try one of these. This example from the Goodell Pratt Tool Company is complete and in excellent working order.* (GOOD) **$155.00**

A4-27. **Starrett Co., The L.S., Athol, Mass. No. 181: Patent Adjustable Scraper. "Buck & Ryan" Tag. Unused Condition. Length: 12 Inches.** *The presence of the original factory wrapping paper and the store tag from London dealers Buck & Ryan are a sure sign that this ca. 1920's scraper has never been used. Brand new, but old.* (FINE) **$85.00**

A4-28. **Pritzlaff Hardware Co., John, Milwaukee: "Everkeen" Set of 12 Chisels. 1/8 Inch to 2 Inch. Length: 14 Inches.** *The Pritzlaff Hardware Company was Milwaukee's very finest. In keeping with their reputation, they offered a full line of high quality tools, produced for them by the major toolmakers, that were marked with their "Everkeen" trademark. Here's a great set of bevel edge chisels in superb condition in their original fitted wooden box. Sets of chisels have become nearly impossible to find.* (FINE) **$545.00**

A4-29. **Sargent, D., (Nashua, N.H.): Beech Smoothing Plane. Rare New Hampshire Maker. Near New Condition. Length: 8 Inches.** *Dana Sargent, who ended his career as Mayor of Nashua, New Hampshire, produced wooden planes in Manchester and Nashua during the 1840's and 1850's. This well preserved smoothing plane is boldly struck with his name. A nice example.* (FINE) **$85.00**

A4-30. **Hudson Tool Company: Transitional Jointer Metallic Plane. Upson Nut Type. Near New Condition. Length: 26 Inches.** *Nearly all of the original yellow lacquer finish remains on this classic transitional plane, which features a most unusual small front knob. The cutting iron is imprinted "Hudson Tool Company", a New York City maker we have not previously encountered. A rare transitional plane in top condition.* (FINE) **$145.00**

A4-31. **Johnson, W., Newark, N.J.: Boxwood Slitting Marking Gauge. Original Brass Wedge. Early and Excellent. Length: 9 Inches.** *Slitting gauges were used for the precise task of cutting veneer to size and could also double as a marking gauge, especially where the knife-like blade could be used when scribing cross grain. This solid Turkish Boxwood example from a prominent New Jersey maker is in superb condition.* (FINE) **$145.00**

A4-32. **Enders, William, St. Louis, Missouri: No. 24: "Oak Leaf" Transitional Metallic Plane. All Original Parts. Uncommon Type. Length: 8 Inches.** *The references that we have indicate that the "Oak Leaf" brand was a "second" line from the E.C. Simmons hardware Company. However, this one is marked with the name "William Enders". A mystery plane in collector qualilty condition.* (GOOD+) **$85.00**

A4-33. **Sargent & Co., New Haven, Conn.: No. 407: No. "2" Size Smooth Metallic Plane. "Sargent V. B. M.". Excellent Condition. Length: 7 Inches.** *Planes manufactured by Sargent & Company are gaining in popularity as additional information on their diverse product line becomes generally available. One need look no further than here to find a superb example of Sargent's best output. This No. 407 smoothing plane is identical to Stanley's No. 2 plane. Sargent was the principal competitor of Stanley in the metallic plane line, but Stanley tools probably outsold Sargent by at least 10 to 1, and probably closer to 25 to 1. A rare Sargent plane in top collector condition. No apologies.* (FINE) **$385.00**

A4-34. **Stanley Rule & Level No. 72: "Razor Edge" Spoke Shave. Rare Cast Iron Type. 2 Inch Cutter. Length: 11 Inches.** *This is the hardest to find of the "Razor Edge" line. 80%+ of the original paint remains.* (GOOD+) **$285.00**

A4-35. **Frog Tool Co. Ltd., Chicago, Illinois: 42 Inch Crosscut Saw. Near New Condition. Original Handles. Length: 48 Inches.** *This two-man/one-man saw is in essentially unused condition and retains nearly all of its original finishes. An excellent working tool in new condition.* (FINE) **$85.00**

A4-36. **Stanley Rule & Level No. 606 C: "Bedrock" Fore Plane. "Sweetheart" Trademark. 99% Original Paint. Length: 18 Inches.** *Some 99% of the original shiny black japan finish remains on this crispy clean "Bedrock" fore plane. The cap is marked with the "Bed Rock" logo and a full cutting iron of the "Type 11" variety (ca. 1910) is in great shape. A great working tool in top condition.* (FINE) **$395.00**

A4-37. **Wright Machine Co., Worcester, Mass.: Patented Quick Adjust Caliper. Patented January 4, 1887. Early and Excellent. Length: 3 1/2 Inches.** *These early spring joint callipers are marked with the 1887 patent date. A rare pair.* (GOOD+) **$65.00**

A4-38. **Record, Sheffield, England: No. 043: Cast Iron Plow Metallic Plane. Complete and Excellent. A Handy Tool. Length: 5 1/2 Inches.** *Designed to fit into the palm of the hand, these miniature plow planes were quite popular in their day and remain so today. This one is in essentially unused condition with 3 original cutting irons in the original box.* (FINE) **$115.00**

A4-39. **Unmarked: Special Double Groove Metallic Plane. For Carriage Work? Most Unusual. Length: 9 Inches.** *Apparently designed for the specialized work of the coachmaker, this is the first example of this specialized grooving plane that we have ever offered for sale. Different.* (GOOD+) **$75.00**

A4-40. **Stanley Rule & Level No. 50: Combination Beading Plane. With Instructions. New Condition, Original Box. Length: 9 1/2 Inches.** *Here's a great example of Stanley's very functional light beading plane in a very well preserved box. These planes can do 95% of the work of the No. 45 combination plane at about half the weight. The plane, complete with all parts and cutters, is about as good as it could get. A very well preserved example. Nice.* (FINE) **$385.00**

A4-41. **Belknap Hardware Co., Louisville: No. 8: Cast Iron Jointer Metallic Plane. Similar to Stanley No. 8. 98% Original Paint. Length: 24 Inches.** *The Belknap Hardware Company produced a wide range of tools under their "Bluegrass" brand name. This pre World War II jointer plane is fitted out with rosewood handles and retains nearly all of its original paint. A rare "Bluegrass" tool.* (FINE) **$225.00**

A4-42. **Goodell-Pratt Company: Hollow Auger Brace. Rare and Excellent. Ready to Use. Length: 18 Inches.** *Much of the nickel plating remains on this example of the Goodell Patent hollow auger brace. A most uncommon patented brace in excellent working order.* (GOOD+) **$145.00**

A4-43. **Stanley Rule & Level No. 66: Patented Scratch Beader. Early Japan Body. Complete and Excellent. Length: 11 1/2 Inches.** *Some 95% of the original black japan finish remains on this complete, early example of the No. 66 scratch beader. All original parts, including both fences and six cutters are included. Ready to use.* (GOOD+) **$155.00**

A4-44. **Goodell-Pratt Company: Engineers Reversible Plumb Bob. Solid Brass Body. Nickel Plated Cap. Length: 4 Inches.** *Here's a nice example of the Goodell-Pratt Company's top-of-the-line "Engineer's" plumb bob. A good one.* (GOOD+) **$125.00**

Group B4

B4-1. Greenfield Tool Co., Greenfield, Mass.: No. 250: 3/4 Inch Dado Molding Plane. With Wooden Stop. Excellent Condition. Length: 9 1/2 Inches. *A straight, sharp and true dado molder from a prolific maker New England maker. A nice plane.* (FINE) **$75.00**

B4-2. Dryburgh, N.E. Hope, Ontario: Moving Filletster Molding Plane. Side Boxed. Very Well Made. Length: 9 1/4 Inches. *This massive and boldly struck molder bears the imprint of Canadian maker Dryburgh. This Canadian classic is in excellent condition and ready to be put to use, if the purchaser chooses.* (GOOD+) **$115.00**

B4-3. Lines, D.: 3/4 Inch Hollow Molding Plane. Excellent Patina. Ca. 1800. Length: 9 1/4 Inches. *A sufficient number of these planes have been discovered as to make it clear that one D. Lines produced woodworking planes for sale. No documentation has yet been found to reveal where the Lines enterprise may have been centered. The Pollaks speculate a working period of ca. 1800. A rare early plane.* (GOOD+) **$65.00**

B4-4. Copeland, M. & A.: Boxed Bilection Molding Plane. Marked 5/8 Inch. Uncommon Type. Length: 9 1/2 Inches. *A superb bilection molder, this from the Hartford planemaking brothers Melvin and Alfred Copeland. No apologies.* (GOOD+) **$145.00**

B4-5. Unmarked: Classic Yankee Plow Plane. Yellow Birch Body. Relieved Wedge. Length: 10 1/2 Inches. *Every carpenter in Colonial New England would have included, among his kit of tools, a plow plane of the type that has come to be known as the "Yankee" plow. Fashioned from native Yellow Birch, riveted together in the fashion of a less technologically complex time and ornamented with carved chamfers, this classic example of that genre has stood the test of time and shows little evidence of its 225+ years of life. A classic woodworking tool and a genuine antique.* (GOOD) **$185.00**

B4-6. Chapin, N., New Hartford, Conn.: No. 10: 5/8 Inch Hollow Molding Plane. Partial Imprint. Owner "H.R. Case". Length: 9 1/2 Inches. *Nathaniel Chapin, the brother of prolific toolmaker Hermon Chapin, made planes in his own right after an internship with his older sibling. This No. 10 hollow is in excellent condition and clearly marked.* (GOOD+) **$45.00**

B4-7. Randall & Cook, Albany, N.Y.: Quirk Ovolo, Bevel Molding Plane. Marked "7/8". Extra Crisp and Clean. Length: 9 1/2 Inches. *Here's an extra wide and crisp complex molder from an Albany, New York, partnership of Samuel Randall and Moses Cook that operated from 1835 to 1839.* (GOOD+) **$155.00**

B4-8. Unmarked: Lignum Vitae Rabbet Molding Plane. From Coastal Maine. Great Grain Pattern. Length: 9 1/2 Inches. *This spectacularly grained rabbet plane of tropical lignum vitae hails from the coast of Maine, where the material from which it was crafted would have been readily available to the ship carpenters who plied their trade in that area. Lignum Vitae, a wood with a density greater than that of water, was used as ballast in the holds of ships sailing north from the tropics. A thoroughly stunning woodworking plane.* (GOOD+) **$225.00**

B4-9. Barton & Co., D.R., Rochester, N.Y.: Solid Boxwood Plow Plane. Excellent Threads. Great Patina. Length: 10 Inches. *This classic boxwood plow has been boldly struck with Barton's semicircular logo, which features a prominent central star. Exotic wood plow planes of this caliber have become increasingly difficult to find.* (GOOD+) **$495.00**

B4-10. Assorted Makers: Side Rabbet Molding Planes. Working Pair. Buck and Stewart. Length: 9 1/2 Inches. *Rescued from the same chest, where they had apparently been committed to a marriage of convenience in a ceremony presided over by a practicing woodworker, these working planes stand ready to return to work.* (GOOD+) **$65.00**

B4-11. Unmarked: Boxwood Smoothing Plane. Mahogany Wedge. Unusual Rounded Escapement. Length: 8 1/2 Inches. *The throat on this craftsman-made boxwood smoothing plane has been rounded out in sculptural fashion by its maker. A boldly contrasting mahogany wedge adds visual appeal to this very well preserved plane. Nice.* (GOOD+) **$110.00**

B4-12. Green, John: Fenced Triple Reed Molding Plane. Fully Boxed. Great Working Order. Length: 9 1/2 Inches. *A prominent and prolific planemaker in the city of York, England, John Green produced a wide range of molding planes, including this fully boxed triple reed molder. A striking molding plane in excellent working condition.* (GOOD+) **$135.00**

B4-13. Marsh, A. & W., Cleveland, Ohio: Boxed Bead Molding Plane. Ca. 1837-1838 Only. Near New Condition. Length: 9 1/2 Inches. *There is evidence that Cleveland planemaker Archibald Marsh, who is recorded as having worked in 1837 and 1838 only, may have started his career as an employee of Hermon Chapin in Connecticut before moving west. An uncommon maker mark on a perfectly preserved molding plane.* (FINE) **$75.00**

B4-14. Carpenter, E. W., Lancaster, Penn.: 1/4 Inch Dado Plane Molding Plane. With 3 Lancaster Marks.. A. Weaver & J. Pusey. Length: 9 1/2 Inches. *A spectacular dado plane in superb condition by Southeastern Pennsylvania maker E.W. Carpenter. Carpenter's planes were distinguished by their oversize prominent wedges. This plane offers ample opportunity to appreciate that feature.* (FINE) **$225.00**

B4-15. Chapin, H., Union Factory: No. 20: 1 1/2 Inch Round Molding Plane. W.G. Grimes New London. Near New Condition. Length: 9 1/2 Inches. *This 1 1/2 inch round molder is double marked with the imprint of Hermon Chapin's Union Factory and one W.G. Grimes of New London, Connecticut, who may have been a dealer in hardware and tools. An uncommon double marked molder.* (FINE) **$85.00**

B4-16. Gleave, Oldham St., Manchester: Spring Set Ogee Molding Plane. With Integral Fence. Extra Bold Imprint. Length: 9 1/2 Inches. *The planemaking firm of Joseph Gleave began operations in Manchester, England in 1832 and continued well into the Twentieth Century. This fenced ogee bearing their imprint has a most unusual variation to its cut.* (GOOD+) **$65.00**

B4-17. Higgs, Edward, (London): 1/2 Inch Dado Molding Plane. With Depth Stop. Ca. 1821-1827. Length: 9 1/2 Inches. *This 1/2 inch English dado plane dates from the first quarter of the Nineteenth Century. Crisp, clean and ready to use.* (GOOD+) **$65.00**

B4-18. H.D.: Early Handled Spar Molding Plane. Wide Flat Chamfers. Distinctive Escapement. Length: 12 Inches. *Everything about this handled spar plane says that it dates from the New England shipbuilding days of some two hundred years ago. Fitted with a rounded iron and a nicely chamfered wedge, this plane is very well preserved and could be put back to use if the new owner so chooses.* (GOOD+) **$115.00**

B4-19. Nurse, C., Walworth Road, London: Massive Quirk Round Molding Plane. Marked "7/8". Near New Condition. Length: 9 1/2 Inches. *The firm of C. Nurse & Co. commenced operation in 1841 and remained in business for nearly 100 years. This oversize quarter round is in nearly new condition and ready for immediate use.* (FINE) **$85.00**

B4-20. Unmarked: Early Handled Sash Molding Plane. Graphic Wedges. Excellent Patina. Length: 11 Inches. *Handled sash molding planes are encountered perhaps once for every example of the unhandled type. This early example is fitted with wedges that suggest it was fashioned by one who learned planemaking in the Eighteenth Century. A classic.* (GOOD+) **$145.00**

B4-21. Unmarked: Early Style Ogee Molding Plane. Wide, Flat Chamfers. Overstruck Imprint. Length: 9 1/2 Inches. *The imprint on this classic ogee molder has been overstruck by an owner's mark, but its functionality has been thoroughly preserved. A great working plane at a bargain price.* (GOOD+) **$65.00**

B4-22. Crow (John), Canterbury: Quirk Ovolo and Astragal Molding Plane. Double Boxed. Ca. 1847-1915. Length: 9 1/2 Inches. *John Crow produced molding planes in Canterbury, England in the last half of the Nineteenth Century. This wide complex molder is boldly struck with his imprint. A nice molder.* (GOOD+) **$225.00**

B4-23. Sutcliffe Brothers: Quirk Ovolo With Bead Molding Plane. Unknown Maker. Extra Crisp and Clean. Length: 9 1/2 Inches. *This perfectly preserved complex molder has been struck with a circular imprint bearing the name "Sutcliffe Brothers", who are not mentioned in American Wooden Planes. A nice plane from undocumented planemakers.* (FINE) **$95.00**

B4-24. Unmarked: Handled Fruitwood Smoothing Plane. Applied Steel Sole. Great Patina. Length: 9 Inches. *The extra flourishes included in the design of this well preserved smoothing plane give reason to suspect that its previous owner (and likely maker) was involved in the coachmaking trade. A strike button of lignum vitae provides a stark contrast to the golden patina of the fruitwood body. A very pretty plane.* (GOOD+) **$165.00**

B4-25. Unmarked: Ebony Smoothing Plane. Fruitwood Wedge. D.R. Barton Iron. Length: 9 Inches. *This solid ebony smoothing plane has been fitted with a contrasting wedge of American fruitwood and a cutting iron imprinted with the logo of Rochester, New York planemaker D.R. Barton & Company. A pretty plane.* (GOOD+) **$135.00**

B4-26. Gregg, I.: Early Tongue Molding Plane. Wide, Flat Chamfers. AWP III: Ca. 1800. Length: 9 1/2 Inches. *Writing in "American Wooden Planes", the Pollaks note that "less than a dozen" examples of this imprint have been reported. This plane was likely produced at the very end of the Eighteenth Century. A good one.* (GOOD+) **$110.00**

B4-27. Sandusky Tool Co., Sandusky, Ohio: No. 36: Beech Toothing Plane. Steep Angle. Superb Condition. Length: 7 1/2 Inches. *A crisp and ready-to-use toothing plane with a clean original iron. Ready to do yeoman service in the veneering business.* (GOOD+) **$115.00**

B4-28. Wentworth: Moving Filletster Molding Plane. With Boxed Side. Undocumented Maker. Length: 9 1/2 Inches. *The professional style of manufacture of this tool leaves little doubt that it was produced by a professional planemaker. We have not previously encountered the "Wentworth" imprint.* (GOOD+) **$75.00**

B4-29. Assorted Makers: Group of Astragal Molding Planes. Sandusky, Ohio, Etc. In Working Order. Length: 9 1/2 Inches. *Here's a working group of four molders including two hollows, a round and a bead. Makers included the Sandusky and Ohio Tool Companies. A nice group.* (GOOD+) **$45.00**

B4-30. Mathieson & Son, A., Glasgow: Double Iron Molding Plane. Astragal, Cove and Bead. Uncommon Profile. Length: 9 1/2 Inches. *This classic double iron Scottish molder combines an astragal, cove and bead in its extra wide profile. A well preserved molder from a prominent Scottish maker.* (GOOD+) **$215.00**

B4-31. Wentworth, J., Worcester, Mass.: Boxed Bead Molding Plane. With Tileston Imprint. Hardware Dealer? Length: 9 1/2 Inches. *This double struck molder from Boston maker Timothy Tileston is also imprinted with the mark of one J. Wentworth of Worcester, Massachusetts, a likely hardware dealer who purchased planes from Tileston for resale.* (GOOD+) **$75.00**

B4-32. Oothoudt, W.: Groove Molding Plane. Rare N.Y.(?) Maker. Extra Crisp Stamp. Length: 9 1/2 Inches. *Enough of the Oothoudt planes show up in central New York to make it fairly clear that the Oothoudts did their work in that area, but documentation remains scarce. This one has the distinctive wedge with elongated finial that suggests that the Oothoudts took pride in their planemaking.* (GOOD+) **$115.00**

B4-33. Jewett, J.C., Waterville, Maine: Adjustable Dado Molding Plane. Marked "3/4". Extra Crisp Mark. Length: 9 1/2 Inches. *This classic dado plane is boldly struck with the imprint of John C. Jewett, who made planes in Waterville, Maine in the 1830's. A nice molding plane.* (GOOD+) **$115.00**

B4-34. Cowell &chapman, New Castle (England): Steep Ogee Molding Plane. With Fence. Most Unusual. Length: 9 1/2 Inches. *Cowell and Chapman were planemakers and ironmongers in the English city of Newcastle-Upon-Tyne in the last half of the Nineteenth Century. This most unusual molder may have been re-cut from a less complex plane, but it looks as though it would be a good working tool.* (GOOD+) **$55.00**

B4-35. Holbrook, Bristol, England: Classic Spar Molding Plane. Ca. 1799-1849. Extra Crisp and Clean. Length: 8 Inches. *A plane such as this would have been used by a ship carpenter for the final planing of any of the many spars and masts that made up a wooden sailing ship. A nice example.* (GOOD+) **$65.00**

B4-36. Stewart: 3/16 Inch Dado Molding Plane. Wood Depth Stop. Scottish Maker. Length: 9 1/2 Inches. *Evidence of a wedge that was once tacked to the side does not distract from the functionality of this uncommon 3/16 inch dado plane. The Stewarts produced planes in Edinburgh, Scotland, from the last quarter of the Eighteenth Century to the middle of the Nineteenth Century.* (GOOD) **$35.00**

B4-37. Copeland, M., Warranted: Steep Quirk Ovolo, Bevel Molding Plane. Marked 5/8 Inch. Owner: I. Ingraham. Length: 9 1/2 Inches. *A nice, narrow yet steep cabinet profile molding profile that works great in the workshop. A crisp clean plane in fine working order. Nice.* (GOOD+) **$135.00**

B4-38. Mathieson & Son, A., Glasgow: Double Iron Molding Plane. Quirk Ovolo With Bevel. Extra Crisp and Clean. Length: 9 1/2 Inches. *Practically nonexistent in the United States, double iron molding planes seem to have been the rule, rather than the exception, in Scotland. This ovolo and bevel combination has been boldly struck and is ready to use or proudly display. A good one.* (FINE) **$155.00**

B4-39. Thompson, Wm. A., Buffalo, N.Y.: 5/8 Inch Dado Molding Plane. Ca. 1839-46. Extra Bold Mark. Length: 9 1/2 Inches. *Scottish born hardware dealer William Thompson imprinted planes sold in his store with this mark for a very few years in the 1840's. An excellent working dado plane that has been boldly struck with the Thompson mark.* (GOOD+) **$45.00**

B4-40. Little, L., (Boston): Quirk Ogee, Astragal Molding Plane. AWP "A" Mark: *. With Lignum Boxing. Length: 9 1/4 Inches.** *This early complex molder is marked with the "A" imprint shown in American Wooden Planes. A nice, early molder.* (GOOD+) **$265.00**

B4-41. Frogatt, B.: Quarter Round Molding Plane. Ca. 1760-1790. 1 Inch Size. Length: 9 1/2 Inches. *This extra large quarter round molder has been boldly struck with the imprint of Eighteenth Century British planemaker Benjamin Frogatt.* (GOOD+) **$115.00**

B4-42. Patt., J.O.: Double Side Rabbet Molding Plane. Very Well Made. Undocumented Maker. Length: 9 1/2 Inches. *The name "J.O. Patt" that has been boldly struck on this most unusual double side rabbet plane is one that we have not previously encountered. The professional quality of this plane makes it obvious, however, that this was not some carpenter's "Saturday Project". A visually striking molding plane in excellent working condition.* (GOOD+) **$385.00**

B4-43. Unmarked: Early Dado Molding Plane. Yellow Birch Body. Dated "1818". Length: 11 Inches. *The contrasting angles of the wedges on this Eighteenth Century Yellow Birch molder make for a striking profile when viewed from the side. The first plane of this configuration that we have encountered.* (GOOD+) **$295.00**

B4-44. Fish, A., Lowell, Mass.: Massive Semicircular Molding Plane. With Bevel Cut. Scarce Type and Excellent. Length: 9 1/2 Inches. *This massive quarter round profile incorporates a side bevel cut. An oversize molder with an uncommon Massachusetts imprint.* (GOOD+) **$95.00**

B4-45. Sleeper, S., (Dover, N.H.): 3/4 Inch Rabbet Molding Plane. Rare New Hampshire Imprint. AWP III: 3 Stars, A Mark. Length: 9 1/2 Inches. *This classic rabbet plane is imprinted with the mark of Vermont-born Dover, New Hampshire maker Sherburn Sleeper, who worked ca. 1830. A rare New Hampshire plane.* (GOOD+) **$145.00**

Group C4

C4-1. Sears, Roebuck & Co.: Set of 3 "Fulton" Chisels. With Socket Handles. Near New Condition. Length: 8 Inches. *These ca. 1930's era chisels bear the "Fulton" trademark of the Sears, Roebuck Company. A nice working set.* (FINE) **$25.00**

C4-2. Sears, Roebuck & Co.: Set of 6 "Craftsman" Chisels. Early Type. Near New Condition. Length: 14 Inches. *There was a time in the 1920's and 1930's when the name "Craftsman" was equivalent in quality to that of the major tool makers. Indeed, most of the early Craftsman tools were produced by America's finest tool makers. That quality standard is evident in this set of six bevel edge paring chisels. An excellent working set in top condition.* (FINE) **$165.00**

C4-3. Witherby, T.H.: Set of Bevel Edge Chisel. Ready to Use. Original Oak Box. Length: 16 Inches. *An exceptionally clean working set of chisels bearing the Witherby trademark that is so prized by woodworkers of every stripe. The original wooden box has kept these tools in top working order. A great set.* (GOOD+) **$595.00**

C4-4. Buck Bros., Millbury, Mass.: Set of 5 Turning Chisels. Short Blade Type. New Condition, Original Box. Length: 15 1/2 Inches. *The original pasteboard box has kept these turning chisels in nearly new condition. New and ready to use, but old.* (FINE) **$95.00**

C4-5. Assorted Makers: Set of 8 Early Chisels and Gouges. Tang Type Handles. Ready to Use. Length: 9 Inches. *These gouges and chisels came from the working kit of a single woodworker. A nicely patinated set of chisels and gouges.* (GOOD+) **$45.00**

C4-6. Unmarked: Early Hand Forged Chisel. Octagonal Socket. Laminated Edge. Length: 6 3/4 Inches. *The octagonal socket of this chisel is evidence of very early manufacture. There are no makers marks of any kind. Found in the vicinity of South Central Connecticut.* (GOOD) **$125.00**

C4-7. Stanley Rule & Level No. 750: Bevel Edge Socket Chisel. 2 Inch Width. Extra Crisp and Clean. Length: 9 3/4 Inches. *This well preserved 2 inch chisel is in excellent working order. A tough size to find.* (GOOD+) **$55.00**

C4-8. Underhill Edge Tool Co.: Heavy Socket Framing Chisel. 2 Inch Size. Ready to Use. Length: 17 Inches. *This well made and extra clean chisel from the Underhill Edge Tool Company is ready to provide a lifetime of service. Choice.* (GOOD+) **$65.00**

C4-9. Stanley Rule & Level No. 720: 2 Inch Bevel Edge Chisel. Near New Condition. Rare and Excellent. Length: 14 Inches. *If you need a chisel to fill out a Stanley set, or if you just want a perfect Stanley 2 inch chisel, here's a great opportunity.* (FINE) **$85.00**

C4-10. Stanley Rule & Level No. 720: 3/4 Inch Bevel Edge Chisel. Near New Condition. Ready to Use. Length: 13 Inches. *This extra long chisel in the desirable 3/4 inch size has been very little used. Crisp, clean and ready to use.* (FINE) **$55.00**

C4-11. Stanley Rule & Level No. 750: Set of 4 Bevel Edge Chisels. Near-New Condition. Ready to Use. Length: 9 1/2 Inches. *This crispy-clean set of Stanley's 750 butt chisels is in near-new condition. Sizes range from 1/4 inch to 1 inch. Ready to use.* (FINE) **$145.00**

C4-12. Ohio Tool Co., Columbus, Ohio: Heavy Socket Corner Chisel. 1 Inch Width. Ready to Use. Length: 15 Inches. *A clean and usable corner chisel from Ohio's largest manufacturer. Straight, sharp and ready to use.* (GOOD+) **$55.00**

C4-13. Unmarked: 1 1/2 Inch Laminated Framing Chisel. Extra Heavy Type. Ready to Use. Length: 17 Inches. *There is no maker mark on this very well made socket framing chisel in the desirable 1 1/2 inch width. A great working tool in top condition.* (FINE) **$65.00**

C4-14. Witherby, T.H.: Socket Mortise Chisel. 1/4 Inch Width. Original Handle. Length: 13 Inches. *This 1/4 inch mortise chisel bears the imprint of respected maker T.H. Witherby of Connecticut.* (GOOD+) **$25.00**

C4-15. Unmarked: Heavy Socket Corner Chisel. 3/4 Inch Size. Extra Crisp and Clean. Length: 16 Inches. *We can't find a maker's mark on this crispy clean corner chisel, but it was very definitely produced by a major edge tool maker. It has seen very little use.* (FINE) **$75.00**

C4-16. Peck, Stow & Wilcox Co. No. 1 EX.: Heavy Socket Framing Chisel. 1 1/4 Inch Size. Ready to Use. Length: 16 Inches. *P. S. & W. were major suppliers to timber framers. This 1 1/4 inch corner chisel is in excellent condition and ready to go back to work.* (GOOD+) **$55.00**

C4-17. Buck Bros., Millbury, Mass.: 1 1/2 Inch Tang Chisel. Bevel Edges. Ready to Use. Length: 12 1/2 Inches. *This bevel edge tang chisel is in excellent working order.* (GOOD+) **$25.00**

C4-18. Lakeside: Heavy Socket Corner Chisel. 1 Inch Size. Superb Condition. Length: 16 1/2 Inches. *This heavy socket corner chisel has been very little used. An excellent working tool.* (GOOD+) **$65.00**

C4-19. Berg, Erik, Eskilstuna, Sweden: 1 1/2 Inch "Shark" Chisel. Wooden Handle. Superb Condition. Length: 8 1/2 Inches. *The handle of the 1 1/2 inch chisel bears the logo of the "Shark" brand trademark of E. Berg, the legendary Swedish edge tool maker.* (FINE) **$45.00**

C4-20. Ohio Tool Co., Columbus, Ohio: Heavy Socket Framing Chisel. 2 Inch Width. Extra Crisp and Clean. Length: 18 Inches. *The Ohio Tool Company distributed their goods nationally from the 1860's to the 1920's and established a strong following with their consistent quality. Here's a superb example of that quality.* (GOOD+) **$65.00**

C4-21. Ward, Sheffield: Set of Bevel Edge Chisels. 1 1/2 Inch and 1 1/4 Inch. From Same Chest. Length: 17 Inches. *These well preserved paring chisels from prominent Sheffield, England maker Ward are ready to provide several more lifetimes of service.* (GOOD+) **$110.00**

C4-22. Swan Co, The James: Heavy Socket Corner Chisel. 3/4 Inch Size. Near New Condition. Length: 16 1/2 Inches. *This practically unused corner chisel is fitted with its original steel capped wooden handle. A perfectly preserved chisel from a highly respected maker.* (FINE) **$95.00**

C4-23. Unmarked: Heavy Socket Framing Chisel. 1 5/8 Inch Size. Extra Crisp and Clean. Length: 17 1/2 Inches. *This extra heavy chisel in the most unusual 1 5/8 inch size features slightly beveled edges. A good working tool.* (GOOD+) **$55.00**

C4-24. Douglass Mfg. Co.: Heavy Socket Framing Chisel. 1 1/2 Inch Size. Applied Steel Edge. Length: 14 1/2 Inches. *This heavy-duty corner chisel is in fine working condition. A good one.* (GOOD+) **$45.00**

C4-25. Witherby, T.H.: Heavy Socket Framing Chisel. 1 1/2 Inch Width. Extra Crisp and Clean. Length: 16 1/2 Inches. *Another nice framing chisel with the much respected Witherby imprint to attest to its quality. This one is in the desirable 1 1/2 inch width.* (FINE) **$85.00**

C4-26. Buck Bros., Millbury, Mass.: 1 Inch Crank Neck Chisel. Extra Clean and Sharp. Ready to Use. Length: 13 1/2 Inches. *This flat, crank-neck chisel features the early style fruitwood handle that was characteristic of Buck Brothers' Nineteenth Century output.* (FINE) **$75.00**

C4-27. Berg, Erik, Eskilstuna, Sweden: 1 3/4 Inch "Shark" Chisel. Wooden Handle. Original Decal. Length: 8 1/2 Inches. *Nearly all of the original decal remains on this classic "Shark" brand chisel from one of Sweden's most respected edge tool makers. Nice.* (FINE) **$55.00**

C4-28. Parr, George, Buffalo, N. Y.: Socket Mortise Chisel. 1/2 Inch Width. Original Handle. Length: 11 Inches. *A good, clean, working chisel by a prominent Buffalo maker noted for the quality of his edge tools. Ready to use.* (GOOD+) **$25.00**

C4-29. Simmons, D., Lockport, N.Y.: Early 1 Inch Corner Chisel. Uncommon Maker. Superb Condition. Length: 17 Inches. *The canal town of Lockport, New York was ideally situated for an edge tool maker sending tools via canal and the Great Lakes to the American Mid-West. This 1 inch corner chisel is in much the same condition it would have been when it left the Simmons factory.* (FINE) **$85.00**

C4-30. Unmarked: Massive Mortise Chisel. 19 Inch Blade Section. Superb Condition. Length: 23 Inches. *This massive mortise chisel was designed for use with extra large joints. Generally, such chisels were for use by bridge builders and the like, but the narrow width of this one suggests some other application. A great working tool in excellent condition.* (GOOD+) **$135.00**

C4-31. Stanley Rule & Level No. 1005: 1 Inch "Everlasting" Chisel. Marbled Ebonite Handle. Rare and Excellent. Length: 8 1/2 Inches. *Clearly imprinted on the shaft of the chisel with its Stanley number designation, the No. 1005 marbled ebonite handle "Everlasting" chisel is so rare that it was not included in the most recent publication of the Stanley Value Guide. A very rare Stanley chisel.* (GOOD+) **$115.00**

C4-32. Unmarked: Early Style Mortise Chisel. Solid Forged Body. Usable Condition. Length: 11 Inches. *A prominent laminated edge is evident in the photograph of this early forged mortise chisel. Most unusual.* (GOOD) **$45.00**

C4-33. Tyzak & Son, S., Railway Arch: Sash Pocket Chisel. Ex. Keillor Collection With Information Tag. Length: 5 Inches. *This sash pocket chisel from prominent English maker Tyzak & Son comes complete with a hand typed tag that distinguishes it as having come from the legendary collection of Long Island collector Archie Keillor. An uncommon chisel with a distinguished provenance.* (GOOD+) **$55.00**

C4-34. Stanley Rule & Level No. 750: Bevel Edge Socket Chisel. 3/4 Inch Width. Near New Condition. Length: 10 Inches. *Nearly all of the original decal remains on the handle of this crispy clean example of Stanley's classic "Red Handle" line.* (FINE) **$55.00**

C4-35. Stanley Rule & Level No. 750: Bevel Edge Socket Chisel. 1/2 Inch Width. With Original Decal. Length: 10 Inches. *The presence of the original decal is prominent testimony to the easy life this chisel has led up to this time. Ready to use or fill out a set. Perfect.* (FINE) **$55.00**

C4-36. Stanley Rule & Level No. 40: Rare 1/4 Inch Everlast Chisel. Uncommon Size. Full Blade. Length: 11 Inches. *This most unusual 1/4 inch "Everlasting" chisel has one small spot of pitting on the side, but it is not situated in such a way that it would affect the use of the tool. A good one.* (GOOD) **$115.00**

C4-37. Buck Bros., Millbury, Mass.: 1 Inch Crank Neck Chisel. Extra Clean and Sharp. Ready to Use. Length: 14 Inches. *This bevel edge crank neck chisel is in new condition. Ready to provide several lifetimes of use.* (FINE) **$65.00**

C4-38. Barton & Co., D.R., Rochester, N.Y.: Set of 6 Socket Chisels. Original Fruitwood Handles. Ready to Use. Length: 15 Inches. *Identical turned fruitwood handles accent these socket chisels that are boldly struck with the imprint of America's premier Nineteenth Century edge tool maker.* (GOOD+) **$265.00**

C4-39. Barton & Co., D.R., Rochester, N.Y.: Set of 3 Framing Chisels. Length: 17 Inches. *Given the hard work that was the life of tools such as these, sets of heavy framing chisels are almost impossible to find. These very well preserved tools from D.R. Barton and Company are in the 1 1/2 inch, 1 3/4 inch and 2 inch sizes. The 1 3/4 inch size has a small crack in the laminated edge, but the others are in perfect condition and ready to use. A great working set from a respected maker.* (GOOD+) **$215.00**

C4-40. Peck, Stow & Wilcox Co. No. 1 EX: Heavy Socket Corner Chisel. 3/4 Inch Width. Unused Condition. Length: 16 Inches. *The owner of this perfectly preserved corner chisel can be the first to use it. Absolutely perfect.* (FINE) **$110.00**

C4-41. Hubbard H. W. Co.: Heavy Socket Framing Chisel. 1 Inch Width. Near New Condition. Length: 16 1/2 Inches. *This one has the characteristic "$" mark of the Hubbard firm. Straight, sharp, clean and ready to last several more lifetimes.* (FINE) **$75.00**

C4-42. Peck, Stow & Wilcox Co. No. 1 EX.: Heavy Socket Corner Chisel. 3/4 Inch Width. Original Handle. Length: 17 Inches. *The original handle remains on this crisp, clean and ready to use 3/4 inch socket corner chisel. A good one.* (GOOD+) **$65.00**

C4-43. Buck Bros., Millbury, Mass.: 3/4 Inch Crank Neck Chisel. Extra Clean and Sharp. Ready to Use. Length: 14 Inches. *The original "Buck" logo remains on the handle of this perfectly preserved crank neck chisel in the desirable 3/4 inch size.* (FINE) **$65.00**

C4-44. Middlesex Mfg. Co., Middletown, Conn.: Heavy Socket Framing Chisel. 2 Inch Width. Ready to Use. Length: 18 Inches. *This well made framing chisel is imprinted with the name of the Middlesex Manufacturing Company of Middletown, Connecticut, a company which we have not previously encountered. They are listed in the Directory of American Toolmakers, but no working dates are shown. This well made chisel is in excellent working condition.* (GOOD+) **$75.00**

C4-45. Union Hardware Co.: 3/4 Inch Corner Chisel. "Samson" Brand. Extra Rare and Crisp. Length: 15 Inches. *This one inch heavy socket framing chisel appears never to have been used. An old tool in new condition.* (FINE) **$75.00**

C4-46. Peck, Stow & Wilcox Co. No. 1 EX: Heavy Socket Framing Chisel. 1 1/4 Inch Width. Great Working Condition. Length: 17 Inches. *There's still plenty of use left in this heavy framing chisel in the desirable 1 1/4 inch size. A nice chisel.* (GOOD+) **$65.00**

C4-47. Greenlee Tool Co., Rockford, Illinois: Bevel Edge Firmer Chisel. 2 Inch Size. Unused Condition. Length: 13 1/2 Inches. *The Greenlee Tool Company of Rockford, Illinois, produced edge tools of the very highest quality for many years. Here's an excellent example.* (FINE) **$45.00**

C4-48. Unmarked: Heavy Socket Corner Chisel. 1 Inch Size. Ready to Use. Length: 16 1/2 Inches. *We can't find a maker's mark on this heavy corner chisel, but it has a decidedly early look about it. A well preserved chisel in excellent working order.* (GOOD+) **$55.00**

C4-49. Peck, Stow & Wilcox Co. No. 1 EX.: Heavy Socket Framing Chisel. 2 Inch Size. Original Handle. Length: 17 1/2 Inches. *Here's an excellent framing chisel in the standard 2 inch width. A good one.* (GOOD+) **$85.00**

C4-50. Witherby, T. H.,Winsted, Conn.: Set of 8 Turning Chisels. Top Quality Maker. Ready to Use. Length: 13 Inches. *We have encountered a wide range of edge tools bearing the mark of T.H. Witherby, the prominent Winsted, Connecticut, maker, but this is the first set of turning chisels bearing their mark that we have been privileged to offer. A rare set in absolutely perfect condition. Highly recommended.* (FINE) **$185.00**

Group D4

D4-1. Stanley Rule & Level No. 278: Rabbet and Filletster Plane. Complete. Replaced Fence Rod. Length: 6 3/4 Inches. *This example of the No. 278 rabbet and filletster is clean and complete. The fence rod is a replacement, which should work equally well. A bargain.* (GOOD+) **$365.00**

D4-2. Stanley Rule & Level No. 79: Double Side Rabbet Plane. First Model. Ready to Use. Length: 5 Inches. *A clean and sound example of the second version of the Stanley double side rabbet plane. Ready to use.* (GOOD) **$115.00**

D4-3. Stanley Rule & Level No. 21: Transitional Smooth Plane. Smallest Size. Ca. 1900. Length: 7 Inches. *The smallest of the Stanley transitional line. Someone has enhanced the original finish, but it is otherwise clean, complete and sound.* (GOOD) **$195.00**

D4-4. Stanley Rule & Level No. 2: 7 Inch Smooth Plane. High Knob. Crisp and Clean. Length: 7 Inches. *Here's a clean and sound example of Stanley's 7 inch smoother to fill out a collection of bench planes. A good one.* (GOOD+) **$245.00**

D4-5. Stanley Rule & Level No. 12 1/4: Narrow Scraper Plane. "Sweetheart" Trademark. Extra Crisp and Clean. Length: 6 Inches. *Substantially more narrow than the other handled scrapers in the Stanley line, the No. 12 1/4 seems not to have been very popular. Examples are quite scarce. This one retains its proper original cutter and some 98% or more of its original paint. Very nice.* (FINE) **$425.00**

D4-6. Stanley Rule & Level No. 71 1/2: Closed Throat Router Plane. With 1/4 Inch Cutter. Patented October 2, 1901. Length: 8 Inches. *Early script lettering with the Stanley imprint and patent date give this well preserved early router plane a most appealing look. Extra early and nice.* (FINE) **$85.00**

D4-7. Stanley Rule & Level No. 3: 9 Inch Smooth Plane. Later Style. Ready to Use. Length: 9 Inches. *This crispy clean bench plane retains nearly all of its original japan finish. An increasingly difficult plane to find, especially in this condition.* (FINE) **$110.00**

D4-8. Stanley Rule & Level No. 239: 1/8 Inch Special Dado Plane. Patented March 30, 1915. Early Type. No Fence. Length: 7 1/2 Inches. *Designed to meet the needs of retrofitting millions of houses with the then-newfangled electrical wiring, they may have proved a bit too specialized for most woodworkers. Used to cut a groove on the back of baseboards to hide the wire, these planes were initially offered without a fence, such as this example, but were later modified and a fence added to increase their utility. Examples of this "Type 1" variety are rare indeed. This one is in top condition.* (FINE) **$445.00**

D4-9. Stanley Rule & Level No. 39: 5/8 Inch Cast Iron Dado Plane. Patented August 12, 1902. Extra Crisp and Clean. Length: 8 Inches. *Examples of the 5/8 inch No. 39 are few and far between. A tough size to find in great shape. Here it is.* (GOOD+) **$325.00**

D4-10. Stanley Rule & Level No. 605 1/2: "Bedrock" Heavy Jack Plane. "Sweetheart" Trademark. 95% Original Paint. Length: 14 Inches. *The No. 605 1/2 added some heft to the basic jack plane by adding 1/2 inch to the width. Tougher to push, but with more momentum. The "Bedrock" mechanism make up for the difference. A nice example of a fine working tool.* (FINE) **$425.00**

D4-11. Stanley Rule & Level No. 603: Early "Bedrock" Plane. Early Type II. 95% Original Paint. Length: 8 Inches. *More than 95% of the original paint remains on this early "Bedrock" smoothing plane. An excellent example of a tough plane to find.* (GOOD+) **$345.00**

D4-12. Stanley Rule & Level No. 10 1/2: Bench Rabbet Plane. Ca. 1930's. Near New Condition. Length: 9 Inches. *This perfectly preserved example of Stanley's "carriage maker's" bench rabbet plane appears to date from the 1930's. A great working tool in top condition. Mint.* (FINE) **$425.00**

D4-13. Stanley Rule & Level No. 194: Fibre Board Beveling Plane. With Adjustable Fence. Near New Condition. Length: 8 1/2 Inches. *One of the first to enter the line of fibre board tools that was uniquely the province of Stanley Tools, this beveling plane was also one of the last to leave. This one is perfectly preserved in top collector-quality condition.* (FINE) **$115.00**

D4-14. Stanley Rule & Level No. 604 C: "Bedrock" Smooth Plane. Corrugated Bottom. Crisp and Clean. Length: 9 Inches. *Stanley's "Bedrock" planes are much in demand for their superior functionality. Here's a clean and sound example that is ready to use.* (GOOD+) **$245.00**

D4-15. Stanley Rule & Level No. 39: Cast Iron Dado Plane. 1/2 Inch Size. Extra Crisp and Clean. Length: 8 Inches. *An excellent example of the 1/2 inch size of the No. 39 series. A good one.* (GOOD+) **$225.00**

D4-16. Stanley Rule & Level No. 78: Duplex Filletster Plane. Sweetheart Trademark. Partial Original Decal. Length: 9 1/2 Inches. *Nearly all of the shiny original paint and much of the Stanley decal remain on this perfect example of Stanley's rabbet plane.* (FINE) **$155.00**

D4-17. Stanley Rule & Level No. 39: Cast Iron Dado Plane. 1/2 Inch Size. Ca. 1907 Trademark. Length: 8 Inches. *This screw on the cap iron of this 1/2 inch dado plane is marked with the ca. 1907 trademark. Nearly all original finishes remain.* (FINE) **$275.00**

D4-18. Stanley Rule & Level No. 602: "Bedrock" Smoothing Plane. Ca. 1915. Clean and Sound. Length: 7 Inches. *Here's a crispy clean example of Stanley's "Bedrock" version of its No. 2, 7 inch smooth plane. The japanning has been lightly "enhanced" but this plane is otherwise without apology. A nice example.* (GOOD+) **$745.00**

D4-19. Stanley Rule & Level No. 190: 1 1/2 Inch Rabbeting Plane. Ready to Use. Early Arch Trademark. Length: 8 Inches. *Here's a good early example of Stanley's 1 1/2 inch fixed rabbeting plane. A good one.* (GOOD) **$55.00**

D4-20. Stanley Rule & Level No. 2 C: 7 Inch Smoothing Plane. Rare Corrugated Sole. Ca. 1930's. Length: 7 Inches. *For some reason, unlike the case with nearly every other Stanley bench plane, purchasers of the diminutive No. 2 smoother seemed not to prefer the corrugated sole version, which was offered beginning in 1897. Despite the 30 year production head start that the smooth bottom variety was given, there seems no apparent explanation for the lack of corrugated sole examples among all No. 2 planes produced since 1900. We proudly offer this well preserved example, which retains some 95% of its original paint. A tough plane to find, especially in this condition.* (GOOD+) **$725.00**

D4-21. Stanley Rule & Level No. 607: "Bedrock" Jointer Plane. Later Type, Square Sides. Extra Crisp and Clean. Length: 22 Inches. *This pristine "Bedrock" jointer plane dates from the 1930's. Nearly new.* (FINE) **$445.00**

D4-22. Stanley Rule & Level No. 40: Beech Handle Scrub Plane. Early "V" Trademark. Superb Condtiion. Length: 11 Inches. *This extra-early scrub plane has much of the bright yellow lacquer on the handles and a good 95% or more of the original paint. A nice example of a great working tool.* (GOOD+) **$145.00**

D4-23. Stanley Rule & Level No. 606: "Bedrock" Fore Plane. Ca. 1907. Later Style. Length: 18 Inches. *This clean No. 606 "Bedrock" fore plane is in excellent working order. Crisp, clean and ready to use.* (GOOD+) **$325.00**

D4-24. Stanley Rule & Level No. 98/99: Pair of Side Rabbet Planes. With Depth Stops. Excellent Condition. Length: 4 Inches. *These side rabbet planes are fitted with the desirable adjustable depth stops that were not added to the tool until after it had been produced for many years. The base of one of the rosewood handles has been modified in a way that will not affect its function, but these planes are otherwise, crisp, clean and ready to use.* (GOOD+) **$325.00**

D4-25. Stanley Rule & Level No. 5 1/4: "Junior Jack" Plane. 1 3/4 Inch Cutter. Rosewood Handles. Length: 11 Inches. *The "Junior" jack plane, was the width of a No. 3 and just a bit shorter than a No. 5. Although these were marketed to manual training schools, these tools have found favor among latter-day woodworkers. This pristine is as nice an example as we have offered in some time.* (FINE) **$195.00**

D4-26. Stanley Rule & Level No. 39: Cast Iron Dado Plane. 3/8 Inch Size. Superb Condiditon. Length: 8 Inches. *This example of the "common" 3/8 inch dado plane is in anything but common condition. Choice.* (FINE) **$275.00**

D4-27. Stanley Rule & Level No. 72: Adjustable Chamfer Plane. Patented April 2, 1885. Extra Crisp and Clean. Length: 9 Inches. *Designed to facilitate the planing of chamfers on the edges of boards and beams, these were a very specific special-purpose tool that would have been purchased by only a very limited number of woodworkers. Examples, accordingly, are rare. This nearly perfectly preserved example retains 98%+ of its original paint. It has the early patent date cast into the body of the plane.* (FINE) **$465.00**

D4-28. Stanley Rule & Level No. 101: "Toy" Block Plane. Ca. 1930's. 99% Original Paint. Length: 3 1/4 Inches. *This shiny clean block plane looks to have been very little used. Nice.* (FINE) **$35.00**

D4-29. Stanley Rule & Level No. 26: Transitional Jack Plane. With Eagle Trademark. Early and Excellent. Length: 15 Inches. *This early prelateral transitional has been boldly struck with the early Stanley "eagle" imprint on the toe of the plane. A tough plane to find in this condition.* (GOOD+) **$95.00**

D4-30. Stanley Rule & Level No. 4 C: 9 Inch Smoothing Plane. With Corrugated Sole. Ca. 1930's Trademark. Length: 9 Inches. *This corrugated sole version of Stanley's 9 inch smoothing plane is in near new condition, retaining some 98% of its original paint. A nice example that is ready to be put back to work.* (GOOD+) **$125.00**

D4-31. Stanley Rule & Level No. 2: Smoothing Plane. Ca. 1930's. 99% Original Paint. Length: 7 Inches. *This magnificent example of the No. 2 smoothing plane retains nearly all of its shiny black paint as well as the nickel plating on the cap iron. Extra nice.* (FINE) **$295.00**

D4-32. Stanley Rule & Level No. 27/35: Pair of Transitional Planes. For Restoration. Worth Working On. Length: 15 Inches. *Here's a bargain for the tool restorationist. These planes are complete, but have some tote damage and a bit of grunge. An opportunity.* (GOOD) **$35.00**

D4-33. Stanley Rule & Level No. 605: "Bedrock" Jack Plane. Rosewood Handles. "Sweetheart" Trademark. Length: 14 Inches. *Bearing the No. 605 designation of Stanley's respected "Bedrock" series, this was, without question the very best jack plane ever offered. Ready to put to use.* (GOOD+) **$255.00**

D4-34. Stanley Rule & Level No. 39: Cast Iron Dado Plane. "3/4" Width. Brand New Condition. Length: 8 Inches. *A picture perfect 3/4 inch cast iron dado plane in the most popular 3/4 inch size. 99% original finishes. Mint.* (FINE) **$345.00**

D4-35. Stanley Rule & Level No. 605: "Bedrock" Jack Plane. Later Type, Square Side. Ca. 1910. Length: 13 1/2 Inches. *As nice an example of the early Bedrock jack plane as you are likely to find. Some 98% of the original paint remains. A good one.* (FINE) **$295.00**

D4-36. Stanley Rule & Level No. 191: 1 1/4 Inch Rabbet Plane. "Sweetheart" Trademark. Ready to Use. Length: 10 1/2 Inches. *The earliest examples of Stanley's fixed and adjustable rabbeting and filletster planes featured this classic Victorian "vine" casting. Missing the depth stop, which could be easily replaced, this is a tough plane to find.* (GOOD) **$35.00**

D4-37. Stanley Rule & Level No. 7: Early "Bedrock" Plane. Earliest Type. Pre "600" Designation. Length: 22 Inches. *The presence of a single patent date is the only distinction between the Type 1 and Type 2 of the "Bedrock" series is the absence of a second patent date on the lateral adjustment lever on the Type 2 planes. This plane, which bears the "No. 7" designation only, predates the bedrock "600" numbering scheme. A well preserved early bedrock plane in top condition.* (GOOD+) **$325.00**

D4-38. Stanley Rule & Level No. 6: "Bedrock" Fore Plane. Early Type 2. Ground Off Patent Date. Length: 18 Inches. *Here's a well preserved example of the early "Type 2" "Bedrock" plane. Clean, complete and sound.* (GOOD) **$325.00**

D4-39. Stanley Rule & Level No. 26: Transitional Jack Plane. "Sweetheart" Trademark. Excellent Working Condition. Length: 15 Inches. *A previous owner of this well preserved transitional has "enhanced" the japanning to improve its appearance. A nice example.* (GOOD+) **$65.00**

D4-40. Stanley Rule & Level No. 608: "Bedrock" Jointer Plane. Early "Type 2". Machined Patent Date. Length: 24 Inches. *The earliest versions of the "Bedrock" planes, which researchers have dubbed "Type 1" and "Type 2", are distinguishable by milling marks on the body where a patent date of September 3, 1895 that was cast into the body was removed after the japanning was in place. The conventional wisdom is that the patent information was removed because the feature was not used on the plane, however, we find it unlikely that Stanley would have gone to the expense of removing the patent date unless some sort of litigation required that it do so. This is a potential gold mine for a researcher willing to dig through civil litigation records of the period. Here's a rare example of one of the reprocessed planes. Rare.* (GOOD+) **$395.00**

D4-41. Stanley Rule & Level No. 607 C: "Bedrock" Jointer Plane. With Corrugated Sole. "Sweetheart" Trademark. Length: 22 Inches. *Here's a good, clean "Bedrock" jointer in excellent overall condition. An increasingly tough plane to find.* (GOOD+) **$325.00**

D4-42. Stanley Rule & Level No. 95: Edge Trim Block Plane. "Sweetheart" Trademark. Ready to Use. Length: 6 Inches. *If you're looking for the No. 95 edge trim block plane, stop here. This one retains more than 95% of its orignal paint and is in excellent overall condition.* (GOOD+) **$165.00**

D4-43. Stanley Rule & Level No. 129: "Liberty Bell Fore Plane. 95% Original Paint. All Original Lacquer. Length: 20 Inches. *The absence of the original cap iron has kept this "Liberty Bell" transitional plane in nearly new condition. An opportunity for a collector with the proper part.* (FINE) **$165.00**

D4-44. Stanley Rule & Level No. 604 1/2: "Bedrock" Smoothing Plane. Ca. 1910. Excellent Condition. Length: 10 Inches. *We highly recommend the Stanley Bedrock series based on numerous testimonials from satisfied customers. Designed to totally eliminate "chatter" when planing— they apparently did just that. This, the wide, heavy smoothing plane evokes near-religious devotion from serious woodworkers who have taken the step up to Bedrock. This nearly perfectly preserved example of the rare and desirable No. 604 1/2 wide, smoothing plane is ready to provide decades of service before being passed on through the family. A superb example.* (FINE) **$785.00**

D4-45. Stanley Rule & Level No. 3: 9 Inch Smooth Plane. "Type 11". Superb Condition. Length: 9 Inches. *Stanley's "Type 11" planes are easily identified by the presence of 3 patent dates cast into the bed of the plane behind the frog and the presence of the early low front knob. These planes have developed a reputation among woodworkers as the high point of utility and aesthetic appeal in Stanley bench planes. Examples are difficult to find and sell very quickly. First come, first serve.* (FINE) **$145.00**

Group E4

E4-1. Bridgeport Hardware Mfg. Co., The: Official "Boy Scout" Hatchet. Uncommon Type. Solid Forged Body. Length: 13 1/2 Inches. *We are unaware of the arrangement by which hatchet makers were certified to provide hatchets to the Scouts. Whatever the case, the B.S.A. crowd apparently didn't do much business with the Bridgeport Hardware Company—these hatchets are rare. A nice example.* (GOOD+) **$85.00**

E4-2. Unmarked: Carpenters Half Hatchet. 4 Inch Hewing Edge. Crisp and Ready to Use. Length: 12 1/2 Inches. *There are no maker's marks on this well preserved hewing hatchet in great working condition. Ready to use.* (GOOD+) **$55.00**

E4-3. Sayre & Co., L.A., Newark, N.J.: Classic "Camp" Hatchet. Graphic Handle. Uncommon Maker. Length: 13 1/2 Inches. *A particularly gracefully formed handle accents this well made hatchet from a most uncommon maker. According to the Directory of American Toolmakers, Sayre worked in Newark, New Jersey from 1884 to 1916.* (GOOD+) **$85.00**

E4-4. Vaughn & Bushnell, Chicago, Illinois: Forged "Boy Scout" Hatchet. "Safthed Axe". Rare and Excellent. Length: 13 Inches. *This special design hatchet is the first of its type that we have encountered. A rare Scouting collectible in collector quality condition.* (GOOD+) **$145.00**

E4-5. Cheney Corp., H., Little Falls, N.Y.: Rare "Cheney" Hatchet. Original Label. Never Seen Another. Length: 14 Inches. *Much of the original label remains on this, the only example of hatchet by the prominent H. Cheney Company that we have ever encountered. If these tools were part of the general production line at Cheney, other examples would have been found over the last two decades. We suspect that a number of these were produced as prototypes and test marketed with discouraging results. An extremely rare hatchet.* (GOOD+) **$475.00**

E4-6. Estwing Mfg. Co., Rockford, Illinois: Rare "Utilax" Hatchet. Earliest Estwing. Multi Purpose Tool. Length: 13 Inches. *The Estwing Company of Rockford, Illinois is well known for their hammers with laminated leather handles. This early "Utilax" incorporates a nail puller and pick into its design. The first example of this uncommon tool that we have ever offered. Rare.* (GOOD+) **$225.00**

E4-7. Unmarked: Carpenter's Half Hatchet. Single Bevel Edge. Ready to Use. Length: 14 Inches. *This classic "Kent Pattern" hatchet features a single bevel edge. It was used for hewing and stands ready to perform that function for the new owner. An excellent working tool.* (FINE) **$65.00**

E4-8. Unmarked: Early Light Duty Hatchet. "Patent Applied For". With Pointed Poll. Length: 11 Inches. *Here's a specialized tool that is unique in my experience. Marked only "Patent Applied For", this was obviously intended for some light-duty function, perhaps even for kitchen use. Different.* (FINE) **$85.00**

E4-9. S.H. Co., St. Louis, Missouri: 4 Inch Hewing Hatchet. Single Bevel Edge. Ready to Use. Length: 15 Inches. *The S.H. Co. is undoubtedly Simmons Hardware, the folks who brought us the "Keen Kutter" hatchet. This one is in essentially unused condition. An excellent working tool.* (FINE) **$65.00**

E4-10. Shapleigh Hardware, St. Louis: Carpenter's Side Hatchet. Near New Condition. With Leather Keeper. Length: 14 Inches. *A fitted leather "keeper" has kept this side hatchet in top working condition. Extra nice.* (FINE) **$85.00**

E4-11. Peck, Stow & Wilcox Co., Conn.: "Pexto" Shingling Hatchet. Uncommon Type. Original Handle. Length: 12 Inches. *We have offered a wide range of "Pexto" tools, but this is the first shingling hatchet we have encountered. A rare P.S. & W. tool.* (GOOD+) **$55.00**

E4-12. Plumb, Fayette R., Philadelphia: Genuine "Boy Scout" Hatchet. Original Handle. Extra Crisp and Clean. Length: 14 Inches. *Someone has removed the lacquer finish from the handle of this classic Boy Scout axe, but the head is in brand new condition. A keepsake collectible.* (FINE) **$45.00**

E4-13. Plumb, Fayette R., Philadelphia: Genuine "Boy Scout" Hatchet. Hickory Handle. "Official Scout Axe". Length: 13 1/2 Inches. *The "Official Scout Axe" inscription is forged into the head of this collectible classic. A nice example.* (GOOD+) **$65.00**

E4-14. Fulton Tool Company: Carpenter's Side Hatchet. 6 Inch Blade. Extra Crisp and Clean. Length: 18 Inches. *The 6 inch blade on this carpenter's side axe is in excellent working order. A nice working tool.* (FINE) **$65.00**

E4-15. Collins & Company, Hartford, Conn.: Classic Lathing Hatchet. Near New Condition. Original Decal. Length: 12 3/4 Inches. *Much of the original decal remains on the handle of this crispy clean lathing hatchet from a legendary Connecticut maker of edge tools.* (FINE) **$85.00**

E4-16. Unmarked: Unusual Bronze Hatchet. With Inset Blade. Original Handle. Length: 15 Inches. *This extraordinary hatchet features a head of cast bronze that has a steel edge fit into it as a "sandwich" inside the bronze. It is unmarked, but may embody a patented design. Never seen another.* (GOOD+) **$295.00**

E4-17. Marble's Arms & Mfg. Co.: No. 3: Folding Camp Hatchet. India Rubber Handle. Near New Condition. Length: 11 Inches. *Here's a great example of the Marble "Camp Hatchet". Only a tight crack in one handle detracts from this otherwise perfect tool. Rare.* (FINE) **$365.00**

E4-18. Acme: Carpenter's Hatchet. Original Labels. Near-New Condition. Length: 15 Inches. *Other than brand his name in the reverse side, the previous owner did nothing at all with this well-preserved tool.* (FINE) **$95.00**

E4-19. Smith & Co., H.D., Plantsville, Conn.: "Perfect Handle" Hatchet. "Patented". Rare and Excellent. Length: 12 Inches. *A nice example of the rare "Perfect Handle" carpenter's hatchet, with its distinctive inlaid grip. A tough tool to find. This one is in excellent condition.* (GOOD+) **$465.00**

E4-20. American Ax & Tool Co., Glassport,: Early Patent Hatchet. Patented April 17, 1900. Rare and Clearly Marked. Length: 15 Inches. *"A.A. & T. Co." is the uncommon maker abbreviation on the head of this patented hatchet, which is also clearly stamped with the patent date. A most unusual patented hatchet.* (GOOD) **$75.00**

E4-21. Champion Fitzall: Salesman's Sample Axe and Hammer Handles. Original Felt Roll. Original Labels. Length: 14 Inches. *We have seen a number of small tools put forward as "salesman's samples" when that was decidedly not the case. Salesman's samples are not small tools, but full size tools made on a small scale to showcase the features of the article without being burdened by the size. These axe and hammer handles are exactly that. Rare and brand new.* (FINE) **$125.00**

E4-22. Kelly Axe Mfg. Co., Charleston, W.V.: Embossed Hammer, Hatchet. Original "Keeper". Near New Condition. Length: 13 1/2 Inches. *Get your sunglasses out for this one. This deeply-etched hatchet retains all of its original factory polish, which has been protected by the leather sheath. Nearly new.* (FINE) **$165.00**

E4-23. Plumb, Philadelphia, Penn.: Official Girl Scout Hatchet. Original Decal. Leather Keeper. Length: 11 1/2 Inches. *No, this one hasn't begun to grow mold from having spent too much time stored in the root cellar. That's the original Girl Scout Green finish on the handle of this official (Scout's Honor) Girl Scouts of America hatchet. Our daughter, who has spent all of her 16 years in the intimate company of tools, has never once asked for an edge tool of any sort. Alas, it could be that the original owner of this one would have preferred something else. This one shows little evidence of use.* (FINE) **$165.00**

E4-24. Bean, L.L., Freeport, Maine: Child's Camp Axe. Original Decal. Near New Condition. Length: 10 Inches. *This 1950's era child's hatchet looks like something Ward and June would have picked up for the Beaver on their trip to Maine. Well, Theodore never got a chance to try this one out on Lumpy Rutherford's father's car—it's as nice and new as the day it left Freeport. An extra-special addition to a collection of small axes.* (FINE) **$165.00**

E4-25. Hults, Swrige: Swedish Child's Hatchet. Original Label. Superb Condition. Length: 10 1/2 Inches. *This undersize child's hatchet is imprinted with the name of a Swedish maker and retains its original paper label. It was acquired in Northern Maine, where children were introduced early to edge tools. A perfect example of a rare collectible hatchet.* (FINE) **$185.00**

E4-26. Germantown Tool Works, Philadelphia, Penn.: No. 2: Lathing Hatchet. Original Paper Label. Near New Condition. Length: 12 Inches. *A nearly perfectly-preserved hatchet, this one comes from the Germantown works of Philadelphia. Lathing hatchets were squared off at the top to facilitate working with laths next to the ceiling. (No extra charge for Tool Facts provided obiter dicta). An extra nice hatchet.* (FINE) **$85.00**

E4-27. Marbles, Gladstone, Mich.: No. 6: "Camp" Hatchet. With Patent Guard. Clean and Sound. Length: 12 Inches. *The protective handle and retractable "keeper" guard are in excellent condition on this clean and sound example of a classic Marbles hatchet.* (GOOD) **$245.00**

E4-28. Hammond, C., Philadelphia, Penn.: Early Carpenter's Hatchet. Kent Pattern. Ready to Use. Length: 16 Inches. *The "Kent Pattern" hatchet is beveled on one side and used for hewing. This example from a prominent and early Philadelphia maker is in excellent working order.* (GOOD+) **$55.00**

E4-29. Plumb, Fayette R., Philadelphia: Genuine "Boy Scout" Hatchet. Original Canvas Case. Original Handle. Length: 13 1/2 Inches. *The original canvas case has kept this Scouting collectible in excellent condition. A nice example.* (GOOD+) **$65.00**

E4-30. Plumb, Fayette R., Philadelphia: No. 2: "Autograph" Model Hatchet. With Gold Infill. Unused Condition. Length: 13 1/2 Inches. *This classic "Autograph" model of the plumb shingling hatchet is in brand new condition. Absolutely perfect.* (FINE) **$115.00**

E4-31. Collins & Company, Hartford, Conn.: No. 2: Carpenter's Hatchet. New Old Stock. Original Decal. Length: 12 3/4 Inches. *Here's a classic Collins carpenter's hatchet in brand new condition. This tool was recently discovered in storage in a Michigan hardware store. Absolutely brand new.* (FINE) **$95.00**

E4-32. Kelly Axe Mfg. Co., Charleston, W.V.: "Hammer" Hatchet. Embossed Image. Rare and Excellent. Length: 13 3/4 Inches. *The hammer and nail puller on this hatchet make it likely that it was intended for the task of splitting and applying cedar shingles. A bold embossed image makes this tool highly collectible.* (GOOD+) **$125.00**

E4-33. Underhill Edge Tool Co., Nashua: Carpenter's Side Hatchet. 5 Inch Blade. Ready to Use. Length: 16 Inches. *Beveled on only one edge, the carpenter's side axe was used for rough shaping of timber before it was sawn or planed to more precise dimensions. This example is marked with the name of the legendary Underhill Edge Tool Company of Nashua, New Hampshire. An excellent working tool.* (GOOD+) **$65.00**

E4-34. Sears, Roebuck & Co.: "Golden Jubilee" Hatchet. With Embossed Logo. Ca. 1936. Length: 14 Inches. *Sears, Roebuck and Company celebrated 50 years in business in 1936 by issuing a line of "Golden Jubilee" tools. A nice example of an increasingly collectible line.* (GOOD+) **$85.00**

E4-35. Plumb, Fayette R., Philadelphia: 4 Inch Carpenter's Hewin Hatchet. Original Handle. Ready to Use. Length: 15 1/2 Inches. *This hewing hatchet from a respected maker is in excellent working order. Ready to use.* (GOOD+) **$55.00**

E4-36. Unmarked: Carpenter's Side Hatchet. Single Bevel Cut. Ready to Use. Length: 13 3/4 Inches. *The 4 inch cutting edge on this side hatchet is in excellent shape and ready to provide years of service.* (GOOD+) **$55.00**

E4-37. Kelly Axe Mfg. Co., Charleston, W.V.: Rare Claw Hatchet. Uncommon Type. Near New Condition. Length: 14 Inches. *Pulling nails with a hatchet head would tend to loosen the head, which may account for the scarcity of hatchets in this pattern. A nice example from a respected maker.* (GOOD+) **$35.00**

E4-38. Witte Hardware Co., St. Louis, Missouri: Deep Embossed Hatchet. With "Ixl" Tradmark. Rare and Excellent. Length: 14 Inches. *The distinctive logo of a St. Louis hardware dealer is embossed on this hatchet. Different.* (GOOD+) **$65.00**

E4-39. Unmarked: Hand-Forged Hatchet. Early Appearance. Superb Patina. Length: 14 Inches. *The handle, the shape of the head and the manner in which this tool was forged all indicate that it is a very early hatchet. The original hand-hewn handle adds an extra element of charm.* (GOOD+) **$45.00**

E4-40. Vaughn & Bushnell, Chicago, Illinois: Embossed Carpenter's Hatchet. With "V. & B." Logo. Crisp and Clean. Length: 13 1/2 Inches. *The imprint of Chicago area hammer and edge tool makers Vaughn & Bushnell is embossed in the surface of this carpenter's hatchet.* (GOOD+) **$65.00**

E4-41. Plumb, Fayette R., Philadelphia: Genuine "Boy Scout" Hatchet. Original Leather Case. Original Handle. Length: 12 1/2 Inches. *Here's an excellent "Boy Scout" hatchet in great condition for the collection, complete with its original belt sheath.* (GOOD+) **$65.00**

E4-42. Unmarked: Early Hand Forged Hatchet. From Phipps Museum. Excellent Condition. Length: 9 1/4 Inches. *This nicely hand forged shingling hatchet was acquired at the dispersal of the Phipps Museum near Cleveland, Ohio. Museum quality.* (GOOD+) **$65.00**

E4-43. Unmarked No. 4: Carpenter's Side Hatchet. Single Edge Bevel. Ready to Use. Length: 15 1/2 Inches. *Green woodworkers use tools such as this for rough hewing of wood to workable size. This one is in excellent condition and ready to be put back to work.* (GOOD+) **$55.00**

E4-44. Rogers, L.: Patented Lathing Hatchet. Patented April 7, 1896. Marked "Ideal". Length: 13 1/2 Inches. *We are not aware of the patent feature embodied in the 1896 patent imprinted on this specialized hatchet. An uncommon patented hatchet.* (GOOD) **$65.00**

E4-45. Plumb, Fayette R., Philadelphia: Genuine "Boy Scout" Hatchet. Original Canvas Case. Exclellent Condition. Length: 14 Inches. *Here's a classic "Boy Scout" hatchet from a prominent edge tool maker. A previous owner, one "W.W." inscribed his initials into the handle on the reverse side, but this hatchet is otherwise in excellent condition.* (GOOD+) **$55.00**

E4-46. Vaughn & Bushnell, Chicago, Illinois: Embossed Lathing Hatchet. Deep Ethced Logo. Rare and Excellent. Length: 13 Inches. *This embossed lathing hatchet has the mark of Chicago dealer Vaughn & Bushnell. Most unusual.* (GOOD+) **$75.00**

E4-47. Unmarked: "Indian Chief" Belt Axe. With "Fire" Pick. With Original Sheath. Length: 14 Inches. *This "Indian Chief" axe/hatchet comes with a sheath for mounting it on a belt. The fact that nearly all Indian chiefs did not wear belts may account for the fact that it is in nearly new condition. A rare collectible hatchet.* (FINE) **$225.00**

Group F4

F4-1. Assorted Makers: Set of 7 Assorted Carving Tools. With Rifflers. Addis, Buck, Etc. Length: 11 Inches. *The names, Addis and Buck are among those included in this group of ready to use carving tools. A nice set.* (GOOD+) **$55.00**

F4-2. Stanley Rule & Level No. 99: Set of "Atha" Cold Chisels. 4 Chisels in Roll. Rare and Near New. Length: 6 Inches. *Four of the original six chisels remain of this set of Stanley's "Atha" brand cold chisels. All are in excellent condition and clearly marked with both the "Atha" and "Stanley" marks.* (FINE) **$135.00**

F4-3. Ibbotson & Co., Thos: Lock Mortise Chisel. 1/2 Inch Width. Ready to Use. Length: 22 Inches. *This lock mortise chisel from Thomas Ibbotson is in great working order. Ready to use, if you choose.* (GOOD+) **$55.00**

F4-4. Millers Falls Company No. 107: Boxed Set of Carving Tools. With Palm Fitted Handles. Original Box. Length: 5 1/2 Inches. *These carving tools were intended to be held in the palm of the hand when in use. All are in excellent condition and ready to be put immediately to use.* (FINE) **$75.00**

F4-5. Berg, Erik, Eskilstuna, Sweden: Set of 5 "Shark" Chisel. Socket and Tang. Ready to Use. Length: 9 Inches. *These classic "Shark" brand chisels came from a single owner, who assembled them for use and kept them in working order. A great working set.* (GOOD+) **$125.00**

F4-6. Barton, D.R., Rochester: No. 15: Bent Gouge Carving Tool. Fruitwood Handle. Extra Crisp and Clean. Length: 5 Inches. *This massive gouge is boldly struck with the trademark "1832" imprint of D.R. Barton & Company, who were renowned for their edge tool making in the 1850's and remain so today.* (GOOD+) **$65.00**

F4-7. Addis, S.J., London: No. 40: 1 1/4 Inch "V" Gouge Carving Tool. Octagon Boxwood Handle. Ready to Use. Length: 6 Inches. *An extra-wide and oversize gouge by a great maker.* (FINE) **$135.00**

F4-8. Berg, Erik, Eskilstuna, Sweden: 1 1/2 Inch "Shark" Chisel. Socket Type. Partial Decal. Length: 8 1/2 Inches. *Other than the initials that a previous owner left in the handle, this 1 1/2 inch "Shark" brand chisel is in top condition. Legendary Swedish quality.* (GOOD+) **$35.00**

F4-9. Stanley Rule & Level No. 750: Bevel Edge Socket Chisel. 1 1/2 Inch Width. Near New Condition. Length: 10 Inches. *This 1 1/2 inch "Red Handle" No. 750 chisel may have been used a time or two, but it shows itself very little worse for wear as a consequence. A tough size to find, especially in this condition.* (FINE) **$55.00**

F4-10. Barton & Co., D.R., Rochester, N.Y.: No. 10: 1 1/2 Inch Tang Gouge. Deep Sweep. Octagon Boxwood Handle. Length: 7 Inches. *Another oversize carving tool. This one has the mark of Rochester, New York maker D.R. Barton & Co. Crisp, clean and ready to use.* (FINE) **$85.00**

F4-11. Stanley Rule & Level No. 50: 3/8 Inch "Everlasting" Chisel. Bevel Edge. Original Decal. Length: 9 Inches. *The amount of the original decal remaining on the handle is testimony to the lack of use this chisel has enjoyed. As a consequence it is in top collector quality condition and ready to fill out a set or be put back to work.* (FINE) **$95.00**

F4-12. Unmarked: Steep Angle "V" Cut Carving Tool. Early Octagon Handle. Ready to Use. Length: 12 Inches. *This unmarked "V" gouge has a steeper than normal slope to its sides. Ready to use.* (GOOD+) **$65.00**

F4-13. Buck Brothers No. 11: Deep Gouge Carving Tool. Crisp and Clean. Ready to Use. Length: 10 Inches. *This wide, deep gouge retains plenty of cutting edge and is ready to be put back into use. Crisp, clean and ready to use.* (FINE) **$45.00**

F4-14. Stanley Rule & Level No. 50: 1/4 Inch "Everlasting" Chisel. Bevel Edge. Original Decal. Length: 9 Inches. *This crispy clean "Everlasting" chisel is in nearly new condition. Most examples in this size were used as screwdrivers or pry bars and consequently met an early end to their useful life. This one didn't.* (GOOD) **$115.00**

F4-15. Veritas: Blind Nailing Tool. With Original Chisel. Ready to Use. Length: 5 1/2 Inches. *Based on the design of Stanley's blind nailing device, which lifted a sliver of wood before a nail or brad was used, this recent reproduction is in great working order.* (FINE) **$15.00**

F4-16. Addis, S.J., London: No. 45: 1 Inch Front Bent "V" Carving Tool. Octagon Boxwood Handle. Ready to Use. Length: 6 1/2 Inches. *This massive "V" gouge is fitted with an octagonal boxwood handle. The condition of the blade is nearly new.* (FINE) **$145.00**

F4-17. Assorted Makers: Assorted Punches and Chisels. Blue Grass, Etc. Ready to Use. Length: 4 Inches. *This opportunity lot includes a grouping of chisels, punches, etc. from a range of makers, including the legendary "Blue Grass" brand name of the Belknap Hardware Company of Louisville, Kentucky. First come, first serve.* (GOOD+) **$25.00**

F4-18. Assorted Makers: Working Set of 10 Carving Tools. Mahogany Handles. Ready to Use. Length: 7 3/4 Inches. *Matching handles of mahogany accent this great working set of carving tools. All are in ready to use condition.* (GOOD+) **$125.00**

F4-19. Simmons Hardware Co., E.C.: 1 1/2 Inch "Keen Kutter" Chisel. Socket Type. Extra Crisp and Clean. Length: 8 1/2 Inches. *This crisp and clean 1 1/2 inch socket chisel bears the distinctive "Keen Kutter" logo of the E.C. Simmons Hardware Company. An excellent working tool from an important tool distributor.* (GOOD+) **$45.00**

F4-20. Berg, Erik, Eskilstuna, Sweden: 1 1/4 Inch "Shark" Chisel. Wooden Handle. Original Decal. Length: 8 1/2 Inches. *The handle of the 1 1/4 inch chisel bears the logo of the "Shark" brand trademark of E. Berg, the legendary Swedish edge tool maker.* (FINE) **$45.00**

F4-21. Howarth, James, Sheffield, England: Early Tang Gouge. 3/8 Inch Width. Ready to Use. Length: 9 1/2 Inches. *This early carving gouge is boldly struck with the imprint of redoubtable English maker James Howarth. An excellent working tool.* (GOOD+) **$25.00**

F4-22. Stanley Rule & Level No. X750 A: "Christmas" Set of Chisels. 3 No. 750 Size. New Conditon, Original Box. Length: 10 Inches. *The original outer sleeve has protected this presentation set of Stanley's No. 750 "red handle" chisels for many years. New and in the box.* (GOOD+) **$125.00**

F4-23. Heller & Bros., Newark, N.J.: No. 4: Horse Tooth File. With Extension. New Condition, Original Box. Length: 12 Inches. *The previous owner of this one apparently let his steeds get a bit long in the tooth, as this one shows nary a bit of wear. The box has been reinforced with some tape, but it is otherwise in great condition, as is the rasp. A most unusual tool.* (FINE) **$95.00**

F4-24. Mix & Co., G.I. No. 1 EX: Heavy Socket Corner Chisel. 1 Inch Width. Superb Condition. Length: 16 Inches. *G.I. Mix & Company produced high quality edge tools in Connecticut during the last century. This well preserved corner chisel is crisp, clean and very clearly marked with the Mix imprint.* (GOOD+) **$75.00**

F4-25. Assorted Makers: Set of 44 Carving Tools. Owner "Gavron". Victrola Carver. Length: 9 Inches. *This extraordinary set of small carving tools belonged to a gentleman who worked at the carving of "Victrola" cases in the years prior to the First World War. These tools come to us from a family member (a nephew) who has kept and treasured them for many, many years. All of the tools are in excellent working condition and could be immediately be put to use. An exceptional working set of carving tools in great condition.* (GOOD+) **$795.00**

F4-26. Wilcox & Co. (Guilford, Conn.): Heavy Socket Framing Chisel. 1 1/4 Inch Width. Near New Condition. Length: 15 1/2 Inches. *The maker's mark of Wilcox & Co. on this Socket framing chisel indicates very early manufacture. A William Wilcox & Co. is listed in the EAIA Directory as working in Guilford, Connecticut in 1851. A rare chisel in near-new condition.* (FINE) **$85.00**

F4-27. Butcher, W.: Set of Early Gouges. Full Set of 11. Extra Long Handles. Length: 17 Inches. *Full sets of gouges have become increasingly difficult to find. Finding sets such as this array of eleven tang handled in-cannel gouges was never an easy task. These have been tucked away in a private corner of a collection for the past 30 years. We would recommend that the next owner do the same with them, although they are in excellent condition to use. A great set in top condition. Highly recommended.* (FINE) **$595.00**

F4-28. Buck Brothers: Set of 8 Crank Neck Gouges. Extra Crisp and Clean. Incannel Grind. Length: 17 Inches. *A set of gouges such as these would have been essential for anyone undertaking the trade of the patternmaker. of primary importance for today's woodworker for scribing, these tools are in excellent working order and ready to be put to use.* (FINE) **$385.00**

F4-29. Unmarked: Set of Lathe Turning Tools. For Brass, Boxwood. Very Well Preserved. Length: 9 1/2 Inches. *These mid-size turning tools are fitted with distinctive turned boxwood handles. An excellent set for the novice or casual turner—or the collector.* (GOOD+) **$125.00**

F4-30. Douglass Mfg. Co.: Heavy Socket Framing Chisel. 2 Inch Size. "Bevel Back" Type. Length: 17 Inches. *This sturdy 2 inch chisel features the desirable "bevel back" design. An excellent tool that is clean, straight, sharp and ready to use.* (GOOD+) **$115.00**

F4-31. Stanley Rule & Level No. 720: 1 1/2 Inch Bevel Edge Chisel. Near New Condition. Rare and Excellent. Length: 14 Inches. *This extra long 1 1/2 inch chisel is ready to go to work or fill our a set, or both. One of the most often used sizes, this is a tough size to find in this condition.* (FINE) **$65.00**

F4-32. Stanley Rule & Level No. 720: 2 Inch Bevel Edge Chisel. Unused Condition. Rare and Excellent. Length: 14 Inches. *This No. 720 "Red Handle" chisel in the largest size offered appears never to have been used. Mint.* (FINE) **$85.00**

F4-33. Reliance, Youngstown, Ohio: Heavy Socket Corner Chisel. 1 Inch Width. Original Hanlde. Length: 16 Inches. *We have had a number of tools imprinted with the "Reliance" brand name in the past and all were of exceptional quality. We suspect that they were made to order for a Youngstown hardware dealers during the 19th Century. A great working tool in top condition.* (FINE) **$75.00**

F4-34. Underhill Edge Tool Co.: Heavy Socket Framing Chisel. 1 1/4 Size. Crisp and Clean. Length: 16 Inches. *This heavy socket framing chisel from the prominent Underhill Edge Tool Company retains its original handle and is in ready to use condition. A good one.* (GOOD+) **$75.00**

F4-35. Addis, S.J., London: Set of 6 Carving Tools. From Single Owner. Near New Condition. Length: 8 1/2 Inches. *Brass ferrules and identically turned handles accent this great working set of carving tools from legendary London maker S.J. Addis. A great set.* (FINE) **$365.00**

F4-36. Assorted Makers: Set of 3 Hand Made Files. Individually Cut. Scarce and Excellent. Length: 12 Inches. *Each of the files in this grouping was hand cut in the classic style by men working long hours with hammer and chisel. All were assembled by a single collector to complement a collection of file makers' tools. A time capsule of early technology.* (FAIR) **$125.00**

F4-37. Addis, S. J., London: No. 19: Deep Hollowing Gouge. 3/4 Inch Width. Ready to Use. Length: 5 Inches. *This 3/4 inch gouge is fitted with a hexagonal handle. An excellent working tool from a top quality maker.* (FINE) **$65.00**

F4-38. Unmarked: Classic Farrier's Butteris. Forged From File. Excellent Patina. Length: 17 Inches. *A supply of used up "horseshoe rasps" would have been the raw materials for this hoof trimming device forged by some forgotten but enterprising farrier.* (GOOD+) **$55.00**

F4-39. Unmarked: Early Strap End Leather Punch. 1 Inch Circle. Very Well Made. Length: 9 1/2 Inches. *We have it on fairly good authority that this is a strap end punch for leatherworking. It is very well made.* (FINE) **$125.00**

F4-40. Barton, D.R., Rochester, N.Y.: No. 18: Bent Gouge Carving Tool. Fruitwood Handle. Superb Condition. Length: 4 1/2 Inches. *The original fruitwood handle adds a touch of class to this perfectly preserved bent gouge carving tool from Rochester, New York maker D.R. Barton & Company.* (FINE) **$65.00**

F4-41. Butcher, W.: Set of Early Tang Gouges. Late 1700's. Ready to Use Condition. Length: 11 Inches. *These extremely early gouges are fitted with the classic octagonal handles employed in the pre-industrial era. A nicely patinated set in excellent working order.* (GOOD+) **$145.00**

F4-42. Stanley Rule & Level No. 720: Set of 10 "Red Handle" Chisel. 1/4 Inch to 2 Inch Width. Superb Condition. Length: 13 1/2 Inches. *Sets of Stanley's long handled No. 720 "Red Handle" chisels have become almost impossible to acquire. These are about as nice as they come. Crisp, clan and ready to last a lifetime.* (FINE) **$625.00**

F4-43. Assorted Makers: Working Set of 4 Carving Tools. Veiners, Gouges, Etc. Addis, Buck, Etc.. Length: 12 1/4 Inches. *These four tools came together from the chest of a single woodworker. All are in excellent working order.* (GOOD+) **$115.00**

F4-44. Barton, D.R., Rochester: Working Set of 3 Carving Tools. From Single Owner. Veiners, Bent Gouge. Length: 11 1/2 Inches. *The carving tools of prominent Rochester, New York maker D.R. Barton & Company were favorites with patternmakers because of the exceptionally good quality of the steel. These 3 tools came from a single owner and all are in excellent condition.* (GOOD+) **$165.00**

F4-45. Butcher, W.: Set of 12 Tang Gouges. Lacquered Beech Handles. Excellent Condition. Length: 14 1/2 Inches. *These exceptionally well preserved tang gouges are fitted with identical turned beech handles accented with brass ferrules. In the mid 1800's, a master craftsman would have owned and cherished as set of tools such as these. The same is true today. A great set.* (FINE) **$445.00**

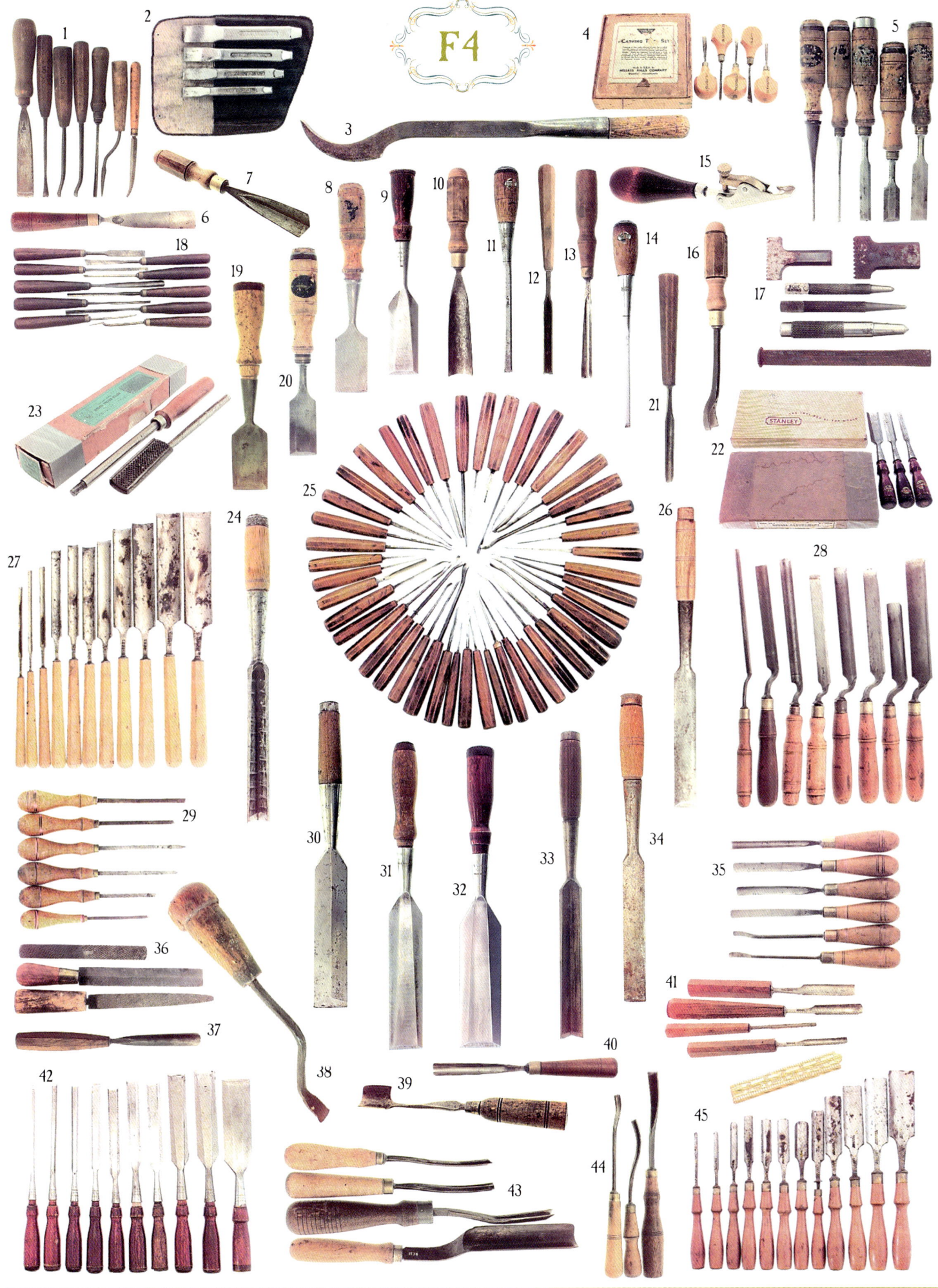

Group G4

G4-1. Searls Mfg. Co.: Cast Iron Advertising Wrench. "Best Drop Nuts". Early and Near New. Length: 9 Inches. *This dramatic cast iron wrench has been cast with the name of the maker and the slogan "Best Drop Nuts" cast into the body. A very rare specialty wrench in superb condition.* (FINE) **$275.00**

G4-2. Boston Wrench Co., Boston, Mass.: Quick Adjust Nut Wrench. Patented October 2, 1906. Schulz No. 480. Length: 6 Inches. *The ring at the base of the sliding jaw locks and releases a wedge that allows positioning of the jaws at the precise adjustment needed. A clean and clearly marked example of a great collectible wrench.* (GOOD+) **$185.00**

G4-3. Schollhorn & Co., Wm., New Haven: Multple Function Combination Tool. Cutter, Riveter, Crimper. Rare and Complete. Length: 9 Inches. *One of the most involved "gizmo" tools we have been privileged to offer, this specialty device incorporates opposing pairs of dies on its paired revolving wheels. Apparently the wheels were turned into position and used for some specialized crimping function. This is the only example of this rare Schollhorn tool we have ever seen available for sale. Rare.* (GOOD+) **$285.00**

G4-4. Simmons Hardware Co., E.C. No. 94: "Keen Kutter" Nut Wrench. Bicycle Type. Rare and Excellent. Length: 4 Inches. *Nearly every tool vendor and tool maker offered a number of "bicycle" wrenches, and the E.C. Simmons company was no exception, but finding surviving examples, especially those as clean and clearly marked as this example is an infrequent occurrence. This one is in fine working order and ready to display in a prominent collection of "Keen Cutter" items or small wrenches.* (GOOD+) **$145.00**

G4-5. Nilson Waters Co., Castleton, S.D.: Patent Alligator Wrench. Patented December 25, 1900. Schultz No. 32. Length: 6 3/4 Inches. *This unusual double alligator wrench hails from a most unusual location. It is in top collector quality condition. A rare wrench.* (FINE) **$195.00**

G4-6. Unmarked: Miniature Nut Wrench. In Leather Case. Marked "Steel". Length: 3 1/2 Inches. *An unusual small wrench in its original leather case. An interesting and mechanically different wrench.* (GOOD) **$65.00**

G4-7. Mc Farland, D., Worcester, Mass.: Screw Adjust Buggy Wrench. Patented December 22, 1874. Schulz No. 206. Length: 10 1/2 Inches. *The McFarland Patent buggy wrench could be locked into position by the screw on the lower jaw. The handle included a standard size open end wrench for good measure. A rare, early wrench in excellent condition.* (GOOD+) **$265.00**

G4-8. Hewett: Hewett Patent Wrench. Patented June 27, 1840. Schulz No. 396. Length: 12 Inches. *A good, clean example of one of the earliest patented wrenches. These have an adjustment mechanism that is decidedly different.* (GOOD) **$325.00**

G4-9. Peck, Stow & Wilcox Co.: 10 Inch Pipe Wrench. Walworth Mechanism. Near New Condition. Length: 10 Inches. *The Walworth adjustment mechanism became the standard for pipe wrench adjustment. The reason? Simplicity. Amazing. This one is hardware-store new.* (FINE) **$55.00**

G4-10. Whitman & Barnes: Twist Handle Monkey Wrench. Patented February 27, 1883. Early and Excellent. Length: 4 3/4 Inches. *This was the smallest of a series that grew to mammoth size. A nice example of a classic wrench.* (GOOD+) **$85.00**

G4-11. Johnson, Iver, Fitchburg, Mass.: Early Bicycle Wrench. With Tire Lever Handle. Near New Condition. Length: 6 Inches. *The Iver Johnson Company made bicycles and supplied them with these and other wrenches. This one, which is in nearly new condition, features a handle that has been forged into the shape of a tire lever. A good one.* (FINE) **$95.00**

G4-12. Erie Tool Works, The, Erie, Penn.: Combination Pipe and Nut Wrench. Wooden Handle. Unusual Maker. Length: 11 Inches. *The Erie Tool Works obviously produced a high quality product, but examples are not often found. This pipe and nut wrench combination is in perfect condition.* (FINE) **$135.00**

G4-13. Armstrong Mfg. Co., Bridgeport, Conn.: Quick Adjust Pipe Wrench. Patented Decmeber 9, 1879. Rare and Excellent. Length: 7 1/2 Inches. *An early and most unusual plier-type pipe wrench. Nicely marked with the patent date and maker name. Ever seen one?* (GOOD+) **$325.00**

G4-14. K.C. Drop Forge Co., Independence, Missouri: Patent Pipe and Nut Wrench. Patented August 4, 1908. Rare and Excellent. Length: 8 Inches. *Somewhere in my files I have an article that recounts the story of the man who patented this wrench and received a number of additional patents for various other devices. I believe that his name was Morris and that at one time he owned the largest barn in the State of Iowa, which was destroyed in a windstorm around the time this wrench was patented. These are rare and very desirable. A wrench with a story, sort of.* (GOOD+) **$345.00**

G4-15. Ellis: Patent Pivot Head Wrench. Patented November 3, 18903. Uncommon 8 Inch Size. Length: 8 Inches. *An extremely well preserved and fully functional example of the "Ellis" patent pivoting jaw wrench in the uncommon 8 inch size.* (FINE) **$365.00**

G4-16. E. Prince Groff Mfg. Co.,, Camden: "Kwik Grip" Patent Wrench. Patented October 15, 1912. Most Unusual. Length: 8 Inches. *This rare wrench of dubious practical value is a most unusual patented wrench and in perfectly preserved condition. A wrench only an alligator could love.* (FINE) **$265.00**

G4-17. Keystone Mfg. Co., Buffalo, N.Y.: No. 74: 4 Inch "Westcott" Wrench. "S" Handle Crescent. Rare, Small Size. Length: 4 Inches. *These "S" wrenches were a popular tool early in this century. Wescott was one of the most prolific makers and produced sizes up to 24 inches. Apparently the 4 inch size was discontinued early on. Examples in this size are extremely rare. Opportunity knocks.* (GOOD+) **$325.00**

G4-18. Columbian Wrench, Brockton, Mass.: "The Columbian" Patented Wrench. Patented September 13, 1892. Very Scarce Size. Length: 8 Inches. *A most unusual smaller size example of the elusive "Columbian" wrench, complete with the seldom seen wood handle. A rare patented wrench in excellent condition. Highly recommended.* (GOOD+) **$395.00**

G4-19. Keystone Mfg. Co., Buffalo, N.Y.: No. 74: 4 Inch "Westcott" Wrench. "S" Handle Crescent. Rare, Small Size. Length: 4 Inches. *The Keystone Manufacturing Company produced a wide range of sizes of this "S" handle wrench. In all likelihood, there was limited demand for examples in this, the smallest size offered. Those that were sold were most likely found impractical and discarded. Whatever the case, these small wrenches are extremely rare and much sought after by knowledgeable wrench collectors.* (GOOD+) **$265.00**

G4-20. I.C.I. No. 3: "Handy" Plier Wrench. Jack of All Trades. "Pat. Pend". Length: 9 Inches. *Another "jack of all trades", I've never seen any of the hype on this one, but one look tells me that the patentee could have provided assurances that it possessed sufficient virtues to be able to care for a farm on its own for weeks on end. The last tool you'll ever need.* (GOOD+) **$95.00**

G4-21. Smith Co., H.D., Plantsville, Conn.: "Perfect Handle" Wrench. 1/2 Inch Open End Size. Superb Condition. Length: 7 Inches. *This one is marked 1/2 inch but the opening seems larger, and it was made that way.* (GOOD) **$35.00**

G4-22. Bonney Vise & Tool Works Inc.: "The Masterpiece" Wrench. Patented March 3, 1900. With Pipe Cutter Jaw. Length: 10 1/2 Inches. *The boys in the Bonney Tool Works Design Department may have dreamed this one up after a long lunch at the local tavern. It features a pipe and nut wrench as well as a pipe cutter, which can be snapped out for sharpening. A masterpiece, we agree; of what, we leave to your judgment. Stupid idea: Great wrench.* (GOOD+) **$365.00**

G4-23. Canuck Tool Co., Toronto, Canada: Pivot Head Nut Wrench. "Canuck Pat." Rare and Excellent. Length: 10 Inches. *A most unusual pivoting head wrench from Canada. Nicely marked with the interesting company name. Never seen another.* (GOOD+) **$265.00**

G4-24. Hammond Mfg. Co., Boston, Mass.: Patent Quick Adjust Wrench. Patented April 3, 1900. Schulz No. 676. Length: 8 Inches. *This turn-of-the-century patent features a lever behind the lower jaw. Pushing on the lever allows the jaw to move freely. Most unusual.* (GOOD+) **$195.00**

G4-25. Gordon: Quick Adjust "Crescent" Wrench. Spring Activated. "Pat. Applied For". Length: 6 Inches. *Most wrench collectors are familiar with the "Gordon Automatic" quick adjust nut wrench, but few are aware the company also offered this pipe wrench version. Extra rare.* (FINE) **$225.00**

G4-26. Craft P.M.I. Co., Conneaut, Ohio: 10 Inch "Craft" Wrench. Patented November 12, 1907. Schulz No. 663. Length: 10 Inches. *The "Craft" wrench has a roller type serrated lower jaw that is tightened in place by a tensioning spring. This example is clean, clearly marked and ready to display.* (GOOD+) **$55.00**

G4-27. Maydole Tool Corp.: "Maydole" Pipe Wrench. Patent No. 1760544. Rare and Excellent. Length: 7 Inches. *Perhaps hoping to expand their operations beyond the hammers which had been their specialty since the 1840's, the Maydole folks in Norwich, New York, produced this adjustable pipe wrench that is imprinted with their name and a patent number. These could not have been commercially successful, and may never have been distributed. A rare Maydole wrench.* (GOOD+) **$225.00**

G4-28. Goodell Pratt Company No. 484: Rare 10 Inch Monkey Wrench. With Aluminum Handle. Manufactured in the 1920's Only. Length: 10 Inches. *A fine working example of the Goodell-Pratt "monkey" wrench. The G.P. automotive tool line featured a number of innovative designs. These tools have finally been discovered by collectors, and for good reason. A nice example of a rare collectible wrench.* (GOOD+) **$115.00**

G4-29. Unmarked No. 73: Cast Iron Nut Wrench. 1/2 Inch Square Nut. Distinctive Form. Length: 6 1/2 Inches. *An exceptionally early and nicely shaped "T" handled nut wrench, purpose unknown. Different.* (GOOD) **$95.00**

G4-30. Clip-Bar Mfg. Co.: The Shuster Speed Wrench. Patented February 2, 1915. 8 Inch Size. Length: 8 Inches. *An interesting variation on the crescent type wrench, this one has a patented quick-adjust feature. Most unusual.* (FINE) **$165.00**

G4-31. Syracuse: Cast Iron Implement Wrench. Marked. "Wood Beam". Uncommon Type. Length: 10 Inches. *This clean and sound plow wrench from Central New York State is marked with the designation "Wood Beam". Never seen another. A rare implement wrench.* (GOOD) **$65.00**

G4-32. Spaulding Mach. Screw Co., Buffalo: "W.B. Dick's Patent" Wrench. Unmarked. Full Nickel Plating. Length: 4 3/4 Inches. *A clean and shiny example of the W.B. Dick patent. No maker imprint, but unmistakable in form. A good clean example.* (GOOD+) **$175.00**

G4-33. Mossberg Wrench Co, Cent.Falls, R.I.: No. C: Bicycle Monkey Wrench. Center Adjust. Patented November 19, 1895. Length: 5 Inches. *Here's a collector-quality example of the Mossberg "C" wrench. Nice.* (FINE) **$95.00**

G4-34. Anderson, A., Boston, Mass.: "Hammer's Pat." Combination Wrench. With Screwdriver, Rule Gauges, Etc. Length: 5 1/2 Inches. *This patented wrench/screwdriver/gauge was marketed as an electrician's tool. Insulated with solid steel. Interesting and unusual.* (GOOD) **$65.00**

G4-35. Mossberg Co., Frank, Attleboro, Mass.: No. D: Early Patented Bicycle Wrench. Patented May 26, 1897. Near New Condition. Length: 4 1/2 Inches. *Nearly all original finishes remain on this example of the Mossberg "D" wrench. Nice.* (FINE) **$95.00**

G4-36. Wakefield Wrench Co. No. 8: Adjustable Nut Wrench. "Indian Motorcycles". Patented September 1, 1900. Length: 6 1/2 Inches. *This adjustable wrench is imprinted with the "Indian Motorcycle" name. It is also marked "No. 8", which is itself quite unusual. A very well preserved example of a rare Indian Motorcycle Wrench.* (FINE) **$135.00**

G4-37. Kenton Brand: Quick Adjust Nut Wrench. Turn Lock Handle. Excellent Working Order. Length: 7 1/2 Inches. *This "Kenton Brand" wrench features a turning handle to adjust the jaws. It is in excellent working order.* (GOOD+) **$65.00**

G4-38. Smith Co., The H.D.: "Perfect Handle" Wrench. 6 Inch Monkey Wrench. Uncommon Size. Length: 6 Inches. *A clean, small monkey wrench. Nicely marked and in working order.* (GOOD+) **$35.00**

G4-39. Hendee Mfg. Co., Springfield, Mass: Indian Motorcycle Wrench. Screw Adjust Type. Schulz No. 124. Length: 6 Inches. *Apparently the purchaser of an Indian motorcycle received a tool kit that included one of these. This one is clearly marked with the Indian name. A nice example of a rare wrench.* (GOOD+) **$85.00**

G4-40. Robert Wrench Co., New York: Self Adjust Wrench. Patented and Patents Pending. Extra Crisp and Clean. Length: 9 Inches. *The parallel jaws on this wrench are designed to tighten when the handle is moved. This one was apparently never used in anger. Nearly new.* (FINE) **$45.00**

G4-41. Elastic Tip Co.: Screw Adjust Bicycle Wrench. Patented March 28, 1895. Uncommon Type. Length: 5 1/2 Inches. *We don't know what else the Elastic Tip Company made, but they made a very nice bicycle wrench. This one is marked with an early patent date. Rare.* (GOOD+) **$135.00**

G4-42. Billings & Spencer Co., The: "Billings Patent" D Wrench. Patented February 13, 1879. Black Metal Finish. Length: 6 Inches. *No telling how far up the B. & S. people went with their alphabetic designation system for wrenches. I would hate to run into the "Z" wrench in a dark alley. This uncommon "number"-ed wrench is in excellent condition.* (FINE) **$45.00**

G4-43. Unmarked: Early Patent Combination Tool. Patented April 19, 1870. For Leatherworking? Length: 10 Inches. *Tools such as this are my very favorites. They are, in general, objects which purportedly provide some added measure of utility by adding additional functionality to a "combination tool"; but which, in practice, diminish the efficacy of the components to such an extent, because of the compromises necessary for them to cohabit with wholly unrelated tools, that the entire device becomes, not a blessing as the obviously inventor intended, but rather a curse upon practitioners of the manual arts. Such tools make great collectibles. This one combines a leather punch, scissors, awl, pliers and God knows what else into a device for which a patent was granted on April 19, 1870. Let the user beware, let the collector rejoice.* (FINE) **$225.00**

G4-44. Wakefield: Bicycle Monkey Wrench. Side Adjust. "Wakefield Cycle Wrench". Length: 5 1/4 Inches. *Nearly all original finishes remain on this early bicycle wrench.* (GOOD+) **$35.00**

G4-45. Schollhorn & Co., New Haven, Conn.: Patent End Cutters. Patented May 2, 1905. Patented April 2, 1907. Length: 5 Inches. *These specialty cutters from the highly collectible Shollhorn Company are marked with 2 separate patent dates. A most unusual Schollhorn tool.* (FINE) **$45.00**

Group H4

H4-1. Winchester Repeating Arms Co. No. 4982: Original Box For 6 Chisels. Original Label. Scarce and Excellent. Length: 12 1/2 Inches. *Pondering the curious nature of collectors and collecting while preparing to write this description, the story of a man who went the the psychiatrist came to mind. "Why are you here?", asked the doctor. "Because my family wants me here.", replied the patent. "Come now, there must be more to it than that", said the shrink. "Well, they wanted me to come here because I like potato pancakes." "Never!", said the doctor. "That's perfectly normal. Why, I myself am particularly fond of potato pancakes." "Really?", replied the patient. "Why don't you come over to my house...I have boxes and boxes full of them in the cellar." A great box for a collection but one not likely to hold potato pancakes without folding.* (GOOD+) **$125.00**

H4-2. Winchester Repeating Arms Co.: Group of 5 "Winchester" Files. Assorted Types. Rare and Unused. Length: 5 Inches. *Winchester offered a wide range of files, but finding marked examples is worse than locating the proverbial Needle in a Haystack. These appear never to have been used. Mint.* (FINE) **$85.00**

H4-3. Sargent & Co., New Haven Conn: "The Steel Square" Catalog. With Instructions. 32 Pages, Ca. 1915. Length: 7 3/4 Inches. *These pamphlets were handed out to prospective purchasers of steel squares. It just happened that in addition to the information about the care and use of squares, there were plenty of reasons why the buyer should select a Sargent square.* (GOOD+) **$35.00**

H4-4. Walters & Sons, William P., Philadelphia: Hand and Treadle Tool Catalog. 448 Pages, Ca. 1908. Extensive Tool Line. Length: 9 Inches. *William Walters was a major Philadelphia dealer in tools. Here's a look at their full line.* (GOOD+) **$165.00**

H4-5. Goodell-Pratt Company No. 7: General Line Catalog. Ca. 1905. 176 Pages. Length: 5 1/2 Inches. *An extra-early G.P. Catalog in clean, sound condition.* (GOOD) **$85.00**

H4-6. Winchester Repeating Arms Co.: Pair of Carpenter's Nippers. Large "W" Logo. Uncommon Type. Length: 8 Inches. *These carpenter's nippers were originally designated as item number F2168M, and later as simple W8. They are not common.* (GOOD+) **$95.00**

H4-7. Gurley, W. & L.E., Troy, N.Y.: No. 22 ED.: "Gurley's Manual" and Catalog. 257 Pages, Ca. 1876. Instructions and How to Use. Length: 6 Inches. *W. & L.E. Gurley published these "Manuals" beginning in the 1860's. They included information on how to use the instruments and engravings of instruments for sale. A great early reference.* (GOOD+) **$225.00**

H4-8. Winchester Repeating Arms Co. No. 3006: No. 4 1/2 Equivalent Metallic Plane. Mahogany Handles. Uncommon Type. Length: 10 Inches. *This No. 4 1/2 size plane retains much of its original paint. Someone has replaced the front handle, but it otherwise in good shape. A front know from a common Sargent plane will fit it nicely.* (GOOD+) **$145.00**

H4-9. Winchester Repeating Arms Co. No. 3010: Rosewood Handle. Metallic Plane. "No. 5" Size. Complete and Proper. Length: 14 Inches. *We are prepared to certify that this Winchester plane is marked in 3 places and therefore qualifies as a Winchester plane. Most original finishes remain on this example, which was produced for Winchester by Sargent & Company, of New Haven, Conn.* (GOOD+) **$165.00**

H4-10. Winchester Repeating Arms Co. No. 4512: 1/4 Inch Cold Chisel. For Steel Work. Unused Condition. Length: 5 Inches. *For an idea of the level of quality that a customer would encounter when entering the Winchester Store, take a look at this brand new cold chisel. A superb quality tool in brand new condition.* (FINE) **$55.00**

H4-11. Winchester Repeating Arms Co. No. 7112: 3 Inch Blade Screwdriver. Crisp and Clean. Brass Ferrule. Length: 7 Inches. *Here's a clean and well preserved example of a Winchester classic.* (GOOD+) **$45.00**

H4-12. Arthur, Henry, New York, N.Y.: Leather Supply Catalog. 48 Pages, Ca. 1879. Many Hand Tools. Length: 9 Inches. *All sort of leatherworking tools and supplies are illustrated and described here.* (GOOD) **$75.00**

H4-13. Henshaw, Edward: Shoemaking Tool Catalog. 40 Pages, Ca. 1881. Excellent Engraving. Length: 9 Inches. *Explore the world of shoe manufacturing as it existed in 1881. An interesting catalog.* (FINE) **$85.00**

H4-14. Winchester Repeating Arms Co. No. 7126: 8 Inch Heavy Duty Screwdriver. With Brass Fittings. Uncommon Size. Length: 14 1/2 Inches. *Winchester screwdrivers are easily recognized by their distinctive brass ferrules. This 8" offering is in excellent condition and quite uncommon.* (GOOD+) **$65.00**

H4-15. Winchester Repeating Arms Co. No. 4532: Octagon Handle Chisel. For Steel Work. Bevel Edge Grind. Length: 5 Inches. *These were known as "round nose" chisels and offered in a variety of sizes. This one has never been used.* (FINE) **$75.00**

H4-16. Winchester Repeating Arms Co.: "Monkey" Type Wrench. "Perfect Handle". Near New Condition. Length: 8 Inches. *This perfectly preserved "Winchester" monkey wrench has a "Perfect Handle" type grip. It appears never to have been used. Mint.* (FINE) **$125.00**

H4-17. Winchester Repeating Arms Co. No. 1032: 10 Inch Screw Adjust Pipe Wrench. Uncmmon Type. Schulz No.640. Length: 10 Inches. *Here's a very nicely kept pipe wrench bearing the Winchester name. A good, clean wrench by a desirable maker.* (GOOD) **$75.00**

H4-18. Stephens Patent Vise Co., New York: Accordion-Fold Catalog. 8 Pages, Ca. 1878. Full Product Line. Length: 9 Inches. *This 8 page fold out illustrates, and describes in great detail, the features of the Stephens Patent vise.* (GOOD+) **$95.00**

H4-19. Winchester Repeating Arms Co.: 8 Inch Curved Jaw Pliers. Full Nickel Plating. With Screwdriver Tip. Length: 8 Inches. *Nearly all of the original nickel plating remains on thise specialty curved jaw pliers from the Winchester gun folks. One of the handles has been forged to function as a screwdriver.* (FINE) **$115.00**

H4-20. Simonds Saw & Steel Co. No. 19: General Line Catalog. 195 Pages, Ca. 1921. Hand Saws and Tools. Length: 9 Inches. *The full Simonds line is illustrated in this full size catalog.* (FINE) **$65.00**

H4-21. Winchester Repeating Arms Co.: Specialty Rust Remover. 2 Ounce Tube. New Condition, Original Box. Length: 5 Inches. *We would suspect that this substance was intended for use on the firearms produced by the Winchester people. The successful purchaser may use it on Winchester tools, or other tools, if he or she so chooses. Different.* (FINE) **$35.00**

H4-22. Winchester Repeating Arms Co. No. 1505: Double Open End Wrench. 1 1/16 Inch and 1 1/4 Inch Sizes. Uncommon Type. Length: 11 Inches. *Much of the original black finish remains on this Winchester open end wrench.* (GOOD+) **$45.00**

H4-23. Goodman, W. L.: The History of Woodworking Tools. Out of Print Book. Original Dust Jacket. Length: 10 Inches. *Long out of print, this book provided my introduction to the world of tools and I recommend it without hesitation to anyone who really wants to understand. A great book from an interesting man.* (FINE) **$115.00**

H4-24. Chandler & Farquar Co., Boston, Mass.: No. 115: Hardware and Machine Catalog. 386 Pages, Ca. 1908. Many Hand Tools. Length: 9 Inches. *Chandler & Farquar were major dealers & suppliers in the Boston area. They carried a wide line of tools, many of which are illustrated here.* (GOOD+) **$145.00**

H4-25. Winchester Repeating Arms Co.: Salesman's Receipt Book. R.C. Bailey, Machias. Ca. 1920'5. Length: 5 Inches. *A customer at the R.C. Bailey Winchester Store in Machias, Maine, would have received a slip from this book with his purchase. The top few pages are loose, but it is otherwise complete and in excellent shape. Extra rare.* (FINE) **$295.00**

H4-26. Wadsworth, Howland & Co., Boston: Artists Supply Catalog. 200 Pages, Ca. 1903. With Drafting Tools. Length: 9 Inches. *Every imaginable drawing and illustrating supply is illustrated in this turn of the century catalog.* (GOOD+) **$95.00**

H4-27. Winchester Repeating Arms Co. No. 9532: One Foot, Four Fold Folding Rule. With Caliper Slide. Rare and Excellent. Length: 12 Inches. *This Winchester classic is clean and clearly marked with the maker name and product number. A rare Winchester rule.* (GOOD+) **$295.00**

H4-28. Winchester Repeating Arms Co. No. 7126: 5 Inch Heavy Duty Screwdriver. With Brass Fittings. Uncommon Type. Length: 10 Inches. *Here's a 5 inch blade version of the Winchester screwdriver. These screwdrivers were apparently quite popular. They are very highly collectible.* (GOOD) **$45.00**

H4-29. Winchester Repeating Arms Co. No. 1030: Screw Adjust Pipe Wrench. Rare 6 Inch Size. Schulz No. 640. Length: 6 Inches. *This small Winchester Stillson-type pipe wrench is clean and clearly marked. This is a very difficult size to find. Finders keepers.* (FINE) **$245.00**

H4-30. Carey & Bros. Co., Thomas, Baltimore: Engines and Supply Catalog. 676 Pages, Ca. 1895. Many Machinists Tools. Length: 9 Inches. *This early catalog features a wide range of tools as well as engines & supplies.* (FINE) **$165.00**

H4-31. Olin: "Winchster" Brand Flashlight. With Flare Tip. Unused Condition. Length: 12 Inches. *Here's a most unusual "Winchester" brand flashlight that has a solid red plastic extension to serve as a beacon. It was most likely used for directing traffic.* (FINE) **$85.00**

H4-32. Goodell-Pratt Company No. 10: General Line Catalog. Ca. 1911. 304 Pages. Length: 5 Inches. *An uncommon edition of the Goodell Pratt series in excellent condition.* (GOOD+) **$115.00**

H4-33. Dietzgen Co., Eugene, Chicago: No. 9th Editon: General Line Catalog. 1910-1911 Edition. 9 Inches X 6 Inches. Length: 6 Inches. *Eugene Dietzgen offered a wide range of tools and supplies for draughtsmen and surveyors. This well preserved book includes their full product line, including a number of slide rules. A great reference.* (GOOD+) **$75.00**

H4-34. Stanley Rule & Level: Carpenters Tools Catalog. Ca. 1890, 20 Pages. 3 Inches X 6 Inches. Length: 6 Inches. *This early catalog has seen some wear but it is complete and makes a great reference. Not a bad book for being more than 100 years old.* (GOOD) **$25.00**

H4-35. Winchester Repeating Arms Co.: Original Box For No. W 84 Folding Rules. Excellent Condition. Extremely Scarce. Length: 6 Inches. *A visitor to the Winchester Store would have seen rows and rows of boxes having labels such as this one. Nearly all have now vanished. This rare example of the Winchester box is in excellent condition and ready to add to a growing Winchester collection.* (GOOD+) **$275.00**

H4-36. Belcher & Loomis, Providence, R.I.: Manual Training School Catalog. Benches Planes, Etc,. 210 Pages, Ca. 1905. Length: 9 Inches. *A most interesting period reference, this catalogue is filled with tools and supplies for the "manual training" schools that turned out carpenters and such at the turn of the century. It includes planes, chisels, saws, workbenches and much, much more.* (GOOD+) **$125.00**

H4-37. Stanley Rule & Level: Carpenters Tools Catalog. Ca. 1907, 24 Pages. 3 1/2 Inches X 6 Inches. Length: 6 Inches. *This 24 page pamphlet showcases the Stanley line as it existed in 1907. An uncommon Stanley promotional pamphlet.* (GOOD+) **$35.00**

H4-38. Stanley Rule & Level: Carpenters Tools Catalog. Ca. 1900, 20 Pages. 3 Inches X 6 Inches. Length: 6 Inches. *This 20 page book illustrates much of the Stanley line as it existed in 1900, or thereabout. It has some slight staining and a few folds, but is otherwise complete and intact.* (GOOD+) **$45.00**

H4-39. Starrett Co., L. S., Athol, Mass.: No. 26: Full Size Dealer Catalog. Copyright 1938. 284 Pages, Supplement. Length: 11 1/2 Inches. *We have seen quite a few of the catalogs that the L.S. Starrett Company distributed to machinists, but this is the first full size dealer catalog we have ever offered. All of the text and illustrations are much larger, and a supplement in the back documents new tools and available spare parts. A rare Starrett catalog.* (GOOD+) **$245.00**

H4-40. Stanley Rule & Level No. 34: General Line Catalog. September, 1942 Edition. 232 Pages. Length: 7 Inches. *Stanley's full product line at a level that would not be continued with post War cutbacks is illustrated in this 1942 edition.* (GOOD) **$85.00**

H4-41. Eagle Square Mfg. Co.: Full Line Catalog. 30 Pages, Ca. 1910. Acquired by Stanley. Length: 8 Inches. *This large pamphlet identifies the full Eagle Square line.* (GOOD+) **$45.00**

H4-42. Pratt & Whitney, W. Hartford, Conn.: No. 16: "Small Tool" Catalog. Taps, Dies, Cutters,. Ca. 1944, 444 Pages. Length: 7 1/2 Inches. *This ca. 1944 catalog includes the precision tools for which Pratt & Whitney were famous.* (FINE) **$35.00**

H4-43. Winchester Repeating Arms Co. No. 1505: Double Open End Wrench. 3/8 Inch and 1/2 Inch Sizes. Uncommon Type. Length: 6 Inches. *This double open end wrench was sold individually or as part of a set. An uncommon Winchester wrench.* (GOOD) **$35.00**

H4-44. Nicholson File Co., Providence, R.I.: File Filosophy and How to Get the Most Out of Files. 1943. Length: 9 Inches. *Most people today don't have the slightest idea how to properly use files. Reading this catalog is a great source of information about files and their uses.* (GOOD) **$15.00**

H4-45. Stanley Rule & Level No. 34: General Line Catalog. 1912 Edition. 128 Pages. Length: 7 1/2 Inches. *One of the earliest of the No. 34 catalogs, this one is in excellent collector-quality condition.* (GOOD+) **$185.00**

Group 14

14-1. Stanley Rule & Level No. 182: Cast Iron Rabbet Plane. 1" Width. Early Vine Casting. Length: 10 1/2 Inches. *Stanley offered its cast iron rabbeting planes with a nicker (the 190 series) or without, as in this early example of the No. 180 series. This one is imprinted with the patent date and the handle has the early and appealing "vine" casting. Missing the depth stop, but otherwise clean and sound. A tough plane to find.* (GOOD) **$55.00**

14-2. Stanley Rule & Level No. 98/99: Pair of Side Rabbet Planes. With Depth Stops. Ready to Use. Length: 4 Inches. *A good clean pair of side rabbet planes, including the desirable depth stops. Ready to add versatility to a woodworker and a woodworking shop. Nice.* (GOOD) **$245.00**

14-3. Stanley Rule & Level No. 22: 8" Transitional Plane. 2nd Smallest Size. Parital Original Decal. Length: 8 Inches. *Part of the original decal remains on this well preserved transitional plane in the second smallest size. A nice example.* (GOOD+) **$115.00**

14-4. Stanley Rule & Level No. 40 1/2: 10 1/2" Scrub Plane. With Pattern Soles. 6 Cutters and 11 Soles. Length: 10 1/2 Inches. *A patternmaker at some point modified this Stanley No. 40 1/2 plane by fitting it with a bronze cap iron and a series of interchangeable soles and irons. A total of 11 soles (including one made of aluminum) and six cutting irons are included. A dramatic functional modification of a Stanley plane. Condition is excellent.* (GOOD+) **$485.00**

14-5. Stanley Rule & Level No. 5 1/4: "Junior" Jack Plane. Ca. 1950's. 95% Original Paint. Length: 13 Inches. *At just a few inches shorter than the No. 5 and the same width as the No. 3, these planes have become the plane of choice for many modern craftsmen. A nice example of a great working tool.* (GOOD+) **$125.00**

14-6. Stanley Rule & Level No. 9 1/4: Cast Iron Block Plane. Non-Adjustable Throat. Ready to Use. Length: 6 Inches. *The 9 1/4 had the same characteristics as the 15 and the 9 1/2 but omitted the adjustable throat. A very nice example.* (FINE) **$45.00**

14-7. Stanley Rule & Level No. 45: Multi Purpose Combination Plane. Complete, Ready to Use. With Original Cutters. Length: 9 Inches. *This example of Stanley's No. 45 combination plane is complete in all respects except that it is missing its long rods. Replacements are available and are interchangeable with the No. 55. An opportunity.* (GOOD+) **$195.00**

14-8. Stanley Rule & Level No. 26: Transitional Jack Plane. Much Original Lacquer. Crisp And Clean. Length: 15 Inches. *Much of the original lacquer remains on this crispy clean transitional plane.* (GOOD+) **$75.00**

14-9. Stanley Rule & Level No. 97: Cabinet Maker's Edge Plane. Ca. 1910 Trademark. 98% Original Paint. Length: 10 Inches. *Another of the Stanley planes with an "Achilles Heel" the Stanley No. 97 might better be referred to as the "cabinetmaker's broken edge plane". This superb example has the later-style high knob and is marked with the trademark in use in 1910 on the shiny cutting iron. Nearly all of the original shiny black japan finish remains on the metal parts and the original lacquer is intact on the rosewood know. A very well preserved example.* (FINE) **$675.00**

14-10. Stanley Rule & Level No. 191: 1 1/4" Rabbet Plane. Early "V" Trademark. 99% Original Paint. Length: 10 1/2 Inches. *Nearly all of the shiny original paint remains on this well preserved Stanley rabbeting plane. Nice.* (FINE) **$75.00**

14-11. Stanley Rule & Level No. 12 1/2: Adjustable Scraper Plane. Rosewood Bottom. "Sweetheart" Trademark. Length: 6 Inches. *Here's a very well preserved example of the rosewood soled No. 12 1/2 in top collector quality condition. Ready to use, if you choose.* (FINE) **$285.00**

14-12. Stanley Rule & Level No. 9 1/4: Cast Iron Block Plane. Non-Adjustable Throat. Near New Condition. Length: 6 Inches. *The No. 9 1/4 block plane was the functional equivalent of the No. 9 1/2, with the exception of the absence of a throat adjustment mechanism. This one is in top shape.* (FINE) **$45.00**

14-13. Stanley Rule & Level No. 12: Early Patent Scraper Plane. With Bulbous Handles. Patent August 31, 1858. Length: 6 1/2 Inches. *Easily identifiable by the sharply angular nose and tail sections, and by the presence of the Bailey patent information on the adjustment nut, these tools were made from 1869 to 1874 only. These tools were fitted with a cutter having the edges filed at an angle of 45 degrees. The cutter in this example is proper, but is quite short. It can, however, be locked in the plane in such a way that it appears complete. A rare, early Stanley plane.* (GOOD+) **$265.00**

14-14. Stanley Rule & Level No. 79: Double Side Rabbet Plane. Earliest Type. "Sweetheart" Trademark. Length: 5 Inches. *This is the first cast iron model with the distinctive dip between the blades. Nearly all nickel plating remains on a very clean plane. Excellent.* (GOOD+) **$145.00**

14-15. Stanley Rule & Level No. 604: Bedrock Smoothing Plane. Early Style. Patent '92 Trademark on Iron. Length: 9 Inches. *Early examples of Stanley's "Bedrock" series are the functional equals of their later and less aesthetically pleasing counterparts. This perfectly preserved example is ready to go back to work or fill out a collection of the "Bedrock" series. A very nice plane.* (FINE) **$295.00**

14-16. Stanley Rule & Level No. 48: Swing Fence Match Plane. Cuts 1/4" Groove. Early Japan Finish. Length: 10 Inches. *Only the very early examples of the No. 48 swinging fence match plane were finished with black japanning and only the early models had the distinctive "vine" casting. Here's an excellent example to fill out a Stanley collection.* (GOOD+) **$325.00**

14-17. Stanley Rule & Level No. 190: 1 1/2" Rabbeting Plane. Near New Condition. 99% Original Paint. Length: 8 Inches. *This crispy clean rabbeting plane is in virtually unused condition. Choice.* (FINE) **$75.00**

14-18. Stanley Rule & Level No. 72: Adjustable Chamfer Plane. Brass Fixing Screw. Ca. 1890's. Length: 7 Inches. *This No. 72 chamfer plane is in superb condition in all respects except that a tight crack in the tote had been properly reglued. A nice working example of a rare Stanley plane.* (GOOD+) **$295.00**

14-19. Stanley Rule & Level No. 604: Bedrock Smoothing Plane. Early Style. Ca. 1907 Trademark on Iron. Length: 9 Inches. *The tote on this early Bedrock series plane has been repaired, and it has been given a liberal coat of lacquer at some point, but it is sound and worthy of restoration. A good one.* (GOOD) **$85.00**

14-20. Stanley Rule & Level No. 39: Cast Iron Dado Plane. 1/4" Size. "Sweetheart" Trademark. Length: 8 Inches. *This was the smallest size of the No. 39 series, and it is one of the scarcest numbers to find, especially in as well-preserved condition as this top shelf example. Shiny black japanning and shiny nickel. No apologies.* (FINE) **$285.00**

14-21. Stanley Rule & Level No. 607 C: "Bedrock" Jointer Plane. Later Type, Square Side. Ready to Use. Length: 22 Inches. *This jointer plane is crisp, clean and complete. It is missing a bit of japanning at the heel and toe, but is functionally perfect. A nice example of an increasingly difficult to find plane.* (GOOD+) **$325.00**

14-22. Stanley Rule & Level No. 605 1/2: "Bedrock" Smoothing Plane. "Sweetheart" Trademark. Near New Condition. Length: 14 Inches. *There is a small mark on one side rail from some oxidation, but this classic late-model "Bedrock" plane is otherwise in immaculate condition. A very well preserved plane from ca. 1925. Nice.* (FINE) **$295.00**

14-23. Stanley Rule & Level No. 75: Bullnose Rabbet Plane. "Sweetheart" Trademark. Extra Crisp and Clean. Length: 4 1/2 Inches. *This pristine example of Stanley's smallest "bullnose" plane is imprinted with the desirable "Sweetheart" logo. Nice.* (FINE) **$65.00**

14-24. Stanley Rule & Level No. 2: 7" Smooth Plane. Later High Knob. Superb Condition. Length: 7 Inches. *This 1930's era example of the No. 2 smooth plane retains 98% of its original finishes. Very nice.* (FINE) **$345.00**

14-25. Stanley Rule & Level No. 112: Handled Scraper Plane. Rosewood Handles. "Stanley" Cutter. Length: 9 Inches. *This Stanley scraper plane is complete with its original cutting iron and ready to go to work. A nice example of a great working tool.* (GOOD+) **$265.00**

14-26. Stanley Rule & Level No. 102: Fixed Angle Plane. Early "Arch" Trademark. Ready to Use. Length: 5 1/2 Inches. *This fixed blade block plane is imprinted with the early "arch" logo of the Stanley Rule & Level Company. A nice early example.* (GOOD+) **$25.00**

14-27. Stanley Rule & Level No. 78: Duplex Filletster Plane. Early Vine Casting. Ready to Use. Length: 9 1/2 Inches. *Somewhere along the line someone applied a coat of lacquer finish to this otherwise excellent duplex rabbet plane. A bargain.* (GOOD+) **$55.00**

14-28. Stanley Rule & Level No. 192: Cast Iron Rabbet Plane. 1" Width. 99% Original Paint. Length: 10 1/2 Inches. *This fixed width 1" rabbeting plane is complete and in nearly new condition.* (FINE) **$65.00**

14-29. Stanley Rule & Level No. 40: Beech Handle Scrub Plane. Sweetheart Trademark. Ready to Use. Length: 11 Inches. *Here's a very well preserved example of Stanley's workaday "scrub" plane. This one is fitted with the desirable beech handles. A good one.* (GOOD+) **$110.00**

14-30. Stanley Rule & Level No. 171: Door Trim Router Plane. Patent December 26, 1911. Complete With 1 Cutter. Length: 11 1/2 Inches. *Introduced by Stanley in the early years of this century, when business was booming, power tools were not even imagined and the average workman could afford such niceties, Stanley may have produced a tool that was a bit too specialized in function for it to achieve any significant market success. This example, which is complete with one of the original 3 cutting irons retains more than 95% of its original shiny black japan finish. An excellent example of a rare Stanley plane.* (GOOD+) **$375.00**

14-31. Stanley Rule & Level No. 31: Transitional Jointer Plane. Partial Original Decal. "Sweetheart" Trademark. Length: 24 Inches. *Much of the original decal remains on the body of this crispy clean transitional. Extra nice.* (FINE) **$195.00**

14-32. Stanley Rule & Level No. 71: Open Throat Router Plane. Patent March 4, 1884. Early Example. Length: 8 Inches. *This early open throat router plane is cast with the 1884 patent date in the body and is in excellent condition with one original cutting iron. A good one.* (GOOD+) **$75.00**

14-33. Stanley Rule & Level No. 4: 9" Smoothing Plane. "Sweetheart" Trademark. Extra Crisp and Clean. Length: 9 Inches. *Some 98% of the original paint and much of the original decal remain on this ca. 1920's smoothing plane. Extra crisp and clean.* (FINE) **$110.00**

14-34. Stanley Rule & Level No. 78: Duplex Filletster Plane. Sweetheart Trademark. Extra Crisp and Clean. Length: 9 1/2 Inches. *Nicely marked with both the patent date (on the body) and the 1920's era "Sweetheart" trademark (on the cutter), this one is ready to provide years of service. A good one.* (FINE) **$95.00**

14-35. Stanley Rule & Level No. 122: "Liberty Bell Smooth Plane. Complete and Original. Uncommon Type. Length: 8 Inches. *The smallest of Stanley's "Liberty Bell" series, this is also the least common. A previous owner has "enhanced" the japanning, but it is otherwise clean and sound.* (GOOD+) **$75.00**

14-36. Stanley Rule & Level No. 113: Adjustable Circular Plane. Embossed Cap. Ready to Use. Length: 10 Inches. *Here's a well used but thoroughly sound example of Stanley's No. 113 circular plane.* (GOOD) **$85.00**

14-37. Stanley Rule & Level No. 45: Adjustable Combination Plane. Complete and Excellent. New Condition, Original Box. Length: 11 1/2 Inches. *Complete and perfect in its original pasteboard box this ca. 1915 era plane features the desirable "micro-dial" fence. A great working plane, complete and in excellent condition.* (FINE) **$395.00**

14-38. Stanley Rule & Level No. 606: Bedrock Fore Plane. Early Style. 95% Original Paint. Length: 18 Inches. *Nearly all of the original paint remains on this classic early "Bedrock" fore plane. A very nice example.* (GOOD+) **$285.00**

14-39. Stanley Rule & Level No. 20: Cast Iron Circular Plane. Ca. 1930's. Ready to Use. Length: 10 Inches. *This heavy duty circular plane is in excellent working order. A previous owner has "enhanced" the japanning to improve its appearance, but it is otherwise clean, sound and complete. A nice working plane.* (GOOD+) **$145.00**

14-40. Stanley Rule & Level No. 40 1/2: 10 1/2" Scrub Plane. Ca. 1915 Trademark. Rare and Excellent. Length: 10 1/2 Inches. *Finding examples of the No. 40 1/2 scrub plane in this condition is nearly impossible. Nearly possible.* (GOOD+) **$225.00**

14-41. Stanley Rule & Level No. 4 C: 9" Smoothing Plane. With Corrugated Sole. Type 11. Length: 9 Inches. *This desirable "Type 11" bench plane is excellent in all respects except that a previous owner has filed a pair of notches in the side to make it easily identifiable. Here's a chance to buy a great working tool with a minor cosmetic blemish for well under the money. An opportunity.* (GOOD+) **$65.00**

14-42. Stanley Rule & Level No. 39: Cast Iron Dado Plane. 1/2" Size. Near New Condition. Length: 8 Inches. *A superb example of the tough to find 1/2" cast iron dado plane in extremely well preserved condition. Nearly all of the shiny nickel plating remains on the fixing screws. Nice.* (FINE) **$245.00**

14-43. Stanley Rule & Level No. 39: Cast Iron Dado Plane. 1/4" Size. First Model. Length: 8 Inches. *The cutting iron in this dado plane has been replaced with a carefully fitted file and it has been given a heavy coat of lacquer at one point, but this plane is otherwise complete and sound.* (GOOD) **$75.00**

14-44. Stanley Rule & Level No. A5: Aluminum Jack Plane. Rosewood Handles. Extra Crisp and Clean. Length: 14 Inches. *Only a small "hang hole" in the back detracts from this otherwise perfect example of Stanley's elusive series of aluminum planes. Rare.* (GOOD+) **$265.00**

14-45. Stanley Rule & Level No. 129: "Liberty Bell Fore Plane. Clean And Sound. Much Original Lacquer. Length: 20 Inches. *Much of the original lacquer finish remains on this example of Stanley's "Liberty Bell" series, which was included in the product line from 1876 to 1919.* (GOOD+) **$125.00**

Group J4

J4-1. **D.B. & S., Providence, R.I.: Machinist's Bench Rule. 24" Length. Early and Excellent. Length: 24 Inches.** *A good clean example of an early machinist's rule from a prominent maker.* (GOOD+) **$95.00**

J4-2. **Assorted Makers: Assortment of Bench Rules. Rabone, Etc. Ready to Use. Length: 6 Inches.** *These steel bench rules were found in the same machinist chest. All are in excellent condition.* (FINE) **$15.00**

J4-3. **Robbins, D.C., Boston: German Silver Bench Rule. Graduated in 1/8ths. Early and Unusual. Length: 4 1/2 Inches.** *The name that appears on this German Silver bench rule is not listed in Cope's Makers of American Machinists Tools. Appearance is ca. 1890.* (FINE) **$65.00**

J4-4. **Unmarked: Owner Made Bench Rule. Extra Crisp and Clean. Owner "G.F. Tyler". Length: 18 Inches.** *We are pleased to offer the tools of one G.F. Tyler, who very likely worked as a machinist in the 1880's or 1890's. This bench rule was obviously something that he personally crafted. It is in new condition.* (FINE) **$25.00**

J4-5. **Stanley Rule & Level No. 39 1/2: Machinist's Bench Level. "Sweetheart" Trademark. Japan Finish Sides. Length: 6 Inches.** *This extra-clean machinist's level features the popular "Sweetheart" trademark. Nice.* (FINE) **$65.00**

J4-6. **Dietzgen Co., Eugene, Chicago: Boxed Set of Divider and Calipers. 4" Length. New Condition, Original Box. Length: 4 1/2 Inches.** *Each of these 4" dividers and calipers is in its own fitted box. Cute.* (FINE) **$65.00**

J4-7. **Moore & Wright, Sheffield (England): Set of 10 Assorted Calipers. Apprentice Kit? Extra Crisp and Clean. Length: 8 Inches.** *Moore & Wright were a principal English maker of precision tools. These assorted calipers and dividers came together from the same chest and were likely purchased together by an apprentice. A great set.* (GOOD+) **$125.00**

J4-8. **Brown & Sharpe Mfg., Providence No. 468: Precision Attachment for Square. With 6" Rule. Uncommon Type. Length: 6 Inches.** *This machinist's accessory was designed to fit on the blade of an engineer's square. Seldom seen.* (FINE) **$45.00**

J4-9. **Sawyer Tool Co., Ashburnham, Mass.: Machinist's Precisio Depth Gauge. Optional Side Mount. Unused Condition. Length: 6 Inches.** *A clean and complete example of Sawyer's multi-purpose depth gauge. It has apparently never been used.* (FINE) **$95.00**

J4-10. **Brown & Sharpe Mfg., Providence: Open Screw Thread Micrometer. Patented April 22, 1878. Extra Early and Rare. Length: 4 1/2 Inches.** *A seldom seen example of the technology of precision measurement as it existed at the very dawn of the industrial age in America, this patented micrometer was the first commercial attempt to mass market a micrometer other than the brass thickness gauge adapted from the Systeme Palmer originated in France at the beginning of the last half of the Nineteenth Century. Patented by George M. Pratt and originally produced by the Victor Sewing Machine Company of Middletown, Connecticut, the mass production of this tool had the effect of revolutionizing manufacturing in a very few years time. Clean, sound, complete and ready to display, we proudly offer this superb example of an extremely historiacly significant early precision tool.* (GOOD+) **$695.00**

J4-11. **Goodell-Pratt Company: Precision Adjust Marking Gauge. With Screw Lock Mechinism. Extra Crisp and Clean. Length: 8 1/2 Inches.** *This special screw-lock scratch gauge was offered in the Goodell-Pratt catalogs, but few examples are known. This one is in superb condition and clearly marked. A rare marking gauge.* (FINE) **$275.00**

J4-12. **Unmarked: Massive Tap Handle. Distinctive Form. Superb Condition. Length: 15 1/2 Inches.** *A great looking early tap handle for working metal. A graphic addition to a display of early machinist's tools.* (FINE) **$55.00**

J4-13. **Amon Spring Needle Works., New Britain: Multi Scribe Marking Gauge. Original Nickel Plating. Scarce and Excellent. Length: 3 Inches.** *A multi-purpose marking gauge that retains most of its original nickel plating. From the home of the Stanley Rule & Level Company. A most interesting and unusual gauge.* (FINE) **$85.00**

J4-14. **Stevens & Co., J., C. Falls, Mass: Machinist's Adjustable Protractor. "Pat. Apl'd. For". Rare and Excellent. Length: 3 1/4 Inches.** *This machinist's protractor and bevel has a notch cut precisely into the tip of the movable arm to allow it to be set precisely at 1 degree increments. Condition is near-new. A great machinist tool.* (FINE) **$265.00**

J4-15. **Starrett Co., L. S., Athol, Mass.: Early Patent Outside Caliper. Patented January 6, 1885. Clear Patent Mark. Length: 4 1/2 Inches.** *A nice, clean and usable example of an early Starrett patent.* (GOOD+) **$35.00**

J4-16. **Unmarked: Early Double Caliper. With Slide Adjust. Near New Condition. Length: 6 Inches.** *This most unusual early caliper is in nearly new condition. Different.* (FINE) **$55.00**

J4-17. **Starrett, L.S., Athol, Mass.: Patented Outside Caliper. Patented June 2, 1885. Positive Lock Mechinism. Length: 6 Inches.** *These early inside calipers are imprinted with the date of the June 2, 1885 patent granted to Charles Fay. Scarce.* (GOOD) **$35.00**

J4-18. **E. & T. Mfg. Co.: Inside and Outside Caliper. Marked "Pat. Pend." Rare and Excellent. Length: 6 Inches.** *There is a passing mention of this company in Ken Cope's "American Machinist's Tools", but not a whole lot of information. This is the only one of these that I have seen. A good one.* (FINE) **$115.00**

J4-19. **Unmarked: Early Outside Caliper. With Overhead Lock. Owner "P.J. Mc Guire". Length: 4 1/2 Inches.** *This well made caliper features an overhead locking mechanism that we have not encountered before. It is imprinted with the name of P.J. McGuire, who may have made it for his own use. Early and excellent.* (FINE) **$75.00**

J4-20. **Mauser: Precision Protractor. With Lock Screw. From Arms Maker. Length: 6 Inches.** *This precision caliper is imprinted with the name of a prominent German maker of firearms. It is in near new condition.* (FINE) **$65.00**

J4-21. **Goodell-Pratt Company: Combination Marking Gauge. With Circular Adjustment. Rare and Excellent. Length: 8 Inches.** *Goodell-Pratt offered a full line of marking gauges, none of which is very common. A gauge similar to this one with a "Y" shaped fence was offered, but this is the only example of an adjustable version of which I am aware. Extra rare.* (FINE) **$295.00**

J4-22. **Brown & Sharpe Mfg. Company No. 260: Precision Inside Micrometer. For Internal Measurement. Near New Condition. Length: 2 1/2 Inches.** *Here's a small inside micrometer in excellent condition.* (FINE) **$35.00**

J4-23. **Starrett Co., The L.S., Athol, Mass.: Machinist's Adjustable Protractor. With Tools Trademark. Patented August 7, 1883. Length: 7 Inches.** *This adjustable protractor will fit on any engineer's square by Starrett or Brown & Sharpe. Ready to use.* (GOOD+) **$35.00**

J4-24. **Dordea Mfg. Co., Detroit, Mich.: Adjustable Beam Trammels. "Pat. Pending". Early Type Knurls. Length: 12 Inches.** *A pair of precision beam trammels that were apparently intended for use in drafting, or possibly by machinists. Clean, complete and clearly marked.* (FINE) **$55.00**

J4-25. **Stevens & Co., J., C. Falls, Mass.: Quick Adjust Caliper. For Threads. "Pat. Appld For". Length: 4 Inches.** *This outside caliper can be quickly moved into the desired position and then precisely adjusted. Scarce.* (FINE) **$45.00**

J4-26. **Brown & Sharpe Mfg., Providence No. 70: Paper Gauge Micrometer. Patented January 22, 1884. Early and Uncommon. Length: 5 Inches.** *The oversize anvil on this early patent micrometer facilitated its use in measuring paper and similar flexible materials. It is imprinted with the date of the 1884 patent granted to C. Carleton of Providence, Rhode Island.* (GOOD+) **$295.00**

J4-27. **Stanley Rule & Level No. 38 1/2: Machinist's Bench Level. Sweetheart Trademark. Excellent Condition. Length: 4 Inches.** *This "Sweetheart" marked level has a lightly stippled casting. Extra crisp and clean.* (FINE) **$75.00**

J4-28. **Goodell-Pratt Company No. 662: Indicating Caliper. 0" to 2" Size. Near New Condition. Length: 3 Inches.** *The Goodell-Pratt Company offered a full line of machinists tools, first after their affiliation with the Massachusetts Tool Company, and, later, on their own. Their line was assumed by Millers Falls after G.P. and M.F. merged. This registering caliper seems to have been offered for only a few years. An uncommon Goodell-Pratt tool.* (FINE) **$65.00**

J4-29. **Unmarked: Early Inside Caliper. With Arm and Hammer. Owner J.M. Jackson. Length: 9 1/2 Inches.** *The only mark on this early tool is an "arm and hammer" device that resembles the logo of the P.S. & W. Company.* (FINE) **$55.00**

J4-30. **Unmarked: Early Brass and Steel Trammels. For Draughtsman. Excellent Condition. Length: 12 Inches.** *These extension bar draughtsman's trammels were the only item remaining in a ca. 1850's boxed set of drafting tools. The set is most unusual and in spectacular condition. Top shelf.* (FINE) **$275.00**

J4-31. **Unmarked: Assorted Reamers. For Drill Press. Ready to Use. Length: 2 1/2 Inches.** *Try buying one of these for this price anyplace else. Ready to use.* (FINE) **$15.00**

J4-32. **Darling Brown & Sharpe: Early Screw-Adjust Caliper. Graduated in 100ths. Crisp and Clean. Length: 5 1/2 Inches.** *Here's an excellent example of a D.B. & S. specialty. Clean and clearly marked.* (GOOD+) **$95.00**

J4-33. **Darling Brown & Sharp, Providence, R.I. No. 7: Flat Steel Bench Rule. 3" Size. Grad in 100'ths. Length: 3 Inches.** *The edge of this early rule has been engine divided into 100ths of an inch. A nice example.* (GOOD+) **$35.00**

J4-34. **Davis Expansion Boring Tool Co.: Special Roller Tip Caliper. Precision Adjust. Most Unusual. Length: 9 1/2 Inches.** *This most unusual caliper is imprinted with the name of a maker we have not previously encountered. The locking central joint is very similar to that on calipers made by J. Stevens & Company. Different.* (GOOD+) **$125.00**

J4-35. **Starrett Co., The L.S.S. No. 51285: Set of Center Punches. Original Wood Case. Near New Condition. Length: 6 Inches.** *Here's a full set of the best center punches ever made. They have been protected by their fitted wooden case. A great set.* (FINE) **$65.00**

J4-36. **Nicholson File Co., Providence, R.I.: Box of Mill Bastard Files. 8" Size. New Condition, Original Box. Length: 8 Inches.** *Here's a full box of top quality files in new condition. Bought a new file lately?* (FINE) **$35.00**

J4-37. **Darling Brown & Sharp, Providence, R.I.: Machinist's Bench Rule. 6" Length. Owner "G.F Tyler". Length: 6 Inches.** *One time owner G.F. Tyler tastefully stamped his name on opposite sides of the D.B. & S. imprint. A nice early rule in near new condition.* (FINE) **$45.00**

J4-38. **Starrett Co., L. S., Athol, Mass. No. 436: Pair of Precision Micrometers. With Decimal Equivalent. Near New Condition. Length: 7 Inches.** *These well made micrometers from America's premier maker are in excellent working condition. Included are a 1" to 2" and 2" to 3" size.* (FINE) **$55.00**

J4-39. **Starrett, L.S., Athol, Mass. No. 85: Patented Combination Divider. Patented September 24, 1889. Near New Condition. Length: 6 Inches.** *A very nice example of Starrett's offering in the combination divider sweepstakes, this pair is in near-new condition.* (FINE) **$85.00**

J4-40. **Starrett Co., The L.S.S. No. 123: "Master" Vernier Caliper. Hardened Stabilizer. New Condition, Original Box. Length: 9 Inches.** *This precision vernier caliper is in unused condition in its original box, complete with instructions and certification papers. Mint.* (FINE) **$95.00**

J4-41. **Starrett Co., L. S., Athol, Mass. No. S 423: Set of Precision Rules. With Handle. New Condition, Original Box. Length: 4 1/2 Inches.** *An extension handle allows these rules to be used in hard to reach places. Condition is as new. Mint.* (FINE) **$25.00**

J4-42. **Brown & Sharpe Mfg., Providence No. 465: Precision Attachment For Square. Machined Stop. For Height Gauge? Length: 3 Inches.** *This accessory was designed to fit on a combination square. An uncommon add on in exdllent condition.* (FINE) **$35.00**

J4-43. **Fay, Charles B., Springfield, Mass.: Early Patent Caliper. Patented June 2, 1885. Rare Quick Adjust. Length: 7 Inches.** *A nice example of the Fay patent, who patented and manufactured these calipers himself before selling them to L.S. Starrett and going to work for them as part of the deal. The tips have been ground a bit, but this one is clean and clearly marked. Rare.* (GOOD) **$45.00**

J4-44. **Assorted Makers: Tools From Machinist's Box. Wrench, Badge, Etc. Owner Sam Valenti. Length: 10 Inches.** *These items occupied one drawer of the machinists chest of Mr. Sam Valenti. A bargain.* (GOOD+) **$35.00**

J4-45. **Adams, Geo. H.: Set of "Mechanic's" Tools. Hamnmers, Dividers. Punches, Etc. Length: 15 Inches.** *All of the tools in this lot came from an estate in Central New Hampshire, where they may have lain unused for nearly a hundred years. All of the tools are so well made as to appear manufactured, yet none bears a makers mark, other than the hand struck "Geo. Adams" imprint. Could it be that these tools were acquired by Mr. Adams for use and then set away and forgotten? Or could it be that Adams was a toolmaker who fashioned these tools for sale? We may never know, but what is certain is that this group of metal working tools provide a snapshot of a time and place that has been all but forgotten. Treasures from the past.* (FINE) **$365.00**

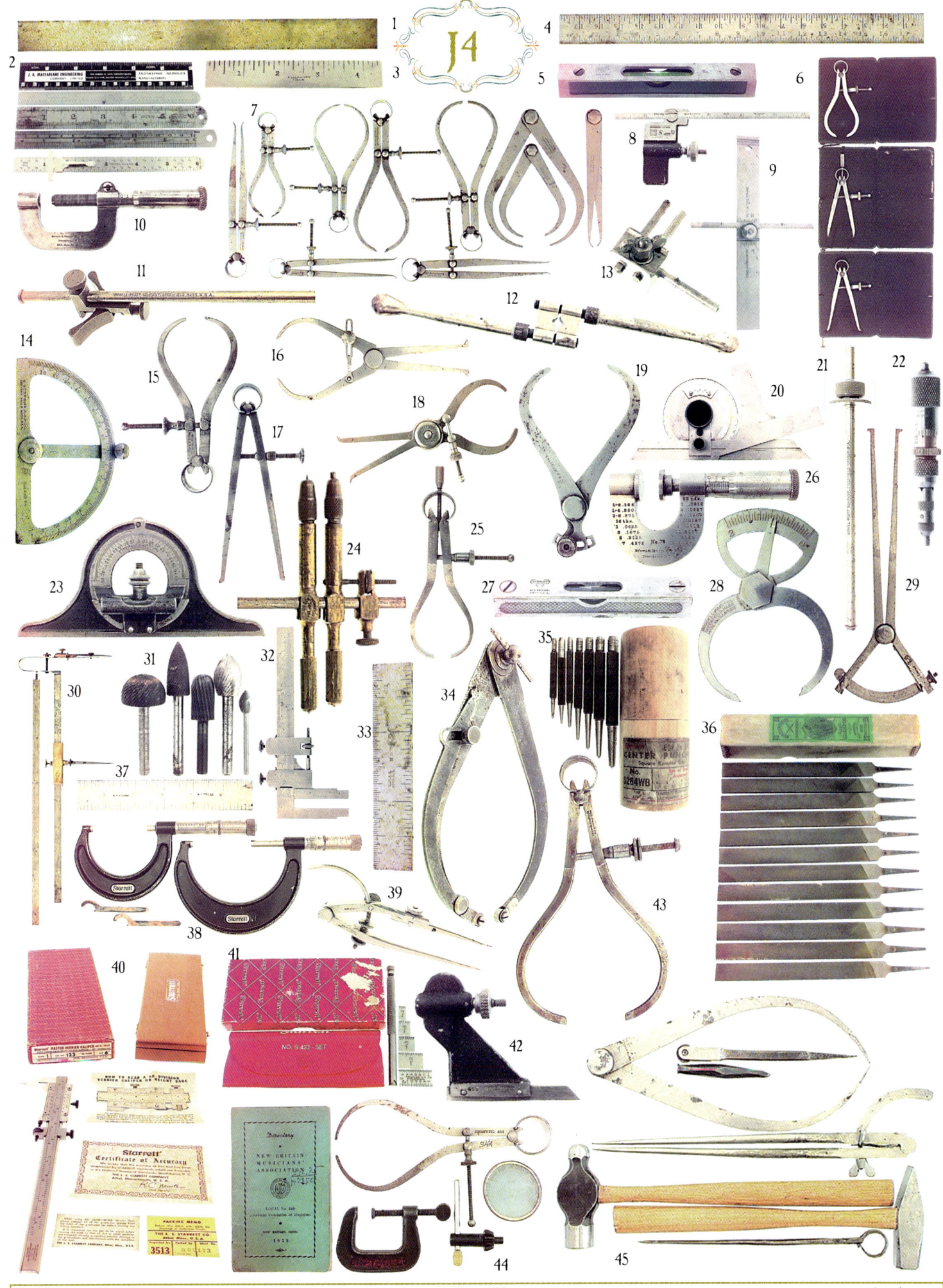

Group K4

K4-1. Olmsted, L.H.: Olmsted's Patent Mitre Box. Patented Apr. 6, 1886. Scarce and Excellent. Length: 17 1/2 Inches. *This cast iron mitre box is cast with the April 6, 1886 patent of one L.H. Olmsted. Patent mitre boxes offer an interesting collecting opportunity. Opportunity knocks.* (GOOD) **$145.00**

K4-2. Unmarked: Cast Iron Block Metallic Plane. Oversize Body. Unknown Maker. Length: 4 Inches. *The pattern of this oversize block plane is one we have not previously encountered. Different.* (GOOD+) **$35.00**

K4-3. Sandusky Tool Co., Sandusky, Ohio: Set of 21 Hollow and Round Molding Planes. Owner H.R. Mclemale. Near New Condition. Length: 9 1/2 Inches. *Still in much the same condition as they were the day they left the factory, this nearly complete set of hollow and round molding planes from the Sandusky Tool Company were once the property of one "H.R. Mc Lemale", who imprinted them with his name. Missing only the No. 5 and 7 hollow and the No. 6 round to make a complete set, this is the most complete and one of the best preserved sets of American made hollows and rounds that we have ever offered. First class.* (FINE) **$1,275.00**

K4-4. Stanley Rule & Level No. 66: Universal Hand Beader. 7 Double Cutters. Complete and Excellent Length: 11 1/2 Inches. *This complete example of Stanley's highly-desirable scratch beader is complete with both fences and seven double-ended cutters. Essentially unused.* (FINE) **$225.00**

K4-5. Stanley Rule & Level No. 75: Bullnose Rabbet Plane. Ready to Use. Owner "Mertz". Length: 4 1/2 Inches. *This Stanley classic is in top working order. A previous owner etched his name in one side, but it is functionally perfect. Ready to use.* (GOOD+) **$35.00**

K4-6. Record, Sheffield, England No. 044: Light Duty Plow Metallic Plane. With Original Cutters. New Condition, Original Box. Length: 8 Inches. *These light duty plows are equally as functional as Stanley's No. 50 beading plane and can be had much cheaper. Complete with all cutters in the original box.* (FINE) **$165.00**

K4-7. Unmarked: Sash Mitre Template. "Pat. App. 16783". Ready to Use. Length: 6 Inches. *Here's a classic sash mitre template for the would-be window maker.* (GOOD) **$45.00**

K4-8. Sears, Roebuck & Co. No. 3728: Combination Metallic Plane. Similar to Stanley 45. Made By Sargent. Length: 11 Inches. *These were made for Sears by Sargent & Company, of New Haven, Connecticut in the 1950's. A great working combination plane at a bargain price. Nearly new.* (FINE) **$165.00**

K4-9. Unmarked: Replacement Handle for Wooden Plane. New Old Stock. Ready to Use. Length: 4 1/2 Inches. *It you have a wooden plane with the all too common chipped tote, here's your chance to make it right. New old stock.* (FINE) **$15.00**

K4-10. Assorted Makers: Drills, Tap Wrench Reamers, Etc. From Tool Box. Bargain Lot. Length: 5 Inches. *Here's a nice group of drill bits, allen wrenches, etc. All came from the same machinist's box.* (GOOD+) **$25.00**

K4-11. Nicholson File Co., Providence, R.I.: Four Faced Rasp. 4 Cutting Edges. Unused Condition. Length: 10 Inches. *This unusual four faced rasp was found in the back of a toolbox where it was set away and never used. Old, but brand new and ready to use.* (FINE) **$15.00**

K4-12. Unmarked: Patternmaker's Bench Dogs. For Joining Wood. Ready to Use. Length: 2 1/2 Inches. *These bench dogs were used in place of clamps for gluing boards edge to edge. Ready to use.* (GOOD+) **$35.00**

K4-13. Stanley Rule & Level No. 22: Dowel Sharpener. For Electric Drill. Original Wrapper. Length: 2 1/4 Inches. *This most unusual "straight shaft" dowel sharpener was apparently intended for use in an electric drill. Condition is unused.* (FINE) **$25.00**

K4-14. Goodell-Pratt Company No. 333: Shepardson's Iron Jointer Gauge. For Metal Planes. Ready to Use. Length: 8 Inches. *Designed to be fitted on the side rail of a metal plane, this early nickel plated gauge is in excellent condition. It will work fine, but is missing its precision adjustment screw from the center.* (GOOD+) **$45.00**

K4-15. Montgomery Ward No. 7: "Lakeside" Jointer Metallic Plane. Made By Stanley. Rosewood Handles. Length: 22 Inches. *The concept of mail order hardware and tools was just coming into its own in the late 1920's when Montgomery, Ward & Company took aim at market leader Sears, Roebuck & Company. By purchasing the very highest quality tools from top makers and selling them under their own brand name as "Master Quality", the folks at Wards hoped to win the battle for the American tool dollar from the Chicago-based Sears. Had the Roosevelt Depression not intervened, they may well have done so. Whatever the case, the Wards venture into high grade tools lasted for but a short time. This well preserved "No. 7" plane is identical in all respects to the Stanley offering for the simple reason that Stanley produced it for Wards with the same attention to quality that they gave to tools produced under their own name. If you're looking for a top quality Stanley No. 7, here's a chance to get one forwell under the money.* (GOOD+) **$65.00**

K4-16. Stanley Rule & Level: 4 Oz. Ball Pein Hammer. Partial Original Decal. Unused Condition. Length: 11 Inches. *This uncommon Stanley hammer appears never to have been used. Traces of the original ca. 1920's orange decal remain. A good one.* (FINE) **$15.00**

K4-17. Unmarked: 1 1/2" Twist Auger Bit. For Boring Machine. Ready to Use. Length: 11 Inches. *Designed to fit in the chuck of a hand crank boring machine, this bit has been drilled to receive the locking screw from the chuck of one of those machines. Ready to use.* (GOOD+) **$45.00**

K4-18. Bruno Tools, Beverly Hills, Ca. No. 304 B: "Bruno" Expansive Auger Bit. Multiple Tips. New Condition, Original Box. Length: 8 1/4 Inches. *When one thinks of Beverly Hills, California, one thinks immediately of auger bits. This boxed set is essentially complete. Unusual.* (FINE) **$35.00**

K4-19. Millers Falls Company: Cutting Iron for Cutting Iron. Fits Stanley No. 75. Unused Condition. Length: 4 1/2 Inches: *This will fit the Millers Falls No. 4 cast iron rabbet plane or Stanley's No. 75 equivalent. New.* (FINE) **$15.00**

K4-20. Record, Sheffield, England No. 044: Light Duty Plow Metallic Plane. With Original Cutters. Unused Condition. Length: 8 Inches. *As a functional working tool, there's no beating this light duty grooving plane from England's now-defunct Record firm. This one is in great condition in its original box.* (FINE) **$135.00**

K4-21. Smith & Son, G.: Early Patent Bench Stop. Patented June 11, 1878. Rare and Excellent. Length: 4 Inches. *This early patent depth stop is marked with the name of a maker we have not encountered before. It is imprinted with the 1878 patent date. A rare and collectible bench stop.* (GOOD+) **$115.00**

K4-22. Stanley Rule & Level No. 40: Beech Handle Scrub Plane. Sweetheart Trademark. Superb Condtiion. Length: 11 Inches. *The roughing out of virgin stock before the jack and smooth plane went to work was the task assigned to these workaday planes, which were fitted with convex cutting irons to literally "scoop" out the wood. A great working example.* (GOOD+) **$115.00**

K4-23. Stanley Rule & Level No. 207: Nickel Plated Bench Stop. With Spring Stop. Scarce and Near New. Length: 3 3/4 Inches. *Here's a pristine example of Stanley's uncommon spring-activated bench stop in new condition. Extra nice.* (FINE) **$35.00**

K4-24. Stanley Rule & Level No. 18: 10" Blade Bevel. Cast Iron Body. Ready to Use. Length: 10 Inches. *Retaining nearly all of its original nickel plating, this example of Stanley's "Eureka Patent Flush T Bevel" is in excellent working condition.* (GOOD+) **$45.00**

K4-25. Stanley Rule & Level No. 30: Angle Divider Bevel. Replaced Screw. "Sweetheart" Trademark. Length: 7 1/2 Inches. *The central screw on this angle divider appears to be a replacement, but it is otherwise in excellent condition. Ready to use, if you choose.* (GOOD) **$45.00**

K4-26. Stanley Rule & Level No. 25: Rosewood Handle Bevel. Unused Condition. Blued Steel Blade. Length: 10 Inches. *All original finishes remain on this pristine bevel. Mint.* (FINE) **$35.00**

K4-27. Buckeye: Cast Iron Jointer Gauge. Nickel Plated Fence. Uncommon Type. Length: 9 Inches. *The "Buckeye" jointer gauge used the cam lock design employed effectively by several other makers. Ready to use.* (GOOD+) **$75.00**

K4-28. Stanley Rule & Level No. 207: Nickel Plated Bench Stop. With Spring Stop. Scarce and Near New. Length: 3 3/4 Inches. *A nice example of Stanley's offering in the bench stop competition. The spring clip was designed to lock the stop into a hole bored in the bench. Tough to find.* (FINE) **$45.00**

K4-29. Standard Tool Co., Athol, Mass.: Chaplin's Patent Combination Square. With Original Rule. Tight Crack In Body. Length: 9 Inches. *This graphic machinist tool has the original offset rule that is often missing. There is a tight crack in the body casting, but it is otherwise excellent.* (GOOD+) **$85.00**

K4-30. Assorted Makers: Group of 5 Palette Knives. For Artist's Use. Assorted Types. Length: 7 Inches. *These specialized tools were used by an artist for mixing oil paints. Appearance is Nineteenth Century.* (GOOD+) **$55.00**

K4-31. Stanley Tools, Australia No. 100 RJ: Russell Jennings Auger Bit. Original Case. Unused Condition. Length: 10 Inches. *These classic Russell Jennings auger bits have apparently never been used. Mint.* (FINE) **$75.00**

K4-32. Stanley Rule & Level No. 3 C: 8" Smoothing Plane. Rosewood Handles. "Sweetheart" Trademark. Length: 9 Inches. *This crisp but slightly dirty "Sweetheart" era molding plane comes to us from a local workshop. More than 90% of the original paint remains and the Brazilian rosewood handles are sound and boldly grained. A nice example of an underrated Stanley plane.* (GOOD+) **$75.00**

K4-33. Horan & Bros., Boston, Mass.: Solid Brass Bench Stop. Marked "Patent". Early and Excellent. Length: 3 1/2 Inches. *This extraordinary brass bench stop is marked with the maker's name and the word "patent". The only one I have ever seen. Near new.* (FINE) **$145.00**

K4-34. Unmarked: Screw Adjust Bench Stop. Cast Iron Body. Near New Condition. Length: 3 1/4 Inches. *Intended to be mortised into a workbench top, the stop on this precision tool could be adjusted with a screwdriver.* (FINE) **$45.00**

K4-35. Unmarked: Stair Builder's Handrail Shave. Ogee Profile. Great Patina. Length: 11 Inches. *This classic stair builder's shave was likely made by the craftsman who used it. It has been carefully kept for perhaps 150 years. Very nice.* (FINE) **$115.00**

K4-36. Unmarked: Mahogany Cased Oilstone. Decorative Box. Early and Near New. Length: 9 1/2 Inches. *The mahogany case for this well preserved oilstone has the the look of fine furniture. An oilstone case that was meant to be better than most and still is.* (FINE) **$145.00**

K4-37. Disston & Sons, Henry, Philadelphia, Penn. No. 338: Early Mason's Trowel. With Original Etching. Near New Condition. Length: 11 Inches. *The acid-etched Disston logo on this one would have lasted about 15 minutes on the job. A great collectible trowel that's never worked a day in its life.* (FINE) **$65.00**

K4-38. Sears, Roebuck & Co. No. 3730: "Craftsman" Duplex Metallic Plane. Rabbet and Filletster. Unused Condition. Length: 8 Inches. *This well made rabbet and filletster plane was made for Sears by the Millers Falls Company. A nice working tool in nearly new condition.* (FINE) **$55.00**

K4-39. Stanley Rule & Level No. 386: Patented Adjustable Jointer Gauge. Complete and Excellent Patented April 1, 1913. Length: 14 Inches. *Stanley's jointer gauge was a great seller for 60 years for the simple reason that it was the best there was. This one is in excellent condition.* (GOOD+) **$145.00**

K4-40. Billings & Spencer Co., Hartford: Canvas Tool Roll. For Wrenches? With Billings & Spencer Mark. Length: 24 Inches. *Apparently this set came filled with a set of wrenches and/or other tools. A project.* (FINE) **$15.00**

K4-41. Spear & Jackson, Sheffield No. 52: 8" Brass-Back Dovetail Saw. Straight and True. Extra Fine Teeth. Length: 12 Inches. *The Spear and Jackson people made saws for well over 100 years. This later-style brass back is clean, straight and true. Ready to use.* (GOOD+) **$85.00**

K4-42. Unmarked: Cast Bronze Lathe Body and Tail Stock Early Appearance. Clean and Sound. Length: 13 1/2 Inches. *We offer the bed and tail stock of this extremely early cast bronze lathe with the expectation that someone will make the proper effort to restore it to its original magnificence. A potentially great tool.* (GOOD+) **$295.00**

K4-43. Disston & Sons, Henry, Philadelphia, Penn.: 10" Dovetail Saw. Straight and True. Ready to Use. Length: 15 Inches. *Here's an excellent working dovetail saw from America's top maker. There is a small chip from the base of the handle, but it is otherwise straight, sharp and ready to use.* (GOOD+) **$65.00**

K4-44. Atkin & Sons, Birmingham (England): 14" Tenon Saw. Early Style Handle. Straight and True. Length: 19 Inches. *Here's an excellent working saw from a prominent English maker. Crisp, clean, straight and ready to use.* (GOOD+) **$55.00**

K4-45. Stanley Rule & Level No. 45: Multi Purpose Combination Plane. Complete, Ready to Use. Owner Made Box. Length: 9 Inches. *An owner made box has kept this combination plane in excellent working order and complete with all original parts. Ready to go to work.* (GOOD+) **$255.00**

Group L4

L4-1. Barlow Hardware Co., Corry, Penn.: Wholesale Iron and Steel, Various Supplies. Net Price List No. 24. 1908, 280 Pages. Length: 8 Inches. *This comprehensive catalog includes a wide range of hardware and tools.* (GOOD+) **$35.00**

L4-2. Millers Falls Company: Langdon Mitre Box Co Price List. Ca. 1907. With Parts List. Length: 6 1/4 Inches. *Here's an early and interesting advertising pamphlet from a company that later merged with the Millers Falls Company.* (GOOD+) **$25.00**

L4-3. Wilkie, Leighton A.: The Story of Measurement. 1957. 32 Pages. Length: 10 Inches. *This interesting book was published by a Midwestern manufacturer of power tools. It traces measurement from the earliest times to the present and is well illustrated.* (FINE) **$15.00**

L4-4. Disston & Sons, H., Philadelphia, Penn.: The File in History Fourth Edition. December 1924. 79 Pages. Length: 8 Inches. *This well done publication traces the history of the saw through time until it was perfected by the folks at the Henry Disston Company.* (FINE) **$65.00**

L4-5. Spence Mfg. Co, S.M., Boston, Mass.: Stamp and Stencil Catalog. 122 Pages, Ca. 1913. Period Engravings. Length: 9 Inches. *All manner of stencils, stamps and engraving accessories are illustrated in this early catalog.* (FINE) **$65.00**

L4-6. Nicholson File Co., Providence, R.I.: File Filosophy Proper Methods of Using Files, 8th Edition. Revised, 1913, 47 Pages. Length: 6 1/4 Inches. *This version of Nicholson's famous "File Filosophy" pamphlet dates from some 90 years ago.* (FINE) **$25.00**

L4-7. Wilkie, Leighton A.: Civilization Through Tools. 1954. 24 Pages. Length: 12 Inches. *Published by the Doall Company, a producer of power tools, this booklet, which was published in 1954, attempted to recount the role of hand tools in the rise of civilization. A rare book in excellent condition.* (GOOD+) **$35.00**

L4-8. Jennings, Russell Mfg. Co., Conn.: Russell Jennings Carpenters' "Precision Tools". 8 Pages, Ca. 1910. Length: 9 Inches. *This uncommon pamphlet was produced by the Russell Jennings Company around the turn of the Century.* (FINE) **$55.00**

L4-9. Sellens, Alvin: "The Stanley Plane" Book. 1st Edition, 1975. Original Dust Jacket. Length: 9 1/2 Inches. *Now out of print, there are no plans for a reprint of Alvin Sellens classic to be issued. This example has been kept in top shape by the presence of a plastic binder. The rare and collectible book that started it all.* (FINE) **$125.00**

L4-10. Audel, Theo. & Co.: Carpenters and Builder's Book Set. 1947 Edition. Hardbound, 4 Volumes. Length: 6 1/2 Inches. *The Audel company produced these "how to" books for carpenters and builders for many years. This complete four volume set dates from 1947. Filled with useful information and interesting to read.* (FINE) **$65.00**

L4-11. Audel, Theo. & Co.: Carpenters and Builder's Book Set. 1947 Edition. Hardbound, 4 Volumes. Length: 6 1/2 Inches. *The Audel company produced these "how to" books for carpenters and builders for many years. This complete four volume set dates from 1947. Filled with useful information and interesting to read.* (FINE) **$65.00**

L4-12. Connecticut Valley Mfg. Co.: Wood Boring Tools. Catalog No. 11. June 1939, 12 Pages. Length: 9 Inches. *This original catalog documents the full product line of this Connecticut maker of wood boring tools. It is in new condition.* (FINE) **$25.00**

L4-13. Bartholomew, H. S., Bristol, Conn: Price-List of Breast Drills, Braces, Ferrules, Etc., Etc. 23 Pages. Length: 5 1/2 Inches. *This original catalog of braces, drills and more dates from around 1880. A great original catalog.* (FINE) **$45.00**

L4-14. Dibner, Bern: Agricola on Metals Book. Publication No. 15. 128 Pages. Length: 10 3/4 Inches. *This well done publication recounts the writings of the ancient writer Agricola, on the subject of metals and mining. A most interesting book that has long been out of print.* (FINE) **$110.00**

L4-15. Roberts, Kenneth D.: Tools For The Trades and Crafts. 1976. 222 Pages. Length: 11 Inches. *A replica of a Nineteenth Century Sheffield "pattern book", this book shows the standard patterns for English tools of that period as well as cutlery and other hardware. Long out of print, we do not expect to have this one for long. First come, first serve.* (FINE) **$95.00**

L4-16. Wilkie, Leighton A.: Civilization Through Tools. 1954. 24 Pages. Length: 12 Inches. *This was the first version of a pamphlet on the history of measurement produced by this Midwestern tool manufacturer. An interesting read that is well illustrated.* (GOOD+) **$25.00**

L4-17. Assorted Makers: Set Of "Mechanic's" Books. Scribner, Ropp, Etc. 1899, 1908, Etc. Length: 6 Inches. *Most "mechanics" had one of these books which included all sorts of tables for performing mathematical calculations. All of the major makers of these tables are represented in this grouping. A bargain.* (GOOD+) **$65.00**

L4-18. Hommell, Rudolf P.: China at Work First M.I.T. Press. Edition, September 1969. 366 Pages, Softbound. Length: 10 Inches. *Here's a most interesting look at trades and the use of tools in the vast nation of China. Illustrated with photographs and well documented.* (FINE) **$45.00**

L4-19. Tunis, Edwin: Colonial Craftsmen Book. 1965 First Edition. 159 Pages. Length: 12 Inches. *There is plenty information about early trades and crafts in this long out of print book.* (GOOD+) **$85.00**

L4-20. Wilkie, Leighton A.: The Story of Measurement. Ca. 1957. 32 Pages, Softbound. Length: 10 Inches. *This interesting book was published by a Midwestern manufacturer of power tools. It traces measurement from the earliest times to the present.* (FINE) **$15.00**

L4-21. Visscher, Albert De, Editor: "L'outil" Book. Classic French Tools. Great Color Photos. Length: 11 1/2 Inches. *Filled with illustrations of classic French tools, this book is a celebration of the blacksmith's art. For a look at true "museum quality" tools, we highly recommend this beautiful but long out of print book.* (GOOD+) **$165.00**

L4-22. Roberts, Kenneth: Set of "Wooden Plane Books. Volume II is Signed. Tough to Find Set. Length: 11 1/2 Inches. *Here's a pair of classic books from legendary tool researcher and bon vivant Kenneth Roberts. Volume II is signed by the author. A great set.* (GOOD+) **$195.00**

L4-23. Davidson, Marshall & Namuth, Hans: American Woodworking. Tool Book. Published 1975. 65 Pages., Illustrated. Length: 12 1/2 Inches. *More art book than tool reference, this out-of-print coffee table book includes some excellent black and white photographs of primarily "primitive" tools, together with commentary. An interesting look at tool collecting.the way it was.* (FINE) **$115.00**

L4-24. Farnham, Alexander: Tool Collector's Hand Book. 3 Early Editions. With Illustrations. Length: 9 Inches. *Perhaps the first attempt to chronicle the values and relative values of antique tools, these books were published by Alexander Farnham, the author of "Early Tools of New Jersey" and other books. Interesting early references and a source of great insight into how tool collecting has changed.* (FINE) **$55.00**

L4-25. Jennings Mfg. Co., The Russell: The Original Russell Jennings Extension. Lip Auger Bits, 45 Pages. Catalog No. 30. Length: 9 Inches. *The full Jennings line is illustrated in this well preserved catalog. An excellent reference.* (FINE) **$85.00**

L4-26. Smith, H. R. Bradley: Blacksmiths' and Farri Book. Museum, Pamphlet #7. 1966, 271 Pages. Length: 9 Inches. *Now out of print, this well done book is an excellent introduction to the tools of the blacksmith and farrier.* (GOOD+) **$35.00**

L4-27. Stanley Rule & Level: 1926 Pocket Catalog. 48 Pages, Softbound. 3 1/2" X 6". Length: 6 Inches. *This 48 page book illustrates much of the Stanley line as it existed in 1926. It has some slight staining and a few tears, but is otherwise complete and intact.* (GOOD) **$25.00**

L4-28. Mercer, Henry: Ancient Carpenters Book. 1960 Edition. 331 Pages, Illustrated. Length: 9 1/2 Inches. *Here's an exceptionally clean copy of the 1960 edition of the book that is credited with getting antique tool collecting started.* (GOOD+) **$95.00**

L4-29. Nicholson File Co., Providence, R.I.: Nicholson File Co. Catalog. 1911 Edition. 92 Pages, Softbound. Length: 6 Inches. *Most people today don't have the slightest idea how to properly use files. Reading this catalog is a great source of information about files and their uses.* (FINE) **$45.00**

L4-30. Disston & Sons, H., Philadelphia, Penn.: Disston Saw, Tool & File Manual, Compliments of Harrison and Gould, 64 Pages. Length: 8 Inches. *These oversize pamphlets include all sorts of information on the proper use of tools. In the back, advertising for Disston products is included.* (FINE) **$35.00**

L4-31. Connecticut Valley Mfg. Co.: Wood Boring Tools Book. Catalog No. 11. 12 Pages. Length: 9 Inches. *This original catalog documents the full product line of this Connecticut maker of wood boring tools. It is in new condition.* (FINE) **$15.00**

L4-32. Union Twist Drill Co., Athol, Mass. No. L2: "Book of Information Catalog. 320 Pages, Ca. 1920's. Near New Condition. Length: 7 1/4 Inches. *This one includes all sorts of tools, machines and more. A nice catalog.* (GOOD+) **$35.00**

L4-33. Millers Falls Co., Mass.: Confidential Resale Prices : Hand and Precision Tools. Effective July 17, 1967. Length: 11 Inches. *These were included with the catalog, which listed retail prices.* (FINE) **$12.00**

L4-34. Sellens, Alvin: "The Stanley Plane" Book. 8th Printing 1986. Original Dust Jacket. Length: 9 1/2 Inches. *This book, which started the Stanley collecting craze, is no longer in print, nor are there any plans to reprint it. A classic.* (FINE) **$115.00**

L4-35. Asher & Adams: Picture Album Industry Book. 1876 Edition. Reprinted 1976. Length: 16 Inches. *This long out of print book is a reprint of an 1876 volume on the subject of American industry.* (GOOD+) **$65.00**

L4-36. Disston & Sons, H., Philadelphia, Penn.: The Saw: How to Keep It in Order, Sold By Oscar Gove. Length: 5 1/2 Inches. *This 1890's era catalog illustrates much of the Disston Saw line from that early period. It is imprinted with the name of the Haverhill, Massachusetts hardware dealer who originally distributed it.* (FINE) **$55.00**

L4-37. Penn. Farm Museum, Landis Valley: The Blacksmith: Artisan Within the Community, 1972. 64 Pages. Length: 11 Inches. *Published by the Landis Valley Museum, this well illustrated book, which is now out of print, includes great photographs and illustrations of the blacksmith, his craft and his work. A great reference.* (FINE) **$115.00**

L4-38. Kebabian, Paul & Whitney, Dudley: Early American Woodworking Tools Book. Published 1978, 213 Pages. Scarce and Excellent. Length: 11 Inches. *An exceptionally well done book on classic woodworking tools, this beautiful book was my first experience with tool collecting. Great color and black and white photos enhance the scholarly but readable text of this classic work. Long out of print and very highly recommended.* (FINE) **$125.00**

L4-39. Deering Harvester Company: Roller Bearings And Light Draft. 1896? 40 Pages. Length: 9 3/4 Inches. *The printing quality of this 19th Century catalog is at least as appealing as its subject. Graphic.* (FINE) **$45.00**

L4-40. Stanley Rule & Level No. 13: Kitchen Cabinet Plans. Ca. 1930's. Rare and Excellent. Length: 10 Inches. *These early plans were part of a Stanley promotion from the 1930's. Scarce.* (GOOD+) **$45.00**

L4-41. Nicholson File Co., Providence, R.I.: Nicholson and X. F. Swiss Pattern Files. Catalog No. N-12. Files, Rasps, 1954. Length: 7 Inches. *Need information about the great variety of files and rasps? Here's an excellent reference.* (FINE) **$25.00**

L4-42. Bittner, Jack: 5 Bittner Auction Catalogs. No.'s 1,3,4 and 5. Early Tool Info. Length: 8 Inches. *Hand in glove with the first antique tool dealers were the first antique tool auctioneers. Beginning at almost the same time Richard Crane and Jack Bittner became legends for all time, selling extraordinary tools in auctions that would make today's auctions pale by comparison. Here are 5 of the early Bittner catalogs, together with their lists of prices realized. This was the cream of the crop the first time New England was picked for tools. Imagine...* (GOOD+) **$65.00**

L4-43. Wyke, John , Liverpool(Eng): A Catalogue of Tools for Watch and Clock. Makers, 1978. 153 Pages. Length: 12 Inches. *Illustrated with great line drawings of every manner of watch and clock makers tool, this hardbound book has been out of print for many years. A great reference.* (GOOD+) **$115.00**

L4-44. Stanley Rule & Level: Framing Squares Brochure. Ca. 1940, 48 Pages. 3 1/2" X 6". Length: 6 Inches. *This brochure provides information on the proper uses of framing squares and strongly suggests that the prospective buyer obtain one from the Stanley Rule & Level Company.* (GOOD+) **$35.00**

L4-45. Stanley Rule & Level No. 53: "Do It Better" Catalog. Published 1953. 48 Pages, Softbound. Length: 9 Inches. *These "Do It Better" catalogs, which included a bit of helpful advice together with all sorts of information about which tools to buy, were distributed as part of an early 1950's Stanley advertising campaign. This one is in excellent condition.* (FINE) **$45.00**

Group M4

M4-1. Stanley Rule & Level No. 36 1/2 L: One Foot, Two Fold Folding Rule. Left Hand Graduation. With Caliper Rule. Length: 12 Inches. *Here's a good, clean example of Stanley's basic one-foot, two-fold caliper rule. The "L" designated the left-hand caliper. Apparently unused.* (FINE) **$35.00**

M4-2. Stanley Rule & Level No. 82: Two Foot, Four Fold Folding Rule. Arch Joint, Full Bound. With Board Tables. Length: 24 Inches. *The arch joint, full bound No. 82 was Stanley's top-of-the-line folding board measure rule. If this one ever found its way to a work site, it was never put into use. A rare lumber rule in nearly perfect condition from America's premier maker.* (FINE) **$485.00**

M4-3. Stanley Rule & Level No. 13: Six Inch, Two Fold Folding Rule. With Caliper. Rare and Excellent. Length: 6 Inches. *This uncommon six inch Stanley rule is in excellent collector quality condition. A scarce Stanley rule.* (GOOD+) **$245.00**

M4-4. Cary, London: Boxwood Marquois Rules. For Military Engineers. Original Mahogany Case. Length: 13 Inches. *These perfectly preserved boxwood rules would likely have been the possession of a student at a military institution learning the rudiments of military engineering. Imprinted with the name of a respected London maker and perfectly preserved by the slide-top mahogany case, this set is as good as they get. Nice.* (FINE) **$225.00**

M4-5. Lufin Rule Co., The, Saginaw, Mich. No. 465: One-Foot, Four-Fold Folding Rule. Round Joint, Unbound. Stanley 69 Equivalent. Length: 12 Inches. *Lufkin's equivalent to Stanley's basic No. 69 is unmistakable as such, owing to the prominent imprinting of the Stanley equivalent number on the face of the rule. A nice example.* (FINE) **$125.00**

M4-6. C-S Co., The, Pine Meadow, Conn. No. 65 1/2: One Foot, Four Fold Folding Rule. Square Joint, Full Bound. Near New Condition. Length: 12 Inches. *This nearly new rule is clearly marked with the C-S Name. Never need to upgrade condition.* (FINE) **$225.00**

M4-7. Preston & Sons, E.: Six Inch, Two Fold Folding Rule. With Caliper Slide. Excellent Patina. Length: 6 Inches. *Only a few small stains detract from this English classic, which is of the pattern of Stanley's No. 13 six-inch rule. Note the "English" pattern of graduations, which move in the opposite direction of American rules.* (GOOD+) **$55.00**

M4-8. Stanley Rule & Level (Unmarked) No. 64: One-Foot, Four-Fold Folding Rule. Square Joint, Unbound. Rare and Excellent. Length: 12 Inches. *One rule that almost never is found with the "Stanley" imprint imprinted in the boxwood is the No. 64, which is distinguished from the No. 65 by the presence of brass edge plates at the center joint. A one-time opportunity for the seeker of "one of each". Nice.* (GOOD+) **$225.00**

M4-9. Stanley Rule & Level No. 36 1/2 R: One Foot, Two Fold Folding Rule. Right Hand Graduations. With Caliper Rule. Length: 12 Inches. *Another nice example of the No. 36 1/2 R. Ready to use or display. No apologies.* (GOOD+) **$25.00**

M4-10. Chapin, H. No. 72: One Foot, Four Fold Folding Rule. Arch Joint, Unbound. As New Condition. Length: 12 Inches. *This equivalent to Stanley's No. 32 caliper rule is in top collector quality condition. A scarce Chapin rule.* (FINE) **$165.00**

M4-11. Stanley Rule & Level No. 36: Six-Inch, Two-Fold Folding Rule. Square Joint, Caliper. Very Early Example. Length: 6 Inches. *This perfectly preserved caliper rule features a very early Stanley imprint. The rule is in nearly new condition. Nice.* (FINE) **$75.00**

M4-12. C-S Co., The, Pine Meadow, Conn. No. 32 1/2: Arch Joint, Full Bound Folding Rule. With Caliper Slide. Extra Crisp and Clean. Length: 12 Inches. *This well preserved caliper rule is clearly marked with the maker name and number. An increasingly tough rule to find, especially in this condition.* (GOOD+) **$55.00**

M4-13. Stanley Rule & Level (Unmarked) No. 64: One-Foot, Four-Fold Folding Rule. Square Joint, Unbound. Rare and Excellent. Length: 12 Inches. *Why the people at Stanley felt that they needed such a wide range of rules that differed only in the manner of joint or binding is not easily comprehensible to modern collectors of antique tools. This uncommon variation on the one foot, four fold theme features the "square" joint and is unbound. A very well preserved example.* (FINE) **$135.00**

M4-14. Rabone & Sons, J., Birmingham: Tapered Boxwood Rule. Graduation in 16ths. Most Unusual. Length: 12 Inches. *We are uncertain as to the function of this well preserved boxwood rule. Most unusual.* (GOOD+) **$85.00**

M4-15. Lufkin Rule Co., The, Saginaw, Mich. No. 386: Arch Joint, Unbound Folding Rule. With Caliper Slide. Near New Condition. Length: 12 Inches. *Here's a perfectly preserved example of Lufkin's unbound 12" caliper rule. Nice.* (FINE) **$95.00**

M4-16. Nicholl, R., High Holborn, London: Engine Divided Rule. 1/2500 Scale and Metric. Solid Boxwood. Length: 12 Inches. *A scale such as this would have been in the kit of either an engineer, surveyor or military officer for the plotting of scale diagrams. Mint.* (FINE) **$20.00**

M4-17. Stearns & Co., E.A., Brattleboro, No. 28: Three Foot, Four Fold Folding Rule. With Yard Measure. Rare and Excellent. Length: 36 Inches. *Pioneering makers of boxwood and ivory folding rules, the E.A. Stearns Company began operations in Brattleboro, Vermont in the 1830's. This three foot yard measure rule is imprinted with the Brattleboro location. The only example of this rare Stearns rule we have seen available for sale. Rare.* (GOOD+) **$365.00**

M4-18. Rabone & Sons, John, Birmingham No. 3261: Folding Shrink Folding Rule. 2/10 Inch to Foot. New Old Stock. Length: 24 Inches. *A good, clean, crisp and only slightly yellowed example of Stanley's 6 inch ivory caliper rule.* (FINE) **$65.00**

M4-19. Stephens & Co., Riverton, Conn. No. 42 1/2: Two Foot, Four Fold Folding Rule. Square Joint, Full Bound. Early and Excellent. Length: 24 Inches. *This uncommon offering from Riverton, Connecticut maker Stephens & Company was the equivalent of Stanley's mainstay No. 84. This one is clean and clearly marked. A good one.* (GOOD+) **$65.00**

M4-20. Stanley Rule & Level No. 76: Two Foot, Four Fold Folding Rule. Arch Joint, Full Bound. "Sweetheart" Trademark. Length: 24 Inches. *The No. 76 arch joint rule features Stanley's top of the line "arch joint" and the extra quality "broad" width. This well preserved example is ready to fill out a serious collection of Stanley rules. Nicely marked with the ca. 1920's "Sweetheart" trademark.* (FINE) **$345.00**

M4-21. Stanley Rule & Level No. 52: Two-Foot, Two-Fold Folding Rule. Arch Joint, Half Bound. Uncommon Type. Length: 24 Inches. *According to Phil Stanley's classic "Boxwood and Ivory: Stanley Traditional Rules, 1855-1975", these were offered from 1859 to 1917 only. This one is in excellent condition, having been lightly cleaned. An uncommon Stanley rule.* (FINE) **$165.00**

M4-22. Stanley Rule & Level No. 78 1/2: Two Foot, Four Fold Folding Rule. Early Trademark. Rare and Extra Clean. Length: 24 Inches. *Here's a very well preserved example of Stanley's top of the line boxwood rule. A nice example.* (GOOD+) **$195.00**

M4-23. C-S Co., The , Pine Meadow Conn. No. 62: Two-Foot, Four-Fold Folding Rule. Square Joint, Full Bound. Architects Scales. Length: 24 Inches. *The Chapin-Stephens equivalent to Stanley's popular No. 62 was similarly numerically designated by their principal competitor. A good, clean example.* (GOOD) **$35.00**

M4-24. Stanley Rule & Level No. 68: Two-Foot, Four Fold Folding Rule. Round Joint, Unbound. Extra Crisp and Clean. Length: 24 Inches. *One of Stanley's most common rules in uncommonly well preserved condition.* (FINE) **$35.00**

M4-25. Chapin, H., U.S. Standard No. 26: Two-Foot, Four-Fold Folding Rule. Square Joint, Full Bound. Boxwood, Metric and English Scales. Length: 24 Inches. *The quality level of the rules produced by Hermon Chapin's Union Factory, in Pine Meadow, Connecticut is immediately apparent at a glance. A number of factors, including the growth of the Stanley Rule & Level Works (who improved upon the manufacturing techniques begun by Chapin), placed the hand made rules of Chapin at a competitive disadvantage. Here's an early example of the very best work of the Chapin enterprise. Clean, crisp and perfect except for a small stain on the reverse side.* (GOOD+) **$85.00**

M4-26. Stanley Rule & Level No. 68: Two-Foot, Four Fold Folding Rule. Round Joint, Unbound. Extra Crisp and Clean. Length: 24 Inches. *This example of Stanley's basic two-foot, four-fold rule has the block lettering that is characteristic of turn-of-the-century output. Perfect.* (FINE) **$35.00**

M4-27. Lufkin Rule Co., The, Saginaw, Mich No. 781: Two-Foot, Four Fold Folding Rule. Square Joint, Full Bound Equivalent Stanley 62. Length: 24 Inches. *This Lufkin two foot, four fold rule was the equivalent to Stanley's No. 62, a fact that the folks at the Lufkin factory noted on the outside of the rule. A very nice example.* (GOOD+) **$35.00**

M4-28. Stanley Rule & Level No. 83 C: Two Foot, Four Fold Folding Rule. With Caliper. "Sweetheart" Trademark. Length: 24 Inches. *The No. 83 C was Stanley's only four-fold caliper rule. This one is clean, sound and without damage. A good one.* (GOOD) **$115.00**

M4-29. Stanley Rule & Level (Unmarked) No. 29: Two-Foot, Two-Fold Folding Rule. Round Joint, Unbound. Excellent Condition. Length: 24 Inches. *These scarce rules were discontinued from the Stanley product line in 1919. Unmarked, but unquestionably Stanley. The pin has slightly pushed though at the joint, but the rule is otherwise excellent. A rare Stanley rule.* (GOOD+) **$185.00**

M4-30. Stephens & Co., Riverton, Conn. No. 60: Two-Foot, Four-Fold Folding Rule. Arch Joint, Full Bound. Architects, Metric and English Scales. Length: 24 Inches. *The presence of the classic arch joint on this broad, full bound rule indicate that it was of the very highest quality. A nice example.* (GOOD) **$55.00**

M4-31. Unmarked No. 18: Two-Foot, Two-Fold Folding Rule. Square Joint, Unbound. Length: 24 Inches. *This very basic two foot, two fold rule was a favorite for household use and in manual training schools. Here's a clean, sound example.* (GOOD) **$25.00**

M4-32. Stanley Rule & Level No. 36 1/2: One Foot, Two Fold Folding Rule. Ca. 1900. Near New Condition. Length: 12 Inches. *This one foot Stanley caliper rule dates from the first quarter of this century, but is in nearly new condition. Choice.* (FINE) **$85.00**

M4-33. Stanley Rule & Level No. 75: Two Foot, Four Fold Folding Rule. Arch Joint, Unbound. "Sweetheart" Trademark. Length: 24 Inches. *Production of Stanley's arch-joint No. 75 rule was discontinued in 1933 and examples are not often found. This one is in top collector quality condition. Extra nice.* (FINE) **$325.00**

M4-34. Stanley Rule & Level No. 66 3/4: Three-Foot, Four-Fold Folding Rule. "Sweetheart" Trademark. Uncommon Type. Length: 36 Inches. *Here's a clean and sound example of Stanley's full bound three foot rule. A bargain.* (GOOD) **$35.00**

M4-35. Stanley Rule & Level No. 18: Two Foot, Two Fold Folding Rule. Square Joint, Unbound. Near New Condition. Length: 24 Inches. *This No. 18 rule was widely marketed to "manual training" schools where young would-be woodworkers could conspire to destroy them without the knowledge of the instructor. This one seems to have been guarded by a particularly zealous pedagogue. Absolutely mint.* (FINE) **$245.00**

M4-36. Stanley Rule & Level No. 79: Folding Board Measure Folding Rule. Early Stanley Mark. Early and Uncommon. Length: 24 Inches. *Stanley offered a range of folding board measure rules, of which this the unbound, square-joint version was the least expensive. As is often the case with specialized rules, which by their nature demanded a premium price, most buyers opted for the fancier, full-bound versions. These are not common. A very nice example.* (GOOD+) **$265.00**

M4-37. Upson Nut Co., Unionville, Conn. No. 72 1/4: Two-Foot, Four-Fold Folding Rule. Square Joint, Half Bound. Drafting Scales. Length: 24 Inches. *The Upson Nut Company offered a full line of folding rules. This is the first example of this number that we have encountered. It has some staining and the binding is a bit loose, but it will do until a better one comes along. Rare.* (FAIR) **$55.00**

M4-38. Steward, 406 Strand (London): Two Foot, Four Fold Folding Rule. London and Metric. Near New Condition. Length: 24 Inches. *Here's a classic English rule that is graduated in both English and metric scales. A very well preserved rule from an obscure London maker.* (FINE) **$85.00**

M4-39. Stanley Rule & Level No. 62: Two-Foot, Four-Fold Folding Rule. Square Joint, Full Bound. Brand New Condition. Length: 24 Inches. *The No. 62 was one of Stanley's best selling rules. This example is nearly 100 years old and looking nearly new. Nice.* (FINE) **$65.00**

M4-40. Stanley Rule & Level No. 27: Two-Foot, Two-Fold Folding Rule. Square Joint, Unbound. Edge Graduations. Length: 24 Inches. *Stanley's No. 27 two-foot carpenter's rule features a Gunter slide for performing mathematical calculations. This example is clean and crisp, noting a slight stain on one outside edge.* (FINE) **$345.00**

M4-41. Lufkin Rule Co., The No. 026: Six Inch Caliper Folding Rule. Unique Configuration. 1 3/8" Wide. Length: 6 Inches. *When Lufkin jumped feet first into the rule making business rather late in the game, they generally copied the Stanley product line. This six inch caliper rule is an example of a rule that was offered by Lufkin and no other maker. Nearly new.* (FINE) **$95.00**

M4-42. Stanley Rule & Level No. 5: Two-Foot, Two-Fold Folding Rule. Architects. Scales. Superb Condition. Length: 24 Inches. *A superb example of a hard to find Stanley rule. Crisp and clean.* (GOOD+) **$265.00**

M4-43. C-S Co., The , Pine Meadow Conn. No. 7: Two-Foot, Four-Fold Folding Rule. Square Joint, Unbound. "Nearsite", Red Numbers. Length: 24 Inches. *The Chapin Stevens equivalent to Stanley's "Blind Man's" rules, the "Nearsite" featured bold red letters. A most uncommon C.S. rule.* (GOOD+) **$115.00**

M4-44. Stanley Rule & Level No. 66 1/2: Three Foot, Four Fold Folding Rule. Arch Joint, Unbound. Near New Condition. Length: 36 Inches. *Stanley basic three-foot rule in uncommonly nice condition. This one dates from the latter days of Stanley production. A very well preserved example.* (FINE) **$45.00**

M4-45. Stanley Rule & Level No. 4: Two Foot, Four Fold Folding Rule. Extra-Thin. Extremely Rare. Length: 24 Inches. *Owing to it's "extra-thin" feature, the No. 4 has the joint plates mounted on the outside of the rule body. Why someone would want a rule that was as susceptible to breakage as these remains a mystery. One of the toughest Stanley rules to find. This example is in top collector quality condition. A very rare Stanley rule.* (FINE) **$465.00**

Group N4

N4-1. Aux Mines De Suede, Paris: 4" Blade Fruitwood Spoke Shave. "Anchor" Trademark. Unused Condition. Length: 12 3/4 Inches. *This French spokeshave is part of an unused set that was recovered from a ca. 1920's house in Upstate New York together with many hundreds more mint condition tools from that era. Absolutely brand new.* (GOOD+) **$125.00**

N4-2. Cahill Forge & Foundry Corp.: Set of 12 Caulking Irons. Unused Condition. Original Packing. Length: 6 Inches. *These shipwright's caulking irons are in absolutely unused condition in their original wooden box. Perfect.* (FINE) **$345.00**

N4-3. Unmarked: Ship Caulking Mallet. With 8 Original Irons. Excellent Condition. Length: 16 Inches. *This well preserved caulking mallet comes complete with a set of 8 irons.* (GOOD+) **$285.00**

N4-4. Sharp, John: Hand Made Bread Rasp. Ca. 1800. Scarce and Excellent. Length: 7 Inches. *Boldly struck with the early imprint of one "John Sharp", this classic bread rasp would have been hand cut using a hammer and chisel.* (GOOD+) **$165.00**

N4-5. Gardner & Brazer, Boston, Mass.: Ship Rabbet Molding Plane. Ca. 1825 Only. Rare and Excellent. Length: 11 Inches. *Listed as having worked in 1825 only, this obscure partnership preceded the prominent association of Gardner & Murdock. This is the only example of this obscure imprint we have ever offered for sale.* (GOOD+) **$285.00**

N4-6. Unmarked: Fruitwood Compass Spoke Shave. Slight Convex Sole. Unused Condition. Length: 10 1/2 Inches. *This brand new convex sole shave came from a major lot of ca. 1920's tools unearthed several years ago. Magnificent.* (GOOD+) **$115.00**

N4-7. Keuffel & Esser Co., New York, N.Y.: Early Artificial Horizon. Lacquered Brass. Original Mahogany Case. Length: 8 1/2 Inches. *This most interesting artificial horizon is pictured in Keuffel & Esser's 1921 catalog together with the notation that these are "..made by us for the United States Navy". All original parts remain as do nearly all original finishes. The leather strap on the mahogany case is a replacement but the box itself retains its original hardware and lacquer finish. We have it on good authority that these were used by early aviators to maintain their relationship to earth even when there was no land or sea visible.* (FINE) **$445.00**

N4-8. Healthways, Los Angeles, Calif.: "Skin Diver" Knife. Solingen Steel. Original Cork Scabbard. Length: 12 Inches. *No idea how old this is, but it sure would be handy to have on the arm of your chair while watching reruns of the Lloyd Bridges classic "Sea Hunt". Somebody probably bought this one about the time the show was airing live.* (FINE) **$55.00**

N4-9. Unmarked No. 42: Ship Bevel Folding Rule. Double Brass Blade. Boxwood. Length: 12 Inches. *These special purpose tools were used by shipwrights who often worked out of plumb in several directions at once. Here's a clean, sound example.* (GOOD) **$35.00**

N4-10. Unmarked: Cooper's Bung Mallet. Flexible Handle. Uncommon Type. Length: 23 Inches. *The keyed handle of this cooper's bung mallet slides out to facilitate its replacement. This one is still in excellent condition and warranted for use by Martin J. Donnelly Antique Tools.* (GOOD) **$75.00**

N4-11. Aux Mines De Suede, Paris: 2 3/4" Blade Fruitwood Spoke Shave. "Anchor" Trademark. Unused Condition. Length: 12 1/2 Inches. *Yet another of a group of tools found in a Mohawk Valley house that had been undisturbed since the 1920's. Brand new, but old.* (FINE) **$115.00**

N4-12. Lufkin Rule Co., The, Saginaw, Mich. No. 42: Shipwrights Bevel. Dual Brass Blade. Unused Condition. Length: 12 Inches. *As wooden shipbuilding became a very minor industry, the need for bevels of this sort became nearly nonexistent. This one apparently never made it beyond the hardware store.* (FINE) **$95.00**

N4-13. Unmarked: Shipwright's Caulk Mallet. Very Little Used. With 6 Original Chisels. Length: 15 1/2 Inches. *A set of six chisels is included with this crispy clean caulking mallet. Ready to use, if you choose.* (FINE) **$245.00**

N4-14. Unmarked: Massive Lignum Mallet. With Retaining Rings. Early and Excellent. Length: 15 1/2 Inches. *A pair of retaining rings were fitted on this early lignum vitae mallet were intended to keep it from splitting. They would have worked better if the tool had ever been used.* (FINE) **$85.00**

N4-15. Lufkin Rule Co., The, Saginaw, Mich. No. 42: Shipwrights Bevel. Dual Brass Blade. Unused Condition. Length: 12 Inches. *These double-blade bevels were intended for use by shipwrights and others who would work with timbers that were fitted out of plumb. This one is in excellent collector quality condition.* (FINE) **$115.00**

N4-16. Bradford, J., Portland, Maine.: Ship Rabbet Molding Plane. With Double Cutter. Carved Escapement. Length: 9 1/2 Inches. *The escapement of this rabbetting plane has a most appealing shape. The double cutting iron indicates that this was intended for use on the long timbers found in the shipyards.* (GOOD+) **$85.00**

N4-17. Edwards & Walker Co., Portland, Maine: Ebony Handle. Sailor's Knife. With Original Sheath. Elaborate Carved Handle. Length: 9 Inches. *This turn of the century sailors knife features a handle of carved ebony and a bold early mark on the blade. The original sheath has kept it in excellent condition.* (GOOD+) **$225.00**

N4-18. Cumings, A., Boston, Mass.: Shipwright's Quarter Round Molding Plane. Ca. 1840's-1850's. 1 1/4" Full Boxed. Length: 9 1/2 Inches. *This wide quarter round molder is of the short, wide type preferred by shipwrights. The presence of full boxing is a sign that this was made to be of the highest quality. A very nice example.* (GOOD+) **$85.00**

N4-19. Unmarked: Ship Caulking Mallet. Rare Small Size. Mesquite Head. Length: 12 1/2 Inches. *This diminutive caulking mallet features a mesquite head and a series of brass rings. Mallets of this size are scarce indeed.* (GOOD+) **$115.00**

N4-20. Unmarked: Classic Caulking Mallet. Solid Oak Head. Excellent Condition. Length: 15 1/2 Inches. *No apologies whatsoever for the well preserved caulking mallet. Crisp clean and ready to use or display.* (GOOD+) **$85.00**

N4-21. Unmarked: Shipwrights Caulk Mallet. Mesquite Head. Excellent Condition. Length: 15 Inches. *A head of dark Mesquite is an indication that this caulking mallet was made to be better than most. A nice example.* (GOOD+) **$85.00**

N4-22. Unmarked: Classic "Travisher" Spoke Shave. Fruitwood Body. Unused Condition. Length: 12 Inches. *Found together with a number of other spokeshaves offered in this volume in a Mohawk Valley, New York home that had been undisturbed since the 1920's, this magnificent deep travisher is in absolutely perfect condition. Highly recommended.* (FINE) **$485.00**

N4-23. Horton, New York, N.Y.: Early Masting Axe. Uncommon Maker. Excellent Condition. Length: 28 Inches. *The handle needs a bit of tightening, but this early masting axe is otherwise in excellent condition. A William Horton produced edge tools in New York City between 1837 and 1853. Clean and clearly marked.* (GOOD+) **$85.00**

N4-24. Unmarked: Shipwrights Caulk Mallet. Mesquite Head. With 8 Assorted Irons. Length: 16 Inches. *This mesquite head cooper's mallet comes complete with a set of 8 caulking mallets. A great set.* (FINE) **$325.00**

N4-25. Watts, L.H., New York: Classic Shipwrights Slick. 2 1/2" Size. Early and Near New. Length: 22 1/2 Inches. *This early slick has a slight sweep to its cut, a pattern that was common for shipwrights. Boldly struck with the Watts name, this tool is in excellent condition. Highly recommended.* (FINE) **$225.00**

N4-26. Unmarked: Massive Wagon Builde Brace. Turned Beech Head. Most Unusual. Length: 27 Inches. *At 27 inches in length, this massive brace is sure to stand out in any collection. Most unusual.* (GOOD) **$225.00**

N4-27. Unmarked: Ship Caulking Mallet. Oak Head. Apparently Unused. Length: 15 1/2 Inches. *This classic caulking mallet appears never to have been used. Nice.* (FINE) **$85.00**

N4-28. Unmarked: Ship Caulking Mallet. Oak Head. Apparently Unused. Length: 15 1/2 Inches. *You could be the first to use this well preserved ship caulking mallet. Extra nice.* (FINE) **$85.00**

N4-29. Marples & Sons, Wm., Hibernia Works.: Rosewood Shipwrights Bevel. Dual Brass Blades. Early And Excellent. Length: 11 1/2 Inches. *Most original factory blued finish remains on this rosewood shipwright's bevel from prominent Sheffield maker William Marples. Extra nice.* (FINE) **$145.00**

N4-30. Unmarked: Miniature Marine Ivory Mallet. Turned Boxwood Handle. From Cape Cod. Length: 6 Inches. *Most likely formed from a whale's tooth, this diminutive mallet was found this past summer on Cape Cod. A nicely turned boxwood handle adds to the overall appeal of this well made tool.* (GOOD+) **$265.00**

N4-31. Bradford, J., Portland, Maine: Cooper's Sun Plane. With Circular Fence. Uncommon Type. Length: 16 Inches. *This specialized cooper's sun plane features a roller to facilitate the cut. It is missing the cutting iron, which may account for the excellent condition in which it remains. A rare cooper's plane from an important Maine maker.* (GOOD+) **$145.00**

N4-32. Unmarked: Set of 9 Caulking Irons. Same Owner Imprint. Excellent Condition. Length: 8 Inches. *Here's a great working set of caulking irons, each of which is imprinted with the name of the original owner. Ready to use or display.* (GOOD+) **$165.00**

N4-33. General Electric Corp., Schenectady: Naval Wavemeter. With Calibration Scale. Unknown Function. Length: 8 1/2 Inches. *Given its association with the General Electric Company, one would surmise that this specialty "Naval Wavemeter", was intended for the measurement of waves of the type associated more with electricity than with the ocean. Whatever its purpose, it is likely that this tool was acquired by the taxpayers for the military at a figure of several thousands of dollars. Close out.* (FINE) **$55.00**

N4-34. Stinson: Laminated Ship Adze. Original Handle. Early and Excellent. Length: 30 Inches. *This high quality shipwright's adze is imprinted with the name of edge tool maker John F. Stinson, who worked in Bath, Maine from 1869 to 1871. A classic.* (GOOD+) **$225.00**

N4-35. Unmarked: Combination Parralel Rule Protractor. For Nautical Use. Superb Patina. Length: 11 1/4 Inches. *This most unusual nautical tool combines a protractor and parallel rule into the same device. No maker marks are present, but this tool is very well made.* (GOOD+) **$375.00**

N4-36. Unmarked: 2 1/4" Blade Spoke Shave. Fruitwood Body. Unused Condition. Length: 10 1/2 Inches. *Part of a grouping of early 20th Century tools that were found intact in Upstate New York several years ago, this fruitwood spokeshave is in absolutely immaculate condition. An opportunity.* (FINE) **$115.00**

N4-37. Lufkin Rule Co., The, Saginaw, Mich. No. 42: Shipwrights Bevel. Dual Brass Blade. Unused Condition. Length: 12 Inches. *If you are planning on building a new ship, why not use a brand new bevel for the event? This Lufkin No. 42 is in brand new condition.* (FINE) **$95.00**

N4-38. Varvill & Sons, York (England): Adjustable Rounding Plane. Full Brass Facing. Superb Condition. Length: 10 Inches. *The opening of this classic rounding plane from a prominent English maker if fully faced with brass. An exceptionally high quality tool.* (FINE) **$345.00**

N4-39. Sheffield, J.M., Stanford, Conn.: Classic Shipwright's Slick. Rare Connecticut Imprint. Excellent Condition. Length: 13 1/4 Inches. *The Directory of American Toolmakers shows J.M. Sheffield as working from 1849 to 1859 only. A well preserved slick from an uncommon maker.* (GOOD+) **$75.00**

N4-40. Unmarked: Shipwrights Caulk Mallet. Mesquite Head. With 8 Assorted Irons. Length: 16 Inches. *Here's another well preserved caulking mallet with a full set of irons. Extra nice.* (GOOD+) **$245.00**

N4-41. Multiform Molding Plane Co.: Massive Ship Rabbet Plane. Marked "16". Most Unusual Type. Length: 19 Inches. *This company is well-known for their planes, produced under an 1850 patent that featured an interchangeable handle. Other planes bearing their imprint are extremely scarce. This is the first example of which we are aware of a double-iron ship rabbet plane bearing their mark. This is the "B" imprint from the Pollak book. A rare plane in superb condition.* (FINE) **$695.00**

N4-42. Cahill Forge & Foundry Corp.: Set of 12 Caulking Irons. Unused Condition. Original Packing. Length: 6 Inches. *These shipwright's caulking irons are in absolutely unused condition in their original wooden box. Perfect.* (FINE) **$345.00**

N4-43. Unmarked: Rosewood Sailor's Fid. For Rope Work. Near New Condition. Length: 10 Inches. *These specialized tools were use for working with large knots. This apparently unused example is formed from Brazilian Rosewood.* (FINE) **$35.00**

N4-44. Unmarked: Classic Joiner's Mallet. Lignum Vitae Head. Ready to Use. Length: 12 1/2 Inches. *A heavy lignum vitae head makes this classic joiner's mallet a very useful tool that just happens to be aesthetically pleasing. Ready to use.* (GOOD+) **$65.00**

N4-45. Unmarked: 2 1/4" Blade Spoke Shave. Fruitwood Body. Unused Condition. Length: 10 1/2 Inches. *Yet another shave from the "miracle lot" of tools found several years ago, this fruitwood spokeshave is in brand new condition.* (FINE) **$115.00**

N4-46. Higgins & Libby, Portland, Maine.: Shipwright's Gouge. Hand Forged. Uncommon Maker. Length: 24 Inches. *This massive shipwright's gouge has been boldly struck with the imprint of Portland, Maine edge tool makers Higgins & Libby who made edge tools there in the 1850's. A classic.* (GOOD+) **$145.00**

Group O4

O4-1. Cumings, A., Boston, Mass.: Quirk Ovolo with Bevel Molding Plane. Double Boxed. Early and Excellent. Length: 9 1/2 Inches. *Wider than normal boxing adds extra appeal to this steep complex molder from Boston. Extra crisp and clean.* (FINE) **$225.00**

O4-2. Pond, W.H., New Haven, Conn.: Handled Coach Molding Plane. Slight Round Shape. Rare and Excellent. Length: 10 Inches. *A unique double-iron handled coachmaker's rounding plane that has very clearly never been modified in any way. Clearly marked on the toe with the Pond imprint, this well-preserved special-purpose plane will nicely complement a collection of coachmaking tools or special-purpose planes. Top shelf.* (FINE) **$325.00**

O4-3. Barton & Co., D.R., Rochester, N.Y.: Carriagemaker's Rabbit Plane. With "1832" Trademark. Rare and Excellent. Length: 6 Inches. *D.R. Barton & Company, of Rochester, New York, specialized in tools for coopers and carriagemakers but this is the first carriage maker's "T" rabbet that we have ever offered. A rare plane from a prominent maker.* (FINE) **$265.00**

O4-4. Hills, S. & H., Springfield, Mass.: Gothic Bead Molding Plane. Double Boxing. Rare and Excellent. Length: 9 1/2 Inches. *One of the most graphic of all molding profiles, the gothic bead is characterized by an acute arched form that was popular in the 1830's. This boldly double-boxed example has been boldly struck with the desirable and graphic "D" imprint of Springfield, Massachusetts makers S. & H. Hills. Extra nice.* (GOOD+) **$355.00**

O4-5. Eastburn R., (N. Brunswick, N.J.): Handled Panel Rasing Plane. With Brass Side Plate. AWP III: 2 Stars (C). Length: 9 1/2 Inches. *Someone has replaced the side fence on this plane, and inserted a brass plate between the fence and the plane while doing so, but this boldly imprinted early New Jersey plane is otherwise in excellent condition. A most unusual configuration for this important maker.* (GOOD) **$195.00**

O4-6. Mc Master, T. J., Auburn, N. Y.: Wedge Arm Beech Molding Plane. Bold Eagle Mark. Early and Excellent. Length: 8 Inches. *The massive Federal eagle imprint of Truman J. McMaster is among the most elaborate of any ever imprinted on a wooden plane. This ca. 1830 brass-tipped, wedge-arm plow has been boldly struck with the easily recognizable mark. An nice plow plane with a great maker imprint.* (GOOD+) **$275.00**

O4-7. Copeland, D.: Steep Quirk, Ovolo & Square Molding Plane. Extra Crisp and Clean. Ready to Use. Length: 9 1/2 Inches. *At least three separate owner's stamps on the toe of this crispy plane attest to the fact that is was a handy molding plane. Crisp, clean and ready to use.* (GOOD+) **$175.00**

O4-8. Bridge, Washington, D.C.: 7/8" Adjustable Dado Molding Plane. Rare D.C. Maker. AWP III: 4 Stars. Length: 9 1/2 Inches. *The least common of the handful of planemakers who imprinted their planes with the District of Columbia designation, Joseph P. Bridge practiced his trade in the Capitol city from 1855 to 1864 only. His planes rate 3 stars for rarity. This is the first example we have ever offered.* (FINE) **$395.00**

O4-9. Schaefer & Cobb, Cincinnati, Ohio: Adjustable Dado Molding Plane. With Applied Handle. AWP III: 1 Star (A1). Length: 9 1/2 Inches. *The obscure partnership of Schaefer and Cobb produced planes and sold hardware in the 1850's boom town of Cincinnati, Ohio. This adjustable dado has an added contoured handle at the rear. A uncommon plane from a rare Mid-West maker.* (GOOD) **$35.00**

O4-10. Rowell, S., Troy, N.Y.: Full Boxed Bead Molding Plane. Rare 3/16" Size. Extra Crisp and Clean. Length: 9 1/2 Inches. *There is something about fully boxed bead planes that says that they were made to be something special. This uncommon 3/16" size example is in nearly new condition and ready to provide several more lifetimes of service. Something special.* (FINE) **$75.00**

O4-11. Copeland, M., Warranted: 2/8" Adjustable Dado Molding Plane. Replaced Nicker Wedge. Ready to Use Condition Length: 9 1/2 Inches. *A fitted piece of wooden stock has been used to replace the nicker wedge on this otherwise perfectly preserved 1/8" dado plane. A nice working tool and a bargain.* (GOOD+) **$45.00**

O4-12. Sargent & Co. (Sandusky) No. 57: Rare Sash Cope Molding Plane. Marked 1/2. Near New Condition. Length: 9 1/2 Inches. *This perfectly preserved sash coping plane is the first such tool bearing the Sargent imprint that we have ever offered. Its low ordinal number in the Sargent numerical listing indicates that it was very likely included in the line of the Sandusky Tool Company, who made it for them, from the very beginning of their production. During the last thirty or forty years of Sandusky's operation, very little window sash was being made by hand, hence such planes would have not been in high demand. A nice example of a most uncommon Sandusky plane produced for Sargent & Company.* (FINE) **$195.00**

O4-13. Fenn & Co., Joel, Wallingford, Conn.: 7/8" Astragal Molding Plane. Thos. Meavity & Co. St. John, N.B. Length: 9 1/2 Inches. *This most unusual astragal molder is imprinted with the name of an uncommon Connecticut maker as well as the imprint of a New Brunswick hardware dealer. Decidedly different.* (GOOD+) **$95.00**

O4-14. Fish, A., Lowell, Mass.: Matched Sash and Cope Molding Planes. Nicely Boxed. Rare and Extra Nice. Length: 9 1/2 Inches. *The fence on this most unusual grooving/molding plane is proper and original. No idea for what purpose it may have been used. Clearly marked with the imprint of a less common New England maker. Different.* (GOOD+) **$485.00**

O4-15. Fox & Son, L., Amherst, Mass.: Double Tounge and Groove Molding Plane. Ca. 1830'3. Absolutely Unused. Length: 8 Inches. *This immaculate double "coming and going" tongue and groove plane bears the imprint of Luther Fox & Son, who produced planes in Amherst, Massachusetts in the 1830's. Absolutely mint and highly recommended.* (FINE) **$165.00**

O4-16. Barton & Co., D.R., Rochester, N.Y: Pair of Table Joint Molding Planes. Marked "4/8". Extra Crisp and Clean. Length: 9 1/2 Inches. *These classic unfenced table joint planes bear the incuse imprint of Rochester, New York planemaker D.R. Barton. Crisp, clean and ready to use.* (GOOD+) **$285.00**

O4-17. Gardner & Murdock, Boston, Mass.: Coachmaker's Rabbet Molding Plane. 7 1/2" Length. Rare and Excellent. Length: 7 1/2 Inches. *Only a very few of these snipe-sided rabbet planes have been found. All known examples are from Boston makers. This one has a bold Gardner & Murdock stamp. A nice mark on a very rare type.* (GOOD+) **$395.00**

O4-18. Gardner, L., Green Street, Boston: Steep Ogee Molding Plane. Marked "Inch 1/4". Extra Crisp and Clean. Length: 9 1/2 Inches. *This steep and wide ogee molder was produced during the heyday of Boston planemaking between 1830 and 1850. A great working tool in top collector quality condition.* (FINE) **$245.00**

O4-19. Farr, J.W., N. York, N.Y.: Quirk, Ovolo and Bevel Molding Plane. Marked "1/2". AWP III: 3 Stars (E). Length: 9 1/2 Inches. *This classic profile of the 1840's is crisp, clean and ready to use. J.W. Farr produced planes in New York City from 1832 to 1852. The imprint on this plane has been designated as the "E" mark in AWP.* (GOOD+) **$110.00**

O4-20. Sandusky Tool Co. (?): Factory Second (?) Molding Planes. Distinctive Wedges. Knotty Beech. Length: 9 1/2 Inches. *The maker marks on these tongue and groove molding planes have been over struck by a "crosshatch" type of mark, which may indicate that they were intended for sale as factory seconds. The distinctive wedge profile leaves no doubt that they were produced by the Sandusky Tool Company. One of the wedges appears to be a replacement, but these planes are otherwise in excellent condition.* (GOOD+) **$85.00**

O4-21. Unmarked: Early Crown Molding Plane. Birch and Fruitwood. Early Pegged Tote. Length: 14 Inches. *This massive crown molder has a classic early look, including an offset tote and a body of native yellow birch. The cutting iron is a likely replacement, but this tool has an overall look that is most appealing. A good one.* (GOOD) **$595.00**

O4-22. Slayton, R.: Yellow Birch Jointer Plane. Rounded Wedge. Decorative Handle. Length: 23 Inches. *There is no documentation of an Eighteenth Century planemaker who use the imprint "J. Slayton", however, this plane has the distinctive look of a professionally made tool. A classic.* (GOOD+) **$145.00**

O4-23. Fish, A., Lowell, Mass.: Classic Sash Cope Molding Plane. With Perpendicular Fence. Extra Crisp and Clean. Length: 9 1/2 Inches. *Sash coping planes were such as this were intended to be used in conjunction with a sash molder for working window sash. This perfectly preserved example is boldly struck at the junction of the two sections. A rare plane in excellent condition.* (FINE) **$125.00**

O4-24. Belcher Bros., Providence, R.I.: Massive Quater Round Molding Plane. Extra Crisp and Clean. AWP III: 2 Stars (A). Length: 9 1/2 Inches. *A well preserved quarter round molder from an obscure Rhode Island hardware dealership that operated from 1857 to 1884. Condition is near new.* (FINE) **$115.00**

O4-25. Hills, H., Springfield, Mass.: Quirk, Ogee, Bevel and Cove Molding Plane. Marked "1 6/8". Extra Wide Cut. Length: 9 1/2 Inches. *A most unusual covetto profile adds interest to this oversize molder from a prominent and early Springfield, Massachusetts planemaker.* (GOOD+) **$285.00**

O4-26. Chapin, H., Union Factory: Rare 3/16" Dado Molding Plane. Tombstone Depth Stop. Extra Crisp and Clean. Length: 9 1/2 Inches. *This crispy clean dado plane bears the imprint of H. Chapin's pioneering Union Factory. Dado planes in this uncommon small size have become increasingly difficult to find. A nice example.* (FINE) **$95.00**

O4-27. Burrowes, E.T. Co., Portland, Maine: Special Screen Fit Plane. With Advertising. Superb Condition. Length: 8 Inches. *The Burrowes Company of Portland Maine supplied these tools with their special patented screens, many of which are still in use on the "camps" that surround the million or so lakes in the state. This great example of the Burrowes screen plane is in collector quality condition.* (FINE) **$65.00**

O4-28. Bensen & Crannell, Albany: Double Door Molding Plane. Adjustable Width. Brass Diamond Plates. Length: 9 1/2 Inches. *This classic door plane is adjustable by means of screws held captive in brass, diamond-shaped plates set in the side of the tool. An excellent example of a rare woodworking tool.* (FINE) **$295.00**

O4-29. Miller, A., New York: 1/2" Groove Molding Plane. Charles Ashley, Ogdens. Rare Double Imprint. Length: 9 1/2 Inches. *This grooving plane is an example of the "double struck" type that provides insight to collectors. Not only is it imprinted with the mark of the obscure "A. Miller", whom Pollak speculates may have worked in upstate New York, but it is also marked with the stamp of Charles Ashley of Ogdensburg(h), New York. A nice example.* (GOOD+) **$65.00**

O4-30. Taylor, J.C., Cincinnati, Ohio: Boxwood Smooth Plane. Ca. 1842-1869. AWP III: 2 Stars (A). Length: 8 Inches. *This extremely well preserved solid boxwood smoothing plane is boldly stamped with the imprint of Cincinnati maker J.C. Taylor. A most unusual Ohio made tool.* (FINE) **$395.00**

O4-31. Ohio Tool Co., Columbus, Ohio No. 68: Large Bilection Molding Plane. With "Plane" Trademark. Extra Crisp. Length: 9 1/2 Inches. *This massive bilection molder is imprinted with the Ohio Tool Company's pictographic "plane" logo. A nice wide molder in collector quality condition.* (GOOD+) **$175.00**

O4-32. Baldwin, A. & E., New York: Boxed Bead Molding Plane. Marked "3/8". Near New Condition. Length: 9 1/2 Inches. *This boxed bead from a prominent pair of New York City planemakers (ca. 1830-1841) has been very little used. A great working plane with a classic heritage.* (FINE) **$55.00**

O4-33. Harris & Shepherd, L. Falls, N.Y. No. 155: 3/4" Quarter Round Molding Plane. Ca. 1868-1869. AWP III: 3 Stars. Length: 9 1/2 Inches. *Rated at 3 Stars for rarity in AWP, this perfectly preserved quarter round molder dates from the years 1868-1869, when Isaac Harris and Alexander Shepherd operated a hardware dealership in Little Falls, New York. Rare.* (FINE) **$115.00**

O4-34. Moss, Wm., Birmingham, England: Cove and Astragal Molding Plane. Ca. 1775-1797. Near New Condition. Length: 9 1/2 Inches. *This classic Eighteenth Century molder and stands ready to be used once again for the purpose for which it was intended. An excellent early molder in top condition.* (FINE) **$215.00**

O4-35. Parkes, W.: Double Iron Nosing Molding Plane. With Adjustable Depth Stop. Marked "3/4". Length: 9 1/2 Inches. *This adjustable dado plane in the desirable 3/4" size is ready to go to work. W. Parkes was a prominent planemaker in Birmingham, England for many years in the 19th Century.* (GOOD+) **$65.00**

O4-36. Harris & Shepherd, L. Falls, N.Y. No. 129: 3/4" Flat Ogee Molding Plane. Ca. 1868-1869. AWP III: 3 Stars. Length: 9 1/2 Inches. *Rated at 3 Stars for rarity in American Wooden Planes, this classic ogee molder dates from the years 1868-1869, when Isaac Harris and Alexander Shepherd operated a hardware dealership in Little Falls, New York. Rare.* (GOOD+) **$125.00**

O4-37. Assorted Makers: Set of 3 Boxed Bead Molding Planes. From Same Chest. Usable Condition. Length: 9 1/2 Inches. *Here's an opportunity lot of 3 molding planes by Mathieson, Sandusky and the English maker Holbrook, all from the same carpenter's chest. A bargain.* (GOOD+) **$35.00**

O4-38. White, L. & I.J., Buffalo, N.Y.: Massive Ogee Molding Plane. Uncommon Maker. Superb Condition. Length: 14 Inches. *Handled molding planes have become extremely difficult to find. Those that appear in the market are generally broken, reworked or have been subjected to such abuse as to be unfit for a serious collection. This extra wide handle ogee from a prominent Buffalo, New York maker has none of those problems, nor any other problems. Extra nice.* (FINE) **$445.00**

O4-39. Dunham & Mc Master\auburn, N.Y.: Fixed Sash 3/16" Dado. Ca. 1821-1825. AWP III: "A" Imprint. Length: 9 1/2 Inches. *S.C. Dunham and T.J. McMaster were the first to contract for use of convict labor to produce planes in Auburn Prison in Auburn, New York. This uncommon 3/16" dado plane bears the earliest imprint used by this pioneering partnership.* (GOOD+) **$85.00**

O4-40. Unmarked: Yellow Birch Bead Molding Plane. Distinctive Form. Early and Excellent. Length: 7 1/4 Inches. *Too often, it seems, when dealing with early molding planes, we become preoccupied with the names of the planemakers who made the tools, the variations of maker's imprints and any of a thousand "inside baseball" facts that lead us to overlook the most important thing about these early tools: They are different—very different from the tools that preceded them by just a few decades and very different from the planes that followed. The wood from which they are made, the style of the wedges, the elaborate ornamentation that was more art than functionality, all of these things are so very different that it is refreshing when a plane such as this, with no makers mark, but all the characteristics of an early plane forces us to look at the tool as a tool and not as one of six example of the work of so and so. A nice tool and unmarked, no buts.* (GOOD+) **$95.00**

O4-41. Harris & Shepherd, L. Falls, N.Y. No. 180: No. 18 Hollow Molding Plane. Ca. 1868-1869. AWP III: 3 Stars. Length: 9 1/2 Inches. *This No. 18 bears the seldom-seen imprint of Little Falls Hardware Dealers Isaac Harris and Alexander Shepherd, who operated from 1868 to 1869 only.* (GOOD+) **$55.00**

O4-42. Sawyer, J., Moravia, N.Y.: Rare Hollow Molding Plane. Rare Type. AWP III: 2 Stars (A). Length: 9 1/2 Inches. *According to the Third Edition of A Guide to American Wooden Planes, by Emil & Martyl Pollak (AWP III), one John Sawyer of Moravia, New York, was the holder of a patent for a miter plane and also produced a number of bench planes and a plow plane. This hollow may well be the first known molding plane bearing the Sawyer imprint, which is the "A" imprint shown in AWP III.* (GOOD) **$115.00**

O4-43. Cumings, A., Boston, Mass.: Double Curved Molding Plane. Round and Bevel. Rare and Near New. Length: 8 Inches. *Planes of this style were intended for the chest of the ship carpenter, where they would have been used to fit out railings and other elements of finish carpentry. This example is in nearly new condition.* (FINE) **$225.00**

O4-44. Baldwin, A. & E., New York: Square Reverse Ogee and Bevel Molding Plane. Marked 6/8". Ca. 1830-1841. Length: 9 Inches. *A pair of "square" cuts at the edges make this early 19th Century molder just a bit different. Condition is near new.* (FINE) **$225.00**

O4-45. Barton & Co., D.R., Rochester, N.Y.: 7/8" Dado Molding Plane. Wooden Depth Stop. Essentially Unused. Length: 9 1/2 Inches. *This classic dado molder has the wooden "tombstone" wedge that was characteristic of early manufacture. It has been very, very little used. Extra nice.* (FINE) **$115.00**

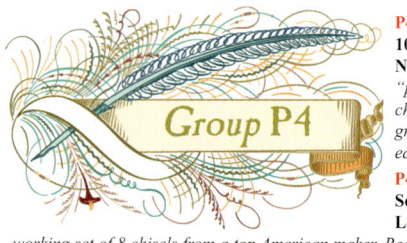

Group P4

P4-1. Stanley Rule & Level No. 740: Set Of 10 "Pocket" Chisels. Original Handles. Near New Condition. Length: 10 Inches. *These "pocket" chisels were Stanley's medium size chisel. These have been very, very little used. A great set in top condition. Highly recommended.* (FINE) **$545.00**

P4-2. Buck Bros., Millbury, Mass.: Set of 8 Socket Chisels. 1/8" to 1 1/2". Ready to Use. Length: 12 Inches. *Here's a well preserved working set of 8 chisels from a top American maker. Ready to use.* (GOOD+) **$195.00**

P4-3. Addis, S. J., London: Massive Fishtail Gouge. 1 1/2" Width. Extra Crisp and Clean. Length: 10 3/4 Inches. *This oversize gouge from the world's most respected maker of carving tools is in top condition. Extra special.* (FINE) **$95.00**

P4-4. Sorby, I. & H., (England): 1/2" Tang Mortise Chisel. Original Handle. Straight and Sharp. Length: 14 1/2 Inches. *English "tang" handle mortise chisels have become quite popular with American woodworkers. This 1/2" example is in excellent working order.* (GOOD+) **$45.00**

P4-5. Buck Brothers, Millbury, Mass.: Set of 7 Bevel Edge Chisels. Fruitwood Handles. Near New Condition. Length: 14 1/2 Inches. *These early Buck Brothers chisels retain their original turned fruitwood handles and the blades are nearly as shiny and clean as the day they were made. The two smallest sizes are so near to each other that they may be identical or one may be 1/16" wider than the 1/4". Whether this is a set of 6 or 7, it is an extremely nice working set of chisels. A set to last a lifetime.* (FINE) **$345.00**

P4-6. Mills Bros., Sheffield: Set Of 8 Paring Chisels. Boxwood Handles. Ready to Use. Length: 11 Inches. *All of the paring chisels in this set are fitted with turned boxwood handles of a distinctive pattern. A nice working set in top condition.* (FINE) **$165.00**

P4-7. Stanley Rule & Level No. 720: Set of 4 Bevel Edge Chisel. White Label Box. New Condition, Original Box. Length: 10 Inches. *The original "Christmas" box has kept these No. 720 "Red Handle" chisels in nearly new condition. A great set.* (FINE) **$155.00**

P4-8. Unmarked: 2" Laminated Framing Chisel. Extra Heavy Type. Ready to Use. Length: 18 Inches. *This clean and sound 2" framing chisel retains its original handle and is in excellent working condition. A good one.* (GOOD+) **$55.00**

P4-9. Unmarked: Heavy Socket Mortise Chisel. 1/2" Size. Ready to Use. Length: 15 1/2 Inches. *There are no visible maker marks on this exceptionally clean mortise chisel, but it is of the very first quality. Nice.* (GOOD+) **$45.00**

P4-10. Unmarked: Massive Framing Chisel. 1 1/4" Width. Near New Condition. Length: 29 Inches. *This extraordinary bevel edge framing chisel is a full 29" in length including the standard size handle. Extraordinary.* (FINE) **$185.00**

P4-11. Unmarked: "Bevel Back" Mortise Chisel. 7/16" Size. Near New Condition. Length: 15 1/2 Inches. *A number of serious woodworkers have recognized a working advantage to the "bevel back" style of mortise chisel. These tools were made by the Douglass Mfg. Company as well as the James Swan Company. This unmarked example is of the quality of the tools produced by those makers.* (GOOD+) **$55.00**

P4-12. Witherby, T.H.: Heavy Socket Framing Chisel. 1 1/4" Size. Extra Crisp and Clean. Length: 16 Inches. *The Witherby name inspires reverent awe from those who have used the tools produced by this Connecticut edge tool maker. This framing chisel is of a size not often encountered.* (FINE) **$85.00**

P4-13. Peck, Stow & Wilcox Co.: Heavy Socket Mortise Chisel. 11/16" Size. Extra Crisp and Clean. Length: 15 1/2 Inches. *This socket mortise chisel in the uncommon 11/16" size is in nearly new condition. Perfect.* (FINE) **$45.00**

P4-14. Jennings & Co., C.E., New York, N.Y. No. 70: Box for Merril & Wilder's Chisels. Original Paper Label. From New Hampshire. Length: 16 Inches. *If you have a set of Merrill & Wilder chisels, this box may be just what you need. Even if you don't, it is well worth having for the graphics alone, including the dramatic label inside the box.* (GOOD+) **$55.00**

P4-15. Marples: 1/2" Lock Mortise Chisel. Ready to Use. Near-New Condition. Length: 13 1/2 Inches. *One needs only to fashion a handle for this crisp and clean lock mortise chisel and it will be as good as new. A bargain.* (FINE) **$45.00**

P4-16. Stanley Rule & Level No. 720: 1" Bevel Edge Chisel. With Leather Cap. Rare and Excellent. Length: 13 Inches. *This No. 720 'Red Handle" chisel in the 1" size appears never to be in excellent condition.* (GOOD+) **$35.00**

P4-17. Union Hardware Co., Torrington, Conn.: Heavy Socket Framing Chisel. 1" Size. New Condition. Length: 16 Inches. *This flat-edge socket chisel has never been used. You can be the first. Exceptional quality.* (FINE) **$75.00**

P4-18. Marples: 1/2" Lock Mortise Chisel. Boxwood Handle. Near New Condition. Length: 15 1/2 Inches. *The presence of a boxwood handles was an indication of a chisel of better quality. This example is in top condition. Choice.* (FINE) **$95.00**

P4-19. Barton, D.R., Rochester, N.Y. No. 3: Flat Gouge Carving Tool. Tang Style Handle. Early and Excellent. Length: 10 Inches. *This flat gouge carving tool has been boldly struck with the imprint of Rochester maker D.R. Barton. A nice example in excellent working order.* (GOOD+) **$55.00**

P4-20. Provost & Williams, Newark, N.J.: Early Hand Forged Chisel. For Framing. 1 3/8" Width. Length: 15 1/2 Inches. *Provost & Williams were edge tool makers in Newark, New Jersey from 1872 to 1874. This example of their work is in top condition. A rare chisel in top condition.* (FINE) **$95.00**

P4-21. Underhill Edge Tool Co.: Heavy Socket Framing Chisel. 1 1/2" Size. Ready to Use. Length: 16 1/2 Inches. *Framing chisels in the most desirable 1 1/2" size have become very difficult to find. This example from a respected New Hampshire maker is in top working condition.* (FINE) **$110.00**

P4-22. Barton & Co., D.R., Rochester, N.Y.: Heavy Socket Gouge. 1 1/2" Size. Crisp and Clean. Length: 15 1/2 Inches. *This D.R. Barton gouge appears to have been very little used. Crisp, clean and clearly marked.* (FINE) **$55.00**

P4-23. Ward: 1/2" Lock Mortise Chisel. Serpentine Form. Most Unusual. Length: 22 Inches. *A serpentine pattern to its form adds to the appeal of this dramatic lock mortise chisel from a principal English maker. Extra nice.* (GOOD+) **$115.00**

P4-24. Groves & Sons, R., Sheffield: 1/2" Lock Mortise Chisel. Bold Early Stamp. Excellent Condition. Length: 21 Inches. *The mark of Sheffield edge tool maker R. Groves and Sons has boldly struck on this well preserved lock mortise chisel. A very nice example.* (GOOD+) **$95.00**

P4-25. P.S. & W. Co. No. 1 EX: 1 1/2" Framing Chisel. Crisp Condition. Ready to Use. Length: 16 1/2 Inches. *This 1 1/2" framing chisel from one of America's top makers is in excellent working condition. Choice.* (GOOD+) **$115.00**

P4-26. Marples: Lock Mortise Chisel. 3/8" Size. Boxwood Handle. Length: 15 1/2 Inches. *The boxwood handle on this well preserved lock mortise chisel has attained a golden patina from use and age. A very nice example.* (GOOD+) **$85.00**

P4-27. Marples: 1/2" Lock Mortise Chisel. Extra Steep Angle. Extra Crisp and Clean. Length: 18 Inches. *The bend at the end of this classic lock mortise chisel is a bit steeper than normal. A good one.* (GOOD+) **$65.00**

P4-28. Unmarked: Heavy Socket Mortise Chisel. 3/8" Size. Ready to Use. Length: 17 3/4 Inches. *The original handle remains with this extra long socket mortise chisel. It is in top working order.* (GOOD+) **$35.00**

P4-29. New Haven Edge Tool Co.: Heavy Socket Corner Chisel. 1 1/2" Size. Near-New Condition. Length: 16 Inches. *Framing chisels in the 1 1/2 inch size are tough to come by in any condition. This one is exceptionally clean and well preserved.* (GOOD+) **$85.00**

P4-30. Unmarked: Heavy Socket Framing Chisel. 1 7/8" Size. Ready to Use. Length: 18 1/2 Inches. *This 1 7/8" framing chisel has no visible maker's mark, but it is in excellent working order. Ready to go to work.* (GOOD+) **$55.00**

P4-31. Peck, Stow & Wilcox Co.: Heavy Socket Framing Chisel. 2" Width. Original Handle. Length: 17 1/2 Inches. *Here's an excellent framing chisel in the standard 2" width. A good one.* (GOOD+) **$75.00**

P4-32. Buck Brothers: Heavy Socket Framing Chisel. 2" Width. Ready to Use. Length: 16 1/2 Inches. *This clean and ready to use Buck Brothers framing chisel retains its original handle. A good one.* (GOOD+) **$55.00**

P4-33. Hicks, J.: Pair Of Early Framing Chisels. Hand Forged Blades. Superb Condition. Length: 17 1/2 Inches. *One J. Hicks is reported as having produced edge tools in Elizabethtown, New Jersey ca. 1870-1871. These chisels, which have the flared shape characteristic of earlier manufacture, appear earlier than that date. Both are in excellent condition and boldly struck with the Hicks imprint.* (FINE) **$295.00**

P4-34. Rockford Tool Co., Kokomo, Ind.: Set of Socket Framing Chisels. 7/8", 1 1/2" and 2". Ready to Use. Length: 17 Inches. *This is our first encounter with the Rockford Tool Company of Indiana, but these framing chisels are of the best quality and ready to go to work. A very nice set.* (FINE) **$265.00**

P4-35. Sorby, I. & H., (England): 1/2" Tang Mortise Chisel. Original Handle. Straight and Sharp. Length: 14 1/2 Inches. *This crispy clean chisel is straight, sharp and ready to use. Mint.* (FINE) **$55.00**

P4-36. Stanley Rule & Level No. 440: Cook's Patent Chisel. Patent September 7, 1926. Scarce 1/8" Size. Length: 8 Inches. *Stanley's "Cook's Patent" chisels are distinguished by a knurled ring at the opening of the socket. This one has some light pitting on the side, but is retains some of its original decal. A rare Stanley chisel.* (GOOD) **$25.00**

P4-37. Union Hardware Co., Torrington, Conn.: Heavy Socket Framing Chisel. 1" Size. New Condition. Length: 16 Inches. *This 1" framing chisel is as nice as they come. Apparently never used, this chisel is ready for a lifetime of service. Mint.* (FINE) **$75.00**

P4-38. Disston & Sons, Henry, Philadelphia: Surgeon's Chisel. For Military Use. Unused Condition. Length: 6 1/2 Inches. *Most likely produced by Disston as part of the war effort in the First World War, this chisel would have been part of a surgeon's kit for working with bone. A rare Disston item in unused condition.* (GOOD) **$65.00**

P4-39. Stanley Rule & Level No. 720: 1/2" Bevel Edge Chisel. Original Handle. Near New Condition. Length: 11 Inches. *The well-regarded Stanley No. 720 "Red Handle" chisels were a very popular item. This nearly new 1/2" bevel edge chisel is ready to use or to fill out a set.* (FINE) **$55.00**

P4-40. Unmarked: Heavy Socket Framing Chisel. 2" Width. Superb Condition. Length: 15 1/2 Inches. *No maker marks on this clean 2" framing chisel. Top quality and top condition.* (FINE) **$75.00**

P4-41. Buck Bros., Millbury, Mass.: Crank Neck Paring Chisel. 1" Width. Extra Crisp and Clean. Length: 16 Inches. *An exceptionally nice, 1" bevel-edge crank neck chisel that has an early-style fruitwood handle imprinted with the Buck's head logo. Nice.* (FINE) **$85.00**

P4-42. Stanley Rule & Level No. 750: Set of 4 Bevel Edge Chisels. Near-New Condition. Ready to Use. Length: 9 Inches. *This crispy-clean set of Stanley's 750 butt chisels is in near-new condition. Sizes range from 1/2" to 1 1/2". A nice set.* (FINE) **$110.00**

P4-43. Underhill Edge Tool Co.: Pair of Socket Framing Chisels. 1 1/2" and 2" Sizes. Near New Condition. Length: 16 1/2 Inches. *These framing chisels from a respected New Hampshire maker are in top working condition. The two most desirable sizes are represented. A great working pair.* (FINE) **$125.00**

P4-44. Sorby, I. & H., England: Set of Massive Paring Chisels. Tropical Hardwood. Handles. 1 1/2", 1 3/4", 1 7/. Length: 17 Inches. *These oversize paring chisels are extra thick throughout their length. All have been fitted with rosewood handles. A dramatic set of special purpose chisels.* (GOOD+) **$165.00**

P4-45. Howarth, James, Sheffield, England: Set of 4 Tang Gouges. Extra Wide Sizes. Ready to Use. Length: 9 1/2 Inches. *Here's a great set of gouges from one of Sheffield's most respected makers. They need a light cleaning, but are in excellent working order and are not pitted.* (GOOD+) **$165.00**

P4-46. Stanley Rule & Level No. 16-600: Set of 6 Bevel Edge Chisels. "Permaloid Handles". "Professional" Series. Length: 7 1/2 Inches. *Here's a full set of bevel edge butt chisels fitted with Stanley's trademark "Permaloid' handles. Ready to provide a lifetime of service. Apparently unused.* (FINE) **$95.00**

P4-47. Sorby, I. & H., England: 5/16" Tang Mortise Chisel. Original Handle. Near New Condition. Length: 13 Inches. *Here's a 5/16" tang handle chisel in nearly new condition. Extra nice.* (FINE) **$55.00**

P4-48. Buck Bros., Millbury, Mass.: 1 1/4" Crank Neck Chisel. Turned Beech Handle. Superb Condition. Length: 14 Inches. *A good, clean, sharp and ready to use bevel-edge chisel with offset handle. Nice.* (GOOD+) **$75.00**

P4-49. Buck Bros., Millbury, Mass.: Set of 5 Crank Neck Chisels. Turned Beech Handles. Rare and Near New. Length: 14 Inches. *It has become nearly impossible to find sets of crank neck chisels in the condition that users and collectors want. Here's a great set of 5 chisels from a top maker in superb Original condition. First come, first serve.* (FINE) **$385.00**

Group Q4

Q4-1. Stanley Rule & Level No. 45: Combination Rabbet Plane. With Instructions. New Condition, Original Box. Length: 12 Inches. *Complete and perfect in its original pasteboard box this ca. 1930's plane features the desirable "micro-dial" fence. A great working plane in nearly new condition.* (FINE) **$425.00**

Q4-2. Stanley Rule & Level No. 101 1/2: "Bullnose" Block Plane. Never In Stanley Catalogue. Crisp and Clean. Length: 3 1/2 Inches. *Never listed in any Stanley catalogs, the miniature "bullnose" block plane is one of the rarest of all Stanley tools. Invariably, examples that are found tend to be either broken, rusted, pitted, missing parts or all of the above. This extraordinarily well preserved example retains more than 95% of its original paint and has never been exposed to the elements in any way. An exceptional example of a rare Stanley block plane.* (GOOD+) **$845.00**

Q4-3. Stanley Rule & Level No. 135: Liberty Bell Smooth Plane. With Lever Adjust. Excellent Condition. Length: 10 Inches. *This classic "Liberty Bell" transitional has been used, but not abused. A very well preserved example.* (GOOD+) **$135.00**

Q4-4. Stanley Rule & Level No. 9 3/4: Tail Handle Block Plane. "Bailey's Patent 1858". Early and Excellent. Length: 6 Inches. *Among the earliest of the tail handle block planes to be produced. This example of the 9 3/4 is imprinted with the "Bailey Patent 1858" trademark on the cutter. More than 90% of the original paint remains and this plane is complete and sound. A nice example of a very rare Stanley plane.* (GOOD+) **$465.00**

Q4-5. Stanley Rule & Level No. 386: Adjustable Jointer Gauge. With Rosewood Handle. 98% Nickel Plating. Length: 14 Inches. *Nearly all of the shiny nickel plating remains on this pristine example of Stanley's popular jointer gauge. Extra nice.* (FINE) **$165.00**

Q4-6. Stanley Rule & Level No. 3 C: 9" Smoothing Plane. Ca. 1950's. Near New Condition. Length: 9 Inches. *This crispy-clean example of Stanley's corrugated sole 8" smoothing plane is proudly offered without apology. A good one.* (FINE) **$85.00**

Q4-7. Stanley Rule & Level No. 10 1/2: Bench Rabbett Plane. Ca. 1930's. 98% Original Paint. Length: 8 1/2 Inches. *This well preserved example of Stanley's "carriage maker's" bench rabbet plane appears to date from the 1930's. There is a small sliver of wood missing from the side of the top of the tote, but it is otherwise excellent. A great working tool in top condition.* (FINE) **$265.00**

Q4-8. Stanley Rule & Level No. 192: Cast Iron Rabbet Plane. 1" Width. Partial Original Decal. Length: 10 1/2 Inches. *Part of the original decal remains on this perfectly preserved 1" rabbeting plane.* (FINE) **$55.00**

Q4-9. Stanley Rule & Level No. 100 1/2: "Toy" Block Plane. With Rounded Sole. New Condition. Length: 3 1/2 Inches. *This curved bottom model maker's plane is essentially in new condition. No apologies for this very nice example. Pristine.* (FINE) **$165.00**

Q4-10. Stanley Rule & Level No. 607: "Bedrock" Jointer Plane. Early Style. 95%+ Original Paint. Length: 22 Inches. *A clean, sound example of the 22" "Bedrock" jointer, this "early style" example retains more than 90% of its original paint. An excellent working plane that is ready to use.* (GOOD+) **$285.00**

Q4-11. Stanley Rule & Level No. 122: "Liberty Bell Smooth Plane. 95% Original Paint. Rare and Excellent. Length: 8 Inches. *The smallest of Stanley's "Liberty Bell" series, this is also the least common. More than 95% of the original paint remains on this well preserved example.* (GOOD+) **$115.00**

Q4-12. Stanley Rule & Level No. 602: "Bedrock" Smoothing Plane. "Sweetheart" Trademark. Rare and Excellent. Length: 7 Inches. *Here's a crispy clean example of Stanley's "Bedrock" version of its No. 2 7" smooth plane. This one is imprinted with the ca. 1920's "Sweetheart" trademark and is in excellent overall condition. A rare Stanley plane.* (GOOD+) **$745.00**

Q4-13. Stanley Rule & Level No. 60 1/2: Low Angle Block Plane. Clean And Useable. With Japanese Cutter. Length: 6 Inches. *Identical to the No. 60, but with japanned cap, this later version is in clean, ready to use condition. The cutting iron has been replaced by a serviceable Japanese replacement.* (GOOD+) **$45.00**

Q4-14. Stanley Rule & Level No. 171: Door Trim Router Plane. Patented December 26, 1911. Complete With 1 Cutter. Length: 11 1/2 Inches. *Introduced by Stanley in the early years of this century, when business was booming, power tools were not even imagined and the average workman could afford such niceties, Stanley may have produced a tool that was a bit too specialized in function for it to achieve any significant market success. This example, which is complete with one of the original 3 cutting irons retains more than 98% of its original shiny black japan finish. A superb example of a rare Stanley plane.* (FINE) **$445.00**

Q4-15. Stanley Rule & Level No. 3: Type 12 Smooth Plane. With High Knob. 3 Patent Dates. Length: 8 Inches. *Here's an exceptionally well preserved example of Stanley's desirable Type 12 smooth plane in the 8" size. Extra crisp and clean.* (FINE) **$145.00**

Q4-16. Stanley Rule & Level No. 12: Adjustable Scraper Plane. With Sweetheart Trademark. Excellent Condition. Length: 6 Inches. *Stanley's basic handled scraper plane in superb condition retaining 99%+ of its original finishes. The original cutting iron is bright, shiny and ready to use. Shiny black japanning and a crispy-clean original Stanley "Sweetheart" era cutting iron. A great plane to use.* (FINE) **$225.00**

Q4-17. Stanley Rule & Level No. 95: Edge Trim Block Plane. 99% Original Paint. Original Decal. Length: 6 Inches. *If you're looking for the No. 95 edge trim block plane, stop here. This one retains all of its original finishes as well as the original decal. Minty crispy nice.* (FINE) **$255.00**

Q4-18. Stanley Rule & Level No. 603 C: "Bedrock" Smoothing Plane. Ca. 1907 Trademark. 90%+ Original Paint. Length: 8 1/2 Inches. *Filling out a series of Stanley's "Bedrock" planes gets tougher as the number you need get smaller. One of the most difficult sizes to find is the corrugated sole No. 603. This one is in excellent collector quality condition and retains more than 90% of its original finishes. A great example.* (GOOD+) **$345.00**

Q4-19. Stanley Rule & Level No. 12 1/2: Adjustable Scraper Plane. Rosewood Bottom. Near New Condition. Length: 6 Inches. *This perfectly preserved scraper plane has been fitted with a later cutting iron from a German maker. Mint.* (FINE) **$235.00**

Q4-20. Stanley Rule & Level No. 81: Nickel Plated Scraper Plane. With Rosewood Bottom. Ready to Use. Length: 10 Inches. *Only a bit of tarnish on the original nickel plating deserves mention on this otherwise clean, complete and proper scraper plane. Ready to use.* (GOOD+) **$75.00**

Q4-21. Stanley Rule & Level No. 9 1/2: Adjustable Throat Plane. With Precision Adjust. Near New Condition. Length: 6 Inches. *Fitted with an adjustable throat mechanism as well as independent lateral adjustment and depth-of-cut features, the No. 9 1/2 block plane was a mainstay of the Stanley line for many years. This one is in excellent condition and ready to go to work. Nice.* (FINE) **$75.00**

Q4-22. Stanley Rule & Level No. 25: Low Angle Transitional Plane. 95% Original Paint. Patented June 9, 1912. Length: 9 1/2 Inches. *Marketed as a "low angle" plane, the mechanism of the No. 25 is distinctively different from the others of the transitional series. Most original finishes remain on this clean example that is destined to fill a hole in a transitional collection. A good one.* (GOOD+) **$365.00**

Q4-23. Stanley Rule & Level No. 78: Duplex Filletster Plane. Sweetheart Trademark. 95% Original Paint. Length: 9 1/2 Inches. *Nicely marked with the 1920's era "Sweetheart" trademark (on the cutter), this one is ready to provide years of service. A good one.* (FINE) **$95.00**

Q4-24. Stanley Rule & Level No. 12 1/4: Narrow Scraper Plane. Applied Rosewood Sole Extra Crisp and Clean. Length: 6 Inches. *For a woodworker looking to obtain a working example of the No. 12 1/4 scraper plane without paying the premium price these tools generally command, we offer this modified version, which has been fitted with a rosewood sole by a previous owner. A nice working tool that is worth the asking price for the parts alone.* (GOOD+) **$175.00**

Q4-25. Stanley Rule & Level No. 70: Cooper's Light Duty Scraper. With Pivoting Head. Ca. 1915. Length: 13 Inches. *Marketed as a "box scraper", for removing stenciled labels from wooden boxes and barrels, these multi-purpose tools are essentially long-handled spokeshaves. This example dates from just before the First World War. Nearly all original finishes remain.* (FINE) **$45.00**

Q4-25. Stanley Rule & Level No. 5 1/2: Wide Jack Plane Plane. Rosewood Handles. Ready to Use. Length: 14 1/2 Inches. *Stanley's No. 5 1/2 plane is approximately the length of the No. 5, but as wide as its big brother, the No. 7 jointer. This "Sweetheart" era example has been used, but not abused. A good working tool.* (GOOD) **$75.00**

Q4-26. Stanley Rule & Level No. 147: Cast Iron Tongue and Groove Plane. Patented January 20, 1903. Rare and Near New. Length: 9 Inches. *The No. 147, for 5/8" stock, and the No. 146, for 3/8" stock, seem to have been generally overlooked by woodworkers of the early part of this Century, who purchased the No. 148, the largest of the series and the size scaled for then-stock lumber, in great quantities. This example the No. 147 plane is clean, complete and retains more than 98% of its original nickel plating. A rare and exceptionally well preserved Stanley classic.* (FINE) **$365.00**

Q4-27. Stanley Rule & Level No. 101: Model Makers Block Plane. "Sweetheart" Trademark. 95% Original Paint. Length: 3 1/4 Inches. *This "Sweetheart" era block plane is in excellent condition. Ready to use or fill out a Stanley collection.* (GOOD+) **$35.00**

Q4-28. Stanley Rule & Level No. 182: Cast Iron Rabbet Plane. 1" Width. Early Vine Casting. Length: 10 1/2 Inches. *Here's an early example of the scarce No. 182 rabbet plane in excellent overall condition. A rare plane, especially in this condition.* (GOOD+) **$195.00**

Q4-29. Stanley Rule & Level No. 140: Skew Blade Block Plane. Patented November 6, 1894. Extra Crisp and Clean. Length: 1 3/4 Inches. *The No. 140 has a skew-set iron and a removable side to facilitate rabbeting. Most of the original nickel plating remains on the cap. A nice example in excellent usable condition.* (GOOD+) **$225.00**

Q4-30. Stanley Rule & Level No. 79: Double Side Rabbet Plane. With Depth Stop. "Made In U.S.A.". Length: 5 1/4 Inches. *This was the second model of the 79, which came fitted with a fence to facilitate its use. Complete and in excellent condition.* (FINE) **$95.00**

Q4-31. Stanley Rule & Level No. 35: Handled Transitional Plane. Ca. 1930. Extra Crisp and Clean. Length: 8 1/2 Inches. *Here's a transitional plane worth saving. Retaining 95%+ of all original finishes, this one is ready to use or display. Crispy clean.* (GOOD+) **$125.00**

Q4-32. Stanley Rule & Level No. 604 1/2 C: "Bedrock" Smoothing Plane. "Sweetheart" Trademark. 99% Original Paint. Length: 10 Inches. *Of all the planes of the "Bedrock" series, it is the 604 1/2 wide smoothing plane that receives the best reviews from serious woodworkers. The distinctive feature of the Bedrock planes was the patented frog designed to eliminate "chatter" when working wood. It is in exactly the types of applications where a wide smoothing plane will be used that this problem is likely to occur. Those who have tried them, in overwhelming numbers, say that this is the tool for the job. This one is in excellent overall condition, noting some very slight pitting on the upper part of one side rail. A very nice example.* (GOOD+) **$695.00**

Q4-33. Stanley Rule & Level No. 10 1/2: Bench Rabbet Plane. Rosewood Handles. Near New Condition. Length: 9 Inches. *This perfectly preserved example of Stanley's "carriage maker's" bench rabbet plane appears to date from the 1930's. A great working tool in top condition. Mint.* (FINE) **$325.00**

Q4-34. Stanley Rule & Level No. 24: 9" Transitional Plane. Ca. 1890's Trademark. Ready to Use. Length: 9 Inches. *If you are looking for a No. 24 transitional plane to fill out a set, this clean and complete example, which dates to the 1890's, will do nicely.* (GOOD) **$45.00**

Q4-35. Stanley Rule & Level No. 180: Cast Iron Rabbet Plane. Early "Vine" Handle. Patented November 18, 1884. Length: 8 1/4 Inches. *Someone has modified this early rabbet plane to accommodate a depth stop. The first example of the No. 180 we have ever offered. Rare.* (GOOD) **$65.00**

Q4-36. Stanley Rule & Level No. 102: Fixed Angle Plane. "Sweetheart" Trademark. Ready to Use. Length: 5 1/2 Inches. *Here's a ready to use example of Stanley's non-adjustable 5 1/2" block plane. A good one.* (GOOD+) **$35.00**

Q4-37. Stanley Rule & Level No. 113: Adjustable Circular Plane. Ca. 1915 Cutter. Ready to Use. Length: 10 Inches. *Here's a well used but thoroughly sound example of Stanley's No. 113 circular plane. Ready to go to work.* (GOOD+) **$125.00**

Q4-38. Stanley Rule & Level No. 40: Beech Handle Scrub Plane. Sweetheart Trademark. Superb Condtiion. Length: 11 Inches. *Here's a crisp and little-used example of Stanley's ready to work "scrub" plane. This ca. 1920's era version is fitted out with handles of lacquered beech. A very nice example of a plane that is difficult to find in this condition.* (FINE) **$145.00**

Q4-39. Stanley Rule & Level No. 112: Handled Scraper Plane. Rosewood Handles. Excellent Condition. Length: 9 Inches. *A nice, clean, working example of Stanley's premier handled scraper plane. Nice rosewood handles on a plane in crisp, sound condition. Ready to use.* (FINE) **$395.00**

Q4-40. Stanley Rule & Level No. 28: Transitional Fore Plane. 99%+ Original Finishes. Unused Condition. Length: 18 Inches. *Finding transitional planes in this condition is like finding a needle in a haystack. Finders keepers. Absolutely perfect.* (FINE) **$445.00**

Q4-41. Stanley Rule & Level No. 7: Rosewood Handle Jointer Plane. Two 1902 Patent Dates. Near New Condition. Length: 22 Inches. *Stanley's basic 22" jointer plane is "basic" because its simplicity of design and functional excellence made it the tool of choice for millions of craftsmen. This ca. 1905 example is in near-new condition. Very nice.* (FINE) **$195.00**

Q4-42. Stanley Rule & Level No. 4: Rosewood Handle. Smooth Plane. Full Nickel Plating. Ready to Use. Length: 10 Inches. *The orange infill on the cap iron of this Stanley No. 4 smoother indicates that is was produced in the 1930's. Condition is near new. A great working plane in top shape.* (FINE) **$95.00**

Q4-43. Stanley Rule & Level No. 98/99: Pair of Side Rabbet Plane. Early Type. Superb Condition. Length: 4 Inches. *Stanley's side rabbet planes are just the tool for cleaning out dados, fitting drawer bottoms or any number of other precise fitting tasks. Handy tools to have. These are in top condition.* (FINE) **$345.00**

Q4-45. Stanley Rule & Level No. 45: Combination Rabbet, Dado Plane. Complete With 17 Cutters. With "Floral" Casting. Length: 9 Inches. *A classic floral casting accents this early example of Stanley's No. 45 plane. Missing only the short rods, this plane is ready to provide many years of service. A very nice example.* (FINE) **$195.00**

Group R4

R4-1. Gee, New York, N.Y.: Early Shoe Measure Rule. Ca. 1825. Decorative Stamp. Length: 14 1/2 Inches. *No idea who "Gee" might have been, but the style of this shoe rule, its manner of embellishment and the style of the lettering suggest that it dates from the first quarter of the Nineteenth Century. A clearly marked early rule by a most uncommon maker.* (GOOD) **$195.00**

R4-2. Assorted Makers: Group of Watchmakers Tools. From Single Shop. Early and Excellent. Length: 6 Inches. *These assorted tools came from the tool kit of a watchmaker. From the looks of the tools, he did his work in the first half of the 19th Century. Interesting.* (GOOD+) **$115.00**

R4-3. Walcott Brothers, Boston, Mass.: "Walcott's Patent" Button Hole Cutter. Patented July 27, 1852. Early and Excellent. Length: 6 Inches. *Another extremely early leather working tool that is clearly marked with the patent date. Very nice.* (GOOD+) **$85.00**

R4-4. Goodell Co., Antrim, N.H.: Early Patent Knife. Patented October 6, 1868. Superb Condition. Length: 10 Inches. *The Goodell Company produced a wide range of products, including a buggy wrench, apple parers, and this early patent knife, which looks as though it was intended for use in the cutting of meat. A well preserved early knife that is clearly marked with the patent date and maker name.* (GOOD+) **$95.00**

R4-5. Unmarked: Early Hand Forged Shears. Ca. 1820's. Excellent Condition. Length: 10 1/2 Inches. *These well made shears date to the first quarter of the Nineteenth Century.* (GOOD+) **$25.00**

R4-6. Walcott Brothers, Boston, Mass.: "Walcott's Patent" Button Hole Cutter. Patented July 27, 1852. Near New Condition. Length: 6 Inches. *Here's an extremely early leather working tool that is clearly marked with the patent date. Very nice.* (FINE) **$95.00**

R4-7. American Leathersupply Co., Providence, R.I.: Textile Mill Supply Catalog. Ca. 1895, 8 VO 260 + xvii pages. Length: 9 Inches. *Everything you needed to outfit a textile mill at the turn of the century.* (GOOD+) **$95.00**

R4-8. Starrett Co., L. S., Athol, Mass. No. 4: Multiple Thread Gauge. 30-.057 to 4-.433. Near-New Condition. Length: 2 1/2 Inches. *This gauge measures threads of a wide range of sizes. It is clean and ready to use, if the new owner so desires.* (FINE) **$15.00**

R4-9. Kerby & Bro. Makers, New York, N.Y.: Slide Adjust Shoe Rule. With Ivory Inlay. Boxwood Body. Length: 19 Inches. *Unquestionably the finest shoe sizing rule ever produced, this boxwood and ivory gauge is in excellent collector quality condition. It was most likely discontinued from use after having disrupted one too many sales by upstaging the shoes. A good one.* (GOOD+) **$175.00**

R4-10. Russell Cutlery Co., John: Patented Circular Glass Cutter. "Alex Rowland Patent". Patented January 22, 1889. Length: 16 Inches. *An interesting circular glass cutter in brass from the famous cutlery maker. Patented and nearly perfect.* (GOOD+) **$115.00**

R4-11. Stanley Rule & Level No. 6 1/2: Sewing Awl Hafts. With Wrenches. New Condition Original Box. Length: 6 Inches. *This most unusual Stanley "in the box" item contains 6 sewing awl hafts and their adjustment wrenches. All tools are in excellent condition and the box is sound, with most of the original labels remaining.* (FINE) **$165.00**

R4-12. Unmarked: Classic Pantograph. For Duplication. New Condition. Original Box. Length: 22 Inches. *A pantograph applied geometric principles to the task of duplicating a two dimensional pattern in a greater of smaller scale. This one is in new condition in its original box.* (FINE) **$45.00**

R4-13. Brown & Sharpe Mfg. Co., The No. 634: Multiple Size Thread Gauge. Extra Fine Threads. Near New Condition. Length: 3 Inches. *Here's a nearly new thread gauge that measures threads up to 74 threads per inch.* (FINE) **$35.00**

R4-14. Unmarked: Turned Brass Glass Cutter. Marked "France". With Diamond Tip. Length: 4 Inches. *The simple designation "France" is the only mark on this well made brass diamond tip glass cutter. A good one.* (FINE) **$25.00**

R4-15. Stanley Rule & Level (Unmarked) No. 212: Hat Measure Rule. Unused Condition. Identical to Stanley. Length: 5 Inches. *We have never seen a hat measure rule imprinted with either the Stanley name or the No. 212 designation. This perfectly preserved example is identical to the one illustrated in, "Boxwood & Ivory", Phil Stanley's classic study of Stanley rules and rulemaking. Nice.* (FINE) **$235.00**

R4-16. Brown & Sharpe Mfg. Co., The No. 636: Multiple Size Thread Gauge. System Internationale. New Condition. Original Box. Length: 3 Inches. *Being relatively unfamiliar with threads and seriously disinclined to learn, I will leave it to one of the readers to brief me on exactly what the "System Internationale" is in the thread measurement world.* (FINE) **$45.00**

R4-17. Ackley, W.H.: Early Patent Hatter' Rule. Patented October 1, 1875. "Combined Rule". Length: 5 Inches. *We have no other information on Mr. W.H. Ackley or what is embodied in the genius of his invention, but a trip to the local library should shed some light on the subject. An extremely early and very clearly marked patented hatter's rule.* (GOOD+) **$385.00**

R4-18. Assorted Makers: Set of 12 Assisstant. Seam Tools. Ready To Use. Gomph, Osborne, Etc. Length: 5 Inches. *Here's a good working set of seam tools from all major makers that came from the same box as many of the other tools on this page. All are in fine working order.* (GOOD+) **$235.00**

R4-19. Page, E.L., Greene, N.Y.: Patent Fabric Rule. With Brass Decoration. Extra Crisp and Clean. Length: 20 Inches. *This decorative rule is imprinted with the name of an obscure Upstate New York maker. It was used in the textile industry to estimate the amount of cloth remaining in a bolt. A scarce rule in excellent condition.* (GOOD+) **$95.00**

R4-20. Bvc: Special Purpose String or Wire Tool. Mechanically Complete. Ca. 1930's. Length: 5 Inches. *This mechanical marvel is meant to be wrapped around the hand and the thumb is inserted in the "Y"-shaped yoke. Moving the thumb causes all manner of flipping, turning, cutting and spinning on the part of the springs, levers and hooks to which it was attached. My guess is that it was for tying and/or cutting string or wire. A mechanical marvel.* (FINE) **$165.00**

R4-21. Macker, D.W., North Grafton, Mass.: Patent Threshold Gauge. Patented August 6, 1889. Complete and Unused. Length: 28 Inches. *This exceptionally nice door threshold gauge was discovered when a multi-generation household was dispersed in North Grafton, Massachusetts four years ago. Complete, proper and clearly marked with the patent date, this is one of those treasures from the past that we see all too infrequently, but truly appreciate when we do. Extraordinary.* (FINE) **$395.00**

R4-22. Chase, D.G., Boston: Early Patent Buttonhole Cutter. Patented December 28, 1869. Scarce and Excellent. Length: 6 1/2 Inches. *There seems to be no end to the wide variety of these ca. 1860's patented buttonhole cutting tools. This offering, from one D.G. Chase of Boston, Massachusetts, is in nearly new condition.* (FINE) **$85.00**

R4-23. Lufkin Rule Co., The (Unmarked): Glass Cutting Rule. "Sommer & Maca". Uncommon Type. Length: 48 Inches. *Sommer & Maca were likely hardware dealers who arranged for the purchase of glass cutting rules from Lufkin imprinted with their name.* (GOOD+) **$55.00**

R4-24. Unmarked: Early Diamond Glass Cutter. Turned Boxwood Handle. Decorative Design. Length: 5 Inches. *This turned boxwood glass cutter has a distinctively shaped handle and incorporates a non-cutting edge into its design that is most unusual.* (GOOD+) **$85.00**

R4-25. Colp, G.: Early Shoe Measure Rule. Dated "1784". From Coastal Conn. Length: 14 Inches. *The edge of this extremely early shoe measure rule is imprinted with the maker name and the Revolutionary War era "1784" date. A great early measuring device.* (GOOD+) **$325.00**

R4-26. Devoe, F.W. & Reynolds, C.T., N.Y.: Diamond Tip Glass Cutter. With Rosewood Tip. Early Leather Case. Length: 7 Inches. *A protective leather case has kept this early diamond tip glass cutter in excellent collector quality condition.* (GOOD+) **$55.00**

R4-27. Millers Falls Company No. 1500: Set of 1/16 Inch Letter Stamps. Complete and Clean. Uncommon Size. Length: 5 1/2 Inches. *Here's an excellent set of 1/16" letter stamps in new condition in their original box.* (FINE) **$55.00**

R4-28. Lowinson, Chas., New York: Patent Fabric Gauge. Patented October 20, 1908. New Condition. Original Box. Length: 4 Inches. *Mr. Lewinson's patent gauge would have been used to count the number of threads in cloth. A number of variations on this theme were produced for the mills of New England. This example is in top collector quality condition.* (FINE) **$115.00**

R4-29. Hesjah: Patent Folding Sewing Kit. With Miniature Scissors. Patented April 14, 1914. Length: 2 Inches. *A nice folding sewing kit complete with scissors that will fit in your pocket safely. Patented.* (FINE) **$35.00**

R4-30. Lufkin Rule Co., The No. 8236: Boxwood Tailor's Square. As New Condition. Rare and Excellent. Length: 12 Inches. *Lufkin offered a wide range of tailor's squares, including this 12 Inch brass tipped configuration. It is in nearly new condition.* (FINE) **$195.00**

R4-31. Unmarked: Early Patent Buttonhole Cutter. Patented September 11, 1868. Chip to Cutter. Length: 8 Inches. *The cutting edge of this early patent buttonhole cutter appears to have been chipped somewhere in its long life, but this tool is otherwise crisp, clean and clearly marked. Unusual.* (GOOD+) **$45.00**

R4-32. Radcliffe: "King of Hearts" Glass Cutter. With Logo. Scarce and Excellent. Length: 6 1/4 Inches. *This most unusual class cutter is imprinted with the designation "King of Hearts" and emblazoned with a "playing card" logo. Never seen another.* (GOOD+) **$55.00**

R4-33. Fowler, Philadelphia, Penn.: Early Tailor's Square. Brass and Maple. Uncommon Early Maker. Length: 24 Inches. *One of the tips of this extremely early rule is missing, but the maker is so obscure that this example is included for its historical significance. An uncommon early Philadelphia rule.* (GOOD) **$65.00**

R4-34. Frasse & Co., New York, N.Y.: Assorted Thread Chasing Tools. For Fine Threads. Early and Scarce. Length: 6 Inches. *Frasse & Company were New York City dealers in high grade machinists tools in the 1890's. These thread chasing tools are in nearly new condition.* (FINE) **$45.00**

R4-35. Unmarked: Collection of Early Buttonhole Cutters. From Connecticut Collection. Rare and Excellent. Length: 5 1/4 Inches. *These exceptionally early buttonhole cutters were assembled some 60 years ago by a prominent collector from the State of Connecticut. A rare opportunity to purchase real antiques in quantity. Very nice.* (GOOD+) **$295.00**

R4-36. Kellogg, Battle Creek, Michigan: Madame Kellogg's Patent Tailor's Square. Patented December 25, 1883. New Condition. Original Box. Length: 24 Inches. *Complete with the original instructions, as well as all rules and charts, this patented layout set for garment makers is in new condition in its original oversize pasteboard box. A most unusual collectible curiosity.* (FINE) **$365.00**

R4-37. Eberhard Faber: Hexagon Lumber Crayons. Assorted Colors. Original Wood Box. Length: 5 1/4 Inches. *This box of lumber crayons originally contained a variety of crayons of assorted colors. It still does.* (GOOD+) **$25.00**

R4-38. Russell Cutlery Co., John: Patented Circular Glass Cutter. "Alex Rowland Patent". Patented January 22, 1889. Length: 13 Inches. *An interesting circular glass cutter in brass from the famous cutlery maker. Patented and perfect.* (GOOD+) **$85.00**

R4-39. Unmarked: Turned Brass Glass Cutter. Marked "France". With Diamond Tip. Length: 4 Inches. *This distinctive glass cutter comes to us from the country of France. Clean and clearly marked.* (FINE) **$25.00**

R4-40. Unmarked: Decorative Brass Square. With Engravings. For Sewing Use? Length: 4 Inches. *This decorated brass square is unmarked in any way, other than the elaborate etching. A most visually appealing small tool.* (GOOD+) **$125.00**

R4-41. Millers Falls Company No. 1550: Set of 1/16 Inch Number Stamps. Complete and Clean. Uncommon Size. Length: 4 Inches. *Finding full sets of letter stamps is a challenge, especially in this small size. These are clean and ready to use.* (FINE) **$45.00**

R4-42. Unmarked: Whitworth Thread Gauge. For 55 Degree Thread. Marked "Foreign". Length: 2 1/4 Inches. *Designed for the 55 degree "Whitworth" threads, this gauge is marked "foreign", which indicates that it was made for export to Great Britain.* (GOOD+) **$15.00**

R4-43. F.W.D. & Co.: Artist's Palette Knife. Ebony Handle. Uncommon Type. Length: 8 Inches. *This early ebony handled palette knife is imprinted with the maker name "F.W.D. & Co.", a maker with whom we are not familiar.* (GOOD+) **$35.00**

R4-44. Roberts, Cushman & Co., New York: Special Purpose Edging Tool. For Hat Making? Most Unusual. Length: 5 Inches. *This most unusual tool is fitted with a cutting iron that appears as if it was designed to work in much the same manner as a cooper's croze. The maker name is stenciled on the body of the tool. Very different.* (GOOD+) **$125.00**

R4-45. Magee, Worral & Richards, N.Y.: Patent Tailor's Square. Patented May 26, 1885. Near New Condition. Length: 24 Inches. *This nearly new folding tailor's square, which was produced under a patent issued on May 26, 1885, features a locking joint as its patented feature. A rare patented rule in new condition.* (FINE) **$345.00**

Group S4

S4-1. Unmarked: Diminutive Frame Saw. 10 Inch Blade. Sculpted Beech Body. Length: 18 1/2 Inches. *At only 18 1/2 inches in length, this smaller than normal frame saw has all of the aesthetic appeal and utility of the classic frame saw without requiring a wall or a barn door on which to hang it. A great working saw in excellent condition.* (GOOD+) **$145.00**

S4-2. Unmarked: Classic Pad Saw. Brazilian Rosewood Handle. Crisp and Clean. Length: 8 1/4 Inches. *A handle of turned rosewood accents this pretty and well preserved pad saw. A nice example.* (GOOD+) **$85.00**

S4-3. Unmarked: Elaborate Early Hack Saw. With Turned Fittings. Most Unusual. Length: 14 Inches. *The high degree of detail in the fittings of this special purpose saw give it a ceremonial look. Never seen another.* (GOOD) **$145.00**

S4-4. Unmarked: Early Style Frame Saw. Ram's Horn Nuts. Pegged Mortise Joints. Length: 34 1/2 Inches. *A pair of ram's horn nuts bracket this early frame saw. The presence of the hand forged nuts and the pegged joints make it likely that this was made in the Eighteenth Century.* (GOOD+) **$145.00**

S4-5. Unmarked: Cast Iron Hack Saw. Open Cast Handle. Decorative Casting. Length: 19 Inches. *The open handle of this early saw has been hollow cast in a decorative pattern. All it needs is a blade to be put back to work or up on a wall. An early and uncommon hack saw.* (GOOD) **$55.00**

S4-6. Unmarked: Early Veneer(?) Saws. With Extension Handles. Superb Patina. Length: 14 Inches. *Of strikingly graphic form, and obviously quite early. These carefully crafted saws are unlike any tool we have ever offered for sale. The teeth of these tools filed in such a way that flush cutting against a flat surface could be achieved, with any kerf being taken on the side away from the edge. Simply a great set of special purpose saws. Highly recommended.* (FINE) **$550.00**

S4-7. Union: Cast Iron Frame Hack Saw. Marked "8 In". Hardwood Handle. Length: 15 Inches. *Nearly all of the original black japan finish remains on this early hack saw. A good one.* (FINE) **$45.00**

S4-8. Disston & Sons, H., Toronto, Ontario: No. 68: Beech Handle. Dovetail Saw. 10 Inch Blade. Ready to Use. Length: 15 1/2 Inches. *This classic dovetail saw is imprinted with the Disston Company's Canadian location. Straight, sharp and nearly new.* (FINE) **$65.00**

S4-9. Stubs, P.S.: Lancashire Pattern Hack Saw. 4 Inch Blade. Rosewood Handle. Length: 10 Inches. *A delicately turned rosewood handle accents this classic "Lancashire pattern" hack saw. Clean and clearly marked with the Stubs name.* (FINE) **$115.00**

S4-10. Unmarked: "Plumber's Friend" Saw. Patented December 31, 1895. With Pivot Handle. Length: 11 1/2 Inches. *The resident genius of this patented keyhole saw is a brass fixing screw that allows the blade to be set at any angle in a 360 degree arc in relation to the handle. Different.* (GOOD+) **$115.00**

S4-11. Unmarked: Lancashire Pattern Saw. Rosewood Handle. Early and Excellent. Length: 14 1/2 Inches. *All one needs is a blade to complete this well preserved hack saw in the classic Lancashire pattern. Early and excellent.* (GOOD+) **$65.00**

S4-12. Unmarked: Classic Pad Saw. Macassar Ebony Handle. Superb Example. Length: 8 1/4 Inches. *The contrasting light and dark pattern of Macassar Ebony is evident in the turned handle of this classic pad saw. Nice.* (GOOD+) **$115.00**

S4-13. Disston & Sons, H., Philadelphia, Penn.: Fruitwood Stair Saw. Near New Condition. All Original Lacquer. Length: 10 Inches. *The Disston imprint is clearly marked on this well preserved stair saw of dark fruitwood. Nice.* (FINE) **$115.00**

S4-14. Unmarked: Unusual Double Handle Hack Saw. Hand Forged Frame. Excellent Patina. Length: 24 1/2 Inches. *What better way to decide who got stuck with the tedious task of hack sawing through metal than to share the misery? This double hack saw was likely made for a specific application, which has long since been forgotten. A graphic saw.* (GOOD) **$145.00**

S4-15. Tyler, Geo. R., Pomona, Calif.: Patent Folding Pruning Saw. Patented April 29, 1907. Rare and Excellent. Length: 12 1/2 Inches. *There were more than a few fruit and nut trees to be trimmed in turn of the Century California. This patented folding saw is the first example of its kind that we have seen. A rare patented saw.* (GOOD+) **$65.00**

S4-16. Mitchell, C.E., Lowell, Mass.: Early Handle For Saw. Patented October 24, 1865. Most Unusual. Length: 6 Inches. *Another early patent keyhole saw handle. This one is missing the blade, but clearly marked with the very early patent date.* (GOOD+) **$45.00**

S4-17. Unmarked: Yellow Birch Saw. With Fishtail Handle. Extra Crisp and Clean. Length: 11 Inches. *The yellow birch body of this shapely saw makes it all but certain that it is of American origin. Graphic.* (GOOD+) **$110.00**

S4-18. Unmarked: Combination Wrench and Saw. Retractable Blade. Brass Fixing Screw. Length: 8 Inches. *When one thinks of wrenches and how to use them, the need for a saw does not come quickly to mind. The same can be said for the inverse of this statement. Whatever the case, some long forgotten genius decided to combine the two for the benefit of tool using consumers. It apparently didn't catch on. These are quite scarce. The best idea since the broom and spatula combination.* (GOOD+) **$45.00**

S4-19. Peace, Harvey W., Brooklyn, N.Y.: 8 Inch Dovetail Saw. Applewood Handle. Ready to Use. Length: 12 Inches. *Here's an early and very well preserved dovetail saw in the desirable 8 Inch size. Crisp, clean and ready to use.* (GOOD+) **$95.00**

S4-20. Starrett Co., The L.S., Athol, Mass.: Advertising Display Sign. Shown In 1919 Catalogue. Brand New Condition. Length: 12 3/4 Inches. *The Starrett catalog of 1919 shows these highly polished display signs and encourages dealers to display them in their shops. A new old stock advertising sign for the tool room.* (FINE) **$85.00**

S4-21. Disston & Sons, H., Philadelphia, Penn.: Beechwood Stair Saw. Near New Condition. Bold Disston Mark. Length: 11 Inches. *Stair saws were used for cutting the sides of the dado cuts to inlay the stair treads. This Disston classic is clean and clearly marked.* (GOOD+) **$65.00**

S4-22. Unmarked: Rosewood Handle. Pad Saw. Original Blade. Extra Crisp and Clean. Length: 8 Inches. *These "pad" saws concealed the blade inside the handle, which could then be extended to form an early type of keyhole saw. They were always beautifully finished, as is this example, which features a turned rosewood handle and decorative brass ferrule.* (FINE) **$85.00**

S4-23. Unmarked: Ebony Pad Saw. Superb Grain. Excellent Condition. Length: 8 Inches. *The nicely turned ebony handle of this classic pad saw is in much the same condition as it was the day it was made. Nice.* (GOOD+) **$115.00**

S4-24. Disston & Sons, H., Philadelphia, Penn.: 10 Inch Dovetail Saw. Straight and True. Ready to Use. Length: 15 Inches. *No apologies whatsoever for this straight, sharp and ready to use 10 Inch dovetail from America's premier saw maker. Ready to go back to work.* (GOOD+) **$75.00**

S4-25. Unmarked: Early Oak Stair Saw. Sculptural Form. Superb Condition. Length: 13 Inches. *This classic stair saw has a most appealing look. A good one.* (FINE) **$125.00**

S4-26. Livingston & Chermfree Mfg. Co.: Early Patent Meat Saw. Patented March 23, 1867. From Johnstown, N.Y. Length: 28 Inches. *The Directory of American Toolmakers lists the working dates of this maker as 1867 to 1882. The patent feature may be the design of the upper part of the frame, which is formed in tubular fashion. A rare and very early patented saw.* (GOOD+) **$195.00**

S4-27. Delta Specialty Co., Milwaukee, Wisconsin: "American" Scoll Saw. Crank Activated. For Bench Mount. Length: 10 Inches. *This hand crank jig saw was intended to be mounted on a bench. Someone has prettied up the paint a bit, but it is in excellent working condition.* (GOOD+) **$85.00**

S4-28. Abercrombie & Fitch, New York: Metal Frame Hack Saw. With Rosewood Handle. Most Unusual. Length: 14 Inches. *Abercrombie & Fitch were outdoor outfitters who apparently were also dealers in hand tools. A rare saw from an uncommon New York City merchant.* (GOOD+) **$95.00**

S4-29. Unmarked: Boxwood Handle Saw. Rare and Extra Nice. Superb Patina. Length: 8 1/2 Inches. *This boxwood handle "pad" saw has been very little used. Extra nice.* (FINE) **$165.00**

S4-30. Unmarked: Decorative Frame Saw. Walnut Body. Carved Tropical Hardwood Handle Length: 17 1/2 Inches. *The owner/maker of this classic frame saw spent a great deal of time carving a decorative grip for the handle. A very nice saw.* (FINE) **$125.00**

S4-31. Unmarked: Rosewood Pad Saw. Superb Grain. Excellent Condition. Length: 8 Inches. *Most of the original finish remains on this well preserved rosewood pad saw. Extra nice.* (GOOD+) **$95.00**

S4-32. Disston & Sons, H., Philadelphia, Penn. No. D 95: Bakelite Handle Saw. With "Victory" Logo. Extra Crisp and Clean. Length: 28 1/2 Inches. *This well preserved bakelite handled saw is etched with Disston's WW II era "Victory" logo. A rare saw in collector quality condition.* (GOOD+) **$115.00**

S4-33. Unmarked: Early Patent Hammer Saw. Patented February 9, 1889. Unused Condition. Length: 6 1/2 Inches. *Clearly marked with its 1889 patent date, this early folding saw was intended to be used in conjunction with a hammer to facilitate sawing holes in plaster and the like. We suspect that the rarity of these in other than unused condition, such as this example, may be attributable to their lack of durability under fire. This example has never been used. Mint.* (GOOD) **$135.00**

S4-34. Unmarked: Early Hand Forged Saw. Ram's Horn Nut. Graphic Form. Length: 13 Inches. *The "ram's horn nut" that adjusts the tension on this early saw is an indication that it was made and used long before the time when standardized hardware was available. Graphic.* (GOOD) **$85.00**

S4-35. Unmarked: Boxwood Pad Saw. With Brass Fitting. Original Blade. Length: 8 Inches. *Here's a classic English pad saw with a nicely turned handle of Turkish Boxwood (Buxus buxus). Ready to use or just admire.* (GOOD+) **$75.00**

S4-36. Disston & Sons, H., Philadelphia, Penn. No. 70: 10 Inch "Dovetail" Saw. Rare Size And Type. Unused Condition. Length: 14 Inches. *These specialty brass backed dovetail saws were advertised in Disston's catalogs, but very few examples are found. This immaculate example is the finest we have ever seen. Perfect, and highly recommended.* (FINE) **$295.00**

S4-37. Disston & Sons, Henry: Adjustable Pocket Saw. With Keystone Design. Patented August 28, 1877. Length: 4 1/2 Inches. *The presence of the "keystone" logo on the adjustment screw of this "pocket" saw is convincing evidence that it was made by Henry Disston & Sons of Philadelphia.* (GOOD) **$35.00**

S4-38. Cunneen Co., N. Rochelle, N.Y. (Unmarked): Adjustable Depth Hack Saw. For Close Work. Bronze Body. Length: 13 Inches. *We are unaware of the existence of any documentation that demonstrates the specific purpose for which these highly specialized hack saws were produced. Evidently there was a need (if only in the perception of the manufacturer and inventor) for a precisely adjustable metal cutting saw to work in close quarters. Having done such work without the benefit of such a device, I can attest to a potential market, as can our neighbors in both adjacent houses, who despair of hearing foul language uttered in loud tones by a frustrated home handyman. Where was this saw when I needed it? A rare patented saw in near new condition.* (GOOD+) **$75.00**

S4-39. Livingston & Chermfree Mfg. Co.: Early Patent Meat Saw. Patented March 23, 1867. From Johnstown, N.Y. Length: 28 Inches. *The Directory of American Toolmakers lists the working dates of this maker as 1867 to 1882. The patent feature may be the design of the upper part of the frame, which is formed in tubular fashion. A rare and very early patented saw.* (GOOD+) **$195.00**

S4-40. Fraley, P.B., Philadelphia, Penn.: Early Butcher's Saw. Ca. 1850's. Rare Philadelphia. Maker. Length: 22 1/2 Inches. *The decorative handle of this saw gives it a decidedly early look. According to the directory of American Toolmakers, Fraley worked in Philadelphia from 1849 to 1859, when he was bought out by Henry Disston.* (GOOD+) **$95.00**

S4-41. Millers Falls Company: Patent Coping Saw. Rosewood Handle. Extra Deep Throat. Length: 12 1/2 Inches. *The extra-deep throat on these tools makes them especially sought after by modern woodworkers. This rosewood handled gem retains much of its original shiny nickel plating. A great saw.* (GOOD+) **$85.00**

S4-42. Atlas Tool Co., Los Angeles, Calif: Patent Folding Hack Saw. Patented July 8, 1924. Near New Condition. Length: 12 Inches. *And now for something completely different...This folding hack saw was meant to take up less room in the tool box. We suspect that most potential buyers of hack saws would not have considered the advantages of this convenience of sufficient merit to by a fancy California saw. Rare.* (FINE) **$165.00**

S4-43. Lantz, E., Paris, France: Massive Veneer Saw. Walnut Handle. Rare and Near New. Length: 21 Inches. *Nearly two feet in length, this specialty veneer saw is larger by far than any veneer saw we have previously encountered. Found together with a massive cache of early Twentieth Century tools in a house in Upstate New York several years ago, this saw, like all others that were found with it, is in absolutely perfect condition. Extraordinary.* (FINE) **$385.00**

S4-44. Unmarked: Precision Jeweler's Saw. With Proper Blade. Ready to Use. Length: 9 Inches. *The frame of this classic jeweler's precision saw has been artfully formed into an aesthetically pleasing form. A pretty saw that will do the job.* (GOOD+) **$65.00**

S4-45. Millers Falls Company No. 357: Turning Saw. New Condition. Original Carton. Length: 21 3/4 Inches. *The original "picture box" has protected this "turning saw" throughout its long life. It may have been assembled for the first time when this photograph was taken.* (FINE) **$225.00**

S4-46. Disston & Sons, Henry: Adjustable Pocket Saw. Patented August 28, 1877. Original Blade. Length: 4 1/2 Inches. *This Disston "pocket saw" is imprinted with the 1877 patent date and appears never to have been used. The tip appears to have snapped off, but it is otherwise perfect.* (FINE) **$55.00**

Group T4

T4-1. Unmarked: Craftsman-Made Scraper. Mahogany Handle. Very Well Made. Length: 8 1/2 Inches. *Very likely one craftsman's project, this mahogany and brass scraper has a most appealing look. It also looks as if it would work extremely well. Special.* (GOOD+) **$85.00**

T4-2. Wiss, Newark, N.J.: No. FH 2: Special Gripping Shears. For Flower Holding? Most Unusual. Length: 7 Inches. *These specialty shears were designed to cut and hold a flower. They were likely used in a greenhouse. A well preserved example.* (FINE) **$35.00**

T4-3. Unmarked: Classic "Stillyard" Scale. Complete and Excellent. Decorative Form. Length: 15 Inches. *These early scales were used for weighing all manner of materials. Clean, complete and very early.* (GOOD+) **$45.00**

T4-4. Ridgeley, London: Precision Wallpaper Trimmer. With Instructions. New Condition, Original Box. Length: 5 1/2 Inches. *We are familiar with the Ridgeley Company who produced wallpaper tools in the United States, but this is our first experience with tools from their London branch. Brand new in the original box.* (FINE) **$35.00**

T4-5. Carborundum Co., Niagara Falls No. 42: Lawn Mower Sharpener. Ca. 1930's. New Condition, Original Box. Length: 6 1/2 Inches. *The reverse side of this unusual tool from the Carborundum Company is covered with abrasive material. It has never been used on a lawnmower. A most unusual "in the box" item.* (FINE) **$35.00**

T4-6. Park & Williams, Williamsburg, Ohio: Early Patent Pruning Tool. Patented March 18, 1872. Scarce and Excellent. Length: 37 Inches. *The lever handle of this early patent pruning device is cast with the maker's name and patent date. Very graphic.* (GOOD+) **$95.00**

T4-7. Unmarked: Cast Iron Candy Hammer. Marked "For Toffee". Different Type. Length: 7 3/4 Inches. *Just so you wouldn't spend the day putting on a roof with this hammer it is marked "For Toffee" on the body of the tool. An interesting and unusual candy hammer.* (GOOD+) **$45.00**

T4-8. Unmarked: Early Style Reamer. With Threaded Tip. Great Patina. Length: 7 1/4 Inches. *The presence of a threaded tip indicates that this reamer was intended to cut holes as well as widen them.* (GOOD+) **$45.00**

T4-9. A.T.F. Co.: Brass Printer's Rule. Leaded and Unleaded. Early and Excellent. Length: 24 Inches. *We are unfamiliar with the A.T.F. Company, who produced this early brass printer's rule. A nice example.* (FINE) **$45.00**

T4-10. Millers Falls Company No. 980: Multiple Speed Hand Drill. Lacquered Mahogany Handle. Top Working Condition. Length: 15 1/2 Inches. *One of the most complex hand drills produced by Millers Falls, this one featured a multiple speed arrangement that could be adjusted by the user. Clean, sound and ready to use.* (GOOD+) **$65.00**

T4-11. Unmarked: Early Hand Forged Clamp. Decorative Filework. Excellent Patina. Length: 12 Inches. *The maker of this early hand forged clamp made an extra effort to fashion a decorative finial on the end of the screw. Graphic.* (GOOD+) **$65.00**

T4-12. Schollhorn Co., W., New Haven, Conn.: "Parrot Head" Pruning Shears. Bernard's Patent. Distinctive Form. Length: 6 Inches. *Here's a collectible classic from a prominent Connecticut maker. Polly want a branch?* (GOOD+) **$35.00**

T4-13. Rogers & Son, Joseph, Sheffield: Special Purpose Hook Knife. Unused Condition. Original Packing. Length: 12 1/2 Inches. *Prominent English cutler Joseph Rogers produced this specialty knife and fitted it out with a wooden "keeper" to safeguard those who handled it. It is in unused condition. Most unusual.* (FINE) **$85.00**

T4-14. Unmarked: Pair of Patent Ladder Locks. Patented July 31, 1894. Early and Unusual. Length: 8 Inches. *Nicely made with the patent date in the body of the casting, these early patent ladder locks could be used, if the purchaser so desires.* (GOOD+) **$45.00**

T4-15. Int. Electric Company: Early Electric Glue Pot. Solid Copper Body. Working Condition. Length: 14 Inches. *This "modern" variation on the classic "double boiler" glue pot adds electricity to the mix. Soon after this was made, changes in the technology of wood gluing made such devices obsolete. An excellent glue pot in very well preserved condition.* (GOOD+) **$85.00**

T4-16. Starrett Co., L.S. No. 86: Adjustable Hand Vise. With Original Handle. Near New Condition. Length: 8 Inches. *As a relentless innovator in the hand tool domain, the L.S. Starrett could not avoid offering a hand vise as long as others were doing the same. Characteristically, theirs was of the very best quality. Here's a nice example.* (FINE) **$55.00**

T4-17. Unmarked: Holder For Scythe Stone. From Cow Horn. Forged Steel Clip. Length: 8 1/2 Inches. *These hollow cow horn devices were used by farmers in Southeastern Pennsylvania and elsewhere for holding scythe sharpening stones. A hand forged hook has been riveted on the horn near the opening for the device to be attached to the belt.* (GOOD+) **$165.00**

T4-18. Unmarked: Hand-Forged Chasing Tool. For Large Lathe. Uncommon Item. Length: 48 Inches. *This oversize edge tool has a hand forged loop at the end that has been honed to an extremely sharp edge. This is the only example of a tool of this sort that we have seen. Different.* (GOOD) **$65.00**

T4-19. Boker & Co., H., Germany: Early Brass Spring Scale. Mared "Germany". 20-400 Pound Scale. Length: 9 Inches. *The only mark on this early scale is the word "Germany". A graphic tool for the scale collector or decorator. Not warranted for use.* (GOOD+) **$45.00**

T4-20. Vaughn & Bushnell, Chicago, Illinois. No. 2865: "House" Axe. Fawn Foot Handle. Original Label. Length: 17 1/2 Inches. *This oversize hatchet is really a small axe, and is described as a "house" axe in V. & B. advertising. The original label remains on the handle as does much of the original decal. A rare axe in nearly new condition.* (FINE) **$125.00**

T4-21. Unmarked: Hand Made Spring Windwer. For 3 Sizes of Wire. Ready to Use. Length: 5 Inches. *An enterprising mechanic made this spring winder to accommodate several gauges of wire. An interesting tool in fine working order.* (GOOD+) **$25.00**

T4-22. Osborne & Co., C.S., Newark, N.J.: Gardener's Dibble. Forged Steel Tip. Original Label. Length: 10 Inches. *This classic gardener's "dibble" was used for forming holes for bulbs, seeds, etc. It is in unused condition and retains its original label.* (FINE) **$45.00**

T4-23. Unmarked: Early Special Purpose Brush. Extra Soft Bristles. Unused Condition. Length: 7 1/4 Inches. *The natural bristles on this specialty brush appear to have been left short for some special application. A well preserved early brush.* (FINE) **$55.00**

T4-24. American Fork & Hoe Company: "Batcheller" Hay Knife. Original Label. Unused Condition. Length: 36 Inches. *A few hours of work would have disposed of the paper label on this well preserved hay knife. This one never made it into the barn.* (FINE) **$85.00**

T4-25. Ridgeley, London: Set of Graining Tools. Full Set of 15. New Condition, Original Box. Length: 5 1/2 Inches. *All of the original graining tools are present and in excellent working order in their original metal container. Just the thing to release the artist in you.* (GOOD+) **$85.00**

T4-26. Assorted Makers: Set of 4 Owner Stamps. Early Lettering. Excellent Condition. Length: 4 1/2 Inches. *Here's a a grouping of four carpenters' name stamps. An increasingly collectible item.* (GOOD+) **$85.00**

T4-27. Norton Grinding Company No. 186: Double India Oilstone. In Fitted Case. Near New Condition. Length: 6 1/2 Inches. *The fitted case has kept this oilstone in new condition. Ready to use.* (FINE) **$25.00**

T4-28. Unmarked No. 2: Hatmaker's Cutting Gauge. With Brass Facing. Graduated Scale. Length: 7 Inches. *This most uncommon tool was used in the manufacture of hats. It could be adjusted to the desired size and then used to trim a hat brim to the desired size. Adjustment screws allowed the brass fence to be precisely adjusted to correspond to the diameter of the hat. A rare and graphic tool in excellent condition.* (FINE) **$225.00**

T4-29. Hazen, E.: Early Strap Type Hammer. Wraparound Poll. Rare and Excellent. Length: 11 1/2 Inches. *The late Fred W. Courser, Jr., of Warner, New Hampshire, whose absence has left a void at every New England tool event, frequently carried one of these with him in his travels. He would thrust it toward you, look you in the eye the way only Fred could, and demand "Who made it!?" If you said "I don't know", he would nod knowingly, as if to say "I didn't think so!" To the best of my knowledge, he never did find out where and how and by whom these came to be, but the search goes on: Who made it?! A rare hammer that stumped The Master Hammer Collector. Chicken Tooth Rare.* (GOOD+) **$335.00**

T4-30. Unmarked: Pair of Rosewood Sash Mitre Templates. Square and Beveled. Early and Unusual. Length: 6 Inches. *Sash mitre templates were used for scribing and cutting the joints of window sash. These beautiful examples are fashioned from solid Brazilian rosewood.* (GOOD+) **$85.00**

T4-31. Russell Cutlery Co., John: Patented Circular Glass Cutter. "Alex Rowland" Patent. Rare Upright Type. Length: 13 Inches. *Nearly all of the original paper label remains on the bottom of this table mounted circular glass cutter from a prominent maker of cutlery. Rare.* (GOOD+) **$295.00**

T4-32. Marples & Sons, Wm., Hibernia Wks.: Adjustable Bench Stop. With "Shamrock" Logo. Rare and Excellent. Length: 3 1/4 Inches. *Bench stops have become increasingly collectible for the simple reason that they are small, visually and mechanically interesting and seemingly infinitely variable. This English offering in the category features the shamrock logo of William Marples of Sheffield.* (FINE) **$115.00**

T4-33. Appleton Mfg. Co., Philadelphia, Penn.: "Challenge" Family Tool Grinder. Original Paper Label. "Patent Applied For". Length: 5 1/2 Inches. *This knife and scissors grinder appears to date from the 1880's. No idea about the maker. An antique.* (FINE) **$95.00**

T4-34. Unmarked: Hand Forged Pig Sticker. With Thimble Ferrule. Very Well Made. Length: 11 Inches. *The maker of this well made and well preserved pig sticker employed a thimble as a ferrule. A tool of the sort not likely to appeal to those who diminish humanity by equating animals with men and women.* (GOOD+) **$55.00**

T4-35. Unmarked: Clamp and Trimmer For Billiard Cue. Patented July 11, 1884; April 23, 1905. Length: 4 Inches. *Many tool collector meetings include a jawboning and showoff event known as a "whatsit" session, where the assembled geniuses attempt to identify the function of mystery tools. We offer here two of the most frequently submitted items: A trimmer for billiard cue tips and a clamp for holding the tip while it is being glued. Both are marked with patent dates and in excellent condition.* (FINE) **$85.00**

T4-36. Millers Falls Company: Early Cast Iron Hand Drill. Early Type Chuck. Superb Condition. Length: 13 1/2 Inches. *We have offered a number of these early Millers Falls drills which date to the late 1890's, and they have sold very quickly. This is by far the best preserved example we have ever been privileged to sell. Extra nice.* (GOOD+) **$195.00**

T4-37. Unmarked: Miner's Candlestick Holder. Early Appearance. Spring Lock Clamp. Length: 11 1/2 Inches. *Also known as a "sticking tommy", these devices were hammered into the walls of mines to hold candles. A nice example.* (GOOD+) **$145.00**

T4-38. Chatillon, New York, N.Y.: Spring Balance Scale. Patented December 10, 1867. 24 Pound Scale. Length: 7 Inches. *This patented spring scale is imprinted with an 1867 patent date. Just for kicks, we took it down to the County Weights & Measures Office and had it tested. They looked at us like we were from Mars. Here's an opportunity to acquire an antique scale from suspected extraterrestrials.* (GOOD+) **$55.00**

T4-39. Roys & Wilcox Co.: Early Manufactured Grafting Froe. Most Unusual Maker. Turned Beech Handle. Length: 10 Inches. *There seems to be no end to the different sizes, styles and maker of grafting froes. Nineteenth Century America was covered with fruit trees of every sort and such tools were much needed. This classic example is from a partnership who worked in Berlin, Connecticut from 1845 to 1870. The were the immediate precursors of the Peck, Stow & Wilcox Company. A rare and early grafting froe.* (GOOD+) **$110.00**

T4-40. Preston & Sons, Edward: Adjustable Bench Stop. With "E.P." Logo. Rare and Excellent. Length: 3 1/4 Inches. *This exceptionally well preserved bench stop has been formed with the distinctive logo of Birmingham, England toolmakers Edward Preston & Sons. Rare and excellent.* (FINE) **$125.00**

T4-41. Alteneder & Sons, Theo, Philadelphia: Draughtsman's Ink Dispenser. Patented December 4, 1900; July 10, 1906. Excellent Condition. Length: 5 Inches. *An interesting tip-up inkwell for the drafting trade. A good one.* (GOOD+) **$85.00**

T4-42. Buck, G., London: Screw Adjust Hand Vise. With Wooden Handle. Excellent Condition. Length: 8 Inches. *Hand vises are another of those specialty tools that lend themselves well to being collectible. The are small, infinitely variable and always just a bit different from each other. This most unusual variation features a wooden handle fitted to a tang in the body.* (GOOD+) **$55.00**

T4-43. Unmarked: Pattern For Core Box Plane. For Foundry Use. Most Unusual Find. Length: 16 Inches. *It is well known that patternmakers made many of their own tools, including the specialized "core box" planes used for hollowing circular patterns. Now, thanks to this original pattern, we have a bit more insight on how those tool were made. All three sections of the original pattern for a massive core box plane are included in this rare opportunity to acquire a unique tool making tool. Very different.* (GOOD+) **$265.00**

T4-44. Unmarked: Special Purpose Cane. With "Dibble" End. Unknown Function. Length: 33 1/2 Inches. *The end of this cane-like device has a bisected cone that apparently functions as a reamer of some sort or possibly as some sort of agricultural device. Never seen another. A mystery.* (GOOD+) **$95.00**

T4-45. Unmarked: Set of 3 Early Pump Tools. For Fitted Wood Pipe. Rare and Excellent. Length: 15 Inches. *In the days before PVC pipe, water was transported in hollow wooden pipes. These tools were used for tapering the joints of the pipes to minimize water loss. Museum quality.* (GOOD+) **$265.00**

Group U4

U4-1. Sandusky Tool Co., Sandusky, Ohio: Set of Plow Plane Cutting Irons. Complete Set. Fitted Leather Roll. Length: 9 Inches. *These plow plane irons are imprinted with the early arch imprint of the Sandusky Tool Company. A fitted leather roll has kept them in top collector quality condition. Mint.* (FINE) **$265.00**

U4-2. Tolman, J.R., Hanover, Mass.: Massive Reverse Ogee Molding Plane. Double Cutter. Scarce and Excellent. Length: 9 1/2 Inches. *This oversize reverse ogee molder has been boldly struck with the Tolman imprint. The side escapement has a square opening in the manner of the coastal planemakers of New England and it is fitted with the cutter/chip breaker combination preferred by shipwrights. A classic Tolman molder in excellent condition.* (GOOD+) **$185.00**

U4-3. Hunt & Wiseman, St. Louis, Mo.: Sash Filletster Molding Plane. Side Boxed. Rare and Sound. Length: 8 1/2 Inches. *This rare sash filletster plane bears the imprint of a pre-Civil War St. Louis, Missouri maker. We have had less than a dozen of these planes with American maker marks over the years. A rare American plane.* (GOOD+) **$185.00**

U4-4. Unmarked: Patternmaker's Plane. Heart Shape Pattern. Mahogany Body. Length: 6 Inches. *The escapement on this well made router plane has been carved into the shape of a heart. Most unusual.* (GOOD+) **$225.00**

U4-5. Varvill & Son, York, England: Classic Ogee Molding Plane. Spring Set Profile. Ready to Use. Length: 9 1/2 Inches. *Here's a crisper than usual reverse ogee molder from a prominent maker from the North of England.* (GOOD+) **$95.00**

U4-6. Tolman, J.R., Hanover, Mass.: Center Bead Molding Plane. Marked "1/4". Full Boxed. Length: 9 1/2 Inches. *This classic fully boxed center bead plane has the characteristic "squared" escapement favored by J.R. Tolman. A very nice molding plane.* (GOOD+) **$85.00**

U4-7. Wilson, H., Newcastle, England: Coach Rabbet Plane. Most Appealing Size. Clean and Sound. Length: 5 Inches. *This compass bottom coachmaker's rabbet plane comes to us from the North of England. A well preserved special purpose plane.* (GOOD+) **$65.00**

U4-8. Chapin, H., Union Factory No. 133: Double Iron Nosing Molding Plane. 1 3/8 Inch Size. Ready to Use. Length: 9 1/2 Inches. *Here's a well preserved double iron nosing plane in the uncommon 1 3/8 Inch size. Extra crisp and clean.* (GOOD+) **$65.00**

U4-9. Unmarked: Coach Rabbet Plane. Decorative Form. French Origin? Length: 7 Inches. *This classic coachmaker's rabbet plane has a decidedly French look. This first impression is reinforced by the name "E.M. Galle" that is imprinted on the body of the tool. C'est magnifique.* (GOOD+) **$75.00**

U4-10. King, Josiah, 373 Bowery, N.Y.: 7/8 Inch Dado Molding Plane. Unusual Depth Stop. Excellent Working Order. Length: 9 1/2 Inches. *The most unusual depth stop on this New York City molding plane consists of a pair of opposing wooden wedges. A well preserved molder in excellent working order.* (GOOD+) **$85.00**

U4-11. Malloch, D., Perth (Scotland): Boxed Bead Molding Plane. Marked "5/8". Appears Unused. Length: 9 1/2 Inches. *No apologies whatsoever for this pristine bead plane from a renowned Scottish planemaker.* (FINE) **$45.00**

U4-12. Bensen & Crannell, Albany: Grecian Ovolo and Bevel Molding Planes. Stepped Set of 4. 1/2, 5/8, 3/4 and 7/8 Inch. Length: 9 1/2 Inches. *We are able to offer far fewer stepped sets of molding planes than the demand in the market could consume. We are able to offer far fewer sets of the quality of these Grecian ovolo and bevel molders from Albany, New York makers Bensen & Crannell. A great set of molding planes in nearly new condition.* (FINE) **$645.00**

U4-13. Gleave, Oldham St., Manchester: Set of Complex Molding Planes. For Fluting Work. Near New Condition. Length: 9 1/2 Inches. *This great working pair of fluting and reeding planes is ready to be put back to work. A nicely boxed set of planes with very uncommon profiles.* (GOOD+) **$245.00**

U4-14. Moir, Glasgow (Scotland): 1/2 Inch Dado Molding Plane. With Adjustable Depth Stop. Very Well Made. Length: 9 1/2 Inches. *James Moir manufactured woodworking planes in Glasgow, Scotland, from 1836 to 1874. This well made plane is in excellent working condition.* (GOOD+) **$75.00**

U4-15. Mockridge & Francis, Newark, N.J.: Quarter Ovolo and Bevel Molding Plane. Marked "3/8". Clean and Near New. Length: 9 1/2 Inches. *A single strip of Turkish Boxwood accents this well preserved complex molder by prominent New Jersey makers Mockridge & Francis. Extra nice.* (FINE) **$65.00**

U4-16. Tolman, J.R., Hanover, Mass.: Full Boxed Bead Molding Plane. Marked "4/8". Double Cutter. Length: 9 1/2 Inches. *Here's a fully boxed bead plane from a prominent maker of shipwright's tools. Absolutely perfect and highly recommended.* (FINE) **$125.00**

U4-17. Malloch, D., Perth (Scotland): Boxed Bead Molding Plane. Marked "1/2". Appears Unused. Length: 9 1/2 Inches. *This well preserved molder from a prominent Scottish maker appears never to have been used. Perfect.* (FINE) **$45.00**

U4-18. Spehr, J.A., Hamburg, Germany: Pair of Miniature Planes. Flat and Compass. Extra Crisp and Clean. Length: 3 1/2 Inches. *These artfully crafted German planes are marked with name of Hamburg maker J.A. Spehr. Nearly new, but old.* (FINE) **$125.00**

U4-19. Tolman, J.R., Hanover, Mass.: Full Boxed Double Bead Molding Plane. Rare Mark, Rare Type. Ready to Use. Length: 9 1/4 Inches. *A massive double bead molder of extraordinary merit. This plane, one of only a few standard size molders from Tolman, is fully boxed, boldly struck and in excellent condition. A rare plane in fine working order.* (GOOD) **$115.00**

U4-20. Tolman, J.R., Hanover, Mass.: Center Bead Molding Plane. Marked "4/8". Full Boxed. Length: 9 1/2 Inches. *No apologies whatsoever for this crispy clean center bead plane from an important Massachusetts maker of shipwright's tools. Nice.* (FINE) **$115.00**

U4-21. Gleave, Manchester: Steep Quarter Ogee Molding Plane. Extra Crisp and Clean. Ready to Use. Length: 9 1/2 Inches. *This oversize quirk ogee molder is in nearly the same condition as it would have been when new. Extra nice.* (FINE) **$145.00**

U4-22. Wallace, Montreal: 3/4 Inch Dado Molding Plane. Slide Depth Stop. Early and Excellent. Length: 9 1/2 Inches. *This professionally made plane plane has a distinctive imprint from a documented Canadian maker. A nice working dado plane in a most desirable size.* (GOOD+) **$65.00**

U4-23. Assorted Makers: Group of 6 Assorted Molding Plane. Assorted Profiles. Stewart, Kellogg, Etc. Length: 9 1/2 Inches. *Here's an opportunity lot of molding planes from a variety of makers including the Scottish maker Stewart, and J. Kellogg of Amherst, Massachusetts.* (GOOD) **$115.00**

U4-24. Jones, Ellis: Wedge Arm Plow Plane. With Ivory Inlay. Graduated Arms. Length: 9 1/2 Inches. *This extraordinary plow plane is fitted with inlaid strips of ivory that are graduated to facilitate the precise adjustment of the width of the fence. The name of the maker, one Ellis Jones, is not documented in American Wooden Planes nor in British Planemaker. A very well made, well preserved and striking plow plane.* (GOOD+) **$975.00**

U4-25. Malloch, D., Perth, Scotland: Boxed Bead Molding Plane. Marked "Inch". Extra Crisp and Clean. Length: 9 1/2 Inches. *One inch bead planes are becoming increasingly difficult to obtain. This one is in excellent working order. Nice.* (GOOD+) **$35.00**

U4-26. Barton & Co., D.R., Rochester, N.Y.: Massive Skew Rabbet Plane. Early Barton Mark. Uncommon Type. Length: 16 Inches. *This oversize skew rabbet plane is imprinted with the mark of Rochester, New York plane and edge tool maker D.R. Barton. It needs only a wedge for the nicker iron to restore it to working order.* (GOOD+) **$165.00**

U4-27. Casey, Kitchell & Co., Auburn, N.Y.: Double Tongue and Groove Molding Plane. Marked "1/2". Ready to Use. Length: 9 1/2 Inches. *Other than a small hang hole through the body, this 1/2" double tongue and groove molder is in excellent condition. Ready to use, if you choose.* (GOOD+) **$75.00**

U4-28. Malloch, D., Perth, Scotland: Full Boxed Bead Molding Plane. Marked "1/8". Scarce and Excellent. Length: 9 1/2 Inches. *Bead planes, especially the narrower widths, have a tendency to wear away their boxing, making them no longer usable. This 1/8" bead is fitted with a full strip of boxwood to minimize the possibility of that eventuality. Ready to use.* (GOOD+) **$35.00**

U4-29. Phillip, T.: Double Iron Sash Molding Plane. From Southeastern Penn. Scarce and Sound. Length: 10 Inches. *This early sash plane has been boldly struck with the imprint of an early planemaker from Southeastern Pennsylvania. A rare plane from a most uncommon maker.* (GOOD) **$345.00**

U4-30. Ohio Tool Co., Auburn, N.Y. U.S.A. No. 282: Double Razee Smooth Plane. With "World" T.M. Near New Condition. Length: 10 Inches. *Many collectors are familiar with this "double-razee" style of plane, but few opportunities exist to actually see them. This one is in excellent condition and clearly marked. Most unusual.* (FINE) **$145.00**

U4-31. Greenslade, W., Bristol, England: Pair of Side Rabbet Molding Planes. Crisp, Clean and Sound. Ready to Use. Length: 9 1/2 Inches. *One of these molders is noticeably darker than the other, but they have obviously been a pair throughout their lives. A nice working set.* (GOOD+) **$110.00**

U4-32. Gleave, Manchester: Quarter Ogee and Bevel Molding Plane. 2 7/8 Inches Overall. Width. Crisp and Clean. Length: 9 1/2 Inches. *The planemaking firm of Joseph Gleave began operations in Manchester, England in 1832 and continued until well into the Twentieth Century. This quirk ogee and bevel bearing their imprint is much wider than the English molders normally encountered.* (GOOD+) **$165.00**

U4-33. Moses, Artemas, Salisbury, Verm.. (?): Side Snipe Molding Plane. Ca. 1815 Appearance. Possible Cabinetmaker. Length: 9 1/4 Inches. *Ethel Hall Bjerkoe's classic "The Cabinetmakers of America" lists an Artemas Moses as working in Salisbury, Vermont ca. 1815. This early molder, which is imprinted with the name "A. Moses" appears to date from around that time and was found in nearby New Hampshire. A likely working tool of a documented American cabinetmaker.* (GOOD) **$345.00**

U4-34. Assorted Makers: Group of 4 Assorted Molding Planes. "V" Groove, Bead. Smoothing Planes. Length: 14 Inches. *All of these wooden planes came together from the same chest, where they were undoubtedly used by the same carpenter. A nice working set.* (GOOD) **$85.00**

U4-35. Nurse, C., 32 Mill St. (London): Pair of Fenced Sash Molding Planes. Marked "1" and "2". Crisp And Clean. Length: 9 1/2 Inches. *These fenced sash molding planes are imprinted with the numbers "1" and "2" and were meant to be worked together. Both are in excellent working order.* (GOOD+) **$145.00**

U4-36. Kellogg, J., Amherst, Mass.: Boxed Bead Molding Plane. Marked "3/16". Extra Crisp and Clean. Length: 9 1/2 Inches. *This boxed bead from a prominent Massachusetts maker is in excellent working order. Nice.* (FINE) **$45.00**

U4-37. Stewart: Double Iron Molding Plane. Torus Bead Profile. Crisp and Clean. Length: 9 1/2 Inches. *This double iron molder was made in the Scottish city of Edinburgh. It is in top collector quality condition and ready to be put immediately to use.* (FINE) **$115.00**

U4-38. Unmarked: Handled Smooth Plane. Sculptural Handle. Most Unusual Type. Length: 8 1/2 Inches. *This most unusual smoothing plane has been sculpted from a single piece of beech and has a most appealing shape to its rear handle. The wood proceeds from the full width of the body at the rear of the plane and then tapers gradually to the tip of the tote. A pretty plane that is a bit dirty, but very sound and worthy of preservation.* (GOOD) **$165.00**

U4-39. Copeland & Co., Warranted: Double Bead Molding Plane. Fully Boxed. Marked "1/4". Length: 9 1/2 Inches. *The base of this 1/4" double bead molder is fitted with "full" boxing, which is wider and covers all wear points to prolong the life of the tool. This well preserved example is in excellent condition.* (GOOD+) **$125.00**

U4-40. Bell, John, Philadelphia, Penn.: Massive Cornice Molding Plane. Classic Ogee Profile. 5 1/4" Overall Width. Length: 14 1/2 Inches. *Fitted with a pull handle to allow others to assist the master carpenter in the planing of cornice moldings, this massive crown molding plane is the sort of tool that only the most successful woodworkers would have owned. Clearly marked with imprint of a prominent Philadelphia planemaker, this tool is ready to serve as the cornerstone of a collection of fine molding planes. Nice.* (GOOD+) **$645.00**

U4-41. Casey & Co., Auburn, N.Y.: Classic Dado Molding Plane. Marked "5/8". Boxwood Depth Stop. Length: 9 1/2 Inches. *According to "American Wooden Planes", Casey & Company produced planes in Auburn Prison for a single year, 1857. This well preserved dado plane is marked with the number "5/8" on the reverse. Crisp, clean and fitted with the early style "tombstone" wedge.* (GOOD+) **$55.00**

U4-42. Dwights & French: Set of Plow Plane Irons. Full Set of Eight. Excellent Condition. Length: 8 1/2 Inches. *Here's a full set of American-made plow plane irons. Seldom seen.* (GOOD+) **$165.00**

U4-43. Whittier & Spear: Handled Razee Try Plane. Extra Bold Mark. AWP III: 4 Examples. Length: 16 Inches. *Writing in "American Wooden Planes", the Pollak's report only four known examples of this imprint. This razee trying plane has been boldly struck with the mark. A rare wooden plane.*(GOOD+) **$135.00**

U4-44. Kellogg, J., Amherst, Mass.: Boxed Bead Molding Plane. Marked "6/8". Extra Crisp and Clean. Length: 9 1/2 Inches. *Here's a 3/4 Inch molding plane in excellent working condition. Nice.* (FINE) **$45.00**

U4-45. Copeland & Co., Warranted: Worrall's Patent Plane. With Bolt Lock Mechinism. Extra Crisp and Clean. Length: 22 Inches. *A bolt runs through the body of this essentially unused molding plane to secure the cutting iron. It is the earliest and best preserved example of the Worrall's patent planes that we have seen. Nearly new and boldly struck with the Copeland name, but not the patent date.* (FINE) **$595.00**

Group V4

V4-1. Stanley Rule & Level: "Arrow" Brand Hammer. With Original Decal. 16 Ounce Size. Length: 13 1/2 Inches. *Nearly all of the original decal remains on this straight claw ripping hammer that was offered under the obscure "Arrow" brand of Stanley. Rare.* (FINE) **$110.00**

V4-2. Stanley Rule & Level No. 0310: 16 Ounce Ball Pein Hammer. "Handyman" Brand. Original Decal. Length: 14 1/2 Inches. *This 16 ounce "Handyman" hammer has never been used. Mint.* (FINE) **$35.00**

V4-3. Maydole, D., Norwich, N.Y. No. 2: 12 Ounce Claw Hammer. With Bell Face. Original Handle. Length: 12 3/4 Inches. *This uncommon claw hammer from the most renowned hammer maker of all time retains its original handle and is clearly marked. A good one.* (GOOD+) **$25.00**

V4-4. Unmarked: 2 Ounce Ball Pein Hammer. "W.R. Adams". With Anchor Device. Length: 9 1/2 Inches. *This unusual hammer from the collection of New Hampshire collector Fred W. Courser, Jr. is in new condition. No idea about who Mr. Adams might have been, or the nautical collection. A great hammer.* (FINE) **$125.00**

V4-5. Unmarked: Precision Jeweler's Hammer. Delicate Handle. Excellent Condition. Length: 7 1/4 Inches. *This specialty hammer is fitted with a handle having a bulbous base and an extremely thin neck. A ver well preserved jewelers hammer.* (GOOD+) **$85.00**

V4-6. Hammer Dry Plate Co., St. Louis, M.O.: Miniature Hammer. With Gold Plating. Excellent Condition. Length: 6 Inches. *This plated hammer with a golden color is made in the manner of a cigar box hammer, but is a bit oversized. Obviously an advertising giveaway to promote Mr. Hammer's dry plate business, whatever that was. A nice advertising hammer.* (FINE) **$65.00**

V4-7. Gilmour & Co., Gatineau Mills, P.Q.: Log Marking Hammer. Initial "G". Original Handle. Length: 17 Inches. *The initial "G" was the imprint used by Gilmour & Company of Gatineau Mills, Quebec. Here's a very well preserved example of that mark.* (GOOD+) **$75.00**

V4-8. Nelson, A.T., Wilton, Iowa: Unusual Patented Hammer. Patented July 28, 1903. Near New Condition. Length: 11 Inches. *The patent papers for this technological marvel describe it as a "hammer for tinners use". This one has not been used by a tinner or anyone else. A scarce patented hammer in great shape.* (FINE) **$85.00**

V4-9. Ross, Beaurivarge, P.Q.: Log Marking Hammer. Imprint "A.R.". Excellent Condition. Length: 27 Inches. *The stylized "A.R." logo on this hammer is for the Quebec based logging concern of Mary C. Simpson Ross.* (GOOD+) **$85.00**

V4-10. Belknap Hardware Co., Louisville. No. 712: 12 Ounce Claw Hammer. Uncommon Size. Extra Crisp and Clean. Length: 12 3/4 Inches. *The original handle remains on this uncommon 12 ounce claw hammer from the "Bluegrass" people at the Belknap Hardware Company.* (GOOD+) **$45.00**

V4-11. Double Claw Hammer Co., The: Patented Double Claw Hammer. Patented November 4, 1902. Maker Name Marked. Length: 12 3/4 Inches. *This example of the elusive double claw hammer is marked with the 1902 patent date and the name of the maker. The condition is as good as we have seen in this elusive tools. A hammer every collector wants. A good one.* (GOOD+) **$345.00**

V4-12. Maydole, D., Norwich, N.Y.: Oversize Farrier's Hammer. Near New Condition. Partial Paper Label. Length: 13 1/4 Inches. *Part of the original paper label remains on this uncommon and uncommonly well preserved farrier's hammer from David Maydole. Nice.* (FINE) **$65.00**

V4-13. Bay State Saw Mfg. Co., Fitchburg: 5 Ounce Carpenter's Hammer. With Bell Face. Uncommon Maker. Length: 11 Inches. *The Bay State Mfg. Company produced this most unusual bell face claw hammer in the rare and desirable 5 ounce size. A most unusual hammer.* (GOOD+) **$35.00**

V4-14. Scott Lumber Co., Fred'ton, N.B.: Double Log Marking Hammer. Single Letter "H". Replaced Handle. Length: 14 1/2 Inches. *The single letter "H" was the imprint used by the Scott Lumber Company of New Brunswick. The choice of letter may have less to do with the name of the company and more to do with ease of forming the character. The handle has been replaced, but the hammer is in good condition.* (GOOD) **$55.00**

V4-15. Sayre, F.E., Ltd., Chipman, N.B.: Log Marking Hammer. Single Letter "E". Nicely Formed Handle. Length: 17 Inches. *The head of this well made lumber stamp is tapered to a head to allow a second hammer to drive it into the log, if necessary. An increasingly difficult to find tool.* (GOOD+) **$125.00**

V4-16. Stanley Rule & Level: "Bell System" Hammer. Extra Heavy Head. Original Decal. Length: 13 1/2 Inches. *Apparently the Stanley Rule & Level Company produced a number of tools especially for the telephone folks working for Ma Bell. This extra heavy hammer, which retains part of its Stanley decal, has the "Bell System" logo boldly stamped in the head. An uncommon hammer in excellent condition.* (GOOD+) **$75.00**

V4-17. Blier, Pierre, St. Eleuthere, P.Q.: Double Log Marking Hammer. Initials "P.B.". Uncommon Type. Length: 13 Inches. *The initials P.B. appear on this double headed log marking hammer. This imprint was used by Pierre Blier of St. Eleuthere, Quebec.* (GOOD+) **$85.00**

V4-18. True Temper: "Papagayo" Hammer. With Parrot Logo. Most Unusual Type. Length: 13 Inches. *Here's a totally different hammer. The maker is True Temper, but the name on the head is "Papagayo" and there is an image of a parrot stamped beside the name. Most unusual.* (GOOD+) **$55.00**

V4-19. Roberts: Upholsterer's Hammer. Mahogany Infill. Very Well Made. Length: 11 Inches. *The name "Roberts" is embossed on this high quality upholsterer's hammer. A very well made tool.* (FINE) **$75.00**

V4-20. Bigelow & Dowse Co., Boston, Mass.: "Worth" Brand 7 Ounce Hammer. Original Handle. Uncommon Type. Length: 12 1/2 Inches. *We have offered a wide range of claw hammers in this highly collectible size, but this is the first bearing the "Worth" imprint used by the Bigelow & Dowse Company of Boston. A nice example.* (GOOD+) **$45.00**

V4-21. Belden Machine Co., The: Slater's Hammer. Extra Crisp and Clean. Leather Handle. Length: 11 Inches. *The Belden Machine Company made the very finest slater's hammers. Here's a classic example.* (FINE) **$165.00**

V4-22. Sayre, F.E., Ltd., Chipman, N.B.: Classic Log Marking Hammer. Single Letter "E". "Stick" Type Handle. Length: 23 1/2 Inches. *This distinctive single "E" log stamp was used by the logging enterprise F.E. Sayre, Ltd. of Chipman, New Bruinswick. The early type handle is formed from a branch inserted in the head. A classic.* (GOOD+) **$75.00**

V4-23. Shapleigh Hardware, St. Louis No. SN 7: 7 Ounce Claw Hammer. Original Handle. "Hammer Forged". Length: 11 Inches. *This Shapleigh 7 ounce claw hammer does not have the distinctive "Keen Kutter" logo that that firm used on many of its tools and hardware items. It is in excellent collector quality condition. A rare 7 ounce claw hammer.* (GOOD+) **$55.00**

V4-24. St. Maurice Lumber Co., Trois Rivieres: Double Log Marking Hammer. Cross "+". From Quebec Province. Length: 18 Inches. *A cross in a circle was the distinctive imprint left by this log marking hammer that was used by the St. Marice Lumber Company of Trois Rivieres, P.Q. It has been fitted with a fawn foot axe handle.* (GOOD+) **$65.00**

V4-25. Sears, Roebuck & Company: 7 Ounce "Dunlap" Hammer. Original Handle. Uncommon Type. Length: 11 1/2 Inches. *Based on the number of surviving tools, one might suspect that Sears sold more of their household line of "Dunlap" tools than they did of their "Craftsman" top of the line brand. Maybe they did. This uncommon 7 ounce claw hammer is in excellent condition.* (GOOD) **$35.00**

V4-26. Unmarked: Multi-Purpose Hammer. Wrenches, Etc. Most Unusual. Length: 8 1/2 Inches. *If these had caught on, we wouldn't need to bother with all these other wrenches and hammers. They didn't, luckily. Early and nice to look at.* (GOOD+) **$125.00**

V4-27. Gillies Bros., Braeside, Ontario: Double End Log Hammer. "M" Within "V". Distinctive Mark. Length: 5 Inches. *This extra heavy log hammer is embossed with the "M" within a letter "V" that was the distinctive imprint of the Gillies Brothers logging enterprise from Braeside, Ontario. A dramatic logging hammer.* (GOOD+) **$55.00**

V4-28. Unmarked: Miniature Claw Hammer. With "Bell" Face. Early Appearance. Length: 9 Inches. *This unmarked hammer has a lean and early look.* (GOOD) **$15.00**

V4-29. Heller Bros. Co., Newark, N.J. No. 523: Adze Eye, Plain Face Hammer. Claw Type. New With Decal. Length: 16 Inches. *Here's a carpenter's hammer from a company who specialized in supplying the blacksmith. This one has never been used. Mint.* (FINE) **$155.00**

V4-30. Stanley Rule & Level No. H0308: 8 Ounce Ball Pein Hammer. "Handyman" Brand. Original Decal. Length: 13 Inches. *All of the original decal remains on this "Handyman" brand hammer from Stanley. Mint.* (FINE) **$35.00**

V4-31. Atha Tool Co., Newark, N.J. No. 553: Rare Nail Holding Hammer. With Horseshoe Trademark. Most Unusual. Length: 12 1/2 Inches. *This nail holding hammer from Newark's Atha Tool Company is the first example so-marked that we have offered. The idea was that the nail head was inserted in the slot and the side of the hammer used to start the nail, after which it could be driven in. A variation on a theme.* (GOOD+) **$245.00**

V4-32. Unmarked: Log Marking Hammer. From British Columbia. Underlined "D 4". Length: 5 1/2 Inches. *This unusual log marking hammer, which was found in the Province of British Columbia, consists of the underlined alphanumeric combination "D 4". We have no information on the company who used it.* (GOOD+) **$45.00**

V4-33. Lakes Timber Co., Ft. Frances, Ontario: Massive Log Marking Hammer. "T" Within "V". Registered 1918. Length: 5 Inches. *The "T" within a "V" imprint of the Lakes Timber Company of St. Frances, Ontario, was more likely a "T" within an angled "L". This imprint was originally registered in 1918.* (GOOD+) **$85.00**

V4-34. Unmarked: Early Log Marking Hammer. Initials "B.P.". Strap Hammer Form. Length: 13 1/2 Inches. *This superb early log marking hammer has distinctively shaped initials forming the letters "B.P." A great early lumbering tool.* (GOOD+) **$265.00**

V4-35. Boyle, J.E. Co., Ltd., Maniwaki, P.Q.: Early Log Marking Hammer. Diamond "J". Distinctive Pattern. Length: 6 1/2 Inches. *A diamond surrounding the letter "J" was the imprint used by the J.E. Boyle Company of Manniwaki, Quebec. The non-embossed head of this example is tapered to allow it to be driven by a hammer.* (GOOD+) **$85.00**

V4-36. J.W.H.: Log Marking Hammer. With "Stick" Handle. Undocumented Maker. Length: 26 1/2 Inches. *The initials "J.W.H." are forged into both sides of this early log marking hammer. The handle has a rustic effect as it is formed from a nicely patinated branch. A classic logging collectible.* (GOOD+) **$75.00**

V4-37. Robertson, A.R., Boston, Mass.: Bill Poster's Hammer. Rare 4-Section Type. Superb Condition. Length: 63 Inches. *Among the rarest of all hammers, we are pleased to offer this, the Robertson four-section bill poster's hammer. When fully extended, a handbill could be hung more than 10 feet in the air with one of these. Only the second example we have ever offered. Rare.* (FINE) **$645.00**

V4-38. Unmarked: Rotating Head Hammer. For Glaziers. Four Sided Head. Length: 10 Inches. *These unusual glaziers hammers were designed in an ergonomic way to make it unnecessary to bend the wrist when the hammer moved across the glass. A good idea and a rare hammer.* (GOOD+) **$155.00**

V4-39. Nutting & Hayden, Concord, N.H.: Early Patent Bush Hammer. Patented October 6, 1889. For Stone Work. Length: 13 1/2 Inches. *This early stone working hammer is marked with the maker's name and early patent date. A nice example of a classic New England tool.* (GOOD+) **$115.00**

V4-40. Garland Mfg. Co.: Decorative Brass Hammer. With Loop Handle. Most Unusual. Length: 9 1/2 Inches. *A most appealing brass hammer with strap handle. This one is clearly marked with the maker's name and has been very little used. Nice.* (FINE) **$65.00**

V4-41. Bailey, John, Widdifield, Ontario: Early Log Marking Hammer. Initials "J.B.". Very Well Preserved. Length: 18 Inches. *The initials "J.B." were the distinctive imprint of John Bailey, the operator of a logging concern in Widdifield, Ontario. This example is in excellent condition.* (GOOD+) **$85.00**

V4-42. Maydole, D., Norwich, N.Y.: Set Of 3 Ball Pein Hammers. Original Decals. Near New Condition. Length: 12 Inches. *These hammers were acquired together by their original owner and then passed into a collection, from whence they were consigned to use. A great set of hammers looking for a new custodian.* (FINE) **$115.00**

V4-43. Rudor, N.Y.C.: "Handi Tool" Hammer. Cast Iron Body. Screwdriver, Etc. Length: 5 Inches. *This specialty hammer incorporates a nail/tack puller into its design. The maker is one we have not previously encountered.* (GOOD+) **$65.00**

V4-44. Robertson, A.R.: Bill Poster's Hammer. Three Section Type. Early and Excellent. Length: 45 Inches. *Not quite so rare as the four-section variety, the three-section bill poster's hammer is not often encountered. This one is in excellent condition and clearly marked.* (GOOD+) **$265.00**

V4-45. Herbert Et Guertin, Ste. Madeleine: Early Log Marking Hammer. Initials "H O". From Quebec. Length: 23 1/2 Inches. *A hammer poll on the reverse of this log marking hammer allows it to do double duty. The "H.O." initials were used by Herbert Et Guertin, a Ste. Madelaine, Quebec partnership.* (FINE) **$115.00**

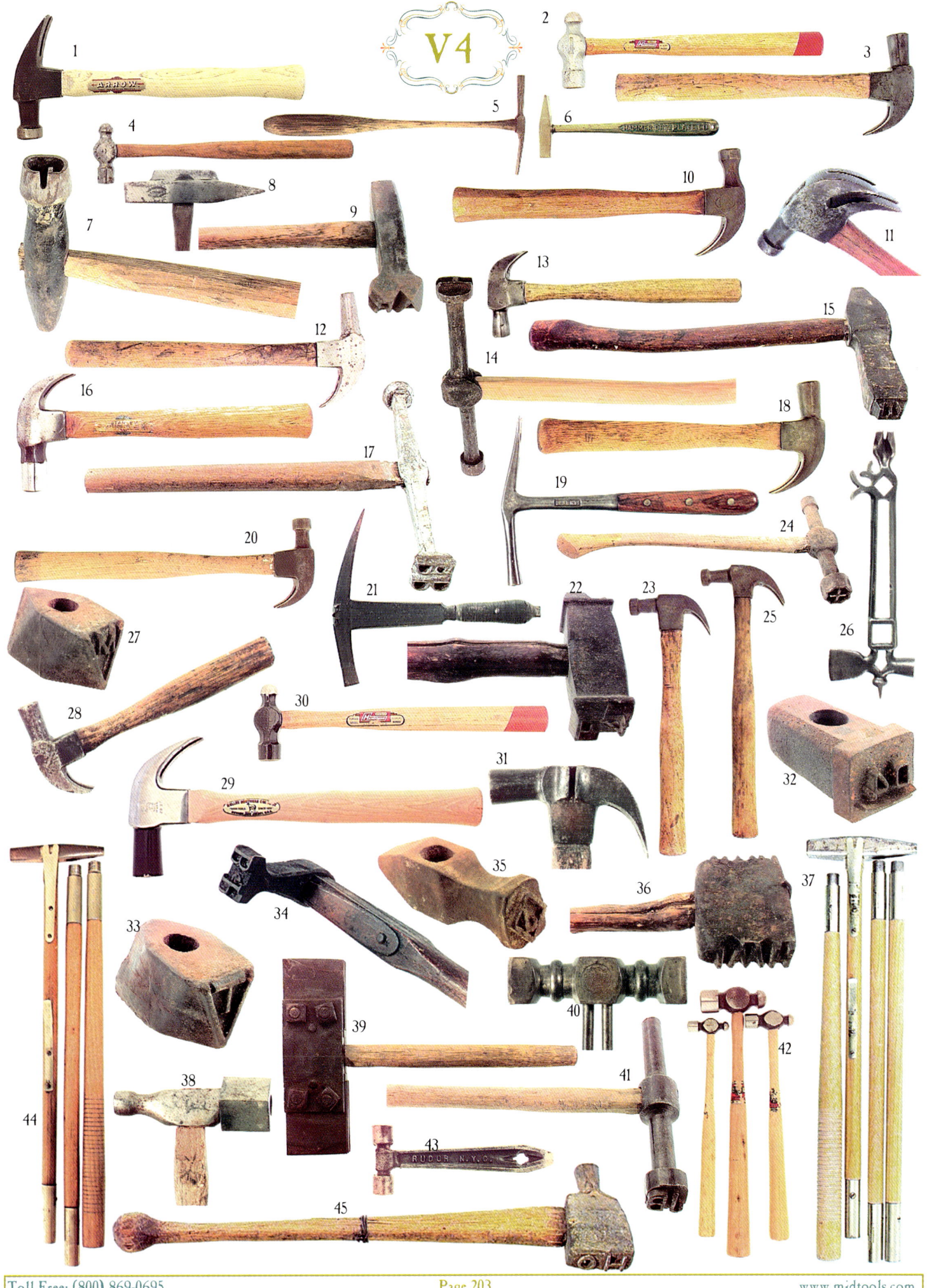

Group W4

W4-1. Vandegrift: Vandegrift Patent Wrench. For Farm Machinery. Rare Size. Length: 5 1/2 Inches. *These were distributed with International Harvester tractors. Examples in this size are tough to come by. A good one.* (GOOD+) **$135.00**

W4-2. Overman Wheel Co., Chicopee Falls: Bicycle Monkey Wrench. Center Adjust. Patented January 6, 1891. Length: 5 Inches. *A nice, early patented wrench with most of its original nickel plating remaining. Top shelf.* (FINE) **$85.00**

W4-3. Whitman & Barnes: Loop Handle Monkey Wrench. Marked "Hercules". Uncommon Type. Length: 4 Inches. *This small loop-handled nut wrench from the Whitman & Barnes Company is not one often encountered. A good one.* (GOOD+) **$85.00**

W4-4. Billings & Spencer Co., The: "Billings Patent" Wrench. Patented February 13, 1879. Very Early Type. Length: 4 Inches. *The markings on this example of the C.E. Billings 1879 patent wrench indicate that it was one of the very first made. Early and excellent.* (GOOD+) **$65.00**

W4-5. Mossberg Co., Frank No. 200: Set of Tappet Wrenches. In Original Pouch. Complete and Perfect. Length: 8 Inches. *Automotive sets in collector quality condition are getting more and more difficult to obtain. This one is as good as they get.* (FINE) **$145.00**

W4-6. Billings & Spencer Co., The No. 97: Bicycle Monkey Wrench. Full Nickel Plating. Near New Condition. Length: 4 1/4 Inches. *Shorter and stubbier than the standard bicycle wrench, these were just the right size to fit in the pocket. Virtually all nickel plating remains. Nice.* (FINE) **$85.00**

W4-7. Peck, Stow & Wilcox Co.: "Solid Bar" Monkey Wrench. 6" Size. Extra Crisp Condition. Length: 6 Inches. *These "Solid Bar" wrenches were offered in every size up to "too big to use". This was the smallest size. Crispy clean.* (GOOD+) **$55.00**

W4-8. Billings & Spencer Co., The: "Billings Patent" Wrench. Patented February 13, 1879. For "Pope Manufacturing.". Length: 4 1/2 Inches. *The Pope Manufacturing was an early maker of bicycles. This Billings & Spencer wrench was apparently given out with those bicycles.* (GOOD) **$65.00**

W4-9. Mossberg Co., Frank No. 11: "Diamond" Bicycle Wrench. Patented November 11, 1900. Superb Condition. Length: 5 Inches. *I've never seen a Mossberg catalog, but they apparently made a bunch of different wrenches. You don't see many of these.* (FINE) **$65.00**

W4-10. Lavigne & Scott Mfg. Co., The: Patented Bicycle Wrench. "Feather" Weight. Patented December 31, 1895. Length: 5 1/2 Inches. *This light-duty wrench was especially appropriate for those whose limited education had not permitted them to learn to read (how's that for a PC way of saying illiterate) to recognize its soft-touch as it was embossed with a "feather" device on the body of the wrench. An uncommon wrench in nice condition.* (GOOD+) **$75.00**

W4-11. Billings & Spencer Co., The: Billings' Patent Nut Wrench. Patented February 18, 1879. Graduted Center Shaft. Length: 6 Inches. *Precise adjustment of the Billings patent was accomplished by reference to the graduations machined into the shaft. Most people probably just screwed it on until it was tight. More wrench than was needed.* (GOOD) **$55.00**

W4-12. Smith & Co., H.D., Plantsville, Conn.: "Perfect Handle" Wrench. 6" Monkey. Rare Cast Handle. Length: 6 Inches. *The wooden handles that were the selling feature of the "Perfect Handle" line are missing from this rare variation. Sorta like chocolate milk with no chocolate. Not exactly plain vanilla.* (GOOD+) **$125.00**

W4-13. Athol Machine Co., Athol, Mass.: Quick Adjust Nut Wrench. Extra Crisp and Clean. Schulz No. 526 (A). Length: 6 Inches. *This one slides quickly and smoothly into place with a push of the button at the rear of the lower jaw. Crisp, clean and clearly marked. The patent was issued to one S.H. Bellows on June 8, 1880. An uncommon mechanical marvel.* (GOOD+) **$245.00**

W4-14. Portland Wrench Company: Combination Nut and Buggy Wrench. Smallest Size. Patented October 16, 1883. Length: 5 1/2 Inches. *This, the smallest size offered by the Portland buggy wrench people is clean, complete and ready to display. A tough size to find.* (GOOD) **$195.00**

W4-15. Standard Tool Co., Athol, Mass.: Quick Adjust Nut Wrench. Rare 8" Wood Handle. Schulz No. 526. Length: 8 Inches. *A crisp and clean example of the Bellows Patent monkey wrench in the unusual 8" size. Unlike the smaller versions, these were fitted with wooden handles. The wooden handle versions of this wrench are extremely scarce. This one is in excellent condition.* (FINE) **$245.00**

W4-16. Universal Wrench Co., Detroit: Quick Adjust Nut Wrench. Patented June 3, 1919, July 22, 1919. Schulz No. 530. Length: 8 Inches. *This locking lever adjustable wrench is in exceptionally nice condition. A good one.* (FINE) **$135.00**

W4-17. Unmarked: Double Open-End Wrench. Forged From a File. Graphic Form. Length: 11 Inches. *Rather than let a farrier's rasp that had seen better days go to the scrap heap, someone made this graphic open-end wrench. A good one.* (GOOD+) **$55.00**

W4-18. Carll: Combination Pipe and Nut Wrench. Patented May 6, 1913. Reversible Jaw. Length: 6 Inches. *The jaw on these patented crescent-type wrenches could be screwed all the way out and reinserted from the other end to change from a pipe to nut wrench. Why not?* (GOOD+) **$55.00**

W4-19. Whitman & Barnes: Railroad Use Wrench. "Santa Fe Route". Uncommon Name. Length: 8 Inches. *This most unusual railroad wrench is imprinted with the designation "Santa Fe Route". There must have been something about these railroad wrenches that made normally honest folks steal them. For every railroad imprinted wrench in an Nineteenth Century railroad shop, there must have been twenty in a home workshop. Once, in an attempt to eliminate this pilfering problem, a severe solution was imposed. Every night, on leaving the shop, the workmen would have their lunch boxes weighed for security reasons. It had previously been determined that the average weight of a lunch box leaving the railroad shops at night was about 14 pounds, so only boxes weighing more than that amount were searched. Despite this draconian solution, very few thieves were apprehended. An uncommon railroad wrench.* (GOOD+) **$45.00**

W4-20. Unmarked: "Mechanicarm" Adjustable Wrench. Double Jaw. European Type. Length: 4 Inches. *A mechanically interesting double jaw wrench that might possibly be from England.* (GOOD+) **$165.00**

W4-21. Unmarked No. 32: Special Purpose Wrench. For Auger Use? Hook Feature. Length: 8 Inches. *This special-purpose wrench has a wicked looking twisting mechanism on one end. Different.* (GOOD) **$35.00**

W4-22. Johnson, Iver, Fitchburg, Mass.: Early Bicycle Wrench. With Embossed Mark. Crisp and Clean. Length: 5 1/2 Inches. *The Iver Johnson Company made bicycles and supplied them with these wrenches. This one is in excellent condition.* (GOOD+) **$55.00**

W4-23. Hammond Mfg. Co., Boston, Mass.: Patent Quick Adjustable Wrench. Patented April 3, 1900. Schulz No. 676. Length: 8 Inches. *The lever beneath the upper jaw allowed free movement to the desired adjustment when depressed. Another idea that didn't catch on. A rare wrench.* (GOOD+) **$195.00**

W4-24. Craft Tool Co., The, Conneaut, Ohio: Rare 24" "Craft" Wrench. Patented November 12, 1907. Schulz No. 663. Length: 24 Inches. *At 24 inches in length, this was the largest of the "Craft" series. A rare wrench in excellent condition.* (GOOD+) **$225.00**

W4-25. Vandegrift Mfg. Co., Shelbyville: Quick Adjust Nut Wrench. Rare Wood Handle. Similar to Schulz No. 546. Length: 10 Inches. *No markings on this one, but the Schulz Book doesn't lie. A rare wood-handled variation of what was once a popular (go figure) style of wrench.* (GOOD+) **$225.00**

W4-26. Billings & Spencer Co., The: Adjustable Nut Wrench. Graduated Shaft. Rare Locking Screw. Length: 7 1/2 Inches. *A bit better than the commonly encountered "S" handle wrench from Billings & Spencer, this variation features a locking screw on the adjustment screw. Most unusual.* (GOOD+) **$65.00**

W4-27. Coes & Co., L., Worcester, Mass.: Mechanic's Improved Wrench. Patented January 1, 1882. Schulz No. 849. Length: 10 Inches. *This was apparently one of the many Taft Patents, which the Coes Company marketed as the "Mechanic's Improved". The slotted adjustment screw apparently kept the adjustment rod from wobbling. Different.* (GOOD+) **$75.00**

W4-28. Smith & Co., H.D., Plantsville, Conn.: 10" "Perfect Handle" Wrench. Uncommon Size. "S" Handle. Length: 10 Inches. *Here's a crispy-clean "S" handle wrench from the Perfect Handle folks.* (GOOD+) **$110.00**

W4-29. Stahl: Ladies Pocket Combination Tool. Hatchet, Pliers, Etc. Leather "Purse". Length: 5 Inches. *While we assign the designation "ladies" to this combined, hammer, screwdriver and hatchet, we do so only tentatively, as there is nothing written on the tool to indicate that it was intended for any specific gender. However, having had sufficient experience on a job site to be able to anticipate the consequences if someone pulled out the doeskin case in which this tool is contained and proceeded to put it to use, we stand behind our assessment. A sissy tool. Ready to go to work.* (FINE) **$185.00**

W4-30. Boos Tool Corp., Kansas City, Missouri: Screw Adjust Nut Wrench. Rare 8" Size. Near New Condition. Length: 8 Inches. *The Boos Patent Wrench was adjusted by turning the handle to regulate the jaws. This one is in nearly new condition.* (FINE) **$65.00**

W4-31. Gordon: Quick-Adjust Nut Wrench. "Gordon Automatic". Schulz No. 493. Length: 7 1/4 Inches. *The spring-loaded "Gordon Automatic" has a mechanism that appears not likely to have tolerated the introduction of dirt and grime. A clean example.* (GOOD+) **$115.00**

W4-32. Simplex Mfg. Co., The, N.Y.: "Anderson Turn-More" Wrench. Patented October 30, 1906. Schulz No. 313. Length: 10 Inches. *Manufactured from folded metal, these do not appear to have been of sufficient durability to withstand life on the job. A nice example.* (GOOD+) **$145.00**

W4-33. Williams & Co., J.H., N.Y. No. 474: Adjustable Spanner Wrench. Black Painted Body. Uncommon Type. Length: 9 1/2 Inches. *Designed to hook into a notch in a lock ring, the spanner wrench was useless for any other purpose. This one appears never to have been used.* (FINE) **$15.00**

W4-34. Peck, Stow & Wilcox Co.: "Solid Bar" Monkey Wrench. 10" Size. Early Peck, Stow & Wilcox Logo. Length: 10 Inches. *This early wrench is in new condition. Choice.* (FINE) **$55.00**

W4-35. Billings & Spencer Co., The: "Billings Patent" Wrench. Patented February 13, 1879. With Graduated Shaft. Length: 7 Inches. *At 7 inches in length, this is a bit longer than the standard Billings patent. A good, clean wrench.* (GOOD+) **$45.00**

W4-36. Crescent Tool Co., Jamestown, N.Y.: 6-8" Double Crescent Wrench. Uncommon Type. Excellent Condition. Length: 8 Inches. *Isn't the idea of an adjustable wrench that you need just ONE wrench instead of several (or even two)? The folks at the Crescent Tool Company probably so despaired of having limited their potential business that they came up with this idea to (in their minds, anyway) double their sales. It didn't work. These wrenches are in scarce supply.* (GOOD+) **$65.00**

W4-37. Alderman: "Alderman" Bicycle Wrench. Patented November 13, 1900. With Tire Iron. Length: 6 Inches. *The Alderman wrench does double duty as its handle is forged in such a way to allow it to serve as a tire iron. A clean and well preserved example.* (GOOD+) **$65.00**

W4-38. Unmarked: Hand Forged "Bed" Wrench. Classic Style. Superb Condition. Length: 6 Inches. *These early-style wrenches were used for disassembling beds. They were supposedly carried by firemen, but I really don't quite understand that whole story. A nice early wrench.* (GOOD+) **$55.00**

W4-39. Cochran: "The Speednut" Wrench. Patented May 2, 1916. Near New Condition. Length: 9 Inches. *These were the standard among self-adjusting wrenches. This clean example is in great working condition.* (FINE) **$35.00**

W4-40. Acme: Twist Handle Monkey Wrench. Patented 1883. Smallest Size. Length: 5 Inches. *This small twist-handle is clearly marked with the early patent date. A good one.* (GOOD+) **$45.00**

W4-41. Bemis & Call Co., Springfield, Mass.: "Briggs' Patent" Wrench. Patented April 28, 1859. Uncommon Small Size. Length: 10 Inches. *The very early patented wrenches of New England can be recognized at once by their bulbous-ended handles. "This display size" example of the Briggs' patent of 1859 is in excellent condition despite its advanced age.* (GOOD+) **$145.00**

W4-42. Tower & Lyon, New York, N.Y.: Boardman's Patent Wrench. 8" Combination Wrench. Very Rare Size. Length: 8 Inches. *At 8 inches in length, this example of the "jack of all trades" Boardman patent is the largest size we have ever offered. An uncommon wrench in a very rare size. A good one.* (GOOD+) **$175.00**

W4-43. Erie Tool Works, The, Erie, Penn.: Adjustable Nut Wrench. With Adjustable Sleeve. Unusual Maker. Length: 10 Inches. *The Great Lakes port city of Erie, Pennsylvania produced more than its share of wrench manufacturers. The highest quality producer of all was the Erie Tool Works. A very well made wrench.* (GOOD+) **$75.00**

W4-44. Unmarked: Quick Adjust Buggy Wrench. Slide Adjust. Most Unusual. Length: 14 Inches. *This slide adjust buggy wrench has seen some hard work, but it is intact and ready to add to a growing collection of these tools.* (GOOD) **$15.00**

W4-45. Trimont Mfg. Co., Roxbury, Mass.: "Trimo" Monkey Wrench. Patented December 19, 1911. Near New Condition. Length: 11 Inches. *Old wrenches in new condition make an interesting collection. Here's one with which to start.* (FINE) **$55.00**

W4-46. Bemis & Call Co., Springfield, Mass.: "Billings" Monkey Wrench. Cast Lead Handle. Uncommon Type. Length: 10 1/2 Inches. *There is no mention of this soft metal handled wrench in any of the Brown & Sharpe catalogs. Different.* (GOOD+) **$25.00**

Group X4

X4-1. Palmer, France: "Systeme Palmer" Micrometer. Pioneer Design. New Condition, Original Box. Length: 3 3/4 Inches. *American precision measurement traces its history to the micrometer developed for gauging the thickness of sheet brass in the country of France and popularized as the "Systeme Palmer". This extraordinary French micrometer dates from the early days of precision measurement and bears the legendary "Palmer" name on the original pasteboard box. A museum quality precision tool. Highly recommended.* (FINE) **$875.00**

X4-2. Modern Products Mfg. Co.: Precision Countour Gauge. For Complex Mouldings. New Condition, Original Box. Length: 4 Inches. *There's more to one of these contour gauges than meets the eye. This one is extremely well made and ready to be put back to work. A good, clean gauge in top condition.* (FINE) **$55.00**

X4-3. Moore & Wright, Sheffield, England: 1-2" Micrometer. With Ratchet Stop. Original Box. Length: 6 Inches. *Moore & Wright were the principal English manufacturers of machinists tools. This 1"-2" micrometer is in excellent condition in its original box.* (GOOD+) **$25.00**

X4-4. Brown & Sharpe Mfg. Co. No. 8: Early Patent Micrometer. Original Pasteboard Box. Patented January 22, 1884. Length: 4 1/2 Inches. *Imprinted with the patent date of 1884, the pasteboard box in which this tool is contained most likely dates from that early period of manufacture. An uncommon patented micrometer in a very rare box.* (GOOD+) **$295.00**

X4-5. Brown & Sharpe Mfg., Providence: Early Inside-Outside Micrometer. Patented January 29, 1907. New Condition, Original Box. Length: 4 Inches. *This patent precision micrometer was intended for both inside and outside measurement. Complete in new condition in the original box with the original adjustment wrench. Perfect.* (FINE) **$145.00**

X4-6. Unmarked: Pair of Specialty Levels. For Machinists Square. Most Unusual. Length: 2 1/2 Inches. *These most unusual levels are of identical design, yet one is made of steel and the other of bronze. Each has two level vials attached and appears to have been designed to fit on an engineer's square with a screw.* (GOOD+) **$165.00**

X4-7. Starrett Co., L. S., Athol, Mass. No. 18-A: Machinist's Center Punch. Spring Loaded. New Condition, Original Box. Length: 5 Inches. *The original sliding top wooden box has kept this precision center punch in nearly new condition. Mint.* (FINE) **$65.00**

X4-8. Westinghouse, G., Schenectady, N.Y.: Hart's Patent Tally Gauge. Patented December 10, 1867. With Paper Label. Length: 8 1/2 Inches. *This early patent gauge was reportedly used for counting bushels of grain that were processed at a mill. The original paper label remains and the tool is in working order. Early and most unusual.* (GOOD+) **$265.00**

X4-9. Brown & Sharpe Mfg. Co. No. 8: Early Patent Micrometer. Original Case. Patented January 22, 1884. Length: 4 1/2 Inches. *This early micrometer is marked with the date of the January 22, 1884 patent issued to one C. Carleton. A nice example of a rare patented American micrometer.* (GOOD+) **$115.00**

X4-10. Starrett Co., The L.S., Athol, Mass. No. 1: Adjustable Jaw Cutnippers. 5 1/2" Size. Original Carton. Length: 5 1/2 Inches. *These were apparently used for nipping off wire, the tips of small bolts and the like. This pair is in new condition. A nice, early example.* (FINE) **$65.00**

X4-11. Koenig, Wm. A., Troy, N.Y.: Precision Depth Gauge. Extra Long Type. New Condition, Original Box. Length: 13 Inches. *This early precision tool is in new condition in its original box. Perfect.* (FINE) **$325.00**

X4-12. Reinhardt: "Reinhardt Profile' Gauge. From A.J. Wilkinson. New Condition, Original Box. Length: 5 Inches. *This turn of the century gauge contains the original instructions bearing the markings of Boston hardware dealer A.J. Wilkinson. New in the box.* (FINE) **$55.00**

X4-13. Unmarked: Machinist Made Trammels. For Graduated Rules. Brass Hex Wrench. Length: 5 Inches. *This combination set of trammels and calipers features a double, central fixture to facilitate the scribing of large circles or measuring wide objects. The carved recesses in the case indicate that this tool once belonged to a practitioner of the patternmaker's trade.* (GOOD+) **$145.00**

X4-14. Starrett Co., L. S., Athol, Mass. No. 436: Precison 0" - 1'" Micrometer. With Decimal Equivalent. Fine Condition, Original Box. Length: 5 Inches. *The outside of the box has weathered a bit, but the micrometer is in excellent condition and ready to be put back to use.* (FINE) **$55.00**

X4-15. Schoenner, Germany No. 2190: German Silver Trammels. For Draughtsman. New Condition, Original Box. Length: 6 Inches. *These precision trammels would have been used in the drafting room for laying out large circles. Generally, these tools were not supplied with the wooden beam with which they were intended to be used. A nice example.* (FINE) **$65.00**

X4-15. Slocomb, J.T., Providence, R.I.: Inside Measure Micrometer. In Fitted Case. Uncommon Type. Length: 4 Inches. *Here's a great inside micrometer set from a prominent Rhode Island maker. Slocomb tools were the equivalent in quality to the major makers and a growing number of collectors are seeking out these tools.* (FINE) **$85.00**

X4-16. Keuffel & Esser Co., N. Y.: German Silver Trammels. Early Keuffel & Esser Mark. Fitted Maple Case. Length: 6 1/2 Inches. *These drafting trammels of German silver have been kept in nearly new condition through many years, thanks to this very well made sliding case having a French fit velvet lined interior and an ivory pull on the "drawer". A great set.* (FINE) **$115.00**

X4-17. Starrett Co., The L.S., Athol, Mass. No. 474: "Special" Screw Pitch Gauge. With Lock Screws. New Condition, Original Box. Length: 3 Inches. *The "Special" designation on the outside of this box indicates that this tool was not a stock item and was likely ordered for a specialized function. The first "Special" tool by this prominent maker that we have encountered.* (FINE) **$115.00**

X4-18. Starrett Co., L. S., Athol, Mass. No. 436RL: 2" - 3" Micrometer. Complete and Near New. New Condition, Original Box. Length: 8 Inches. *Examples of the 2"-3" micrometer are much less common than their smaller cousins. This one is in new condition in its original box.* (FINE) **$55.00**

X4-19. Starrett Co., The L.S., Athol, Mass. No. 279: Folding Radius Gauge. Graduation In 10ths. New Condition, Original Box. Length: 2 3/4 Inches. *This perfectly preserved radius gauge is graduated in 10ths of an inch. New and in the box.* (FINE) **$35.00**

X4-20. Starrett Co., The L.S., Athol, Mass. No. 178 A: Folding Radius Gauge. Multiple Size. New Condition, Original Box. Length: 3 Inches. *These inside/outside radius gauges served a number of purposes in the machinist and patternmaking trades. This extra-crispy clean examplè is in new condition in its original box.* (FINE) **$45.00**

X4-21. Starrett Co., The L.S., Athol, Mass. No. 124 A: Inside Micrometer. Multiple Sizes. Fitted Wood Case. Length: 8 Inches. *It appears that the longest section is missing from this otherwise perfect inside micrometer. Unless you're planning to build a submarine, you probably will never need it.* (FINE) **$25.00**

X4-22. Starrett Co., L. S., Athol, Mass. No. 436: Precison 0" - 1'" Micrometer. With Decimal Equivalent Complete, Original Box. Length: 5 Inches. *Here's an excellent precision tool in excellent condition in its original box. A good one.* (GOOD+) **$25.00**

X4-23. Starrett Co., L. S., Athol, Mass. No. 436: Precison 1" - 2'" Micrometer. With Ratchet, Lock Nut. New Condition, Original Box. Length: 6 Inches. *We know of at least one individual who uses a micrometer to evaluate the width and thickness of Stanley planes before purchasing. Not exactly the kind of guy you would want next to you in an airline seat on a flight to Australia. This one is in excellent working order.* (FAIR) **$75.00**

X4-24. Starrett Co., L. S., Athol, Mass. No. 203 C.: 0" to 1" Micrometer. With Ratchet and Lock. New Condition, Original Box. Length: 5 Inches. *Here's a well preserved micrometer in new condition in its original box. Complete with instruction manual and adjustment wrench. Perfect.* (FINE) **$45.00**

X4-25. Brown & Sharpe Mfg. Co.: Precision Indicator Gauge. Patented July 24, 1906. Original Box. Length: 6 Inches. *An early precision indicator gauge in its original wooden case. Crisp and clean.* (GOOD) **$65.00**

X4-26. Starrett Co., L. S., Athol, Mass. No. 2 M: 1" -2" Micrometer. With Attachment. Fine Condition, Original Box. Length: 7 Inches. *This early micrometer includes a precision attachment to allow it to function as either a 1"-2" size or as a 0"-1" size. Scarce and excellent.* (GOOD+) **$145.00**

X4-27. Stanley Rule & Level No. 49: Auger Bit Depth Gauge. Nickel Plated Finish. Original Box. Length: 2 1/2 Inches. *These were used for boring holes of a fixed depth, such as those used for stopped mortises. A perfectly preserved example in new condition in the original box.* (GOOD+) **$35.00**

X4-28. Starrett Co., L.S., Athol, Mass. No. 245: Engineer's Pocket Gauge. Taper, Wire and Thickness. New Condition, Original Box. Length: 5 1/4 Inches. *These "engineer's" gauges were designed to be carried by a practitioner of that profession. Included in one tool are a taper gauge, feeler gauges and a thickness gauge. A very well made and uncommon Starrett item.* (FINE) **$85.00**

X4-29. Lufkin Rule Co., The No. 891: Machinist's Protractor. With Screw Lock. New Condition, Original Box. Length: 8 Inches. *Lufkin's machinist tool line was of the very best quality. Both box and tool are in new condition.* (FINE) **$55.00**

X4-30. Lufkin Rule Co., The, Saginaw, Mich. No. 513: Micrometer Adjust Depth Gauge. Complete and Excellent. New Condition, Original Box. Length: 7 1/2 Inches. *The Lufkin people did things right. This old but brand new depth micrometer is a nice example of their high standard of quality.* (FINE) **$55.00**

X4-31. Starrett Co., The L.S., Athol, Mass. No. 364: Vernier Read Protractor. All Original Blades. New Condition, Original Box. Length: 12 Inches. *This perfect and complete example of Starrett's vernier protractor includes two blades and the original instructions in the original leather covered case. A classic precision tool in top condition.* (FINE) **$115.00**

X4-33. Moore & Wright, Sheffield, England: 0"-1" Micrometer. With Ratchet Stop. New Condition, Original Box. Length: 5 Inches. *This precision micrometer from a prominent English maker is in nearly new condition. A good one.* (FINE) **$35.00**

X4-34. Lufkin Rule Co., The, Saginaw, Mich. No. 79 B: Telescoping Gauge. 3/4" to 1 1/4" Size. New Condition, Original Box. Length: 3 1/2 Inches. *to precisely measure the inside diameter of an opening, this was inserted and the screw at the base of the handle was turned to allow the telescoping tips to expand. A micrometer was then used to measure the width. Mint.* (FINE) **$25.00**

X4-35. Lufkin Rule Co., The No. 455 EM: 5" Slide Caliper Rule. Metric and English. New Condition, Original Box. Length: 5 Inches. *The "EM" designation on this Lufkin caliper rule refers to its English and metric graduations. It appears never to have been used. Perfect.* (FINE) **$75.00**

X4-36. Goodell-Pratt Company No. 340: Clapboard Marking Gauge. Patented October 18, 1904. Original Box. Length: 8 Inches. *The Goodell Pratt Company produced a wide range of innovative tools, many of which were unlike anything of their type that had proceeded them. This clapboard gauge is a classic example of such a tool. Fitted with a pair of levers to facilitate locking and holding the work in place, it is not likely that many of these were sold. This one is in clean and sound condition in its original picture label pasteboard box. Most unusual.* (GOOD+) **$85.00**

X4-37. Chesterman & Co., Ltd., Sheffield No. 600: Precision Slide Caliper. 0" - 7". Original Case. Length: 9 Inches. *This English made caliper is in nearly new condition, thanks to its protective case. Ready to be used again.* (FINE) **$45.00**

X4-38. Atkins & Co., Indianapolis, Ind. No. 32: Rare Pulp Wood Gauge. Double Screw Adjust. New Condition, Original Box. Length: 4 Inches. *This tool was apparently used in setting the teeth of a pulp wood saw. Never seen another.* (FINE) **$45.00**

X4-39. Starrett Co., The L.S., Athol, Mass No. 186: Drill and Wire Gauge. Unused Condition. Original Envelope. Length: 5 1/2 Inches. *The original sleeve has kept this wire gauge in new condition. Perfect.* (FINE) **$25.00**

X4-40. B. & J. Mfg. Co., Detroit, Mich.: "Schieber" Beam Compass. For Yard Sticks. New Condition, Original Box. Length: 4 1/2 Inches. *For those of you needing to lay out a shuffleboard court or basketball key for the driveway, we recommend the "Schieber" beam compass for yardsticks. A most unusual collectible tool.*(FINE) **$45.00**

X4-41. Brown & Sharpe Mfg. Co.: Precision Inside Micrometer. Original Case. Near New Condition. Length: 11 Inches. *In an era where precision measurement has become the exclusive province of laser devices, tools such as this inside micrometer have become increasingly collectible. This one is in new condition in its original case. Perfect.* (FINE) **$85.00**

X4-42. Starrett Co., The L.S., Athol, Mass. No. 454: 10" Vernier Height Gauge. With "Tools" Trademark. New Condition, Original Box. Length: 10 Inches. *This vernier adjust height gauge was designed to be mounted on the bench. All of the original attachments are present and in new condition in the original box. An uncommon Starrett tool in top condition.* (FINE) **$225.00**

X4-43. Starrett Co., The L.S., Athol, Mass. No. 122: Precision Vernier Caliper. Original Wood Case. Near New Condition. Length: 15 1/2 Inches. *The original leather covered wooden case has kept this precision vernier caliper in nearly new condition. The original instructions remain. Choice.* (FINE) **$165.00**

X4-44. Starrett Co., L. S., Athol, Mass. No. 45 C: Adjustable Depth Gauge. Extra Long Body. Uncommon Item. Length: 10 Inches. *Starrett's basic, adjustable depth gauge is relatively common. This is the first example in this size that we have seen.* (FINE) **$85.00**

X4-45. Brown & Sharpe Mfg. Co. No. 55: Multiple Size Micrometer. Patented November 6, 1894. Original Wood Case. Length: 11 1/2 Inches. *Through the use of the various spindles, this early patent micrometer could be adjusted to accommodate the precision measurement of a wide range of work. Complete and in excellent condition in the original wooden case.* (FINE) **$165.00**

Group Y4

Y4-1. Dikeman Mfg. Co., The, So. Norwalk: Hollow Handle Tool Handle. Machined Steel Body. 7 Original Blades. Length: 5 Inches. *The Dikeman Company manufactured these in at least three different sizes of which we are aware. A quality product in excellent condition.* (FINE) **$65.00**

Y4-2. Unmarked: Nickel Plated Tool Handle. With 10 Original Tools. Near New Condition. Length: 4 1/2 Inches. *There are no maker marks on this most unusual tool handle which has a knurled lip on the chuck. The tools are stored under the metal cap in individual slots. Condition is nearly new.* (FINE) **$45.00**

Y4-3. Unmarked: Precision Tool Handle. With 10 Original Tools. Very Well Made. Length: 6 Inches. *Similar in many respects to the high grade machined tool handles sold by the Dikeman Tool Company, this well preserved example retains 10 of its original complement of bits.* (FINE) **$45.00**

Y4-4. Hibbard, Spencer & Bartlett Co.: Rosewood Handle. Tool Handle. With 6 Original Bits. "O.V.B." Brand. Length: 7 1/2 Inches. *We have seen a wide range of tool handles, but this is the first we have encountered that is marked with the "O.V.B." (Our Very Best) logo of the Hibbard, Spencer & Bartlett Company. Compete with 6 original tools.* (GOOD+) **$65.00**

Y4-5. Assorted Makers: Group of 4 Screwdrivers. Early Appearance. Flather Bros., Etc. Length: 10 1/2 Inches. *All of these early screwdrivers came from the same collection. An opportunity lot.* (GOOD+) **$35.00**

Y4-6. Millers Falls Company No. 600: Solid Steel Tool Handle. With 8 Original Tools. Excellent Condition. Length: 5 Inches. *A most uncommon example of the only all-steel tool handle manufactured by Millers Falls. This one is marked in a circular pattern around the top of the cap. Chicken Tooth Rare.* (GOOD+) **$185.00**

Y4-7. Millers Falls Company No. 1: Ratchet Screwdriver. 3 Original Blades. Early and Excellent. Length: 9 1/2 Inches. *One of the earliest of ratcheting screwdrivers, this example of the Millers Falls No. 1 is complete in its original box, which retains its cobalt blue paper label with period graphics. Finding these 19th Century screwdrivers in their original boxes in this condition is something that happens very, very seldom. A rare collectible screwdriver from an important early toolmaker.* (GOOD+) **$385.00**

Y4-8. Millers Falls Company: Rosewood Handle Tool Handle. Patented January 14, 1868. Complete and Near New. Length: 7 1/2 Inches. *The Millers Falls Company was a prolific producer of tool handles, but very few are found today in this high level of condition. Nearly all original finishes remain on the tool and the 10 original bits, which show their original tempering marks. A very nice example.* (FINE) **$125.00**

Y4-9. Fray & Co., John S. (?): "Dunham's Cocoanut" Tool Handle. With 6 Original Tools. Advertising Gift? Length: 6 Inches. *The ferrule of this early rosewood tool handle is marked with advertising for "Dunham's Cocoanut". The tool was likely made by the John Fray Company. Six original tools remain with this most unusual advertising tool handle.* (GOOD+) **$95.00**

Y4-10. Aiken: "Aiken's Patent" Tool Handle. 11 Original Tools. With Original Wrench. Length: 5 Inches. *The Aiken firm produced, among other things, wrenches, saw sets and these tool handles, all of which were apparently quite successful. An exceptionally clean example, complete with the wrench for the jaw mechanism in the hollow handle.* (GOOD+) **$55.00**

Y4-11. Unmarked: Combination Hammer and Tool Handle. Mahogany Body. With All Original Tools. Length: 4 1/2 Inches. *The knurled cap screws off of this unusual mahogany handled tool handle to reveal a series of chambers where a range of square shafted tools are held. Most unusual.* (GOOD+) **$85.00**

Y4-12. Peck, Stow & Wilcox Co. No. 50: Rare Small Expansion Auger Bit. 1/2 Inches to 1 1/2 Inches Size. New Condition, Original Box. Length: 7 1/2 Inches. *Much smaller than the adjustable auger bits one normally encounters, this nearly new offering from the Peck, Stow & Wilcox Company is an interesting variation on the adjustable auger bit theme.* (FINE) **$85.00**

Y4-13. Unmarked: Rosewood Handle Tool Handle. Most Unusual Chuck. With 8 Original Tools. Length: 5 1/4 Inches. *Here's a most unusual rosewood handled tool handle with a distinctive chuck mechanism.* (GOOD+) **$125.00**

Y4-14. Kutmaster, Utica, N.Y.: Genuine "Girl Scout" Knife. Excellent Condition. Very Little Used. Length: 3 3/4 Inches. *Among the many things one associates with girls and Girl Scouting, the pocket knife is generally not included. The previous owner of this dandy apparently found it as appealing as snakes and toads. It appears never to have been used.* (FINE) **$25.00**

Y4-15. Armco: "Scroo Grip" Screwdriver. Screw Holding Claws. Ca. 1950's? Length: 10 Inches. *This is our first experience with the "Scroo Grip" driver. Different.* (GOOD+) **$35.00**

Y4-16. Unmarked: Early Patent Tool Handle. Patened August 12, 1884. Cocobolo Handle. Length: 7 Inches. *The early patent date is imprinted on the chuck of this well made tool handle. Nine original tools remain.* (GOOD+) **$45.00**

Y4-17. Fray & Co, C.S., Bridgeport, Ct.: Rosewood Handle Tool Handle. With 7 Original Tools. Excellent Condition. Length: 5 3/4 Inches. *The Fray Company was eventually bought out by Stanley, who assumed manufacture of their line of braces and tool handles. A nice example.* (FINE) **$65.00**

Y4-18. Stanley Rule & Level No. 2: "Excelsior" Tool Handle. Patented March 27, 1867. Excellent Condition. Length: 3 1/2 Inches. *More than 95% of the original japanning remains on this exceptionally clean example of the "Exelsior" tool handle. Complete with 12 original bits. Extra special.* (GOOD+) **$145.00**

Y4-19. Stanley Rule & Level No. 300: Rosewood Tool Handle. 11 Original Tools. " Sweetheart" Trademark Length: 6 Inches. *Nearly all original finishes remain on this rare and complete Stanley tool handle. It is imprinted with the ca. 1920's "Sweetheart" trademark.* (FINE) **$225.00**

Y4-20. Stanley Rule & Level No. 2: "Excelsior" Tool Handle. Patented March 29, 1867. Excellent Condition. Length: 3 1/2 Inches. *A crisp and clean example of Nathan Clement's 1867 patented design, which was marketed extensively by the Stanley Rule & Level Company. A decorative Victorian tool in very well preserved condition.* (GOOD+) **$85.00**

Y4-21. Millers Falls Co. (Unmarked): Rosewood Handle Tool Handle. With Floral Design. Most Unusual. Length: 7 1/2 Inches. *The head of this most unusual tool handle has a brass cap having an embossed Victorian design. Never seen another. Rare.* (GOOD+) **$115.00**

Y4-22. Aiken: "Aiken's Patent" Tool Handle. With All Original Tools. Rare Marked Chuck. Length: 5 Inches. *The Aiken firm produced, among other things, wrenches, saw sets and these tool handles, all of which were apparently quite successful. An exceptionally clean example, complete with the wrench for the jaw mechanism in the hollow handle.* (GOOD+) **$75.00**

Y4-23. Stanley Rule & Level No. 2: "Excelsior" Tool Handle. Patented March 29, 1867. Missing Tools. Length: 3 1/2 Inches. *Someone has lost the tools from this example of the Clement Patent tool handle, but it is otherwise clean and sound.* (GOOD) **$45.00**

Y4-24. Millers Falls Company No. 1: Hollow Handle Tool Handle. Near New Condition. Cocobolo Handle. Length: 6 Inches. *Here's a pristine example of a big-seller from Millers Falls. Complete and excellent.* (FINE) **$55.00**

Y4-25. Holt Mfg. Co. (Unmarked.): Rosewood Handle Tool Handle. With 9 Original Tools. Scarce and Excellent. Length: 5 1/2 Inches. *The Holt Manufacturing Company produced a full line of quality tools, of which this unusual variation is an excellent example. An uncommon type in excellent condition.* (GOOD+) **$45.00**

Y4-26. Stanley Rule & Level No. 306: Maple Handle Tool Handle. With All Original Tools. "Sweetheart" Trademark. Length: 4 1/4 Inches. *This maple handled tool handle dates from the "Sweetheart" era when Stanley briefly offered these tool handles after acquiring the Fray Company.* (GOOD+) **$65.00**

Y4-27. Unmarked: "Arm & Hammer" Tool Handle. Cocobolo Handle. Excellent Condition. Length: 6 1/4 Inches. *This was likely intended to be given away as part of some sort of baking soda promotion. The tools very likely were made for the '"Arm & Hammer" people by the Millers Falls Tool Company.* (GOOD+) **$95.00**

Y4-28. Millers Falls Company No. 5: Mahogany Tool Handle. Original Box. New Condition. Length: 7 1/2 Inches. *Nearly all of the original decal remains on this Millers Falls classic. It is in new condition in its original box. Mint.* (FINE) **$245.00**

Y4-29. Hull Co., L.L., Clinton, Conn., USA: Beechwood Tool Handle. With 11 Original Tools. Solid Brass Chuck. Length: 4 Inches. *Eleven original tools are stored beneath the brass chuck of this Connecticut made tool handle.* (GOOD+) **$55.00**

Y4-30. Stanley Tools No. 8: Long Handled Tool Handle. 2 Original Tips. New Condition, Original Box. Length: 9 Inches. *Three original bits remain with this well preserved multi purpose tool. New in the original box.* (FINE) **$95.00**

Y4-31. Crescent Tool Co., Jamestown, N.Y. No. K101 1/2: Slotted Screwdriver. 1 1/2 Inches Blade. New Condition. Length: 4 Inches. *Crescent's catalogs refer to this diminutive gem as the "Infant" screwdriver. It has never been used.* (FINE) **$45.00**

Y4-32. Irwin: "Perfect Handle" Screwdriver. Square Shank Blade. Brand New Condition. Length: 11 Inches. *The inlaid wood handle style was introduced by the H.D. Smith Company of Plantsville, Connecticut, but was imitated by many others for the simple reason that it was a great idea. This fifty year old example bears the name of the Irwin Auger Bit Company. Brand New.* (FINE) **$35.00**

Y4-33. Buck Bros., Millbury, Mass.: 1 Inch Crank Neck Chisel. Fruitwood Handle. Near New Condition. Length: 14 Inches. *"Crank neck" chisels are so versatile around the shop that finding an adequate supply is a major challenge—no one wants to let go of one. This 1 inch size from Buck Brothers has beveled edges, the original fruitwood handle and is ready to be put immediately to work. Extra nice.* (FINE) **$95.00**

Y4-34. Millers Falls Company No. 1405: Heavy Duty Awl. Black Painted Handle. Unused Condition. Length: 7 Inches. *This hardwood handle awl from the Millers Falls Company is in brand new condition. A very nice example.* (FINE) **$15.00**

Y4-35. Unmarked: Bronze File Handle. Decorative Pattern. Beehive Design. Length: 4 1/4 Inches. *This cast bronze file handle looks almost too good to use. A showy tool handle from bygone days.* (GOOD+) **$35.00**

Y4-36. Jennings & Co., C.E., New York, N.Y. No. 71: Patent Adjustable Auger Bit. Patented October 3, 1911. New Condition, Original Box. Length: 10 1/2 Inches. *If you are one of the many who have taken to collecting these seemingly infinitely variable and mechanically interesting tools, then you will surely need an example from the C.E. Jennings Company. This one is in new condition in its original box.* (FINE) **$45.00**

Y4-37. Marples & Co., William, Sheffield: Set of Plow Plane Cutting Iron. With "Shamrock" Trademark. Extra Crisp and Clean. Length: 9 Inches. *An excellent set of Marples high-grade irons in perfect shape.* (FINE) **$135.00**

Y4-38. Unmarked: Beech Handle Tool Handle. With 9 Original Tools. Unused Condition. Length: 6 Inches. *Combination tools were present in nearly every home and in many workshops. This unmarked beech handle version apparently was not to be found when it was needed. It is in nearly new condition.* (FINE) **$25.00**

Y4-39. Stanley Rule & Level (Unmarked): Clement's Patent Tool Handle. Patented March 19, 1867. Rare Boxwood Handle. Length: 4 Inches. *Stanley's "Excelsior" tool handle in decorative cast iron employs the same patent as does this boxwood handled version, which was also listed in early Stanley catalogs. Six original bits remain with this rare Stanley tool handle.* (GOOD+) **$145.00**

Y4-40. Bridgeport H.M. Corp., Bridgeport: Cocobolo Handle Tool Handle. With All Original Tools. Unused Condition. Length: 7 Inches. *The Bridgeport Hardware Company was one of the survivors in the competition for the tool handle dollar. They apparently stayed until the tool handle dollar disappeared. Extra nice.* (FINE) **$65.00**

Y4-41. Aiken: "Aiken's Patent" Tool Handle. With All Original Tools. Excellent Condition. Length: 5 Inches. *The Aiken firm produced, among other things, wrenches, saw sets and these tool handles, all of which were apparently quite successful. An exceptionally clean example, complete with the wrench for the jaw mechanism in the hollow handle and twenty original bits.* (FINE) **$75.00**

Y4-42. Holt Co., The G.L., Hartford, Conn.: Multi Purpose Tool Handle. With Cavity Handle. Extra Narrow Type. Length: 5 1/4 Inches. *The handle of this uncommon Holt tool handle has been hollowed out to hold the bits. A steel cap can easily be removed to obtain the proper bit.* (GOOD+) **$55.00**

Y4-43. Millers Falls Company: Cocobolo Handle Tool Handle. With 9 Original Tools. Near New Condition. Length: 6 1/2 Inches. *The Millers Falls Company was a prolific producer of tool handles, but very few are found today in this high level of condition. Nearly all original finishes remain on the tool and the 10 original bits, which show their original tempering marks. A very nice example.* (FINE) **$75.00**

Y4-44. North Bros Mfg. Co., Philadelphia No. 95: "Yankee" Slotted Screwdriver. 1 1/2 Inches Blade. Unused Condition. Length: 4 Inches. *This early "Yankee" screwdriver is in brand new condition. A nice example of a very well made screwdriver.* (FINE) **$45.00**

Y4-45. Millers Falls Company No. 1: Hollow Handle Tool Handle. Near New Condition. Original Decal. Length: 6 Inches. *The full complement of 8 original bits are included with this classic cocobolo tool handle from Millers Falls. Much of the original M.F. decal remains on the handle. Extra nice.* (FINE) **$75.00**

Group Z4

Z4-1. Unmarked: Pair Of Handled Tounge and Groove Molding Planes. Owner "A. Heise". Near New Condition. Length: 14 3/4 Inches. *The owner's name "A. Heise" which has been stamped on each of these planes is the only mark to be found. These classic handled tongue and groove planes are in nearly new condition. Choice.* (FINE) **$145.00**

Z4-2. Preston & Sons, Edward: Miniature Beech Router Plane. Original Iron. Extra Crisp and Clean. Length: 4 Inches. *Boldly imprinted with the classic Preston logo, this miniature router has been preserved in much the same condition as it was when new. A rare plane in top condition.* (FINE) **$125.00**

Z4-3. Stevens, J., Boston, Mass.: Quirk Ovolo and Bevel Molding Plane. Nicely Boxed. Marked "3/8". Length: 9 1/2 Inches. *James Stevens made planes in Boston between 1822 and 1860. This well preserved molder has a steeper than usual cut. Nice.* (GOOD+) **$165.00**

Z4-4. Unmarked: Classic "Fielding" Plane. Yellow Birch Body. Superb Condition. Length: 14 1/2 Inches. *This classic "fielding" or panel raising plane of native Yellow Birch is in great working order and ready to be put back to use. A classic.* (FINE) **$345.00**

Z4-5. Mutter, George, (London): Full Boxed Bead Molding Plane. 1/2 Inch Size. Ready To Use. Length: 9 1/2 Inches. *George Mutter, who was the successor to the planemaking enterprise of William Madox, made planes from 1766 to 1799 at various working locations in London. This fully-boxed bead is an excellent, ready-to-use example of his work.* (GOOD+) **$55.00**

Z4-6. Assorted Makers: Group of 8 Tounge and Groove Molding Planes. Barton, Stewart. Hendrickson, Ohio. Length: 9 1/2 Inches. *Here's an opportunity lot of 8 assorted tongue and groove planes. Represented makers include Barton, Stewart, the Ohio Tool Company and more. A bargain.* (GOOD) **$115.00**

Z4-7. Mathieson & Son, A., Glasgow No. 17: Fully Boxed Sash and Moving Filletster Plane. Boxwood Wedges. Extra Crisp and Clean. Length: 9 Inches. *This extraordinary combination moving filletster and sash filletster from Scottish maker A. Mathieson is fitted with a dovetailed sole of Turkish Boxwood. The brass tips retain their original lacquer and the plane is in excellent overall condition. A showstopper.* (GOOD+) **$365.00**

Z4-8. Hoey, R., New York, N.Y.: Quirk Ovolo, Bead Molding Plane. Ca. 1834-1836 Only. Uncommon Profile. Length: 9 1/2 Inches. *Robert Hoey's planemaking business lasted from 1834 to 1836. This complex molder of uncommon cut has outlasted him by far. A good one.* (GOOD) **$145.00**

Z4-9. Unmarked: Early Complex Molding Plane. Cove Quirk Ogee. Most Unusual Profile. Length: 9 1/2 Inches. *With molding plane profiles, it's the "something extra" that separates the good planes from the great ones. This one has it.* (GOOD+) **$225.00**

Z4-10. Dunham & Mc Master\Auburn, N.Y.: Fixed Sash Molding Plane. Ca. 1821-1825. AWP III: "B" Imprint. Length: 9 1/2 Inches. *S.C. Dunham and T.J. McMaster were the first American planemakers to produce wooden planes using prison convict labor. Their working dates were from 1821 to 1825. An uncommon and historically significant molding plane.* (GOOD) **$75.00**

Z4-11. Odell, Charles, Salem, Mass.: Skew Rabbet Molding Plane. Side Boxed. AWP III: 3 Stars. Length: 10 1/2 Inches. *Side boxing adds to the appeal of this perfectly preserved skew blade rabbet plane. Odell worked in Salem, Massachusetts from 1869 to 1876. Highly recommended.* (FINE) **$85.00**

Z4-12. Ohio Tool Co. (Unmarked) No. 139 3/4: Double Door Molding Plane. With Boxwood Arms. Extra Crisp and Clean. Length: 9 1/2 Inches. *Only the manufacturers number, which corresponds to the numbering scheme used by the Ohio Tool Company, is imprinted on this well preserved double door plane. Well preserved boxwood arms and nuts are an indication that this plane was made to be very special. It still is.* (FINE) **$245.00**

Z4-13. Copeland, M., Warranted: Steep Quirk Ogee Molding Plane. Marked 5/8 Inch. Uncommon Profile. Length: 9 1/2 Inches. *Here's an extra-steep ogee molder with a bold Copeland mark. A nice clean plane.* (GOOD+) **$145.00**

Z4-14. Stothert, Bath (England): Quirk Ovolo, Astragal Molding Plane. Marked "4/8". Ca. 1784-1841. Length: 9 1/2 Inches. *A steep and crisp complex molder from England that has developed a dark brown patina from having been oiled over the years. A nice plane.* (GOOD+) **$125.00**

Z4-15. Weifs, J.: Continental Round Molding Plane. Austrian? Decorative Form. Length: 10 1/2 Inches. *We have little documentation regarding the planemakers of the European continent, and it may well be that little such documentation exists. This classic round of sculptural form is imprinted with the maker name "J. Weifs".* (GOOD+) **$35.00**

Z4-16. Mathieson & Son, A., Glasgow: Set of 8 Boxed Bead Molding Planes. Nicely Boxed. Ready To Use. Length: 9 1/2 Inches. *Here's a great working set of boxed beads bearing the imprint of respected Scottish maker Alexander Mathieson. Crisp, clean and ready to use. A nice set.* (GOOD+) **$445.00**

Z4-17. Greenslade, W., Bristol (England): Ogee, Bevel/Bead Molding Plane. 3 Inch Width. Most Unusual Profile. Length: 9 1/2 Inches. *This extra-wide English molder has that extra element of variation that makes for a truly great molding plane. A nut brown patina of age adds to its appeal. Choice.* (GOOD+) **$255.00**

Z4-18. Parry, 325 Old Street (London): Center Fluting Molding Plane. Double Boxed. Elaborate Profile. Length: 9 1/2 Inches. *For the latter day woodworker, planes such as this one offer exceptional utility and the opportunity to incorporate an element of personal style in woodworking that modern methods will not abide. Crisp, clean and nicely boxed. A great plane.* (GOOD+) **$145.00**

Z4-19. Sanborn, D.P., Littleton, N.H.: 3/4 Inch Dado Molding Plane. Crisp and Clean. Undocumented Imprint. Length: 9 1/2 Inches. *Only a small chip from the head of the wedge deserves mention as an apology for this otherwise excellent dado plane in the desirable 3/4 inch size. Nice.* (GOOD+) **$85.00**

Z4-20. Hills & Wolcott, Amherst, Mass.: Quirk Ovolo and Bevel Molding Plane. Extra Steep Profile. Marked 6/8 Inch. Length: 9 1/2 Inches. *A crisp and steep complex molder from an obscure Connecticut Valley planemaking partnership that lasted for but one year, 1829. A great plane with a very rare mark.* (GOOD+) **$225.00**

Z4-21. Carter, C., Syracuse, N. Y.: 3/8 Inch Dado Molding Plane. With Brass Depth Stop. AWP III: 4 Stars. Length: 9 1/2 Inches. *Syracuse maker C. Carter had previously worked in Utica, New York and later was a toolmaker in the Auburn Tool Company shops in Auburn Prison. Planes with this imprint are extremely rare, receiving the four star rating from The Pollaks in their essential reference American Wooden Planes. This 3/8 inch dado is marked with the Syracuse imprint and is in excellent working order.* (GOOD+) **$115.00**

Z4-22. Unmarked: Early Yellow Birch Molding Plane. Relieved Wedge. Reverse Ogee Profile. Length: 10 Inches. *This classic 18th Century reverse ogee molder is fitted with a Jo Fuller type wedge and is in excellent working order. The 10 inch length indicates very early manufacture.* (GOOD+) **$85.00**

Z4-23. Reed, Utica N.Y.: Handle Sash Molding Plane. Uncommon Type. Extra Crisp and Clean. Length: 15 Inches. *This fixed size handled sash molder is boldly struck with the imprint of Utica, New York planemaker John Reed. Extra special.* (FINE) **$275.00**

Z4-24. Lindenberger, I.: Early Bead Molding Plane. Yellow Birch Body. Marked "3/4". Length: 9 Inches. *A characteristically boldly struck imprint adds character to this 3/4 inch bead of native Yellow Birch. A classic Eighteenth Century plane.* (GOOD+) **$155.00**

Z4-25. Green, John: Reverse Ogee Molding Plane. Marked 3/8. Ready To Use. Length: 9 1/2 Inches. *A prominent and prolific planemaker in the city of York, England, John Green produced a wide range of molding planes, including this classic reverse ogee. A striking molding plane in excellent working condition.* (GOOD+) **$55.00**

Z4-26. Greenfield Tool Co., Greenfield, Mass. No. 378: Pair of 2 Inch Hollow and Round Molding Planes. Marked "24". Extra Large Size. Length: 9 1/2 Inches. *Here's an excellent working pair of hollow and round planes in the desirable No. 24 size. Ready to use.* (GOOD+) **$95.00**

Z4-27. Taber, John M., New Bedford, Mass.: Rare Flooring Raglet Molding Plane. Scottish Type. Rare American Mark. Length: 7 1/4 Inches. *Considered rare in Scotland, where the form originated, this plane is the only known example of the Scottish flooring raglet plane by an American maker. It is clearly marked with the imprint of New Bedford maker John M. Taber. Designed to cut a groove along the edge of a room for inserting a kickboard, the visually-appealing plane of diminutive size features an offset handle fitted to the side in a sculptural fashion. One of a kind.* (GOOD+) **$795.00**

Z4-28. Hunt & Wiseman, St. Louis, Missouri: Bevel, Reverse Ogee Molding Plane. Rare Double Iron. Near New Condition. Length: 9 1/2 Inches. *Double iron molding planes with American maker marks are extremely rare. Finding such a plane bearing the imprint of a pre-Civil War St. Louis, Missouri maker is an occasion for celebration. A superb quality complex molding plane. Highly recommended.* (FINE) **$375.00**

Z4-29. Brown, J.T., (Baltimore): Wedge Lock Sash Molding Plane. AWP III: 3 Stars. Ca. 1825. Length: 9 1/2 Inches. *Here's an early wedge lock sash molder from an uncommon early Baltimore maker. A good one.* (GOOD) **$95.00**

Z4-30. Dwights & French: Set of Plow Plane Irons. Full Set of Eight. Ready to Use. Length: 8 1/4 Inches. *Here's a full set of American-made plow plane irons. Seldom seen.* (GOOD) **$95.00**

Z4-31. Bensen & Crannell, Albany, N.Y.: Adjustable Sash Molding Plane. Diamond Side Plates. Essentially Unused. Length: 9 1/2 Inches. *Nearly all of the original finishes remain on this perfectly preserved sash molding plane from a prominent Albany, New York planemaking partnership. Mint.* (FINE) **$225.00**

Z4-32. Mathieson & Son, A., Glasgow No. 99: Steep Quirk Ogee and Bevel Molding Plane. Scottish Double Iron. Crisp and Clean. Length: 9 1/2 Inches. *This classic double iron Scottish molder has been boldly struck with the imprint of Scotland's largest toolmaker, A. Mathieson & Son of Glasgow. A crisp, clean molder from a quality maker.* (GOOD+) **$165.00**

Z4-33. Wetherell, H., Chatham: Cabinet Ogee Molding Plane. With "Cartouche". Early and Excellent. Length: 9 1/2 Inches. *This classic complex molder from Massachusetts maker H. Wetherell is imprinted with the distinctive "cartouche" device used on his planes. A nice molding cut on a clean early plane.* (GOOD+) **$185.00**

Z4-34. Melhuish, Fetter Lane (London): Wedge Arm Plow Plane. With Brass Depth Stop. Ready to Use. Length: 8 Inches. *A gracefully arched skate adds to the appeal of this very well preserved wedge arm plow plane from a prominent London maker. A pretty plane in excellent working order. Nice.* (GOOD+) **$110.00**

Z4-35. Way, William, New York: Pair of Handled Tounge and Groove Planes. Ca. 1848 Only. APW III: 2 Stars. Length: 14 Inches. *The fence on the tongue plane of this set is a later replacement, but the planes are otherwise in excellent condition and clearly marked with the imprint of New York City maker William Way. A nice set.* (GOOD+) **$85.00**

Z4-36. Ward, William, 8th Ave., N.Y.: Coachmaker's "T" Molding Plane. Bull Boxwood Sole. Dovetailed Joint. Length: 6 1/2 Inches. *This "T" bottom coachmaker's rabbet bears the imprint of a most desirable New York City planemaker and has a full boxwood sole that is fitted to the body of the plane with a prominent dovetail joint. Clean, most uncommon and visually appealing.* (GOOD+) **$195.00**

Z4-37. Smith, A., Rehoboth, Mass.: Skew Rabbet Molding Plane. Bold Imprint. Great Patina. Length: 9 1/2 Inches. *Someone has removed the nickers from this boldly marked rabbet plane that bears the unmistakable logo of Aaron Smith of Rehoboth, Massachusetts.* (GOOD+) **$135.00**

Z4-38. King & Co., Hull (England): Classic Chamfer Plane. With Depth Stop. Extra Crisp and Clean. Length: 7 Inches. *Brass fittings protect the side of this classic chamfer plane from the screws that regulate the travel of the stop wedge. It is in excellent condition and ready to use.* (GOOD+) **$95.00**

Z4-39. Hills, H., Springfield, Mass.: Classic Bilection Molding Planes. Marked "6/8". Extra Crisp and Clean. Length: 9 1/2 Inches. *This classic "bilection" molder, or bead and cove, is in very nice working order. A good one.* (GOOD+) **$195.00**

Z4-40. Malloch, D., Perth (Scotland): Boxed Bead Molding Plane. Marked "1/4". Appears Unused. Length: 9 1/2 Inches. *Bead planes, especially the narrower widths, have a tendency to wear away their boxing, making them no longer usable. This 1/4 inch bead is in excellent condition and ready to provide years of service.* (FINE) **$35.00**

Z4-41. Tolman, J.R., Hanover, Mass.: Group Of 13 Bead Molding Planes. Fully Boxed. Rare and Excellent. Length: 9 1/2 Inches. *This extraordinary set of fully boxed bead planes was assembled by a collector from the Pacific Northwest. All are marked with the imprint of planemaker J.R. Tolman, who specialized in tools for shipwrights. There are a few duplicates, but this is essentially a full set of fully boxed beads from a very rare and desirable maker. A great set.* (GOOD+) **$695.00**

Z4-42. Jones, J.T., Philadelphia, Penna: Quirk Ovolo With Bead Molding Plane. Double Lignum Boxing. B2 Mark With Stars. Length: 9 1/2 Inches. *Here's an extra-complex profile with prominent dark lignum vitae or rosewood boxing. A gentle cleaning should make this one shine. A nice plane.* (GOOD+) **$285.00**

Z4-43. Bensen, D., Albany, N.Y.: Boxed Astragal Molding Plane. Marked "3/4". Ca. 1827-1850. Length: 9 1/2 Inches. *Boxed astragal molders in any condition are difficult to find. Finding one in this condition is rare indeed. A great working plane in top condition.* (FINE) **$95.00**

Z4-44. Marley: N.Y.: Special Purpose Bead Molding Plane. Extra Deep Profile. Most Unusual. Length: 9 1/2 Inches. *This most unusual molder from New York City maker Luke Marley features an extended strip of boxing, adjacent to which is a cutter that would cut a deep groove. A most unusual plane in excellent condition.* (GOOD+) **$115.00**

Z4-45. Sandusky Tool Co., Sandusky, Ohio No. 92: Set of 18 Hollow and Round Molding Planes. Sizes 1 to 9. Early Sandusky Imprint. Length: 9 1/2 Inches. *This ready to use set of 9 pairs of hollow and round molding planes are imprinted with the designations 1 through 9 on the heel of each plane. One plane is fitted with a wedge that lacks the distinctive relief of the Sandusky style, but otherwise fits perfectly and one of the round planes has a slightly steeper than normal concavity, most likely owing to honest use. An excellent and ready to use set of American-made hollow and round molding planes.* (GOOD+) **$785.00**

Group A5

A5-1. Sears, Roebuck & Co., Chicago: "Dunlap" Brand Valve Grinder. Original Decal. New Condition, Original Box. Length: 7 Inches. *Here's a never need to upgrade addition to a growing collection of valve grinding tools.* (GOOD+) **$45.00**

A5-2. K.D. Mfg. Co., Lancaster, Penn.: "Kay Dee" Valve Spring Compressor. Patented November 23, 1920. Marked "Special". Length: 6 Inches. *The early days of motoring brought this patented valve spring compressor to the market. Automobile enthusiasts know that this tool inspired as many stupid inventions as any other. There is something about needing to improvise in automotive maintenance that spurs the inventive spirit. Clean and clearly marked.* (GOOD+) **$55.00**

A5-3. Nash No. 2: Open End Auto Wrench. For Nash Car. Uncommon Type. Length: 5 1/2 Inches. *All of Stanley's threads on their line of planes were non-standard. Perhaps the Nash automobile people had a similar trick and used only prime number sizes for their fasteners. I haven't measured, but this may be a 13/53". Fill out your set.* (GOOD+) **$35.00**

A5-4. Nash No. 1: Open End Auto Wrench. For Nash Car. Uncommon Size. Length: 5 1/2 Inches. *Don't try using a standard open end wrench on your Nash automobile. They will not work, or at least that seems to have been the idea behind providing wrenches with the car. Whatever the case, we have been left with a hot collectible. A rare automotive wrench.* (GOOD+) **$45.00**

A5-5. Ford Motor Co., Dearborn, Mich.: "Fordson" Factory Tool Check. Used In Factory. With Worker ID. Length: 1 1/2 Inches. *The use of specialized tools from the Fordson Tractor plane required that you provide the keeper of the "tool cage" with one of these checks, which were marked with your ID number. If you didn't bring the tool back, they knew where to find you. Fordson ceased United States operations in 1926. A rare tool and tractor collectible.* (FINE) **$15.00**

A5-6. Nash No. 2: Open End Auto Wrench. For Nash Car. Uncommon Type. Length: 5 1/2 Inches. *All of Stanley's threads on their line of planes were non-standard. Perhaps the Nash automobile people had a similar trick and used only prime number sizes for their fasteners. I haven't measured, but this may be a 13/53". Fill out your set.* (GOOD+) **$35.00**

A5-7. Maxwell No. 2: Maxwell Automotive Wrench. Double Open End. 5 Inch Size. Length: 5 Inches. *Don't blame me if you're out driving your Maxwell automobile tomorrow and it blows a head gasket. You'll need one of these to get it going again. Tomorrow may be too late.* (GOOD) **$45.00**

A5-8. Rowe, L.L., Boston, Mass.: Special Purpose Crimper. Patented December 21, 1885. For Metalwork? Length: 10 Inches. *This patented crimping device was likely used for fitting pieces of stovepipe. An unusual special purpose patented tool.* (GOOD+) **$125.00**

A5-9. Unmarked: Set of Cast Iron Wrenches. 98% Original Paint. With Driver Device. Length: 6 Inches. *These cast iron "socket" wrenches come complete with their own auger handle type driver, or they can be used in a brace. An interesting set.* (FINE) **$65.00**

A5-10. Keystone Mfg. Co., Buffalo, N.Y.: No. 1: Patent Ratchet Wrench. Patented November 6, 1883. New Condition, Original Box. Length: 9 1/2 Inches. *One of the earliest attempts at producing a practical ratchet wrench, the "Keystone" patent of 1883 employed adjustable jaws, rather than the interchangeable sockets that were to become the standard. A number of original attachments are included. Clean, clearly marked and and in the original box.* (FINE) **$395.00**

A5-11. Tadwell, R., Boston, Mass.: Early Soldering Iron. With Copper Tip. Distinctive Form. Length: 11 3/4 Inches. *A wedge shaped copper tip on the end of this specialty soldering iron was designed to fit into tight places by pivoting on the end of the handle. A graphic and unusual soldering iron.* (GOOD) **$15.00**

A5-12. Goodell-Pratt Company: Special Purpose Scraper. Imprinted Name. Near New Condition. Length: 6 Inches. *Finding "one of each" of the diverse Goodell Pratt line can be a challenge. This specialty scraper is in new condition.* (FINE) **$15.00**

A5-13. Borden Tool Co., Warren, Ohio: Combination Pipe Reamer and Cutter. "Beaver" Brand. Most Unusual. Length: 6 Inches. *This specialty tool combines a reamer and pipe cutter in the same device. Leave it to Beaver.* (GOOD+) **$55.00**

A5-14. Mossberg Co., Frank, Attleboro, Mass.: Pair of Early "Ford" Wrenches. 5-Z-828 and 3z-2034. Ratchet Adjust. Length: 8 Inches. *Both of these early fixed size ratchet wrenches are imprinted with the "Ford" logo. They were probably sold to dealers rather than provided with cars.* (GOOD+) **$65.00**

A5-15. Marvel, Cleveland, Ohio: "Marvel" Brand Valve Grinder. "Patent Pending". Uncommon Type. Length: 4 1/2 Inches. *We really can't figure out how to hold this thing while it is being used, which may account for its rarity: nobody else could either. Rare.* (GOOD) **$45.00**

A5-16. Boston Brass, Waltham, Mass.: Cast Bronze Die Stock. With 3/4 Inch Die. Graphic Form. Length: 14 Inches. *This solid bronze die stock accepts a variety of dies. This maker is new to us. Different.* (FINE) **$65.00**

A5-17. May, Atlanta, Georgia: May's Cotter Pin Puller. Patented March, 1912. Rare and Excellent. Length: 6 Inches. *Anyone who has ever had to remove a bent and rusted cotter pin whilst contorted into some inhuman position in the absence of adequate light and heat will appreciate the genius of this one. You just grab the loop, squeeze and you're done.* (GOOD+) **$45.00**

A5-18. Unmarked: Wagon Spring Grease Tool. Original Nickel Plating. Scarce and Excellent. Length: 5 Inches. *One of the most frequently submitted "whatsit" items, this wagon spring greaser is in excellent condition.* (GOOD+) **$25.00**

A5-19. Goodell-Pratt Company No. 747: Rack and Pinion Valve Grinder. Excellent Condition. Rare and Fine. Length: 12 Inches. *There seems to be no end to the different designs that were applied to facilitate the tedious task of grinding valves for early automobile engines. This oscillating version from the Goodell-Pratt Company incorporates the extraordinarily high standard of craftsmanship that was the stock in trade of that underrated company. An excellent example of an increasingly collectible category of tools.* (FINE) **$275.00**

A5-20. Buffum Tool Co., Louisiana, Missouri: Cast Iron Gear Puller. With "Swastika" Mark. Ca. 1930's. Length: 6 Inches. *The story of how the Buffum Tool Company came to adopt this "Indian Good Luck" symbol in the 1930's only to have it preempted by a bunch of leiderhosen wearing, mustachioed, seig heiling, book burning and goose stepping pretenders from the Rhine valley has been recounted too many times to repeat it here. As loyal Americans, the symbol was quickly dropped. We have no information about the success of the replacement logo, which employed two tools, a hammer and a sickle, arranged on a red background. A most unusual gear puller.* (GOOD+) **$185.00**

A5-21. Adamson Mfg. Co., E. Pales. Ohio: Patent Vulcanizer. Patented April 1, 1913. Original Box and Papers. Length: 7 Inches. *If you have a mind to remake your office or living room and choose as the theme a 1920's era gas station, this patented vulcanizing tool in new condition will help contribute to the overall effect. An early and unusual automotive tool.* (GOOD+) **$15.00**

A5-22. Bernz Co., Otto, Rochester, N.Y.: Solid Brass Blowtorch. Bakelite Adjustment. Original Decal. Length: 9 1/2 Inches. *All of the original decal remains on this very little used oval shaped blowtorch. Nice.* (GOOD+) **$85.00**

A5-23. Buffum Tool Co., Louisiana, Missouri: Cast Iron Gear Puller. With "Swastika" Mark. Ca. 1930's. Length: 6 Inches. *The Buffum Tool Company apparently offered a wide range of tools. This is the first example of a gear puller imprinted with their logo of which we are aware. Rare.* (GOOD) **$165.00**

A5-24. Schild Mfg. Co., Milwaukee, Wisc.: Special Purpose Cutter. With Hammer Driver. For Metal Ripping? Length: 10 Inches. *This specialized tool looks to have been designed for cutting sheet metal by hitting it with a hammer.* (GOOD+) **$25.00**

A5-25. Unmarked: Massive Chain Drill. Ratchet Mechanism. Most Unusual Type. Length: 16 1/2 Inches. *This oversize chain drill is unlike any example of the genius that we have encountered. It is unmarked with any maker name. Different.* (GOOD+) **$165.00**

A5-26. Atwood, Geo. F., Brockton, Mass. No. 190: Automotive Mud Guard Cleaner. Full Nickel Plating. New Condition, Original Box. Length: 9 1/2 Inches. *There may have been more ludicrously specialized tools offered, but this "Mud Guard Cleaner" ranks in the upper echelon of those devices on style alone. Fully nickel plated and fitted with a brass hose junction, it appears that the original owner found no compelling reason to gear up and clean his mud guards. New and in the original box. A great automotive tool collectible.* (FINE) **$145.00**

A5-27. Millers Falls Company No. 238: Universal Valve Grinder. Cast Iron Body. 98% Original Paint. Length: 12 1/2 Inches. *Looking not unlike an egg beater, this tool was used to grind automobile engine valves in the early days of motoring. A nice example.* (GOOD+) **$65.00**

A5-28. North Bros. Mfg. Co., Philadelphia, Penna. No. 500: "Yankee" Brand Chain Drill. 3 Jaw Chuck. Near New Condition. Length: 10 Inches. *As was the case with all of North Brothers' "Yankee" line, this chain drill is of the highest quality. It has been very little used.* (FINE) **$55.00**

A5-29. Flexible Carbon Scraper Co., Los Angeles, Calif.: Patent Carbon Scraper. Patented March 28, 1916. Unusual California Tool. Length: 11 1/2 Inches. *A series of spring wires are the genius behind this unusual California patented tool. Never seen another.* (GOOD+) **$35.00**

A5-30. Maxwell No. 1/2/3/4: Set of Open End Auto Wrench. Full Working Set. Superb Condition. Length: 9 Inches. *Those of you who have great-grandpa's Maxwell automobile under a piece of canvas in the barn will want this full set of original equipment wrenches to go with it. The only full set I've ever seen. Apparently unused.* (GOOD+) **$110.00**

A5-31. Unmarked: Patent Leaf Spring Separator. Patented June 8, 1915. Near New Condition. Length: 5 1/2 Inches. *Whether for the springs of buggies or the newer, "horseless" carriages, these separated the leaf springs to facilitate the insertion of grease. Condition is as new.* (FINE) **$45.00**

A5-32. Heller Bros. Co., Newark, N.J.: Auto Body Work Hammer. Uncommon Type. Original Handle. Length: 12 Inches. *This Heller Brothers tool needed to be substantial enough to hammer the fenders of 1920's and 1930's era cars back into shape. It was. A well made hammer.* (GOOD+) **$15.00**

A5-33. Radio Lectric No. 480: "Radio Lectric" Wrench. With Interchangeable Sockets. New Condition Original Box. Length: 6 1/2 Inches. *An interesting special purpose radio wrench in its original box.* (FINE) **$35.00**

A5-34. Ford Motor Co., Dearborn, Mich.: Set of C.E. Johansso Gage Blocks. In Fitted Case. With Ford Logo. Length: 8 Inches. *The Johansson gauge blocks have been kept in nearly new condition by their protective wooden case. All are imprinted with the Ford Motor Company logo.* (FINE) **$195.00**

A5-35. Wakefield Wrench Co. No. 17: Adjustable Nut Wrench. "Indian Motorcycles". Uncommon Type. Length: 7 Inches. *This "Indian Motorcycle" wrench is in excellent condition and, no, it doesn't have a tattoo on the back.* (GOOD+) **$115.00**

A5-36. Millers Falls Company No. 718: Automatic Feed Chain Drill. For Cast Pipe. New Condition, Original Box. Length: 8 1/2 Inches. *A number of makers offered these "chain" drills, which could be incrementally tightened as the bit dug into the post or cast iron pipe on which it was being used. This example is in new condition in its original box.* (FINE) **$55.00**

A5-37. Goodell-Pratt Company No. 740: Hardwood Handle Bearing Scrapers. Original Leather Case. Very Little Used. Length: 10 Inches. *The original leather pouch has kept these special purpose bearing scrapers in new condition. A great set in new condition.* (FINE) **$135.00**

A5-38. Vlchek Tool Co., The: "Four Edge" Bearing Scraper. With Leather Cap. New Condition Original Box. Length: 16 Inches. *A leather cover protects the working edges of this uncommon bearing scraper. It has never been used.* (FINE) **$95.00**

A5-39. Unmarked No. 3: "Todd Patent" Nippers. For Metal Work? Replaceable Jaws. Length: 10 Inches. *The genius embodied in the "Todd Patent" nippers seems to have been their replaceable tips. Different.* (FINE) **$35.00**

A5-40. Tobrin Tool Co., Plantsville, Conn.: "Perfect Handle" Type. Tire Tool? Successor to Smith? Extra Wide Body. Length: 13 Inches. *We have seen screwdrivers with the "Perfect Handle" handle style, but this flat, wide tool is totally new to us. The fact that Tobrin was located in Plantsville, Connecticut where the H.D. Smith Company began the "Perfect Handle" line is reason to suspect that Tobrin took over at least part of the business from Smith. A rare "Perfect Handle" tool.* (GOOD) **$125.00**

A5-41. Bridgeport Hardware Mfg. Co., The: Early Patent Valve Spring Compressor. Patented January 11, 1927. With Ratchet Device. Length: 7 Inches. *There seems to be no end to the different forms that a valve spring compressor can assume. This one is in fine working order and clearly marked.* (FINE) **$55.00**

A5-42. W.W. Co., Brooklyn, N.Y.: Patent Valve Spring Compressor. Patented October 4, 1921. Early and Excellent. Length: 8 1/2 Inches. *The collecting of valve spring compressors shows promise as a potential area for collectors. The first cousins of Rube Goldberg were quite active in this area. Here's one I've never seen before.* (FINE) **$85.00**

A5-43. Vlchek Tool Co., The: "The Auto" Hammer. With Pry Bar. Uncommon Type. Length: 10 Inches. *This company made automotive tools of very high quality for a brief period in the 1920's and 1930's. I believe they were located in Cleveland, Ohio.* (GOOD+) **$55.00**

A5-44. Millers Falls Company No. 238: Universal Valve Grinder. Cast Iron Body. New Condition, Original Box. Length: 12 1/2 Inches. *The original box has kept this Millers Falls valve grinder in nearly new condition. Nearly all of the original decal remains on this perfectly preserved example of a Millers Falls tool that didn't last long in the product line.* (GOOD+) **$145.00**

A5-45. Unmarked: Early Brass Blowtorch. Oval Body. Uncommon Type. Length: 9 Inches. *We have it on good authority that the oval shaped body of this brass blowtorch is an important departure from the norm. A graphic torch of a collectible configuration.* (GOOD+) **$225.00**

Group B5

B5-1. Stanley Rule & Level No. 644: Victor Zig Zag Folding Rule. 4 Foot Length, 4 Inch Section. Sweetheart Trademark. Length: 48 Inches. *Stanley's Zig-Zag rules attracted little interest early on, and were not addressed in Phil Stanley's classic Boxwood & Ivory: Stanley Traditional Rules, 1855-1975. By the time of the publication of the Stanley Value Guide these rules were covered in detail. At four feet in length, the No. 644 was the longest size offered in the rare and short-lived 4 inch section zig zag series offered by Stanley.* (GOOD+) **$225.00**

B5-2. Lufkin Rule Co., The, Saginaw, Mich.: No. 172: 6 Inch, Two Fold Folding Rule. Similar to Stanley's 13 1/2. Uncommon Type. Length: 6 Inches. *In their zeal to match Stanley number for number in the rule competition, Lufkin began making some rules at about the same time that Stanley was ceasing production. This Lufkin equivalent of the Stanley No. 13 1/2 is one example.* (GOOD+) **$95.00**

B5-3. Master Rule Mfg. Co. No. X-4: Rare 2 Foot "Interlox" Folding Rule. Sliding Zig Zag. Scarce and Excellent. Length: 24 Inches. *The "Interlox" rule features a sliding adjustment that is handy for inside measurements. This well preserved example has only is in the seldom seen 2 foot configuration. Rare.* (GOOD+) **$65.00**

B5-4. Stanley Rule & Level No. 32: One-Foot, Four-Fold Folding Rule. Arch-Joint, Unbound. Ca. 1900 Trademark. Length: 12 Inches. *Nearly every carpenter kept a rule such as this in his (or her, if you insist) vest pocket. This one is marked with the Stanley trademark in use at the very beginning of the Twentieth Century.* (FINE) **$45.00**

B5-5. Lufkin Rule Co., The, Saginaw, Mich.: No. 1176: 6 Foot Zig-Zag Folding Rule. Large Black Numbers. New Condition, Original Box. Length: 72 Inches. *This 6 foot folding steel rule is in unused condition in its original box. Extra special.* (FINE) **$95.00**

B5-6. Starrett Co., L. S., Athol, Mass. No. 451: Steel "Zig Zag" Folding Rule. Patented March 14, 1911. Scarce and Near New. Length: 36 Inches. *Made up of heavy gauge steel sections that were etched with dark graduations, this Starrett rule was produced under a March 14, 1911 patent. It is in nearly new condition.* (FINE) **$65.00**

B5-7. Stanley Rule & Level No. 156 F: "Read Rite" Folding Rule. With Original Wrapper. Manufactured 1932-1935 Only. Length: 72 Inches. *Stanley's "Read Rite" series featured graduations that went in the opposite direction from the standard rules. They lasted just a few short years. A rare zig-zag rule.* (FINE) **$185.00**

B5-8. Stephens & Co., Riverton, Conn.: No. 60: Two-Foot, Four-Fold Folding Rule. Arch Joint, Full Bound Architect, Metric and English Scales. Length: 24 Inches. *We have long believed that rules by Stephens and the other early Stanley competitors are one of the neglected areas of collecting. This No. 60 arch joint rule shows some wear, but is sound and presentable.* (GOOD) **$55.00**

B5-9. Stanley Rule & Level No. 856 F: "Victor" Zig Zag Folding Rule. White Enamel Finish. Near New Condition. Length: 72 Inches. *The No. 856 F was distinguished from the standard No. 856 rule in having its graduations arranged for inside reading. This example is in nearly new condition.* (FINE) **$35.00**

B5-10. Royal No. X-672: "Royal Eagle" Zig Zag Folding Rule. With Extension. Most Unusual. Length: 72 Inches. *The Royal Rule company offered this "Royal Eagle" rule for those who didn't want to spring for the Stanley equivalent. A well preserved "zig-zag" rule from an obscure Twentieth Century maker.* (FINE) **$35.00**

B5-11. Eagle Rule Mfg. Corp., N.Y.: No. 072 W: Columbia Zig-Zag Folding Rule. 6 Foot Size. Uncommon Type. Length: 72 Inches. *The Eagle Rule Manufacturing Company produced a wide range of "zig-zag" rules in direct competition with the principal rule makers. This "Columbia" brand offering is in the 6 foot length. As new.* (FINE) **$25.00**

B5-12. Stanley Rule & Level No. 798 M: "Zig Zag" Folding Rule. Metric and Werschock, Etc. Patented May 22, 1917. Length: 76 Inches. *Patented in 1917 and imprinted with the patent date, this most unusual Stanley "Zig-Zag" rule is graduated in both Metric and Werschock scales. The latter scale was, I believe, a Russian measurement. The last of the White Russian rules.* (FINE) **$295.00**

B5-13. Stanley Rule & Level No. 72 1/2: Two-Foot, Four-Fold Folding Rule. Square Joint, Full Bound. Uncommon Type. Length: 24 Inches. *The block letter trademark on this broad full bound rule dates it to ca. 1900. It has been used, but is not in bad shape for a 100 year old tool.* (GOOD) **$55.00**

B5-14. Lufin Rule Co., The, Saginaw, Mich. No. 626: "Plumber's" Folding Rule. With 40 Degree Scale. Unused Condition. Length: 72 Inches. *Anyone who has seen a plumber at the end of a workday will know immediately that this rule never went out on the job. Brand new.* (FINE) **$35.00**

B5-15. Chapin-Stephens Co.: Rare "Flexifold" Folding Rule. "Zig Zag" Type. Marked "Patented". Length: 36 Inches. *A late entrant to the "Zig-Zag" rule market, the Chapin Stephens Company apparently jumped in and then quickly jumped out. These are very rare. The only example we have ever offered.* (GOOD+) **$135.00**

B5-16. Unmarked: Set Of Sample Advertising Rules. Tinner's Rules, Etc. Most Unusual. Length: 9 Inches. *When the advertising vendor came to your place of business, he would bring one of these to show you the different configurations of yardstick on which you could have your advertising printed. The grateful customers who received the sticks would then break them up to be used for stirring paint. Different.* (FINE) **$35.00**

B5-17. Lufkin Rule Co., The No. X 46: Zig-Zag Folding Rule. With Extension Slide. "Red End" Style. Length: 72 Inches. *The "x" designation on Lufkin rules indicated the presence of a sliding extension. This example has been well cared for.* (GOOD+) **$15.00**

B5-18. Auburn Lumber Co., Auburn, C.A.: Advertising Folding Rule. "Let Us Figure". Excellent Condition. Length: 24 Inches. *This giveaway from a California hardware dealer is imprinted with the slogan "Let us figure" on the reverse. An interesting advertising item.* (GOOD+) **$25.00**

B5-19. Master Rule Mfg. Co.: "Interlox" Folding Rule. Sliding Zig Zag. Patented November 24, 1916. Length: 48 Inches. *This early four foot example of these interesting slide-lock rules is imprinted with the November 24, 1916 patent date. A good one.* (GOOD) **$25.00**

B5-20. Stanley Rule & Level No. 426: Aluminum Zig-Zag Folding Rule. 6 Foot Size. Excellent Condition. Length: 72 Inches. *Aluminum zig-zag rules from Stanley were discontinued early on. This one is in excellent condition for the collector.* (GOOD+) **$45.00**

B5-21. Lufkin Rule Co., The No. 523: Zig-Zag Log Scale Folding Rule. Patented June 13, 1916. Doyle Log Scales. Length: 36 Inches. *Graduated in the same way as the larger board measure rules, this folding version was protected by a United States Patent issued in 1916. A hook on the end was used to grab the edge of the log.* (GOOD+) **$25.00**

B5-22. Stanley Rule & Level No. 05: Early "Zig-Zag" Folding Rule. With "ZZ" Logo. Ca. 1900-1942. Length: 60 Inches. *This early zig-zag is imprinted with Stanley's block letter trademark and the "ZZ" inside a shield that appeared on the earliest rules of this series.* (GOOD+) **$45.00**

B5-23. Lufkin Rule Co., The No. 524: Zig-Zag Log Scale Folding Rule. With Hook End. Doyle Log Scales. Length: 48 Inches. *This well preserved folding log measure rule is graduated with the standard "Doyle" scale. An uncommon rule in uncommonly nice condition.* (GOOD+) **$25.00**

B5-24. Casartelli & Son, J., Manchester: Sectional Steel Rule. Strange Alphabet. Unused Condition. Length: 78 Inches. *The number markings on this most unusual folding steel rule are of a form with which I am totally unfamiliar. Having begun to speculate that they might come from the world of the Near East, I pondered what Arabic numerals might look like, then quickly thought better of that notion. Approximately 2 meters in length, the rule is broken into units of measurement that are not at all metric. This tool is in great shape and appears to date from the 1920's or 1930's. A curiosity.* (FINE) **$95.00**

B5-25. Lufkin Rule Co., The: Early "Zig Zag" Folding Rule. Patented May 14, 1912. Rare 3 foot Size. Length: 36 Inches. *Collector's Tip No. 575: Zig Zag rules in the 2 foot and 3 foot sizes are quite scarce. Here's a chance to obtain a 3 footer in excellent condition.* (GOOD+) **$85.00**

B5-26. Grant & Co., W.T. No. 83: "Gold Label" Folding Rule. With Extension. 6 Foot Length. Length: 72 Inches. *No collector of zig-zag rules should be without an example imprinted with the name of the W.T. Grant Company, once a prominent retail chain.* (GOOD+) **$15.00**

B5-27. Unmarked: Narrow Metric Rule. Also Marked "Groningen". Unused Condition. Length: 39 1/2 Inches. *Designed to allow the conversion of measurements from one standard to another, this rule is graduated in both metric scales and the "Groningen" standard, which apparently relates to the area of Germany by the same name. This rule has never been used. Mint.* (FINE) **$110.00**

B5-28. Lufin Rule Co., The, Saginaw, Mich. No. 626: "Plumber's" Folding Rule. With 40 Degree Scale. Unused Condition. Length: 72 Inches. *The inside of this specialty zig-zag rule is graduated with a scale that reads diagonal inches per linear inch. Euclid would have had a field day with this thing. Brand new, but old.* (FINE) **$35.00**

B5-29. Master Rule Mfg. Co. No. 106: "Interlox" Folding Rule. Sliding Zig Zag. Unused Condition. Length: 72 Inches. *These are set up to slide out, one section at a time, to facilitate inside measure. When it is time to slide the sections back in, each section releases the catch on the joint as it as pushed toward the rule. Warning: folding these like a standard "zig-zag" rule is not recommended. Different.* (FINE) **$45.00**

B5-30. Lufkin Rule Co., The No. 8616: Zig-Zag Folding Rule. 6 Foot Length. Near New Condition. Length: 72 Inches. *Here's a 6 foot Lufkin Zig-Zag in brand new condition. Nice.* (FINE) **$25.00**

B5-31. Starrett Co., The L.S., Athol, Mass.: No. 450: 30 Centimeter Metric Folding Rule. Black Enamel Finish. Rare and Excellent. Length: 12 Inches. *The reverse side of this most unusual Starrett folding rule is graduated in centimeters. A rare Starrett metric rule in brand new condition.* (FINE) **$65.00**

B5-32. Stanley Rule & Level No. X 226: 6 Foot Zig Zag Folding Rule. 100 Plus Series. New Condition, Original Box. Length: 96 Inches. *The presence of the box is an indication that this specially packaged zig-zag rule was intended for sale as a Christmas gift, hence the "X" designation on the number. Brand new in the original box. Merry Christmas.* (FINE) **$145.00**

B5-33. Unmarked: "Pit Prop Gauge" Rule. For Mine Tunnels. Solid Boxwood. Length: 13 1/2 Inches. *When cutting or measuring the adequacy of wood to be used for overhead support in a mining tunnel, one of these would have come in handy. This one is in new condition is marked with the "Pit Prop Gauge" designation, but no maker mark.* (FINE) **$85.00**

B5-34. Stephens & Co. No. 9: Two-Foot, Two-Fold Folding Rule. Square Joint, Unbound. With Extension Slide. Length: 24 Inches. *The No. 9 was Stephens' basic unbound calculating rule. This one is complete and sound, but shows some evidence of use.* (GOOD) **$65.00**

B5-35. C-S Co., The No. 36: Six Inch, Two Fold Folding Rule. With Caliper Slide. Near New Condition. Length: 6 Inches. *Identical in all respects to Stanley's 6 inch unbound caliper rule, the Chapin-Stephens example appears never to have been used. Perfect.* (FINE) **$95.00**

B5-36. Lufkin Rule Co., Cleveland, Ohio: 12 Inch, 3 Fold Folding Rule. Spring Steel. "Tiffany Glass Co. Length: 12 Inches. *Over the years, we have offered a few rules imprinted with the early mark of the Lufkin Rule Company before they relocated to Saginaw, Michigan. Any rule bearing the "Cleveland" imprint is justifiably rare. Much less common, however are Cleveland marked rules having promotional advertising printed on them. Rarer still are rules bearing advertising for the "Tiffany Glass Company", as does this early example. An art glass rule at a tool price.* (GOOD+) **$225.00**

B5-37. Stanley Rule & Level No. 62: Two-Foot, Two-Fold Folding Rule. Square Joint, Full Bound. Extra Crisp and Clean. Length: 24 Inches. *This extra-clean example of one of Stanley's more popular rules has an early trademark. No apologies.* (FINE) **$55.00**

B5-38. F. Mc C.: Engine Divided Rule Set. Graduated In Chains. Boxwood and Mahogany. Length: 12 Inches. *Most likely intended for the offices of a surveyor in the years preceding the First World War, the five graduated boxwood rules and matching offsets in this set are numbered 1A through 1E. The set, which would have been used by surveyors and mapmakers to precisely chart boundaries, appears never to have been used. All of the scale and offset rules are in pristine condition with nary a chip or crack (offset rules were used when drafting lines that deviated at a precise slope from a given line). Having been protected throughout its long life by a carefully crafted mahogany case, which itself shows little, if any wear, this magnificent set is ready to accent any serious colleIlection of antique tools. A find not likely to be repeated for some time. Superb.* (FINE) **$165.00**

B5-39. Engert & Rolfe, London, England: Boxwood "Zig-Zag" Folding Rule. With Advertising. Original Leather Case. Length: 36 Inches. *This most interesting boxwood zig-zag is imprinted with advertising for roofing materials. Complete with the original leather case and in unused condition.* (FINE) **$35.00**

B5-40. Stanley Rule & Level No. 04: Early "Zig-Zag" Folding Rule. With "ZZ" Logo. Ca. 1900-1942. Length: 48 Inches. *This early Zig-Zag rule was included with many of Stanley's early tool kits. A tough rule to find, especially in this condition.* (GOOD+) **$145.00**

B5-41. C-S Co., The No. 51: One Foot, Four Fold Folding Rule. Square Joint, Unbound. Uncommon Number. Length: 12 Inches. *The Chapin-Stephens Company matched Stanley's rule production nearly item for item, including this uncommon arch joint offering. An uncommon Chapin-Stephens rule.* (GOOD) **$35.00**

B5-42. Stanley Rule & Level No. 36 1/2 L: One Foot, Two Fold Folding Rule. Left Hand Graduation. With Caliper Rule. Length: 12 Inches. *Here's a good, clean example of Stanley's basic one-foot, two-fold caliper rule. The "L" designated the left-hand caliper.* (GOOD) **$25.00**

B5-43. Lufkin Rule Co., The, Saginaw, Mich.: No. 1176: 6 Foot Zig-Zag Folding Rule. Large Black Numbers. Unused Condition. Length: 72 Inches. *This 6 foot folding steel rule is in unused condition. Mint.* (FINE) **$45.00**

B5-44. Stanley Rule & Level No. 84: Two Foot, Four Fold Folding Rule. Square Joint, Half Bound. Clean and Sound. Length: 24 Inches. *Perhaps the second most common of Stanley's better-grade rules (to the full bound No. 62), the No. 84 was protected by brass binding on its outer edges only. This example has seen some use, but is in sound, presentable condition.* (GOOD) **$35.00**

B5-45. Unmarked: Narrow Metric Rule. Solid Boxwood. Unused Condition. Length: 39 1/2 Inches. *Apparently never used in anger, or any other way, for that matter, this boxwood metric four-fold rule is in exactly the same condition as it would have been when it was first produced.* (FINE) **$65.00**

Group C5

C5-1. Stanley Rule & Level No. 112: Handled Scraper Plane. 99%+ Original Paint. Near New Condition. Length: 9 Inches. *Virtually all original finishes remain on this perfectly preserved handled scraper plane. Someone put it back and forgot about it. An absolutely perfect example of a highly desirable Stanley plane.* (FINE) **$525.00**

C5-2. Stanley Rule & Level No. 16: Adjustable Throat Block Plane. With Nickel Plated Cap. Early "Arch" Trademark. Length: 6 Inches. *Another Stanley plane that was offered for a relatively long period, but is seldom seen. This extra-clean example is in excellent condition. A very nice example of a most uncommon Stanley tool.* (FINE) **$110.00**

C5-3. Stanley Rule & Level No. 39: Cast Iron Dado Plane. 1 Inch Size. Missing Nickers. Length: 8 Inches. *It is a little known fact that the depth stops and cap irons are not interchangeable on the various sizes of Stanley's No. 39 series of dado planes. Another important fact regarding these planes is that the side nickers are interchangeable, one to the other. This example of the rare 1 inch size is missing its nickers, but is otherwise complete.* (GOOD+) **$175.00**

C5-4. Stanley Rule & Level No. 92: Cabinetmaker's Rabbet Plane. 3/4 Inch Cutter. Near New Condition. Length: 5 Inches. *This 3/4 inch shoulder plane is practically perfect in every way. The way it would be at the woodworkers store, if only they could get them. A great working plane in great shape.* (FINE) **$225.00**

C5-5. Stanley Rule & Level No. 95: Edge Trim Block Plane. Early "Arch" Trademark. Ready to Use. Length: 6 Inches. *More than 95% of the shiny black japanning remains on this clean and complete edge trim block plane. A nice clean with the early "arch" trademark.* (GOOD+) **$145.00**

C5-6. Stanley Rule & Level No. 98/99: Pair Of Side Rabbet Plane. With Depth Stops. Excellent Condition. Length: 4 Inches. *These side rabbet planes are the third production model, which featured cast iron depth stops, a significant functional improvement. Clean, complete and ready to use. A pretty pair.* (GOOD+) **$325.00**

C5-7. Stanley Rule & Level No. H104: "Handyman" Smooth Plane. Manufactred 1964 Only. Unused Condition. Length: 9 Inches. *All references indicate that this distinctively different Stanley plane was produced for a very, very short time in 1964 and then discontinued. A rare later day Stanley plane in new condition.* (FINE) **$225.00**

C5-8. Stanley Rule & Level No. 2: Smoothing Plane. "Sweetheart" Trademark. Superb Condition. Length: 7 1/4 Inches. *This, the smooth bottom variety of the No. 2 is imprinted with Stanley's ca. 1925 "Sweetheart" trademark on the cutter and seems to have been put away for storage at about that time. Extra crisp and clean.* (FINE) **$415.00**

C5-9. Stanley Rule & Level No. 3: 9 Inch Smooth Plane. Rosewood Handles. Near New Condition. Length: 9 Inches. *A woodworker looking for a great working example of Stanley's 9 inch smoothing plane need look no further. Fitted with rosewood handles and retaining 98%+ of its original finishes, this one is ready to go back to work. Nice.* (FINE) **$125.00**

C5-10. Stanley Rule & Level No. 603: Early "Bedrock" Plane. 99%+ Original Paint. Ca. 1905. Length: 14 Inches. *This pristine example of Stanley's early "Bedrock" series has passed through some 90 years of existence with very minimal evidence of use. A great example in excellent working order.* (FINE) **$285.00**

C5-11. Stanley Rule & Level No. 4 1/2: Heavy Smoothing Plane. Ca. 1950's. Superb Condition. Length: 10 Inches. *Here's an excellent example of Stanley's mainstay wide, heavy smoothing plane in ready to use condition. A great tool that is becoming almost impossible to find.* (FINE) **$155.00**

C5-12. Stanley Rule & Level No. 100: Squirrel Tail Plane. With Flat Sole. Extra Crisp and Clean. Length: 4 Inches. *The working partner of the 101 1/2, this version has the squirrel tail handle, but with a flat sole. A scarce and underrated Stanley plane in top condition.* (FINE) **$75.00**

C5-13. Stanley Rule & Level No. 72: Adjustable Chamfer Plane. Patented April 2, 1885. Extra Crisp and Clean. Length: 9 Inches. *Designed to facilitate the planing of chamfers on the edges of boards and beams, these were a very specific special-purpose tool that would have been purchased by only a very limited number of woodworkers. Examples, accordingly, are rare. This well preserved example retains more than 95% of its original japan finish. A nice example.* (FINE) **$425.00**

C5-14. Stanley Rule & Level No. 12: Rosewood Handle Plane. New Proper Cutter. Ready to Use. Length: 6 Inches. *Stanley's basic rosewood handled scraper plane in ready to go to work condition. More than 90% of the shiny black japanning remains on this ready to use example. The brand new cutting iron is the same thickness and temper of the original Stanley iron and is guaranteed to perform as well as the original. A bargain.* (GOOD+) **$115.00**

C5-15. Stanley Rule & Level No. 18: Knuckle Joint Block Plane. Adjustable Throat. Crisp, Clean and Sound. Length: 6 Inches. *An extra-clean example of Stanley "knuckle-joint" block plane. These featured a two-section cap that functioned as a spring to lock the cutter into position. Nearly all original nickel plating remains on this example which is marked with the Stanley name on the cap iron.* (GOOD+) **$55.00**

C5-16. Stanley Rule & Level No. 78: Duplex Rabbet, Fillet Plane. Early "Vine" Casting. Complete and Excellent. Length: 10 Inches. *Graced with Stanley's early "vine" casting on the handle, this No. 78 plane is clean and complete. A previous owner has "enhanced" some of the japanning, but it is otherwise excellent and ready to be put back to work.* (GOOD+) **$55.00**

C5-17. Stanley Rule & Level No. 140: Skew Rabbet Block Plane. "Sweetheart" Trademark. Removable Side. Length: 7 Inches. *A clean and complete skew bladed block plane that is complete and in excellent working order.* (GOOD) **$125.00**

C5-18. Stanley Rule & Level No. 113: Adjustable Circular Plane. Early Model. Painted Black. Length: 10 1/2 Inches. *Early versions of Stanley's No. 113 circular plane are among the most visually appealing of all Stanley metallic planes. Unfortunately, someone has applied a coat of black paint to this one and the front screw is tight. However, of the many salvageable parts, very few would sell for less than our asking price. A big bargain.* (GOOD) **$45.00**

C5-19. Stanley Rule & Level No. 12 1/2: Adjustable Scraper Plane. Proper Stanley Blade. Superb Condition. Length: 6 1/4 Inches. *Here's a very well preserved example of the rosewood soled No. 12 1/2 in top collector quality condition. Ready to use, if you choose.* (FINE) **$285.00**

C5-20. Stanley Rule & Level No. 48: Swing Fence Match Plane. "Sweetheart" Trademark. Near New Condition. Length: 10 Inches. *This swinging fence plane is marked with the "Sweetheart" trademark and retains all of its shiny nickel plating. A nice example.* (FINE) **$225.00**

C5-21. Stanley Rule & Level No. 65: Low Angle Block Plane. Nickel Plated Cap. Superb Condition. Length: 7 Inches. *Only a few specks of nickel plating are missing from this cap of this otherwise perfect Stanley block plane. A good one.* (GOOD+) **$110.00**

C5-22. Stanley Rule & Level No. 101: "Toy" Block Plane. Red Lever Cap. 99% Original Paint. Length: 3 1/4 Inches. *As a handy tool for use around the shop, these Stanley planes can't be beat. Essentially unused.* (FINE) **$35.00**

C5-23. Stanley Rule & Level No. 604: "Bedrock" Smoothing Plane. Later Style. Ca. 1915 Trademark. Length: 9 Inches. *Here's an excellent working example of the classic "Bedrock" series in a most desirable size. A great working tool in ready to use condition. No apologies.* (GOOD+) **$235.00**

C5-24. Stanley Rule & Level No. 101: Early "Toy" Block Plane. "Football" Trademark. 95% Original Paint. Length: 3 1/4 Inches. *This extremely early No. 101 block plane has the Stanley Rule & Level "football" mark. At least 110 years old. A very early plane in top condition.* (FINE) **$95.00**

C5-25. Stanley Rule & Level No. 5 1/4: "Junior Jack" Plane. World War II Type. 95% Original Paint. Length: 11 Inches. *The "Junior" jack plane, was the width of a No. 3 and just a bit shorter than a No. 5. Although these were marketed to manual training schools, these tools have found favor among latter-day woodworkers. This clean example has a very tight crack in the rear handle which could be easily glued to be invisible.* (GOOD+) **$65.00**

C5-26. Stanley Rule & Level No. 386: Adjustable Jointer Gauge. 100% Original Japan Finish World War II Type. Length: 11 Inches. *Here's a crispy clean example of Stanley's jointer gauge—the best ever produced. This one was made sometime between 1941 and 1945 when the use of nickel plating was restricted due to wartime exigencies. Nearly new.* (FINE) **$225.00**

C5-27. Stanley Rule & Level No. 192: Cast Iron Rabbet Plane. 1 Inch Width. Extra Crisp and Clean. Length: 10 1/2 Inches. *The No. 192 was the narrowest size of the Stanley rabbet plane series. This one is in nearly new condition.* (FINE) **$65.00**

C5-28. Stanley Rule & Level No. 11 1/2: Adjustable Floor Plane. Early "Patented '92" Trademark. Rare and Excellent. Length: 7 1/2 Inches. *Stanley offered the No. 11 1/2 floor plane in its catalogues beginning in 1909 and continuing for a brief period of fourteen years. It differs from the No. 11 beltmaker's plane in having a nose extension with the "No. 11 1/2" cast into the extension. Most planes of this type, which were intended to do the hard and dirty work of floor planing, show considerable evidence of abuse. This plane is in extremely well preserved condition and has been very, very little used. A nice example of a rare Stanley plane.* (GOOD+) **$695.00**

C5-29. Stanley Rule & Level No. 90: Cast Iron Bullnose Plane. Very Early Type. Patented August 3, 1897. Length: 4 Inches. *The cutting iron of this extra early example of the No. 90 bullnose rabbet plane is marked with the August 3, 1897 patent date of Justus Traut. A one hundred year old plane in nearly new condition.* (FINE) **$155.00**

C5-30. Stanley Rule & Level No. 71 1/2: Closed Throat Router Plane. Early Script Trademark. Patented October 29, 1901. Length: 8 Inches. *Two orignal cutters remain with this tough to find closed throat router plane. It is marked with the 1901 patent date. Crisp, clean and ready to use.* (GOOD+) **$95.00**

C5-31. Stanley Rule & Level No. 4 C: "Type 11" Smooth Plane. With Corrugated Sole. Early "V" Trademark. Length: 9 Inches. *This desirable "Type 11" bench plane is excellent in all respects. Nearly all of the original cutting iron remains and the rosewood handles are in excellent condition. Ready to last a lifetime.* (GOOD+) **$115.00**

C5-32. Stanley Rule & Level No. 30: Transitional Jointer Plane. Uncommon Size. Complete and Sound. Length: 22 Inches. *Stanley offered a full range of these "transitional" planes, beginning at No. 21 and continuing in increments of one to No. 34, with a half size thrown in for good measure. This example of the No. 30 is complete and sound, but shows some evidence of having been used. A good one.* (GOOD) **$55.00**

C5-33. Stanley Rule & Level No. 6: 18 Inch Fore Plane. Ca. 1950's. 99% Original Finishes. Length: 18 Inches. *Half jack plane and half jointer, the 18 inch No. 6 can do some of the work of each. This one is about as good as they get. Mint.* (FINE) **$165.00**

C5-34. Stanley Rule & Level No. 82: Adjustable Head Scraper. Partial Original Decal. Patented January 29, 1907. Length: 12 Inches. *Part of the original decal remains on this well preserved adjustable scraper. A nice example of an increasingly difficult to find Stanley tool.* (GOOD+) **$35.00**

C5-35. Stanley Rule & Level No. 4: Cast Iron Smooth Plane. With 1910 Patent Date. Original Decal. Length: 9 Inches. *The "Sweetheart" trademark and the presence of a single patent date confirm that this is a "Type 13" plane and was made in the period before compromises in quality began to be incorporated into the Stanley line. A great working tool in excellent condition.* (GOOD+) **$85.00**

C5-36. Stanley Rule & Level No. 83: Adjustable Scraper Plane. With Lignum Wheel. Patented February 4, 1896. Length: 9 1/2 Inches. *Here's a complete and ready to use example of Stanley's elusive No. 83 rolling wheel scraper plane.* (GOOD+) **$115.00**

C5-37. Stanley Rule & Level No. 40: Beech Handle Scrub Plane. Early "V" Logo. Ready To Use. Length: 11 Inches. *The logo on this beech handled No. 40 scrub plane indicates that it was made just before the First World War. It is clean, complete and ready to use. A nice example.* (GOOD+) **$95.00**

C5-38. Stanley Rule & Level No. 289: Skew-Blade Rabbet Plane. Complete and Original. "Sweetheart" Trademark. Length: 8 1/2 Inches. *Here's a clean and complete working example of Stanley's skew-blade rabbet. These planes were much more heavily cast than the No. 78 rabbet plane, and were well-suited to working with figured woods and end grain. A ready to use precision tool in excellent condition.* (GOOD+) **$445.00**

C5-39. Stanley Rule & Level No. 9 1/2: Adjustable Throat Plane. "Sweetheart" Trademark. New Condition, Original Box. Length: 6 Inches. *A bit of cellophane tape over the label of the box is the only "apology" we can find for this otherwise perfectly preserved example of Stanley's mainstay precision block plane. Extra crisp and clean.* (FINE) **$85.00**

C5-40. Stanley Rule & Level No. OH 20: "Two Tone" Block Plane. Maroon and Yellow. Scarce and Excellent. Length: 6 1/2 Inches. *Stanley had the good fortune to tool up for production of the "Two Tone" line about six months before the entire country tooled up to produce arms and war materials for a sustained period. A perfect example of a tool that was casually swept aside by the winds of war. A rare plane in excellent condition.* (GOOD+) **$55.00**

C5-41. Stanley Rule & Level No. 10: Bench Rabbet Plane. Early Trademark. Near New Condition. Length: 12 Inches. *This early example of the No. 10 bench rabbet plane, or carriagemaker's plane is in nearly new condition. All edges are sharp and all original finishes remain. Superb.* (FINE) **$325.00**

C5-42. Stanley Rule & Level No. 45: Patent Combination Plane. Shiny and Near New. New Condition, Original Box. Length: 11 1/2 Inches. *This superb example of Stanley's No. 45 combination is complete and perfect in the original pasteboard box, which retains its original label. All original parts as well as a reprint of the instruction manual are included. Extra crisp & clean.* (FINE) **$395.00**

C5-43. Stanley Rule & Level No. 120: Adjustable Block Plane. Rosewood Knob. Patented April 18, 1876. Length: 7 1/2 Inches. *A lever mechanism precisely regulates the depth of cut of this Stanley classic. This one is marked with the 1876 patent date. A nice early example.* (GOOD+) **$45.00**

C5-44. Stanley Rule & Level No. 7 C: 22 Inch Jointer Plane. Rosewood Handles. Ca. 1923. Length: 22 Inches. *This crisp but slightly dirty jointer plane comes to us as-found in a local woodworking shop. The 1915 era "V" shaped trademark appears on the cutter of this high knob (ca. 1920's) plane, an indication that the boys in the Stanley factory were about as enthused about "type studies" as we are here at Martin J. Donnelly Antique Tools. An excellent working plane that is ready to go back to work.* (GOOD+) **$145.00**

C5-45. Stanley Tools (England) No. 50 S: Combination Rabbet Plane. With All Original Cutters. Rosewood Handle. Length: 8 Inches. *The No. 50 S included the rabbeting cutters, but not the beading cutters that were included with the full fledged No. 50. New and in the box. Mint.* (FINE) **$125.00**

Group D5

D5-1. Braime, England: Braime's Double Slide Oil Can. With Grit Excluder. Classic Style. Length: 12 Inches. *Here's a classic English oiler in excellent condition. These graphic tool accessories are becoming increasingly difficult to find.* (GOOD+) **$65.00**

D5-2. Unmarked: Violin Maker's Metallic Plane. With Globular Handle. Bronze Body. Length: 4 1/4 Inches. *A globular handle of beech is attached to this well preserved instrument makers plane.* (GOOD+) **$110.00**

D5-3. Unmarked: Specialty Jeweler's Anvil. Conical Base. For Hardy or Vise. Length: 4 1/2 Inches. *The cone shaped base of this early "stake" anvil indicates that it was meant to fit in a specialized receiver—either a hole on a larger anvil or a holder produced especially for this anvil. Never seen another.* (FINE) **$225.00**

D5-4. Braime, England: Braime's Double Slide Oil Can. With Grit Excluder. Classic Style. Length: 12 Inches. *This classic English oil can is fitted with a "grit excluder" to minimize the possibility of dirt getting mixed in with the oil.* (GOOD+) **$65.00**

D5-5. Unmarked: Rare "Hardy Hole" Anvil. With Movable Shaft. Early and Unusual. Length: 4 Inches. *This most unusual and very early miniature anvil was designed to fit into the hardy hole on a standard anvil. Rare and well preserved.* (GOOD) **$245.00**

D5-7. Unmarked: Miniature Oil Can. Egg Shape Form. Early and Excellent. Length: 3 1/2 Inches. *When oil can collectors get together, they might call this an "ovaform" oil can. It is in excellent condition and retains the fluted cover for the spout. A good one.* (GOOD+) **$65.00**

D5-8. Unmarked: Cast Iron Block Metallic Plane. Screw Lock Cap. Unknown Maker. Length: 3 1/4 Inches. *We have sold a number of planes of this configuration over the past several years. They appear early, but are unmarked in any way. Graphic.* (GOOD) **$115.00**

D5-9. Unmarked: M.L. Sperry Patent Oil Can. Patented January 23, 1894. Near New Condition. Length: 3 1/2 Inches. *This can is not marked in any way, but its distinctive shape and rectangular foot leave no question that this is the M.L. Perry patent oil can. The patent was issued on January 23, 1894. A scarce oil can in nearly new condition.* (FINE) **$55.00**

D5-10. Unmarked: "The Model" Hand Vise. Patented July 31, 1883. Early and Excellent. Length: 4 1/4 Inches. *The early patent date is imprinted on the locking screw of this most unusual patented hand vise. The patent feature was apparently the oversize circular nut, which would lock the wing nut adjustment positively into place. A rare patented hand vise.* (GOOD+) **$165.00**

D5-11. Lockwood, Taylor Hardware Co., Clevland, Ohio: Bronze Advertising Anvil. Marked "1900". Uncommon Type. Length: 3 3/4 Inches. *The reverse side of this well preserved bronze advertising is cast with the date "1900" which may correspond to the founding date of the company or the date the anvil was made. An uncommon advertising anvil in excellent condition.* (GOOD+) **$165.00**

D5-12. Unmarked: Bronze Double Anvil. European Style. Excellent Patina. Length: 5 Inches. *Formed in the style of the classic French anvil, this bronze miniature is in nearly new condition. Judging from the patina of the brass it is quite old indeed.* (FINE) **$145.00**

D5-13. Stanley Rule & Level No. 101: Early "Toy" Block Plane. Ca. 1900 Trademark. 98% Original Paint. Length: 3 1/4 Inches. *Nearly all of the shiny original japan finish remains on this crispy clean "toy" block plane. The trademark indicates that this plane was made ca. 1900. Nice.* (FINE) **$55.00**

D5-14. Billings & Edmands Mfg. Co.: Forged Steel Hand Vise. Rocky Hill, Conn. Rare and Excellent. Length: 5 Inches. *Nearly all original finishes remain on this graphic hand vise from an uncommon Connecticut maker.* (FINE) **$65.00**

D5-15. Fisher & Norris, Trenton, N.J.: Miniature Working Anvil. Great Condition. Rare and Excellent. Length: 6 Inches. *Fisher & Norris marked their products with a distinctive "eagle" trademark, which appears on the reverse side of this early bench anvil. A very well preserved small bench anvil.* (GOOD+) **$245.00**

D5-16. Tower & Lyon, New York, N.Y.: Stephens' Patent Vise. Patented March 12, 1868. With Cam Gear Adjust. Length: 5 Inches. *These were offered in a variety of sizes of which this was the smallest. It is clearly marked with the patent dates and the quick-adjust mechanism is in fine working order. Nice.* (GOOD+) **$285.00**

D5-17. J.H.S., Devon: Set of Letter, Number Stamps. With Seriph Characters. New Conditon, Original Box. Length: 3 Inches. *This group of matching number and letter stamps is complete and ready to put to work. The letters have the seriphs characteristic of late 19th or early 20th Century styles.* (FINE) **$55.00**

D5-18. Unmarked: "Victor" Patent Oil Can. Patented October 5, 1886. With Locking Cap. Length: 4 Inches. *These were made by the same people who gave us the Overman Wrench (w.s.). A patented oil can that is clean and clearly marked.* (GOOD+) **$95.00**

D5-19. Overman Wheel Co., Chicopee Falls: Early Patent Oil Can. Marked Patent Applied For. Near New Condition. Length: 4 Inches. *The Overman Wheel Company produced a number of wrenches for bicycles and this special purpose oil can, which features a locking cap. A nice example.* (FINE) **$135.00**

D5-20. Unmarked: "All Brass" Oil Can. British Make. Near New Condition. Length: 4 Inches. *Because nearly all of the original nickel plating remains, the printing on this British made oil can is necessary to know that it is "All Brass". A graphic oil can in top condition.* (FINE) **$65.00**

D5-21. Unmarked: Machined Bronze Anvil. Distinctive Form. Extra Crisp and Clean. Length: 2 Inches. *This diminutive bronze anvil was made to be something special...it still is. Nice.* (FINE) **$55.00**

D5-22. Stanley Rule & Level No. 101: "Toy" Block Plane. Ca. 1930's. Unused Condition. Length: 3 1/4 Inches. *Here's a crispy-clean example of Stanley's popular "toy" size block plane. A handy tool in top condition.* (FINE) **$45.00**

SD5-23. Stanley Tools No. 101 PA: Low Angle Block Plane. Steel Body. Unused Condition. Length: 3 1/4 Inches. *This is the sort of tool that Stanley has taken to making. We invite the purchaser of this tool to crush it with one of Stanley's garage door openers. Sad, but true.* (FINE) **$15.00**

D5-24. Fanner Mfg. Co.: Cast Iron Glue Pot. Extra Small Size. Excellent Condition. Length: 3 Inches. *The cover of this miniature glue pot has been cast in a decorative pattern. Condition is near new.* (FINE) **$95.00**

D5-25. Unmarked: Advertising Hatchet. Marked "A, C". Excellent Condition. Length: 7 3/4 Inches. *A stylized logo featuring the letters "A" & "C" is forged into the head of this special purpose hatchet. Graphic.* (FINE) **$45.00**

D5-26. Unmarked: Miniature Oil Can. Turned Brass Cap. Near New Condition. Length: 3 1/2 Inches. *A decorative turned brass cap accents this well made miniature oil can.* (FINE) **$35.00**

D5-27. Arrow No. 1: Polished Steel Anvil. With Cast Iron Base. Near New Condition. Length: 4 Inches. *"Arrow No. 1" is the designation stamped into this very well made steel anvil. The fitted cast iron base retains all of its original finish. A nice example.* (FINE) **$65.00**

D5-28. Columbian Hardware. Co., Cleveland, Ohio: Miniature Advertising Anvil. Very Well Made. Most Unusual Type. Length: 3 1/2 Inches. *Among the most desirable of all small anvils are those that were produced as advertising promotional items by the anvil makers themselves. We have, in the past, sold such anvils made by both Hay Budden and Norris. This well made anvil is the first we have been privileged to offer bearing the imprint of anvil maker the Columbian Hardware Company. Crisp, clean and offered without apology. A very rare advertising anvil.* (FINE) **$445.00**

D5-29. Unmarked: Miniature English Oil Can. "Use Berkle's Oil". Brass Screw Cap. Length: 7 Inches. *The slogan "Use Berkle's Oil" is imprinted on the side of this undersize English oil can. A good one.* (GOOD+) **$45.00**

D5-30. Millers Falls Company No. 3: Spring Tension Hand Vise. 5 Inch Size. New Conditon, Original Box. Length: 5 Inches. *A new old stock example of the M.F. No. 3 hand vise in its original pasteboard box. Nice.* (FINE) **$95.00**

D5-31. Stanley Rule & Level No. 101: "Toy" Block Plane. Red Lever Cap. 99% Original Paint. Length: 3 1/4 Inches. *As a handy tool for use around the shop, these Stanley planes can't be beat. Nearly new condition.* (FINE) **$35.00**

D5-32. Unmarked: Precision Nickel Plated Anvil. Very Well Made. Superb Condition. Length: 4 1/4 Inches. *Here's a very well made nickel plated anvil that is not marked with a maker's name or advertising.* (FINE) **$65.00**

D5-33. Stubs, P.S.: Special Function Hand Vise. With Loop For Strap. Oversize Nut. Length: 7 Inches. *This Stubs hand vise has a loop handle for securing it to the bench, or whatever. The fixing screw is most unusual.* (GOOD+) **$65.00**

D5-34. Stanley Rule & Level No. 741: "Victor" Patent Vise. Patented January 28, 1908. Sweetheart Trademark. Length: 6 1/2 Inches. *The upper jaw of this patented bench vise is imprinted with its ca. 1920's era trademark. It has apparently never been used. Perfect.* (FINE) **$165.00**

D5-35. Kinsley, J.R., Cincinnati, Ohio: Advertising Anvil. Mounted on Base. Nicely Replated. Length: 4 Inches. *Someone has replated this advertising anvil and mounted it on a wooden base. Different.* (GOOD) **$45.00**

D5-36. J.G. & J.M.: Specialty Clamp and Anvil. Extremely Early. Near New Condition. Length: 5 1/2 Inches. *Marked only with the paired initials "J.G. & J.M." this graphic anvil and clamp combination is unlike any tool we have previously offered. The appearance of the tool, including the fittings on the clamp and the shape of the anvil indicate that this tool dates, at the latest, to the first quarter of the Nineteenth Century. A rare miniature anvil, with a twist.* (FINE) **$385.00**

D5-37. Unmarked: Bronze Fillet Metallic Plane. Turned Cherry Handle. From J.J. Kjelleberg. Length: 6 1/2 Inches. *This most unusual and well made bronze fillet cutting plane came together with a grouping of tools from the patternmaker's tool chest of J.J. Kjelleberg of Fitchburg, Massachusetts. A very well made miniature plane.* (FINE) **$165.00**

D5-38. Lufkin Rule Co., The No. 584: Tape Measure Clamp Handle. Nickel Plated Brass. Most Unusual. Length: 3 Inches. *Try holding a steel tape measure while walking across a field on an icy morning without one of these to grab it with. A curiosity.* (GOOD+) **$45.00**

D5-39. Stanley Rule & Level No. 101: Early "Toy" Block Plane. Ca. 1907 Trademark. 98% Original Paint. Length: 3 1/4 Inches. *This ca. 1915 era block plane is in excellent condition, retaining 98% of its shiny original paint. Ready to use or fill out a Stanley collection.* (FINE) **$45.00**

D5-40. D.B. Co.: Bronze Advertising Anvil. Dated "1915". Excellent Patina. Length: 3 Inches. *We have no idea who the D.B. Company might have been. Thanks to the use of carbon dating we have estimated that tool was produced between the first and second decades of the Twentieth Century. A nice looking bronze anvil.* (GOOD+) **$85.00**

D5-41. Unmarked: Early Patent Cap Popper. Patented June 13, 1876. 90% Original Nickel. Length: 2 Inches. *This looks to have been a toy used to teach children the benefits of pyrotechnic devices, a practice of which we approve. An early patented toy.* (GOOD+) **$85.00**

D5-42. Unmarked: Miniature Steel Anvil. Excellent Detail. Extra Small Size. Length: 2 3/4 Inches. *This well preserved steel anvil has been formed with an eye for detail by its makers.* (FINE) **$95.00**

D5-43. Bleckman: Miniature Hand Vise. Nicely Chamfered. Early and Excellent. Length: 3 Inches. *We believe that Bleckman was a German exporter. The quality of this tool is excellent.* (GOOD+) **$75.00**

D5-44. Unmarked: German Miniature Oil Can. Marked D.R.P. & D.R.G. Scarce and Excellent. Length: 2 Inches. *The bottom of this specialty miniature oil can is marked with the initials D.R.P. and D.R.G., which will mean something to people who understand German acronyms. Very cute.* (FINE) **$145.00**

D5-45. Unmarked: Early Patent Oil Can. Patented June 19, 1894. Early and Excellent. Length: 3 Inches. *The patent date of June 19, 1894 is printed on the bottom of this graphic early oil can. A nice example.* (GOOD+) **$45.00**

Group E5

E5-1. Wilkinson & Co., A. J., Boston, Mass: 8 Inches Patent Folding Handle. Draw Knife. Patented July 16, 1886. Near New Condition. Length: 12 1/2 Inches. *A superb example of the Wilkinson patent folding drawknife. Nicely complemented with fruitwood handles.* (FINE) **$175.00**

E5-2. Barton, D.R. & Smith, Wm. P., Roch: Early Coachmaker's Draw Knife. With 8 Inch Blade. Undocumented Partnership. Length: 22 Inches. *Sometimes something as simple as a maker's mark on a tool can change the one element of the perception of the history, as we know it, of tool manufacturing in the United States and lead to greater understanding. Writing in American Wooden Planes, the Pollaks have speculated that the toolmaking partnership of Barton & Smith consisted of D.R. Barton and one Albert H. Smith. However, this draw knife is very clearly marked D.R. Barton & Wm. P. Smith, a totally different name and a reason for researchers to begin anew the search to document the Barton & Smith partnership. A rare and significant drawknife.* (GOOD) **$285.00**

E5-3. Wilkinson & Co., A. J., Boston, Mass: 7 Inch Patent Folding Handle. Draw Knife. Patented July 16, 1886. Fruitwood Handles. Length: 11 1/2 Inches. *This 7 inch folding handle drawknife from A.J. Wilkinson has a pair of fruitwood handles and is in excellent working condition.* (GOOD+) **$95.00**

E5-4. Unmarked: Massive Coach Draw Knife. Owner "J.R. Graves". Uncommon Type. Length: 20 Inches. *This specialized coachmaker's tool comes to us from a prominent Connecticut collection—a state where the building of carriages was once the principal occupation. A nice example.* (GOOD+) **$115.00**

E5-5. Winsted Edge Tool Works No. 8: Folding Handle Draw Knife. 8 Inch Blade. Extra Crisp and Clean. Length: 14 Inches. *The Winsted Edge Tool Works was the producer of the T.H. Witherby chisels. This uncommon folding handle draw knife is in excellent condition and ready to use.* (GOOD+) **$65.00**

E5-6. Riverside Tool Co., New York, N.Y. No. 8: 8 Inch Blade Draw Knife. Uncommon Imprint. Excellent Condition. Length: 14 1/2 Inches. *The Riverside Tool Company was a hardware dealer and seller of high quality tools in New York City in the first quarter of the Nineteenth Century. This well preserved draw knife is clearly marked with their distinctive "anvil" logo.* (GOOD+) **$55.00**

E5-7. Kimball & Son, C. J., N. H.: Beech Handle Draw Knife. 6 Inch Blade. Extra Crisp and Clean. Length: 11 1/2 Inches. *The manufactures of the New Hampshire makers C.J. Kimball & Son are characterized by an exceptionally high standard of finish. This example, clearly marked with the Kimball mark, is in top condition. Extra nice.* (FINE) **$85.00**

E5-8. Ohio Tool Co., Columbus, Ohio: 7 Inch Cutting Edge Draw Knife. Very Little Used. Near New Condition. Length: 12 1/2 Inches. *No apologies whatsoever for this crispy clean 7 inch drawknife from the Ohio Tool Company. A nice example.* (FINE) **$75.00**

E5-9. Peck, Stow & Wilcox Co. No. 1 EX.: 4 1/2 Inch Blade Draw Knife. Early Appearance. Rare and Excellent. Length: 8 1/2 Inches. *This is the smallest P.S. & W. draw knife that we have ever seen. Rare and near new.* (FINE) **$155.00**

E5-10. Wilkinson & Co., A. J., Boston, Mass.: 8 Inch Folding Handle Draw Knife. Applewood Handles. Near New Condition. Length: 13 Inches. *The first time I sold tools at the markets in Brimfield, Massachusetts, a man came to my booth and bought all of the folding handle drawknives I had. A student of the business opportunity, I returned to Brimfield the next show loaded down with drawknives. The man returned and bought every single one of them once again. Needless to say, by the time the next show rolled around, I was the folding drawknife king. Back he came and buy he did. Dumbfounded, I had to ask. What do you do with them? He looked from side to side, as if to make certain that no one would hear, then said, in a low voice, "I coat them with oil." "Then", he continued, "I put them in a barrel, cover them with sawdust and start another layer." Before I could stammer out a response, he finished, "I'm working on my sixth barrel." While we place no requirements on the tools purchased here, we would recommend this one for a place of honor in the workshop or collection and that it be spared any time in the barrell. A nice tool and a true story.* (FINE) **$145.00**

E5-11. Wilkinson & Co., A. J., Boston, Mass.: 8 Inch Folding Handle Draw Knife. Patented July 16, 1895. Ready to Use. Length: 13 1/2 Inches. *This folding handle drawknife from A.J. Wilkinson features a pair of fruitwood handles and it is in great working condition. An excellent example.* (GOOD+) **$95.00**

E5-12. Swan Co. The James: 7 Inch Adjustable Angle Draw Knife. With "Swan" Trademark. Excellent Condition. Length: 13 Inches. *Nearly all of the original black paint remains on the non-working surfaces of this well preserved folding handle 7 Inch drawknife from the highly respected James Swan Company.* (GOOD+) **$125.00**

E5-13. Wilkinson & Co., A. J., Boston, Mass.: 6 Inch Patent Folding Handle Draw Knife. Patented July 16, 1895. Rare and Excellent. Length: 10 1/2 Inches. *The adjustable joints are imprinted with the July 16, 1895 patent date, a likely indicator that the joint was the subject of the patent. This uncommon 6 inch blade size is in excellent overall condition and ready to use.* (GOOD+) **$125.00**

E5-14. Cantelo, J. S., Boston, Mass.: Early Folding Handle. Draw Knife. Multiple Adjust. Rare Type and Excellent. Length: 18 Inches. *J.S. Cantelo of Boston patented and manufactured a number of unusual folding handle drawknives. This variation features a pair of wing nuts that, when released, allow the handles to pivot as well as swivel to a wide variety of positions. We have seen very, very few examples of this rare adjustable draw knife. Rare.* (GOOD+) **$185.00**

E5-15. Wilkinson & Co., A. J., Boston, Mass. No. 8: 8 Inch Patent Folding Handle. Draw Knife. Patented July 16, 1886. Fruitwood Handles. Length: 12 1/2 Inches. *Here's a well preserved and ready to use folding handle drawknife from the undisputed leader in the making of these tools. A nice example.* (GOOD+) **$85.00**

E5-16. Jennings & Co., C.E., New York, Ny No. 10: "Arrowhead Brand" Draw Knife. 8 Inch Cutting Blade. Patented February 20, 1906. Length: 15 Inches. *A wooden "keeper" has done its job in protecting the blade of this well preserved folding handle drawknife. Extra crisp & clean.* (GOOD+) **$95.00**

E5-17. Unmarked: Coachmaker's Router Draw Knife. Multiple Cut. Rare and Excellent. Length: 22 Inches. *The building of carriages and wagons required specialized tools including drawing knives that would reach into grooves cut for panels. We have observed a number of variations on this them, including tools such as the example shown here, which includes interchangeable blades. However, this is, without question, the finest example of the interchangeable blade carriage maker's draw knife that we have encountered for sale anywhere. Complete with four original blades and in excellent collector quality condition, we highly recommend this classic tool.* (GOOD+) **$345.00**

E5-18. Peck, Stow & Wilcox Co.: Folding Handle Draw Knife. With 8 Inch Blade. Near New Condition. Length: 14 Inches. *This folding handle drawknife from P.S. & W. is in excellent condition and offered without apology. A good one.* (FINE) **$95.00**

E5-19. Jennings & Co., C.E., New York, N.Y.: "Arrowhead Brand" Draw Knife. 8 Inch Cutting Blade. Patented February 20, 1906. Length: 13 Inches. *New York City toolmakers C.E. Jennings & Company imprinted all of their tools with their "Arrowhead" brand. This one is also marked with a 1906 patent date. It has what appears to be dried black grease on the handles, which should remove easily. A most uncommon folding-handle drawknife in excellent condition.* (FINE) **$115.00**

E5-20. Peck, Stow & Wilcox Co.: Folding Handle Draw Knife. With 10 Inch Blade. Unused Condition. Length: 16 Inches. *This folding handle drawknife from P.S. & W. is in excellent condition and offered without apology. Mint.* (FINE) **$135.00**

E5-21. Nobles Mfg. Co., (Elmira, N.Y.) No. 6: 6 Inch Patent Adjustable Draw Knife. Double Bevel Edge. Early and Near New. Length: 12 1/2 Inches. *These ca. 1860's pivoting handle drawknives were adjusted by loosening the perforated fixing screw on the end to allow the geared handles to move into position while disengaged from the identical gearing on the blade. The early working dates of this firm would indicate that this was one of the very first folding handle drawknives manufactured in the United States.* (FINE) **$115.00**

E5-22. Sears, Roebuck & Co. No. 3678: "Dunlap" 10 Inch Draw Knife. Extremely Well Made. New Condition, Original Box. Length: 16 Inches. *You can't go to Sears and buy a draw knife anymore. The next best thing is to buy one from Martin J. Donnelly Antique Tools. New and in the box.* (FINE) **$65.00**

E5-23. Witherby, T.H.: Folding Handle Draw Knife. With 8 Inch Blade. Near New Condition. Length: 14 Inches. *Here's an extra-clean folding handle drawknife from T.H. Witherby, the edge tool people.* (FINE) **$155.00**

E5-24. Unmarked: Classic Coachmaker's Draw Knife. Triple Adjustment. Wedge Lock Blade. Length: 16 Inches. *This specialized draw knife is in nearly perfectly preserved condition and retains all of its interchangeable blades. A stunningly well preserved example.* (FINE) **$225.00**

E5-25. Morrill, J.J.: Handle Maker's Draw Knife. With Semi-Circle. Blade. Early and Excellent. Length: 12 1/2 Inches. *This specialized tool made short work of the process of turning a piece of hickory stock into a handle for a pitchfork. Crisp, clean and ready to use.* (GOOD+) **$85.00**

E5-26. Peck, Stow & Wilcox Co.: Folding Handle Draw Knife. With 10 Inch Blade. Fruitwood Handles. Length: 15 1/2 Inches. *Here's a shiny, clean and nearly new 10 Inch blade drawknife from a respected maker. The previous owner, one "A.M.C." stamped it with his initials, but it is otherwise in excellent condition. Crisp.* (FINE) **$65.00**

E5-27. Unmarked: Curve Blade Draw Knife. Distinctive Form. Most Unusual. Length: 14 Inches. *This slightly arched draw knife must have been intended for a very specialized task, but we are uncertain as to what that task might have been. A nice example.* (GOOD+) **$115.00**

E5-28. Witherby, T.H. No. 8: Beech Handle Draw Knife. With 8 Inch Blade. Near New Condition. Length: 14 Inches. *This T.H. Witherby is made from the same high-grade steel as their chisels. Simply the best.* (FINE) **$65.00**

E5-29. Winsted Edge Tool Works: Massive 12 Inch Blade Draw Knife. Uncommon Size. Near New Condition. Length: 18 Inches. *The 12 Inch blade of the Connecticut made draw knife was designed for trimming spars to form the masts of ships. It is in absolutely superb condition and has been very little used. Extra nice.* (FINE) **$75.00**

E5-30. Unmarked: Adjustable Chamfer Guides. Working Condition. Ready to Use. Length: 5 Inches. *Most of the original nickel plating is missing from these chamfer guides, but they are otherwise in excellent working order and ready to use.* (GOOD) **$35.00**

E5-31. Spring & Robinson, Hyde Park, Mass.: Early Patent Draw Knife. Patented March 11, 1879. 3 Inch Blade. Length: 5 1/2 Inches. *This one is in generally great condition, except it is missing one of the original wing nuts. A superb small tool in great shape. An opportunity for the fixer upper.* (GOOD+) **$375.00**

E5-32. Kimball & Company?: Rare 3 Inch Draw Knife. Near New Condition. Ca. 1860's. Length: 6 1/2 Inches. *This early 3 Inch drawknife is of the form of tools made by Kimball & Company of New Hampshire. A nice example in a very rare and desirable size.* (GOOD+) **$285.00**

E5-33. Unmarked: "Black Prince" Draw Knife. Black Handles. Most Unusual. Length: 14 1/2 Inches. *The only imprint on this very well preserved drawknife is the designation "Black Prince". We believe this to have been a trade name and that this tool was never owned by royalty. More truth in advertising from Martin J. Donnelly Antique Tools and a very well preserved and uncommon drawknife.* (FINE) **$65.00**

E5-34. Jennings & Co., C.E., New York, N.Y.: Patternmaker's Draw Knife. 4 Inch Blade. Near New Condition. Length: 10 1/2 Inches. *As a handy shop tool, there's no beating the Jennings 4 Inch drawknife. This one is crisp, clean and ready to go to work. Nice.* (FINE) **$75.00**

E5-35. Unmarked: Carriagemaker's Draw Knife. With 4 Original Blades. Usable Condition. Length: 13 1/2 Inches. *Here's a very well preserved example of a coachmaking classic. Complete with four original blades. A bit dirty, but extra special.* (GOOD+) **$265.00**

E5-36. Unmarked: Adjustable Drawshave Guides. Similar to Goodell Prat. Ready to Use. Length: 3 1/2 Inches. *Drawshave guides were used in conjunction with a drawknife to cut stopped chamfers on boards and beams. A nice working example.* (GOOD+) **$45.00**

E5-37. Jennings & Co., C.E., New York, N.Y.: Patternmaker's Drawknife. Brass Ferrules. 4 Inch Blade. Length: 4 Inches. *The Jennings Company offered two small drawknives that remain popular today. The "patternmaker's" short-handled version, and this type with longer handles. These are significantly less common. This one is ready to go back to work.* (GOOD+) **$95.00**

E5-38. Jennings & Griffin Mfg. Co. No. 42: 7 Inch Blade Draw Knife. Marked. "J. & G. Mfg. C." Near New Condition. Length: 12 Inches. *Jennings & Griffin manufactured a full line of quality tools in the New York City area around the turn of the Century. Their quality was second to none. A exceptionally nice example in ready to use condition.* (FINE) **$55.00**

E5-39. Smith & Co., H.D., Plantsville, Conn.: "Perfect Handle" Draw Knife. 8 Inch Blade. Rare and Excellent. Length: 14 Inches. *One of the least common of the "Perfect Handle" tools, this 8 Inch blade drawknife was one of 3 sizes of this tool that they offered. A rare drawknife from a highly respected maker.* (GOOD+) **$115.00**

E5-40. Unmarked: Massive Mast Maker's. Draw Knife. 12 Inch Cutting Edge. Scarce and Usable. Length: 21 1/2 Inches. *This oversize drawknife comes to us from the unlikely location of St. Simon's Island in the State of Georgia. A good one.* (GOOD) **$45.00**

E5-41. Stanley Rule & Level No. 66: Universal Hand Beader. With 5 Cutters. Straight Fence Only. Length: 11 1/2 Inches. *Five double-ended cutters should give a would-be traditional woodworker a great start on mastery of the art of beading. The straight edge fence only is provided with this tool.* (FINE) **$145.00**

E5-42. Unmarked: Folding Handle Draw Knife. Forged From a File. Very Well Made. Length: 12 Inches. *We have had a goodly number of folding-handle drawknives these past few years, and more than our share of tools made from files, but this is the first example of a combination of the two that we have been privileged to offer. Different.* (GOOD+) **$110.00**

E5-43. White, L. & I.J., Buffalo, N.Y.: Massive 10 Inch Cut Draw Knife. Near New Condition. Uncommon Type. Length: 20 Inches. *This well preserved draw knife has extra wide blade and was intended for the use of the shingle maker. It is in nearly new condition.* (FINE) **$75.00**

E5-44. Winsted Edge Tool Works: 14 Inch Masting Draw Knife. Marked "U.S.N.". New Condition. Length: 20 Inches. *The 14 Inch blade of the Connecticut made draw knife was designed for trimming spars to form the masts of ships. It is in absolutely brand new condition and has never been used. Mint.* (FINE) **$115.00**

E5-45. Unmarked: Curved Blade Draw Knife. 5 Inch Blade. Superb Patina. Length: 9 1/2 Inches. *This might well have been used in a wheelwright's shop for trimming spokes. An unusual and uncommon curved draw knife.* (GOOD+) **$65.00**

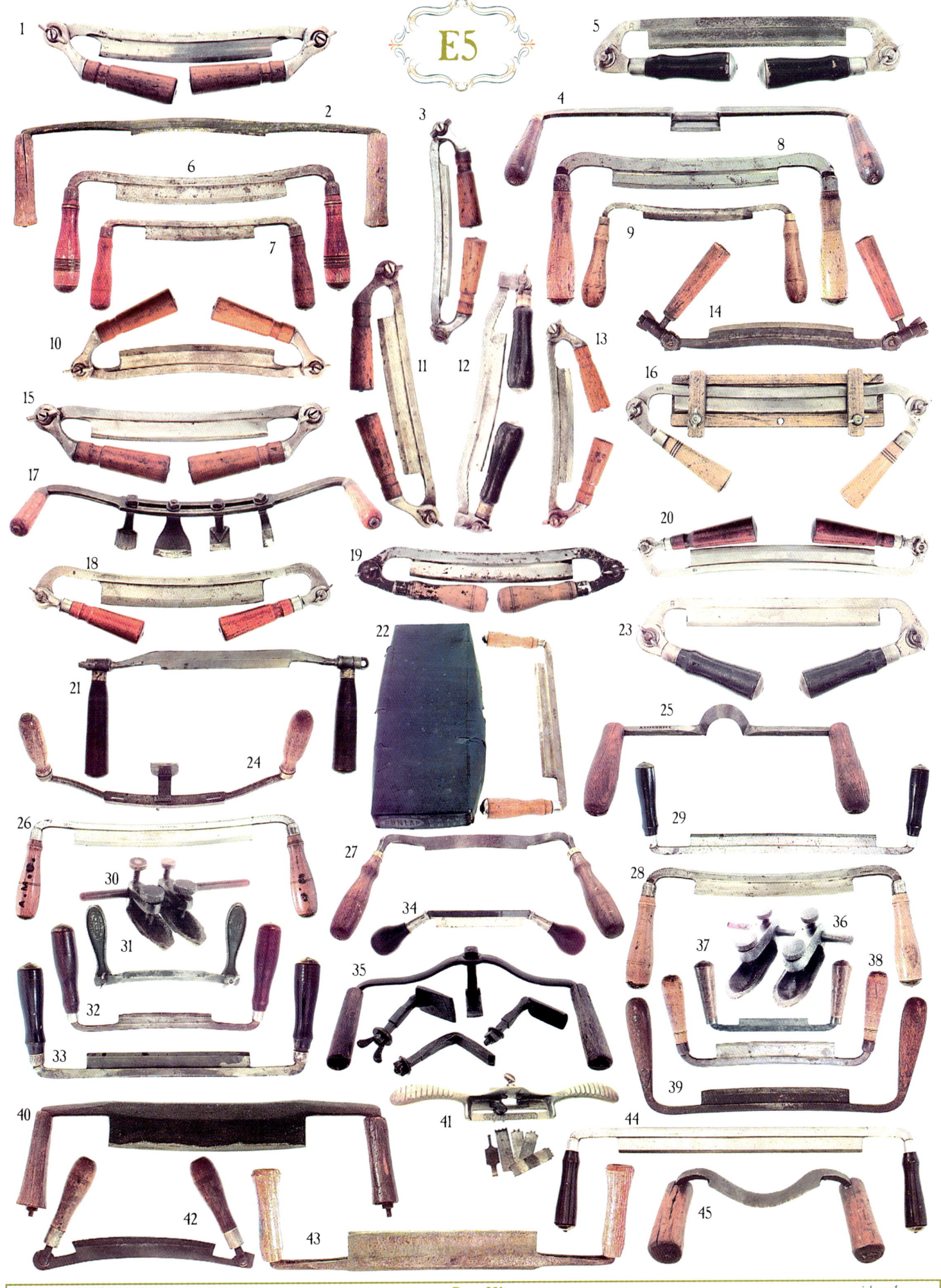

Group F5

F5-1. **Stanley Rule & Level No. 20: 6 Inch Rosewood Handle. Try Square. "Notched" Trademark. New Condition, Original Box. Length: 7 Inches.** *Protected from time and the elements by the presence of its original box, this Stanley classic is in brand new condition. Mint.* (FINE) **$85.00**

F5-2. **Topp & Co., G.A., Indianapolis, Indiana: Topps Framing Tool Try Square. With Horsehead Trademark. Extra Crisp Condition. Length: 9 1/2 Inches.** *More than 90% of the original etching is visible on this patented tool. All original finishes on the body. Nice.* (FINE) **$195.00**

F5-3. **Unmarked: Rosewood and Brass Try Square. Blued Steel Blade. Near New Condition. Length: 4 Inches.** *There are no marks on this one...no marks of any kind. It is in new condition. Mint.* (FINE) **$45.00**

F5-4. **Disston & Sons, Henry, Philadelphia Penn.: No. 1: Rosewood Handle Try Square. 8 Inch Blade. New Old Stock. Length: 8 Inches.** *This Disston offering has yet to be used. Of equal quality to any square ever made, this one is ready to complement the tool kit of a modern woodworker. Perfect.* (FINE) **$55.00**

F5-5. **Stanley Rule & Level No. 20: Rosewood Handle Try Square. Rare 15 Inch Size. "Sweetheart" Trademark. Length: 16 1/2 Inches.** *Nearly all of the original decal remains on this extra clean example of Stanley's second largest size of the No. 20 try square. Rare and near new.* (FINE) **$165.00**

F5-6. **Unmarked: Combination Level and Try Square. With Notches at 1/8 Inch. Most Unusual. Length: 10 Inches.** *This specialty try square has seen a bit of use, but it incorporates a sufficient number of unusual features to merit inclusion in a collection. Different.* (GOOD) **$15.00**

F5-7. **Brown & Sharpe, J.R.: "Ames Patent" Try Square. "Patented 1852". Early and Excellent. Length: 11 Inches.** *This example of the Ames Patent square, has a very light dusting of oxidation, but it should clean easily. It is marked with the 1852 patent date.* (GOOD) **$95.00**

F5-8. **Goodell-Pratt Company: Patternmaker's Try Square. Oval Cutout Handle. Rare and as New. Length: 10 Inches.** *One of the least common of all manufactured try squares, the G.P. patternmaker's square was of such high quality and price that very few were apparently sold. Nearly new.* (FINE) **$225.00**

F5-9. **Stanley Rule & Level No. 2: 10 Inch Traut's Patent Try Square. Patented May 26, 1874. Rare Type 1. Length: 10 Inches.** *This is a most unusual size in which to find this, the first model of the Justus Traut 1874 patent, which featured a riveted joint fixed with molten soft metal. A rare square.* (GOOD) **$65.00**

F5-10. **Hall & Knapp, New Britain, Conn.: Rosewood and Brass Try Square. 12 Inch Size. Extra Crisp Mark. Length: 12 Inches.** *A superb example of the work of the Hall and Knapp Company, the firm that Stanley acquired to get into the rule and level business. The rest is history. This one is clearly marked with the bold, circular Hall & Knapp logo. A rare square in great condition. Extra nice.* (GOOD+) **$265.00**

F5-11. **Disston & Morss, Philadelphia Penn.: Mahogany and Brass Try Square. With Integral Level. Missing Scribe. Length: 10 Inches.** *These early combination tools from Disston & Morss combined a level, try square and scribe. This one is missing the scribe, but is otherwise excellent. A rare square.* (GOOD) **$185.00**

F5-12. **Disston & Sons, H., Philadelphia Penn.: Early Patent Combonation Try Square. Patented January 6, 1885. Very Rare Type. Length: 8 Inches.** *The 1885 patent imprinted on this tool apparently applied to the notch cast into the handle, which would allow it to scribe a 45 degree bevel when placed over the end of a squarely cut piece of wood. An integral level adds functionality. A very rare Disston square.* (GOOD) **$345.00**

F5-13. **Nelson & Hubbard, Middletown, Conn.: Rosewood and Brass Try Square. Extra Bold Imprint. Ca. 1850's. Length: 6 Inches.** *This well preserved square is imprinted with the mark of Nelson & Hubbard who were tool and hardware dealers in the Middletown, Connecticut area in the 1850's. A very nice example.* (FINE) **$125.00**

F5-14. **D.B. & S., Providence, R.I.: Solid Steel Try Square. Ungraduated. 4 Inch Size. Length: 4 Inches.** *A good clean example with a clear D.B. & S. mark. A bargain.* (GOOD+) **$35.00**

F5-15. **: Patent Adjustable Combination Square. Patented February 13, 1917. Near New Condition. Length: 12 Inches.** *This uncommon combination square includes a locking protractor and a level, which would allow it to function as an inclinometer. Scarce and near new.* (FINE) **$75.00**

F5-16. **Starrett, L.S., Athol, Mass. No. 55: 4 Inch Machinist's Try Square. With Beveled Edges. "Tools" Trademark. Length: 4 Inches.** *A later-style square, this one has Starrett's ca. 1915 "Tools" Trademark. Square and true.* (GOOD+) **$55.00**

F5-17. **Bridge City Tool Co., Portland, Oregon: No. TB-2: Rosewood Infill Bevel. Brass Blade and Bind. Extremely Well Made. Length: 7 Inches.** *This Bridge City classic is in absolutely perfect condition. Highly recommended.* (FINE) **$125.00**

F5-18. **Stanley Rule & Level No. 1: Nickel Plated Try Square. Early "Arch" Trademark. Most Unusual. Length: 4 Inches.** *The metal parts of this early Stanley try square are fully nickel plated. This example, which features the early "arch" trademark was obviously produced with the nickel plating. A most unusual variation.* (FINE) **$245.00**

F5-19. **Johnson & Conway, Philadelphia Penn.: Brass Handled Try Square. 6 Inch Blade. Most Unusual Type. Length: 6 Inches.** *An early brass-handled machinist's try square with a clear, early mark.* (GOOD+) **$145.00**

F5-20. **Stanley Rule & Level No. 18: Adjusable Cast Iron Bevel. 8 Inch Size. Unused Condition. Length: 8 Inches.** *This classic example of Stanley's mainstay "Eureka" patent flush t bevel is in essentially unused condition. Ready to provide several lifetimes of use for a discriminating woodworker. Nice.* (FINE) **$45.00**

F5-21. **Stanley Rule & Level No. 30: Angle Divider Bevel. All Original Nickel Plated. Complete and Excellent. Length: 7 1/2 Inches.** *A superb example of Stanley's best selling angle divider bevel. This one is in nearly new condition. A tough tool to find in this condition.* (FINE) **$125.00**

F5-22. **Starrett Co., The L. S. No. 20: 1 1/2 Inch Ungraduated Try Square. Early Starrett Box. New Condition, Original Box. Length: 1 1/2 Inches.** *This ungraduated square has been kept in absolutely perfect condition by the presence of its original box. Mint.* (FINE) **$65.00**

F5-23. **Starrett, L.S., Athol, Mass.: Early Machinists Try Square. Early Starret Marked. Excellent Condition. Length: 4 Inches.** *The earliest work of Laroy S. Starrett was marked only with his name and his working location. This early try square bears the early Starrett imprint.* (GOOD+) **$55.00**

F5-24. **Union Tool Co., Orange, Mass. No. 625: 4 Inch "Double" Try Square. With Beveled Blade. New Condition, Original Box. Length: 4 Inches.** *The Union Tool Company produced a high quality line of machinists tools at the beginning of the Twentieth Century. This try square is in brand new condition in its original box. Mint.* (FINE) **$65.00**

F5-25. **Bridge City Tool Co., Portland, Oregon: No. TB-1: Rosewood Infill Bevel. Brass Blade and Bind. Extremely Well Made. Length: 5 Inches.** *Closer by far in their commitment to finish, quality and presentation among all contemporary makers to the toolmakers of old, the Bridge City Tool Company of Portland, Oregon produces products that are, and should be, highly collectible. This rosewood and brass bevel, which is marked with the number designation TB-1, is a classic example of their work.* (FINE) **$145.00**

F5-26. **Stanley Rule & Level No. 12: Cast Iron Nickel Plated. Try Square. Black Japan Finish. "Sweetheart" Trademark. Length: 4 Inches.** *Here's a crispy clean try square from Stanley's immediate post-WW I production. Extra nice.* (FINE) **$65.00**

F5-27. **Disston & Sons, Henry (Unmarked.): 15 Centemeters. Metric Try Square. Rosewood Handle. Rare and Near New. Length: 4 Inches.** *There is no mistaking the pattern of the triple circular escutcheon on this well preserved try square: It was produced by Henry Disston & Sons of Philadelpha. The 15 cm. size is one we have not seen before. Rare and nearly new.* (FINE) **$165.00**

F5-28. **Challenge Cutlery Corp., Bridgeport: Patent Steel Try Square. Patented 1904. Near New Condition. Length: 12 Inches.** *This early patent try square retains virtually all of its original nickel plating. The blade is clearly imprinted with the maker mark. An uncommon square in uncommonly nice condition.* (FINE) **$75.00**

F5-29. **Marples & Co., William, Sheffield: Massive Rosewood Try Square. 12 Inch Blade. Near New Condition. Length: 13 3/4 Inches.** *This straight, clean and true try square is in essentially the same condition as it would have been when it left the Marples factory. An excellent joiner's try square in top condition.* (FINE) **$135.00**

F5-30. **Stanley Rule & Level No. 2: Combined Mitre and Try Square. "Sweetheart" Trademark. Crisp and Clean. Length: 4 Inches.** *A excellent example of Stanley's combined mitre and try square. This one has been marked with the initial "Z" by a previous owner, and not, we would venture, by a Spanish swordsman. A nice working tool.* (GOOD+) **$25.00**

F5-31. **Winterbottom, Philadelphia Penn.: 6 Inch Early Patent Try Square. Patented June 22, 1860. Acquired by Stanley. Length: 6 Inches.** *The Stanley Rule & Level Company purchased the rights to the Winterbottom patent square and incorporated it into their product line. Here's a rare example of the tool before it was sold to Stanley. Early and excellent.* (GOOD+) **$145.00**

F5-32. **Starrett Co., L. S., Athol, Mass. No. 14: Adjustable Locking Try Square. No. 4 Graduations. Near New Condition. Length: 2 1/2 Inches.** *The No. 14 locking try square was marketed as a "double steel square" by Starrett, perhaps because you could use it from both ends simultaneously. A nice example.* (FINE) **$35.00**

F5-33. **Kennedy & Co., Hartford, Conn.: Rare Joiner's Try Square. 18 Inch Blade. Ca. 1820's. Length: 20 Inches.** *Collectors of wooden planes are well familiar with the work of Leonard Kennedy of Hartford, a pioneering manufacturer of planes and the patriarch of a family of planemakers who manufactured these tools in Connecticut and New York State. Unlike England, where the making of other tools by planemakers was commonplace, in the United States, it was an exception for a planemaker to produce anything but wooden planes. Those planemakers who dabbled in other tools are relatively well known. When a tool is found that expands the range of planemakers known to have made or sold tools other than planes, it is cause for celebration among the rhykenologically inclined, as that discovery adds, incrementally, to the picture of planemaking in America. This boldly marked try square, which bears the imprint of Kennedy & Company, who made planes in Hartford in the 1820's, is an example of such a tool. However, the dearth of other examples raises the possibility that this might possibly have been a tool used in the Kennedy shop as part of the planemaking process. Whether it was intended for sale or use, there can be no question that this is a rare and important planemaker imprinted tool. Important.* (GOOD+) **$395.00**

F5-34. **Starrett Co., L. S., Athol, Mass. No. 453: Adjustable Locking Try Square. With Screw Lock. Uncommon Type. Length: 4 Inches.** *This special locking square was marketed by Starrett as a "Die Maker's Square". A nice example.* (GOOD+) **$35.00**

F5-35. **Siewers, Charles G., Cincinnati: Rosewood and Brass Try Square. Original Blue Finish. Ca. 1850. Length: 15 Inches.** *C.G. Siewers, in addition to being the son-in-law of planemaker E.W. Carpenter, also made planes, bevels, gauges and this try square. An uncommon example of a non-plane made by a planemaker.* (GOOD+) **$165.00**

F5-36. **Stanley Rule & Level No. 16: Filled Miter Try Square. Extra Early Trademark. Superb Condition. Length: 8 Inches.** *These were designed for laying out mitre joints at fixed angles. This one is in excellent condition and has a bold and early Stanley mark. A good one.* (GOOD+) **$125.00**

F5-37. **Unmarked: Early 10 Inch Try Square. Birdeye Maple Handle. Very Well Preserved. Length: 10 Inches.** *The hand filed diamond shaped escutcheons are an indication that this hand made try square dates from approximately 1800. Its birdseye maple handle is in excellent condition for a tool of this age.* (GOOD+) **$65.00**

F5-38. **Cresson, W., Philadelphia: Rosewood and Brass Try Square. For Mitre Cuts. Early U.S. Imprint. Length: 12 Inches.** *W. Cresson was making tools in Philadelphia before Henry Disston started making saws, which is a long time ago. This one is nicely marked with the Cresson name.* (GOOD) **$65.00**

F5-39. **D.B. & S., Providence, R.I.: "Ames Patent" Try Square. Marked "W.H.A.". 6 Inch Size. Length: 6 Inches.** *A nice example of the "Ames Patent" centering square in the next-to-smallest size. A good, clean example.* (GOOD+) **$65.00**

F5-40. **Unmarked: Combination Plumb, Level and Bevel. With Brass Fittings. Most Unusual. Length: 19 Inches.** *This unmarked combination bevel and level is a sign that the need to create tools with a high gizmocity factor did not end with the 19th Century. A gizmo.* (GOOD) **$45.00**

F5-41. **Lufkin Rule Co., The, Saginaw, Mich. No. 138: Machinists Precision Try Square. With Attachments. Near New Condition. Length: 2 1/2 Inches.** *All of the original attachments are present with this immaculate Lufkin die maker's square. Perfect.* (FINE) **$65.00**

F5-42. **D.B. & S., Providence, R.I.: Rosewood Infill Try Square. Patented October 6, 1857. Excellent Condition. Length: 8 Inches.** *An extra crisp example of a D.B. & S. main line item. Early, and marked with the 1857 patent date.* (FINE) **$115.00**

F5-43. **Disston & Sons, Henry (Unmarked.): Rosewood Mitre and Try Square. Patented April 27, 1909. Rare and Excellent. Length: 4 1/2 Inches.** *Here's a well preserved and ready to use try and mitre square from an important toolmaker. Unmarked, but unquestionably by Disston.* (GOOD+) **$45.00**

F5-44. **D.B. & S., Providence, R.I.: Solid Steel Try Square. With Graduations. 6 Inch Size. Length: 6 Inches.** *This early try square is clearly marked and ready for show and tell.* (GOOD) **$15.00**

F5-45. **Disston & Morss (Unmarked): Combination Try Square and Bevel. Blued Steel Blades. Early and Excellent. Length: 10 Inches.** *These bevel & try square combination tools were offered by Disston & Morss in their early catalogs. As is the case with most examples encountered, this one is not imprinted with the maker's name. A rare combination tool from an important early maker.* (GOOD+) **$115.00**

Group G5

G5-1. D. & S., Bangor, Maine: Early 6 Inch Square Rule. Graduated in 64ths. Early and Excellent. Length: 6 Inches. *This crispy clean example of the work of pioneering precision machinist tool makers Darling & Swartz, of Bangor, Maine, is in very well preserved condition.* (GOOD+) **$85.00**

G5-2. Goodell-Pratt Company: Rare Circular Marking Gauge. Cast Iron Head. Near New Condition. Length: 8 Inches. *Goodell-Pratt offered a full line of marking gauges, none of which is very common. This one has a "Y" shaped fence for circular work. All of the Goodell Pratt marking gauges are quite scarce. This one is in essentially unused condition. Mint.* (FINE) **$295.00**

G5-3. Boulet's Fine Tool Works: Dial Indicator Gauge. Patented October 2, 1900. From Sebago Lake, Maine. Length: 8 Inches. *This precision tool was made in Sebago Lake, Maine, where frightfully long winters would give ample opportunity to conceive of such intricate devices as this. Complete in the original box.* (FINE) **$195.00**

G5-4. Darling, Brown & Sharpe: 6 Inch Bench Rule Rule. Graduated in 64ths. Near New Condition. Length: 6 Inches. *No apologies whatsoever for this pristine bench rule from D.B. & S. Mint.* (FINE) **$65.00**

G5-5. Bemis & Call Co., Springfield, Mass.: Massive Tinsmith's Divider. Early and Well Made. Ready to Use. Length: 23 Inches. *At 23 inches in length, these dividers would have been well suited for laying out patterns in sheet metal by a tinsmith. They are clean, straight and ready to use once again for that purpose.* (GOOD+) **$115.00**

G5-6. Stanley Rule & Level No. 46: Pocket Square Level. Rare Marked Example. Excellent Condition. Length: 3 Inches. *A collector-quality example of Stanley's seldom-seen No. 46 square level. Marked examples are very hard to find.* (FINE) **$115.00**

G5-7. Assorted Makers: Assorted Steel Rules and Gauges. Ready to Use. Length: 6 Inches. *Another grab bag from the bottom of a machinists chest, these steel rules and gauges are in excellent condition. Nice.* (FINE) **$25.00**

G5-8. Stevens A. & T. Co., Chicopee Falls, Mass.: Patent Thread Caliper. Patented February 14, 1888. Superb Condition. Length: 5 1/4 Inches. *A most unusual thread gauge caliper marked with both the maker name and the early patent date. Nice.* (FINE) **$75.00**

G5-9. Darling, Brown & Sharpe: "Ames Patent" Square. Rare 4 Inch Size. Crisp and Clean. Length: 4 Inches. *This is the smallest size of the "Ames Patent" that was offered. A good, clean and clearly marked example. Nice.* (GOOD+) **$145.00**

G5-10. Grau, G.: Early Outside Caliper. With Wing Adjust. Nicely Chamfered. Length: 11 Inches. *A betting man would venture that this early appearing caliper came here by way of Germany. A well preserved caliper with a very early look. Nice.* (GOOD+) **$55.00**

G5-11. Boker & Co., H., Germany: Massive 10 Inch Outside Caliper. Early Spring Joint. Excellent Condition. Length: 10 Inches. *The Boker firm was known for the high quality of its metalworking. This is a superb example of that quality, with crisp edges and a forged spring joint that is a wonder of workmanship. Crispy clean.* (GOOD) **$65.00**

G5-12. Stevens A. & T. Co., J.: 3 Inch Outside Caliper. Patented November 20, 1888. Early Spring Joint. Length: 3 Inches. *A nice precision caliper clearly marked with maker name and patent date.* (FINE) **$35.00**

G5-13. Darling, Brown & Sharpe: "Ames Patent" Square. 8 Inch Size. Extra Crisp and Clean. Length: 10 1/2 Inches. *This example of the classic "Ames Patent" square is in nearly new condition. Choice.* (FINE) **$135.00**

G5-14. Unmarked: Unusal Patent Caliper. Patented January 4, 1887. Quick Release. Length: 8 1/4 Inches. *The patent date on these quick release calipers is 1/4/1887, but I can't find it in the Cope book. These are in superb condition. A rare pair.* (FINE) **$95.00**

G5-15. Stevens & Co., J., C. Falls, Mass.: Early Spring Joint Caliper. Patented November 20, 1888. For Outside Use. Length: 6 Inches. *An excellent example of the early Stevens forged spring joint type caliper.* (GOOD+) **$45.00**

G5-16. Assorted Makers: Assortment of Bench Rules. Lufkin, Etc. Ready to Use. Length: 18 Inches. *This assortment of rules and accessories came from the same machinist's box. A bargain.* (GOOD+) **$35.00**

G5-17. Stoddard, O., Detroit, Mich.: Patented Bronze Divider. With Adjust Points. "Pat. Appl'd. For". Length: 17 Inches. *This O. Stoddard divider was eventually patented in the late 1870's and later in the 1880's. The locking mechanism for the leg was also used on trammel points produced under the same patent. Compete with 3 sets of legs. Extra nice.* (FINE) **$225.00**

G5-18. Stevens & Co., J.: Early Spring Joint Caliper. For Inside Measure. "F. H. Phillips". Length: 5 Inches. *A clean and clearly marked example of the early work of the Stevens firm.* (GOOD+) **$65.00**

G5-19. Sawyer Tool Co., Fitchburg, Mass.: Thread Constant Gauge. With Tables. Uncommon Type. Length: 6 3/4 Inches. *Most likely produced as an advertising giveaway rather than a catalog item, this Sawyer gauge is boldly imprinted with their advertising.* (GOOD+) **$45.00**

G5-20. Sawyer Tool Mfg Co.: Precision Adjust Caliper. With Extension Leg. Most Unusual Type. Length: 9 Inches. *An extension tip adds additional utility to this well preserved hermaphrodite caliper.* (FINE) **$85.00**

G5-21. Starrett Co., L. S., Athol, Mass.: No. 14: Adjustable Locking Try Square. No. 4 Graduations. With Two Blades. Length: 2 1/2 Inches. *Two original blades remain with this well preserved "double" try square from Starrett.* (FINE) **$85.00**

G5-22. Wiete-Goethe Co., San Francisco, Calif.: Patent Caliper and Protractor. Patented March 21, 1905. Rare and Complete. Length: 4 1/2 Inches. *Patented in 1905, this combination caliper, protractor, bevel and rule was invented by Eugene Wiet of San Francisco, California, who was apparently one of the manufacturers. These didn't catch on. A rare machinists tool.* (GOOD+) **$85.00**

G5-23. Kellogg, Battle Creek, Mich.: Madame Kellogg's Patent Square. Patented December 25, 1883. Near New Condition. Length: 24 Inches. *This patented maple and brass square was used for laying out clothing patterns. It is in nearly new condition.* (FINE) **$125.00**

G5-24. Chesterman & Co., Ltd., Sheffield: Adjustable Metal Gauge. With Slide Adjust. Uncommon Type. Length: 5 Inches. *The markings on this example of the C.E. Billings 1879 patent wrench indicate that it was one of the very first made. Early and excellent.* (GOOD+) **$45.00**

G5-25. Brown & Sharpe, J. R.: Circular Wire Gauge. With Eagle Stamp. Uncommon Size. Length: 2 1/4 Inches. *An early example of the work of the Providence firm, complete with an appealing eagle imprint. Extra crisp and clean.* (GOOD+) **$45.00**

G5-26. Sawyer Tool Co., Fitchburg, Mass.: 4 Inch Bench Rule. Multiple Graduates Tempered. No. 10. Length: 4 Inches. *The Sawyer "script" trademark is boldly imprinted on this perfectly preserved rule. Mint.* (FINE) **$25.00**

G5-27. Starrett Co., The L.S., Athol, Mass.: Machinist's Adjustable Protractor. Ready to Use. Nicely Rejapanned. Length: 6 Inches. *Here's an excellent working protractor head for a Starrett Combination square. Someone has touched up the paint, but tastefully so. Ready to use.* (GOOD) **$25.00**

G5-28. Dodd, Wm. & Co.: Leather Worker's Compass. With Hooked Tip. Early and Excellent. Length: 5 1/4 Inches. *This extremely early leather worker's compass was used for scribing circles in leather. The tip is formed into a sharpened hook. According to Alexander Farnham's "Early Tools of New Jersey", Dodd worked in the 1850's in Newark, New Jersey.* (GOOD+) **$95.00**

G5-29. D.B. & S., Providence, R.I.: Narrow One Foot Rule. Extra Thick Body. Uncommon Type. Length: 12 Inches. *Of a configuration not often encountered, this D.B. & S. rule has an exceptionally thick body. It is clean and very clearly marked.* (GOOD+) **$65.00**

G5-30. Starrett Co., The L.S., Athol, Mass.: Group of 3 Shrink Rules. 1/8 Inch, 1/4 Inch and 1/10 Inch. Ready to Use. Length: 24 Inches. *Purchased new, shrinkage rules are extremely expensive. A bargain.* (GOOD+) **$45.00**

G5-31. D.B. & S., Providence, R.I.: Double Gauge Printer Rule. Nonpareil and Agate. German Silver Body. Length: 7 1/4 Inches. *A superb example of one of the lesser known products of the D.B.& S. product line. Rare, clean and clearly marked.* (FINE) **$295.00**

G5-32. Unmarked: Precisison Adjust Divider. With Brass Adjust Screw. Most Unusual Type. Length: 6 Inches. *This divider features a captive central screw that positively locks the adjustment of the tips. Different.* (GOOD) **$55.00**

G5-33. Sawyer Tool Co., Fitchburg, Mass.: Decimal Equivalent Gauge. With Tables. Copyright 1908. Length: 6 3/4 Inches. *The prominence of the Sawyer name on this tool indicates that it was likely provided to machinists as a promotional item rather than as a stock catalog item. Condition is near new.* (FINE) **$45.00**

G5-34. Sawyer Tool Co., Fitchburg, Mass.: Machinists Feeler Gauge. Graduated in 1000ths. Near New Condition. Length: 4 1/2 Inches. *This Sawyer classic includes the fixing screw for the blade, which was left out of the picture. Mint.* (FINE) **$35.00**

G5-35. Darling, Brown & Sharpe: "Ames Patent" Square. Largest Size. Extra Crisp and Clean. Length: 12 Inches. *An extra crisp and clean example of the Ames Patent in the largest size. A good one.* (GOOD+) **$165.00**

G5-36. Sawyer Tool Co., Ashburnham, Mass.: Machinists Center Gauge. Graduated in 32nds. Unused Condition. Length: 1 3/4 Inches. *These arrow-shaped gauges have threads cut into each side of the arrow tip. A graphic machinist's tool.* (FINE) **$45.00**

G5-37. Stevens & Co.: Early Keyhole Caliper. With Spring Joint. Crisp and Clean. Length: 6 Inches. *This keyhole caliper features the early wing nut adjustment. A graphic tool in excellent condition.* (FINE) **$65.00**

G5-38. Starrett Co., The L.S., Athol, Mass.: No. 22: 59 Degree Drill Angle Gauge. Patented December 19, 1922. Uncommon Type. Length: 2 1/2 Inches. *The patent feature of this adjustable drill gauge is likely the locking screw at the base. An uncommon Starrett item.* (GOOD+) **$65.00**

G5-39. Union Tool Co., Orange, Mass.: Patent Quick Adjust Caliper. Patented June 13, 1914. Uncommon Type. Length: 7 Inches. *Produced under a 1914 a patent one Emory Ellis, these mechanically different calipers feature a quick adjustment feature quite unlike anything produced before or since.* (FINE) **$45.00**

G5-40. Stevens & Co., J., C. Falls, Mass.: Patent Quck Adjust Divider. Patented February 14, 1888. Rare and Excellent. Length: 7 Inches. *Holding the legs together on this early patent divider allows the adjustment screw to be moved nearly effortlessly into position, where it will lock once pressure is applied. Clean and clearly marked with the patent date.* (FINE) **$115.00**

G5-41. Unmarked: Machinsts Precision Try Square. With Fine Adjust. Very Well Made. Length: 2 1/4 Inches. *Most likely the shop made product of a tool and die maker, this precision square is in perfect condition. Mint.* (FINE) **$55.00**

G5-42. Stoddard, O., Detroit, Mich.: Patented Bronze Divider. With Adjust Points. Patented March 31, 1885. Length: 9 Inches. *This O. Stoddard divider was patented on March 31, 1885. The screw adjust mechanism on the tip of the leg was also used on trammel points produced under the same patent. A rare and early divider in excellent condition.* (FINE) **$145.00**

G5-43. Moore & Wright, Sheffield (England): Inside and Out Radius Gauge. On Locking Ring. Excellent Condition. Length: 2 1/4 Inches. *A handy ring keep these radius gauges both organized and accessible. A nice set from a prominent English maker.* (FINE) **$15.00**

G5-44. Sawyer Tool Mfg Co.: Group of 3 Calipers. Inside, Outside, Etc. Extra Crisp and Clean. Length: 5 Inches. *These calipers were likely purchased together by an apprentice machinist. A nice set.* (FINE) **$75.00**

G5-45. Assorted Makers: 3 Small Machinists Tools. Calipers and Gauge. Extra Crisp and Clean. Length: 3 Inches. *These tools came from a single drawer of one machinist's tool chest. A bargain.* (FINE) **$25.00**

Group H5

H5-1. Lufkin Rule Co., The, Saginaw, Mich. No. 3851: Three-Foot, Four Fold Folding Rule. Arch Joint, Unbound. Equal to Stanley 66 1/2. Length: 36 Inches. *Here's a clean and sound example of Lufkin's answer to Stanley's No. 66 1/2 three-foot, four-fold rule.* (GOOD) **$25.00**

H5-2. Mathieson & Sons, A.: Boxwood Meter Folding Rule. Metric and English. Unused Condition. Length: 39 1/2 Inches. *No one has ever used this pristine one meter, four fold rule from respected Scottish makers A. Mathieson & Sons. Absolutely brand new.* (FINE) **$145.00**

H5-3. Unmarked No. 90: One- Foot, Four-Fold Folding Rule. Ivory and Brass. Clean and Sound. Length: 12 Inches. *Only the designation "No. 90" is marked on the brass and ivory folding rule. A previous owner has imprinted the initial "W" on the edge, but it is otherwise clean, sound and ready to display.* (GOOD+) **$135.00**

H5-4. Rabone & Sons, John, Birmingham No. 1166: Two Foot, Four Fold Folding Rule. Round Joint, Unbound. New Condition, Original Box. Length: 24 Inches. *This pristine boxwood rule is in new condition in its very graphic green and yellow pasteboard box. Mint.* (FINE) **$95.00**

H5-5. Nicholl & Co., J.A.: "Capt. Field's Improved" Rule. For Navigation. Boxwood and Brass. Length: 12 Inches. *Parallel rules such as this were used for navigational route charting. This boxwood and brass example is imprinted with the designation "Capt. Field's Improved" and is marked with the maker's name. A great special function rule in nearly new condition.* (FINE) **$115.00**

H5-6. C-S Co., The, Pine Meadow, Conn.: No. 65 1/2: One Foot, Four Fold Folding Rule. Square Joint, Full Bound. Crisp and Clean. Length: 12 Inches. *This well preserved one foot, four fold rule is marked with the C-S imprint and product number.* (GOOD+) **$55.00**

H5-7. Rabone Chesterman, England, No. 1190: Protractor Combination Folding Rule. With Level. Crisp and Clean. Length: 24 Inches. *These multi-purpose rules were a mainstay of the Rabone line for many years. This one is in new condition in its very well preserved condition.* (GOOD+) **$115.00**

H5-8. Unmarked: Narrow Metric Rule. Also Marked"Groningen". Unused Condition. Length: 39 1/2 Inches. *Graduated with metric scales and another scale known as "Groningen", which is new to us, this specialized comparative scale rule has never been used. Mint* (FINE) **$110.00**

H5-9. Stanley Rule & Level No. 163: Light Duty Folding Rule. 1941 To 1943 Only. Rare and Excellent. Length: 24 Inches. *These light-duty rules were produced during WW II and discontinued after a short run. This one appears never to have been used.* (FINE) **$45.00**

H5-10. Stanley Rule & Level No. 54: Two-Foot, Four-Fold Folding Rule. Arch Joint, Full Bound. Extra Early Imprint. Length: 24 Inches. *Here's an early example which has no stains, tight joints and clear marks inside and out. The inside mark is the very early "Stanley Rule & Level" mark in small lettering.* (GOOD+) **$75.00**

H5-11. Stanley Rule & Level No. 54: Two-Foot, Four-Fold Folding Rule. Arch Joint, Full Bound. Extra Early Imprint. Length: 24 Inches. *This No. 54 arch joint rule was just a notch better than the much more common No. 62, which featured a "square" joint. This extra early example is clean and sound. A nice Stanley rule.* (GOOD+) **$55.00**

H5-12. Unmarked: Boxwood Comparitive Folding Rule. Gamla, Nya and London. Unused Condition. Length: 24 Inches. *Comparative rules were used frequently in Europe to contend with the differing units of measurement in use within short distances. This unused example, which is not imprinted with any maker's mark, is graduated in inches (London) as well as the Scandinavian scales of Gamla and Nya. Rare and perfect.* (FINE) **$65.00**

H5-13. Stanley Rule & Level No. 36 1/2 R: One Foot, Two Fold Folding Rule. With Caliper Rule. Near New Condition. Length: 12 Inches. *This right hand caliper rule is in nearly perfectly preserved condition. A nice example.* (FINE) **$45.00**

H5-14. Chapin, H., No. 2: One Foot, Four Fold Folding Rule. Square Joint, Unbound. Rare and Excellent. Length: 12 Inches. *This No. 2 Chapin rule is the functional equivalent of Stanley's No. 65. A rare and early folding boxwood rule.* (GOOD+) **$95.00**

H5-15. Smallwood, I. & D., Birmingham: One Meter Folding Rule. Solid Boxwood. Unused Condition. Length: 39 1/2 Inches. *No apologies whatsoever for this pristine one meter folding rule from respected Birmingham (England) rulemakers I. & D. Smallwood.* (FINE) **$85.00**

H5-16. C-S Co., The, No. 65: One Foot, Four Fold Folding Rule. Square Joint, Unbound. Suberb Condition. Length: 12 Inches. *The equivalent of Stanley's No. 65 square-joint, boxwood rule is in top collector-quality condition. A nice example.* (FINE) **$75.00**

H5-17. Stanley Rule & Level No. 36 1/2: One Foot, Two Fold Folding Rule. With Caliper. Ca. 1910. Length: 12 Inches. *This one foot Stanley caliper rule dates from the first quarter of this century. A common but clean Stanley rule.* (GOOD) **$25.00**

H5-18. Stanley Rule & Level No. 32: One-Foot, Four-Fold Folding Rule. Arch-Joint, Unbound. With Caliper. Length: 12 Inches. *Nearly every carpenter kept a rule such as this in his (or her, if you insist) vest pocket. This one is marked with the Stanley trademark in use at the very beginning of the Twentieth Century.* (GOOD) **$25.00**

H5-19. Chapin-Stephens Co., The, No. 78 1/2: Double Arch Joint Folding Rule. Full Bound. Rare and Excellent. Length: 24 Inches. *Double arch joint rules were the very best offered by all makers. This early Chapin Stephens example is clean, sound and ready for inclusion in a principal collection.* (GOOD+) **$115.00**

H5-20. Unmarked: Two Foot, Four Fold Folding Rule. London and Paris Graduated. German Silver Fittings. Length: 12 Inches. *This unmarked rule features fittings of German silver and comparative scales of Paris and London measurements. Only a few minor stains detract from this otherwise well preserved rule.* (GOOD+) **$85.00**

H5-21. Smallwood, I. & D., Birmingham: One Meter Folding Rule. Solid Boxwood. Unused Condition. Length: 39 1/2 Inches. *No apologies whatsoever for this pristine one meter folding rule from respected Birmingham (England) rulemakers I. & D. Smallwood.* (FINE) **$85.00**

H5-22. Stanley Rule & Level No. 51: 2 Foot, 4 Fold Folding Rule. With Arch Joint. "English" Graduates. Length: 24 Inches. *The original purchaser of this rule ordered the optional "English" graduations, hence the numbering proceeds from left to right, rather than the standard right to left. It is marked with Stanley's early block letter trademark.* (GOOD+) **$65.00**

H5-23. Stanley Rule & Level (Unmarked) No. 69: One Foot, Four Fold Folding Rule. With Round Joint. Early and Excellent. Length: 12 Inches. *The smaller sizes of Stanley's folding rules were seldom marked with the maker mark. This one is unmarked, but unmistakable because of the distinctive "pentagon pin" in the joint.* (FINE) **$55.00**

H5-24. Unmarked: Broad Boxwood Folding Rule. Unfinished Graduates. Very Well Made. Length: 24 Inches. *For some reason this early appearing arch joint, half-bound boxwood rule did not complete the manufacturing process. It has no apparent defects and is in excellent condition. An interesting unfinished symphony from the world of folding rules.* (FINE) **$115.00**

H5-25. Chapin, H.: No. 5: One Foot, Four Fold Folding Rule. Sqare Joint, Full Bound. Rare and Excellent. Length: 12 Inches. *Fully bound and fitted with a "square" joint, this H. Chapin No. 5 rule, which retains nearly all of its original finishes, is the only example of this rare rule that we have ever offered for sale. Rare and excellent.* (FINE) **$185.00**

H5-26. Lufkin Rule Co., The, Saginaw, Mich.: No. 014: 4 Inch Caliper Folding Rule. With Caliper Slide. Near New Condition. Length: 4 Inches. *This Lufkin rule was produced late in their cycle of boxwood production. As were many Lufkin rules from this period, it is imprinted with the equivalent Stanley number in parentheses. It has never been used.* (FINE) **$35.00**

H5-27. Unmarked: English Novelty Folding Rule. Better Than Rule of Thumb. Near New Condition. Length: 6 Inches. *"Better than Rule of Thumb" is the inscription imprinted on the leather case for this two fold, one foot rule from England. Cute.* (FINE) **$35.00**

H5-28. Stanley Rule & Level No. 36: Six-Inch, Two-Fold Folding Rule. Ca. 1890's. Near New Condition. Length: 6 Inches. *This perfectly preserved caliper rule features a very early Stanley imprint. The rule is in as new condition. Nice.* (FINE) **$65.00**

H5-29. Rabone & Sons, J., Birmingham: No. 1040: Boxwood 1/2 Yard Rule. With Bevel Edge. Scarce and Near New. Length: 18 Inches. *Half yard rules in any configuration are seldom seen about. Far fewer are found in this condition. Crispy clean and clearly marked with the Rabone imprint.* (FINE) **$65.00**

H5-30. Preston & Sons, Edward: Extra Thick Boxwood Folding Rule. Dated "1916". For Military Use. Length: 24 Inches. *Unlike any rule from Preston that we have encountered and not shown in any Preston catalogs, it is likely that this extra thick folding boxwood rule was produced for military use during the First World War. The military use theory is made more likely by the "1916" date imprinted on the rule. A rare Preston rule in top collector quality condition.* (FINE) **$110.00**

H5-31. Stanley Rule & Level No. 66 1/2: Three Foot, Four Fold Folding Rule. Arch Joint, Unbound. Superb Condition. Length: 36 Inches. *Stanley basic three-foot rule in uncommonly nice condition. This one dates from the period shortly after the style of the "arch" joint was modified. A superb example of a Stanley rule not often found in this condition.* (FINE) **$95.00**

H5-32. C-S Co., The, Pine Meadow, Conn.: No. 84: Two Foot, Four Fold Folding Rule. Square Joint, Half Bound. Near New Condition. Length: 24 Inches. *Identical in all respects to the Stanley numerical equivalent, this Lufkin rule is in nearly new condition, noting a small black stain on the reverse side. A very nice rule.* (FINE) **$95.00**

H5-33. Rule Tool Co., Newark, N.J.: Cam Lock Rule Accessory. Patented October 1, 1907. With Cam Lock. Length: 3 Inches. *This device was affixed by a cam lock to your standard carpenter's rule where it facilitated the laying out of miter cuts. An uncommon patented rule accessory.* (GOOD+) **$65.00**

H5-34. Lufkin Rule Co., The: No. 372: One Foot, Two Fold Folding Rule. Similar to Stanley 36 1/2. Near New Condition. Length: 12 Inches. *The Lufkin equivalent to a common Stanley rule that is not near so common in this line. It appears never to have been used. Mint.* (FINE) **$35.00**

H5-35. Lufkin Rule Co., The, England: No. 372: One Foot, Two Fold Rule. With Caliper. Extra Wide Body. Length: 12 Inches. *Lufkin's later rules were made in England. Unlike the consequences of Stanley's venture into English manufacturing, the quality of the Lufkin rules went up. This example is in new condition.* (FINE) **$45.00**

H5-36. Stanley Rule & Level No. 36: Six-Inch, Two-Fold Folding Rule. Square Joint, Caliper. Early Example. Length: 6 Inches. *The patina on the outside of this rule is a consequence of having spent some time in the pocket of its original owner. An early Stanley rule with character.* (GOOD) **$25.00**

H5-37. Stanley Rule & Level No. 66 3/4: Three-Foot, Four-Fold Folding Rule. "Sweetheart" Trademark. Near New Condition. Length: 36 Inches. *No yard measure scales on this one, but it does have Stanley's 1920's era "Sweetheart" trademark and nearly all of its original finishes. A tough rule to find in this condition.* (FINE) **$175.00**

H5-38. Lufkin Rule Co., The, England: No. 3851: Three-Foot, Four Fold Folding Rule. Arch Joint, Unbound. Equal to Stanley 66 1/2. Length: 36 Inches. *Three foot rules tended to have their joints become "sprung" after limited use. This one avoided that fate by never having been used. Mint.* (FINE) **$35.00**

H5-39. Chapin-Stephens Co., The, No. 78 1/2: Double Arch Joint Folding Rule. Full Bound. Uncommon Type. Length: 24 Inches. *This double arch joint rule has a few stains, but it is otherwise clean and sound. A tough rule to find.* (GOOD) **$75.00**

H5-40. Lufkin Rule Co., The, Saginaw, Mich.: No. 388: Arch Joint, Full Bound Folding Rule. With Caliper Slide. Near New Condition. Length: 12 Inches. *This arch joint, full-bound caliper rule is the equivalent to Stanley's 32 1/2. A tough rule to find in any condition and rare when found like this. Perfect.* (FINE) **$95.00**

H5-41. Smallwood, I. & D., Birmingham: Broad Arch Joint Folding Rule. With Architect Scales. Uncommon Type. Length: 24 Inches. *This unmarked rule from English rulemakers I. & D. Smallwood of Birmingham is of the wider than normal "broad" type. It is fitted with the higher quality arch joint. A very nice example.* (GOOD+) **$75.00**

H5-42. Stanley Rule & Level No. 18 E: Two Foot, Two Fold Folding Rule. Square Joint, Unbound. "English" Graduates. Length: 24 Inches. *Stanley offered all of its rules with optional "English" graduations. The original purchaser of this well preserved rule exercised that option and the "English" designation is imprinted on the body of the rule.* (FINE) **$135.00**

H5-43. Stanley Rule & Level No. 18: Two Foot, Two Fold Folding Rule. Square Joint, Unbound. "Sweetheart" Trademark.. Length: 24 Inches. *This No. 18 rule was widely marketed to "manual training" schools where young would-be woodworkers could conspire to destroy them without the knowledge of the instructor. This one seems to have been guarded by a particularly zealous pedagogue. A nice example that is marked with Stanley's "Sweetheart" trademark.* (GOOD+) **$65.00**

H5-44. Stearns & Co., E.A., No. 22: Two Foot, Four Fold Folding Rule. With Board Scales. Early and Uncommon. Length: 24 Inches. *The inside of this uncommon Stearns rule is marked with board measure tables. A scarce Stearns rule.* (GOOD) **$125.00**

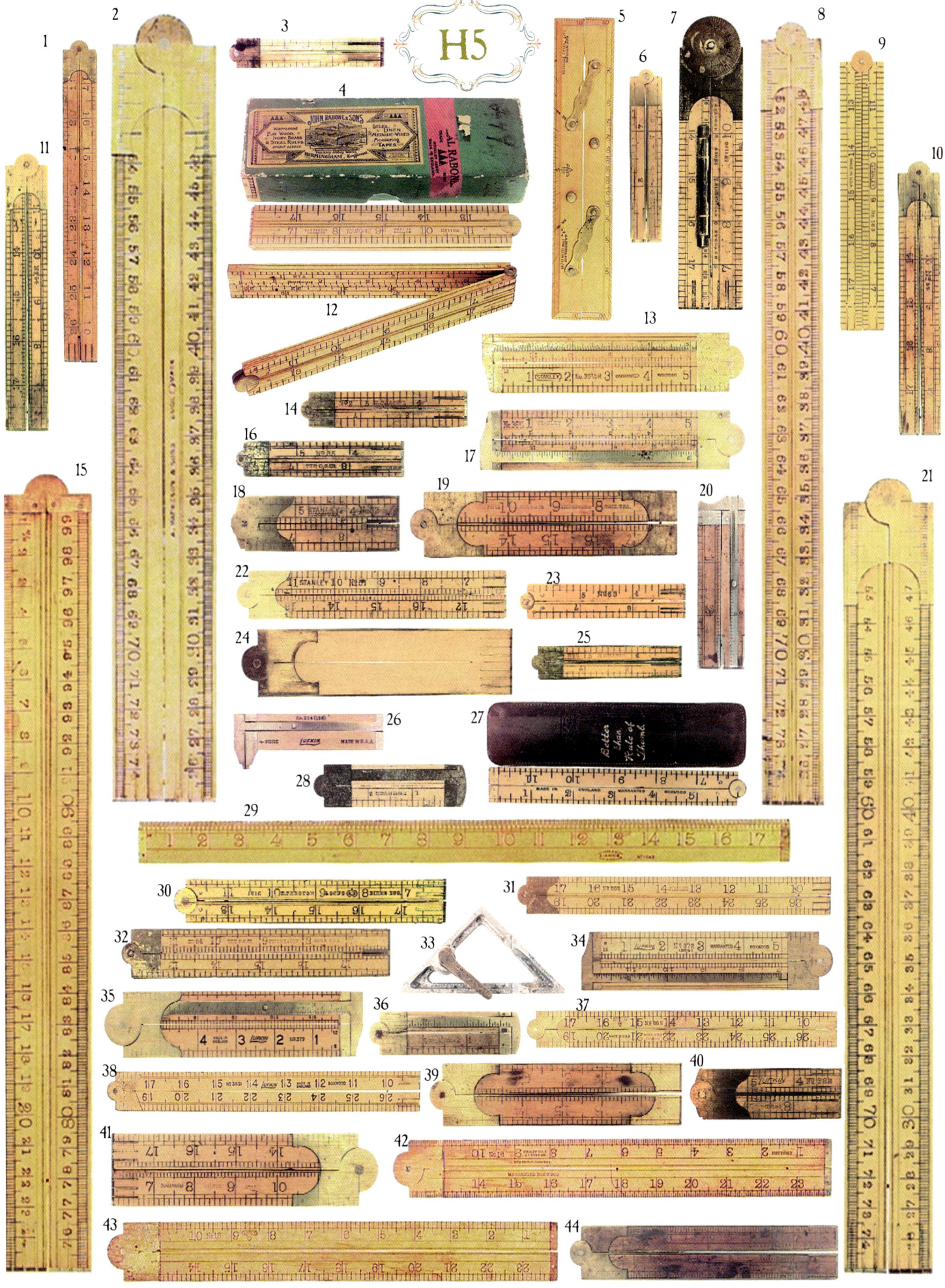

Group 15

15-1. Osborne & Co., C.S., Newark, N.J.: Group of 14 Oval Leather Punches. Assorted Sizes. Ready to Use. Length: 4 1/2 Inches. *These oval punches would have been used for cutting holes in leather for straps to pass through. All are marked with the C.S. Osborne imprint and are in excellent working order.* (GOOD+) **$365.00**

15-2. Unmarked: Advertising Crate Hammer. "Buy Arm & Hammer". Excellent Condition. Length: 8 1/2 Inches. *Why someone opening a wooden crate would have an interest in baking soda is not readily apparent to those of us with a 21st Century perspective. As an inducement to buy, we offer a box of Arm & Hammer Baking Soda to the purchaser of this tool. Two for one.* (GOOD+) **$65.00**

15-3. Assorted Makers: Group of 10 Round and Oval Punches. Assorted Sizes. Ready to Use. Length: 4 1/2 Inches. *All of these leather punches are in excellent working order and ready to use.* (GOOD+) **$45.00**

15-4. Osborne & Co., C.S., Newark, N.J.: Group of 17 Strap End Punches. Assorted Sizes. Ready to Use. Length: 4 1/2 Inches. *Obtained this past fall in the State of Maine, these leather punches were part of a cache of tools disbursed from a private museum.* (GOOD+) **$325.00**

15-5. Unmarked: Forged Iron Combination Tool. Hammer, Wrench, Etc. Most Unusual. Length: 13 Inches. *There may be tasks that this tool is incapable of performing. If you are able to identify one or more, please do not tell the inventor or he will likely produce an "improved" model that is even more of a monstrosity. A great collectible combination tool.* (GOOD) **$145.00**

15-6. Peck, Stow & Wilcox Co.: Massive Masting Draw Knife. With 12 Inch Blade. Near New Condition. Length: 23 Inches. *An oversize drawknife of this sort would have been used for poles or masts. It has never been used. Absolutely perfect.* (FINE) **$135.00**

15-7. Unmarked: "Star" Patent Nail Puller. Patented December 27, 1898. Unique Double Shaft. Length: 18 Inches. *As a collector of nail pullers, I would like to offer an invitation for others to take an interest in these quintessentially American tools. In early times, houses were often burned in order to save the nails. Later on, the disassembly of existing structures was facilitated by a series of seemingly endless variations on this simple theme. Here is a mechanically interesting early patent, which bears the designation "Star" but there are no maker markings. It is in excellent condition.* (GOOD+) **$75.00**

15-8. Assorted Makers: Group of 7 Round Leather Punches. Assorted Sizes. Ready to Use. Length: 4 1/2 Inches. *Some of these round punches have been well used, but all are in excellent working order.* (GOOD+) **$35.00**

15-9. Kraeuter & Co., Newark, N.J.: No. 337: Forged Steel Hammer. Full Nickel Plating. Uncommon Type. Length: 11 Inches. *As was the case with everything that they made, the crate opening hammer from Kraeuter & Company is of the very first quality.* (FINE) **$55.00**

15-10. Drew & Co., C., Kingston, Mass.: Crate Opening Hammer. Uncommon Type. Important Maker. Length: 9 Inches. *C. Drew & Company specialized in drop forged tools of the highest quality. This crate opener is consistent with that standard. A good one.* (GOOD+) **$35.00**

15-11. Osborne & Co., C.S., Newark, N.J.: No. 28: Rosewood Handle Cigar Box Opener. Integral Hammer. Most Unusual Type. Length: 7 Inches. *The last time cigars were trendy, they came packed in cedar boxes sealed with small nails. Opening and sealing the box required one of these specialized tools. This example is from from leather working tool giant C.S. Osborne & Company. Different.* (GOOD+) **$45.00**

15-12. Unmarked: Side Nail Puller Hammer. Bell Face. Excellent Condition. Length: 13 Inches. *The side of this claw hammer is fitted with a slot to start and extract nails. We would suspect that too much use of the nail extraction feature would have resulted in a two piece hammer.* (GOOD+) **$65.00**

15-13. Unmarked: Hand Forged Cutting Wheel. Solid Steel Head. With Shoulder Grip. Length: 23 Inches. *Unlike anything else we have ever offered, this specialty cutting wheel has a heavy, sharp edged roller of unknown function. From the appearance of this thing it seems likely that it was meant to be pushed with the shoulder. Different.* (GOOD) **$85.00**

15-14. Mohler Mfg. Co., E.M., Champaign,: Early Patent Crate Hammer. Patented March 5, 1901. Uncommon Large Size. Length: 9 Inches. *We have seen this patented box opening hammer in a 6 inch version, but never in this size. This one is clearly marked with the name and patent date.* (GOOD+) **$55.00**

15-15. Unmarked: Forged Iron Nail Puller. Patented January 2, 1900. Early and Unusual. Length: 18 Inches. *This patented nail pulling device is unlike any other animal of this genus that we have seen before. Decidedly different.* (GOOD+) **$65.00**

15-16. Unmarked: Uncommon Small Size Nail Puller. "B" Casting. Most Unusual. Length: 16 Inches. *Only a letter "B" inside of a diamond is imprinted on the body of this unusual nail puller. It is about two inches shorter than standard nail pullers. Different.* (GOOD+) **$85.00**

15-17. Unmarked: Combination Hatchet and Hammer. With Nail Puller. Similar to Thayer Patent. Length: 9 1/2 Inches. *This early hammer, hatchet and nail puller combination looks to have its original handle intact. It is very similar to the Thayer Patent shown in "The Hammer: The King of Tools".* (GOOD) **$395.00**

15-18. Geiger, G, Philadelphia Penn.: Nickel Plated Crate Hammer. With Nail Puller. Uncommon Maker. Length: 8 Inches. *The Directory of American Toolmakers makes no mention of a G. Geiger in Philadelphia or anywhere else. A well preserved crate hammer from an undocumented maker.* (FINE) **$65.00**

15-19. Unmarked: Early Hand Forged Nail Puller. With Pivot End. Very Old Type. Length: 13 3/4 Inches. *For the serious collector of nail pullers, we recommend this very early forged iron example. The hook handle appears to have been designed to do double duty as a hanger and for beginning the process of extracting nails.* (GOOD) **$145.00**

15-20. Bridgeport Hardware Mfg. Corp.: Cast Iron Nail Puller. "Jumbo". Patent January 9, 1902. Length: 18 Inches. *The Bridgeport Hardware Manufacturing Company was a major producer of nail pullers. This early Twentieth Century patent has the designation "Jumbo" cast into the body.* (GOOD+) **$65.00**

15-21. Millers Falls Company No. 3: Wood Handle Nail Puller. Patented October 25, 1898. Rivet Plate Fulcrum. Length: 20 Inches. *Millers Falls offered several nail pullers, of which these are the least common. A rare nail puller in excellent condition.* (GOOD+) **$195.00**

15-22. Herculever Co., New York: "Herculever" Patented. Nail Puller. Spring Action Fulcrum. Patented May 1, 1906. Length: 20 Inches. *The patented "Herculever" nail puller features a spring activated prybar tip with an extended fulcrum. Totally unlike anything else we have seen in the nail puller line, we have it on good authority that this was used to remove stray nails from the Augean Stables. A rare nail puller in excellent condition.* (GOOD+) **$125.00**

15-23. Kilborn & Bishop: Crate Opening Hammer. Original Nickel Plating. Uncommon Maker. Length: 9 Inches. *Kilborn and Bishop are new to us, but they sure made a nice crate hammer. Nice.* (GOOD+) **$35.00**

15-24. Bailey, L., Boston, Mass.: Cooper's Heavy Spoke Shave. 18 Inch Length. 4 Inch Cutter. Length: 18 Inches. *A rare example of the pre-planemaking of Leonard Bailey, the uncontested champion of metallic plane innovation this massive cooper's spokeshave is marked with the "L. Bailey, Boston" mark dating from the 1850's. Early and well preserved.* (GOOD+) **$115.00**

15-25. E.T.F. Ltd., St. Catharines, Canada No. 3775: Forged Steel Nail Puller. Uncommon Type. Very Well Preserved. Length: 18 Inches. *There has to be a first for everything and we are pleased to make this our very first Canadian made nail puller. The red paint on the handle, of which about 80% remains, looks to have been original.* (GOOD+) **$35.00**

15-26. Kelley, J.P., Erie, Penn.: "Giant Grip" Staple Puller. Crate Opener Style. Uncommon Type. Length: 11 Inches. *Staple pullers, box openers and nail pullers are one of those "easy to enter, fun to participate" areas of tool collecting that don't require a million dollars to participate. This "giant grip" puller comes from an obscure Erie, Pennsylvania maker.* (GOOD+) **$35.00**

15-27. Unmarked: Early Ratchting Wrench. Spring Lock Ratchet. Hand Forged Body. Length: 19 1/2 Inches. *When scholars get around to documenting the history of the ratchet wrench, this is one that will end up in Chapter 1. A very well made and mechanically interesting hand forged ratchet wrench.* (GOOD+) **$225.00**

15-28. Bridgeport Hardware Mfg. Co., The No. 88: Multi Purpose Crate Opener. With Hatchet Head. Nail Puller Tip. Length: 12 1/2 Inches. *Bridgeport made more types of crate opening tools than almost anybody. This "tomahawk" type incorporates a nail puller at the top of the head. A good one.* (GOOD+) **$35.00**

15-29. Barnes: "Barnes Patent" Pipe Cutter. Patented January 9, 1877. Early and Unusual. 12 Inches. *This same patent was applied to an uncommon early pipe wrench. I haven't looked at the patent papers, but the cutting mechanism and the pipe jaw may have been interchangeable. An uncommon tool.* (GOOD) **$55.00**

15-30. Millers Falls Company No. 52: Ratcheting Joist Brace. Black Metal Finish. Rare and Excellent. Length: 19 Inches. *Designed for the rough and tumble work of boring through floor joists to fit electrical wire and pipe, these tools were subjected to much abuse. This example has survived intact and in excellent working order.* (GOOD+) **$165.00**

15-31. Bridgeport Hardware Mfg. Co., The No. 120: Multi Purpose Crate Opener. "Wool Soap Flakes". Unused Condition. Length: 12 1/2 Inches. *While we have yet to see a "Crate Opener Collectors Association" promoting itself, we are aware that there are many of you out there endeavoring to find "one of each" in this seemingly endlessly variable field. It is our pleasure to offer this, the finest such tool that we have ever offered. Obviously never used for the task for which it was designed, this Bridgeport No. 120 is imprinted with advertising for "Wool Soap Flakes", a product the time of whose demise may help to date this device. Crate openers were subjected to hard use and many show signs of abuse, however, as in every area of collecting, examples in new condition are those that are the most eagerly sought out and the most treasured. A quintessential crate opener. Highly recommended.* (FINE) **$165.00**

15-32. Johnson, W., Newark, N.J.: Hardwood Handle Tack Puller. Ca. 1920's. Uncommon Maker. Length: 6 1/2 Inches. *William Johnson of Newark, New Jersey made all sorts of tools and hardware. This nail puller is in excellent condition.* (GOOD+) **$15.00**

15-33. Drew & Co., C., Kingston, Mass.: Heavy Duty Slate Ripper. Quality Maker. Near New Condition. Length: 25 Inches. *C. Drew and Company are renowned for the quality of their ship caulking tools and kindred nautical accessories. This slater's ripper is up to their standard. Ready to use.* (FINE) **$65.00**

15-34. Billings & Spencer Co., The: Multi Purpose Wire Cutter. Early Appearance. Very Well Made. Length: 10 Inches. *This distinctively different wire cutter is of the kind of quality you would expect from Billings & Spencer. A rare collectible tool.* (GOOD) **$45.00**

15-35. Jacobs Bros., Inc., New York, N.Y.: Crate Opening Hatchet. With Nail Pullers. Uncommon Type. Length: 12 1/2 Inches. *This crate opener is imprinted with the name of a maker we have not previously encountered. Working dates are not listed in the Directory of American Toolmakers.* (GOOD+) **$55.00**

15-36. Assorted Makers: Group of 11 Round Leather Punches. Assorted Sizes. Ready to Use. Length: 4 1/2 Inches. *A wide array of sizes are represented among these well preserved punches. Crisp, clean and ready to use.* (GOOD+) **$45.00**

15-37. Osborne & Co., C.S., Newark, N.J.: Group of 3 Oval Leather Punches. Uncommon Type. Ready to Use. Length: 5 Inches. *Here's an excellent stepped set of oval punches from the most prominent maker of leather working tools. Ready to use.* (GOOD+) **$145.00**

15-38. Berylco: Special Purpose Beryllium Tool. With Chipping Head. Scarce and Excellent. Length: 18 Inches. *Nearly every tool under the sun was fashioned from beryllium at some point, including some that we were not previously aware existed, such as this spade end hammer. Most unusual.* (GOOD+) **$115.00**

15-39. Osborne & Co., C.S., Newark, N.J.: Group of 9 Strap End Punches. Assorted Sizes. Ready to Use. Length: 4 1/2 Inches. *Semicircular punches such as these were used to form the rounded end on a belt, such as that used for horse harnesses. These are in excellent order and ready to use.* (FINE) **$325.00**

15-40. Unmarked: Assorted Rosewood Leather Burnishers. Various Shapes. Excellent Condition. Length: 10 1/2 Inches. *A cut above the standard leather burnishers, those made of rosewood has a durability beyond other woods as well as natural oil for lubrication. Here's a nice assortment from the tools of a single leather worker.* (GOOD+) **$65.00**

15-41. Unmarked: Assorted Hardwood Leather Burnishers. Various Shapes. Excellent Condition. Length: 10 1/2 Inches. *If you're looking to start a burnisher collection, or maybe just want to start a small fire, here's an affordable opportunity.* (GOOD+) **$35.00**

15-42. Assorted Makers: Group of 11 Round Leather Punches. Assorted Sizes. Ready to Use. Length: 5 1/2 Inches. *These graduated round punches were part of the working tools of a harness maker. A nice set.* (GOOD+) **$45.00**

15-43. Unmarked: Early Specialty Hammer. With Tack Puller. Very Well Made. Length: 12 Inches. *This extra long specialty hammer is fitted with a steel ferrule at the head and a tack puller on the end of the handle. It appears never to have been used.* (FINE) **$65.00**

15-44. Assorted Makers: Group of 10 Round and Serrated Punches. Assorted Sizes. Ready to Use. Length: 4 1/2 Inches. *Here's a bargain lot of leather punches with a pinking iron or two thrown in for good measure.* (GOOD+) **$35.00**

15-45. Osborne & Co., C.S., Newark, N.J.: Group of 13 Strap End Punches. Assorted Sizes. Ready to Use. Length: 4 1/2 Inches. *Here's an excellent set of strap end punches for harness work in excellent overall condition. Ready to use.* (GOOD+) **$325.00**

Group J5

J5-1. Stanley Rule & Level No. 55: Patent Combination Plane. With 4 Boxes of Cutters. Owner Made Box. Length: 9 Inches. *This "Patent Universal Combination Plane" is complete with its full complement of cutters in a substantial craftsman-made box.* (GOOD) **$625.00**

J5-2. Stanley Rule & Level No. 78: Duplex Filletster Plane. Sweetheart Trademark. 99%+ Original Paint. Length: 9 1/2 Inches. *This shiny and crispy clean example of Stanley's No. 78 duplex rabbet and filletster plane retains 99% of its original shiny black japan finish. It is marked with the ca. 1920's "Sweetheart" trademark. Perfect.* (FINE) **$95.00**

J5-3. Stanley Rule & Level No. 40: Beech Handle Scrub Plane. Sweetheart Trademark. Excellent Condition. Length: 11 Inches. *This 1930's era scrub plane is in great condition with more than 95% of its original paint. The lacquered beech handles are clean and sound. A great working tool.* (GOOD+) **$115.00**

J5-4. Stanley Rule & Level No. 12-250D: Combination Plane. Made in England. New Condition, Original Box. Length: 12 Inches. *A very late manifestation of the Stanley combination plane, these tools were made in England, perhaps as late as the 1970's or 1980's. This one is in new condition in its original box. We shudder to think of what one of these would cost if produced new today.* (FINE) **$125.00**

J5-5. Tyzack & Son, Joseph, Sheffield: Miniature Boxwood Spoke Shave. 1 1/2 Inch Cutting Edge. Near New Condition. Length: 8 Inches. *This narrow spokeshave is imprinted with the mark of Joseph Tyzak and fitted with a 1 1/2 Inch cutting iron. It has been very little use. Extra nice.* (FINE) **$85.00**

J5-6. Preston & Sons, Edward: Decorative Cast Iron Spoke Shave. Precision Adjust. Elaborate Casting. Length: 10 Inches. *With few exceptions, American manufactured tools were seldom the equal of their English counterparts in pure visual appeal. This elaborately cast spoke shave is a showpiece of the English toolmakers' art.* (FINE) **$75.00**

J5-7. Stanley Rule & Level No. 4: 9 Inch Smoothing Plane. Original Decal. Near New Condition. Length: 9 Inches. *Virtually all of the shiny original japan finish remains on this pristine example of the "Type 13" No. 4 smoothing plane. Nearly all of the original decal remains.* (FINE) **$135.00**

J5-8. Buckeye: Cast Iron Jointer Gauge. Nickel Plated Fence. Uncommon Type. Length: 9 Inches. *The "Buckeye" jointer gauge used the cam lock design employed effectively by several other makers. Ready to use.* (GOOD) **$45.00**

J5-9. Record, Sheffield, England No. 043: Cast Iron Plow Metallic Plane. Complete and Excellent. Fitted Felt Pouch. Length: 5 1/2 Inches. *Designed to fit into the palm of the hand, these miniature plow planes were quite popular in their day and remain so today. This one is in essentially unused condition in a fitted felt pouch, complete with some wood shavings at no extra charge.* (FINE) **$135.00**

J5-10. Preston & Sons, Edward: Cast Iron Quirk Router. With 3 Cutters. 3 Original Fences. Length: 13 Inches. *An excellent example of the Preston patent quirk router, complete with many original parts. A mechanically interesting tool.* (GOOD+) **$145.00**

J5-11. Stanley Rule & Level No. 5: Rosewood Handle Jack Plane. Ca. 1920. 98% Original Paint. Length: 14 Inches. *Nearly all of the original paint and much of the decal remains on this crisp and clean jack plane of the "type 12" variety. Ready to use.* (FINE) **$95.00**

J5-12. Record, Sheffield, England No. 050: Improved Combination Metallic Plane. With Original Cutters. New Condition, Original Box. Length: 9 Inches. *Complete in its original box with a full set of rabbeting and the optional beading cutters, this light duty combination plane is destined to be put back into use. Extra-nice.* (FINE) **$295.00**

J5-13. Red Devil Tools, Union, N.J. No. 12: Handled Paint Scraper. Lacquered Red Handle. New Condition, Original Box. Length: 11 Inches. *An interesting handled scraper in new condition in its original carton. We will all remember the days when Red Devil stuff could be had for a pittance. Different.* (FINE) **$35.00**

J5-14. Stanley Rule & Level No. 78: Duplex Rabbet, Fillet Plane. Patented June 7, 1910. New Condition, Original Box. Length: 10 Inches. *A great early example of the popular No. 78 rabbet and filletster plane in absolutely pristine condition it the desirable "picture box". An increasing number of collectors are seeking out these early and visually appealing pasteboard boxes for their visual appeal. Those who have seen a shelf or two of these boxes assembled together know what I mean. A great plane in a great box.* (FINE) **$135.00**

J5-15. Graves, J.D., Sheffield: Solid Boxwood Spoke Shave. 2 1/2 Inch Cutting Edge. Excellent Condition. Length: 10 1/2 Inches. *This boxwood spokeshave is in excellent working order and ready to use. A good one.* (GOOD+) **$75.00**

J5-16. Stanley Rule & Level No. 192: Cast Iron Rabbet Plane. 1 Inch Width. Extra Crisp and Clean. Length: 10 1/2 Inches. *The No. 192 was the narrowest size of the Stanley rabbet plane series. This one is in extra clean condition and ready to be put immediately to use.* (GOOD+) **$55.00**

J5-17. Stanley Rule & Level No. 65: Low Angle Block Plane. Patented October 12, 1897. Uncommon Type. Length: 7 Inches. *The No. 65 was Stanley's basic wide-body low angle block plane for many years. The knuckle joint cap provides a positive lock and the screw adjustment will precisely adjust the cut. Clean, sound and ready to use.* (GOOD+) **$95.00**

J5-18. Stanley Rule & Level No. 608: Bedrock Jointer Plane. Later Style. Smooth Bottom. Length: 24 Inches. *One of the most popular of all the Bedrock series, the No. 608 would perform work under circumstances where the "chatter" that it was supposed to prevent would be most likely to occur. The original owner touched up the paint on this one so it appears nearly new. A great working plane in ready to use condition.* (GOOD) **$225.00**

J5-19. Stanley Rule & Level No. 12 1/2: Adjustable Scraper Plane. Rosewood Bottom. Extra Crisp and Clean. Length: 6 Inches. *The cutting iron on this rosewood sole scraper plane is a proper recent replacement, but the plane is otherwise perfect and ready to use. A nice working tool.* (FINE) **$155.00**

J5-20. Record, Sheffield, England No. 044: Light Duty Plow Metallic Plane. With Original Cutters. New Condition, Original Box. Length: 8 Inches. *As a functional working tool, there's no beating this light duty grooving plane from England's now-defunct Record firm. This one is in great condition in its original box.* (FINE) **$165.00**

J5-21. Stanley Rule & Level No. 39: 3/4 Inch Cast Iron Dado Plane. "Sweetheart" Trademark. Superb Condition. Length: 8 Inches. *More than 99% of the original shiny black japan finish remains on this 3/4 inch dado plane from Stanley's ca. 1920's "Sweetheart" era. The 3/4 inch size is particularly desirable as it is the same size as nominal 1 inch lumber. A sweetheart.* (FINE) **$325.00**

J5-22. Marples & Sons, Wm., Hibernia Wks.: Solid Boxwood Spoke Shave. 2 1/2 Inch Cutting Edge. Excellent Condition. Length: 10 1/2 Inches. *The imprint of Sheffield toolmakers William Marples & Sons appears on the handle of this narrow boxwood spokeshave. A nice example in excellent working order.* (GOOD+) **$65.00**

J5-23. Stanley Rule & Level: Box of 6 Cutting Irons. For No. 102 Plane. New Condition, Original Box. Length: 4 Inches. *The original paper seal remains in place on this box of cutting irons for the No. 102 block plane. Perfect.* (FINE) **$45.00**

J5-24. Record, Sheffield, England No. 075: Bullnose Block Metallic Plane. With Original Decal. New Condition, Original Box. Length: 4 Inches. *This equivalent to Stanley's No. 75 bullnose rabbet is in new condition in its original box. Perfect.* (FINE) **$65.00**

J5-25. Stanley Rule & Level No. 6: 18 Inch Fore Plane. Orange Infill Cap. 99% Original Finish. Length: 18 Inches. *Half jack plane and half jointer, the 18 inch No. 6 can do some of the work of each. This one is about as good as they get. Mint.* (FINE) **$145.00**

J5-26. Abington, Sheffield: Classic Beechwood Spoke Shave. With Brass Wear Plate. Extra Tight Throat. Length: 11 3/4 Inches. *A brass wear plate has been mortised into the sole of this beech spokeshave as part of the manufacturing process to prolong its longevity. Extra crisp and clean.* (GOOD+) **$45.00**

J5-27. Stearns & Co., E.C., Syracuse, N.Y.: Cast Iron Jointer Gauge. Nickel Plated Fence. Extra Crisp and Clean. Length: 9 Inches. *of essentially the same design as the jointer gauges offered by the Millers Falls Company, those made by the E.C. Stearns Company are equally useful. A nice example of an excellent working tool.* (GOOD+) **$75.00**

J5-28. Stanley Rule & Level No. 66: Universal Scratch Beader. With Straight Fence. 6 Double Cutters. Length: 11 Inches. *This complete example of Stanley's highly-desirable scratch beader is complete with the straight fence and six double-ended cutters. Extra crisp and clean.* (FINE) **$165.00**

J5-29. Stanley Rule & Level No. 69: Patent Hand Beader. With Set of Cutters. Super Rare and Early. Length: 4 3/4 Inches. *Produced by Stanley for only a few short years, from 1898 to 1917, when it was discontinued "temporarily" for wartime purposes and then unceremoniously dumped, as were a number of slow selling items, when peacetime conditions again prevailed, the No. 69 beader is a rare and very collectible Stanley tool. Designed to be used in conjunction with a fixed fence of wood to cut decorative beading and fluting on wood, these tools apparently failed to produce sufficient demand in the marketplace. Accordingly, examples are quite rare. This example is in excellent collector-quality condition, complete with cutters and is ready to proudly display.* (GOOD+) **$595.00**

J5-30. Stanley Rule & Level No. 78: Duplex Rabbet, Fillet Plane. Absolutely Unused. New Condition, Original Box. Length: 10 Inches. *This example of Stanley's classic combination bullnose and rabbet plane is clean, complete and has been protected throughout its long life by the presence of its original box. Absolutely unused.* (FINE) **$135.00**

J5-31. Record No. 042: 3/4 Inch Shoulder Metallic Plane. With Screw Adjustment. Superb Condition. Length: 10 Inches. *These 3/4 inch rabbet planes are becoming extremely difficult to find at any price. Extra nice.* (FINE) **$245.00**

J5-32. Mathieson, (Glasgow, Scotland): Brass Bench Level. Mirrored Lining. Rare and Near New. Length: 6 Inches. *Those who have seen the buffed and ruined tools offered for sale at London markets will appreciate this rare solid brass Mathieson bench level, which has never been polished and, apparently, was very little used. A mirrored finish underlies the original level vial. A rare Mathieson level in excellent condition.* (FINE) **$255.00**

J5-33. Preston & Sons, Edward No. 1394: Cast Iron Quirk Router Plane. With 2 Fences, Cutters. Rare and Complete. Length: 5 Inches. *This well preserved Preston router comes with two depth stops and three cutting irons. A tough Preston tool to find.* (GOOD+) **$145.00**

J5-34. Stanley Rule & Level No. 66: Universal Scratch Beader. Complete With 2 Fences. 6 Double Cutters. Length: 11 Inches. *Complete, with shiny nickel plating, both original fences and a total of 6 different double-ended cutters, this one is ready to go to work. A choice tool for the yuppie woodworker or the discerning collector.* (GOOD+) **$145.00**

J5-35. Stanley Rule & Level No. 604 C: "Bedrock" Smooth Plane. Corrugated Bottom. Ready to Use. Length: 9 Inches. *Our experience has been that purchasers of Stanley's "Bedrock" planes opted, in overwhelming proportions, for those without corrugated soles. The original buyer of this well preserved example took the road not taken. An excellent working tool.* (GOOD+) **$225.00**

J5-36. Stanley Rule & Level No. 39: Cast Iron Dado Plane. 3/8 Inch Size. Superb Condition. Length: 8 Inches. *Supposedly the "most common" of the No. 39 series, this 3/8 inch example is in uncommonly nice condition. Crisp.* (FINE) **$225.00**

J5-37. Sargent & Co., New Haven, Conn. No. 217: Cast Iron Block Metallic Plane. Early Fixing Screw. Crisp and Clean. Length: 7 1/4 Inches. *This uncommon block plane was more or less the equivalent of Stanley's No. 220 block plane. An uncommon Sargent plane.* (FINE) **$45.00**

J5-38. Sargent & Co., New Haven, Conn. No. 107: Cast Iron Block Metallic Plane. Early Example. New Condition, Original Box. Length: 6 Inches. *The original box has kept this Sargent block plane in top collector quality condition. Mint.* (FINE) **$95.00**

J5-39. Stanley Rule & Level No. 45: Adjustable Combination Plane. Complete and Excellent. New Condition, Original Box. Length: 11 1/2 Inches. *No apologies whatsoever for this crispy clean and complete No. 45 combination plane. All original parts, including the instruction manual and the screwdriver are included. Pristine.* (FINE) **$425.00**

J5-40. Record, Sheffield, England No. 044: Light Duty Plow Metallic Plane. With Original Cutters. New Condition, Original Box. Length: 8 Inches. *These light duty plows are equally as functional as Stanley's No. 50 beading plane and can be had much cheaper. Complete with all cutters in the original box.* (FINE) **$165.00**

J5-41. Preston & Sons, Edward: Miniature Cast Iron Router Plane. With 3 Original Irons. Scarce and Excellent. Length: 4 1/2 Inches. *An enterprising craftsman replaced the original screws with knurled replacements of his own, but was kind enough to keep the originals around to preserve the collectible value of this tool. Complete with its full complement of 3 cutting irons, this rare Preston router is ready for the shelf, or use, or both.* (FINE) **$165.00**

J5-42. Stanley Rule & Level No. 7: "Type 12" Jointer Plane. 3 Patent Dates. Near New Condition. Length: 22 Inches. *A few flakes of japanning are missing from the heel and toe of this pristine jointer plane, but it is otherwise picture perfect. An extra clean example of the desirable "Type 12" plane, which has the 3 patent dates cast in the body and features the high rosewood front knob.* (FINE) **$225.00**

J5-43. Sorby, I. , (England): Classic Boxwood Spoke Shave. 2 Inch Cutter. Extra Crisp and Clean. Length: 10 Inches. *This boxwood spokeshave appears to have been very little used. Crisp, clean and ready to use. Nice.* (FINE) **$65.00**

J5-44. Stanley Rule & Level No. 5: Rosewood Handle Jack Plane. Crisp and Clean. Length: 14 Inches. *The color of the tote on this jack plane seems not to match that of the front knob, but the plane is otherwise in excellent condition and ready to use.* (GOOD+) **$55.00**

J5-45. Stanley Rule & Level No. 1299: "Defiance" Carpenter Knife. Cast Iron Body. Near New Condition. Length: 4 1/4 Inches. *These cast iron knives are the preferred choice of drywall workers. They are much sturdier than the cheap knives produced today. This one is in nearly new condition. Heavy duty.* (FINE) **$35.00**

Group K5

K5-1. Sandusky Tool Co., Sandusky, Ohio, No. 102: Pair of 7/8 Inch Tongue and Groove Molding Planes. Right Hand Handles. Extra Crisp and Clean. Length: 11 1/2 Inches. *Each of these Sandusky handled tongue and groove planes was contoured at the factory to fit the hand of a right handed user.* (GOOD+) **$125.00**

K5-2. Cumings, A., Boston, Mass.: Handled Spar Molding Plane. With Side Boxing. With Rope Hole. Length: 14 Inches. *A hole for a rope through the front of this plane is a sure sign that this tool was used for the work for which it was designed. The throat is a bit open from some of that use, but it is otherwise clean, sound, clearly marked and ready to display.* (GOOD) **$125.00**

K5-3. Nurse, C., 32 Mill St. (London): Set of 9 Boxed Bead Molding Planes. With Slip Sides. Near New Condition. Length: 9 1/2 Inches. *These slip sided bead planes from prominent maker C. Nurse are in nearly new condition. Simply a great set.* (FINE) **$445.00**

K5-4. Sandusky Tool Co., Sandusky, Ohio, No. 149: Skew Blade Rabbet Plane. With Offset Handle. 1 3/4 Inch Size. Length: 9 1/2 Inches. *The handle on this Sandusky classic was mounted at an angle to save the knuckles of the user when planing large rabbet or joints in close proximity to other boards. It is in very well preserved condition.* (GOOD+) **$85.00**

K5-5. Smith, E.: Handled Rabbet Molding Plane. With Dual Nickers. AWP III: 1 Star (A). Length: 14 1/2 Inches. *This classic handled rabbet and dado plane is crisp, clean and boldly marked with the E. Smith mark.* (GOOD+) **$195.00**

K5-6. Howland & Co., A., Auburn, N.Y. No. 73: Pair of Tongue and Groove Molding Planes. Marked "7/8". Near New Condition. Length: 10 1/2 Inches. *These planes were made by A. Howland & Company at Auburn Prison in Auburn, New York in the 1860's. Condition is near new. Mint.* (FINE) **$185.00**

K5-7. Unmarked: Early Gunstock Molding Plane. Yellow Birch Body. Wide Flat Chamfers. Length: 10 3/4 Inches. *Here's a classic 18th Century plane in yellow birch. It was used for hollowing out the recess for the barrel of a rifle. There is a hang hole in the body, but the tool is otherwise excellent. A classic collectible plane.* (GOOD+) **$225.00**

K5-8. Reed, Utica (N. Y.): Classic Ogee Molding Plane. Marked "8/8". Ready to Use. Length: 9 1/2 Inches. *to facilitate the use of this wide ogee molder, a previous owner bored a hole through the body for a rope or dowel to be used to pull the plane along the wood. A plane with character.* (GOOD+) **$110.00**

K5-9. Smith, E.: Pair of Handled Tongue and Grove Molding Planes. For 1 Inch Lumber. Near New Condition. Length: 11 1/2 Inches. *These are as nice a pair of handled tongue and groove planes as we have ever offered. Absolutely perfect and highly recommended.* (FINE) **$195.00**

K5-10. Cumings, A., Boston, Mass.: Boxed Double Bead Molding Plane. Marked "4/8". Ready to Use. Length: 9 1/2 Inches. *This 1/2 inch double bead plane is fully boxed to maximize wear. Crisp, clean and ready to use.* (GOOD+) **$225.00**

K5-11. Hide, A., (Norwich, Conn.): Yellow Birch Rabbet Molding Plane. Earliest Conn. Maker. AWP III: 5 Stars (B). Length: 10 1/2 Inches. *One of the least common and most sought after of all Eighteenth Century planemakers marks, this imprint of Asa Hide, who worked in Norwich, Connecticut in the mid-1700's, has been designated as the "B" mark and rates 5 stars for rarity. The plane is well worn, but the imprint is clean and clear. An extremely rare 18th Century plane from the State of Connecticut.* (GOOD) **$1,445.00**

K5-12. Jenkins & Clark, Birmingham, England: Set of Plow and Molding Planes. 5 Stepped Beads. Original Name Stamp. Length: 9 1/2 Inches. *The original owner of this perfectly preserved set of bead planes and a plow stamped each with his "R.R.R." initials and a distinctive "hand" device. The stamps for both the initials and the hand are included with the tools. A most interesting set of tools in top condition.* (FINE) **$465.00**

K5-13. Gilbert, J., (New Haven, Conn.): Fenced Panel Molding Plane. Robt. Sorby Iron. Rare and Extra Clean. Length: 15 Inches. *A John Gilbert was listed as a jointer in New Haven, Connecticut in 1840. This plane, which has been boldly struck with the Gilbert mark, is of a decidedly English pattern. An excellent example of a rare Connecticut planemaker's mark.* (GOOD+) **$550.00**

K5-14. Tileston, T., Boston (Front St.): Ovolo Sash Molding Plane. Fully Boxed. Extra Crisp and Clean. Length: 9 1/2 Inches. *The planes of Timothy Tileston were of the very finest quality. This fully boxed sash molder is an excellent example of his best work.* (GOOD+) **$145.00**

K5-15. Sandusky Tool Co., Sandusky, Ohio, No. 109: Fenced Tongue Molding Plane. With Screw Adjust. Extra Crisp and Clean. Length: 14 Inches. *This classic handled tongue plane is in excellent collector quality condition. A nice example.* (GOOD+) **$75.00**

K5-16. Spencer: Boxed Center Bead Molding Plane. Marked ""1/4". Extra Crisp and Clean. Length: 9 1/2 Inches. *This 1/4 inch center Connecticut maker Benjamin Spencer of Saybrook is in excellent working order. A nice plane.* (GOOD+) **$85.00**

K5-17. Reed, Utica (N. Y.): Boxed Bead Molding Plane. Marked "7/8". Extra Crisp and Clean. Length: 9 1/2 Inches. *If you have a 3/4 inch cutting iron for a bead plane, or are inclined to grind your own, here's a bargain. Nice.* (FINE) **$15.00**

K5-18. Sandusky Tool Co., Sandusky, Ohio No. 113: Double Iron Nosing Molding Plane. Marked "1 1/8". Uncommon Size. Length: 9 1/2 Inches. *This classic nosing plane is in nearly new condition. Choice.* (FINE) **$95.00**

K5-19. Reed, Utica (N. Y.): Steep Quirk Ogee, Bevel Molding Plane. Marked "7/8". Near New Condition. Length: 9 1/2 Inches. *A number of the planes in this Edition of the Catalogue of Antique Tools are from the Collection of James Cooley of Frankfort, New York, who was an avid seeker of all manner of tools throughout his native Mohawk Valley, and beyond. Among the tools that he kept for himself were those made by planemaker Reed, of nearby Utica, New York. This pristine molder has been carefully kept for the last 30 years. Ex-Cooley collection and nearly new.* (FINE) **$145.00**

K5-20. Desforges, I.B.: Rare Matchstick Molding Plane. N.Y. and Canadian Maker. Most Unusual Type. Length: 9 1/2 Inches. *One of a very few planemakers who worked in more than one country, I.B. Desforges reportedly working in both the State of New York and in Canada. This "matchstick" molder appears as an octuple reeding plane. An extraordinary molding plane profile from that has been boldly struck with the maker name. Highly recommended.* (GOOD+) **$645.00**

K5-21. Doscher Plane & Tool Co., The No. 22: Hollow Molding Plane. H.S. & Co. Imprint. Uncommon Dual Maker. Length: 9 1/2 Inches. *This double struck plane is imprinted with the name of its maker and that of Hammacher Schlemmer, the New York City tool and hardware merchants.* (GOOD+) **$45.00**

K5-22. Reed, Utica (N. Y.): Boxed Bead Molding Plane. Marked "3/4". Near New Condition. Length: 9 1/2 Inches. *If you ever wondered what woodworking planes looked like when they first came off the toolmaker's bench, take a look at this pristine bead plane. Mint.* (FINE) **$65.00**

K5-23. Sawheag Works, Wallingford, Conn.: 1 3/4 Inch Round Molding Plane. Extra Bold Imprint. AWP III: 1 Star (A). Length: 9 1/2 Inches. *The distinctive "crossed arrow" mark of the Sawheag Works has been boldly struck on the end of this 1 3/4 inch molder.* (GOOD+) **$35.00**

K5-24. Reed, Utica (N. Y.): Set of 3 Boxed Bead Molding Planes. 5/8 Inch, 3/4 Inch and 7/8 Inch. Near New Condition. Length: 9 1/2 Inches. *The same owner's initials "J.N." is marked on each of these perfectly preserved bead planes. A great set. Ex-Cooley collection.* (FINE) **$145.00**

K5-25. Reed, Utica (N. Y.): Boxed Bead Molding Plane. Marked "3/8". Ready to Use. Length: 9 1/2 Inches. *Here's a clean 3/8 inch bead in ready to use condition.* (FINE) **$35.00**

K5-26. Reed, Utica (N. Y.): Massive Quirk Ovolo, Bevel Molding Plane. Marked "8/8". Crisp and Clean. Length: 9 1/2 Inches. *This oversize molder has been boldly struck with the Reed/Utica imprint. Extra nice.* (FINE) **$135.00**

K5-27. Fish, J., New York, No. 18: Round Molding Plane. Uncommon N.Y.C. Imprint. AWP III: 3 Stars (A). Length: 9 1/2 Inches. *The J. Fish name has been boldly struck on the end of this 3 star New York City molding plane.* (GOOD+) **$65.00**

K5-28. Reed, Utica (N. Y.): Boxed Bead Molding Plane. Marked "8/8". Near New Condition. Length: 9 1/2 Inches. *One inch bead planes by American makers are not often encountered, especially when they are in this kind of condition.* (FINE) **$65.00**

K5-29. Reed, Utica (N. Y.): Boxed Bead Molding Plane. Marked "1/2". Ready to Use. Length: 9 1/2 Inches. *This 1/2 inch bead has an extra bold imprint and is in ready to use condition.* (GOOD+) **$35.00**

K5-30. Reed, Utica (N. Y.): Boxed Bead Molding Plane. Marked "5/8". Near New Condition. Length: 9 1/2 Inches. *No apologies for this crispy clean bead from Reed of Utica. A nice working tool.* (FINE) **$45.00**

K5-31. Bridge, Washington, D.C.: 1 1/4 Inch Hollow Molding Plane. Rare D.C. Maker. AWP III: 4 Stars. Length: 9 1/2 Inches. *The least common of the handful of planemakers who imprinted their planes with the District of Columbia designation, Joseph P. Bridge practiced his trade in the Capitol city from 1855 to 1864 only. His planes rate 3 stars for rarity. Only the second example of his work that we have offered.* (FINE) **$265.00**

K5-32. Webb, Wm. P., Washington, D.C.: 1 1/8 Inch Round Molding Plane. Rare D.C. Maker. AWP III: 3 Stars (A). Length: 9 1/2 Inches. *The least common of the Washington, D.C. makers, William Webb's planes rate 3 stars for rarity. Seldom seen.* (GOOD+) **$275.00**

K5-33. Reed, Utica (N. Y.): Set of 3 Quirk Ovolo, Bevel Molding Planes. 1/2 Inch, 5/8 Inch and 3/4 Inch. Extra Crisp and Clean. Length: 9 1/2 Inches. *Finding stepped sets of molding planes is becoming an increasingly difficult task. These molders from planemaker Reed of Utica, New York are in excellent condition. The 5/8 inch size is missing its cutting iron, but all planes are otherwise clean, complete and excellent.* (GOOD+) **$325.00**

K5-34. Copeland & Co., Warranted: Quirk Ogee, Bevel Molding Plane. Marked "2 1/4". Near New Condition. Length: 9 1/2 Inches. *The number "2 1/4" is marked on the back of this massive and well preserved complex molding plane. Choice.* (FINE) **$265.00**

K5-35. Reed, Utica (N. Y.): Quirk Ovolo and Bevel Molding Plane. Marked "5/8". Ready to Use. Length: 9 1/2 Inches. *This clean molder features the Grecian ovolo and bevel cut that was popular in the 1830's and 1840's—a period that coincided with the working dates of Reed.* (GOOD+) **$85.00**

K5-36. Reed, Utica (N. Y.): Steep Quirk Ogee, Bevel Molding Plane. Marked "7/8". Near New Condition. Length: 9 1/2 Inches. *This classic molder has steeper than normal cut and is in much the same condition it would have been in when it left the Reed factory. A great complex molding plane.* (FINE) **$225.00**

K5-37. Bywater, Richard, London: Steep Quirk Ogee Molding Plane. Ca. 1790-1814. Excellent Condition. Length: 9 1/2 Inches. *Richard Bywater made planes in Eighteenth and Early Nineteenth Century London. This molder has a much steeper than normal profile. A good one.* (GOOD+) **$145.00**

K5-38. Extra Quality No. 72: Round Molding Plane. Uncommon Mark. From Ohio Tool? Length: 9 1/2 Inches. *For the collector of "one of each" among planemaker's marks we offer this well preserved molder, which is imprinted "Extra Quality". Different.* (GOOD+) **$35.00**

K5-39. Reed, Utica (N. Y.), No. 14: Hollow Molding Planes. 7/8 Inch Size. Ready to Use. Length: 9 1/2 Inches. *If you need to fill an inside straight on a nearly new set of hollows and rounds, there's a 1 in 18 chance that this plane is for you.* (FINE) **$25.00**

K5-40. Reed, Utica (N. Y.): Set of 4 Classic Ogee Molding Planes. 5/8 Inch, 3/4 Inch, 7/8 Inch and 1 Inch. Near New Condition. Length: 9 1/2 Inches. *We sell more ogee planes to woodworkers than any other profile. These ca. 1830's steep ogee's are in much the same condition as they were the day they were made. Extra nice. Ex-Cooley Collection.* (FINE) **$685.00**

K5-41. Taber, L.H.: 5/8 Inch Cove Molding Plane. Ca. 1830's-1850. AWP III: 2 Stars. Length: 9 1/2 Inches. *Cove molders in this condition have become almost impossible to find. A nice example.* (FINE) **$85.00**

K5-42. Reed, Utica (N. Y.): Set of 3 Assorted Holler and Round Molding Planes. No.'s 2, 4 and 8. Ready to Use. Length: 9 1/2 Inches. *If you need some odd "hollers and rounds" to fill out a set, here's an opportunity knocking.* (GOOD+) **$55.00**

K5-43. Reed, Utica (N. Y.): Boxed Bead Molding Plane. Marked "5/8". Ready to Use. Length: 9 1/2 Inches. *Here's an excellent working bead plane in the uncommon 5/8 inch size. Ready to use.* (GOOD+) **$35.00**

K5-44. Reed, Utica (N. Y.): Set of 4 Quirk Ogee, Bevel Molding Planes. 1/2 Inch, 5/8 Inch, 3/4 Inch and 1 Inch. Near New Condition. Length: 9 1/2 Inches. *These pristine quirk ovolo and bevel planes have a steeper than normal cut to the ovolo. Condition is near new. A spectacular set. Ex-Cooley Collection.* (FINE) **$595.00**

K5-45. Reed, Utica (N. Y.): Set of 3 Boxed Bead Molding Planes. 3/4 Inch, 7/8 Inch, 1 Inch. Ready to Use. Length: 9 1/2 Inches. *These three bead planes came together in a single carpenter's chest and will remain together. Crisp, clean and ready to use.* (GOOD+) **$145.00**

Group L5

L5-1. Griffin, Ravenna, Ohio: 1 1/2 Inch Skew Rabbet Molding Plane. Extra Crisp Imprint. Ready to Use. Length: 9 1/2 Inches. *Orlando Griffin made planes in Ravenna, Ohio in the 1850's. This skew bladed rabbet is in excellent condition.* (GOOD+) **$55.00**

L5-2. Tolman, J.R., Hanover, Mass.: Group of 5 Assorted Molding Planes. Beads, Hollow, Etc. Have Been Used. Length: 9 1/2 Inches. *All of these molding planes from Hanover, Massachusetts maker J.R. Tolman have been well used, but are sound and presentable. Most are fully boxed. An opportunity.* (GOOD) **$115.00**

L5-3. Dalpe S., Roxton Pond, Quebec: Double Tounge and Groove Molding Plane. Marked "1/2". Ready to Use. Length: 9 1/2 Inches. *S. Dalpe was one of a number of planemakers who worked in Roxton Pond, Quebec. This double tongue and groove plane, which bears their mark, is in excellent working order.* (GOOD+) **$55.00**

L5-4. Owasco Tool Co., New York No. 72: Adjustable Sash Molding Plane. Fruitwood Arms, Nuts. Crisp, Clean and Sound. Length: 9 1/2 Inches. *The Owasco Tool Company was the name given to a line of planes produced by the Auburn Tool Company. Scholars have speculated that this was not a "second quality line", but rather an attempt to disguise the fact that the tools were produced using prison convict labor—a practice that would soon be outlawed owing to widespread public disapproval. This extra-clean sash appears has been very little used. Nice.* (FINE) **$145.00**

L5-5. Gardner & Murdock, Boston, Mass.: Special Purpose Rabbet Molding Plane. Adjustable Fence. With Steel Stops. Length: 9 1/2 Inches. *This most unusual molder was designed to cut some special rabbet cut. It has a dab of tar on the toe, but is otherwise in excellent condition.* (GOOD+) **$95.00**

L5-6. Mockridge & Son, Newark, N.J. No. 18: Hollow Molding Plane. 1 1/2 Inch Size. Uncommon Mark. Length: 9 1/2 Inches. *This 1 1/2 inch hollowing plane is in top condition. A well preserved plane from an uncommon New Jersey maker.* (FINE) **$35.00**

L5-7. Kellogg, J., Amherst, Mass.: Adjustable Dado Molding Plane. Tombstone Depth Stop. Marked "2/8". Length: 9 1/2 Inches. *This 1/4 inch dado features the early style friction fit "tombstone" depth stop. Ready to use.* (GOOD+) **$55.00**

L5-8. M.C.: Classic Ogee Molding Plane. Sleeper Style Wedge. Early and Excellent. Length: 9 1/2 Inches. *Only the initials "M.C." appear on the end of this classic ogee molder, which has a Sleeper-style wedge profile.* (GOOD+) **$65.00**

L5-9. Nurse, C., 32 Mill St. (London): Beechwood Mitre Plane. With Boxwood Throat. Rare and Excellent. Length: 11 1/2 Inches. *Wooden mitre planes of any sort are rare indeed. Finding a maker-marked example, especially one imprinted with the name of prominent and respected London maker, C. Nurse and Company, is cause for celebration. Nicely fitted with an adjustable boxwood throat and clearly marked with the Nurse imprint and "Invicta" trademark, this one is ready to put to use or proudly display.* (GOOD+) **$265.00**

L5-10. Birch & Co., John, (Birmingham, England): Pair of Hollow and Round Molding Planes. Marked "12". Skew Set Blades. Length: 9 1/2 Inches. *Here's a nice working pair of hollow and round molding planes from a prominent English maker.* (GOOD+) **$65.00**

L5-11. Sandusky Tool Co., Ohio: Weatherstrip Molding Plane. With Slide Depth Stop. Uncommon Type. Length: 9 1/2 Inches. *The Sandusky Tool Company produced a wide range of tools for weatherstrip work. This "armor plated" grooving plane is fitted with an adjustable side stop of steel.* (GOOD+) **$45.00**

L5-12. Assorted Makers: Group of 6 Assorted Molding Planes. Assorted Profiles. Stewart, Kellogg, Etc. Length: 9 1/2 Inches. *Here's an opportunity odd lot of molding planes, all having been considerably used and missing boxing, etc.* (GOOD) **$115.00**

L5-13. Kellogg, J., Amherst, Mass.: Fenced Cove Molding Plane. Marked "5/8". Scarce and Excellent. Length: 9 1/2 Inches. *Cove molding planes have become increasingly difficult to obtain and are eagerly sought out by those adding traditional tools to their workshop. A nice clean 5/8 inch cove plane. Ready to use.* (GOOD+) **$65.00**

L5-14. Auburn Tool Co., Auburn, N.Y. No. 189: Double Iron Nosing Molding Plane. Marked "Inch 3/8". Crisp and Clean. Length: 9 1/2 Inches. *Nosing planes were used for rounding the edges of wide boards, such as stair treads. This example, which was intended for use with 1 3/8 inch stock lumber, is in very crisp, clean condition.* (FINE) **$75.00**

L5-15. Shiverick & Malcom, Brooklyn: Fixed Gothic Bead Molding Plane. With Integral Fence. AWP III: 2 Stars. Length: 9 1/2 Inches. *An exceptionally crisp and clean gothic bead molding plane with the "B" mark of this prominent Brooklyn maker. Superb patinated adds extra appeal to this massive and unusual profile. Nice.* (FINE) **$275.00**

L5-16. Casey & Co., Auburn, N.Y. No. 144: Massive Quirk Ovolo, Beveled Molding Plane. Marked "Inch". Extra Crisp and Clean. Length: 9 1/2 Inches. *According to "American Wooden Planes", Casey & Company produced planes in Auburn Prison for a single year, 1857. This complex molder is marked with the designation "inch" on the reverse. Crisp and clean.* (FINE) **$235.00**

L5-17. Hills & Winship, Springfield, Mass.: Quirk Ovolo With Bevel Molding Plane. Marked "1 1/2". Ready to Use. Length: 9 1/2 Inches. *Hills & Winship were prolific planemakers in Springfield, Massachusetts in the 1830's. This complex molder bearing their mark is in excellent condition.* (GOOD+) **$85.00**

L5-18. Booth Brothers, Dublin (Ireland): Fenced Ogee Molding Plane. Rare Irish Imprint. Marked "3/4". Length: 9 1/2 Inches. *What better way to add to the collectibility of an uncommon Irish imprinted plane than by having the previous owner stamp it with his quintessentially Irish name: "J. Fitzpatrick".* (GOOD+) **$95.00**

L5-19. Elsworth, John, Glasgow (Scotland): Cock Bead Molding Plane. Fully Boxed. Ready to Use. Length: 7 1/2 Inches. *This steep angled cock bead plane has seen some hard use, but appears to be in working order. The full boxing on the base is fully intact.* (GOOD) **$55.00**

L5-20. Sandusky Tool Co., Ohio: Weatherstrip Molding Plane. With Steel Fence. Reworked Body. Length: 9 1/2 Inches. *An enterprising previous owner was apparently troubled by the sharp corners on this weatherstripping plane and took pains to remove them.* (GOOD) **$15.00**

L5-21. Unmarked: Shop Made Wooden Router. Extra Thick Iron. Decorative Knobs. Length: 9 Inches. *This shop-made router plane has the look of a tool that was made to be used...for a long time. A great working tool.* (GOOD+) **$25.00**

L5-22. Sandusky Tool Co., Sandusky, Ohio No. 54: Quarter Round Molding Plane. Marked "7/8". Extra Crisp and Clean. Length: 9 1/2 Inches. *Here's a clean and thoroughly usable quarter round maker from a venerable American maker.* (GOOD+) **$65.00**

L5-23. Sandusky Tool Co., Ohio: Weatherstrip Molding Plane. With Steel Fence. Early Incuse Mark. Length: 9 1/2 Inches. *A fixed fence of steel was applied in the Sandusky factory to this well preserved molding plane.* (FINE) **$65.00**

L5-24. Unmarked: Classic Smoothing Plane. Owner L.S. Bumpus. Near New Condition. Length: 8 Inches. *The owner/maker of this classic smoother marked his creation with his name: "L.S. Bumpus". Condition is near new.* (FINE) **$35.00**

L5-25. Watson (England): Set of 7 Boxed Bead Molding Planes. Slight Skew Cut. Near New Condition. Length: 9 1/2 Inches. *These bead planes have their irons set at a skew angle to facilitate their use with hardwoods. A great working set of beads.* (FINE) **$285.00**

L5-26. Unmarked: Early Yellow Birch Molding Plane. Owner "S. Stephens". Great Lettering. Length: 9 1/2 Inches. *An early owner of this Yellow Birch molder, one "S. Stephens", carved his name very tastefully in the side. A graphic Eighteenth Century plane.* (GOOD) **$45.00**

L5-27. Martin & Shaw, (Birmingham, England): Quirk Ogee and Bevel Molding Plane. Ca. 1840's. Marked "7/8". Length: 9 1/2 Inches. *This wide molder is also imprinted with the stamp of a Welsh ironmonger. A well made plane in excellent condition.* (GOOD+) **$95.00**

L5-28. Tileston, T., Boston: Pair of Special Purpose Molding Planes. Fully Boxed. For Door Panels? Length: 7 1/2 Inches. *At only 7 1/2 inches in length, these specialty molders from Boston planemaker Timothy Tileston make their presence known immediately. The complex profiles are fully boxed and in excellent working order. These planes may have been used in conjunction with each other to form complex door panels in early Nineteenth Century Boston. A pretty pair.* (GOOD+) **$585.00**

L5-29. Unmarked: Handled Dado Molding Plane. Primitive Construction. 3/4 Inch Size. Length: 12 Inches. *The maker of this handled rabbet plane apparently ran out of steam as he got to the handle, as it lacks the level of finish as the rest of the plane. A graphic woodworking tool.* (GOOD+) **$45.00**

L5-30. Unmarked: Decorative Bead Molding Plane. Decorative Form. French Influence? Length: 12 1/2 Inches. *This specialty molder has a decided Continental appearance and may be of French manufacture. The decorative profile cuts a raised bead on the edge of a board. Different.* (GOOD+) **$55.00**

L5-31. Reed, Utica (N. Y.): Quirk Ogee, Bevel Molding Plane. With Boxing. Ready to Use. Length: 9 1/2 Inches. *This ogee and bevel plane has a steeper than normal cut. A nice example.* (GOOD+) **$125.00**

L5-32. Assorted Makers: Group of 4 Asstorted Molding Planes. Handled Tongue and Groove. Tolman, N. Nutting. Length: 12 Inches. *Here's a nice assortment of odd handled tongue and groove planes by J.R. Tolman, N. Nutting and others.* (GOOD) **$75.00**

L5-33. Dibb, W., York: Moving Filletster Molding Plane. Fully Boxed. Near New Condition. Length: 9 1/2 Inches. *This classic English filletster plane is in nearly new condition. A solid brass screw-adjust depth stop adds aesthetic appeal. Ready to use, if you choose.* (FINE) **$155.00**

L5-34. Reed, Utica (N. Y.): Quirk Ogee and Bevel Molding Plane. Marked "5/8". Near New Condition. Length: 9 1/2 Inches. *Here's a quick ogee and bevel combination in nearly new condition. Ex-Cooley collection.* (FINE) **$125.00**

L5-35. Unmarked: Early Compass Molding Plane. Owner "T.O. Martin". Skew Set Blade. Length: 9 1/4 Inches. *The owner/maker of this early compass plane boldly stamped it with his name. One Thomas Martin is known to have worked as a cabinetmaker in Salem, Massachusetts in 1816. A plane of uncommon configuration from an early cabinetmaker.* (GOOD+) **$85.00**

L5-36. Denison, J.: Set of 4 Boxed Bead Molding Planes. 3/16, 1/4, 3/8, and 1/2. Near New Condition. Length: 9 1/2 Inches. *Here's a nice working set of boxed bead planes in the desirable small sizes. Ready to use.* (FINE) **$225.00**

L5-37. Reed, Utica (N. Y.) No. 14: Pair of Hollow and Round Molding Planes. Owner "C. Morris". Ready to Use. Length: 9 1/2 Inches. *A nice working pair of hollow and round planes from a respected Utica, New York planemaker.* (GOOD+) **$75.00**

L5-38. Unmarked: Yellow Birch Toothing Plane. I. and H. Sorby Iron. Early and Nice. Length: 6 3/4 Inches. *The wide chamfers and early style round top iron date this yellow birch toothing plane to ca. 1800. A very early woodworking plane in excellent working order.* (FINE) **$185.00**

L5-39. Unmarked: Early Panel Raising Molding Plane. Moulson Bros. Iron. Pegged Tote. Length: 13 Inches. *An inlaid diamond strike button and a tote that is secured to the body with a wooden peg indicate that this plane was made by one whose planemaking skills had their nexus in the Eighteenth Century. A nice example of a difficult to find plane.* (GOOD+) **$155.00**

L5-40. Auburn Tool Co., Auburn, N.Y. No. 144: Quirk Ovolo, Bevel Molding Plane. Marked "3/4". Extra Crisp and Clean. Length: 9 1/2 Inches. *Here's a crispy clean wide molder having a classic Grecian ovolo profile. A nice plane.* (FINE) **$85.00**

L5-41. Unmarked: Cuban Mahogany Molding Plane. Ogee and Bevel Profile. From Shipwright's Kit. Length: 9 1/2 Inches. *This crisp ogee and bevel molder is formed from solid Cuban Mahogany, a particularly dense wood. The grain pattern is spectacular.* (GOOD+) **$85.00**

L5-42. Brown & Barnard: Quirk Ovolo, Bevel Molding Plane. Marked "5/4". Ca. 1815. Length: 9 1/2 Inches. *A previous owner of this crisp and clean complex molder fitted it with a recessed finger grip using a gouge. Another possibility might be that it once bore the name of another woodworker. Ready to use.* (GOOD+) **$65.00**

L5-43. Bensen & Crannell, Albany: Double Iron Sash Molding Plane. Classic Profile. Ready to Use. Length: 9 1/2 Inches. *This fixed blade sash molder is in top condition and ready to be put immediately to work.* (FINE) **$110.00**

L5-44. Assorted Makers: Group of 12 Hollow and Round Molding Planes. Ring, Kelly. Stewart, Kellogg. Length: 9 1/2 Inches. *A wide range of planemakers are represented in this assortment of odd hollow and round planes. Opportunity knocks.* (GOOD+) **$145.00**

L5-45. Assorted Makers: Group of 3 Asstorted Molding Planes. Parrish Mold, Etc. Massive Yellow Birch Groove. Length: 12 Inches. *Here's an assortment of planes from one collection, including a massive Yellow Birch grooving plane. All have seen considerable use.* (GOOD) **$95.00**

Group M5

M5-1. Hjorth & Co., W., Jamestown, N.Y.: Combination Plier Wrench. Patented September 8, 1903. Schulz No. Length: 6 Inches. *This collectible classic retains nearly all of its shiny nickel plating. Extra nice.* (FINE) **$55.00**

M5-2. Unmarked: Slide Jaw Nut Wrench. With Spring Mechinism. As-New Condition. Length: 9 Inches. *This one is identical to a quick-adjust wrench from the Providence Tool Company, but is unmarked. A good one.* (FINE) **$45.00**

M5-3. Unmarked: Patent Combination Wrench. Patented August 3, 1897. Uncommon Type. Length: 5 1/2 Inches. *Take one pair of pliers, add an alligator wrench, a pair of screwdrivers and you have the recipe for a patent. An early patented gizmo that must have been painful to use for any of its intended functions.* (GOOD) **$45.00**

M5-4. Crescent Tool Co., Jamestown, N.Y. No. AC 16: Adjustable "Crescent" Wrench. Chromed Finish. New Condition, Original Box. Length: 6 Inches. *The corners of this graphic picture box have been repaired with cellophane tape, but both wrench and box are otherwise excellent. Nice.* (FINE) **$35.00**

M5-5. Perfection No. 2: Perfection Wagon Wrench. Patented April 14, 1896. Schulz No. 224. Length: 11 Inches. *Here's a nice example of the larger size of this spring locking buggy wrench from the state of Maine. For those of you here for the information, rather than the bargains, this was the patent of G.E. Wood (No. 558,246). A good one.* (GOOD+) **$85.00**

M5-6. Mossberg Co., Frank No. 1: Bicycle Monkey Wrench. "Sterling". Near New Condition. Length: 5 Inches. *This was Mossberg's biggest-selling product, judging by the surviving examples. Very few of them are this well-preserved. Picture perfect.* (FINE) **$45.00**

M5-7. Acme: Twist Handle Monkey Wrench. Uncommon Imprint. Clean and Sound. Length: 9 Inches. *The Acme Wrench Company made a full line of twist handle wrenches, including an 18 inch behemoth . This was their next to smallest offering. A well preserved example.* (GOOD) **$45.00**

M5-8. Ohio State: Early Patented Bicycle Wrench. Patented January 7, 1901. Scarce and Sound. Length: 4 1/2 Inches. *As a collector of bicycle wrenches myself, I pay careful attention to them. This is the only "Ohio State" wrench I have seen. A rare patented bicycle wrench in clean, sound condition.* (GOOD+) **$125.00**

M5-9. Chantrell, Felix: Early Patent Wrench. Patented February 28, 1882. Pearson: "A" Rating. Length: 12 Inches. *Incorporating the same patented adjustment mechanism as that found on the elusive Chantrell braces, this early patented "T" wrench is very likely less common than its extremely rare cousin. Nicely marked with the patent date and in essentially new condition. A most unusual carriage wrench.* (FINE) **$385.00**

M5-10. Unmarked: Early Patent Bicycle Wrench. Patented March 26, 1895. As-New Condition. Length: 5 1/2 Inches. *The extension behind the upper jaw apparently fit into a socket, perhaps to adjust the handlebars. Nearly new.* (FINE) **$65.00**

M5-11. Walworth & Co., Boston No. 0: "Hex" Pipe Wrench. "Pat. Appld. For". Scarce and Near New. Length: 8 Inches. *This "Hex" wrench was apparently intended for use with angular pipe fittings, as it does not appear that it work on round pipe. Perhaps that is the reason it is in such nice shape.* (FINE) **$55.00**

M5-12. Overman Wheel Co., Chicopee Falls: Bicycle Monkey Wrench. Center Adjust. Patented January 6, 1891. Length: 5 Inches. *This offering from the Overman Wheel Company would have been used on the very first bicycles. A good one.* (FINE) **$95.00**

M5-13. Climax No. 2: Double Jaw Alligator Wrench. "Pat. Appl'd For". Not In Schulz Book. Length: 10 Inches. *Generally, the makers of alligator wrenches were content to place pipe and nut-mangling serration's on only one jaw. With one of these safely in hand, you could be fairly well make certain that the local plumber could destroy a serious amount of metalwork in an afternoon of modest effort. An unusual and graphic wrench.* (FINE) **$135.00**

M5-14. Billings & Spencer Co., The No. A: Bicycle Monkey Wrench. Center Adjust. Crisp and Clean. Length: 4 1/4 Inches. *Billings & Spencer offered wrenches in A, B, and C designations as well as others. Here's a crispy-clean example of letter "A".* (FINE) **$35.00**

M5-15. Mossberg Co., Frank, Attleboro, Mass. No. 10: "Diamond" Bicycle Wrench. Patented March 11, 1902. Near New Condition. Length: 4 1/2 Inches. *The Frank Mossberg Company made a full series of special purpose and bicycle wrenches. All of the tools were of the highest quality and produced with an extra emphasis on finish. Here's a great example of their "Diamond" bicycle wrench.* (FINE) **$55.00**

M5-16. Simmons Hardware Co., E.C.: "Keen Kutter" Crescent Wrench. 10 Inch Size. Rare and Excellent. Length: 10 Inches. *We have sold a few "Keen Kutter" wrenches in our day, but this is the first "Crescent" type we have offered. Extra clean and clearly marked with the Keen Kutter logo.* (FINE) **$75.00**

M5-17. Wakefield Wrench Co.: Patented Lever Action Wrench. Spring Activated. Patented June 30, 1891. Length: 9 Inches. *Pushing on the lever of this quick adjust dandy serves to tighten the jaws. A well made patented wrench.* (GOOD+) **$95.00**

M5-18. Billings & Spencer Co., The: Patent Bicycle Wrench. Patented September 29, 1896. 70% Nickel Plating. Length: 4 1/4 Inches. *Much of the original nickel plating remains on this early patent bicycle wrench. A nice example.* (GOOD+) **$15.00**

M5-19. Unmarked: Multi Function Pocket Wrench. "Mobiloil". Full Nickel Plating. Length: 4 Inches. *File, pipe wrench, nut wrench, tack puller and nail puller are just a few of the task for which this specialty tool was designed. This example is imprinted with advertising from a prominent oil company. A rare tool in new condition.* (FINE) **$55.00**

M5-20. Mossberg Co., Frank, Attleboro, Mass. No. 1: " Junior No. 1" Wrench. Metric and English. Original Nickel Plating. Length: 3 Inches. *At only 3 inches in length. These were literally "vest pocket" wrenches. This one has nearly 100% of its original nickel finish. Mint.* (FINE) **$165.00**

M5-21. F.M.R. & Co.: "Newleva" Wrench. Adjustable Angle. Rare and Near New. Length: 13 1/2 Inches. *And now for a horse of a very different color...Unlike anything we have previously offered or even seen, this "Newleva" wrench is adjusted by means of a lever-like handle attached to a pair of bars that are riveted to the "Crescent" type head. Marked only with the name of the obscure "F.M.R. & Co.", this amazing wrench is in essentially new condition. Extra rare and very graphic. A great wrench.* (FINE) **$385.00**

M5-22. Eastern Machine Screw Corp., N.H.: "H. & G." Brand Socket Wrench Set. With Ratchet Adjust. Complete, Original Box. Length: 11 3/4 Inches. *All of the sockets and accessories are present in this fitted box, which still retains its original decal. A great wrench set from the early days of automobiles.* (GOOD) **$145.00**

M5-23. Petersen Mfg. Co., Dewitt, Nebr. No. 9 R: "Vise-Grip" Wrench. For Sheet Metal. Uncommon Type. Length: 9 Inches. *If you're planning to spot weld some sheet metal, you may want one of these. Even if you're not, it could be handy around the shop. First come, first serve.* (GOOD+) **$15.00**

M5-24. Ampco, Milwaukee, Wisc. No. W-213: Screw Adjust Pipe Wrench. Beryllium Body. Near New Condition. Length: 18 Inches. *The Ampco people made a full line of non-sparking tools. This one is in great shape. A good one.* (FINE) **$55.00**

M5-25. Unmarked: Souvenir Quick Adjust Wrench. "Hudson Fulton 1909". Commemmorative Tool. Length: 4 Inches. *Henry Hudson and Robert Fulton were both important in the history of New York State. Why a celebration, complete with commemorative wrenches, needed to be held in their honor 1909 is a mystery to me. We will offer two tickets to the person to the Martin Van Buren/Hulk Hogan Commemorative Jamboree to anyone who can provide some insight. A rare wrench.* (GOOD+) **$85.00**

M5-26. Zip Grip, Los Angeles, Calif.: Quick Adjust Pipe Wrench. "Zip Grip" Brand. Similar to Schulz No 53. Length: 8 Inches. *Differing only in name from an identical wrench of Eastern origin, this L.A. classic employs a central worm gear with driver to facilitate adjustment of the width of the jaws. A scarce quick adjust wrench in nearly new condition.* (FINE) **$225.00**

M5-27. Bay State Tool Co.: Slide Adjust Nut Wrench. Patented June 7, 1904. Schulz No. 476. Length: 10 Inches. *This one has a spring-activated quick adjustment that is a joy to use. Picture perfect, and a reluctant deaccession from the Donnelly Collection. Highly recommended.* (FINE) **$245.00**

M5-28. Wakefield Wrench Co., Worcester No. 8: Patent Nut Wrenches. Patented September 4, 1900. Uncommon Type. Length: 7 Inches. *This design is very similar to those that were imprinted with the "Indian Motorcycle" name and marked "Hendee Mfg. Co." This one is only marked "No. 8", which is itself quite unusual.* (GOOD+) **$75.00**

M5-29. Peugot Freres: Double Coach Wrench. Octagonal Handle. Rare Size and Type. Length: 11 3/4 Inches. *This well made wrench France features an octagonal wood handle an two sets of jaws for the price of one. A nice example.* (GOOD+) **$65.00**

M5-30. Speednut Wrench Corp., Chicago: Quick Adjust Nut Wrench. 8 Inch Size. Extra Crisp and Clean. Length: 8 Inches. *The "Speednut" wrench was one of the most popular of all quick adjust wrenches. This crispy clean example is in nearly new condition.* (FINE) **$35.00**

M5-31. Scholler Mfg. Co., Buffalo, N.Y.: Double "Crescent" Wrench. Uncommon Maker. 6 Inch and 8 Inch Size. Length: 8 Inches. *Other products give their wannabe imitators names like "gelatin dessert" or "adhesive bandage strip". Here at Martin J. Donnelly Antique Tools, we'll just call this lookalike a double end Crescent wrench, then hunker down and wait for the lawsuit. These are much less common than their "real" counterpart.* (GOOD+) **$55.00**

M5-32. Tower & Lyon, New York, N.Y.: Baxter's Patent Wrench. Early Type. Rare Hardware. Imprint. Length: 8 1/2 Inches. *We have seen a number of these early "Baxter Patent" wrenches, many marked with obscure maker names, but this is the first we have seen from the venerable Tower & Lyon, a major tool and hardware dealer in New York City. Rare and crispy clean.* (GOOD+) **$225.00**

M5-33. Unmarked: Advertising Quick Adjust Wrench. Eclipse Supply Company Struthers, Ohio. Length: 3 Inches. *The Ohio-based manufacturer of these quick-adjust wrenches apparently targeted a wide range of companies as buyers for the purpose of advertising in seeking to expand their market. This extremely well preserved wrench is imprinted with the advertising of a Struthers, Ohio company.* (FINE) **$95.00**

M5-34. Buffum Tool Company: Double Alligator Wrench. With "Swastika" Symbol. Unused Condition. Length: 8 Inches. *The Buffum Tool Company of Louisiana made a full line of high quality wrenches and metal working tools marked with their trademark "Swastika" symbol. Just the thing for the Klansman or the collector. Extra rare.* (FINE) **$85.00**

M5-35. Mossberg Wrench Co, Central Falls, R.I. No. C: Bicycle Monkey Wrench. Center Adjust. Patented November 19, 1895. Length: 5 Inches. *This Mossberg "C" wrench dates from their earliest days in Central Falls, Rhode Island. Rare, especially in this condition.* (FINE) **$95.00**

M5-36. Boston Wrench Co., Boston, Mass.: Quick Adjust Nut Wrench. Patented October 2, 1906. Schulz No. 480. Length: 6 Inches. *The ring at the base of the sliding jaw locks and release a wedge that allows positioning of the jaws at the precise adjustment needed. A clean and clearly marked example of a great collectible wrench.* (GOOD+) **$145.00**

M5-37. Williams & Co., J.H., N.Y. No. AP-6: 6 Inch "Crescent" Wrench. Uncommon Maker. New Condition, Original Box. Length: 6 Inches. *By the time this wrench was being manufactured, nearly every wrench maker offered their version of the "Crescent" wrench. This 6 inch example from J.H. Williams is in new condition in its original box. Mint.* (FINE) **$35.00**

M5-38. Billings & Spencer, Hartford, Conn. No. B: Screw Adjust Nut Wrench. Full Nickel Plating. Near New Condition. Length: 5 1/2 Inches. *That's a reflection, not rust on the handle of the wrench. All of the shiny nickel plating remains.* (FINE) **$65.00**

M5-39. Unmarked: Patent Bicycle Wrench. Patented May 11, 1897. With Spanner Handle. Length: 5 Inches. *The spanner handle was intended to tighten or loosen those notched lock nuts that more practical souls dealt with using a hammer and dad's best screwdriver. A nice example of an early patent bicycle wrench.* (GOOD+) **$115.00**

M5-40. Bethlehem Wrench Co., Bethlehem, Penn.: "The Duffy" Wrench. Marked "Patented". Schulz No. 625. Length: 10 Inches. *A most unusual pivoting head pipe wrench from Southeastern, Pennsylvania. This is a nice example in a desirable size. Visibly different.* (GOOD+) **$165.00**

M5-41. Erie Tool Works, The, Erie, Penn.: Set of Stillson Pipe Wrenches. 6 Inches to 24 Inches. Unused Condition. Length: 24 Inches. *There was a time when someone would purchase a set of wrenches such as these and actually use them. We couldn't recommend that that be done with this magnificent set of unused "Stillson" type pipe wrenches. A great set of collectible wrenches in brand new condition.* (FINE) **$225.00**

M5-42. Mossberg Co., Frank No. 2: Bicycle Monkey Wrench. "Sterling". Patented January 13, 1900. Length: 6 1/2 Inches. *The No. 2 version of the "Sterling" was 1 1/2 inches longer than the No. 1. These are far less common than the No. 1 incarnation.* (GOOD+) **$45.00**

M5-43. Peck, Stow & Wilcox Co., Conn.: "Solid Bar" Monkey Wrench. With "Fist" Trademark. Near New Condition. Length: 10 1/2 Inches. *Monkey wrenches were intended for hard, dirty work, and most saw their share of it. This one didn't. Nearly all original finishes remain on this classic example of the genre from the Peck, Stow & Wilcox Company.* (FINE) **$45.00**

M5-44. Boos Tool Corp. (Unmarked): Screw Adjust Nut Wrench. Rare 8 Inch Size. Crisp and Clean. Length: 8 Inches. *Turning the handle moves the jaws into position. A nice clean but unmarked example.* (GOOD+) **$45.00**

M5-45. Wade Wrench Co., White Pigeon, Mich.: Patent Plier Lever Wrench. With Alligator Jaws. Potential Mangler. Length: 8 Inches. *Anybody who could use one of these for a day without pinching his hand between the handles probably wasn't working very hard. White Pigeon's finest wrench was a failure as a tool, but has great potential as a collectible.* (GOOD+) **$75.00**

Group N5

N5-1. Stanley Rule & Level No. 36 G: Double Plumb and Level. 99% Original Paint. Near New Condition. Length: 6 Inches. *Stanley's cast iron levels were designed to be used. Finding an example in the pristine, collector-grade condition that this one is in is not a common happening. Choice.* (FINE) **$75.00**

N5-2. Unmarked: Lacquered Bench Level. Fitted Metal Case. Unused Condition. Length: 4 1/2 Inches. *All of the original lacquer remains on both the level and its protective metal case. A classic English level in uncommonly nice condition.* (FINE) **$30.00**

N5-3. Smith, E.G., Columbia, Penn.: Early Patent Machinists Level. Patented October 18, 1898. Rare and Excellent. Length: 1 1/2 Inches. *Designed to be placed on a flat surface, this level would read "level" when the solitary bubble was centered in the middle of the circular opening. The base is marked with the name of the maker, who also produced calipers and dividers. The base is also imprinted with the 1898 patent date. The bubble seems not as precise as it once might have been, but the level is otherwise excellent. A rare patented pocket level.* (GOOD+) **$145.00**

N5-4. Pfister, Cincinnati, Ohio: Bronze Machinists Level. Uncommon Imprint. Original Box. Length: 7 Inches. *Nearly identical in form to a bronze machinists level produced by L.S. Starrett, this well preserved bench level is imprinted with the name of an obscure Cincinnati maker.* (GOOD+) **$85.00**

N5-5. Davis & Cook, Watertown, N.Y.: 26 Inch Wooden Level. Patented December 7, 1886. Cleaned and Polished. Length: 26 Inches. *A previous owner has cleaned and polished this visually different level from a short-lived but important Upstate New York maker.* (GOOD) **$85.00**

N5-5. Huber Mfg. Co., The, Marion, Ohio: Beechwood Level. With Brass Top. Uncommon Maker. Length: 8 Inches. *A Huber Manufacturing Company is documented in the Directory of American Toolmakers as having produced machinists tools, including the Woodman Patent speed indicator, in Marion, Ohio in the 1870's. It is likely that this small level was intended as an advertising promotion for their business. A rare level.* (GOOD+) **$65.00**

N5-6. Starrett Co., The L.S., Athol, Mass. No. 133: Engineers, Plumbers Level. 10 Inch Size. Unused Condition. Length: 10 Inches. *This example of the Starrett cast iron No. 133 level in the 10 inch size is in pristine condition. As sharp and clean as it was when new. Nice.* (FINE) **$95.00**

N5-7. Starrett Co., The L.S.S. No. 136: Cross Test Level. With Dual Vials. Uncommon Type. Length: 2 3/4 Inches. *These served a multiplicity of shop functions. This example is in very well preserved condition.* (GOOD+) **$45.00**

N5-8. Unmarked: Rosewood and Brass Level. "Torpedo" Type. Near New Condition. Length: 12 Inches. *Many English and Scottish tools were not marked with a maker's name. Here's an example of why that practice might be though of as "leaving well enough alone". Nearly new and very pretty.* (FINE) **$65.00**

N5-9. Smallwood, I. & D., Birmingham No. 756: Combination Rule and Level. Boxwood and Brass. Unused Condition. Length: 6 Inches. *Nearly all of the 6 inch examples of these desirable boxwood rule and level combinations found their way into the pockets of their owners and degraded rapidly. This one apparently never made it out of the factory. Mint.* (FINE) **$145.00**

N5-10. Stratton Bros., Greenfield, Mass. No. 1: Brass Bound Mahogany Level. With Eagle Mark. Patented May 26, 1886. Length: 28 Inches. *The Stratton "eagle" imprint has been boldly struck on the top plate of this, their classic full bound mahogany level. A very nice example.* (GOOD+) **$265.00**

N5-11. Stanley Rule & Level No. 38 1/2: Nickel Plated Machinists Level. "Sweetheart" Trademark. Superb Condition. Length: 4 Inches. *This "Sweetheart" marked level has a lightly stippled casting. Extra crisp and clean.* (FINE) **$75.00**

N5-12. Starrett Co., L. S., Athol, Mass. No. 442: Hexagon Machinists Level. Full Nickel Plating. Near New Condition. Length: 2 3/4 Inches. *All original finishes remain on this uncommon Starrett "pocket" level.* (FINE) **$45.00**

N5-13. Robinson, M.W., Brooklyn, N.Y. No. 8: Cast Iron Plumb and Level. L.L. Davis Patent. 95%+ Original Paint. Length: 18 Inches. *Identical in all respects to the No. 9 version offered elsewhere in this section, the No. 8 was 6 inches shorter at 18 inches. Nearly all of the original paint remains on this graphic example.* (FINE) **$225.00**

N5-14. Stratton Bros., Greenfield, Mass. No. 1: Brass Bound Plumb and Level. Brazilian Rosewood. Near New Condition. Length: 24 Inches. *No apologies whatsoever for this magnificently grained brass bound level of Brazilian Rosewood. Extra nice.* (GOOD+) **$385.00**

N5-15. Rabone & Sons, J., Birmingham: Brass Machinists Level. With "Keeper" Plate. Extra Clean and Nice. Length: 10 Inches. *Produced by Birmingham makers John Rabone & Son, this brass machinists level was of a form uniquely British. This example is in nearly new condition.* (FINE) **$65.00**

N5-16. Stratton Bros., Greenfield, Mass. No. 2: Mahogany Plumb and Level. With Eagle Trademark. Patented October 4, 1887. Length: 28 Inches. *The No. 2 was Stratton's "second quality" level, behind their No. 1 fully brass bound offering, but there's nothing second quality about this one.* (GOOD+) **$145.00**

N5-17. Unmarked: Rosewood Bench Level. Full Brass Facing. Unused Condition. Length: 12 Inches. *Only the words "Warranted Correct" appear on this perfectly preserved brass topped bench level. A showy level in new condition.* (FINE) **$185.00**

N5-18. Starrett Co., L. S., Athol, Mass.: Double Plumb Level. Cast Iron Body. As New Condition. Length: 6 Inches. *This example of the Starrett cast iron No. 133 double plumb and level in the 6 inch size is in pristine condition. As sharp and clean as it was when new. Nice.* (FINE) **$45.00**

N5-19. Robinson, M.W., Brooklyn, N.Y. No. 9: Cast Iron Plumb and Level. L.L. Davis Patent. Elaborate Casting. Length: 24 Inches. *Continuing the tradition of the Davis Level & Tool Company, M.W. Robinson produced these graphic plumb and level combinations. The casting of this example, which bears the designation "No. 9", has been rejapanned by a previous owner. A graphic level.* (GOOD+) **$110.00**

N5-20. Smallwood, I. & D., Birmingham: Boxwood Rule and Level. Extra Small Size. Unused Condition. Length: 4 Inches. *Someone must have put this miniature level and rule away many years ago for safe keeping. Absolutely perfect.* (FINE) **$65.00**

N5-21. Unmarked: Classic English Bench Level. "Best Improved Level Tube" Mahogany Body. Length: 9 Inches. *The inscription "Best Improved Level Tube" is imprinted on the brass top plate of this mahogany bench level of English origin.* (GOOD+) **$45.00**

N5-22. Unmarked: Scottish Ebony Level. With Sliding Covers. Very Well Preserved. Length: 8 Inches. *A pair of sliding brass covers can be brought in from the outside edges to protect the vial of this very well made Scottish spirit level. A striking Nineteenth Century level.* (GOOD+) **$145.00**

N5-24. Stratton Bros., Greenfield, Mass. No. 11: Brass Bound Mahogany Level. Narrow Width. Clean and Sound. Length: 24 Inches. *Full brass binding and a body of reddish brown mahogany give this narrow-bodied level from Stratton Brothers a striking visual appeal.* (GOOD+) **$175.00**

N5-25. Tower & Lyon, New York, N.Y.: Wood's Patent Level. Patented June 14,1887. Brass Bound Rosewood. Length: 28 Inches. *The Wood's Patent level featured a spring activated "pop up" sighting feature which could be locked out of the way when it was not needed. This example is clearly marked with the patent date and both the brass and the rosewood are in excellent condition.* (GOOD+) **$345.00**

N5-26. Smallwood, I. & D., Birmingham No. 756: Combination Rule and Level. Boxwood and Brass. Unused Condition. Length: 10 Inches. *Those who have followed the chronicling of tools in these pages over the years are aware that we have been suspect of so-called "combination" tools. We generally approach these items as having made compromises to the better qualities of the tools included in the mix, while adding nothing to the utility of the resulting hybrid. Such is decidedly not the case with this combined boxwood rule and spirit level. Produced by I. & D. Smallwood in their Birmingham tool factory, this pristine example of a thoroughly practical combination tool is in absolutely unused condition.* (FINE) **$115.00**

N5-27. Stratton Bros., Greenfield, Mass. No. 11 1/2: 18 Inch Carpenter's Level. Full Brass Bound. Crisp and Clean. Length: 18 Inches. *This narrow-gauge brassbound Stratton level was apparently intended for lighter duty work than its full sized cousins. A well preserved example of an uncommonly configured Stratton level.* (GOOD+) **$195.00**

N5-28. Starrett Co., L. S., Athol, Mass. No. 134: Cross Test Level. Angle Shape. Unused Condition. Length: 3 1/4 Inches. *An extremely well preserved example of a Starrett level of uncommon form. Very nice.* (FINE) **$55.00**

N5-29. Ibbotson & Co., Thos: Precision Rosewood Level. Full Brass Face. Rare and Excellent. Length: 12 Inches. *This classic English brass topped rosewood bench level from Thomas Ibbotson & Company has been lightly cleaned to restore its original brilliance. Extra nice.* (FINE) **$165.00**

N5-30. I.G. No. 188: Classic Scottish Level. Full Brass Face. With Plumb Vial. Length: 8 Inches. *Marked only with the maker's mark "I.G." and its number designation, this small level has an artfully shaped full brass top plate and a plumb vial surrounded by a brass facing. A particularly pretty Scottish level.* (GOOD+) **$135.00**

N5-31. Stanley Rule & Level No. 10: Laminated Plumb and Level. Patented June 2, 1891. Scarce and Excellent. Length: 28 Inches. *The date of the 1891patent of Justus Traut for Stanley's "Hand-y" feature has been boldly stamped into the side of this level. The tool is in very well preserved condition and ready to display.* (GOOD+) **$115.00**

N5-32. Davis Level & Tool Co.: Rare 12 Inch Carpenter's Level. Double Plumb Vials. Near New Condition. Length: 12 Inches. *Unmarked in any way with a maker's mark, this graphic carpenter's level was undoubtedly produced by the Davis Level & Tool Company of Springfield, Massachusetts. A very pretty small level.* (FINE) **$225.00**

N5-33. Unmarked: Combination Rule and Level. Boxwood Body. Full Brass Face. Length: 4 Inches. *These are no maker marks on this unusual 4 inch boxwood rule and level combination.* (GOOD+) **$15.00**

N5-34. Stratton Bros., Greenfield, Mass.: No. 1: Brass Bound Plumb and Level. Cuban Mahogany. Patented May 22, 1886. Length: 30 Inches. *Later levels of mahogany were much lighter in weight than those produced in the 1880's, when this tool was made, owing to the fact that the heavier Cuban Mahogany, an entirely different species, was used at that time. This fully bound example is in excellent condition, noting the beginning of some narrow separation at the laminations. A nice level.* (GOOD+) **$165.00**

N5-35. Stanley Tools No. 34 V: Machinist's Level. Scarce 4 Inch Size. New Condition, Original Box. Length: 4 Inches. *No apologies for this one. This specimen of Stanley's smallest machinist level is still in its original box. Pristine.* (FINE) **$55.00**

N5-36. Corcoran, Bryan, 31 Cork Lane: Mahogany Bench Level. With Brass Top. Mark Inside Glass. Length: 7 3/4 Inches. *The underside of the vial of this interesting mahogany level is printed with the maker's name and location. A British classic.* (GOOD) **$35.00**

N5-37. Mulliken & Stackpole, Boston, Mass. No. 10: Early Mahogany Level. Brass Top Plate. Early and Excellent. Length: 22 Inches. *Milliken and Stackpole were makers of high quality levels in the bustling 1850's City of Boston. This unbound mahogany example is in excellent condition.* (GOOD+) **$85.00**

N5-38. Rabone & Sons, Makers, Birmingham: Combination Rule and Level. Solid Boxwood Body. Patent No. 22017. Length: 12 Inches. *A good, sound example of Rabone's boxwood rule and level combination. A bargain.* (GOOD+) **$35.00**

N5-39. Stratton Bros., Greenfield, Mass. No. 10: 10 Inch Rosewood Level. Full Brass Bound. Scarce and Excellent. Length: 10 Inches. *This early Stratton brass bound level has a body of Brazilian Rosewood. It has been used, but it is fully intact and very presentable.* (GOOD) **$365.00**

N5-40. Stratton Bros., Greenfield, Mass. No. 10: Rosewood Plumb and Level. Patented July 16, 1872. Early and Excellent. Length: 8 Inches. *A "gentleman's tool" from the very beginning, the Stratton No. 10 brass bound level was made to be beautiful. This 8 inch example has been very tastefully cleaned and refinished to showcase the dramatic effect these tools would have had when new. Marked with the 1872 patent date and ready to proudly display.* (GOOD+) **$445.00**

N5-41. Starrett Co., L.S., Athol, Mass.: No. 130: Bench Level. 3 1/2 Inch Size. Original Carton. Length: 3 1/2 Inches. *An excellent example of Starrett's 4 inch bench level. All original finishes remain on this "in the box" example. Perfect.* (FINE) **$45.00**

N5-42. Chapin, H., Union Factory: Patent Fruitwood Level. Patented June 6, 1870. Early and Excellent. Length: 28 Inches. *An early patent date is imprinted on this classic carpenter's level from H. Chapin's Union Factory. A well preserved plumb and level combination.* (GOOD+) **$55.00**

N5-43. Stanley Rule & Level No. 38: 4 Inch Machinist's Level. Full Nickel Plating. 98% Original Paint. Length: 4 Inches. *Stanley saved a lot of us a lot of work by providing these "oil burner levels" with the orange paint already applied. I remember as a child how it was always my job to get out the orange enamel and get the painting done whenever we got a new level for the oil burner. Boy, was I glad when we switched to Stanley! This one's in nice shape, honest.* (FINE) **$45.00**

N5-44. Stanley Rule & Level: Solid Rosewood Level. With Hand-E Feature. Scarce and Excellent. Length: 28 Inches. *We can find a number designation on this Stanley Rosewood level, but would suspect that it is a No. 11, which was discontinued in 1917. A nice example of an uncommon Stanley rosewood level.* (GOOD+) **$195.00**

N5-45. Millers Falls Company No. 24: Cast Iron Plumb And Level. 12 Inch Size. Stippled Web Body. Length: 12 Inches. *In their early days, the Millers Falls Company competed with each other for the cast iron level dollar. Davis made a prettier level, but Millers Falls stayed in business for 75 more years than Davis. This early 12 inch level is sound but has seen some use and has been exposed to the elements. An uncommon Millers Falls level.* (GOOD) **$65.00**

Group O5

O5-1. Brown, G.: Early "Carcase" Saw. Disston Brand Name. Uncommon Type. Length: 17 Inches. *Henry Disston & Son's marketed saws under various names, including "Jackson" and "G. Brown". In most cases, those were the trade names of companies that Disston had bought out. This "G. Brown" saw may date to the days before their incorporation into the Disston empire.* (GOOD+) **$75.00**

O5-2. Unmarked: Special Purpose Saw. With Double Blade. For Stairs? Length: 13 Inches. *A pair of dowels regulate the width of this double blades saw, which was likely used for cutting the shoulders for stair treads simultaneously. This interesting saw is early and nicely patinated.* (GOOD+) **$115.00**

O5-3. Riverside Tool Co., New York, N.Y. No. 5: 8 Inch Dovetail Saw. Elaborate Logo. Extra Crisp and Clean. Length: 12 1/4 Inches. *Nearly all of the original factory etching remains on this 8 inch dovetail saw from the New York City based Riverside Hardware Company. The saw is straight, true and sharp and could be put immediately to use, if the user so desired. An exceptionally well preserved saw.* (FINE) **$155.00**

O5-4. Peace & Co., J., Sheffield No. 2238: Etched Imported Saw. Registered April 29, 1850. Butler, Keith & Hill. Length: 30 Inches. *The etching on the blade of this ca. 1850's saw from a prominent Sheffield maker is of a speeding locomotive. Only a very early glued repair on the top of the handle horn deserves mention on this otherwise perfect saw.* (GOOD+) **$485.00**

O5-5. Bishop & Co., Geo. H.: Cabinetmaker's Combination Saw. Patended January 9, 1906. Uncommon 8 Inch Size. Length: 13 Inches. *This example of the Bishop patent cabinet maker's saw has a triple-edged blade that can be precisely adjusted to regulate the depth of cut. A carved fruitwood handle accents this handsome saw. A versatile tool for the shop.* (GOOD+) **$85.00**

O5-6. Disston & Sons, H., Philadelphia, Penn.: Beech Handle. Dovetail Saw. Straight and True. Ready To Use. Length: 11 Inches. *For the woodworker who wishes to work intimately with wood, the cutting and fitting, by hand, of dovetail joints is highly recommended. For those so inclined, we recommend this clean, straight, sharp and very well-preserved saw from top maker Henry Disston & Sons. Quality handsaws being made today are infinitely more expensive, while the ordinary offerings from woodworking supply companies have a "clunkiness" about them that spoils the communion between man and wood. A classic woodworking tool in great shape for the contemporary woodworker.* (GOOD+) **$55.00**

O5-7. Richardson Brothers, Newark, N.J. No. 5: "Diamond" Dovetail Saw. Early Open Handle. Superb Condition. Length: 15 Inches. *The manner in which the handle extends over the back of this early dovetail saw is characteristic of the work of the Richardson Brothers, Newark sawmakers of the 19th Century. A great early American saw.* (GOOD+) **$145.00**

O5-8. Bishop & Co., Geo. H.: Cabinetmaker's Combination Saw. Patented January 9, 1906. Rip and Crosscut Blades. Length: 17 1/2 Inches. *A crisp, clean and ready to use example of the 1906 Bishop Patent Cabinet Saw. These would serve as a back saw, cut stopped dados, dovetails or whatever. They still will. A nice saw in great condition.* (GOOD+) **$135.00**

O5-9. Richardson Brothers, Newark, N.J.: 12 Inch Tenon Saw. Blued Steel Back. Straight and True. Length: 17 Inches. *Richardson Brothers produced a line of very high quality saws that were marketed both under their own name and sold to hardware dealers with "custom etching". This 12 inch tenon saw is imprinted with the Richardson name and is straight, true and ready to use.* (GOOD+) **$45.00**

O5-10. Sorby, Robt., Sheffield (England): 8 Inch Open Handle Dovetail Saw. With Kangaroo Device. Straight and True. Length: 12 1/2 Inches. *Here's a great working dovetail saw with the early type open handle from respected Sheffield maker Robert Sorby. The sort of classic saw has become increasingly difficult to find.* (FINE) **$95.00**

O5-11. Sorby, Robt., Sheffield (England): 8 Inch Open Handle Dovetail Saw. With Kangaroo Device. Straight and True. Length: 12 1/2 Inches. *The classic "Kangaroo" logo of Sheffield maker Robert Sorby has been stamped on this perfectly preserved dovetail saw. Crisp, clean and ready to use.* (FINE) **$95.00**

O5-12. Tillotson, Sheffield: 14 Inch Tenon Saw. Early Style Screws. Shapely Handle. Length: 18 Inches. *An interesting handle accents this clean tenon saw from a respected Sheffield maker. There is some light pitting on the front section of the blade, but the offending oxidation was removed many years ago.* (GOOD+) **$65.00**

O5-13. Disston & Sons, H., Philadelphia, Penn. No. 150: "Keystone" Panel Saw. Orange, Black Handle. Ca. 1920's. Length: 19 1/2 Inches. *Much of the original etching remains on this ca. 1920's Disston saw, which probably was included as part of a kit of tools.* (GOOD+) **$35.00**

O5-14. Disston & Sons, Henry No. 68: 16 Point Dovetail Saw. 12 Inch Blade. Straight and True. Length: 17 1/4 Inches. *The Disston No. 68 saw has become very popular among modern woodworkers for the simple reason that it is very good at the job for which it was designed.* (GOOD+) **$75.00**

O5-15. Spear & Jackson, Sheffield: Open Handle Dovetail Saw. Blued Steel Blade. Near New Condition. Length: 14 1/2 Inches. *Open handle dovetail saws in this condition have become nearly impossible to find. Nearly all of this original finishes remain on this early open handle saw from Sheffield's most respected sawmaker.* (FINE) **$225.00**

O5-16. Sears & Co., W.B., Middletown, N.Y.: Early 8 Inch Dovetail Saw. Open Handle Type. Straight and True. Length: 12 Inches. *One of the many sawmakers who operated in and around Middletown, New York in the 1850's W.B. Sears & Company produced this excellent quality open handle dovetail saw. Ready to use, if you choose.* (GOOD+) **$155.00**

O5-17. Ives, W.A. & Co., New Haven, Conn.: Adjustable Compass' Saw. "Mephisto" Brand. Original Paper Label. Length: 16 Inches. *The "Mephisto" brand name appears on this uncommon compass saw from an obscure Connecticut maker better known for their auger bits. Nearly all of the original paper label remains.* (GOOD+) **$35.00**

O5-18. Osborne, H.G.: "Mitrewright" Saw. Patended 1906. Rare and Near New. Length: 16 1/2 Inches. *Produced under a patent granted in 1906, it is not likely that many of these "Mitrewright" saws were ever sold. This example is in nearly new condition. Choice.* (FINE) **$225.00**

O5-19. Disston & Sons, H., Philadelphia, Penn. No. K1: "Keystone" Dovetail Saw. 10 Inch Blade. Straight and True. Length: 15 Inches. *A later Disston brass-backed back saw in superb condition. Most original etching remains, as does most original finish. No apologies.* (GOOD+) **$55.00**

O5-20. Tyzak Sons & Turner, Sheffield: 8 Inch Open Handle Dovetail Saw. Full Brass Back. Straight and True. Length: 13 Inches. *For many years, the name Tyzak & Turner, has been synonymous with saws of the very highest quality. Here's a classic dovetail saw in excellent working order. Ready to use.* (FINE) **$145.00**

O5-21. Sorby, Robt., Sheffield (England): 8 Inch Open Handle Dovetail Saw. Full Brass Back. Straight and True. Length: 12 1/2 Inches. *In much the same condition as it was when put away for the last time some 100 years ago, this classic brass back dovetail saw is as nice as they come. A classic.* (FINE) **$155.00**

O5-22. Montgomery Ward No. 84-3995: 14 Point Tenon Saw. Ready To Use. New Condition, Original Box. Length: 22 Inches. *Apparently never removed from its original box, this ca. 1950's saw is in brand new condition.* (FINE) **$65.00**

O5-23. Disston & Sons, Henry, Philadelphia, Penn. No. 68: 8 Inch Blade Dovetail Saw. With Beech Handle. All Original Etching. Length: 8 Inches. *An excellent working example of Disston's best dovetail saw. All original etching remains on the straight, sharp blade.* (GOOD+) **$95.00**

O5-24. Bishop & Co., Geo. H., Lawrencebur No. 8: 10 Inch Blade Tenon Saw. Straight and True. Ready To Use. Length: 14 1/2 Inches. *George Bishop operated two saw manufacturing facilities, one in Cincinnati and the other in Lawrenceburg, Indiana. This example is straight, true and ready to use.* (GOOD+) **$55.00**

O5-25. Roberts, L.T., London: 8 Inch Dovetail Saw. Extra Fine Teeth. Straight and True. Length: 12 Inches. *The handle has been carfeully carved in the factory to a decorative pattern on this rare and ready to use dovetail saw from a prominent London maker. Straight, sharp and ready to use.* (GOOD+) **$65.00**

O5-26. Unmarked: Miniature Dovetail Saw. 28 Points Per Inch. Ready to Use. Length: 9 Inches. *At 28 points per inch, this qualifies under any criteria as a fine point saw. Very well made and ready to use.* (GOOD+) **$65.00**

O5-27. Atkins & Co., E.C., Indianapolis No. 25: 10 Inch Handled Dovetail Saw. Sharp and Straight. Ready to Use. Length: 14 1/2 Inches. *All of the original etching remains on this straight and sharp dovetail saw from a renowned maker. Nice.* (GOOD+) **$45.00**

O5-28. Cheeseman, James: Brass-Backed Tenon Saw. Mahogany Handle. Straight and True. Length: 14 Inches. *Another brass-backed tenon saw, this on from the English maker James Cheesman. A fancier than usual mahogany handle compliments this super-clean, straight and sharp example. There is a very tight crack in the handle, but the tool is otherwise excellent.* (GOOD+) **$95.00**

O5-29. Jackson: Open Handle Dovetail Saw. 10 Inch Blade Length. Extra Crisp and Clean. Length: 14 1/2 Inches. *"Jackson" was the trademark of a secondary line carried by the firm of Henry Disston & Sons, but there's nothing second quality about this straight, clean and early-appearing dovetail saw.* (GOOD+) **$65.00**

O5-30. Gardner, T.J., Narrow Wine, Bristo: 8 Inch Open Handle Dovetail Saw. Early Split Screws. Straight and True. Length: 12 1/2 Inches. *The blade on this extra nice dovetail saw is affixed to the handle by the "split" screws that were characteristic of early manufacture. A nice saw.* (GOOD+) **$95.00**

O5-31. Drabble & Sanderson, London: 8 Inch Brass Back Dovetail Saw. Early Open Handle. Straight and True. Length: 13 1/2 Inches. *One of the last Enlglish sawmakers to remain in operation, this classic dovetail saw is an excellent example of the early work of Drabble and Sanderson. A great working saw with a decidedly early look. Nice.* (FINE) **$155.00**

O5-32. Sorby, Robt., Sheffield (England): 8 Inch Open Handle Dovetail Saw. With Kangaroo Device. Straight and True. Length: 12 1/2 Inches. *Only an easily removed spot of tarnish detracts from this otherwise perfect English dovetail saw. A nice example in ready to use condition.* (GOOD+) **$75.00**

O5-33. Disston & Son, Henry, Philadelphia, Penn.: Brass Backed Tenon Saw. Ca. 1900. As New Condition. Length: 16 1/2 Inches. *Nearly all original finishes remain on this rare brass backed dovetail saw from Henry Disston & Sons. Mint.* (FINE) **$265.00**

O5-34. Spear & Jackson, Sheffield: 10 Inch Brass Back Dovetail Saw. Early Open Handle. Early and Excellent. Length: 14 3/4 Inches. *Here's a ready to use brass back dovetail saw from Sheffield's most respected maker. Straight, sharp and ready to use.* (GOOD+) **$145.00**

O5-35. Disston & Sons, Henry, Phila, Pa No. 12: 22 Inch London Spring Steel Saw. 8 Point Crosscut. Early and Near New. Length: 26 Inches. *This immaculate No. 12 saw was produced from "London Spring Steel" and was among the very best that Disston offered. Extra crisp and highly recommended.* (FINE) **$225.00**

O5-36. Peace, Harvey W., Brooklyn, N.Y.: "Marvin Gauge" Saw. Patented June 14, 1881. Rare and Unusual. Length: 17 1/2 Inches. *This is unquestionably the earliest example of an adjustable-depth back saw of which I am aware. Patented on June 14, 1881 and manufactured by the Harvey W. Peace Company of Brooklyn, this saw has a most appealing profile, despite the ancient application of a brass plate to effect a repair. A patented saw that started a trend.* (GOOD) **$275.00**

O5-37. Atkins & Co., E. C. No. 100: Flooring Saw. Applewood Handle. Crisp and Clean. Length: 22 Inches. *These special purpose saws were curved to allow a cut to be started on a flat surface. The pointed tip could also start a cut from a small hole. This example never participated much, if at all, in the dirty and difficult work of installing flooring. Much original etching remains. An uncommon saw in very well preserved condition.* (GOOD+) **$115.00**

O5-38. Disston & Son, Henry, Philadelphia, Penn.: Brass Back Dovetail Saw. Ca. 1890's. Straight and True. Length: 14 1/2 Inches. *Disston's brass backed tenon saws are as common as chicken teeth. This one is in excellent overall condition.* (GOOD+) **$145.00**

O5-39. Frost, Dove Street, Norwich: 9 Inch Open Handle Dovetail Saw. Early Split Screws. Straight and True. Length: 14 Inches. *The name of a sawmaker from the Northeast of England is imprinted on the blade of this crisp, clean and arrow straight dovetail saw. Extra nice.* (FINE) **$145.00**

O5-40. Atkins & Co., E. C. No. 63: 6 Point Crosscut Saw. Decorative Handle. Slight Bow to Blade. Length: 22 1/2 Inches. *Only the very highest quality saws were embellished with the "wheat" carving on the handle that was symbolic of the very best. This "four button" Atkins has a slight bow to the blade, but is otherwise excellent. A nice saw.* (GOOD+) **$35.00**

O5-41. Marples & Co., William, Sheffield: 8 Inch Dovetail Saw. Straight and Sharp. Ready to Use. Length: 12 3/4 Inches. *This 8 inch dovetail saw from renowned Sheffield makers William Marples & Company features the extra fine teeth needed for the specialized task for which it was intended.* (FINE) **$65.00**

O5-42. Stanley Rule & Level No. 835: 12 Point Dovetail Saw. From Tool Kit. "Sweetheart" Trademark. Length: 15 Inches. *Produced exclusively for the tool kits that were produced as part of a 1920's marketing promotion, this 12 point dovetail saw retains nearly all of its original etching, which features the "Sweetheart" trademark. A rare Stanley saw.* (FINE) **$145.00**

O5-43. Sorby, I., Sheffield: 8 Inch Open Handle Dovetail Saw. With "Jester" Device. Straight and True. Length: 12 1/2 Inches. *The classic "Jester" logo of I. Sorby has been boldly struck on the back of this classic brass back dovetail saw. A very nice saw in top condition.* (FINE) **$165.00**

O5-44. Jackson: Open Handle Dovetail Saw. 10 Inch Blade Length. Near New Condition. Length: 14 1/2 Inches. *Jackson was the name used on Disston's craftsman grade saws. They picked up the trademark when they acquired the Jackson & Gorham Saw Co. A nice saw in great shape. First come, first serve.* (FINE) **$85.00**

O5-45. Disston & Sons, H., Philadelphia, Penn. No. D 8: 26 Inch 5 1/2 Point Rip Saw. With Contour Handle. Near New Condition. Length: 29 Inches. *Disston's rip saws were fitted with a patented contour handle to facilitate overhand rip sawing. This pristine example in the 5 1/2 point size has had its applewood handle fitted with the distinctive Disston grip. Straight, sharp and ready to use.* (FINE) **$75.00**

Group P5

P5-1. Stanley Rule & Level No. 54: Two-Foot, Four-Fold Folding Rule. Arch Joint, Full Bound. Architect's Scales. Length: 24 Inches. *This No. 54 arch joint rule was just a notch better than the much more common No. 62, which featured a "square" joint. This one is in crisp condition, but just a bit dirty. It should clean to fine condition.* (GOOD+) **$45.00**

P5-2. Lufkin Rule Co., The, No. 771: Two-Foot, Four-Fold Folding Rule. Square Joint, Half Bound. Equivalent to a Stanley 84. Length: 24 Inches. *This example of Lufkin's answer to Stanley's popular half-bound No. 84 rule was their No. 771. This one has been well used, but is sound and clearly marked.* (FAIR) **$35.00**

P5-3. Lufkin Rule Co., The, Saginaw, Mich. No. 851: Two Foot, Four Fold Folding Rule. With Arch Joint. Similar to Stanley No. 51. Length: 24 Inches. *Lufkin's No. 851 was the equivalent to Stanley's arch joint, unbound No. 51. An uncommon Lufkin rule.* (GOOD) **$55.00**

P5-4. Stanley Rule & Level (Unmarked.) No. 78 1/2: Two Foot, Four Fold Folding Rule. Use Frictionless Metal. Rare Advertising Rule. Length: 24 Inches. *Advertising from the Frictionless Metal Company is imprinted on this high quality double arch joint rule, which was made by Stanley for that company. A rare Stanley advertising rule.* (GOOD+) **$135.00**

P5-5. Rabone & Sons, Makers, Birmingham No. 1167: Two-Foot, Two-Fold Folding Rule. "Blindman's Rule". Uncommon Type. Length: 24 Inches. *Here's a clean and sound example of Rabone's classic "blind man's" rule in the 2 foot size. A tough rule to find in this condition.* (GOOD+) **$45.00**

P5-6. Stanley Rule & Level No. 27: Two Foot, Four Fold Folding Rule. With "Sweetheart" Trademark. Ca. 1920's-1940. Length: 24 Inches. *Offered as a low-end rule in the 1930's, these were generally used up and thrown away. This one was neither. A great example of an uncommon Stanley rule.* (FINE) **$65.00**

P5-7. Stanley Rule & Level No. 72 1/2: Two Foot, Four Fold Folding Rule. Square Joint, Full Bound. "Sweetheart" Trademark. Length: 24 Inches. *The No. 72 1/2 is distinguished from the No. 72 by being fully brass-bound. This one is in excellent condition and clearly marked with the ca. 1920's "Sweetheart" trademark.* (FINE) **$195.00**

P5-8. Stearns & Co., E.A. No. 37: Two-Foot, Four Fold Folding Rule. Square Joint, Unbound. Graduated in 8ths and 1/4s. Length: 24 Inches. *Somewhat worse for wear after 140 years of existence, we offer this uncommon rule as a rare example of this obscure Stearns configuration. Different.* (FAIR) **$25.00**

P5-9. Stanley Rule & Level No. 163: Light Duty Folding Rule. 1941 to 1943 Only. Rare and Excellent. Length: 24 Inches. *These light-duty rules were produced during World War II and discontinued after a short run. This one appears never to have been used.* (GOOD+) **$45.00**

P5-10. Stanley Rule & Level No. 18: Two Foot, Two Fold Folding Rule. Square Joint, Unbound. As New Condition. Length: 24 Inches. *Once derided as "common", serious collectors have come to realize that examples of the No. 18 two fold rule in collector quality condition are very difficult to obtain. This example, which is imprinted with an early Stanley maker mark has never been used. Absolutely perfect.* (FINE) **$265.00**

P5-11. Lufkin Rule Co., The, Saginaw, Mich. No. 172: 6 Inch, Two Fold Folding Rule. Similar to Stanley 13 1/2. Uncommon Type. Length: 6 Inches. *When Lufkin got into the folding rule business they offered an equivalent to nearly every item in the Stanley line. Most of the obscure numbers, such as this one, were probably produced in a single production run. A rare Lufkin item.* (GOOD+) **$115.00**

P5-12. Stanley Rule & Level No. 53 1/2: Two-Foot, Four-Fold Folding Rule. Arch Joint, Unbound. Near New Condition. Length: 24 Inches. *Always a collector's favorite, the No. 53 1/2 is fitted with beveled inside edges for close work, such as would have been required by an architect. This one is in new condition. Perfect.* (FINE) **$165.00**

P5-13. Stanley Rule & Level No. 30 1/2: 1/16 Inch Per Foot Shrinkage Rule. Uncommon Size. Near New Condition. Length: 24 Inches. *Stanley's early patternmaker's shrinkage rules were all designated as the No. 30 1/2, with a shrinkage amount included to designate different configurations. This early example of the rare 1/16 inch size appears never to have been used.* (FINE) **$125.00**

P5-14. Rabone & Sons, J., Birmingham: Rope Caliper Rule. Shroud, Hawser, Etc. 99% Original Finish. Length: 4 3/4 Inches. *Rules such as this were used in the marine trades and by merchants who sold rope and cable. This example is marked with the name of English makers John Rabone & Sons and is in top condition. Choice.* (FINE) **$165.00**

P5-15. Unmarked: Patented Cam-Lock Rule Attachment. Patented October 1, 1907. Bronze Body. Length: 3 Inches. *This device was affixed by a cam lock to your standard carpenter's rule where it facilitated the laying out of miter cuts. An uncommon patented rule accessory.* (GOOD+) **$85.00**

P5-16. Chapin-Stephens Co., The No. 036: Patent Inclinometer Folding Rule. With Level, Bevel, Etc. Crisp, Clean and Sound. Length: 12 Inches. *The Chapin Stephens Company was the last of a series of makers who produced the Stephens Patent Combination Rule that was originally patented by L.C. Stephens in 1858. This example is in excellent overall condition.* (GOOD+) **$275.00**

P5-17. Stanley Rule & Level No. 62 1/2: Two Foot, Four Fold Folding Rule. Square Joint, Fully Bound. As New Condition. Length: 24 Inches. *This example of the narrow, full bound, square-joint rule is in just-out-of-the-box condition. Mint.* (FINE) **$195.00**

P5-18. Rustless Rule Co., Buffalo, N.Y. No. W-5: 6 Inch Caliper Rule. Brass Jaws. "Pat. Appl'd. For". Length: 6 Inches. *This company offered a series of rolled aluminum rules, of which this is the least common. A good one.* (FINE) **$55.00**

P5-19. Stanley Rule & Level No. 68: Two-Foot, Four-Fold Folding Rule. Round Joint, Unbound. Horizontal Read. Length: 24 Inches. *As nice an example of this so-called "common" Stanley rule as we have offered, this example of the No. 68 is in never-need-to-upgrade condition. Choice.* (FINE) **$25.00**

P5-20. Sampson Aston Maker: Two Foot, Two Fold Folding Rule. With Gunter Slide. Early Steel Tips. Length: 24 Inches. *This calculating rule from a prominent English maker is fitted with early style steel tips and has a Gunter slide for computation. A well preserved early calculating rule.* (GOOD+) **$135.00**

P5-21. Stanley Rule & Level No. 62: Two-Foot, Two-Fold Folding Rule. Square Joint, Full Bound. "Sweetheart" Trademark. Length: 24 Inches. *The No. 62 was one of Stanley's best selling rules. This "Sweetheart" era rule is 75 years old and still looking young. Extra crisp and clean.* (GOOD+) **$55.00**

P5-22. Unmarked: 3 Foot "Blind Man's" Folding Rule. Midland Lumber. Windsor, Ontario. Length: 36 Inches. *The advertising of the Midland Lumber Company of Windsor, Ontario is imprinted on this classic "Blind Man's" rule.* (GOOD) **$75.00**

P5-23. Stanley Rule & Level (Unmarked) No. 57: One Foot, Four Fold Folding Rule. Arch Joint, Full Bound. Near New Condition. Length: 12 Inches. *Stanley may have made the No. 57 with its imprint applied thereto, but I have yet to see one. This example is as crisp and new as the day it left the factory. No apologies and highly recommended.* (FINE) **$285.00**

P5-24. Keuffel & Esser Co., N.Y.: Broad Architect's Folding Rule. Solid Boxwood. Manufactured By Rabone. Length: 24 Inches. *The Keuffel & Esser Company was always one with an international vision, and it is therefore not surprising to see this English-made architect's rule included as part of their diverse line. An uncommon rule in excellent condition.* (GOOD+) **$115.00**

P5-25. Unmarked: Two Foot, Two Fold Folding Rule. Unused Condition. Early Steel Tips. Length: 24 Inches. *There are no maker marks on this perfectly preserved rule. The presence of steel tips indicates quite early manufacture. It appears never to have been used.* (FINE) **$85.00**

P5-26. Stanley Rule & Level No. 63: Two Foot, Four Fold Folding Rule. Square Joint, Unbound. Clean, Sound Example. Length: 24 Inches. *A step up from Stanley's No. 61 square-joint rule, the No. 63 added the stronger "bitted" joints on its central hinge. A good one.* (GOOD+) **$35.00**

P5-27. Rabone & Sons, John, Birmingham No. 1171: Two Foot, Four Fold Folding Rule. Extra Narrow. Crisp and Clean. Length: 24 Inches. *This Rabone rule features the "arch" joint that was characteristic of better quality rules. A nice example.* (GOOD+) **$45.00**

P5-28. Lufkin Rule Co., The, Saginaw, Mich. No. 171: Six Inch, Two Fold Folding Rule. With Caliper. Stanley No. 36 Equivalent. Length: 6 Inches. *Lufkin's answer to the No. 36 caliper rule, this one has seen some light wear, but is sound and clearly marked with the maker name.* (GOOD+) **$35.00**

P5-29. Stanley Tools No. 36 1/2 R: One-Foot, Two-Fold Folding Rule. Square Joint, Unbound. Crisp Condition. Length: 12 Inches. *This right hand caliper rule is in nearly perfectly preserved condition. A nice example.* (GOOD+) **$25.00**

P5-30. Stanley Rule & Level No. 31 1/2: Early Shrinkage Folding Rule. Early Stanley Mark. 1/10 Inches Per Foot. Length: 24 Inches. *This rare Stanley folding shrinkage rule has graduations that correspond to 1/10" per foot. A tough rule to find, especially in the 1/10 inch size.* (GOOD) **$185.00**

P5-31. Stanley Rule & Level No. 61 1/2: Two Foot, Four Fold Folding Rule. Square Joint, Unbound. Rare and Excellent. Length: 24 Inches. *The No. 61 1/2 is graduated on both its face and sides. Clean examples are hard to come by. This is a good one.* (GOOD+) **$115.00**

P5-32. Stanley Rule & Level No. 32 1/2: Arch Joint, Full Bound Folding Rule. With Caliper Slide. Near New Condition. Length: 12 Inches. *Here's an unused example of Stanley's top of the line full-bound, arch-joint caliper rule. This one features the later style arch joint. Near mint.* (FINE) **$85.00**

P5-33. Lufkin Rule Co., The, Saginaw, Mich. No. 388: Arch Joint, Full Bound Folding Rule. With Caliper Slide. Crisp and Clean. Length: 12 Inches. *This arch joint, full-bound caliper rule is the equivalent to Stanley's 32 1/2. A tough rule to find in any condition. This one has some light stains, but is otherwise crisp and sound.* (GOOD+) **$75.00**

P5-34. Stanley Rule & Level No. 31 1/8: Early Shrinkage Folding Rule. Early Stanley Mark. Extra Crisp and Clean. Length: 24 Inches. *An early Stanley mark is imprinted on this rare folding shrinkage rule. A shrinkage of 1/8 inch was the standard for cast iron. A nice example.* (GOOD+) **$325.00**

P5-35. Stanley Rule & Level No. 32: One-Foot, Four-Fold Folding Rule. Arch Joint, Unbound. "Sweetheart" Trademark. Length: 12 Inches. *Nearly every carpenter kept a rule such as this in his (or her, if you insist) vest pocket. This one is marked with the Stanley trademark in use in the 1920's. A nice, clean rule.* (GOOD+) **$45.00**

P5-36. Stanley Rule & Level No. 61: Two Foot, Four Fold Folding Rule. Square Joint, Unbound. Apparently Unused. Length: 24 Inches. *This pristine and early example may never have had its joint opened. New.* (FINE) **$35.00**

P5-37. C-S Co., The, Pine Meadow, Conn. No. 63: Two Foot, Four Fold Folding Rule. Round Joint, Unbound. Unused Condition. Length: 24 Inches. *This perfectly preserved Chapin Stephens rule features the "low end" round joint. An old rule, but new.* (FINE) **$45.00**

P5-38. Stanley Rule & Level No. 65 1/2: One Foot, Four Fold Folding Rule. Square Joint, Full Bound. Crisp and Clean. Length: 12 Inches. *Word has it that the principal makers of boxwood rules toward the end of the last century would pool their production and exchange supplies of the smaller, more common rules, all of which were not marked with a maker imprint. I have never seen any proof of this, but it would certainly explain why so few examples of the one-foot, four-fold rules are marked with maker names. This No. 65 1/2 by Stanley is a crisp and clean example of a rare maker marked rule. No apologies.* (GOOD+) **$155.00**

P5-39. Chapin-Stephens Co., Pine Meadow, No. 54: Two Foot, Four Fold Folding Rule. Arch Joint, Full Bound. Uncommon Type. Length: 24 Inches. *A step above the "basic" full bound rule, the No. 54 is fitted with an arch joint for durability. Owing to the added expense of the fancy joint, far fewer of these rules were sold. This one has some outside wear, but is otherwise crisp, clean and clearly marked.* (GOOD+) **$65.00**

P5-40. Stanley Rule & Level No. 26: Two-Foot, Two-Fold Folding Rule. Middle, Edge Scales. Excellent Condition. Length: 24 Inches. *Stanley's No. 26 folding rule features a Gunter slide on a square joint, full bound rule. This example is crisp, clean and clearly marked. A nice example of an increasingly difficult rule to find.* (GOOD+) **$185.00**

P5-41. Unmarked No. 10: Two Foot, Four Fold Folding Rule. Round Joint, Unbound. Early Chapin No.? Length: 24 Inches. *The equivalent in form to Stanley's No. 68 rule, this No. 10 rule is not imprinted with any maker's mark, but was likely made by H. Chapin at the Union Factory. A clean and early folding rule.* (GOOD+) **$45.00**

P5-42. Stanley Rule & Level No. 36: Six-Inch, Two-Fold Folding Rule. Square Joint, Caliper. Early Stanley Mark. Length: 6 Inches. *The patina on the outside of this rule is a consequence of having spent some time in the pocket of its original owner. An early Stanley rule with character.* (GOOD+) **$35.00**

P5-43. Rust Craft, Boston, Mass.: Nickel Plated Folding Rule. Original Pasteboard Box. Ca. 1915. Length: 12 Inches. *This nickel-plated rule looks to date from the very early years of this century. A cute little collectible.* (FINE) **$65.00**

P5-44. Stanley Rule & Level (Unmarked) No. 69: One Foot, Four Fold Folding Rule. With Round Joint. Early and Excellent. Length: 12 Inches. *The smaller sizes of Stanley's folding rules were seldom marked with the maker mark. This one is unmarked, but unmistakable because of the distinctive "pentagon pin" in the joint.* (GOOD+) **$45.00**

P5-45. Stanley Rule & Level No. 36: Six-Inch, Two-Fold Folding Rule. "Sweetheart" Trademark. Unused Condition. Length: 6 Inches. *The next time someone tells you that the No. 36 is a "common" rule, give them a month to show you one in this condition. You won't hear that again unless they call here before you do. Mint.* (FINE) **$85.00**

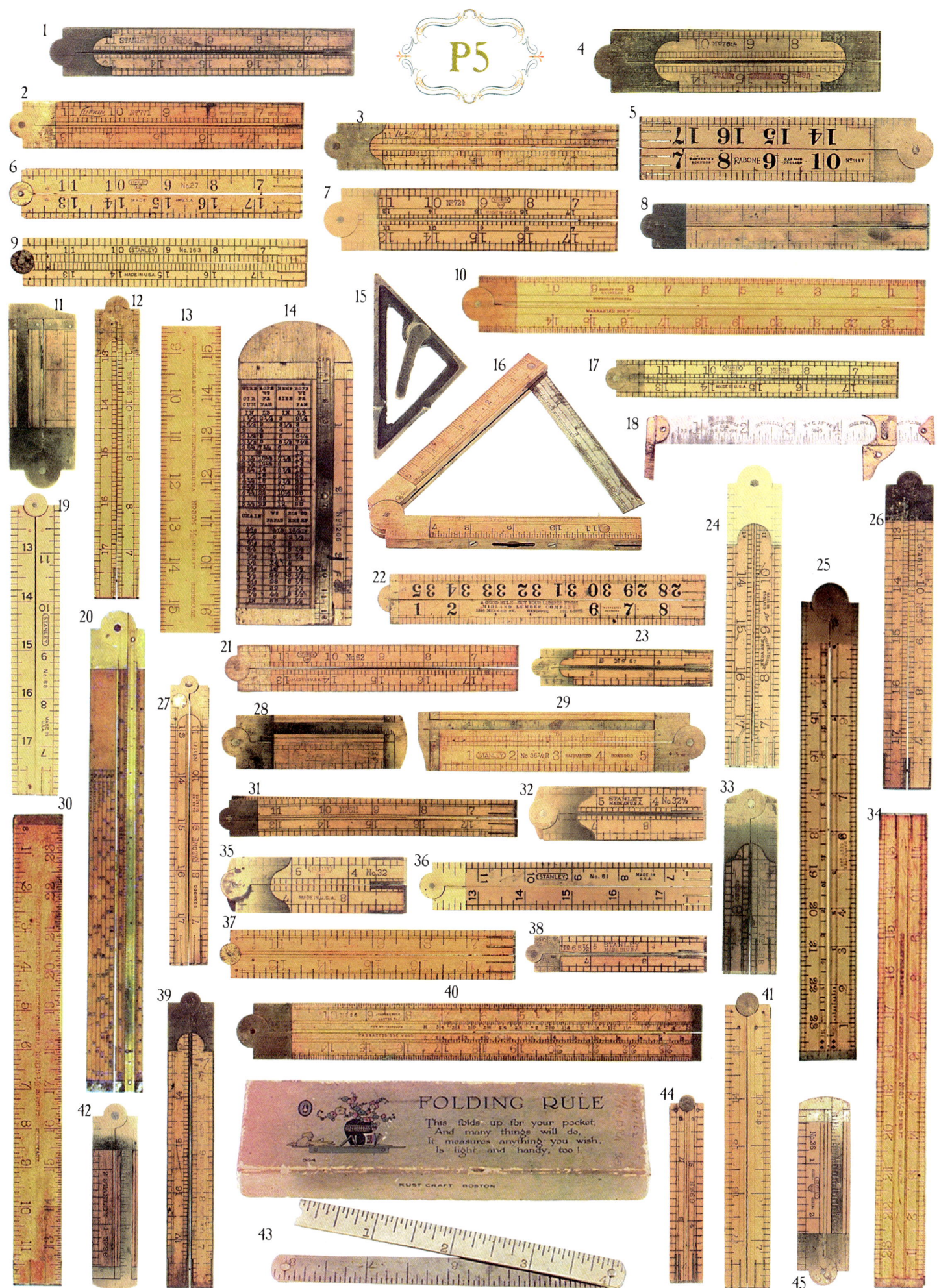

Group Q5

Q5-1. Stanley Rule & Level No. 50: Combination Beading Plane. Complete and Excellent. New Condition, Original Box. Length: 8 Inches. *Stanley's very functional light beading plane in a box that has seen some wear, but is complete and intact. These planes can do 95% of the work of the No. 45 combination plane at about half the weight. The plane, complete with all parts and cutters, is about as good as it could get. A very well preserved example. Nice.* (FINE) **$335.00**

Q5-2. Stanley Rule & Level No. 100 1/2: "Toy" Block Plane. With Rounded Sole. Unused Condition. Length: 3 1/2 Inches. *Topped off with a nicely-contrasting red lever cap, this example of Stanley's convex bottom model maker's block plane is in mint condition. Perfect.* (FINE) **$165.00**

Q5-3. Stanley Rule & Level No. 4 C: 8 Inch Smoothing Plane. Ca. 1930's. Extra Crisp and Clean. Length: 9 Inches. *This one is a bit dirty, but appears to have nearly all of its original paint. A nice working plane.* (GOOD) **$85.00**

Q5-4. Stanley Rule & Level No. 39: Cast Iron Dado Plane. 7/8 Inch Size. "Sweetheart" Trademark. Length: 8 Inches. *This was the next to largest size of the No. 39 series, and it is one of the scarcest numbers to find, especially in as well-preserved condition as this example. Shiny black japanning and shiny nickel. No apologies.* (GOOD+) **$245.00**

Q5-5. Stanley Rule & Level No. 55 E: Patented Universal Combination Plane. Complete With Cutters. Rare Metal Box. Length: 11 1/2 Inches. *Apparently produced exclusively for export to the British Isles, the "55 E" differs in no particular way from the American version of the 55. This boxed 55 E plane does however, differ markedly from most No. 55 planes one sees due to the exceptionally well preserved condition it is in. Nearly all of the shiny nickel plating remains and all original parts are present. The flip top metal box was designed to allow the 55 to be stored inside while assembled, thus resolving a longstanding problem with 55's that led to most of the original boxes being discarded. A spectacularly well preserved example of a rare Stanley plane. Extra special.* (FINE) **$1,650.00**

Q5-6. Stanley Rule & Level No. 4: 9 Inch Smoothing Plane. Ready to Use. With Rosewood Handles. Length: 9 Inches. *Nearly all original finishes remain on this crispy clean No. 4 smooth plane, which features the orange infill cap iron that was introduced in the 1930's. Top shelf.* (FINE) **$65.00**

Q5-7. Stanley Rule & Level No. 6: 18 Inch Fore Plane. Ca. 1930's. 98% Original Finishes. Length: 18 Inches. *This Type 2 No. 6 plane is in about as nice condition as one could hope for in such an early plane. 98% of original finishes on the metal and the nicely grained rosewood handles. Very nice.* (FINE) **$125.00**

Q5-8. Stanley Rule & Level No. 40: Rosewood Handle. Scrub Plane. Ca. 1935. Ready to Use. Length: 9 1/2 Inches. *This 1930's era scrub plane is in great condition with more than 90% of its original paint. A great working tool.* (GOOD+) **$110.00**

Q5-9. Stanley Rule & Level No. 39: Cast Iron Dado Plane. 5/8 Inch Size. Extra Crisp and Clean. Length: 8 Inches. *A superb example of the tough to find 5/8 inch cast iron dado plane in extremely well preserved condition. Ready to fill out a collection that will never need an upgrade. Nice.* (FINE) **$335.00**

Q5-10. Stanley Rule & Level No. 15: Early "Type 4" Block Plane. 95% Original Paint. Scarce Type and Size. Length: 7 Inches. *The No. 15 is the same as the 9 1/2, only 1/2 inch longer. This early example is in excellent condition and ready to use or fill out a collection, or both.* (GOOD+) **$145.00**

Q5-11. Stanley Rule & Level No. 19: Knuckle Joint Plane. Patented December 28, 1886. Early and Excellent. Length: 7 Inches. *The bigger brother of the much more common No. 18 knuckle joint block plane, this one is 1/2 inch longer. Nearly all original nickel plating remains on the cap iron. Nice.* (FINE) **$75.00**

Q5-12. Stanley Rule & Level No. 20: Cast Iron Circular Plane. Ca. 1935. 95% Original Paint. Length: 10 Inches. *By far the best of Stanley's three models of circular planes to use, the No. 20 is a direct descendent of the "Victor" planes of Leonard Bailey. This later version is in great working condition and retains more than 95% of its original shiny black japan finish. All of the original nickel plating remains on the cap iron. Crisp, clean and ready to use.* (FINE) **$275.00**

Q5-13. Stanley Rule & Level No. 9 1/2: Adjustable Throat Plane. With Precision Adjustment. Near New Condition. Length: 6 Inches. *This "basic" block plane is in anything but basic condition. Extra crisp and ready to use.* (FINE) **$55.00**

Q5-14. Stanley Rule & Level No. 5 1/4: "Junior Jack" Plane. 1 3/4 Inch Cutter. Rosewood Handles. Length: 11 Inches. *The "Junior" jack plane, was the width of a No. 3 and just a bit shorter than a No. 5. Although these were marketed to manual training schools, these tools have found favor among latter-day woodworkers. This pristine is in top condition and is ready to use or fill out a Stanley collection. Nice.* (FINE) **$165.00**

Q5-15. Stanley Rule & Level No. 10: Bench Rabbet Plane. Early Trademark. Crisp, Clean and Sound. Length: 12 Inches. *Here's a good working carriage maker's rabbet plane that retains more than 90% of its original finishes on both wood and metal. A previous owner has identified the plane by cutting an "x" in the top of the tote, but the tool is otherwise excellent. A nearly full cutting iron remains.*(GOOD+) **$225.00**

Q5-16. Stanley Rule & Level No. 8 C: Cast Iron Jointer Plane. Ca. 1905 Era. Clean and Sound. Length: 24 Inches. *The two patent dates cast in the bed of this clean jointer plane date its manufacture to approximately 1905. A sliver of wood is missing from the side of the top of the tote, but the plane is otherwise mechanically perfect and retains 95%+ of its original paint.* (GOOD+) **$185.00**

Q5-17. Stanley Rule & Level No. 93: 1 Inch Shoulder Rabbet Plane. "Made in USA". Near New Condition. Length: 6 Inches. *A crisp, clean and ready to use example of Stanley's 1 inch shoulder plane. Extra nice.* (FINE) **$245.00**

Q5-18. Stanley Rule & Level No. 182: Cast Iron Rabbet Plane. 1 Inch Width. Early Vine Casting. Length: 10 1/2 Inches. *Stanley offered its cast iron rabbeting planes with a nicker (the 190 series) or without, as in this early example of the No. 180 series. This one is marked with the early "arch" trademark and the handle has the early and appealing "vine" casting. An increasingly difficult plane to find. This one is in great collector-quality condition.* (GOOD+) **$115.00**

Q5-19. Stanley Rule & Level No. 16: Adjustment Throat Block Plane. With Nickeled Cap. Chip in Cap Iron. Length: 6 Inches. *Another Stanley plane that was offered for a relatively long period, but is seldom seen. This extra-clean example is in excellent condition, noting a pinhead sized flake from the inside of the cap iron. A very nice example of a most uncommon Stanley tool.* (GOOD) **$35.00**

Q5-20. Stanley Rule & Level No. 40: Beech Handle Scrub Plane. "Sweetheart" Trademark. Superb Condition. Length: 11 Inches. *This extra-early scrub plane has all of the bright yellow lacquer on the handles and a good 98% or more of the original paint. Highly recommended.* (FINE) **$165.00**

Q5-21. Stanley Rule & Level No. 606 C: "Bedrock" Fore Plane. "Sweetheart" Trademark. 98% Original Paint. Length: 18 Inches. *Some 98% of the original shiny black japan finish remains on this crispy clean "Bedrock" fore plane. The cap and cutter are a bit dirty, but they are neither rusty nor pitted. A great working tool in top condition.* (FINE) **$345.00**

Q5-22. Stanley Rule & Level No. 7 C: 22 Inch Jointer Plane. Rosewood Handles. Near New Condition. Length: 22 Inches. *Nearly all original finishes remain on this shiny clean jointer plane produced in the 1930's by Stanley. A superb example of Stanley's best selling jointer plane.* (FINE) **$215.00**

Q5-23. Stanley Rule & Level No. 15: Adjustable Throat Plane. Ready to Use. Excellent Condition. Length: 7 Inches. *The No. 15 is the same as the 9 1/2, only 1/2 inch longer. It is in clean, complete and thoroughly usable condition.* (GOOD+) **$65.00**

Q5-24. Stanley Rule & Level No. 71: Open Throat Router Plane. Ready to Use. Complete and Extra Nice. Length: 8 Inches. *This open throat router is complete with all original parts and the original Stanley instruction manual. Absolutely complete and perfect.* (FINE) **$125.00**

Q5-25. Stanley Rule & Level No. 70: Cooper's Light Duty Scraper. With Pivoting Head. Ca. 1930's. Length: 13 Inches. *Marketed as a "box scraper", for removing stenciled labels from wooden boxes and barrels, these multi-purpose tools are essentially long-handled spokeshaves. This example dates from the immediate post-Sweetheart era of Stanley production. Nearly all original finishes remain.* (FINE) **$65.00**

Q5-26. Stanley Rule & Level No. 46: Combination Dado Plane. Full Nickel Plating. Fitted Pine Box. Length: 12 Inches. *Stanley's No. 46 plane did everything that the No. 45 did (except cut beads) and did it with a skew-set iron. These have recently been recognized by woodworkers as a better choice than the No. 45 for rabbet and dado work. This crispy clean example comes with all original parts and a full set of cutting irons. It has been protected through some 100 years of existence by a fitted pine box. Extra nice.* (FINE) **$485.00**

Q5-27. Stanley Rule & Level No. 39: 1/2 Inch Width Dado Plane. "Sweetheart" Trademark. Crisp and Clean. Length: 8 Inches. *A picture perfect 1/2 inch cast iron dado plane in a popular size. 95% of all original finishes remain. Very nice.* (FINE) **$215.00**

Q5-28. Stanley Rule & Level No. 3: Rosewood Handle. Smooth Plane. Orange Lever Cap. Unused Condition. Length: 9 Inches. *More than 99% of the original finishes remain on this 1950's era example of Stanley's rosewood handle smoothing plane. Ready to provide a lifetime of service. Mint.* (FINE) **$110.00**

Q5-29. Stanley Rule & Level No. 6: 18 Inch Fore Plane. Ca. 1950's. 99% Original Finishes. Length: 18 Inches. *Half jack plane and half jointer, the 18 inch No. 6 can do some of the work of each. This one is about as good as they get. 99% of the shiny original finishes remain. Mint.* (FINE) **$125.00**

Q5-30. Stanley Rule & Level No. H 101 P: Model Maker's Plane. "Handyman" Brand. Extra Crisp and Clean. Length: 3 1/2 Inches. *A later version of Stanley's No. 101 plane, this is offered as an example of the depths to which this once great toolmaker has sunk. The name goes on before the quality goes in.* (GOOD+) **$5.00**

Q5-31. Stanley Rule & Level No. 607 C: "Bedrock" Jointer Plane. With Corrugated Sole. Extra Crisp and Clean. Length: 22 Inches. *This later style corrugated sole Bedrock is in crisp, sound condition. The cutting iron is marked with the ca. 1915 era "V" trademark. A good one.* (GOOD+) **$285.00**

Q5-32. Stanley Rule & Level No. 4: 9 Inch Smoothing Plane. Ca. 1930's. 99% Original Finishes. Length: 9 Inches. *Nearly all of the original finishes remain on this pristine smoothing plane that dates from the 1930's, or thereabout. Bold grain patterns accent the Brazilian Rosewood handles. A pretty plane.* (FINE) **$95.00**

Q5-33. Stanley Rule & Level No. 101: Early "Toy" Block Plane. Circular Trademark. 98% Original Paint. Length: 3 1/4 Inches. *Nearly all of the shiny original japan finish remains on this crispy clean "toy" block plane. The trademark indicates that this plane was made ca. 1890. Nice.* (FINE) **$95.00**

Q5-34. Stanley Rule & Level No. 148: Tongue and Groove Plane. "Sweetheart" Trademark. Length: 9 Inches. *No apologies for this pristine example of Stanley's stock-lumber version of its 140 series of double tongue and groove plane. These are becoming increasingly difficult to find. Examples in this condition have always been scarce. A good one.* (FINE) **$175.00**

Q5-35. Stanley Rule & Level No. 4 1/2: Wide Heavy Smooth Plane. Scarce Type 12. "Sweetheart" Trademark. Length: 10 Inches. *Looking for a great working heavy smoothing plane. Here's an exceptionally nice No. 4 1/2 fitted out with handles of Brazilian Rosewood. A great working tool that is ready to provide several lifetimes of service. Part of the original decal remains on the handle of this "Type 12" version.* (GOOD+) **$225.00**

Q5-36. Stanley Rule & Level No. 191: Cast Iron Rabbet Plane. Clean and Complete. Ready to Use. Length: 10 1/2 Inches. *More than 95% of the original paint remains on this well preserved Stanley rabbeting plane. A good one.* (GOOD+) **$55.00**

Q5-37. Stanley Rule & Level No. 80: Cast Iron Cabinet Scraper. Early "V" Trademark. Ready to Use. Length: 12 Inches. *Stanley's basic cast iron scraper can be adjusted for depth of cut as well as tension by three separate adjustment screws. This example is in excellent working condition.* (GOOD+) **$45.00**

Q5-38. Stanley Rule & Level No. 55: Patented Universal Combination Plane. Complete with Cutters. Oak Carry Case. Length: 11 1/2 Inches. *Advertised as "A Planing Mill Within Itself", the Stanley No. 55 Patent Universal Combination Plane can, with a bit of practice, be made to duplicate any molding profile ever made. This one is complete with all of the original parts, including more than 50 specialized cutting irons. It comes in a fitted wooden box. Much original nickel plating remains and the rosewood fences and handles are in excellent condition. Were it possible to make these planes today, a working approximation of much lesser quality would cost thousands of dollars. A bargain.* (FINE) **$645.00**

Q5-39. Stanley Rule & Level No. 5 1/2: Wide Jack Plane Plane. Type 11, 3 Patent Dates. Ca. 1910 Trademark. Length: 14 1/2 Inches. *Stanley's No. 5 1/2 plane is approximately the length of the No. 5, but as wide as its big brother, the No. 7 jointer. This "Type 11" example has been used, but not abused. An excellent working tool.* (GOOD+) **$145.00**

Q5-40. Stanley Rule & Level No. 100: Squirrel Tail Block Plane. Red Lever Cap. 99% Original Paint. Length: 3 1/4 Inches. *The working partner of the 101 1/2, this version has the squirrel tail handle, but with a flat sole. Nearly new.* (FINE) **$85.00**

Q5-41. Stanley Rule & Level No. 45: Patent Combination Plane. Complete and Excellent. New Condition, Original Box. Length: 12 Inches. *This superb example of Stanley's No. 45 combination has been sheltered from the elements by its original pasteboard box. A great working tool that is complete and in ready to go to work order.* (FINE) **$465.00**

Q5-42. Stanley Rule & Level No. 78: Duplex Filletster Plane. "Sweetheart" Trademark. Crisp and Clean. Length: 9 1/2 Inches. *This early version of Stanley's duplex bullnose rabbet and filletster plane is marked on the body with the early "Old English" casting and on the cutting iron with the "Sweetheart" tradmark. Extra crisp and clean.* (GOOD+) **$95.00**

Q5-43. Stanley Rule & Level No. 65: Low Angle Block Plane. Nickel Plated Cap. Ready to Use. Length: 7 Inches. *Here's a good clean working example of Stanley's wide, low angle block plane. A good one.* (GOOD+) **$95.00**

Q5-44. Stanley Rule & Level No. 8: Cast Iron Jointer Plane. With 3 Patent Dates. New Stanley Iron. Length: 24 Inches. *A previous owner has ensured that no one else would ever get his "Type 11" No. 8 jointer plane by placing two small file marks in the side rail. Unfortunately, this didn't keep us from getting it and it shouldn't keep you. This plane is in excellent condition. A good one.* (GOOD+) **$155.00**

Q5-45. Stanley Rule & Level No. 604 C: "Bedrock" Smoothing Plane. Later Type. Square Sides. Patented. Length: 9 Inches. *Our experience has been that purchasers of Stanley's "Bedrock" planes opted, in overwhelming proportions, for those without corrugated soles. The original buyer of this well preserved example took the road not taken. An excellent working tool.* (GOOD+) **$265.00**

Group R5

R5-1. Utica Drop Forge & Tool Corp. No. 50: 6 Inch Side Cutting Pliers. Fully Polished. New Condition, Original Box. Length: 6 Inches. *These ca. 1950's side cutting pliers are in new condition in their original picture box. Perfect.* (FINE) **$25.00**

R5-2. Utica Tools, Utica, N.Y. No. 98: Pair of End Cutting Nippers. Early Appearance. Very Little Used. Length: 5 1/2 Inches. *The Utica Tool Company produced a wide range of high quality pliers, nippers and wrenches. These end cutting nippers have been very little used. Nice.* (FINE) **$15.00**

R5-3. Proto Tools, Los Angeles, C.A. No. 238: Angle Head Pliers. Multiple Adjust. Near New Condition. Length: 7 Inches. *Automotive tools have become increasingly collectible. If you're thinking of adding a few to your collection, these angle headed adjustable pliers from a prominent Los Angeles maker would be a good place to start.* (FINE) **$25.00**

R5-4. Unmarked: Special Function Pliers. Patented October 28, 1880. Rare and Excellent. Length: 2 1/4 Inches. *Measuring only 2 1/4 inches in length, these special purpose ppatented pliers are marked with a very early patent date. As The Ol' Perfessor, Casey Stengel, used to say "you culd look it up". Most unusual.* (FINE) **$65.00**

R5-5. Crescent Tool Co., Jamestown, N.Y. No. 20: 5 Inch Flat Nose Pliers. With Cushion Grip. New Condition, Original Box. Length: 5 Inches. *These speical purpose pliers have been fitted with rubber "cushion grips". Both the tool and the graphic picture box are in new condition.* (FINE) **$35.00**

R5-6. Clark, Alfred: Patent Shoe Lasting Pliers. Patented April 4, 1871. Early and Excellent. Length: 8 Inches. *We are unaware of the specific "improvements" of the 1871 patent, the date of which has been stamped on these early shoe lasting pliers. The name of Alfred Clark is missing from the Directory of American Toolmakers. A rare pair from an undocumented maker.* (GOOD+) **$45.00**

R5-7. Schollhorn Co., W., New Haven, Conn.: Combination Punch And Pliers. "H.L. Judd Co., N.Y.". Unusual and Excellent. Length: 8 Inches. *This "Bernard" brand combination tool was produced by William Schollhorn for the H.L. Judd Company of New York City. Different.* (GOOD+) **$45.00**

R5-8. Peck Stow & Wilcox Company No. 20: 6 Inch Flat Jaw Pliers. With Etched Logo. Near New Condition. Length: 6 Inches. *A classic example of P.S. & W.'s diverse line, these pliers are in top collector quality condition.* (FINE) **$35.00**

R5-9. Schollhorn & Co., Wm., New Haven: Combination Punch and Rivet Pliers. B. Lawr. Stationary. Patented May 6, 1890. Length: 4 3/4 Inches. *A punch and riveter make this pair of Schollhorn specialty pliers a formidable tool for office work. The jaw is imprinted with the name of a New York City office supply company. Different.* (GOOD+) **$75.00**

R5-10. Kraeuter & Co., Newark, N.J.: Early Slip Joint Pliers. "Pat. Appd. For". Crisp and Clean. Length: 6 1/2 Inches. *The tip of one end of these well made Kraeuter pliers is formed to function as a screwdriver.* (GOOD+) **$25.00**

R5-11. Stanley Rule & Level: Rare Slip Joint Pliers. "Sweetheart" Trademark From Tool Kit. Length: 7 Inches. *No apologies whatsoever for these crispy clean Stanley pliers. Extra nice.* (FINE) **$285.00**

R5-12. Danielson Co., J.P., Jamestown, N.Y.: Slip Joint Pliers. Crescent Precursor. Superb Condition. Length: 7 Inches. *J.P. Danielson was one of the early producers in the tool making city of Jamestown, New York. These pliers are in excellent collector quality condition and clearly marked with the Danielson name.* (FINE) **$15.00**

R5-13. Stanley Tools No. 1500: "Handyman" Pliers. For Tool Kit. Near New Condition. Length: 6 1/2 Inches. *These pliers from Stanley's post World War II "Handyman" line are in nearly new condition.* (FINE) **$25.00**

R5-14. Unmarked: Pair of Pin Joint Pliers. Early Type Joint. Near New Condition. Length: 6 Inches. *These early round nose pliers are in excellent working order. Nice.* (FINE) **$15.00**

R5-15. Stanley Rule & Level: 6 Inch Slip Joint Pliers. With Sweetheart Trademark. Rare and Excellent. Length: 6 Inches. *Here's a crispy clean pair of Stanley's uncommon "Sweetheart" era pliers. These tools were offered exclusively in tool boxes and are consequently rare. If you have a Stanley tool box to fill, you may well need this tool.* (GOOD+) **$185.00**

R5-16. Forged Steel Prod., Newport, Penn. No. 27: "Vacuum Grip" Pliers. Patented March 8, 1927. Excellent Condition. Length: 7 Inches. *This company produced an extremely high grade line of automotive tools that were marketed under the name "Vacuum Grip". These patented pliers are in excellent collector quality condition.* (GOOD+) **$35.00**

R5-17. T.T.T., Hockanum, Conn.: Special Purpose Pliers. Patented July 19, 1910. Tooth Like Jaws. Length: 7 1/2 Inches. *Looking not unlike a particularly fearsome creature of the deep, these patented pliers have extremely sharp teeth (some of which are chipped) that performed some unknown function. As always, a search through the patent papers will tell us more about them than we really want to know. Most unusual.* (GOOD+) **$45.00**

R5-18. Unmarked: Early Set of 7 Pliers. File Fitted Joint. Most Unusual. Length: 5 Inches. *All of these small pairs of pliers came from the same toolkit. An early set of pliers of excellent quality.* (GOOD) **$115.00**

R5-19. Utica Drop Forge & Tool Corp. No. 1-7: 7 Inch Wide Jaw Pliers. Fully Polished. Near New Condition. Length: 7 Inches. *The jaws of these special-purpose pliers would have been parallel at only one setting. Different.* (FINE) **$15.00**

R5-20. Triple Grip: Patented "Triple Grip" Pliers. Patented June 17, 1924. With Center Jaw. Length: 8 Inches. *Someone serious about determining the function of these unusual patented pliers need only to consult the patent papers to determine the genius that they have captured in their form. An initial examination indicates that they were intended to hold and crimp something simultaneously. Most unusual.* (GOOD+) **$115.00**

R5-21. Stanley Rule & Level: Rare Slip Joint Pliers. "Sweetheart" Trademark From Tool Kit. Length: 7 Inches. *Apparently produced only for inclusion in Stanley's ca. 1920's tool kits, these "Sweetheart" imprinted pliers are eagerly sought after by collectors. First come, first serve.* (FINE) **$245.00**

R5-22. Diamond Horseshoe Caulk Co. No. DH 16: Combination Pliers and Wrench. With Screwdriver. With Seized Screw. Length: 6 Inches. *The folks at the Diamond Horseshoe Company must have figured it wasn't hard enough to use a pair of pliers to loosen the object of its use, so they added a "crescent" wrench to the end of one of the handles at the precise location where the application of force in the use of the pliers would cause the most pain. As for the adjustable wrench, these things are imprecise enough without the added burden of a pair of pliers to stick you in the eye. Offered as an historical curiosity unless you're stupid enough to try and use this thing. The adjustment screw on the wrench is a bit tight, but the tool is otherwise in good shape. Caveat Emptor.* (GOOD) **$15.00**

R5-23. Danielson Co., J.P., Jamestown, N.Y.: Early Manufactured Pliers. Distinctive Pattern. Extra Crisp and Clean. Length: 6 1/2 Inches. *Having a much narrower and longer nose that the commonly encountered sorts of pliers, this unusual tool from an early Jamestown, New York maker was undoubtedly produced for some special application. Different.* (FINE) **$20.00**

R5-24. Hibbard, Spencer & Bartlett Co.: "O.V.B." Brand Pliers. With Long Nose. Near New Condition. Length: 7 Inches. *When the H.S. & B. people marked a tool with their "Our Very Best" trademark, they meant it. A great pair of pliers in top condition.* (FINE) **$45.00**

R5-25. M. & M.: Patent Fencing Pliers. Patented May 22, 1900. Uncommon Type. Length: 10 Inches. *These early fencing pliers combine a multiplicity of functions into a single tool. Different.* (GOOD) **$95.00**

R5-26. Schollhorn Co., W., New Haven, Conn.: Bernard Patent Pliers. Interlock Brass Jaw. Patented December 27, 1892. Length: 5 Inches. *The Schollhorn Company specialized in special-application pliers, some of which appear to have been designed after a six martini lunch. These feature a series of interlocking brass teeth that may have been intended for holding and pulling wire. Different.* (GOOD+) **$85.00**

R5-27. Proto Tools, Los Angeles, C.A. No. 234: Multiple Adjustable Pliers. With Cam Feature. United States Patent 2600512. Length: 8 Inches. *These multiple size parallel jaw pliers are in new condition. A most unusual pair of patented pliers.* (FINE) **$35.00**

R5-28. Schollhorn & Co., Wm., New Haven No. 102: 6 1/2 Inch Parallel Pliers. With Wire Cutters. Full Nickel Plating. Length: 6 1/2 Inches. *We receive a large number of requests for parallel jaw pliers. This "Bernard Patent" classic also includes a wire cutter.* (FINE) **$45.00**

R5-29. Schollhorn & Co., New Haven, Conn.: Bernard's Patent End Nippers. Patented October 24, 1899. Uncommon Type. Length: 8 1/2 Inches. *One of the bolts that fixes the upper jaw to the arm is a replacement, but these early patented end cutters are otherwise in excellent condition. An uncommon "Bernard's Patent" tool.* (GOOD) **$15.00**

R5-30. Johnson: Special Purpose Pliers. Patented July 22, 1913. For Hog Rings? Length: 8 Inches. *These specialty patent pliers feature a forged lower jaw of circular form that has a series of notches cut into it, possibly for bending chain or shaping hog rings. Very different.* (GOOD+) **$55.00**

R5-31. Ross Mfg. Co., San Francisco, C.A.: "Lock Line" Pliers. For Electrical Use? Uncommon Type. Length: 7 1/4 Inches. *Looking for something different? Try these "Lock Line" pliers from a California maker. Different.* (GOOD+) **$35.00**

R5-32. Schollhorn & Co., Wm., New Haven No. 180: Parallel Jaw Pliers. Extra Heavy Jaw. Full Nickel Plating. Length: 5 Inches. *These most unusual parallel jaw pliers appear to have been designed for particularly heavy work. Unusual.* (FINE) **$65.00**

R5-33. Billings & Spencer Co., Hartford: Special Purpose Pliers. With Curved Tip. Screwdriver Function. Length: 6 Inches. *This particular set is not marked, but there is a pair in the original box in the Legendary Donnelly Collection. The patent date is in the 1870's, as I recall. An uncommon pair of pliers.* (GOOD) **$35.00**

R5-34. Smith Co., H.D., Plantsville, Conn.: Patent Offset Pliers. With Slip Joint. Patented June 9, 1907. Length: 7 Inches. *These rare offset pliers were produced by the H.D. Smith Company of Plantsville, Connecticut, the makers of the "Perfect Handle" line of tools. A rare pair of patented pliers from a prominent Connecticut maker.* (GOOD+) **$85.00**

R5-35. Utica Drop Forge & Tool Co.: "Hall's Patent" Nippers. Classic Pattern. Scarce and Excellent. Length: 5 Inches. *The "Hall's Patent" nippers were apparently very successful. This is the first pair we have seen bearing the Utica Tool imprint.* (GOOD+) **$35.00**

R5-36. Schollhorn & Co., Wm., New Haven: Dynamite Crimping Pliers. Military Use. Excellent Condition. Length: 7 Inches. *Produced by Connecticut maker William Schollhorn for military use, these Dynamite crimping pliers were apparently carefully used by the person to whom they were last assigned, as they show no evidence of powder burns or of having been hurled several hundred feet into the air. Different.* (FINE) **$35.00**

R5-37. Parrot Head Tool Co., Oklahoma City: "Parrot Head" Pliers. Screwdriver Tip. Very Little Used. Length: 7 Inches. *These are certainly a well made pair of pliers, but the idea of starting a company to market a single product seems a bit excessive. It is just those excesses that have made our tool collecting hobby so endlessly interesting. A classic collectible.* (FINE) **$55.00**

R5-38. Hayden's Patent: Hayden "Shank Laster" Pliers. Patented January 11, 1881. Scarce and Near New. Length: 9 Inches. *A pivoting fulcrum was apparently the patent feature of these early shoe lasting pliers. Crisp, clean and clearly marked with both the name and the patent date.* (FINE) **$85.00**

R5-39. Kraeuter & Co., Newark, N.J. No. 1611: 6 Inch Ring Pliers. Ready to Use. Unused Condition. Length: 6 Inches. *We have had much to say in the past about the consistently high quality of the tools produced by Kraeuter & Company of Newark, New Jersey. These well made round joint pliers are in new condition.* (FINE) **$15.00**

R5-40. Unmarked No. S-64: Special Purpose Pliers. For Crimping. Unique Design. Length: 6 Inches. *Pressing the handles together on these specialty pliers causes the jaws to move apart. A puzzle.* (GOOD+) **$45.00**

R5-41. Unmarked: Early Patent Lasting Pliers. Patented October 25, 1887. Hammer, Puller, Etc. Length: 8 Inches. *A keen observer might speculate that the manner of making of the joint is the patented feature on these unusual lasting pliers. There is no maker's mark, but they are clearly imprinted with the patent date.* (GOOD+) **$25.00**

R5-42. Kraeuter & Co., Newark, N.J.: 100th Anniversary Pliers. Decorative Casting. New Condition, Original Box. Length: 5 3/4 Inches. *To commemorate their 100th Anniversary in 1960, Kraeuter offered these specially boxed pliers. A rare commemorative tool.* (FINE) **$85.00**

R5-43. Kraeuter & Co., Newark, N.J. No. 2601-6: 6 Inch Side Cutting Pliers. Embossed Grip. Excellent Condition. Length: 6 Inches. *Looking for something really well made and not too expensive to be on the lookout for, while participating in the Great Weekend Tool Hunt? Check out the line of Kraeuter & Company of Newark, New Jersey. Early examples of their tools have elaborate hand grips forged into the handles, as does this pair. Crispy-clean.* (FINE) **$35.00**

R5-44. Unmarked No. K25: "Motor Spec." Pliers. From Duluth, Minn. Uncommon Type. Length: 5 1/2 Inches. *These "Motor Spec." pliers were likely a product of the Marshall Wells Hardware Company, a prominent tool maker and dealer in Duluth.* (FINE) **$25.00**

R5-45. Utica Drop Forge & Tool Corp. No. 43: Diagonal and Wire Strip Pliers. Fully Polished. New Condition, Original Box. Length: 6 Inches. *The notch in the jaws of these cutters did not come from carelessly cutting through a live electrical wire, but was put there intentionally for the purpose of stripping wire. New in the original picture label box.* (GOOD+) **$35.00**

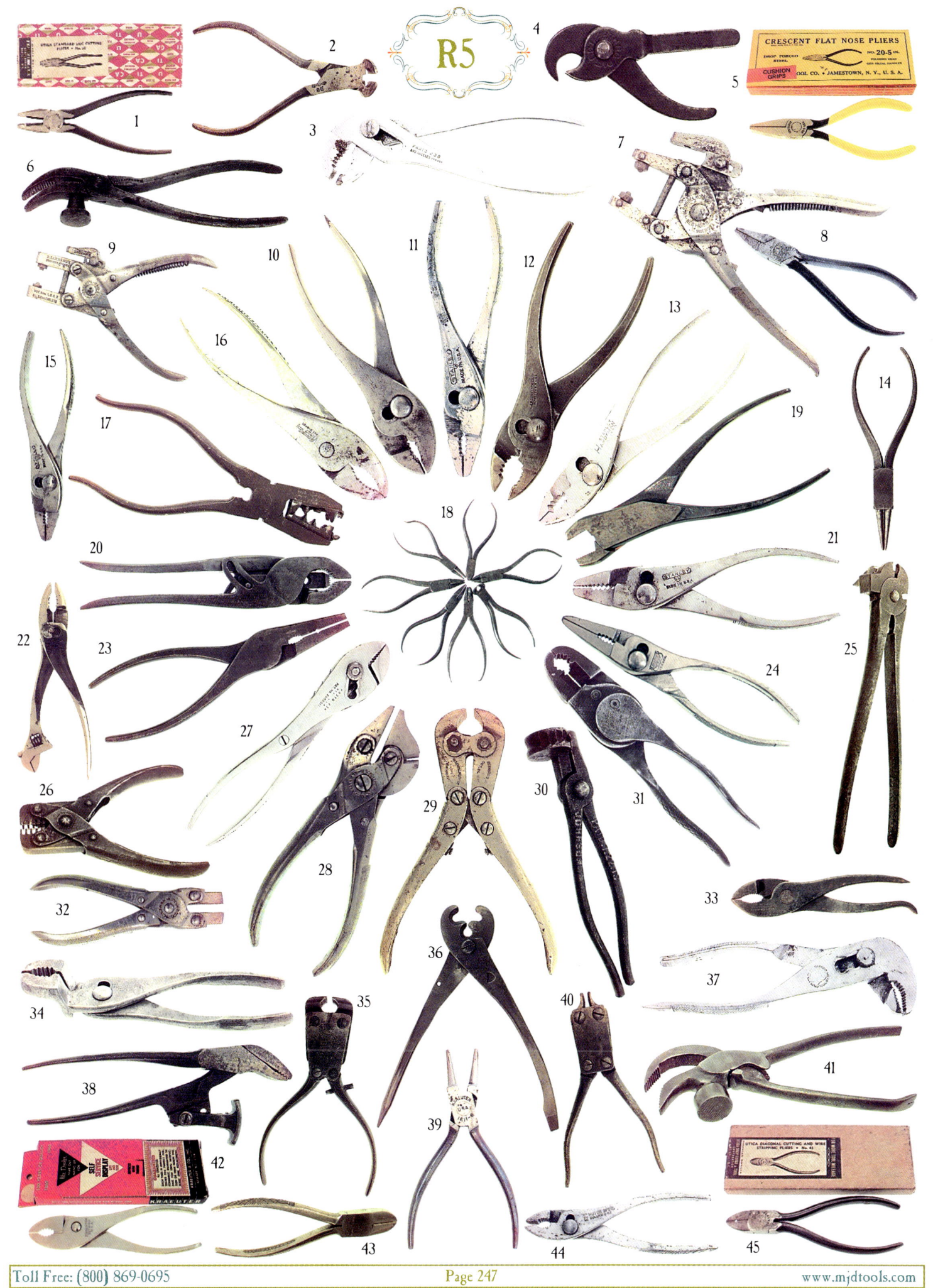

Group S5

S5-1. Sawyer Belt Hook Co., R.I.: No. 1970: Hammer and Axe Wedges. Different Sizes. New Condition, Original Box. Length: 2 1/2 Inches. *Every once in a while, usually after selling some tool for thousands of dollars, it dawns on me how I got started in the tool business. Visiting every yard sale for miles around, I would use my limited funds to buy usable tools, fix them up and take them to the flea market sixty miles away to sell them. Much of the "fixing up" involved putting new handles on hammers, hatchets, etc. It was not particularly financially rewarding but it was business and it was hard work, and that's what you do to get ahead. So now, sometimes, when those tools sell at once unimaginable prices, I head for the shop with a back saw, a spoke shave, some hammer heads and handles and undertake a ritual of remembering as I saw wooden wedges from hardwood, cut a kerf in the handle and carefully fit the head to the handle, driving in a metal wedge at the very end to finish the process. While the process is calculated to promote humility, its actually a lot of fun, so please, buy some more multiple thousand dollar tools. Here's a start up kit for someone thinking about getting in to the tool business on the ground floor.* (FINE) **$25.00**

S5-2. Cheney Corp., H., Little Falls, N.Y.: Early 2 Pound Flooring Hammer. Factory Reject? Cut Nail Holder. Length: 12 3/4 Inches. *This extra heavy duty flooring hammer has a wider than normal notch in its nail holding device, which may have held some specialized flooring nail. The back of the claw has a marked recess in the metal that has been there since the tool was made. This tool was found in Little Falls, where Cheney was located, and may have originally have been a factory reject.* (GOOD+) **$145.00**

S5-3. Double Claw Hammer Co., The: Patent Double Claw Hammer. Patented November 4, 1902. Rare Solid Head. Length: 13 Inches. *Generally, the double claw hammers produced by the Double Claw Hammer Company have a head formed of two separate sections. The fact that this hammer has a single piece head would normally have caused suspicion as to its authenticity; however, the patent date has been struck across the area of the head where the joint would have been, leaving no doubt that this is a most unusual variation of this collectible classic.* (GOOD+) **$365.00**

S5-4. Barton & Co., D.R., Rochester, N.Y.: Rare Veneer Hammer. With Nail Puller. Original Handle. Length: 11 1/4 Inches. *One of the most unusual hammers we have offered in some time, this specialized veneer hammer from D.R. Barton & Company has a slot milled into its extended face. Very different.* (GOOD+) **$345.00**

S5-5. Unmarked: Classic Veneer Hammer. Smooth Polish Face. Ready to Use. Length: 9 Inches. *This early veneer hammer is in essentially unused condition and ready to be put back to work. A good one.* (FINE) **$115.00**

S5-6. Unmarked: Early Ball Pein Hammer. Owner "J.F. Back". Original Handle. Length: 14 Inches. *The owner's name "J.F. Back" is the only mark on this ball pein hammer. Tools such as this were likely filed and hardened by the maker/owner as part of the apprenticeship training.* (GOOD+) **$25.00**

S5-7. Cheney Corp., H., Little Falls, N.Y.: No. 938: 16 Ounce Claw Hammer. With Original Label. Crisp and Clean. Length: 13 Inches. *Nearly all of the original label remains on the handle of this classic Cheney nail holding hammer.* (GOOD+) **$85.00**

S5-8. Unmarked: Massive Log Marking Hammer. Initial "G". From South Central N.H. Length: 22 1/2 Inches. *The single initial "G" is the uncompromising message of this early log marking hammer. It was found in South Central New Hampshire.* (GOOD+) **$85.00**

S5-9. Stanley Rule & Level No. 213: "Ladies" Defiance" Hammer. 7 Ounce Size. Original Paper Label. Length: 12 Inches. *We understand that the current President of Stanley Tools is planning a public apology and will issue reparations to those whose lives were ruined as a consequence of Stanley having offered this 7 ounce claw hammer as a "Ladies" hammer in the 1930's. A great collectible hammer that retains nearly all of its original paper label and which stands as a monument to the insensitivity of our non-politically correct forbears.* (FINE) **$115.00**

S5-10. Plumb, Fayette R., Philadelphia.: No. L 83: 7 Ounce "Leader" Hammer. Original Handle. Superb Condition. Length: 13 Inches. *This 7 oz. classic from Fayette R. Plumb retains its original handle and is in excellent collector quality condition.* (FINE) **$45.00**

S5-11. Robertson, A.R.: Advertising Tack Hammer. Patended November 2, 1886. Durfee Embalming Fluid Compny. Length: 11 3/4 Inches. *This early tack hammer is imprinted with an 1886 patent date as well as advertising for the Durfee Embalming Fluid Company. Funeral directors would likely have used such a tool in outfitting a casket for public viewing. A most interesting patented advertising hammer.* (GOOD+) **$65.00**

S5-12. Unmarked: Hand Forged Slaters Hammer. Made From a Rasp. Great Patina. Length: 12 Inches. *We have offered a wide range of tools made from discarded files and rasps over the years, and we are aware of a growing body of collectors who seek out tools produced from this medium. This is the first slater's hammer made from a rasp that we have ever offered. This classic collectible hammer is in excellent overall condition and still shows much of the rasp pattern. Extra nice.* (GOOD+) **$225.00**

S5-13. Cheney Corp., H., Little Falls, N.Y.: No. 4: Tinsmith's Hammer. As New Condition. Scarce Type. Length: 11 3/4 Inches. *Should the new user choose to put this hammer to work at the task for which it was designed, he (or she) would be the first to ever use it. Brand new.* (FINE) **$55.00**

S5-14. Cheney, Little Falls, N.Y.: No. 777: Adze Hammer. Original Decal. Near New Condition. Length: 15 Inches. *This is as fine an example of the Cheney Adze/Hammer combination as we have been privileged to offer. Its sharp adze edge was apparently never used in anger against a recalcitrant piece of lumber. Nice.* (FINE) **$225.00**

S5-15. Unmarked: Early "Strap" Hammer. With Integral Straps. "S.P. Guilford". Length: 12 Inches. *The straps on this early carpenter's hammer are integral to the head, unlike more common patterns for these tools where the straps are riveted to both the head and to the handle. A most interesting early hammer.* (GOOD) **$75.00**

S5-16. Atha Tool Co. No. 309: 16 Ounce Ball Pein Hammer. Original Handle. Unused Condition. Length: 14 Inches. *Nearly all of the original finish remains on this hammer from the days before the Atha Tool Company was purchased by Stanley. Mint.* (FINE) **$35.00**

S5-17. Unmarked: Early Patent Shoe Hammer. Patented April 13, 1884. Distinctive Form. Length: 7 Inches. *This patented shoe hammer has a distinctively different look, which must be the patent feature. The general concept of a piece of metal on the end of a stick had, by this time, been established as belonging in the public domain, and would not, in and of itself, constitute a patentable feature.* (FINE) **$155.00**

S5-18. Riverside Tool Co., New York, N.Y.: No. 16: 12 Ounce Claw Hammer. With "Anvil" Logo. Uncommon Maker. Length: 13 Inches. *Apparently very little used for the task for which it was produced, this ca. 1900 hammer retains its original handle and is marked with the Riverside Tool Company logo. A nice hammer.* (GOOD+) **$35.00**

S5-19. Niagara Machine & Tool Works: Slater's Hammer. Extra Crisp and Clean. Leather Handle. Length: 11 Inches. *A good, clean, ready to go to work slater's hammer with the desirable "leather washer" handle.* (FINE) **$155.00**

S5-20. Cheney H., Little Falls, N.Y.: "Hard Hitter" Hammer. Early Appearance. Uncommon Type. Length: 13 Inches. *The head of this hammer is imprinted with the Cheney name and the trademark "Hard Hitter". The handle is a replacement. A rare Cheney hammer.* (GOOD) **$55.00**

S5-21. Utica Drop Forge & Tool Co.: "Third Hand" Hammer Nail Clip. With Cardboard Back. Rare and Excellent. Length: 14 Inches. *This hardware store display features the "Third Hand" device marketed by the Utica Drop Forge & Tool Company. This device would be fixed on the head of a hammer where it could be used for holding nails in place as they were being set. The idea never caught on. A rare advertising display.* (GOOD+) **$245.00**

S5-22. Lampert, France: Classic Jeweler's Hammer. Original Handle. Near New Conditoin. Length: 8 1/2 Inches. *This graphic French jeweler's hammer has apparently never been used. Mint.* (FINE) **$45.00**

S5-23. Unmarked: Early Claw Hammer. Strap Type. Excellent Patina. Length: 13 1/2 Inches. *Here's a classic early "strap" hammer with a most appealing dark golden patina to its handle.* (GOOD+) **$115.00**

S5-24. Unmarked: Early Patent Claw Hammer. With Nail Holder. Early and Excellent. Length: 12 1/2 Inches. *The side of this hammer was designed to hold nails when starting them over one's head. An uncommon claw hammer that retains its original handle.* (GOOD) **$225.00**

S5-25. Stanley Rule & Level: "Stanley Standard" Hammer. With Original Decal. 16 Ounce Size. Length: 13 1/2 Inches. *Stanley offered this "second line" of hammers in the 1920's and 1930's. This one retains most of its original label. Uncommon.* (GOOD+) **$65.00**

S5-26. H. Cheney Hammer Co.: Early "Cheney" Hammer. Marked "Tool Steel". Original Handle. Length: 12 3/4 Inches. *This bell faced hammer dates from the days before Cheney produced its trademark nail holding feature. A rare Cheney hammer* (GOOD+) **$55.00**

S5-27. Stanley Rule & Level No. 12: 10 Ounce Claw Hammer. Early "V" Trademark. Original Handle. Length: 12 1/2 Inches. *Here's a crispy clean Stanley hammer that dates from around 1915. A nice example.* (GOOD+) **$45.00**

S5-28. Unmarked: Early Upholstery Hammer. With Side Straps. Tack Puller End. Length: 12 Inches. *A pair of straps are riveted to the handle of this uncommon upholstery hammer to ensure that the head and handle stay together. The tip of the handle is fitted with a puller to facilitate the removal of tacks.* (GOOD+) **$45.00**

S5-29. Maydole, D., Norwich, N.Y.: Bell Face Claw Hammer. 9 Ounce Head. Extra Crisp and Clean. Length: 9 1/2 Inches. *This 9 ounce carpenter's hammer is clearly marked with the D. Maydole imprint. The lack of markings at the end of the handle may indicate that this handle is not original, but overall condition is excellent.* (FINE) **$55.00**

S5-30. Roberts: Upholsterer's Hammer. Mahogany Infill. Very Well Made. Length: 11 Inches. *The equivalent in form, function and quality of manufacture to the upholsterer's hammer made by C.S. Osborne of Newark, New Jersey, this one is marked only with the name "Roberts". A great working tool in top condition.* (FINE) **$75.00**

S5-31. Unmarked: Miniature Jeweler's Hammer. Extra Long Handle. Distinctive Form. Length: 11 1/2 Inches. *The handle on this miniature hammer is so long that it is questionable whether or not the narrow neck would withstand a full blow against a hard surface. This graphic hammer is in excellent condition.* (GOOD+) **$45.00**

S5-32. Osborne & Co., C.S., Newark, N.J.: No. 5: Rosewood Handle Hammer. Unused Condition. Rare and Excellent. Length: 11 Inches. *These were marketed as "saddler's hammers" or "upholsterer's hammers" depending on which section of the catalog you were looking in. We offer a "tool collector's hammer", and a good one. Nearly new condition.* (FINE) **$135.00**

S5-33. Unmarked: Early Claw Hammer. Pre "Adze Eye". Chamfered Poll. Length: 11 1/2 Inches. *The nose of this early hammer has been nicely chamfered to an octagonal form. A classic.* (GOOD+) **$35.00**

S5-34. Berezeiat, Paris No. 14: Early Strap Hammer. Distinctive Form. Uncommon Type. Length: 11 Inches. *The name "Berezeiat" is imprinted on this distinctively shaped Continental hammer. Different.* (GOOD+) **$65.00**

S5-35. Unmarked: Specialty Metalwork Hammer. Original Handle. Superb Condition. Length: 10 1/2 Inches. *The rearward facing poll of this specialty hammer is virtually flat. Its exact function is not known.* (FINE) **$15.00**

S5-36. Stanley Tools No. 221: Floor Layer's Hammer. 32 Ounce Size. Unused Condition. Length: 13 1/2 Inches. *Nearly all of the original Stanley decal remains on this 2 pound flooring hammer. It appears never to have been used.* (FINE) **$95.00**

S5-37. Cheney Corp., H., Little Falls, N.Y.: 20 Ounce Claw Hammer. Partial Original Decal. Black Japan Finish. Length: 13 1/2 Inches. *Here's an extra heavy claw hammer from H. Cheney. It is fitted with the trademark nail puller and retains most of its original decal.* (GOOD+) **$115.00**

S5-38. Atha Tool Co. No. 52: 12 Ounce Claw Hammer. Original Handle. Near New Condition. Length: 13 Inches. *The Atha Tool Company was eventually bought out by the Stanley Rule & Level Company. This 12 ounce hammer is in nearly new condition. Choice.* (FINE) **$55.00**

S5-39. Unmarked: Early Claw Hammer. Pre "Adze Eye". Excellent Patina. Length: 13 Inches. *David Maydole's invention of the "adze eye", an extension of the head of the hammer to hold it more securely to the handle, probably save more than a few carpenter's from the loss of their front teeth or worse as a consequence of wayward hammer heads. The classic example of what used to be the standard for carpenters hammers likely dates from the 1830's or 1840's.* (GOOD+) **$45.00**

S5-40. Stanley Rule & Level: 7 Ounce Bell Face Claw Hammer. Uncommon Type. Early Handle. Length: 13 Inches. *This well made 7 ounce hammer is clearly marked on the head with the Stanley logo. An uncommon Stanley hammer.* (GOOD+) **$25.00**

S5-41. Maydole, D., Norwich, N.Y.: No. 77: Early Ball Pein Hammer. Original Handle. Excellent Condition. Length: 12 1/2 Inches. *The bottom of the handle is imprinted with the Maydole product number on this clean ball pein hammer, a guarantee that the handle is the one that began life with the tool. A nice example.* (GOOD+) **$35.00**

S5-42. Stanley Rule & Level No. 6020: Upholsterer's Hammer. With Tack Puller. Unused Condition. Length: 11 Inches. *Nearly all of the original decal remains on this Stanley upholsterer's hammer. The end of the handle is fitted with a tack puller to increase its functionality. An uncommon Stanley hammer in nearly new condition.* (FINE) **$75.00**

S5-43. Atha Tool Co.: Bell-Face Claw Hammer. 10 Ounce Size. Original Handle. Length: 11 1/2 Inches. *This light-duty claw hammer is imprinted with the distinctive "horseshoe" trademark of the Atha Tool Company. An excellent collectible hammer.* (GOOD+) **$45.00**

S5-44. Unmarked: Early "Strap" Hammer. Extra Long Nose. For Upholstery? Length: 12 1/2 Inches. *A pair of side straps have been soldered on the sides of the head and riveted to the handle to keep this tool in one piece. It has the look of an upholstery hammer.* (GOOD+) **$45.00**

S5-45. Stanley Rule & Level: Cross Pein Hammer. Original Paper Label. "Atha Horseshoe". Length: 11 1/2 Inches. *Dating from the earliest days following Stanley's acquisition of the Atha Tool Company, this cross pein hammer retains its entire Stanley decal advertising its newly-acquired "Atha Horseshoe" line. A great hammer.* (FINE) **$165.00**

Group T5

T5-1. **Taber, J.M., New Bedford, Mass.: Double Bead Molding Plane. 1/2" Size. Ready to Use. Length: 9 1/2 Inches.** *Here's a most appealing boxed double bead plane. This ready to use plane bears the imprint of New Bedford maker John M. Taber.* (GOOD+) **$135.00**

T5-2. **Mc Master & Co., T. J., Auburn, N.Y.: Steep Quirk Ovolo, Astragal Molding Plane. Extra Bold Mark. Superb Condition. Length: 9 1/2 Inches.** *This extra steep molder dates from the ca. 1830's planemaking enterprise of Auburn, New York entrepreneur Truman J. McMaster, who contracted with the State of New York for the use of prison labor in planemaking.* (FINE) **$335.00**

T5-3. **Unmarked: Early Quarter Round Molding Plane. Scalloped Edge. From Mohawk Valley. Length: 10 1/2 Inches.** *This specialized quarter round molding plane has been decorated with a "scalloped" pattern around the front and rear edges. It apparently was once fitted with a side handle. Both the round topped iron and rounded wedge are consistent with very early planemaking. It was found in the Mohawk Valley approximately 30 years ago. A distinctively different and early appearing molding plane. Ex-Cooley Collection.* (GOOD+) **$425.00**

T5-4. **Reed, Utica (N. Y.): Handled Beech Plow Plane. Boxwood Arms and Nuts. Ex-Cooley Collection. Length: 10 Inches.** *We have seen a number of planes from Reed of Utica, including a large number from the Jim Cooley collection, but this is the first handled plow we have observed with the Reed imprint. A scarce American plow plane in excellent condition. Ex-Cooley Collection.* (GOOD+) **$265.00**

T5-5. **Unmarked: Workaday Toothing Plane. Refitted Sole. Ready to Use. Length: 7 1/4 Inches.** *Someone has replaced the sole on this toothing plane, and it is good enough for the job. A bargain.* (GOOD) **$35.00**

T5-6. **Cox & Luckman, Birmingham, England: Beechwood Toothing Plane. Ready to Use. Extra Crisp and Clean. Length: 6 1/2 Inches.** *Cox & Luckman produced planes in Birmingham, England from 1839 to 1876. This toothing plane is in excellent working order and clearly imprinted with their mark.* (GOOD+) **$95.00**

T5-7. **Routledge, 64 Bull St., Birmingham: Classic Toothing Plane. Near New Condition. Ready to Use. Length: 7 1/2 Inches.** *If you're looking for a great working toothing plane for veneer work, this one is in excellent condition and ready for whatever tasks you have for it. Extra nice.* (FINE) **$95.00**

T5-8. **Unmarked: Miniature Lignum Smooth Plane. Great Grain Pattern. Slightly Rounded Sole. Length: 7 Inches.** *A slightly convex contour has been formed on the sole of this spectacular miniature smoothing plane, which has been formed of dramatically grained lignum vitae. Simply a great plane.* (FINE) **$165.00**

T5-9. **Hubbard, D., (Royalston, Mass.): Early Beech Smooth Plane. Circa. 1820's. AWP III: 3 Stars. Length: 6 Inches.** *Daniel Hubbard is known to have worked as a housewright and carpenter in Royalston, Massachusetts. He also dabbled in planemaking, but very few of his planes are known to exist. This smoothing plane has been boldly struck on the toe with the distinctive Hubbard mark.* (GOOD+) **$425.00**

T5-10. **Assorted Makers: Set of 7 Bead Molding Planes Plus 1 Center Bead. 5 By Copeland & Co. Length: 9 1/2 Inches.** *Each of the planes in this working set of bead planes is imprinted with the name of their original owner, one "A. Dixon". A nice set.* (GOOD+) **$245.00**

T5-11. **Reed, Utica (N. Y.): Pair of Tongue and Groove. Molding Planes. Marked "8/8". Extra Crisp and Clean. Length: 9 1/2 Inches.** *The grooving cutter is missing, but these uncommon 1" tongue and groove planes are otherwise in superb condition. Extra crisp and clean. Ex-Cooley Collection.* (FINE) **$75.00**

T5-12. **Tileston, T., Harrison St., Boston: Quarter Ogee and Bead Molding Plane. Double Boxed. Most Unusual Profile. Length: 9 1/2 Inches.** *This well preserved molder has been boldly struck with the "Harrison Street" imprint of prominent Boston maker Timothy Tileston. An excellent molder from a top maker.* (GOOD+) **$245.00**

T5-13. **Angier M' Intire: Wedge Arm Plow Plane. Extra Bold Stamp. Turned Grips. Length: 8 Inches.** *The name "Angier M'Intire" has been boldly struck on the toe of this most unusual plow plane, which was found in the State of Maine. The original wedge and iron are missing, but could be replaced. A distinctively shaped plow plane having a dramatic maker's mark.* (GOOD+) **$345.00**

T5-14. **Marples & Sons, Wm., Hibernia Wks.: Handled Smooth Plane. Adjustment Throat Mechanism. Near-New Condition. Length: 9 Inches.** *The throat of this extra clean handled smoothing plane was fitted at the factory with a brass adjustment mechanism to regulate its width. The toe has been boldly struck with the Marples imprint.* (FINE) **$95.00**

T5-15. **Harrison, J. & H., Newcastle (England): Adjustable Chamfer Plane. Ironmonger Mark. Extra Crisp and Clean. Length: 6 3/4 Inches.** *J. & H. Harrison were ironmongers (hardware dealers) in Newcastle, England and probably purchased this plane from a major maker. It is in superb condition.* (FINE) **$165.00**

T5-16. **Burt, G.W.: Handled Sash Molding Plane. Early New England Maker. Applied Brass Sole. Length: 14 Inches.** *The name "G.W. Burt" has been boldly struck on the toe of this massive early sash plane. The working face of the tool has been fitted with a full brass facing to minimize wear. Burt does not appear in the Third Edition of American Wooden Planes, but the quality of this early Nineteenth Century tool is strong evidence that it was produced by a professional planemaker.* (GOOD+) **$495.00**

T5-17. **Greenfield Tool Co., Greenfield, Mass. No. 529: Beechwood Plow Plane. Boxwood Arms and Nuts. Extra Crisp and Clean. Length: 10 1/2 Inches.** *This well marked plow plane is in excellent working order and could be put immediately to use if the new owner so desires. A classic.* (GOOD+) **$185.00**

T5-18. **Smith, A., Lowell (Mass.): Steep Quarter Ovolo and Astragal Molding Plane. Full Double Boxed. Awp III: 1 Star. Length: 9 1/2 Inches.** *The presence of full boxing at the wear points indicates that this superb molder was intended to be something very special when it was made. It still is. Highly recommended.* (FINE) **$375.00**

T5-19. **Marples & Co., William, Sheffield: Beechwood Smooth Plane. Original Cutter. Ready to Use. Length: 7 3/4 Inches.** *This toothing plane from English maker William Marples is in excellent working order. Crisp, clean and ready to use.* (GOOD+) **$75.00**

T5-20. **Auburn Tool Co., Auburn, N.Y.: Handled Rosewood Plow Plane. Boxwood Arms, Nuts. Superb Condition. Length: 11 Inches.** *A handled rosewood and boxwood plow plane would have been acquired at great expense by a woodworker of considerable accomplishment in the 1860's or 70's when this tool was produced. A full week's wages for a master cabinetmaker would have been required to purchase such a tool. To own such a plow plane would have been a way of making a statement about one's commitment to quality and pride in craftsmanship. It still is. A great plane in excellent condition.* (GOOD+) **$595.00**

T5-21. **Preston & Sons, Edward: Miniature Beech Plane. Rich Dark Patina. Excellent Condition. Length: 4 Inches.** *This miniature beech smoothing plane his imprinted with the mark of prominent British maker Edward Preston & Sons. A nice example of a maker marked miniature plane.* (GOOD+) **$95.00**

T5-22. **Unmarked: Early Style Nosing Plane. Newbould Iron. Ca. 1780's. Length: 10 1/2 Inches.** *The presence of a cutting iron by Eighteenth Century maker Newbould is a sure sign of the age of this chunky nosing plane. The tote has been repaired by a wood screw, but could be removed and attended to otherwise. A classic.* (GOOD) **$35.00**

T5-23. **Colton, J., Market St./Philadelphia: Handled Bilection Molding Plane. Marked "1 1/2". Near New Condition. Length: 13 1/2 Inches.** *Having experienced, at Martin J . Donnelly Antique Tools, the indignity of having our trademark logo appropriated by fly-by night planemakers from the Philadelphia slums, we appreciate the contribution of the elaborate D. Colton logo to his success. This extra steep handled molder in the classic "bilection" profile has been boldly struck and is in fine working order. The type of handled complex molding that is generally unavailable in today's market. Choice.* (FINE) **$550.00**

T5-24. **Marples & Co., William, Sheffield: Adjustable Compass Plane. Screw Adjustment Stop. Near New Condition. Length: 8 Inches.** *A brass screw serves to adjust a steel plate mortised into the sole so as to regulate the degree of curvature of this unusual compass plane from William Marples. A most unusual plane in top condition.* (GOOD) **$95.00**

T5-25. **Providence Tool Co.: Set of 8 Early Plow Plane Irons. Marked "Cast Steel". Ready to Use. Length: 9 Inches.** *The Providence Tool Company provided plane irons for a large number of American planemakers. Here's a well preserved full set of 8 cutting irons for a plow plane. A nice set.* (GOOD+) **$145.00**

T5-26. **Copeland, M.: Massive Skew Rabbet Plane. Double Nickers. Extra Crisp and Clean. Length: 14 Inches.** *This oversize skew rabbet plane has been boldly struck with the Copeland mark. Nice.* (GOOD) **$95.00**

T5-27. **Nurse, C., Walworth Road, London: Adjustable Chamfer Plane. Stallion Trademark. "Sole Inventor". Length: 6 1/4 Inches.** *Nicely fitted with an adjustable throat and clearly marked with the Nurse imprint and "Invicta" trademark, this classic chamfer plane is ready to put to use or proudly display.* (FINE) **$135.00**

T5-28. **Unmarked: Miniature Rabbet Plane. Graphic Form. Replaced Iron. Length: 3 1/2 Inches.** *The iron for this carved miniature smoothing plane appears to be a replacement, but the plane is otherwise in excellent condition.* (GOOD+) **$55.00**

T5-29. **Ohio Tool Co., Columbus, Ohio: Classic Toothing Plane. Original Lacquer. Unused Condition. Length: 7 Inches.** *Only a minor ding at the base of the toe detracts from this otherwise perfect toothing plane. It is functionally perfect. A great working tool in new condition.* (FINE) **$125.00**

T5-30. **Auburn Tool Co., Auburn, N.Y. No. 176: 5/8 Inch Dado Molding Plane. With Brass Depth Stop. Extra Crisp and Clean. Length: 9 1/2 Inches.** *Here's a crisp, clean and ready to use dado plane in the uncommon 5/8 inch size. A good one.* (GOOD+) **$55.00**

T5-31. **Kellogg, J., Amherst, Mass.: Fully Boxed Bead Molding Plane. Marked "5/8". Near New Condition. Length: 9 1/2 Inches.** *The highest quality bead planes were those that were fitted with full boxwood strips on their wear surfaces to ensure t hat the tough work for which they were intended did not wear them out. Because of the extra hand work involved in making these planes, they were prohibitively expensive in their day, making the ownership of such tools the exclusive province of highly successful craftsment. This 5/8" bead from prominent maker J. Kellogg, of Amherst, Massachusetts, had been fitted with "full boxing" that is keyed into the beechwood body of the plane. A superb example of a top of the line bead plane.* (FINE) **$75.00**

T5-32. **Phillips, N., Boston: Ovolo, Astragal. and Cove Molding Plane. Massive Form. Most Unusual Profile. Length: 9 1/2 Inches.** *American Wooden Planes lists only the working dates for Phillips (1807-1823). This very complex molder is characteristic of that early period. It is well preserved and boldly marked. An extra complex molding plane by a rare Boston maker.* (GOOD+) **$465.00**

T5-33. **Marley, N. York: Steep Quarter Ogee and Bead Molding Plane. Uncommon Profile. AWP III: "B" Imprint. Length: 9 1/2 Inches.** *This well preserved wide molder has the uncommon combination of an ogee and bead to its profile. A well made plane from a desirable maker.* (GOOD+) **$265.00**

T5-34. **King, S., Hull (England): Quarter Ovolo and Astragal Molding Plane. Ca. 1800-1817. Early and Excellent. Length: 9 1/2 Inches.** *Samuel King produced planes in Hull, England in the late 18th and early 19th Centuries. This crispy complex molder has been boldly stuck with his imprint. A nice early molder.* (GOOD+) **$185.00**

T5-35. **Andruss, Newark, N.J.: Carriagemaker's Rabbett Plane. Ca. 1821-1841 Only. Rare and Excellent. Length: 6 1/2 Inches.** *Imprinted with the mark of Newark planemaker George W. Andruss, who specialized in coachmaker's tools, this compass sole carriagemaker's rabbet is in excellent collector quality condition. A good one.* (GOOD+) **$125.00**

T5-36. **Reed, Utica, N. Y.: Screw Arm Filletster Plane. Double Side Boxed. Ex-Cooley Collecttion Length: 10 1/2 Inches.** *Screw arm filletster planes by American makers are scarce indeed. This example, from Utica planemaker Reed, features boxing on both working edges. The original wedge has been replaced, but the tool is otherwise in excellent condition. A rare type of tool from a respected New York State maker. Ex-Cooley Collection.* (GOOD+) **$345.00**

T5-37. **Dawson, J., Montreal, Quebec, Canada: Special Purpose Molding Plane. For Window Sash. Double Iron. Length: 9 1/2 Inches.** *One of the two wedges has been sheared, but is worthy of restoration on this unusual sash molder from a prominent Canadian maker.* (GOOD) **$85.00**

T5-38. **Hathersich, George, Manchester: Classic Toothing Plane. For Veneer Work. Near New Condition. Length: 7 1/4 Inches.** *If you are looking for a toothing plane in great working order, we heartily recommend this superb example, which is imprinted with the mark of Manchester (England) maker George Hathersich. Nice.* (FINE) **$95.00**

T5-39. **Moseley & Son, London: Wedge Arm Filletster Plane. Nicely Boxed. Clean and Complete. Length: 8 Inches.** *This nicely boxed sash filletster plane has been professionally cleaned and is ready to use or display. A nice example.* (GOOD+) **$125.00**

T5-40. **Goodale, J.W., Amherst, Mass.: Compass Smooth Plane. Dual Lignum Strike. AWP III: 3 Stars. Length: 9 Inches.** *The Lignum Vitae strike buttons on both the body and wedge of this compass bottom plane make it stand out in a crowd. It bears the imprint of Amherst, Massachusetts planemaker J.W. Goodale, who rates 3 stars for rarity. Rare.* (GOOD+) **$165.00**

T5-41. **Unmarked: Double Razee Jack Plane. 99% Original Finish. Scarce and Near New. Length: 14 Inches.** *Nearly all original finishes remain on this classic "double razee" smoother, which is fitted with a turned front knob. A graphic plane. Ex-Riley Collection.* (FINE) **$95.00**

T5-42. **Steele, A.P.: Set of Wooden Planes. With "Geer" Scale. Dated "1867". Length: 7 Inches.** *One of the endlessly fascinating things about antique tools is that the history of the tools, those who used them and those who made them is so much more than the object itself. Here are several tools from the kit of one "A.P. Steele". Many of the tools are dated with the year "1867". The undersize hollow and rounding planes appear to have been designed for a specific task. The rule, carefully laid out and marked by hand, has the word "Geer scale" written over it in pencil. Who was this forgotten artisan? What did he do? What has become of his other tools? Perhaps by printing this here, the likelihood that more of the story will become known will be enhanced. A great set, with a story only partly told.* (GOOD+) **$345.00**

T5-43. **Eastburn R., (N. Brunswick, N.J.): Quarter Ovolo and Bevel Molding Plane. Ca. 1815. AWP III: 2 Stars (C). Length: 9 1/2 Inches.** *The original India ink price marking is still visible on the toe of the early New Jersey complex molding plane. Early and excellent. Ex-Cooley Collection.* (GOOD+) **$125.00**

T5-44. **Eastwood, G., York: Pair of Tongue and Groove Molding Plane. For 7/8 Inch Stock. Unusual Side Escapement. Length: 9 1/2 Inches.** *The side escapement of these 7/8 inch tongue and groove planes from York maker G. Eastwood is in the form of a "port hole". A most unusual set of planes in top condition.* (FINE) **$95.00**

T5-45. **Kieffer & Auxer, Lancaster, Penn.: Rare Double Iron Jointer Plane. Patent Design. Uncommon Maker. Length: 22 1/2 Inches.** *This double wedge wooden plane was produced under a ca. 1840's patent granted to E.W. Carpenter. An uncommon patented plane.* (GOOD+) **$85.00**

Group U5

U5-1. Simmons Hardware Co., St. Louis: "Keen Kutter" Axe. Embossed Logo. Rare Double Bit. Length: 35 Inches. *As nice an example of the embossed "Keen Kutter" double bit axe as we have been privileged to offer.* (GOOD+) **$195.00**

U5-2. Simmons Hardware Co., St. Louis No. K 112: Empty Box For Blacksmith Drills. Great Graphics. Clean and Sound. Length: 7 Inches. *Many collectors display their collections in the format of a "hardware store". A Keen Kutter collector seeking to replicate a Simmons dealership may need this to stock the shelves. An uncommon Keen Kutter item.* (FINE) **$45.00**

U5-3. Simmons Hardware Co., St. Louis No. 5: "Keen Kutter" Axe. Embossed Logo. With "No. 5" Mark. Length: 8 Inches. *The "No. 5" was apparently the designation of this uncommon pattern of axe head. A most uncommon embossed axe.* (GOOD) **$195.00**

U5-4. Simmons Hardware Co., St. Louis: "Keen Kutter" Hatchet. For Shingling. Near New Condition. Length: 13 Inches. *This "Keen Kutter" brand shingling hatchet is in nearly new condition. Rare and excellent.* (FINE) **$115.00**

U5-5. Simmons Hardware Co., St. Louis No. K 32: "Keen Kutter" Jack Knife. Celluloid Handle. Chips to Small Blade. Length: 3 1/4 Inches. *The smallest blade has a few chips, which could be easily ground out, but the rest of this knife is otherwise in excllent condition.* (GOOD+) **$115.00**

U5-6. Simmons Hardware Co., St. Louis No. 55: "Keen Kutter" Jointer Gauge. Full Nickel Plated. Rare and Excellent. Length: 9 Inches. *Here's an excellent example of the E.C. Simmons company's earnest effort to make "one of each" with the Keen Kutter logo emblazoned upon it. A rare tool in excellent shape.* (GOOD+) **$185.00**

U5-7. Simmons Hardware Co., St. Louis No. KLL 2: "Keen Kutter" Side Hatchet. 4 Inch Cutting Edge. Ready to Use. Length: 14 Inches. *This Keen Kutter side hatchet is beveled on only a single edge. It is in excellent working order and could be put immediately to use.* (FINE) **$65.00**

U5-8. Simmons Hardware Co., St. Louis No. K 195: "Keen Kutter" Jack Knife. Staghorn Handle. Crisp and Clean. Length: 2 3/4 Inches. *A handle of genuine staghorn graces this double blade pocketknife from E.C. Simmons.* (FINE) **$145.00**

U5-9. Simmons Hardware Co., E.C. No. K 23: "Keen Kutter" Metallic Plane. Transitional Type. Near New Condition. Length: 9 Inches. *Transitional planes deteriorated very rapidly once they were used. This Keen Kutter example retains nearly all of its original finishes. The way you wish they all were. Mint.* (FINE) **$345.00**

U5-10. Simmons Hardware Co., St. Louis: "Keen Kutter" Shovel Handle. Original Paper Label. Uncommon Item. Length: 29 1/2 Inches. *Here's just the thing for the serious Keen Kutter collector: a replacement handle for a shovel. Much of the original paper label remains.* (FINE) **$35.00**

U5-11. Simmons Hardware Co., E.C. No. KK 65: "Keen Kutter" Block Metallic Plane. Similar to Stanley 65. Rare and Near New. Length: 7 Inches. *The equivalent to Stanley's No. 65 low angle block plane, this well preserved Keen Kutter No. 65 was likely made for the Simmons Hardware Company by the Ohio Tool Company of Columbus. Nearly all original finishes remain.* (FINE) **$295.00**

U5-12. Simmons Hardware Co., St. Louis No. 312: "Keen Kutter" Metallic Plane. Similar to Stanley 112. Rare and Sound. Length: 9 Inches. *The equivalent in form and function to Stanley's No. 112 scraper plane, this Keen Kutter offering is marked No. 312 and is much less common by several orders of magnitude. The cutting iron is marked "Anderson Tool Company" and may be a replacement. A rare Keen Kutter plane.* (FINE) **$325.00**

U5-13. Simmons Hardware Co., St. Louis No. K100 MG: "Keen Kutter" Marking Gauge. Solid Boxwood. Near New Condition Length: 8 1/2 Inches. *A nice Keen Kutter marking gauge in solid boxwood. Very pretty and clearly marked.* (FINE) **$75.00**

U5-14. Simmons Hardware Co., E.C. No. KK115: "Keen Kutter" Circular Metallic Plane. Similar to Stanley 113. Rare and Excellent. Length: 10 Inches. *The folks at E.C. Simmons have been accused of thinking their products were better than those of anyone else. Now is the time to correct an historical misapprehension: the folks at E.C. Simmons KNEW their tools were better. In many cases, they were right. "Keen Kutter" tools, which were made for Simmons by the principal toolmakers of the day, often had features that the professional quality lines of the toolmakers themselves did not have. This magnificent plane, the K.K. answer to Stanley's No. 113 (only 2 numbers better) is as rare a "Keen Kutter" item as you will find. A rare and highly collectible plane in superb condition.* (GOOD+) **$795.00**

U5-15. Simmons Hardware Co., E.C.: "Keen Kutter" Transitional Metallic Plane. Similar to Stanley 24. Rare and Excellent. Length: 9 Inches. *Much of the original finish remains on this well preserved Keen Kutter transitional plane. A nice example.* (FINE) **$145.00**

U5-16. Simmons Hardware Co., St. Louis: "Keen Kutter" Saw Set. With Keen Kutter Logo. Scarce and Excellent. Length: 7 Inches. *This plier-type set was manufactured under the patent of William Potter, which was assigned to the E.C. Stearns Company of Syracuse, New York. There can be little doubt that Stearns produced this tool for Simmons. A nice example.* (GOOD+) **$25.00**

U5-17. Simmons Hardware Co., St. Louis No. K 85: "Keen Kutter" Hammer. For Upholstery. Original Handle. Length: 12 Inches. *The end of the handle of this well preserved upholstery hammer is imprinted with the K 85 designation. An uncommon Keen Kutter hammer.* (GOOD+) **$35.00**

U5-18. Simmons Hardware Co., St. Louis No. KR6: "Keen Kutter" Brace. Ratcheting Type. Rare 6 Inch Sweep. Length: 12 1/2 Inches. *Six inch braces by any maker are tough to find. This one is marked with the Keen Kutter name and product number. A good one.* (GOOD) **$55.00**

U5-19. Simmons Hardware Co., St. Louis: "Keen Kutter" Steel Square. Copper Plate Finish. With Keen Kutter Logo. Length: 9 Inches. *Nearly all of the original copper plating remains on this unusual steel square. Rare.* (FINE) **$85.00**

U5-20. Simmons Hardware Co., St. Louis: "Keen Kutter" Back Saw. Applewood Handle. Superb Condition. Length: 15 1/2 Inches. *This Keen Kutter back saw was likely made for Simmons by Henry Disston & Sons. It is straight, sharp and retains nearly all original finishes. Nice.* (FINE) **$115.00**

U5-21. Simmons Hardware Co., St. Louis No. K734773/4: "Keen Kutter Kattle" Knife. With Longhorn Logo. Scarce and Excellent. Length: 3 1/2 Inches. *The reverse side of the Keen Kutter classic has a longhorn steer etched on the handle. A rare Keen Kutter knife.* (GOOD+) **$345.00**

U5-22. Simmons, E. C., St. Louis, Mo.: "Keen Kutter" Pruning Saw. Double Edge Blade. Scarce and Excellent. Length: 23 Inches. *Here's a double sided pruning saw marked with the Keen Kutter logo. It is in excellent condition.* (FINE) **$65.00**

U5-23. Simmons Hardware Co., St. Louis No. 88: 26 Inch "Keen Kutter" Saw. Applewood Handle. 6 Point Rip. Length: 30 Inches. *Most of the original etching and most of the original finishes remain on this "Keen Kutter" hand saw, which features a carved applewood handle—the sure sign of a high quality saw. No apologies.* (GOOD+) **$75.00**

U5-24. Simmons Hardware Co., E.C.: "Keen Kutter" Pipe Wrench. 9 Inch Size. Crisp and Clean. Length: 9 Inches. *The handle of this Simmons pipe wrench has been forged with the "Keen Kutter" name. A nice wrench.* (GOOD+) **$35.00**

U5-25. Simmons Hardware Co., E.C. No. 8: "Keen Kutter" Draw Knife. 8 Inch Blade. Near New Condition. Length: 13 3/4 Inches. *Nearly all original finishes remain on this crispy clean Keen Kutter drawknife. A nice example.* (FINE) **$85.00**

U5-26. Simmons Hardware Co., St. Louis: "Keen Kutter" Nail Puller. "Pat. Appl'd. For". 85% Original Paint. Length: 18 1/2 Inches. *A growing number of collectors are seeking out the wide range of nail pulling devices produced over the past several hundred years. This "Keen Kutter" offering was apparently the subject of a patent application. Most of the original paint remains.* (GOOD+) **$95.00**

U5-27. Simmons Hardware Co., E.C.: "Keen Kutter" Draw Knife. 10 Inch Blade. Brand New Condition. Length: 16 Inches. *This E.C. Simmons "Keen Kutter" drawing knife is in unused, hardware store new condition. Crispy.* (FINE) **$225.00**

U5-28. Simmons Hardware Co., St. Louis No. K 2288: Empty Box For Pocket Knives. Great Graphics. Clean and Sound. Length: 4 Inches. *If you were wondering what to do with those six brand new Keen Kutter No. K 2288 pocket knives, why not buy this box for them? Even if you don't have the knives, the box is pretty enough to keep for itself. Graphic.* (FINE) **$85.00**

U5-29. Simmons Hardware Co., E.C. No. KK 3: "Keen Kutter" Metallic Plane. Rosewood Handles. Superb Condition. Length: 9 Inches. *The Brazilian Rosewood handles of this Keen Kutter KK 3 smoothing plane have a particularly striking grain pattern. Some 98% of the original japan finish remains. A great smoothing plane.* (FINE) **$115.00**

U5-30. Simmons Hardware Co., St. Louis: "Keen Kutter" Razor Hone. Enameled Tin Box. Embossed Stone. Length: 5 1/2 Inches. *This Keen Kutter razor hone has never been used. The original tin box has a most appealing wood grain pattern.* (FINE) **$85.00**

U5-31. Simmons Hardware Co., E.C. No. KK 71: "Keen Kutter" Router Plane. With Cast Logo. Made by Stanley? Length: 7 1/2 Inches. *One of the less common Keen Kutter planes, this No. KK 71 features the same "open throat" configuration as the Stanley equivalent. One original cutting iron remains.* (GOOD) **$55.00**

U5-32. Simmons Hardware Co., E.C.: "Keen Kutter" Auger Bit. For Countersinking. Near New Condition. Length: 4 3/4 Inches. *No one has ever used this perfectly preserved Keen Kutter auger bit.* (FINE) **$25.00**

U5-33. Simmons Hardware Co., St. Louis No. KK 79: "Keen Kutter" Scraper. Similar to Stanley 80. Full Nickel Plating. Length: 11 Inches. *We are please to offer an example of the plane that recently took top honors at the Annual Meeting of the Kape Kod Keen Kutter Kollectors Klub. For additional information about Keen Kutter Kollecting in the East, Kontact Dale Lumsden, Klub Kommander. Retaining nearly all of its original nickel plating and clearly marked with the Keen Kutter product number, which is cast into the body of the tool, this example, the cutting iron of which is not marked, is a superb example of an elusive Keen Kutter item. Rare, and extra-nice.* (GOOD+) **$135.00**

U5-34. Simmons Hardware Co., St. Louis: "Keen Kutter" 6 Inch Bevel. Patended October 29, 1907. Made by Sargent. Length: 6 Inches. *The body of this cast iron bevel has been cast with the Keen Kutter name and logo. The 1907 patent date is proof that this tool was made for Simmons by Sargent & Company of New Haven, Connecticut.* (GOOD+) **$75.00**

U5-35. Simmons Hardware Co., St. Louis: "Keen Kutter" Marking Gauge. Rosewood Body. Near New Condition Length: 8 1/2 Inches. *A very nice Keen Kutter marking gauge, this one is solid rosewood. Very pretty and clearly marked.* (FINE) **$185.00**

U5-36. Simmons Hardware Co., St. Louis: "Keen Kutter" Jack Knife. With Pearl Handle. Diminutive Size. Length: 2 1/2 Inches. *This "Keen Kutter" knife features pearl handles and a shield inlay of mother of pearl. Most unusual.* (GOOD+) **$125.00**

U5-37. Simmons Hardware Co., St. Louis No. K85-8: "Keen Kutter" Pliers. Lineman Type. With Keen Kutter Logo. Length: 8 Inches. *The joint of these uncommon Keen Kutter lineman's pliers has been boldly struck with the Keen Kutter logo. Uncommon.* (GOOD+) **$35.00**

U5-38. Simmons Hardware Co., St. Louis: "Keen Kutter" Side Hatchet. 4 Inch Cutting Edge. Ready to Use. Length: 14 Inches. *The "Keen Kutter" trademark was intended to be a symbol of the highest quality. It still its.* (GOOD+) **$65.00**

U5-39. Simmons Hardware Co., St. Louis: "Keen Kutter" Drill Bit. 9/32 Inch Size. Unused Condition. Length: 5 1/2 Inches. *The shaft of this unusual brace mounted drill bit has been boldly struck with the Keen Kutter logo.* (FINE) **$15.00**

U5-40. Simmons Hardware Co., St. Louis: "Keen Kutter" Saw Jointer. Patended May 3, 1898. Full Nickel Plating. Length: 5 1/2 Inches. *Designed to hold a file firmly in place when leveling the teeth of saws prior to filing, this nickel plated device has been cast with the "Keen Kutter" logo. An uncommon Keen Kutter tool.* (FINE) **$45.00**

U5-41. Simmons Hardware Co., E.C. No. K240: "Keen Kutter" Block Metallic Plane. From Ohio Tool? Brand New Condition. Length: 7 Inches. *Undoubtedly produced by the Ohio Tool Company for Simmons, this "Keen Kutter" block plane employs the lever depth of cut adjustment that was an Ohio Tool trademark. A perfectly preserved "Keen Kutter" block plane.* (FINE) **$115.00**

U5-42. Simmons Hardware Co., St. Louis No. 55: "Keen Kutter" Jointer Gauge. Full Nickel Plated. Near New Condition. Length: 9 Inches. *Here's an excellent example of the E.C. Simmons company's earnest effort to make "one of each" with the Keen Kutter logo emblazoned upon it. A rare tool in excellent shape, complete with the original store tag.* (FINE) **$195.00**

U5-43. Simmons Hardware Co., St. Louis No. K624: 24" "Keen Kutter" Level. 98% Original Paint. Scarce and Excellent. Length: 24 Inches. *Nearly all of the original paint remains on this classic two foot Keen Kutter level. Extra nice.* (FINE) **$145.00**

U5-44. Simmons Hardware Co., St. Louis: "Keen Kutter" Hatchet. Embossed Head. Uncommon Size. Length: 4 1/2 Inches. *The head of this well preserved hatchet is embossed with the Keen Kutter logo. Graphic.* (GOOD+) **$25.00**

U5-45. Simmons Hardware Co., E.C. No. KK 27: "Keen Kutter" Transitional Metallic Plane. Similar To Stanley 27. Nicely Relacquered. Length: 15 Inches. *The E.C. Simmons Company offered nearly every plane being offered by the major manufacturers. This transitional jack plane was probably made for Simmons by Stanley. A previous owner has touched up the lacquer finish, but it is clean and complete.* (GOOD) **$55.00**

Group V5

V5-1. Jennings Mfg. Co., The Russell: Early Set of 13 Auger Bits. 3 Tiered Box. Near New Condition. Length: 10 Inches. *A great working set of auger bits by a highly-respected maker. A flip-top wooden box has kept this full set in nearly new condition. All of the original paper label remains. Ready to go to work.* (FINE) **$265.00**

V5-2. Marples & Co., William, Sheffield: Rare Wide Spur Auger Bits. Full Set of 8. Near New Condition. Length: 5 Inches. *These wide spur type auger bits were featured in many some of the catalogs of the early English tool makers, but this is the first such set we have encountered. Rare, early and near new.* (FINE) **$115.00**

V5-3. Unmarked: Boring Machine Auger Bit. 2 Inch Width. Near New Condition. Length: 12 Inches. *There are no maker marks on this boring machine auger bit, but it appears to be of excellent quality. Condition is near new.* (FINE) **$45.00**

V5-4. Swan Co., The James: Boring Machine Auger Bit. 1 Inch Size. Near New Condition. Length: 13 Inches. *This uncommon 1 inch boring machine bit is imprinted with the name of respected Connecticut edge tool maker James Swan.* (FINE) **$45.00**

V5-5. Unmarked: 2 Inch Twist Auger Bit. For Boring Machine. Ready to Use. Length: 11 Inches. *This 2 inch auger bit is ready to build a barn or two. Condition is excellent.* (GOOD+) **$35.00**

V5-6. Jennings Mfg. Co., The Russell: Set of 13 Auger Bit. Fitted Wood Box. Near New Condition. Length: 10 Inches. *The fitted wooden box has kept these classic Russell Jennings bits in top condition. A great set of the best auger bits ever made.* (FINE) **$145.00**

V5-7. Assorted Makers: Group of Specialty Auger Bits. Countersink, Etc. Usable Condition. Length: 4 Inches. *This assortment of auger bits includes a most unusual double screwdriver bit that can be reversed in the chuck to change the size of the screw bit. A bargain.* (GOOD+) **$15.00**

V5-8. Assorted Makers: Group of 8 Spoon Auger Bits. Assorted Sizes. Ready to Use. Length: 6 Inches. *Here's a working set of spoon bits that came from the same tool chest. These are becoming increasingly difficult to find.* (GOOD+) **$75.00**

V5-9. Assorted Makers: Group of 8 Spoon Auger Bits. Assorted Sizes. Ready to Use. Length: 6 Inches. *Large size spoon bits, such as those offered here, are particularly useful when doing furniture work as they do not "follow the grain" the way other bits do. These are in excellent working order.* (GOOD+) **$0.00**

V5-10. Unmarked: 1 3/4 Inch Twist Auger Bit. For Boring Machine. Ready to Use. Length: 11 Inches. *We get about two 1 3/4 inch bits for every ten of the 2 inch and 1 1/2 inch sizes. First come, first serve.* (GOOD+) **$35.00**

V5-11. Stanley Rule & Level: Countersink Auger Bit. Early Patent. Uncommon Type. Length: 4 Inches. *This one is clearly marked with the Stanley imprint, but the shaft is slighly bent from demanding use. A bargain.* (GOOD) **$15.00**

V5-12. Irwin, Charles: "Dimitt's Patent" Auger Bit. Patented October 21, 1884. Early and Rare Type. Length: 9 1/2 Inches. *The patentee for this bit was William Dimmit of Martinsville, Ohio, who assigned it to Charles Irwin. The patent papers describe it as a "solid center bit". Different.* (FINE) **$45.00**

V5-13. Ladd, V.J. Edge Tool Co.: Boring Machine Auger Bit. 2 Inch Size. Unused Condition. Length: 11 1/2 Inches. *The purchaser of this bit will have the pleasure of being the first to use it. As new.* (FINE) **$55.00**

V5-14. Snell Mfg. Co., Fiskdale, Mass.: 1 1/2 Inch Boring Machine Auger Bit. Upward Set Spurs. Ready to Use. Length: 12 Inches. *This 1 1/2 inch auger bit from a major New England maker is in excellent condition and ready to use.* (FINE) **$55.00**

V5-15. Ives, William A., New Haven, Conn.: Early Patented Expansion Auger Bit. Patented October 13, 1868. Rare and Excellent. Length: 7 3/4 Inches. *A slotted screw locks the cutter in place on this very early adjustable auger bit. A rare patented auger bit.* (GOOD+) **$165.00**

V5-16. Backus, Q.S, Holyoke, Mass.: Patent Ratchet Attachment. For Barber Chucks. Patented November 5, 1872. Length: 7 1/4 Inches. *The folks at the Quimby Backus Company took advantage of an opportunity when they saw one, even if one didn't really exist. At the time they introduced this marvel to the market, most braces were of the older, non-ratcheting type. Perhaps by reasoning that folks would prefer to keep their tried and true brace, they came up with the idea to market this chuck and ratchet attachment as a separate add on for a brace. The market response can be judged by the number of these available in the collector market today, which is very, very few. A rare tool that embodies an idea whose time never came.* (GOOD+) **$115.00**

V5-17. Snell Mfg. Co., Fiskdale, Mass.: 1 Inch Boring Machine Auger Bit. Upward Set Spurs. Ready to Use. Length: 12 Inches. *Here's a well preserved 1 inch boring machine auger bit in top working order.* (GOOD+) **$45.00**

V5-18. Griswold & Co., G.G.: Boring Machine Auger Bit. 2 Inch Size. Near New Condition. Length: 12 1/2 Inches. *This boring machine auger bit is in top condition and ready to use. Nice.* (FINE) **$35.00**

V5-19. Wedgeway: 1 1/2 Inch Boring Machine Auger Bit. Double Spur Tip. Ready to Use. Length: 12 1/2 Inches. *You can't go to the store and buy a 1 1/2 inch boring machine auger bit. Even if you could, it wouldn't be as nice as this one. Ready to use.* (GOOD+) **$45.00**

V5-20. Snell Mfg. Co., Fiskdale, Mass.: Boring Machine Auger Bit. 2 Inch Width. Near New Condition. Length: 12 Inches. *This 2" auger bit from a top maker has been little if ever used. Nice.* (FINE) **$55.00**

V5-21. Conn. Valley Mfg. Co.: Wrights Patent Auger Bit. Patented March 18, 1913. Original Sleeve. Length: 10 Inches. *This example of the Wright Patent of 1913 includes two cutting blades and a special screwdriver for adjustment—all in new condition in the original pouch.* (FINE) **$45.00**

V5-22. Unmarked: Boxed Set of Drill Bits. For Bit Brace. Missing One Bit. Length: 6 3/4 Inches. *These gimlet style bits are in excellent working order. One bit is missing, but could be easily replaced.* (GOOD) **$25.00**

V5-23. Greenlee Tool Co., Rockford, IL. No. 900: Extension Shaft For Auger Bit. 18 Inch Size. Original Leather. Case. Length: 18 Inches. *Believe me, when you need one of these, you need it. I've been there. An excellent usable tool in collector quality condition.* (FINE) **$45.00**

V5-24. Assorted Makers: Boxed Set of Auger Bits. Enderes, Irwin, Etc. Ready to Use. Length: 10 Inches. *This was a working set of bits assembled by a woodworker. It still is. Ready to use.* (GOOD+) **$45.00**

V5-25. Assorted Makers: Working Set of Countersink Bits. B.M.C., Holt, Etc. Excellent Condition. Length: 4 Inches. *Here's a small collection of countersink bits from major makers. An interesting diversion.* (FINE) **$35.00**

V5-26. Morse Twist Drill & Machine Co.: Patent Mahogany Drill Case. Patented June 24, 1902. Excellent Condition. Length: 4 1/2 Inches. *Retaining much of its original finish on both the mahogany body and the nickeled steel top, this patented drill index is clearly marked with the 1902 patent date. Scarce.* (GOOD+) **$165.00**

V5-27. Hood Bros., Philadelphia: Set of 6 Early Auger Bits. Apparently Unused. "V" Shape Point. Length: 5 Inches. *These "V" shaped auger bits have a decidedly early look. They have never been used. Mint.* (FINE) **$95.00**

V5-28. Assorted Makers: Group of 25 Stone Cutting Tools. Assorted Shapes and Sizes. Ready to Use. Length: 12 Inches. *These chisels were part of the working tools of a stonecutter. All are in excellent condition and ready to use.* (GOOD+) **$95.00**

V5-29. Gibbs, L.H., N.Y.: Early Patent Auger Bit. With Pin Adjustment. Patented June 27, 1855. Length: 9 Inches. *One of the earliest of expansion auger bits, this mechanically interesting tool from a Washington, D.C. inventor was also one of the most complex. A great example of a rare auger bit.* (GOOD+) **$165.00**

V5-30. National Tube Wks., Boston, Mass.: Universal Joint Auger Handle. Early Appearance. Distinctive Form. Length: 11 Inches. *The markings on this most unusual angle auger device were individually stamped, so this may not be a manufactured tool, but it is so very well made that it deserves to be included in a collection. Special.* (GOOD+) **$55.00**

V5-31. Jennings Mfg. Co., The Russell: Set of 13 Auger Bit. Tiered Wooden Box. Extra Crisp and Clean. Length: 10 1/2 Inches. *All of the original Russell Jennings bits are present in this classic three tiered box. A great set of bits in a handy box.* (GOOD+) **$175.00**

V5-32. Bruno Tools, Beverly Hills, Calif.: No. 200-B: "Bruno" Expansive Auger Bit. Bulldog Trademark. "Auger of the Stars". Length: 7 1/2 Inches. *When one thinks of Beverly Hills, California, one thinks immediately of auger bits. This adjustable example is in excellent condition.* (GOOD+) **$25.00**

V5-33. Excelsior Mfg. Co.: George Hill's Patent Auger Bit. Patented March 10,1885. With Lever Lock. Length: 8 Inches. *This cam-lock auger bit was produced under George Hill's 1885 patent. We are unsure of the working location of the Exelsior Manufacturing Company. A very rare patented auger bit.* (GOOD+) **$145.00**

V5-34. Ladd, V.J. Edge Tool Co.: Boring Machine Auger Bit. Rare 13/16 Inch Size. New Condition, Original Box. Length: 11 1/2 Inches. *We have handled a number of boring machine auger bits, but this is the first one in the original box that we have seen. A brand new bit in a must unusual size.* (FINE) **$85.00**

V5-35. Conn. Valley Mfg. Co.: Wrights Patent Auger Bit. Patented March 18, 1913. Original Sleeve. Length: 10 Inches. *This example of the Wright Patent of 1913 includes two cutting blades and a special screwdriver for adjustment—all in new condition in the original pouch.* (GOOD+) **$35.00**

V5-36. Assorted Makers: Group of 26 Stone Cutting Tools. Assorted Shapes and Sizes. With Caliper. Length: 10 Inches. *These stone cutting tools are in excellent working condition. Also included is an early caliper that was most likely used by the stoneworker who owned these tools.* (GOOD+) **$110.00**

V5-37. Cleveland Twist Drill Co., The: Set of Square Shank Drill Bits. Celluloid Case. Unused Condition. Length: 6 Inches. *A clear case of an early plastic material has kept this set of "square shank" bits in new condition. A nice set.* (FINE) **$35.00**

V5-38. Assorted Makers: Group of 7 Spoon Auger Bits. Assorted Sizes. Ready to Use. Length: 6 Inches. *Here's a nice assortment of spoon bits in some of the larger sizes. Tough to find.* (GOOD+) **$75.00**

V5-39. New Process Drill, Taunton, Mass.: Cast Iron Drill Stand. "Pat. Applied For". Nickel Plated Casting. Length: 5 Inches. *Because of their graphic form and seemingly infinite variety, drill stands have attracted a growing number of specialized collectors. This nickel plated offering from the New Process Drill Company is a classic example of why these stands are in such demand.* (GOOD+) **$115.00**

V5-40. Assorted Makers: 8 Countersink Auger Bit. Various Styles. Ready to Use. Length: 5 Inches. *Why a single carpenter would have had 8 separate countersink bits in his kit of tools is a mystery. Whatever the case, here they are. A bargain.* (GOOD+) **$35.00**

V5-41. Nurse, C., 32 Mill St. (London): "Rosette" Countersink Auger Bit. Original Straw Temper. Unused Condition. Length: 4 1/4 Inches. *This classic countersink bit retains every bit of its original "straw temper finish". Absolutely brand new.* (FINE) **$25.00**

V5-42. Wilson, John, Sheffield: Full Set of Auger Bits. Spoon, Spur, Etc. New Condition, Original Roll. Length: 7 Inches. *In essentially the same condition as it would have been when it left the shop of an English "ironmonger" perhaps 120 years ago, this rare full set of bits will serve as a perfect compliment to a Sheffield or Ultimatum brace. Absolutely perfect and ready to show or use.* (FINE) **$385.00**

V5-43. Cleveland Twist Drill Co.: Package of Twist Drills. 1/2 Dozen 1/2 Inch Size. New Condition, Original Box. Length: 7 Inches. *If you went to the hardware store in the 1920's, you could have bought a package of 1/2 inch drills just like this one—or you could buy it here. Brand new.* (FINE) **$15.00**

V5-44. Assorted Makers: Group of 26 Stone Cutting Tools. Assorted Shapes and Sizes. Ready to Use. Length: 11 Inches. *All of these stone cutting tools are in excellent working order. Just the thing for the would-be sculptor. Tough tools to find.* (GOOD+) **$95.00**

V5-45. Assorted Makers: Group of 7 Spoon Auger Bits. Assorted Sizes. Ready to Use. Length: 6 Inches. *Don't go to the hardware store looking for spoon bits. They will either look at you like you're from Mars or refer you to Martin J. Donnelly Antique Tools. A great working set.* (GOOD+) **$75.00**

Group W5

W5-1. Stanley Rule & Level No. 71: Open Throat Router Plane. "Sweetheart" Trademark. New Condition, Original Box. Length: 8 Inches. *Nearly all original finishes remain on this clean and complete router plane. The original "Sweetheart" era box has kept it in top condition. Choice.* (FINE) **$155.00**

W5-2. Stanley Rule & Level No. 98/99: Pair of Side Rabbet Plane. With Depth Stops. Extra Crisp and Clean. Length: 4 Inches. *These side rabbet planes are fitted with the desirable adjustable depth stops that were not added to the tool until after it had been produced for many years. These well preserved planes are crisp, clean, ready to use and offered without apology. A great working pair.* (FINE) **$345.00**

W5-3. Stanley Rule & Level No. 100 1/2: Squirrel Tail Block Plane. With Convex Sole. Near New Condition. Length: 3 1/2 Inches. *Topped off with a nicely-contrasting red lever cap, this example of Stanley's convex bottom model maker's block plane is in mint condition. Perfect.* (FINE) **$165.00**

W5-4. Stanley Rule & Level No. H104: "Handyman" Smooth Plane. Manufactured 1964 Only. Unused Condition. Length: 9 Inches. *All references indicate that this distinctively different Stanley plane was produced for a very, very short time in 1964 and then discontinued. A rare later day Stanley plane in new condition.* (FINE) **$195.00**

W5-5. Stanley Rule & Level No. 55: Patent Combination Plane. With 4 Boxes of Cutters. Clean and Complete. Length: 11 1/2 Inches. *Advertised as "A Planing Mill Within Itself", the Stanley No. 55 Patent Universal Combination Plane can, with a bit of practice, be made to duplicate any molding profile ever made. This one is complete with all of the original parts, including the four boxes containing more than 50 specialized cutting irons. It comes in a fitted wooden box, which has served to protect it through more than 90 years of existence. Nearly all original nickel plating remains and the rosewood fences and handles are in excellent condition. Were it possible to make these planes today, a working approximation of much lesser quality would cost thousands of dollars. A bargain.* (FINE) **$585.00**

W5-6. Stanley Rule & Level No. 37: "Jenny" Transitional Plane. Early "Arch" Trademark. Scarce and Excellent. Length: 13 Inches. *One of the most difficult to find of all Stanley transitional planes, the "Jenny" was the length of a Jack plane, but much wider. It reportedly took its name from the female mule, called a "Jenny". This example has been used, but not abused. It retains more than 90% of its original japan finish and is clean and intact. The early "Arch" trademark is imprinted on the cutting iron.* (GOOD+) **$345.00**

W5-7. Stanley Rule & Level No. 4: 9 Inch Smoothing Plane. "Sweetheart" Trademark. Extra Crisp and Clean. Length: 9 Inches. *A ca. 1920's era trademark is imprinted on the cutting iron of this crispy clean smoothing plane. Ready to use.* (FINE) **$115.00**

W5-8. Stanley Rule & Level No. 78: Duplex Rabbet, Fillet Plane. Near New Condition. Complete and Excellent Length: 10 Inches. *A Stanley mainstay for many years, this plane was designed to serve as both a rabbet plane and a bullnose plane. In the last years of the manufacture of this tool, a severe degradation in quality took place. This one dates from the 1930's, when the quality of Stanley tools was at its peak. Choice.* (FINE) **$85.00**

W5-9. Stanley Rule & Level No. 190: 1 1/2 Inch Rabbeting Plane. Near New Condition. 99% Original Paint. Length: 8 Inches. *Stanley's 190 series of fixed-width rabbeting planes are handy tools for the home shop. At 1 1/2 inch in width, the No. 190 is extremely versatile. Mint.* (FINE) **$65.00**

W5-10. Stanley Rule & Level No. 140: Skew Blade Block Plane. Patented November 6, 18894. Early Arch Trademark. Length: 6 1/2 Inches. *The No. 140 has a skew-set iron and a removable side to facilitate rabbeting. Most of the original nickel plating remains on the cap. A nice example in fine usable condition.* (GOOD+) **$235.00**

W5-11. Stanley Rule & Level No. 39: 3/4 Inch Width Dado Plane. "Sweetheart" Trademark. Unused Condition. Length: 8 Inches. *All of the following in the No. 39 series are in superb condition and strongly recommended to the serious collector. This 3/4 inch size is essentially unused with shiny nickel plating. Nice.* (FINE) **$325.00**

W5-12. Stanley Rule & Level No. 101: "Toy" Block Plane. Red Lever Cap. 99% Original Paint. Length: 3 1/4 Inches. *As a handy tool for use around the shop, these Stanley planes can't be beat. Unused condition.* (FINE) **$45.00**

W5-13. Stanley Rule & Level No. 81: Cabinetmaker's Scraper Plane. "Sweetheart" Trademark. Portion of Decal Remains. Length: 10 Inches. *A portion of the original Stanley decal remains on the cutting iron of this rosewood sole scraper plane. Missing a bit of nickel, but in fine working condition.* (GOOD+) **$95.00**

W5-14. Stanley Rule & Level No. 2: Smoothing Plane. "Sweetheart" Trademark. Original Decal. Length: 7 1/4 Inches. *This superb example of Stanley's No. 2 smoothing plane retains virtually all of the original decal on the handle—a sure sign that it was used very, very little.* (FINE) **$345.00**

W5-15. Stanley Rule & Level No. 20: Cast Iron Circular Plane. Ca. 1930's. Near New Condition. Length: 10 Inches. *This japan-finished example of Stanley's most popular adjustable compass plane is in top condition. Some 98% of all original finishes remain. A great working tool in superb condition.* (FINE) **$285.00**

W5-16. Stanley Rule & Level No. 9 1/4: Cast Iron Block Plane. Non-Adjustable Throat. Excellent Condition. Length: 6 Inches. *The No. 9 1/4 block plane was the functional equivalent of the No. 9 1/2, with the exception of the absence of a throat adjustment mechanism. This one is in top shape.* (FINE) **$55.00**

W5-17. Stanley Rule & Level No. 603: Bedrock Smoothing Plane. Later Style. Ca. 1930's. Length: 8 Inches. *This crisp and clean example of Stanley's later "Bedrock" series has passed through some 75 years of existence with very minimal evidence of use. Only a sliver from the side of the top of the tote deserves mention as a "flaw". A great example in excellent working order.* (FINE) **$295.00**

W5-18. Stanley Rule & Level No. 5: Rosewood Handle Jack Plane. Rosewood Handles. Superb Condition. Length: 14 Inches. *All of the shiny black japan finish remains on this excellent rosewood handled jack plane. A great example.* (FINE) **$85.00**

W5-19. Stanley Rule & Level No. 9 1/2: Adjustable Throat Plane. With Precision Adjust. New Condition, Original Box. Length: 6 Inches. *Here's a great working example of Stanley's mainstay No. 9 1/2 block plane in nearly new condition in its original box. Extra crisp and clean.* (FINE) **$115.00**

W5-20. Stanley Rule & Level No. 4 1/2: Heavy Smoothing Plane. Ca. 1930's. 98% Original Paint. Length: 10 Inches. *This is the first example of Stanley's No. 4 1/2 wide, heavy smoothing plane that we have offered in some time. These planes have become nearly impossible to find. This one has nearly all of its original shiny black paint and the handles are sound and ready to go to work. A good one.* (FINE) **$215.00**

W5-21. Stanley Rule & Level No. 289: Skew-Blade Rabbet Plane. Original Decal. "Sweetheart" Trademark. Length: 8 1/2 Inches. *There is no question that these skew-bladed rabbet and filletster planes would have become the standard had they not required such precise machining and hand-fitting in the Stanley factory, resulting in what proved to be a prohibitively expensive plane for the average woodworker. This example retains nearly all of its original paint and most of the original ca. 1920's decal. The finest example of this plane that we have ever offered.* (FINE) **$545.00**

W5-22. Stanley Rule & Level No. 80: Cast Iron Cabinet Scraper. Early "V" Trademark. Ready to Use. Length: 12 Inches. *A Stanley classic, these workaday scraper planes are great on the job. This pristine example is marked with the 1915 era "V" trademark.* (GOOD+) **$45.00**

W5-23. Stanley Rule & Level No. 39: Cast Iron Dado Plane. 1/4 Inch Size. Early Type I. Length: 8 Inches. *Distinguished from the later versions of the No. 39 series by having the number and size cast into the machined face of the tool, the "Type 1" versions of the No. 39 are dramatically more graphic in appearance than the later versions. This example, in the 1/4 inch size retains some 95% of its original paint. Nice.* (GOOD+) **$265.00**

W5-24. Stanley Rule & Level No. 82: Adjustable Head Scraper. Beechewood Handles. Patented January 29, 1907. Length: 12 Inches. *This example of Stanley's pivoting head scraper is in sound condition, but someone at a flea market somewhere sprayed it with a coat of lacquer. Ready to use.* (GOOD+) **$35.00**

W5-25. Stanley Rule & Level No. 10 1/2: Bench Rabbet Plane. Ca. 1915 Trademark. Ready to Use. Length: 9 Inches. *Only a light spot of pitting on the side rail detracts from this otherwise excellent carriage maker's rabbet plane. The minor cosmetic flaw does not affect the utility of this tool.* (GOOD+) **$185.00**

W5-26. Stanley Rule & Level No. 45: Patent Combination Plane. "Sweetheart" Trademark. Ready to Use. Length: 12 Inches. *All original parts and cutters are present with this excellent working example of the No. 45 combination plane.* (GOOD+) **$165.00**

W5-27. Stanley Rule & Level No. 12: Adjustable Scraper. With Rosewood Handles. Brand New Blade. Length: 11 Inches. *Here's an excellent working example of Stanley's No. 12 scraper plane. The blade is not marked with the Stanley name but it is of the same dimensions and in perfect condition. Ready to use.* (GOOD+) **$135.00**

W5-28. Stanley Rule & Level No. 4 C: 9 Inch Smoothing Plane. With Corrugated Sole. "Sweetheart" Trademark. Length: 9 Inches. *The rosewood handles of this well preserved "Type 12" smooth plane have a particularly dramatic grain pattern. A great working plane in nearly new condition.* (FINE) **$125.00**

W5-29. Stanley Rule & Level No. 45: Early "Type 3" Combination Plane. With Floral Casting. Early and Excellent. Length: 12 Inches. *This early No. 45 is of the type designated by studies as "Type 3". Its dramatically graphic floral casting adds aesthetic appeal to an excellent working tool. Includes two boxes of cutting irons.* (GOOD+) **$245.00**

W5-30. Stanley Rule & Level No. 20: "Victor" Compass Plane. 85% Original Nickel. Ca. 1900. Length: 9 1/2 Inches. *Most of the shiny nickel plating remains on this ready to use example of Stanley's top of the line No. 20 circular plane. If you're looking for a circular plane to put to work, you need look no further.* (GOOD+) **$195.00**

W5-31. Stanley Rule & Level No. 604: "Bedrock" Smoothing Plane. Later Style. Excellent Condition. Length: 9 Inches. *If you're looking for a good, clean "Bedrock" smoother, look no further. Crisp, clean and ready to use.* (GOOD+) **$265.00**

W5-32. Stanley Rule & Level No. 605: "Bedrock" Jack Plane. Later Style. "Sweetheart" Trademark. Length: 14 Inches. *As nice an example of the early Bedrock jack plane as we have ever offered. A full 99% of the original finishes remain on this super clean plane which retains much of its original decal. Offered without apology and highly recommended.* (FINE) **$285.00**

W5-33. Unmarked: Hand Carved Replica of Stanley No. 20. Nicely Detailed. Length: 10 Inches. *Perhaps the consequence of a combination of a long winter and a slow year for work, a woodworker with an eye for detail carved this full scale working model of a Stanley No. 20 circular plane. Complete with all original parts and a wooden cutter that indicates he may also have been working on a No. 78 plane in the same medium, this is one of the most unusual collectible tools we have ever offered. Decidedly different.* (FINE) **$185.00**

W5-34. Stanley Rule & Level No. 192: Cast Iron Rabbet Plane. 1 Inch Width. Unused Condition. Length: 10 1/2 Inches. *The No. 192 was the narrowest size of the Stanley rabbet plane series. This one is in essentially unused condition. Mint.* (FINE) **$75.00**

W5-35. Stanley Rule & Level No. 45: Early Type Combination Plane. With Floral Casting. Original Cutters. Length: 11 Inches. *In its early days, the Stanley No. 45 combination plane was a horse of a different color. The first production models were made especially attractive, in High Victorian fashion, to lure woodworkers steeped in centuries of tradition to abandon their tried and true methods. An excellent example of a classic hand plane. This one is missing the slitter and rear depth stop, but is otherwise in excellent condition.* (GOOD+) **$165.00**

W5-36. Stanley Rule & Level (Canada) No. 3 C: 8 Inch Smoothing Plane. Rosewood Handles. New Condition, Original Box. Length: 9 Inches. *Someone has run a bit of tape over the bottom of the label of this early Stanley box, but the plane is in perfect condition. The cutting iron is marked with the "Made in Canada" logo. Absolutely perfect.* (FINE) **$215.00**

W5-37. Stanley Rule & Level No. 6: 18 Inch Fore Plane. With Sweetheart Trademark. 98% Original Finishes. Length: 18 Inches. *Half jack plane and half jointer, the 18 inch No. 6 can do some of the work of each. This one is about as good as they get. 98% of all original finishes remain.* (FINE) **$185.00**

W5-38. Stanley Rule & Level No. 3: 9 Inch Smooth Plane. Sweetheart Trademark. 99%+ Original Paint. Length: 9 Inches. *Virtually all of the shiny original japan finish remains on this pristine smoothing plane. Rosewood handles add aesthetic appeal to this perfectly preserved tool.* (FINE) **$125.00**

W5-39. Stanley Rule & Level No. 40: Cast Iron Scrub Plane. With Beech Handles. Ca. 1890's Trademark. Length: 9 1/2 Inches. *The roughing out of virgin stock before the jack and smooth plane went to work was the task assigned to these workaday planes, which were fitted with convex cutting irons to literally "scoop" out the wood. A great working example.* (GOOD+) **$95.00**

W5-40. Stanley Rule & Level No. 283: Adjustable Cabinet Scraper. With Rosewood Handles. Sweetheart Trademark. Length: 9 1/2 Inches. *Among the least common of all of Stanley's scraper planes, the No. 283 features a pair of rosewood handes, one of which is attached to the cutting edge by a steel bracket that positively locks it into place. A rare Stanley tool in nearly new condition.* (GOOD+) **$425.00**

W5-41. Stanley Rule & Level No. 45: Combination Rabbet Plane. With Instructions. New Condition, Original Box. Length: 12 Inches. *This superb example of Stanley's No. 45 combination has been sheltered from the elements by its original pasteboard box. All original parts, including the screwdriver and original instruction manual remain with this top shelf example. Extra nice.* (FINE) **$495.00**

W5-42. Stanley Rule & Level No. 78: Duplex Rabbet, Fillet Plane. Complete and Excellent. New Condition, Original Box. Length: 10 Inches. *Here's a superb working example of an increasingly desirable Stanley classic in never-need-to-upgrade condition. The original box has kept it in perfect condition throughout its life.* (FINE) **$125.00**

W5-43. Stanley Rule & Level No. 7: Rosewood Handle Jointer Plane. "Sweetheart" Trademark. Near New Condition. Length: 22 Inches. *Virtually all of the shiny black japanning remains on this pristine jointer plane from Stanley's "Sweetheart" era. Mint.* (FINE) **$245.00**

W5-44. Stanley Rule & Level No. 78: Duplex Rabbet, Fillet Plane. Near New Condition. Complete and Excellent Length: 10 Inches. *Here's a good, clean working example of Stanley's mainstay bullnose/rabbet and filletster plane. This plane was made ca. 1935 and is in top condition.* (FINE) **$95.00**

W5-45. Stanley Rule & Level No. 65: Low Angle Block Plane. Nickel Plated Cap. Superb Condition. Length: 7 Inches. *Crisp and clean example of Stanley's No. 65 wide-body low-angle block plane have become almost impossible to find. The art of the possible.* (FINE) **$115.00**

Group X5

X5-1. Eastwood, G., York: Pair of Tongue and Groove Molding Planes. Marked "5/8". Unusual Side Escapement. Length: 9 1/2 Inches. *A most unusual "window" escapement adds to the character of these perfectly preserved tongue and groove planes from a prominent Scottish maker.* (FINE) **$85.00**

X5-2. Auburn Tool Co., Auburn, N.Y.: No. 72: Double Tongue and Groove Molding Plane. Marked "Inch". Extra Crisp and Clean. Length: 9 1/2 Inches. *No apologies whatsoever for this nearly new double tongue and groove plane in the uncommon 1 inch size. A 135 year old plane in new condition.* (FINE) **$110.00**

X5-3. Panton, James, Aberdeen (Scotland): Handled Sash Scribe Molding Plane. Nicely Boxed. Near New Condition. Length: 10 Inches. *An exceptionally clean and nicely boxed handled sash scribing plane with applied offset handle. Boldly stamped with the maker of Scottish maker James Panton. A great plane.* (FINE) **$325.00**

X5-4. Mathieson & Son, A., Glasgow: Cove, Astragal/Cove Molding Plane. Massive Proportion. Unused Condition. Length: 9 1/2 Inches. *This massive complex molding plane is imprinted with the Quarter Moon logo of Scottish planemakers Mathieson & Company. It appears never to have been used. Absolutely perfect.* (FINE) **$525.00**

X5-5. Booth, R.W., Cincinnati, Ohio: 3/4 Inch Double Tongue and Groove Molding Planes. Ca. 1849-1850 Only. AWP III: 2 Stars (A). Length: 9 1/2 Inches. *Here's a clean double tongue and groove plane in the desirable 3/4 inch size from an uncommon Cincinnati maker. Nice.* (GOOD+) **$115.00**

X5-6. Booth, R.W., Cincinnati, Ohio: 1 Inch Dado Molding Plane. Ca. 1849-1850 Only. AWP III: 2 Stars (A). Length: 9 1/2 Inches. *This well preserved dado plane is marked with the imprint of Cincinnati maker R.W. Booth. Condition is near new. A rare 1 inch dado plane in top condition.* (FINE) **$95.00**

X5-7. Harwood, C.: Grecian Ogee Molding Plane. Extra Bold Stamp. AWP III: 2 Stars. Length: 9 1/2 Inches. *The elusive imprint of American 18th Century planemaker C. Harwood has been boldly struck on the toe of this well preserved complex molding plane. A great example from a very rare maker.* (GOOD+) **$265.00**

X5-8. Gouch, F.J., Worcester, Mass.: Skew Rabbet Molding Plane. Ca. 1847-1868. Extra Steep Angle. Length: 9 1/2 Inches. *The cutting angle of this skew rabbet molder is set at a particularly acute angle indicating that it may have been intended primarily for use with hardwood lumber. It is in nearly new condition.* (FINE) **$85.00**

X5-9. Preston & Sons, Edward: Set of 18 Hollow and Round Molding Planes. Skew Set Irons. Near New Condition. Length: 9 1/2 Inches. *From their headquarters in the industrial city of Birmingham, England, toolmakers Edward Preston & Sons produced a wide range of tools of the very highest quality. These skew bladed hollow and round molding planes are boldly imprinted with the Preston mark and appear to have been very little used. Whether you are a discriminating woodworker looking for a first class set of hollows and rounds or a collector seeking the very best of the best, you will not be disappointed by these planes. Extra nice.* (FINE) **$985.00**

X5-10. Andruss, Newark, N.J.: Coachmakers's Rabbet Molding Plane. With Curved Sole. Owner C.L. Morse. Length: 6 1/2 Inches. *Imprinted with the mark of Newark planemaker George W. Andruss, who specialized in coachmakers' tools, this compass sole carriagemaker's rabbet is in excellent collector quality condition. A rare and clearly marked compass soled molding plane.* (GOOD+) **$225.00**

X5-11. Taber, John M., New Bedford, Mass.: Quirk Ovolo, Bevel Molding Plane. Marked 1/2 Inch. Crisp and Clean. Length: 9 1/2 Inches. *This clean complex molder is in excellent working order. A nice example.* (GOOD+) **$85.00**

X5-12. Hathersich, George (Manchester): Adjustable Stair Rail Molding Plane. Ca. 1820-1840. Unusual Size and Type. Length: 6 Inches. *Much less common in England than they are in the United States, stair rail molding planes are quite rare on either side of the Atlantic. This squat adjustable fence example bears the imprint of George Hathersich, who worked in the second quarter of the Nineteenth Century.* (GOOD+) **$225.00**

X5-13. Mathieson & Son, A., Glasgow: Astragal and Cove Molding Plane. Massive Proportion. Unused Condition. Length: 9 1/2 Inches. *Boldly struck with this Mathieson imprint, this massive molder may never have left the factory. Absolutely perfect.* (FINE) **$425.00**

X5-14. Unmarked: 1/16 Inch Tongue and Groove Molding Planes. Most Unusual Size. Ready to Use. Length: 7 Inches. *At only 7 inches in length, these special tongue and groove planes are some 40% smaller than a standard molding plane. They were designed to form tongue and groove joints of 1/16 inch size. The smallest tongue and groove planes we have ever seen in excellent working order. Very different and highly recommended.* (GOOD+) **$225.00**

X5-15. Wells, G.F., Bolton: Special Purpose Molding Plane. Most Unusual Cut. Bevel, Ogee, Etc. Length: 9 1/2 Inches. *This unusual molding plane has a cut unlike anything we have ever seen. Most unusual.* (GOOD+) **$185.00**

X5-16. Heald, Addison, Milford, N.H.: No. 19: Massive Round Molding Plane. With Trademark Cap. Bold "A" Imprint. Length: 9 1/2 Inches. *This oversize round plane is fitted with the distinctive cap iron used by planemaker Addison Heald of Milford, New Hampshire.* (GOOD+) **$135.00**

X5-17. Callendar & Co., B., Boston, Mass.: No. 12: Pair of Tongue and Groove Molding Planes. Superb Condition. AWP III: "A" Imprint. Length: 11 1/2 Inches. *These handled tongue and groove planes from an uncommon Boston maker are in essentially new condition. Absolutely perfect.* (FINE) **$125.00**

X5-18. Moon, Lincoln Inn Fields: Coach Rabbet Molding Plane. Most Unusual Form. Excellent Condition. Length: 9 1/2 Inches. *This most unusual coachmaker's rabbet plane has the form of a standard molding plane above, but the lower section is cut away to form a 4" rabbeting plane having contoured sides. Unlike any carriage maker's plane we have previously encountered, this plane was obviously made originally produced in this configuration. A rare and graphic carriage maker's plane. Highly recommended.* (GOOD+) **$165.00**

X5-19. Sandusky Tool Co., Ohio: No. 60: Skew-Blade Dado Molding Plane. Marked 1/4 Inch. Brass Depth Stop. Length: 9 1/2 Inches. *A nice example of an adjustable depth stop dado from toolmaking giant Sandusky Tool in the desirable 1/4" size.* (GOOD) **$45.00**

X5-20. Barton & Co., D.R. Rochester, N.Y.: No. 44: Fenced Quirk Round Molding Plane. Marked "7/8". Scarce and Excellent. Length: 9 1/2 Inches. *This fenced quarter round from Rochester, New York maker D.R. Barton is in virtually new condition. Extra nice.* (FINE) **$75.00**

X5-21. Stothert, Bath (England): Massive Cove and Astragal Molding Plane. Marked "8/8". Ca. 1784-1841. Length: 9 1/2 Inches. *A major exporter of planes to the fledgling United States, most Stothert planes found in the U.S. are complex molders. This massive cove and astragal is in excellent working order. Early and excellent.* (GOOD+) **$185.00**

X5-22. Kinnear, Dundee (Scotland): Boxed Bead Molding Plane. Marked "3/4". Extra Crisp and Clean. Length: 9 1/2 Inches. *This 3/4" boxed bead comes to us from an obscure Scottish maker, who worked in Dundee from 1829 to 1845.* (FINE) **$55.00**

X5-23. Barton & Co., D.R., Rochester, N.Y: Classic Astragal Molding Plane. Marked "7/8". Ready to Use. Length: 9 1/2 Inches. *Here's a very well preserved astragal molder that has been stamped with the early imprint of D.R. Barton. A nice plane.* (GOOD+) **$85.00**

X5-24. Sandusky Tool Co., Sandusky, Ohio: No. 36: Beech Toothing Plane. Steep Angle. Ready to Use. Length: 7 1/2 Inches. *A crisp and ready-to-use toothing plane with a clean original iron. Ready to do yeoman service in the veneering business.* (GOOD+) **$75.00**

X5-25. Gladwin & Appleton, Boston: Boxed Center Bead Molding Plane. Marked "3/4." Extra Crisp and Clean. Length: 9 1/2 Inches. *This double boxed center bead has been boldly struck with the imprint of Gladwin & Appleton, Boston planemakers from 1873 to 1877. A great working plane.* (GOOD+) **$65.00**

X5-26. Berry, G., Old Street, London: Classic Hook Joint Molding Plane. For Airtight Case. Fully Boxed. Length: 10 Inches. *Hook joint planes were used for cutting of the grooves for joints in air tight cases. This superb example is fully boxed and fitted with a sliding stop that is arched to accommodate escapement of the shavings. A rare special purpose plane in top collector quality condition.* (GOOD+) **$285.00**

X5-27. Chapin, H., Union Factory No. 1: Steep Quirk Ovolo and Astragal Molding Plane. Marked 1 1/4 Inch. Near New Condition. Length: 9 1/2 Inches. *Hermon Chapin's Union Factory produced tools of every sort for a rapidly expanding America. This extra steep complex molding plane is in essentially unused condition. Absolutely perfect.* (FINE) **$395.00**

X5-28. Fuller, C., Causeway St., Boston: Double Iron Sash Molding Plane. With Integral Fence. Most Unusual Cut. Length: 9 1/2 Inches. *This perfectly preserved double iron sash molding plane is fitted with an integral fence. Most unusual.* (FINE) **$225.00**

X5-29. Unmarked No. 155: Quarter Round Molding Plane. 3/4 Inch Size. Ready to Use. Length: 9 1/2 Inches. *Only the designation "No. 155" appears on this 3/4" quarter round molder, which matches the numbering scheme of the Auburn Tool Company. It once had a fence applied to the side, but it is in great working order.* (GOOD+) **$35.00**

X5-30. Auburn Tool Co., Auburn, N.Y.: No. 155: Massive Quirk Round Molding Plane. Marked "Inch 1/4". Crisp and Clean. Length: 9 1/2 Inches. *A clean and usable quarter round molding plane from a prominent Upstate New York maker in an extra wide size. Ready to use.* (GOOD+) **$95.00**

X5-31. Kennedy, Utica: Ovolo With Astragal Molding Plane. Marked "3/8". Near New Condition. Length: 9 1/2 Inches. *Leonard Kennedy, Jr. produced planes in Utica, New York, from 1825 to 1832. Examples of this imprint are not common, especially when they appear on extra crisp complex molders such as this. Very nice. Ex-Cooley Collection.* (FINE) **$185.00**

X5-32. Eastwood, G., York: Pair of Hollow and Round Molding Planes. Marked "14". Ready to Use. Length: 9 1/2 Inches. *These No. 14 hollow and round planes are in excellent working order.* (GOOD+) **$55.00**

X5-33. Malloch, D., Perth (Scotland): Pair of Tongue and Groove Molding Planes. Marked "3/8". Near New Condition. Length: 9 1/2 Inches. *These nearly new tongue and groove planes from Scottish maker D. Malloch have a most unusual carved escapement. A great set in top condition.* (FINE) **$95.00**

X5-34. Kellogg, J., Amherst, Mass.: Set of Bead Molding Planes. 1/4 Inch, 3/8 Inch and 7/8 Inch. Owner: W.H. Hartwell. Length: 9 1/2 Inches. *Here's a working set of bead planes, all bearing the owner's stamp of one W.H. Hartwell. A nice set.* (GOOD+) **$95.00**

X5-35. Nurse, C., Walworth Road, London: Fishing Rod Maker's Molding Plane. Skew Set Iron. Extra Rare and Nice. Length: 7 3/4 Inches. *This semicircular plane has its cutting iron set at a skew and was intended for use in the making of fishing rods. It is in unused condition. Rare and excellent. Highly recommended.* (FINE) **$345.00**

X5-36. Burnham Jr., George, Amherst, Mass: Pair of Tongue and Groove. Molding Planes. Marked "1/2". Extra Crisp and Clean. Length: 9 1/2 Inches. *These 1/2" tongue and groove planes are in top condition and ready to use, if you choose.* (FINE) **$75.00**

X5-37. Gladwin & Appleton, Boston: Pair of Handled Tongue and Groove Molding Planes. Marked "7/8". Near New Condition. Length: 11 1/2 Inches. *Here's a great pair of handle tongue and groove molding planes from a Boston partnership which operated from 1872 to 1877. Nearly new.* (FINE) **$165.00**

X5-38. Ohio Tool Co., Columbus, Ohio: No. 48: Fixed Dado Molding Plane. 7/8 Inch Size. Brass Depth Adjust. Length: 9 1/2 Inches. *An extra crisp and clean dado plane by a prominent maker. A brass screw adjustment regulates the depth of cut on this nearly new molding plane. Nice.* (FINE) **$125.00**

X5-39. Nurse, C., Walworth Road, London: Set of Plow Plane Cutting Irons. Felt Roll. Near New Condition. Length: 9 Inches. *A fitted felt roll has kept these cutting irons in nearly new condition. A great set of plow plane irons.* (FINE) **$165.00**

X5-40. Kellogg, J., Amherst, Mass.: Quarter Round Molding Plane. Marked "4/8". Ready to Use. Length: 9 1/2 Inches. *This 1/2" quarter round molder is in excellent working order.* (GOOD+) **$45.00**

X5-41. Chapin, H., Union Factory: No. 171: Double Tongue and Groove Molding Plane. Marked "7/8". Crisp and Ready to Use. Length: 9 1/2 Inches. *This crispy clean double tongue and groove molder is marked with the imprint of H. Chapin's Union Factory, which produced wooden planes from 1828 to 1860. A classic example in excellent condition.* (GOOD+) **$75.00**

X5-42. Chapin, H., Union Factory: No. 217 1/4: Fence Quirk Round Molding Plane. Owner "J.E. Durgin". Extra Crisp and Clean. Length: 9 1/2 Inches. *The owner imprint of one J.E. Durgin has been stamped on the toe of the fenced quarter round molder from H. Chapin's Union Factory. A boldly marked plane from and important maker.* (GOOD+) **$85.00**

X5-43. Preston & Sons, Edward: Set of 7 Boxed Bead Molding Planes. 1/4 Inch to 1 Inch. Ready to Use. Length: 9 1/2 Inches. *Here's a nice working set of boxed bead planes for the woodworker. Extra crisp and ready to work.* (FINE) **$345.00**

X5-44. Smith, E., Warranted: Double Bead Molding Plane. Marked "1/2". Extra Crisp and Clean. Length: 9 1/2 Inches. *No apologies whatsoever for this extraordinarily well preserved boxed double bead from a prominent Massachusetts maker. Nice.* (FINE) **$165.00**

X5-45. Sandusky Tool Co., Ohio: No. 152: Quadruple Reed Molding Plane. Marked "3/16". Rare and Excellent. Length: 9 1/2 Inches. *One of the most visually striking of all wooden planes, the quadruple reed quickly captures the attention of anyone perusing a shelf filled with those tools. This Sandusky classic is in top collector quality condition. Choice.* (FINE) **$345.00**

Group Y5

Y5-1. North Bros. Mfg. Co., Philadelphia, Penn.: No. 1251: Long Handle Tap Wrench. Largest Size. New Condition, Original Box. Length: 13 Inches. *This, the largest size of three ratcheting tap wrenches offered by the North Brothers Company, is also the least common. New and in the original box.* (FINE) **$165.00**

Y5-2. P.T. Co.: "A.B.C." Double Pipe and NutWrench. Patented May 6, 1913. Length: 8 Inches. *This jack of all trades allowed the jaw to be inserted from one direction to serve as a pipe wrench and from the other to function as a nut wrench.* (GOOD+) **$45.00**

Y5-3. Disston & Sons, H., Philadelphia, Penn.: Double Edge Saw. With Adjustable Depth Stop. Most Unusual Type. Length: 18 Inches. *This most unusual double saw is fitted with Disston's depth stop that appeared on back saws and a few panel saws. Never seen another.* (GOOD+) **$135.00**

Y5-4. Disston & Sons, Henry: No. D 23: 8 Point Crosscut Saw. 26 Inch Blade. Straight and Sharp. Length: 29 Inches. *Nearly all of the original etching remains on this pristine panel saw. Mint.* (FINE) **$65.00**

Y5-5. Unmarked: Quintuple Scribe Race Knife. Octagon Boxwood Handle. Early and Unusual. Length: 5 Inches. *Unlike any other race knife we have previously offered for sale. this early manufactured tool of early appearance has a scribing head with four individual scribes, which may have been intended for working in pairs in the scribing of parallel lines. The boxwood handle has attained a most appealing golden patina and the tool is in excellent overall condition. An extraordinary collectible race knife.* (FINE) **$365.00**

Y5-6. Assorted Makers: Group of 27 Stone Cutting Tools. Assorted Shapes and Sizes. Length: 10 Inches. *If you have a mind to do some stonecutting, this well preserved set of chisels will get you into the game. All are in excellent working order.* (GOOD+) **$95.00**

Y5-7. P.T. Co.: "The Carll" Wrench. Double Pipe and Nut. Patented May 6, 1913. Length: 8 Inches. *This jack of all trades allowed the jaw to be inserted from one direction to serve as a pipe wrench and from the other to function as a nut wrench. A good one.* (GOOD+) **$45.00**

Y5-8. Disston & Sons, Henry, Philadelphia, Penn.: No. D 115: 26 Inch 6 Point "Victory" Saw. Rosewood Handle. Ca. World War I. Length: 29 1/2 Inches. *This is the earlier variety of "Victory" saw, much more elaborately decorated than the World War II version. Clean, clearly etched and very nice.* (GOOD+) **$165.00**

Y5-9. Smith, Phineas, New York, N.Y.: Early Cast Steel Saw. Open Type Handle. Decorative "Nib". Length: 17 Inches. *The blade of this classic early "carcase" saw is imprinted with the name of sawmaker Phineas Smith of New York City, a maker we have not encountered before.* (GOOD+) **$145.00**

Y5-10. Shapleigh Hardware, St. Louis: 16 Inch Cabinetmaker's Saw. "Diamond Edge" Logo. Rare and Near New. Length: 21 1/2 Inches. *No apologies whatsoever for this straight, sharp and crispy clean saw from the "Diamond Edge is a Quality Pledge" people at the Shapleigh Hardware Company.* (FINE) **$225.00**

Y5-11. Graves, J., Bangor, Maine: Multiple Scribe Race Knife. Rare Maine Maker. Early and Excellent. Length: 7 Inches. *The imprint of an undocumented Maine maker is imprinted on the shaft of this graphic race knife. There is a "hang hole" through the handle, but the tool is otherwise in excellent condition.* (GOOD+) **$265.00**

Y5-12. American Wrench Co., Augsta, Maine: 9 Inch Screw Adjust Buggy Wrench. Patented September 8, 1885. Schulz No. 231 (B). Length: 9 Inches. *This screw adjust buggy wrench is marked on the top of the head. A nicely fluted handle adds to its appeal. A classic collectible buggy wrench.* (GOOD+) **$125.00**

Y5-13. Bemis & Call Co., Springfield, Mass.: Early Patent Pipe Wrench. Patented August 1866. Near New Condition. Length: 12 Inches. *The earliest wrenches have a distinctly non-angular look about them that clearly distinguishes them at a glance from the homogeneity of Twentieth Century wrenches. This early example from Bemis and Call is clearly marked with the 1866 patent date. A rare, early wrench in top condition.* (FINE) **$225.00**

Y5-14. Unmarked: Combination Log Mark and Ice Axe. Original Handle. Most Unusual. Length: 26 1/2 Inches. *Given the climates in which most American logging took place, we are surprised that we haven't seen a log marking hammer and ice axe before now. A very rare combination tool.* (GOOD) **$225.00**

Y5-15. Hjorth & Co., W., Jamestown, N.Y.: Rare 4 Inch "Crescent" Wrench. Preceded Crescent. Excellent Condition. Length: 4 Inches. *We have sold a large number of 4 inch size "Crescent" wrenches, but this example from Jamestown maker Hjorth & Company is the first to come our way. It may well be that this is a pre-Crescent Crescent. Say that five times really fast. A rare 4 inch wrench.* (GOOD+) **$85.00**

Y5-16. Disston & Sons, Henry, Philadelphia, Penn.: No. 7: 24 Inch 5 1/2 Point Rip Saw. Original Label. Straight and True. Length: 28 Inches. *This is the way they made Disston saws when Henry Disston was on hand to supervise production. This one has the classic 1880's era shape, with characteristic "nib" and a lacquered applewood handle that still has much of its original finish. A nice, early saw in excellent working order.* (GOOD+) **$95.00**

Y5-17. Heller Bros. Co., Newark, N.J.: Self-Adjusting Wrench. "Masterwrench". Smallest Size. Length: 6 Inches. *Heller offered these "Masterwrench" tools in a number of sizes. This was the smallest size they offered. A nice example.* (GOOD+) **$45.00**

Y5-18. Unmarked: Classic Cooper's Scorp. Fruitwood Handle. Ca. 1850's. Length: 10 1/4 Inches. *Here's a very well preserved scorp that has been fitted with a handle of turned fruitwood. Very nice.* (GOOD+) **$55.00**

Y5-19. Jennings Mfg. Co., The Russell: Set of 13 Auger Bits. 3 Tiered Box. Near New Condition. Length: 10 Inches. *The outside of the box has weathered a bit, all of the bits inside are in excellent condition. A well preserved set of Jennings bits in a handy box.* (FINE) **$225.00**

Y5-20. Starrett Co., L. S., Athol, Mass.: No. 11: Machinist's Metric Combination Square. With Center Head. Near New Condition. Length: 6 Inches. *This most unusual Starrett square is fitted with a blade having metric graduations. It is in nearly new condition.* (FINE) **$95.00**

Y5-21. Goodell-Pratt Company: Screw Adjust Nut Wrench. Aluminum Handle. Schulz No. 394. Length: 6 Inches. *The Goodell-Pratt Company's consistently high quality level is evident in this small adjustable nut wrench. A rare wrench in great shape.* (FINE) **$175.00**

Y5-22. Williams & Co., J.H., N.Y. No. AP-6: 6 Inch "Crescent" Wrench. Uncommon Maker. New Condition, Original Box. Length: 6 Inches. *By the time this wrench was being manufactured, nearly every wrench maker offered their version of the "Crescent" wrench. This 6 inch example from J.H. Williams is in new condition in its original box. Mint.* (FINE) **$35.00**

Y5-23. Marples & Sons, Wm., Hibernia: Staghorn Handle Race Knife. Uncommon Type. Very Little Used. Length: 3 1/2 Inches. *This English style folding race knife has a staghorn handle and is in superb condition. Well marked and well preserved.* (FINE) **$115.00**

Y5-24. Richardson Brothers, Newark, N.J.: 10 Inch Dovetail Saw. Chandler & Barber. Clean and Straight. Length: 14 1/2 Inches. *The blade of this clean and straight dovetail saw is engraved with the advertising of Chandler & Barber, who were dealers in hardware and tools at 15 and 17 Eliot Street in Boston. Both the saw back and the applewood handle are stamped with the number "22", an indication that this was used in a trade school. A good one.* (GOOD+) **$115.00**

Y5-25. Smyth Co., John M.: Smyth's "Washington" Saw. From Washington State. Great Etching. Length: 31 1/2 Inches. *The decorative etching on this saw was apparently designed to appeal to regional pride. The absence of the Smyth from the Directory of American Toolmakers indicates that he was likely a hardware dealer who purchased this saw from a major maker to sell in his store. A classic collectible saw.* (GOOD+) **$145.00**

Y5-26. Ferdin: Early Dutch Chisel. 3 Inch Cutting Edge. Original Handle. Length: 19 Inches. *This classic Continental chisel is still in working order and it retains what appears to be its original handle. A great example of a classic form.* (GOOD+) **$115.00**

Y5-27. American Saw Co., Newark, N.J.: "The Curtis" Pipe Wrench. Patented April 9, 1890. Schulz No. 33. Length: 15 Inches. *Just to demonstrate why they were in the saw business, the folks at the American Saw Company tried their hand at making a pipe wrenchs. We have a well known aversion to the so-called "alligator" wrenches and this is a classic example of why that is the case. A wrench that the paired muses of Ignorance and Invention decreed would someday be collectible. A stupid idea makes a great wrench.* (GOOD+) **$285.00**

Y5-28. Sorrento Wood Carving Co., Boston: Early Patent Fret Saw. Patented December 13, 1870. Rosewood Handle. Length: 22 Inches. *This Sorrento saw is retains much of its original finishes on all surfaces. It is fitted with a rosewood handle and clearly marked with both the maker name and patent date. A graphic saw in great shape.* (GOOD+) **$195.00**

Y5-29. Millers Falls Company No. 4: Pratt's Ratchet Auger Handle. Complete and Sound. Removeable Handle. Length: 15 Inches. *These ratchet handle augur handles were produced by Millers Falls as "Pratt's Patent Auger Handle" for many years. The longevity of this tool is solely attributable to the fact that it performed the work for which it was designed very well. A great working tool.* (GOOD+) **$45.00**

Y5-30. Unmarked: Dramatic Hand Forged Saw. With Lever Lock Adjust. Early Appearance. Length: 28 1/2 Inches. *Fitted out with a locking arm to precisely tension the blade, this early hand forged saw of oversize proportions is unlike any other saw we have ever offered. Most unusual.* (GOOD) **$225.00**

Y5-31. Unmarked: Early Hand Forged Scorp. Original Handle. Sharp and Usable. Length: 5 1/2 Inches. *Designed for the hollowing tasks that a chairmaker or cooper might encounter, the scorp was a very handy tool for which there is no contemporary equivalent. This one is in excellent condition and could be put back to use immediately.* (GOOD+) **$55.00**

Y5-32. Moulson Brothers, (England): Extra Long Paring Chisel. 3/4 Inch Width. Ready to Use. Length: 19 Inches. *Here's an excellent oversize paring chisel in the desirable 3/4 inch size from a respected English maker.* (GOOD+) **$65.00**

Y5-33. Unmarked: Pennsylvania Style Splitting Wedge. Original Handle. Superb Patina. Length: 12 3/4 Inches. *This early splitting wedge retains its original handle, complete with the ring that kept it from splitting. A classic early tool.* (GOOD+) **$85.00**

Y5-34. Stanley Rule & Level No. 21 1/2: 6 Inch Patent Combination Square. Marked Patented January 23, 1917. Also Marked Patent Pending. Length: 6 Inches. *This cast iron combination square is marked with the "Sweetheart" logo and the patent date. Much less common than its first cousin, the No. 21, this one has an open cast body with the "Stanley" name cast in raised lettering. A rare square.* (FINE) **$295.00**

Y5-35. Boker & Co., H., Germany: Boxwood Handle Race Knife. Early Appearance. Unused Condition. Length: 7 Inches. *A boxwood handle adds aesthetic appeal to this well preserved race knife of German manufacture. Perfect.* (FINE) **$75.00**

Y5-36. Atkins & Co., E.C., Indianapolis: No. 65: 26 Inch 8 Point Crosscut Saw. With Apple Handle. New Condition, Original Box. Length: 29 1/2 Inches. *Saws don't get any better than this classic crosscut from E.C. Atkins. Brand new in the original oiled paper in the original box. Absolutely perfect and highly recommended.* (FINE) **$345.00**

Y5-37. Bay State Tool Co.: Quick Adjust Nut Wrench. Patented June 7, 1904. Schulz No. 476. Length: 8 Inches. *This one has a spring-activated quick adjustment that is a joy to use. A thumb activated lever at the top of the handle frees the jaw to travel freely. A nice example of a great gizmo.* (FINE) **$225.00**

Y5-38. Wescott: Massive 14 Inch Pipe Wrench. Early Appearance. Rare Type and Size. Length: 14 1/2 Inches. *The Wescott Company was a prolific manufacturer of "S" handle wrenches, which were apparently distributed Nation-wide. This obviously early example in the rare 14 inch size is fitted with the serrated "pipe" jaw. Anyone who has attempted to disassemble a pipe fitting with one of these knows why these tools are not included in the "utilitarian" category and are know as pure collectibles. A nice example of a deservedly rare wrench.* (GOOD+) **$85.00**

Y5-39. Disston & Sons, Henry, Philadelphia, Penn.: No. K 4: 20 Inch 11 Point Cutoff Saw. "Air Master" Logo. With Etched Plane. Length: 23 1/2 Inches. *Disston produced a wide range of elaborately etched saws for household use. This "Air Master" saw is one of the many variations on the theme.* (FINE) **$95.00**

Y5-40. Assorted Makers: Group of 20 Stone Cutting Tools. Length: 10 Inches. *Many of the chisels in this set have extra long shanks. All are in excellent working condition. Tough tools to find.* (GOOD+) **$75.00**

Y5-41. Perry, C.T. No. A: "Perry's Saw Protector". 24 Inch Size. Rare and Excellent. Length: 24 Inches. *Imprinted with the maker's intention to patent, this most unusual device was intended to protect the sharpened blade of a carpenter's hand saw. It may not have dawned on the inventor that few carpenters worth their salt would be seen with a tool that most of them learned to make, early-on, by sawing a kerf through a strip of wood. The only example we have encountered, this example of Perry's saw protector has a graphic appearance that will complement any collection of uncommon antique tools. Different.* (GOOD+) **$185.00**

Y5-42. Cleveland Wrench Co., Cleveland, Ohio: "The Cleveland" Wrench. Self Adjusting. Marked "Patented". Length: 10 Inches. *This is our first encounter with the "Cleveland Wrench". It applies the general principle that wrenches intended to eliminate the need for multiple sizes of the same wrench are able to destroy the object of their work far more quickly and efficiency than would a tool specifically made to deal with a single size. A mangler.* (GOOD+) **$35.00**

Y5-43. Bishop & Co., Geo. H., Lawrencebur: "Bishop's Bull Dog" Saw. With Dog Etching. Rare and Excellent. Length: 26 1/2 Inches. *Apparently designed for very heavy work, this "Bulldog" saw has the blade integrated into the handle, perhaps to minimize the bending of the saw. A bulldog logo is clearly etched on the blade of this rare and perfectly preserved saw. Rare.* (FINE) **$255.00**

Y5-44. Starrett Co., The L.S., Athol, Mass.: Precision Combination Square. Complete and Excellent. With Protractor Head. Length: 12 Inches. *Looking for a great combination square for the home shop? This complete and apparently unused example dates from the period when the subject of compromising on quality was never raised at the Starrett Company. Perfect. Nearly new.* (FINE) **$165.00**

Y5-45. Billings & Spencer, Hartford, Conn.: "S" Handle Nut Wrench. Patented November 14, 1905. Uncommon Type. Length: 8 Inches. *This embossed-forging "S" wrench from the B. & S. people is not one often encountered. Clean and in fine working order.* (GOOD+) **$45.00**

Group Z5

Z5-1. Unmarked: Early Watchman's Rattle. Owner "Wm. Tupman". Excellent Condition. Length: 7 Inches. *These devices were used by night watchmen to sound an alarm if necessary. We have observed examples of these devices imprinted with the names of planemakers. this one has the name "Wm. Tupman" set into the top of the body. A nice example.* (GOOD+) **$195.00**

Z5-2. Unmarked: Lignum Vitae Mallet. For Wood Carving. Early Appearance. Length: 9 1/2 Inches. *This well preserved mallet of lignum vitae has a form of sculptural effect. It is ready to use or decorate a shop or both.* (GOOD+) **$65.00**

Z5-3. Unmarked: "Double Razee" Jointer. Plane. Early Rounded Iron. Excellent Condition. Length: 24 Inches. *Recently deaccessioned from the collection of Granite State collector, mystic and marketing genius Richard J. Riley, this classic "double razee" jointer has a sculpted shape at the point it begins its razee curve that we have not previously observed. The rounded wedge is indicative of early manufacture. A classic. Ex-Riley Collection.* (GOOD+) **$145.00**

Z5-4. Unmarked: Classic Double Coach Router Plane. Boxwood Wedges. Owner "N.T. Hall". Length: 18 Inches. *The owner's imprint "N.T. Hall" that appears on this plane was the proprietor of a carriage shop in the State of Vermont. These tools were acquired nearly 50 years ago by a Connecticut collector and are offered in this volume. This classic "double pistol" router is clean, complete and ready to show. A classic coachmaker's tool with a history.* (GOOD+) **$325.00**

Z5-5. Unmarked: Massive Double Razee Plane. Sculptural Form. Rare Type. Length: 29 Inches. *By far the most visually appealing of all wooden bench planes, the "double razee" style plane is markedly narrower at the heel and toe than it is at the throat. This most unusual variation features a sculpted front knob formed above the razee section. A most unusual double razee plane. Ex-Riley Collection.* (GOOD) **$165.00**

Z5-6. Hickock, W.O., Harrisburg, Penn.: Bookbinder's Clamp. For Trimming. Excellent Condition. Length: 39 Inches. *This massive bookbinder's tool was used for holding the sheets of paper while they were being worked on by someone with a bookbinder's plow. The imprint of Harrisburg, Pennsylvania maker W.O. Hickock is boldly struck on the end of this uncommon tool.* (GOOD+) **$245.00**

Z5-7. Unmarked: Carpenter's Mallet. With Lignum Head. Crisp and Clean. Length: 9 1/2 Inches. *This smaller than normal mallet is fitted with a graphic head of lignum vitae sapwood.* (GOOD+) **$15.00**

Z5-8. Unmarked: "Double Razee" Plane. Faceted Wedge. Lignum Strike Button. Length: 30 Inches. *Many a visitor to New England over the past decade has made the pilgrimage to the tiny village of New Ipswich, New Hampshire for the opportunity to view the legendary collection of "double razee" planes painstakingly assembled and displayed there by Rhkenological scholar, gourmand and all around good guy Richard J. Riley. We are pleased to offer in the pages of this volume many of the planes from that distinguished collection. This extraordinary example, fitted with a dramatic diamond-shaped lignum vitae strike button and a faceted wedge, was one of the standouts of this standout collection. Dating perhaps to the 1820's or 1830's, this perfectly preserved and perfectly proportioned jointer plane is guaranteed to attract the admiration of even the non-tool collector. We highly recommend this classic jointer plane. Ex-Riley Collection.* (GOOD+) **$385.00**

Z5-9. Hammond, I., New Haven, Conn.: Coachmaker's Double Router Plane. All Original Parts. Rare and Excellent. Length: 17 Inches. *Isaac Hammond produced planes in New Haven Connecticut from 1840 to 1845. A number of coachmaking tools have been found bearing his imprint, an indication that this was a specialty. This classic double coachmaker's router or "double pistol router" is clearly marked with the Hammond name on the end grain of one handle. All original wedges and fences remain. This graphic tool ready to proudly display in the tool room. Highly recommended.* (GOOD+) **$285.00**

Z5-10. Unmarked: Turned Lignum Vitae Mallet. Original Handle. Ready to Use. Length: 12 Inches. *Apparently turned from a selected piece of Lignum vitae heartwood, this mallet was apparently burnished to protect its edges by a previous owner. A great working tool.* (GOOD+) **$25.00**

Z5-11. Unmarked: Massive Winged Core Box Plane. Most Unusual Form. Missing Iron, Wedge. Length: 17 Inches. *Missing its cutter and somewhat worn by time and use, this massive corebox plane is nonetheless deserving of restoration and conservation. A graphic plane from the days when American factories produced durable goods for a waiting world.* (GOOD) **$35.00**

Z5-12. Unmarked: Massive Burl Mallet. Original Handle. For Timber Frames? Length: 34 Inches. *This massive and heavy mallet was likely used for driving together the joints of post and beam buildings.* (GOOD+) **$65.00**

Z5-13. Unmarked: Classic Rounding Witchet. Brass Facing. Excellent Condition. Length: 19 1/2 Inches. *Designed for the necessary task of forming rounded shafts from squared stock, the witchet is a tool that has no real equivalent in the modern shop. This extra quality example can be precisely adjusted by a pair of wood screws and the mouth is protected by a pair of cast brass faces. A great example in excellent working order.* (GOOD+) **$265.00**

Z5-14. Unmarked: Primitive Handmade Brace. Very Short Sweep. Classic Early Repair. Length: 12 1/2 Inches. *This massive brace has a look that suggests a story is trapped somewhere within. Darkly patinated from years of use, and possessed of an early repair to its chuck that was successful in extending its useful life, this was most certainly a cherished tool of some long-forgotton craftsman. A tool with a secret.* (GOOD) **$165.00**

Z5-15. Unmarked: Massive Lignum Joint Plane. Rosewood Tote, Wedge. Moulson Brothers Iron. Length: 29 1/2 Inches. *Undoubtedly used in one of the nearby shipyards, this extraordinary solid lignum vitae jointer plane was recently found in the seacoast city of Camden, Maine. It is fitted with a clean Moulson Brothers cutting iron and darkly contrasting wedge and tote of Brazilian Rosewood. A classic.* (FINE) **$245.00**

Z5-16. Unmarked: Multiple Scribe Marking Gauge. Very Early Appearance. Initials "H.Z.". Length: 10 Inches. *The paired beams on this marking gauge are locked into place by a single wedge which pushes against a pair of opposing wedges inside the head. A very early gauge in great condition having a most interesting design.* (FINE) **$85.00**

Z5-17. Unmarked: Miniature Burl Mallet. Early Handle. Superb Patina. Length: 6 Inches. *One can imagine this miniature burl mallet on the bench of a Colonial woodworker. A classic early mallet.* (GOOD+) **$115.00**

Z5-18. Unmarked: Tapered Rounding Device. Full Brass Inlay. Boxwood Arms, Handles. Length: 9 Inches. *The finest example of this type of tool that we have ever seen, this rounding plane has been fitted with adjustment screws of turned boxwood and the mouth opening has been fitted with a lining of precisely turned brass. An extremely showy and well preserved special purpose plane. Highly recommended.* (GOOD+) **$345.00**

Z5-19. Dickinson & Co.: Classic Broom Maker's Hammer. Uncommon Type. Working Condition. Length: 9 Inches. *Never having watched brooms being made, I am uncertain as to how these tools are used. This marked example in in very well preserved condition.* (GOOD+) **$85.00**

Z5-20. Unmarked: Early Burl Mallet. Hickory Handle. Superb Patina. Length: 11 Inches. *The handle on this early burl mallet appears to have started life with the tool. A classic antique tool, in the tradition of Eric Sloane.* (GOOD+) **$55.00**

Z5-21. Unmarked: Early Cooper's Joint Plane. Yellow Birch Body. I. & H. Sorby Iron. Length: 48 Inches. *The chamfered edge on the side of this early Yellow Birch cooper's jointer comes from the selection of stock that followed the contour of the tree. A classic early cooper's plane in excellent collector quality condition.* (GOOD+) **$145.00**

Z5-22. Unmarked: Pair of Mahogany "Winking" Sticks. Ebony and Ivory. Scarce and Excellent. Length 15 Inches. *"Winking" sticks were used for sighting down a piece of wood to determine the amount of "wind" in the wood. To make the sighting process easier, one of this pair has been fitted with inlays of ivory. A pretty pair.* (GOOD+) **$55.00**

Z5-23. Atkins & Co., E.C., Indianapolis: Adjustable Ram's Horn Scraper. Near New Condition. Ready to Use. Length: 12 Inches. *This adjustable scraper of distinctive form is in excellent order and ready to go back to work. Nearly all original finishes remain.* (FINE) **$125.00**

Z5-24. Unmarked: Massive 42 Inch Try Plane. Razee Back. Usable Condition. Length: 42 Inches. *Only a sheared tip on the tote detracts from this spectacular 42 inch trying plane. The longest jointer plane we have ever offered. Extraordinary.* (GOOD+) **$115.00**

Z5-25. Unmarked: Classic Turpentine Hack. With Cast Weight. Unused Condition. Length: 19 1/2 Inches. *Those who seek to collect the wide range of specialized tools that were used in the harvesting of naval stores and the making of turpentine are confronted with a challenge: these tools got dirty and degraded very rapidly. Being covered with pine pitch and laid on a nest of termites does not do much for the longevity of tools. Luckily this classic turpentine hack was spared such a fate by never having been taken into the woods. The end of the tool is fitted with a lead weight to facilitate its use. Whether you're planning to boil up a batch of turpentine or just looking for a graphic tool for the toolroom, we highly recommend this American classic.* (FINE) **$165.00**

Z5-26. Howarth, James, Sheffield, England: Classic Sash Trim Gouge. With Wood Frame. Uncommon Type. Length: 9 1/2 Inches. *These specialized gouges have a handle that extends down the blade to function as a stop. We are not certain as to how they were actually used. A nice example.* (GOOD+) **$95.00**

Z5-27. Unmarked: Special Leveling Plane. For Shaker Boxes? Great Patina. Length: 25 Inches. *One needs only to visit the collections of Shaker memorabilia at former Shaker sites in New York, Massachusetts and Maine to understand that everything in the lives of those who followed the Shaker way followed basic principles. The architecture and woodwork of the Shakers has been studied intensely by those captivated by its simplicity and proportionality. The lives of the Shakers were devoted both to religion and to industry. Their manufactures, including stylized round wooden boxes, were sold to support the colonies in which they lived. The tool offered here may well be, we believe, a tool made and used by the Shakers in the construction of wooden boxes. Approximately two feet in length and delicately chamfered in the characteristic shaker style, the sole of this specialized planing device has a circular wear pattern that indicates it may have been used for precise planing of the tops of shaker boxes. While we have no documentation of provenance to support this theory, the unique style of this tool leaves one to question what else it might possibly be. A beautiful tool of precise proportions and possible Shaker origin. Extra special.* (GOOD+) **$645.00**

Z5-28. Unmarked: Diminutive Maple Mallet. Figured Maple Handle. Owner "A. Johnson". Length: 8 Inches. *This solid maple mallet has a handle that was selected with a view to its appearance. A great working tool in top condition.* (FINE) **$145.00**

Z5-29. Unmarked: Classic Carriage Router Planes. Right and Left Hand. Superb Patina. Length: 14 1/2 Inches. *These coachmaker's shaves are set up in a right and left hand pattern. Both are clean, complete and in excellent overall condition. A pretty pair.* (GOOD+) **$115.00**

Z5-30. Lignum Vitae Products Corp., N.J.: Rosewood and Brass Gavel. Unusual Type. New Condition, Original Box. Length: 9 1/2 Inches. *Thinking of a gift for that judge in your life? How about a gavel in the original box? Decidedly different.* (FINE) **$45.00**

Z5-31. Swan Co., The James, (Unmarked): Cooper's Bung Auger. Largest Size. Rare and Near New. Length: 15 Inches. *This oversize cooper's bung auger was undoubtedly made by the James Swan Company, but it is not imprinted with their name. A bit of the red paint is missing from the casting, but it is otherwise in excellent condition.* (FINE) **$65.00**

Z5-32. Unmarked: Special Purpose Clamp. With Wire Mechanism. Most Unusual. Length: 9 1/2 Inches. *We don't have a whatsit table at Martin J. Donnelly Antique Tools, but when we find an object of unknown function we acquire that object, when possible, for inclusion within the pages of these volumes. This special purpose clamp, which is fitted with a wire loop that is tightened by turning the clamp handle is just such a tool. It was obviously not designed for heavy use and looks to have been made to accommodate a wide range of sizes within its wire loop. A puzzler. We invite your input.* (GOOD+) **$45.00**

Z5-33. Unmarked: Double Reverse Ogee Router Plane. With Ivory Sole. From Coach Shop. Length: 13 Inches. *This extraordinary coachmaker's double reverse ogee shave is fitted with wear plates of elephant ivory on its sole. All original parts are present on this perfectly preserved and showy coachmaker's tool.* (FINE) **$375.00**

Z5-34. Unmarked No. 1: Solid Lignum Mallet. For Joiner. Superb Condition. Length: 12 1/2 Inches. *The head of this superb joiner's mallet is formed from the extra dense tropical vine lignum vitae.* (FINE) **$95.00**

Z5-35. Unmarked: Special Purpose Rounding Plane. With Brass Inlay. Mathieson Iron. Length: 11 Inches. *This specialized plane, which is fitted with a Mathieson iron and may have been made by Mathieson, was used for the rounding of dowels and spars. A most unusual specialized plane.* (GOOD) **$125.00**

Z5-36. Unmarked: Pair of Special Purpose Clamps. Turned Wood Screws. Most Unusual. Length: 18 Inches. *These clamps came together, and so they shall stay. The double arm example looks as though it was used to hold something that was then sawn or pared. Graphic.* (GOOD+) **$65.00**

Z5-37. Unmarked: Cooper's Double Plane. Uncommon Type. 7 1/2 Inch Width. Length: 42 Inches. *This double cooper's jointer would have been used for trimming the edges of barrel staves as they were being fit. A nice example of a classic cooper's tool.* (GOOD+) **$225.00**

Z5-38. Unmarked: Hand Forged Nut Wrench. Forged from File. Distinctive Form. Length: 11 1/2 Inches. *Not content to employ the classic "double end" style when fashioning this wrench, its maker added an extra opening on one end, just to be different. A graphic file forged tool.* (GOOD+) **$65.00**

Z5-39. Unmarked: American Birch Mitre Jack. Classic Form. Near New Condition. Length: 28 Inches. *Designed to be held in the bench vise of a woodworking bench, the mitre jack was used for precise planing of end grain joints for moldings, picture frames and the like. This superb example, which shows only minimal evidence of use, is formed from a series of laminated blocks of American Birch. The threads are in excellent condition and the tool is in perfect working order. As nice an example as we have ever offered.* (FINE) **$225.00**

Z5-40. Unmarked: Coachmaker's Double Router. With Center Fence. Owner "H. Weston". Length: 12 Inches. *A pair of ebony wedges accent this well preserved double coachmaker's router, which has been stamped with the name of a previous owner, one "H. Weston". Nice.* (GOOD+) **$75.00**

Z5-41. Unmarked: "Double Razee" Jointer. Plane. Raised Throat Section. Unusual Form. Length: 22 Inches. *A recent deaccession from the collection of the Granite State and the world's preeminent collector of double razee planes, this example has a decidedly different squared off pattern to its razee form. Art, for the price of wood. Ex-Riley Collection.* (GOOD) **$135.00**

Z5-42. Langley, London, England: Massive Cooper's Spoke Shave. For Inshave Work. Original Decal. Length: 15 Inches. *Nearly all of the original decal remains on this well preserved cooper's spoke shave from a prominent London toolmaker.* (GOOD+) **$95.00**

Z5-43. Unmarked: Pair of "Winking" Sticks. With Ivory Inlay. Solid Rosewood. Length: 15 3/4 Inches. *Used to sight down a piece of sawn lumber to determine the degree of "wind" in the wood, the use of these tools was facilitated by the application of sighting marks of inlaid ivory. A superb example of a classic woodworking accessory.* (GOOD+) **$55.00**

Z5-44. Unmarked: Early Picture Frame Clamp. Exhibited at Phipps Museum. Graphic Form. Length: 24 Inches. *Assembled by some long forgotten craftsman, this specialized framing clamp was on display at the Phipps Museum in Burton, Ohio until it was de-accessioned last fall following the death of the proprietor. An early and graphic tool in excellent working order.* (GOOD+) **$225.00**

Z5-45. Unmarked: Classic Burl Mallet. Original Handle. Usable Condition. Length: 9 Inches. *This well preserved burl mallet has what appears to be its original handle. A classic woodworking tool.* (GOOD+) **$85.00**

Group A6

A6-1. Marples & Sons, Wm., Hibernia Works.: Massive Beech Spoke Shave. 4 Inch Cutting Edge. Near New Condition. Length: 13 1/2 Inches. *This crispy beech spokeshave is in excellent working order and ready to use. Nice.* (GOOD+) **$55.00**

A6-2. Stanley Rule & Level No. 53: Adjustable Throat Spoke Shave. Early "Arch" Trademark. Ready to Use. Length: 10 1/2 Inches. *The early ca. 1880's "arch" trademark is imprinted on the cutting iron of this adjustable throat spokeshave. A good one.* (GOOD) **$45.00**

A6-3. Weston, C.H., Yarmouth, Maine: Cast Iron Spoke Shave. Uncommon Type. Clean and Sound. Length: 10 Inches. *C.H. Weston produced these graphic tools, which have his name cast into the cap, in Yarmouth, Maine, in the middle of the Nineteenth Century. A rare spokeshave from an uncommon Maine maker.* (GOOD) **$85.00**

A6-4. Stanley Rule & Level No. 66: Precision Hand Beader. With 7 Original Cutters. Complete and Excellent. Length: 12 Inches. *This beader has seen some use, but it is complete and could be put into working order quickly. Ready to go back to work.* (FAIR) **$125.00**

A6-5. Ellsworth, Geo., S. Garder (Mass.): Cabinet Scraper Spoke Shave. 1868-1871 Only. Not in Lamond. Length: 13 Inches. *George Ellsworth is listed in the Directory of American Toolmakers as an edge tool maker in Gardner, Massachusetts from 1868 to 1871. This cabinet scraper is clearly marked with his imprint. A rare scraper from a tool maker with a brief working history.* (GOOD+) **$285.00**

A6-6. Stanley Rule & Level No. 69: Patent Hand Beader. With Set of 6 Cutters. Super Rare and Early. Length: 4 3/4 Inches. *Nearly all original finishes remain on this example of Stanley's elusive No. 69 hand beader. A rare Stanley tool that is proudly offered without apology.* (FINE) **$645.00**

A6-7. Geral: Pair of Carriagemaker Spoke Shaves. Bronze Bodies. Adjustable Fences. Length: 9 Inches. *The product line of the "Geral" line of coachmakers tools is well documented in "Manufactured and Patented American Spokeshaves and Similar Tools", but little is known about who actually made these handsome and well made fine woodworking tools. These unmarked right and left hand shaves are unmarked, but fit the classic Geral pattern. A very pretty pair.* (FINE) **$285.00**

A6-8. Jennings & Co., C.E., New York, N.Y.: Patternmaker's Draw Knife. 4 Inch Blade. Near New Condition. Length: 10 1/2 Inches. *As a handy shop tool, there's no beating the Jennings 4 inch drawknife. This one is crisp, clean and ready to go to work. Nice.* (FINE) **$65.00**

A6-9. Buck, Tottenham Conn. Rd: Coachmaker's Double Router. Adjustable Depth of Cut. Brass Adjust Screw. Length: 16 Inches. *This specialty tool of the coach maker features a brass adjustment screw to regulate the depth of cut. A most unusual coachmaker's tool in excellent collector quality condition.* (GOOD+) **$75.00**

A6-10. Geral: Carriagemaker's Spoke Shave. Double Cutters. Adjustable Fence. Length: 13 1/2 Inches. *The recently published Patented and Manufactured American Spokeshaves lists many of the coachmaking tools produced under the "Geral" brand name. Very little is known about who made these tools, when they made them and where they were produced. This double carriagemaker's shave is a classic Geral tool. Unmarked, but unmistakable.* (GOOD+) **$145.00**

A6-11. White, L. & I.J., Buffalo, N.Y.: Rubadeaux Patent Spoke Shave. "Pat. 1869". For Cooper's Use. Length: 18 1/2 Inches. *Marked with the inscription "Pat. 1869" on the body of the tool, this is spokeshave is an example of the Rubadeaux Patent cooper's spokeshave. It is clean, sound and clearly marked.* (GOOD+) **$115.00**

A6-12. Unmarked: Coachmaker's Router Spoke Shave. With Double Blades. Adjustable Fence. Length: 14 1/2 Inches. *This coach router has an adjustable steel fence, a carved, circular escapement and a dual cutting iron arrangement. It is in excellent condition.* (GOOD+) **$125.00**

A6-13. Stanley Rule & Level No. 65: Adjustable Chamfer Spoke Shave. "Sweetheart" Trademark. Near New Condition. Length: 10 Inches. *This 1920's version of the adjustable chamfer spokeshave is in unused condition. Pristine.* (FINE) **$225.00**

A6-14. Unmarked: Set of 3 Coach Beaders. With Ivory Fences. From "W.T. Hall", Vermont. Length: 12 1/2 Inches. *The fences for this stepped set of 3 coachmakers beaders are made of solid ivory. All came from the coachmaking shop of one W.T. Hall, a carriagemaker in the State of Vermont. A dramatic set of tools that were gathered in the early days of tool collecting.* (GOOD+) **$465.00**

A6-15. Bailey, L., Boston, Mass. No. 9: Adjustable Throat Spoke Shave. Rare Early Version. With "Boston" Imprint. Length: 10 Inches. *Tool collectors familiar with Leonard Bailey's spectacular success in his later years sometimes forget that at one time he was a beginning inventor and manufacturer, offering products that were totally different than the standards of the woodworker's trade as it was then being practiced. This example of his earliest work is clearly marked with Bailey's name and Boston location. A classic example of the work of a bold, young genius of American manufacturing.* (GOOD+) **$265.00**

A6-16. Preston & Sons, Edward No. 77: Precision Adjust Spoke Shave. Gull Wing Handles. Scarce and Near New. Length: 10 Inches. *A precision screw at the top of the blade allows the depth of cut to be finely adjusted. An uncommon Preston spokeshave in nearly new condition.* (FINE) **$55.00**

A6-17. Unmarked: Brass Scraper Spoke Shave. With Hook Edge. Most Unusual. Length: 7 Inches. *A turned brass handle serves to guide the hook edge scraper clamped in the center of this craftsman made tool. A very showy and well made tool.* (GOOD+) **$65.00**

A6-18. Unmarked: Screw Adjust Spoke Shave. With Brass Screws. Ready to Use. Length: 11 Inches. *These screw adjust spokeshaves are a bit more convenient to use than the friction fit types. This one is in great working order.* (GOOD+) **$65.00**

A6-19. Mathieson & Sons, Glasgow: Solid Boxwood Spoke Shave. 2 1/2 Inch Cutter. Great Patina. Length: 11 Inches. *This extra clean boxwood spokeshave is boldly marked with the imprint of Scottish tool giant A. Mathieson. A great working tool.* (GOOD+) **$55.00**

A6-20. Pond, W.H., New Haven, Conn.: Double Coach Beader. Excellent Condition. Missing Fence. Length: 13 1/2 Inches. *This extra narrow coachmaker's beader is set up to cut in either direction. The fence is missing, but could be easily replaced.* (GOOD+) **$55.00**

A6-21. Millers Falls Company No. 2: "Four Faced" Spoke Shave. Removeable Handles. Near-New Condition. Length: 11 Inches. *This "four faced" spokeshave was so named because its series of blades and fixing screws were ordered in such a way as to permit exactly that many adjustments. Here's an example in great working order that retains more than 95% of its original finishes.* (FINE) **$165.00**

A6-22. Stanley Rule & Level No. 80: Cast Iron Cabinet Scraper. Patented May 2, 1914. Near New Condition. Length: 12 Inches. *Probably one of the most popular tools ever produced by Stanley, these were successful for the simple reason that they worked, and worked very well. Ready to use.* (FINE) **$65.00**

A6-23. Unmarked: Quadruple Coach Beader. Fruitwood Body. Uncommon Type. Length: 12 1/2 Inches. *A fixed fence set at 90 degrees works with the quadruple beading iron in this coachmaker's tool, which was used to apply the final details to panels. Whether or not you intend to build a carriage, it has plenty of potential for woodworking applications today.* (GOOD+) **$75.00**

A6-24. Pond, W.H., New Haven, Conn.: Coachmaker's Double Beader. With Adjustable Fence. Uncommon Type. Length: 13 1/2 Inches. *The end of the handle is marked with the Pond imprint. An adjustable brass fence can be locked into place to improve the utility of the tool.* (GOOD) **$85.00**

A6-25. Pond, W.H., New Haven, Conn.: Reversible Coach Beader. "Made For Brown Brothers". Excellent Patina. Length: 13 1/2 Inches. *This extra narrow Pond coach beader is marked "Made for Brown Bros.", who were likely coach builders. The adjustable fence is missing, but could be easily replaced.* (GOOD+) **$65.00**

A6-26. Unmarked: Beechwood Spoke Shave. 4 Inch Blade. Ready to Use. Length: 14 Inches. *Here's an extra wide beechwood spokeshave in excellent working order. Ready to use.* (GOOD+) **$45.00**

A6-27. Unmarked: Gull Wing Spoke Shave. Solid Brass Body. Precision Adjustment. Length: 11 Inches. *A massive gull wing shave in solid bronze, most likely from a pattern or carriage works. This one is fitted with an early Stanley cutting iron.* (GOOD+) **$110.00**

A6-28. Stanley Rule & Level No. 53: Adjustable Throat Spoke Shave. "Sweetheart" Trademark. Near New Condition. Length: 10 1/2 Inches. *A crisp and clean "Sweetheart" era example of the No. 53 adjustable spokeshave.* (FINE) **$55.00**

A6-29. Marples & Sons, Wm., Hibernia Works.: Solid Boxwood Spoke Shave. 3 Inch Cutter. Unused Condition. Length: 11 1/2 Inches. *You can be the first to use this pristine boxwood spokeshave from Sheffield makers William Marples & Sons. Mint.* (FINE) **$75.00**

A6-30. Windsor Mfg. Co., Windsor, Vermont: Patent Scratch Beader. Patented March 10, 1885. Complete With 2 Cutters. Length: 10 1/4 Inches. *Produced in several different styles during the course of its production, the Windsor Patent beader is one of the most collectible of shave-like tools. This, the second production model has a rotating circular blade with various beading cutters filed into the edge. Loosening of an adjustment screw allows the blade to be set precisely into place for use. A well preserved example of a classic collectible tool.* (GOOD+) **$295.00**

A6-31. Unmarked: Birdseye Maple Scraper. With Stanley "Sweetheart" Blade. Ready to Use. Length: 13 1/2 Inches. *The blade in this homemade scraper is marked with the Stanley "Sweetheart" trademark, giving us a clue as to when it was made. The body is formed of highly figured birdseye maple.* (GOOD+) **$85.00**

A6-32. Preston & Sons, E.: Registered Nickel Plated Spoke Shave. Registered No. 322021. Superb Condition. Length: 7 Inches. *All of the original shiny nickel plating remains on this diminutive spokeshave from Edward Preston & Sons. Even the tool heathens will be impressed with this one. A showstopper.* (FINE) **$165.00**

A6-33. Unmarked: Set of 8 Coachmakers Beaders. Flutes and Beads. Owner "N.T. Hall". Length: 14 1/2 Inches. *Each of these well preserved fluting and beading shaves came together from the undisturbed Vermont coachmaker's shop of one N.T. Hall. A great set of tools from a practitioner of a now nearly lost art. Highly recommended.* (GOOD+) **$645.00**

A6-34. Cincinnati Tool Co., The: "Martin's" Spoke Shave. Curved Sole. Excellent Condition. Length: 11 Inches. *The curved sole on this unusual spokeshave from the Cincinnati Tool Company would have improved its ability to work with concave shapes. The innovative owner made use of the top of the cutting iron to form it into a special purpose scraper. A seldom seen spokeshave with character.* (GOOD+) **$85.00**

A6-35. Bailey, L., Boston, Mass.: Double Cutter Spoke Shave. Flat and Concave. Early and Excellent. Length: 10 Inches. *A rare example of the pre-planemaking of Leonard Bailey, the uncontested champion of metallic plane innovation this paired flat and circular spokeshave is marked with the "L. Bailey, Boston" mark dating from the 1850's. Early and well preserved.* (GOOD+) **$85.00**

A6-36. Cincinnati Tool Co., The: Convex Bottom Spoke Shave. 2 Inch Wide Cutter. Excellent Condition. Length: 11 Inches. *A great convex soled spokeshave that's just waiting for an ambitious would-be chairmaker to put it to use. There is a small "hang hole" through one handle. A clean and handsome tool.* (FINE) **$145.00**

A6-37. Stanley Rule & Level No. 51: Cast Iron Spoke Shave. With Screw Cap Lock. Early Type 1. Length: 10 Inches. *This example of the No. 51 shave has the flattened turnscrew locking mechanism for the cutting iron that was unique to the "Type 1" version of this number. A nice example of an early Stanley spokeshave.* (GOOD+) **$45.00**

A6-38. Stanley Rule & Level: "Universal" Spoke Shave. Patented February 25, 1896. Removable Handles. Length: 9 1/2 Inches. *For nearly 50 years, beginning in the mid-1890's and ending with the onset of the Second World War, Stanley produced this, the uncontested winner of the "Jack of all Spokeshaves" contest. Fitted with removable rosewood handles and interchangeable flat and concave soles, the handles can be removed and repositioned in the center for working in tight corners. A great working tool in excellent condition.* (GOOD+) **$115.00**

A6-39. Unmarked: Classic Boxwood Spoke Shave. 3 Inch Cutting Edge. Ready to Use. Length: 11 1/2 Inches. *Part of the original decal remains on this extra crisp boxwood spokeshave. Crisp, clean and ready to use.* (GOOD+) **$55.00**

A6-40. Unmarked: Boxwood Coachmaker's Beader. Excellent Condition. Great Patina. Length: 11 Inches. *Formed from a solid piece of knotty boxwood and aged to a golden patina from many years of careful use, This coachmaker's beading plane is one of the prettiest tools offered in this volume. Magnificent and highly recommended.* (FINE) **$225.00**

A6-41. Stanley Rule & Level No. 65: Adjustable Chamfer Spoke Shave. "Sweetheart" Trademark. Unused Condition. Length: 10 Inches. *This 1920's version of the adjustable chamfer spokeshave is in unused condition. Pristine.* (FINE) **$245.00**

A6-42. Preston & Sons, Edward No. 77: Precision Adjust Spoke Shave. Gull Wing Handles. Scarce and Near New. Length: 10 Inches. *A precision screw at the top of the blade allows the depth of cut to be finely adjusted. An uncommon Preston spokeshave in nearly new condition.* (FINE) **$55.00**

A6-43. Humphrey Tool Co., Warren, Mass.: Early Patent Spoke Shave. Unmarked Example. With Handle Adapters. Length: 10 1/2 Inches. *The Humphrey Tool Company manufactured this, their so-called "cavity plane" under a patent granted in 1882. This example is clean, complete and ready to display. An opportunity investment for the potential collector of early spokeshaves.* (GOOD) **$145.00**

A6-44. Stanley Rule & Level No. 55: Concave Bottom Spoke Shave. "Sweetheart" Trademark. Crisp and Clean. Length: 10 Inches. *These work great for trimming handles and other similar work. This clean example is marked with the ca. 1920's "Sweetheart" trademark.* (GOOD+) **$55.00**

A6-45. Stanley Rule & Level No. 60: Concave, Convex Spoke Shave. 1 1/2 Inch Cutters. "Sweetheart" Trademark. Length: 11 Inches. *This convex and straight-blade shave was produced in Stanley's heyday in the 1920's and bears the famous "Sweetheart" trademark. Crisp, clean and ready to use.* (GOOD+) **$55.00**

A6-46. Bailey, L., New Britain, Conn.: Early Cast Iron Spoke Shave. Distinctive Mark. Rare and Sound. Length: 9 1/2 Inches. *A most unusual and interesting shave. Unlike most of Bailey's other spokeshaves, which bear a Boston mark from his pre-Stanley days, this one is clearly imprinted with the New Britain mark, indicating either that he continued his private business after associating with Stanley or recommenced the production of spokeshaves after falling out with Stanley in the mid-1870's. A historically significant spokeshave.* (GOOD) **$145.00**

Group B6

B6-1. Eagle Square Mfg. Co. No. 11: 12 Inch Framing Square. With Eagle Imprint. Crisp and Clean. Length: 12 Inches. *A bold eagle touchmark is visible at the joint of this uncommon 12 inch "framing" square. It is in excellent condition.* (GOOD+) **$45.00**

B6-2. Stanley Rule & Level No. 21: 12 Inch Nickel Plated Combination Square. Patented January 23, 1917. New Condition, Original Box. Length: 12 Inches. *Stanley's patented adjustable 12 inch combination square, complete and perfect in its original box. A most unusual "in the box" item. Nice.* (FINE) **$245.00**

B6-3. Marples & Co., William, Sheffield: 3 Inch Rosewood and Brass Try Square. Diamond Brass Escutcheon. Extra Crisp and Clean. Length: 4 1/4 Inches. *Here's a crisp, clean pocket sized try square from a highly respected English maker. Pretty to look at and handy to use.* (GOOD+) **$35.00**

B6-4. Starrett Co., L. S., Athol, Mass.: No. 492: Protractor Head For Combination Square. Near New Condition. Ready to Use. Length: 6 Inches. *If you have a Starrett combination square, it can be easily upgraded to an engineer's square simply by adding one of these.* (FINE) **$55.00**

B6-5. Starrett Co., L. S., Athol, Mass.: No. 11 H: Machinist's Combination Square. Graduated in 64ths. New Condition, Original Box. Length: 6 Inches. *The original box has kept this Starrett classic in perfect condition.* (FINE) **$95.00**

B6-6. Stanley Rule & Level (Unmarked) No. 2: Combined Mitre and Try Square. Patented April 16, 1872. Excellent Condition. Length: 4 1/2 Inches. *The patent date is stamped in a circular pattern on this early example of the No. 2 try square. A maker's name has been tastefully stamped in the handle, otherwise excellent.* (GOOD+) **$65.00**

B6-7. Unmarked: Classic English Try Square. Rosewood Handle. Decorative Escutcheon. Length: 11 Inches. *Here's a classic English try square having a decorative, polished brass escutcheon plate.* (GOOD) **$15.00**

B6-8. Howell Tool Co., Orange, Mass.: Machinist's 4 Inch Try Square. Obscure Maker. Ca. 1900. Length: 4 1/2 Inches. *This small square is imprinted with the name of the Howell Tool Company. Writing in "American Machinist's Tools", Ken Cope speculates that the company worked ca. 1900. A rare square.* (GOOD) **$45.00**

B6-9. Disston & Sons, Henry, Philadelphia, Penn.: No. 10: Beech Handled Try Square. Patented April 27, 1909. Unused Condition. Length: 6 Inches. *The handles of this patented mitre square are fastened securely in position by a series of massive rivets. Condition is as new. Mint.* (FINE) **$65.00**

B6-10. Starrett Co., The L.S., Athol, Mass.: No. 134: Cross Test Level. Dual Vial. New Condition, Original Box. Length: 3 Inches. *An extremely well preserved example of a Starrett level of uncommon form. New and in the box.* (FINE) **$85.00**

B6-11. Standard Tool Co., Athol, Mass.: "Chaplin's Patent" Combination Square. With Both Heads. Offset Groove Rule. Length: 12 Inches. *This extra-clean example of the Chaplin's patent combination square needs only its original scribe to make it complete. A tough tool to find in this condition.* (GOOD+) **$195.00**

B6-12. Stanley Rule & Level No. 20: Rosewood and Brass Try Square. Rare 3 Inch Size. Patented December 29, 1896. Length: 4 1/4 Inches. *The December 29, 1996 patent imprinted on this square was for the application of the "Hand-y" feature to this type of tool. This feature was a groove in the handle to facilitate the grip of the user. This turn of the century square is in excellent condition.* (GOOD+) **$55.00**

B6-13. Starrett Co., L. S., Athol, Mass.: Engineer's Combination Square. With Protractor Head. Ready to Use. Length: 12 Inches. *Both the protractor head and the center finder head are present on this extra clean combination square. A precision tool in top condition.* (FINE) **$85.00**

B6-14. Stanley Rule & Level No. 20: Rosewood and Brass Try Square. 12 Inch Size. Ca. 1915. "V" Trademark. Length: 13 1/2 Inches. *The ca. 1915 "V" shaped trademark of the Stanley Rule & Level Company is imprinted on this well preserved 12 inch try square. Crisp, clean and ready to use.* (GOOD+) **$35.00**

B6-15. Stanley Rule & Level No. 20: 6 Inch Rosewood Handle. Try Square. "Notched" Trademark. Unused Condition. Length: 7 Inches. *The Stanley No. 20 was their biggest and best seller, this is an example of why. This unused example is ready to be put to work for the first time.* (FINE) **$45.00**

B6-16. Brown & Sharpe Mfg., Providence: Precision 6 Inch Combination Square. No. 4 Graduated. Missing Scribe. Length: 6 Inches. *If you can make do without the original scribe, this high-quality square is a bargain. Ready to use.* (GOOD+) **$45.00**

B6-17. Starrett Co., The L.S., Athol, Mass.: No. 10: Adjustable Inclinometer Level. With 18 Inch Blade. Rare and Excellent. Length: 18 Inches. *These inclinometer squares were included in the Starrett line for many years. This clean example is in excellent working order. A previous owner has touched up the paint and it appears as new. Nice.* (GOOD+) **$185.00**

B6-18. Adjustable Gauge Co., Lexington, Kentuky: Patent Angle Divider Gauge. Patented August 11, 1908. Extra Crisp and Clean. Length: 8 1/4 Inches. *This was designed to simplify the complex mathematical task of figuring the angles needed when fitting out the framing for the Victorian-style houses that grace every small town East of the Mississippi. complete in all respects and very well preserved, this rare tool is one of just a few patented by residents of the State of Kentucky.* (FINE) **$225.00**

B6-19. Stanley Rule & Level No. 20: Rosewood and Brass Try Square. 8 Inch Size. Unused Condition. Length: 9 Inches. *The Stanley No. 20 was their biggest and best seller, this is an example of why. This one has apparently never been used. Mint.* (FINE) **$45.00**

B6-20. Houle: "Houle" Try Square and Bevel. "Pat. Appl'd For". Replaced Fixing Screw. Length: 10 Inches. *One of the fixing screws has been replaced, but this "Houle" combination tool is otherwise clean and sound. A rare combination tool.* (GOOD) **$85.00**

B6-21. Turner & Co, Thomas: 6 Inch Rosewood Try Square. Brass Diamond Escutcheon. Early and Excellent. Length: 7 1/4 Inches. *The name of the English maker Thomas Turner & Company is boldly marked on this early try square. Crisp, clean and ready to use.* (GOOD+) **$25.00**

B6-22. Stanley Rule & Level No. 2: Combined Mitre and Try Square. Patented February 8, 1898. Crisp and Clean. Length: 4 Inches. *No apologies for the 1898 patent version of Stanley's combined try and mitre square. The patent applies to a further modification of the "Hand-y" feature first used on Stanley levels in 1891. A very well preserved 100 year old square.* (GOOD+) **$35.00**

B6-23. Stanley Rule & Level No. 21 1/2: 6 Inch Patent Combination Square. Marked Patented 1-23-17. "Sweetheart" Trademark. Length: 6 Inches. *This cast iron combination square is marked with the "Sweetheart" logo and the patent date. Much less common than its first cousin, the No. 21, this one has an open cast body. A rare square.* (GOOD+) **$185.00**

B6-24. Stanley Rule & Level No. 20: Rosewood and Brass Try Square. 8 Inch Size. Unused Condition. Length: 9 Inches. *This 8 inch American made rosewood handle try square is in brand new condition. Ready to use, if you choose.* (FINE) **$45.00**

B6-25. Stanley Rule & Level No. 14: Type I Adjustable Try Square. Early Japan Finish. Patented October 24, 1882. Length: 6 Inches. *Stanley apparently sold very few of these adjustable try squares. This japan finished version would have been produced before 1909. It is clearly marked with the patent date. A rare square.* (GOOD) **$115.00**

B6-26. Stanley Rule & Level (Unmarked) No. 15: Early "Type I" Try Square. Cast Brass Handle. Early and Unusual. Length: 7 1/2 Inches. *Among the least common of Stanley's try squares, the No. 15 featured a cast brass handle. This "Type I" example, which is not imprinted with the Stanley mark, would date from the 1870's or thereabout.* (GOOD) **$65.00**

B6-27. Unmarked: Draughtsman's Try Square. Macassar Ebony. Ivory Inserts. Length: 31 Inches. *Intended from the beginning to be something very special, this spectacular draughtsman's adjustable "T" square has been artfully formed from rich Macassar Ebony and ornamented with German silver fittings and ivory inserts. It is in spectacularly well preserved condition and will serve as a focal point of a collection of drafting tools. Simply extraordinary.* (FINE) **$385.00**

B6-28. Disston & Sons, Henry: Early Machinist's Try Square. Cast Iron Handle. Scarce and Excellent. Length: 6 Inches. *These graphic squares were produced in the 1870's and 1880's when Disston first began to market accessory tools. A nice example of an uncommon try square that is clearly marked with the Disston name.* (GOOD+) **$65.00**

B6-29. Stanley Rule & Level No. 20: Rosewood Handle Try Square. Rare 18 Inch Size. Patented June 2, 1891. Length: 18 Inches. *The Stanley No. 20 was their biggest and best seller. However, there are very few examples of this, at 18 inches in length, the largest size offered in this series. A rare Stanley square in top collector quality condition.* (FINE) **$295.00**

B6-30. Stanley Rule & Level (Unmarked) No. 20: Rosewood and Brass Try Square. 3 Inch Size. With Hang Hole. Length: 4 1/4 Inches. *A "hang hole" through the blade does not detract from the utility of this clean try square. A bargain.* (GOOD) **$15.00**

B6-31. Topp & Co., G.A., Indianapolis, Indiana: Topps Framing Tool Try Square. Patented November 1, 1892. With Horsehead Trademark. Length: 9 1/2 Inches. *This example of the Topp's 1892 patent is clean and complete, but just a bit dark.* (GOOD) **$115.00**

B6-32. Starrett Co., L. S., Athol, Mass.: Machinist's Combination Square. With Center Head. Ready to Use. Length: 12 Inches. *This Starrett Square is missing the scribe, but is otherwise in excellent condition. Extra nice.* (FINE) **$35.00**

B6-33. Disston & Sons, Henry: No. 5 1/2: Nickel Plated Cast Iron Try Square. With Cast Logo. Excellent Condition. Length: 8 Inches. *The Disston logo is cast into the handle of this well preserved try square. A good one.* (GOOD+) **$45.00**

B6-34. Starrett Co., L.S.: Nickel Plated Patent Combination Square. Early Starrett Mark. With Perforations. Length: 12 Inches. *The edges of the head of this early Starrett combination square were originally nickel plated—a most unusual variation. The blade is fitted with the perforations specified in Starrett's 1879 patent, but the blade is not marked with the patent date. Missing the scribe, but otherwise excellent. A rare and early combination square from L.S. Starrett.* (GOOD+) **$115.00**

B6-35. Unmarked: Massive Tiger Maple Try Square. With Ogee Ends. Owner "C.C. Mitchell. Length: 21 1/2 Inches. *This extraordinary oversize try square was artfully formed from a highly figured piece of tiger maple by one C.C. Mitchell, whose name is imprinted on the tool. The central joint is a fitted dovetailed mortise of the sort that only a very accomplished woodworker could produce. The end of the square is formed into an ogee shape, and a secondary ornamental shape is applied halfway down the blade. A dramatic early woodworking tool.* (FINE) **$785.00**

B6-36. Stanley Rule & Level No. 10: 8 Inch Machinist's Try Square. With Hand- E Feature. Uncommon Type. Length: 9 Inches. *Although these squares were included in the Stanley product line for nearly 50 years, they were nowhere near as popular as the more common carpenter's squares. This clean and well marked example is in excellent working order.* (GOOD+) **$55.00**

B6-37. D. & S., Bangor, Maine: Patented Solid Steel Try Square. Patented October 6, 1857. Rare 2 Inch Size. Length: 2 Inches. *The ca. 1860 imprint of pioneering precision tool makers Darling & Swartz of Bangor, Maine is printed on the blade of this early try square. An clean and collectible example of the work of an historically important maker.* (GOOD) **$85.00**

B6-38. Disston & Sons, H., Philadelphia, Penn. No. 1: Rosewood Handle Try Square. Blued Steel Blade. Near New Condition. Length: 4 Inches. *This Disston offering has yet to be used. Of equal quality to any square ever made, this one is ready to complement the tool kit of a modern woodworker.* (FINE) **$45.00**

B6-39. Stanley Rule & Level No. 122: "Defiance" Combination Square. Full Nickel Plating. Filled Level Casting. Length: 12 Inches. *The "Defiance" combination square featured dual level vials set into the casting. This one is in superb condition. Nice.* (FINE) **$45.00**

B6-40. Disston & Sons, H., Philadelphia, Penn. No. 1: Rosewood Handle Try Square. Blued Steel Blade. Unused Condition. Length: 10 Inches. *A new old stock example of Disston's best try square. As good as anything made before or since. Perfect.* (FINE) **$65.00**

B6-41. Disston & Sons, H., Philadelphia, Penn. No. 1: Rosewood Handle Try Square. Blued Steel Blade. Near New Condition. Length: 10 Inches. *The graduated 10 inch blade on this Disston try square retains nearly all of its original blued finish. Minty crispy nice.* (FINE) **$45.00**

B6-42. Unmarked: Rosewood and Brass Try Square. Blued Steel Blade. Near New Condition. Length: 6 Inches. *A solid brass plate serves to fix the blade at its proper angle on this essentially unused rosewood and brass try square. Ready to use.* (FINE) **$35.00**

B6-43. Thrall & Son, Willis, Hartford, Conn.: 5 Inch Rosewood Handle Try Square. Distinctive Logo. Etched Graduations. Length: 6 Inches. *The Willis Thrall firm of Hartford was active in the years preceding the Civil War. Their products were of exceptional quality, of which this square is an excellent example. Nicely marked with their distinctive oval imprint and featuring a level of precision graduation to the blade that we have not previously encountered.* (GOOD+) **$115.00**

B6-44. Stanley Tools (England): Rosewood Handle Try Square. 12 Inch Blade. Unused Condition. Length: 14 Inches. *Stanley moved much of their production of tools to England in 1962. This English made Stanley try square is in unused condition.* (FINE) **$35.00**

B6-45. Stanley Rule & Level No. 2: Combined Mitre and Try Square. Ca 1915 Trademark. Extra Crisp and Clean. Length: 9 Inches. *Stanley's classic "V" shaped trademark that was introduced ca. 1915 is stamped on the blade of this well preserved combination square. A nice example in excellent working order.* (GOOD+) **$35.00**

B6-46. Nicholls Mfg. Co., Ottumwa, Iowa: 12 Inch Advertising Square. "Since 1896". Rare and Excellent. Length: 12 Inches. *This square was apparently an advertising giveaway from this prolific Iowa based maker of squares and accessory tools. The "hang hole" in the body looks to be original. An uncommon toolmaker's promotional item.* (GOOD+) **$65.00**

Group C6

C6-1. Stanley Rule & Level No. 45: Combination Plane. 99% Nickel Plating. Near New Condition. Length: 12 Inches. *If you're looking for a clean, complete example of Stanley's No. 45 combination plane at a bargain price, here it is. As your first project, you can make a fitted box to hold the plane. Extra nice.* (FINE) **$345.00**

C6-2. Stanley Rule & Level No. 190: Cast Iron Rabbet Plane. 1 1/2 Inch Width. 98% Original Paint. Length: 10 1/2 Inches. *Stanley's 190 series of fixed-width rabbeting planes are handy tools for the home shop. At 1 1/2 inch in width, the No. 190 is extremely versatile. Nearly new.* (FINE) **$55.00**

C6-3. Stanley Rule & Level No. 4 1/2: Wide, Heavy Smooth Plane. Rosewood Handle and Knob. Ca. 1930's. Length: 10 1/2 Inches. *Looking for a great working heavy smoothing plane. Here's an exceptionally nice No. 4 1/2 fitted out with handles of Brazilian Rosewood. A great working tool that is ready to provide several lifetimes of service. The rosewood handles have a particularly striking grain pattern. A great working tool.* (GOOD+) **$195.00**

C6-4. Stanley Rule & Level No. 55: Patent Combination Plane. With 4 Boxes of Cutters. Early Chestnut Box. Length: 11 1/2 Inches. *Dating from the very earliest days of the manufacture of the No. 55, this example of Stanley's "Planing Mill Unto Itself" is complete in the original chestnut box with all original parts, including the screwdriver. A copy of the "Stanley Combination Plane" book, which includes a reprint of the instructions, will be provided to the purchaser. A perfect example that has been very little used.* (GOOD+) **$845.00**

C6-5. Sargent & Co., New Haven, Conn.: No. 710: "Autoset" Patent Metallic Plane. "V.B.M." Trademark. Near New Condition. Length: 10 Inches. *Sargent's "Autoset" planes were a later, but most interesting, entry in the competition to produce the most involved adjustment mechanism on a metallic plane. This example of the equivalent of Stanley's No. 4 plane, which features an extraordinarily long, sloping horn to the tote, is in nearly new condition. For a great collectible plane, we recommend this Autoset No. 10.* (FINE) **$325.00**

C6-6. Stanley Rule & Level No. 65: Low Angle Block Plane. Nickel Plated Cap. Excellent Condition. Length: 7 Inches. *The No. 65 was Stanley's basic wide-body low angle block plane for many years. The knuckle joint cap provides a positive lock and the screw adjustment will precisely adjust the cut. The nickel on the cap of this one has dulled a bit, but the plane is in excellent condition.* (GOOD+) **$85.00**

C6-7. Stanley Rule & Level No. 5 1/4: "Junior Jack" Plane. 1 3/4 Inch Cutter. Rosewood Handles. Length: 11 Inches. *The "Junior" jack plane, was the width of a No. 3 and just a bit shorter than a No. 5. Although these were marketed to manual training schools, these tools have found favor among latter-day woodworkers. This pristine example is ready to be put immediately to work or used to fill out a collection of top quality Stanley tools.* (FINE) **$185.00**

C6-8. Stanley Rule & Level No. 7: Cast Iron Jointer Plane. 95% Original Paint. Rosewood Handles. Length: 22 Inches. *Nearly all of the original paint remains on this crispy clean jointer plane that dates from the late 1930's. The rosewood handles are sound and there is plenty of cutting iron remaining. A great working plane in excellent condition.* (GOOD+) **$165.00**

C6-9. Stanley Rule & Level No. 9 1/2: Adjustable Throat Plane. With Precision Adjust. Ready to Use. Length: 6 Inches. *Fitted with an adjustable throat mechanism as well as independent lateral adjustment and depth-of-cut features, the No. 9 1/2 block plane was a mainstay of the Stanley line for many years. This one is in excellent working order.* (GOOD+) **$45.00**

C6-10. Stanley Rule & Level No. 4 1/2 C: Heavy Smoothing Plane. Corrugated Sole. Ready to Use. Length: 10 Inches. *The corrugated sole version of the Stanley No. 4 1/2 is far less common than its smooth soled counterpart. This one is in excellent condition and ready for a lifetime of use.* (GOOD+) **$215.00**

C6-11. Stanley Rule & Level No. 4 1/2: Heavy Smoothing Plane. World War II Era Example. Near New Condition. Length: 10 Inches. *The depth of cut adjustment screw on this World War II era heavy smoothing plane is made of Bakelite as a consequence of wartime limitations on the use of brass. Condition is nearly new. Extra nice.* (FINE) **$125.00**

C6-12. Stanley Rule & Level No. 604 1/2: "Bedrock" Smoothing Plane. Early Type. Rare and Excellent. Length: 10 Inches. *As a usable, working, heavy smoothing plane, there is simply no equal amone American-manufactured tools to the Bedrock No. 604 1/2. This example of the "early" style is clean, sound and ready to use.* (GOOD+) **$445.00**

C6-13. Stanley Rule & Level No. 10: Bench Rabbett Plane. Ca. 1907 Trademark. Near New Condition. Length: 13 Inches. *Nearly all original finishes remain on this well preserved example of Stanley's longer carriage maker's rabbet plane. An increasingly difficult plane to find, especially in this kind of condition.* (FINE) **$285.00**

C6-14. Stanley Rule & Level No. 65: Low Angle Block Plane. Knuckle Joint Cap. Unused Condition. Length: 7 Inches. *Here's a crispy clean example of Stanley's best wide, low-angle block plane. All of the shiny nickel plating remains on the knuckle joint cap. An increasingly difficult plane to find. Absolutely perfect.* (FINE) **$1,651.00**

C6-15. Stanley Rule & Level No. 7: Cast Iron Jointer Plane. Rosewood Handles. 99% Original Paint. Length: 22 Inches. *Virtually all of the shiny original paint remains on this well preserved Stanley Jointer plane. The blade is a bit dirty, but it is not rusted or corroded in any way. A great working tool.* (FINE) **$185.00**

C6-16. Stanley Rule & Level No. 4 1/2: Wide, Heavy Smooth Plane. Rosewood Handle and Knob. "Sweetheart" Trademark. Length: 10 1/2 Inches. *The cutting iron of this woodworking classic is marked with Stanley's "Sweetheart" trademark, which dates from the 1920's. Nearly all original paint and a full cutting iron remain. Ready to go back to work.* (FINE) **$225.00**

C6-17. Stanley Rule & Level No. 604 1/2: "Bedrock" Smoothing Plane. Later Type, Square Sides. Ready to Use. Length: 10 Inches. *As a usable, working, heavy smoothing plane, there is simply no equal among American-manufactured tools to the Bedrock No. 604 1/2. These planes are as wide as the No. 7, yet stocky as the No. 4. In working large flat surfaces, the "Bedrock" frog mechanism serves its purpose extremely well. This well preserved example retains 85% of its original paint and is ready to be put immediately to work.* (GOOD+) **$645.00**

C6-18. Stanley Rule & Level No. 7: 22 Inch Jointer Plane. Rosewood Handles. Ca. 1890's. Length: 22 Inches. *These early Stanley planes often have handles of exceptionally darkly-grained and highly-figured rosewood. This early example is one such plane. An early example that is still in fine working condition. Needs a light cleaning, but is crisp and ready to use.* (GOOD+) **$115.00**

C6-19. Stanley Rule & Level No. 9 1/4: Cast Iron Block Plane. Non-Adjustable Throat. 95% Original Paint. Length: 6 Inches. *The No. 9 1/4 block plane was the functional equivalent of the No. 9 1/2, with the exception of the absence of a throat adjustment mechanism. This one is in excellent working order.* (GOOD+) **$55.00**

C6-20. Stanley Rule & Level No. 65: Low Angle Block Plane. Ca. 1915. Near New Condition. Length: 7 Inches. *This pre World War I version of the Stanley No. 65 block plane is in brand new condition. Choice quality on a very hard to find plane.* (FINE) **$145.00**

C6-21. Stanley Rule & Level No. 4: Cast Iron Smooth Plane. With 3 Patent Dates. Type "12" Pattern. Length: 9 Inches. *This classic "Type 12" smoothing plane has the characteristic 3 patent dates cast into the sole and is fitted with the later style "high" front knob. A great working Stanley plane.* (FINE) **$155.00**

C6-22. Stanley Rule & Level No. 4 1/2: Wide, Heavy Smooth Plane. Ca. 1890's - 1900. Later Style Cutter. Length: 10 1/2 Inches. *Looking for a great working heavy smoothing plane. Here's an exceptionally nice No. 4 1/2 fitted out with handles of Brazilian Rosewood. This plane was made ca. 1890, but is fitted with a full ca. 1930's cutting iron. A great working tool.* (GOOD+) **$185.00**

C6-23. Stanley Rule & Level No. 386: Patent Adjustable Jointer Gauge. Rosewood Knob. 99% Nickel Plating. Length: 14 Inches. *Nearly all of the shiny nickel plating remains on this pristine example of Stanley's popular jointer gauge. Nearly new.* (FINE) **$165.00**

C6-24. Stanley Rule & Level No. 603: Early "Bedrock" Plane. Complete and Sound. Ca. 1905. Length: 14 Inches. *A great working example of Stanley's early style "Bedrock" smother in the tough to find 8 inch size. It is a bit dirty, but will clean up nicely.* (GOOD+) **$155.00**

C6-25. Stanley Rule & Level No. 40: Beech Handle Scrub Plane. Ca. 1930's. 95% Original Paint. Length: 11 Inches. *Nearly all of the original paint remains on this beech handled scrub plane. A tough tool to find in this condition. Nice.* (FINE) **$115.00**

C6-26. Stanley Rule & Level No. 5: Rosewood Handle Jack Plane. Sweetheart Trademark. Superb Condition. Length: 14 Inches. *This classic "Type 13" jack plane is in virtually unused condition. A great working tool in top condition.* (FINE) **$115.00**

C6-27. Stanley Rule & Level No. 45: Multi Purpose Combination Plane. With 27 Cutting Irons. "Sweetheart" Trademark.. Length: 9 Inches. *The original owner of this combination plane apparently added to the original assortment of irons by acquiring a few extras. A nice working plane with more than enough blades.* (GOOD+) **$295.00**

C6-28. Stanley Rule & Level No. 78: Duplex Filletster Plane. Sweetheart Trademark. New Condition, Original Box. Length: 9 1/2 Inches. *The bottom of the box has kept this "Sweetheart" era duplex bullnose, rabbet and filletster plane in nearly new condition. Extra nice.* (FINE) **$115.00**

C6-29. Ohio Tool Co., Columbus, Ohio: No. 09 1/2: Adjustable Block Metallic Plane. With Lever Adjust. Uncommon Type. Length: 6 Inches. *This early Ohio Tool Company Block plane features their distinctive throat adjustment mechanism. More than 90% of the original paint remains.* (GOOD+) **$165.00**

C6-30. Stanley Rule & Level No. 603 C: "Bedrock" Smoothing Plane. Ca. 1915 Trademark. 95% Original Paint. Length: 8 1/2 Inches. *Nearly all of the original paint remains on this "Bedrock" smoother, which dates from ca. 1910. A great working tool in top condition.* (GOOD+) **$235.00**

C6-31. Stanley Rule & Level No. 78: Duplex Rabbet, Fillet Plane. Early "Vine" Casting. Patented January 30, 1883. Length: 10 Inches. *Both of dates of the early patent that introduced the Stanley No. 78 rabbet and filletster plane are marked on the cutting iron of this extremely well preserved early example.* (GOOD+) **$110.00**

C6-32. Stanley Rule & Level No. 607 C: "Bedrock" Jointer Plane. With Corrugated Sole. 99% Original Paint. Length: 22 Inches. *This later style bedrock with corrugated bottom is in superb condition with more than 99% of the original shiny black japanning and most of the original Stanley decal. Highly recommended.* (FINE) **$445.00**

C6-33. Stanley Rule & Level No. 71 1/2: Nickel Plated Router Plane. Patented October 29, 1901. With 2 Original Irons. Length: 7 1/2 Inches. *Stanley's "closed throat" router plane is much less common than the later "improved" model, and much more in demand by contemporary woodworkers. This clean example comes with a pair of cutting irons in the 1/4 inch and 1/2 inch size. Ready to use.* (FINE) **$125.00**

C6-34. Stanley Rule & Level No. 45: Multi Purpose Combination Plane. Complete and Ready to Use. New Condition, Original Box. Length: 9 Inches. *Complete and shiny in its original pasteboard box, this ca. 1920's plane features the desirable "micro-dial" fence, two full boxes of cutters and the original instruction manual. A great working plane in excellent condition.* (FINE) **$365.00**

C6-35. Stanley Rule & Level No. 5: Classic "Type 12" Plane. High Front Knob. 98% Original Paint. Length: 14 Inches. *Nearly all of the shiny original black japan finish remains on this jack plane of Stanley's highly desirable "Type 12" series, which featured the recently-invented throat adjustment screw and the "high" front knob. Crisp, clean and ready to use.* (FINE) **$125.00**

C6-36. Unmarked: Early Cast Iron Scraper. "Pat. Apl'd. For". Distinctive Handles. Length: 10 1/2 Inches. *There seems to be no end to the number of variations on the theme of scrapers and spokeshaves. No matter how many tools one sees, and how many collections are visited, it is simply not possible to see everything. This adjustable cast iron scraper, easily distinguished by its uplifted cast iron handles formed into flat, circular finials, is marked "Pat. Apl'd For" in the casting. A series of 3 screws fix the unmarked cutting iron in place and adjust the tension. A classic Victorian scraper that we have not previously encountered. Rare.* (GOOD+) **$245.00**

C6-37. Stanley Rule & Level No. 71 1/2: Closed Throat Router Plane. With Script Logo. 1 Original Cutter. Length: 8 Inches. *One original cutter remains with this crispy clean closed throat router plane. The body is cast with the 1901 patent date. Nice.* (GOOD+) **$65.00**

C6-38. Stanley Rule & Level No. 60 1/2: Low Angle Block Plane. 95% Original Paint. Ready to Use. Length: 6 Inches. *Identical to the No. 60, but with japanned cap, this later version is in clean, ready to use condition. A full cutting iron will provide a lifetime of use. A tough plane to come by.* (FINE) **$65.00**

C6-39. Stanley Rule & Level No. 8: Cast Iron Jointer Plane. Rosewood Handles. 99% Original Paint. Length: 24 Inches. *More than 99% of the shiny original japan finish remains on this ca. 1930's era 24 inch jointer plane. Mint.* (FINE) **$295.00**

C6-40. Stanley Rule & Level No. 71 1/2: Closed Throat Plane. Early "Script" Trademark. Excellent Condition. Length: 8 Inches. *Here's a clean "closed throat" router with the original 1/2 inch cutting iron. Ready to use.* (GOOD+) **$85.00**

C6-41. Stanley Rule & Level No. 8: Cast Iron Jointer Plane. Orange Infill Cap. Virtually New. Length: 24 Inches. *Virtually all of the original finishes remain on this pristine jointer plane. A tight crack to the tote has been professionally glued and the plane is ready to be put immediately to use.* (FINE) **$245.00**

C6-42. Stanley Rule & Level No. 45: Combination Rabbett, Dado Plane. Fitted Wood Box. "Sweetheart" Trademark. Length: 9 Inches. *The original owner of this plane, Mr. H.C. Wisner of Indiantown Gap, Pennsylvania made a protective box for it which kept it very clean and completely intact. Nearly all original nickel plating remains on this crispy clean and ready to use example. A nice plane in a box with character.* (GOOD+) **$285.00**

C6-43. Stanley Rule & Level No. 19: Knuckle Joint Block Plane. 7 Inch Length. 85%+ Nickel Plating. Length: 7 Inches. *The bigger brother of the much more common No. 18 knuckle joint block plane, this one is 1/2 inch longer. It is clean, sound and in excellent working order.* (GOOD+) **$65.00**

C6-44. Stanley Rule & Level No. 8: Cast Iron Jointer Plane. Ca. 1900. Crisp and Clean. Length: 24 Inches. *This extra clean jointer plane dates from ca. 1900 and features the early style beaded front knob. A great working tool.* (GOOD+) **$145.00**

C6-45. Stanley Rule & Level No. 4 1/2: "Type 12" Smooth Plane. Rosewood Handle and Knob. Ca. 1915 Trademark. Length: 10 1/2 Inches. *Looking for a great working heavy smoothing plane? Here's an exceptionally nice No. 4 1/2 fitted out with handles of Brazilian Rosewood. A great working tool that is ready to provide several lifetimes of service.* (GOOD+) **$215.00**

C6-46. Stanley Rule & Level No. 605: "Bedrock" Jack Plane. Later Style. Square Sides. Length: 14 Inches. *If you can live with a bit of dirt and a dab or two of paint, this "Bedrock" jack plane, which is otherwise in excellent working condition, is a great buy.* (GOOD+) **$165.00**

C6-47. Stanley Rule & Level No. 45: Multi Purpose Combination Plane. Complete and Ready to Use. New Condition, Original Box. Length: 9 Inches. *This superb example of Stanley's No. 45 combination has been sheltered from the elements by its original pasteboard box. A great working tool that is complete and in ready to go to work order.* (FINE) **$365.00**

Group D6

D6-1. Coes & Co., L., Worcester, Mass.: Early Monkey Wrench. Patented March 29, 1869. Schulz No. 872. Length: 4 1/2 Inches. *This example of the "Coes No. 1" is marked with the 1869 patent date. A rare wrench in excellent condition.* (FINE) **$185.00**

D6-2. Capitol: Early Patent Bicycle Wrench. Patented March 11, 1884. Rare and Excellent. Length: 4 1/2 Inches. *We have seen a great variety of patented bicycle wrenches of every shape, size and color, but this is the first "Capitol" wrench to ever grace these pages. A rare bicycle wrench.* (GOOD+) **$145.00**

D6-3. American Plierench Corp., Chicago: Eifel Geared Plier Wrench. Unused Condition. With Instructions. Length: 8 1/2 Inches. *One of the most successful "gizmos" of all time, the Eifel Geared Plierench had been in the Popular Invention Hall of Fame long before the Veg-o-Matic and the Pocket Fisherman arrived. This pristine example is in new condition in its original case, complete with instructions.* (FINE) **$85.00**

D6-4. Unmarked: Massive Twist Handle Wrench. For Pipes and Nuts. Rare Size and Type. Length: 15 Inches. *Twist handle wrenches are about, but finding a double pipe and nut combination wrench with a twist handle is an occasion to write home about. Start writing.* (GOOD+) **$165.00**

D6-5. Bonney Forge & Tool Works: Set of "Zenel" Wrenches. Double Open End. Original Pouch. Length: 4 1/2 Inches. *These open end wrenches have been kept in top condition due to the presence of their original pouch. A great set from an increasingly collectible category.* (FINE) **$65.00**

D6-6. Billings & Spencer Co., The: "Billings Patent" Wrench. Patented February 13, 1879. "For Pope Mfg.". Length: 5 Inches. *Pope Manufacturing Company was a maker of bicycles, so it is likely that this wrench was provided to the purchaser of a bicycle as part of a tool kit. Other than a very slight spring to the jaw, this wrench is in excellent condition.* (GOOD+) **$35.00**

D6-7. Peck, Stow & Wilcox Co.: "Solid Bar" Monkey Wrench. 6 Inch Size. Near New Condition. Length: 6 Inches. *These "Solid Bar" wrenches were offered in every size up to "too big to use". This was the smallest size. Crispy clean.* (FINE) **$45.00**

D6-8. Coes Wrench Co.: Steel Handle Wrench. Patented December 24, 1901. Extra Crisp and Clean. Length: 5 Inches. *The companion to Coes' early wood handle 4 3/8 inch wrench, we know of at least one unscrupulous dealer who surgically removes the handles from these and replaces them with wood. Caveat Emptor. A scarce Coes wrench in top condition.* (FINE) **$75.00**

D6-9. Wakefield Wrench Co., Worcester, Mass.: No. 19: Patent Nut Wrench. Patented November 14, 1922. Uncommon Type. Length: 9 Inches. *It is not readily apparent what the patented feature of this screw adjust nut wrench might have been. A nice example, nonetheless.* (FINE) **$15.00**

D6-10. Standard Tool Company, Athol, Mass.: Quick Adjust Nut Wrench. Patented 1880. Rare and Excellent. Length: 6 Inches. *This one slides quickly and smoothly into place with a push of the button at the rear of the lower jaw. It was produced under the Bellows Patent of 1880. Crisp, clean and clearly marked. A good one.* (GOOD+) **$225.00**

D6-11. Robinson: "Robinson Pat." Nut Wrench. Patented June 16, 1885. Early and Excellent. Length: 6 1/2 Inches. *The Robinson's Patent wrench has a distinctive recessed receiver for the adjustment nut, which may be the patented feature. Incidentally, Antique & Unusual Wrenches by Al & Lucille Schulz is, once again, nearly sold out. Don't miss your chance to own this classic.* (GOOD+) **$55.00**

D6-12. Petersen Rapid Wrench Co.: Rare "Petersen" Wrench. Patented November 3, 1908. With Lever Lock. Length: 10 Inches. *One of the most mechanically interesting of all patented wrenches, the "Petersen Rapid Wrench" is locked in place and adjusted by means of a toggle switch like lever that is immediately below the lower jaw. Clean, mechanically perfect and ready to proudly display. The only example of this rare wrench that we have ever offered.* (GOOD+) **$645.00**

D6-13. Bullard No. 0: Self-Adjusting Pipe Wrench. Spring Activated. Patented October 27, 1903. Length: 5 1/2 Inches. *According to Antique & Unusual Wrenches, the Bullard wrench was offered in a wide range of sizes. This, the smallest size ever offered, and by far the rarest of the bunch, is crisp, clean and ready to add to a collection of small wrenches.* (GOOD+) **$195.00**

D6-14. H. & E. Wrench Co., New Bedford, Mass.: Adjustable Nut Wrench. "Hande" Wrench. Patented September 21, 1921. Length: 10 Inches. *The mathematicians would put it this way: (High Quality Manufacture+Exceptional Materials) x Stupid Idea=Great Collectible. The equation balances for this sliding jaw gizmo in new condition.* (FINE) **$65.00**

D6 15. Billings & Spencer Co., The: Bicycle Monkey Wrench. Unique Side Adjust. Made for Pope Manufacturing Company. Length: 5 1/2 Inches. *Here's a great example of a tool that is completely different from everything else. There are literally hundreds, if not thousands of variations on the bicycle wrench theme, but this seems to be the only one to have found it necessary to use the face of the wrench as a receiver for the adjustment screw. These were specially made for the Pope Manufacturing Company, undoubtedly for inclusion with their line of bicycles. A rare and unusual wrench.* (GOOD) **$185.00**

D6-16. Simmons Hardware Co. No. K 94: "Keen Kutter" Wrench. Bicycle Type. Rare and Excellent. Length: 3 Inches. *Nearly every tool vendor and tool maker offered a number of "bicycle" wrenches, and the E.C. Simmons company was no exception, but finding surviving examples, especially those as clean and clearly marked as this example is an infrequent occurrence. This one is in fine working order and ready to display in a prominent collection of "Keen Kutter" items or small wrenches.* (GOOD+) **$145.00**

D6-17. Reinhard-Mc Cabe Co., Minneapolis No. 1 C: Lever Adjust Wrench. "Pat. Pend". Uncommon Type. Length: 10 Inches. *In the days before the "Vise Grip" wrench joined the hammer and duct tape as the Three Universal Tools, a number of wannabes appeared on the scene, including this lever locking dandy from a Minnesota maker. An uncommon universal plier wrench.* (FINE) **$55.00**

D6-18. Unmarked: "The Teddy" Combination Wrench. Screwdriver, Hammer. Most Unusual. Length: 9 Inches. *Whether or not the name of this ca. 1900 era wrench had anything to do with Theodore Roosevelt is anyone's guess. This device combines a hammer, alligator wrench and screwdriver into the same tool with about the same degree of efficiency as a modern inventor would combine a toothbrush, shower head and lemon squeezer. All combination tools embody one of the the eternal truths of tool collecting: Stupid Ideas Make Great Collectible Tools.* (GOOD+) **$115.00**

D6-19. Crescent Tool Co., Jamestown, N.Y.: 4-6 Inch Crescent Wrench. Extra Crisp and Clean. Rare and Excellent. Length: 6 Inches. *Isn't the idea of an adjustable wrench that you need just ONE wrench instead of several (or even two)? The folks at the Crescent Tool Company probably so despaired of having limited their potential business that they came up with this idea to (in their minds, anyway) double their sales. It didn't work. These wrenches are in scarce supply.* (GOOD+) **$125.00**

D6-20. Perfection No. 3: 14 Inch "Perfection" Wrench. Patented April 14, 1896. Schulz No. 224. Length: 14 Inches. *A most interesting carriage wrench, this one dubbed the "Perfection" wrench.. Apparently, other inventors were not properly informed that the marketers of this one had arrived at the apotheosis, so the kept on churning out "improvements" of their own. This, the largest size offered of this uncommon wrench is the least common of all. Rare.* (GOOD+) **$275.00**

D6-21. Wescott, Geo. W., Homer, N.Y.: Early Style Pipe Wrench. Pre-Buffalo. Rare Wescott Mark. Length: 14 Inches. *The Wescott Company was a prolific manufacturer of "S" handle wrenches, which were apparently distributed Nation-wide. This obviously early example of the Wescott pipe wrench is marked with Wescott's first working location, Homer, New York. An early wrench from a prominent maker in excellent condition.* (GOOD+) **$165.00**

D6-22. Hoe Corp., Poughkeepsie, N.Y.: Self Adjusting Pipe Wrench. Patented February 21, 1922. Schulz No. 361. Length: 6 Inches. *The idea behind this patented wrench was that the spring mechanism would combine with the action of the user to keep the jaws tight on the work. They apparently didn't catch on.* (GOOD+) **$65.00**

D6-23. Parker Co., The Charles, Meriden, No. 4: Special Vise Wrench. For Parker Vises. Uncommon Type. Length: 7 1/4 Inches. *The vices produced by the Charles Parker Company are sought out as among the best ever made. This wrench, which is imprinted with the Parker name, was used to adjust the angle of the vise on the bench. A rare wrench.* (GOOD+) **$45.00**

D6-24. Bergman Tool Mfg. Co., Buffalo, N.Y. No. 4: 4 Inch "Queen City" Wrench. "Bergman O' Buffalo". With 3/16 Inch Socket. Length: 4 Inches. *The "Queen City" wrench was a "crescent" wrench with a twist. Additional functionality was added adding a 5/16 inch square wrench at the base of the tool. A tough wrench to find in this small size.* (GOOD+) **$45.00**

D6-25. Simplex Wrench Co., New York, N.Y. No. 14: "Simplex Ratchet" Wrench. Patented January 1, 1924. Most Unusual. Length: 6 1/4 Inches. *We have seen a number of stupid ideas masquerading as tools, but this "Simplex" scores as both simplistic and stupid. The general idea here was to allow one open end wrench to function as several sizes by cutting a series of notches in the same opening. Anyone who has ever used one of these tools to simultaneously break the head off from a bolt and remove a substantial amount of skin from the knuckles knows what I mean. Looks more like the Simpleton wrench to me.* (GOOD+) **$35.00**

D6-26. Unmarked: Miniature Cast Iron Wrench. Brass Adjust Screw. Uncommon Type. Length: 4 Inches. *This 4 inch wrench looks not to have been of the highest quality, but its different than many wrenches that we have seen, so we include it here. A bargain.* (GOOD+) **$15.00**

D6-27. M.W. & Co., Framingham, Mass.: Patent Pivot Jaw Wrench. Patented June 15, 1897. Superb Condition. Length: 10 Inches. *This most unusual patented wrench features a spring-activated upper jaw that locks on to the pipe or nut before final adjustments are made. Crisp, clean and clearly marked. A rare wood-handled quick adjust wrench. Extra crisp and clean.* (GOOD+) **$185.00**

D6-28. Unmarked: Early Patent Pipe Wrench. Marked "Springfield". From Bemis & Call? Length: 12 1/2 Inches. *This extremely early wrench has a form we have not previously encountered. The upper jaw is marked "Springfield", but the patent date is not legible.* (GOOD) **$115.00**

D6-29. C & F Mfg. Co.: "The Marshalltown" Wrench. Combination Alligator and Nut. Patented August 26, 1913. Length: 8 1/2 Inches. *"...if you can keep your head while all about you are losing theirs..." Kipling, I think. Anyway, these apparently came with different sizes of nut wrenches to fit in the end, but I've only seen them with one. An interesting patented wrench in superb condition.* (FINE) **$165.00**

D6-30. Diamond Tool And Horseshoe Co.: Double "Crescent" Wrench. 4 Inch-6 Inch Sizes. Rare Size and Type. Length: 6 Inches. *This company turned its attention to wrench making when the market for its previous principal product, horseshoe caulks, disappeared with the horses. For those left clueless by the pace of change, horseshoe caulks were metal inserts that were screwed into the base of horseshoes to facilitate transit on snow and ice—equine tire chains, if you would. These double ended wrenches are tough to find by any maker.* (GOOD) **$85.00**

D6-31. Mephisto: Patent Angle Wrench. Patented June 23, 1914. Rare and Excellent. Length: 8 Inches. *The maker name has been forged into this most unusual pivot head wrench in a Germanic script pattern. A rare wrench in excellent condition.* (GOOD+) **$165.00**

D6-32. Mc I. H. Co.: "Steel Bicycle" Wrench. Wooden Handle. Extra Crisp and Clean. Length: 5 3/4 Inches. *These "Steel Bicycle" wrenches were one of the few bicycle wrenches that were not made completely of steel. Go figure. This example is in excellent condition and ready to add to a collection of small wrenches.* (GOOD+) **$165.00**

D6-33. Benton: Twist Handle Wrench. Full Nickel Plating. Near New Condition. Length: 7 Inches. *The handle of this well made nickel plated wrench can be turned to facilitate its adjustment. An uncommon wrench in nearly new condition.* (FINE) **$185.00**

D6-34. Unmarked: Hand Filed "Alligator" Wrench. Square Nut Holes. Early and Excellent. Length: 5 Inches. *One can imaging that the relentless output of the drop forge would produce a pricing level driven by economy of scale that would have made even the wisest of mechanics susceptible to buying and trying an "alligator" wrench. How someone possessed of the level of mechanical skill as the maker of this tool could have convinced himself that he needed an example of the Worst Wrench Ever Made challenges the imagination. Whatever the case, this hand-filed wrench is very well made and in nearly new condition. When artists make mistakes, they throw the work away, when the same happens with the mechanical genius, the item finds its way to Martin J. Donnelly Antique Tools.* (FINE) **$45.00**

D6-35. Coes Wrench Co.: Steel Handle Wrench. Patented December 24, 1901. Smallest Size. Length: 5 Inches. *This, the smallest size offered in the steel handle Coes monkey wrench series, is in excellent collector quality condition.* (GOOD+) **$55.00**

D6-36. Unmarked: 4 Inch "Crescent" Wrench. "Jamestown, N.Y.". "Made In U.S.A.". Length: 4 Inches. *A growing number of collectors have begun seeking out the wide variety of 4 inch size "Crescent" wrenches. Here's the Real Thing.* (GOOD+) **$35.00**

D6-37. Red Chief Mfg. Co., Louisville, Kentucky: Patent Self Adjust Wrench. Patented November 16, 1915. Rare and Excellent. Length: 8 Inches. *A sufficiently wide range of makers offered these "self adjusting" wrenches that they have their own page in Al Schulz' book on wrenches. This Kentucky made wrench is the first example of the "Red Chief" that we have seen.* (GOOD+) **$245.00**

D6-38. Unmarked: Early Patent Buggy Wrench. Patented 1881. "Propeller" Handle. Length: 10 Inches. *We have it on good authority that the flat back on this patented "buggy" wrench was intended for placement of an oil can. Having seen several of the wrenches, but no oil cans, we will offer two possibilities for consideration by the tool collecting community. The first is that the wrenches were sold without oil cans with the understanding that they be added by the owner. The second, and more likely, theory is that those few who bought these ridiculous excuses for tools got poked in the eye with the spout of the oil can while trying to turn a stubborn nut and personally saw to it that the oil can was removed, most likely with a hammer. A rare wrench that is better than a poke in the eye with a sharp oil can.* (GOOD) **$245.00**

D6-39. Williams & Co., J.H., Brooklyn No. BC-5: Crow's Foot Crescent Wrench. Most Unusual Type. Near New Condition. Length: 1 1/2 Inches. *Wrenches of this type are referred to as crow's foot wrenches, but they are generally of fixed sizes. This example features a "Crescent" type adjustment. Unusual and in unused condition. Something to carry in your pocket and amaze your friends (assuming that you have any if you're the kind of person to carry a wrench in your pocket for entertainment purposes).* (FINE) **$55.00**

D6-40. Hartford Hardware Co., Hartford, Conn.: Set of 3 "Tryon" Patent Wrenches. Patented January 29, 1901. Sizes 5 Inch, 7 Inch, and 9 Inch. Length: 9 Inches. *Not to be outdone by the double jawed pipe and nut wrenches that were the standard of complexity for the time, the Hartford Hardware Company introduced the Tryon Patent wrench, which included all of that plus a buggy wrench jaw on the same wrench. This stepped set of these wrenches came from one individual's tool kit. A great set of rare combination wrenches.* (GOOD+) **$445.00**

D6-41. Diamond Tool and Horseshoe Co. No. DH16: "Handyboy" Plier and Wrench. 6 Inch Size. New Condition, Original Box. Length: 6 Inches. *Perhaps the most salable feature of this monstrosity was that your couldn't lose the Crescent wrench while working with the pliers (or vice versa). Unfortunately, for the People at The Diamond Tool and Horseshoe Co., most people preferred to stick with two tools. An interesting collectible wrench in great condition in its original box.* (FINE) **$95.00**

D6-42. Bonney Forge & Tool Works No. BW-KIT: Repair Parts For Wrenches. "Crescent" Type. New Condition, Original Box. Length: 6 Inches. *If your Bonney "Crescent" type wrench ever breaks down, these will put you in position to have it back on the job in no time. Most unusual.* (FINE) **$75.00**

D6-43. Smith, S.: Early Patent Saw Set. Patented October 4, 1859. Rare and Excellent. Length: 12 Inches. *This example of the Seymour Smith patent has spent some time in the woods, but it is clean, complete and ready to display. A graphic saw set of very early manufacture.* (GOOD+) **$245.00**

D6-44. Unmarked: Hand Forged Ratchet Wrench. With Spring Catch. Excellent Patina. Length: 19 1/2 Inches. *This ratcheting wrench was hand forged by a blacksmith and fitted with a tempered spring to engage the ratchet. A dramatic hand forged wrench.* (GOOD+) **$85.00**

D6-45. Crescent Tool Co., Jamestown, N.Y.: 4-6 Inches "Crestoloy" Wrench. Extra Crisp and Clean. Most Unusual Size. Length: 6 Inches. *In the 1920's, the folks at the Crescent Tool Company introduced the "Crestoloy" finish, their own version of nickel plating. This double end classic has been Crestoloyed.* (GOOD+) **$115.00**

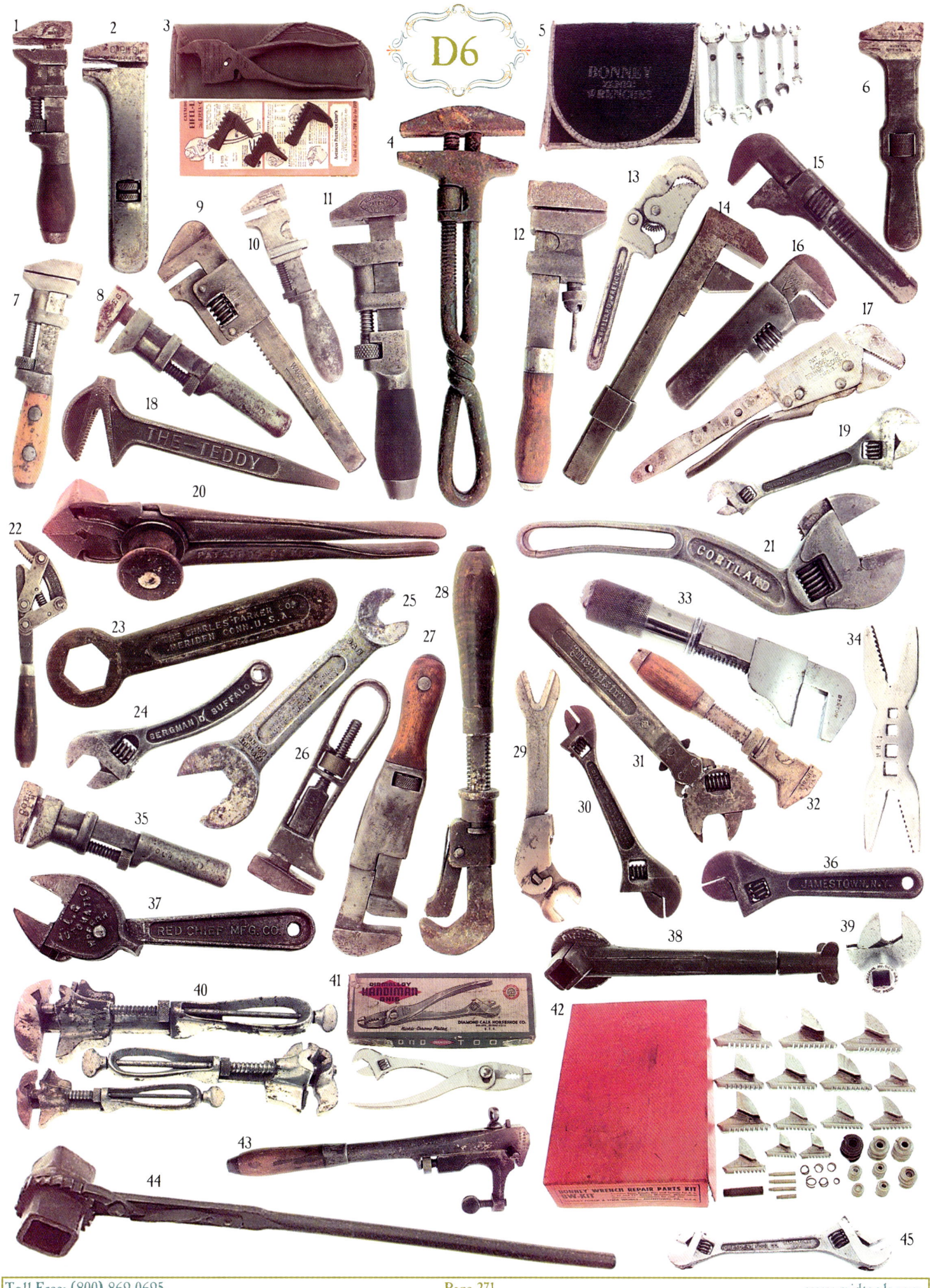

Group E6

E6-1. Lufkin Rule Co., The, Saginaw, Michigan: No. 171: Six Inch, Two Fold Folding Rule. With Caliper. Near New Condition. Length: 6 Inches. *Lufkin's answer to the No. 36 caliper rule, this pristine example is clearly marked with the Lufkin name and number. Nearly new.* (GOOD+) **$35.00**

E6-2. Stanley Rule & Level No. 36 1/2: One Foot, Two Fold Folding Rule. With Caliper. "Sweetheart" Trademark. Length: 12 Inches. *A bold "Sweetheart" stamp adds appeal to this well preserved Stanley caliper rule. Rules with this mark were made during the 1920's.* (FINE) **$45.00**

E6-3. Stephens & Co., Riverton, Conn.: No. 59: Double Arch Joint Folding Rule. Uncommon Type. Some Staining. Length: 24 Inches. *Double arch joint rules were the most expensive at the time they were made and they are consequently the least common today. This example, from Stephens & Company of Riverton, Connecticut, has some staining, but is sound and presentable.* (GOOD+) **$45.00**

E6-4. C-S Co., The, Pine Meadow, Conn.: No. 84: Two Foot, Four Fold Folding Rule. Square Joint, Half Bound. Unused Condition. Length: 24 Inches. *Identical in all respects to the Stanley numerical equivalent, this Chapin-Stephens rule is in brand new condition. A superb example.* (FINE) **$75.00**

E6-5. Unmarked: Broad Boxwood Folding Rule. Unfinished Graduates. Very Well Made. Length: 24 Inches. *For some reason this early appearing arch joint, half-bound boxwood rule did not complete the manufacturing process. It has no apparent defects and is in excellent condition. An interesting unfinished symphony from the world of folding rules.* (FINE) **$115.00**

E6-6. Chapin, H., U. S. Standard No. 39: Two Foot, Two Fold Folding Rule. Square Joint, Unbound. Scarce and Excellent. Length: 24 Inches. *A scarce rule under any circumstances, this H. Chapin No. 39 is brand new from old hardware stock and is in immaculate condition, despite its 150 odd years of existence. A great rule.* (FINE) **$245.00**

E6-7. Stanley Rule & Level No. 804 E-M: Metric "Zig-Zag" Folding Rule. 4 Foot Length. Ca. 1930's. Length: 48 Inches. *Here's an early example with both English and metric graduations that were offered in the catalogs but are seldom seen. A nice example.* (GOOD+) **$95.00**

E6-8. Stanley Rule & Level (Unmarked). No. 32 1/2: One Foot, Four Fold Folding Rule. With Caliper Slide. Near New Condition. Length: 12 Inches. *Here's a nearly new example of Stanley's top of the line full-bound, arch-joint caliper rule. This one features the later style rounded arch joint. Near mint.* (FINE) **$65.00**

E6-9. Lufkin Rule Co., The No. 651: Two Foot, Four Fold Folding Rule. Round Joint, Unbound. Brand New Condition. Length: 24 Inches. *Lufkin's equivalent to the Stanley No. 68, this rule is much less common, especially in unused condition, as is this pristine example.* (FINE) **$35.00**

E6-10. Stanley Rule & Level No. 34 1/4 VR: Two Way Bench Rule. Dual Brass Tips. Unused Condition. Length: 12 Inches. *Stanley's vertical read bench rules were sold primarily to schools where they were promptly defaced and destroyed by enterprising students. This one is in brand new condition. An uncommon Stanley rule.* (FINE) **$35.00**

E6-11. Preston & Sons, Edward: One Foot, Four Fold Folding Rule. Early Round Joint. Presentation Case. Length: 12 Inches. *A gold trimmed leatherette case has kept this Preston presentation rule in brand new condition. Choice.* (FINE) **$75.00**

E6-12. Unmarked: Advertising Folding Rule. Listers, Newark, N.J. For Fertilizer Maker. Length: 24 Inches. *In place of the graduations on the outside edge, the makers of this rule (most likely H. Chapin) imprinted it with advertising for a Newark, New Jersey fertilizer manufacturer. The fact that the rule's usefulness was thus compromised may or may not have been noticed by the customers who received the rule for free.* (GOOD+) **$35.00**

E6-13. Stanley Tools No. 66 1/2: Three-Foot, Four Fold Folding Rule. Square Joint, Unbound. With "Sweetheart" Trademark. Length: 36 Inches. *A new and unused example of Stanley's basic 3 foot, four fold rule. This "Sweetheart" era example features the "printed" lettering introduced in the 1920's.* (FINE) **$45.00**

E6-14. Stanley Rule & Level: Advertising Caliper Rule. Montello Heel Co. New Conditon, Original Box. Length: 6 Inches. *The original presentation box from Stanley has preserved the original condition of this advertising rule from a supplier to the shoe industry. The first Stanley advertising rule with this mark that we have seen.* (FINE) **$55.00**

E6-15. Unmarked: Unfinished Boxwood Folding Rule. Round Joint, Unbound. Most Unusual. Length: 24 Inches. *This round joint rule is perfect in all respects, save for the fact that the graduations were never applied at the factory. A collectible curiosity.* (FINE) **$65.00**

E6-16. Unmarked: Broad Boxwood Folding Rule. Unfinished Graduates. Very Well Made. Length: 24 Inches. *For some reason this early appearing arch joint, half-bound boxwood rule did not complete the manufacturing process. It has no apparent defects and is in excellent condition. An interesting unfinished symphony from the world of folding rules.* (FINE) **$115.00**

E6-17. Lufkin Rule Co., The: No. 34 1/4 V: Vertical Reading Rule. Uncommon Type. Unused Condition. Length: 12 Inches. *Lufkin's equivalent in both configuration and numeric designation to Stanley's 34 1/4 V was intended for the same high school and college market. This one is in brand new condition.* (FINE) **$35.00**

E6-18. Lufkin Rule Co., The No. 651: Two Foot, Four Fold Folding Rule. Round Joint, Unbound. Brand New Condition. Length: 24 Inches. *No one has ever used this perfectly preserved equivalent to the Stanley No. 68 rule. Brand new.* (FINE) **$35.00**

E6-19. Lufkin Rule Co., The, Saginaw, Mich. No. 171: Six Inch, Two Fold Folding Rule. With Caliper. Clean and Sound. Length: 6 Inches. *This one has some staining, but is otherwise clean and sound.* (GOOD+) **$45.00**

E6-20. Unmarked: Narrow Metric Rule. Also Marked "Groningen". Unused Condition. Length: 39 1/2 Inches. *This comparative scale includes both metric and a North German scale. A rare comparative measure in brand new condition.* (FINE) **$110.00**

E6-21. Stanley Rule & Level No. 62: Two-Foot, Four-Fold Folding Rule. Square Joint, Full Bound. "Sweetheart" Trademark. Length: 24 Inches. *This extra-clean example of one of Stanley's more popular rules has an early trademark. No apologies.* (GOOD+) **$45.00**

E6-22. Unmarked: Broad Boxwood Folding Rule. Unfinished Graduates. Very Well Made. Length: 24 Inches. *For some reason this early appearing arch joint, half-bound boxwood rule did not complete the manufacturing process. It has no apparent defects and is in excellent condition. An interesting unfinished symphony from the world of folding rules.* (FINE) **$115.00**

E6-23. Stanley Rule & Level No. 36 1/2: One Foot, Two Fold Folding Rule. With Caliper. Ready to Use. Length: 12 Inches. *This one foot Stanley caliper rule dates from the second quarter of the Twentieth Century, but is in very well preserved condition.* (GOOD) **$15.00**

E6-24. Stanley Rule & Level No. 643: Victor Zig Zag Folding Rule. 3 Foot Length, 4 Inch Section. "Sweetheart" Trademark. Length: 36 Inches. *The most rare and desirable of all zig zag rules are those having sections of only four inches instead of the standard six. This 3 footer is marked with the Sweetheart trademark. A good one.* (GOOD+) **$245.00**

E6-25. Chapin, H., U. S. Standard No. 38: Two Foot, Two Fold Folding Rule. Double Arch Joint. Full Bound. Clean and Sound. Length: 24 Inches. *Double arch joint rules were the top of the line for every maker. This one is marked with the imprint of pioneering maker Hermon Chapin.* (GOOD) **$245.00**

E6-26. C-S Co., The, Pine Meadow, Conn. No. 36 1/2: One Foot, Two Fold Folding Rule. With Caliper. Near New Condition. Length: 12 Inches. *This Chapin-Stephens caliper rule is crisp, clean and ready to fill out a collection. This configuration by Chapin Stephens is much less common than similar rules by Stanley or Lufkin.* (GOOD+) **$85.00**

E6-27. Ricks, J., London: Narrow Boxwood Folding Rule. With Architect Scales. Near New Condition. Length: 24 Inches. *This is our first meeting with "J. Ricks", the maker of this rule, but it is very well made and in brand new condition. A most unusual narrow architect's rule.* (FINE) **$115.00**

E6-28. Lufkin Rule Co., The, England No. 3851: Three-Foot, Four Fold Folding Rule. Arch Joint, Unbound. Equal to Stanley 66 1/2. Length: 36 Inches. *Three foot rules tended to have their joints become "sprung" after limited use. This one avoided that fate by never having been used. Mint.* (FINE) **$45.00**

E6-29. Scovill Mfg. Co., New York, N.Y.: Early Button Caliper. Ivory and German Silver. Owner "R.S. Ould". Length: 3 1/2 Inches. *Fitted with a German silver caliper graduated in the 1/40th of an inch scale that somehow became the standard for measuring buttons, this extra early ivory rule is engraved on the caliper side with the owner's name "R.S. Ould". The reverse side, which is graduated in inches, is marked with the maker's name "Scovill Mf'g. Co., N.Y. in early style lettering. Appearance is ca. 1850's. A tight longitudinal crack shows on one side of the ivory for about one inch. An extra early special purpose ivory caliper rule in excellent condition.* (GOOD+) **$325.00**

E6-30. Stanley Tools No. 66 1/2: Three-Foot, Four Fold Folding Rule. Square Joint, Unbound. With "Sweetheart" Trademark. Length: 36 Inches. *Stanley basic three-foot rule in very nice condition. This one features the 1920's era "Sweetheart" trademark.* (GOOD+) **$35.00**

E6-31. Lufkin Rule Co., The, Saginaw, Mich. No. 372 R: One Foot, Two Fold Folding Rule. Stanley 36 1/2 Equivalent. Near New Condition. Length: 12 Inches. *Not to be outdone by Stanley, Lufkin offered their caliper rules in both Left and Right hand sizes. This right hand size offering is in excellent condition.* (FINE) **$45.00**

E6-32. Stearns & Co., E.A., Brattleboro, No. 32: Two Foot, Four Fold Folding Rule. Square Joint, Unbound. Metric and English Scales. Length: 24 Inches. *The E.A. Stearns Company advertised their rules as being of "extra quality". One look at this well preserved four foot rule is to know that they meant what they said. Extra quality.* (GOOD+) **$165.00**

E6-33. Stanley Rule & Level (Unmarked) No. 68: Two Foot, Four Fold Folding Rule. Round Joint, Unbound. Early Example. Length: 24 Inches. *Among the most rare and desirable of all "Ultimatum" braces are those that have as the material of their "stuffing" the horn of the Cape Buffalo. This example is so stuffed and remains in top collector quality condition. A very rare and desirable brace.* (GOOD+) **$35.00**

E6-34. Lufkin Rule Co., The, Saginaw, Mich.: No. 651: Two Foot, Four Fold Folding Rule. Round Joint, Unbound. New Condition, Original Box. Length: 24 Inches. *Lufkin's equivalent to the Stanley No. 68, this rule is much less common, especially in unused condition, as is this "new in the box" example.* (FINE) **$95.00**

E6-35. Stanley Rule & Level No. 61: Two Foot, Four Fold Folding Rule. Square Joint, Unbound. Near New Condition. Length: 24 Inches. *This pristine and early example may never have had its joint opened. Nearly new.* (FINE) **$35.00**

E6-36. Unmarked: Comparitive Caliper Rule. "London" and "Metric". Unused Condition. Length: 4 Inches. *This pristine caliper rule is imprinted on one side with metric scales and on the reverse with the more civilized English measurements.* (FINE) **$65.00**

E6-37. Stanley Rule & Level No. 96: "Defiance" Zig-Zag Folding Rule. 6 Foot Length. Excellent Condition. Length: 72 Inches. *Stanley's "Defiance" series is becoming increasingly collectible. Here's an excellent example of the No. 96 zig-zag rule.* (FINE) **$55.00**

E6-38. Stanley Rule & Level No. 34 1/4 VR: Two Way Bench Rule. Dual Brass Tips. Unused Condition. Length: 12 Inches. *No one has ever used this scarce "vertical read" bench rule. Brand new.* (FINE) **$35.00**

E6-39. Stanley Rule & Level No. 36 1/2 L: One Foot, Two Fold Folding Rule. Left Hand Graduation. With Caliper Rule. Length: 12 Inches. *Here's a good, clean example of Stanley's basic one-foot, two-fold caliper rule. The "L" designated the left-hand caliper. Apparently unused.* (FINE) **$35.00**

E6-40. Stanley Rule & Level No. 36: Six-Inch, Two-Fold Folding Rule. "Sweetheart" Trademark. New Condition. Length: 6 Inches. *The next time tells you that the No. 36 is a "common" rule, give them a month to show you one in this condition. You won't hear that again unless they call here before you do. Mint.* (FINE) **$65.00**

E6-41. Sawyer Tool Co., Ashburnham, Mass.: Bench and Key Seat Rules. Near New Condition. Hard to Find. Length: 4 Inches. *These perfectly preserved tools from the Sawyer Tool Company came together and will stay together. Scarce and early new.* (FINE) **$65.00**

E6-42. Lufkin Rule Co., The No. 651: Two Foot, Four Fold Folding Rule. Round Joint, Unbound. Brand New Condition. Length: 24 Inches. *Rules of this quality have practically disappeared from the market. Absolutely perfect.* (FINE) **$35.00**

E6-43. Lufin Rule Co., The, Saginaw, Mich. No. 626: "Plumber's" Folding Rule. With 40 Degree Scale. Unused Condition. Length: 72 Inches. *Zig-Zag rules were produced with specialized graduations for nearly any conceivable trade. This "plumber's" rule has its inside edge imprinted with a scale that estimates the number of diagonal inches for every horizontal inch. I haven't really figured it out, but, then again, I haven't really tried. Brand new.* (FINE) **$35.00**

E6-44. Lufkin Rule Co., The No. 651: Two Foot, Four Fold Folding Rule. Round Joint, Unbound. Brand New Condition. Length: 24 Inches. *No apologies whatsoever for this brand new Lufkin rule in the two foot, four fold configuration. Mint.* (FINE) **$35.00**

E6-45. Rabone & Sons, John, Birmingham: Three Foot, Four Fold Folding Rule. Half Bound Type. Mowat's Stores, Ayr. Length: 36 Inches. *Imprinted with the name of an "ironmonger" in Ayr, Scotland, the home town of Stewart Spiers, this three foot folding rule from John Rabone & Sons is in brand new condition. An early rule in new condition.* (FINE) **$115.00**

E6-46. Stanley Rule & Level No. 163: Light Duty Folding Rule. 1941 to 1943 Only. Rare and Excellent. Length: 24 Inches. *These light-duty rules were produced during World War II and discontinued after a short run. This one appears never to have been used.* (FINE) **$65.00**

E6-47. Lufkin Rule Co., The No. 34 1/4 V: Vertical Reading Rule. Uncommon Type. Unused Condition. Length: 12 Inches. *The vertical read scales on this rule were used in school laboratories and the like. This one has never been used anywhere. Brand new.* (FINE) **$35.00**

E6-48. Unmarked: "Pit Prop Gauge" Rule. For Mine Tunnels. Solid Boxwood. Length: 13 1/2 Inches. *This most unusual rule was used in the mining industry to gauge the size of wooden props used in mining. It is made of solid boxwood, unmarked with any maker's name and in unused condition.* (FINE) **$85.00**

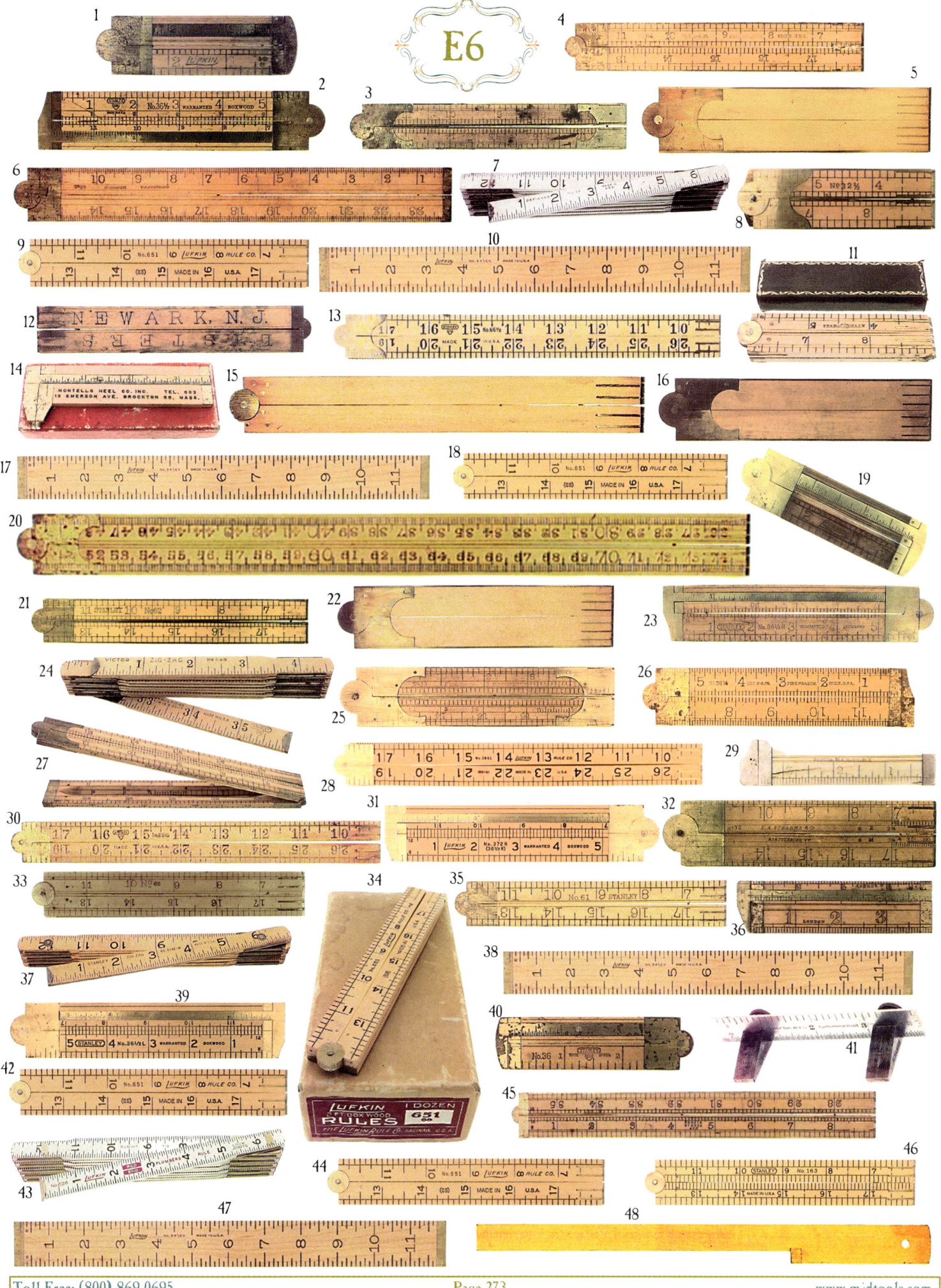

Group F6

F6-1. Smith, B.W.: Side Rabbet Molding Plane. Right Hand Cut. Ready to Use. Length: 9 1/2 Inches. *Pairs of side rabbet planes sell for up to $200.00. Why not get halfway there for a fraction of the cost? A nice working plane.* (GOOD+) **$35.00**

F6-2. Reed, Utica (N. Y.) No. 2: Pair of Hollow and Round Molding Planes. Uncommon Size. Ready to Use. Length: 9 1/2 Inches. *Hollow and round planes in the No. 2 size are the most difficult to find. These are in excellent working order. A pretty pair.* (GOOD+) **$95.00**

F6-3. Reed, Utica (N.Y.): Special Sash Molding Plane. With Integral Fence. Uncommon Type. Length: 9 1/2 Inches. *This unusual plane apparently performed some specialized sash making function. Ex-Cooley Collection.* (GOOD+) **$95.00**

F6-4. Assorted Makers: Group of 7 Assorted Molding Planes. Assorted Profiles. Stewart, Kellogg, Etc. Length: 9 1/2 Inches. *Here's an interesting assortment of profiles from a range of planemakers. Some have been modified and all have been well used.* (GOOD) **$55.00**

F6-5. Copeland, M., Warranted: 3/8 Inch Center Bead Molding Plane. Inlaid Boxing. Extra Crisp and Clean. Length: 9 1/2 Inches. *Center beads are handy shop tools for modern woodworkers. This one is in excellent working order.* (GOOD+) **$45.00**

F6-6. Sargent & Co. (Sandusky): No. 626: Boxed Center Bead Molding Plane. 3/8 Inch Size. Ready to Use. Length: 9 1/2 Inches. *Wooden planes marketed by Sargent & Company of New Haven, Connecticut were made for them by the Sandusky Tool Company. This one is clean, clearly marked and ready to use.* (GOOD+) **$35.00**

F6-7. Auburn Tool Co., Auburn, N.Y.: No. 105: Boxed Bead Molding Plane. Marked "1/2". Extra Crisp and Clean. Length: 9 1/2 Inches. *Here's a ready to use bead plane in the desirable 1/2 inch size. Extra crisp and clean.* (FINE) **$45.00**

F6-8. Chapin, N., Eagle Factory: Shipwright's Bead Molding Plane. Fully Boxed. Rare Double Iron. Length: 9 1/2 Inches. *The double cutting iron on this plane is a sure indication that it was intended for marketing to shipwrights where work with extra long timbers required the minimization of splintered shavings. This one has been fully boxed to promote longevity.* (GOOD+) **$85.00**

F6-9. Reed, Utica (N.Y.): Quirk Ovolo and Bevel Molding Plane. Marked "1/2". Excellent Condition. Length: 9 1/2 Inches. *This narrow molder is crisp, clean and ready to use.* (GOOD+) **$85.00**

F6-10. Gabriel, (London): Massive Ogee Molding Plane. Early Flat Chamfers. Eighteenth Century. Length: 9 1/2 Inches. *Distinguished both by his prodigious output and the quality of his work, Christopher Gabriel is perhaps best remembered as the planemaker who provided the tools for the "Seaton Chest" a rare, intact example of an Eighteenth Century cabinetmaker's tool kit. This massive and boldly struck molder has the wide, flat chamfers that were characteristic of the earliest work of this important maker. For an excellent discussion of the Seaton Chest, Christopher Gabriel and the History of British planemaking, we highly recommend British Planemakers From 1700, edited by Mark and Jane Rees. A great complex molding plane in top condition.* (GOOD+) **$245.00**

F6-11. Auburn Tool Co., Auburn, N.Y.: No. 108: Center Bead Molding Plane. Marked "1/4". Extra Crisp and Clean. Length: 9 1/2 Inches. *Here's a clean and ready to use center bead plane produced in the 1860's by convict labor in New York State's Auburn Prison.* (FINE) **$55.00**

F6-12. Reed, Utica (N. Y.): Classic Ogee Molding Plane. Marked "3/4". Near New Condition. Length: 9 1/2 Inches. *No apologies whatsoever for this immaculately preserved reverse ogee molder. Crisp and clean.* (GOOD+) **$95.00**

F6-13. Ohio Tool Co., Columbus, Ohio: No. 62: Massive Handled Ogee Molding Plane. Marked 2 1/4 and 7/8. Uncommon Type. Length: 13 Inches. *This massive handled ogee molder has a distinctive razee shape that is uncommon among makers other than along the East Coast. A nice plane.* (GOOD) **$225.00**

F6-14. Unmarked: Classic Bilection Molding Plane. Early Flat Chamfers. 18th Century Appearance. Length: 9 1/2 Inches. *This bilection molder has wide, flat chamfers and a rounded wedge that are characteristic of Eighteenth Century planemaking. A classic early plane.* (GOOD+) **$95.00**

F6-15. Reed, Utica (N.Y.): Cove and Astragal Molding Plane. Marked "7/8". Extra Crisp and Clean. Length: 9 1/2 Inches. *This spectacular cove and astragal molder is in nearly new condition. Absolutely perfect. Ex-Cooley Collection.* (FINE) **$225.00**

F6-16. Reed, Utica (N.Y.): 5/16 Inch Dado Molding Plane. Brass Screw Adjust. Extra Crisp and Clean. Length: 9 1/2 Inches. *The easily replaced nicker iron is missing from this plane, which may account for its extraordinarily well preserved condition. Choice.* (FINE) **$45.00**

F6-17. Moss, Wm., Birmingham, England: Early 5/8 Inch Astragal Molding Plane. Ca. 1775-1797. Excellent Condition. Length: 9 1/2 Inches. *This classic Eighteenth Century molder and stands ready to be used once again for the purpose for which it was intended. An excellent early molder in working condition.* (GOOD+) **$85.00**

F6-18. Composition of Artists: 3/4 Inch Dado Molding Plane. Early Round Chamfers. Strange Mark. Length: 9 1/2 Inches. *"American Wooden Planes" notes reports of other planes similarly marked, but there is no documentation on the location or working dates of this curiously named enterprise. This dado plane appears to date from the 1840's.* (GOOD+) **$215.00**

F6-19. Auburn Tool Co., Auburn, N.Y.: No. 155 1/2: Fence Quarter Round Molding Plane. Uncommon Type. Near New Condition. Length: 9 1/2 Inches. *An uncommon profile, this fenced quarter round molding plane bears an unusual number designation. It is in top condition for the collection or the shop.* (FINE) **$65.00**

F6-20. Hills & Winship, Springfield, Mass.: Fixed Width Sash Molding Plane. Fully Boxed. Extra Crisp and Clean. Length: 9 1/2 Inches. *Here's an excellent, fully boxed sash molding plane from a prominent Central Massachusetts maker.* (GOOD+) **$75.00**

F6-21. Sandusky Tool Co., Sandusky, Ohio: No. 639: Adjustable Dado Molding Plane. Marked "3/4". Extra Crisp and Clean. Length: 9 1/2 Inches. *This clean and complete dado plane is ready to go to work. As nice as they come.* (FINE) **$85.00**

F6-22. Elsworth, John, Glasgow (Scotland): Pair of Hollow and Round Molding Planes. Marked "14". Ready to Use. Length: 9 1/2 Inches. *Here's a well preserved working pair of hollow and round molding planes from a top Scottish maker.* (GOOD+) **$65.00**

F6-23. Gardner & Murdock, Boston, Mass.: Pair of Table Joint Molding Planes. With Integral Fences. Rare and Excellent. Length: 9 1/2 Inches. *This pair of fenced table planes are in great working condition. A super pair with a respected maker's mark. Ready to use, if you choose.* (GOOD+) **$375.00**

F6-24. Reed, Utica (N.Y.): Quirk Ogee and Bevel Molding Plane. Marked "1/2". Excellent Condition. Length: 9 1/2 Inches. *Here's a clean and thoroughly usable molder from a respected Upstate New York planemaker.* (FINE) **$95.00**

F6-25. Reed, Utica (N.Y.): Flat Ogee Molding Plane. Marked "1/2". Ready to Use. Length: 9 1/2 Inches. *A piece of leather was tacked on to the edge of this plane many, many years ago. It is in excellent condition and ready to use. Choice.* (FINE) **$85.00**

F6-26. Unmarked: Pair of Special Function Molding Planes. With Hollowing Cut. Most Unusual. Length: 9 1/2 Inches. *These special function molding planes have a distinctive convex cut. They are not marked, appear professionally made and are in nearly new condition. It is possible that they served some planemaking function. Ex-Cooley Collection.* (FINE) **$95.00**

F6-27. Copeland, M., Warranted: Boxed Bead Molding Plane. Marked "3/16". Uncommon Size. Length: 9 1/2 Inches. *A nice crisp mark on a clean bead plane in a most uncommon 3/16 inch size. Ready to use.* (GOOD+) **$45.00**

F6-28. Baldwin, A & E: Boxed Bead Molding Plane. Marked "7/8". Ca. 1830-1841. Length: 9 1/2 Inches. *Here's a clean and ready to use extra wide boxed side bead plane. A good one.* (GOOD+) **$35.00**

F6-29. Hayden, Syracuse, N.Y.: No. 4: Hollow Molding Plane. With "Arm" Trademark. Uncommon Maker. Length: 9 1/2 Inches. *The distinctive "arm and hammer" device that was used on the W.H. Blye patent plane also appears on this molding plane. A rare variation on the Hayden imprint.* (GOOD+) **$85.00**

F6-30. Fish, A., Lowell, Mass.: 3/4 Inch Cove Molding Plane. Uncommon Profile. Extra Crisp Condition. Length: 9 1/2 Inches. *"Covetto" is the proper name for the profile cut by this classic molder. It is in excellent working order.* (GOOD+) **$75.00**

F6-31. Howland & Co., A., Auburn, N.Y.: No. 96: Rosewood and Boxwood Plow Plane. Boxwood Arms and Nuts. Crisp and Clean. Length: 9 1/2 Inches. *The last of New York State's planemakers who used the labor force of "volunteers" from Auburn Prison, in Auburn, New York, A. Howland & Company made a specialty of plow planes of exotic woods. This rosewood and boxwood example is in superb collector quality condition.* (GOOD+) **$495.00**

F6-32. Taber Plane Co., New Bedford: No. 107: 3/4 Inch Boxed Bead Molding Plane. Owner "C.H. Fogg". Ca. 1866-1872. Length: 9 1/2 Inches. *No apologies for this clean and honest bead plane that once belonged to a Mr. C.H. Fogg.* (GOOD+) **$35.00**

F6-33. Mathieson & Son, A., Glasgow: Miniature Smooth Plane. With Original Decal. Extra Crisp and Clean. Length: 9 1/4 Inches. *Among the most sought-after of all wooden planes are miniature molders imprinted with the maker's mark. This well-preserved example has the added appeal of retaining most of its original decal. Choice.* (GOOD+) **$135.00**

F6-34. Crane, D.O., Utica, N.Y.: 7/8 Inch Astragal Molding Plane. Uncommon Type. Near New Condition. Length: 9 1/2 Inches. *David Orville Crane was a former apprentice planemaker to Leonard Kennedy in Hartford, Connecticut, who relocated to Utica, New York where he was self-employed as a planemaker in the 1830's. This perfectly preserved astragal molder is boldly struck with his imprint and is in top, collector quality condition.* (FINE) **$85.00**

F6-35. Reed, Utica (N.Y.): Classic Ogee Molding Plane. Marked "7/8". Extra Crisp and Clean. Length: 9 1/2 Inches. *Molding planes in this type of condition have become increasingly difficult to find. Crisp, clean and ready to use.* (GOOD+) **$95.00**

F6-36. Greenfield Tool Co., Greenfield, Mass.: No. 526: Handled Beech Plow Plane. Boxwood Arms and Nuts. Extra Crisp and Clean. Length: 11 Inches. *This crisp and clean handled plow plane was found in England. How it got there is anybody's guess. I brought it back so we could sell it in this catalogue to someone from England. First come, first serve.* (FINE) **$235.00**

F6-37. Assorted Makers: Group of 7 Assorted Molding Planes. Assorted Profiles. Stewart, Kellogg, Etc. Length: 9 1/2 Inches. *All of these planes have seen quite a bit of use, but are mostly intact and clearly marked with maker's name.* (GOOD) **$95.00**

F6-38. Kellogg, J., Amherst, Mass.: Side Rabbet Molding Plane. Left Hand Cut. Near New Condition. Length: 9 1/2 Inches. *If you have the other half of this pristine side rabbet set then this is a big time bargain. Nearly new.* (FINE) **$45.00**

F6-39. Gladwin & Appleton, Boston: Boxed Center Bead Molding Plane. 3/16 Inch Size. Ready to Use. Length: 9 1/2 Inches. *This center bead is nicely boxed and ready to go to work. Extra crisp and clean.* (GOOD+) **$35.00**

F6-40. Routledge, Birmingham: Fully Boxed Filletster Molding Plane. Rare Type. Near New Condition. Length: 9 1/2 Inches. *The entire sole of this spectacularly well preserved filletster plane is a solid 2 inch piece of boxwood that has been fitted to the body by means of a dovetailed key. Planes of this sort were offered as an option by some planemakers, but the historical evidence indicates that very few were sold. When such planes were made, it was likely for such hard use that they deteriorated quickly, despite the extra effort in their making. A pristine example of a most unusual wooden plane configuration.* (FINE) **$425.00**

F6-41. Tileston, T., Boston (Front St.): Astragal and Cove Molding Plane. Most Unusual Profile. Extra Crisp and Clean. Length: 9 1/2 Inches. *The 1830's in Boston was a time of economic prosperity and plenty. One thing of which they had more than plenty was wood. Clean pine from the forests of New England was everywhere and it was used to fashion great houses in a great city. Planemaker Timothy Tileston was one of the principal providers of tools to the builders who fashioned the homes of the city. This extra steep molder from that early period is in excellent condition, noting a hang hole in back through the body. A dramatic early molding plane.* (GOOD+) **$365.00**

F6-42. Carter, R., Troy, N.Y.: 3/4 Inch Boxed Bead Molding Plane. Ca. 1833-1841. Extra Crisp and Clean. Length: 9 1/2 Inches. *Dual strips of boxing are an indication that extra care was taken to make this boxed bead last longer than most. It has now survived for nearly 170 years. Not a bad job. Crisp, clean and ready to use.* (GOOD+) **$35.00**

F6-43. Preston, W., London: Cove, Bead/Cove Molding Plane. 2 7/8 Inch Over All Width. Uncommon Profile. Length: 9 1/2 Inches. *This massive English molder has a dramatic cascading profile in a highly unusual cove, bead and cove pattern. It is in excellent condition.* (GOOD+) **$385.00**

F6-44. Unmarked No. 135: Steep Quirk Ovolo, Bevel Molding Plane. Appears Manufactured. Marked "3/4". Length: 9 1/2 Inches. *This extra steep molding plane is marked with the designation "3/4" on the heel as well as the mark "No. 135", but has no makers mark. A crisp, clean and ready to use complex molding plane.* (GOOD+) **$115.00**

F6-45. Reed, Utica (N. Y.): Wide Flat Ogee Molding Plane. Marked "3/4". Near New Condition. Length: 9 1/2 Inches. *This classic ogee with bevel molder is in essentially unused condition. Choice.* (FINE) **$135.00**

Group G6

G6-1. Starrett Co., L. S., Athol, Mass.: No. 18-A: Machinist's Center Punch. Spring Loaded. Near New Condition. Length: 5 Inches. *This precision center punch is in nearly new condition. Nice.* (FINE) **$25.00**

G6-2. Stanley Rule & Level No. 5: Saddler's Hammer. Patented December 12, 1867. Extra Rare. Length: 12 Inches. *Offered by Stanley from 1872 to 1898, but apparently never marked with the Stanley name, this tool was manufactured under a patent granted to Thomas Conklin on December 10, 1867. A rare Stanley hammer.* (GOOD) **$95.00**

G6-3. Rustless Rule Co., Buffalo, N.Y.: No. W-5: 6 Inch Caliper Rule. Brass Jaws. "Pat. Appl'd. For". Length: 6 Inches. *Part of a line of aluminum rules from this obscure Buffalo, New York-based company, this, the 6 inch version is the only offering to feature a caliper. This one is in crisp, clean condition. A very nice example.* (FINE) **$65.00**

G6-4. Unmarked: Precision Brass Level. Original Case. Near New Condition. Length: 5 Inches. *This lacquered brass level is in excellent condition, thanks to the presence of it protective tin case. A showy small level.* (FINE) **$65.00**

G6-5. Dietzgen Co., Eugene, Chicago: Draughtsman's Trammels. Velvet Lined Case. Marked "D.R.P.". Length: 12 Inches. *Thanks to the protective presence of the original box, these trammels, which were made for use at the drafting table, are in nearly new condition. A nice set.* (FINE) **$85.00**

G6-6. Starrett Co., The L.S., Athol, Mass.: Bronze Advertising Sign. Raised Cast Letters. Unused Condition. Length: 3 1/2 Inches. *This small sign was used for mounting on the Starrett Display cases that hung in hardware stores. It is made of cast bronze. The background is unfinished and the raised letters have been highly polished. It is in unused condition. A great Starrett advertising item.* (FINE) **$25.00**

G6-7. Snap On Tools Corp, Kenosha, Wisconsin.: Large Open, Hex Wrench Tie Clasp. Marked 1/4 Inch. Crisp and Clean. Length: 2 3/4 Inches. *The fellow at the garage across the street used to wear a tie and used it when checking the oil to clean the dipstick. He would have had no use for this fancy tie clasp. A well preserved Snap On collectible.* (GOOD+) **$25.00**

G6-8. Goodell-Pratt Company: 6 Inch Machinist's Combination Square. With Center Head. Ready to Use. Length: 6 Inches. *Goodell-Pratt produced machinists tools under their own name for a brief period which bracketed the First World War. This uncommon 6" combination square is missing the original scribe, but is otherwise clean and complete. A good one.* (GOOD+) **$25.00**

G6-9. North Bros Mfg. Co., Philadelphia: No. 41: Automatic Push Drill. All Original Bits. New Condition, Original Box. Length: 10 Inches. *This example of the workhorse of the North Bros. line is in New Condition in the original box. What more could one ask? Nice.* (FINE) **$45.00**

G6-10. Warlow, Bristol: Ebony and Brass Spirit Level. Top and Bottom Facing. Int. Side Plate. Length: 8 Inches. *The English port city of Bristol, from whence Jim Hawkins sailed, was the home of the maker of this classic level. A very well preserved brass and ebony level.* (GOOD+) **$145.00**

G6-11. Unmarked: Massive Hand Forged Calipers. With Roman Numerals. Very Well Made. Length: 21 1/2 Inches. *The beam that regulates the adjustment of these oversize hand forged calipers is graduated in inches, but marked with Roman numerals. A graphic set of early calipers.* (GOOD+) **$295.00**

G6-12. Goodell-Pratt Company No. 92: Machinist's Brass Hammer. 4 Ounce Size. Superb Condition. Length: 7 1/4 Inches. *Goodell Pratt made a full range of these wooden handled brass hammers. This one is in nearly new condition. Practically perfect.* (FINE) **$85.00**

G6-12. Unmarked: Quick Adjust Pipe Wrench. Needs Cleaning. Uncommon Type. Length: 12 Inches. *If you are inclined to do some grunge removal, there is a very interesting wrench under what is there. Most unusual.* (FAIR) **$55.00**

G6-13. D.B. & S., Providence, R.I.: Triangular Steel Rule. 6 Inch Size. Near New Condition. Length: 6 Inches. *These triangular rules are a marvel of the toolmaker's art. This one is perfectly preserved and very clearly marked.* (FINE) **$75.00**

G6-14. Starrett Co., The L.S., Athol, Mass.: Pair of Key Seat Gauges. Near New Condition. Ready to Use. Length: 1 1/2 Inches. *All of the original blued finish remains on these classic machinists accessories from L.S. Starrett.* (FINE) **$15.00**

G6-15. North Bros Mfg. Co., Philadelphia: No. 95: "Yankee" Slotted Screwdriver. 5 1/2 inch Blades. New Condition, Original Box. Length: 9 1/2 Inches. *This early "Yankee" screwdriver is in new condition in its original box. Absolutely top shelf.* (FINE) **$95.00**

G6-16. Lufkin Rule Co., The: No. 910 B: Toolmaker's Clamps. 1 1/4 Inch Size. New Condition, Original Box. Length: 3 1/4 Inches. *These machinists clamps are in new condition in their original yellow and purple Lufkin box. Nice.* (FINE) **$65.00**

G6-17. Brown & Sharpe Mfg., Providence: Patent Precision Combination Square. Patented December 2, 1890. Original Case. Length: 6 1/2 Inches. *The original box has kept this early patent machinists precision combination square in top condition. Crisp, clean and clearly marked.* (FINE) **$115.00**

G6-18. Goodell-Pratt Company No. 91: 3 Ounce Brass Machinist Hammer. Checkered Steel Handle. Excellent Condition. Length: 5 1/2 Inches. *This was the smallest size of the Goodell Pratt hammer line. It is the only example we have ever seen. Rare.* (GOOD+) **$185.00**

G6-19. Millers Falls Company No. 1405: Heavy Duty Awl. Black Painted Handle. Unused Condition. Length: 7 Inches. *This hardwood handle awl from the Millers Falls Company is in brand new condition. A very nice example.* (FINE) **$15.00**

G6-20. Howard & Son, F. A., Belfast, Maine: Patent Reverse Spiral Screwdriver. Patented March 1, 1892. Uncommon Type. Length: 10 1/2 Inches. *Perhaps the shipbuilding industry along the Maine coast was responsible for the plethora of patented screwdrivers originating in that area in the last quarter of the 19th century. Simple artistry combined with a mechanically complex form.* (GOOD) **$35.00**

G6-21. Snap On Tools Corp, Kenosha, Wisconsin.: Ratchet Wrench Tie Clasp. Original Case. Unused Condition. Length: 2 3/4 Inches. *If you were an auto mechanic and your wife made you dress up to go out to dinner, you might feel a bit more comfortable knowing there was a wrench within reach just below the table top. A well preserved Snap On collectible.* (FINE) **$35.00**

G6-22. Starrett Co., The L.S., Athol, Mass: Advertising Pin. With Tools Trademark. Early and Excellent. Length: 0 3/4 Inches. *This advertising pin is bright red in color and is decorated with the famous "tools" logo. Crisp, clean and graphic. It appears to date from the 1920's.* (FINE) **$25.00**

G6-23. Starrett Co., L.S., Athol, Mass.: No. 570: Multiple Blade Screwdriver. With 4 Blades. Near New Condition. Length: 8 Inches. *This crispy clean Starrett screwdriver comes complete with four original blades. Scarce and near new.* (FINE) **$115.00**

G6-24. North Bros Mfg. Co., Philadelphia: Early Patent Ratchet Screwdriver. Patented November 2, 1897. Pre-Numbered Type. Length: 11 Inches. *This early ratchet screwdriver from North Brothers is marked only with an 1897 patent date and precedes the North Bros. numbering scheme, indicating that it was one of the first screwdrivers they produced. The ratchet mechanism is not in perfect working order. A rare and early screwdriver.* (GOOD+) **$35.00**

G6-25. Unmarked: Early Style Knurling Set. With 8 Original Knurls. Brass Ferrule and Tip. Length: 9 Inches. *A series of original knurls are included with this rosewood handle knurling set. Early and excellent.* (GOOD+) **$65.00**

G6-26. Starrett Co., The L.S., Athol, Mass.: Advertising Display Sign. Shown in 1919 Catalogue. Brand New Condition. Length: 12 3/4 Inches. *This highly polished new old stock advertising sign was featured in Starrett's 1919 catalog to encourage dealers to display the sign in their store. This sign is in nearly new condition.* (FINE) **$95.00**

G6-27. Johnson Rule Mfg. Co., E.P.: No. 46: Patent Protractor Folding Rule. Patented January 8, 1907. German Silver Body. Length: 6 Inches. *This example of the Johnson patent rule is in excellent collector quality condition. A superb example of an uncommon patented German silver rule.* (FINE) **$65.00**

G6-28. Unmarked: Early Double Caliper. With Distinctive Form. Hand Filed. Length: 10 Inches. *This early pair of calipers has a unique profile accented by the presence of a pair of "boots" immediately above the caliper tips. Very different.* (GOOD+) **$55.00**

G6-29. Assorted Makers: Rules and Whitworth Gauge. Chesterman, Etc. From Single Chest. Length: 7 Inches. *Here's an opportunity lot of rules and gauges from the same drawer of a machinists chest. A bargain.* (FINE) **$25.00**

G6-30. Millers Falls Company No. 92: Machinist's Brass Hammer. 4 Ounce Head. Near-New Condition. Length: 7 Inches. *Millers Falls produced a full line of these attractive brass headed hammers. This one has the M.F. name imprinted on the handle in gold lettering. Nearly new, and nice.* (FINE) **$75.00**

G6-31. Unmarked: Quick Adjust Caliper. For Outside Measure. Similar to Stevens Patent. Length: 4 Inches. *No maker or owner marks on this one, given the difference in condition from the other tools, this may have been acquired from another workman at some point.* (GOOD) **$25.00**

G6-32. Wyke & Co., E. Boston, Mass.: "Wyke's Patent" Gauge. Patented September 11, 1882. Complete and Excellent. Length: 4 Inches. *A clean, complete and clearly marked example of the Wyke multi-purpose machinist's gauge of 1882. A rare and mechanically interesting tool in excellent condition.* (GOOD+) **$115.00**

G6-33. Millers Falls Company: Augur Bit Depth Gauge. With Rolling Ball Stop. Patented May 25, 1900. Length: 5 1/2 Inches. *Tools for use in bit braces or as accessories thereto have become increasingly collectible in recent years. This depth gauge from the Millers falls company features a ball bearing in a socket to serve as the stop. Early and excellent.* (FINE) **$55.00**

G6-34. Starrett Co., L. S., Athol, Mass.: No. 414: Polished Steel Bench Rule. 8ths and 16ths Graduates. As New Condition. Length: 12 Inches. *This one is as crisp and clean as the day it was made. An uncommon Starrett rule.* (FINE) **$25.00**

G6-35. Stearns & Co., E.C., Syracuse, N.Y.: No. 85: Cast Iron Marking Gauge. Full Nickel Plating. Near New Condition. Length: 3 Inches. *We have offered a wide range of the tools produced by Syracuse, New York maker E.C. Stearns & Company, but this is the first butt marking gauge we have encountered. Rare & as new.* (FINE) **$45.00**

G6-36. D.B. & S., Providence, R.I.: Machinist's Bench Rule. 6 Inch Length. Early and Excellent. Length: 6 Inches. *The early mark of the Darling, Brown & Sharpe Company is imprinted on this well preserved bench rule. A nice example.* (GOOD+) **$35.00**

G6-37. Starrett, L.S., Athol, Mass.: No. 108: Precision Line Level. Aluminum Body. New Condition, Original Box. Length: 3 1/4 Inches. *You could go to the hardware store and get a junky Japanese line level for a pittance or spend a day's pay on the best one made from L.S. Starrett. The top of the line in new condition in its original box.* (FINE) **$45.00**

G6-38. Brown & Sharpe Mfg. Co.: Early Patent Micrometer. Patented April 23, 1878. Complete and Excellent. Length: 3 3/4 Inches. *The body of this early patent micrometer is engraved with tables of decimal equivalents. The patent was granted to G.M. Pratt on April 23, 1878. A nice example.* (GOOD+) **$55.00**

G6-39. Sawyer Tool Co., Ashburnham, Mass.: Precision Bench Rule. Graduated in 100ths. Near New Condition. Length: 2 Inches. *This early precision bench rule is in unused condition. Mint.* (FINE) **$25.00**

G6-40. Starrett Co., L.S., Athol, Mass.: No. 97: Precision Bench Level. With Cross Test Vial. New Condition, Original Box. Length: 8 Inches. *The original pasteboard box has kept this high precision level from America's premier makers of machinists tools in top condition. New and in the box.* (FINE) **$65.00**

G6-41. Stanley Rule & Level No. 122: Try and Mitre Combination Square. With Integral Level. New Condition, Original Box. Length: 12 Inches. *The original box has protected this example of the No. 122 Combination Square throughout its long life. An uncommon tool in a seldom-seen box. Missing the label, but otherwise perfect.* (FINE) **$85.00**

G6-42. Mason, New Haven, Conn.: "Pat. Appl'd. For" Stamp. Ca. 1890's. Most Unusual. Length: 3 1/2 Inches. *This "Pat. appl'd. For" stamp has a decidedly early appearance.* (GOOD+) **$145.00**

G6-43. Starrett Co., L. S., Athol, Mass.: Early Patent Outside Caliper. Patented January 6, 1885. Rare and Excellent. Length: 6 Inches. *A good, clean example of Starrett's precision adjust 1885 patent.* (GOOD+) **$75.00**

G6-44. American Plierench Corp., Chicago: Eifel Geared Plier Wrench. Complete with Instructions. Original Case. Length: 8 1/2 Inches. *One of the most successful "gizmos" of all time, the Eifel Geared Plierench had been in the Popular Invention Hall of Fame long before the Veg-o-Matic and the Pocket Fisherman arrived. This pristine example is in new condition in its original case.* (FINE) **$115.00**

Group H6

H6-1. Lively Lad Mfg. Co., Clarksville: Genuine Original Fish Axe. With Leather Scabbard. Original Decal. Length: 10 Inches. *Years on the tool trail can take the passion out of a collector. The once rare becomes "oh, another one of those" and the other stuff is just stuff. Once in a while, however, there comes a tool that brings back the passion of the very early days when every tool was a discovery and every maker a mystery. Produced by the Lively Lad Manufacturing Company, this "Fish Axe" is the first of its kind we have seen. A tool to bring a tear to the eye of even the most hardened collector.* (FINE) **$55.00**

H6-2. Plumb, Fayette R., Philadelphia: Carpenter's Hewing Hatchet. Original Handle. Near New Condition. Length: 15 1/2 Inches. *This Plumb hewing hatchet looks as though it has been little if ever used. Perfect, and ready to go to work.* (FINE) **$75.00**

H6-3. Fulton Tool Company: Early No. 4 1/2 Size Metallic Plane. Rosewood Handles. Made by Sargent? Length: 10 Inches. *Collectors of bench planes who despair of the rising cost of "No. 2" size planes would be well advised to consider seeking out and collecting those of the No. 4 1/2 size. These are insufficiently common to keep the search interesting and make an excellent display when grouped together. This example from the Fulton Tool Company is fitted with dramatically grained handles of Brazilian Rosewood and is in excellent overall condition. The pin that fixes the yoke on the depth of cut adjustment has been replaced by a cotter pin, but this could easily be put right. A rare No. 4 1/2 plane.* (FINE) **$145.00**

H6-4. Iron Age No. E38: Cast Iron "Cutout" Wrench. With Hammer End. Largest Size. Length: 9 Inches. *This graphic "cutout" is marked with the number "E 38" cast into the body in addition to the hard to miss maker name.* (GOOD+) **$65.00**

H6-5. Belden Machine Co., New Haven, Conn.: Non-Mar Jaw Pipe Wrench. Patented August 19, 1885. J.T. Hayden's Patent. Length: 9 Inches. *This early patented wrench comes with three of the interchangeable wraparound jaws. Nicely marked with the maker name and patent date.* (GOOD+) **$165.00**

H6-6. Lufkin Rule Co., The: Machinist's Combination Square. With Center Head. Original Decals. Length: 4 Inches. *Here's a pristine Lufkin try square complete with its original center head. A great working tool.* (FINE) **$75.00**

H6-7. Bishop & Co., Geo. H., Lawrenceburg: No. B 80: 26 Inch 5 Point Rip Saw. With Hand Grip. Superb Condition. Length: 29 Inches. *Fitted with a handle equivalent in form and function to those supplied by Henry Disston's 7 Sons, this classic rip saw from George Bishop is imprinted with the Lawrenceburg, Indiana working location of that company. An uncommon saw in uncommonly nice condition.* (FINE) **$85.00**

H6-8. Stanley Rule & Level No. 66: Universal Scratch Beader. With Straight Fence. 7 Double Cutters. Length: 11 Inches. *Seven double-ended cutters should give a would-be traditional woodworker a great start on mastery of the art of beading. The straight edge fence only is provided with this tool.* (FINE) **$165.00**

H6-9. Lufkin Rule Co., The: No. 588: Oil Gauge Plumb Bob. Cast Brass Body. New Condition, Original Box. Length: 2 1/2 Inches. *A new old stock plumb bob, this one has an ovate shape and was used at the end of a reel for gauging the depth of oil in a tank. The box is in great shape.* (FINE) **$65.00**

H6-10. Stanley Rule & Level No. 289: Skew-Blade Rabbet Plane. Complete and Original. Ca. 1910 Trademark. Length: 8 1/2 Inches. *Here's a clean and complete working example of Stanley's skew-blade rabbet. These planes were much more heavily cast than the No. 78 rabbet plane, and were well-suited to working with figured woods and end grain. Someone has "enhanced" the japanning so that this plane appears as new. A ready to use precision tool.* (FINE) **$395.00**

H6-11. Buck & Ryan Ltd., London: Boxwood Handle. Dovetail Saw. Octagonal Grip. Near New Condition. Length: 13 Inches. *Fitted with an octagonal-shaped handle of Turkish boxwood that has achieved a bright, golden patina, this saw is in essentially unused condition. Straight, sharp and ready to use. Extra nice.* (FINE) **$95.00**

H6-12. Stanley Rule & Level No. 5 C: "Type 14" Jack Plane. Ca. 1920's. 98% Original Paint. Length: 14 Inches. *This ca. 1920's jack plane is in superb condition. Nearly all of the original shiny black japan finish remains. The early type Brazilian Rosewood handles have a spectacular grain pattern. A nice plane in top working condition.* (FINE) **$115.00**

H6-13. Diamond Edge: Aluminum Handle Draw Knife. 5 Inch Gauge. Near New Condition. Length: 7 Inches. *The maker or product name "Diamond Edge" is the only writing on this most unusual aluminum leather draw gauge. A rare gauge in top condition.* (FINE) **$85.00**

H6-14. Greenlee Tool Co., Rockford, Illinois: No. 265: Heavy Socket Framing Chisel. 1 1/2 Inch Size. Unused Condition. Length: 16 1/2 Inches. *This ca. 1920's framing chisel has been kept in new condition by the presence of the original cosmoline covering, which I do not care to remove ever again. A brand new framing chisel in a most desirable size.* (FINE) **$55.00**

H6-15. Keuffel & Esser Co., New York: No. 999026: "Linemaster" Plumb Bob Reel. Crank Reel Type. New Condition, Original. Box. Length: 3 1/4 Inches. *If you were one of those unfortunate enough to have a plumb bob without an internal winding reel (most were), this gizmo would provide you with additional functionality. An uncommon accessory to the world of Plumb Bobbery.* (FINE) **$65.00**

H6-16. Chapin, H., Union Factory: No. 244: Applewood Plow Plane. Boxwood Arms, Nuts. Near New Condition. Length: 8 Inches. *Complete and in nearly the same condition as it was the day it left the Hermon Chapin's Union Factory in Pine Meadow, Connecticut, this spectacular applewood plow plane is absent any evidence of wear or abuse on either its boxwood arms or the body of the plane. A full set of Moulson Brothers cutting irons, which undoubtedly were sold with the plow, are also in new condition. If you are looking for an extra special plow plane, this pristine example from a prominent and highly respected Connecticut maker may be just what you need. Extra special.* (FINE) **$585.00**

H6-17. Union Hardware Co.: Set of 3 Socket Chisel. Square Side Type. 1/2 Inch, 1 Inch and 1 1/2 Inch. Length: 17 Inches. *The fact that these well made chisels were sheltered by a wooden box and, in the case of two of the tools, by fitted leather "keepers", accounts for the reason they are in such well preserved condition. A great working set that is ready to be put to work.* (GOOD+) **$155.00**

H6-18. Fulton Tool Company No. 5264: "no. 4" Size Metallic Plane. Mahogany Handles. Made By Sargent? Length: 10 Inches. *This early example of the "Fulton" line dates from the immediate pre-WW I period and was likely made for Fulton by Sargent & Company of New Haven, Connecticut.* (FINE) **$75.00**

H6-19. Disston & Sons, H., Philadelphia, Penn.: No. D 8: 26 Inch 8 Point. Crosscut Saw. Original Etching. Near New Condition. Length: 29 Inches. *Nearly all of the original factory etching remains on this classic "sway back" crosscut saw. Straight, sharp and ready to use.* (FINE) **$75.00**

H6-20. Hall, Robinson, Sheffield: Adjustable Beech Spoke Shave. With Original Decal. Near New Condition. Length: 10 Inches. *Nearly all of the original decal remains on this well made English spokeshave of Sheffield manufacture. Nearly new.* (FINE) **$45.00**

H6-21. Caspers, J., Lancaster, Wisc.: Plier Type Wrench. "Pat. Appl'd. For". Uncommon Type. Length: 13 Inches. *This plier-type wrench from an obscure Wisconsin maker is marked "Pat. Appl'd. for" at the pivot joint. Never seen another.* (GOOD+) **$65.00**

H6-22. Keuffel & Esser Co., New York: No. 83 0036: Surveyor's Brass Plumb Bob. With Green Box. New Condition, Original Box. Length: 5 Inches. *This K. & E. classic is absolutely mint in its original box.* (FINE) **$65.00**

H6-23. Starrett Co., L. S., Athol, Mass.: No. 465: Brass Blacksmith's Rule. With Handle & Hook. Uncommon Type. Length: 16 1/2 Inches. *These hook end rules from Starrett were designed for gauging hot metal. They are far from common. This one is in unused condition.* (FINE) **$145.00**

H6-24. Overman Wheel Co., Boston, Mass.: Combination Screwdriver and Wrench. Patented February 2, 1886. "Cycle Brush Tool". Length: 5 1/2 Inches. *One of the most unusual tools offered here: A bone handled, combination parts brush, spanner wrench and reamer for early bicycles. Marked with the patent date and maker's mark.* (GOOD) **$95.00**

H6-25. Millers Falls Company No. 1: Rosewood Handle Spoke Shave. Original Red Paint. Extra Crisp and Clean. Length: 10 Inches. *Early tools by the Millers Falls Company are noted for their exceptional finish and workmanship. This circular spokeshave is a classic example. Most original finishes remain on clean example of the nickel plating, classic rosewood handles and period red infill in the throat. A nice example.* (GOOD+) **$95.00**

H6-26. Unmarked: Classic Nailmaker's Bench. For Hand Cut Nails. Early and Excellent. Length: 26 Inches. *The user of this early American classic would likely have sat on top of a barrel working through winter days cutting nails by hand to earn extra "hard money". A museum quality example found in the vicinity of Madison, New York many years ago.* (GOOD+) **$165.00**

H6-27. Record No. 722: Miniature Router Metallic Plane. Stanley 171 Equivalent. New Condition, Original Box. Length: 3 1/4 Inches. *The equivalent in form an function to Stanley's No. 171 router, this example from English maker Record is in new condition in its original box. Mint.* (FINE) **$65.00**

H6-28. Stanley Rule & Level No. 4 1/2: "Type 12" Smooth Plane. Rosewood Handle and Knob. 98% Original Paint. Length: 10 1/2 Inches. *Looking for a great working heavy smoothing plane. Here's an exceptionally nice No. 4 1/2 fitted out with handles of Brazilian Rosewood. A great working tool that is ready to provide several lifetimes of service. Part of the original decal remains on the handle of this "Type 12 inch version.* (FINE) **$245.00**

H6-29. Stanley Rule & Level No. 78: Duplex Filletster Plane. "Sweetheart" Trademark. New Condition, Original Box. Length: 9 1/2 Inches. *This example of Stanley's classic combination bullnose and rabbet plane is clean, complete and has been protected throughout its long life by the presence of its original box. A Stanley classic in top working order.* (FINE) **$145.00**

H6-30. Keuffel & Esser Co., New York: No. 6490: Surveyor's Brass Plumb Bob. Unused Condition. New Condition, Original Box. Length: 5 Inches. *The original box has kept this classic surveyor's plumb bob in top collector quality condition. Choice.* (FINE) **$35.00**

H6-31. Stanley Rule & Level No. 604: "Bedrock" Smoothing Plane. Original Decal. 98% Original Paint. Length: 9 Inches. *Much of the original decal and more than 98% of the shiny black japan finish remains on this exceptionally clean smoothing plane from Stanley's "Bedrock" series. If you are looking for a top quality smoothing plane to last a lifetime or two, this is it. Extra nice.* (FINE) **$345.00**

H6-32. Unmarked: Solid Boxwood Spoke Shave. Sharp and Clean. Ready to Use. Length: 11 1/2 Inches. *This well made boxwood spokeshave is in excellent working order and ready to use.* (FINE) **$65.00**

H6-33. Stanley Rule & Level No. 53: Adjustable Throat Spoke Shave. "Sweetheart" Trademark. Near New Condition. Length: 10 1/2 Inches. *Turning the adjustment screw at the top regulates the adjustment of the throat of this precision Stanley spokeshave. Nearly new and ready to use.* (FINE) **$55.00**

H6-34. Dudly Mfg. Co., A., Menominee, Mich.: Large Size Spoke Wrench. For High Wheelers? Patented May 29, 1904. Length: 4 Inches. *The Dudly company also made a series of pipe and nut wrenches. This is the largest size of their spoke wrench series. It is of such large size as to lead one to speculate that it may have been intended for high wheel bicycles. Boldly marked with the maker name and patent date.* (FINE) **$55.00**

H6-35. Disston & Sons, H., Philadelphia: No. 68: Beech Handle. Dovetail Saw. 8 Inch Blade. Straight and True. Length: 13 Inches. *Here's a clean and straight example of Disston's classic handled dovetail saw. Sharp and straight.* (GOOD+) **$45.00**

H6-36. Lufkin Rule Co., The: No. 25: Precision Combination Square. No. 4 Graduation. Unused Condition. Length: 6 Inches. *This crispy clean combination square is ready to be used...for the first time. Nice.* (FINE) **$55.00**

H6-37. Osborne & Co., C.S., Newark, N.J.: Set of 9 Round Leather Punches. 1/4 Inch To 1 Inch. Original Roll. Length: 6 Inches. *The original roll has kept this set of circular punches from C.S. Osborne in brand new condition. A great set.* (FINE) **$125.00**

H6-38. Jennings Mfg. Co., The, Russell: Set of 13 Auger Bits. 3 Tiered Box. Near New Condition. Length: 10 Inches. *The original box has kept these classic Russell Jennings auger bits in top working order. All of the shiny factory polish remains on this pristine set.* (FAIR) **$185.00**

H6-39. Hart Mfg. Co.: Heavy Socket Framing Chisel. Scarce 1 7/8 Inch Size. Extra Crisp and Clean. Length: 17 Inches. *No apologies from this quarter, nor complaints from any other for this exceptionally well preserved working tool. Crisp, clean and ready to use.* (GOOD+) **$75.00**

H6-40. Lufkin Rule Co., The, (Canada): No. 8512: "Zig Zag" Folding Rule. Rare 2 Foot Size. Clean and Sound. Length: 24 Inches. *The least common of all "Zig-Zag" rules are those in this, the two foot size. The utility to be gained from a folding rule that extended only as long as a ruler was likely determined to be negligible by potential users and the rules were either not stocked or discontinued early on. A rare Lufkin rule.* (GOOD) **$95.00**

H6-41. United States Government: Military Issue Chisel Roll. For Wheelwrights. Scarce and Excellent. Length: 18 Inches. *Back in the days when the U.S. Army had "wheelwrights", they were issued this canvas roll to keep track of their tools. The roll is empty, but intact and clearly marked. An unusual crossover collectible for tools and militaria.* (GOOD+) **$45.00**

H6-42. Copeland, D.: Steep Quirk Ovolo Molding Plane. Marked "6/8". Extra Crisp and Clean. Length: 9 1/2 Inches. *This Copeland molder has an extra steep cut and is in excellent working order.* (GOOD+) **$155.00**

H6-43. Stanley Rule & Level No. 49: Early Tongue and Groove Plane. 3/16 Inch Cutter. 99% Original Paint. Length: 10 Inches. *Early examples of Stanley's swinging fence match plane with the 3/16" cutter are seldom found, especially examples that retain some 99% of their original shiny japan finish, as does this example. The fence is imprinted with the date of the July 6, 1875 patent granted to Charles G. Miller, the same Miller whose patents were applied to Stanley's 41-44 series of combination planes. A rare and early plane in new condition.* (FINE) **$285.00**

H6-44. Unmarked: London Spring Steel Saw. 10 Point. Crosscut. With Bear Logo. Length: 27 Inches. *A most unusual "Bear" logo appears on the blade of this crispy clean 10 point crosscut saw. The handle has been formed with the thumb notch to accommodate overhand sawing.* (FINE) **$125.00**

Fresh Tools Every Tuesday and Thurday at 1:00 Eastern Time

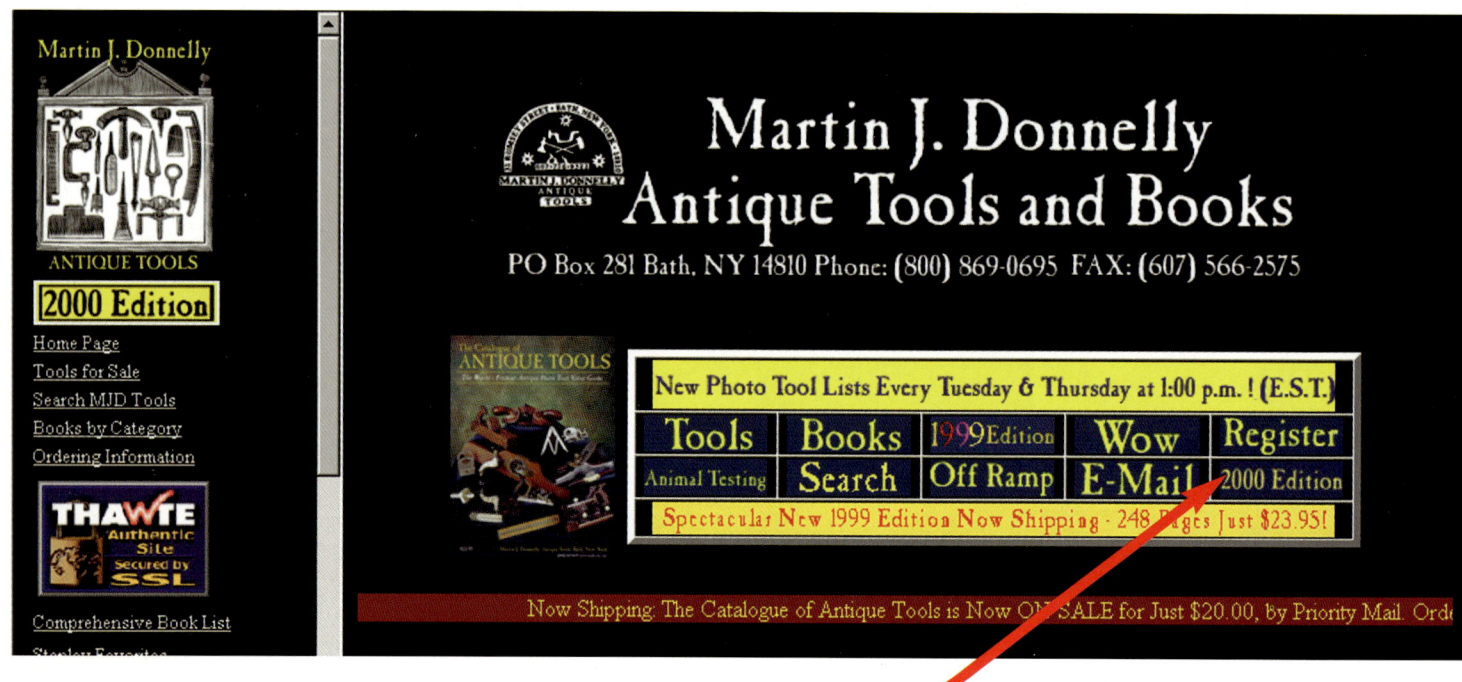

www.mjdtools.com

Click HERE to Register for Immediate Notice of New Lists

AN INTERNATIONAL MILLENIUM YEAR
TOOL AUCTION

Tony Murland in conjunction with Tyrone Roberts announces an outstanding International Sale of Antique and Useable Woodworking Tools

FRIDAY 28TH JULY 2000

THE LIMES HOTEL, NEEDHAM MARKET, SUFFOLK, ENGLAND

This auction contains a fantastic set of miniature ivory Carpenters' tool, a 19c apprentice piece; over 50 **NORRIS** and SPIERS metal and infill planes; a **STANLEY** No. 9 and other rare **STANLEY** planes; and dozens of twin-iron; the finest Collection of complex moulders we have ever auctioned; a solid rosewood plough by MATHIESON; a 22 1/2" **NORRIS** jointer, virtually unused; a **NORRIS** 20E in the original box
….and too much more to mention….

For fully illustrated and indexed colour catalogue, absentee bidding instructions and prices realized in due course please send US $35 (credit card details, cheque, money order) to:

TOOL SHOP AUCTIONS 78 HIGH STREET,
NEEDHAM MARKET, SUFFOLK, IP6 8AW, UK

Tel: 011-44-1449-722992 FAX: 011-44-1449-722683
E-mail: tony@toolshop.demon.co.uk Website: http://www.toolshop.demon.co.uk

PLEASE BE SURE TO VISIT OUR WEBSITE……25 FRESH TOOLS ADDED EVERY FRIDAY
AND SO MUCH MORE TO INTEREST EVERY TOOL ENTHUSIAST

The Collector's Bookshelf

Value Guides to Antiques   Books About Tools Trades & Technology

Martin J. Donnelly Antique Tools   www.mjdtools.com   Toll Free: (800) 869-0695

The Catalogue of Antique Tools *Millennium Edition*
Now Shipping! · 6500 Tools · Fully Indexed · All Items for Sale

175 New Titles in Stock!

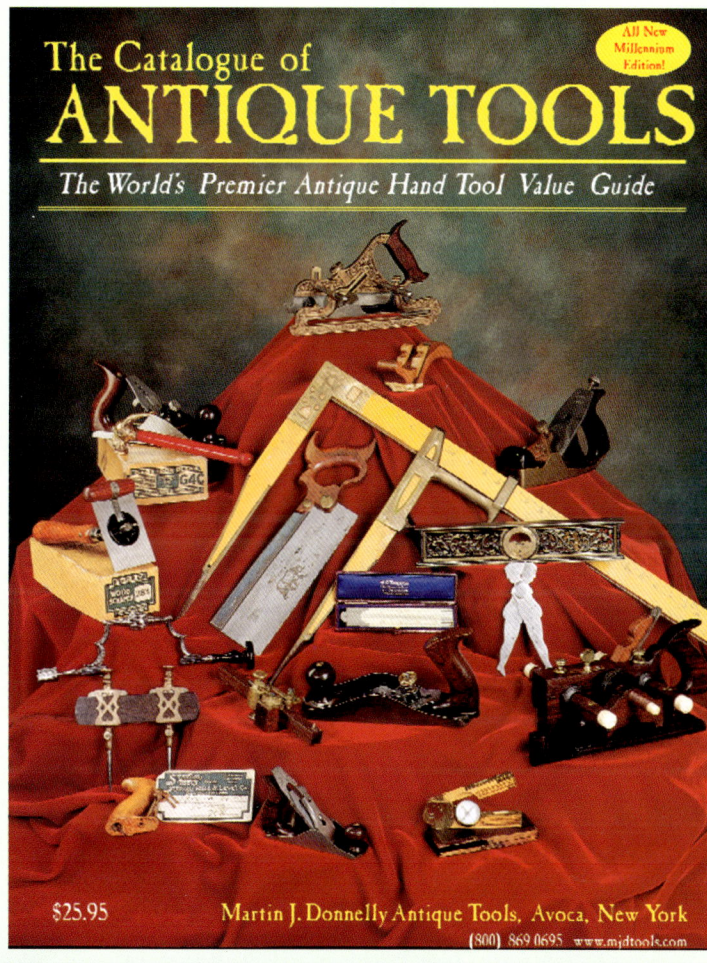

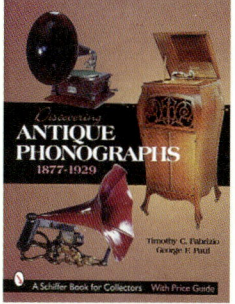
BK 366 · Page 5

BK 326 · Page 3

BK 367 · Page 5

Books Make GREAT Gifts for Father's Day, Birthdays & More!

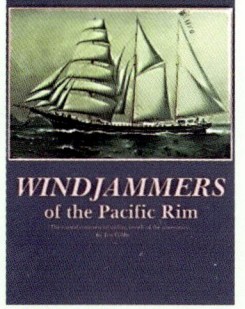
BK 415 · Page 7

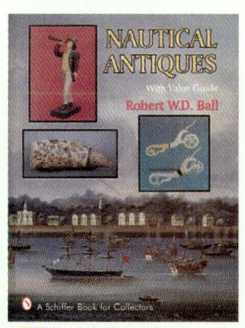
BK 450 · Page 3

BK 415 · Page 3

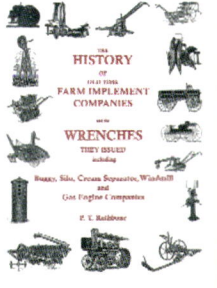
BK 323 · Page 8

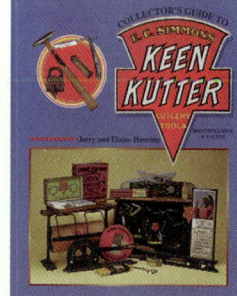
BK 453 · Page 3

Bk 357 · Page 3

Free Shipping · Orders: Page 17 · Index: Page 30 · Toll Free: (800) 869-0695

A Personal Note...From the Publisher

First, on behalf of all of our team here at Martin J. Donnelly Antique Tools, I would like to thank you for the support you have given to our continuing expansion of our inventory of books about tools, trades and technology. As part of our commitment to becoming your sole source for books, we have added a wide range of titles about tools, trades, woodworking, and antiques. Consistent with this expansion of focus, we have changed the title of this publication to *The Collector's Bookshelf*. In the coming months we will be expanding our scope even more. If you don't see a book that you would like, just let us know and we will do everything we can to obtain it for you and add it to our inventory.

We are particularly excited about the Millennium Edition of the Catalogue of Antique Tools. This year's Edition is, once again, bigger and better than those that have preceded it. Included in this year's volume are 6,662 tools, all photographed in full color, carefully described and priced to sell. During the past year, we moved to our new location in Avoca, New York. Our greatly expanded facilities include a 300 foot climate controlled warehouse, a modern office building and a *circa* 1865 home in the country. We have hired five more employees as part of our longstanding commitment to provide the best and most professional service in the business. We look forward to serving you.

During 1999 we have expanded our ability to serve you through our internet site at www.mjdtools.com. If you are interested in ordering books, please consider making use of our new Secure Online Ordering Facility. This fully secure system uses state of the art SSL Encryption Technology to ensure that your online transactions are as safe and efficient as ordering by mail, fax or phone. For details about how to order online, just check out the easy directions on page 16 of this catalog. If you do decide to order online, feel free to call with questions, or just to say hello. We pride ourselves on the personal level of our service and we never want to lose touch with you.

Finally, a word to the many collectors of antique tools who have supported the Catalogue of Antique Tools. If you are considering selling some or all of your antique tools, we invite you to consider the services we provide. During 1999, thousands of copies of the Catalogue of Antique Tools were sold in a total of 34 countries. In addition, our twice-weekly lists of tools on our internet site, www.mjdtools.com, have produced an ever-expanding array of potential buyers. During the month of March of this year alone, our site registered 928,000 "hits". We are eager to talk to you about purchasing your antique tools or accepting them for consignment. Please give us a call at (800) 869-0695. We look forward to discussing with you how we can help you obtain the best possible return for your investment in antique tools.

Martin J. Donnelly
Spring, 2000

Special Offer: Back Issues Just $10.00
With Any Order

1999: BK 172   1998: BK 62

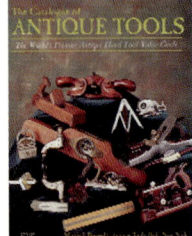

The Catalogue of Antique Tools, Millennium Edition, by Martin J. Donnelly. 320 Pages. 8 1/2" x 11". *Our biggest and best catalogue ever, the much anticipated Millennium Edition is bigger by 25% than the 1999 Edition. Included in the 320 page volume are 6,662 tools, each photographed in full color, carefully described and priced to sell. An expanded six-page index listing both manufacturers and types of tools makes the Catalogue of Antique Tools a long lasting reference for collectors, antique dealers and those with an interest in the history of technology. If you have not previously ordered the Catalogue, we encourage you to do so. We absolutely guarantee that you will be delighted.* **$25.95 (BK 364)**

Makes A Great Gift!

New Books in Stock - Just Published!

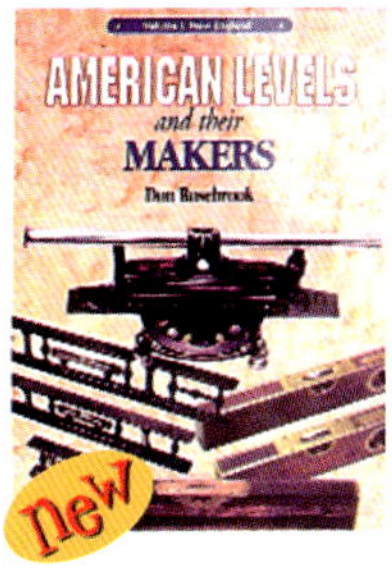

American Levels and Their Makers - New England, by Don Rosebrook. 297 Pages. 8 1/2" x 11". *In this work on the level makers of New England, the first volume of a planned series covering all American level makers, author Don Rosebrook, the premier researcher and collector of American-made levels, has produced a book that substantially expands the range of knowledge of tool collectors, not only about levels, but also about a large number of previously undocumented New England manufacturers. Rosebrook has masterfully combined the results of years of research in New England libraries and archives with his personal knowledge of manufactured levels gleaned from years of collecting and study of the great American collections to produce a work that is informative, very readable, useful as a reference work and beautiful to behold. Superb color and black and white photographs by kindred spirit level collector Dennis Fisher contribute significantly to the overall appeal of the work. As a principal New England maker, the Stanley Rule & Level Company is prominently featured in more than 30 pages, which contain much previously unpublished information. All of the other great New England makers, such as L.L. Davis, Stratton Brothers, the early Boston makers and many, many more are thoroughly covered together with illustrations from early catalogs, photographs and advertising. Without question, this book stands without peer as the best tool book of the new millennium. Highly recommended.* **$65.00 (BK 326)**

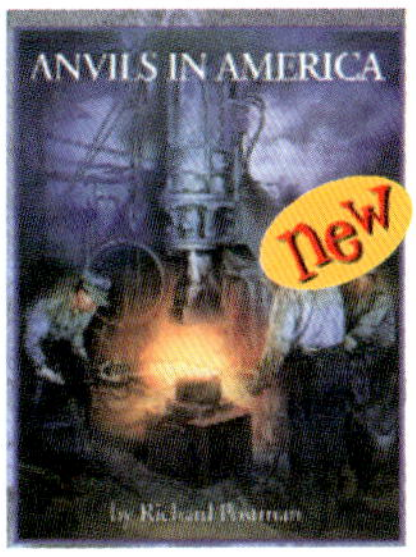

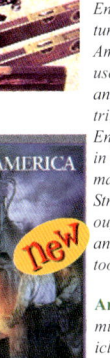

Anvils In America, by Richard Postman. 550 Pages. 9" x 11.25". *A culmination of fifteen years of meticulous research, Anvils in America chronicles the evolution of the historically important implement that was integral to the Iron Age. Early American and European anvils, English anvils, and American cast anvils are discussed in great detail. Blacksmiths, anvil collectors, and anyone interested in historical tools will enjoy this unique book.* **$60.00 (BK 422)**

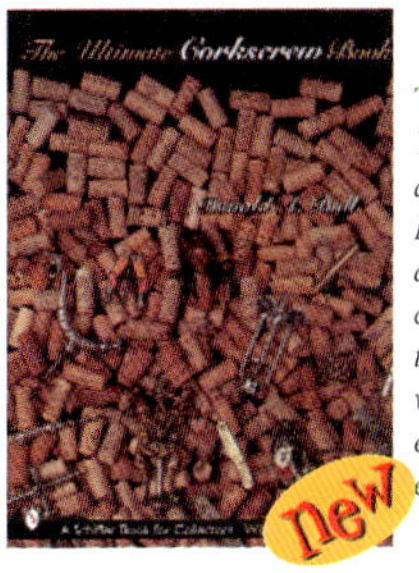

The Ultimate Corkscrew Book, by Onald A. Bull. 318 Pages. 9.5" x 12.25". *An armchair guide to corkscrews with over 700 color photographs and 3600 illustrated and documented examples, The Ultimate Corkscrew Book showcases the diversity and creativity that has occurred in the production of corkscrews over the last several hundred years. Eclectic corkscrews, figural corkscrews, corkscrew knives, and many others reflect the labors of a most relentless and diligent pursuit on the author's part, which has resulted in the most comprehensive collection of corkscrews ever amassed. This book will open the eyes of every devotee of this twisted hobby.* **$89.95 (BK 372)**

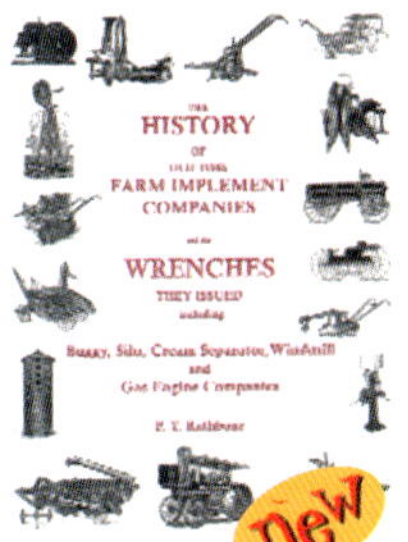

The History of Old Time Farm Implement Companies and the Wrenches They Issued, by P. T. Rathbone. 513 Pages. 8 1/2" x 11". *Antique tool collectors and dealers in antiques who might not otherwise have an interest in cast iron implement wrenches begin to change their focus when they learn that the two highest prices ever paid for wrenches were for tools of this type. Long considered incomprehensible by many collectors, P.T. Rathbone has put together a work that makes sense of the vast array of wrenches produced and issued with plows, cultivators, buggies, silos, cream separators, windmills and more. Organized in encyclopedic fashion by manufacturer, Rathbone's documents in "time line" fashion, the history of each maker and includes illustrations of known examples adjacent to each maker history. Especially helpful to collectors and dealers is the supplement included with this volume that allows wrenches marked only with numbers to be linked to manufacturers and also includes a summary of recent auction prices. In all likelihood, the cost of this book will be covered by the first wrench in the top of a box of similar items in the garage. A necessary reference that will more than pay its own way.* **$55.00 (BK 453)**

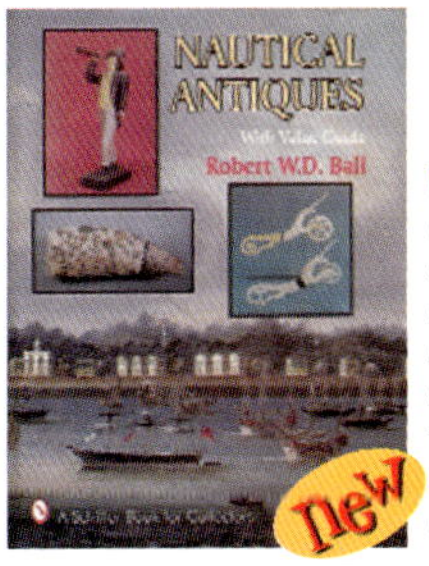

Nautical Antiques, by Robert W.D. Ball. 238 Pages. 9" x 11.25". *This beautiful volume illustrated the hundreds of nautical items sought after by collectors. Scrimshawed items, sailor-made ship models, nautical instruments and aids, nautical and whaling implements, furnishings and accessories, ship's figureheads, sternboards, and much more. The selection is endless, with many venues to pursue, limited only by the contents of one's wallet and one's patience to search the dusty corners of some antique shop. Collectors and old salts alike will enjoy this fascinating look at the artifacts of our nautical past (complete with price guide).* **$39.95 (BK 382)**

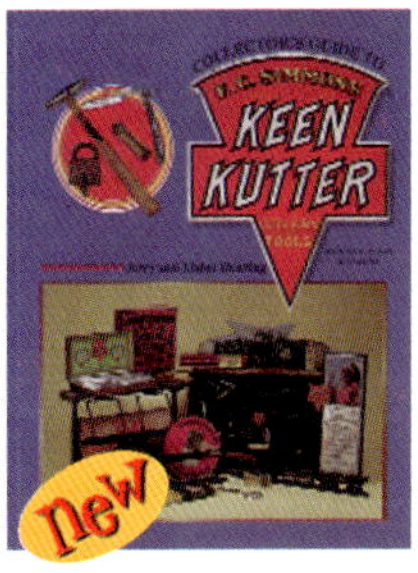

Collector's Guide to Keen Kutter, by Jerry and Elaine Heuring. 192 Pages. 8 1/2" x 11". *Recently released by America's foremost "Keen Kutter" Kouple, Jerry and Elaine Heuring, this very well done and thoroughly illustrated book provides background information for collectors at every level and includes superb photographs, all in full color, of Keen Kutter Kollectibles of every sort. The "Keen Kutter" line, produced over many years by the E.C. Simmons Hardware Company of St. Louis, Missouri, was characterized by an uncompromising level of quality and the inventiveness with which the "Keen Kutter" trademark was incorporated into the products. For a look at a Great American Collectible through the eyes of two noted experts, we heartily recommend the Collector's Guide to Keen Kutter* **$19.95 (BK 357)**

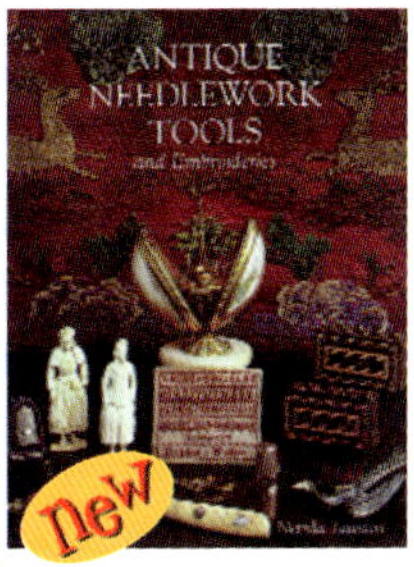

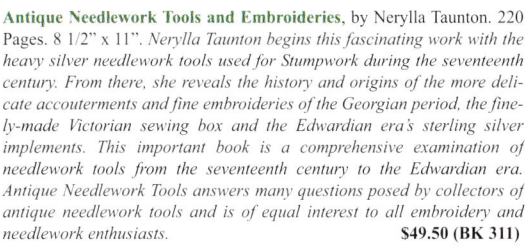

Antique Needlework Tools and Embroideries, by Nerylla Taunton. 220 Pages. 8 1/2" x 11". *Nerylla Taunton begins this fascinating work with the heavy silver needlework tools used for Stumpwork during the seventeenth century. From there, she reveals the history and origins of the more delicate accouterments and fine embroideries of the Georgian period, the finely-made Victorian sewing box and the Edwardian era's sterling silver implements. This important book is a comprehensive examination of needlework tools from the seventeenth century to the Edwardian era. Antique Needlework Tools answers many questions posed by collectors of antique needlework tools and is of equal interest to all embroidery and needlework enthusiasts.* **$49.50 (BK 311)**

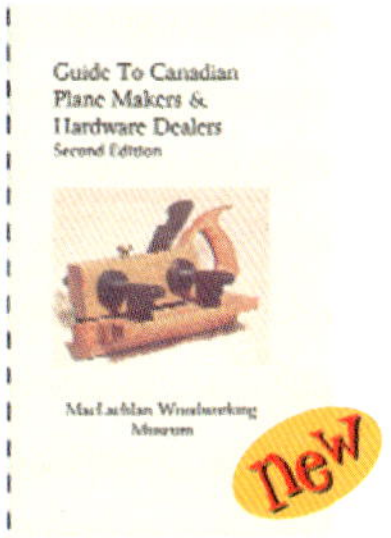

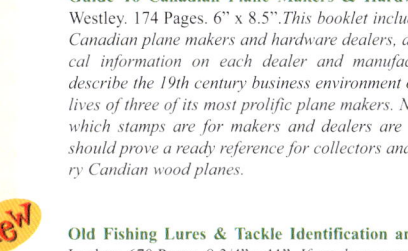

Guide To Canadian Plane Makers & Hardware Dealers, by Robert Westley. 174 Pages. 6" x 8.5".*This booklet includes the imprints of known Canadian plane makers and hardware dealers, as well as brief biographical information on each dealer and manufacturer. Interesting essays describe the 19th century business environment of the times as well as the lives of three of its most prolific plane makers. Notes on how to determine which stamps are for makers and dealers are also included. This book should prove a ready reference for collectors and historians of 19th century Candian wood planes.* ***$14.50 (BK 450)***

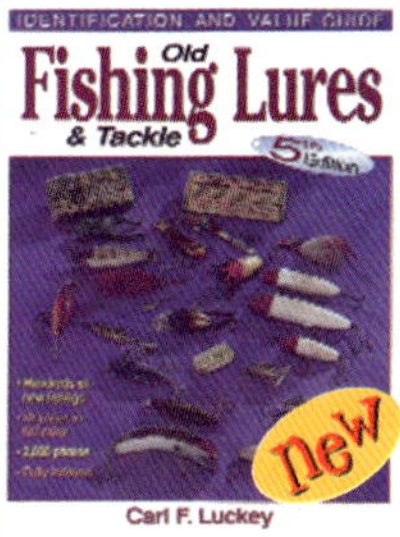

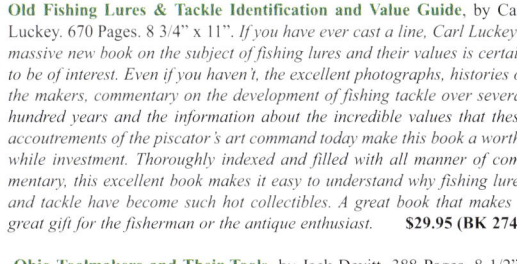

Old Fishing Lures & Tackle Identification and Value Guide, by Carl Luckey. 670 Pages. 8 3/4" x 11". *If you have ever cast a line, Carl Luckey's massive new book on the subject of fishing lures and their values is certain to be of interest. Even if you haven't, the excellent photographs, histories of the makers, commentary on the development of fishing tackle over several hundred years and the information about the incredible values that these accoutrements of the piscator's art command today make this book a worthwhile investment. Thoroughly indexed and filled with all manner of commentary, this excellent book makes it easy to understand why fishing lures and tackle have become such hot collectibles. A great book that makes a great gift for the fisherman or the antique enthusiast.* **$29.95 (BK 274)**

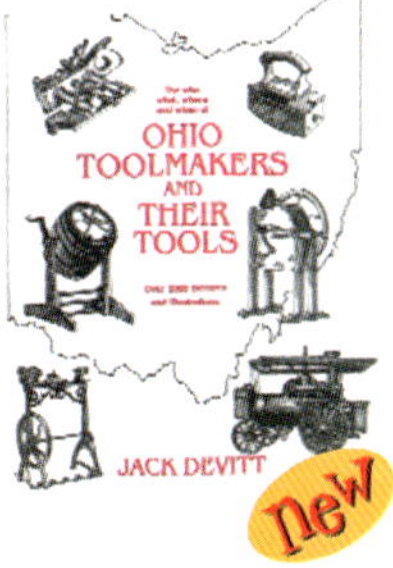

Ohio Toolmakers and Their Tools, by Jack Devitt. 388 Pages. 8 1/2" x 11". *More than twenty years in the making, Jack Devitt's groundbreaking study of Ohio Toolmakers is unique among tool publications in its approach, its scope and its content. Organized alphabetically by village and town, this work lists in alphabetical order under each town or city name all of the tool makers who worked there as well as the tools they produced, their working dates and sources for additional information. To make the book easy to use and fun to peruse, the author has kept the city and villages listings in the left hand facing pages of the book and filled the opposite pages with illustrations of tools produced in those towns. A total of 2500 illustrations, including several pages in color, make this book a very interesting way to spend a rainy evening. A secondary index in the back lists every documented maker and allows the user of the book to quickly find the entries for that maker. While not for everyone, "Ohio Toolmakers and Their Tools" belongs in the library of every serious tool collector. Hats off to Jack Devitt for this great new book. Now we only need 49 more like this one.* **$32.50 (BK 459)**

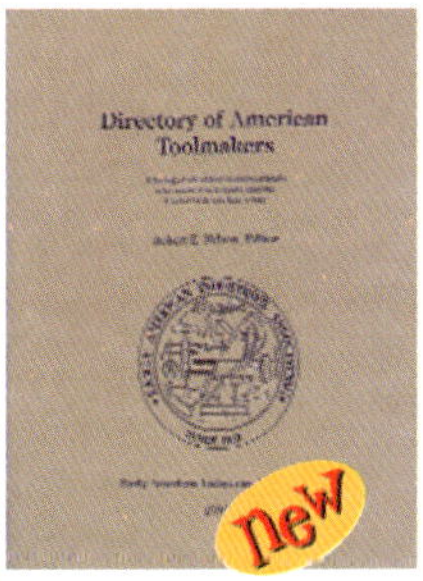

Directory of American Tool Makers, by Early American Industries Assn.. 1176 Pages. 8 1/2" x 11". *Just weeks after its issuance as the First Edition, we are pleased to offer, by special arrangement, this superb new reference work. First conceived more than 20 years ago, this massive volume of more than 1100 pages contains an encyclopedic listing of more than 14,000 documented American toolmakers who worked before 1900. Masterfully edited by Robert E. Nelson with an investment of self not seen since Michaelangelo got down from the scaffold, this book will be consulted often by tool collectors, antique dealers and students of history. Each listing contains the maker name, working location, working dates, birth and death dates, types of tools produced, notes on variations in maker marks used and narrative text entries that relate specific details of the maker's products. For the collector this information is the key to appreciating tools to a greater degree; and for the dealer, this essential reference provides valuable insight into value. Only a limited number of copies were printed and we have no assurance of a continued supply. We encourage you to order soon.* **$65.00 (BK 023)**

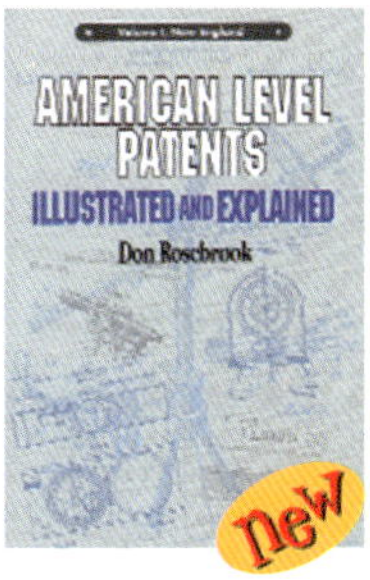

American Level Patents, by Don Rosebrook. 244 Pages. 7" x 10". *Those who would understand the phenomenon of antique tool collecting need only to look to the United States Patent System. To encourage innovative technology, the patent laws made it easy for anyone, at very little cost, to protect and document one's innovation, even if it was of questionable utility. In this new reference book, level maven Don Rosebrook has documented, illustrated and explained the technology of more than 200 levels patented in the New England States, including many by the Stanley Rule & Level Company. If you are a serious collector of antique tools, or an antique dealer with an interest in tools, this volume belongs in your library.* **$34.95 (BK 452)**

More Great New Titles on a Variety of Topics

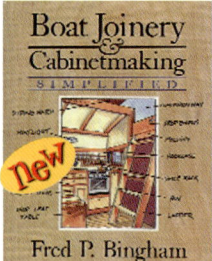

Boat Joinery & Cabinetmaking, by Fred Bingham. 289 Pages. 7 1/4" x 9 1/4". This three-part book takes boat building to an entirely different level. Part One provides a woodworker with a complete education on basic hand tools, electric hand tools, and stationary power tools needed for the job. Part Two reveals the methods and techniques needed in the building process-from shaping the hulls, laying down the deck, and constructing all the niceties and necessities of the yacht interior. Part Three provides the reader with projects from within the home as well as instructions to build your own trifle dinghy. A necessity for both the casual weekend tinkerer and the experienced sailor. **$24.95 (BK 303)**

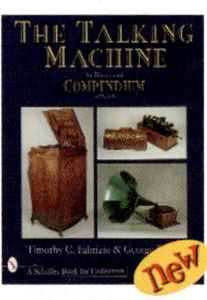

The Talking Machine Illustrated Compendium, by Timothy C. & George F. Fabrizio. 251 Pages. 9" x 11.25". Antique talking machines are among today's most popular collectibles. Names like "Edison" and "Victor" call to mind an era of polished wood, brightly painted morning glory horns and fascinating machinery. The Talking Machine contains over 550 color illustrations showing an incredible variety of these external-horn and internal-horn players as well as other related items. The authors with over 50 years of combined experience in the field make this book the most accurate and complete work on antique talking machines for the novice or the advanced collector. **$69.95 (BK 383)**

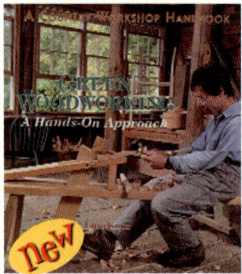

Green Woodworking, by Drew Langsner. 176 Pages. 8 1/2" x 10". Learn to work with wood, bark, or root in its natural "green" state. Instead of power tools, learn to sue the maul and froe, the broad axe and adze, the drawknife and carving knife to create handsome and serviceable pieces to use and display. Langsner provides basic tips in selecting trees for logging as well as instruction in the various methods used in working with green wood-hewing, riving, shaving, boring, bending, and joinery. Complete with a profile of contemporary workers of green wood, this book is of practical use to any carpentry devotee. **$18.95 (BK 313)**

Encyclopedia of American Silver Manufacturers, by Dorothy T. Rainwater & Judy Redfield. 418 Pages. 6" x 9". With more than 2,200 marks illustrated and brief histories and cross-references of more than 1,600 manufacturers, this is the most comprehensive reference source on the subject. This 4th edition contains many new trademarks as well as revisions to existing listing bring them up to date. Over ten years of research has resulted in the information presented here, from such sources as U.S. Patent Office records, city directories, census records, newspapers, magazines, silver and jewelry catalogs, company records, and various pieces examined in antique shops across the country. **$19.95 (BK 404)**

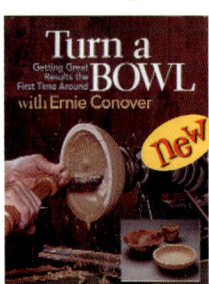

Turn a Bowl: Get Great Results, by Ernie Conover. 8 1/2" x 11". Most beginners are daunted by the task of turning a bowl and don't know where to begin. Veteran teacher Ernie Conover reveals that the act of turning a bowl is easy, it's the tools and procedures to do the job that are not generally understood. Step-by-step photo essays show every part of the process. Detailed drawings show how to sharpen tools and make the correct cuts. Conover also provides information on how to find wood, prepare bowl blanks, and correctly chuck them. This book will help the beginner get great results the first time around. **$19.95 (BK 349)**

Great Wood Finishes A Step-by-step Guide, by Jeff Jewitt. 8 1/2" x 11". Good information on finishing wood is hard to find. What type of finish should you use? What's the best way to apply it? How do you match the finish on another piece of furniture in your house? This book provides the answers that you need. Jewitt gives a thorough explanation of all tools used and over 400 photos illustrate each finishing step. Timesaving tips and charts show how to avoid or solve common mistakes. From specialty finish to cleaning a repair, this book gives advice even an amateur can follow. **$22.95 (BK 348)**

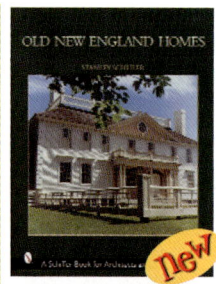

Old New England Homes, by Stanley Schuler. 224 Pages. 9" x 11.25". Stanley Schuler shares his first-hand knowledge of Yankee architecture and sensibility through his study of their homes. Color photographs of formal and informal interiors and exteriors, drawings of floor plans, and the historical connections of many homes are woven in the comprehensive volume. Architectural details are pointed out and their significance explained. The pictures are large and attractive to inspire present-day home remodelers, builders and architects; or just to help the nostalgic dreamers slide into a distant time. **$35.00 (BK 370)**

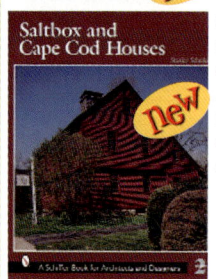

Saltbox and Cape Cod Houses, by Stanley Schuler. 160 Pages. 9" x 11 1/4". The Saltbox, or Catslide, house was first built in America about 1650 and goes back three centuries before that in England. The old Cape Cod House has a history as old as well. Yet this book is not just about the past. Within its pages, Schuler brings history to the present day for anyone hoping to build or remodel an attractive, comfortable, and reasonably authentic Saltbox or Cape. **$29.95 (BK 368)**

Building & Restoring the Hewn Log House, by Charles Mcraven. 162 Pages. 8 1/2" x 11". Charles McRaven, an expert on hewn log houses, shares his years of experience as well as numerous tips for solid craftsmanship in creating - or restoring - your own hewn log structure. You'll find instruction on how to...select and sharpen appropriate tools, construct the foundation and frame, select appropriate logs, replace rotting wood, notching corners to avoid buildup of moisture inside the wood, building the roof and final touches. This book is for anyone interested in building a hewn log house evocative of the early American landscape. **$21.99 (BK 299)**

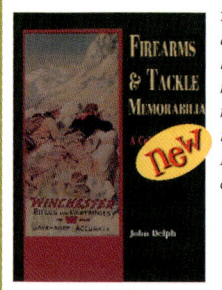

Firearms & Tackle Memorabilia, by John Delph. 141 Pages. 9" x 11.25". Among the most beautiful executed and highly collectible advertising art is related to firearms and fishing tackle. Companies like Winchester, Remington, Colt, Du Pont, Marlin, Bristol, and many others took great care and went to a great expense to promote their products. Among the artists engaged to create these images were N.C. Wyeth, A.B. Frost, Remington, A. Russell, and Philip R. Goodwin. This book, complete with value guide, provides concise and accurate information for any enthusiast or collector. **$39.95 (BK 381)**

Stonework Techniques and Projects, by Charles Mc Raven. 184 Pages. 8 1/2" x 11". Beginning with a pictorial survey of stonework of every sort, and proceeding to a detailed analysis of the properties of stone of every sort, author Charles McRaven gives up the secrets gathered in some fifty years of working with stone. Throughout this book, McRaven stresses that adherence to basic principles can make the difference between a wall that will stand virtually forever and one that will soon be just a pile of rubble. By examining the building of a wide range of stonework projects, such as walls, steps, waterfalls, bridges, seats and more, the author illustrates the various techniques of the master stoneworker and makes them comprehensible to those who would try their hand at this timeless craft. Whether you intend to build, or are simply interested in a nearly forgotten skilled trade, Charles McRaven's Stonework will be a worthwhile read. **$18.95 (BK 281)**

Lighthouses of the Pacific, by Jim Gibbs. 256 Pages. 9" x 11.25". Travel along the coasts of Washington, Oregon, California, Hawaii, Alaska, and British Columbia as Jim Gibbs takes you on a tour of the lighthouses of the Pacific. This wonderful historical reference explains everything from the United States' earliest attempts to light the capes of the coast to the development of the technology that made navigation in perilous waters possible. No history is complete without exciting tales of ghosts, mysteries, and shipwrecks and Gibb knows how to tell 'em. Within this book, one will find the drama, history, color and action that have been so much a part of lore of the lighthouse and nautical Americana. **$29.95 (BK 377)**

Domestic Crafts & Collectibles

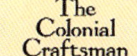

The Colonial Craftsman, by Carl Bridenbaugh. 140 Pages. 5 3/8" x 8 1/2". In colonial America, craftsman comprised the largest segment of the population, after farmers. Cabinetmakers, silversmiths, pewterers, printers, painters, engravers, blacksmiths, brass button-makers, shipwrights, hatters, shoemakers, and other artisans manufactured the tools, clothing, and housegoods necessary to sustain life and trade in the New World. This fascinating study examines the lives and work of craftsmen in the years prior to the Revolution-the golden age of colonial craftmanship-showing them at work, play, worship, school, home, competing at their trade, striving to get ahead and playing a vital role as citizens, especially in its fight for independence. Students of American history, culture, arts and crafts will enjoy this authorative, well-researched, and highly readable book. **$12.95 (BK 209)**

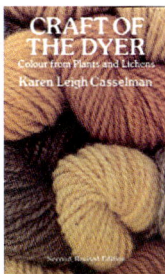

Craft Of The Dyer Colour From Plants and Lichens, by Karen Leigh Casselman. 256 Pages. 5 3/8" x 8 1/2". Those interested in traditional crafts and their methods will welcome this complete guide to making and using dyes from the very plants in their backyard. This book educates its reader about the necessary equipment, mordants, and dyeing procedures. An enormous variety of plants are discussed including identification and location, suitability for dyeing, the parts to use, how to process them, the color obtained, fastness of the dye, and much more. This book contains valuable indexes-plants by common and botanical name and by colors produced, a list of suppliers, metric conversion tables, and a great deal of other useful information in this practical guide to safe, ecologically friendly dyeing methods. **$12.95 (BK 208)**

The Dyer's Companion, by Elijah Bemiss. 319 Pages. 5 3/8" x 8 1/2". In this complete reprinting of Bemiss's 1815 edition, the reader can find dye recipes for all shades and varieties for reds, blues, yellows, browns, and blacks for woolens, linens and cottons, for both hot and cold dye processes. The early sections give 119 recipes and nearly all the dyes a dyer could want the use. The second part, an appendix added in the 1815 edition, Bemiss give information on setting up vats, on equipment and tools, on the choosing certain dye materials and methods were chosen, on European methods, and much more. A final section gives recipes for inks, dyes for feathers, miracle cures, recipes for beer and mead and other curiosities of the dyers repertoire. This book is a must for anyone interested in the craftmen of the early years of the American republic. **$13.95 (BK 213)**

Zalkins' Handbook of Thimbles & Sewing Implements, by Estelle Zalkin. 304 Pages. 6" x 9". This fact-packed and impressively illustrated handbook finds values for collectible sewing implements from needlework tools to pin cushions, clamps, workboxes, and more. You'll find a wealth of information on research sources, and learn how to spot variations and reproductions, catalog a collection, and located other valuable collectible objects. **$24.95 (BK 245)**

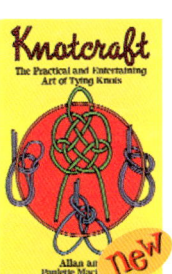

Knotcraft: The Practical and Entertaining Art of Tying Knots, by Allan & Paulette Macfarlan. 186 Pages. 5 3/8" x 8 1/2". Knowing how to tie a variety of different knots is a necessity for weekend sailors and campers, rockclimbers and horseback riders, and any other outdoor enthusiast. Hundred of knots are explained with clear illustrations: stopper knots and hitches, toggled knots, whipping, seizings, loop knots, decorative knots, lashing and splicing. Practical applications such as rappelling, raft building, log rolling, tents, bed and bunks are also discussed. Knots and ropes in history and literature, games, tricks, and stunts also reveal the entertaining end of the craft. A classic required by boaters, campers, boy scouts, and any lover of the outdoors. **$7.95 (BK 212)**

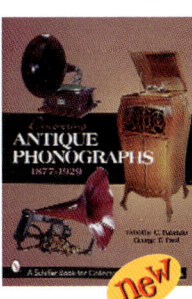

Discovering Antique Phonographs, by Timothy C. Fabrizio & George F. Paul. 244 Pages. 8 1/2" x 11". Out of collections far and wide come these spectacular survivors of the phonographs early years. Through over 400 beautiful color illustrations, Timothy Fabrizio and George Paul follow the progress of the acoustic talking machine from its crude beginnings in the 1870s to its most splendid and sophisticated heights in the early 20th century. The story behind the beautiful, bright machinery is told through clear and insightful descriptions and a value guide will further enlighten the reader on the modern marketplace. Prepare to discover the variety and charm of the antique phonograph. **$49.95 (BK 366)**

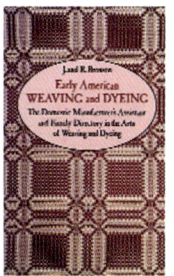

Early American Weaving and Dying, by J. And R. Bronson. 212 Pages. 5 3/8" x 8 1/2". This landmark work, first published in 1817, is a practical and historical guide to hand-weaving patterns and dye recipes. It revolutionized 19th-century practices by revealing closely held trade secrets to home weavers and dyers, and giving recipes the home craftsman could use. While not intended for the beginner, this book is a great source for weaving drafts. Included here are instructions for 35 of them: Bird Eyes, Herring Bone, Eight Shaft Coverlet, Diamond Coverlet, Plain Block Carpet, Damask Diaper, Curtain Diaper, and more. The dye recipes and methods for cotton and wool use natural dyes. Tables and calculations are included for size and amount of yarn for various projects, dye-woods and drugs are descibed, as well as recipes for varnishes and stains. With only a few adaptions, the modern home weaver and dyer can make great practical use of the valuable book. **$10.95 (BK 211)**

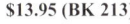

Old-time Tools & Toys of Needlework, by Gertrude Whiting. 364 Pages. 6 1/8" x 9 1/4". This book is a gem. Not only does it describe and illustrate nearly all the paraphernalia, accoutrements, appliances, accessories, and doodads associated with all yarn and thread handicrafts from knitting, embroidery, and dressmaking to warp weaving, batik making, and lace making from such widely scattered cultures as Java, ancient Egypt, Victorian England, and pre-revolutionary Russia, but its etymology as well. For each artifact, the author gives us the history of its invention, age, lore, use, and a variety of literary and artistic sources in which it's mentioned or depicted. This book will definitely be desired by any needlework practitioner and will awaken a new world of possibilities for those who already collect tools. **$16.95 (BK 221)**

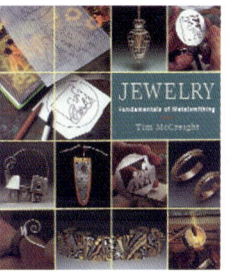

Jewelry: Fundamentals of Metalsmithing, by Tim Mc Creight. 144 Pages. 9" x 10 1/4". In this beautifully illustrated new publication, artist-metalworker and instructor Tim McCreight shares his vast experience as he analyzes the metalworking techniques that underly every aspect of the making of jewelry. Specatcular color photos of jewelry of every sort ornament this book and accent the clear topical treatment of each technique. Covered are fusing & soldering, cold joining, finishing & patinas, casting, stone setting & more. A list of tools is only one of many appendices that provide added value to this very well done new book. **$29.99 (BK 282)**

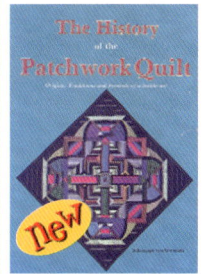

The History of the Patchwork Quilt, by Schnuppe Von Gwinner. 196 Pages. 8" x 10.5". Anyone who enjoyed creating or collecting patchwork quilts will enjoy this book celebrating the creative artistry and history of this medium. Schnuppe von Gwinner traces the history from its earlier beginning known around 1000 BC to the present. Asiatic, European, African, and Indian patchwork traditions are examined. The development of various popular patchwork patterns, such as the log cabin, friendship and Amish quilts are explored. This unique history reveals the patchwork quilt for the high art that it really is. **$16.95 (BK 405)**

The Story of Antique Needlework, by Bridget Mc Connel. 252 Pages. 9" x 11 1/4". Covering the simple and the sumptuous, this delightful book chronicles the history and diversity of needlework tools dating from ancient Egypt through the twentieth century. Nearly 500 color and black-and-white photographs beautifully illustrate tools such as needles, bodkins, pincushions, thimbles, bobbins, chatelaines, etuis, clamps, hooks, shuttles, measuring tapes, waxers, winders, and more. Both the new and experienced will be fascinated by the range of items described within this captivating book. A necessary reference for any collector **$59.95 (BK 367)**

Folk Art In America, by Adele Earnest. 192 Pages. 9" x 11.25". This book reveals the story of the roots of America's passion for art that is uniquely its own. Adele Earnest acquaints the reader the history of the folk art movement, with folk artists and their masterpieces, and the founding of the Museum of American Folk Art. Earnest also reminisces about the early collectors who blazed place for folk art in the art world: Henry Francis duPont, Titus Geesey, Mme. Gamma Walska, to name a few. Her narrative blends anecdote with history as she recounts triumphs and tragedies of the art, the feature exhibits to be admired, and the exhilaration of finding a new piece. **$35.00 (BK 376)**

The Stanley Rule & Level Company & More

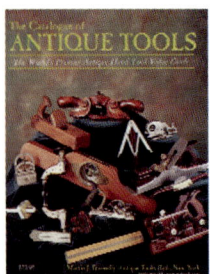

The Catalogue of Antique Tools, 1999 Edition, by Martin J. Donnelly. 220 Pages. 8 1/2" x 11". *Unlike any publication available anywhere else in the antique world, The Catalogue of Antique Tools, 1999 Edition, contains more than 5500 individual items, each priced for sale and photographed in full color. The wide scope of the tools included and the comprehensive index have made this book the first choice as a price guide for antique dealers around the world. Woodworkers, tool collectors and those with an interest in tools and technology eagerly await the publication of each annual edition. More than just a price guide, all of the tools in The Catalogue of Antique Tools are for sale on a "first come, first serve" basis.* **$23.95 (BK 172)**

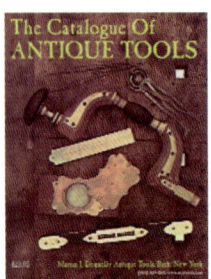

The Catalogue Of Antique Tools: 1998 Edition, by Martin J. Donnelly. 180 Pages. 8 1/2" x 11". *The Catalogue of Antique Tools, from Martin J. Donnelly Antique Tools, has become the first choice when looking to purchase antique tools of exceptional quality and rarity. The high degree of detail, informative commentary and lively wit provided in the descriptions have made The Catalogue of Antique Tools the de facto reference guide for thousands of collectors worldwide. With less than one hundred copies of several of these classics now remaining, this represents what could be the final opportunity to fill out your collection.* **$22.95 (BK 062)**

General Line Catalog Ca. 1939, by The Stanley Rule & Level Company. 254 Pages. 7 1/2" x 10 1/2". *This, Stanley's last great pre-WW II dealer catalogue, illustrates the Stanley line including the wide line of Atha Tool Company products, including metalworking tools and hammers of every sort. Many of the tools illustrated in this book would be discontinued following the war, and the quality level of Stanley Tools would never again retain their pre-war peak. A superb reference.* **$24.50 (BK 071)**

Stanley Rule & Level Company: Catalog No. 34, 1915 Edition, by The Stanley Rule & Level Company. 147 Pages. 5 1/2" x 7 1/2". *This was the general line catalog provided to carpenter and woodworkers. Included in this volume is the full Stanley line at the peak of its variety. An excellent reference to Stanley's diverse and innovative line of tools.* **$12.00 (BK 026)**

Antique & Collectible Stanley Tools: Guide to Identity & Value, by John Walter. 885 Pages. 6" x 9". *This eagerly-anticipated expansion and revision of the 1990 Edition is an absolute must-have for anyone with an interest in antique tools. The documentation in this massive volume expands the knowledge of even the most advanced collectors, and the realistic price guidelines will be a frequent and invaluable reference for collectors and dealers alike. Every tool known to have been produced by the Stanley Rule & Level Company is included in this thoroughly illustrated and documented volume. Collectors looking to value a tool will find each item in order of Stanley number designation. Those interested in gaining greater familiarity with the wide range of tools produced by Stanley can study the topical sections for a thorough overview. A major added benefit is the complete numerical index in the back, which allows an obscure tool of which only the Stanley number marking is known to be quickly and easily identified and priced. Highly recommended.* **$45.00** **(BK 041)**

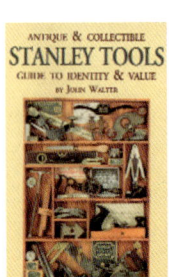

Boxwood & Ivory: Stanley Traditional Rules, 1855-1975, by Philip E. Stanley. 188 Pages. 8 3/4" x 11 1/4". *This major contribution to tool research by Philip Stanley would be invaluable if it contained only the detailed analysis of the design and function of every rule ever produced by the Stanley Rule & Level Company, which it does. Stanley's book goes much further, however, to include commentary on relative scarcity and value. Stanley's text brings life to the seemingly dull topic of rules and scales. Additional chapters detail the rule manufacturing process, the principal competitors of Stanley in the last half of the Nineteenth Century, and reviews some of the specialized patented rule modifications that command great collector interest. The superb photographs illustrate the many features of the Stanley rule line. A book not to be without.*

Out of Print: Less Than 20 Copies Remain! **$45**

The Stanley Calalog Collection, Volume I, by Stanley Rule & Level Co.. 390 Pages. 6 1/4" x 9 1/4". *This one volume contains complete reprints of catalogs issued by the Stanley Rule & Level Company in 1855, 1859, 1867, 1870, 1888 and 1898. Collectors can follow the development of different elements of the Stanley line and make reference easily through the use of the full volume index. This documented reference to the full Nineteenth Century Stanley line includes all of the early and sometimes short-lived innovations that have become today's hottest collectibles. All illustrations are early engravings from the peak period of that illustrative art. An essential reference and a good old fashioned "good read." Makes a great gift for the tool enthusiast. Highly recommended.* **$30.00 (BK 004)**

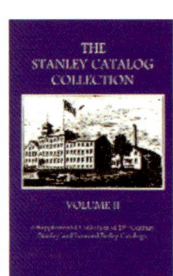

The Stanley Catalog Collection, Volume II, by Stanley Rule & Level Co.. 408 Pages. 6 1/4" x 9 1/4". *This just-off the press publication would be well worth adding to the collector's library if it contained only the full text of the 1872, 1874, 1877, 1884 and 1892 Stanley catalogs, which it does. Also included are the Leonard Bailey Catalogs of 1876 and 1883, both of which have long been out of print. The Bailey catalogs, which document the beginning and end of Bailey's independent manufacture, including the celebrated "Victor" planes are a must-have for the serious collector. This volume fills out the area not covered by Volume I and nicely complements the Stanley Value Guide.* **$30.00 (BK 045)**

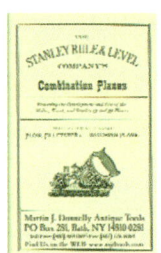

The Stanley Combination Plane, by The Stanley Rule & Level Company. 80 Pages. 5 1/2" x 6 1/2". *If you own a Stanley No. 45 or 55 plane and don't have the original instructions, this book is for you. Instructions for both the 45 and the 55 are reprinted in their original format. Also included is information on the changes in these planes over the course of their production, important patent information and detailed information on Stanley's other combination planes including the highly-collectible Miller's Patent series. Whether for the professional craftsman, the Saturday woodworker or the beginning or advanced collector of antique tools, this is a reference that you will consult often.* **$12.00 (BK 033)**

Edward Preston & Son: 1909 General Line Catalog, by Edward Prestons & Sons. 224 Pages. 8" x 11 1/2". *The English tool making giant, Edward Preston & Sons, were perhaps the most comparable to The Stanley Rule & Level Company in the United States. Their diverse line included tools of every conceivable type. These tools were numbered and marked in a way that feeds the collecting mentality. This very well done reprint includes an introduction by Mark Rees, who, together with his wife Jane have produced the only price guide and collector's guide to British Tools, "Tools: A Guide for Collectors." Discover another world.* **$22.50 (BK 034)**

General Line Catalog Ca. 1920, by The Stanley Rule & Level Company. 151 Pages. 8 1/2" x 11 1/4". *This beautiful full size catalog illustrates the complete Stanley line at the peak of Stanley's production of hand woodworking tools. Originally produced for use by hardware dealers, this catalog is illustrated with color plates of many tools and includes in-depth information on many of the tools and product lines. Highly recommended.* **$29.95 (BK 070)**

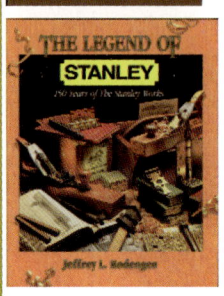

The Legend of Stanley: 150 Years of the Stanley Works, by Jeffrey L. Rodengen. 191 Pages. 9 1/2" x 11 1/2". *Produced in close cooperation with The Stanley Works, Jeffrey Rodengen's corporate history of Stanley traces the development of the tool making giant from its earliest years before the Civil War to the multi-national giant that it has become. Included are an overview of Stanley's many marketing campaigns, biographies of the men who have led Stanley through the years and an excellent treatment of Stanley's hand tool division. In preparing the book, Rodengen was given access to the Stanley corporate archives and many photographs and advertising items not previously published are included here for the first time. For those who wish to look beyond the tools and examine in detail, America's most prolific producer, The Legend of Stanley will serve that purpose well.* **$39.50 (BK 019)**

Ships & Sailing - Nautical Topics

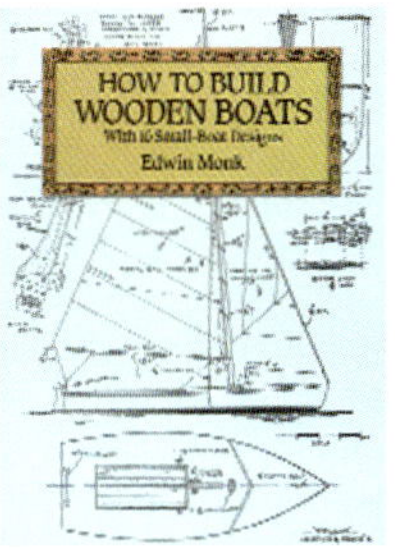

How To Build Wooden Boats: With 16 Small Boat Designs, by Edwin Monk. 90 Pages. 9" x 12". *Written especially for the amateur boat builder, this guidebook contains clear, practical directions and designs for building 16 modern small boats, rowboats, sailboats, outboards, a 125-class hydroplane and a runabout. The standardized techniques are used in boat yards and can be used to construct a variety of other crafts not included in this volume. Monk, a noted naval architect, presents guidelines for choosing and assembling building material, building and finishing the craft. This book is perfect for the carpentry and sailing enthusiasts who will derive as much pleasure from building their boats as using them.* **$12.95 (BK 194)**

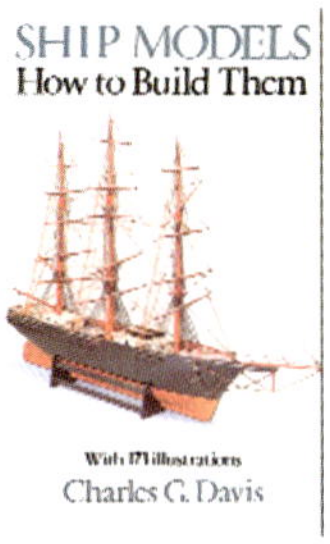

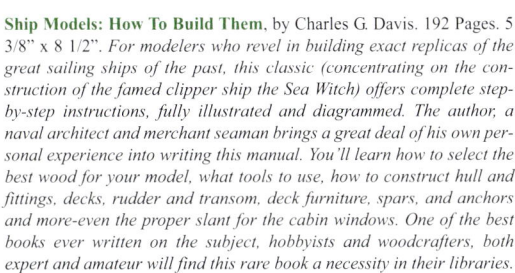

Ship Models: How To Build Them, by Charles G. Davis. 192 Pages. 5 3/8" x 8 1/2". *For modelers who revel in building exact replicas of the great sailing ships of the past, this classic (concentrating on the construction of the famed clipper ship the Sea Witch) offers complete step-by-step instructions, fully illustrated and diagrammed. The author, a naval architect and merchant seaman brings a great deal of his own personal experience into writing this manual. You'll learn how to select the best wood for your model, what tools to use, how to construct hull and fittings, decks, rudder and transom, deck furniture, spars, and anchors and more-even the proper slant for the cabin windows. One of the best books ever written on the subject, hobbyists and woodcrafters, both expert and amateur will find this rare book a necessity in their libraries.* **$10.95 (BK 206)**

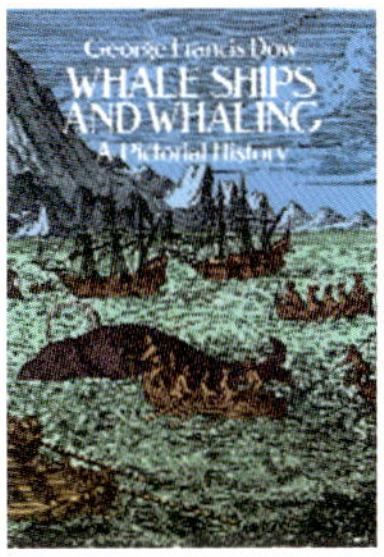

Whale Ships & Whaling, by George Francis Dow. 288 Pages. 6" x 9". *This pictorial history shows us that the mystery, excitement and romance of whaling have fired the human imagination since ancient times. Although many books have been written about whales and whaling, this one is unique. Few have presented a pictorial view of whaling ships as the present volume. Over 200 vintage illustrations, including woodcuts dating from 1555, 18th-century engravings, 19th-century lithographs, and photographs from the late 19th and early 20th centuries, depict a fleet of barks, brigs, cutters, and other whaling vessels, from the inside as well as out. Whaling implements, guns, and other tools are also revealed. These prints, collected from private sources and meticulously reproduced, are now to be enjoyed by interested in this intriguing chapter of maritime history.* **$14.95 (BK 217)**

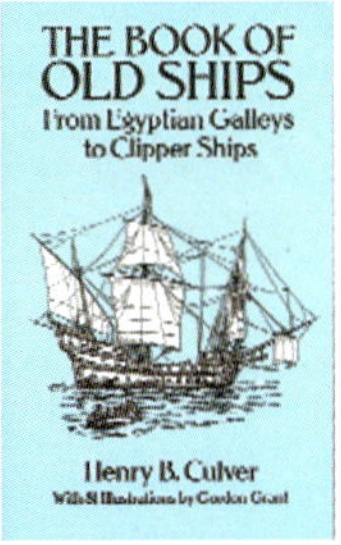

The Book of Old Ships: From Egyptian Galleys To Clipper Ships, by Henry B. Culver. 256 Pages. 5 3/8" x 8 1/2". *In this classic review, noted maritime artist Gordon Grant has created 80 magnificent line illustrations of some of history's most important sailing ships. Henry B. Culver, well-known naval historian, has provided a detailed and meticulously researched text for each of Grants illustrations. Culver describes for us not only the material and details of the construction each vessel, but also its period of popularity and function and the romance and lore surrounding the individual craft as well. This book Begins with the graceful Egyptian galley (c.1600 B.C.) and ends with the splendid 5-masted clipper ship of 1921. Also depicted are the Roman trireme, the Viking longship, a 16th-century caravel, an East Indiaman of 1750, a 19th brigantine, a New Bedford whaling ship, and well as dozens of other lesser know vessels. This book will be enjoyed by naval historians, sailing enthusiasts and model shipbuilders alike.* **$10.95 (BK 203)**

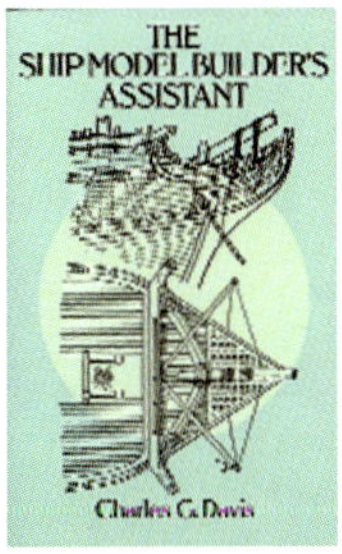

The Ship Model Builder's Assistant, by Charles G. Davis. 288 Pages. 5 3/8" x 8 1/2". *Every serious model builder should have this book beside him as he prepares to untake building a replica of any American clipper ship or packet ship of the Great Age of Sail, as it offers hobbyists a true understanding of the workings of a fully rigged and appointed sailing ship. Davis, a well-known naval architect and seaman, describes various types of ship models and devotes individual chapters to the various aspects of the ship: masting and mastheads, standing and running rigging, foot-ropes, the blocks, steering wheels, the galley, pumps, ship ironwork, copper sheathling, ground tackle, gun ports, boats, and davits. This book provides a valuable treasury of information for any model builder, historian, or sailing enthusiast. An absolute must have!* **$10.95 (BK 216)**

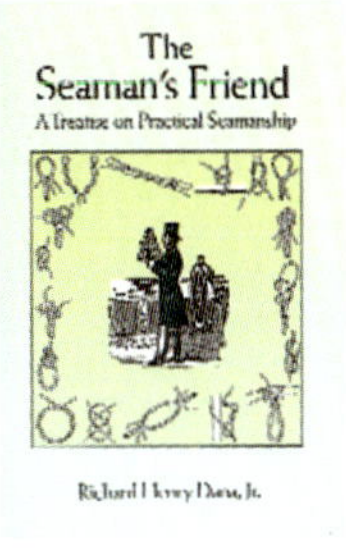

The Seaman's Friend: A Treatise On Practical Seamanship, by Richard Henry Dana Jr. 240 Pages. 5 3/8" x 8". *Best known for his realistic account of a sailor's life aboard a 19th-century sailing vessel, Richard Henry Dana also wrote this treatise on practical seamanship and the duties of masters and mariners. Reproduced from a rare 1879 edition of the text, it offers a wealth of information on the actual operations of a sailing ship. Part one concerns the practical details of seamanship-fitting the rigging, setting and taking in sails, getting under way, tacking, lying to, coming to anchor-and includes an extensive dictionary of nautical terms. Part Two discusses customs and usages of the merchant service, the duties of the crew, and the particulars of life on a ship. Part Three examines the duties of master and mariners relating to vessels-it cargo, passangers, officers, and seaman. Based on the author's own experience, this volume offers a fascinating look at the seafaring world of the 19th century.* **$10.95 (BK 205)**

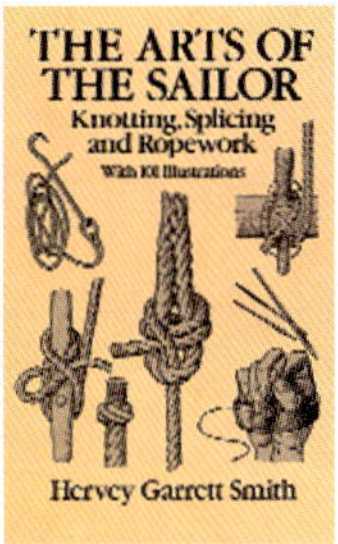

The Arts of the Sail: Knotting, Splicing, and Ropework, by Hervey Garrett Smith. 256 Pages. 5 3/8" x 8 1/2". *This excellent handbook on basic shipboard skills offers boating and yachting enthusiasts a complete course in rigging, working, and maintaining a ship. More than a 100 illustrations help the reader grasp the fundamentals and fine points of handling a ship while the author describes in detail the sailors tools, basic knots and useful hitches as well as splicing, hand sewing and canvas work. Boat maintenance and management are also discussed-such as belaying, coiling and stowing; towing procedures; chafing gear; etc. Fashioning decorative knots, ornamental coverings, and nettings are made easy with Smith's step-by-step instructions. This is the perfect book to keep aboard as a ready reference, but may also entertain many an armchair sailor or landlubber as well.* **$10.95 (BK 204)**

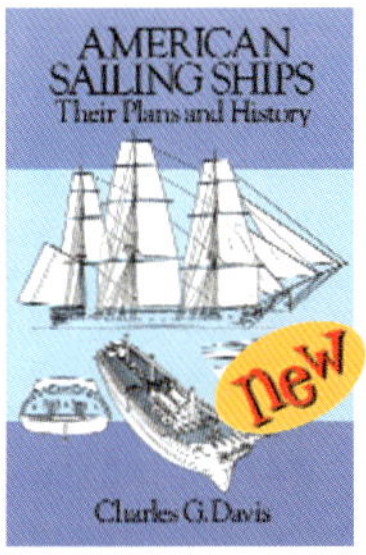

American Sailing Ships: Their Plans and History, by Charles G. Davis. Pages. 6 1/8" x 9 1/4". *Seaman extraordinaire Charles G. Davis plots a course through America's rich nautical history. With nearly 140 photographs, prints and plans, Davis reveals not only the technical details for a wide range of sailing ships from the 18th through the 20th centuries, but the history and lore of each of these vessels as well. Filled with entertaining historical accounts of famous vessels, shipbuilders, and the men who sailed them, this book will be enjoyed by sailing enthusiasts, historians, American buffs and model builders alike.* **$8.95 (BK 347)**

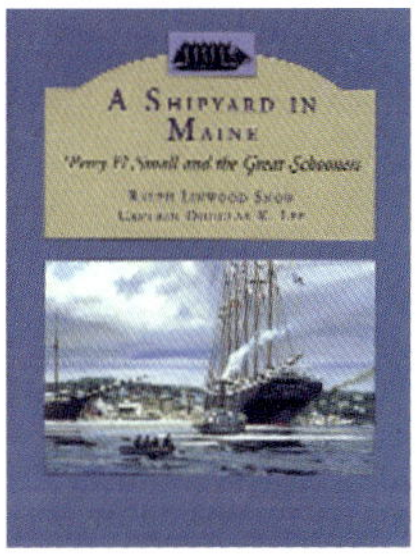

A Shipyard in Maine: Percy & Small and the Great Schooners, by Ralph Linwood Snow & Douglas Lee. 391 Pages. 8 3/4" x 11". *Virtually the last of the great plank on frame wooden ship builders, the Bath, Maine shipbuilding enterprise of Percy & Small built some 70% of all the six-masted schooners ever produced in the United States. In a work that is thoroughly documented and beautifully illustrated with early photographs and superbly detailed line drawings, the authors have captured the spirit of the last great days of sail. Set against the backdrop of a changing world of commerce, this well written book examines every aspect of wooden shipbuilding during the last years of the last century and the early 1900's. Included is much information about the actual construction of the ship, including the day to day duties of the workers in the yard and photographs of every stage of the construction of the great ships. For a romantic journey to a forgotten world of wooden ships, we recommned A Shipyard in Maine.* **$49.95 (BK 279)**

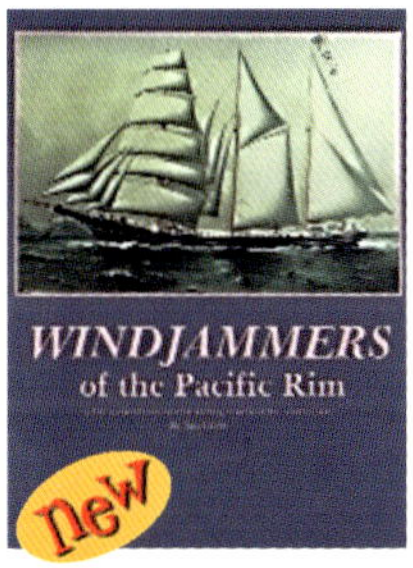

Windjammers of the Pacific Rim, by Jim Gibbs. 232 Pages. 8 1/2" x 11". *For the early settlers of California, Oregon and Washington, the commercial sailing schooner was common sight. In the late 1800s, this sturdy ship was a necessary means of transportation for both the people and the growing industries of the West Coast. Through many old photographs and stirring true stories, Jim Gibbs shares his deep appreciation for the schooners, barkentines, brigs, and brigintines of the times as well as the fearless crews that manned them. This fascinating history brings the golden age of wind ships alive.* **$19.95 (BK 415)**

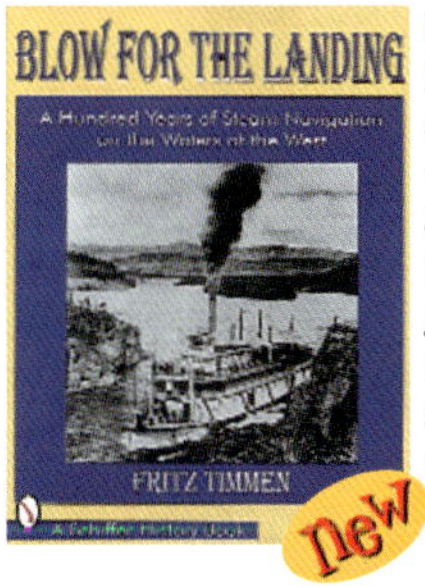

Blow For The Landing 100 Years of Steam, by Fritz Timmen. 235 Pages. 8 1/2" x 11". *From Lewiston down through the desert of eastern Oregon and the rich green of the Cascades, the colorful paddlewheelers carried their goods and passengers and did their share to develop the pioneer American West. Some of the boats were exquisitely ornate and provided complete luxury for the excursion passengers while others had only the bare necessities and carried miners, their animals and supplies. Although the steamers are all but gone now, Timmen relives the glory days of steamboating in the book full of history, photographs and terrific tales.* **$29.95 (BK 414)**

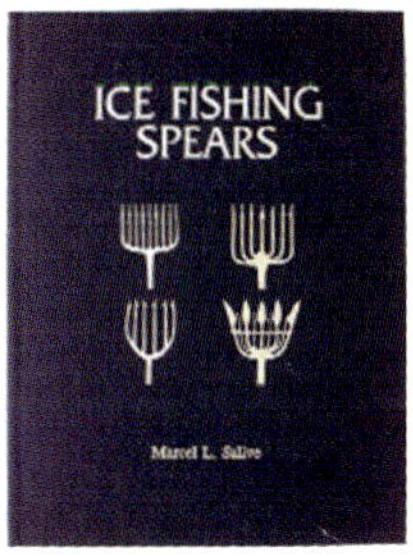

Ice Fishing Spears, by Marcel Salive. 300 Pages. 8 1/2" x 11". *Looking back at the history of collecting in the last twenty or thirty years, there is one very obvious truth: Almost without exception, each area of collecting has within it a solitary individual whose personal passion for the subject has generated infectious enthusiasm among others. Through research and writing, as well as personal persuasion, that person has been responsible for opening the eyes of others to the object of his enthusiasm. In the fascinating area of fishing spears, that individual is Marcel Salive. In this ground breaking work, Salive has chronicled every aspect of this obscure area including the history, regional differences, uses and even information about how to display the spears. A nicely illustrated and well documented work. The definitive reference.* **$90.00 (BK 061)**

Three Centuries of Furniture

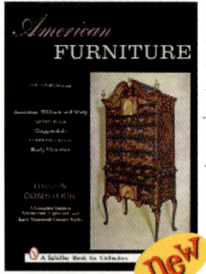

American Furniture Guide To 17th,18th,&19th Century Furniture, by Helen Comstock. 336 Pages. 8.5" x 11.25". *Examples of Jacobean and William and Mary styles, Queen Anne, Chippendale, Classical, and Early Victorian can all be found within this comprehensive guide to 17th-, 18th-, and 19th-century American furniture. Over 700 illustrations of individual pieces from both collectors and house collections are described in full with its history, style, region, wood, and probable date. A must for collectors or lovers of the furniture craft.*
$44.95 (BK 384)

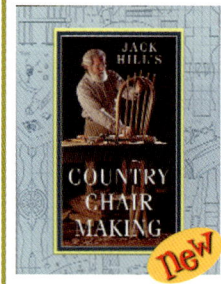

Jack Hill's Country Chair Making, by Jack Hill. 152 Pages. 8 1/2" x 11". *Village craftsman originally made these elegant chairs for the cottage or farmhouse during the 18th and 19th centuries. This practical guide for the making of traditional country chairs from master craftsman Jack Hill includes 13 complete projects including simple stools, woven-seat chairs and Windsor chairs. With information on materials, tools and techniques, superb photography and clear step-by-step instructions, anyone from the raw beginner to the expert will find this book informative and enjoyable.*
$19.95 (BK 342)

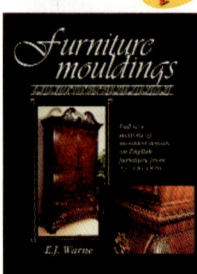

Furniture Mouldings: Sections of Moulded Details 1574-1820, by E.J. Warne. 140 Pages. 8 1/2" x 11". *While not for the casual reader, the study of the moulding profiles from furniture produced between 1574 and 1820 will give the serious student a great deal of insight into the evolution of style over this period. A helpful cross reference guide allows this work, which is arranged in chronological order, to be used as a study guide to the evolution of various types of furniture. An inexpensive opportunity to develop insight into the world of early furniture.*
$16.95 (BK 135)

The Chairmaker's Workshop, by Drew Langsner. 304 Pages. 9" x 11". *Ever dreamed of handcrafting a handsome, gleaming, graceful chair? An American bow-back Windsor, say, or set of ladder-backs for the dining room? How about a comfortable rocker...a child's highchair...a sack-back settee? Here's the handbook to take you there. With more than 500 photographs and figures and to-scale plans for eleven chairs and five pieces of basic chairmaking equipment, Drew Langsner takes you from log to finished chair.*
$34.95 (BK 323)

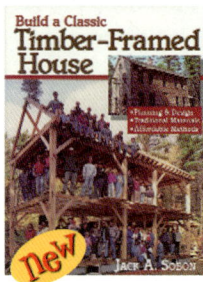

Build a Classic Timber-framed House, by Jack A. Sobon. 202 Pages. 8 1/2" x 11". *Following the traditional "hall-and-parlor" home design, architect and builder Jack Sobon reveals how to build an attractive timber-framed house able to meet the needs of any growing family. The basic house design taught in this book is easily adapted to meet different needs and Sobon's practical advice incorporates the latest knowledge on building a healthy house, integrating natural systems, and finding effective home heating solutions.*
$21.95 (BK 298)

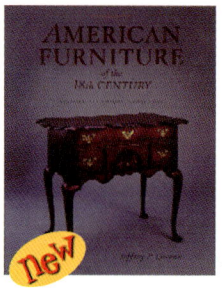

American Furniture of the 18th Century, by Jeffrey Greene. Pages. 9 1/2" x 11 1/4". *American Furniture by Jeffrey P. Greene. American Furniture of the 18th century is prized for its historical and artistic value by museums and collectors, as well as a benchmark in design and craftsmanship by modern day furniture makers. Jeffrey Greene chronicles the evolution of design and construction, historical influences and tastes of the period. He explains and illustrates techniques of the period and examines 24 important original examples in detail for their design, construction and merit. The book is an essential reference for anyone with an interest in 18th century furniture and provides a detailed guide to connoisseurship and the historical methods of the period.*
$45.00 (BK 341)

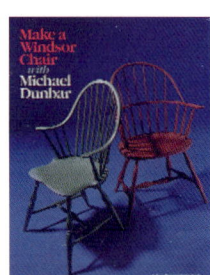

Make A Windsor Chair With Michael Dunbar, by Michael Dunbar. 165 Pages. 8 1/2" x 11". *Tool collectors may be familiar with Michael Dunbar from his books on tuning and using traditional tools. Woodworkers are very familiar with Dunbar, who is one of the best known makers of Windsor chairs and a renowned teacher of the craft of chair making. In this superb new book from the publishers of Fine Woodworking magazine, Dunbar has captured the making of these fascinating chairs in words and pictures. Written with a strong emphasis on the use of hand tools and superbly illustrated with photographs and line drawings, this book will be of interest to the collector of tools, the woodworker or the student of furniture. Highly recommended.*
$19.95 (BK 265)

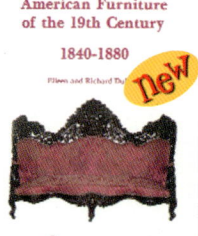

American Furniture of the 19th Century, by Ileen&richard Dubrow. 247 Pages. 9" x 11.25". *This is an important study of the fine handcrafted furniture made in America between 1840 and 1880, considered to be the most productive period of American furniture making. Most pieces are identified by the cabinetmakers, which made them. Biographies of the leading cabinetmakers from all over America are presented. Most of the examples in the book have not been seen before in any publication. Filled with hundreds of photographs of furniture from Rococco to Neo-Greco, this book is a must for historian and collectors.*
$59.95 (BK 373)

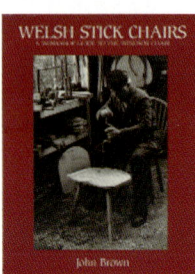

Welsh Stick Chairs, by John Brown. 97 Pages. 7 1/2" x 9 1/2". *All too often, the "experts" on woodworking subjects are pretentious and unapproachable yuppies who may or may not have the experience and training to qualify as such. There can be no doubt that the subject of this book, Welsh chairmaker John Brown, is as authentic as they come. In a work that is illustrated with photographs of Brown at work in his home workshop, this book addresses not only how to make traditional chairs, but also their history, traditions and tips for how not to make mistakes. If you're interested in trying your hand at chairmaking and can't quite justify $1600.00 to attend some wine and cheese New England seminar, we recommend "Welsh Stick Chairs".*
$14.95 (BK 129)

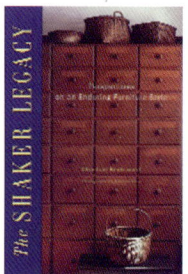

The Shaker Legacy: Perspectives of an Enduring Tradition, by Christian Becksvoort. 234 Pages. 8 1/4" x 12". *To truly understand and appreciate the distinctive Shaker furniture that has attracted such enthusiastic interest from collectors, one must first come to know who the Shakers were and what was their perspective on life and work. In this spectacular new book, author Christian Becksvoort offers as compelling a portrait of Shaker life and work as has ever been assembled. Filled with superb color photographs of great examples of Shaker woodwork, the book also includes a detailed history of the Shakers in America with an emphasis on the concepts of "harmony" and "order" that governed their lives and their work. If you are to read only one book this month or this year, we heartily recommend The Shaker Legacy.*
$40.00 (BK 259)

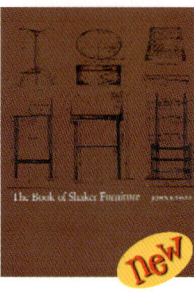

The Book of Shaker Furniture, by John Kassay. 265 Pages. 9 1/2" x 12 1/2". *John Kassay, an accomplished draftsman, furniture maker, and photographer, began compiling the photographs and measured drawing that make up this amazing book more than 10 years ago. Kassay's sensitive attention to detail in this comprehensive study makes this book the standard reference work on this small but distinctive group of artifacts of the nineteenth century. The Book of Shaker Furniture is an asset for people who are attracted to things Shaker and especially those interested in reproducing Shaker furniture for use in everyday life.* **$60.00 (BK 325)**

Shaker Architecture, by Herbert Schiffer. 190 Pages. 8 1/2" x 11". *Nearly everyone who has ever visited one of the many Shaker communities in the Northeastern United States has come away in awe of the simple and perfectly proportioned style of the artifacts and buildings created by these enigmatic people. In this recently published work, author Herber Schiffer includes a wide range of black and white photographs of 16 Shaker communites, some of which no longer exist. Each photograph includes commentary on the function of the structure shown, including the original plans, in some instances. A thorough introduction traces the history of the Shaker people and relates the teachings of the Shaker way of life to the structures they created. For a look at how a religious movement changed the landscape of America, we strongly recommend this new book.* **$24.95 (BK 269)**

Toll Free: (800) 869-0695 — Secure Online Ordering at www.mjdtools.com

Classic Reference Books About Antique Tools

The Wooden Plane: Its History, Form and Function, by John M. Whelan. 513 Pages. 7" x 10". A thorough and comprehensive reference for the student of tools. Collector and craftsman Jack Whelan traces the history and development of different classes of planes in this work that is destined to become a classic. Copiously illustrated with line drawings by the author, The Wooden Plane provides the first-ever systematic study of molding plane profiles and explains in straightforward prose the relationship between planes and the work they produced. The Wooden Plane gives the collector or woodworker an in-depth understanding of the why and how of wooden planes in a way that will add tremendous enjoyment to their use or collection. Included are sections dealing with specific trades: the Cooper; Sashmaker, Coachmaker, Wheelwright, Planemaker, Organ Builder, Staircase Builder, Basketmaker, Rulemaker, Chairmaker, Patternmaker and more. Also includes an overview of the types of planes used by the French, Dutch, Germans, Japanese and Chinese. For the student of trades, for the collector of tools, for the artist-craftsperson, The Wooden Plane is a book that will change the way you view your tools. An essential reference for the library. **$37.50 (BK 014)**

Makers of American Wooden Planes, 3rd Edition, by Emil & Martyl Pollak. 462 Pages. 7" x 10". Since the publication of the 1st Edition in 1983, this essential reference by the late Emil Pollak and his wife Martyl has transformed the way collectors viewed collecting. By opening the door of discovery to the rich harvest of history that lay behind the maker imprints on wooden planes, the Pollaks began, and led, an ever-growing search for information about the men who made the tools that built this country. This edition adds some 600 documented makers to the previous edition and includes an updated rating system for judging the relative scarcity and value of American maker-imprinted wooden planes. The one absolutely necessary reference that no collector or dealer should be without. **$35.00 (BK 001)**

Wooden Planes In 19th Century America Volume II, by Kenneth D. Roberts. 452 Pages. 8 1/2" x 11". Long thought to be out of print, a cache of these books were recently discovered in New England. This extraordinary book, rendered in the inimitable style of Ken Roberts, one of the true greats of tool collecting, features great color photographs, commentary by Roberts, reproduced original documents and catalogs, an inventory of the planemaking tools of Solon Rust, inventories of tools and materials and much, much more. If you wish to see the world of the Nineteenth Century as it was when some 2000 wooden planemakers competed with each other, we highly recommend Ken Roberts classic work. We do not expect to be able to fill all orders for this book. **$65.00 (BK 252)**

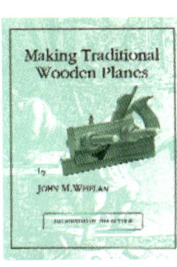

Making Traditional Wooden Planes, by John M. Whelan. 128 Pages. 8 1/2" x 11". As the author of The Wooden Plane „Jack Whelan knows a thing or two about these tools and the techniques used in making them. In this book, which is intended to serve as a working guide for the would-be amateur planemaker, Whelan provides step-by-step instructions for making a number of different types of wooden planes. For the woodworker with an interest in hand tools or for the collector seeking a deeper understanding of the tools he collects, Making Traditional Wooden Planes provides a fascinating reference. **$19.95 (BK 021)**

Patented Transitional & Metallic Planes in America, Volume I, by Roger K. Smith. 340 Pages. 8 1/2" x 11". This initial volume of the series covers developments from the very first patented metallic planes through the beginning of the Twentieth Century. Chapters covering Stanley, Leonard Bailey, Stanley's principal competitors, patented combination planes and more are included. This book also includes type studies of Stanley planes, patent drawings and illustrations from early catalogs. A treasure trove of information for the antique tool enthusiast. The publication of this book sparked a collecting frenzy that continues to this day. **$90.00 (BK 017)**

Patented Transitional & Metallic Planes in America, Volume II, by Roger K. Smith. 400 Pages. 8 1/2" x 11". Includes the full harvest of new information unearthed as a result of the publication of Volume I. Filled with photographs of tools not known to exist at the time the first Volume was published. Chapters include updated information on Stanley & Bailey, New York City planemakers, Stanley's competitors and much more. Appendices include detailed listings of all patented planes, updated type studies and a guide to hardware dealers who marketed planes in their own names. Together with Volume I, these books provide a crystal clear image of the world of industry and invention in the last century. **$90.00 (BK 018)**

The Handplane Book, by Garrett Hack. 264 Pages. 9 1/2" x 11 1/2". The divergence between "users" and "collectors" is one of the underlying themes of the search for antique tools. Author Garrett Hack is thoroughly credentialed as both a user, through his mastery of his profession as a maker of fine furniture; and as a collector, by virtues of the passion with which he pursues his avocation. In his superb "Handplane Book," Hack brings together those two groups in a way that helps each to an understanding and appreciation of the other. At first glance, As with all Taunton Press publications, but especially so with this work, the quality of the color and black & white photographs is superb. Planes of every sort, from the common to the very, very rare, are photographed in ways that capture the spirit that both craftsmen and collectors feel for them. Whether you have a thousand planes or have never touched one in your life, The Handplane Book will provide countless hours of delight.
Softbound $24.95 (BK 266)
Clothbound $34.95 (BK 050)

British Planemakers From 1700, by W. L. Goodman. 530 Pages. 7" x 10". In their superb new edition of William Goodman's classic work, British collectors Jane and Mark Rees have more than doubled the number of planemakers listed and updated the 1978 edition with 15 years of additional research. The Rees' introductory chapters are the best analysis of early wooden planemaking ever written. Early and obscure British planes have recently sold at auction for prices exceeding those of contemporary American tools and the market for early English and Scottish planes is developing rapidly. Large numbers of 18th Century English planes were exported to the colonies. If you are a collector or dealer, can you afford to be without this important source of information? A necessary reference. **$39.50 (BK 015)**

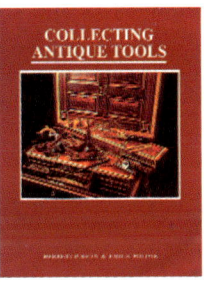

Collecting Antique Tools, by Emil Pollak & Herb Kean. 201 Pages. 8 1/2" x 11". When Herb Kean and the late Emil Pollak began work on this book, it was their intention to provide a general reference that would serve as an introduction to the wide range of hand tools that were produced and to provide new collectors with enough of a working knowledge of the various sorts of tools to begin exploring on their own. Their efforts resulted in this volume, which has been an unqualified success in achieving its intended purpose. Illustrated with superb black and white photographs of hundreds of tools, As a gift for the woodworker to provide understanding of the rich history of that craft or as a gift for a son or daughter who has expressed an interest in the mysterious array of objects that Dad drags home, we heartily recommend this book. **$24.95 (BK 032)**

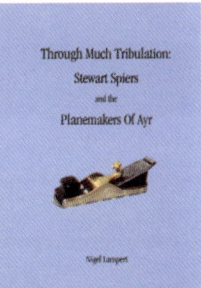

Stewart Spiers and the Planemakers of Ayr, by Nigel Lampert. 128 Pages. 8 1/4" x 10 3/4". In producing this work, which is certain to become a model for future historical monographs of important toolmakers, Australian author Nigel Lampert has contributed mightily to the range of knowledge not only about Stewart Spiers and his planemaking enterprise, but also to the broader subject of toolmaking in the Nineteenth Century. By tracing though historical records, reviewing every known document, examining every Spiers tool to be found and following up on each and every clue thus derived, Lampert has brought to life the story of Stewart Spiers, those who worked with him and the trials and tribulations they endured. Illustrated with superb black & white as well as a number of color photographs, maps, catalog illustrations, patent drawings and geneological charts, Lampert's book is certain to take an important place among the literature of antique tool collecting. Highly recommended. **$34.50 (BK 175)**

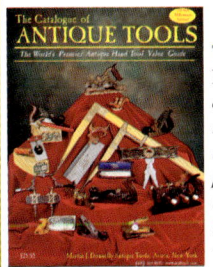

The Catalogue of Antique Tools, Millennium Edition, by Martin J. Donnelly. 320 Pages. 8 1/2" x 11". Our biggest and best catalogue ever, the much anticipated Millennium bigger by 25% than the 1999 Edition. Included in the 320 page volume are 6, 662 tools, each photographed in full color, carefully described and priced to sell. An expanded six-page index listing both manufacturers and types of tools makes the Catalogue of Antique Tools a long lasting reference for collectors, antique dealers and those with an interest in the history of technology. If you have not previously ordered the Catalogue, we encourage you to do so. We absolutely guarantee that you will be delighted. **$25.95 (BK 364)**

Anvils In America, by Richard Postman. 550 Pages. 9" x 11.25". A culmination of fifteen years of meticulous research, Anvils in America chronicles the evolution of the historically important implement that was integral to the Iron Age. Early American and European anvils, English anvils, and American cast anvils are discussed in great detail. Blacksmiths, anvil collectors, and anyone interested in historical tools will enjoy this unique book. **$60.00 (BK 422)**

Woodworking Ways: East, West & Long Ago

The Conversion and Seasoning of Wood, by William H. Brown. 222 Pages. 6" x 9". *For the woodworker interested in truly understanding the properties of the raw material of his craft, William Brown's The Conversion and Seasoning of Wood fully addresses processes through which wood passes at every stage from tree to finished product. Filled with information about techniques and methods used for various types of wood, a thorough reading of Brown's book gives a perspective to the woodworker that may well lead to a decision to being harvest and season a tree or two. A number of charts and tables document the properties to look for in various types of wood. Whether you are ready to stick and store a forest full of freshly sawn timber or just want to know a bit more about this subject, this book will prove well worth reading.*
$16.95 (BK 136)

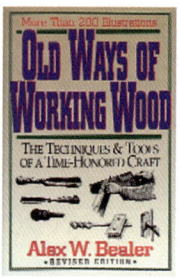

Old Ways of Working Wood, by Alex W. Bealer. 255 Pages. 6 1/4" x 9 1/4". *The recent return to print of this long time classic should be cause for celebration by all who have an interest in traditional woodworking. Bealer's excellent line drawings are completely and accurately reproduced in the durable and affordable volume that virtually gives away the secrets of old time woodworking. Arranged topically by the type of woodwork to be performed, Bealer's book moves the student through the process of harvesting the timber, splitting, sawing and planing it to size, and then to working it into a wide range of objects. Throughout the book, the author digresses to explain the process of making tools from the very same wood, and his illustrations bring the art of toolmaking to life. This classic work belongs on the bookshelf of every woodworker and antique tool enthusiast.*
$14.50 (BK 291)

The Complete Woodworker, by Bernard E. Jones, Editor. 408 Pages. 6" x 9". *If you are interested in learning more about hand woodworking than how to use a circular saw, then this ca. 1920's reprinted instruction manual is for you. In a work that goes well beyond a superficial treatment of its subject, Editor Bernard Jones has compiled a series of articles that illustrate, in detailed line drawings and photographs, how the tools that are now collectible were actually used. Included are chapters on the use and adjustment of tools, the cutting and fitting of all manner of wood joints, and a series of projects for the home woodworker, including detailed instructions on "aeroplane woodwork". A thorough chapter on the types and properties of wood adds real value. Perhaps the most valuable section is the 20 page chapter on the use of the Stanley No. 55 plane. If you enjoy woodwork and wish to benefit from the wisdom of the ages, we highly recommend this book.*
$16.95 (BK 124)

The Complete Manual of Wood Veneering, by William A. Lincoln. 400 Pages. 6" x 9". *A total of 274 photographs and drawings illustrate this well researched and thoroughly documented book that will stand as the definitive reference on the subject of veneering. Covering every aspect from the harvesting of the tree to finishing, this book begins with an historical overview of veneering, continues to the harvesting and preparation of veneers and then throughway examines every aspect of their use from the home woodworker to commercial veneering. Appendices include a 20 page table in the rating more than one hundred species of woods for their suitability for veneering, a glossary of terms and a detailed index. If you wish to gain a thorough understanding of veneering, we highly recommend this book.*
$21.95 (BK 127)

The Complete Dovetail Handmade Furniture's Signature Joint, by Ian Kirby. 151 Pages. 6" x 9". *Ian Kirby, who teaches all aspects of woodworking at Kirby Studios in Norwalk, Conn., reveals the long-lost art of dovetailing and shows why the dovetail is the signature of fine furniture making. Sharp photographs, clear drawings, and Kirby's detailed explanations take the reader step by step through four major corner dovetails (through, single-lap, double-lap, secret miter) and three rail joints (dovetail halving, dovetail housing, drawer top rail). Kirby's practice exercises allow woodworker's to build skill with hand tools. A must for amateur and accomplished carpenters!*
$14.95 (BK 331)

Modern Practical Joinery, by George Ellis. 486 Pages. 6" x 9". *Originally published in 1908 as a guide for would-be woodworkers, this comprehensive work of nearly 500 pages is filled with information and insights into all manner of woodworking, from the fundamental skills to the making of complex wooden joints. The work draws heavily upon Ellis' broad experience in the use of tools for woodworking tasks of every sort. Covered are the building of staircases, cabinets, the installation of wainscoting and much, much more. For a look at the world of woodworking at the high point of the use of hand tools, this book will more than fill the bill.*
$21.95 (BK 147)

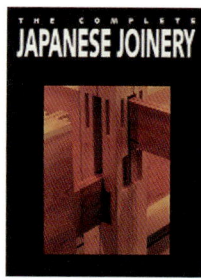

The Complete Japanese Joinery, by Koichi Paul Nii. 397 Pages. 7 1/4" x 9 1/4". *This splendid new book by Koichi Nii unlocks the secrets of the long admired but mysterious craft of Japanese joinery and offers even the novice woodworker an opportunity to create complex joints, the secrets of which were guarded by Japanese guilds for more than a thousand years. Beginning with an an analysis of the tools and techniques of the Japanese woodworker, Nii proceeds to explain the spiritual relationship between joiner and wood that is at the heart of Japanese joinery. In the subsequent chapters, the author examines every detail of modern and traditional japanese carpentry, including the spectacularly complex joints for which it is noted. Nii shows the intricacies of Japanese timber framing, flooring, roofing and more. If you are interested in woodworking, or architecture, or simply in undertaking a bit more, The Complete Japanese Joinery will prove a most worthwhile investment.*
$29.95 (BK 292)

The Wood Wright's Eclectic Workshop, by Roy Underhill. 238 Pages. 8 1/2" x 10 3/4". *Longtime master housewright at Colonial Williamsburg, Roy Underhill is the leading authority on old-time woodworking techniques. In his fourth book, Underhill features many of the popular projects featured on his television series, such as the Adirondack chair, tavern table, folding ladder, rocking horse, lathe, and kayak. Along with step-by-step instructions for each project, Underhill provides colorful descriptions of what it was like to be a tradesperson who made a living by hand.*
$16.95 (BK 301)

The Woodwright's Work Book, by Roy Underhill. 248 Pages. 8 1/2" x 11". *Roy Underhill returns with his third woodworking book. In The Woodwright's Work Book features step-by-step instructions for a selection of projects aired on his popular PBS series "The Woodwright's Shop." All projects are illustrated with photographs and measured drawings. Included here are plans for tool chests, workbenches, lathes, and historical reproductions of items for the home: a six-board chest, rustic chairs with cattail seats, a churn for the kitchen, and the Rittenhouse hygrometer. Let Roy be your guide to the world of traditional woodworking.*
$18.95 (BK 327)

The Woodwrights Shop Trad. Woodcraft, by Roy Underhill. 202 Pages. 8 1/2" x 11". *Currently master housewright at Colonial Williamsburg, Roy Underhill has made a living for more than 10 years as a woodworker, lecturer, and museum consultant. In this book, he brings to woodworking the intimate relationship with wood that craftsmen enjoyed in the days before power tools. Combining historical background, folklore, alternative technology, and humor he provides a great source of information as well as step-by-step instructions for a great selection of projects-from chairs to dough bowls, dove-tails to log houses.*
$16.95 (BK 304)

The Woodwright's Apprentice: 20 Favorite Projects, by Roy Underhill. 196 Pages. 8 1/2" x 11". *If you can't wait for the next episode of "The Woodwright's Shop" this compilation of projects from America's favorite traditional woodworker is just the thing get you through. Arranged around the building of twenty woodworking projects, in the same manner as Underhill's popular television show, this book shows how to make all sorts of things, including a tool tote, folding workbench, bookshelf, music stand, blacksmith bellows and more. Appendices on sharpening and the uses of traditional tools round out this fine new book from Roy Underhill.*
$18.95 (BK 270)

Furniture And Its Makers of Chester County, Pennsylvania, by Margaret Berwind Schiffer. 400 Pages. 9" x 11 1/4". *This book is a complete survey of furniture craftsmen working in Chester County, Pa., from its founding in 1682 to 1850 when there was a recognized decline in the handicraft tradition. Every kind of local record-old newspapers, letters, wills, inventories, land transfers, tax records, diaries and journal-was sought to create this volume. Along with an alphabetical list of craftsmen, one will find information of the characteristics and peculiarities of Chester County Furniture, as well as photographs of many signed and attributed furniture made in the area. A wonderful reference for any historian, preservationist, or collector.*
$35.00 (BK 365)

More Great Books About Wood & Woodworking

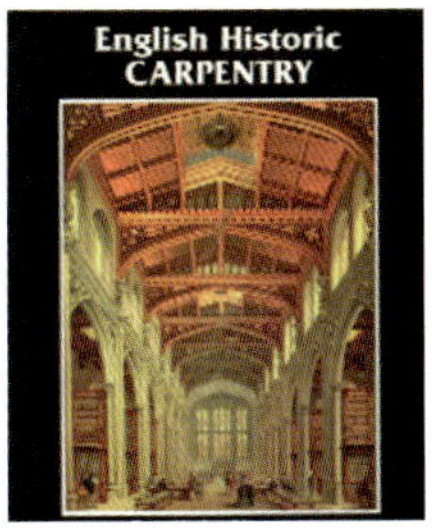

English Historical Carpentry, by Cecil A. Hewett. 338 Pages. 8" x 10". *Cecil Hewett's English Historical Carpentry looks beyond the superficial treatment of classic English buildings found in architecture books and conducts a virtual dissection of those edifices from the perspective of the woodworker. Hewett's book is filled with detailed line drawings showing the details of the framing of buildings both great and small. For the timber framer seeking inspiration, for the student of architecture or the antique tool collector interested in the work created using classic hand tool, English Historical Carpentry is a fascinating book that will be consulted often.* **$24.95 (BK 140)**

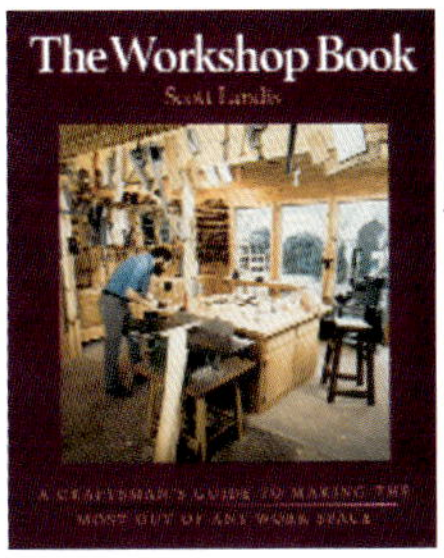

The Workshop Book, by Scott Landis. 224 Pages. 9" x 11". *Whether you have resigned yourself to forever doing your woodworking in a cramped corner of your garage or cellar or you are contemplating the building of a Dream Workshop, this new publication from the author of the popular Taunton Press "Workbench Book" is the book for you. Lavishly illustrated with great color photographs and detailed shop diagrams, this book is the result of the author's travels to some of the most interesting and unusual workshops in the country. Included are great historical shops, such as those of the Dominy craftsmen of Long Island, Windsor chairmaking shops, fully equipped power workshops, carving shops, turning shops and much more. Why reinvent the wheel when you can learn from the genius (and mistakes) of others. A most enjoyable book written in a very appealing style.* **$22.95 (BK 092)**

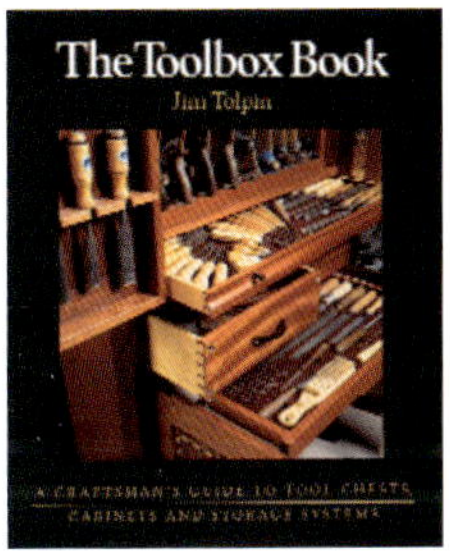

The Toolbox Book, by Jim Tolpin. 200 Pages. 9 1/2" x 11 1/2". *Collectors of antique tools are particularly well aware that the survival in collector quality condition of the tools they treasure has, in most cases, been the result of effective storage that has sheltered them from the ravages of time. In his guide to toolboxes, both past and present, author Jim Tolpin takes the reader on a tour through some of the great tool chests of the past, including the legendary H.O. Studley tool cabinet, as well as addressing the design and function of a working toolbox. Illustrated with superb color and black & white photographs as well as exploded drawings of all sorts of chests, The Toolbox Book is guaranteed to make it difficult to look at your collection or working tools without thinking about how they would fit together in a chest. Whether you come to tools as a craftsman or collector, this insightful book will bring hours of pleasure.* **$22.95 (BK 051)**

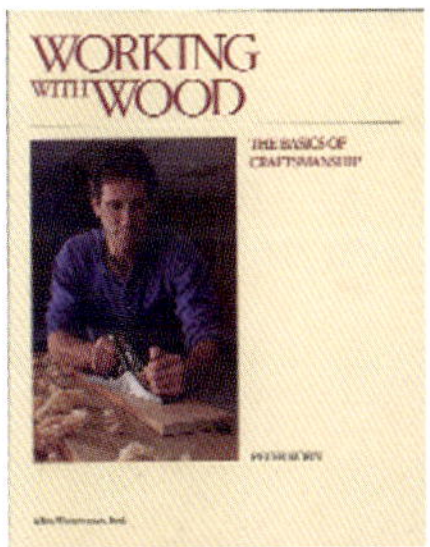

Working With Wood: The Basics of Craftsmanship, by Peter Korn. 200 Pages. 8" x 10". *Peter Korn's background of nearly 20 years as an instructor of woodworking is apparent in the text of this excellent new book from the publishers of Fine Woodworking magazine. Offering insight into every aspect of the working of wood from the selection of material to the final finishing of the work, the author accents each step with practical real world experience for both the beginner and experienced woodworker. Illustrated with excellent line drawings and clear photographs, this affordable book has much to offer to anyone interested in working with wood.* **$19.95 (BK 263)**

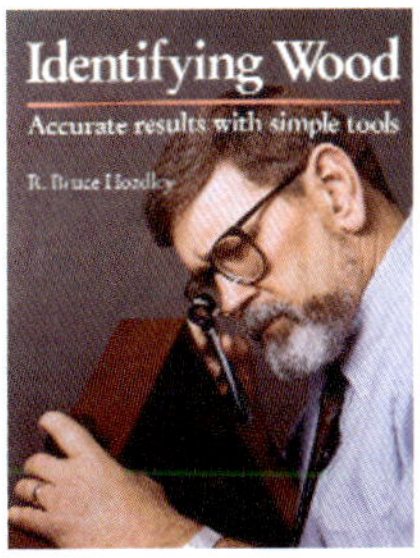

Identifying Wood: Accurate Results With Simple Tools, by R. Bruce Hoadley. 223 Pages. 9" x 11 1/2". *While not for the casual reader, this new publication from the "Fine Woodworking" folks at the Taunton Press is unquestionably the best book available on this subject for anyone other than a practicing dendrologist. Lavishly illustrated with intricately detailed microphotographs of wood specimens, this publication is much more than just a picture book. The author provides a thorough introduction to the properties of various woods and describes how the serious amateur can identify all manner of wood with nothing more than a magnifying glass and razor blade. Included among the color illustrations are all domestic and European timbers as well as a wide range of tropical hardwoods. If you're serious about wood, this book is for you.* **$39.95 (BK 095)**

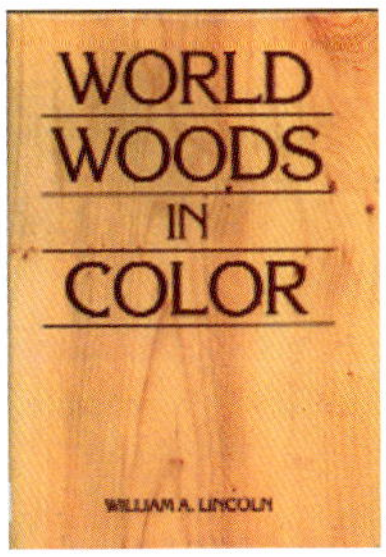

World Woods in Color, by William A. Lincoln. 320 Pages. 7" x 10". *Written by William Lincoln, the former president of The Art Veneers Co., Ltd., a major international dealer in exotic woods, this superb reference work is the definitive reference to more than 275 species of common and exotic woods. Organized in encylopedic fashion with a full page devoted to each species of tree, with half of each page containing a superb full color photograph of actual size (3" x 4") specimens of the heartwood of each timber, this beautiful book is enjoyable just to sit down and read. Each entry contains information about the names by which the wood is known, its properties and uses. A series of appendices provide information for further research and a detailed index of botanical and vernacular names makes finding a specific type of wood extremely easy. We heartily recommend World Woods in Color to any woodworker.* **$49.95 (BK 137)**

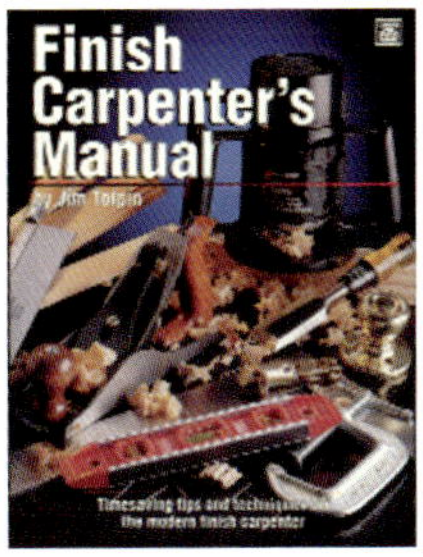

The Finish Carpenter's Manual, by Jim Tolpin. 204 Pages. 8 1/2" x 11". *Jim Tolpin, who is known to many readers as the author of "The Toolbox Book" from Taunton Press, has produced this highly informative guide that chronicles, in a well-organized and highly readable way, the tips and tricks used by professional finish carpenters to achieve perfect results with a minimum of effort. Whether you are an advanced professional woodworker or a home handyman beginning a kitchen renovation, Jim Tolpin's "Finish Carpenter's Manual" will provide insights that were previously available only after years of mistakes and on-the-job experience.* **$22.50 (BK 139)**

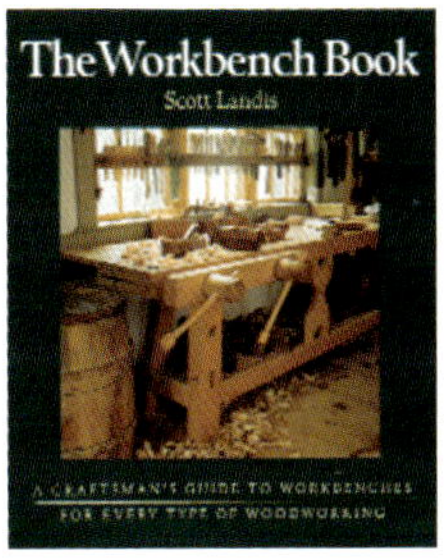

The Workbench Book, by Scott Landis. 248 Pages. 9 1/2" x 11 1/2". *In this, the first of the Taunton Press "Book" series, Scott Landis began this exciting series that combines the great tools of long ago with modern woodworking in a way that brings contemporary craftsment to an appreciation of the past and antique tool collectors to an understanding of the function and history of the accouterments of traditional craftsmanship. In a work that set the continuing standard for this superb series, Landis looks at the workbench in every imaginable form, with a special eye toward the historical development of this essential accessory to woodworking. The Workbench Book is filled with superb color and black & white photographs, including many of classic workbenches of the past. Included are plans for making traditional workbenches for the home shop, information on the many uses of the workbench; a survey of the use of workbenches in non-Western cultures and, finally a chapter that sings the praises of the latter day workbench, the Black & Decker Workmate. For a book that looks at its subject in more ways than you could imagine, and does so in an entertaining and informative way, we recommend Scott Landis' excellent b ook.* **$22.95 (BK 049)**

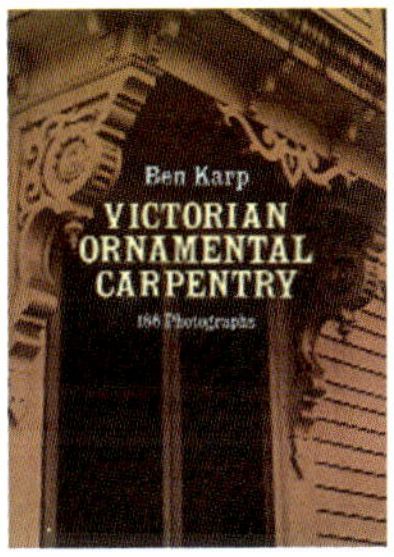

Victorian Ornamental Carpentry, by Ben Karp. 144 Pages. 8 1/4" x 11". *Sawn ornamentation-the "gingerbread" of the 19th-century Victorian homes-expressed not only the skills of the carpenter but the desires and attitudes of the owner. A growing middle class wanted a functional family home with affordable architectural embellishments and, in the realization of their dreams, they made the saw into an artist's tool. This study focuses on such sawn-wood ornamentation (i.e. designs rendered with the handsaw and without the use of chisels or planes to bevel the edges) and in 186 sharp, and detailed photographs reveals not only its recognizable elements, but the skill of the craftmen who produced it. This book is a must for carpentry enthusiasts, historians of Americana, and anyone who can appreciate an art that was of the people, by the people, and for the people.* **$17.95 (BK 189)**

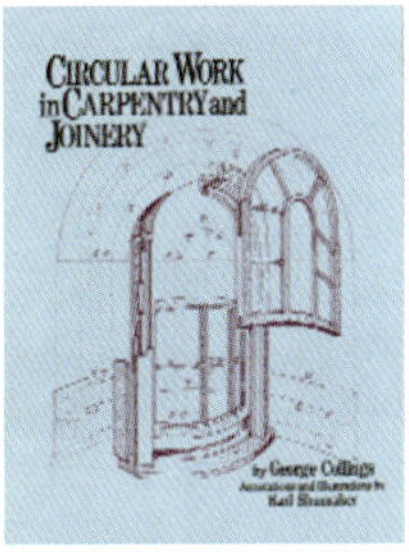

Circular Work in Carpentry, by George Collings. Pages. " x ". *A drive or walk through a town that developed during the last quarter of the Nineteenth Century is made all the more interesting through observation of the windows of the Victorian homes. Many of these houses feature elaborate circular and oval windows. On the inside of the house additional examples of curved woodwork stand as a testament to the commitment to complexity of the carpenters and jointers of the Gilded Age. This reprint of George Collings ca. 1886 book on the subject of circular woodworking captures the technical underpinnings of this complex subject as it was understood at the height of its popularity. Filled with superb period line drawings, Collings' book addresses the complex geometry of such work in a way that is at once thoroughly readable and inspiring to the potentially creative. For a look behind the scenes in the construction of a Victorian mansion, we heartily recommend George Collings superb book.* **$21.95 (BK 138)**

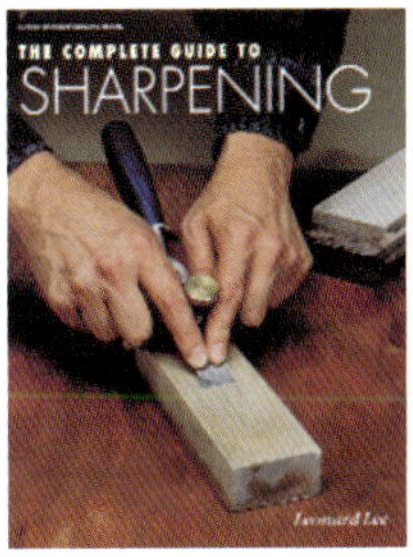

The Complete Guide to Sharpening, by Leonard Lee. 246 Pages. 9" x 11 1/2". *Whether you are interested in tools as a collector or as a craftsman, there is no reason why you should not have this book and countless reasons why you should. As the president of Veritas Tools and Lee Valley Tools, Leonard Lee has learned a few things about sharpening. This book, long overdue to the market addresses the techniques used in the sharpening of nearly every tool, including chisels, gouges, axes, adzes, saws, planes and on and on. In addition to the practical information, a great deal of technical data is provided to demonstrate why the time-tested techniques work as they do. We highly recommend this thoroughly illustrated and very well organized book.* **$34.95 (BK 077)**

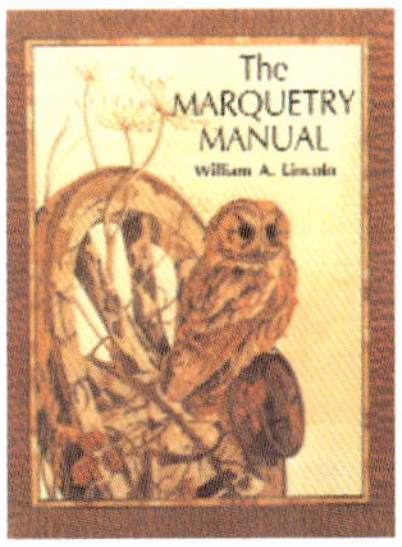

The Marquetry Manual, by William A. Lincoln. 272 Pages. 7 1/2" x 10". *Expanding upon the work begun in The Veneering Manual, author William Lincoln covers in detail every aspect of marquetry and parquetry from the selection and care of the woods to the tools employed to the techniques used to the display of the finished work. If you are interested in learning the art of marquetry, this book places a strong emphasis on the use of wood for artistic expression. Thoroughly indexed, well illustrated with photographs and line drawing and filled with helpful advice, The Marquetry Manual serve as a reference for may years to come.* **$21.95 (BK 133)**

The Ways and Workings of Hand Tools

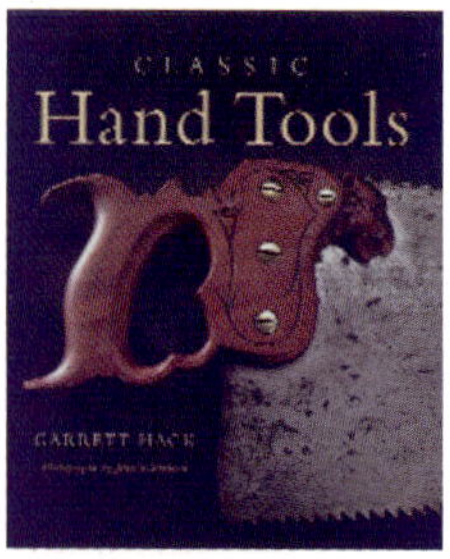

Classic Hand Tools, by Garrett Hack. 218 Pages. 9 1/4" x 11". *Expanding upon the theme begun in his classic "Handplane Book", author Garrett Hack continues his exploration of the world of classic hand tools. In this delightful new book, which is filled with superb color photographs of all sorts of highly collectible tools, Hack offers commentary for the woodworker on the traditions and uses of classic tools. The combination of great collectible tools with common sense information is the true genius of this work, as it brings together the distinct groups of tool enthusiasts who find their way to antique tool collecting. Whatever your perspective, even if you don't care at all about tools, you are certain to enjoy this beautiful new book from the publishers of Fine Woodworking magazine.*
$34.95 (BK 184)

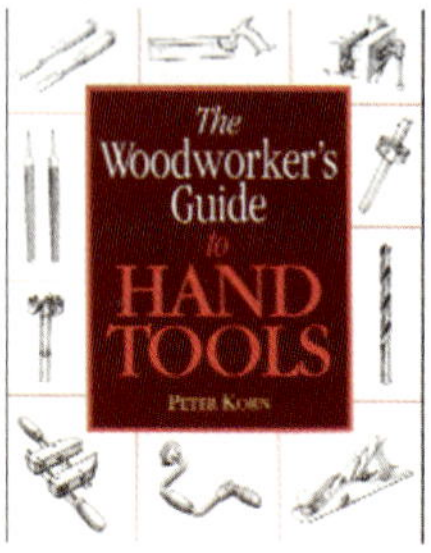

The Woodworker's Guide to Hand Tools, by Peter Korn. 200 Pages. 8" x 10". *Recently published by the "Fine Woodworking" folks at the Taunton Press, this book is crammed full of tips about every hand tool likely to be encountered by the contemporary craftsperson. The author, Peter Korn, is the Director of the Center for Furniture Craftsmanship, a provider of a hands-on workshop in the use of traditional woodworking tools. Chapters cover boring, sawing, scraping, marking and measuring, striking, planing and much, much more. Superb line drawings illustrate the various tools described and their uses. While not primarily intended for the advanced collector or cabinetmaker, there is no one who would not benefit from studying this excellent new book.* **$22.95 (BK 079)**

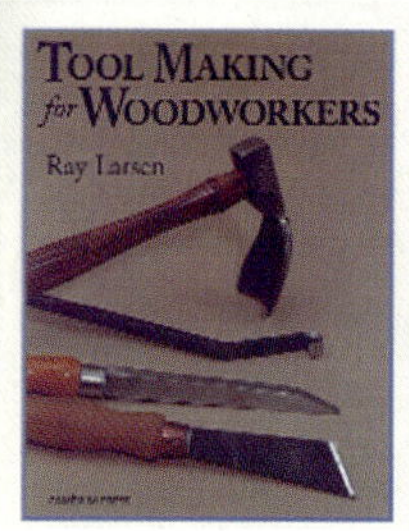

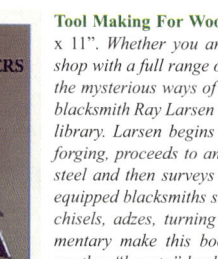

Tool Making For Woodworkers, by Ray Larsen. 160 Pages. 8 1/2" x 11". *Whether you are interested in fitting out your woodworking shop with a full range of hand forged tools or are simply interested in the mysterious ways of the toolmaker, this new publication by master blacksmith Ray Larsen is guaranteed to be a valuable addition to your library. Larsen begins with an introduction to the raw materials of forging, proceeds to an analysis of the heating and tempering of the steel and then surveys in detail the tools and equipment of the well equipped blacksmiths shop. Subsequent chapters detail the making of chisels, adzes, turning tools and more. The great photos and commentary make this book seem more like a hands-on session than another "how to" book.* **$22.95 (BK 273)**

The Hammer: The King of Tools, by Ron Baird & Dan Comerford. 352 Pages. 5 1/2" x 8 1/2". *Subtitled "A Collector's Handbook," this book, written by two of the World's foremost experts in the field of percussion tool technology, succeeds in its avowed task of making sense of an implement that ranges from the simplicity of a stone on the end of a stick to the complexity of patented special purpose hammer that only an inventor's mother could love. Divided into two distinct sections, the book begins with a pictorial analysis of hammers of every sort, and includes photographs of mallets, double claw hammers, stoneworking hammers, tack hammers and many, many, more. The second section, and the one that will prove most worthwhile to collectors and dealers, features an index of all known hammer patents together with the original patent drawings as submitted to the U.S. Patent Office. Included are patents for hammers for the one-armed man, nail holding hammers, double claw hammers, combination tools of every sort (including a hammer/wrench combination that is an insult to the integrity of each of its components) and much more. If you have an interest in tools, "The Hammer" will open the Door of Discovery to an interesting and infinitely variable world. An essential reference.*
$26.50 (BK 126)

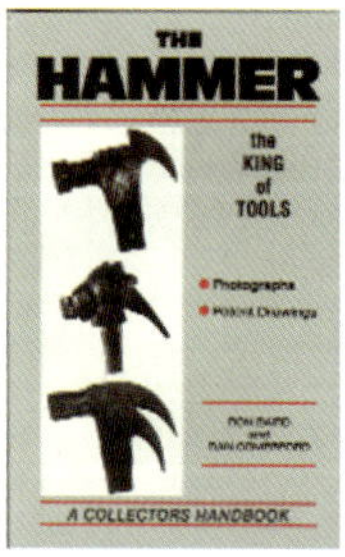

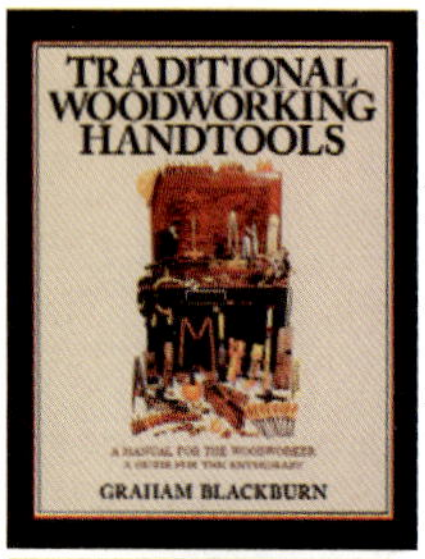

Traditional Woodworking Handtools, by Graham Blackburn. 364 Pages. 8 1/2" x 11". *In a book that draws upon a lifetime of woodworking experience in the United States as well as insights gained through professional training at that craft as a youth in Author Graham Blackburn has produced an excellent guide for today's woodworker to use in bringing traditional tools into use in the modern woodworking shop. Filled with excellent line drawings that illustrate the tools and the techniques of their use, this book follows upon a number of succesful publications by this author. For the woodworker who has learned about tools and wishes to use them effectively or the collector wishing to gain insight into how classic tools were intended to be used, this work will be a welcome addition to the library.* **$29.95 (BK 171)**

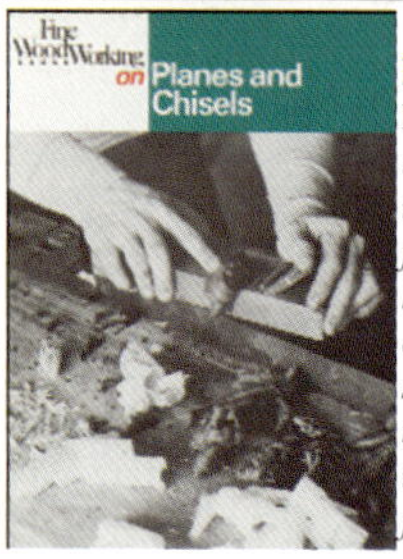

Fine Woodworking on Planes & Chisels, by The Taunton Press. 90 Pages. 8" x 11". *As hand tools became increasingly obsolete for working carpenters and jointers, many of the secrets of the maintenance and use of those tools were in danger of being forgotten. This superb book from the Fine Woodworking people captures much of that endangered knowledge and presents it in a thoroughly readable and well illustrated "how to" guide. A total of 29 articles address such diverse topics as sharpening, the use of the No. 55 plane, tuning planes and much, much more. Whether you intend to use your classic hand tools or just want to understand more about them, this excellent and affordable work is right for you.*
$9.95 (BK 058)

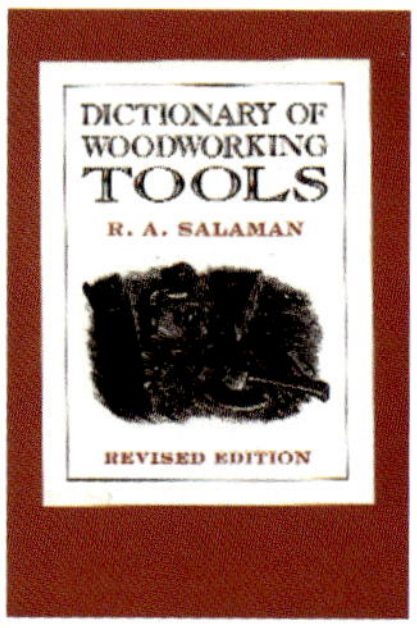

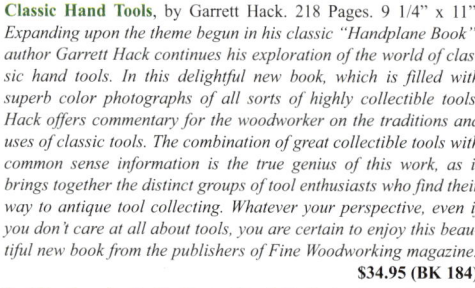

The Dictionary of Woodworking Tools, by R.A. Salaman. 546 Pages. 7" x 10". *We are extremely pleased to once again be able to offer this important and essential work to the tool collecting public. Raphael Salaman dedicated his life to the study of hand tools and the crafts in which they were used. This volume, and his equally fascinating Dictionary of Leather Working Tools are among the most frequently consulted and referenced sources for tool collectors. To truly understand and appreciate the trades and crafts and the multifarious tools that they spawned, the Salaman books are absolutely essential. Highly recommended.*
$39.95 (BK 046)

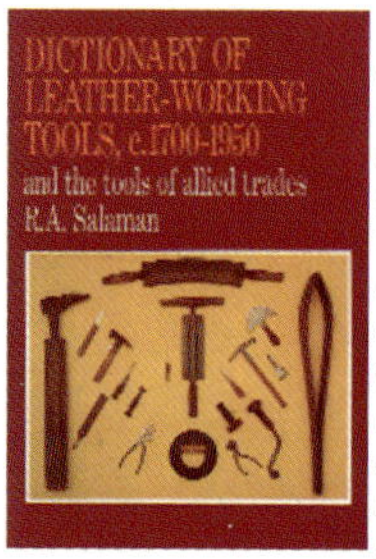

Dictionary of Leather Working Tools, by R.A. Salaman. 377 Pages. 7" x 10". *Anyone who has stared blankly into a box of leather working tools without a clue as to the function of many of the specialized implements would be well advised to add a copy of this recently republished masterpiece to his or her library. Copiously illustrated with line drawings prepared especially for this work as well as period engravings from Nineteenth Century catalogs, this work addresses in detail more than 1100 individual leather-working tools and the specialized crafts in which they were used. An index of more than 25 pages allows for easy cross-referencing when looking for a specific tool in this work that is organized around the function of specific leather-working trades. Included are the bookbinder, shoemaker, glove maker, harness maker, hatmaker and saddler. Whether you are a collector of leather working tools, an antique dealer or someone with a general interest in hand tools, this book is guaranteed to entertain and to be a valuable and frequently consulted reference.*
$37.50 (BK 022)

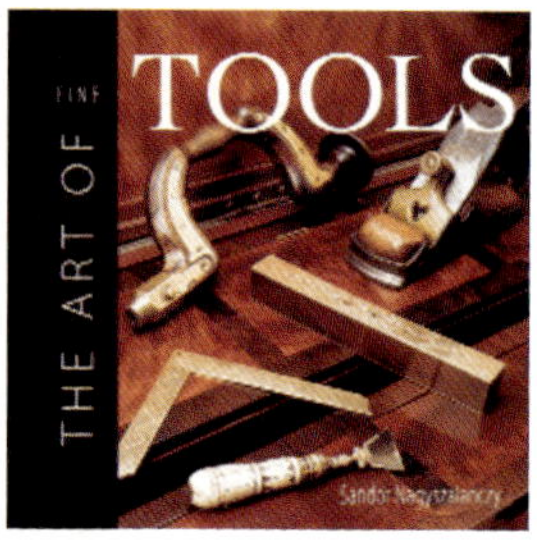

The Art of Fine Tools, by Sandor Nagyszalanczy. 240 Pages. 10" x 10". *Over the past several years, the author of this spectacularly beautiful book traveled to every corner of this country to visit and photograph the great collections of American tools. As a result of his efforts, novice collectors now have the opportunity to view an extraordinary number of extremely rare and beautiful antique tools, all from the comfort of home. Stunningly photographed in full color, topically arranged and filled with informative commentary, Sandor Nagyszalanczy's The Art of Fine Tools is for today's tool enthusiast what the Sears "Wish Book" was all too many years ago. A great book. Highly recommended.*
$37.00 (BK 094)

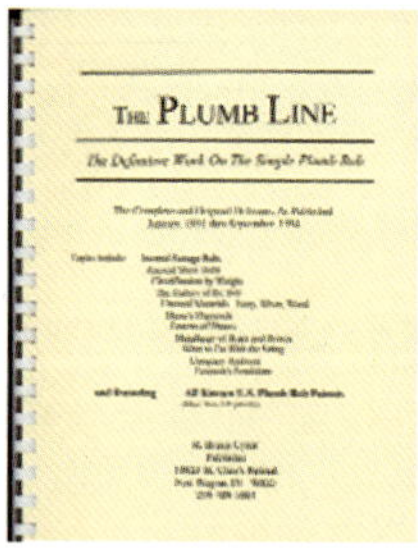

The Plumb Line Compendium, by Bruce Cynar. 176 Pages. 8" x 11 1/2". *Bruce Cynar's publication,"The Plumb Line", produced between 1991 and 1994 was truly a labor of love. During the course the years that the magazine was produced, Mr. Cynar assembled and published information on all known makers of plumb bobs, all patented bobs and shared historical research on notable makers. The back issues have long been out of print. Those of you who missed the first chance to obtain this treasure trove of information would be well advised not to delay—our supply is limited. A great reference and entertaining reading.*
$45.00 (BK 112)

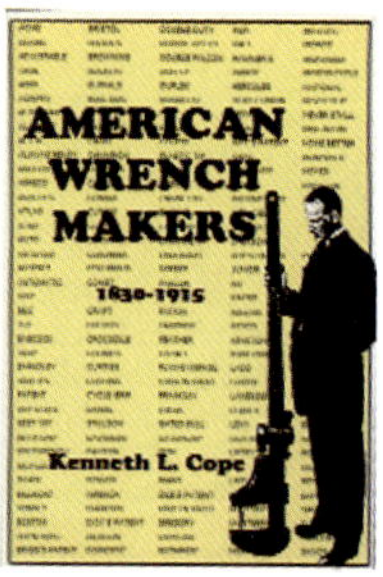

American Wrench Makers, by Kenneth L. Cope. 290 Pages. 7" x 10". *Destined to become a classic, this new work from Kenneth L. Cope, the world's most prolific antique tool researcher, uses the same format employed in his highly successful American Machinists Tools and applies it to the manufacturers and patentees of wrenches. Arranged in encyclopedic fashion and copiously illustrated with original period advertising, "American Wrench Makers" captures the spirit of inventiveness that was the Nineteenth Century. Each entry includes the known working dates of the maker(s) and biographical information, much of which is available nowhere else. Includes a valuable and innovative "Wrench Identifier" that links patent dates to manufacturers, patentees and the all-important Schulz book on wrenches. Certain to be the biggest tool book success of 1999, this one is not to be missed.*
$24.95 (BK 180)

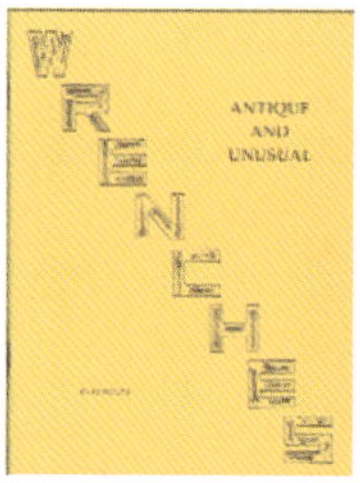

Antique and Unusual Wrenches, by Alfred & Lucille Schulz. 90 Pages. 8 1/2" x 11". *The essential picture guide to the Wrench Kingdom. Wrenches are grouped by the type or function and assigned a reference number to facilitate communication among collectors. This is the only wrench reference, and the book the collectors all carry. This publication has been out of print for more than a year. We have been allocated a limited number of copies of the reprinting that was done last winter as a tribute to the late Al Schulz. Don't miss a chance to add this American classic to your antique tool library.*
$22.50 (BK 005)

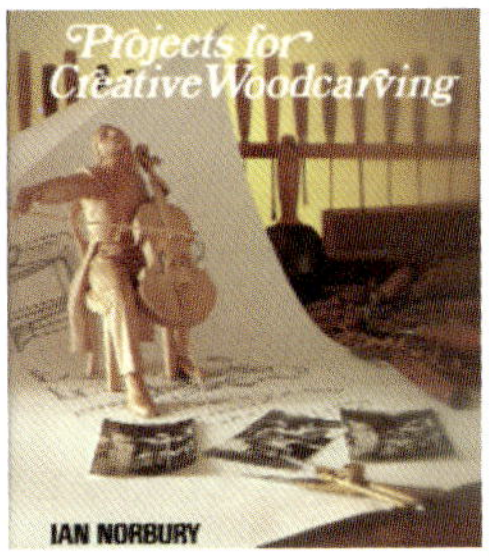

Projects For Creative Woodcarving, by Ian Norbury. 187 Pages. 8 1/2" x 9 1/2". *In this examination of some fifty woodcarving projects, author Ian Norbury includes the entire process that led to each work, including the original concept drawings, measured outline drawings, photographs of the works in progress and of the final project. In so doing, he provides much helpful commentary on the elements of design and the specific challenges encountered in each project. The novice or experienced carver has much to gain from following in the footsteps of a master and reading this well done book.* **$19.95 (BK 128)**

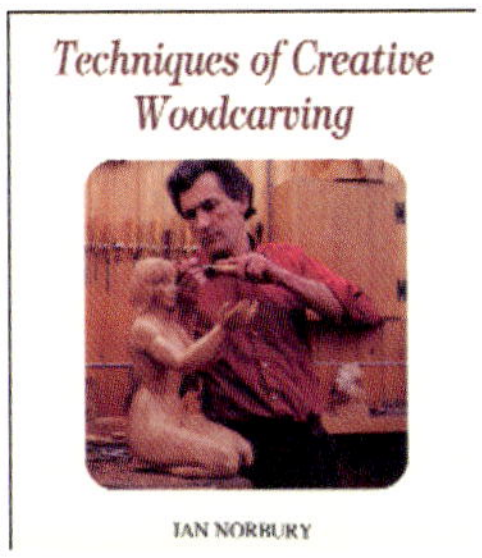

Techniques of Creative Woodcarving, by Ian Norbury. 159 Pages. 8 1/2" x 9 1/2". *The first of what was to be a continuing series of books on the subject of woodcarving, this volume by Ian Norbury begins with a series of chapters that analyze the essential components of any woodcarving project: Design, wood, equipment (including an in-depth treatment of carving tools), sharpening and polishing & mounting. The balance of the book addresses a number of woodcarving projects, each of which is broken down into an analysis of the basic components and how they varied depending upon the challenges of the specific work. Each project section ends with a photograph of the finished work, a listing of the tools used and the specifics of the timber employed in the project. For an introductory look at woodcarving from the perspective of a master, this fine book has no peer.* **$19.95 (BK 132)**

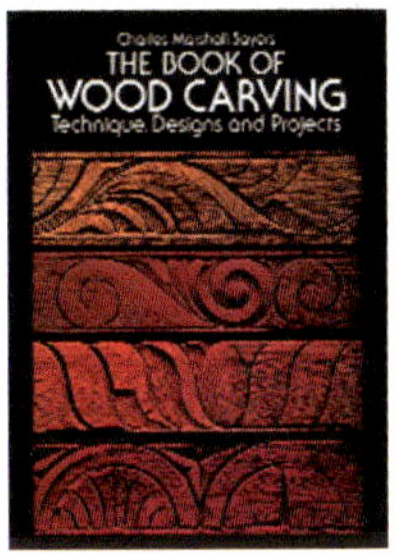

The Book of Wood Carving, by Charles Marshall Sayers. 118 Pages. 7 1/4" x 10 1/2". *'Cut the grain, and stop frequently!' This an absolutely first rate book for beginners in woodcarving. Sayers' clear, straighforward language guides the reader through the fundamentals: the woods suitable for carving, the tools and how to use them. In seven easy lessons, Sayers instructs the reader in relief carving, incised carving, and other cutting methods. Stains and finishes, preliminary and advanced methods of preparing wood for finishing are also included. There are 34 illustrated designs for over 34 projects-panels for cabinets, chests, and doors; borders, bookends, footstools, bookcovers, shelves,etc.-and all projects employ only four tools (one straight parting tool, three different sizes of straight gouges). If you have any interest in carving, you need this book.* **$9.95 (BK 191)**

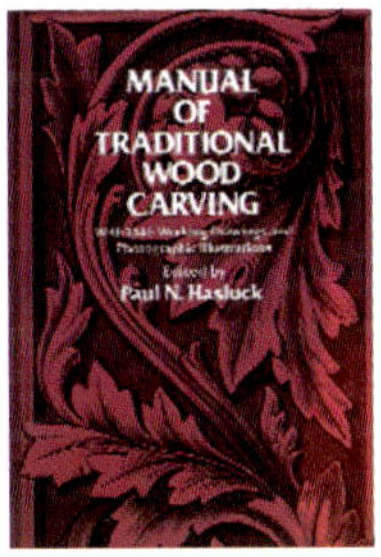

Manual of Traditional Wood Carving, by Paul N. Hasluck. 576 Pages. 6 1/2" x 9 1/4". *Want to make an exact replica of a 16th-century carved table? An armchair in carved oak? How about a 17th century chest or an Italian cassone or coffer? This book combines precise and easy-to-follow instructions along with numerous illustrations and diagrams for even the serious-minded beginner. The author begins with the basics: the tools and appliances necessary, what wood to use, how to design, trace, and outline your project. The various methods of carving are described: incised, pierced, and chip carving; carving in the round; Gothic carving; carved ornaments; etc. Many simple projects are offered-small boxes, platters, chairs, stools as well as the more complex, such as tables, cabinets, beds and even staircases-any item you can imagine in wood. Filled with a wealth of information, there is much here you could find nowhere else* **$17.95 (BK 192)**

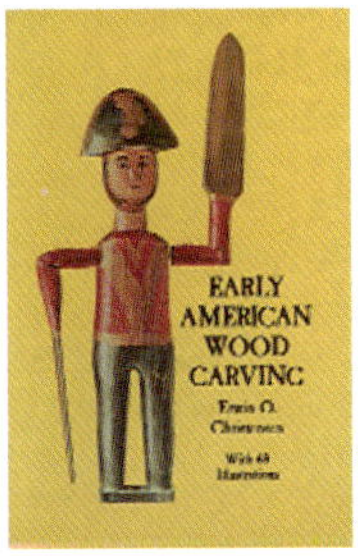

Early American Wood Carving, by Erwin O. Christensen. 160 Pages. 6 1/8" x 9 1/4". *In folk-art, American woodcarving has long been overlooked by critics and art historians. In this survey, drawn from the widely acclaimed 'Index of American Design', many of the earliest examples of American primitive art are examined, including works from the 17th-century to the end of the 19th. Every section of the Continental United States is covered with considerable attention to native Spanish, Swiss, Quebecois, German, and Scandinavian arts which influenced many regional styles. Many categories of woodcarving are discussed: portraits, monuments, shop figures, household articles, etc. with many evaluations of unexplored areas of folk art such as the religious carvings of the French Canadians, and the traditional ship figurehead carving of the Atlantic seaboard. Collectors, historian, woodcarving enthusiasts, and amateurs will find this book informative and entertaining.* **$7.95 (BK 220)**

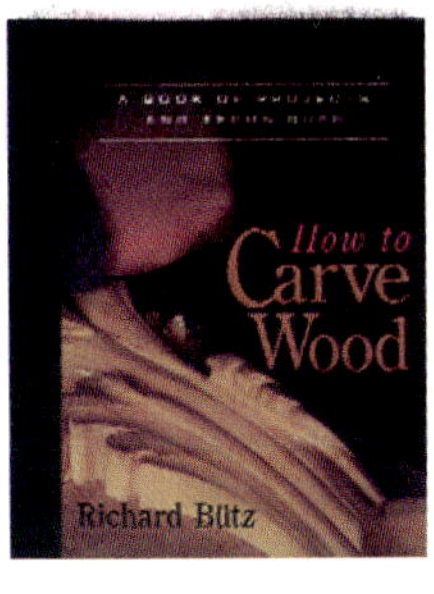

How to Carve Wood, by Richard Butz. 216 Pages. 8" x 10". *Subtitled "A book of projects and techniques", this new offering from the publishers of Fine Woodworking Magazine is exactly that. Beginning with a thorough overview of the tools needed by the woodcarver and a primer on the importance of proper work space and equipment to the production of quality work, Butz then devotes a full chapter to the importance of proper sharpening and the techniques necessary to sharpen properly. Subsequent chapters cover the types of wood for carving, finishes for the work and project design. Finally, the author demonstrates the proper techniques for whittling, chip carving and relief carving through specific projects. If you are a wood carver, or think you might like to be one, you will thoroughly enjoy this new book.* **$19.95 (BK 262)**

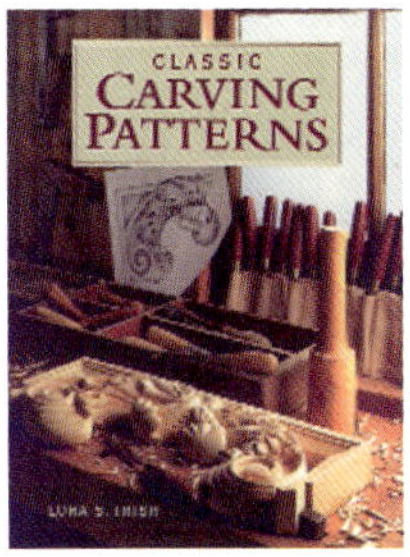

Classic Carving Patterns, by Lora S. Irish. 186 Pages. 8 3/4" x 11 1/2". *Lora Irish was an accomplished freelance artist before she turned her attention to woodcarving. One benefit of that early experience is this superb new book from the publishers of Fine Woodworking Magazine. Filled with templates in every classic style, the book includes instructions on the use of these designs to facilitate carving and provides commentary on the element of design in adding carved ornamentation to furniture. Whether you are a master carver or a novice, these classic designs will be a welcome addition to your working library.* **$19.95 (BK 264)**

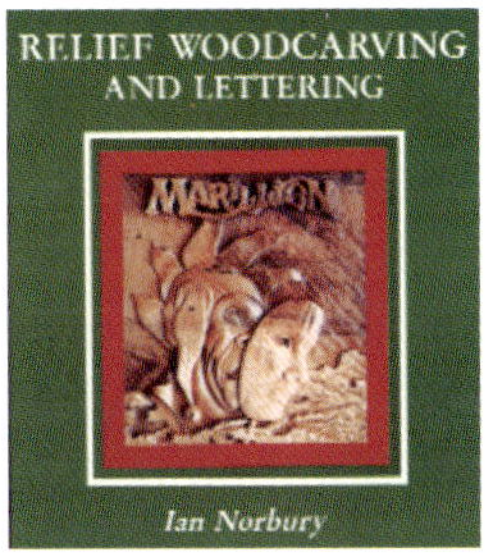

Relief Woodcarving and Lettering, by Ian Norbury. 157 Pages. 8 1/2" x 9 1/2". *Very likely the most comprehensive work in print on the subject of the ancient art of relief carving, Ian Norbury's treatment of the subject, as is the case with all of his works, is historical, analytical, technical and thoroughly readable. Beginning with a history of relief carving through the ages, Norbury then proceeds to a treatment of the uses of the vee tool and other tools in relief carving. Additional chapters address the specific requirement of low relief carving, high relief work and the challenges of letter carving. For a detailed treatment of a complex subject that is at the same an enjoyable read, this well written and well illustrated book can't be beat.* **$18.95 (BK 141)**

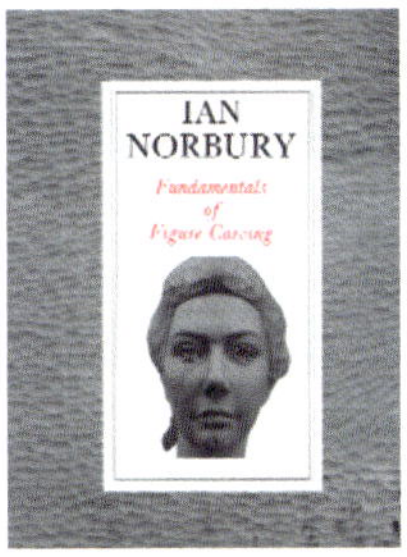

Fundamentals of Figure Carving, by Ian Norbury. 160 Pages. 9" x 11". *The sculpture of the human form has been a challenge to carvers since before the time of Michaelangelo. In "Fundamentals of Figure Carving", master carver Ian Norbury provides a course of study for the carver that leaves nothing to guesswork. Beginning with a treatment of the special tools and equipment necessary when working with human forms, Norbury proceeds to the topic of appropriate timbers and then to the techniques of carving. Focusing heavily on the exact replication of the human form, the book is copiously illustrated with line and measured drawings, photographs and anatomical drawings. A series of projects are examined in great detail to illustrate the specific challenges and rewards carving the human figure. For the woodcarver, the sculptor, the student of art or the casual reader, Ian Norbury's "Fundamentals of Figure Carving" is filled with insights that will prove invaluable.* **$31.95 (BK 144)**

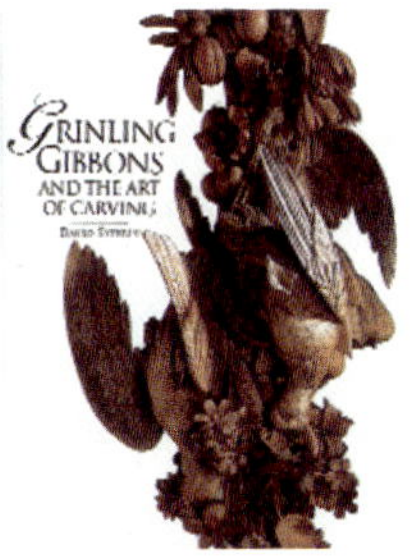

Grinling Gibbons and the Art of Carving, by David Esterly. 221 Pages. 8 3/4" x 11 1/4". *Described by Horace Walpole as "An original genius, a citizen of nature", English woodcarver Grinling Gibbons, who lived from 1648 to 1721 was all of that, and more. Gibbons' spectacular carving style, which ornaments, among other places, Windsor Castle, St. Paul's Cathedral and many of the great country homes of England, has influenced woodcarving in the British Isles and beyond to this day. Here in this beautifully presented and well researched work author David Esterly recounts the life of Gibbons, including his early failures and, later, his spectacular success. Spectacular color photographs of his greatest carvings, commissioned especially for this volume, make this a book that will be consulted form years to come. Esterly's background as a woodcarver himself is especially helpful and evident in his analysis of Gibbons' carving style. Whether you are a student of history, a lover of art, a carver of wood or all of the above, this book will provide countless hours of enjoyment.* **$49.50 (BK 287)**

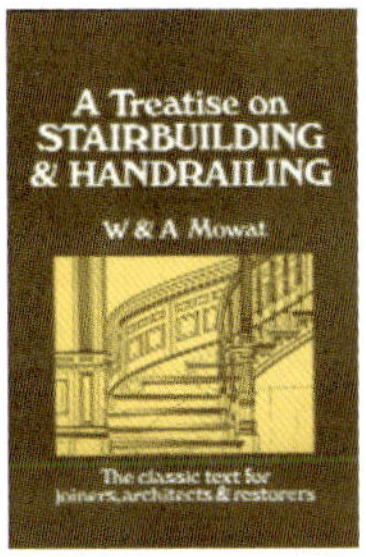

Treatise on Stairbuilding & Handrailing, by W. & A. Mowat. 390 Pages. 7 1/2" x 13". *This work, originally published in 1900, might well be subtitled "Everything You Ever Wanted to Know About Stairs". The authors, both instructors at the School of Science and Art in Barrow-in-Furness, England, produced, at the turn of the Century, what Fine Homebuilding magazine recently referred to by saying "...there is simply no better book available on the subject." Included in this comprehensive volume that is thoroughly illustrated with superb line drawings, are a history of stairbuilding and a detailed analysis of how to build stairs of every kind from simple steps to complex winding staircases. Sections on on the building of stone steps, stairbuilding for ships and the fine art of handrailing round out this comprehensive and well written book. Definitive.* **$24.95 (BK 176)**

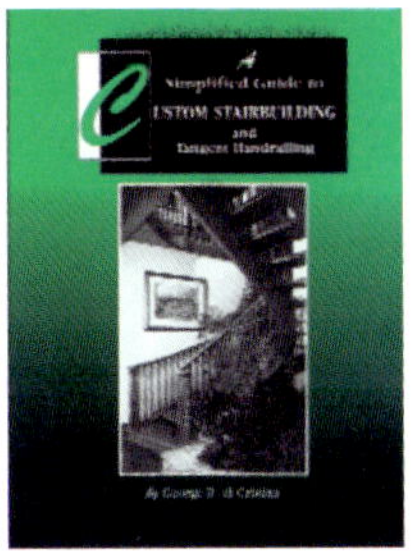

Simplified Guide to Custom Stairbuilding, by George R. Di Cristina. 278 Pages. 9" x 11 2/8". *What does the tangent system offer today's stairbuilder? It gives one the ability to construct distinctive, personalized, innovative stair and handrail designs which are not subject to the limits of stock chair and handrail parts. It allows construction of hand rails from solid stock where the finest wood grain can be featured. The continuous incline turns can be produced for any possible condition. There are no forms to build, one can make full round wall type rails fast, as well as solid wood handrail sections in the shop to fit existing metal sub-railing on the job site. George di Christine has been building stairs for nearly 50 years and presents a comprehensive text that is accessible to all who have the desire to learn this art.* **$34.95 (BK 145)**

The Turner's Art & The Carriage Trade

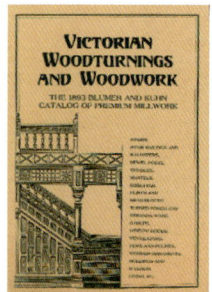

Victorian Woodturning, by Blumer & Kuhn, St. Louis, Missouri. 144 Pages. 7" x 10". One lasting reminder of the Victorian "Gilded Age" with which nearly everyone is familiar, and which is of particular interest to woodworkers and tool collectors, is the elaborate woodwork that graced nearly every home built during that period. Featuring everything from moldings (of every sort that can be imagined), mantels, staircases, balusters and verandas, this period catalogue from one of the premier producers of the day is a fascinating tour through a period that was certainly the high water mark of America's Wooden Age. For a look at the building blocks of late-Nineteenth Century America, we heartily recommend this book. **$16.95 (BK 056)**

Ornamental Turning, by John Henry Evans. 344 Pages. 5 1/2" x 8 1/2". Here, in a reprint of the 1886 Edition of this classic work by J.H. Evans are the secrets of the arcane art of ornamental turning. Beginning with a survey of the hand tools, as well as the machinery needed to produce the elaborate turnings, this book addresses every aspect of this obscure subject. Illustrated with 192 engravings and 17 plates, this book allows the reader to understand how man and machine could produce the extraordinarily complex output that now graces museums and collections. While not for the casual reader, Ornamental Turning, is guaranteed to be a worthwhile experience for those with a general interest in the subject. **$22.50 (BK 053)**

Beyond Basic Turning, by Jack Cox. 256 Pages. 9" x 9 1/2". Anyone who has ever stared in wonder at an example of the work of a master woodturner will look at that work in an entirely different way after reading Jack Cox's "Beyond Basic Turning". In a very high quality book that is copiously illustrated with superb color and black and white photographs, Cox takes the reader through the creation of a series of complex turned objects, and in so doing illustrates the basic techniques used in every sort of artistic turning. Whether you are a beginner at the lathe or a seasoned veteran, Jack Cox's well written book on this subject is certain to provide insight and enjoyment. **$28.95 (BK 146)**

Techniques of Creative Spiral Work, by Stuart Mortimer. 176 Pages. 9" x 9 1/2". Not for the casual woodworker, Mortimer Stuart's "Techniques of Spiral Work" is, however a thoroughly well put together work that clearly explains how the seemingly impossible creations featured on the cover and within the book can be produced by a committed turner. **$24.95 (BK 142)**

Turning Lathes, by James Lukin, Ed.. 432 Pages. 6" x 9". The subtitle of this period book "A guide to turning, screw-cutting, metal-spinning, ornamental turning, etc." gives a more precise idea of what the reader will find here. Most collectors, and a large number of woodworkers are only generally familiar with the fine art of turning. Here, in the pages of this book that was originally published in 1894, one will find all of the secrets of the many specialized forms of turning and spinning, as well as the special sharpening techniques for the tools used in those crafts. In addition to the thoroughly entertaining and well-illustrated text, the catalogue of the Brittania Company, a period dealer in metalworking tools, complete with original engravings, is included. For a look at the lost world of metalworking as it existed at the dawn of the Industrial Age, we wholeheartedly recommend this book. **$24.95 (BK 054)**

A Treatise on Lathes and Turning, by W. Henry Northcott. 310 Pages. 5 1/2" x 8 1/2". Originally published in 1876, this book by Henry Northcott is as comprehensive a work on the lathe as can be found in a single volume. Beginning with a study of the various lathes then in use, both for the turning of wood and metal, the author then proceeds to an overview of the tools of the turner, again, both for wood or metal. Succeeding chapters address simple wood turning, the basics of metal turning, screw cutting, wheel cutting and ornamental turning. This comprehensive volume is filled with period engravings that bring life to the well written text. For a look at the state of the art of turning 125 years ago that is still useful today, we heartily recommend this classic book. **$14.95 (BK 130)**

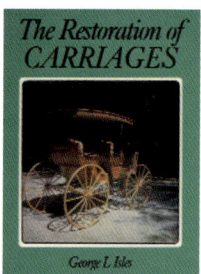

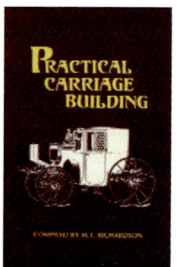

Wheelmaking: Wagon Wheel Design and Construction, by Don Peloubet, Editor. 246 Pages. 9" x 12". Compiled from the information in the library of The Carriage Museum of America, this book captures nearly everything that was known of wheels and traditional wheelmaking at its late 19th Century peak. Incorporating period writings on all manner of topics relating to wheels, the book is organized by chapters which address, wheelmaking, dishing, hubs, spokes, rims, tires, wheel repair and much more. Thoroughly illustrated with period engravings and line drawings, including a wealth of patented wheelwrights tools and machinery, this book will turn a novice into an expert about this arcane yet interesting subject in a single sitting. **$32.50 (BK 116)**

The Restoration of Carriages, by George L. Isles. 190 Pages. 7 1/2" x 9 1/2". Written by the former curator of the Carriage Museum at Stony Brook, this work includes a series of chapters that explain in detail exactly how to take a battered and broken relic of a carriage and make it into a vehicle fit for a Sunday stroll. Covered are such things as the replacing of panels, wheelwright work, roof repair, paining and finishing and much more. A series of appendices address the work of the wheelwright, the reminiscences of a coach painter and the organization of the coach house. A well done introduction that is well illustrated with photographs and period engravings. **$24.95 (BK 131)**

Practical Carriage Building, by M.T. Richardson, Compiler. 285 Pages. 5 1/2" x 8 1/2". Originally published in 1891, this reprinted book by the author of Practical Blacksmithing, Vol. I and Practical Blacksmithing, Vol. II, this book represents an attempt to compile in a single volume, all that was then known about the art and practice of carriage building. In chapters that address the tools, techniques, materials and essential elements of design, Richardson succeeds mightily at his avowed goal. Addressing every thing from the wheels to the trimmings and also carriages without wheels, this book is filled with practically lost information about a nearly forgotten age. Whether you are a student of trades or a would-be carriage builder, "Practical Carriage Building" will undoubtedly entertain and enlighten. you. **$27.95 (BK 117)**

The Coach Maker's Illustrated Hand-Book, by The Carriage Museum of America. 368 Pages. 6" x 9". A reprint of one of the earliest known books about the subject of carriage building, this work is reprinted from a ca. 1875 original in the collection of The Carriage Museum of America. Addressing every aspect of the art and science of the construction and finish of horse drawn conveyances as it was then know, this book is thoroughly illustrated with illustrations and engravings of every sort. Beginning with an assessment of the tools and techniques of the draughtsman in the design of carriages, the book proceeds to analyze actual construction, smith work for the carriage shop, painting, trimming and final outfitting. Special emphasis is devoted to the restoration and repair of existing vehicles. For those who wish to understand the ways and workings of the horse-drawn age, this book will contribute substantially. **$27.95 (BK 119)**

Bristol Wagon & Carriage Illustrated Catalog, by Bristol Wagon & Carriage Works Co. 178 Pages. 8 1/4" x 11". This invaluable book, reprinted from a rare original catalog, advertises commercial carts, wagons, vans and drays built by the prosperous wagon and carriage works in Bristol, England at the turn of the 20th century. Bristol Wagon & Carriage Works built and sold vehicles customized for many different occupations and trades people: farmers, dairymen, bakers, butchers, wine merchants, cabinet makers, coal merchants and many more. Filled with over 270 detailed line drawings accompanied by descriptive copy, the book with is a delight to peruse and study. **$12.95 (BK 329)**

Horse Drawn Sleighs, by Susan Green. 268 Pages. 8 1/2" x 11". Produced by the curator of the Carriage Museum of America, this book is a compendium of 19th Century catalogs of horse drawn sleighs. Profusely illustrated with period engravings and line drawings, each of which is accompanied by the period catalog description, this book encompasses a virtual Museum of Sleighs between its covers. Arranged in chapters that are topically devoted to the type and function of the sleigh, the regional variations in design, as well as the functional uses of winter horse-drawn vehicles become quickly apparent to the modern student. If you wish to be able to distinguish between a Portland Cutter or an Albany Swell-Body Sleigh, or if you are thinking of building your own, this book will surely get you well on your way. **$29.95 (BK 115)**

More Antique Value Guides

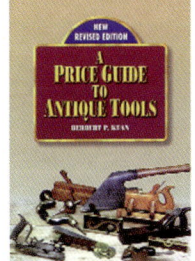

Price Guide to Antique Tools, by Herbert P. Kean. 184 Pages. 7" x 10". In a major revision of this work that was designed as a companion to "Collecting Antique Tools", Herb Kean has once again put together a book that does exactly what a price guide should do: It includes a picture of the tool and an easy way to find an estimate of its current value. In compiling this work, Kean has undertaken a great deal of research, including auction results, private sales, dealer offerings and general market trends. More than just a list of tools and prices, this book also includes chapters on the classification of "condition", the all-important factor in evaluating value, as well as a key to the important names to look for in wooden planes. For the collector, the dealer or the sometime garage sale visitor, this new price guide is guaranteed to pay its own way many times over.
$17.95 (BK 048)

Prices Realized on Rare Imprinted American Wooden Planes, by Emil & Martyl Pollak. 151 Pages. 7" x 9 1/2". For the new collector or the casual observer, one of the most perplexing aspects of antique tool collecting is the wide variation in prices for wooden molding planes. Given two planes that appear identical to the unitiated, one might sell for $15.00 and the other for $1500. In this eye opening book that is virtually guaranteed to pay for itself, the late Emil Pollak and wife Martyl chronicle a full range of planes sold at auction or in private sales, including the specific maker imprint, type of plane and the date of the sale. Whether you're an avid collector of 18th Century molding planes or just interested in the value of the tools in Great Grandpa's tool chest, this book will be a welcome addition to the library.
$16.95 (BK 277)

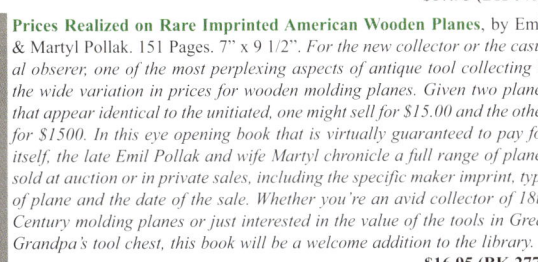

Care & Repair of Antiques & Collectables, by Albert Jackson & David Day. 144 Pages. 8 1/4" x 10". While targeted toward the general antique collector or dealer, this work is filled with volumes of information for the antique tool restorer and preservationist. By addressing the basic techniques for use in cleaning, preserving and repairing objects made of every conceivable material, the authors have covered every possible component of any antique hand tool. Whether it be information about the treatment of rusted metal, dented or damaged wood, stained paper or damaged jewelry, the tips contained in this book will certainly help you bring your tools up a grade or two in condition. The introductory sections about spotting fakes and evaluating potential purchases are well worth reading. Nicely illustrated in full color. A quality Taunton Press publication.
$27.95 (BK 090)

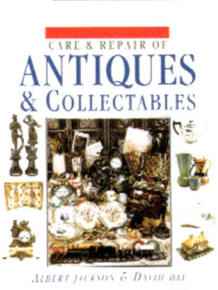

Restoring Antique Tools, by Herbert P. Kean. 122 Pages. 5 1/2" x 8 1/2". Normally a shy and reticent man, former auctioneer and long time antique tool collector Herb Kean has finally been persuaded to offer his opinion to others. In "Restoring Antique Tools", Kean articulates a philosophy of restoration and then carefully spells out specific restoration techniques that, with practice, will allow the beginning or advanced collector to transform broken or battered antique tools into those worthy of collection and display. This book, which virtually "gives away the secrets" of tool restoration, will provide insight to all who are interested in antique tools, whether they intend to implement the suggestions contained within or not. Being aware of the tricks of the tool fixer-upper can lead collectors to purchase with a much more practiced eye. Whether it is your intention to make old tools look new again or to be able to tell the difference, "Restoring Antique Tools" will be well worth reading.
$17.95 (BK 165)

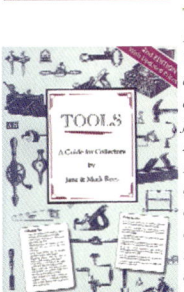

Tools: A Guide For Collectors, by Mark & Jane Rees. 238 Pages. 8" x 11". Mark and Jane Rees are well known as the Editors of the Third Edition of William Goodman's British Planemakers From 1700. This new revision and expansion of their enormously successful first edition of this book is an attempt to provide a general guide to the collecting of antique tools. Written from a British perspective, which provides even experienced collectors of American tools with a thorough introduction to the tools produced in England and Scotland, the Rees' draw heavily upon their personal experiences of some thirty years of collecting and share anecdotes of personal experience, analysis of general market trends, advice for the beginner and expert alike, and provide pricing information on tools from the most common to the very rare. This book is thoroughly illustrated with period engravings of hand tools of every sort and it addresses, in a topical analysis of each type of tool, what collectors should look for (and avoid) when considering the purchase of tools of that type. Highly recommended.
$28.95 (BK 020)

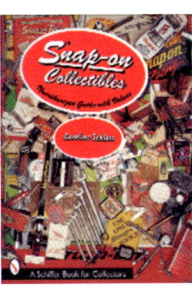

Snap-on Collectibles: Unauthorized Guide with Prices, by Caroline Schloss. 160 Pages. 8 1/2" x 11". Since 1920, the Snap-On Wrench Company has provided the world with tools that combine state-of-the-art design with classic American style. The Snap-On Company has also ventured far beyond the workbench, appearing on everything from toys to T-shirts. This collection of Snap-On items will send any automotive enthusiast into his garage to rummage around for those old calendars, mugs, model cars, and commemorative sets that may be worth a pretty penny. If you're interested in buying, selling, or simply enjoying the world of Snap-On collectibles, the book is the right tool for you.
$29.95 (BK 223)

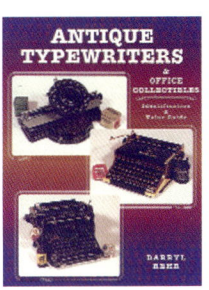

Antique Typewriters & Office Collectibles Identification & Value Guide, by Darryl Rehr. 176 Pages. 8 1/2" x 11". The origins and evolutions of a now defunct office landmark are covered in great detail in Darryl Rehr's new Antique Typewriters and Office Collectibles Identification and Value Guide. Not only does Rehr provide excellent histories of the machines and their makers, but he also includes up to date values for many of the machines, including those that look like they might be valuable, but aren't and those that look like they might be valuable and are. Arranged alphabetically by manufacturer, this book also includes chapters on the development of typewriters, the mechanics of typewriters, information on pencil sharpeners, calculators, typewriter ribbon tins and a thorough index with hundreds of entries. For a frequently consulted reference on the world of office collectibles, we highly recommend this new book.
$19.95 (BK 268)

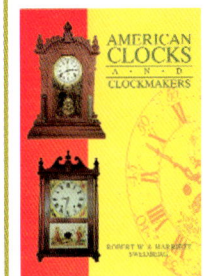

American Clocks and Clockmakers, by Robert W. & Harriett Swedberg. 192 Pages. 7" x 10". Pass the times by browsing through more than 350 clocks available and indeed desired by today's collector. Learn fascinating historical information on each clock and its maker, as well as each clocks worth.
$16.95 (BK 244)

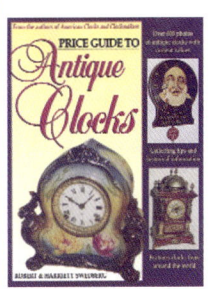

Price Guide to Antique Clocks, by Robert & Harriett Swedberg. 320 Pages. 8 1/2" x 11". Whether you are a seasoned collector with a house full of clocks, a beginner to this fascinating hobby or just interested in what great grandma's clock might be worth, this new publication will more than meet your needs. Beginning with an overview of the various types of clocks, the book then traces the clockmaking profession from the earliest days. Subsequent chapters cover every notable and many obscure American clockmakers and their work and provide value ranges for each. Final chapters analyze each of the principal types of clocks and provide photos and values for examples through every price range. If you are not interested in clocks, don't by this book or you soon will be.
$27.95 (BK 293)

Cowboy Equipment With Values, by Joice Overton. 158 Pages. 9" x 11.25". From saddles to silverware, this book reveals the various and diversified items that were so essential to the cowboy way of life. Containing over 500 photographs along with helpful text and captions and value guide, this book will serve as an invaluable historical reference, as well as a present day guide for collectors, antique dealers, traders, and modern day cowboys. Cowboy Equipment is guaranteed to bring the Old West back to life, and will be enjoyed by all lovers of Western Lore.
$39.95 (BK 378)

Cowboys, by John Eggen. 128 Pages. 11" x 8.5". In the frontier of Colorado in 1903, Frank Sherman had a photography studio and souvenir shop in Colorado Springs. He decided he needed more postcards to sell to the tourists, so he visited his brothers who worked at the Holt Livestock Co., in Hugo, Colorado. His timing was fortuitous. Just before the roundup was to start, word came that President Theodore Roosevelt would be stopping into Hugo on his western trip. Frank Sherman got the pictures and John Eggen shares these picture with you for the first time. This wonderful volume reveals a rare glimpse of the Old West and will be enjoyed by anyone who revels in the romance of the West.
$19.95 (BK 391)

The Art of the Decoy: American Bird Carvings, by Adele Earnest. 208 Pages. 8.5" x 11". The carved bird decoy was first used as a hunting aid by the American Indians and has grown as a useful art since the days of the Colonists. This book, full of stunning photographs, shows the best examples from both public and private collections and gives the reader an idea of the great range, vigor and variety of the birds.
$19.95 (BK 398)

Shop Online at www.mjdtools.com: It's Easy and it's Safe!

Step One:
Click Here
To Bring Up the Search Page

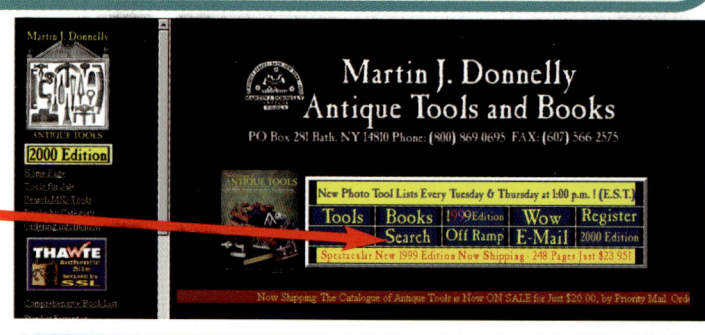

Step Two:
Type in the Book Information
for example BK 005 or BK 225. Adding the author's name can help, such as BK 001 Pollak

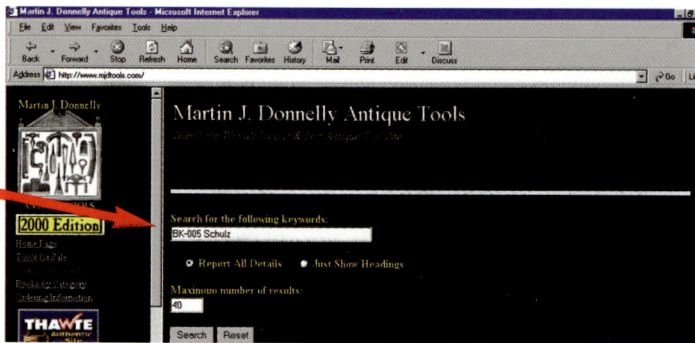

Step Three:
Click Here
to Bring up the Book Description

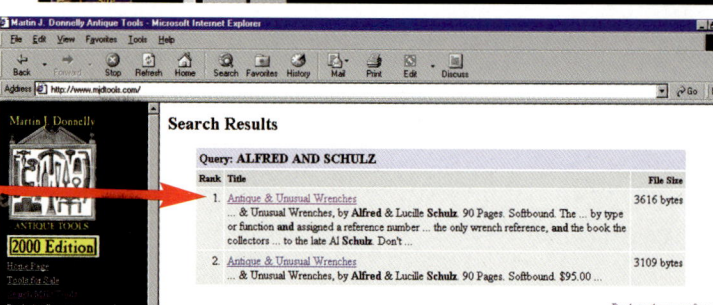

Step Four:
Click Here
to Order the Book

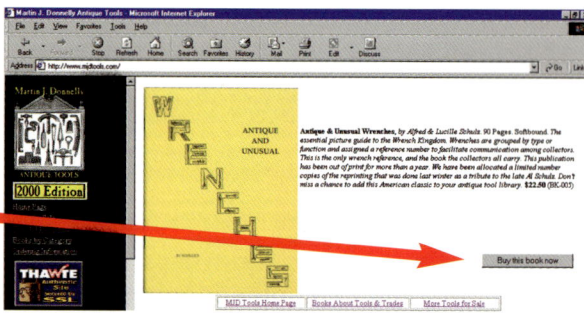

Step Five:
Enter Information
*All Credit Card Information is Transmitted Using 100% Secure SSL Encryption.
You will receive confirmation by email almost immediately after the sale.*

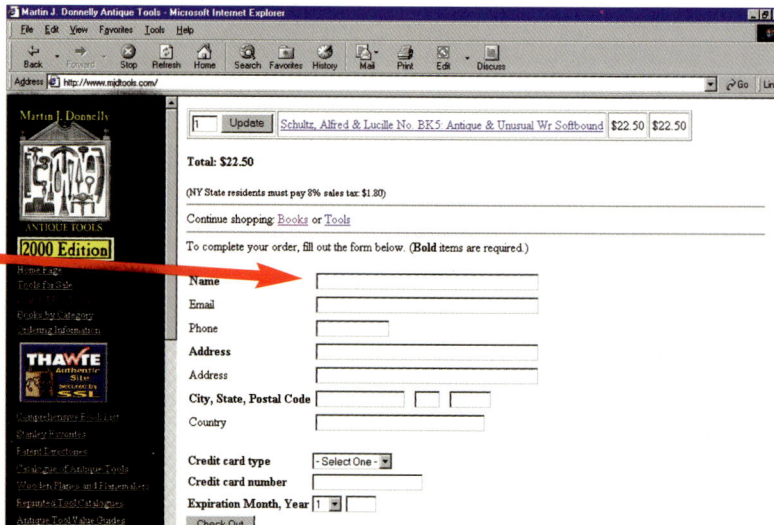

Toll Free: (800) 869-0695   Page 16   Secure Online Ordering at www.mjdtools.com

Call, Mail, Fax or Click

Toll Free: 1-800-869-0695 Fax: (607) 566-2575 Secure Online Ordering: www.mjdtools.com

Available From: **MARTIN J. DONNELLY ANTIQUE TOOLS**

P.O. Box 281 Bath, N.Y. 14810-0281 *Please...Share Our Booklist With a Friend*

Phone: (800) 869-0695 or (607) 566-2617 • FAX: (607) 566-2575 • E-Mail: mjd@mjdtools.com

We Invite You to Visit our Expanding Book Gallery on the World Wide Web! www.mjdtools.com

Quantity:	Book Number:	Book Name:	Per Book:	Total:

Subtotal

Shipping (free within the Continental United States unless noted. Actual cost elsewhere)

New York State Residents Must Add N.Y.S. Sales Tax @ 8%

Total

Name:
Shipping Address:
City/State/Zip/Country:
Telephone:

Credit Card Type: _____ No: _____
Expiration Date: _____

Special Offer: Back Issues Just $10.00
With Any Order
1999: BK 172   1998: BK 62

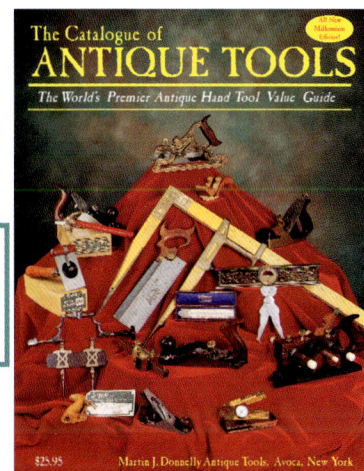

Don't Miss It!!!
Just $25.95 ➔ BK 364

Avoid Delay: *Call Today!*
Toll Free: (800) 869-0695
FAX: (607) 566-2575

Don't Miss Our Internet Tool Lists: Every Tuesday & Thursday at 1:00 p.m. E.S.T.
www.mjdtools.com

Collectibles of Every Sort

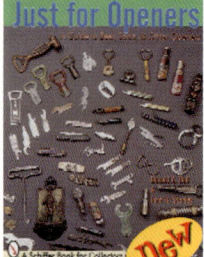

Just For Openers: A Guide to Beer, Soda and Other Openers, by Donald A. Bull & John R. Stanley. 160 Pages. 8.5" x 11". *Although every household in America has at least one "opener" in their home, this ultimate guidebook may convince you one may not be enough. Grouped categorically as well as alphabetically, this guide offers collectors over 850 remarkable examples of collectible advertising cap lifters, can piercers, and corkscrews, along with their history and current market value.* **$29.95 (BK 395)**

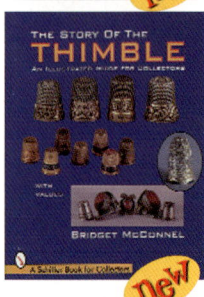

The Story of the Thimble, Illustrated, by Bridget McConnel. 175 Pages. 9" x 11.25". *In this second edition, the world's foremost authority on the history of thimbles tells all, outlining the little tools long romantic history, from ancient Egypt to today. The thimble's history is interwoven with that of women, such as the Victorian seamstress or the French Court lady, giving glimpses of a private and domestic world history books often overlook. This book also supplies practical tips on cataloging, maintenance, and display. With more than 2,000 thimbles illustrated in full-color, this book is a must for anyone with a fascination for sewing tools.* **$49.95 (BK 374)**

Scales a Collector's Guide, by Bill & Jan Berning. 160 Pages. 8.5" x 11". *In almost any business or home at least one scale can be found. This book features hundreds of color photographs of the most collectible scales ever made: diamond scales, egg scales, bathroom scales, martini scales, toy scales, gold club scales, coin-operated scales, and many others, all described in detail including their values. If you love mechanical gadgets or you just love scales, this collector's guide cannot be missed.* **$29.95 (BK 387)**

Cigarette Lighters Book For Collectors, by Stuart Schneider & George Fischler. 176 Pages. 9" x 11.25". *Although most households may possess a cigarette lighter of some sort, very few may truly appreciate them for the collectible items that they are. Schneider & Fischler have created a book that will certainly remedy that situation. With over 500 color illustrations, Cigarette Lighters reveals interesting and unusual examples of lighters from well-known companies like Dunhill, Ronson, and Zippo as well as lighters from companies that have long since been lost in obscurity. Complete with collecting tips and values, this book is the ultimate guide for collectors in the fun and challenging hobby.* **$39.95 (BK 379)**

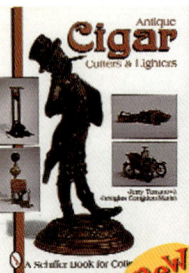

Antique Cigar Cutters & Lighters, by Jerry Terranova & Douglas Congdon-Martin. 174 Pages. 9" x 11.25". *From the end of the Civil War until the explosive popularity of the cigarette in the early 20th-century, the cigar was king. A wide variety of accessories were manufactured for the pleasure and convenience of cigar smokers, including cigar cutters and lighters-the subject of this book. Cutters ranged from simple pocket models to large mechanical contraptions, in between they took the shape of sculpted Vienna bronzes or bicycles. Lighters were made of anything from blown glass to pierced tin. With 513 color illustrations and value guide, this book is a must for anyone who appreciates a fine cigar.* **$69.95 (BK 385)**

Pocket Guide to Corkscrews, Book, by Onald A. Bull. 190 Pages. 6" x 9". *Rack and pinion, double lever, frame, and flynut- these are just some of types of corkscrews that can be found in this fascinating book. This guide, Bull's Guide to Corkscrews, invites collectors and dealers once again to explore remarkable examples of corkscrews, from figurals and eclectic corkscrews to corkscrew knives: rare and novelty varieties are well represented. For easy reference, all corkscrews are classified categorically along with their current market value.* **$19.95 (BK 403)**

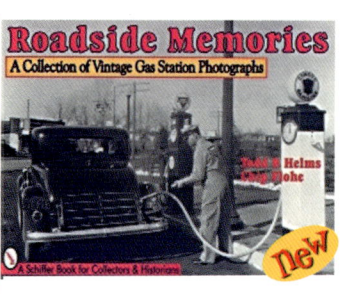

Roadside Memories Collection of Vintage Gas Station Photographs, by Todd P. Helms & Chip Floe. 159 Pages. 11" x 8.5". *This rare collection of photographs takes the reader on a trip down memory lane to a much simpler time in American history. Since its inception in the early 1900s, the service station has been an icon of the American roadside and a catalyst of childhood memories. Included is a brief history of the development of the gasoline station in the United States and details about the many companies which marked the roadside with their building- the Standard companies, Cities, Mobil, Phillips, Gulf, Shell, Texaco, and Sonoco. These nostalgic black-and-white photos, dating from the 1920s to the 1970s, will aid both the collector and historian interested in the aspect of American life.* **$29.95 (BK 407)**

Sporting Collectibles, by Jim & Vivian Karsnitz. 160 Pages. 8.5" x 11". *The lure of the outdoors is universal, and the items associated with its pleasure are cherished by all. Old shells, decoys, advertising signs, books, prints, traps, licenses and the like are featured in many varieties here. A rarities scale is provided for each item illustrated. Unusual and interesting sport-hunting collectibles are presented through over 400 clear color photos, an informative text and identifying captions. The readers will quickly become fascinated with this exciting field of collecting interest.* **$29.95 (BK 408)**

Hoard's Dairyman Dairy Collectibles, by James Baird. 72 Pages. 5.5" x 6.5". *Compiled and edited by prominent collector Jim Baird, who also designed the dairy exhibit at the Hoard Historical Museum in Fort Atkinson, Wisconsin, this book is a treasure trove of dairy farming collectibles. Filled with clear black and white photos of churns, creamery items, scales, milking stools, household items and more, this small book provides a fond look back to those whose families have a farming background. An interesting read for anyone interested in the "Good Old Days".* **$8.50 (BK 439)**

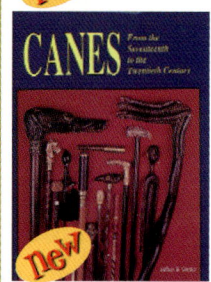

Canes From The Seventeenth to the Twentieth, by Effery B. Snyder. 288 Pages. 9.5" x 12.25". *Canes is a magnificent tour of canes and staffs from the late seventeenth through the twentieth century in both folk art and formal forms. Nine hundred eye-catching photos provide a sweeping survey of the varying cane forms available to collectors today from around the globe. Discussion travels far afield, leaping across time from 300,000 years ago to the 1930s, discovering relics from the carriage of George Washington and investigating the connection between agriculture, organized warfare and weapon canes.* **$69.95 (BK 375)**

Stick Making A Complete Course, by Andrew and Clive George Jones. 152 Pages. 8 1/4" x 11". *This complete introduction to the art and craft of stickmaking shows how to make a wide range of traditional walking stick, market sticks and crooks. The twenty-two sticks presented in this book reflect a diversity that includes knob handles, round handles, nose-in and nose-out handles, Cardigan sticks, and carved sticks. From sourcing and seasoning wood, and shaping, carving and shanking handles, to coloring and finishing methods, all aspects are covered to provide a thorough course in stickmaking.* **$17.95 (BK 309)**

Walkingsticks Book For Collectors, by Ulrich Klever. 244 Pages. 8.5" x 11". *The multitude of ideas that find expression in the shapes of canes is amazing. Canes were made of whalebone, glass, paper disks, or wood. Their handles were formed in silver, ivory, porcelain or horn and were carved into the shapes of skulls, hands, animal heads, or balls and could be opened to reveal compasses, watches, dice or cigarette lighters. The functions of the cane were endless. Filled with hundred of color photographs and pages of fascinating history, Walkingsticks is a book to be enjoyed by collectors and craftsmen alike.* **$29.95 (BK 402)**

Traditional Tools and Trades

Early Tools of New Jersey and the Men Who Made Them, by Alexander Farnham. 190 Pages. 8 1/2" x 11". Clothbound. Sometimes our focus as collectors seems unduly fixed on the prominent manufacturers who came to dominate the market and whose products are consequently very well known. Many beginning collectors, who naturally gravitate toward Stanley tools because of the large amount of information available, are unaware of the rich history of manufacturing before the scale of production that national distribution made possible had the effect of bringing a sterile homogeneity to those hand tools still being produced. In his masterful historical account of the many specialized toolmakers of Nineteenth Century New Jersey, Alexander Farnham has provided the means for collectors to focus on the distinctive and varied products of literally hundreds of manufacturers. Illustrated with photographs and early advertising and thoroughly indexed, this book carefully examines the many makers of tools of every sort. A superb reference.
$22.50 (BK 027)

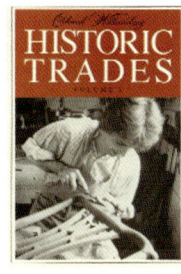

The Search For New Jersey Toolmakers, by Alexander Farnham. 148 Pages. 8 1/2" x 11". Following up on new information unearthed as a result of the publication of the first volume on Garden State Toolmakers, this book includes all new information and illustrations, including many original early advertisements. An excellent resource for the collector.
$25.00 (BK 028)

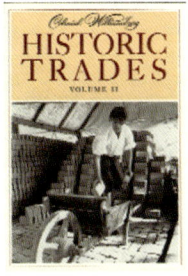

Historic Trades Annual Volume I, by The Colonial Williamsburg Foundation. 77 Pages. 7" x 10". This, the first volume of what promises to be an important series of publications from the Colonial Williamsburg Foundation, set out to document "...the people and the processes of historical trades and technology." It succeeds mightily. Included in this volume are articles on chair-building, the Bloomery Process of smelting iron, the art of gilding, taps and dies and much more. If you are interested in traditional methods, American history or both, this book makes a great addition to a library.
$9.50 (BK 101)

Historic Trades Annual Volume II, by The Colonial Williamsburg Foundation. 91 Pages. 7" x 10". The second volume of the Colonial Williamsburg Foundations "Historic Trades" series, this work continues in the tradition of the first volume with an eclectic collection of articles. Included are sections on the contributions of black craftsmen to the American Revolution, a detailed article on traditional brickmaking, a chapter on making knotted rugs and the inventory of an early builder. Nicely illustrated with black & white photographs and early engravings.
$7.95 (BK 102)

Eighteenth-Century Woodworking Tools, Volume III, by The Colonial Williamsburg Foundation. 248 Pages. 6" x 9 1/2". Unlike the first two volumes of the "Historic Trades" series, this third volume is devoted to the publication of a number of important and thoroughly readable papers presented at the symposium on Eighteenth Century Tools held at Colonial Williamsburg in the Spring of 1994. Included are articles on the processes of woodworking and chair-making shops; planemaking in 18th Century America; the marketing and distribution of English tools in America; an article on Eighteenth Century toolmaking by Paul Kebabian and a range of other articles, for a total of fifteen in all. Highly recommended. **$19.95 (BK 103)**

Instruments of Change: New Hampshire Hand Tools and Their Makers 1800-1900, by James L. Garvin. 113 Pages. 9" x 12". Originally put together for a 1984 exhibition of New Hampshire hand tools held at the New Hampshire Historical Society, to this day it remains virtually without peer as a history of regional toolmaking (with the notable exception of Alexander Farnham's fine works on New Jersey toolmakers). The author's love of tools, history and art is apparent in the photographs and layout of this beautiful book. Each page contains several photographs of historically significant tools together with detailed commentary on their manufacturers. Includes a 25 page descriptive index of all known New Hampshire toolmakers. A thoroughly enjoyable reference and read.
$22.50 (BK 097)

Christopher Gabriel and the London Tool Trade, by Mark & Jane Rees. 92 Pages. 8 1/4" x 10 1/2". Christopher Gabriel a prominent London planemaker of the late Eighteenth and early Nineteenth Century kept a "book" of his transactions throughout his working career. Fortunately for students of the history of tools and toolmaking, this book has survived. Using the Gabriel journals as a principal reference and knitting them together with other documented information about Gabriel and his times, English tool historians Jane and Mark Rees have brought the life and times of Cristopher Gabriel to life for contemporary readers. Beautifully illustrated with photographs and period illustrations.
$22.50 (BK 105)

Tools: Working Wood in Eighteenth Century America, by James Gaynor & Nancy Hagedorn. 126 Pages. 8 1/2" x 11". Produced in conjunction with the Colonial Williamsburg exhibition "Tools: Working Wood in Eighteenth Century America" by the Wallace Gallery of Decorative Arts, this beautiful book is filled with superb color photographs of important tools and period oil paintings. Accompanied by a text written for the dual purpose of documenting the history of early tools and serving as an introduction to the world of early tools for visitors to the Exhibition, this work succeeds mightily at its task. For those who wish to understand early history of woodworking in this Nation, we heartily recommend this book.
$22.95 (BK 075)

Patent Sourcebook for Bitstock Tools, by Dr. James E. Price. 175 Pages. 8 1/2" x 11". In a work that required five years of research, Jim Price, whose professional training as an anthropologist is apparent in the quality of this work, has assembled a collector's guide to nearly every type of tool that could be used in a brace and bit. In so doing he has revealed a fascinating world of invention set against the backdrop of the industrial dynamism of the last century. Illustrated with period engravings and patent drawings, and including tables grouped by date, patentee and type of tool, this book is the key to understanding the fascinating world of bitstock tools. **$25.00 (BK 025)**

The Ultimate Brace: A Unique Product of Victorian Sheffield, by Reg Eaton. 180 Pages. 8 1/2" x 10 1/2". Those who know Reg Eaton and his passion for braces, particularly the Ultimatum Brace, know very well that this book was a labor of love; those who do not need only to examine the contents of this thoroughly researched and lavishly illustrated volume. Included are histories of all the major manufacturers, including Marples, Pilkington, Marsden and scores of others; color and black and white photographs of important examples; engravings from period catalogs and patent drawings; and a text which essentially "gives away the secrets" of those who have studied and collected these fascinating and beautiful tools. For those who wish to see beyond the spectacular outward beauty of these tools, we heartily recommend this fascinating book. **$37.50 (BK 031)**

The American Patented Brace, by Dr. Ronald Pearson. 185 Pages. 8 1/2" x 11". Finally, a way to make sense of the complex subject of patented braces. Using actual patent drawings and indexes grouped by date, maker and patentee, this new book will be a tremendous asset for the collector or dealer. Includes a detailed introduction, and a rating system to serve as a valuation guide. **$22.95 (BK 016)**

Manufactured and Patented Spokeshaves, by Thomas C. Lamond. 442 Pages. 9" x 11". In publishing this long awaited work, the result of more than 20 years of research and collecting, author Tom Lamond has expanded the horizons of tool collectors in a way that has as its only comparison the publication of Roger Smith's Patented Metallic and Transitional Planes in America. Beginning with an introduction to the early history of spokeshaves and the evolution of the technology of those tools and proceeding through a topical analysis, chapter by chapter, of the various types of shaves and their use in specialized crafts, this book is certainly the defininitive work on these tools. It is, however, much more than just a history of spokeshaves. In identifying hundreds of obscure manufacturers in every corner of this country, and carefully researching their working dates, the author has assembled a portrait of the development of American enterprise from the focal point of these fascinating tools. Thoroughly indexed, copiously illustrated in color and black and white and filled with all manner of useful and entertaining information, this work deserves a place on the bookshelf of every serious collector. **$90.00 (BK 109)**

Axes, Timber and Logging

Building The Timber Frame House: The Revival of a Forgotten Craft, by Tedd Benson with James Gruger. 211 Pages. 8 1/4" x 10 3/4". Authors Tedd Benson and James Gruger make no effort to conceal their enthusiasm for the timber framed structure in this excellent celebration of the craft. Beginning with an historical overview of timber frame construction and proceeding to an analysis of the modern application of the style, the authors cover every conceivable aspect for the would-be practitioner. Every possible joint is defined and examined in detail, with an emphasis on the process for actually doing the work. Black and white photographs of recent and historical drawings complement the excellent illustrations by Jamie Page. The book culminates in a thorough explication of the process of "raising" a frame by hand. **$21.95 (BK 288)**

The Handsaw Catalog Collection, by Assorted Handsaw Makers. 136 Pages. 7" x 10". Excerpts from the catalogs of America's three premier sawmakers, E.C. Atkins, Henry Disston & Sons and Simonds Mfg. Co. are included as well as the principal English maker, Spear & Jackson of Sheffield. A handy reference to a hot collectible. **$18.50 (BK 036)**

Grimshaw On Saws, by Robert Grimshaw. 172 Pages. 7" x 10". A reprint of the 1880 Edition of this classic work, this book was an attempt to incorporate, in one volume, all that was then known about saws and their use. Profusely illustrated with period line drawings of saws, saw tools, machinery and the techniques discussed in the text, Grimshaw's book captures the science of sawcraft at the height of America's Wooden Age. The text addresses the history of saws, the innumerable types of saws then available, the setting and filing of saws, the arcane science of straightening saws and includes elaborate engravings of the then state of the art sawmill machinery. If you are interested in saws, early technology or American history, we strongly recommend this interesting and enlightening book. **$22.50 (BK 113)**

The Axe And Man: The History of Man's Early Technology, by Charles A. Heavrin. 174 Pages. 8 1/2" x 11 1/4". Heavrin traces the history of the ax from its early ancient beginnings 2.5 million years ago to the present. This fascinating book takes the reader through the evolution of this ancient tool-from the pebble tool of early man, the Paleolithic flint hand-axe, the Neolithic ground axe, early copper, bronze and iron axes of the Greek and Romans, and the various trade axes of the 16th to 19th centuries. Filled with over 100 illustrations, this book is a most for axe-lovers everywhere! **$27.00 (BK 294)**

Axe Makers of North America, by Allan Klenman. 112 Pages. 8 1/2" x 11". Finally, there is a reference available for tool collectors on the topic of axes. Canadian axe collector and researcher Allan Klenman has shared the many discoveries of his years of dedicated scholarship in this well writted and well illustrated book. Worth its purchase price just for the index of American and Canadian axe makers contained in the appendices, Axe Makers of North America also inlcudes histories of the major, and some minor, axe makers, information on axe manufacture and a chart of various axe head patterns. Whether you are an antique dealer, a tool collector or interested in the history of tools and technology, this new book is certain to be consulted often. **$18.95 (BK 170)**

This Was Logging: Drama In The Northwest Timber Country, by Ralph W. Andrews. 157 Pages. 8 1/2" x 11". With 200 superb photographs by Darius Kinsey, Andrews recalls lumbering's great days in the Pacific Northwest's "Big Woods," a place now remembered as a fog-blurred memory. Shown in detail are the first axes, 12-foot crosscut saws, the first oxen and horses, the first donkey engines and "lokeys." The story continues on into the "highball" days of high production with steel tower skidders and miles of steel rigging. Ralph Andrews research, together with Kinsey's photographs, makes a book of fascinating true stories of America's exciting logging industry. **$14.95 (BK 236)**

Timber: Loggers Challenge The Great Northwestern Forests, by Ralph W. Andrew. 182 Pages. 8 1/2" x 11". The photographs in this book will instantly transport the reader into the early world of logging. Here was the greatest stand of Douglas fir timber in existence and here was labor for the Poles, Finns, Swedes, and Norskies lured out of the Midwest to make lumber that helped build the West Coast cities. Ralph Andrews, the timber historian of the West, brings you some nostalgic scenes bringing you the high climbers, fallers balanced on high spring boards, rivers and salt water, early donkey engines, railroads on steep grades, logging camps as well as devastating fires. For a look at the lost world of America as it was, we invite you to peruse this fascinating book. **$12.95 (BK 235)**

Glory Days of Logging, by Ralph W. Andrews. 176 Pages. 8 1/2" x 11". In this chronicle of logging in Northwestern U.S. and Canada, bunk house ballads, humorous sketches and eyewitness accounts of work and life help recreate the logging atmosphere with the best photos drawn from a dozen famous collections: David and Benson rafts, river drives, hand logging spar topping big wheels in the pine, saw mills of 1890 to 1915, historical ox teams, tractors, blumes. This chronicle of the Big Woods will transport the readers back to witness for themselves a fascinating piece of pioneer history. **$15.95 (BK 237)**

Simonds Saw Mfr. Co. General Line Catalog, by Simonds Saw Mfr. Co., Fitchburg, Massachusetts. 195 Pages. 6 1/4" x 9 1/4". Their relatively early demise has left many collectors unaware that the Simonds Company was one of the largest and best makers of all manner of saws up until the time of the Roosevelt Depression. Illustrated here are all sorts of hand saws, from the standard types to specialty sorts now seldom seen. Also included are sharpening tools, saw makers' tools and much more. A superb catalog. **$14.50 (BK 074)**

This Was Sawmilling, by Ralph W. Andrews. 176 Pages. 8 1/2" x 11". The first whistle wailed at 5:20 AM, second at 5:40. Boiled beans, ham, hot cakes, and 12 hours later $1.50. The circle saw was its symbol. Boards and ship planking were its bid to immortality. This was sawmilling. The vital, true story of the triumphant growth and promise of the sawmill industry is shown with superb photography and told with exciting text. Anecdotes of the men who transformed logs into the building materials of a nation is augmented with thorough research, bringing to life the industry which has persevered since 1825. **$15.95 (BK 238)**

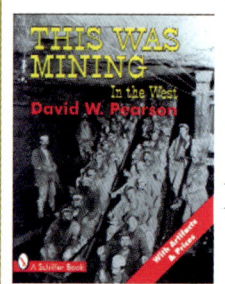

This Was Mining In The West, by David W. Pearson. 166 Pages. 8 1/2" x 11". Within this book the real lives of the brave '49ers of the California Gold Rush are exposed and followed throughout the expansion of mining to other states and to silver, and copper. Significant mines in California, Nevada, Utah, Oregon, Washington, Montana, Wyoming, South Dakota, Idaho, Colorado, and Arizona are discussed, including their dates of operation and production records. Mining stock certificates, currency, and newspapers from the day are also shown, along with antique mining tools. With over 225 period photographs revealing the difficulties and peticularities faced by miners, this book is a must for anyone interested in the realities of Gold Rush life. **$24.95 (BK 234)**

Redwood Classics Stories And, by Ralph W. Andrews. 174 Pages. 8.25" x 10.5". This book is one man's memorial to the magnificent natural redwood Sequoia trees in California which today number only a fraction of the groves of 125 years ago. These trees, once used to build lumbering empires, kept thousands employed in their destruction. Many of the lumbermen themselves are quoted in memories of their work on old trees-hardships, inventions, earthquakes, fires, sawmills, logging camps and shipping are remembered. With over 239 haunting photographs, this book is a testament to the hard work that men and women required, logging these natural giants. **$12.95 (BK 399)**

Technical Topics, Tools and Trades

A History of the Logarithmic Slide Rule and Allied Instruments, by Florian Cajori. 178 Pages. 6 1/4" x 9 1/2". *Slide rules and calculators have become one of the fastest growing areas of collecting. This work, originally published in 1920, provides insight into the development of these tools.* **$24.95 (BK 037)**

Tools & Trades of America's Past: The Mercer Museum Collection, by Marilyn Arbor. 124 Pages. 8 1/2" x 11". *Finally back in print, this excellent and affordable publication from the Mercer Museum of Doylestown, Pennsylvania documents the Henry Chapman Mercer collection of artifacts relating to American material culture. Organized in much the same way that the museum is arranged, the book documents the trades, professions, and accoutrements of everyday life. Each trade or topic features a series of line drawings of artifacts and then the function of each is explained in detail. This volume chronicles much nearly forgotten information about our "primitive" heritage and a thorough index makes it very accessible. This book will add much to the library of any tool enthusiast.* **$14.95 (BK 280)**

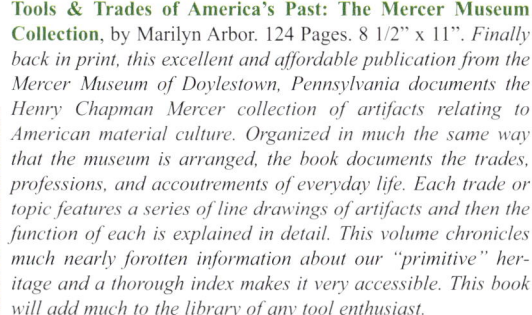

Collecting Figural Tape Measures, by E. & D. Arbittier; J. & J. Morphy. 128 Pages. 6" x 9". *This book contains over 700 sewing tape measures in brass, wood, celluloid and porcelain figural shapes, dating from the 1820s to the present. Photos show hundred of variations from animals and birds to people and houses. Each caption describes the items particular winding mechanism and value. This work offers an interesting perspective on antique tool collecting and is a must for any sewing enthusiast, collector of the whimsical or anyone interested in expanding his or her knowledge of these endlessly variable tools.* **$19.95 (BK 227)**

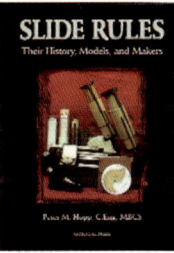

Slide Rules: Their History, Models, and Makers, by Peter M. Hopp. 316 Pages. 8 1/2" x 11". *The rise of collectibility of slide rules has been a phenomenon that has confounded even the most knowledgeable antique tool collectors. Now, in this important new book, author Peter Hopp unlocks the mysteries of slide rules and lays out the fascinating history of calculation in a way that expands the knowledge of the advanced collector and also brings the novice up to speed. Included is a thorough history of slide rules, biographies of important figures, patent information, important innovations and much, much more. An important new reference.* **$35.00 (BK 181)**

Scientific Instruments 1500-1900: An Introduction, by Gerard L'e Turner. 142 Pages. 7 1/4" x 9 3/4". *This extraordinary new book fills a long time void in the literature of tools and technology. In this one volume, author Gerard L'e Turner covers the basics and much more about the precision instruments of every principal profession. Arranged topically by the trade or profession in which the instruments were used, the author describes the need for the specific instruments, their historical development and variations, and includes spectacular photographs of instruments from the great museums and collections from Britain, Europe and the United States. Covered are astronomy, surveying, optical, medical navigational and philosophical instruments. A chapter on calculators and measuring instruments is particularly well done. The instruments featured, particularly those in the color plates are alone worth the price of this great new book. Highly recommended.* **$45.00 (BK 289)**

The Construction and Principal Uses of Mathematical Instruments, by N. Bion. 400 Pages. 9" x 12". *First published in 1758, this book reviews every measuring tool and gauging instrument then in use. This book is not for the casual reader, but if you are interested in understanding the science of measurement, this is an essential source.* **$59.50 (BK 038)**

1874 Gurley Catalog, by W. & L.E. Gurley, Troy, New York. 256 Pages. 5 1/2" x 8 1/2". *W. & L.E. Gurley, the manufacturers of surveying instruments employed a highly successful marketing ploy which led them to their unquestioned status as America's premier manufacturer of such instruments. Beginning in the 1860's they produced, annually, a "Manual" which included descriptions of the function and operation of all manner of surveying and mapping instruments. Conveniently located in the back of these "Manuals" was a catalog of Gurley instruments offered for sale. This edition of the Manual is thoroughly documented with period engravings, including an exceptional illustration of a miners plummet in use. For a look at the state of the surveyor's art in the third quarter of the last century, we recommend the Gurley Manual.* **$22.95 (BK 076)**

The Berger Handbook, by C.L. Berger & Sons, Boston, Mass.. 224 Pages. 7" x 10". *This 1900 catalog was the first ever published by this important Boston-based maker of surveying instruments and other precision tools. If you wish to be able to tell a solar compass from a theodolite and a wye level from a transit, the detailed descriptions are extremely helpful. And if you've ever yearned to be able to match the instrument oriented folks technical term for technical term, a study of the drawings will get you on the right path. Includes an introduction and historical commentary by David Garcelon.* **$22.95 (BK 093)**

Make A Chair From A Tree Video, by John D. Alexander Jr. Pages. 4" x 7". *Don't look for any hidden meaning in the title of this new video from Baltimore based woodworker and wooworking instructor John Alexander. It's about what it says it's about--making a chair from a tree. Sharing nearly 50 years of experience, Alexander takes the viewer through all of the steps necessary to make a chair, from the felling of the tree to cutting, riving, shaping and shaving the components to their final form. As the project proceeds, Alexander shares insight into the properties of green wood and advises the viewer on how to take advantage of the shrinking and swelling properties of wood to produce a long lasting piece of furniture.* **24.95 (BK 455)**

Stanley Planes By The Numbers, by Patrick Leach. Pages. 4" x7". *More and more woodworkers are becoming aware of the great hand tools produced by Stanley Tools of New Britain, Connecticut over the past 150 years. Now, thanks to this new video featuring woodworker and antique tool collector Patrick Leach, even those who have never before seen a Stanley plane can get the inside story on how the planes were meant to be used and what to look for when evaluating a Stanley plane for purchase. Virtually the entire range of Stanley planes are covered in this exciting new production, including many worth thousands of dollars in the collector market. Being aware of what is rare and what is not in antique tools can make the Sunday morning trip to the local flea market to look for tools much more interesting.* **$24.95 (BK 456)**

Hand Saw Sharpening Video, by Tom Law. Pages. 4" x 7". *If you have ever been frustrated by the difficulty of finding a competent professional to sharpen your hand saw, or if you're a woodworker or tool user who would like to learn to do things "the old way", this new video featuring Tom Law is just what you need. Clad in denim overalls and possessed with an easy and folksy manner, Law guides the viewer through the finer points of saw sharpening, including jointing, shaping, setting and filing. Law explains what tools are needed and how to use them. Just be careful not to start watching this one too late at night. We guarantee you'll be out in the shop with a saw shortly after you finish viewing this video.* **$24.95 (BK 458)**

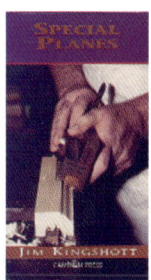

Special Planes Video Tape, by Jim Kingshott. N.A. Pages. 4" x 7 1/2". *Woodworkers with hundreds of tools, the use of some of which they may have no conception, and woodworkers who might be unaware of these traditional tools that will add style and interest to their work will all delight in this great new video from English master craftsman Jim Kingshott. Kingshott, whose style has earned him an enthusiastic following among hand tool and woodworking enthusiasts, shares the secrets learned in 50 years of woodworking in this superb new video. Everything from buying, tuning and sharpening is covered for a full range of planes, including rebates, molding planes, hollows & rounds, filletster planes, spokeshaves, shoulder planes and many more. Whatever your perespective, we recommend "Special Planes" for as in interesting, entertaining and educational investment.* **$24.95 (BK 271)**

Bench Planes Video Tape, by Jim Kingshott. N.A. Pages. 4" x 7 1/2". *For the antique tool collector whose interest in the functionality of tools is of secondary consideration, or for the woodworker, whose grasp of the traditions and history of classic tools may be of secondary interest to their utility, Jim Kingshott's great new video on bench planes is a great meeting place. A traditional woodworker of British heritage who has made furniture for British royalty, Kingshott has an on-camera style that is certain to please. In this offering, he covers every aspect of bench planes, including tuning, sharpening, selection and use. Covering the full range of tools from Stanley-Bailey type planes to the legendary Norris planes of England, Kingshott will make a traditional woodworker out of Norm Abrams and make the current enthusiast even more enthusiastic.* **$24.95 (BK 272)**

The Material Culture of Country Living

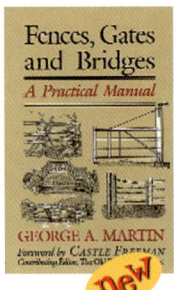

Fences, Gates And Bridges, by George A. Martin. 191 Pages. 5 1/2" x 8 1/2". *This practical manual of fencing for every home and farm purpose makes putting up fences less difficult. As useful today as in 1887, when it was first published, this book explains the principles and procedures necessary in building fences. Three hundred illustrations aid in comprehension and demonstrate how to build primitive fences, stone and sod fences, board fences, picket fences, barbed wire fence and many other fence types and appurtenances.*
$12.50 (BK 319)

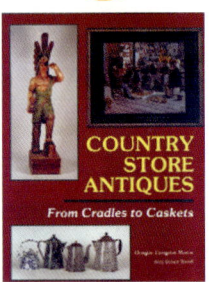

Country Store Antiques: From Cradles to Caskets, by Douglas Condon-Martin with Bob Biondi. 160 Pages. 8 1/2" x 11". *From birth to death, country stores provided every human need. On the shelves were food, tobacco, clothing, whiskey, hardware, farm and home goods, and patent medicines. Advertising signs and posters promised the wonderful and impossible. Hundreds of ordinary household items originally found for sale at the old country store are found here, from kitchen, bath, and table wares, advertising, candy containers, tobacco products, and much more. This book not only contains the history of such items, but the history of the country and general stores themselves. A must for any antique enthusiast or historian of bygone days.* **$29.95 (BK 228)**

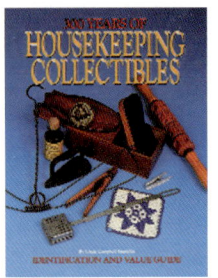

300 Years of Housekeeping Collectibles, by Linda Campbell Franklin. 645 Pages. 8 1/2" x 11". *This book sweeps through 3 centuries of domestic innovation. With sections on laundering, house cleaning, closeting, bathrooms, and more, you'll quickly discover what those "whatzit" gadgets were used for and what they are worth to the avid collector today.* **$22.95 (BK 241)**

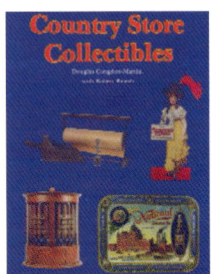

Country Store Collectibles, by Douglas Congdon-Martin with Bob Biondi. 160 Pages. 8 1/2" x 11". *The "General Store" or "Mom and Pop" played an important role in small towns, prairies, and frontiers of America providing items the people could not produce themselves: tools, gadgets, clothing, shoes, food, medicine. This book contains nearly 600 fixtures from American country stores of the 19th and early 20th century. Fully illustrated, it contains not only valuable information on each item sold therein, but a great deal of history on the stores themselves and the people who worked in them as well. Dating from the turn of the 20th century, many of the illustrations provide historical references to actual everyday life. A must for the library of any antique lover, collector or student of history.* **$24.95 (BK 229)**

Apple Parers, by Don Thornton. 239 Pages. 8 1/2" x 11". *Those who have spent any time in the serious pursuit of antiques have likely encountered mechanical apple parers in their travels. Almost without exception, those parers would have been of the more popular and commonly encountered types. In producing this superb book, author Don Thornton has opened the door of discovery to a world that was previously known only to the most advanced collectors of these uniquely American mechanical devices. In a work that covers the full range of these tools from early wooden handmade devices to the most complex Victorian gadgetry, Thornton not only documents what is known of each parer, but includes a series of extraordinarily well done black and white photographs that reveal the details of each device. Whether you are already an advanced collector of these tools or a student for the sake of study, or anywhere in-between, Don Thornton's "Apple Parers" is guaranteed to provide hours of enjoyment and be consulted often.* **$55.00 (BK 169)**

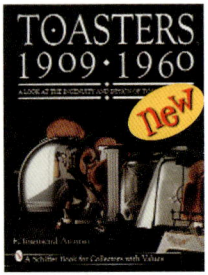

Toasters 1909-1960 Ingenuity & Design, by E. Townsend Atrman. 176 Pages. 8.5" x 11". *For anyone who enjoys finely toasted bread, this is definitely the book for you! Within one will find over a hundred fine examples of kitchen ingenuity. From the history and evolution of the toaster to recognizing toaster patterns on bread, Toasters is the definitive reference for information on this underrated appliance. Mr. Artman inspires a new appreciation for the toaster, whether it is a percher or a pop-up.*
$29.95 (BK 390)

American Country Store, by Don & Carol Raycraft. 160 Pages. 6" x 9". *This perfect price guide and reference for anything and everything you can find in a country store. Hundreds of detailed photographs help identify and price tins, glass, advertising, textiles, tools, and more.*
$14.95 (BK 239)

American Family Farm Antiques, by Terri Clemens. 208 Pages. 6" x 9". *Clemens digs through 100 years of farm life, farm tools, and other items granting us a peek as life on the family farm. See how thousands of items were used, how they changed over time, and what they are worth to the avid collector today.* **$17.95 (BK 243)**

Groovy Kitchen Designs For Collectors, by Michael J. Goldburg. Pages. 8.5" x 11". *For anyone who grew up with chrome and Bakelite in the kitchen, this book is your ticket to nostalgia. With over 300 illustrations of appliances and kitchenware plus lots of wonderful advertising, Groovy Kitchen Designs researches different types of metal and their applications as well as historical background on the companies behind the products. This introduction into the world of vintage electric and metal kitchen collectibles, with special emphasis on current values, will be treasured by collectors and flea market frequenters alike.* **$29.95 (BK 388)**

Collecting Household Linens, by Frances Johnson. 160 Pages. 8.5" x 11". *Whether you are an experienced collector or a novice in collecting linens, this book by Frances Johnson will prove to be an invaluable resource. Afghans, alter clothes, bedspreads, centerpieces, curtains, doilies, decorative pillows, and napkins are described in full detail. Johnson shows how to distinguish between old loom and factory fabrics as well as provides tips for caring for your linen and salvaging damaged linen. Complete with values and over 100 pictures, this book will be enjoyed by all lovers of needlework.* **$29.95 (BK 397)**

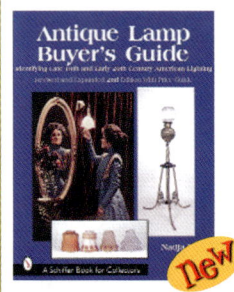

Antique Lamp Buyers Guide, by Nadja Maril. 144 Pages. 8 1/2" x 11". *Do you own an old lamp? Do you want to know who made it, how it was originally used, and how to restore it? Then this is the guide for you. The Lamp Buyer's Guide covers examples of American lighting made between the mid-1850s and the 1950s, a time period when lighting technology changed from oil to kerosene, gas, and finally electricity. Designed for both the beginner and the advanced collector, this fully illustrated guide will provide a wealth of information for anyone interested in buying or selling old lighting.*
$29.95 (BK 418)

Garden Tools, by Pellerin, Cliff, Rozenszt Slesin. 160 Pages. hardbound. 8 3/4" x 9 3/4". *Filled with beautiful color photographs and illustrations, Garden Tools tells the fascinating story of the basic implements used by the human race to cultivate nature. The book follows the gardening cycle from "Preparing the Earth" to "Harvesting," and each chapter features the traditional tools in that phase of gardening—from dibbers to trowels, and seeders to pruners. This book places the tools the gardener may have taken for granted in a whole new light. For those who love to till the soil, this book will be hard to put down.* **$35.00 (BK 353)**

Firearms and Hunting

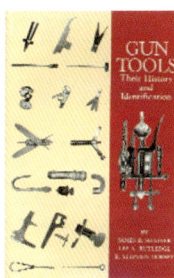

Gun Tools: Their History And Identification, Volume I, by James Shaffer, Lee Rutledge, and S. Dorsey. 377 Pages. 5 1/2" x 8 1/2". *Anyone who has ever attended a "whatsit session" at a tool collectors meeting, where attempts are made to collectively identify tools of indeterminate function, will find this recently published volume especially helpful. Chock full of photographs and documentation on every conceivable tool ever provided with, or used primarily for, the maintenance of firearms this book will stand as the definitive work on this subject. Beginning with a survey of the various types of gun tools, the book then proceeds to review, in great detail, many examples of each of those types. Excellent black and white photographs, line drawings and early photographs illustrate this comprehensive book. Of special interest to the tool collector with an interest in firearms, but also to the general collector, particularly the section on combination tools for guns, this book will fill a void in any collectors library.* **$30.00 (BK 167)**

Gun Tools : Their History And Identification, Volume II, by James Shaffer, Lee Rutledge, and S. Dorsey. 396 Pages. 5 1/2" x 8 1/2". *Published in response to a wealth of new information that came to light following the publication of Volume I of this series, this book greatly expands the range of tools contained in the first book and showcases some spectacular military tools not previously known to exist. Organized into sections based on the different types of gun tools, each section is chock full of excellent photographs and detailed commentary. As was the case with the first volume, the wide range of combination tools for use in firearms maintenance are a delight to the tool collector. For a look at a world of tools beyond the commonplace, Gun Tools offers an expansive view.* **$30.00 (BK 168)**

Illustrated Catalog of Civil War Military Goods, by Schuyler, Harley, & Graham. 146 Pages. 8 1/2" x 11". *Schuyler, Hartley, & Graham, military suppliers during the Civil War, were a major source of material for the Union Army, Navy, Marines and Revenue Corps. This unabridged edition of their catalog is brimming with uniform and dress regulations, arms and ammunition, horse "furniture," tables of military pay, an organizational chart of the Navy Dept. and much, much more. Here one can find military sundries of every kind. You'll find detailed descriptions of coats, "trowsers," hats, boots, spurs, sashes, foils and fencing masks, saddles, bits, bridles, field glasses, gauntlets, epaulette ornaments, coat sleeve trimmings, medal, buttons, knives, canteens, candlesticks, musical instruments, and much more. A vital source of authentic information and illustrations and a must for Civil War buffs, military historians, and collectors.* **$14.95 (BK 195)**

The Archaeology of Weapons, by R. Ewart Oakeshott. 384 Pages. 5 3/8" x 8 1/2". *Covering a period of 30 centuries, this book gives a very detailed and thorough account of the development of arms and armor beginning with the weapons of the Bronze and Iron Ages, through the breakup of the Roman Empire and the ethnic migrations of the period; the age of the Vikings; and finally, the Age of Chivalry. Oakeshott, a noted authority on medieval arms in Europe, describes in detail the awesome array of weapons and accoutrements of war: swords, spears, shield, helmets, daggers, longbows, crossbows, axes, chain mail, plate armor, gauntlets, etc. This illustrated and meticulously researched volume is indispensible resource for military historians, archeologists, and anyone interest in weaponry of old.* **$14.95 (BK 207)**

The Book of the Sword, by Richard F. Burton. 336 Pages. 6 1/8" x 9 1/4". *"The history of the sword is the history of humanity." With these words, British author, Victorian scholar and world traveler, Sir Richard Burton begins his eloquent and exceptionally erudite history of the "Queen of Weapons." Spanning centuries, and a wide range of cultures, Burton illuminates the sword as both ornamental and potent symbol. Drawing from a wealth of literary, archaeological, anthropological, and other sources, the author traces the sword's origins, from its birth as a charred and sharpened stick, through its diverse stages of development, to its full growth in the early Roman Empire. This text provides an incredible wealth of detailed data about the sword and its variations: sabres, broadsword, cutlass, scimitar, rapier, foil as well as dirks, dagger, knives, flails. Any military and social historian, scholar, or armchair adventurer will find this volume a fascinating account of this symbol of power.* **$13.95 (BK 218)**

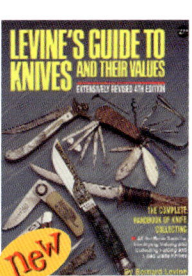

Levine's Guide To Knives & Their Value, by Bernard Levine. 512 Pages. 9 1/4" x 10 3/4". *For those who collect knives or are thinking about collecting knives, Levine offers the reader much more than a simple value guide. Within these pages the reader will find tips on collecting knife lore, proper knife show etiquette, and recognizing fakes. This handy and fully illustrated reference contains hundreds of examples of both folding and fixed blade knives including the histories of various types of knives and their makers.* **$27.95 (BK 300)**

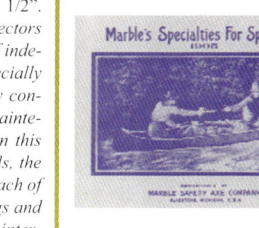

Marble's Specialities For Sportsman, by Marbles Arms & Mfg. Co., Gladstone, Mich.. 56 Pages. 7" x 5". *Not only does this catalog reprint by the Marble Safety Axe Company serve as a guide to the highly collectible tools produced by this company, but it is the perfect reference for anyone interested in tools used by outdoorsman in the early part of this century. Included are an assortment of Marble's Safety Pocket Axes and Hunting Knives, fishing gaffs, pedometers, compasses, rifles, pistols, hunting jackets, and the original "Ever Ready" Light. An excellent guide to a hot collectible.* **$7.00 (BK 254)**

Marble's Outing Equiptment, by Marbles Arm & Mfg. Co, Gladstone, Mich.. 32 Pages. 4" x 7". *In September of 1898, Webster L. Marble finished his first Safety pocket axe. This reprint of Marples Arms & Manufacturing Co. 1933 catalog features an assortment of these fine Marble axes, folding claw axes, and folding pick axes, as well as the Marble line of high quality hunting, woodcraft, and fishing knives. In addition to the axes and knives, this volume is filled with illustrations of all manner of necessities for the outdoorsman, including compasses, waterproof matchboxes, rifle sights, cartridges and more.* **$7.00 (BK 255)**

Baskets And Basketmakers In Southern Appalachia, by John Rice Irwin. 192 Pages. 8 1/2" x 11". *American baskets made by people in Tennessee, Kentucky, North Carolina, and their surroundings are lovingly shared with readers by a man who knows and respects their heritage. Egg gathering baskets, feather baskets, chicken coop baskets, garden and clothing baskets are examined. Indian baskets, especially Cherokee, also are included. Related items are also described such as grass brooms, winnowing sieves, fish basket traps, bed mattresses and donkey muzzles. Numerous photos detail every step in the basket making process: from the time the tree is cut until the time the basket is completed. This book is a warm personal account of these mountain people and their love, care and dependence upon their baskets.* **$14.95 (BK 232)**

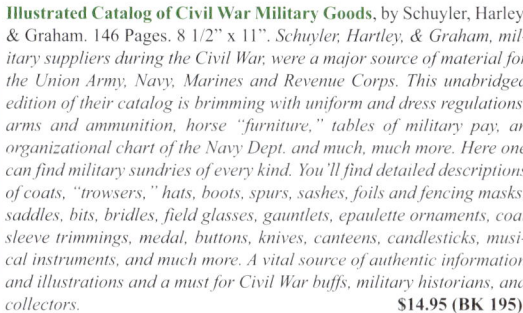

Guns And Gunmaking Tools of Southern Appalachia, by John Rice Irwin. 118 Pages. 11" x 8 1/2". *Gunmakers have a culture in their traditions, tools, and products which this book exposes in very human terms. Vivid photographs display the gun anvils, gunboring machines, rifling guides, bow drills, bullet molds, powder horns, chargers, flasks and other tools used by such famous makers as Hacker Martin and Will Howell. The story told in this fascinating book is one shared by the people of the isolated mountain valleys of Appalachia as each family tells the reader how they make and use the Kentucky and related firearms and the supplies that go with them, both in the past and today as tradition continues.* **$9.95 (BK 231)**

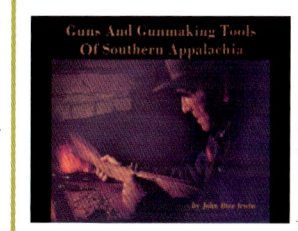

Flayderman's Guide Antique Amer Firearm, by Norm Flayderman. 654 Pages. 8 1/4" x 10 5/8". *Now in its 7th edition, Flayderman's Guide is the definitive text for any firearm collector. With over 1,700 illustration, it provides easy identification including values for over 4,000 antique American firearms. The histories of the makers as well as dates and locations of manufacture are discussed. Flayderman covers every aspect of collecting from value and condition to restoration and fakes. Present day collecting trends are reviewed as well. This book will be treasured by anyone interested in truly old guns.* **$32.95 (BK 302)**

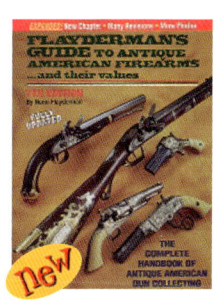

Cowboy Collectibles And Western, by Robert W.d. And Ed Vebell Ball. 160 Pages. 8 1/2" x 11". *The cowboy's adventures have been the conjured about countless tales about the West. In this wonderful price guide, Robert Ball and Edward Vebell focus on the reality of the cowboy's life. Here one will find artifacts essential to life on the range-rifles, pistols, saddles, clothing, boots, hats, and gun rigs. For the lover of the Old West and collector of artifacts, this is a wonderful book that will help the era come alive.* **$29.95 (BK 417)**

Traditional Trades and Crafts

Hand Bookbinding: A Manual of Instruction, by Aldren A. Watson. 160 Pages. 8.5" x 11". *Before the advent of mass-production, books were bound by hand to remarkably high standards of quality. People bought books not for just what they contained, but the craftsmanship of its binding. Unfortunately, machine-binding methods have made this craft practically a lost art. This guide offers an opportunity to save the secrets of bookbinding. Within its pages, the reader learns the traditional methods of bookbinding through detailed instruction and over 270 helpful illustrations. Eight binding projects are included: dust jacket; blank book; single signiture; folio; four signiture; manuscript binding; music binding; rebinding an old book and much more. This manual is a valuable reference for those involved in publishing and its allied trades, but will also be enjoyed by any lover of books.* **$12.95 (BK 193)**

Pictorial Encyclopedia of Trades and Industries, Volume II, by Denis Diderot. 535 Pages. 9" x 12". *This, the Second Volume of Denis Diderot's "Encyclopedie" is a continuation of the first volume. Included are collection of plates on trade and industry taken from the 'Encyclopedie.' Its chapters include plates of glass making; masonry and carpentry; textiles; paper and printing; leather; gold, silver, and jewelry; fashion; and other trades. The plates are so clear and detailed that an engineer could actually use them as working drawings—and many did. An excellent opportunity to add this essential reference to the library at an opportunity price.* **$31.95 (BK 187)**

Pictorial Encyclopedia of Trades and Industries Volume I, by Denis Diderot. 472 Pages. 9" x 12". *Denis Diderot's 'Encyclpedie' was the crowning venture of the 18th-century's Enlightenment. It included contributions from such intellectual greats as Rousseau, Montesquieu, and Voltaire. Its purpose was to publicize trade secrets in the hope it would lead to more rational industrial processes. This is volume I of a collection of plates on trade and industry taken from the 'Encyclopedie.' Its chapters include plates on agricultural and rural arts, the art of war, the iron foundry and forge, extractive industries, and metal working. Each plate is so clear and detailed that an engineer could construct any machine or plant and go into 18th-century production. This wonderfully inexpensive book is an invaluable and fascinating reference for any craftsman or student of Europe before the Industrial Revolution.* **$27.95 (BK 186)**

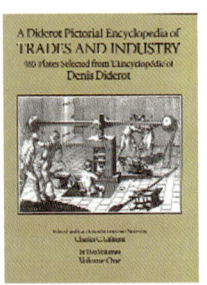

The Book of Trades, by Amman Jost & Hans Sachs. 176 Pages. 5 1/2" x 8 1/2". *Priest, Pilgrim, Prince, Physician, Astronomer, Lawyer, Typefounder, Bookbinder, Godsmith, Coin, Stamp, Peddler, Belt Maker, Butcher, Huntsman, Farmer, Tailor, Weaver, Shoemaker, Thimble Maker, Needlemaker, Gunsmith, Joiner, Wagonwright, Cooper, Tapestry Weaver, and 89 other tradesmen of Renaissance Europe are captured in Jost Amman and Hans Sach's Book of Trades. First published in 1568 in Frankfurt, Germany, this book features descriptions by Hans Sachs, the shoemaker poet, made famous today by Wagner's operatic masterpiece Meistersinger von Nurnberg. Jost Amman's woodcuts not only reveal in intricate detail the tools and machinery of the Renaissance tradesman, but the furniture, costume, and nuances of everday life. A classic that celebrates the work ethic as well as the talents of its practitioners and an absolute necessity for anyone interested in the crafts and trades of earlier times.* **$9.95 (BK 188)**

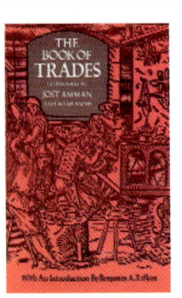

Build a Classic Timber-framed House, by Jack A. Sobon. 202 Pages. 8 1/2" x 11". *Following the traditional "hall-and-parlor" home design, architect and builder Jack Sobon reveals how to build an attractive timber-framed house able to meet the needs of any growing family. The basic house design taught in this book is easily adapted to meet different needs and Sobon's practical advice incorporates the latest knowledge on building a healthy house, integrating natural systems, and finding effective home heating solutions.* **$21.95 (BK 298)**

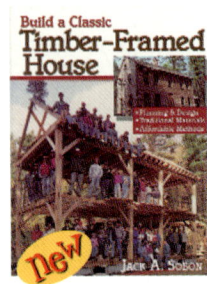

Secrets of Green Sand Casting, by International Correspondence School. 40 Pages. 5 1/2" x 8 1/2". *The first page of this reprinted textbook from 1906 explains that green sand casting is "...the making of castings in molds that are composed entirely of sand in a damp state." The rest of this volume goes on to explain the now nearly lost techniques brought that practice to a high art. Illustrated with superb engraved illustrations, "Secrets of Green Sand Casting" provides insight into a lost world of men, molds and metal. If you're interested in metallurgy or thinking about making some brass plumb bobs, this book will give you all the information you need.* **$9.95 (BK 148)**

The Colonial Printer, by Lawrence C. Wroth. 368 Pages. 5 3/8" x 8". *Lawrence Wroth, considered by many to be the leading authority on the subject, has written the definitive study of the American printer and his craft. The Colonial Printer explores every aspect of the printing trade from 1639, when the first press was established in the Colonies, until the end of the Colonial Period—approximately1800. All the tools, materials, and conditions of America's early printing trade are discussed, including presses, type, ink, paper, apprenticeship, bookbinding, working conditions, labor issues, and more. In the final chapter, Wroth describes both the content and the look of finished books, pamphlets, and papers of the times. Finely reproduced illustrations show presses and pressmen, typefaces and typefoundries, printed pages, and decorated bindings. This classic is an absolute necessity for any historian, bibliophile, typographic artist or printer, as well as any one with a general interest in books.* **$13.95 (BK 201)**

Papermaking, by Dard Hunter. 672 Pages. 5 1/2" x 8 1/2". *Practically every aspect of papermaking is covered in this book, from its invention in China to its introduction in Europe and in America—a chronology spanning 4500 years. Hunter examines the development of different materials and tools of papermaking: the different types of hand moulds, dipping or pouring liquid paper onto the mould; pressing, sizing, the paper. Hunter compares techniques both old and new, by hand or machine. Early and modern watermarking styles are also discussed. Bibliophiles, papermakers, artists, engravers, printers, bookbinders, and workers in watermarking will find this volume a useful addition to their library.* **$13.95 (BK 183)**

The Cooper and His Trade, by Kenneth Kilby. 192 Pages. 6" x 9". *Now back in print after many years, this classic book might well be subtitled "Everything You Might Possibly Want to Know About Coopering". Kilby's classic is a very well written book that is filled with excellent photographs of coopers at work, line drawings showing every imaginable tool of the cooper and historical prints of coopers from ancient times to the recent past. Its 192 pages are divided roughly in half between an exposition on the many aspects of the coopers' trade and a detailed history of coopering. We recommend this important book for the library of every antique tool collector and every student of technology. A classic.* **$21.95 (BK 179)**

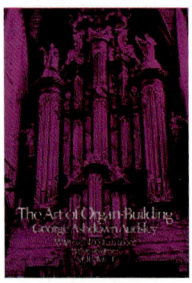

The Art of Organ-Building, by George Ashdown Audsley. 610 Pages. 6 1/2" x 9 1/4". *Over a half a century ago, this work stood as the standard treatise in the field of pipe organ construction. This is volume I of a two volume set, reproduced with care from the 1905 first edition. It opens with the history of the organ and treats various descriptive matters, such as external design and decoration of the organ, acoustical matters in regard to organ pipes, tonal structure and appointment, the compound stops of the organ, etc. Audsley gives an extensive description of all the organ's components, and set out the differences in structure among church, concert-room, and chamber instruments. This book contains a wealth of information that cannot be found at any other source; the illustrations alone have made it one of the most sought-after books in musical literature.* **$24.95 (BK 219)**

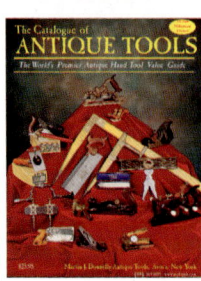

The Catalogue of Antique Tools, Millennium Edition, by Martin J. Donnelly. 320 Pages. 8 1/2" x 11". *Our biggest and best catalogue ever, the much anticipated Millennium bigger by 25% than the 1999 Edition. Included in the 320 page volume are 6,662 tools, each photographed in full color, carefully described and priced to sell. An expanded six-page index listing both manufacturers and types of tools makes the Catalogue of Antique Tools a long lasting reference for collectors, antique dealers and those with an interest in the history of technology. If you have not previously ordered the Catalogue, we encourage you to do so. We absolutely guarantee that you will be delighted.* **$25.95 (BK 364)**

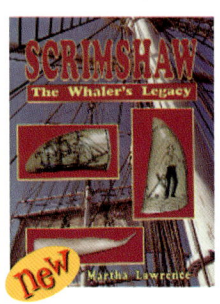

Scrimshaw The Whaler's Legacy, by Martha Lawrence. 227 Pages. 9" x 11.25". *Scrimshaw has always evoked the romance and mystique of the great age of sail. The combination of idle hours and the desire for artistic expression resulted in many wonderful pieces of scrimshaw by sailors. Martha Lawrence covers every facet of the art of scrimshaw, from it origins to the daily life of the scrimshander, to the materials, themes, and tools used in creating these objects. Complete with over 400 illustrations, collectors and those with an interest in the sea will find this book a joy to read.* **$69.95 (BK 380)**

Metalworking Tools and Mechanical Devices

American Machinists Tools: An Illustrated Directory of Patents, by Kenneth L. Cope. 424 Pages. 7" x 10". *Soft bound. Early and unusual machinists tools are one of the most popular areas of collecting in today's market. Chief among such tools sought out by serious collectors are those reflecting significant technological innovation and tools invented by the principal figures in the development of the industry. Using this guide only, collectors and dealers can identify a tool, its manufacturer and other important historical information. Includes three separate indexes and illustrations of every tool patented through 1904, and many thereafter. In combination with the other Cope Book, it leads to an understanding of early machinists tools.*
$35.00 (BK 003)

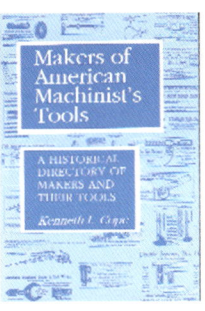

Makers of American Machinist's Tools, by Kenneth L. Cope. 320 Pages. 7" x 10". *Ken Cope's encyclopedic reference broadens the range of understanding of an area of antique tools in a way that has as its only parallel the publication of the First Edition of American Wooden Planes in 1983. By providing collectors with detailed information about the tool makers who produced precision tools for the metalworkers of the 19th Century, Cope has provided the impetus for thousands of collectors to preserve for posterity the history of technological innovation in this important area of economic development. A Must Have.*
$30.00 (BK 002)

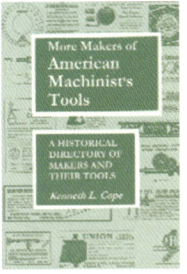

More Makers of American Machinists Tools, by Kenneth L. Cope. 185 Pages. 7" x 10". *The publication of Ken Cope's seminal work, "Makers of American Machinist Tools", produced a flood of new information about previously undocumented makers. This book documents more than a hundred new makers and expands information about the products of major manufactures. A series of indices includes supplemental patent information omitted from Cope's Patent Guide, new information on early makers Darling & Swartz, several previously unknown catalogs and much more. The newly-discovered tools include a wide variety of the increasingly collectible speed indicator gauges. An excellent new book from America's most prolific tool author.*
$22.50 (BK 098)

Power and Machinery Employed in Manufactures, by Paul N. Hasluck. 440 Pages. 9" x 11". *Compiled by the United States Government in conjunction with the 1880 census, this work was meant to document and to encourage the innovative use of machinery in every industry. Filled with engraved illustrations that provide detailed insight into the state of the art of manufacturing in nearly every industry, this massive work also contains detailed commentary on the processes employed. Produced at a time when there was justifiable faith in the potential of power and machines to elevate the standard of living of man, this celebratory work may be a bit of a revelation to those whose "education" in history has led them to view this vibrant industrial age as one inimical to the interests of the common man. A great book that captures the dynamic, industrial spirit of a nation on the rise.* **$49.95 (BK 163)**

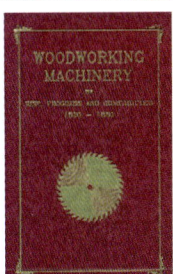

Woodworking Machinery, by M. Powis Bale, C.E.. 362 Pages. 5 1/2" x 8 1/2". *Originally published in 1880, this work was intended to be a primer on the former State of the Art in the application of power to the processing of timber. Every aspect of machine woodworking is covered, but the subtitle "with hints on the management of saw mills and the economical conversion of lumber" accurately prepares the reader for the focus of the work. Illustrated with superb period engravings that are complemented by a thoroughly readable, informative and interesting text, Woodworking Machinery offers the reader a glimpse of a nearly forgotten time when the Great American Forest drove nearly every aspect of manufacturing and commerce.*
$16.50 (BK 267)

Vintage Woodworking Machinery, by Dana M. Batory. 138 Pages. 8 1/2" x 10 1/2". *This important new book on woodworking machinery concentrates on the products of four principal manufacturers: the J.A. Fay & Egan Company of Cincinnati, Ohio; the Yates-Amerian Machine Company of Berlin, Wisconsin; the Defiance Machine Works of Defiance, Ohio; and the Oliver Machine Company of Grand Rapids, Michigan. Filled with illustrations from the mid-1800 through the early part of the Twentieth Century, this book provides detailed histories of the makers, commentary on their principal products and much information about restoration, use and the moving of woodworking machinery. Whether you're fitting out a shop or just out for a look, there's something in Vintage Woodworking Machinery for you.*
$21.95 (BK 278)

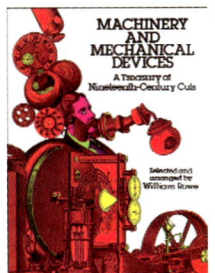

Machinery and Mechanical Devices: A Pictorial Archive, by William Rowe. 64 Pages. 9 1/4" x 12 1/4". *Lovers of Victoriana and the vintage machines, contraptions, and gizmos of the past, will love this book. Each page is an eye-catching collection of old-fashioned cuts selected and arranged by noted illustrator William Rowe. Reproduced from 19th-century books and periodicals, this book contains such whimsical devices as "Ericsson's Solar Engine," "Compound Engines of the Ozone," "New and Gigantic Telescope," "Craik's Improved Turbine Press for Treating Beet Pulp" and many more items of questionable function. Each page contains hundred of illustrations and offers an unusual perspective of man and machine in Victorian Times.*
$10.95 (BK 185)

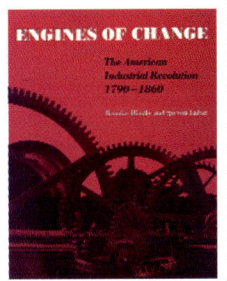

Engines of Change: The American Industrial Revolution 1790-1860, by Brooke Hindle & Steven Lubar. 309 Pages. 8" x 10". *Collectors of tools who marvel and wonder at the dramatic changes in the objects of their interest in the course of just a few decades will find in this classic book from the Smithsonian Institution some insight into the dramatic changes wrought by the rise of technology in America. A latecomer to industrialization, especially in comparison to the British, the unconquered New World was fertile soil in which to sow the seeds of innovation. Moving topically through the various industries, the authors document the incredible changes in the material culture brought about by inventions, factories and mass production. Covering every topic, including clocks, guns, textiles and transportation. A culminating chapter details the rousing reception given to American products at the Crystal Palace Exhibition of 1851. For a look at the dynamism of pre-Civil War America, we recommend this well written and well illustrated book.*
$22.95 (BK 283)

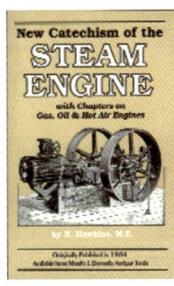

New Catechism of the Steam Engine, by N. Hawkins, M.E.. 432 Pages. 5 1/2" x 8 1/2". *The "Catechism" title of this classic work, which is reprinted from an early edition, comes from its question and answer form of organization. Meant to serve as a self-instruction manual for those who need to master the maintenance and use of the steam engine, Hawkins "Catechism" is filled with information for modern students of the state of the art of power and machinery in the last century. In addition to addressing every aspect of steam engine use and the technology that supports the application, this book also provides the student with a detailed history of the steam engine and its development. Whether you're thinking of setting up your own colliery or you are simply curious about the ways and workings of steam engines, Hawkins' "Catechism of the Steam Engine" will be and enjoyable and rewarding investment.*
$15.95 (BK 158)

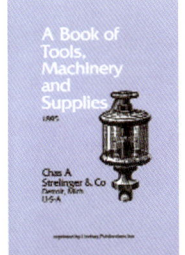

The Book of Tools, Machinery and Supplies 1895, by C. Strelinger & Co., Detroit, Mich. 521 Pages. 6" x 9". *This reprint of Chas A Strelinger's 1895 Cataloginventories all six floors of Strelinger's store in Detroit, Michigan. Within, one will find calipers, drop presses, blacksmiths' hammers, polishing wheels, wrenches, lathes, trowels, hand oilers, lamps, pulleys, carving tools, saws, and much much more. This is a book that will be enjoyed by metalworker and carpenter alike, as well as any lover of tools.*
$22.95 (BK 251)

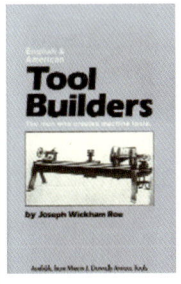

English and American Tool Builders, by Joseph Wickham Roe. 315 Pages. 5 1/2" x 8 1/2". *In his classic work, English and American Tool Builders, author Joseph Wickam Roe examines the lives of some of the great men of the machine tool industry, and in so doing, accurately recounts the development of the art of metalworking from the early 1800's into this century. Included in this well written book are accounts of the lives of Henry Maudslay, Samuel Bentham, James Nasmyth, Joseph Whitworth, Eli Whitney, Samuel Colt, Brown & Sharpe, and more. Roe's theme is that the great inventions all were built upon the previous inventions and that machine tools, once they were created, led to the building of more complex tools that could build even more complex tools. Illustrated with diagrams of machinery and portraits of the great inventors who produced them, "Tool Builders" is as much about the ascent of man as it is about tools and machines. A very well written and inspiring book. Highly recommended.*
$18.95 (BK 157)

Barns, Sheds & Outbuildings, by Byron D. Halsted. 236 Pages. 5 1/2" x 8 1/2". *Originally published in 1881, this book is filled with plans and instructions for building barns, poultry houses, piggeries, carriage houses, dog kennels, bird houses, smokehouses, and root cellars. Filled with hundreds of charming drawings, Barns, Sheds & Outbuildings provides a real, practical understanding not only of materials and construction but also farming and farm economics, weather, geography, history, and especially the animals of the farm.*
$14.00 (BK 316)

The Art of the Metalsmith

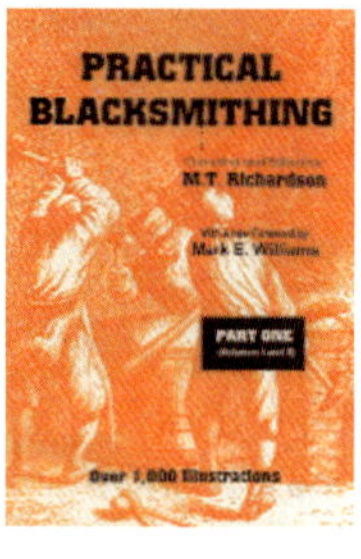

Practical Blacksmithing, Part I, by M.T. Richardson, Ed.. 528 Pages. 6" x 9". *We are pleased to be able to offer in a set of two volumes, the contents of the 4 volume series on blacksmithing by M.T. Richardson. There was a time when even the smallest village had several smiths and a would-be practitioner could learn this ancient art by observation and practice. Today, except among a very few remaining practitioners, the art is practically lost. Richardson's books have captured the blacksmith's craft and its arcane secrets between their pages. Volumes I & II, contained in this section, detail the tools and equipment, discuss the layout of a well organized shop and address the basic techniques of the blacksmith's craft. For those with an interest, either as a practitioner or as a collector, we highly recommend these excellent books.* **$24.95 (BK 059)**

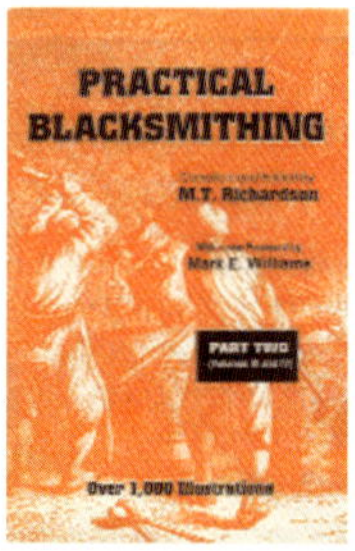

Practical Blacksmithing, Part II, by M.T. Richardson, Ed.. 608 Pages. 6" x 9". *Continuing where Volume I leaves off, and including the original Volumes 3 and 4 of the Richardson series, this massive and thoroughly illustrated work guides the potential smith through the processes of welding, brazing, soldering, forging, cutting, bending, setting and tempering. Also included is a section on carriage repair, and for those preparing for the next Winter Games, a section on how to make a bobsled. An excellent reference for the artist/craftsman or the general reader.* **$27.95 (BK 060)**

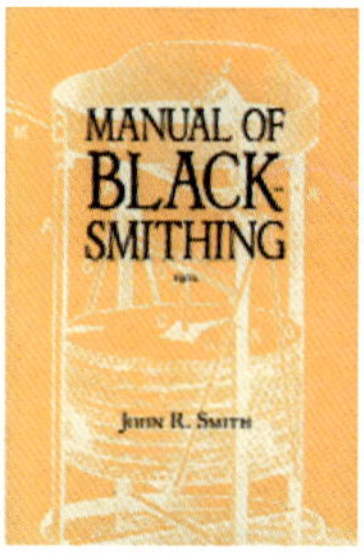

Manual of Blacksmithing, by John R. Smith. 158 Pages. 5" x 7". *Originally published in 1902, this comprehensive and very well illustrated small book begins with a review of the various appliances of the smithy's shop, including swages, cone mandrels, forges, cranes and anvils. A thorough treatment of the hand tools of the blacksmith is next, followed by succeeding chapters on the fundamental techniques of forge work including drawing, welding, upsetting and punching. Later chapters examine examples of the day to day work of the practicing smith and provide instructions for the crafting of a forge and forge tools. A handy little book that is filled with information.* **$9.95 (BK 161)**

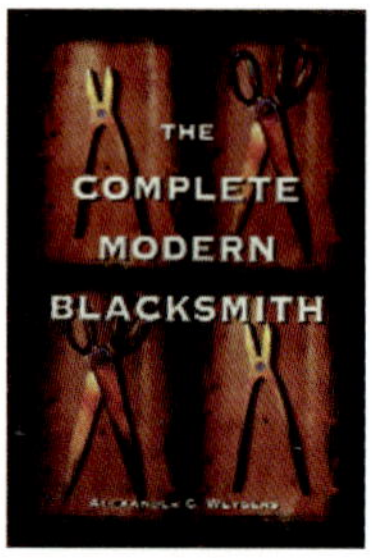

The Complete Modern Blacksmith, by Alexander G. Weygers. 300 Pages. 8" x 11". *This delightful book is a step-by-step guide to assembling a complete blacksmith shop for a limited investment, and then putting it to use making the tools you will need to complete other projects. Thoroughly illustrated with superb line drawings by the author, this book begins with an introduction to metallurgy, surveys the tools necessary for a modern shop and then proceeds to detail, in step-by-step fashion, how to make all of the tools necessary for use in the shop including hammers, chisels and even the anvil. The balance of the book is devoted to illustrating the various techniques of the experienced smith by detailing the processes for making a number of useful household and shop necessities, such as hinges, woodworking tools, fireplace tools and many more. The final section addresses the "recycling & repair of tools" and includes many tips of use to the antique tool restorationist or home handyman. Whether to understand the ways of metalwork or to actually begin the practice of the craft, "The Complete Modern Blacksmith" will prove and enjoyable and frequently consulted reference.* **$22.50 (BK 125)**

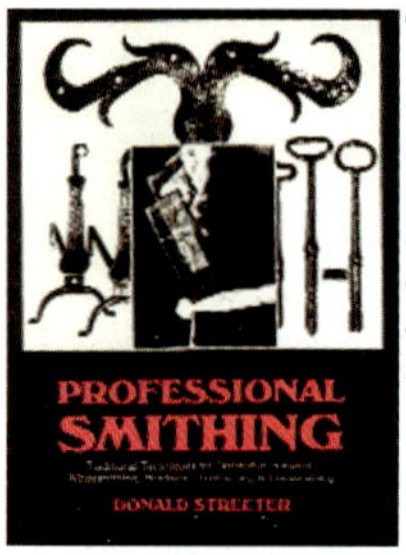

Professional Smithing, by Donald Streeter. 144 Pages. 8 1/2" x 11". *If you've ever yearned to fire up the forge somewhere not far from the spreading chestnut tree, then this is the book for you. While its name "professional smithing" implies that this is a book for the advanced blacksmith, it begins with an overview of the tools needed in the shop of the modern artist blacksmith and addresses the techniques for their use. The balance of this well illustrated work is devoted to the detailed review of the forging of specific objects, each of which employs a range of techniques. By studying the tricks used in making hinges, forks, locks and much more, the reader will become well versed in the art of the blacksmith.* **$24.95 (BK 080)**

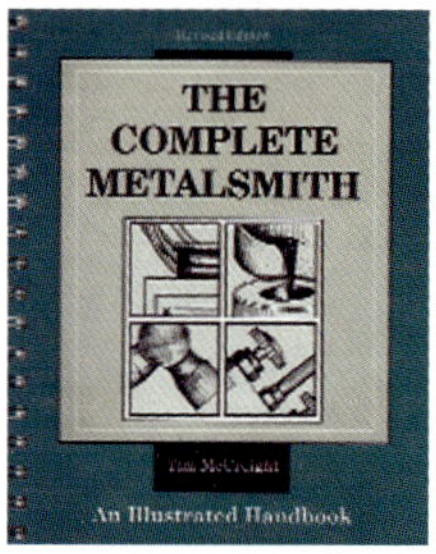

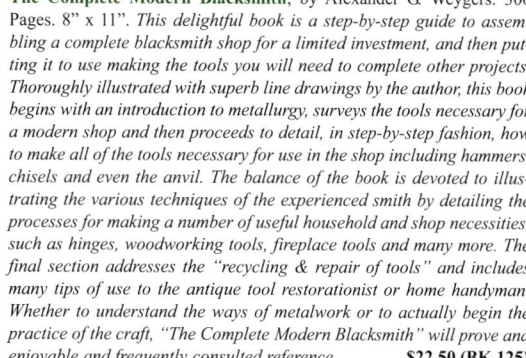

The Complete Metalsmith: An Illustrated Handbook, by Tim Mc Creight. 198 Pages. 7 1/2" x 9". *Appropriately subtitled "An Illustrated Handbook", Tim McCreight's new book covers every aspect of the metalworker's craft. A working metalsmith and a professor at the Portland School of Art in Maine, McCreight puts his background to work in this "how to" book. Topics include casting, forging, riveting, repousse, raising and many, many others. In fact, no aspect of metalworking appears to have been omitted. Each topic is carefully presented, with detailed explanations of techniques, accompanied by illustrations. Tips for the novice and the experienced metalworker are included for each subject. Whether you intend to try your hand at some aspect of metalwork or simply have an academic interest, The Complete Metalsmith will more than fill the bill.* **$14.95 (BK 284)**

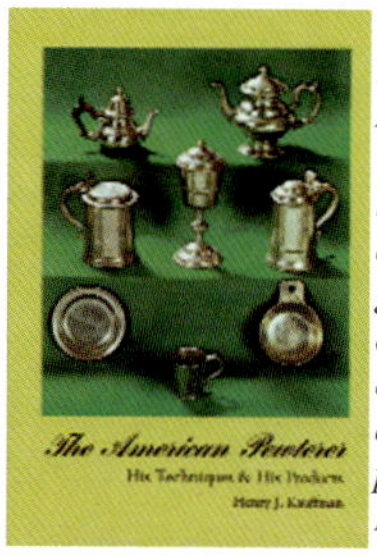

The American Pewterer: His Techniques & His Products, by Henry J. Kauffman. 132 Pages. 7" x 10". *A complement to his other works "Early American Copper, Tin & Brass", "The Colonial Silversmith" and "Metalworking Trades in Early America", this Kauffman classic focuses on the history, methods, materials and artifacts of those who worked with the classic colonial material, pewter. Illustrated with black and white photographs of all manner of classic American pewter, this book provides a thorough introduction to this all but forgotten craft. Beginning with an historical overview of the metal and its properties, the book then reviews the layout of a colonial pewterer's shop and proceeds to a topical analysis of the types of products that were produced. Additional chapters address the pewterer in England, factory production of pewter and much more. A thorough bibliography and index make this a most useful addition to the library.* **$24.95 (BK 121)**

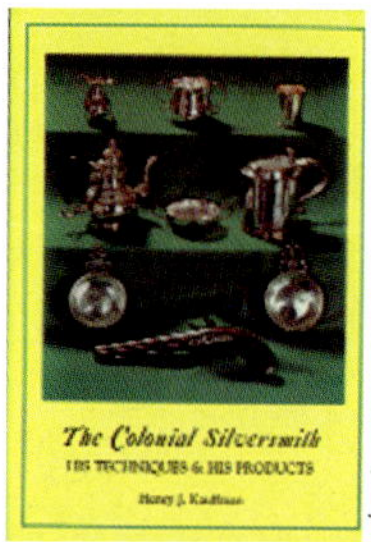

The Colonial Silversmith: His Techniques and His Products, by Henry J. Kauffman. 175 Pages. 7" x 10". *A complement to his other works "Early American Copper, Tin & Brass", "The Colonial Pewterer" and "Metalworking Trades in Early America", this Kauffman classic focuses on the history, methods, materials and artifacts of Paul Revere and his contemporaries. Illustrated with black and white photographs of all manner of classic American silver, this book provides a thorough introduction to this ancient and thriving. Beginning with an historical overview of the metal and its properties, the book then reviews the layout of a colonial silversmith's shop and proceeds to a topical analysis of the types of products that were produced. Additional chapters address the use of silver ornamentation in firearms and presentation items. A thorough index make this a most useful addition to the library.* **$24.95 (BK 123)**

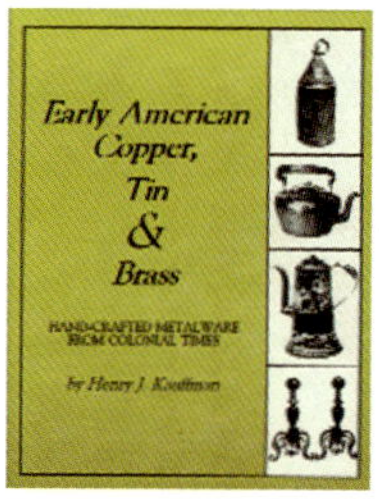

Early American Copper Tin and Brass, by Henry J. Kauffman. 108 Pages. 8 1/2" x 11". *A complement to his other works "The American Pewterer", "The Colonial Silversmith" and "Metalworking Trades in Early America", this Kauffman classic focuses on the history, methods, materials and artifacts of colonial metalworkers. Illustrated with black and white photographs of all manner of classic Americana, this book is a virtual museum tour. Chapters include decorated tinware, lighting fixtures, the craftsmen and their trade and much more. A most enlightening and entertaining book.* **$22.50 (BK 114)**

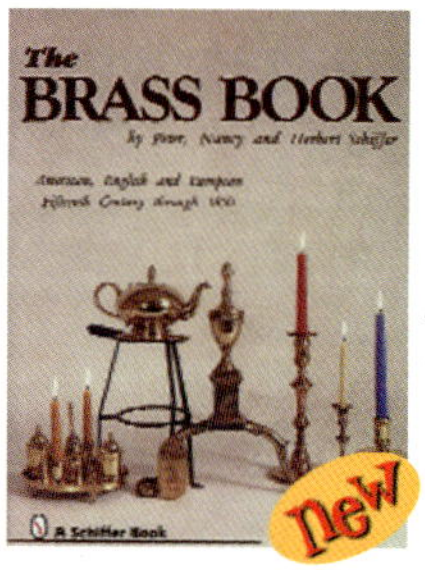

The Brass Book: American, English and European by Herbert, Peter, & Nancy Schiffer. 447 Pages. 9" x 11.25". *As the title implies, this book is the definitive reference on brass objects. Chapters are devoted to andirons, candlesticks, fireplace accessories, kettles and tobacco boxes. Even horse brasses, scientific and occupational instruments, and table wares can be found here. The development of artistic styles in brass are fully illustrated and explained. The accompanying text explains the composition of brass, eighteenth century method of sand casting, and ways to identify old copies and fakes. An eighteenth century catalog is even reproduced at the end of the book. A must for any lover of brass things!* **$60.00 (BK 371)**

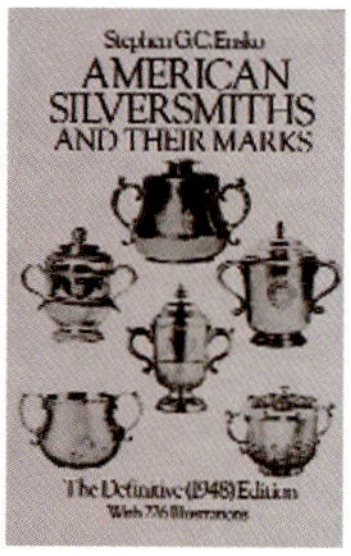

American Silversmith and Their Marks, by Stephen G.C. Ensko. 287 Pages. 5 3/8" x 8 1/2". *Foresaking the flourishes and ornamental design of their European contemporaries, early American gold and silversmiths pioneered a new luxurious metalware for the table marked by simplicity and forthrightness of design. For serious connoisseurs of American gold and silver ware, Ensko provides the definitive directory. Its an exhaustive list of over 3000 gold and silversmiths working between the years of 1650 and 1850. Biographical details of these silversmiths, their marks, and shop location (complete with maps) are given wherever possible. Over 200 of the finest examples of work of these early American artisans are displayed in sharp black and white photographs. Historians as well as American history buffs, will find this book a necessity for its unique perspective on culture, lifestyle, and value of a young America.* **$16.95 (BK 210)**

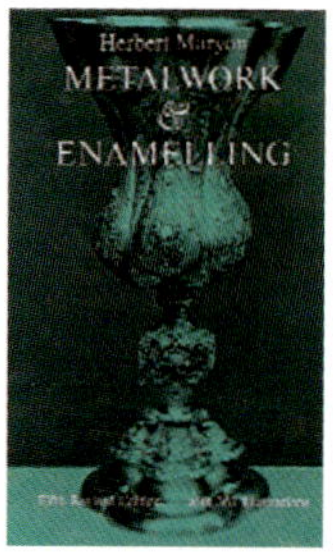

Metalwork & Enamelling, by Herbert Maryon. 347 Pages. 5 3/8" x 8 1/2". *All those concerned with goldsmithing, silversmithing, rare metal objects, metal scientific instruments, or their repair or restoration, will be delighted with this professional's handbook. Maryon, well known for his reconstruction work in the field, treats every aspect of the craft in detail, discussing materials and tools, soldering of rare metals, filigree work, setting of stones, raising and shaping, spinning, repousse work, wire twisting, hinges and joints, inlaying and overlaying, niello, alloys and stratified fabrics, enameling, metal casting, construction, setting out, polishing and coloring, design, assaying and hallmarking. Where ever possible, he analyzes examples of fines craftsmanship, ancient and modern, in order to better illustrate the processes he explains. This definitive work is required on the shelf of any metal workshop, laboratory, or any enthusiast or collector.* **$13.95 (BK 214)**

More Metalworking Topics

Practical Metal Plate Work, by Paul N. Hasluck. 160 Pages. 5 1/2" x 8 1/2". *The title of this work is a bit confusing to Americans who do not know the British term "metal plate" to mean "sheet metal". The confusion begins and ends with the title, however, as Hasluck's book addresses nearly every aspect of the universal techniques of sheet metal fabrication. In a book that was originally published in 1907 for the training of students, Hasluck begins with the basics, including a thorough overview of the tools used and continues through a series of projects that employ many of the skills and techniques required of a master sheet metal worker. Filled with great period drawings showing the use of tools and demonstrating techniques, this book will be valuable for anyone interested in learning about sheet metal work and the tools used to accomplish that work.*
$9.95 (BK 150)

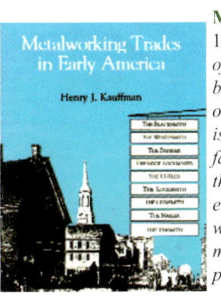

Metalworking Trades in Early America, by Henry J. Kauffman. 168 Pages. 8 1/2" x 10 1/2". *Long out of print, this classic survey of the way metalworking was accomplished in the various trades before the advent of large factories is a must-have for the collector or the general reader. Kauffman's thoroughly researched and lavishly illustrated book addresses the blacksmith, the whitesmith, the farrier, the edge toolmaker, the cutler, the locksmith, the gunsmith, the nailer, the tinsmith and wheelwright. In addition, there are several chapters on forges, furnaces and early iron making. Anyone with an interest in the world in which the tools we treasure were made will find delight in this excellent work that is finally back in print.*
$24.95 (BK 057)

Hardening, Tempering, Annealing and Forging of Steel, by Joseph V. Woodworth. 288 Pages. 5 1/2" x 8 1/2". *The secrets of tempering and hardening of steel were once closely guarded secrets on which the security of nations rested. Today, that information can be readily obtained by consulting this comprehensive and extremely affordable volume. Covering every aspect of its complex subject in great detail, this work, which is reprinted from the 1907 original by Joseph Woodworth, covers the chemical processis of hardening, addresses the metallurgical properties of iron and steel and is filled with superb period engravings to complement the text. Whether you are a dedicated blacksmith or an interested layman, Woodworth's book will prove an interesting and frequently consulted reference.*
$9.95 (BK 151)

Blacksmith Shop & Iron Forging, by International Correspondence Schools. 53 Pages. 5 1/2" x 8 1/2". *This ca. 1906 manual is filled with detailed engraved illustrations showing blacksmith and forge tools and the techniques for using them. For the would-be smith, there is an excellent chapter on setting up a forge on either a large or small scale. Each chapter is organized in encyclopedic fashion, with careful attention given to detailed explanation of terms and techniques. As an introduction to the work of the smith or as a primer in the tools and language of the forge, this affordable book will more than fill the bill.*
$9.95 (BK 153)

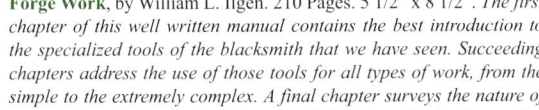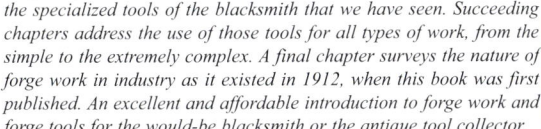

Forge Work, by William L. Ilgen. 210 Pages. 5 1/2" x 8 1/2". *The first chapter of this well written manual contains the best introduction to the specialized tools of the blacksmith that we have seen. Succeeding chapters address the use of those tools for all types of work, from the simple to the extremely complex. A final chapter surveys the nature of forge work in industry as it existed in 1912, when this book was first published. An excellent and affordable introduction to forge work and forge tools for the would-be blacksmith or the antique tool collector.*
$9.95 (BK 159)

Elementary Forge Practice, by Robert H. Harcourt. 148 Pages. 5" x 7". *Originally put together by the author as a "how to" manual for students interested in learning the art of the blacksmith, it serves equally well at that task today. A series of excellent line drawings illustrate the techniques and methods of the metalworker as well as the uses of specialized tools for each task. One aspect of this book that recommends it for the home blacksmith is that Harcourt has focused on the making of tools as a course of study in the use of the forge. A modern would-be smith can follow Harcourt's course of study and end up with many of the tools he will need to expand upon what was learned.*
$9.95 (BK 160)

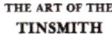

The Art of The Tinsmith: English and American, by Shirley Spalding Devoe. 222 Pages. 8 1/2" x 11". *Tin, the most useful of all metals, has been used since ancient times to make vessels of many sorts. England's Cornwall was an early source and manufacturing center for tin; and in the 19Th century Cornish miners and English and Welsh metal workers immigrated to the United States where the tin industry flourished. This book provides a rich history of the manufacturing processes and methods for decoration of antique, utilitarian tinwares on both sides of the Atlantic. The examples demonstrate a variety of wares and details which help identify English and American products. This book will be an asset to the library of any collector or anyone who can appreciate the artistry of the craft.*
$27.50 (BK 226)

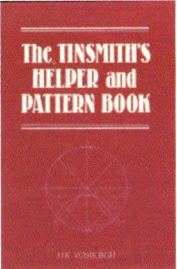

The Tinsmith's Helper and Pattern Book, by H.K. Vosburgh. 120 Pages. 6" x 9". *A reprint of the 1910 Edition of a work that was originally published in 1910, this small but information filled book features a series of line drawings that illustrate the methods for laying out everyday articles and fittings of tin and also provide insight for the smith into techniques that might be innovatively applied later in actual practice. A series of appendices cover the mathematical formula necessary for the working tinsmith as well as a series of tables that allow one to quickly ascertain the dimensions of working stock necessary for construction of vessels of specific sizes. If you hated geometry, you will loathe this book, but if you have an interest in traditional crafts, or if you would like to try your hand at "tin knocking", this book is a great place to start.*
$14.50 (BK 120)

Silversmithing, by Rupert Finegold & William Seitz. 480 Pages. 8 1/4" x 10 7/8". *Discover the basics of silversmithing in this complete guidebook. This book provides you with all the basics from the types and properties of metal used, to the required tools, and numerous easy-to-understand techniques.*
$39.95 (BK 246)

The Art of Coppersmithing, by John Fuller, Sr.. 327 Pages. 6" x 9". *Now largely abandoned in favor of other materials, copper was widely used in the last century for everything from the making of kitchen utensils to roofing to plumbing materials. Originally published in 1893, this work by John Fuller, Sr., who was then one of the leading authorities in the copper industry, addresses every aspect of this important metal. Beginning with an historical overview of the use of copper, the author proceeds to a review of ancient and modern methods of mining. Subsequent chapters trace the development of copper working by smiths from the earliest times to the then-modern era. In addition to the voluminous information about hand work (including a thorough review of the tools of the trade), there is a detailed overview of the use of copper in every industry from brewing to ship building. Nearly 500 superb Victorian engravings accent this classic work. Whether you are a modern metallurgist or a latter-day smith, this book will surely enlighten and entertain.*
$27.50 (BK 118)

Metalworking: A Book of Tools, Materials & Processes for the Handyman, by Paul N. Hasluck. 760 Pages. 6" x 9". *Written by British author, Paul Hasluck, and originally published in 1907, this book is subtitled "A Book of Tools, Materials and Processes for the Handyman" and it fully lives up to its billing. Nearly every aspect of metalworking of every sort is covered in great detail in this comprehensive reference, as are the tools used in those trades. A wide range of subjects are brought more clearly into focus thanks to Hasluck's well written explication and a series of period line drawings. Whether you are an aspiring metalworker, a collector of tools or a student of industry, Paul Hasluck's "Metal Working" will prove to be a fequently consulted reference.*
$29.95 (BK 162)

The Early Ironwork of Charleston, by Alston Deas. 110 Pages. 8 1/2" x 11". *Originally published in 1941, this book would be well worth having were it no more than a virtual walking tour of Charleston's great homes and buildings and their unique and decorative ironwork. That walking tour is contained within this well illustrated book, but so is much more, including a historical overview of the founding and settlement of Charleston and a history of some of the great blacksmiths of that city. Whether or not you're planning a trip to Charleston, we recommend this well written and well illustrated book. When you have finished reading it, you will definitely be planning a trip to Charleston.*
$19.95 (BK 143)

Toll Free: (800) 869-0695 — Secure Online Ordering at www.mjdtools.com

Specialized Work in Iron and Wood

Antique Iron, English and American: 15th Century through 1850, by Herbert, Peter, & Nancy Schiffer. 320 Pages. 8 1/2" x 11". *Within this informative book the reader will find architectural hardware, lighting devices, andirons and fireplace equipment, tools, toys, weathervanes, firemarks, kitchen utensils, fences, and gates. Concise descriptions indicate regional products from the South, Midwest, and Northeastern United States, as well England and Europe. A short history of the manufacturing process is also presented. Ironworks and their functions are discussed focusing on three particular locations: Saugus, Mass. in the 17th century; Batsto, N.J. in the 18th century; and Hopewell, Penn. in the 19th Century. The importance of the blacksmith in townlife is made clear by the numerous examples present in this book, which is sure to be enjoyed by historians, iron buffs, and antique collectors alike.* **$59.95 (BK 224)**

The Pattern Maker's Assistant, by Joshua Rose. 249 Pages. 6" x 9". *Originally published in 1889 as a guide for those learning the demanding art of creating patterns for metal castings. Rose's classic work addresses nearly every aspect of the trade in a thoroughly readable and profusely illustrated work. Beginning with an overview of the trade, including its earliest history, Rose's work proceeds to a detailed analysis of the tools of the trade, with particular emphasis on their maintenance. Subsequent chapters address the actual practice of shop work, including core construction, lathe work, the making of gear wheels and much, much more. Anyone who has ever been left in awe when contemplating the complexity of an old mahogany casting pattern or who has looked into an undisturbed chest of pattern maker's tools will find this book an interesting read and helpful resource.* **$22.50 (BK 122)**

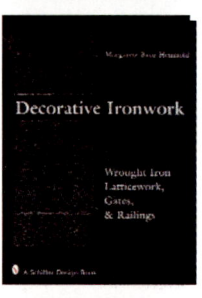

Decorative Antique Ironwork: A Pictoral Treasury, by Henry Rene D'allemagne. 417 Pages. 8 1/2" x 11". *The 4500 examples of decorative ironwork in this volume, taken from the 1924 French catalogue of the extensive collection in the Le Secq des Tournelles Museum in Rouen, date from Roman times on to the first part of the 19th-century. The first part of the text discusses architectural ironwork such as grilles, locks and padlocks, keys, door knocker, door knobs, hinges, handles and pulls, signs and brackets. The second part deals with small iron and steel objects, including jewelry, toilet accesories, key rings and handbag frames, scissors, religious symbols, sundials, clocks, furniture, lighting fixtures, and various other tools and equipment. Informative captions provide historical facts connected with the pieces. This is an ideal book for craftman, dealers, collectors, and any one who appreciates the beauty of this craft.* **$27.95 (BK 198)**

The Pattern Maker's Assistant, by Joshua Rose. 324 Pages. 5 1/2" x 8 1/2". *Written by an accomplished machinist and pattern maker, this classic work was originally pubished in 1877. In a thorough, comprehensive and very readable book, author Joshua Rose examines, in great detail, the hand tools of the patternmaker and how they are used, the uses of lathes, the techniques of foundry work, the machine tools found in a shop and the techniques used in the making of all manner of patterns from the simple to the very complex. Copiously illustrated with hundreds of line drawings showing tools, machines and examples of the patternmaker's craft, Rose's The Pattern Maker's Assistant is a step back in time to the world of the last century. An interesting and enjoyable read.* **$14.95 (BK 156)**

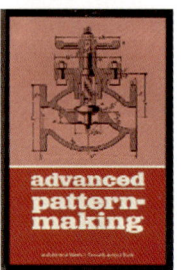

Decorative Ironwork: Wrought Iron Gratings, Gates and Railings, by Margarete Baur Heinhold. 176 Pages. 9" x 12". *Many centuries worth of ornamental design in wrought iron are brought to us in this book, including the restrained English works, the tasteful Italian and French, the elegant Spanish, and the lively German types, some of which overflow with rocaille, flowers, leaves and ribbon decor. Each is depicted in all particulars in this fascinating work. From the gratings, entries, and gates of medieval Europe, to the artistic creations of the 17th and 18th century, and finally to the works of today, Heinhold provides valuable historical information about these items as well as their restoration. With hundreds of photos with book, this book with be appreciated by any enthusiast.* **$49.95 (BK 225)**

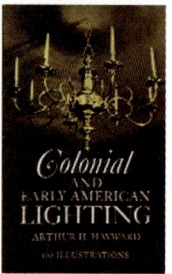

Colonial & Early American Lighting, by Arthur H. Hayward. 229 Pages. 5 3/8" x 8 1/2". *Beginning with the rushlight holders used by the earliest settlers and ranging up to the elaborate chandeliers of the Federal period, this book is a unique retelling of the fascinating story of lamps and other lighting devices in America. Although the main emphasis is on the Colonial era, work up until the 1880's is also considered. Along with valuable information and collecting hints about these early lamps, each chapter tells of Colonial life, custom and habits not available elsewhere. This volume has probably the largest selection of antique lamps ever illustrated and will indeed fill a long-felt need of any antique collector, designer, historian, and Americana enthusiast.* **$14.95 (BK 215)**

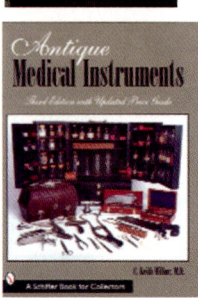

Advanced Patternmaking, by International Correspondence School. 43 Pages. 5 1/2" x 8 1/2". *Written for the working patternmaker, this book examines in detail the techniques used for making casting patterns for some extremly complex castings. By studying this book, the modern student can gain an undertanding of what was involved in the making of patterns for everything from giant pot-belly stoves to church bells. to steam engines. An interesting and affordable journey to a forgotten time.* **$9.95 (BK 149)**

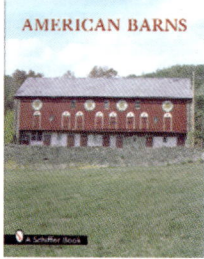

American Barns, by Stanley Schuler. 224 Pages. 8 1/2" x 11". *This handsome and richly illustrated book takes a look at 240 barns from throughout the United States. Here you'll find huge barns and small barns, rustic barns and ornate barns, round barns and octagonal barns, Pennsylvania Dutch barns and New England barns, stables and carriage houses, and countless others are presented with gorgeous pictures and detailed information and descriptions. This is the perfect book for barn lovers everywhere, and may even make the indifferent observer an enthusiast.* **$24.95 (BK 233)**

Antique Medical Instruments, by Keith Wilbur, M.D.. 156 Pages. 8 1/2" x 11". *This book, with its carefully drawn illustrations and precise hand lettered text, will be a beautiful addition to the libraries of historians, medical professionals, and collectors. A wide range of antique medical instruments, both diagnostic and therapeutic, are examined in detail. Microscopes, reflex hammers, stethoscopes, blood pressure instruments, electro cardiographs, ophthalmoscopes, otoscopes, endoscopes, vaginal specula, thermometers, etc. are described from the most early example to the present. Superb line drawings by the author illustrate this essential reference. The indices within include an insightful price guide and a listing of American Dental, Medical, and Apothecary Museums, each of which is more than worth the price of this book.* **$23.95 (BK 230)**

Early Illustrations Views of American Architecture, by Edmund V. Gillon Jr. 308 Pages. 9 1/2" x 12". *Here are streets, squares and business blocks of numerous cities as they appeared in the 1800s, with their people going about their everyday affairs. Among its 742 illustrations you'll find churches and lodge buildings; log cabins and slave quarters; city halls and state houses; police stations and courthouses; stores and shops; banks and theatres; Yale college as it looked in 1884, along with many other school and colleges of the time; prisons; hospitals and libraries; hotels and breweries; mills and factories; fire towers; windmills and lighthouses. All major architectural styles are represent: Colonial, Federal, Greek Revival, Gothic Revival, and Victorian "eclectic;" as well 26 states and 249 cities. For any lover of America's architectural history, this collection of illustrations is a rare find.* **$21.95 (BK 199)**

Handicrafts of the Southern Highlands, by Allen S. Eaton. 392 Pages. 5 3/8" x 8". *This is the only comprehensive book written about the crafts of Southern Appalachia. It contains a wealth of information on this region's traditional handicrafts, such as log cabin building; spinning and weaving out of cotton, wool, and flax; natural dyes; quilt making; pottery; woodcarving; furniture and doll making; musical instruments and mountain music. Every aspect of the matieal culture of this region as it has been practiced since the earliest settlers came from Virginia and other parts of the coast. Many of these craft practices can be traced back to their roots in England, Scotland, and Ireland. Eaton's classic study, complimented by photos by the great social photographer, Doris Ulmann, is one of the most important documents to have come out of the Roosevelt Depression and a must for anyone interested in American traditional music and craft.* **$17.95 (BK 202)**

Horseless Vehicles Automobiles and Motorcycles, by Gardner D. Hiscox. 460 Pages. 5 1/2" x 8 1/2". *This treatise, published in 1900, offers a discourse on everything powered by steam, hydrocarbon, electric and pneumatic motors at the turn of the century. Hiscox wrote this book to satisfy the interest of many people, who were just beginning to realize the potentiality of automobiles for common road locomotion. Within it, he analyzes the various mechanisms of automotive power and construction of many of the vehicles used as the time from the Gurney Steam Carriage to the Hansom Cab. Complete with a list of various patent numbers, this book with be enjoyed by any automobile fanatic!* **$24.95 (BK 345)**

Reprints of Early Trade Catalogues

Henry Disston & Sons Company General Line Catalog Ca. 1874, by Henry Disston & Sons Company. 86 Pages. 6 1/2" x 10". *Those who think that the Henry Disston Company made only hand saws are in for a real surprise when they leaf through the pages of this early and nicely illustrated catalog. The saws are here, of course, and every sort imaginable. Also included are bevels, levels, squares, marking gauges, masons' tools and much, much more. A superb early catalog.* **$14.50 (BK 073)**

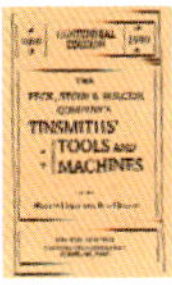

The Peck, Stow & Wilcox Company Centennial Catalog of Tools and Machines, by Peck, Stow & Wilcox Company. 144 Pages. 6" x 9 1/4". *The Peck, Stow & Wilcox Company was the unquestioned leader in the manufacture of tools for tinsmiths and sheet metal workers. This massive catalog reprint illustrates their full product line at the peak of their production. .* **$15.95 (BK 091)**

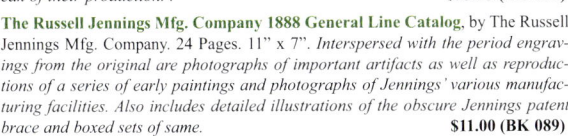

The Russell Jennings Mfg. Company 1888 General Line Catalog, by The Russell Jennings Mfg. Company. 24 Pages. 11" x 7". *Interspersed with the period engravings from the original are photographs of important artifacts as well as reproductions of a series of early paintings and photographs of Jennings' various manufacturing facilities. Also includes detailed illustrations of the obscure Jennings patent brace and boxed sets of same.* **$11.00 (BK 089)**

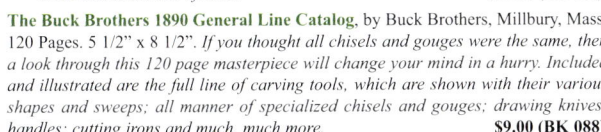

The Buck Brothers 1890 General Line Catalog, by Buck Brothers, Millbury, Mass. 120 Pages. 5 1/2" x 8 1/2". *If you thought all chisels and gouges were the same, then a look through this 120 page masterpiece will change your mind in a hurry. Included and illustrated are the full line of carving tools, which are shown with their various shapes and sweeps; all manner of specialized chisels and gouges; drawing knives; handles; cutting irons and much, much more.* **$9.00 (BK 088)**

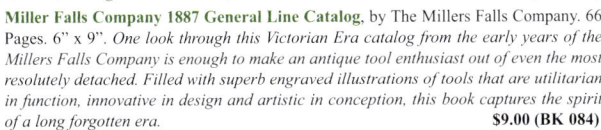

Miller Falls Company 1887 General Line Catalog, by The Millers Falls Company. 66 Pages. 6" x 9". *One look through this Victorian Era catalog from the early years of the Millers Falls Company is enough to make an antique tool enthusiast out of even the most resolutely detached. Filled with superb engraved illustrations of tools that are utilitarian in function, innovative in design and artistic in conception, this book captures the spirit of a long forgotten era.* **$9.00 (BK 084)**

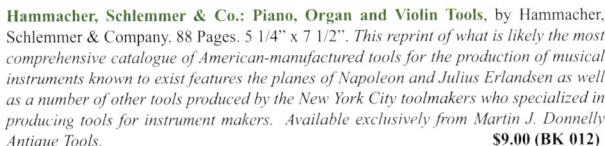

Hammacher, Schlemmer & Co.: Piano, Organ and Violin Tools, by Hammacher, Schlemmer & Company. 88 Pages. 5 1/4" x 7 1/2". *This reprint of what is likely the most comprehensive catalogue of American-manufactured tools for the production of musical instruments known to exist features the planes of Napoleon and Julius Erlandsen as well as a number of other tools produced by the New York City toolmakers who specialized in producing tools for instrument makers. Available exclusively from Martin J. Donnelly Antique Tools.* **$9.00 (BK 012)**

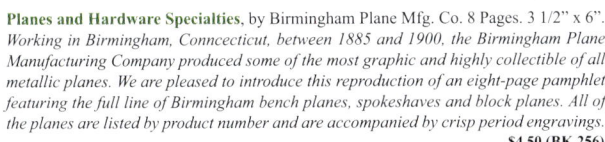

The Sandusky Tool Company 1925 General Line Catalog, by Sandusky Tool Company. 72 Pages. 5 1/2" x 8 1/2".*Nicely illustrated with the full Sandusky line, including an extensive line of coopers tools, this book will be an oft-consulted reference.* **$11.50 (BK 086)**

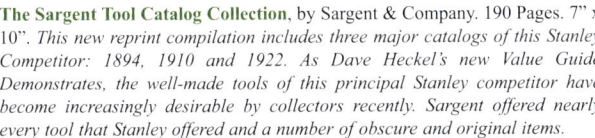

Planes and Hardware Specialties, by Birmingham Plane Mfg. Co. 8 Pages. 3 1/2" x 6". *Working in Birmingham, Conncecticut, between 1885 and 1900, the Birmingham Plane Manufacturing Company produced some of the most graphic and highly collectible of all metallic planes. We are pleased to introduce this reproduction of an eight-page pamphlet featuring the full line of Birmingham bench planes, spokeshaves and block planes. All of the planes are listed by product number and are accompanied by crisp period engravings.* **$4.50 (BK 256)**

The Sargent Tool Catalog Collection, by Sargent & Company. 190 Pages. 7" x 10". *This new reprint compilation includes three major catalogs of this Stanley Competitor: 1894, 1910 and 1922. As Dave Heckel's new Value Guide Demonstrates, the well-made tools of this principal Stanley competitor have become increasingly desirable by collectors recently. Sargent offered nearly every tool that Stanley offered and a number of obscure and original items.* **$20.00 (BK 010)**

"The Level You Need", by Davis & Cook, Watertown, N.Y.. 14 Pages. 5 1/2" x 7 1/4". *Situated in the unlikely location of Watertown, New York, the Davis & Cook Level Company produced some of the most visually striking and collectible levels ever produced. In addition to their distinctive pretzel filligree cast iron bench levels, this innovative company also produced a line of aluminum levels long before that metal became as commonly available as it is today. Nicely illustrated and filled with well written period commentary, this book will make a nice helpful addition to the reference shelf.* **$6.00 (BK 030)**

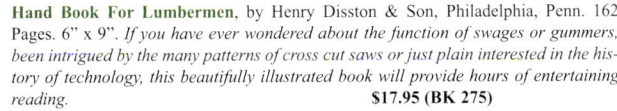

Hand Book For Lumbermen, by Henry Disston & Son, Philadelphia, Penn. 162 Pages. 6" x 9". *If you have ever wondered about the function of swages or gummers, been intrigued by the many patterns of cross cut saws or just plain interested in the history of technology, this beautifully illustrated book will provide hours of entertaining reading.* **$17.95 (BK 275)**

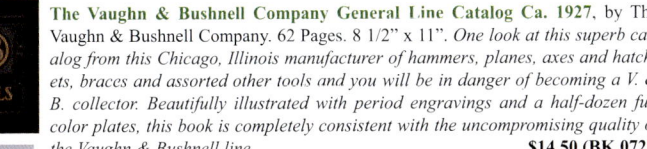

The Vaughn & Bushnell Company General Line Catalog Ca. 1927, by The Vaughn & Bushnell Company. 62 Pages. 8 1/2" x 11". *One look at this superb catalog from this Chicago, Illinois manufacturer of hammers, planes, axes and hatchets, braces and assorted other tools and you will be in danger of becoming a V. & B. collector. Beautifully illustrated with period engravings and a half-dozen full color plates, this book is completely consistent with the uncompromising quality of the Vaughn & Bushnell line.* **$14.50 (BK 072)**

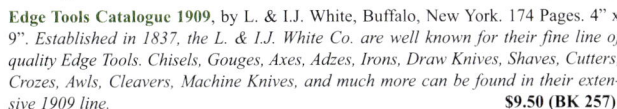

Edge Tools Catalogue 1909, by L. & I.J. White, Buffalo, New York. 174 Pages. 4" x 9". *Established in 1837, the L. & I.J. White Co. are well known for their fine line of quality Edge Tools. Chisels, Gouges, Axes, Adzes, Irons, Draw Knives, Shaves, Cutters, Crozes, Awls, Cleavers, Machine Knives, and much more can be found in their extensive 1909 line.* **$9.50 (BK 257)**

The Tower & Lyon Company General Line Catalog, by The Tower & Lyon Company. 111 Pages. 6" x 9". *This full line catalog from the marketing arm of the Union Hardware Company includes all manner of specialty tools, including the full line of "Chaplin's Patent" planes, Stephens' patent vises, all manner of rare wrenches and much, much more. A great reference to the obscure patented tools that are on the top of every collector's wish list.* **$11.50 (BK 066)**

The Greenfield Tool Company 1872 General Line Catalog, by The Greenfield Tool Company, Greenfield, Mass. 86 Pages. 5" x 7 1/2".*Nicely illustrated with line drawings of all manner of planes, this book also includes illustrations of a full line of levels, try squares and folding carpenters rules. An interesting read and one for the reference shelf.* **$8.00 (BK 087)**

The H.D. Smith & Company General Line Catalog, by The H.D. Smith & Company. 36 Pages. 6" x 8". *Collector's of the "Perfect Handle" line of tools from this Plantsville, Connecticut manufacturer are quite familiar with the line of extremely high quality wrenches and related tools they produced. An extremely well done catalog that illustrates the entire "Perfect Handle" line.* **$9.50 (BK 065)**

A Brown & Sharpe Catalogue Collection, by Brown & Sharpe Mfg. Company. 291 Pages. 6" x 9". *Comprised of significant offerings from the 1868, 1887 and 1899 catalogs of this important early manufacturer of machinists tools, this book provides the reader with a survey of the development of hand machinist tools over a dynamic period of American industrial expansion.* **$22.95 (BK 083)**

The Chapin-Stephens Company General Line Catalog No. 114, by The Chapin-Stephens Company. 84 Pages. 6" x 9". *As the final surviving major manufacturer of folding rules other than the Stanley Rule & Level Company. Chapin-Stephens was the successor, through mergers and acquisitions to every other Nineteenth Century maker of boxwood & ivory rules. This catalog dates from their pre-WW I peak and includes their full line of folding rules, wooden planes, levels, marking gauges, plane irons and much more. Nicely illustrated with extra sharp line drawings.* **$8.50 (BK 096)**

Millers Falls Company General Line Catalog Ca. 1915, by Millers Falls Company. 183 Pages. 6" x 9". *This early catalog illustrates their full line of braces, drills, levels, saws, treadle powered tools and much more. Superb period engravings bring these tools to life.* **$12.00 (BK 067)**

The James Swan Company General Line Catalog, by The James Swan Company. 104 Pages. 6 3/4" x 9 3/4". *Recently reprinted by ATTIC, the Connecticut tool collectors organization, this reprint from the first quarter of this century illustrates and documents the full product line of respected edge tool maker James Swan & Company at the peak of their production. In addition to chisels, slicks, gouges and drawknives, this book includes a wide range of auger handles, boring machines, hollow augers and a number of other obscure hand tools. An excellent reference.* **$9.50 (BK 177)**

Millers Falls Company Catalog No. 74, by Millers Falls Co., Mass. 49 Pages. 4 1/4" x 7". *This reprint of the 1878 Catalog by No. 74 Chambers Street, N.Y. features their newly improved "steel" Barber's bit brace, as well as many other braces, bit stocks, chucks, vises, mitre boxes, glass cutters, hand and breast drills, bracket sets, carving tools, scroll saws and planes. But if one is interested in mosquito netting, clock movements, camp stools, and toy cannons, this may also be the source.* **$7.00 (BK 249)**

The Sandusky Tool Company 1877 General Line Catalog, by Sandusky Tool Company, Sandusky, Ohio. 68 Pages. 6" x 9". *This early reprint from the increasingly collectible manufacturer the Sandusky Tool Company includes a complete listing of the product line as available in 1877, including a full line of edge tools, gauges, handles and coopers tools and much more.* **$11.50 (BK 085)**

The Belcher Bros. & Company Catalog of Boxwood & Ivory Rules, by Belcher Bros. & Company, New York. 44 Pages. 5 1/2" x 8 1/2". *One of the first manufacturers of measuring instruments in the United States, the Belcher Brothers Company is known to have operated as early as 1822. This reprint of their 1860 catalog documents and illustrates their full line of folding rules in both boxwood and ivory, as well a full range of other tools. Rounding out this essential period reference are several pages of historical commentary on the history of Belcher Brothers by noted author Kenneth D. Roberts.* **$7.50 (BK 082)**

Sargent Combination Planes (1080 and 1085), by Sargent & Company. 20 Pages. 5" x 8 1/2".*This recent reprint includes full parts listings and instructions for both the No. 1080 (Stanley 45 equivalent) and the No. 1085 (Stanley No. 55 equivalent). For the collector, woodworker or dealer, this affordable volume is an excellent addition to the library.* **$8.50 (BK 104)**

The Atha Tool Company General Line Catalog, 1883, by Atha Tool Company, Newark, New Jersey. 62 Pages. 10 1/4" x 6 3/4".*This catalog is one of the hightest quality reprints to be produced in recent years. All of the Victorian era engravings of the tools are reproduced in sharp, full detail. For an excellent overview of the world of edge tools in the last century, we highly recommend this excellent reprinted catalog.* **$11.50 (BK 164)**

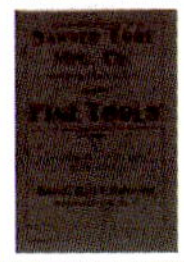

Sawyer Tool Company: 1892 General Line Catalog, by The Sawyer Tool Company. 54 Pages. 3 3/4" x 5 1/2". *The full product line ca. 1900 from this important, early maker of precision tools for the machinist..* **$6.00 (BK 013)**

Comprehensive Topical Index

Antique Tool Price Guides
- Antique & Collectible Stanley Tools: Guide to Value — 6
- Collector's Guide To Keen Kutter — 3
- Old Fishing Lures & Tackle Identification & Value Guide — 3
- Price Guide to Antique Tools — 15
- Snap-on Collectibles: Unauthorized Guide with Prices — 15
- The Catalogue Of Antique Tools, 1999 Edition — 6
- The Catalogue Of Antique Tools: 1998 Edition — 6
- The Catalogue of Antique Tools, Millennium Edition — 2
- Tools: A Guide For Collectors — 15

Achitecture and Building
- American Barns — 28
- Barns, Sheds & Outbuildings — 25
- Build A Classic Timber-framed House — 24
- Building & Restoring Hewn Log House — 4
- Building The Timber Frame House — 20
- Early Illustrations Views Of American Architecture — 28
- English Historical Carpentry — 11
- Fences, Gates And Bridges — 22
- Lighthouses Of The — 4
- Saltbox And Capecod Houses — 4

Axes, Saws & Lumbering
- Axe Makers Of North America — 20
- Glory Days Of Logging — 20
- Grimshaw On Saws — 20
- Hand Book For Lumbermen — 29
- Simonds Saw Mfr. Co. General Line Catalog — 20
- The Axe And Man: — 20
- The Handsaw Catalog Collection — 20
- This Was Logging: Drama In The Northwest — 20
- This Was Mining In The West — 20
- This Was Sawmilling — 20
- Timber: Loggers Challenge Great Northwestern Forests — 20

Beautiful Books
- The Art Of Fine Tools — 12
- Patented Transitional & Metallic Planes, Volume I — 9
- Patented Transitional & Metallic Planes, Volume II — 9
- Manufactured and Patented Spokeshaves — 19
- Windjammers of The Pacific Rim — 7
- Wooden Planes In 19th Century America Volume II — 9

Blacksmithing & Metal Work
- American Silversmith And Their Marks — 26
- Antique Iron, English & American — 28
- Blacksmith Shop & Iron Forging — 27
- Decorative Antique Ironwork: A Pictoral Treasury — 28
- Decorative Ironwork: Gratings, Gates & Railings — 28
- Early American Copper Tin and Brass — 26
- Elementary Forge Practice — 27
- Encyclopedia Of American Silver — 4
- Forge Work — 27
- Hardening, Tempering, Annealing & Forging Of Steel — 27
- Jewelry: Fundamentals Of Metalsmithing — 5
- Manual Of Blacksmithing — 26
- Metalwork & Enamelling — 26
- Metalworking Trades in Early America — 27
- Metalworking: Tools, Materials & Processes — 27
- Practical Blacksmithing, Part II — 26
- Practical Metal Plate Work — 27
- Professional Smithing — 26
- Silversmithing — 27
- The American Pewterer: His Techniques & His Products — 26
- The Art of Coppersmithing — 27
- The Brass Book American, english, & — 26
- The Colonial Silversmith: His Techniques and His Products — 26
- The Complete Metalsmith: An Illustrated Handbook — 26
- The Complete Modern Blacksmith — 26
- The Early Ironwork of Charleston — 27

British Tools
- Christopher Gabriel and the London Tool Trade — 19
- Stewart Spiers and the Planemakers of Ayr — 9
- The Ultimate Brace: — 19
- Tools: A Guide For Collectors — 15

Carriages
- Bristol Wagon & Carr Illustrated Catalog, — 14
- Horse Drawn Sleighs — 14
- Horseless Vehicles Automobiles & Motor — 28
- Practical Carriage Building — 14
- The Coach Maker's Illustrated Hand-Book — 14

- The Restoration Of Carriages — 14
- Wheelmaking: Wagon Wheel Design and Construction — 14

Carving
- Classic Carving Patterns — 13
- Early American Wood Carving — 13
- Fundamentals of Figure Carving — 13
- Grinling Gibbons And The Art Of Carving — 13
- How To Carve Wood — 13
- Manual Of Traditional Wood Carving — 13
- Projects For Creative Woodcarving — 13
- Relief Woodcarving and Lettering — 13
- Techniques Of Creative Spiral Work — 14
- Techniques of Creative Woodcarving — 13
- The Book Of Wood Carving — 13

Catalogue of Antique Tools
- The Catalogue Of Antique Tools, 1999 Edition — 6
- The Catalogue Of Antique Tools: 1998 Edition — 6
- The Catalogue of Antique Tools, Millennium Edition — 2

Clocks
- American Clocks And Clockmakers — 15
- Price Guide To Antique Clocks — 15

Country Store
- American Country Store — 22
- American Family Farm Antiques — 22
- Country Store Antiques: From Cradles to Caskets — 22
- Country Store Collectibles — 22

Crafts, Needlework & Sewing
- Antique Needlework Tools & Embroideries — 3
- Craft Of The Dyer Colour From Plants and Lichens — 5
- Early American Weaving & Dying — 5
- Knotcraft: The Practical and Entertaining Art of Tying Knots — 5
- Old-time Tools & Toys Of Needlework — 5
- The Dyer's Companion — 5
- The History Of The Patchwork Quilt — 5
- The Story Of Antique Needlework — 5
- The Story Of The Thimble, Illustrated — 18
- Zalkins' Handbook Of Thimbles & Sewing Implements — 5

Domestic & Kitchen Related
- 300 Years Of Housekeeping Collectibles — 22
- American Clocks And Clockmakers — 23
- American Country Store — 22
- American Family Farm Antiques — 22
- Apple Parers — 22
- Baskets And Basketmakers In Southern Appalachia — 23
- Collecting Household Linens — 22
- Colonial & Early American Lighting — 28
- Country Store Antiques: From Cradles to Caskets — 22
- Country Store Collectibles — 22
- Craft Of The Dyer Colour From Plants and Lichens — 5
- Early American Weaving & Dying — 5
- Garden Tools Hardbound — 22
- Groovy Kitchen Designs For — 22
- Old-time Tools & Toys Of Needlework — 5
- The Dyer's Companion — 5
- Toasters 1909-1960 Ingenutiy & Design — 22
- Zalkins' Handbook Of Thimbles & Sewing Implements — 5

Firearms and Military
- Firearms & Tackle Memorabilia — 4
- Flayderman's Guide Antique Amer Firearm — 23
- Gun Tools : Their History And Identification, Volume II — 23
- Gun Tools: Their History And Identification, Volume I — 23
- Guns And Gunmaking Tools Of Southern Appalachia — 23
- Illustrated Catalog Of Civil War Military Goods — 23
- Levine's Guide To Knives & Their Value — 23
- Marble's Outing Equiptment — 23
- Marble's Specialities For Sportsman — 23
- The Archaeology Of Weapons — 23
- The Book Of The Sword — 23

Furniture
- American Furniture Guide To 17th, 18th, & — 8
- American Furniture Of The 18th Century — 8
- American Furniture Of The 19th Century — 8
- Furniture And Its Makers Of — 10
- Furniture Mouldings: 1574-1820 — 8
- Jack Hill's Country Chair Making — 8
- Make A Windsor Chair With Michael Dunbar — 8
- The Chairmaker's Workshop — 8
- The Shaker Legacy: Perspectives of an Enduring Tradition — 8

- Welsh Stick Chairs — 8

Gift Books
- Classic Hand Tools — 12
- Collecting Antique Tools — 9
- Directory Of American Tool Makers — 3
- Edward Preston & Son: 1909 General Line Catalog — 6
- Hammacher, Schlemmer & Co.: — 29
- Manufactured and Patented Spokeshaves — 19
- Pat. Transitional & Metallic Planes in America, Volume I — 9
- Pat. Transitional & Metallic Planes in America, Volume II — 9
- Planes And Hardware Specialties — 29
- The Sandusky Tool Company 1925 General Line Catalog — 29
- Sargent Combination Planes (1080 & 1085) — 29
- The Sargent Tool Catalog Collection — 29
- General Line Catalog Ca. 1920 — 6
- General Line Catalog Ca. 1939 — 6
- The Art Of Fine Tools — 12
- The Handplane Book — 9
- The Tower & Lyon Company General Line Catalog — 29
- The Vaughn & Bushnell Company General Line Catalog — 29

Hand Tools
- Classic Hand Tools — 12
- Dictionary of Leather Working Tools — 12
- Ice Fishing Spears — 7
- The Hammer: The King of Tools — 12
- The Handplane Book — 9
- Traditional Woodworking Handtools — 12
- Tools: A Guide For Collectors — 15

History of Tools
- American Levels & Makers - New England — 3
- Anvils In America — 3
- Christopher Gabriel and the London Tool Trade — 19
- Directory Of American Tool Makers — 3
- Early Tools of New Jersey and the Men Who Made Them — 19
- Eighteenth-Century Woodworking Tools, Vol III — 19
- Engines Of Change: The American Industrial Revolution — 25
- Historic Trades Annual Volume I — 19
- Historic Trades Annual Volume II — 19
- New Hampshire Hand Tools & Makers 1800-1900 — 19
- Stewart Spiers and the Planemakers of Ayr — 9
- The Dictionary of Woodworking Tools — 12
- The Plumb Line Compendium — 12
- The Search For New Jersey Toolmakers — 19
- The Talking Machine Illustrated Compendi — 4
- The Ultimate Brace — 19
- Tools & Trades Of America's Past: The Mercer Museum Collection — 21
- Tools: Working Wood in Eighteenth Century America — 19

"How-To" Books
- Care & Repair of Antiques — 15
- How To Build Wooden Boats With 16 Small Boat Designs — 7
- How To Carve Wood — 13
- Jack Hill's Country Chair Making — 8
- Make A Windsor Chair With Michael Dunbar — 8
- Making Traditional Wooden Planes — 9
- Restoring Antique Tools — 15
- Ship Models: How To Build Them — 7
- Stonework Techniques & Projects — 4
- The Complete Guide to Sharpening — 11
- The Restoration Of Carriages — 14
- Tool Making For Woodworkers — 12
- Wheelmaking: Wagon Wheel Design and Construction — 14

Japanese Tools & Techniques
- The Complete Japanese Joinery — 10

Lathes & Turning
- A Treatise On Lathes and Turning — 14
- Beyond Basic Turning — 14
- Ornamental Turning — 14
- Turn A Bowl Get Great Results — 4
- Turning Lathes — 14
- Victorian Woodturning — 26

Machines of Every Sort
- Engines Of Change: The American Industrial Revolution — 25
- English & American Tool Builders — 25
- Machinery And Mechanical Devices: A Pictorial Archive — 25
- New Catechism Of The Steam Engine — 25
- Power & Machinery Employed in Manufactures — 25
- The Book Of Tools, Machinery & Supplies 1895 — 25
- Vintage Woodworking Machinery — 25

Woodworking Machinery	25
Machinists Tools	
A Brown & Sharpe Catalogue Collection	29
American Machinists Tools: Directory of Patents	25
English & American Tool Builders	25
Henry Disston & Sons Company General Line Catalog	29
Makers of American Machinist's Tools	25
More Makers of American Machinists Tools	25
Sawyer Tool Company: 1892 General Line Catalog	29
The Book Of Tools, Machinery & Supplies 1895	25
Nautical Topics	
A Shipyard In Maine: Great Schooners	7
American Sailing Ships Their Plans	7
Blow For The Landing 100 Years Of Steam	7
How To Build Wooden With 16 Small Boat Designs	7
Nautical Antiques	3
Scrimshaw The Whaler's	24
Ship Models: How To Build Them	7
The Arts Of The Sail: Knotting, Splicing, & Ropework	7
The Book Of Old Ships: Egyptian Galleys To Clipper Ships	7
The Seaman's Friend: A Treatise On Practical Seamanship	7
The Ship Model Builder's Assistant	7
Whale Ships & Whaling	7
Patent Guides	
American Levels Patents	3
American Machinists Tools: Directory of Patents	25
Manufactured and Patented Spokeshaves	19
Patent Sourcebook for Bitstock Tools	19
The American Patented Brace	19
Price Guides to Collectibles	
Antique Cigar Cutters & Lighters	18
Antique Lamp Buyers Guide	22
Antique Typewriters & Office Collectibles	15
Canes From The 17th To The	18
Cigarette Lighters Book Forcollectors	18
Cowboy Collectibles And Western	23
Cowboy Equipment With Values	15
Cowboys Stories And	15
Discovering Antique Phonographs	5
Hoard's Dairyman Dairy Collectibles	18
Just For Openers Guide To Beer, Soda,	18
Pocket Guide To Corkscrews, Book	18
Roadside Memories Collection Of Vintag	18
Scales A Collector's Guide	18
Sporting Collectable Stories And	18
Stick Making A Complete Course	18
The Ultimate Corkscrew Book	3
Walkingsticks Book For Collectors	18
Regional Studies	
Baskets And Basketmakers In Southern Appalachia	23
Early Tools of New Jersey and the Men Who Made Them	19
Engines Of Change: The American Industrial Revolution	25
Handicrafts Of The Southern Highlands	28
New Hampshire Hand Tools & Makers 1800-1900	19
Ohio Toolmakers And Their Tools	3
Old New England Homes 2nd Ed For	4
Stewart Spiers and the Planemakers of Ayr	9
The Search For New Jersey Toolmakers	19
Tools & Trades Of America's Past:	21
Reprinted Catalogs	
1874 Gurley Catalog	21
"The Level You Need"	29
A Brown & Sharpe Catalogue Collection	29
Edge Tools Catalogue 1909	29
Edward Preston & Son: 1909 General Line Catalog	6
Stanley General Line Catalog Ca. 1920	6
Stanley General Line Catalog Ca. 1939	6
Hammacher, Schlemmer & Co.:	29
Henry Disston & Sons Company Catalog Ca. 1874	29
Marble's Outing Equiptment	23
Marble's Specialities For Sportsman	23
Miller Falls Company 1887 General Line Catalog	29
Millers Falls Company Catalog No. 74	29
Millers Falls Company General Line Catalog Ca. 1915	29
Planes And Hardware Specialties	29
Sargent Combination Planes (1080 & 1085)	29
Sawyer Tool Company: 1892 General Line Catalog	29
Simonds Saw Mfr. Co. General Line Catalog	20
The Atha Tool Company General Line Catalog, 1883	29
The Belcher Bros. & Co.: Boxwood & Ivory Rules	29
The Book Of Tools, Machinery & Supplies 1895	25
The Buck Brothers 1890 General Line Catalog	29
The Chapin-Stephens Company Catalog No. 114	29
The Greenfield Tool Company 1872 General Line Catalog	29
The Handsaw Catalog Collection	20
The H.D. Smith & Company General Line Catalog	29
The James Swan Company General Line Catalog	29
The Peck, Stow & Wilcox Co. Catalog of Tools	29
The Russell Jennings Mfg.	29
The Sandusky Tool Company 1877 General Line Catalog	29
The Sandusky Tool Company 1925 General Line Catalog	29
The Sargent Tool Catalog Collection	29
The Tower & Lyon Company General Line Catalog	29
The Vaughn & Bushnell Company Catalog Ca. 1927	29
Shaker Life	
Shaker Architecture	8
The Book Of Shaker Furniture	8
The Shaker Legacy: Perspectives of an Enduring Tradition	8
Specialized Woodworking	
Boat Joinery & Cabinetmaking	4
Circular Work In Carpentry	11
English Historical Carpentry	11
Fine Woodworking on Planes & Chisels	12
Simplified Guide To Custom Stairbuilding	13
The Complete Japanese Joinery	10
The Complete Manual of Wood Veneering	10
The Finish Carpenter's Manual	11
The Marquetry Manual	11
The Pattern Maker's Assistant	28
Treatise On Stairbuilding & Handrailing	13
Victorian Ornamental Carpentry	11
Stanley Tools	
Antique & Collectible Stanley Tools	6
Boxwood & Ivory: Stanley Traditional Rules, 1855-1975	6
General Line Catalog Ca. 1920	6
General Line Catalog Ca. 1939	6
Stanley Rule & Level Company: Catalog No. 34, 1915 Edition	6
The Legend of Stanley: 150 Years of the Stanley Works	6
The Stanley Calalog Collection, Volume I	6
The Stanley Catalog Collection, Volume II	6
The Stanley Combination Plane	6
Tinsmithing	
Metalworking: A Book of Tools, Materials & Processes for the Handyman	27
Practical Metal Plate Work	27
The Art Of The Tinsmith: English & American	27
The Complete Metalsmith: An Illustrated Handbook	26
The Tinsmith's Helper and Pattern Book	27
Technical Topics	
1874 Gurley Catalog	21
A History of The Logarithmic Slide Rule and Allied Instruments	21
American Clocks And Clockmakers	15
Antique Medical Instruments	28
Collecting Figural Tape Measures	21
New Catechism Of The Steam Engine	25
Restoring Antique Tools	15
Scientific Instruments 1500-1900: An Introduction	21
Slide Rules: Their History Models And Makers	21
The Berger Handbook	21
The Construction and Principal Uses of Mathematical Instruments	21
Tool Value Guides	
Antique & Collectible Stanley Tools: Guide to Identity & Value (Softbound)	6
Collecting Antique Tools	9
Edward Preston & Son: 1909 General Line Catalog	6
Hammacher, Schlemmer & Co.:	29
Price Guide to Antique Tools	15
Prices Realized on Rare American Wooden Planes	15
Snap-on Collectibles: Unauthorized Guide with Prices	15
Tools: A Guide For Collectors	15
Trades of Every Sort	
Advanced Patternmaking	28
Dictionary of Leather Working Tools	12
Early American Copper Tin and Brass	26
Folk Art In America	5
Hand Bookbinding: A Manual Of Instruction	24
Handicrafts Of The Southern Highlands	28
Historic Trades Annual Volume I	19
Historic Trades Annual Volume II	19
Marble's Outing Equiptment	23
Marble's Specialities For Sportsman	23
Metalwork & Enamelling	26
Metalworking Trades in Early America	27
Metalworking: Tools, Materials & Processes	27
Papermaking	24
Pictorial Encyclopedia of Trades & Industries Volume I	24
Pictorial Encyclopedia of Trades and Industries, Volume II	24
Secrets Of Green Sand Casting	24
Silversmithing	27
Stonework Techniques & Projects	4
The American Pewterer: His Techniques & His Products	26
The Art Of Organ-Building	24
The Art Of The Decoy: American	15
The Book Of Trades	24
The Colonial Craftsman	5
The Colonial Printer	24
The Cooper And His Trade	24
The Pattern Maker's Assistant	28
This Was Mining In The West	20
Video Tapes	
Bench Planes Video Tape	21
Special Planes Video Tape	21
Stanley Planes by The Numbers	21
Hand Saw Sharpening Video	21
Make A Chair From A Tree Video Tape	21
Wood	
Great Wood Finishes A Step-by-step Guide	4
Identifying Wood: Accurate Results With Simple Tools	11
Old Ways Of Working Wood	10
Redwood Classics Stories And	20
The Complete Manual of Wood Veneering	10
The Conversion and Seasoning of Wood	10
Working With Wood The Basics Of Crafts	11
World Woods in Color	11
Wooden Planes	
British Planemakers From 1700	9
Edward Preston & Son: 1909 General Line Catalog	6
Guide To Canadian Plane Makers And	3
Makers of American Wooden Planes, 3rd Edition	9
Making Traditional Wooden Planes	9
Prices Realized on Imprinted American Wooden Planes	15
The Greenfield Tool Company 1872 General Line Catalog	29
The Sandusky Tool Company 1877 General Line Catalog	29
The Sandusky Tool Company 1925 General Line Catalog	29
The Wooden Plane: Its History, Form and Function	9
Wooden Planes In 19th Century America Volume II	9
Woodworking	
Circular Work In Carpentry	11
Green Woodworking	4
Identifying Wood: Accurate Results With Simple Tools	11
Modern Practical Joinery	10
Simplified Guide To Custom Stairbuilding	13
The Complete Dovetail Handmade Furniture's	10
The Complete Guide to Sharpening	11
The Complete Japanese Joinery	10
The Complete Manual of Wood Veneering	10
The Complete Woodworker	10
The Conversion and Seasoning of Wood	10
The Dictionary of Woodworking Tools	12
The Finish Carpenter's Manual	11
The Marquetry Manual	11
The Pattern Maker's Assistant	28
The Toolbox Book	11
The Wood Wright's Eclectic Workshop	10
The Woodworker's Guide to Hand Tools	12
The Woodwright's Apprentice: 20 Favorite Projects	10
The Woodwright's Work Book	10
The Woodwrights Shop Trad. Woodcraft	10
The Workbench Book	11
The Workshop Book	11
Tool Making For Woodworkers	12
Treatise On Stairbuilding & Handrailing	13
Working With Wood The Basics Of Crafts	11
World Woods in Color	11
Wrenches	
American Wrench Makers	12
Antique & Unusual Wrenches	12
The History of Old Time Farm Implement Wrenches	3

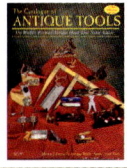

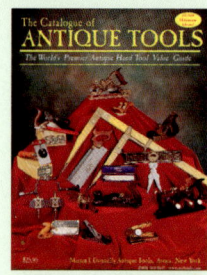 

Don't Miss Our Spectacular
MILLENNIUM EDITION

Now Shipping   6500 Tools   Details: Page 2

Books Make Great Gifts...
for Father's Day, Birthdays and More

175 New Titles in Stock!

Great Gift Ideas for Antique Enthusiasts

Martin J. Donnelly Antique Tools
PO Box 281 Bath NY 14810-0281

Toll Free: (800) 869-0695
Phone: (607) 566-2617
FAX: (607) 566-2575
E-Mail: mjd@mjdtools.com
Find Us On The Web: www.mjdtools.com

www.mjdtools.com

BULK RATE
U.S. POSTAGE
PAID
Bath, New York
PERMIT NO. 43

Index

A. & M., Buffalo, New York ... 114
A.M. Tool Co., Cleveland, Ohio ... 28
A.P.W. Paper Co., Albany, New York ... 122
A.T.F. Co. ... 198
Abercrombie & Fitch, New York ... 196
Abingdon ... 114
Abington, Sheffield, England ... 230
Ackley, W.H. ... 194
Acme ... 168, 204, 236
Acme Level Company, Toledo, Ohio ... 32
Acme Rule Company ... 26
Adams, Geo. H. ... 178
Adams, Z., Philadelphia, Pennsylvania ... 78
Adamson Mfg. Co., E. Pales. Ohio ... 212
Addis & Sons, J. B., Sheffield, England ... 54, 98
Addis, J.B., Sheffield, England ... 98
Addis, S.J., London ... 54, 98, 146, 170, 190
Adjustable Gauge Co., Lexington, Kentucky ... 266
Adzes ... 44, 70, 112, 186
Aiken ... 208
Aiken, F.H. ... 78
Ainsley, J.D., South Shields ... 40
Air, Living On ... See Riley, Richard J.
Alaska Freezer Co., Winchendon, Massachusetts ... 86
Albertson & Co., Pokeepsie, New York ... 96
Alderman ... 204
Aldrich, Milton., Lowell, Massachusetts ... 86
Allen & Co., (Providence, Rhode Island) ... 146
Alteneder & Sons, Theo, Philadelphia, Pennsylvania ... 42, 198
Amer. Circular Loom Co., Chelsea, Massachusetts ... 48
American. Mfg. Concern, Rochester, New York ... 36
American Plierwrench Co., Chicago, Illinois ... 114
American Ax & Tool Co., Glassport, Pennsylvania ... 56, 168
American Fork & Hoe Company ... 82, 198
American Institute, New York ... 36
American Leathersupply Co., Providence, Rhode Island ... 194
American Plierench Corp., Chicago, Illinois ... 270, 276
American Ratchet ... 150
American Saw Co., Newark, New Jersey ... 260
American Steel & Wire Company ... 110
American Tool. Co., Pawtucket, Rhode Island ... 124
American Wrench Co., Augusta, Maine ... 260
Amon Spring Needle Works., New Britain, Connecticut ... 178
Amos, John P., Rochester, New York ... 30
Ampco, Milwaukee, Wisconsin ... 236
Anderson, A., Boston, Massachusetts ... 172
Andruss, Newark, New Jersey ... 250, 258
Angier M' Intire ... 250
Anvils ... 74, 218
Apple Parers ... 122
Appleton Mfg. Co., Philadelphia, Pennsylvania ... 198
Appleton, Thos., Boston, Massachusetts ... 130
Archimedian Drills ... 156
Arlindo ... 78
Armco ... 208
Armstrong Mfg. Co., Bridgeport, Connecticut ... 172
Arnold & Walker, London, England ... 82
Arrow ... 218
Arthington, Manchester ... 46
Arthur, Edinburgh (Scotland) ... 20, 108
Arthur, Henry, New York, New York ... 174
Ash & Co., Wm. ... 54, 98
Asher & Adams ... 182
Aston & Mander, Soho, London ... 30
Atha Tool Co. ... 96, 248
Atha Tool Co., Newark, New Jersey ... 96, 202
Athol Machine Co., Athol, Massachusetts ... 32, 66, 80, 204
Atkin & Sons, Birmingham (England) ... 130, 180
Atkins & Co., E.C., Indianapolis, Indiana 36, 64, 70, 74, 92, 118, 150, 206, 240, 260, 262
Atlas Tool Co., Los Angeles, California ... 196
Attwood Mfg. Co., The, Conneaut, Ohio ... 100
Atwood, Geo. F., Brockton, Massachusetts ... 212
Auburn Lumber Co., Auburn, California ... 214
Auburn Tool Co., Auburn, New York68, 108, 130, 148, 234, 250, 258, 274
Audel, Theo. & Co. ... 182
Augur Bits36, 62, 66, 84, 86, 126, 144, 180, 208, 252, 254, 260, 278
Augur Handles ... 84, 126, 260
Aux Mines De Suede, Paris ... 186
Auxer & Remley, Lancaster, Pennsylvania ... 154
Auxer, Samuel, Lancaster, Pennsylvania ... 160
Awls ... 84, 120, 156, 208, 276
Axes ... 44, 56, 62, 70, 168, 186, 198, 252, 260, 278
B. & J. Mfg. Co., Detroit, Michigan ... 206
B. Mfg. Assoc. ... 64
B.W. Co., Newark, New Jersey ... 48
Bach & Co., S.F.L., Boston, Massachusetts ... 64
Backus, Q.S, Holyoke, Massachusetts ... 254
Bailey And Company, L., Hartford ... 16
Bailey Tool Co., Woonsocket, Rhode Island ... 136
Bailey, John, Widdifield, Ontario ... 202
Bailey, L., Boston, Massachusetts ... 112, 228, 264
Bailey, L., New Britain, Connecticut ... 264
Bailey, Leonard ... 16, 18, 58, 94
Baker, Hamilton & Co., San.Francisco., California ... 56
Baldwin, A. & E., New York ... 52, 188, 274
Bargains, Big Time ... Throughout
Barlow Hardware Co., Corry, Pennsylvania ... 182
Barlow, S.H., Lacona, New York ... 4
Barnes ... 228
Barnes, L.P. ... 28
Barnes, R. (Orange, Massachusetts) ... 68
Bartholomew, H. S., Bristol, Connecticut ... 182
Bartlett & Co. ... 70
Bartlett, A.C. ... 46, 52
Bartlett, S.B., Watertown, New York ... 46
Barton & Co., D.R., Rochester, New York 54, 68, 98, 112, 162, 164, 170, 188, 190, 200, 248, 258
Barton, D.R. & Smith, Wm. P., Rochester, New York ... 220
Bauer, P. ... 78
Bauge, J.L. ... 16
Bauman & Sons, Frank W. ... 114
Baxter, William, Newark, New Jersey ... 48, 152
Bay State Saw Mfg. Co., Fitchburg, Massachusetts ... 202
Bay State Tool Co. ... 236, 260
Beaders ... 18, 58, 106, 146, 158, 160, 180, 220, 230, 264, 278
Bean, L.L., Freeport, Maine ... 168
Beatty & Co., W., Chester, Pennsylvania ... 56
Beatty, J. ... 44
Bedini, Silvio A. ... 110
Bee, Wm., Sheffield, England ... 20
Belcher & Loomis, Providence, Rhode Island ... 174
Belcher Bros. & Co., New-York ... 26, 76
Belcher Bros., Providence, Rhode Island ... 188
Belcher, Z., Sheffield, England ... 140
Belden Machine Co., New Haven, Connecticut ... 202, 278
Belknap Hardware Co., Louisville, Kentucky56, 72, 88, 98, 160, 202
Bell, J. ... 80
Bell, John, Philada., Pennsylvania ... 200
Bemis & Call Co., Springfield, Massachusetts 114, 132, 152, 204, 224, 260
Benjamin, G., Avoca, New York ... 20
Bensen & Crannell, Albany ... 188, 200, 210, 234
Bensen, D., Albany, New York ... 210
Benson & Mockridge ... 52
Benton ... 270
Berezeiat, Paris ... 248
Berg, Erik, Eskilstuna, Sweden ... 54, 164, 170
Berger, C.L. ... 34
Bergman Tool Mfg. Co., Buffalo, New York ... 270
Bernz Co., Otto, Rochester, New York ... 212
Berry, G., Old Street, London ... 258
Berylco ... 228
Bessey ... 100
Bethlehem Wrench Co., Bethlehem, Pennsylvania ... 236
Bevels ... 80, 86, 94, 120, 132, 158, 180, 186, 222, 252, 266
Bewley, Warranted ... 68
Bigelow & Dowse Co., Boston, Massachusetts ... 36, 56, 202
Billings & Edmands Mfg. Co. ... 218
Billings & Spencer Co., The, Hartford, Connecticut 48, 88, 100, 104, 114, 134, 172, 180, 204, 228, 236, 246, 260, 270
Billings, J.P., Clinton, Maine ... 112
Birch & Co., John,(Birmingham, England ... 234
Birmingham Plane Manufacturing Company ... 16, 58
Bishop & Co., Geo. H., Cincinnati, Ohio ... 92, 240
Bishop & Co., Geo. H., Lawrenceburg, Indiana ... 240, 260, 278
Bittner, Jack ... 182
Blaisdell, A.H. ... 102
Bleckman ... 218
Blier, Pierre, St. Eleuthere, P.Q. ... 202
Blood, I., Ballston, New York ... 56
Bloomer & Phillips ... 20
Blue Point ... 48, 54
Boardman, B., Norwich, Connecticut ... 152
Boes Co., The W.W., Dayton, Ohio ... 42
Boker & Co., H., Germany ... 198, 224, 260
Boker, H., Germany ... 124
Bonney Forge & Tool Works ... 270
Bonney Vise & Tool Works Inc. ... 172
Boos Tool Corp., Kansas City, Missouri ... 204, 236
Booth & Mills, Philadelphia, Pennsylvania ... 104
Booth & Son, John, Philadelphia, Pennsylvania ... 104
Booth Brothers, Dublin, Ireland ... 234
Booth, J.,(Philadelphia) ... 122
Booth, R.W., Cincinnati, Ohio ... 258
Borden Tool Co., Warren, Ohio ... 212
Boring Machines ... 44, 84
Bornstein, H. ... 48
Borthwick, John, Atlantic City, New Jersey ... 64
Boston Brass, Waltham, Massachusetts ... 212
Boston Wrench Co., Boston, Massachusetts ... 172, 236
Boudreau & Co., L. ... 78
Boulet's Fine Tool Works ... 224
Bow Drills ... 10, 138
Bower, W. ... 20
Bowser & Co., S.F., Fort Wayne, Indiana ... 104
Boyle, J.E. Co., Ltd., Maniwaki, Quebec, Canada ... 202
Boynton, E.M. ... 64
Braces .. 8, 20, 62, 84, 118, 138, 150, 158, 160, 186, 228, 252, 262
Bradford, J., Portland, Maine ... 186
Bradley Smith Co. ... 36
Braime, England ... 218
Braunsdorf-Mueller Co. ... 34
Breast Drills ... 20, 62, 138
Bridge City Tool Co., Portland, Oregon ... 222
Bridge Tool Co., St. Louis, Missouri ... 128
Bridge, Washington, D.C. ... 188, 232
Bridgeport Gun Implement Co., The ... 146
Bridgeport H.M. Corp., Bridgeport, Connecticut ... 208
Bridgeport Hardware Mfg. Co., The ... 168, 212, 228
Bridgeport Hdwe. Mfg. Corp. ... 228
Brinkerhoff & Son, Upper Sandusky, Ohio ... 122
Bristol, C.B. ... 48
Brooks, P. ... 46
Brooks, P., E. Hartford (Connecticut.) ... 108
Brown & Barnard ... 234
Brown & Sharpe Mfg. Co., Providence, Rhode Island 18, 44, 50, 66, 78, 80, 82, 124, 132, 146, 178, 194, 206, 222, 224, 266, 276
Brown Quality Machine Company ... 72
Brown, C. ... 44
Brown, G. ... 240
Brown, J.T.,(Baltimore) ... 210
Brown, Jas., St. Vincent St., Glasgow, Scotland ... 50
Bruin & Co., Bristol (England) ... 40
Bruno Tools, Beverly Hills, California ... 180, 254
Bryan Plow ... 152
Buck & Hickman, London, England ... 66, 126
Buck & Ryan Ltd., London ... 278
Buck Bros., Millbury, Massachusetts . 44, 54, 82, 98, 164, 190, 208
Buck Brothers ... 54, 58, 98, 160, 170, 190
Buck Brothers, Millbury, Massachusetts ... 190
Buck, G., London ... 198
Buck, Tottenham Road, London, England ... 264
Buckeye ... 180, 230
Buell, F.A., St. Paul, Minnesota ... 68
Buffum Tool Co., Louisiana, Missouri ... 212, 236
Bullard ... 48, 100, 114, 270
Buller ... 64
Burge ... 44
Burke Tobacco Co., R.M., Utica, New York ... 122
Burnham Co., The George, Worcester ... 96
Burnham Jr., George, Amherst, Massachusetts ... 258
Burrowes, E.T. Co., Portland, Maine ... 188
Burt, G.W. ... 250
Bush, George W., President of the United States ... 43rd
Butcher, W. ... 170
Butcher, W., Sheffield (England) ... 98
Butterises ... 170
Button Hole Cutters ... 194
B.V.C. ... 194
Bywater, Richard, London ... 232
C & F Mfg. Co. ... 270
Cahill Forge & Foundry Corp. ... 186
Calculators ... 4, 10, 50
Calef ... 114
Calipers4, 6, 10, 12, 28, 30, 74, 80, 96, 132, 140, 160, 178, 206, 224, 272, 276
Callendar & Co., B., Boston, Massachusetts ... 156, 258
Campbell, J. ... 18
Canastota Knife Company, The ... 122
Cantelo, J. S., Boston, Massachusetts ... 220
Canuck Tool Co., Toronto, Canada ... 114, 172
Capitol ... 270
Carabel, Carlo ... 48
Carborundum Co., Niagara Falls, New York ... 198
Card, S.W., Mansfield, Massachusetts ... 100
Carey & Bros. Co., Thomas, Baltimore, Maryland ... 174
Carll ... 204
Carlson & Sullivan, Monrovia, California ... 60
Carpenter's Slicks ... 44, 186
Carpenter, D. H. ... 114
Carpenter, E.W., Lancaster, Pennsylvania ... 12, 154, 162
Carter, C., Syracuse, New York ... 210
Carter, Edward, Troy, New York ... 108
Carter, R., Troy, New York ... 274
Carving Tools ... 54, 98, 146, 170, 190
Cary, London ... 184
Casartelli & Son, J., Manchester ... 214
Casella, L., London, England ... 6
Casey & Co., Auburn, New York ... 68, 200, 234
Casey, Clark & Co., Auburn, New York ... 148
Casey, Kitchell & Co., Auburn, New York ... 148, 200

Caspar, A., Sooutah, Illinois 70
Caspers, J., Lancaster, Wisconsin. 278
Catalogues 18, 50, 82, 96, 144, 158, 174, 182, 194
Catalogue of Antique Tools, Hierarchial Ranking 1
Cedarberg Mfg. Co., Minneapolis. 34
Chadwick, J., Manchester, England 10
Challenge Cutlery Corp., Bridgeport, Connecticut 222
Chamfer Guides 220
Champion Dearment, Meadville, Pennsylvania. 78
Champion Fitzall 56, 168
Chandler & Farquar Co., Boston, Massachusetts. 174
Chandler Co, Cedar Rapids, Iowa. 114
Chandler, C.E., Boston, Massachusetts 134
Chantrell, Felix. 236
Chapin's Son Co., H. 26
Chapin, A., Troy, New Hampshire 54
Chapin, E.M. 10
Chapin, E.M., Pine Meadow, Connecticut. 26
Chapin, Frank, Pine Meadow, Connecticut. 4
Chapin, H., U.S. Standard. 184
Chapin, H., Union Factory. 26, 30, 68, 102, 142, 162, 184, 188, 200, 226, 238, 258, 272, 278
Chapin, N., Eagle Factory. 274
Chapin, N., New Hartford, Connecticut. 162
Chapin-Stephens Co., The . 26, 40, 76, 142, 184, 214, 226, 242, 272
Charlton, J., Newark, New Jersey 78
Chase, D.G., Boston 194
Chase, R.G. 64
Chatillon, New York, New York 122, 198
Cheeseman, James 240
Chelor, Ce., Living In Wrentham 6
Chelor, Ce., Wrentham 46
Cheney Corp., H., Little Falls, New York 88, 168, 248
Chesterman & Co., Ltd., Sheffield, England 132, 206, 224
Chesterman, Sheffield, England 36
Chevillon A Auxerre. 70
Child, J. E., Providence, Rhode Island 108
Chisels 44, 54, 62, 86, 98, 146, 160, 164, 170, 174, 190, 208, 260, 278
Chloride Of Silver Battery Co., ... 50
Christensen, A.M., Brockton, Massachusetts. 78
Cincinnati Tool Co., The 86, 124, 136, 264
Clamps. 20, 60, 86, 124, 198, 262, 276
Clark, Alfred. 246
Clark, D.. 108
Clark, H., Utica, New York. 46
Clark, William A. 126
Clerline, Weedsport, New York. 86
Cleveland Autmatic Machine Co. 50
Cleveland Twist Drill Co., The 36, 254
Cleveland Wrench Co., Cleveland, Ohio 260
Climax 236
Clip-Bar Mfg. Co. 172
Clipper Tool Co., Buffalo, New York 118
Cochran 152, 204
Coes & Co., A.G., Worcester, Massachusetts. 152
Coes & Co., L., Worcester, Massachusetts. 48, 204, 270
Coes Wrench Co. 100, 114, 152, 270
Coes Wrench Co., Worcester, Massachusetts 36, 48, 66, 100
Collins & Company, Hartford, Connecticut. 44, 56, 112, 168
Collins & Robbins, Utica, New York 130, 148
Collins, Utica, New York 52, 130, 148
Colp, G. 194
Colton, J., Market St., Philadelphia, Pennsylvania. 130, 250
Columbian Hdwe. Co., Cleveland, Ohio 218
Columbian Wrench, Brockton, Massachusetts. 172
Combination Squares 42, 86, 180, 222, 260, 266, 276, 278
Comp. Of Artists 274
Compasses 28, 42, 50, 66, 70, 80, 132, 206, 224
Concise 30
Connecticut Valley Mfg. Co. 66, 110, 182, 254
Consolidated Tool Co., New York, New York 132, 138
Cook, J.F. & Keller, A., New York,. 26
Cooper, Joseph 20
Copeland & Co., Warranted 200, 232
Copeland, D.. . . . . 188, 278
Copeland, D. & M. 52
Copeland, M. & A. 162
Copeland, M.. . . . . 162, 188, 210, 250, 274
Corcoran, Bryan,31 Cork Lane 238
Corgi Toys, Ltd., Swansea (England 120, 158
Corning, Arthur W., New York 80
Cornwell Quality Tools Co. 100
Coughtry, J., Albany, New York 130
Cowell &chapman, New Castle (England) 162
Cowgill, C.D. 10
Cox & Luckman, Birmingham, England. 250
Cox, I.,(Birmingham, England). 46
Craft P.M.I. Co., Conneaut, Ohio 172
Craft Tool Co., The, Conneaut, Ohio. 204
Crafts & Co., Arthur A., Boston, M 82
Craftsman Tool Co., Conneaut, Ohio. 48
Crane, D.O., Utica, New York. 108, 274
Crawford, J., Newark, New Jersey 78
Creagh & Pickard, Cincinnati, Ohio. 52
Creagh & Williams, Cincinnati, Ohio. 108
Crescent Tool Co., Jamestown, New York . 66, 100, 156, 204, 208, 236, 246, 270
Cresson, W., Philadelphia. 222
Cressy, J. 114
Croissant & Bro., C., Albany, New York. 64
Crosby Steam Gage & Valve, Boston, Massachusetts 50
Crossman & Co., C.P., Fitchburg, Massachusetts 126
Crossman, A.W. 98
Crow (John), Canterbury, England 162
Cumings & Gale,(Providence, Rhode Island.). 68
Cumings, A., Boston, Massachusetts 186, 188, 232
Cumings, S.,(Providence, R.I.) 46
Cunneen Co., N. Rochelle, New York (Unmarked) 196
Currie, Glasgow, Scotland 52
Currier- Koeth Mfg. Co. 146
Curtis, F., Stockbridge, Massachusetts. 102, 154
Cushman & Denison 28
Cutters 146
D. & S., Bangor, Maine. 80, 224, 266
D.B. & S., Providence, Rhode Island 80, 178, 222, 224, 276
D.B. Co. 218
Dalpe S., Roxton Pond, Quebec 234
Danberry, E., N. Brunswick, N. J. 52, 68
Danielson Co., J.P., Jamestown, New York 246
Darling, Brown & Sharpe, Providence, Rhode Island 80, 132, 178, 224
Dasco 88
Davenport. 98
Davidson, Marshall & Namuth, Hans 110, 182
Davis & Cook, Watertown, New York 32, 238
Davis Expansion Boring Tool Co.. 178
Davis Instrument Mfg. Co., Baltimore, Maryland 122
Davis, G., Birmingham, England. 68
Davis, L.L., Springfield, Massachusetts 32, 142
Davis, Level & Tool Co., Springfield, Massachusetts . 16, 18, 32, 58, 142, 150, 238
Dawson, J., Montreal, Quebec, Canada. 250
De Lacy, G., New York 78
De Sancon, B.F. 88
De Wolf, Lucien 42
Dean, S., Dedham (Massachusetts) 18, 108
Decatur Coffin Co., Decatur, Illinois 104, 156
Deering Harvester Company. 182
Deforest, Birmingham (Connecticut) 46
Delta Specialty Co., Milwaukee, Wisconsin 196
Delve, I. 148
Deming, F.B., Calais, Maine. 42
Denison & Co., G.W., Winthrop, Connecticut. 68
Denison, C.H., Freeport, Maine 108
Denison, J. 234
Denison, J. & L., Saybrook, Connecticut. 52
Dentist Supply Co., The, New York,. 42
Depth Gauges 50, 66, 80, 120, 132, 158, 178, 206, 276
Derby Bit Co., Ansonia, Connecticut 126
Desforges, I.B. 232
Detroit Lock & Variety Works 28
Detroit Shear Co. 122
Devoe, F.W. & Reynolds, C.T., New York 194
Diamond Edge 278
Diamond Tool And Horseshoe Co. 66, 152, 246, 270
Diamond Wrench Co., Portland, Maine. 152
Dibb, W., York 234
Dibner, Bern. 182
Dickinson & Co. 262
Die Stocks 124, 212
Dietzgen Co., Eugene, Chicago 30, 60, 174, 178, 276
Dikeman Mfg. Co., The, South Norwalk, Connecticut 208
Disston & Morss, Philadelphia, Pennsylvania 94, 222
Disston & Son, Henry, Philadelphia, Pennsylvania. 156, 240
Disston & Sons, Henry, Philadelphia, Pennsylvania 36, 60, 64, 82, 92, 94, 118, 122, 142, 180, 182, 190, 196, 222, 240, 260, 266, 278
Disston, Henry, Philadelphia. 92
Disston-Carlson, Philadelphia., Pennsylvania 60
Dividers. 42, 80, 132, 144, 178, 224
Dixon Crucible Co., Jersey City, New Jersey 42
Dixon, William, Newark, New Jersey 82, 138
Dobson 124
Dodd, Wm. & Co. 224
Dole, I.A, Salem, O. 90
Dordea Mfg. Co., Detroit, Michigan. 178
Doscher Plane & Tool Co., The. 108, 130, 232
Double Claw Hammer Co., The 202, 248
Douglass Mfg. Co. 54, 90, 98, 164, 170
Douglass, New York. 46
Dowel Machines. 24
Doweling Jigs. 66, 86, 120
Drabble & Sanderson, London 240
Drafting Sets 42
Draw Gauges 78
Draw Knives 86, 112, 144, 220, 228, 252, 264, 278
Drew & Co., C., Kingston, Massachusetts. 112, 228
Drill Presses 90, 160
Drummond, J., Edinburgh. 92
Dryburgh, N.E. Hope, Ontario. 162
Dryburgh, Toronto (Canada). 108
Dudly Mfg. Co., A., Menominee, Michigan 278
Dumont Tool Co. 150
Dunbar, D. 102
Dunham & Mc Master, Auburn, New York 188, 210
Dunham, S.C. & Mc Master, T.J. 130
Dunn Edge Tool Co., Oakland, Maine 36
Dwights & French 200, 210
E. & T. Mfg. Co. 178
E. Prince Groff Mfg. Co., Camden, New Jersey 172
E.F.B. & Co.. 74
E.R: 148
E.T.F. Ltd., St. Catharines, Canada 228
Eagle Mng. Co. 68
Eagle Pencil Co., New York 80
Eagle Rule Mfg. Corp., New York 214
Eagle Square Mfg. Co. 36, 44, 174, 266
Early American Industries Association.. 36
Eastburn R., (New Brunswick, New Jersey) 188, 250
Eastern Machine Screw Corp., New Haven, Connecticut 236
Eastwood, G., York 250, 258
Eberhard Faber 194
Eden Specialty Co., The 66
Edgerton, H.S., German, New York 138
Edmonds-Metzel Mfg. Co., Chicago 114
Edwards & Walker Co., Portland, Maine 186
Efficient Wrench Co., Cleveland, Ohio 152
Elastic Tip Co. 172
Elgin 100
Ellis 48, 172
Ellsworth, Geo., S. Garder (Massachusetts) 264
Elsworth, John, Glasgow (Scotland) 234, 274
Emir, London 68
Enders, William, St. Louis, Missouri. 160
Engert & Rolfe, London, England 214
Engineering Products Ltd., London, England 134
Erie Tool Works, The, Erie, Pennsylvania. 172, 204, 236
Erlandsen, N., New York 4, 16
Escher & Sons, J.G. 36
Esterbrook Steel Pen Mfg. Co. 66
Estwing Mfg. Co., Rockford, Illinois 168
Evans & Co., Old Change, London. 50
Evansville Tool Works, Evansville 70, 88
Excelsior Mfg. Co. 254
Extra Quality 232
F. Mc C. 50, 214
F.M.R. & Co. 236
F.W.D. & Co. 194
F.W.S., New York 90
Faber, A.W., Newark, New Jersey. 30
Faber-Castell, Germany 30
Fabian Son, Derby, Maine 140
Fanner Mfg. Co. 218
Farmar 30
Farnham, Alexander 182
Farr, J.W., New York, New York. 188
Farrand Sales Corp., New York, New York 60
Farrand, Hiram A., Inc., Berlin, New Hampshire. 60
Favor, Ruhl & Co., Chicago, Illinois. 66
Fay, Charles B., Springfield, Massachusetts 178
Federal Land Bank Of Springfield 140
Fenn & Co., Joel, Wallingford, Connecticut. 188
Fenn, J., Newgate St. (London, England) 8, 20
Fenton & Marsden, Sheffield (England) 20, 102
Ferdin. 260
Field, Alfred, Sheffield, England. 136
Fish, A., Lowell, Massachusetts 162, 188, 274
Fish, J., New York 232
Fisher & Norris, Trenton, New Jersey. 218
Fisk, S. 52
Fitch, W.. 148
Fitchburg Tool Co. Fitchburg, Massachusetts 32
Flash Sales Corp., The, Chicago, Illinois 146
Flather & Sons, D., Sheffield, England 20
Flather, D., Solly Works, Sheffield, England. 20
Flexible Carbon Scraper Co., La, C 212
Folding Rules . 4, 6, 10, 26, 30, 40, 42, 50, 62, 76, 86, 96, 120, 140, 158, 174, 184, 186, 214, 226, 242, 272, 276, 278
Ford Motor Co., Dearborn, Michigan. 36, 212
Fordham, J., Sag Harbor (New York) 96
Forged Steel Prod., Newport, Pennsylvania. 246
Fowler & Co., Manchester (England. 50
Fowler, Philadelphia. 194
Fox & Son, L., Amherst, Massachusetts 188
Fraley, P.B., Philadelphia, Pennsylvania 196
Frasse & Co., New York, New York 194
Fray & Co, C.S., Bridgeport, Connecticut. 208
Fray & Co., John S. 138, 150
Fray & Co., John S. (?) 150, 208
Fray & Co., John S., Bridgeport, Connecticut. 150
Fray, J.S. 150
Frisk, O., Kiron, Iowa. 64
Froes 70
Frog Tool Co. Ltd., Chicago, Illinois. 160
Frogatt, B. 162
Frost, Dove Street, Norwich, England. 240

Entry	Pages
Fuller & Field.	18
Fuller, C., Causeway St., Boston, Massachusetts	68, 112, 258
Fuller, Jo., Providence, Rhode Island.	14, 22, 46, 52, 68
Fulton Tool Company	58, 168, 278
Fulton, New York, New York	58, 72, 98
Furbish & Hamlin, Augusta, Maine	156
G.E.	96
G.T.L.	58
Gabriel,(London).	274
Gage Tool Co., Vineland, New Jersey.	58, 72
Gardam & Son, Wm., New York, New York.	42
Gardner & Brazer, Boston, (Massachusetts)	186
Gardner & Murdock, Boston, Massachusetts	130, 188, 234, 274
Gardner, L., Green Street, Boston, Massachusetts	188
Gardner, T.J., Narrow Wine, Bristol, England	240
Gargory, James.	10
Garland Mfg. Co.	202
Gauges	42, 50, 74, 78, 80, 96, 102, 124, 126, 132, 194, 198, 206, 224, 266, 276
Gearench Mfg. Co., Houston, Texas	100
Gee, New York, New York	194
Geer, D.S. & S.P., Syracuse, New York.	130
Geer, John, Holden, Massachusetts	64
Geiger, G., Philadelphia, Pennsylvania	228
Gellman Wrench Corp.	48, 114
General Electric Corp., Schenectady, New York	50, 186
General Hardware Mfg. Co.	50, 118
George, M.	108
Geral.	136, 264
Gerber Scientific Co., The, Hartford, Connecticut.	30
Germantown Tool Works, Philadelphia, Pennsylvania.	168
Gesch, E.S., Germany.	152
Gibbs, I.H., New York	126, 254
Gibson, J., Albany (New York)	68, 148
Gilbert, J.,(New Haven, Connecticut.)	232
Gillies Bros., Braeside, Ontario.	202
Gilmour & Co., Gatineau Mills, P.Q.	202
Gilson (Unmarked).	30
Gladding, R.	148
Gladwin & Appleton, Boston, Massachusetts	258, 274
Glass Cutters.	74, 194, 198
Gleave, Manchester	200
Gleave, Oldham St., Manchester	162, 200
Gocher, George	14
Gohm Mfg. Co., Saginaw, Michigan.	66
Goodale, J.W., Amherst, Massachusetts	250
Goodell Bros. Company, Greenfield, Massachusetts	138, 150
Goodell Co., Antrim, New Hampshire	194
Goodell Tool Co., Shelburne Falls, Massachusetts.	86, 138, 150
Goodell-Pratt Company	20, 32, 44, 74, 80, 82, 90, 94, 96, 124, 128, 138, 142, 160, 172, 174, 178, 180, 206, 212, 222, 224, 260, 276
Goodman, W. L.	110, 174
Gordon	100, 172, 204
Gouch, F.J., Worcester, Massachusetts	258
Gouges	54, 98, 160, 170, 186, 190, 262
Gould Products Co., Oakland, California.	36
Grafting Froes	198
Grangeret A Paris	8
Grannis, J.	100
Grant & Co., W.T.	214
Grant, Thomas,(New York, New York)	18
Grau, G.	224
Graves, J., Bangor, Maine	260
Graves, J.D., Sheffield, England.	230
Great Stuff.	All Pages
Greble, Turner & Co., Hamilton, O.	10
Green, Iohn.	162, 210
Greene, Tweed & Co., New York, New York	134
Greenfield Tap & Die Corp., Massachusetts	124
Greenfield Tool Co., Greenfield, Massachusetts.	148, 162, 210, 250, 274
Greenleaf, F.M., Littleton, New Hampshire	10
Greenlee Tool Co., Rockford, Illinois.	44, 126, 146, 164, 254, 278
Greenslade, W., Bristol (England)	130, 148, 200, 210
Gregg, I.	162
Grier, William.	110
Griffin, Ravenna, Ohio.	234
Griffiths, Norwich (England).	108, 130
Griplock, Norfolk, Nebraska.	152
Griswold & Co., G.G.	254
Groves & Sons, R., Sheffield, England	92, 190
Guild Machine Co., C.D., Attleboro, Massachusetts	48
Gurley, W. & L.E., Troy, New York	42, 50, 140, 174
H. & E. Wrench Co., New Bedford, Massachusetts	114, 152, 270
H. Gerstner & Sons, Dayton, Ohio	146
H.D.	162
Hack Saws	196
Haines & Smith, Portland (Maine)	46
Halden & Co., Ltd., Manchester, England.	26
Halden & Company	26
Haley & Son, London, England	50
Hall	114
Hall & Knapp, New Britain, Connecticut.	94, 222
Hall Co., The Chas. E., Buffalo, New York	152
Hall, Robinson, Sheffield, England.	278
Hammacher Schlemmer & Co., New York	82, 146
Hammer Dry Plate Co., St. Louis, Missouri	202
Hammers	12, 14, 36, 62, 66, 70, 74, 78, 88, 96, 124, 180, 198, 202, 212, 228, 248, 252, 262, 276
Hammond Mfg. Co., Boston, Massachusetts	172, 204
Hammond, C., Philadelphia, Pennsylvania	168
Hammond, I., New Haven, Connecticut.	46, 262
Hand Drills.	42, 74, 84, 120, 138, 146, 156, 158, 198
Hand Vises	42, 74, 126, 146, 198, 218
Hanna, Roger	45 Only
Hanover, J. C., Cincinnatti., Ohio.	78
Harling, W.H., London, England.	50
Harris & Shepherd, L. Falls, New York.	148, 188
Harrison, J. & H., Newcastle (England)	124, 250
Hart Mfg. Co.	278
Hartford Hardware Co., Hartford, Connecticut	270
Harwood,	258
Haselton, R. B., Contoocook, New Hampshire.	140
Haselton, R.B., Groton, New Hampshire.	140
Hatchets	44, 56, 62, 144, 168, 218, 228, 252, 278
Hathersich, George (Manchester, England)	250, 258
Haw Hdwe. Co., Ottumwa, Iowa	56
Hawke, H., Solly Works, Sheffield, England.	20
Hayden's Patent	100, 246
Hayden, Syracuse, New York.	68, 274
Hazen, E.	198
Heald, Addison, Milford, New Hampshire.	46, 258
Healthways, Los Angeles, California.	186
Healy, Chas., Sheffield, England.	136
Hebert, J.R., Brooklyn, New York.	134
Helb, Edward, Railroad, Pennsylvania.	32, 142
Heller Bros. Co., Newark, New Jersey.	66, 170, 202, 212, 260
Hemsley, R., Montreal, P.Q., Canada.	74
Hendee Mfg. Co., Springfield, Massachusetts	172
Henshaw, Edward	174
Herbert Et Guertin, Ste. Madeleine	202
Herculever Co., New York	228
Herring Bros., London (England)	54
Hesjah	194
Hewett	172
Hibbard, Spencer & Bartlett Co.	32, 56, 58, 208, 246
Hickock, W.O., Harrisburg, Pennsylvania	262
Hicks, J.	56, 190
Hide, A. , Norwich, Connecticut.	232
Hields, William, Nottingham, England	22
Higgins & Libby, Portland, Maine	186
Higgs, Edward,(London)	162
Hildreth, S.W., Athol Depot, Massachusetts	150
Hill, J.V., Gray's Inn Road, London, England	46
Hills & Winship, Springfield, Massachusetts	68, 234, 274
Hills & Wolcott, Amherst, Massachusetts	210
Hills, H., Springfield, Massachusetts	188, 210
Hills, S. & H., Springfield, Massachusetts	188
Hinckley, A.	44
Hinkle, J.N., Columbus, Ohio.	100
Hjorth & Co., W., Jamestown, New York	236, 260
Hjorth Lathe and Tool Company	50, 134
Hoe Corp., Poughkeepsie, New York	270
Hoerner, John S., Highland, Illinois.	42
Hoey, R., New York, New York	210
Hoffa Sr., James.	Not Found
Holbrook, Bristol, England.	162
Hollow Augurs	86, 90, 144, 160
Holt Co., The G.L., Hartford, Connecticut.	48, 64, 208
Holt Mfg. Co., Springfield, Massachusetts	86, 150, 208
Hommell, Rudolf P.	182
Hood Bros., Philadelphia.	254
Horan & Bros., Boston, Massachusetts	180
Houle	266
Howard & Son, F. A., Belfast, Maine	156, 276
Howard, L.D.	94
Howard, L.D. (Unmarked)	94
Howarth, James, Sheffield, England.	20, 128, 170, 190, 262
Howell Tool Co., Orange, Massachusetts	266
Howland & Co., A., Auburn, New York	46, 52, 130, 232, 274
Hubbard H. W. Co.	164
Hubbard, D., (Royalston, Massachusetts)	250
Huber Mfg. Co., The, Marion, Ohio.	142, 238
Hudson Tool Company	160
Hugenot, L., Tussot (France)	126
Hugh Tools	None
Hull Co., L.L., Clinton, Connecticut., USA.	208
Hull, Grummond & Company	36
Hults, Swrige	168
Humphrey Tool Co., Warren, Massachusetts	264
Hunt & Wiseman, St. Louis, Missouri	200, 210
I.C.I.	172
I.D.F.	148
I.G.	238
Ibbotson & Co., Thos	170, 238
Ideal	152
Igpay Atinlay, Index Entries in	1
Imperial, Bloomington, Illinois.	48
Indicators	134
Int. Electric Company.	198
Internet, Inventor of	See Gore, Al
Iowa Novelty Co., Burlington, Iowa.	70
Iron Age	114, 278
Irwin	104, 156, 208
Irwin Auger Bit Co., Wilmington, Ohio.	36, 126, 156
Irwin, Charles.	254
J. & J. Gibson, Albany, New York	68
J.G. & J.M.	218
J.H.S., Devon, England.	218
J.T.O.	68
J.W.H.	202
Jackson.	92, 240
Jackson & Gorham	92
Jacobs Bros., Inc., New York, New York	228
Jenkins & Clark, Birmingham, England.	232
Jennings & Co., C.E., New York, New York	32, 58, 92, 126, 142, 190, 208, 220, 264
Jennings & Griffin Mfg. Co.	220
Jennings Mfg. Co., The Russell	126, 182, 254, 260, 278
Jessop.	54
Jewett, J.C., Waterville, Maine	162
Jo Mfg. Co., So. Gate, California.	138
Johnson.	122, 246
Johnson & Conaway, Philadelphia, Pennsylvania.	94, 222
Johnson & Tainter.	138
Johnson Rule Mfg. Co., E.P.	26, 76, 276
Johnson Tool Co., Warren, Pennsylvania.	146
Jointer Gauges	58, 72, 84, 86, 158, 180, 192, 216, 230, 252, 268
Jones & Co., M.H., Cohoes, New York.	56
Jones & Co., S.A., Hartford, Connecticut.	40, 154
Jones, Ellis	200
Jones, J.T., Philadelphia, Pennsylvania.	210
Jones, John N.	108
Josef, E.E., Buffalo, New York	124
Joy, A.P., Rockingham, New Hampshire.	48, 152
K. & D.	74
K.C. Drop Forge Co., Indiana., Missouri	172
K.D. Mfg. Co., Lancaster, Pennsylvania	212
Karle, Geo. J., Buffalo, New York.	118
Kearney & Foote	66
Kebabian, Paul & Whitney, Dudley	182
Keen Kutter Kollectors, Kape Kod	See Lumsden, Dale
KKellett.	128
Kelley, A.D.	78
Kelley, J.P., Erie, Pennsylvania.	228
Kelley-How-Thomson Co., Duluth, Minnesota	56, 72
Kellogg, Battle Creek, Michigan.	194, 224
Kellogg, J., Amherst, Massachusetts	108, 148, 200, 234, 250, 258, 274
Kelly Axe & Tool Works, Charleston	56
Kelly Axe Mfg. Co., Charleston, West Virginia	168
Kendall, I., Bristol, England	130
Kennedy & Co., Hartford, Connecticut.	222
Kennedy, L., Hartford, Connecticut	46
Kennedy, Utica, New York	258
Kenney	14, 102, 154
Kenton Brand	172
Kerby & Bro., New York	26, 140, 194
Kershaw Bros. Mfrs., Cleveland, Ohio.	94
Keuffel & Esser Co., New York	30, 34, 42, 50, 60, 66, 82, 206, 242, 278
Keuffel & Esser Co., New York, New York.	30, 50, 186
Keystone Mfg. Co., Buffalo, New York	152, 172, 212
Keyworth	20
Kieffer & Auxer, Lancaster, Pennsylvania.	250
Kilborn & Bishop	228
Kimball & Company?.	220
Kimball & Son, C. J., New Hampshire.	220
King & Co., Hull (England)	210
King, Arthur H., New York, New York	16
King, Josiah,373 Bowery, New York.	130, 200
King, S., Hull (England)	250
King, W.H., Athol, Massachusetts	80
Kinnear, Dundee (Scotland)	258
Kinsley, J.R., Cincinnati, Ohio.	218
Kirk & Asling, Nottingham, England	52
Klein, Hilary	48
Knives	36, 42, 70, 78, 120, 122, 158, 180, 186, 194, 198, 208, 230, 252
Koenig, Wm. A., Troy, New York.	206
Kohler, F.	64
Kone, G.W.	48
Kraeuter & Co., Newark, New Jersey.	78, 228, 246
Kraut, Henry, Summit, New Jersey.	48
Kruse & Baulmann Hardware. Co., Cincinnati, Ohio	56
Kuker- Ranken Inc., Seattle, Washington.	34
Kunz	128
Kutmaster, Utica, New York.	208
L. & S. Company, Cleveland, Ohio.	48
La Gripper Wrench Co., Battle Creek, Michigan.	100
Ladd, V.J. Edge Tool Co.	254
Lagomarcino-Grupe Co., Iowa	122
Lakes Timber Co., Ft. Frances, Ontario, Canada	202
Lakeside	164
Lakeside Saw & Tool Co., Chicago, Illinois	92
Lampert, France	248

Lancaster . . . 36
Lane, E.S., Upton, Maine . . . 4
Langdon Mitre Box Co., M.F., Massachusetts. . . . 72
Langlais . . . 94
Langley, London, England . . . 262
Lantz, E., Paris (France) . . . 196
Larkin. . . . 122
Lavigne & Scott Mfg. Co., The. . . . 100, 204
Lawrence Eng. Svce., Peru, Indiana . . . 30
Leather Tools . . . 78
Lee, Coit & Anderson Hardware., Omaha. . . . 56
Lenk Mfg. Co., Newton Lower. Falls,. . . . 66
Leopold . . . 64
Levels . 6, 8, 18, 22, 32, 36, 42, 50, 62, 66, 120, 142, 144, 158, 160, 178, 206, 224, 230, 238, 252, 266, 276
Lever Wrench Co.. . . . 114
Lewin. . . . 72
Leypoldt, F.C., Philadelphia., Pennsylvania . . . 78
Lignum Vitae Products Corp., Jersey City, New Jersey . . . 262
Lindenberger, I. . . . 210
Lindsey, J.F. & G.M., Warranted. . . . 68
Lines, D.. . . . 162
Lintner & Sporborg, Gloversville, New York . . . 134
Littell, T. & Atkinson, T., Louisville, Kentucky . . . 130
Little, L., Boston, Massachusetts. . . . 130, 162
Lively Lad Mfg. Co., Clarksville,. . . . 278
Livingston & Chermfree Mfg. Co. . . . 196
Lloyd, W.S. . . . 64
Lockwood, Taylor Hardware. Co., Cleveland.. . . . 218
Lorsch, Albert & Co., New York, New York . . . 132
Losee Wrench Works, Corry, Pennsylvania . . . 118
Lothrop, G.M., Norwood, Massachusetts . . . 124
Lourie, Edinburgh, Scotland. . . . 68
Lovell Mfg. Co., The A.K., New York, New York . . . 18
Lovell Wrench Co., Bridgeport, Connecticut. . . . 48
Lowell Plane & Tool Co. . . . 8
Lowinson, Chas., New York, New York . . . 194
Lowntraut Mfg. Co., P., Newark, New Jersey . . . 48, 114, 118
Lozier Mfg. Co., Cleveland, Ohio. . . . 48
Lufkin Rule Co., Cleveland, Ohio. . . . 214
Lufkin Rule Co., Saginaw, Michigan. 26, 30, 36, 40, 42, 50, 60, 66, 76, 80, 86, 94, 96, 110, 124, 140, 146, 184, 186, 194, 206, 214, 218, 222, 226, 242, 272, 276, 278
Lukin, James, Ed. . . . 110
Lutz . . . 30
Lyon & Co., D.M., Newark, New Jersey. . . . 102, 142
Lyon & Smith, Cincinatti, Ohio . . . 52
Lyon, D.M., Newark, New Jersey. . . . 154
M. & M. . . . 246
M.C. . . . 234
M.W. & Co., Framingham, Massachusetts. . . . 114, 270
Machin, Thos., Toronto (Canada) . . . 108
Macker, D.W., North Grafton, Massachusetts . . . 194
Maddock, E., Watertown (New York) . . . 44
Magee, Worral & Richards, New York . . . 194
Maiers, C.. . . . 54
Malloch, D., Perth (Scotland) . . . 46, 52, 200, 210, 258
Manchester, P.H.. . . . 46
Manchester, P.H., Providence, Rhode Island . . . 52
Mandery, Joseph, Rochester, New York . . . 36
Mann, J.B., Bridgewater, Massachusetts. . . . 78
Mann, William, Lewistown, Pennsylvania . . . 44
Marble's Arms & Mfg. Co., Gladstone, Michigan. . . . 28, 168
Marking Gauges 14, 20, 52, 62, 84, 86, 102, 120, 154, 158, 160, 178, 224, 252, 262, 276
Marley, N. York . . . 52, 210, 250
Marples . . . 190
Marples & Co., William, Sheffield, England32, 68, 98, 102, 124, 154, 208, 222, 240, 250, 254, 266
Marples & Sons, Wm., Hibernia Wks., Sheffield, England 20, 54, 64, 82, 156, 186, 198, 230, 250, 260, 264
Marples, Robert, Hermitage Works, Sheffield, England . . . 20
Marsh. . . . 58
Marsh & Sons, Oakland, Maine . . . 44
Marsh, A. & W., Cleveland, Ohio. . . . 162
Marshall Wells Hardware Co. . . . 40, 58
Marshall, I. . . . 50
Martin & Corey (Made For) . . . 148
Martin & Shaw,(Birmingham, England) . . . 46, 234
Marvel, Cleveland, Ohio. . . . 212
Mascot . . . 30
Mason, New Haven, Connecticut.. . . . 276
Massachusetts Tool Co., Greenfield., Massachusetts. . . . 80
Master Rule Mfg. Co. . . . 60, 76, 214
Matchless . . . 56
Mateaux, C. L. . . . 110
Mathews, Dayton, Ohio. . . . 114, 152
Mathieson & Son, A., Glasgow, Scotland 22, 46, 102, 124, 130, 136, 142, 148, 162, 210, 226, 230, 258, 264, 274
Mauser . . . 178
Maxwell . . . 212
May, Atlanta, Georgia. . . . 212
Maydole Tool Corp. . . . 172
Maydole, D., Norwich, New York. . . . 88, 202, 248
Maydole, David, Norwich, New York. . . . 88
Mayhew Co., H.H., Shelburne Falls, Massachusetts . . . 126
Mayhew Steel Prod. Co., Shelburne Falls, Massachusetts . 54, 60, 66
Mc Bee. . . . 122
Mc Gillis, Brown & Pratt Mfg. Co.. . . . 66, 122
Mc Grath, St. Paul, Minnesota . . . 132
Mc I. H. Co. . . . 270
Mc Master & Co., T. J., Auburn, New York. . . . 102, 188, 250
Mc Master, Z. J., Auburn, New York. . . . 52, 130
Melhuish Sons & Co., Fetter Lane . . . 94
Melhuish, Fetter Lane (London) . . . 210
Melick, W.B. . . . 32
Mephisto. . . . 98, 270
Mercer, Henry . . . 182
Merrick, S. . . . 48
Metallic Plane Co., Auburn, New York. . . . 8, 72, 160
Metallic Planes . 4, 6, 8, 14, 16, 18, 22, 46, 58, 62, 72, 84, 106, 144, 146, 160, 174, 180, 218, 230, 252, 268, 278
Micrometers . . . 18, 50, 66, 74, 80, 132, 178, 206, 276
Middlesex Mfg. Co., Middletown, Connecticut. . . . 164
Miller, A., New York . . . 188
Millers Falls Company 20, 32, 34, 36, 42, 66, 74, 80, 84, 86, 90, 94, 104, 118, 122, 128, 136, 138, 146, 150, 156, 160, 170, 180, 182, 194, 196, 198, 208, 212, 218, 228, 238, 260, 264, 276, 278
Mills Bros., Sheffield, England. . . . 190
Mitchell & Co., Hudson, New York.. . . . 72
Mitchell, C.E., Lowell, Massachusetts . . . 196
Mitre Boxes . . . 44, 84, 86, 180
Mitteldorfer Straus . . . 14
Mix & Co., G.I. . . . 170
Mockridge & Francis, Newark, New Jersey . . . 200
Mockridge & Son, Newark, New Jersey. . . . 234
Modern Products Mfg. Co. . . . 206
Modern Tools, Japan. . . . 132
Modern Utilities Co., Harrisburg, Pennsylvania . . . 32
Modern Woodmen of America . . . 36
Mohler Mfg. Co., E.M., Champaign, Illinois. . . . 228
Moir, G.D. . . . 132
Moir, Glasgow (Scotland). . . . 200
Molding Planes 4, 6, 12, 18, 22, 46, 52, 68, 108, 130, 146, 148, 162, 180, 186, 188, 200, 210, 232, 234, 250, 258, 274, 278
Mongomery Ward & Company. . . . 72
Montague, Woodrough Saw Co. . . . 92
Montgomery Ward . . . 180, 240
Montgomery Ward & Co. . . . 60
Moon, Lincoln Inn Fields . . . 258
Moore & Wright, Sheffield (England) . . . 134, 178, 206, 224
Moore, William,(New York) . . . 52
Morrill, B., Bangor, Maine . . . 136
Morrill, Charles, Jersey City, New Jersey . . . 64
Morrill, J.J. . . . 220
Morse Twist Drill & Machine Co.. . . . 126, 254
Moseley & Son, John, London, England . . . 108, 130, 250
Moses, Artemas, Salisbury, Vermont (?) . . . 200
Moss, Wm., Birmingham, England . . . 52, 130, 188, 274
Mossberg Co., Frank, Attleboro, Massachusetts48, 114, 124, 152, 172, 204, 212, 236
Mossberg, Frank. . . . 48, 152
Moulson Brothers, Sheffield, England. . . . 102, 260
Mowry, B.R., Union, Maine . . . 112
Mulliken & Stackpole, Boston, Massachusetts . . . 238
Multiform Molding Plane Co. . . . 46, 186
Munks, John & Sons, Sheffield, England . . . 18
Murcott, John H., Inc., St. Albans. . . . 66
Mustbewinchesterifitsmarkedinthismanyplaces. . . . 3
Mutter, George, London, England. . . . 210
New York M'f'g'r's Co., New York . . . 104
Nail Pullers. . . . 228, 252
Nash. . . . 212
Nash Co., George, New York, New York . . . 132
National Tube Wks., Boston, Massachusetts. . . . 254
Natural Ice Associationn. of America . . . 26
Nelson & Hubbard, Middletown, Connecticut. . . . 222
Nelson (Richard), York, England . . . 108
Nelson, A.T., Wilton, Iowa . . . 202
Nester. . . . 154
Nestler, Albert . . . 30
New Haven Edge Tool Co. . . . 44, 54, 190
New Process Drill, Taunton, Massachusetts . . . 254
Niagara Machine & Tool Works . . . 248
Nicholl & Co., J.A.. . . . 226
Nicholl, R., High Holborn, London. . . . 140, 184
Nicholls & Co., J.A., London . . . 30
Nicholls Mfg. Co., Ottumwa, Iowa. . . . 266
Nicholson File Co., Providence, Rhode Island . 33, 66, 82, 110, 124, 146, 174, 178, 180, 182
Nicholson, F., Wrentham, Massachusetts . . . 18
Nilson Waters Co., Castleton, South Dakota. . . . 172
Nobles Mfg. Co., Elmira, New York. . . . 220
Noepal & Assman, Newark, New Jersey. . . . 64
Norris, London, England . . . 6, 22
North Bros. Mfg. Co., Philadelphia, Pennsylvania . 42, 66, 82, 90, 100, 104, 124, 138, 146, 150, 156, 160, 208, 212, 260, 276
Norton Tool Co. . . . 56
Norton, S.S., Colchester, Connecticut. . . . 154
Numberall Stamp & Tool Co. . . . 66
Nurse, C., Walworth Road, London, England130, 136, 162, 250, 258
Nurse, C.,32 Mill St. (London, England)126, 136, 200, 232, 234, 254
Nutting & Hayden, Concord, New Hampshire. . . . 202
Nylint. . . . 120
O.W.B. & Co. . . . 74
Odell, Charles, Salem, Massachusetts. . . . 210
Ogden, R.C., New York . . . 44
Ogontz Tool Company . . . 68
Ohio State. . . . 236
Ohio Tool Company4, 6, 16, 58, 72, 108, 130, 164, 188, 200, 210, 220, 250, 258, 268, 274
Oil Cans . . . 28, 218
Olin . . . 174
Oliver Chilled Plow Works . . . 110
Olmsted, L.H.. . . . 180
Onions & Co. . . . 124
Oothoudt, J. . . . 52
Oothoudt, W. . . . 162
Osborn, Henry, Southhampton (England) . . . 108
Osborne & Co., C.S., Newark, New Jersey 78, 86, 88, 118, 198, 228, 248, 278
Osborne, H.G. . . . 240
Osborne, Late Dodd, Newark, New Jersey . . . 78
Otto & Reynders, New York. . . . 42
Otto & Sons, F.C.,64 Chatham, N.Y . . . 42
Overman Wheel Co., Boston, Massachusetts . . . 278
Overman Wheel Co., Chicopee Falls. . . . 204, 218, 236
Owasco Tool Co., New York. . . . 234
P.S. & W. Co. . . . 190
P.T. Co.. . . . 260
Page, E.L., Greene, New York . . . 194
Palmer, A.J. . . . 118
Palmer, France . . . 206
Panton, James, Aberdeen (Scotland) . . . 258
Park & Williams, Williamsburg, Ohio. . . . 198
Park Metalware Co., Inc. . . . 48
Parker Co., The Charles, Meriden, Connecticut . . . 270
Parker Hubbard & Co., Conway, Massachusetts . . . 68
Parkes, W. . . . 188
Parkhurst, J., Springfield, New Jersey. . . . 52
Parmenter, Geo. A., Boston, Massachusetts . . . 48
Parr, Geo., Buffalo, New York. . . . 164
Parrot Head Tool Co., Oklahoma City, Oklahoma. . . . 246
Parry, 325 Old Street, London, England . . . 210
Parsons Bros. Slate Co., Pen Argyl, Pennsylvania. . . . 96
Patent Level Co., Bridgeport, Connecticut . . . 6, 32
Patt., J.O. . . . 162
Pazzano Wrench Co., Waltham, Massachusetts . . . 114
Peace & Co., J., Sheffield, England . . . 240
Peace, Harvey W., Brooklyn, New York . . . 92, 196, 240
Peck & Smith Co, Southington. . . . 96
Peck Stow & Wilcox Company. . . . 246
Peck, Obed & Powers, D. . . . 150
Peck, Stow & Wilcox Co. 44, 54, 88, 90, 98, 122, 126, 138, 146, 156, 164, 168, 172, 190, 204, 208, 220, 228, 236, 270
Peckham, P.M., Fall River, Massachusetts . . . 52
Penn Saw Co., Frackville, Pennsylvania. . . . 92
Penn. Farm Museum, Landis Valley, Pennsylvania . . . 182
Perfection . . . 34, 236, 270
Perfection & Columbia Novelty Co. . . . 10
Perry, C.T. . . . 260
Peters, P.F., Natick, Massachusetts . . . 88
Petersen Mfg. Co., Dewitt, Nebraska . . . 66, 236
Petersen Rapid Wrench Co. . . . 270
Petersen Tool Co., Eldorado, Kansas . . . 100
Peugot Freres . . . 236
Pfister, Cincinnati, Ohio . . . 238
Phillip, T. . . . 200
Phillips. . . . 154
Phillips (Unmarked) . . . 154
Phillips, George B., Albany, New York. . . . 48
Phillips, J., Cincinnati, Ohio. . . . 154
Phillips, N., Boston, Massachusetts. . . . 250
Pierce & Co. . . . 92
Pierce, W.F. . . . 96
Pike Mfg. Co., Pike, New Hampshire, U.S.A. . . . 118
Pilkington, C. T., Sheffield, England . . . 20
Pirce, J.W. . . . 68
Planes, Wurwartwotype, When Made. . . . 1941-1945
Platt Co., The Frank S. . . . 82
Pliers . . . 14, 62, 66, 74, 78, 144, 174, 246, 252
Plumb. . . . 56
Plumb Bobs . . . 18, 34, 50, 134, 160, 278
Plumb, Fayette R., Philadelphia, Pennsylvania. 44, 56, 168, 248, 278
Pond, W.H., New Haven, Connecticut. . . . 72, 188, 264
Ponder, S., London . . . 108
Pool, H.M., Easton, Massachusetts. . . . 8
Pope, W., Pralph. . . . 20
Portland Wrench Company . . . 48, 100, 114, 204
Potter, C. . . . 130
Powell Tool Co., Cleveland, Ohio. . . . 44
Pratt & Whitney, W. Hartford, Connecticut. . . . 174
Prefer . . . 100
Preston & Sons, Edward 20, 22, 28, 32, 40, 58, 90, 184, 198, 210, 226, 230, 250, 258, 264, 272

Preston, W., London, England. . . . 274
Preveron, Pontarion . . . 56
Proto Tools, Los Angeles, California. . . . 246
Protractors . . . 42, 50, 132, 178, 186, 206, 224
Proudfoot, Christopher & Walker, Phillip . . . 110
Providence Tool Co. . . . 46, 250
Provost & Williams, Newark, New Jersey . . . 190
Prutton Mfg. Co., D.H., Cleveland, Ohio . . . 118
Push Drills. . . . 66, 138, 156, 158, 276
Putz, J., New York . . . 42
Rabone & Sons, John, Birmingham, England10, 30, 40, 76, 140, 142, 160, 184, 226, 238, 242, 272
Rabone Chesterman, England . . . 226
Race Knives . . . 260
Radcliffe. . . . 194
Radio Lectric . . . 212
Ralph Williams, Inc., Boston, Mass . . . 60
Randall & Cook, Albany, New York . . . 162
Raphaels, Ltd. . . . 30
Rast Prod. Corp., New York, New York . . . 100
Read, M., Boston, Massachusetts . . . 108
Reading Hardware Co., The . . . 122
Record, Sheffield, England . . . 58, 146, 160, 180, 230, 278
Red Chief Mfg. Co., Louisville, Kentucky . . . 270
Red Devil Tools, Union, New Jersey . . . 230
Reed & Co., Higganum, Connecticut . . . 152
Reed Mfg. Co., Erie, Pennsylvania . . . 48
Reed, Utica (N. Y.) . . . 52, 108, 148, 210, 232, 234, 250, 274
Reedman & Co., C.H., Newark, New Jersey . . . 114
Reid, A. H., Philadelphia, Pennsylvania . . . 104, 156
Reinhard-Mc Cabe Co., Minneapolis . . . 152, 270
Reinhardt . . . 206
Reizenstein & Moller . . . 80
Reliance, Youngstown, Ohio. . . . 170
Remington Tool & Mch. Co., Boston . . . 126
Renchall . . . 152
Rex Wrench Co., Boston, Massachusetts . . . 42
Rice, Royal B., Williamsburg, Massachusetts . . . 4
Richards & Co., J.F., Kansas City, . . . 56
Richards, W.G. . . . 134
Richardson . . . 46
Richardson Brothers, Newark, New Jersey . . . 240, 260
Richardson, C.F., Athol, Massachusetts. . . . 32, 50, 142
Ricks, J., London . . . 272
Ridgeley, London . . . 198
Riverside Tool Co., New York, New York . . . 58, 160, 220, 240, 248
Rixford, O. S. . . . 110
Robbins, D.C., Boston, Massachusetts . . . 178
Robert Wrench Co., New York . . . 172
Roberts . . . 202, 248
Roberts, Cushman & Co., New York . . . 194
Roberts, Edw., Grocers Alley, London . . . 6
Roberts, Kenneth . . . 182
Roberts, Kenneth D. . . . 110, 182
Roberts, L.T., London. . . . 240
Robertson & Sons, James L. . . . 42
Robertson, A.R. . . . 202, 248
Robertson, A.R., Boston, Massachusetts . . . 202
Robinson . . . 270
Robinson, M.W., Brooklyn, New York . . . 238
Rockford Tool Co., Kokomo, Indiana. . . . 190
Roe & Sons, Justus, Patchogue, New York . . . 60
Rogers & Son, Joseph, Sheffield, England . . . 198
Rogers, L. . . . 168
Root Co., The C.J., Bristol, Connecticut. . . . 122
Ross Mfg. Co., S.F., California . . . 246
Ross, Beaurivarge, P.Q. . . . 202
Router Planes . . . 18, 70, 72, 84, 210, 230, 234, 252, 262
Routledge, 64 Bull St., Birmingham, England . . . 52, 112, 250, 274
Rowe, L.L., Boston, Massachusetts . . . 212
Rowell, S., Albany, New York . . . 130
Rowell, S., Troy, New York . . . 52, 188
Rown, W., Sheffield, England. . . . 100
Royal . . . 214
Roys & Wilcox Co. . . . 198
Rubelmann, Geo., St. Louis, Missouri . . . 58
Rudor, New YorkCity. . . . 202
Rule Attachments . . . 242
Rule Products Co., Stratford, Connecticut. . . . 60
Rule Tool Co., Newark, New Jersey . . . 226
Rules 10, 26, 30, 36, 40, 42, 50, 66, 76, 80, 84, 122, 124, 132, 140, 178, 184, 194, 198, 206, 214, 224, 226, 242, 272, 276, 278
Nikslitslepmur . . . See Grimm, Brothers
Rural Industries Bureau . . . 110
Russell Cutlery Co., John . . . 194, 198
Rust Craft, Boston, Massachusetts . . . 242
Rust, W.O., Great Falls, New.Hampshire . . . 64
Rustless Rule Co., Buffalo, New York. . . . 242, 276
S.D. . . . 152
S.H. Co. . . . 92
S.H. Co., St. Louis, Missouri . . . 168
S.M. . . . 124
Salmen's, A.B. Successors, Ltd. . . . 130
Sampson Aston Maker . . . 242
Sanborn, D.P., Littleton (New HampshireS . . . 46, 210
Sandusky Tool Co., Sandusky, Ohio 52, 68, 112, 148, 162, 180, 188, 200, 210, 232, 234, 258, 274
Sandvik, Sweden . . . 66
Sandvikens Jernverks, A.B. . . . 92
Sanford, Levi, East Solon, New York . . . 14
Sanger, Karl, Consecutive Years in Index . . . 3
Sargent & Compan7, New Haven, Connecticut. . . 6, 44, 78, 90, 130, 144, 160, 174, 188, 230, 268, 274
Sargent, D., Nashua, New Hampshire . . . 160
Sarjent, W., West Street, Reading . . . 130
Saunders' Sons, D. . . . 124
Saw Sets . . . 36, 64, 86, 252, 270
Saw Vises . . . 118
Sawheag Works, Wallingford, Connecticut. . . . 232
Saws . 4, 42, 62, 74, 84, 92, 120, 122, 160, 180, 196, 240, 252, 260, 278
Sawyer Belt Hook Co., Rhode Island . . . 248
Sawyer Tool Company, Ashburnham, Massachusetts . 178, 224, 272, 276
Sawyer Tool Co., Fitchburg, Massachusetts. . . . 42, 66, 224
Sawyer Tool Mfg Co. . . . 80, 224
Sawyer, J., Moravia, New York. . . . 188
Saybarger, J., Cincinnati, Ohio . . . 70
Sayre & Co., L.A., Newark, New Jersey. . . . 168
Sayre, F.E., Ltd., Chipman, N.B., Canada . . . 202
Schaefer & Cobb, Cincinnati, Ohio. . . . 188
Schmidt & Moellenhoe. . . . 80
Schoenner, Germany. . . . 206
Scholl, C. . . . 20, 102, 154, 160
Scholler Mfg. Co., Buffalo, New York . . . 236
Schollhorn & Co., Wm., New Haven, Connecticut. . . . 172, 198, 246
Schrader, Frederick, Bridgeport, Connecticut . . . 48
Scientific American . . . 110
Scott Lumber Co., Fred'ton, N.B, Canada. . . . 202
Scott, W., Pittsburg, Pennsylvania. . . . 52
Scott, W., Pittsburg. Allegany Town, Pennsylvania . . . 108
Scovill Mfg. Co., New York, New York . . . 272
Scovill, J. (Johnstown, New York) . . . 52
Scrapers. 12, 24, 58, 70, 84, 106, 112, 120, 158, 192, 198, 212, 216, 230, 244, 252, 256, 262, 264, 268
Scrarm . . . See Therapy, Speech
Screwdrivers . . . 62, 84, 86, 104, 120, 144, 156, 160, 174, 208, 276
Seabers Mach.Co., J.A.W., Malden, Massachusetts. . . . 114
Searls Mfg. Co. . . . 172
Sears & Co., W.B., Middletown, New York . . . 240
Sears, Roebuck & Co.. . . . 54, 72, 86, 98, 118, 164, 168, 180, 220
Sears, Roebuck & Co., Chicago, Illinois . . . 212
Sears, Roebuck & Company . . . 202
Sears, Roebuck And Company . . . 64, 66
See, C. S.,(New York). . . . 130
Sellens, Alvin . . . 110, 182
Semple & Bro., A.B., Louisville, Kentucky . . . 52
Shapleigh Hardware, St. Louis, Missouri . 58, 72, 98, 134, 168, 202, 260
Sharp, John. . . . 186
Shaw Propeller Co. . . . 152
Shears . . . 122, 194, 198
Sheffield Machine & Tool Co., Dayton, Ohio . . . 134
Sheffield, J.M. & Palmer, Stanford, Connecticut. . . . 56
Sheffield, J.M., Stanford, Connecticut. . . . 186
Sheldon Axle Company . . . 152
Shelton . . . 156, 160
Sheneman & Bro., B., Phildelphia, Pennsylvania . . . 46
Shephardson & Co., Shelburne Falls, Massachusetts. . . . 150, 156
Sherman, S.J., New York, New York . . . 42
Shiverick & Malcom, Brooklyn . . . 234
Shiverick, Brooklyn, New York . . . 46
Shurly - Dietrich- Atkins . . . 92
Siegley Tool Company . . . 18, 58, 72, 128
Siewers, Charles G., Cincinnati, Ohio . . . 222
Simmons Hardware Co., E.C., St. Louis, Missouri 20, 44, 74, 76, 92, 118, 156, 170, 172, 236, 252, 270
Simmons, D., Lockport, New York . . . 164
Simonds Saw & Steel Co., Fitchburg, Massachusetts36, 92, 118, 174
Simplex Mfg. Co., The, New York . . . 204
Simplex Wrench Co., New York, New York . . . 100, 270
Sims, London . . . 68
Slayton, R. . . . 188
Sleeper, S., Dover, New Hampshire . . . 162
Slide Rules . . . 6, 30
Slip Lens . . . 30
Sloane, Eric . . . 110
Slocomb, J.T., Providence, Rhode Island. . . . 132, 206
Smallwood, I. & D., Birmingham, England . . . 40, 142, 226, 238
Smith & Co., E.S., Rockford, Illinois . . . 28
Smith & Co., H.D., Plantsville, Connecticut 48, 104, 156, 168, 204, 220
Smith & Hemenway, Jamestown, New York. . . . 86
Smith & Son, G. . . . 180
Smith Co., The H.D., Plantsville, Connecticut. . . 100, 122, 156, 172, 246
Smith, A., Lowell, Massachusetts . . . 250
Smith, A., Rehoboth, Massachusetts . . . 210
Smith, B.W. . . . 274
Smith, E. G., Columbia, Pennsylvania. . . . 80
Smith, E., Warranted. . . . 258
Smith, E.B., St. Louis, Missouri. . . . 18
Smith, E.G., Columbia, Pennsylvania . . . 132, 238
Smith, H. R. Bradley . . . 182
Smith, Joseph . . . 110
Smith, Otis A., Rockfall, Connecticut. . . . 118
Smith, Phineas, New York, New York. . . . 260
Smith, Joseph . . . 110
Smith, Otis A., Rockfall, Connecticut. . . . 118
Smith, Phineas, New York, New York. . . . 260
Smith, S. . . . 64, 270
Smyth Co., John M. . . . 260
Snap On Tools Corp, Kenosha, Wisconsin. . . . 36, 100, 276
Snell & Atherton, Brockton, Massachusetts . . . 136
Snell & Co., L.S., Bridgeport, Connecticut . . . 78
Snell Mfg. Co., Fiskdale, Massachusetts. . . . 126, 254
Solidhed Company, Hoboken, New Jersey . . . 78
Sorby, I (England). . . . 126, 240
Sorby, I. & H., Sheffield, England . . . 126, 190
Sorby, I., Sheffield, England . . . 240
Sorby, Robert, Sheffield, England . . . 44, 102, 112, 240
Sorrento Wood Carving Co., Boston . . . 260
Soule, L.S., Waldoboro (Maine) . . . 52
Southington Hardware Co. . . . 44, 94
Spalding . . . 120
Spaulding Mach. Screw Co., Buffalo . . . 172
Spear & Jackson, Sheffield, England. . . . 180, 240
Speed Indicators . . . 134
Speednut Wrench Corp., Chicago . . . 236
Spehr, J.A., Hamburg . . . 200
Spence Mfg. Co, S.M., Boston, Massachusetts . . . 182
Spencer. . . . 68, 232
Spiers, Stewart, Ayr, Scotland . . . 8, 22, 132
Spoke Pointers . . . 86, 90, 124
Spoke Shaves 16, 20, 62, 70, 86, 106, 112, 120, 136, 158, 160, 186, 212, 228, 230, 262, 264, 278
Spot Bob, Santa Ana, California. . . . 34
Spring & Robinson, Hyde Park, Massachusetts. . . . 220
Spring, T. . . . 148
Springfield Drop Forging Co. . . . 100
Springfield Level & Tool Co. . . . 32
Squangle Corporation, Lynwood, Washington. . . . 60
Squares . . . 36, 40, 42, 44, 62, 144, 158, 194, 224, 252, 266
St. Johnsbury Tool Co. . . . 94
St. Maurice Lumber Co., Trois Rivieres, P.Q.. . . . 202
Staatsburg, Staatsburg, New York . . . 44
Stackpole, Greenleaf, New York, New York . . . 150
Stahl . . . 204
Standard Engineering Works. . . . 50
Standard Rule Co., Unionville, Connecticut . . . 26, 40, 58
Standard Tool Co., Athol, Massachusetts 80, 114, 180, 204, 266, 270
Stanley Rule & Level 4, 6, 8, 10, 12, 14, 16, 18, 20, 22, 24, 26, 28, 30, 32, 34, 36, 38, 40, 42, 44, 48, 50, 54, 56, 60, 64, 66, 76, 82, 86, 88, 90, 92, 94, 96, 98, 102, 104, 106, 110, 116, 120, 124, 126, 128, 134, 136, 138, 140, 142, 146, 150, 152, 154, 156, 158, 160, 164, 166, 170, 174, 176, 178, 180, 182, 184, 190, 192, 194, 202, 206, 208, 212, 214, 216, 218, 220, 222, 224, 226, 230, 238, 240, 242, 244, 246, 248, 254, 256, 260, 264, 266, 268, 272, 276, 278
Stanley Rule & Level (Canada). . . . 106, 256
Stanley Tools (England) . . . 116, 216, 266
Stanley Tools, Australia . . . 180
Stanley Works. . . . 120
Stanley, W. F., London (England) . . . 10, 50, 76
Star Tool Company . . . 102, 154
Star Tool Company (Unmarked) . . . 94
Stark, Molly, Bennington, Vermont . . . 122
Starrett Co., The L.S.S., Athol, Massachusetts 32, 36, 42, 60, 66, 76, 80, 82, 100, 124, 126, 132, 134, 142, 146, 160, 174, 178, 194, 196, 198, 206, 214, 222, 224, 238, 260, 266, 276, 278
Stearns & Co., E.A., Brattleboro, Vermont 10, 26, 40, 184, 226, 242, 272
Stearns & Co., E.C., Syracuse, New York . . 58, 64, 86, 90, 230, 276
Stearns, E.C. (Unmarked) . . . 90
Stearns, G.N., Syracuse (Unmarked) . . . 136
Stearns, George, H., Syracuse, N.Y . . . 90
Steele, A.P. . . . 250
Stephens & Co., Riverton, Connecticut 26, 40, 76, 94, 184, 214, 272
Stephens Patent Vise Co., New York. . . . 174
Stephenson Mfr., A.M., Joliet, Illinois. . . . 50
Stevens A. & T. Co., The, Chicopee. Falls, Mass . . 34, 74, 80, 132, 178, 224
Stevens Walden, Inc., Worcester, Massachusetts . . . 146
Stevens, G.M., Portland, Maine. . . . 118
Stevens, J., Boston, Massachusetts . . . 46, 210
Steward, 406 Strand (London) . . . 184
Stewart . . . 148, 162, 200
Stickeley, I. . . . 68
Stiles, J., Kingston, New York . . . 108
Stinson . . . 186
Stoddard, O., Detroit, Michigan. . . . 224
Storer, J.P., Brunswick, Maine . . . 46
Stortz, J., Philadelphia., Pennsylvania . . . 112
Stothert, Bath (England) . . . 148, 210, 258
Stover Mfg. Co., Freeport, Illinois. . . . 118
Strange, J.W., Bangor, Maine . . . 50

Name	Pages
Stratton Bros., Greenfield, Massachusetts	32, 142, 238
Strelinger & Co., Charles, Detroit, Michigan	82
Stubs, P.S.	72, 74, 80, 132, 196, 218
Suffell, 132 Long Acre (London)	42
Sun Hemmi, Japan	30
Superior	86
Surface Gauges	80, 134
Sutcliffe Brothers	162
Sutton, Charles D., Kensico, New York	6
Swan Co., The James	44, 54, 86, 98, 164, 220, 254, 262
Sym, I.	46
Syracuse	114, 172
T.T.T., Hockanum, Connecticut	246
Taber Plane Co., New Bedford, Connecticut	274
Taber, John M., New Bedford, Massachusetts	210, 250, 258
Taber, L.H.	232
Tabor Mfg. Co., New York	134
Tack Pullers	228
Tadwell, R., Boston, Massachusetts	212
Taggart, Thomas, Grasmere, New Hampshire	10
Taintnor Mfg. Co., New York	64
Tanner & Davenport, Albany, New York	4
Tap Wrenches	100, 260
Tape Measures	36, 50, 60, 120
Tavella Sales Co., New York	30
Taylor Ltd., Henry, Sheffield, England	54, 98
Taylor, J.C., Cincinnati, Ohio	188
Taylor, W.W.	108
Taylor, Wm.	148
Teneyck Mfg. Co., Cohoes, New York	56
Thackeray, J.W., Armley, Yorks.	22
Thayer, W.E.	104
The Simonds Saw Works	86
Thompson, A.L. Mfr., Lowell, Massachusetts	134
Thompson, Wm. A., Buffalo, New York	162
Thrall & Son, Willis, Hartford, Connecticut	40, 266
Thread Gauges	194
Tiffany & Co.	36
Tileson, T., Boston, Massachusetts	68, 130, 232, 234, 250, 274
Tileston & Hollingsworth, Boston	26
Tillotson, Sheffield, England	240
Tite Grip Wrench Co., Milwaukee, Wisconsin	100
Tobey, C., Hudson (New York)	12
Tobrin Tool Co., Plantsville, Connecticut	212
Toledo Plow Co.	152
Tollner, C., 209 Bowery, New York	138
Tolman, J.R., Hanover, Massachusetts	130, 200, 210, 234
Tolor Mfg. Co., J.L., Poughkpsie, New York	124
Tool Boxes	36, 146
Tool Catalogue, Greatest of All Time	You're Looking at It
Tool Chests	4, 146
Tool Handles	124, 158, 208
Tool Kits	42, 80, 122, 146
Tools You've Never Seen Before	All Pages
Topp & Co., G.A., Indianapolis, Indiana	42, 94, 222, 266
Tower & Lathrop	94
Tower & Lyon, New York, New York	14, 32, 58, 72, 114, 204, 218, 236, 238
Trammels	12, 18, 28, 42, 178, 206, 276
Travelers	96
Trimont Mfg. Co., Roxbury, Massachusetts	48, 100, 114, 204
Triple Grip	246
True Temper	202
True, Moses, Oakfield, New York	64
Truth, The Absolute	All Pages
Try Squares	10, 14, 18, 42, 44, 62, 94, 120, 158, 222, 224, 266
Tunis, Edwin	110, 182
Turner & Co., Thomas	266
Tyler, Geo. R., Pomona, California	196
Tyzack & Son, Joseph, Sheffield, England	230
Tyzak & Son, S., Railway Arch	164
Tyzak & Son, S., Sheffield, England	96
Tyzak & Son, S., 34 Old St, London	124
Tyzak Sons & Turner, Sheffield, England	240
Underhill	54
Underhill Bros., Boston (Massachusetts)	98
Underhill Edge Tool Co., Nashua, New Hampshire	98, 164, 168, 170, 190
Union	196
Union Hardware Co., Torrington, Connecticut	54, 98, 122, 146, 164, 190, 278
Union Mfg. Co., New Britain, Connecticut	8, 58, 72, 160
Union Steel Chest Corp., Leroy, New York	146
Union Tool Co., Orange, Massachusetts	222, 224
Union Twist Drill Co., Athol, Massachusetts	182
United States Government	278
Universal Wrench Co., Detroit	114, 204
Upson Nut Co., Unionville, Connecticut	26, 40, 76, 184
Utica Drop Forge & Tool Corp, Utica, New York	66, 246, 248
Utica Tools, Utica, New York	100, 246
Utility Wrench Co., New York	48, 114
Valve Grinders	124, 212
Van Camp Hdwe. & I. Co.	118
Vandegrift	204
Vandegrift Mfg. Co., Shelbyville, Illinois	100, 152, 204
Varvill & Son, York (England)	186, 200
Vaughn & Bushnell, Chicago, Illinois	58, 138, 150, 168, 198
Veal, I.,(England)	108
Veeder Mfg. Co., Hartford, Connecticut	134
Veritas	170
Vernier, J.J., Toledo, Ohio	74
Victor	100
Vigor, Switzerland	74
Vinall, J.J., Cleveland, Ohio	154
Vincent, J., Stratford on Avon	130
Vises	74, 86, 90, 120, 124, 218
Visscher, Albert De, Editor	182
Vlchek Tool Co., The	104, 212
Vom Berg, Gebr	150
Vulcan	88
W.W. Co., Brooklyn, New York	212
Wade Wrench Co., White Pigeon, Michigan	236
Wadsworth, Howland & Co., Boston, Massachusetts	174
Wagor, D.	80
Wakefield	172
Wakefield Wrench Co., Worcester, Massachusetts	100, 114, 172, 212, 236, 270
Walcott Brothers, Boston, Massachusetts	194
Walden, Worcester, Massachusetts	114, 152
Walker Turner Co., Plainfield, New Jersey	110
Walker, Isaac, Peoria, Illinois	44
Walters & Sons, William P., Philadelphia	174
Waltham Watch Co., Waltham, Massachusetts	74
Walworth & Co., Boston, Massachusetts	152, 236
Wantage Rods	50
Ward	190
Ward & Payne	146
Ward, Sheffield, England	164
Ward, Vern	82
Ward, William, 8th Ave., New York, New York	210
Warlow, Bristol	276
Warren Paint Co., Warren, Ohio	36
Warren, C., Nashua, New Hampshire	108
Washer Cutters	118, 124
Watkins & Son, Bristol, Connecticut	22
Watson (England)	234
Watts, G.	154
Watts, L.H., New York	186
Way, William, New York	210
Waycott, Paignton	146
Wayne Mfg. Co. (Unmarked.)	126
Weaver L. & Leiser, Z., Lock Haven	26
Webb, C.H., New York (Unmarked)	50
Webb, Wm. P., Washington, D.C.	232
Webster, W., E. Jaffrey, New Hampshire	78
Wedgeway	254
Weifs, J.	210
Welch Mfg. Co., W.M., Chicago, Illinois	140
Wells Tool Co., Greenfield, Massachusetts	124
Wells, G.F., Bolton, Massachusetts	258
Wells, R.	46, 130
Wentworth	118, 162
Wentworth, J., Worcester, Massachusetts	162
Wescott	260
Wescott, Geo. W., Homer, New York	270
Westinghouse, G, Schenectady, New York	206
Weston, C.H., Yarmouth, Maine	264
Wetherell, H., Chatham, Massachusetts	46, 52, 210
Wheatcroft, George, Newark, New Jersey	154
Wheatcroft, I., New York, New York	154
Whitcher Co., Frank W., Boston, Massachusetts	140
Whitcher, Boston, Massachusetts	78
White Dental Mfg. Co., The S.S.	42
White, H.G.	56
White, H.O., Hebron, Connecticut	150
White, L. & I.J., Buffalo, New York	54, 96, 98, 112, 148, 188, 220, 264
Whitman & Barnes	48, 152, 172, 204
Whitman & Barnes Mfg. Co., Boston, Massachusetts	100, 152
Whitney Metal Tool Co., Rockford, Illinois	66
Whittier & Spear	200
Wiard Plow Company	152
Wickmann, W.	94
Wiete-Goethe Co., San Francisco, California	224
Wilcox & Co., Guilford, Connecticut	170
Wiley & Russell Manufacturing Company	124
Wilkie, Leighton A.	182
Wilkinson & Co., A. J., Boston, Massachusetts	28, 220
Williams & Co., J.H., Brooklyn, New York	96, 114, 204, 236, 260, 270
Williams, Brown & Earle, Inc.	50
Williams, J.L., Philadelphia., Pennsylvania	56
Williamsburg Mfg. Co., Williamsburg, Massachusetts	142
Wilson, H., Newcastle, England	130, 200
Wilson, John, Sheffield, England	254
Winchester, Number of Places Marked	3
Winchester Repeating Arms Co.	62, 174
Windsor Mfg. Co., Windsor, Vermont	114, 264
Winsted Edge Tool Works	220
Winterbottom, Philada., Pennsylvania	222
Wiser, C., Cincinnati, Ohio	112
Wiss, Newark, New Jersey	198
Witherby, T.H., Winsted, Connecticut	44, 164, 190, 220
Witte Hardware Co., St. Louis, Missouri	168
Wms. Mfg. Co., H.A., Boston, Massachusetts	34
Woburn Machine Co., Woburn, Massachusetts	80
Wood & Reynolds, Boston, Massachusetts	132
Wood & Sons Co., The A.A., Atlanta, Georgia	86, 90, 124
Wood Mfg. Co.	90
Wooden Planes	4, 6, 8, 12, 14, 16, 18, 22, 46, 52, 68, 72, 108, 112, 116, 130, 148, 160, 162, 186, 188, 200, 210, 232, 234, 250, 258, 262, 274, 278
Woodman	134
Woodrough & Mc Parlin, Cincinnati, Ohio	4
Woods, A.W., Lincoln, Nebraska	50
Wrenches	16, 18, 42, 48, 56, 66, 84, 100, 114, 144, 146, 152, 172, 174, 204, 212, 228, 236, 246, 252, 260, 262, 270, 276, 278
Wright Machine Co., Worcester, Massachusetts	160
Wright Wrench Forging Co., The	48, 100
Wright, S.J., Ellsworth, New York	138, 150
Wyke & Co., E. Boston, Massachusetts	132, 276
Wyke, John , Liverpool (England)	182
Yerkes & Plumb, Philadelphia, Pennsylvania	56
Youglove, G.T., Fitchburg, Massachusetts	140
Youngstown Kitchens	122
Ziegler & Mc Curdy, Philadelphia, Pennsylvania	4
Zip Grip, Los Angeles, California	236

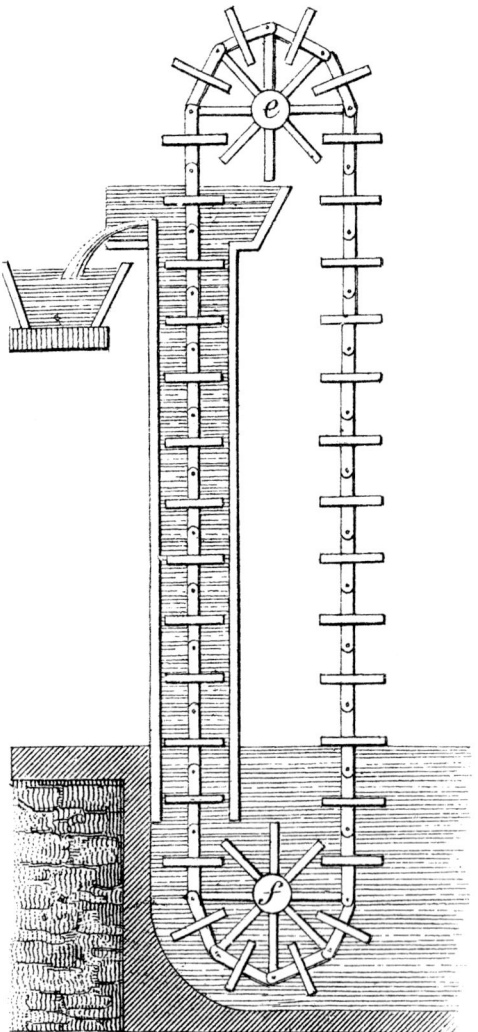

Extra Order Form for Books (Booklist Begins After Page 280)

Call, Mail, Fax or Click

Toll Free: 1-800-869-0695 Fax: (607) 566-2575 Secure Online Ordering: www.mjdtools.com

Available From: **MARTIN J. DONNELLY ANTIQUE TOOLS**

P.O. Box 281 Bath, N.Y. 14810-0281 *Please...Share Our Booklist With a Friend*

Phone: (800) 869-0695 or (607) 566-2617 • FAX: (607) 566-2575 • E-Mail: mjd@mjdtools.com

We Invite You to Visit our Expanding Book Gallery on the World Wide Web! www.mjdtools.com

Quantity:	Book Number:	Book Name:	Per Book:	Total:

Subtotal
Shipping (free within the Continental United States unless noted. Actual cost elsewhere)
New York State Residents Must Add N.Y.S. Sales Tax @ 8%
Total

Name: _____
Shipping Address: _____
City/State/Zip/Country: _____
Telephone: _____

Credit Card Type: _____   No: _____
Expiration Date: _____

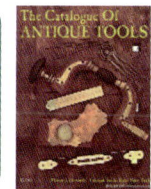

Special Offer: Back Issues Just $10.00
With Any Order
1999: BK 172   1998: BK 62

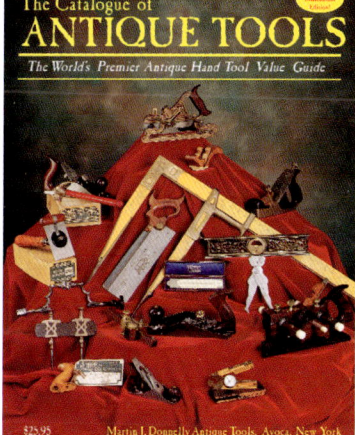

Avoid Delay: *Call Today!*
Toll Free: (800) 869-0695
FAX: (607) 566-2575

Don't Miss It!!!
Just $25.95 ➔ BK 364

Don't Miss Our Internet Tool Lists: Every Tuesday & Thursday at 1:00 p.m. E.S.T.
www.mjdtools.com

Let's Talk About...
Marketing Your Antique Tools

At Martin J. Donnelly Antique Tools, we are committed to helping you to realize the most value from your investment in antique tools. As leaders in direct mail marketing through the medium of this Catalogue and through our web site at www.mjdtools.com, we have the ability to place your tools in front of tens of thousands of eager potential buyers worldwide.

Because of our unique market position, we won't be selling the treasures of your lifetime collection in "box lots". We will assess each item individually and then provide proper documentation, photograph each tool, and provide a description based on nearly twenty years of antique tool marketing experience. Our 300 foot climate controlled warehouse has storage capacity for more than 80,000 antique tools and our inventory tracking system is the finest in the antique business. Thanks to our state of the art computer system, once an item is documented and photographed, it is very carefully packed away and need not be handled again until it is shipped to its new owner.

If you are considering selling some or all of your antique tools, we are eager to speak with you to about the many advantages of marketing your tools through Martin J. Donnelly Antique Tools. Please, give us a call, toll free, at (800) 869-0695.

We Can Sell Your Antique Tools!

- **Unique Print Catalogue: Sold in 34 Countries Last Year**
- **Dynamic Web Site: 900,000 Monthly Hits (www.mjdtools.com)**
- **Competitive Commission**
- **Climate Controlled Storage Facilities**
- **State of the Art Computer System**
- **Risk Free Marketing**

Martin J. Donnelly Antique Tools
PO Box 281 Bath, New York 14810-0281

Toll Free: (800) 869-0695 Phone: (607) 566-2617 Fax: (607) 566-2575 EMail: mjd@mjdtools.com